GEOGRAPHY OVERVIEW

Maps are among the most powerful of human inventions, showing us where we are, where we have been, and where we might go in the future. They are essential tools in nearly every aspect of social life, enabling politicians to govern their people, soldiers to defend against invasions, and merchants to conduct trade and commerce. As noted in the *Introducing World History* essay, maps also create mental images of the world and, hence, help shape the way people look at the world and their place in it.

Maps are especially useful for the historian or student of history. Historical maps show us where different peoples lived and interacted, at one point in time or over long periods. Typically, they use lines, symbols, shading, and text to present a combination of physical and political information. The physical part pertains to the natural world—the shape of landmasses and bodies of water—and serves as a kind of background or screen onto which political information is projected. Categories of political information commonly featured on historical maps include the location and names of important cities and states, the changing borders of nations and empires, and the routes people traveled as they explored, migrated, traded, or fought with one another. In order to read a historical map, one must first understand its legend. The legend provides a key for interpreting the map's graphical symbols.

The first map in this overview, Map 1.3: The Indo-European Migrations and Eurasian Pastoralism, uses colored shading to show that around 4000 B.C.E. a people called the Indo-Europeans lived by the Caucasus Mountains in western Asia, and blue arrows to show that over the next three thousand years various Indo-European tribes migrated into western and northern Europe, Central and southwestern Asia, and northern India. Black capital letters are used to name important regions of human settlement, such as Anatolia and Mesopotamia, and black italic capitals for topographical features, such as mountains and desert. Red italic capitals indicate how people in different parts of Eurasia and Africa sustained themselves at this time—whether by raising livestock, farming, hunting and gathering, or some combination of these.

Every map is designed to convey only selected categories of information and, therefore, may leave certain questions about the geographical area and its inhabitants at either the same or different points in history unanswered. Thus, Map 1.3 tells us very little about the other human populations that lived in Eurasia between 4000 and 1000 B.C.E. The names *Sumer* and *Akkad* appear, but their status as regions where the world's first urban societies arose is something the student will only discover by reading the beginning of Chapter 2 and looking at Map 2.1 Ancient Mesopotamia. Arrows show the probable routes taken by different Indo-European tribes as they migrated from their homeland, but these tribes are not named, and the student must read the rest of Chapter 2 and all of Chapter 3 before learning that they included the Greeks in Europe and the Aryans in northern India.

To introduce you to the maps in this text, and the world history they help to illuminate, seven maps have been reproduced in this section, each provided with an analytical introduction and set of questions. Every part of the world is covered, and every historical period is represented by one map—except for the Early Modern Era, which is represented by two maps. The introductions help explain the content of each map by placing it in its broader historical context. That context includes the other maps in this text, and these are referenced whenever possible. For almost any subject about which the student would like to learn more, there are several maps that should be consulted. A list of all the maps in this text follows the table of contents.

THE INDO-EUROPEAN MIGRATIONS AND EURASIAN PASTORALISM

After the first human communities learned to domesticate native plants and animals, between 11,500 and 7,000 years ago, two types of cultures arose: farming societies in fertile river basins and pastoral societies in areas dominated by grassland, mountainous terrain, or desert (see Map 1.2). Important early farming societies include the city-states of Sumer and Akkad in Mesopotamia (see Map 2.1), the Harappan cities of the Indus Valley in India (see Map 2.2), the Egyptian and Nubian states along the Nile River in Africa (see Map 3.1), and the Shang state by the Yellow River in China (see Map 4.1). Bordering these peoples were pastoral societies who raised livestock as their main source of food and raw material and lived in smaller, dispersed groups over large areas of Eurasia, Africa, and Arabia. One such society, or collection of tribes, were the Indo-Europeans, who lived near the Caucasus Mountains around 4000 B.C.E. Over the next three thousand years, various Indo-European peoples migrated from their homeland: the Greeks settled in the eastern Mediterranean, the Hittites in central Anatolia, and the Aryans in northern India. Most European languages and many languages of southwestern Asia, Central Asia, and India are direct descendants of the prehistoric language spoken by the Indo-Europeans.

Maps referenced

e **Visit the website and eBook for additional study material and interactive tools:**
www.cengage.com/history/lockard/globalsocnet2e

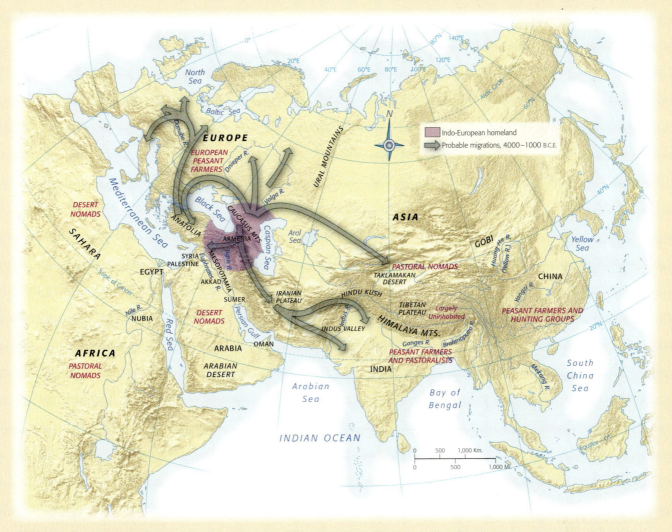

MAP 1.3
The Indo-European Migrations and Eurasian Pastoralism
Some societies, especially in parts of Africa and Asia, adapted to environmental contexts by developing a pastoral, or animal herding, economy. One large pastoral group, the Indo-Europeans, eventually expanded from their home area into Europe, southwestern Asia, Central Asia, and India.

Questions

1. The Indo-Europeans were pastoral nomads, most of whom later became farmers. Which regions on this map are suited to pastoralism and which to farming economies?

_____

_____

_____

2. The blue arrows on this map show the probable migration routes taken by various Indo-European tribes from 4000 to 1000 B.C.E. Identify the main geographical features (rivers, seas, mountain ranges, etc.) of the Indo-European homeland and the regions settled by Indo-Europeans during their migrations.

_____

_____

_____

THE ROMAN EMPIRE, CA. 120 C.E.

Rome was founded in the eighth century B.C.E. by the Latin people, a tribe of Indo-European pastoralists. In 509 B.C.E., influenced by the cultures of the neighboring Greek and Etruscan city-states (see Map 8.1), the Romans established a republic—a form of government in which political power is exercised by elected representatives of the people. The Roman Republic became a great military power, defeating the trading empire of the Carthaginians, and, by 58 B.C.E., under Julius Caesar, the Celtic tribes in Gaul (modern France). With the rise to power of Octavian, who defeated Mark Antony and Queen Cleopatra of Egypt at the naval Battle of Actium in Greece in 31 B.C.E., the Republic became a military dictatorship. At the time of Emperor Hadrian's death in 138 C.E., the Roman Empire dominated the whole of the Mediterranean basin, bounded in the west by the Atlantic Ocean, in the south by the Sahara Desert, to the north by Germanic and Celtic tribes, and to the east by the Parthian empire and the Arabian Desert. The Roman Empire was unified by a network of over 150,000 miles of roads and linked to the peoples of Africa and Asia by numerous land and sea trade routes (see map on page 233, "Great Empires and Trade Routes").

Maps referenced

MAP 8.1   **Italy and the Western Mediterranean, 600–200** B.C.E. (p. 182)

SNT 2   **Great Empires and Trade Routes** (p. 233)

 Visit the website and eBook for additional study material and interactive tools: www.cengage.com/history/lockard/globalsocnet2e

MAP 8.2
The Roman Empire, ca. 120 C.E.
The Romans gradually expanded until, by 120 C.E., they controlled a huge empire stretching from Britain and Spain in the west through southern and central Europe and North Africa to Egypt, Anatolia, and the lands along the eastern Mediterranean coast.

Questions

1. Which three rivers helped define the borders of the Roman Empire by the death of Augustus (Octavian) in 14 C.E.?

2. Which Roman emperor had a 73-mile wall built to secure the province of Britain from Celtic tribes to the north?

Dar al-Islam and Trade Routes, ca. 1500 c.e.

The rise and spread of Islam in the Intermediate Era is paralleled by that of Christianity in Europe and Buddhism in Asia (see the map on page 378, "World Religions and Trade Routes, 600–1500"). By 750 c.e. the Umayyad Caliphate had conquered Spain and North Africa in the west (see Map 10.1), and a year later Arab armies defended their conquest of Central Asia by defeating Chinese forces from the Tang Empire at the Battle of Talas (see Map 11.1). From its capital in Baghdad, the Abbasid Caliphate ruled an empire stretching from Egypt to the Indus River (see Map 10.2). Like Latin culture in Europe, Arabic literature and science flourished during this period; new long-distance trade routes enriched Arab merchants and rulers and stimulated interest in the wider world. The confidence and curiosity of Islamic culture at this time are shown by the life and writings of the fourteenth-century Moroccan jurist and explorer Ibn Battuta. Logging more than 60,000 miles in thirty years, Ibn Battuta traveled to the far reaches of the Islamic world, from Timbuktu in the West African empire of Mali (see Map 12.1) to the Delhi Sultanate in India (see Map 13.1) and the cities of Pasai and Melaka in Southeast Asia (see Map 13.3).

Maps referenced

e **Visit the website and eBook for additional study material and interactive tools:** www.cengage.com/history/lockard/globalsocnet2e

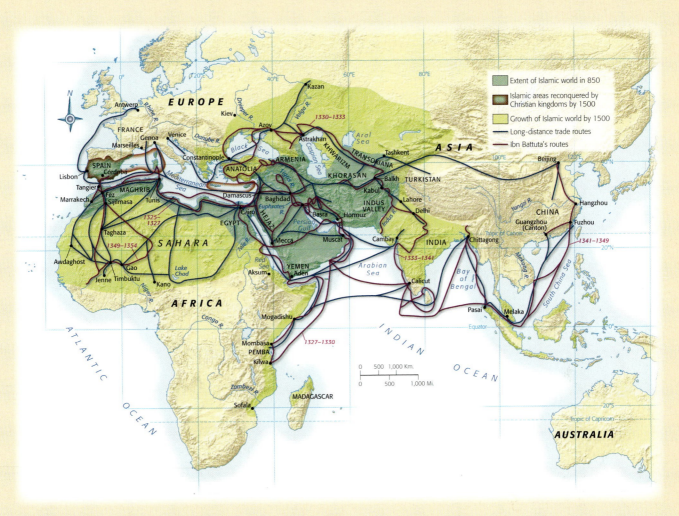

MAP 10.3
Dar al-Islam and Trade Routes, ca. 1500 C.E.
By 1500 the Islamic world stretched into West Africa, East Africa, and Southeast
Asia. Trade routes connected the Islamic lands and allowed Muslim traders to
extend their networks to China, Russia, and Europe.

Questions

1. Which European cities conducted maritime trade with Islamic societies in the
Intermediate Era?

_____

_____

_____

2. Islam spread to which western European land during the early Intermediate
Era? (See also Map 10.1.)

_____

_____

_____

THE ATLANTIC ECONOMY

The rise of European political and economic power in the Early Modern Era was made possible by maritime exploration (see Map 15.1) and missions of conquest in the Americas (see Map 17.1). In four voyages between 1492 and 1504, Christopher Columbus crossed the Atlantic Ocean and surveyed much of the Caribbean Basin, claiming it for Spain. Hernán Cortés sailed from Cuba to eastern Mexico and conquered the Aztec Empire in 1521, and in 1535 the Inca Empire in South America was conquered by Francisco Pizarro. By 1700, Portugal controlled Brazil, while England, France, and Spain claimed most of North America (see Map 17.2). European colonization was devastating to indigenous peoples. The introduction of infectious diseases like smallpox, to which Native Americans had no immunity, reduced their population by 90 percent from 1500 to 1700. Millions of West Africans were enslaved and transported to the Americas, where they mined gold and silver and produced sugarcane and tobacco on plantations (see Map 16.2). European states prospered from the development of capitalist economies, and the revenue from colonial slave labor and increased global trade put them in a position to dominate the world.

Maps referenced

 Visit the website and eBook for additional study material and interactive tools: www.cengage.com/history/lockard/globalsocnet2e

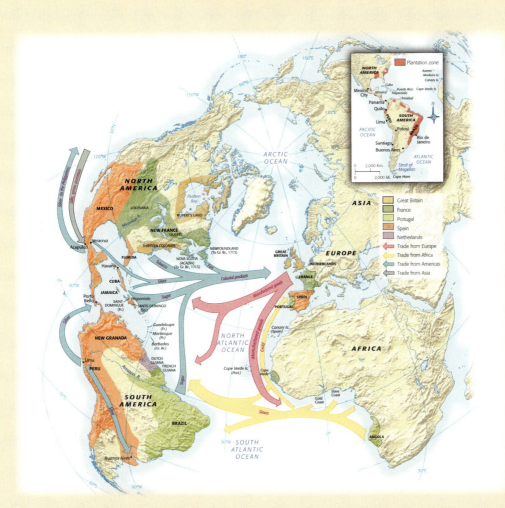

MAP 17.3
The Atlantic Economy
The Atlantic economy was based on a triangular trade in which African slaves were
shipped to the Americas to produce raw materials that were chiefly exported to
Europe, where they were turned into manufactured goods and exported to Africa
and the Americas.

Questions

1. Which Caribbean islands were colonized by Spain, France, and Great Britain?

2. Which Spanish American port imported silks, spices, and porcelain from Asia?

3. Settlers from which American colony exported furs to Europe?

U.S. EXPANSION THROUGH 1867

The successful revolution in 1776 of Great Britain's thirteen North American colonies inaugurated a series of revolutions throughout the Western Hemisphere. Apart from Cuba and Puerto Rico, all of Spain's Latin American colonies achieved independence by 1840 (see Map 19.2). In 1783 the United States extended as far west as the Mississippi River; in 1803 its territory was doubled by the Louisiana Purchase; by 1848, after a war with Mexico, the territories of Texas, New Mexico, and California were annexed. Beginning in England in the 1770s, the Industrial Revolution had—and continues to have—far-reaching effects on the social and political history of the world. Europe's population soared, and industrial capitalism enriched nations and wealthy investors, but also impoverished and dislocated millions of people. From 1821 to 1920 more than 30 million Europeans emigrated to the United States (see Map 20.1). In 1865, after a bloody Civil War, slavery was abolished in the southern states. Only four years later, a large and diverse workforce, including African Americans and Chinese immigrants, completed the first transcontinental railroad. Immigrants from Britain also settled Oceania during the Modern Era (see Map 20.3), seizing the lands of Aborigines in Australia and Maori in New Zealand, just as European colonists had seized the lands of Native Americans two centuries before.

Maps referenced

 Visit the website and eBook for additional study material and interactive tools: www.cengage.com/history/lockard/globalsocnet2e

MAP 20.2
U.S. Expansion Through 1867
The United States expanded in stages after independence, gaining land from Spain, France, Britain, and Mexico until the nation stretched from the Atlantic to the Gulf and Pacific coasts by 1867. During the same period Canadians expanded westward from Quebec to British Columbia.

Questions

1. First mapped in 1811, the Oregon Trail became the primary overland route for settlers migrating to the Pacific Northwest. Which future states did it pass through?

2. Which cities in the western United States benefited from the California Gold Rush of 1849?

3. The first transcontinental railroad was a joint effort of the Union Pacific and Central Pacific Railroads. What two cities did it join by 1869?

AFRICA IN 1914

After losing their American colonies, European nations projected their power to the south and east, and by 1914 they had colonized most of Africa, India, and Southeast Asia (see Map 19.4). Numerous Africans resisted European colonization, such as the Mandinka king Samory Toure, who fought the French in West Africa, and the confederation of Shona and Ndebele peoples, who fought the British in Southern Rhodesia. Ultimately, however, a combination of deceitful diplomacy and superior firearms made the Europeans unstoppable. Belgium seized the Congo River Basin, France took control of most of West Africa, and Great Britain conquered lands in a north-south band stretching from Cairo to Cape Town. The remaining African territories, with the exception of independent Ethiopia and Liberia, were colonized by Germany, Italy, and Portugal. The spread of Muslim culture beyond the Middle East and Central Asia, begun in the Intermediate Era, was unaffected by European colonialists and Christian missionaries: today Islam is the majority religion in northern Africa and Southeast Asia (see Map 26.3 and Map 30.2).

Maps referenced

MAP 19.4 **The Great Powers and Their Colonial Possessions in 1913** (p. 541)

MAP 26.3 **World Religions** (p. 759)

MAP 30.2 **The Islamic World** (p. 877)

 Visit the website and eBook for additional study material and interactive tools: www.cengage.com/history/lockard/globalsocnet2e

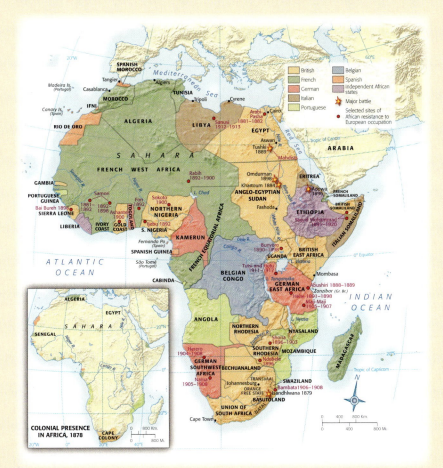

MAP 21.1
Africa in 1914
Before 1878 the European powers held only a few coastal territories in Africa, but in that year they turned to expanding their power through colonization. By 1914 the British, French, Belgians, Germans, Italians, Portuguese, and Spanish controlled all of the continent except for Ethiopia and Liberia.

Questions

1. Which European state had a single African colony?

_____

_____

_____

2. What world religions are predominant in northern and southern Africa, respectively (see also Map 26.3)?

_____

_____

_____

3. Around which two African river basins did the British and French base their colonies?

_____

_____

_____

WORLD POPULATION GROWTH

World population increased more rapidly in the contemporary era than at any time in history: from 2.5 billion to more than 6.5 billion. This map shows the relative size of nations as measured by their populations in 2002. It also shows their projected average annual growth rates between 2002 and 2015. Currently, population growth is moderate in the world's five largest nations, and higher in developing nations like Pakistan, Nigeria, and Mexico. For a number of reasons, including women's desire to work outside the home and to prevent pregnancy by using birth control, Japan and many European nations have declining birthrates and aging populations. Since 1900 there has been a massive increase in global industrial output, consumption of resources, and all forms of pollution. Although the developing nations of Asia have the largest populations, most of the world's wealth is concentrated in North America, western Europe, and Japan (see the map on page 938, "Global Distribution of Wealth"). In 2000, over 1 billion people were desperately poor. People living in wealthier nations consume a much greater share of the earth's raw materials and cause more damage to the environment than those in developing nations. The average American consumes some twenty times the resources of the average Pakistani.

Map referenced

SNT 6   Global Distribution of Wealth (p. 938)

 Visit the website and eBook for additional study material and interactive tools:
www.cengage.com/history/lockard/globalsocnet2e

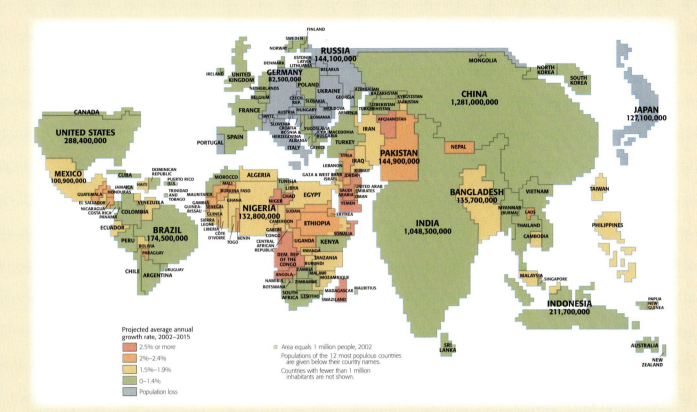

MAP 26.2
World Population Growth

This map shows dramatically which nations have the largest populations: China, India, the United States, Indonesia, and Brazil. It also shows which regions experience the most rapid population growth: Africa, South Asia, and Central America.

Questions

1. In 2002, the population of India was how many times greater than that of the United States? How many times greater was the population of China?

2. What challenges confront developing nations with large and growing populations?

3. What are some things developing nations can do to meet these challenges?

SOCIETIES, NETWORKS, AND TRANSITIONS

A GLOBAL HISTORY

Second Edition

Volume C: Since 1750

Craig A. Lockard

University of Wisconsin—Green Bay

WADSWORTH
CENGAGE Learning

Australia • Brazil • Japan • Korea • Mexico • Singapore • Spain • United Kingdom • United States

Societies, Networks, and Transitions, 2e, Volume C
Craig A. Lockard

Senior Publisher: Suzanne Jeans

Senior Acquisitions Editor: Nancy Blaine

Development Manager: Jeff Greene

Senior Development Editor: Tonya Lobato

Assistant Editor: Lauren Floyd

Editorial Assistant: Emma Goehring

Senior Media Editor: Lisa Ciccolo

Senior Marketing Manager: Katherine Bates

Marketing Coordinator: Lorreen Pelletier

Marketing Communications Manager:
Christine Dobberpuhl

Senior Content Project Manager: Carol
Newman

Senior Art Director: Cate Rickard Barr

Print Buyer: Becky Cross

Senior Rights Acquisition Account Manager:
Katie Huha

Text Permissions Editor: Tracy Metivier

Senior Photo Editor: Jennifer Meyer Dare

Photo Researcher: Carole Frohlich

Production Service: Lachina Publishing Services

Text Designer: Henry Rachlin

Cover Designer: Dutton & Sherman Design

Cover Image: Mosque of Touba: Galen Fry

Compositor: Lachina Publishing Services

For product information and technology assistance, contact us at
Cengage Learning Customer & Sales Support, 1-800-354-9706
For permission to use material from this text or product,
submit all requests online at **www.cengage.com/permissions**
Further permissions questions can be emailed to
permissionrequest@cengage.com

Library of Congress Control Number: 2009935606

Student Edition:

ISBN-13: 978-1-4390-8534-9

ISBN-10: 1-4390-8534-X

Wadsworth
20 Channel Center Street
Boston, MA 02210
USA

Cengage Learning is a leading provider of customized learning solutions with office locations around the globe, including Singapore, the United Kingdom, Australia, Mexico, Brazil, and Japan. Locate your local office at:
international.cengage.com/region

Cengage Learning products are represented in Canada by Nelson Education, Ltd.

For your course and learning solutions, visit **academic.cengage.com**

Purchase any of our products at your local college store or at our preferred online store **www.ichapters.com**

Printed in the United States of America
1 2 3 4 5 6 7 13 12 11 10 09

BRIEF CONTENTS

CONTENTS

MAPS

FEATURES

PREFACE

> Awareness of the need for a universal view of history—for a history which transcends national and regional boundaries and comprehends the entire globe—is one of the marks of the present. Our past [is] the past of the world, our history is the first to be world history.[1]
>
> —GEOFFREY BARRACLOUGH

British historian Geoffrey Barraclough wrote these words over two decades ago, yet historians are still grappling with what it means to write world history, and why it is crucial to do so, especially to better inform today's students about their changing world and how it came to be. The intended audience for this text is students taking introductory world history courses and the faculty who teach them. Most of these students will be taking world history in colleges, universities, and community colleges, often with the goal of satisfying general education requirements or building a foundation for majoring in history or a related field. Like the contemporary world, the marketplace for texts is also changing. Both students, many of whom have outside jobs, and instructors, often facing expanded workloads, have increasing demands on their time. New technologies are promoting new pedagogies and a multiplicity of classroom approaches. Hence, any textbook must provide a sound knowledge base while also enhancing teaching and learning whatever the pedagogy employed.

To make this second edition even more accessible than the first edition, we have changed from a two-column to a more reader-friendly one-column format, streamlined and shortened the narrative, and added a brand-new map program. We believe that these changes will make the text more visually dynamic, easier to follow, and even more user friendly. Furthermore, students and many faculty are more interested in technology than ever before, and this second edition places more emphasis on the many website resources that are available through icons that tell students where to find online primary sources and interactive maps related to the text, as well as through a suggested list of online resources at the end of each chapter. I believe that these changes and additions enhance the book's presentation and clarity and enable it to convey the richness and importance of world history for today's students and tomorrow's leaders while also making the teaching of the material easier for both high school and college instructors using this text.

Twenty-first-century students, more than any generation before them, live in multicultural countries and an interconnected world. The world's interdependence calls for teaching a wider vision, which is the goal of this text. My intention is to create a meaningful, coherent, and stimulating presentation that conveys to students the incredible diversity of societies from earliest times to the present, as well as the ways they have been increasingly connected to other societies and shaped by these relationships. History may happen "as one darn thing after another," but the job of historians is to make it something more than facts, names, and dates. A text should provide a readable narrative, supplying a content base while also posing larger questions. The writing is as clear and thorough in its explanation of events and concepts as I can make it. No text can or should teach the course, but I hope that this text provides enough of a baseline of regional and global coverage to allow each instructor to bring her or his own talents, understandings, and particular interests to the process.

I became involved in teaching, debating, and writing world history as a result of my personal and academic experiences. My interest in other cultures was first awakened in the multicultural southern California city where I grew up. Many of my classmates or their parents had come from Asia, Latin America, or the Middle East. There was also a substantial African American community. A curious person did not have to search far to hear music, sample foods, or encounter ideas from many different cultures. I remember being enchanted by the Chinese landscape paintings at a local museum devoted to Asian art, and vowing to one day see some of those misty mountains for myself. Today many young people may be as interested as I was in learning about the world, since, thanks to immigration, many cities and towns all over North America have taken on a cosmopolitan flavor similar to my hometown.

While experiences growing up sparked my interest in other cultures, it was my schooling that pointed the way to a career in teaching world history. When I entered college, all undergraduate students were required to take a two-semester course in Western Civilization as part of the general education requirement. Many colleges and universities in North America had similar classes that introduced students to Egyptian pyramids, Greek philosophy, medieval pageantry, Renaissance art, and the French Revolution, enriching our lives. Fortunately, my university expanded student horizons further by adding course components (albeit brief) on China, Japan, India, and Islam while also developing a study abroad program. I participated in both the study abroad in Salzburg, Austria, and the student exchange with a university in Hong Kong, which meant living with, rather than just sampling, different customs, outlooks, and histories.

Some teachers and academic historians had begun to realize that the emphasis in U.S. education on the histories of the United States and western Europe, to the near exclusion of the rest of the world, was not sufficient for understanding the realities of the mid-twentieth century. Young Americans were being sent thousands of miles away to fight wars in countries, such as Vietnam, that few Americans had ever heard of. Newspapers and television reported developments in places such as Japan and Indonesia, Egypt and Congo, Cuba and Brazil, which had increasing relevance for Americans. Graduate programs and scholarship directed toward Asian, African, Middle Eastern, Latin American, and eastern European and Russian history also grew out of the awareness of a widening world, broadening conceptions of history. I attended one of the new programs in Asian Studies for my MA degree, and then the first PhD program in world history. Thanks to that program, I encountered the stimulating work of pioneering world historians from North America such as Philip Curtin, Marshall Hodgson, William McNeill, and Leften S. Stavrianos. My own approach, developed as I taught undergraduate world history courses beginning in 1969, owes much to the global vision they offered.

To bring some coherence to the emerging world history field as well as to promote a global approach at all levels of education, several dozen of us teaching at the university, college, community college, and secondary school levels in the United States and Canada came together in the early 1980s to form the World History Association (WHA), for which I served as founding secretary and, more recently, as a member of the Executive Council. The organization grew rapidly, encouraging the teaching, studying, and writing of world history not only in the United States but all over the world. The approaches to world history found among active WHA members vary widely, and my engagement in the ongoing discussions at conferences and in essays, often about the merits of varied textbooks, provided an excellent background for writing this text.

THE AIMS AND APPROACH OF THE TEXT

Societies, Networks, and Transitions: A Global History provides an accessible, thought-provoking guide to students in their exploration of the landscape of the past, helping them to think about it in all its social diversity and interconnectedness and to see their lives with fresh understanding. It does this by combining clear writing, special learning features, current scholarship, and a comprehensive, global approach that does not omit the role and richness of particular regions.

There is a method behind these aims. For forty years I have written about and taught Asian, African, and world history at universities in the United States and Malaysia. A cumulative seven years of study, research, or teaching in Southeast Asia, East Asia, East Africa, and Europe gave me insights into a wide variety of cultures and historical perspectives. Finally, the WHA, its publications and conferences, and the more recent electronic listserv, H-WORLD, have provided active forums for vigorously discussing how best to think about and teach world history.

The most effective approach to presenting world history in a text for undergraduate and advanced high school students, I have concluded, is one that combines the themes of connections and cultures. World history is very much about connections that transcend countries, cultures, and regions, and a text should discuss, for example, major long-distance trade networks such as the Silk Road, the spread of religions, maritime exploration, world wars, and transregional empires such as the Persian, Mongol, and British Empires. These connections are part of the broader global picture. Students need to understand that cultures, however unique, did not emerge and operate in a vacuum but faced similar challenges, shared many common experiences, and influenced each other.

The broader picture is drawn by means of several features in the text. To strengthen the presentation of the global overview, the text uses an innovative essay feature entitled "Societies, Networks, and Transitions." Appearing at the end of each of the six chronological parts, this feature analyzes and synthesizes the wider trends of the era, such as the role of long-distance trade, the spread of technologies and religions, and global climate change. The objective is to amplify the wider transregional messages already developed in the part chapters and help students to think further about the global context in which societies are enmeshed. Each "Societies, Networks, and Transitions" essay also makes comparisons, for example, between the Han Chinese, Mauryan Indian, and Roman Empires, and between Chinese, Indian, and European emigration in the nineteenth century. These comparisons help to throw further light on diverse cultures and the differences and similarities between them during the era covered. Finally, each essay is meant to show how the transitions that characterize the era lead up to the era discussed in the following part. In addition, the prologues that introduce each of the six eras treated in the text also set out the broader context, including some of the major themes and patterns of wide influence as well as those for each region. Furthermore, several chapters concentrate on global rather than regional developments.

However, while a broad global overview is a strongly developed feature of this text, most chapters, while acknowledging and explaining relevant linkages, focus on a particular region or several regions. Most students learn easiest by focusing on one region or culture at a time. Students also benefit from recognizing the cultural richness and intellectual creativity of specific societies. From this text students learn, for instance, about Chinese poetry, Indonesian music, Arab science, Greek philosophy, West African arts, Indian cinema, Latin American economies, and Anglo-American political thought. As a component of this cultural richness, this text also devotes considerable attention to the enduring religious traditions, such as Buddhism, Christianity, and Islam, and to issues of gender. The cultural richness of a region and its distinctive social patterns can get lost in an approach that minimizes regional coverage. Today most people are still mostly concerned with events in their own countries, even as their lives are reshaped by transnational economies and global cultural movements.

Also a strong part of the presentation of world history in this text is its attempt to be comprehensive and inclusive. To enhance comprehensiveness, the text balances social, economic, political, and cultural and religious history, and it also devotes some attention to geographical and environmental contexts as well as to the history of ideas and technologies. At the same time, the text highlights features within societies, such as economic production, technological innovations, and portable ideas that had widespread or enduring influence. To ensure inclusiveness, the text recognizes the contributions of many societies, including some often neglected, such as sub-Saharan Africa, pre-Columbian America, Southeast Asia, and Oceania. In particular, this text offers strong coverage of the diverse Asian societies. Throughout history, as today, the great majority of the world's population has lived in Asia.

ORGANIZING THE TEXT

All textbook authors struggle with how to organize the material. To keep the number of chapters corresponding to the twenty-eight or thirty weeks of most academic calendars in North America, and roughly equal in length, I have often had to combine several regions into a single chapter to be comprehensive, sometimes making decisions for conveniences sake. For example, unlike texts that may have only one chapter on sub-Saharan Africa covering the centuries from ancient times to 1500 C.E., this text discusses sub-Saharan Africa in each of the six chronological eras, devoting three chapters to the centuries prior to 1500 C.E. and three to the years since 1450 C.E. But this sometimes necessitated grouping Africa, depending on the era, with Europe, the Middle East, or the Americas. Unlike texts that may, for example, have material on Tang dynasty China scattered through several chapters, making it harder for students to gain a cohesive view of that society, I want to convey a comprehensive perspective of major societies such as Tang China. The material is divided into parts defined as distinct eras (such as the Classical and the Early Modern) so that students can understand how all regions were part of world history from earliest times. I believe that a chronological structure aids students in grasping the changes over time while helping to organize the material.

For the second edition I have reorganized Part II. The chapter on southern and Central Asia now leads off this part as Chapter 5, introducing the development and beliefs of Buddhism as well as examining Central Asian societies such as the Sogdians and Huns. This makes the discussion of Buddhism and of the Silk Road in Chapter 6 on East Asia more understandable. The coverage of the Greeks and Persians in the Eastern Mediterranean (Chapter 7) is now followed immediately by the chapter on the Western Mediterranean and Roman Empire (Chapter 8).

DISTINGUISHING FEATURES

Several features of *Societies, Networks, Transitions: A Global History* will help students better understand, assimilate, and appreciate the material they are about to encounter. Those unique to this text include the following.

Introducing World History World History may be the first and possibly the only history course many undergraduates will take in college. The text opens with a short essay that introduces students to the nature of history, the special challenges posed by studying world history, and why we need to study it.

Balancing Themes Three broad themes—uniqueness, interdependence, and change—have shaped the text. They are discussed throughout in terms of three related concepts—societies, networks, and transitions. These concepts, discussed in more detail in "Introducing World History," can be summarized as follows:

- **Societies** Influenced by environmental and geographical factors, people have formed and maintained societies defined by distinctive but often changing cultures, beliefs, social forms, institutions, and material traits.
- **Networks** Over the centuries societies have generally been connected to other societies by growing networks forged by phenomena such as migration, long-distance trade, exploration, military expansion, colonization, the spread of ideas and technologies, and webs of communication. These growing networks modified individual societies, created regional systems, and eventually led to a global system.
- **Transitions** Each major historical era has been marked by one or more great transitions sparked by events or innovations, such as settled agriculture, Mongol imperialism, industrial revolution, or world war, that have had profound and enduring influences on many societies, gradually reshaping the world. At the same time, societies and regions have experienced transitions of regional rather than global scope that have generated new ways of thinking or doing things, such as the expansion of Islam into India or the European colonization of East Africa and Mexico.

Through exposure to these three ideas integrated throughout the text, students learn of the rich cultural mosaic of the world. They are also introduced to its patterns of connections and unity as well as of continuity and change.

"Societies, Networks, and Transitions" Minichapters A short feature at the end of each part assists the student in backing up from the stories of societies and regions to see the larger historical patterns of change and the wider links among distant peoples. This comparative analysis allows students to identify experiences and transitions common to several regions or the entire world and to reflect further on the text themes. These features can also help students review key developments from the preceding chapters.

Historical Controversies Since one of the common misconceptions about history is that it is about the "dead" past, included with each "Societies, Networks, and Transitions" feature is a brief account of a debate among historians over how an issue in the past should be interpreted and what it means to us today. For example, why are the major societies dominated by males, and has this always been true? Why and when did Europe begin its "great divergence" from China and other Asian societies? How do historians evaluate contemporary globalization? Reappraisal is at the heart of history, and many historical questions are never completely answered. Yet most textbooks ignore this dimension of historical study; this text is innovative in including it. The Historical Controversy essays will help show students that historical facts are anything but dead; they live and change their meaning as new questions are asked by each new generation.

Profiles It is impossible to recount the human story without using broad generalizations, but it is also difficult to understand that story without seeing historical events reflected in the lives of men and women, prominent but also ordinary people. Each chapter contains a Profile that focuses on the experiences or accomplishments of a woman or man, to convey the flavor of life of the period, to embellish the chapter narrative with interesting personalities, and to integrate gender into the historical account. The Profiles try to show how gender affected the individual, shaping her or his opportunities and involvement in society. Several focus questions ask the student to reflect on the Profile. For instance, students will examine a historian in early China, look at the spread of Christianity as seen through the life of a pagan female philosopher in Egypt, relive the experience of a female slave in colonial Brazil, and envision modern Indian life through a sketch of a film star.

Special Coverage This text also treats often-neglected areas and subjects. For example:

- It focuses on several regions with considerable historical importance but often marginalized or even omitted in many texts, including sub-Saharan Africa, Southeast Asia, Korea, Central Asia, pre-Columbian North America, ancient South America, the Caribbean, Polynesia, Australia, Canada, and the United States.
- It includes discussions of significant groups that transcend regional boundaries, such as the caravan travelers and traders of the Silk Road, Mongol empire builders, the Indian Ocean maritime traders, and contemporary humanitarian organizations such as Amnesty International and Doctors Without Borders.
- It features extensive coverage of the roots, rise, reshaping, and enduring influence of the great religious and philosophical traditions.
- It blends coverage of gender, particularly the experiences of women, and of social history generally, into the larger narrative.

- It devotes the first chapter of the text to the roots of human history. After a brief introduction to the shaping of our planet, human evolution, and the spread of people around the world, the chapter examines the birth of agriculture, cities, and states, which set the stage for everything to come.
- It includes strong coverage of the world since 1945, a focus of great interest to many students.

Witness to the Past Many texts incorporate excerpts from primary sources, but this text also keeps student needs in mind by using up-to-date translations and addressing a wide range of topics. Included are excerpts from important Buddhist, Hindu, Confucian, Zoroastrian, and Islamic works that helped shape great traditions. Readings such as a collection of Roman graffiti, a thirteenth-century tourist description of a Chinese city, a report on an Aztec market, and a manifesto for modern Egyptian women reveal something of people's lives and concerns. Also offered are materials that shed light on the politics of the time, such as an African king's plea to end the slave trade, Karl Marx's *Communist Manifesto,* and the recent *Arab Human Development Report.* The wide selection of document excerpts is also designed to illustrate how historians work with original documents. Unlike most texts, chapters are also enlivened by brief but numerous excerpts of statements, writings, or songs from people of the era that are effectively interspersed in the chapter narrative so that students can better see the vantage points and opinions of the people of that era.

Learning Aids

The carefully designed learning aids are meant to help faculty teach world history and students actively learn and appreciate it. A number of aids have been created, including some that distinguish this text from others in use.

Geography Overview Located at the front of the textbook, the Geography Overview pairs key maps found in the text with critical-thinking questions that help students interpret the variety of geographic and historical information that a map can convey.

Part Prologue and Map Each part opens with a prologue that previews the major themes and topics—global and regional—covered in the part chapters. An accompanying world map shows some of the key societies discussed in the part.

Chapter Outline, Primary Source Quotation, and Vignette A chapter outline shows the chapter contents at a glance. Chapter text then opens with a quotation from a primary source pertinent to chapter topics. An interest-grabbing vignette or sketch then funnels students' attention toward the chapter themes they are about to explore.

Focus Questions To prepare students for thinking about the main themes and topics of the chapter, a short list of thoughtfully prepared questions begins each chapter narrative. These questions are then repeated before each major section. The points they deal with are revisited in the Chapter Summary.

Special Boxed Features Each chapter contains a Witness to the Past drawn from a primary source, and a Profile highlighting a man or woman from that era. The Historical Controversy boxes, which focus on issues of interpretation, appear at the end of each part and before each "Societies, Networks, and Transitions" essay. Questions are also placed at the end of the primary source readings, historical controversies, and profiles to help students comprehend the material.

Maps and Other Visuals Maps, photos, chronologies, and tables are amply interspersed throughout the chapters, illustrating and unifying coverage and themes.

Section Summaries At the end of each major section within a chapter, a bulleted summary helps students to review the key topics.

Chapter Summary At the end of each chapter, a concise summary invites students to sum up the chapter content and review its major points.

Annotated Suggested Readings and Endnotes Short lists of annotated suggested readings, mostly recent, and websites providing additional information are also found at the end of each chapter. These lists acknowledge some of the more important works used in writing as well as sources of particular value for undergraduate students. Direct quotes in the text are attributed to their sources in endnotes, which are located at the end of the book.

Key Terms and Pronunciation Guides Important terms likely to be new to the student are boldfaced in the text and immediately defined. These key terms are also listed at the end of the chapter and then listed with their definitions at the end of the text. The pronunciation of foreign and other difficult terms is shown parenthetically where the terms are introduced to help students with the terminology.

New to this Edition

In developing this new edition, I have also benefited from the responses to the first edition, including correspondence and conversations with instructors and students who used the text. Incorporating many of their suggestions, this second edition is somewhat shorter than the first. The chapter structure is now streamlined by combining some materials and hence eliminating superfluous heads. Yet the new one-column format also allows for short call-outs of paragraph topics to be placed in the margins, along with key terms and definitions, helping students to organize the material and study for exams. New "eBook and Website Resources" sections at the end of every chapter indicate important corresponding online assets, including Primary Sources and Interactive Maps. I have also eliminated redundancies, corrected factual errors, and revised the suggested readings lists.

In addition to all these changes, I have updated the narrative to incorporate new scholarly knowledge and historical developments since the first edition was completed in 2006. Hence, many chapters include new information. Paleontology, archaeology, and ancient history are lively fields of study that constantly produce new knowledge, and the chapters in Part I include updates on subjects such as human evolution, the spread of modern humans, the rise of agriculture, the emergence of states, and early human settlement in the Americas. Later chapters incorporate new material on such subjects as politics in Muslim Spain, the invention of the Cherokee alphabet, and the contributions of the abolitionist Frederick Douglass. As most readers know, many important developments have occurred in the last few years, and hence the chapters in Part VI have required the most revision. As a result, Chapter 26 on the Global System includes, among other topics, new material on the 2008–2009 global recession, increasing global warming, the spread of Christianity (especially Pentacostalism), political protests and instant messaging (especially in China and Iran), and the world response to the death of Michael Jackson. Chapter 27 on East Asia examines economic challenges, human rights protests in China, violence in Tibet and Xinjiang, Japanese politics, and North Korean developments and regional tensions. The discussion of Europe and Russia in Chapter 28 ponders recent economic challenges, immigration issues, Russian-Georgian tensions, Vladimir Putin's government, and changing attitudes toward the European Union. In Chapter 29 on the Americas, I have added material on such topics as the Reagan and Bush legacies, the 2008–2009 economic meltdown, the election of Barack Obama, the wars in Iraq and Afghanistan, politics in various Latin American nations, the drug wars in Mexico and Colombia, and Chinese investment. New material in Chapter 30 on the Middle East and Africa includes Turkish politics, continuing Israel-Arab conflicts, the 2009 Iran elections, Iraq and Afghanistan updates, conflicts in Somalia, politics in varied African nations, the spread of Christianity, and the growing Chinese economic presence. Finally, Chapter 31 addresses the 2009 Indian elections, India's challenges, Pakistani politics, the Sri Lankan defeat of Tamil rebels, the Southeast Asian economic crisis, and politics and violence in various Southeast Asian nations. These chapters should give students a good introduction to the world in which they live.

Ancillaries

A wide array of supplements accompany this text to help students better master the material and to help instructors teach from the book.

Instructor Resources

PowerLecture CD-ROM with ExamView® and JoinIn® This dual-platform, all-in-one multimedia resource includes the Instructor's Resource Manual; a Test Bank (developed by Candace Gregory-Abbott of California State University, Sacramento; includes key term identification and multiple-choice, short answer/essay, and map questions); Microsoft® PowerPoint® slides of lecture outlines and of images and maps from the text, which can be used as offered or customized by importing personal lecture slides or other material; and JoinIn® PowerPoint® slides with clicker content. Also included is ExamView®, an easy-to-use assessment and tutorial system that allows instructors to create, deliver, and customize tests in minutes. Instructors can build tests with as many as 250 questions using up to 12 question types; using ExamView®'s complete word-processing capabilities, they can enter an unlimited number of new questions or edit existing ones.

HistoryFinder This searchable online database allows instructors to quickly and easily download thousands of assets, including art, photographs, maps, primary sources, and audio/video clips. Each asset downloads directly into a Microsoft® PowerPoint® slide, allowing instructors to easily create exciting PowerPoint presentations for their classrooms.

eInstructor's Resource Manual Prepared by Rick Gianni of Purdue University Calumet, this manual has many features, including instructional objectives, annotated chapter outlines, chapter summaries, lecture suggestions, suggested debate and discussion topics, and writing and research assignments. It is available on the instructor's companion website.

WebTutor™ on Blackboard®, WebTutor™ on WebCT®, and WebTutor™ on Angel® With WebTutor™'s text-specific, preformatted content and total flexibility, instructors can easily create and manage their own custom course website. Its course management tool gives instructors the ability to provide virtual office hours, post syllabi, set up threaded discussions, track student progress with the quizzing material, and much more. For students, WebTutor™ offers real-time access to a full array of study tools, including animations and videos that bring the book's topics to life, plus chapter outlines, summaries, learning objectives, glossary flashcards (with audio), practice quizzes, and weblinks.

Student Resources

Book Companion Site This website features a wide assortment of resources to help students master the subject matter. Prepared by Jason Ripper of Everett Community College, it includes a glossary, flashcards, crossword puzzles, learning objectives, preclass quizzes, tutorial quizzes, critical thinking exercises, and matching exercises. Throughout the text, icons direct students to relevant exercises and self-testing material located on the student companion website, which can be accessed at: *www.cengage.com/history/lockard/globalsocnet2e.*

CL eBook This interactive multimedia ebook links out to rich media assets such as Internet field trips and MP3 chapter summaries. Through this ebook, students can also access self-test quizzes, chapter outlines, focus questions, fill-in-the-blank exercises, chronology puzzles, essay questions (for which the answers can be emailed to their instructors), primary source documents with critical thinking questions, and interactive (zoomable) maps. Available on iChapters.

iChapters The website *www.iChapters.com* saves students time and money by giving them a choice in formats and savings and a better chance to succeed in class. iChapters.com, Cengage Learning's online store, is a single destination for more than 10,000 new textbooks, eTextbooks, eChapters, study tools, and audio supplements. Students have the freedom to purchase a-la-carte exactly what they need when they need it. They can save 50 percent on the electronic textbook and can pay as little as $1.99 for an individual eChapter.

Wadsworth World History Resource Center Wadsworth's World History Resource Center gives students access to a "virtual reader" with hundreds of primary sources, including speeches, letters, legal documents and transcripts, poems, maps, simulations, timelines, and additional images that bring history to life, along with interactive assignable exercises. A map feature including Google Earth™ coordinates and exercises will aid in student comprehension of geography and use of maps. Students can compare the traditional textbook map with an aerial view of the location today. It's an ideal resource for study, review, and research. In addition to this map feature, the resource center also provides blank maps for student review and testing.

Writing for College History, 1e Prepared by Robert M. Frakes, Clarion University, this brief handbook for survey courses in American history, Western Civilization/European history, and world civilization guides students through the various types of writing assignments they encounter in a history class. Providing examples of student writing and candid assessments of student work, this text focuses on the rules and conventions of writing for the college history course.

The History Handbook, 1e Prepared by Carol Berkin of Baruch College, City University of New York, and Betty Anderson of Boston University, this book teaches students both basic and history-specific study skills, such as how to read primary sources, research historical topics, and correctly cite sources. Substantially less expensive than comparable skill-building texts, *The History Handbook* also offers tips for Internet research and evaluating online sources.

Doing History: Research and Writing in the Digital Age, 1e This text was prepared by Michael J. Galgano, J. Chris Arndt, and Raymond M. Hyser of James Madison University. Whether they are starting down the path as a history major or simply looking for a straightforward and systematic guide to writing a successful paper, students will find it an indispensable handbook to historical research. This text's "soup to nuts" approach to researching and writing about history addresses every step of the process, from locating sources and gathering information to writing clearly and making proper use of various citation styles to avoid plagiarism. It enables students to learn how to make the most of every tool available—especially the technology that helps them conduct the process efficiently and effectively.

The Modern Researcher, 6e Prepared by Jacques Barzun and Henry F. Graff of Columbia University, this classic introduction to the techniques of research and the art of expression is used widely in history courses but is also appropriate for writing and research methods courses in other departments. Barzun and Graff thoroughly cover every aspect of research, from the selection of a topic through the gathering, analysis, writing, revision, and publication of findings. The research process is presented not as a set of rules but through actual cases that put the subtleties of research in a useful context. Part One covers the principles and methods of research; Part Two covers writing, speaking, and getting one's work published.

Reader Program Cengage Learning publishes a number of readers, some containing exclusively primary sources, others a combination of primary and secondary sources, and some designed to guide students through the process of historical inquiry. A complete list of readers can be found at *www.cengage.com*.

CUSTOM OPTIONS

Cengage Learning offers custom solutions for this course that can tailor-fit students' learning needs—whether it's making a small modification to *Societies, Networks, and Transitions* to match the syllabus or combining multiple sources to create something truly unique. Instructors can pick and choose chapters, include their own material, and add additional map exercises along with the *Rand McNally Historical Atlas of the World* to create a text that fits the way they teach. They can ensure that students get the most out of their textbook dollar by giving them exactly what they need. A Cengage Learning representative can help instructors explore custom solutions.

Rand McNally Historical Atlas of the World, 2e This valuable resource features over seventy maps that portray the rich panoply of the world's history from preliterate times to the present, illustrating how cultures and civilizations were linked and interacted. The maps make it clear that history is not static; rather, it is about change and movement across time, a process of expansion, cooperation, and conflict. This atlas includes maps that display the world from the beginning of civilization; the political development of all major areas of the world; Africa, Latin America, and the Middle East in increased detail; the current Islamic World; and the world population change in 1900 and 2000.

Document Exercise Workbook Prepared by Donna Van Raaphorst, Cuyahoga Community College, this is a two-volume collection of exercises based around primary sources.

FORMATS

The text is available in a one-volume hardcover edition, a two-volume paperback edition, a three-volume paperback edition, and as an interactive ebook. *Volume I: To 1500* includes Chapters 1–14; *Volume II: Since 1450* includes Chapters 15–31; *Volume A: To 600* includes Chapters 1–9; *Volume B: From 600 to 1750* includes Chapters 10–18; and *Volume C: Since 1750* includes Chapters 19–31.

ACKNOWLEDGMENTS

The author would like to thank the following community of instructors who, by sharing their teaching experiences and insightful feedback, helped shape the final textbook and ancillary program:

Susan Autry, Central Piedmont Community College
Brett Berliner, Morgan State University
Edward Bond, Alabama A & M University
Gayle K. Brunelle, California State University, Fullerton
Clea Bunch, University of Arkansas at Little Rock
Steve Corso, Elwood-John Glenn High School
Gregory Crider, Winthrop University
Jodi Eastberg, Alverno College
Eve Fisher, South Dakota State University
Rick Gianni, Purdue University Calumet
Candace Gregory-Abbott, California State University, Sacramento
Gregory M. Havrilcsak, University of Michigan–Flint
Linda Wilke Heil, Central Community College
Mark Hoffman, Wayne County Community College District
Bram Hubbell, Friends Seminary
Frances Kelleher, Grand Valley State University
Kim Klein, Shippensburg University
Rachel Layman, Lawrence North High School
Christine Lovasz-Kaiser, University of Southern Indiana
John Lyons, Joliet Junior College
Mary Ann Mahony, Central Connecticut State University
Laurence Marvin, Berry College
Patrick McDevitt, University at Buffalo SUNY
David K. McQuilkin, Bridgewater College
Bill Mihalopoulos, Northern Michigan University

W. Jack Miller, Pennsylvania State University–Abington
Edwin Moise, Clemson University
Aarti Nakra, Salt Lake Community College
Peter Ngwafu, Albany State University
Melvin Page, East Tennessee State University
Craig Patton, Alabama A & M University
William Pelz, Elgin Community College
Paul Philp, John Paul II HS/Eastfield Community College
Jason Ripper, Everett Community College
Rose Mary Sheldon, Virginia Military Institute
Anthony Steinhoff, University of Tennessee–Chattanooga
Bill Strickland, East Grand Rapids High School
Kurt Waters, Centreville High School

The author would also like to acknowledge the following instructors who lent their insight and guidance to the previous edition: Siamak Adhami, Saddleback Community College; Sanjam Ahluwalia, Northern Arizona University; David G. Atwill, Pennsylvania State University; Ewa K. Bacon, Lewis University; Bradford C. Brown, Bradley University; Gayle K. Brunelle, California State University–Fullerton; Rainer Buschmann, California State University, Channel Islands; Jorge Canizares-Esguerra, State University of New York–Buffalo; Bruce A. Castleman, San Diego State University; Harold B. Cline, Jr., Middle Georgia College; Simon Cordery, Monmouth College; Dale Crandall-Bear, Solano Community College; Cole Dawson, Warner Pacific College; Hilde De Weerdt, University of Tennessee, Knoxville; Anna Dronzek, University of Minnesota, Morris; James R. Evans, Southeastern Community College; Robert Fish, Japan Society of New York; Robert J. Flynn, Portland Community College; Gladys Frantz-Murphy, Regis University; Timothy Furnish, Georgia Perimeter College; James E. Genova, The Ohio State University; Deborah Gerish, Emporia State University; Kurt A. Gingrich, Radford University; Candace Gregory-Abbott, California State University, Sacramento; Paul L. Hanson, California Lutheran University; A. Katie Harris, Georgia State University; Gregory M. Havrilcsak, University of Michigan–Flint; Timothy Hawkins, Indiana State University; Don Holsinger, Seattle Pacific University; Mary N. Hovanec, Cuyahoga Community College; Jonathan Judaken, University of Memphis; Thomas E. Kaiser, University of Arkansas at Little Rock; Carol Keller, San Antonio College; Patricia A. Kennedy, Leeward Community College–University of Hawaii; Jonathan Lee, San Antonio College; Thomas Lide, San Diego State University; Derek S. Linton, Hobart and William Smith Colleges; David L. Longfellow, Baylor University; Erik C. Maiershofer, Point Loma Nazarene University; Afshin Marashi, California State University, Sacramento; Robert B. McCormick, University of South Carolina Upstate; Doug T. McGetchin, Florida Atlantic University; Kerry Muhlestein, Brigham Young University–Hawaii; Peter Ngwafu, Albany State University; Monique O'Connell, Wake Forest University; Annette Palmer, Morgan State University; Nicholas C. J. Pappas, Sam Houston State University; Patricia M. Pelley, Texas Tech University; John Pesda, Camden County College; Pamela Roseman, Georgia Perimeter College; Paul Salstrom, St. Mary-of-the-Woods; Shar-lene Sayegh, California State University, Long Beach; Michael Seth, James Madison University; David Simonelli, Youngstown State University; Peter Von Sivers, University of Utah; Anthony J. Steinhoff, University of Tennessee–Chattanooga; Nancy L. Stockdale, University of Central Florida; Robert Shannon Sumner, University of West Georgia; Kate Transchel, California State University, Chico; Sally N. Vaughn, University of Houston; Thomas G. Velek, Mississippi University for Women; and Kenneth Wilburn, East Carolina University.

The author has incurred many intellectual debts in developing his expertise in world history, as well as in preparing this text. To begin with, I cannot find words to express my gratitude to the wonderful editors and staff at Wadsworth, Cengage Learning—Nancy Blaine, Tonya Lobato, Carol Newman, and Jean Woy—who had enough faith in this project to tolerate my missed deadlines and sometimes grumpy responses to editorial decisions or some other crisis. I also owe an incalculable debt to my development editor on the first edition, Phil Herbst, who prodded and pampered and helped me write for a student, rather than scholarly, audience. Tonya Lobato adroitly supervised the second edition. Carole Frohlich ably handled photos; Charlotte Miller, maps; Susan Zorn, copyediting; Jake Kawatski, indexing; and Katherine Wetzel, general project management. Katherine Bates provided great help with marketing. I also owe a great debt to Pam Gordon, whose interest and encouragement got this project started. Ken Wolf of Murray State University prepared the initial drafts of several of the early chapters and in other ways gave me useful criticism and advice. I am grateful to Edwin Moise, Michelle Pinto, Rick Gianni, and Ibrahim Shafie for pointing out factual errors in the first edition. I would also like to acknowledge the inspiring mentors who helped me at various stages of my academic preparation: Bill Goldmann, who introduced me to world history at Pasadena High School in California; Charles Hobart and David Poston, University of Redlands professors who sparked my interest in Asia; George Wong, Bart Stoodley, and especially Andrew and Margaret Roy, my mentors at Chung Chi College in Hong Kong; Walter Vella, Robert Van Niel, and Daniel Kwok, who taught me Asian studies at Hawaii; and John Smail and Philip Curtin, under whom I studied comparative world history in the immensely exciting PhD program at Wisconsin. My various sojourns in East Asia, Southeast Asia, and East Africa allowed me to meet and learn from many inspiring and knowledgeable scholars. I have also been greatly stimulated and influenced in my approach by the writings of many fine global historians, but I would single out Philip Curtin, Marshall Hodgson, L. S. Stavrianos, William McNeill, Fernand Braudel, Eric Hobsbawm, Immanuel Wallerstein, and Peter Stearns. Curtin, Hobsbawm, and McNeill also gave me personal encouragement concerning my writing in the field, for which I am very grateful.

Colleagues at the various universities where I taught have been supportive of my explorations in world and comparative history. Most especially I acknowledge the friendship, support, and intellectual collaboration over three and a half decades of my colleagues in the interdisciplinary Social Change and Development Department at the University of Wisconsin-Green Bay (UWGB), especially Harvey Kaye, Lynn Walter, Larry

Smith, Andy Kersten, Kim Nielsen, Andrew Austin, and the late Tony Galt, as well as members of the History faculty. I have also benefited immeasurably as a world historian from the visiting lecture series sponsored by UWGB's Center for History and Social Change, directed by Harvey Kaye, which over the years has brought in dozens of outstanding scholars. My students at UWGB and elsewhere have also taught me much.

I also thank my colleagues in the World History Association (WHA), who have generously shared their knowledge, encouraged my work, and otherwise provided an exceptional opportunity for learning and an exchange of ideas. I am proud to have helped establish this organization, which incorporates world history teachers at all levels of education and in many nations. Among many others, I want to express a special thank-you to longtime friends and colleagues in the WHA from whom I have learned so much and with whom I have shared many wonderful meals and conversations.

Finally, I need to acknowledge the loving support of my wife Kathy and our two sons, Chris and Colin, who patiently, although not always without complaint, for the many years of the project put up with my hectic work schedule and the ever-growing piles of research materials, books, and chapter drafts scattered around our cluttered den and sometimes colonizing other space around the house. Kathy also spent many hours selflessly helping me to complete chapter revisions to meet deadlines for the second edition.

About the Author

Craig A. Lockard is Ben and Joyce Rosenberg Professor of History in the Social Change and Development Department at the University of Wisconsin–Green Bay, where since 1975 he has taught courses on Asian, African, comparative, and world history. He has also taught at SUNY-Buffalo, SUNY-Stony Brook, and the University of Bridgeport, and twice served as a Fulbright-Hays professor at the University of Malaya in Malaysia. After undergraduate studies at the University of Redlands, during which he was able to spend a semester in Austria and a year as an exchange student at a college in Hong Kong, the author earned an MA in Asian Studies at the University of Hawaii and a PhD in Comparative World and Southeast Asian History at the University of Wisconsin–Madison. His published books, articles, essays, and reviews range over a wide spectrum of topics: world history; Southeast Asian history, politics, and society; Malaysian studies; Asian emigration and diasporas; the Vietnam War; and folk, popular, rock, and world music. Among his major books are *Southeast Asia in World History* (2009); *WORLD* (2009); *Dance of Life: Popular Music and Politics in Modern Southeast Asia* (1998); and *From Kampung to City: A Social History of Kuching, Malaysia, 1820–1970* (1987). He was also part of the task force that prepared revisions to the U.S. National Standards in World History (1996). Professor Lockard has served on various editorial advisory boards, including the *Journal of World History* and *The History Teacher,* and as book review editor for the *Journal of Asian Studies* and the *World History Bulletin*. He was one of the founders of the World History Association, served as the organization's first secretary, and is currently a member of the Executive Council. He has lived and traveled widely in Asia, Africa, and Europe.

Note on Spelling and Usage

Transforming foreign words and names, especially those from non-European languages, into spellings usable for English-speaking readers presents a challenge. Sometimes, as with Chinese, Thai, and Malay/Indonesian, several romanized spelling systems have developed. Generally I have chosen user-friendly spellings that are widely used in other Western writings (such as *Aksum* for the classical Ethiopian state and *Ashoka* for the classical Indian king). For Chinese, I generally use the *pinyin* system developed in the People's Republic over the past few decades (such as *Qin* and *Qing* rather than the older *Chin* and *Ching* for these dynasties, and *Beijing* instead of *Peking*), but for a few terms and names (such as the twentieth-century political leaders *Sun Yat-sen* and *Chiang Kai-shek*) I have retained an older spelling more familiar to Western readers and easier to pronounce. The same strategy is used for some other terms or names from Afro-Asian societies, such as *Cairo* instead of *al-Cahira* (the Arabic name) for the Egyptian city, *Bombay* instead of *Mumbai* (the current Indian usage) for India's largest city, and *Burma* instead of *Myanmar*. In some cases I have favored a newer spelling widely used in a region and modern scholarship but not perhaps well known in the West. For example, in discussing Southeast Asia I follow contemporary scholarship and use *Melaka* instead of *Malacca* for the Malayan city and *Maluku* rather than *Moluccas* for the Indonesian islands. Similarly, like Africa specialists I have opted to use some newer spellings, such as *Gikuyu* rather than *Kikuyu* for the Kenyan ethnic group. To simplify things for the reader I have tried to avoid using diacritical marks within words. Sometimes their use is unavoidable, such as for the premodern Chinese city of *Chang'an;* the two syllables here are pronounced separately. I also follow the East Asian custom of rendering Chinese, Japanese, and Korean names with the surname (family name) first (e.g., *Mao Zedong, Tokugawa Ieyasu*). The reader is also referred to the opening essay, "Introducing World History," for explanations of the dating system used (such as the Common Era and the Intermediate Era) and geographical concepts (such as Eurasia for Europe and Asia, and Oceania for Australia, New Zealand, and the Pacific islands).

INTRODUCING WORLD HISTORY

A journey of a thousand miles begins with the first step.

—CHINESE PROVERB

This introduction helps you take the important "first step" toward understanding the scope and challenge of studying world history. By presenting the main concepts and themes of world history, it serves as your guide in exploring the story of the world presented in the rest of the book while providing a foretaste of the lively debates among historians as they try to make sense of the past, especially how societies change and how their contacts with one another have created the interconnected world we know today. By examining world history, you can better understand not only how this connection happened, but also why.

WHAT DO HISTORIANS DO?

History is the study of the past that looks at all of human life, thought, and behavior and includes both a record and an interpretation of events, people, and the societies they developed. Therefore, the job of the historian is to both describe *and* interpret the past. Although beginning students generally see history as the story of "what happened," most professional historians want to make sense of historical events. Two general concepts help historians in these efforts. When they look at humans in all their historical complexity, historians see both changes and continuity. The legal system in the United States, for example, is unlike any other in the world, and yet it has been shaped in part by both English and ancient Roman legal practices.

Historians face their greatest challenges in their role as interpreters of the past. Although historians agree on the need for extensive evidence to support their generalizations, they often disagree on how an event should be interpreted. Often the disagreements reflect political differences. In 1992 a widely publicized disagreement took place on the occasion of the 500-year anniversary of the first cross-Atlantic voyage of Christopher Columbus to the Western Hemisphere in 1492. Some historians pictured Columbus as a farsighted pioneer who made possible communication between the hemispheres, while others saw him as an immoral villain who mistreated the local peoples, beginning a pattern of exploitation by Europeans. Similar debates have raged about whether it was necessary for the United States to drop atomic bombs on Japan in 1945, killing thousands of Japanese civilians but also ending World War II.

While the events of the past do not change, our understanding of them does, as historians both acquire new information and use the old information to answer new questions. Only within the past fifty years, for example, have historians studied the diaries and journals that reveal the important role of women on the home front during the American Civil War. Recently historians have used long-neglected sources to conclude that, a millennium ago, China had the world's most dynamic economy and sophisticated technology. Similarly, historians have recently discovered, in the West African city of Timbuktu, thousands of old books written in African languages, forcing a rethinking of literacy and scholarship in West African societies hundreds of years ago.

What history "tells us" is constantly evolving. New evidence, changing interests, and the asking of new questions all add up to seeing things in a new light. As you read the text, remember that no text contains the whole or final truth. Historical revision, or changing understanding of the past, is at the heart of historical scholarship. This revision and the difficulties of interpretation also make history controversial. In recent years heated debates about what schools should teach about history have erupted in many countries, including Japan, India, France, and the United States.

Historians bridge the gap between the humanities and the social sciences. As humanists, historians study the philosophies, religions, literatures, and arts that people have generated over the ages. As social scientists, historians examine political, social, and economic patterns, though frequently asking questions different from those asked by anthropologists, economists, political scientists, and sociologists, who are generally more concerned with the present and in theoretical questions. Historians also study people in their many roles and stations in life—the accomplishments of the rich and famous as well as the struggles and dreams of common women and men—and must be familiar with the findings of other relevant academic disciplines.

WHY STUDY WORLD HISTORY?

World or global history is the broadest field of history. It studies the human record as a whole and the experiences of people in all the world's inhabited regions—Africa, the Americas, Asia, Europe, and the Pacific Basin—and also helps us better understand individual societies by making it easier to look at them comparatively. Studying history on a global scale also brings out patterns of life, cultural traditions, and connections between societies that go beyond a particular region, such as the spread of Buddhism, which followed the trade routes throughout southern and eastern Asia nearly two thousand years ago. World history takes us through the forest of history in which the individual societies represent the individual trees. World history helps us comprehend both the trees and the forest, allowing us to situate ourselves in a broader context.

This helps us understand our increasingly connected world. Decisions made in Washington, D.C., Paris, or Tokyo influence citizens in Argentina, Senegal, and Malaysia, just as events elsewhere often affect the lives of people in Europe and North America. World historians use the widest angle of vision to comprehend how diverse local traditions and international trends intermingle. International trends spread from many directions. Western phenomena such as McDonald's, Hard Rock Cafes, French wines, Hollywood films, churches, the Internet, cell phones, and text messaging have spread around the world but so have non-Western products and ideas, among them Mexican soap operas, Chinese food, Japanese cars, Indonesian arts, African rhythms, and the Islamic religion. When we study individual nations, we must remember that, for all their idiosyncrasies, each nation develops in a wider world.

Along with the growing interconnectedness of the world, a global perspective highlights the past achievements of all peoples. The history of science, for example, shows that key inventions—printing, sternpost rudders, the compass, the wheelbarrow, gunpowder—originated in China and that the modern system of numbering came from India, reaching Europe from the Middle East as "Arabic" numerals. Indeed, various peoples—Mesopotamians, Egyptians, Greeks, Chinese, Indians, Arabs—built the early foundation for modern science and technology, and their discoveries moved along the trade routes. The importers of technology and ideas often modified or improved on them. For example, Europeans made good use of Chinese, Indian, and Arab technologies, as well as their own inventions, in their quest to explore the world in the fifteenth and sixteenth centuries. The interdependence among and exchanges between peoples is a historical as well as a present reality.

THE WORLD HISTORY CHALLENGE

When we study world history, we see other countries and peoples, past and present. We do not, however, always see them accurately. Nevertheless, by studying the unfamiliar, world history helps us to recognize how some of the attitudes we absorb from the particular society and era we live in shape, and may distort, our understanding of the world and of history. Coming to terms with this mental baggage means examining such things as maps and geographical concepts and acquiring intellectual tools for comprehending other cultures.

Broadening the Scope of Our Histories

During much of the twentieth century, high school and college students in North America were often taught some version of a course, usually called Western Civilization, that emphasized the rise of western Europe and the European contributions to modern North American societies. This course recognized the undeniably influential role of Western nations, technologies, and ideas in the modern world, but also reflected historians' extensive acquisition of data on Europe and North America compared with the rest of the world. This approach often exaggerated the role that Europe played in world history before modern times, pushing Asian, African, and Native American peoples and their accomplishments into the background while underplaying the contributions these peoples made to Europe. Students usually learned little about China, India, or Islam, and even less about Africa, Southeast Asia, or Latin America.

In the 1960s the teaching of history began to change in North America. The political independence of most Asian, African, and Caribbean nations from Western nations fostered a more sophisticated understanding of African, Asian, Latin American, Native American, and Pacific island history in North America and Europe. The increased knowledge has made it easier to write a history of the entire globe. As a result, world history courses, rare before the 1960s, became increasingly common in U.S. universities, colleges, and high schools by the late twentieth century and have been proliferating in several other countries, such as Australia, Canada, South Africa, China, and the Netherlands.

Revising Maps and Geography

Maps not only tell us where places are; they also create a mental image of the world, revealing how peoples perceive themselves and others. For example, Chinese maps once portrayed China as the "Middle Kingdom," the center of the world surrounded by "barbarians." This image reflected and deepened the Chinese sense of superiority over neighboring peoples. Similarly, 2,500 years ago, Greek maps showed Greece at the center of the inhabited world known to them.

Even modern maps can be misleading. For example, the Mercator projection (or spatial presentation) still used in many school maps in North America and elsewhere and standard in most atlases, is based on a sixteenth-century European model that distorts the relative size of landmasses, greatly exaggerating Europe, North America, and Greenland while diminishing the lands nearer the equator and in the Southern Hemisphere. Hence, Africa, India, Southeast Asia, China, and South America look much smaller than they actually are. In the United States, maps using a Mercator projection have often tellingly placed the Americas in the middle of the map, cutting Asia in half, suggesting that the United States, appearing larger than it actually is, plays the central role in the world. Some alternative maps give a more accurate view of relative size. For example, the oval-shaped Eckert projection uses an ellipse that shows a better balance of size and shape while minimizing distortion of continental areas. A comparison between the Mercator and Eckert world maps is shown on the following spread.

The same shaping of mental images of geography found in maps is also seen in concepts of geographical features and divisions, such as continents, the large landmasses on which most people live. The classical Greeks were probably the first to use the terms *Europe, Africa,* and *Asia* in defining their world 2,500 years ago, and later Europeans transformed these terms into the names for continents. For centuries Western peoples have taken for granted that Europe is a continent although Europe is not a separate landmass, and the physical barriers between it and Asia are not that significant. If mountains and other geographical barriers define a continent, one can make a better case for India (blocked off by truly formidable mountains) or Southeast Asia than for Europe. At the same time, seeing Asia as a single continent is also a problem, given its spectacular size and geographical diversity. Today world geographers and historians usually consider Europe and Asia to constitute one huge continent, Eurasia, containing several subcontinental regions, such as Europe, South Asia, and East Asia.

Popular terms such as *Near East, Middle East,* or *Far East* are also misleading. They were originally formulated by Europeans to describe regions in relationship to Europe. Much

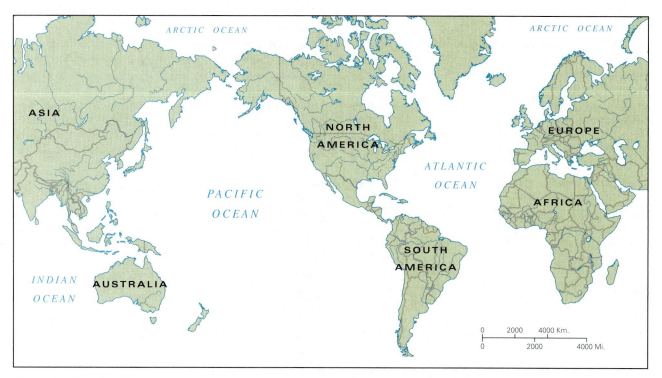

Mercator Projection

depends on the viewer's position; Australians, for example, often label nearby Southeast and East Asia as the "Near North." Few Western scholars of China or Japan today refer to the "Far East," preferring the more neutral term *East Asia*. This text considers the term *Near East*, long used for western Asia, as outdated, but it refers to Southwest Asia and North Africa, closely linked historically (especially after the rise of Islam 1,400 years ago), as the Middle East, since that term is more convenient than the alternatives. The text also uses the term *Oceania* to refer to Australia, New Zealand, and the Pacific islands.

Rethinking the Dating System

A critical feature of historical study is the dating of events. World history challenges us by making us aware that all dating systems are based on the assumptions of a particular culture. Many Asian peoples saw history as moving in great cycles of birth, maturation, and decay (sometimes involving millions of years), while Westerners saw history as moving in a straight line from past to future (as can be seen in the chronologies within each chapter). Calendars were often tied to myths about the world's creation or about a people's or country's origins. Hence, the classical Roman calendar was based on the founding of the city of Rome around 2,700 years ago, reflecting the Romans' claim to the territory in which they had recently settled.

The dating system used throughout the Western world today is based on the Gregorian Christian calendar, created by a sixteenth-century Roman Catholic pope, Gregory XIII. It uses the birth of Christianity's founder, Jesus of Nazareth, around 2,000 years ago as the turning point. Dates for events prior to the Christian era were identified as B.C. (before Christ); years in the Christian era were labeled A.D. (for the Latin *anno domini*, "in the year of the Lord"). Many history books published in

Europe and North America still employ this system, which has spread around the world in recent centuries.

The notion of Christian and pre-Christian eras has no longer been satisfactory for studies of world history because it is rooted in the viewpoint of only one religious tradition, whereas there are many in the world, usually with different calendars. Hence, the Christian calendar has little relevance for the non-Christian majority of the world's people. Muslims, for example, who consider the revelations of the prophet Muhammad to be the central event in history, begin their dating system with Muhammad's journey, within Arabia, from the city of Mecca to Medina in 622 A.D. Many Buddhists use a calendar beginning with the death of Buddha around 2,500 years ago. The Chinese chronological system divides history into cycles stretching over 24 million years. The Chinese are now in the fifth millennium of the current cycle, and their system corresponds more accurately than does the Gregorian calendar to the beginning of the world's oldest cities and states, between 5,000 and 6,000 years ago. Many other alternative dating systems exist. Selecting one over the others constitutes favoritism for a particular society or cultural tradition.

Therefore, most world historians and many specialists in Asian, African, and European history have moved toward a more secular, or nonreligious, concept, the Common Era. This system still accepts as familiar, at least to Western readers, the dates used in the Western calendar, but it calls the period after the transition, identified by Christians with the birth of Jesus, a "common" era, since many influential, dynamic societies existed two millennia ago throughout the world, not only in the Judeo-Christian Holy Land. Two millennia ago, the beginning of the Common Era, the Roman Empire was at its height, Chinese and Indian empires ruled large chunks of Asia, and many peoples in the Eastern Hemisphere were linked by trade and religion to a greater extent than ever before. Several African societies also flourished, and states and cities had long before

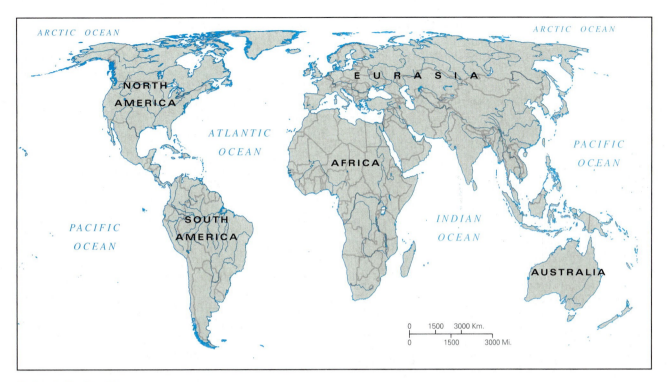

Eckert Projection

developed in the Americas. Hence this period makes a useful and familiar benchmark. In the new system, events are dated as B.C.E. (before the Common Era) and as C.E. (Common Era, which begins in year 1 of the Gregorian Christian calendar). This change is an attempt at including all the world's people and avoiding preference for any particular religious tradition.

Rethinking the Division of History into Periods

To make world history more comprehensible, historians divide long periods of time into smaller segments, such as "the ancient world" or "modern history," each marked by certain key events or turning points, a process known as **periodization**. For example, scholars of European, Islamic, Chinese, Indonesian, or United States history generally agree among themselves on the major eras and turning points for the region they study, but world historians need a system that can encompass all parts of the world, no easy task since most historic events did not affect all regions of the world. For instance, developments that were key to eastern Eurasia, such as the spread of Buddhism, or to western Eurasia and North Africa, such as the spread of Christianity, did not always affect southern Africa, and both the the Americas and some Pacific peoples remained isolated from the Eastern Hemisphere for centuries.

Given the need for an inclusive chronological pattern, this book divides history into periods, each of which is notable for significant changes around the world:

1. **Ancient (100,000–600 B.C.E.)** The Ancient Era, during which the foundations for world history were built, can be divided into two distinct periods. During the long centuries known as Prehistory (ca. 100,000–4000 B.C.E.), Stone Age peoples, living in small groups, survived by hunting and gathering food. Eventually some of them began simple farming and living in villages, launching the second period, the era of agrarian societies. Between 4000 and 600 B.C.E., agriculture became more productive, the first cities and states were established in both hemispheres, and some societies invented writing, allowing historians to study their experiences and ideas.

2. **Classical (600 B.C.E.–600 C.E.)** The Classical Era is marked by the creation of more states and complex agrarian societies, the birth of major religions and philosophies, the formation of the first large empires, and the expansion of long-distance trade, which linked distant peoples.

3. **Intermediate (600–1500 C.E.)** The Intermediate Era comprises a long middle period or "middle ages" of expanding horizons that modified or displaced the classical societies. It was marked by increasing trade connections between distant peoples within the same hemisphere, the growth and spread of several older religions and of a new faith, Islam, and oceanic exploration by Asians and Europeans.

4. **Early Modern (1450–1750 C.E.)** During the Early Modern Era, the whole globe became intertwined as European exploration and conquests in the Americas, Africa, and southern Asia fostered the rise of a global economy, capitalism, and a trans-Atlantic slave trade while undermining American and African societies.

5. **Modern (1750–1945 C.E.)** The Modern Era was characterized by rapid technological and economic change in Europe and North America, Western colonization of many Asian and African societies, political revolutions and ideologies, world wars, and a widening gap between rich and poor societies.

6. **Contemporary (1945–present)** The Contemporary Era has been marked by a more closely interlinked world, including the global spread of commercial markets, cultures, and communications, the collapse of Western colonial empires, international organizations, new technologies, struggles by poor nations to develop economically, environmental destruction, and conflict between powerful nations.

Understanding Cultural and Historical Differences

The study of world history challenges us to understand peoples and ideas very different from our own. The past is, as one writer has put it, "a foreign country; they do things differently there."[1] As human behavior changes with the times, sometimes dramatically, so do people's beliefs, including moral and ethical standards. For example, in Asia centuries ago, Assyrians and Mongols sometimes killed everyone in cities that resisted their conquest. Some European Christians seven hundred years ago burned suspected heretics and witches at the stake and enjoyed watching blind beggars fight. Across the Atlantic, American peoples such as the Aztecs and Incas engaged in human sacrifice. None of these behaviors would be morally acceptable today in most societies.

Differences in customs complicate efforts to understand people of earlier centuries. We need not approve of empire builders, plunderers, human sacrifice, and witch burning, but we should be careful about applying our current standards of behavior and thought to people who lived in different times and places. We should avoid **ethnocentrism**, viewing others narrowly through the lens of one's own society and its values. Historians are careful in using value-loaded words such as *primitive, barbarian, civilized,* or *progress* that carry negative or positive meanings and are often matters of judgment rather than fact. For instance, soldiers facing each other on the battlefield may consider themselves civilized and their opponents barbarians. And progress, such as industrialization, often brings negative developments, such as pollution, along with the positive.

Today anthropologists use the term **cultural relativism** to remind us that, while all people have much in common, societies are diverse and unique, embodying different standards of proper behavior and thought. For instance, cultures may have very different ideas about children's obligations to their parents, what happens to people's souls when they die, or what constitutes music pleasing to the ear. Cultural relativism still allows us to say that the Mongol empire builders in Eurasia some eight hundred years ago were brutal, or that the mid-twentieth-century Nazi German dictator, Adolph Hitler, was a murderous tyrant, or that laws in some societies today that blame and penalize women who are raped are wrong and should be protested. But cultural relativism discourages us from criticizing other cultures or ancient peoples just because they are or were different from us. Studying world history can make us more aware of our ethnocentric biases.

THE MAJOR THEMES

Determining major themes is yet another challenge in presenting world history. This text uses certain themes to take maximum advantage of world history's power to illuminate both change and continuity as we move from the past to the present. Specifically, in preparing the text, the author asked himself: What do educated students today need to know about world history to understand the globalizing era in which they live?

Three broad themes help you comprehend how today's world emerged. These themes are shaped around three concepts: societies, networks, and transitions.

1. **Societies** are broad groups of people that have common traditions, institutions, and organized patterns of relationships with each other. The societies that people have organized and maintained, influenced by environmental factors, were defined by distinctive but often changing cultures, beliefs, social forms, governments, economies, and ways of life.

2. **Networks** are arrangements or collections of links between different societies, such as the routes over which traders, goods, diplomats, armies, ideas, and information travel. Over the centuries societies were increasingly connected to other societies by growing networks forged by phenomena such as population movement, long-distance trade, exploration, military expansion, colonization, the diffusion of ideas and technologies, and communication links. These growing networks modified individual societies, connected societies within the same and nearby regions, and eventually led to a global system in which distant peoples came into frequent contact.

3. **Transitions** are passages, changes, events, or movements that reshape societies and regions. Each major historical era was marked by one or more great transitions that were sparked by events or innovations that had profound, enduring influences on many societies and that fostered a gradual reshaping of the world.

The first theme, based on societies, recognizes the importance in world history of the distinctiveness of societies. Cultural traditions and social patterns differed greatly. For example, societies in Eurasia fostered several influential philosophical and religious traditions, from Confucianism in eastern Asia to Christianity, born in the Middle East and later nourished both there and in Europe. Historians often identify unique traditions in a society that go back hundreds or even thousands of years.

The second theme, based on networks, acknowledges the way societies have contacted and engaged with each other to create the interdependent world we know today. The spread of technologies and ideas, exploration and colonization, and the growth of global trade across Eurasia and Africa and then into the Western Hemisphere are largely responsible for spurring this interlinking process. Today networks such as the World Wide Web, airline routes, multinational corporations, and terrorist organizations operate on a global scale. As this list shows, many networks are welcome, but some are dangerous.

The third theme, transitions, helps to emphasize major developments that shaped world history. The most important include, roughly in chronological order, the beginning of agriculture, the rise of cities and states, the birth and spread of philosophical and religious traditions, the forming of great empires, the linking of Eurasia by the Mongols, the European seafaring explorations and conquests, the Industrial Revolution, the forging and dismantling of Western colonial empires, world wars, and the invention of electronic technologies that allow for instantaneous communication around the world.

With these themes in mind, the text constructs the rich story of world history. The intellectual experience of studying world history is exciting and will give you a clearer understanding of how the world as you know it came to be.

KEY TERMS

history	ethnocentrism	societies	transitions
periodization	cultural relativism	networks	

SUGGESTED READING

After each chapter and essay, you will find a short list of valuable books and useful websites to help you explore history beyond the text. The books listed below will be of particular help to beginning students of world history because they examine the field of world history, offer an overview of history, or place key themes in a broad context for the general reader. The websites listed are megasites containing links to many essays, primary readings, and other sources.

Books

Bender, Thomas. *A Nation Among Nations: America's Place in World History*. New York: Hill and Wang, 2006. Looks at the history of the United States as part of modern world history.

Bentley, Jerry H. *Shapes of World History in 20th Century Scholarship*. Washington, DC: American Historical Association, 1996. A brief presentation of the scholarly study of world history.

Buschmann, Rainer F. *Oceans in World History*. Boston: McGraw-Hill, 2008. An innovative overview of how oceans connected distant societies.

Chanda, Nayan. *Bound Together: How Traders, Preachers, Adventurers, and Warriors Shaped Globalization*. New Haven: Yale University Press, 2007. A lively examination by an Indian journalist.

Christian, David. *Maps of Time: An Introduction to Big History*. Berkeley: University of California Press, 2004. A detailed but pathbreaking study by an Australian scholar that mixes scientific understandings into the study of world history.

Crossley, Pamela Kyle. *What Is Global History?* Malden, MA: Polity Press, 2008. Briefly examines approaches to understanding world history.

Dunn, Ross, ed. *The New World History: A Teacher's Companion*. Boston: Bedford/St. Martin's, 2000. A valuable collection of essays on various aspects of world history and how it can be studied. Useful for students as well as teachers.

Fernandez-Armesto, Felipe. *Pathfinders: A Global History*. New York: W.W. Norton, 2006. Readable survey of exploration.

Headrick, Daniel R. *Technology in World History*. New York: Oxford University Press, 2009. Good summary of this important topic.

Hodgson, Marshall G. S. *Rethinking World History: Essays on Europe, Islam, and World History*. Edmund Burke III, ed. New York: Cambridge University Press, 1993. Written by one of the most influential world historians for teachers and scholars but also offering many insights for students.

Manning, Patrick. *Migration in World History*. New York: Routledge, 2005. Explores population movements from prehistory to today.

McNeill, J. R., and William H. McNeill. *The Human Web: A Bird's-Eye View of World History*. New York: W.W. Norton, 2003. A stimulating overview of world history using the concept of human webs to examine interactions between peoples.

McNeill, William H., et al., eds. *Berkshire Encyclopedia of World History*, 5 vols. Great Barrington, MA: Berkshire, 2005. One of the best of several fine encyclopedias, with many essays on varied aspects of world history.

Nieberg, Michael S. *Warfare in World History*. New York: Routledge, 2001. Focuses on wars as agents of long-term change.

Ponting, Clive. *A New Green History of the World: The Environment and the Collapse of Great Civilizations*. New York: Penguin, 2007. Provocative study by a British scholar for a general audience.

Stavrianos, Leften S. *Lifelines from Our Past: A New World History*. rev. ed. Armonk, NY: M. E. Sharpe, 1997. A brief but stimulating reflection on world history by a leading scholar.

Stearns, Peter N. *Western Civilization in World History*. New York: Routledge, 2003. A brief examination of how Western civilization fits into the study of world history.

Wiesner-Hanks, Merry E. *Gender in World History*. Malden, MA: Blackwell, 2001. A pioneering thematic survey of a long-neglected subject.

WEBSITES

Bridging World History (*http://www.learner.org/courses/world history/*). Rich site with essays and multimedia presentations.

The Encyclopedia of World History (*http://www.bartleby.com/67/*). A valuable collection of thousands of entries spanning the centuries from prehistory to 2000.

Internet Global History Sourcebook (*http://www.fordham.edu/halsall/global/globalsbook.html*). An excellent set of links on world history from ancient to modern times.

Internet History Sourcebooks Project (*http://www.fordham.edu/halsall/*). Huge invaluable collection of public domain historical readings on many topics and regions.

Women in World History (*http://chnm.gmu.edu/wwh/*). Invaluable collection of links covering many societies and all eras.

World Civilizations (*http://www.wsu.edu/~dee*). An Internet anthology maintained at Washington State University.

World History Connected (*http://worldhistoryconnected.press/illinois.edu)/*). This e-journal contains essays of use to both students and teachers.

World History for Us All (*http://worldhistoryforusall.sdsu.edu*). A growing site with useful essays and other materials, sponsored by San Diego State University.

World History Sources (*http://worldhistorymatters.org*). Valuable annotated links on different subjects, based at George Mason University.

GLOBAL IMBALANCES: INDUSTRY, EMPIRE, AND THE MAKING OF THE MODERN WORLD, 1750–1945

The Early Modern Era from the mid-1400s to the mid-1700s, discussed in Part IV, constituted a key stage in the building of today's world. During that era European overseas expansion established permanent communication between the Eastern and Western Hemispheres, building ever closer political and economic ties between Europe, the Americas, the West and East African coasts, and some Asian societies. These ties in turn fostered a global economy while dramatically altering the lives, for better or worse, of many people.

The next key stage in creating the world we live in today came during the Modern Era, between around 1750 and 1945, which was marked by revolutions in political, intellectual, economic, and social life around the world. In countries such as France, Britain, the United States, and Japan, political revolutions or major reforms replaced old governments with more democratic or progressive governments, inspiring other peoples to seek similar changes. Latin Americans became independent from Spanish and Portuguese colonialism. In many countries political change went hand in hand with new ideas about the relationship between citizens and governments, new visions of a better life, and more skeptical attitudes toward organized religions. At the same time, Western nations transformed world politics by asserting their power in Asia, Africa, and Latin America, a few of them establishing huge colonial empires. The peoples they colonized, however, often resisted Western rule. Meanwhile, in the economic realm, the Industrial Revolution, which produced unprecedented goods and fostered technological advances, reshaped Western economic life. In some societies assertive workers', peasants', and women's movements challenged old aristocratic social orders. Overall, great progress was made toward improving social and economic conditions, especially in providing material goods. But the progress was purchased at a high cost in the dislocation of human lives, the suppression of colonized peoples, the ravaging of the natural environment, growing antagonism toward the powerful Western nations, and the deadliest wars in history.

The increasing military, political, and economic domination of the rest of the world by several European nations, soon joined by the United States, was a major trend in the nineteenth and early twentieth centuries. While Western peoples controlled some

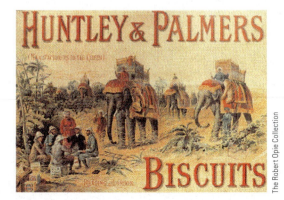

Colonial Advertisement As imperialism became a part of European life, advertisers capitalized on the interest in the colonial realm. This nineteenth-century advertisement for a British biscuit company shows a scene of the British in India.

The Robert Opie Collection

35 percent of the world's land surface in 1800, they controlled over 84 percent by 1914. This domination encouraged European emigration and helped to spread capitalism, Western languages, and Western ideas such as Christianity and Marxism. It also contributed to huge changes in the world economy. Strongly shaped by Western activity, the world economy reshuffled natural resources, so that rubber, for example, a plant native to Brazil, became a major cash crop in Southeast Asia, often grown by Indian or Chinese immigrants. Around the world men and women now often worked for wages to produce goods primarily for sale in distant markets rather than the local community.

But Western expansion and domination also created imbalances. The major imbalance was a growing gap by the early 1900s between rich nations and poor societies. Rich nations enjoyed industrialization and, in some cases, imperial expansion. The poor societies, by contrast, were usually colonies of Western nations, economically subordinate to the West, or, like China and Latin America, subject to informal Western power. Most Asian societies powerful in the Early Modern Era, including China and India, declined. The West, including North America, increasingly exported industrial and consumer goods while people elsewhere largely exported raw materials. Six hundred years ago many Chinese and Southeast Asians and some Native Americans lived longer and healthier lives than did most Europeans. By the early twentieth century, however, the balance had changed and most societies in western Europe and North America were far richer and healthier, and had far more influence on the world, than other peoples.

By the first decade of the twentieth century Western imperialism had generated global integration, the increasing connections between societies. Sparked partly by these connections, major changes came to the world during the first half of the twentieth century, some of them creating widespread misery. The hopes for a more democratic, equitable world were undermined by two ruinous world wars, the decade-long collapse of the world economy, and some of history's most brutal, despotic governments. Meanwhile, people in Asia, Africa, and Latin America increasingly challenged Western power and unpopular local governments. These developments set the stage for a new world order to emerge after 1945.

NORTH AND CENTRAL AMERICA
In the later 1700s, the thirteen British colonies along the Atlantic coast revolted and established a new democratic nation, the United States, that gradually expanded across the continent. After a civil war ended slavery, the United States rapidly industrialized; as it became the world's major political and economic power in the later 1800s, it attracted immigrants. U.S. military power proved decisive in World Wars I and II. Meanwhile, Canada spread west to the Pacific and achieved self-government. After overthrowing Spanish rule, Mexico was reshaped by liberalism, dictatorship, and revolution.

SOUTH AMERICA
During the early 1800s the Latin American societies overthrew colonialism by force and became independent nations, but they also retained close economic links to Europe, reinforcing their natural resources-based economies and limiting industrialization. The struggles between liberal reformers and conservatives often led to military dictatorship. As European and Asian immigrants reshaped Latin American societies, Latin Americans created distinctive cultures by combining imported and local traditions.

EUROPE
The Industrial Revolution, which began in Britain in the later 1700s, sparked dramatic economic, social, and political change. The French Revolution and the rise of parliamentary democracy in nations such as Britain benefited the middle classes and fostered new national loyalties. Russia conquered Siberia and Central Asia. Britain, France, and Germany renewed imperialism in the later 1800s, forging large empires in Asia and Africa. After 1914 Europe was reshaped by World War I, communist revolution in Russia, economic collapse, the rise of fascism, and World War II.

WESTERN ASIA
Although gradually losing its grip on southeastern Europe and North Africa, the Ottoman Empire maintained control of much of western Asia until after World War I, when Britain and France acquired the Arab territories and the Ottomans collapsed, replaced by a modernizing Turkish state. Persia attempted reforms but still fell under Western domination. Arab nationalism challenged Western power, while secular reformers and pro- and antimodern Muslims struggled for influence throughout the region.

EASTERN ASIA
China remained strong until the early 1800s, when, unable to reform and thwart Western ambitions, it lost several wars to the West and experienced rebellions. After a revolution ended the imperial system in the early 1900s, China lapsed into warlordism and then civil war, opening the door for Japanese invasion. Fearing Western power, the Japanese had rapidly industrialized and modernized their society in the later 1800s but, ravaged by economic depression, came under military rule in the 1930s, which eventually led to their defeat in World War II.

AFRICA
Although some African states, such as Ashante, Buganda, and Egypt, remained strong into the 1800s and instituted reforms, they could not halt increasing Western power. The ending of the trans-Atlantic slave trade by the mid-1800s opened the door to Western colonization of the entire continent. The British and French built large empires in both sub-Saharan Africa and North Africa. Western imperialism created artificial countries, undermined traditional societies, and drained Africa of resources. After World War I African and Arab nationalist movements struggled against Western domination.

SOUTHERN ASIA AND OCEANIA
Overcoming local resistance, the British gradually conquered India, and their rule exploited India's resources, reshaped Indian life, and generated opposition from Indian nationalists seeking independence. Dynamic Southeast Asian states repulsed the West until the mid-1800s, when the British, French, and Dutch colonized all of these resource-rich societies, except Thailand, often against fierce resistance, and the United States replaced Spanish rule in the Philippines, crushing a local independence movement. To the east, Western powers colonized the Pacific islands and Europeans settled in Australia and New Zealand.

MODERN TRANSITIONS: REVOLUTIONS, INDUSTRIES, IDEOLOGIES, EMPIRES, 1750–1914

British Museum/Laurie Platt Winfrey, Inc.

Crystal Palace Exposition of 1851
Attracting more than 6 million visitors, the Great Exhibition, held at the Crystal Palace in London in 1851, showcased industrial products and the companies that produced them from all over the world but especially from Europe.

*F*rom this foul drain the greatest stream of human industry flows out to fertilize the whole world. From this filthy sewer pure gold flows. Here humanity attains its most complete development and its most brutish.

—French writer Alexis de Tocqueville on Manchester, England, 1835[1]

On a spring day in 1851 Londoners celebrated their era's technological achievements. People of all social classes, from bankers and nobles to sailors, day laborers, and barmaids, headed for the spectacular new Crystal Palace in Hyde Park to see the official opening, led by Queen Victoria herself, of the Great Exhibition. The less affluent walked while the wealthy rode in horse-drawn carriages or steam-powered buses. Some came by railroad from other British cities or by steamships from France and Belgium to honor "The Works of Industry of All Nations," with Progress as the organizing theme. The first "world's fair" was dazzling. Some 14,000 firms had displays showcasing British industrial leadership and the mineral basis for British industry such as coal and iron ore. The hall of machinery contained inventions that had revolutionized British life: power textile looms, hydraulic presses, printing presses, marine engines, and locomotives that had attained the unimaginable speed of 60 miles per hour. Another hall featured industrial products that British merchants sold all over the world, including fine textiles made from wool, cotton, linen, and silk. Many of these products were made in Manchester, the city condemned as a "foul drain" but praised for fostering development. Nearly half of the exhibitors represented other countries of Europe and North America, illustrating the spread of industrialization.

The Great Exhibition celebrated the industrialization that had begun three-quarters of a century earlier and was already transforming the social and physical landscapes in parts of Europe. The British, enamored with the idea of progress, saw in modern industry, a growing economy, and creative science humanity's triumph over the natural world. Industrialization gave Britain and other European and North American countries the economic and military power to increase their influence around the world. Political revolutions and new ideologies also redefined Europe and the Americas between 1750 and 1914. Historians refer to an "age of revolutions," violent conflicts that spurred the rise of modern European, North American, and Latin American nations. In turn, the economic and political changes resulting from industrialization and revolutions fostered new political ideas. Great Britain, France, Germany, and Russia emerged as the main powers in Europe while the United States became the strongest American country. But the trends yielded mixed blessings. The British writer Charles Dickens, commenting on the French Revolution, summed up the era: "It was the best of times, it was the worst of times. It was the age of wisdom, it was the age of foolishness, it was the season of light, it was the season of darkness, it was the spring of hope, it was the winter of despair."[2] These trends had also sparked a renewal of the imperialism that resulted in various European nations acquiring or expanding empires in Asia and Africa.

FOCUS QUESTIONS

1. How did the Caribbean and Latin American revolutions compare with those in North America and Europe?

2. How did industrialization reshape economic and social life?

3. How did nationalism, liberalism, and socialism differ from each other?

4. What factors spurred the Western imperialism of the later 1800s?

e Visit the website and eBook for additional study materials and interactive tools:
www.cengage.com/history/lockard/globalsocnet2e

517

THE AGE OF REVOLUTION

How did the Caribbean and Latin American revolutions compare with those in North America and Europe?

Age of Revolution The period from the 1770s through the 1840s when revolutions rocked North America, Europe, the Caribbean, and Latin America.

The **Age of Revolution** refers to the period from the 1770s through the 1840s, when violent upheavals rocked North America, Europe, the Caribbean, and Latin America as revolutionaries employed armed violence to seize power (see Chronology: The North American and European Revolutions, 1770–1815). While political revolutions changed the personnel and structure of government, social revolutions transformed both the political and social order. The Age of Revolution began when the American Revolution ended British colonial rule and led to a new democratic form of government. The French Revolution, the major social revolution, overthrew a discredited old order of royalty and aristocratic privilege and also inspired other peoples to seek radical change. As in British North America, dissatisfaction with colonialism was common in the Caribbean and Spanish America and led to revolutions and wars of independence in these regions. For the next two centuries revolutions transformed states, ideologies, and class structures in Europe, Latin America, and Asia.

These revolutions were brutal but momentous events in modern world history and had much in common. Though often well educated and from middle-class or upper-class backgrounds, revolutionary leaders mobilized followers from among disenchanted peasants and urban workers. Many revolutions, including the French, moved from moderate to more extreme actions such as purging dissidents, rivals, or opponents. Although they replaced repressive and inequitable systems, few revolutionaries satisfied the demands of their people.

British Colonialism and the American Revolution

Resentments had festered for decades between American colonists and the imperial British government. Then in the late 1700s Europeans and Latin Americans watched fascinated as the disaffected citizens in the thirteen British colonies in North America ended British rule and established the United States. The American revolutionary leaders proclaimed Enlightenment political theories, such as democracy and personal freedom, while forming their new representative government.

Colonial Governments

In the mid-1700s the British hold on these colonies seemed strong. Each colony from New Hampshire to Georgia had unique institutions and economies. The southern colonies depended largely on plantation slavery, while the northern colonies combined commerce and manufacturing with farming, a more balanced economy. Only 2 million persons lived in the colonies in the 1760s, and the largest town, Boston, had only 20,000 residents. A fifth of the colonial population was African American, mostly slaves concentrated in the southern plantation zone. The white American colonists were generally prosperous, enjoyed considerable self-government and religious toleration, could vote for local assemblies and mayors if they were adult white males who owned sufficient property, and faced much lighter taxes than did people in Britain. Most colonists eagerly consumed British culture.

But tensions increased between the governing British and many colonists who, claiming for themselves the label of Americans, felt divorced from Britain and increasingly resented British policies, such as taxation without representation in the British Parliament. The British also placed more restrictions than before on local American manufacturing. Clumsy British attempts to raise taxes, enforce long-ignored laws, and reserve the coveted land west of the Appalachians for Indians angered many colonists, who mounted boycotts of British goods. In 1773, protesters of a higher tax on tea, dressed as Indians, raided three British ships in Boston harbor and dumped their cargo of tea overboard, an event known as the Boston Tea Party.

Patriots and Loyalists

Colonists favoring independence, known as Patriots, and those opposed, called Loyalists, increasingly clashed. Most of the Patriot and Loyalist leaders were wealthy lawyers, physicians, journalists, merchants, and landowners. Patriot leaders admired European Enlightenment thinkers such as John Locke in England and Baron de Montesquieu in France and favored democracy and a republic. The Patriots were also stirred by the writings of the antiroyalist Englishman Tom Paine (1737–1809), a sailor and teacher turned journalist who settled in Philadelphia and promoted independence, separation of church and state, social equality, women's rights, abolition of slavery, and other ideas then considered radical. Paine's passionate pamphlet *Common Sense*, which urged Americans to oppose tyranny and free themselves by force in order to "begin the world over again," helped galvanize public opinion against colonialism.

CHRONOLOGY

	Europe	The Americas
1750	**1770s–1870s** First Industrial Revolution **1789–1815** French Revolution	**1776–1783** American Revolution **1791–1804** Haitian Revolution
1800	**1815** Congress of Vienna	**1810–1826** Spanish-American wars of independence
1850	**1859–1870** Unification of Italy **1862–1871** Unification of Germany **1870s–1914** Second Industrial Revolution	

The colonies' many competing churches and schools of thought fostered intellectual diversity. Some of the Patriots were devout Protestants or Catholics; others were free thinkers. Some, including Paine, Thomas Jefferson, James Madison, Benjamin Franklin, and George Washington, were deists, believing in an impersonal creator who left humanity alone, and were often suspicious of organized churches. Patriot leaders also reflected their times: some owned slaves, smuggled, took mistresses, had illegitimate children, and, like many other male colonists, drank heavily.

After preliminary American-British skirmishes, delegates met and declared that the thirteen colonies ought to be free and independent states, with no allegiance to the British crown. On July 4, 1776, the delegates approved the Declaration of Independence, written largely by Thomas Jefferson (1743–1826), a Virginia planter, which stated, "We hold these truths to be self-evident, that all men are created equal, that they are endowed by their Creator with certain inalienable Rights, that among these are Life, Liberty and the pursuit of Happiness."[3] Perhaps a third of the colonists remained Loyalists, and many others, especially less-affluent white colonists, were neutral or apathetic. A revolutionary army organized and commanded by George Washington (1732–1799), a wealthy Virginia farmer and decorated veteran of earlier wars against France and its Indian allies, then fought the British and their allies for six bitter years, famously described by Tom Paine as "the times that try men's souls."

Struggle for Independence

Women aided the Patriot cause by raising funds for the army, serving as cooks and nurses in army camps, and engaging in sabotage and spying. A few women disguised themselves as men to join the combat. Britain's rivals, France and Spain, aided the Patriot cause. The British enjoyed support from many Indians, who resented the colonists for aggressively occupying Indian lands, and from some black slaves, who were promised their freedom by a British general. Some Loyalists and British officials accused the Patriots of hypocrisy, wanting freedom for themselves while maintaining slavery for nonwhites. The American defeat of British forces at Yorktown, Virginia, in 1781 proved decisive, and Britain recognized American independence in 1783. Despite their democratic values, the Patriots treated the Loyalists harshly, confiscating their land and jailing them. Ultimately 100,000 Loyalists were expelled or fled to Canada, and many others left for England.

The thirteen former colonies formed an independent federation, the United States of America. The new country's founders debated the relative powers of the states and of a national government that could unite them. The first weak confederation proved unworkable. Seeking a stronger central government, in 1787 delegates met in Philadelphia and approved a constitution, mostly written by James Madison (1751–1836), a well-educated Virginian, that established an elected president and congress presiding over a federal system that granted the states many powers. The delegates then elected the war hero Washington (g. 1789–1797), admired for his integrity and managerial skills, as the republic's first president. The first elected congress approved ten constitutional amendments, known as the Bill of Rights, which enshrined Enlightenment values such as freedom of speech, assembly, press, and religion.

However, the founders of the new republic made no effort to transform the American social order. Despite their rhetoric, they did not challenge slavery, recognize Native American claims to land, or expand voting rights even to all white men, much less to persons other than white men. Although some Patriots, including

CHRONOLOGY
The North American and European Revolutions, 1770–1815

1770s–1840s Age of Revolution

1773 Boston Tea Party

1776 American Declaration of Independence

1783 Britain's recognition of United States independence

1787 United States constitutional convention; Northwest Ordinance for forming new states

1789–1815 French Revolution

1791–1792 Constitutional state in Poland-Lithuania

1804 Crowning of Napoleon as emperor of France

1810–1811 Height of Napoleon's empire

1815 Defeat of Napoleon at Battle of Waterloo; Congress of Vienna

Washington, freed their slaves, and most northern states gradually abolished slavery, blacks who fought for Britain were often executed or reenslaved, and some left with other Loyalists for Canada. Indians could only watch bitterly as the government claimed and promoted settlement of most of the Indian land east of the Mississippi River and as the U.S. Congress approved the Northwest Ordinance, allowing frontier settlements to join the United States. Women did not gain equal rights with men, even though they too had sacrificed to win independence and had managed their absent husbands' shops, businesses, and farms during the war. However, new laws made it somewhat easier for women to obtain a divorce, a right long enjoyed by men.

American "Exceptionalism"

Americans also believed they had formed a society unique to history, an idea known as American "exceptionalism." They viewed themselves as the most democratic, individualistic, enterprising, prosperous, technological, and self-determining society on earth, unhindered by the burdens of history that held down other peoples. Yet, Americans also argued that their ideas and institutions were relevant for the whole world, agreeing with the Puritan Massachusetts governor, John Winthrop, who claimed in 1630 that his new society constituted a "City upon a Hill, [with] the eyes of all people upon us."[4] A century and a half later, Jefferson declared that America was a standing monument and example for the world. These attitudes have remained powerful in American thought.

The French Revolution

The French Revolution electrified Europe by replacing the monarchy with a republic and spreading values of liberty and social equality, but it also generated terrible violence, the rise of despotic leaders, and long years of war. The shock waves it generated strongly shaped nineteenth-century Europe. The Revolution was traumatic but also inspiring: it preached "liberty, equality, and fraternity" and a fairer distribution of wealth, and the middle classes took over the government in the name of the common people. But the Revolution also plunged Europe into a prolonged crisis and a series of wars between France and its European rivals, who feared the spread of radical ideas and sought to restore royal government to France.

Causes

The Revolution had many causes. France's participation in the American War of Independence, aiding the Patriot's anti-British cause, worsened long-standing financial problems rooted in an unjust economic system that badly needed reform. The Roman Catholic clergy and the privileged nobility were exempt from most direct taxes, putting the entire burden on artisans and peasants. While several bad harvests increased hunger and misery, high prices, food shortages, and high unemployment spurred resentment. The difficulty the poor had in buying bread led Marie-Antoinette, the king's wife, to contemptuously remark: "Let them eat cake."

To calm rising passions, King Louis XVI (1754–1793) called the Estates General, a long-dormant consultative body that included representatives of the clergy, the nobility, and finally a Third Estate comprising the middle classes and peasants. Every town debated political issues and then elected delegates to the Estates General. The leaders of the Third Estate, who represented over 90 percent of the population, demanded influence reflecting their numbers. Many middle-class men and women had read the works of Enlightenment thinkers and had found the American Revolution inspirational. Stalemated in the Estates General, the Third Estate delegates formed a rival national assembly and began writing a new French constitution. In response, the king called in the army to restore order, provoking anger and violence.

Eruption of Conflict

The Revolution erupted in Paris in 1789 after armed crowds stormed the Bastille, the royal prison and a hated symbol of tyranny, to release the prisoners and seize gunpowder and cannon. The bloody Bastille attack proved so inspirational that the date (July 14) later became France's national holiday. Both men and women took up arms to oppose royal power, and the terrified nobility fled. Members of the Third Estate formed a new Constituent Assembly, which voted to destroy the social order and then adopted the Declaration of the Rights of Man and of the Citizen, a document strongly influenced by the English Bill of Rights of 1689 and the new United States constitution. The Declaration announced that all people everywhere had a natural right to liberty, property, equality, security, religious toleration, and freedom of expression, press, and association. A new constitution made the king bound by laws and subject to an elected assembly, outlawed slavery, and reorganized and weakened the church, confiscating the vast wealth of the higher clergy. The French example inspired other Europeans to adopt political reform. In 1791 reformers in Poland-Lithuania reshaped the state and expanded voting rights. But Russia, supported by the Polish nobility, invaded and crushed the reformist government.

Continental War

With several European states demanding a restoration of royal power in France, French leaders who thought that war might unify the nation behind the revolution declared war in 1792. The

Kunsthistorisches Museum Vienna/The Bridgeman Art Library International

Storming the Bastille This painting celebrates the taking of the Bastille, a castle prison in Paris that symbolized hated royal rule, by armed citizens and soldiers. The governor and his officials are led out and will soon be executed.

army recruited volunteers, identifying the defense of France with revolutionary ideals and proclaiming that "young men shall go forth in battle, married men shall forge weapons, women shall make tents and clothing, and shall serve in hospitals."[5] A national convention, elected by universal male suffrage, made France a republic, ending the monarchy. In the name of all the world's people, the French began a crusade to end absolute monarchies and social inequality in Europe. With patriotic enthusiasm the French public rallied behind the revolutionary government, singing a song, the *Marseillaise* (mar-sye-EZ), that was written as a call to oppose tyranny and is now France's national anthem. In 1793 the revolutionaries executed King Louis XVI for treason.

Military conflict intensified internal dissent and worsening economic problems in France. Some leaders emphasized preserving the Revolution's libertarian principles, such as freedom of speech and assembly. However, a more radical faction known as **Jacobins** (JAK-uh-binz), who believed these rights had to be set aside in the crisis, took control of the state and imposed a dictatorship to promote internal security. The Jacobins' Committee of Public Safety used terror against real or imagined opponents, often cutting off their victims' heads in public using the gruesome guillotine. Perhaps 40,000 French citizens, mostly rebellious peasants and provincial leaders, were executed, and tens of thousands more were arrested, often on flimsy evidence, to restore internal order. The Jacobins' leader, Maximilien Robespierre (1758–1794), a lawyer and dedicated republican, started as an idealistic humanist but became the most zealous promoter of the terror against alleged counterrevolutionaries, some of them his former allies. As the violence and radicalism intensified, sowing dissension, some Jacobin leaders themselves, including Robespierre, were executed in factional disputes. The terror abated when the Jacobins lost power in 1795, but several constructive Jacobin policies endured, including guaranteeing the right to public education for all children.

Although not all its accomplishments proved long-lasting, the French Revolution showed that a new order could be created, inspiring generations of revolutionaries to come. Ultimately the Revolution constructed a middle class–dominated state much more powerful than that of the Bourbon kings. During these years much of the vocabulary of modern politics emerged, including terms such as *conservative* and *right-wing*, referring to those who favored retaining the status quo or restoring the past, and *liberal* and *left-wing*, meaning progressives wanting faster change. Revolutionary France also transformed warfare by introducing conscription and promotion through the ranks. The countries occupied or conquered by France, such as Belgium, were turned into "sister republics," where new revolutionary governments promoted human rights.

Revolutionary Divisions and Terror

Jacobins A radical faction in the French Revolution that believed civil rights had to be set aside in a crisis and that executed thousands of French citizens.

Legacies

But the Jacobins' terrible violence undermined personal liberty and dampened the Revolution's appeal. The French trauma turned North Americans against revolutions, which they now feared too often degenerated into anarchy and then despotism. Observers also debated whether the "Rights of Man" included women. Olympe de Gouges (1748–1793), a French butcher's daughter, published a manifesto complaining that women were excluded from decision making and tried to organize a female militia to fight for France, arguing that needles and spindles were not the only weapons women knew how to handle. For her efforts she was executed by the Jacobins. A British campaigner for women's rights, Mary Wollstonecraft (1759–1797), moved to Paris and wrote the *Vindication of the Rights of Women* in 1792, calling for equal opportunities for women in education and society. But despite the efforts of reformers such as de Gouges and Wollstonecraft, women remained excluded from active citizenship in France and nearly everywhere else.

The Napoleonic Era and a New European Politics

Rise of Bonaparte

Although the republican system had inspired many, the terror and the shifting fortunes of war led to a resurgence of pro-monarchy feelings and prompted antiroyalists to turn to the ambitious General Napoleon Bonaparte (BOW-nuh-pahrt) (1769–1821), a lawyer's son and a brilliant military strategist from the French-ruled island of Corsica, whose rise to power was astounding. A lowly artillery officer once imprisoned for alleged Jacobin ties, through political connections and his forceful personality he rapidly rose through the ranks to command major military victories in France, Italy, Austria, and Egypt. In 1799 Bonaparte gained the most powerful political office in revolutionary France, that of First Consul. In 1804, responding to a widespread belief that only a dictator could provide stability, Bonaparte crowned himself emperor in a regal coronation, attended by the pope, that harked back a millennium to the crowning of Charlemagne. Quickly promoting reconciliation and economic prosperity within France, he standardized revolutionary laws, including the equality of all citizens before the law, thus making permanent the Revolution's core values. However, Bonaparte's dictatorial tendencies betrayed French liberty, and he developed a taste for the trappings of royal power. Wanting an heir, he divorced his childless wife, the popular Empress Josephine, and married an eighteen-year-old Austrian princess, Marie-Louise.

Napoleonic Wars

The wars soon began again. In 1805 Britain, the world's dominant sea power, forged a coalition with Austria, Prussia, and Russia to defeat France. France won most of the land battles, enabling it to occupy much of western Europe. Bonaparte's family now ruled Spain, Naples, and some German states. But armed resistance in Spain and the German states, a costly invasion of Russia resulting in humiliating retreat, and an invasion of France by rival powers all sapped Bonaparte's military strength. In 1814 allied armies entered Paris. Bonaparte abdicated and was imprisoned on an Italian island. He escaped and regrouped his forces, but was finally overcome by British and Prussian armies at Waterloo, a Belgian village, in 1815. While the Bourbon family reclaimed the French throne, Bonaparte spent his remaining years in exile on St. Helena, a remote, British-ruled South Atlantic island.

The demise of revolutionary France and Napoleon's empire allowed for a partial return to the European status quo. The victorious allies met in 1815 at the Congress of Vienna to remold the European state system (see Map 19.1). Europeans who preferred monarchy and church-state alliance rejoiced at French defeat. The men who overthrew French control in Naples sang, "Naples won't stay a republic. Here's an end to equality. Here's an end to liberty. Long live God and his Majesty."[6] Dominated by Austria, Britain, Russia, and the revived royalist government of France, the Congress reaffirmed pre-Napoleonic borders and restored most of the former rulers displaced by revolutionaries and reformers. However, thirty-nine German states began moving toward national unity by forming the German Confederation. Russia invaded Poland-Lithuania, destroying the constitutional government and partitioning the nation between Russia and Prussia.

Later Upheavals

Once the revolutionary genie was out of the bottle, however, all the best efforts of the established order could not put it back again. Revolutionary ideas combined with popular discontent and frequent wars continued to unsettle Europe as various revolutions broke out in 1830–1831 because of discontent with despotic political systems. The French overthrew the despotic Bourbon king, Charles X, and installed his more progressive cousin, Louis-Philippe (1773–1850), as a constitutional monarch who recognized some liberties. Uprisings in several German and Italian states and in Poland sought voting rights, and a peasant rebellion caused by poverty and unemployment rocked Britain.

Even more turbulent European revolts erupted in 1848, a result of poor harvests, rising unemployment, massive poverty, and a desire for representative government. These upheavals began

Map 19.1 Europe in 1815
With the Napoleonic wars ended, the Congress of Vienna redrew the map of
Europe. France, Austria, Spain, Britain, and a growing Prussia were the dominant
states, but the Ottoman Turks still ruled a large area of southeastern Europe.

Interactive Map

in France, forcing the increasingly unpopular King Louis-Philippe to abdicate, and soon spread
to Austria, Hungary, and many German and Italian states. In German cities students met in city
marketplaces to demand elected parliaments and civil liberties such as free speech and a free press.
But conservative regimes violently crushed the uncoordinated dissident movements within a few
months. A French observer said that "nothing was lacking" in the repression in Paris, "not grape-
shot, nor bullets, nor demolished houses, nor martial law, nor the ferocity of the soldiery, nor the
insults to the dead."[7] Still, the uprisings helped further spread democratic ideas, and parliamentary
power increased in countries such as Denmark and the Netherlands. To prevent revolutionary out-
bursts, many European governments also began to consider social and economic reforms, such as
higher wages, to improve people's lives.

Caribbean Societies and the Haitian Revolution

In the Caribbean, the first successful movement to overthrow colonialism came in Haiti, where
slaves of African ancestry fought their way to power. Most of the small Caribbean islands and the

Guianas in northeast South America were colonies of Britain, France, or the Netherlands, inhabited chiefly by African slaves working on plantations. The Afro-Caribbean peoples mixed European cultural forms and languages with African traditions. In British-colonized islands such as Jamaica, Barbados, and Antigua, for example, most slaves adopted Christianity and Anglo-Saxon names.

Haitian Conflicts

Slave revolts were common throughout the colonial era, but only the Haitian Revolution overthrew a regime. In 1791 some 100,000 Afro-Haitian slaves, inspired by the French Revolution and its slogans of liberty and equality, rose up against the oppressive society presided over by French planters (see Chronology: The Caribbean and Latin American Revolutions, 1750–1840). Toussaint L'Ouverture (too-SAN loo-ver-CHORE) (1746–1803), a freed slave with a vision of a republic of free people, became the insurgent leader. Raised a Catholic, Toussaint learned French and Latin from an older slave.

The Haitian revolution went from triumph to tragedy. For a decade the Afro-Haitians fought the French military and anti-French British and Spanish forces hoping to capitalize on the turmoil, and by 1801 Toussaint's forces controlled Haiti and freed the slaves. But Napoleon Bonaparte sent in a larger French force and French soldiers captured Toussaint, who died in a French prison. In 1804 Afro-Haitians defeated Napoleon's army and established the second independent nation in the Western Hemisphere after the United States. Around the Americas the Haitian Revolution cheered slaves and abolitionists but alarmed planters, who became more determined to preserve slavery, and the United States, still a slave-owning nation, withheld diplomatic recognition of the black Haitian republic. In Haiti, French planters were either killed or fled, and the ex-slaves took over sugar production. The promise of a better life for Haiti's people proved short-lived, however. Toussaint's successor as revolutionary leader, the Africa-born Jean Jacques Dessalines (de-sah-LEEN) (1758–1806), ruled despotically, beginning two centuries of tyranny.

Latin America's Independence Wars

Spanish and Portuguese Empires

The Spanish and Portuguese ruled much larger and more populous American empires than did the British. By 1810 some 18 million people lived under Spanish rule from California to South America's southern tip, including 4 million Europeans, 8 million Indians, 1 million blacks, and 5 million people of mixed descent. Corruption ran deep, and the planters, ranchers, mine owners, bureaucrats, and church officials who benefited from Spanish rule opposed any major change, preferring a system that sent raw materials, such as silver and beef, to Spain rather than developing domestic institutions or markets.

The Spanish ruled their colonies differently than did the British in North America, allowing little self-government, maintaining economic monocultures, and imposing one dominant religion: Roman Catholicism. Latin American social conditions did not promote unity or equality. The creoles, whites born in the Americas, resented the influential newcomers from Spain, but they also feared that resistance against Spain might get out of control and threaten their position. The huge underclass of Indians, enslaved Africans, and mixed-descent people faced growing unemployment and perhaps the world's most inequitable distribution of wealth. In contrast to British America, a rigid Catholic Church wary of dissent discouraged intellectual diversity. The Inquisition denounced as seditious any literature espousing equality and liberty and punished "heretics." Local critics accused the government and church of "[keeping] thought in chains."[8]

Given the political and social inequalities, revolts punctuated Spanish colonial rule. For instance, in Mexico the Maya revolted against high taxes and church repression of Maya customs in 1761, leading to Spanish reprisals. A mass uprising led by Tupac Amaru II (1740–1781), the wealthy, well-educated mestizo who claimed to be a descendant of an Inca king, spread over large areas of Peru in the 1780s. Tupac and Michaela Bastidas, his wife and a brilliant strategist, organized a broad-based coalition that quickly overran much of the colony. They hoped to establish an independent state, with Tupac as king, where Indians, mestizos, and creoles would live in harmony. Many of Tupac's peasant followers revived the Inca religion and attacked Catholic churches and clergy. However, the better-armed Spanish defeated the rebel bands and executed Tupac and his family.

Eventually, dissatisfaction in Spanish America exploded into wars of national independence. Creole merchants and ranchers criticized Spain for its commercial monopoly, increasing taxes, and the colonial government's favoritism toward those

CHRONOLOGY

The Caribbean and Latin American Revolutions, 1750–1840

1791–1804 Haitian Revolution

1808 Move of Portuguese royal family to Brazil

1810–1826 Wars of independence in Spanish America

1810–1811 First Mexican revolution

1816 Argentine independence

1821 Founding of Gran Colombian republic by Bolivar

1822 Mexican independence; Dom Pedro emperor of Brazil

1830 Independence of Colombia, Venezuela, and Ecuador

1839 Division of Central American states

born in Spain. They also wanted a role in government. Creoles also often felt more loyalty to their American region than to distant Spain, and some were influenced by the Enlightenment and the American and French Revolutions. The British, who were pressuring the Spanish and Portuguese to open Latin American markets to British goods, also secretly aided anticolonial groups. At the same time, Spain experienced political problems at home, including French occupation during the Napoleonic wars.

Since Spain refused to make serious political concessions, middle-class creole revolutionaries waged wars of independence between 1810 and 1826. Two separate independence movements began in Venezuela and Argentina, led respectively by Simon Bolivar **(bow-LEE-vahr)** and Jose de San Martin. Born into a wealthy Caracas family that owned slaves, land, and mines, Bolivar (1783–1830) had studied law in Spain, was a free thinker who admired rationalist Enlightenment thought, and had a magnetic personality that inspired loyalty. He offered an inclusive view of his Latin American people: "We are a microcosm of the human race, a world apart, neither Indian nor Europeans, but a part of each."[9] Bolivar also spent time in Haiti and Jamaica, where he gained sympathy for blacks. He formed an army in 1816 to liberate northern South America, offering freedom to slaves who aided his cause. After many setbacks, Bolivar's forces triumphed and created the republic of Gran Colombia in 1821, uniting Colombia, Ecuador, and Venezuela. San Martin (1778–1850), a former colonel in the Spanish army, helped Argentina gain independence in 1816 and Chile in 1818. In 1824 San Martin and Bolivar cooperated to liberate Peru, where royalist sympathies were strongest.

But the wars damaged economies and caused people to flee the fighting. The creoles who now governed these countries often forgot the promises made to the Indians, mestizos, mulattos, and blacks who had provided the bulk of the revolutionary armies. And although some slaves were freed, slavery was not abolished. Some women enthusiastically served the revolution as soldiers and nurses. For example, Policarpa Salavarrieta helped Bolivar as a spy until she was captured by the Spanish. Before she was executed in Bogota's main plaza, she exclaimed: "Although I am a woman and young, I have more than enough courage to suffer this death and a thousand more."[10] But women still lived in patriarchal societies that offered them few new legal or political rights. Finally, unlike the founders of the United States, Latin America's new leaders were largely unable to form democratic governments. Bolivar could not hold his own country together, and in 1830 Gran Colombia broke into Colombia, Ecuador, and Venezuela. Meanwhile, Uruguay and Paraguay split off from Argentina, and Bolivia separated from Peru. Disillusioned, Bolivar concluded that Latin America was ungovernable.

Political change also came to Mexico and Brazil but less violently (see Map 19.2). In 1810 two progressive Mexican Catholic priests, the creole Manuel Hidalgo and the mestizo Jose Maria Morelos **(moh-RAY-los)**, mobilized peasants and miners and launched a revolt promoting independence, the abolition of slavery, and social reform. Creole conservatives and royalists suppressed that revolt, but a compromise between various factions brought Mexico independence in 1822 under a creole general, Agustin de Iturbide **(ah-goos-TEEN deh ee-tur-BEE-deh)** (1783–1824), who proclaimed himself emperor. However, the anti-Spanish alliance of creoles, mestizos, and Indians unraveled and a republican revolt ousted Iturbide. The Central American peoples split off from Mexico and by 1839 had splintered into five states.

Portuguese Brazil also experienced dissension. By the late 1700s Brazil was the wealthiest part of the Portuguese colonial realm, but only the white plantation and gold mine owners benefited from the prosperity. Since Brazil was the major importer of slaves, accounting for a quarter to a

akg-images

Simon Bolivar The main leader of the anti-Spanish war of independence in northern South America, Bolivar came to be known as "the Liberator," a symbol of Latin American nationalism and the struggle for political freedom.

Primary Source: The Jamaican Letter Simon Bolivar shares his thoughts in 1815 on the present and future of the Latin American independence movement.

Brazilian Political Change

OREGON COUNTRY
(Joint U.S.-British occupation)

BRITISH NORTH AMERICA (CANADA) (Gr. Br.)

Mississippi R.

Colorado R.

UNITED STATES

New York
Philadelphia
Washington, D.C.
Charleston

MEXICO 1821

Rio Grande

San Antonio
New Orleans

Gulf of Mexico

ATLANTIC OCEAN

BAHAMA IS. (Gr. Br.)

Havana

CUBA (Spain)

HAITI 1804

PUERTO RICO (Spain)

Mexico City
Veracruz

BRITISH HONDURAS (Gr. Br.)
GUATEMALA
Guatemala City

JAMAICA (Gr. Br.)

Caribbean Sea

UNITED PROVINCES OF CENTRAL AMERICA 1823–1839

Panama

TRINIDAD (Gr. Br.)

Caracas

VENEZUELA
Socorro
Bogotá

Magdalena R.

Orinoco R.

BR. GUIANA (Gr. Br.)
DUTCH GUIANA (Neth.)
FRENCH GUIANA (France)

GRAN COLOMBIA 1819–1830

Quito

ECUADOR

Galápagos Islands

Equator 0°

Amazon R.

EMPIRE OF BRAZIL 1822

PACIFIC OCEAN

Lima

PERU 1824

BOLIVIA 1825
La Paz
Sucre

Salvador

Paraná R.

20°S

PARAGUAY 1811

Rio de Janeiro
São Paulo

CHILE 1817

UNITED PROVINCES OF THE RIO DE LA PLATA 1816

URUGUAY 1828
Montevideo

Valparaíso
Santiago

ARGENTINA
Buenos Aires
Bahía Blanca

PATAGONIA
(Disputed between Argentina and Chile)

0   500   1000 Km.
0   500   1000 Mi.

Islas Malvinas
(Falkland Islands)

80°W   60°W

1811 Year independence gained
Colony

40°W

40°N

20°N

Map 19.2 Latin American Independence, 1840

By 1840 all of Latin America except for Cuba and Puerto Rico, still Spanish colonies, had become independent, with Brazil and Mexico the largest countries. Later the Central American provinces and Gran Colombia would fragment into smaller nations, and Argentina would annex Patagonia.

 Interactive Map

third of all Africans arriving in the Americas, blacks vastly outnumbered Native Americans. Disgruntled Afro-Brazilians demanded a better life, but they faced many setbacks, including the defeat of a 1799 revolt in the northeastern state of Bahia (buh-HEE-uh). Yet, Brazil enjoyed a nearly bloodless transition to independence. In 1808 the Portuguese royal family and government sought refuge in Brazil to escape the Napoleonic wars, and Brazilians increasingly viewed themselves as separate from Portugal. A member of the royal family still in Brazil, Dom Pedro (1798–1834), severed ties with Portugal completely in 1822 and became emperor of Brazil as Pedro I. However, although an elected parliament was set up, most Brazilians had no vote and Pedro I governed autocratically. Politics involved a small group of merchants, landowners, and the royal family.

SECTION SUMMARY

- Many people in the North American colonies chafed against British rule and, inspired by Enlightenment thinkers, pushed for independence, while others, including many Indians and black slaves, sided with the British.

- After a first failed attempt at confederation, the thirteen American colonies agreed upon a system that balanced federal and state powers, but the American Revolution did little to change the social order and did not extend equal rights to blacks, women, and Indians.

- The French Revolution, which aimed to wrest control from the nobility and the clergy, achieved some of its progressive goals and was an inspiration to some societies, but it led to a period of war and widespread terror, and its excesses turned others away from revolution.

- In the tumultuous aftermath of the French Revolution, Napoleon Bonaparte seized power, implemented some of the Revolution's egalitarian ideals in law, and waged a series of overly ambitious wars that eventually led to his defeat and the Congress of Vienna, at which many pre-Revolution

boundaries were restored. Throughout the first half of the nineteenth century, other revolutions against despotic regimes rose up and were usually crushed, but nevertheless democratic ideals made gradual progress.

- After over a decade of revolutionary struggle, the Afro-Haitian slaves won their freedom from the French, but they soon fell under the control of an African-born despot.

- Spain controlled its American colonies extremely tightly, leaving little room for intellectual freedom or economic mobility, and put down many revolts through the end of the eighteenth century.

- Rising dissatisfaction among South Americans, particularly creoles, led to successful independence movements throughout the continent, though the newly free nations had trouble forming representative and democratic governments.

- After Mexico obtained its independence, the coalition that had opposed the Spanish fell apart, while members of the Portuguese royal family who fled to Brazil helped it to obtain its independence peacefully.

THE INDUSTRIAL REVOLUTION AND ECONOMIC GROWTH

How did industrialization reshape economic and social life?

The **Industrial Revolution**, a dramatic transformation in the production and transportation of goods, was a major force reshaping the economic, political, and social patterns of Europe and later of North America and Japan. For the first time in history, the shackles were taken off the productive power of societies. Henceforth, people became capable of the rapid, constant, and seemingly limitless increase of goods and services. This revolution was perhaps the greatest transformation in society since settled farming, urbanization, and the first states arose thousands of years ago. In the late 1700s breakthroughs in productivity were made in Britain and then spread across the English Channel to western Europe and the Atlantic to North America, eventually transforming the limited European power of 1750 into Western domination over much of the world by 1914.

Industrial Revolution A dramatic transformation in the production and transportation of goods.

The Age of Machines

The Industrial Revolution and the changes it generated had deep roots. The Renaissance, Reformation, Scientific Revolution, and Enlightenment had generated new ways of thought and understandings of the natural and physical world, and the discovery of new lands, animals, plants, peoples, and cultures stimulated curiosity about the world. Commercial capitalism and conquest overseas formed political and economic links between the Americas, the African coast, some Asian societies, and western Europe, allowing Europeans to acquire natural resources and great wealth overseas for investment in new technologies and incentives for producing more commodities for the world market.

Rise of British Industries

Great Britain became the world's leading trading nation. By the early 1700s British inventors experimented with steam power and spinning machines, and accelerating world demand spurred Britain to replace India as the main supplier of cotton textiles. Britain had many advantages over rival countries, including a diverse intellectual atmosphere, a reasonably democratic political system, favorable terrain on which to build transportation networks, abundant raw materials like coal and iron, and many water sources to run machines. As a result, between the 1780s and 1830s Britain dominated European industrialization. Profits from the British-controlled Caribbean islands and North American colonies and from British trading posts in India were particularly crucial in funding the Industrial Revolution. Some British companies made vast fortunes from the trans-Atlantic slave trade, and companies owning sugar, cotton, and tobacco plantations in the Americas often invested their excess capital in new British industries. The English Midlands region east of Liverpool, a slave trade port, and northern Wales, near rich coal and iron ore fields, became the center of British industry (see Map 19.3).

Map 19.3 Industrial Transformation in England
British industrialization mostly occurred near coalfields and iron ore deposits, spurring the rise of cities such as Birmingham, Leeds, Liverpool, and Manchester.

e Interactive Map

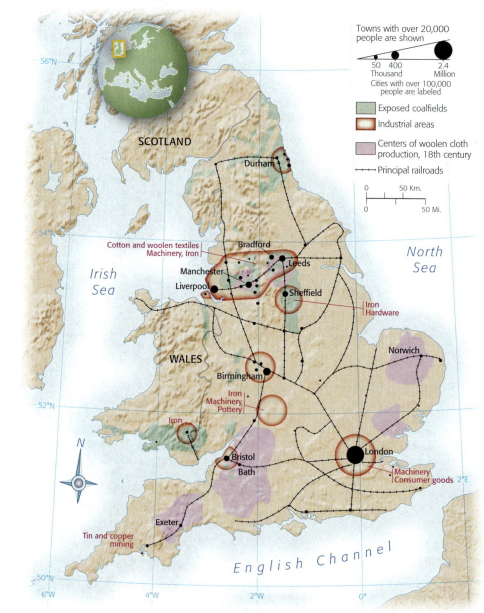

The Industrial Revolution introduced an era in which machines produced goods and increasingly performed more human tasks, reshaping peoples' lives. Instead of making things by hand with the aid of simple tools, workers now used increasingly complicated chemical processes and machines moved by energy derived from steam and other inanimate sources rather than people or animals. By tapping the resources of the earth's crust and turning them into commodities, the Industrial Revolution created great material richness and great misery. Between the 1770s and 1914 a Europe of peasant holdings, country estates, and domestic workshops became a Europe of sprawling and polluted industrial cities such as Manchester, with a wide gap between the few rich and the many poor (see Chronology: European Politics and Economy, 1750–1914). In the past 250 years the material culture of Europe changed more than it had in the previous 750 years. Today citizens of industrialized nations use transportation, wear fabrics, and employ building materials inconceivable in 1750. As one measure of how the world changed, one need only consider some of the words that first appeared in the English language between 1780 and 1850: *industry, factory, middle class, working class, engineer, crisis, statistics, strike,* and *pauper.*

The Industrial Revolution triggered continual technological innovations and a corresponding increase in economic activity. Inventions in one industry stimulated inventions in others. New cotton machines created a demand for more plentiful and reliable power than could be provided by traditional water wheels and horses. The steam pump invented in England in 1712 was inefficient, but in 1774 James Watt (1736–1819), a Scottish inventor who gained financial support from a wealthy merchant, produced the first successful rotary steam engine. Useful in many types of industrial activities, steam engines provided power for the textile mills, iron furnaces, flour mills, and mines. When used in railroads and steamships, steam power conquered time and space, bringing the world much closer together. Watt's backer, Matthew Boulton, argued that he had to sell steam engines to all the world to make money.

The new machines and engines required increased supplies of iron, steel, and coal, spurring improved mining and metalworking and then transportation facilities to move the coal and ore. After a while technological and economic growth came to be accepted as normal. The British novelist William Thackeray celebrated the changes in 1860: "It is only yesterday, but what a gulf between now and then! *Then* was the old world. Stagecoaches, riding horses, pack-horses, knights in armor, Norman invaders, Roman legions. But your railroad starts a new era."[11] Mechanization also provoked fear. Between 1815 and 1830 anti-industrialization activists in Britain known as **Luddites**, mostly skilled textile workers, invaded factories and destroyed machines in a mass protest against the effects of mechanization. Ultimately the Luddite cause proved futile. The British government sent in troops to stop the destruction and made the wrecking of machines a crime punishable by death.

For decades Britain was the world's richest, most competitive nation, with a reputation as the workshop of the world. The new factories mass-produced goods of better quality and lower price than traditional handicrafts, giving British merchants marketable goods and a powerful need to sell them to the world to recoup their heavy investments in machinery and materials. By the mid-1800s Britain produced two-thirds of the world's coal, half the iron, and half the cotton cloth and other manufactured goods. A British poet boasted that "England's a perfect World, hath Indies, too, Correct your Maps, Newcastle [a center of the coal industry] is [silver rich] Peru."[12] No other state could substantially threaten Britain's economic and political position.

However, the British also invested some of their huge profits in western Europe, spreading the Industrial Revolution across the English Channel between the 1830s and 1870s. Industrial operations became concentrated in regions rich in coal and iron ore. Capitalizing on its mineral reserves, prosperous trading cities, and a strategic location, Belgium industrialized in the early 1800s, building an ambitious railroad system to transport coal, iron, and manufactured goods. By the 1830s France, where the government helped fund industrial activity, also begun constructing a national railroad network. In the German states, political fragmentation before 1870 discouraged industrialization, except in several coal-rich regions, and some countries, including Portugal, Spain, and Austria-Hungary, remained largely agricultural. By 1914, however, industrialization was widespread around Europe and had also taken root in North America and Japan, and large numbers of people lived in cities and worked in factories.

CHRONOLOGY
European Politics and Economy, 1750–1914

1770s Beginning of Industrial Revolution in England

1774 James Watt's first rotary steam engine

1776 Adam Smith's *The Wealth of Nations*

1800 British Act of Union

1821–1830 Greek war of independence

1830–1831 Wave of revolutions across Europe

1831 Formation of Young Italy movement by Mazzini

1845–1846 Irish potato famine

1848 Wave of revolts across Europe; *The Communist Manifesto* by Marx and Engels

1851 Great Exhibition in London

1859–1870 Unification of Italy

1862–1871 Unification of Germany

1870s–1914 Second Industrial Revolution

Luddites Anti-industrialization activists in Britain who destroyed machines in a mass protest against the effects of mechanization.

Spreading the Industrial Revolution

Industrial Sheffield
This painting of one of the key British industrial cities, Sheffield, in 1858 shows the factories, many specializing in producing steel and metal goods, that dominated the landscape.

Courtesy, Sheffield Archives and Local Studies Library

Industrial Capitalism and Society

Industrialization and the vast increase in manufactured goods transformed commercial capitalism, dominated by large trading companies, into industrial capitalism centered around manufacturing. European industrial firms made and exported manufactured goods and imported raw materials, such as iron ore, to make more goods. Since economic success depended on a large and steady turnover of goods, advertising developed to create demand, and banking and financial institutions expanded their operations. Governments supported the industrialists, bankers, and financiers by fostering policies to maximize private wealth.

Economic Philosophers

Economic philosophers emerged to praise and justify British-style capitalism. The Scottish professor and Enlightenment supporter Adam Smith (1723–1790) helped formulate modern economics theory, known as neoclassical economics, in his book *The Wealth of Nations* (1776), which advocated the principle of **laissez faire**. Rather than allowing government to interfere in the marketplace through laws regulating business and profits, Smith believed in self-interest, arguing that the "invisible hand" of the marketplace would turn the entrepreneur's individual greed into a rising standard of living for all. He also introduced the new idea of a permanently growing economy, reinforcing the long-standing Western view of progress. History was going somewhere.

laissez faire Restriction of government interference in the marketplace, such as laws regulating business and profits.

Smith's free trade philosophy refuted medieval Christian attitudes that condemned mercantile activity and also helped end the mercantilism of the Early Modern Era. The free traders believed that Britain should serve as the world's industrial center, into which flowed raw materials and out of which flowed manufactured goods. But Smith saw the potential for both good and evil in capitalism, acknowledging that free enterprise did not necessarily generate prosperity for all, since the interests of the manufacturers were not necessarily those of society. Hence, he encouraged businesses to pay their employees high wages, writing that "no society can surely be flourishing and happy of which the far greater part of its members are poor and miserable. [They should be] well fed, clothed and lodged."[13]

Second Industrial Revolution

Around 1870, the Second Industrial Revolution, characterized by technological change, mass production, and specialization, commenced, led by the United States and Germany. The increasing application of science to industry spurred improvement in the electrical, chemical, optical, and automotive industries and brought new inventions such as electricity grids, radio, the internal combustion engine, gasoline, and the flush toilet. By 1900 Germany was Europe's main producer of electrical goods and chemicals. Factory production was now often done on an assembly line of separate specialized tasks; for example, a worker in an automobile assembly line might only install wheels. The Second Industrial Revolution promoted a shift from many competitive enterprises to giant monopolies, led by tycoons with unprecedented wealth.

The concentration of capital in "big business" gave a few businessmen and bankers, such as the Krupp family in Germany and the Rockefellers in the United States, vast economic power and control over many industries. For instance, Alfred Krupp (1812–1887) became Europe's leading manufacturer of arms and also owned steel mills and mines. The monopolies emerged because the factories, including new industries producing such useful innovations as aluminum and electrical power, required a heavy capital investment to start, eliminating many small businesses. A long depression in the late 1800s also undermined competition, encouraging businesses to merge or cooperate and to moderate slumps by fixing prices. These economic changes reshaped government policies and generated a drive to colonize more of the world to ensure access to resources and markets.

Social Consequences

The Industrial Revolution also affected both men and women and all social and economic classes (see Chapter 20). In 1800 Europe remained mainly agricultural. A century later there was a greater division of labor, growing social problems, most people living in cities, and the replacement of human workers by machines. The factory system compelled the migration of millions of people from the countryside into cities, which were overcrowded and unhealthy, with high rates of alcoholism, prostitution, and crime. City people crowded into festering slums, worked long hours for low wages, and learned new lifestyles. French writer Alexis de Tocqueville **(TOKE-vill)** described the atmosphere of Manchester in 1835:

> *The footsteps of a busy crowd, the crunching wheels of machinery, the shriek of steam from boilers, the regular beat of the looms, the heavy rumble of carts, these are the noises from which you can never escape in the somber half-light of these streets. Crowds are ever hurrying this way and that, but their footsteps are brisk, their looks preoccupied, and their appearance somber and harsh.*[14]

Factories, mines, and cities reshaped European life. Many factory workers labored fourteen- or even eighteen-hour days in a system of rigid discipline, with no insurance for accidents, ill health, or old age. Many children worked seven days a week in mines or factories. In the mid-nineteenth-century English cotton mills, about one-quarter of workers were adult men, over half were women and girls, and the rest were boys younger than eighteen. Workers such as the English coal miner Tommy Armstrong sometimes used songs to express their solidarity with each other and resentment of those they worked for (see Profile: Tommy Armstrong, Bard of the English Coal Mines). Gradually many people began to think of themselves as members in a social and economic class that had interests of its own in opposition to other classes. The working classes, such as the coal miners and factory workers, were the largest group. The middle classes included businesspeople, professionals, and prosperous farmers. A salaried labor force, today known as "white-collar" workers, emerged to handle sales and paperwork. For example, some 90,000 women worked as secretaries in Britain by 1901. The middle class prided itself on a keen work ethic and attributed poverty to poor work habits and lack of initiative. Meanwhile, in many countries the beleaguered aristocrats struggled to maintain their dominance over the governments and churches. Crime increased as the gap between the haves and the have-nots became more apparent.

Industrial Workers

SECTION SUMMARY

- The Industrial Revolution began in England, which had great stores of capital derived from overseas trade, an openness to new ideas, and abundant natural resources, and the revolution gradually spread throughout western Europe and North America.

- As technology played an increasingly important role in the economy and in people's lives, with machines constantly evolving and being put to new uses, some people marveled at the technological change while others, such as the Luddites, resisted it.

- Commercial capitalism was changed into industrial capitalism centered on manufacturing, and economic philosophers such as Adam Smith advocated laissez faire, the idea that the market, if left alone, would improve everyone's standard of living and create ever-increasing wealth and progress.

- The Second Industrial Revolution ushered in an age of specialization and mass production, and it favored monopolistic corporations that could afford enormous investments in new technology.

- The Industrial Revolution brought many people from the countryside to cities, where they encountered crowding, noise, new social problems, and hard labor conditions.

- As a result of the revolution, new classes arose—the working class; the middle classes, including a new secretarial force; and the aristocrats—and the gap between the haves and the have-nots widened.

TOMMY ARMSTRONG, BARD OF THE ENGLISH COAL MINES

Tommy Armstrong (1849–1919) was one of the most famous song-makers who came out of the new industrial working class of Britain. From a poor family and with little formal schooling, Armstrong began working in the mine pits around Durham in the Northumbrian region of north England at age nine. Since the youngster was born with crooked legs, his older brother William carried him to work on his back. Tommy worked first as a trapper-boy, opening the ventilation doors for coal and miners to pass through. Later he went on to more demanding jobs in the pits.

In the later nineteenth century many miners in Durham and elsewhere composed rhymes and songs. Armstrong was already writing song lyrics at age twelve. Eventually he married, but miners' wages barely covered expenses for his large family—his overworked wife and fourteen children—prompting Armstrong to seek additional money by writing songs and having them printed. Single sheets, known as broadsides, containing lyrics were then sold in pubs to raise money for his family but also to buy beer for himself. The balladeer of Tyneside, as he was known, referring to the nearby Tyne River, developed a legendary thirst. His son claimed, "Me dad's Muse was a mug of beer." Armstrong engaged in song duels with rival songwriters and even made up verses about the people in the houses he passed on his way home from work or pub. His songs usually had a strong sense of social class and social criticism. One of them encouraged educating the young, in part to avoid trouble with the law: "Send your bairns [children] to school, Learn them all you can. Make scholarship your faithful friend, and you'll never see the school-board man [truant officer]." He set his songs to folk and music-hall tunes as well as to Irish melodies brought by the thousands of Irish immigrants to the mines.

Armstrong became renowned for writing songs reflecting the miner's increasingly radical views and ballads to memorialize mining disasters, usually to raise money for union funds or the relief of orphans and widows. For example, in 1882, after an explosion killed seventy-four miners, Armstrong produced a song commemorating the lost men: "Oh, let's not think of tomorrow lest we disappointed be. Our joys may turn to sorrow as we all may daily see. God protect the lonely widow and raise each dropping head; Be a father to the orphans, never let them cry for bread." Conscious of his responsibility, he claimed that "when you're the Pitman's [coalminer's] Poet and looked up for it, if a disaster or a strike goes by without a song from you, they say: What's with Tommy Armstrong? Has someone let out all the inspiration?"

Armstrong was especially productive in the last two decades of the 1800s when strikes were common and the Miners' Union grew rapidly from 36,000 to over 200,000 members. As the struggles between miners and mine owners became more bitter, the union grew more assertive and organized. Armstrong wrote strike songs to give information and courage to miners, but also to collect money for hungry families of strikers. Some of the worst conflicts erupted in 1892, when the Durham miners were asked to take a large pay cut. When the union refused, the workers were locked out of their workplaces, prompting one of Armstrong's most famous songs: "In our Durham County I am sorry for to say, That hunger and starvation is increasing every day. For want of food and coals, we know not what to do, But with your kind assistance, we will stand the battle through. Our work is taken from us now, they care not if we die, For they [the mine owners] can eat the best of food, and drink the best when dry." After months of labor strife, the union pragmatically agreed to a lower pay reduction. The songs of Tommy Armstrong and other industrial balladeers provide a chronicle of the Industrial Revolution and the ways it shaped the lives of millions of people.

THINKING ABOUT THE PROFILE

1. How did Armstrong's life reflect the working conditions and often hardships imposed on workers by the Industrial Revolution?

2. What did the songs of industrial balladeers like Armstrong tell us about how working-class people confronted the realities of industrial society?

Note: Quotations from A. L. Lloyd, *Folk Song in England.* Copyright © 1967 by International Publishers. Reprinted with permission of International Publishers Co./New York.

Courtesy, Northern Recording Company, UK

Tommy Armstrong Known as the "Pitman's (coalminer's) Poet," Armstrong worked in the coalfields around Durham, in England, and wrote many songs celebrating the miners' struggles for a better life.

NATIONALISM, LIBERALISM, AND SOCIALISM

How did nationalism, liberalism, and socialism differ from each other?

Modern Europe also produced three new ideologies—nationalism, liberalism, and social-ism—that influenced societies and that continue to shape our world. An **ideology** is a coherent, widely shared system of ideas about the nature of the social, political, and economic realm. Nationalism fostered unified countries, liberalism encouraged democratic governments, and socialism sparked movements to counteract the power of industrial capitalism and the social dislocations generated by industrialization.

ideology A coherent, widely shared system of ideas about the nature of the social, political, and economic realm.

Nations and Nationalism

Nationalism, a primary loyalty to, and identity with, a nation bound by a common culture, government, and shared territory, greatly influenced Europe and the Americas in this era. Nationalists insisted that support for country transcended loyalty to family, village, church, region, social class, monarch, or ethnic group. Many peoples had a growing sense of belonging to a nation, such as France or Italy, that shared a common identity separate from, and often better than, those of other nations. For example, a Swiss newspaper proclaimed in 1848 that the "nation [Switzerland] stands before us as an undeniable reality. The Swiss of different cantons [small self-governing states] will henceforth be perceived and act as members of a single nation."[15] Some historians conceive of the nation as an "imagined community" that grew in the minds of people living in the same society.

nationalism A primary loyalty to, and identity with, a nation bound by a common culture, government, and shared territory.

Nationalist Visions

Nationalism provided a cement that bonded all citizens to the state but also fostered wars with rival nations. With its vision of uniting people who shared many traditions and a sense of common destiny, nationalism became a popular, explosive force, appealing particularly to the rising middle classes and intellectuals struggling to gain more political power while claiming that the nation included all the people, regardless of social status. This perception of collective identity and the nation's special nature was captured by the India-born English poet Rudyard Kipling: "If England was what England seems, An' not the England of our dreams, But only putty, brass an' paint, 'Ow quick we'd drop 'er! But she ain't!"[16]

Most historians credit the birth of modern nationalism to France and Great Britain in the late eighteenth and early nineteenth centuries. The French revolutionaries proclaimed that all sovereignty emanated from the nation, rather than from individuals or groups, and the British began to conceive of themselves as one nation composed of several peoples. England and Wales had united in 1536 under English monarchs, joined by Scotland in 1707, but there was not yet a Britain; the peoples who shared the island identified themselves as English, Scottish, or Welsh. But the spread of English power led to the suffocation of the Scottish and Welsh cultures and languages. Although some Welsh and Scots remained wary of England, eventually most accepted being part of Great Britain, a linking formalized in the British Act of Union in 1800.

Changing Political Landscape

Nationalism also transformed Europe's political landscape. In 1750 large parts of Europe were dominated by multinational states with ethnically diverse populations. One royal family, the Vienna-based Habsburgs, ruled Austria, Hungary, the Czech lands, Belgium, and parts of Italy. In contrast, nationalism fostered **nation-states**, politically centralized countries with defined territorial boundaries, such as Italy, Belgium, and Norway. By 1914 only the Russian and Habsburg-ruled Austro-Hungarian empires remained major multinational states in Europe.

nation-states Politically centralized countries with defined territorial boundaries.

Greeks, Italians, and Germans made some of the most dramatic efforts to create unified nations. The Greeks, long a part of the Turkish-dominated Ottoman Empire, claimed nationhood through violence. While Greeks served in the Ottoman government and Greek merchants dominated commerce in Ottoman-ruled western Asia, some Greeks sent their sons to western Europe to study. Returning home with nationalist ideas, they organized an uprising for independence in 1821, killing many Turks. The Ottomans responded by massacring Greek villages, pillaging churches, and hanging the leader of the Greek Orthodox Church in Istanbul, inflaming western European opinion. Aided by the intervention of Britain, France, and Russia, Greece became independent in 1830, inspiring other restless Ottoman subjects. In 1862 Romania also became independent.

Making Greece and Italy

Unlike the Greeks, Italians long cultivated a dream of unity. The Italian speakers were divided into many small states ruled by the Habsburgs, the Holy Roman Empire, or the pope. In 1831 the fiery Giuseppi Mazzini (jew-SEP-pay mots-EE-nee) (1805–1872), an exiled Genoese political philosopher, founded the Young Italy movement, which advocated one Italian nation. He also promoted a republican government and women's rights, radical ideas in Italy. Mazzini's example inspired nationalists and democrats elsewhere in Europe, who formed imitative organizations such as Young Poland. In 1859 Italian nationalists began an armed struggle for Italian unity. Forces under Giuseppi Garibaldi **(gar-uh-BOWL-dee)** (1807–1882), who had nurtured his passion for Italy during years of exile in South America, created the kingdom of Italy in 1861. In 1870 Italian troops entered the last Papal State, Rome, reuniting Italy for the first time since the Roman Empire. The job of creating Italians who shared a common national vision would take longer.

German Unification

German unification also came in stages. In 1862 the Prussian prime minister, Otto von Bismarck (1815–1898), brought together many northern German states under Prussian domination. Bismarck came from the landed nobility and had spent his youth gambling and womanizing before beginning a rapid political ascent. Hostile to business and democratic political rights, he united the Germans through warfare, a policy he characterized as "blood and iron." War with Denmark added to Prussian territory, and the defeat of Austria in 1866 drove the Habsburgs out of all their German holdings west of Austria. A war with France added southern Germany and the Alsace-Lorraine border region. In 1871 King William I of Prussia was declared *kaiser* (emperor) of a united Germany, by now one of Europe's major powers.

Frustrated Nationalisms

Some peoples could not satisfy their nationalist aspirations. The Poles frequently but unsuccessfully rebelled against their Russian and German rulers. Jewish minorities, scattered around Europe and often having little in common, faced daunting barriers. Many east European and Russian Jews had been restricted to all-Jewish villages and urban neighborhoods known as ghettoes, where they often maintained conservative cultural and religious traditions. Yet, many Jews, especially in Germany, France, and Britain, adopted a secular approach, moving toward assimilation with the dominant culture. Reacting against widespread anti-Semitism, other Jews gravitated to revolutionary groups or to **Zionism**, a movement founded by Hungarian-born journalist Theodor Herzl **(HERT-suhl)** (1860–1904) that sought a Jewish homeland. In 1948 the Zionists formed the state of Israel in Palestine.

Zionism A movement that sought a Jewish homeland.

Ireland had been a colony of England for centuries, and Irish opposition to harsh English rule simmered, sometimes erupting in violence. The English attempted to destroy the language, religion, poetry, literature, dress, and music of the Irish people. As an Irish folk song from 1798 protested, "She's the most distressful country that ever yet was seen. [The English] are hanging men and women for the wearing of the green [Ireland's unofficial national color]."[17] Much of Ireland's farming land belonged to rich English landlords, and after 1800 the English mounted even more laws restricting Irish rights, deporting thousands who resisted to Australia. Many Irish men, with few job prospects, were recruited into the British army, to fight in England's colonial wars abroad. Irish ballads are filled with men going out to fight, of mothers or wives greeting their wounded men when they returned, or of families grieving for those who would never return. Then during the 1840s the potato crop failed for several successive years because of a fungus blight. One and a half million

Battle of Langhada
The Greek war for independence from the Ottoman Turks gained strong support from liberals and nationalists all over Europe. This painting, by the Greek artist Panagiotis Zographos, uses Byzantine art traditions to show Greek soldiers riding to fight the Turks in the Battle of Langhada.

Irish died from starvation while English landlords ejected Irish peasants from the land so that they could replace subsistence food growing with more profitable sheep raising. As a result, millions of Irish sought escape from poverty and repression by emigrating to the Americas and Australia.

But the Irish still rebelled against British rule. The Fenians (FEE-nians), a secret society dedicated to Irish independence, were transformed by 1905 into Sinn Fein (shin FANE) (Gaelic for "Ourselves Alone"), which turned to violence against English targets. Sinn Fein extremists formed the Irish Republican Army, which organized a rebellion on Easter Monday, 1916, in which some 1,500 volunteers seized key buildings in Dublin and proclaimed a republic in Ireland. The English quickly crushed the rising, executed the ringleaders, and jailed 2,000 of the participants, but Sinn Fein, the IRA, and terrorism continued to bedevil the English colonizers.

Liberalism and Parliamentary Democracy

While nationalism reshaped states, another ideology offered a vision of democracy and individual freedom. Influenced by Enlightenment thinkers such as John Locke and Baron de Montesquieu, **liberalism** favored emancipating the individual from all governmental, economic, or religious restraints. Liberals, mainly of middle-class background, favored representative government, the right to vote, and basic civil liberties such as freedom of speech, religion, assembly, and the press. The Scottish philosopher John Stuart Mill (1806–1873) offered the most eloquent defense of free expression, writing that no one should restrict what arguments a legislature or executive should be allowed to hear. Liberal politicians fought against slavery, advocated religious toleration, and worked for more popular participation in government.

Democratic decision making is an old and widespread idea. Village democracies that allowed many residents to voice their opinions and shape decisions had long existed in various tribal and stateless societies of Asia, Africa, and the Americas. The classical Greeks and Romans had also introduced democratic institutions, but political rights were restricted to a small minority of male citizens. Representative institutions later appeared in England, the Netherlands, Switzerland, Iceland, and Poland. By the nineteenth century liberal democracy came to mean choice and competition, usually between contending political parties and policies, within a constitutional framework that allows free choice for the electorate. Eventually some nations such as Britain adopted **parliamentary democracy**, government by representatives elected by the people. Liberalism proved particularly popular in Britain and the United States, providing the bedrock for the United States' democratic Constitution and Bill of Rights. To protect against tyranny, the nation's founders mandated a separation of executive, legislative, and judicial powers.

Democracy had gradually grown in Britain as royal power declined over several centuries. The popular Queen Victoria (r. 1837–1901) reigned over Britain for sixty-four years after becoming queen at eighteen, and, with her German-born husband, Prince Albert, provided a model of morality and stability. But the British monarch, even one as respected as Queen Victoria, was no longer very powerful, exercising influence mostly behind the scenes. Prime ministers, elected by the majority of Parliament members, now made national and foreign policy. The base of democracy gradually widened as the elected House of Commons exercised more power than the appointed and hereditary House of Lords. Both houses featured lively debate between political parties.

But democratic access remained somewhat limited in Britain, and British reformers wanted average people to have more voice in the electoral system. While the Reform Act of 1832 increased the number of voters, all voters were upper- and middle-class males. The major working-class protest movement, Chartism, called for universal adult male suffrage, a secret ballot, and paying members of Parliament so that people without wealth could run for office. Some Chartists, led by Elizabeth Neesom, advocated the right of women to participate in government. Chartists used demonstrations, strikes, boycotts, and riots to support their demands; however, because the wealthy feared that radical ideas such as wealth redistribution might be proposed, these measures had little success.

Socialism, Marxism, and Social Reform

While liberals favored preservation of wealth and property rights and feared radical popular movements, a third ideology encouraged protest. In contrast to liberalism's promotion of individual liberty, **socialism** offered a vision of social equality and the common, or public, ownership of economic institutions such as factories. Socialism grew out of the painful social disruption that accompanied the Industrial Revolution. Utopian socialists in Britain, France, and North America, many influenced by Christian ideals, offered visions of perfect, cooperative

Democracy and Freedom

liberalism An ideology that favored emancipating the individual from all restraints, whether governmental, economic, or religious.

parliamentary democracy Government by representatives elected by the people.

British Democracy

Socialist Visions

socialism An ideology offering a vision of social equality and the common, or public, ownership of economic institutions such as factories.

societies shaped by the common good. A few even founded communal villages based on service to the community and renunciation of personal wealth. The British industrialist Robert Owen (1771–1858) set up a model factory town around his cotton mill and later founded a model socialist community, New Harmony, in Indiana. Some proponents of women's rights, such as Emma Martin (1812–1851) in Britain and Flora Tristan (1801–1844) in France, promoted socialism as the solution to end female oppression, stirring controversy. Clergymen opposed to feminism and socialism urged their congregations to disrupt Martin's speeches, and outraged mobs chased and stoned her.

Karl Marx

Karl Marx (1818–1883) had the most long-lasting influence on socialist thought, and his ideas, known as Marxism, became one of the major intellectual and political influences around the world. Marx, a German Jew with a passion for social justice, studied philosophy at the University of Berlin and then worked as a journalist before settling in London. He worked closely with his German friend, Friedrich Engels (1820–1895), who managed his father's cotton factory in England. Engels, who collaborated in writing and editing some of Marx's books, introduced Marx to the degraded condition of English industrial workers. In *The Communist Manifesto* (1848), Marx developed a scenario in which the downtrodden could redress the wrongs inflicted upon them by rising up in a violent socialist revolution, seizing power from the capitalists, and creating a new society (see Witness to the Past: The Communist View of Past, Present, and Future). Marx argued that, through violent revolution, peoples can change the inequitable political, social, and economic patterns inherited from the past. He also opposed nationalism, writing that working people had common interests and needed to cooperate across borders. In 1864 Marx helped form the International Workingmen's Association to work toward those goals.

Marx was a product of his scientific age and considered his ideas as laws of history. In his most influential work, the three-volume *Capital*, he argued that historical change resulted from struggle between antagonistic social classes. All social and economic systems, he suggested, contain contradictions that doom them to conflict, which generates a higher stage of development. For example, feudalism was undermined by the confrontation between nobles, merchants, and serfs, leading to capitalism. Eventually, Marx predicted, this process would replace capitalism with socialism, where all would share in owning the means of production and the state would serve the interests of the masses rather than the privileged classes. Finally would come communism, where the state would wither away and all would share the wealth, free to realize their human potential without exploitation by capitalists or governments. Such a vision of redistributing wealth and power proved attractive to many disgruntled people in Europe and later around the world.

Marxian Ideas

Marx offered ideas that economists and historians have debated ever since. He believed that the nature of the economic system and technology determined all aspects of society, including religious values, social relations, government, and laws. In each system, such as feudalism or capitalism, the ways in which land and labor were allocated to production, work was organized (such as on medieval manors or in capitalist factories), and products were distributed, as well as the tools used, determined such patterns as family relationships and the gods people worshiped. Marx also argued that religion was the "opiate of the people," encouraging people not to protest but to fatalistically accept their lot in life in hopes of earning a better afterlife. He criticized capitalism for fostering extremes of wealth and poverty and for separating workers from ownership and management of the means of production—the farms, mines, factories, and businesses where they labored—to furnish wealth to the owners as well as to the urban-based, mostly commercial, middle class that Marx called the bourgeoisie. Marx observed that the industrial working class, the **proletariat**, grew more miserable as wealth became concentrated in giant monopolies in the later 1800s.

proletariat The industrial working class.

Spread of Marxism

Marxist ideas attracted a wide following, first in Europe and later in various American, Asian, and African countries. In Europe they stimulated unrest. In 1871, in the aftermath of a disastrous war with Germany and the election of a conservative government, a people's government comprising Marxists, republicans, and other groups briefly gained control of Paris. The Paris Commune, as this government was called, experimented with some socialist programs such as better wages and working conditions. The French government attacked Paris with ruthless force, and in response the Commune supporters (Communards) burned public buildings and killed the Catholic archbishop. The brutality of the French government troops prompted a horrified British reporter to conclude that "Paris the beautiful is Paris the ghastly, the battered, the burning, the blood-splattered."[18] When the dust had cleared, 38,000 Communards had been arrested, 20,000 executed, and 7,500 deported to the South Pacific. Later rebels across Europe would hoist the Marxist banner for radical redistribution of power and privilege.

With its promise of a more equitable society, Marxism became a major world force. Socialist parties were formed all over Europe in the late 1800s and early 1900s, and more radical socialists

The Communist View of Past, Present, and Future

In 1848 Karl Marx and Friedrich Engels published *The Communist Manifesto* as a statement of beliefs and goals for the Communist League, an organization they had founded. In this excerpt Marx and Engels outlined their view of history as founded on class struggle, stressed the formation of the new world economy, and offered communism as the alternative to an oppressive capitalist system. They ended their summary of the problems of contemporary society by inviting the working class to take its future into its own hands through unity and revolution.

A specter is haunting Europe—the specter of communism. All the powers of old Europe have entered into a holy alliance to excise this specter. . . . Where is the party in opposition that has not been decried as communistic by its opponents in power? . . . The history of all hitherto existing society is the history of class struggles. . . . Oppressor and oppressed stood in constant opposition to one another, carried on in an uninterrupted, now hidden, now open fight, a fight that each time ended, either in a revolutionary reconstitution of society at large, or in the common ruin of the contending classes.

In the earlier epochs of history, we find almost everywhere a complicated arrangement of society into various orders, a manifold gradation of social rank. In ancient Rome we have patricians, knights, plebeians, slaves; in the Middle Ages, feudal lords, vassals, guild-masters, journeymen, apprentices, serfs; in almost all these classes, again, subordinate gradations. The modern bourgeois [middle class] society that has sprouted from the ruins of feudal society has not done away with class antagonisms. It has but established new classes, new conditions of oppression, new forms of struggle in place of the old ones.

Our epoch, the epoch of the bourgeoisie, possesses, however, this distinctive feature: it has simplified the class antagonisms. Society as a whole is more and more splitting up into two great hostile camps, into two great classes directly facing each other: bourgeoisie and proletariat (working class). . . . The discovery of America, the rounding of the Cape [of Good Hope], opened up fresh ground for the rising bourgeoisie.

The East Indian and Chinese markets, the colonization of America, trade with the colonies, the increase in the means of exchange and in commodities generally, gave to commerce, to navigation, to industry, an impulse never before known, and, thereby, a rapid development to the revolutionary element in the tottering feudal society. . . . Meantime the markets kept ever growing, the demand ever rising. Even manufacture no longer sufficed. Thereupon, steam and machinery revolutionized industrial production. The place of manufacture was taken by the giant, modern industry, the place of the industrial middle class, by industrial millionaires. . . .

Modern industry has established the world market, for which the discovery of America paved the way. . . . The bourgeoisie, by the rapid improvement of all instruments of production, by the immensely facilitated means of communication, draws all, even the most barbarian, nations into civilization. The cheap prices of its commodities are the heavy artillery with which it batters down all Chinese walls. . . . It compels all nations, on pain of extinction, to adopt the bourgeois mode of production. . . . It creates a world after its own image. . . .

[The Communists] have no interests separate from those of the proletariat as a whole. . . . The immediate aim of the Communists is . . . the formation of the proletariat into a class; the overthrow of the bourgeois supremacy; and the conquest of political power by the proletariat. . . . The Communists disdain to conceal their views and aims. They openly declare that their ends can be attained only by the forcible overthrow of all existing social conditions. Let the ruling classes tremble at a Communistic revolution. The proletarians have nothing to lose but their chains. They have a world to win. WORKING MEN OF ALL COUNTRIES, UNITE!

THINKING ABOUT THE READING

1. What did Marx and Engels identify as the opposing classes in European history?
2. What developments aided the rise of the bourgeoisie to power?
3. What is the goal of the communists?

Source: From *The Communist Manifesto*, trans. 1880. *http://www.anv .edu.au/polisci/marx/classics/manifesto.html.*

soon split off to establish parties that called themselves communist. But while many poor people or industrial workers envied the rich and thought life unfair, they were also inhibited by family, religion, and social connections from joining radical movements or risking their lives in a rebellion that might fail. An English pub toast reflected the desires of people for more immediate pleasures: "If life was a thing that money could buy, the rich would live and the poor might die. Here's oceans of wine, rivers of beer, a nice little wife and ten thousand a year."[19] North Americans had a weaker sense of social class, and Marxism never became as influential in the United States as in parts of Europe. Furthermore, Marx mistakenly believed that socialist revolution would first occur in leading capitalist nations such as Britain and Germany. Instead the first successful socialist revolution came, over three decades after Marx had died, in Russia.

SECTION SUMMARY

- With the rise of nationalism, the inhabitants of a given country came to identify with each other as distinct from, and often better than, the inhabitants of other countries.

- Greece attained nationhood through revolution, Italy through a unification movement, and Germany through war against others, while the Poles, the Irish, and the Jews struggled unsuccessfully to form nations.

- Liberalism, which favored maximizing individual liberty, was particularly influential in Britain and the United States of America.

- Socialism aimed to achieve economic equality through common ownership of industry, and its major proponent, Karl Marx, argued that history is driven by class struggle and that capitalism would inevitably give way to a communist society.

- Marx's ideas exerted a strong influence on the Paris Communards and the founders of labor unions.

- Social Democrats, who rejected Marx's revolutionary ideas and instead favored working to better the lot of workers within a capitalist democracy, managed to

In contrast to the call for revolution, some Marxists favored a more gradual, evolutionary approach of working within constitutional governments and establishing social democracy, a system mixing capitalism and socialism within a parliamentary framework. The first Social Democratic Party was formed in Germany in 1875. Criticizing Marxist revolutionaries, a German Social Democratic leader, Eduard Bernstein (1850–1932), argued that socialists should work less for the better future and more for the better present. Socialists often felt a kinship with people of shared views and class backgrounds in other countries, leading in 1889 to the founding of the Second International Workingmen's Association by nonrevolutionary socialist parties, with the goal of working for world peace, justice, and social reform.

Social Democrats and Marxists actively supported labor unions and strikes to promote worker demands. Although most employers were opposed, unions gradually gained legal recognition as representatives of the work force in many nations. In Britain, France, Germany, the Netherlands, and Sweden, trade unions and labor parties acquired enough political influence to force governments to legislate better working conditions. In the later 1800s governments implemented social reforms to address the ills of the Industrial Revolution, laying the foundation for state-run welfare systems. Many European nations legislated the length of the working day, working conditions, and safety rules. To tackle poverty, Germany and Britain introduced health and unemployment insurance and created old-age pensions. Thus, contrary to Marx's expectations, life for many European workers improved considerably by the early 1900s. But many people still worked in dangerous and unhealthy conditions or faced a ten-hour working day, and child labor continued.

THE RESURGENCE OF WESTERN IMPERIALISM

What factors spurred the Western imperialism of the later 1800s?

The Industrial Revolution provided economic incentives, and nationalism provided political incentives, for European merchants and states to exploit the resources of other lands to enrich their own nations and thwart the ambitions of rival nations. Initially the British were most successful in dominating the growing world economy. But economic, political, and ideological factors eventually fostered a resurgence of imperialism, leading European nations to colonize and dominate much of Asia and Africa, reshaping the global system. With the entire world connected by economic and political networks, history now transcended regions and became truly global.

British Trade, Industrialization, and Empire

British Economic Power

The quest for colonies diminished somewhat in the first phase of the Industrial Revolution, even for Great Britain, who feared no competitor in world trade because it had none. The British free traders, wanting neither economic nor political barriers to their operations, viewed the acquisition of more colonies as too expensive. Britain already controlled or had gained access to valuable territories in the Americas, Africa, Asia, and the Pacific. Although it lost its thirteen North American colonies, it took control of French Canada and Australia. Furthermore, Britain's Spanish and Portuguese rivals suffered even graver losses; most of their Latin American colonies became independent, opening doors for British commercial activity.

British merchants also benefited from new technologies that enabled them to compete all over the world. Steam power meant that sailors were no longer dependent on trade winds, allowing British ships to reach distant shores faster. The first exclusively steam-powered ships, in 1813, took 113 days to travel from England around Africa to India, in contrast to eight or nine months by sailing ships. The completion of the Suez Canal linking the Mediterranean Sea and the Red Sea in 1869 dramatically cut the travel time, and Britain, the canal's major shareholder, extended its influence to East Africa and Southeast Asia. By 1900 the England-India trip took less than twenty-five days, making for more efficient transport of resources, goods, and people.

Despite a pragmatic preference for peaceful commerce, Britain did obtain some colonies between 1750 and 1870, taking over territories or fighting wars when local governments refused to trade or could not protect British commerce. For example, as states in India grew weaker and banditry increased, the British began expanding the territory under their influence and gradually gained direct control or indirect power over most of India. They also established footholds in Malaya, Burma, China, and South Africa. But the British preferred to undercut the economic power of their rivals, as they did in Argentina, Brazil, and Chile. They could flood a society with cheap manufactured goods, as shown when they greatly diminished India's crafts and industries for their own benefit. British industrialists and merchants also opposed any attempts to foster rival enterprises, such as textile mills, in Asian and African states.

However, the British advantage in world markets gradually diminished as world economic leadership changed during the later 1800s. The British invested many of the profits that they earned from India and their Caribbean colonies in other nations, especially in the United States, Canada, and Australia, all countries settled largely by British immigrants. This investment helped the United States become a serious competitor. British investment also benefited some European nations, and increasingly the United States and Germany were able to gain on Britain. Because British investors found it more profitable to invest abroad rather than at home, British industrial plants became increasingly obsolete. In 1860 Britain had been the leading economic power, with France a distant second followed by the United States and Germany. By 1900, however, the hierarchy had changed: the United States was now at the top, followed by Germany and then a fading Britain and France.

As industrializing Germany, France, and the United States became more competitive with Britain, their growing economic and political competition renewed the quest for colonies abroad. The shift to domestic economies dominated by large monopolies stimulated empire building by piling up huge profits and hence excess capital that needed investment outlets abroad to keep growing. Furthermore, by the 1880s some of the wealth generated by the industrial economy began to filter down to the European working classes, stimulating new consumer interests in tropical products such as chocolate, tea, soap, and rubber for bicycle tires. Businessmen in Britain, Germany, Italy, France, Belgium, and the United States looked for new opportunities to exploit environments in Africa, Asia, and the Pacific and then pressured their governments to pursue colonization to assist their efforts.

National rivalries also motivated imperialism. Nations often seized colonies to prevent competing nations from gaining opportunities. While expanding British control in southern Africa, the British imperialist Cecil Rhodes (1853–1902) was moved by the words of his Oxford University professor, the philosopher and art critic John Ruskin: "This is what England must either do, or perish: found colonies as fast and as far as [it] is able, seizing every piece of waste ground [it] can get [its] foot on."[20] The national rivalries and the intense competition for colonies also planted the roots of conflict in Europe. By the early 1900s Germany and Austria-Hungary had forged an alliance, prompting Britain, France, and Russia to do likewise and setting the stage for future wars.

The conflicts between European powers led to a resurgence of Western imperialism between 1870 and 1914, often resulting in colonialism or, less commonly, neocolonialism. Seizure of colonies not only brought profits for business interests but also strengthened a nation's power in competition with rival nations. The result was the greatest land grab in world history: a handful of European powers dividing up the globe between themselves.

Challenges to Britain

Revival of Imperialism

The Scramble for Empire and Imperial Ideologies

With the resurgent Western imperialism, millions of Africans, Asians, and Pacific islanders were conquered or impacted by Western nations and thus brought into the Western-dominated world economic system. Many peoples fiercely resisted conquest. The Vietnamese, Burmese, and various Indonesian and African societies held off militarily superior European armies for decades, and even after conquest guerrilla forces often continued to attack European colonizers. For fifteen years after the French annexed Vietnam, anticolonial fighters refused to surrender, preferring to fight to the death. Countless revolts punctuated colonial rule, from West Africa to the Philippines, and Western ambitions were sometimes frustrated. Ethiopians defeated an Italian invasion force bent on conquest, while the slaughter of British occupiers by Afghans discouraged direct colonization. The Japanese prevented Western political domination by modernizing their own government and economy, and the Siamese (Thai) used skillful diplomacy and selective modernization to deflect Western power.

New Conquests and Resistance

Lipton Tea   European imperial expansion brought many new products to European consumers. Tea, grown in British-ruled India, Sri Lanka (Ceylon), and Malaya, became a popular drink, advertised here in a London weekly magazine.

The Illustrated London News Library

Despite these efforts, by 1914 Western colonial powers controlled 90 percent of Africa, 99 percent of Polynesia, and 57 percent of Asia (see Map 19.4). The British Empire, the world's largest, included fifty-five colonies containing 400 million people, ten times Britain's population, inspiring the boast that "the sun never sets on the British Empire." France acquired the next largest empire of twenty-nine colonies. Germany, Spain, Belgium, and Italy joined in the grab for African colonies. Between 1898 and 1902 the United States took over Hawaii, Samoa, Puerto Rico, and the Philippines. Russia also continued its expansion in Eurasia that had begun in the Early Modern Era (see Chapter 23).

New Technologies

New technologies permitted and stimulated imperial expansion. The Industrial Revolution gave Europeans better weapons to enforce their will, including the repeating rifle and the machine gun, such as the lightweight, quick-firing Maxim Gun. A British writer boasted: "Whatever happens we have got the Maxim Gun, and they have not."[21] These weapons gave Europeans a huge advantage against Asians and Africans, and the discovery of quinine to treat malaria enabled European colonists and officials to survive in tropical Africa and Southeast Asia. Later, better communication and transportation networks, such as steamship lines, colonial railroads, and undersea telegraph cables, helped consolidate Western control and more closely connected the world. In 1866 a speaker at a banquet honoring Cyrus Field, the American most responsible for building the trans-Atlantic cable linking Europe and North America, noted that on the statue of Christopher Columbus in Genoa, Italy, was the inscription: "There was one world; let there be two." Now, with the cable, the speaker boasted, "There were two worlds and [now] they [are] one."[22]

Imperial Networks

Western imperialism forged networks of interlinked social, economic, and political relationships spanning the globe. Hence, decisions made by a government or business in London or Paris affected people in faraway Malaya or Madagascar, and silk spun in China was turned into dresses worn by fashionable women in Chicago and Munich. Westerners also enjoyed advantageous trade relations with, or strong influence over countries such as China, Siam, Persia, and Argentina, a condition known as neocolonialism. The scope of this imperialism changed world power arrangements. In 1750 China and the Ottoman Empire remained among the world's strongest countries, but by 1914 they could not match Western military and economic power. In 1500 the wealth gap between the more economically developed and the less developed Eurasian and African societies was small, and China and India dominated world trade and manufacturing. By 1914 the gap in total wealth and personal income between industrialized societies, whether in Europe or North America, and most other societies, including China and India, had grown very wide.

Social Darwinism

Supporters of imperialism embraced a new ideology, Social Darwinism, based on the ideas about the natural world developed by the British scientist Charles Darwin, who described a struggle for existence among species (see Chapter 20). Social Darwinists concluded that this struggle led to

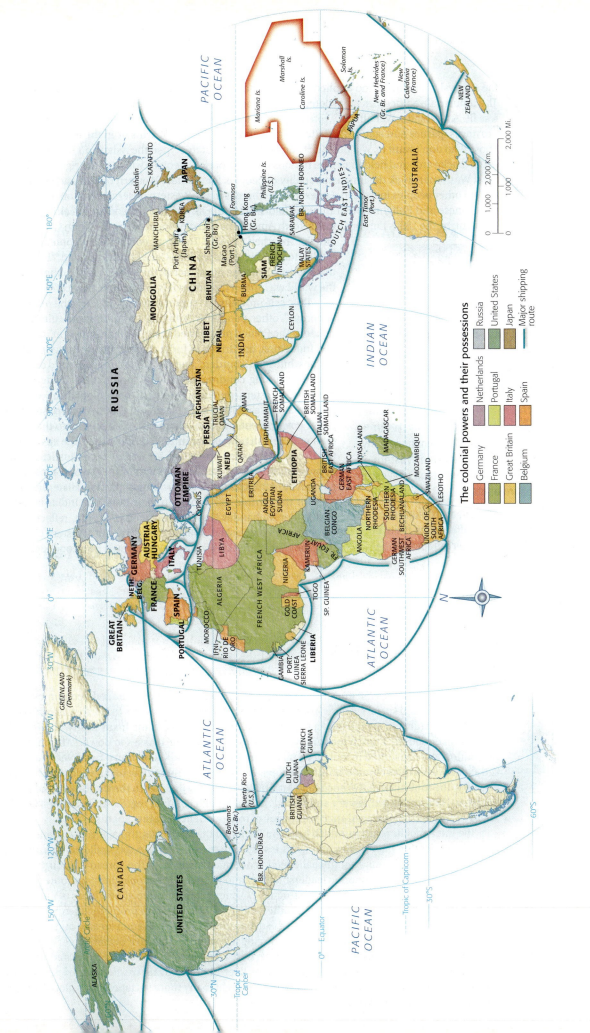

Map 19.4 The Great Powers and Their Colonial Possessions in 1913
By 1913 the British and French controlled huge empires, with colonies in Africa, southern Asia, the Caribbean zone, and the Pacific Basin. Russia ruled much of northern Eurasia, while the United States, Japan, and a half dozen European nations controlled smaller empires.

e Interactive Map

The colonial powers and their possessions

- Germany
- France
- Great Britain
- Belgium
- Netherlands
- Portugal
- Italy
- Spain
- Russia
- United States
- Japan
- Major shipping route

CHANGING SOCIETIES IN EUROPE, THE AMERICAS, AND OCEANIA, 1750–1914

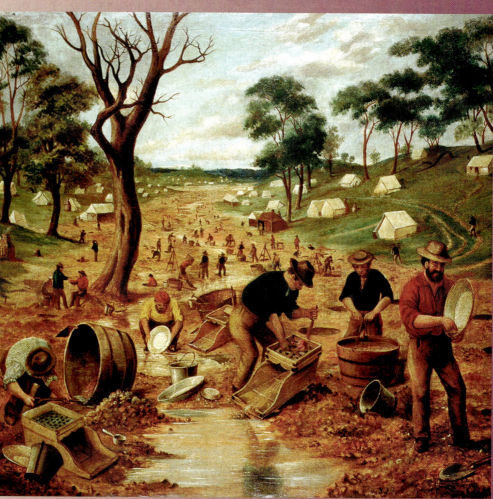

Australian Gold Rush
The discovery of gold in southeastern Australia set off a gold rush in the 1850s. Hoping to strike it rich, miners, often from other countries, among them Chinese, flocked to the gold fields, and immigration to Australia boomed.

The Art Archive

KEY TERMS

Age of Revolution	laissez faire	nation-states	parliamentary democracy
Jacobins	ideology	Zionism	socialism
Industrial Revolution	nationalism	liberalism	proletariat
Luddites			

EBOOK AND WEBSITE RESOURCES

e PRIMARY SOURCE
The Jamaica Letter

e INTERACTIVE MAPS
Map 19.1 Europe in 1815
Map 19.2 Latin American Independence, 1840
Map 19.3 Industrial Transformation in England
Map 19.4 The Great Powers and Their Colonial Possessions in 1913

LINKS

The American Revolution (http://revolution.hnet.msu.edu/intro.html). An excellent collection of links, essays, and other resources.

BBC Outline: History (http://www.bbc.co.uk/history/). Offers valuable information by topic and time.

British History (http://www.british-history.com/). Contains links to short essays on various periods of British history.

Internet Resources for Latin America (http://lib.nmsu.edu/subject/bord/laguia/). An outstanding site with links to many resources.

Modern History Sourcebook (http://www.fordham.edu/halsall/). An extensive online collection of historical documents and secondary materials.

Plus flashcards, practice quizzes, and more. Go to: www.cengage.com/history/lockard/globalsocnet2e.

SUGGESTED READING

Abernethy, David B. *The Dynamics of Global Dominance: European Overseas Empires, 1415–1980.* New Haven, CT.: Yale University Press, 2002. Classic study of Western imperialism.

Anderson, Benedict. *Imagined Communities: Reflections on the Origin and Spread of Nationalism,* rev. ed. London: Verso, 1991. An influential scholarly examination of the rise of nationalism.

Anderson, M. S. *The Ascendancy of Europe, 1815–1914,* 3rd ed. Harlow, UK: Pearson, 2003. A good overview of the era by a British historian.

Baumgart, Winfried. *Imperialism: The Idea and Reality of British and French Colonial Expansion, 1880–1914.* New York: Oxford University Press, 1986. A readable analysis of the imperial quest.

Connelly, Owen, and Fred Hembree. *The French Revolution and Napoleonic Era,* 3rd ed. New York: Harcourt, 1999. A thoughtful survey emphasizing the Revolution's long-term consequences.

Countryman, Edward. *The American Revolution,* rev. ed. New York: Hill and Wang, 2003. An excellent treatment of the conflict and its context.

Grosby, Steven. *Nationalism: A Very Short Introduction.* New York: Oxford University Press, 2005. Highlights social, historical, and philosophical perspectives.

Headrick, Daniel R. *The Tools of Empire: Technology and European Imperialism in the Nineteenth Century.* New York: Oxford University Press, 1981. A pathbreaking study of the role of technology in European expansion.

Heilbroner, Robert L. *The Worldly Philosophers: The Lives, Times and Ideas of the Great Economic Thinkers,* 7th ed. New York: Simon and Schuster, 1999. A classic and readable introduction to these thinkers.

Hobsbawm, Eric. *The Age of Revolution, 1789–1848; The Age of Capital, 1848–1875; The Age of Empire, 1875–1914.* New York: Vintage, 1996. This outstanding trilogy by an esteemed British historian remains the standard survey of the period.

Martin, Cheryl E., and Mark Wasserman. *Latin America and Its People,* 2nd ed. New York: Longman, 2007. An introductory survey, especially strong on this era.

Samson, Jane. *Race and Empire.* New York: Longman, 2005. Examines the relationship of racism and imperialism.

Sperber, Jonathan. *Revolutionary Europe, 1780–1850.* Harlow, UK: Pearson, 2000. A good overview of these turbulent decades.

Stearns, Peter N. *The Industrial Revolution in World History,* 3rd ed. Boulder, CO: Westview Press, 2007. An overview from a global perspective.

Wesseling, H. L. *The European Colonial Empires, 1815–1919.* Harlow, UK: Pearson, 2004. A useful overview of the entire colonial enterprise by a Dutch scholar.

CHANGING SOCIETIES IN EUROPE, THE AMERICAS, AND OCEANIA, 1750–1914

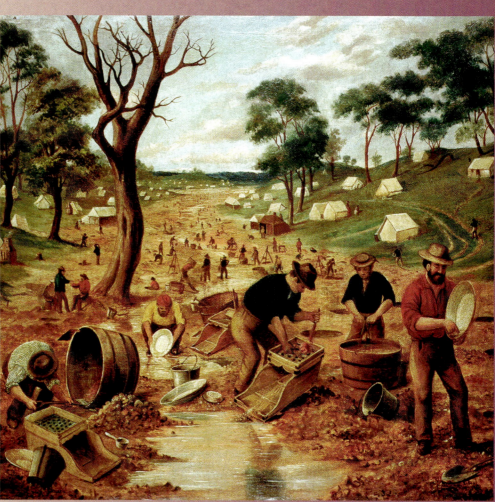

The Art Archive

Australian Gold Rush
The discovery of gold in southeastern Australia set off a gold rush in the 1850s. Hoping to strike it rich, miners, often from other countries, among them Chinese, flocked to the gold fields, and immigration to Australia boomed.

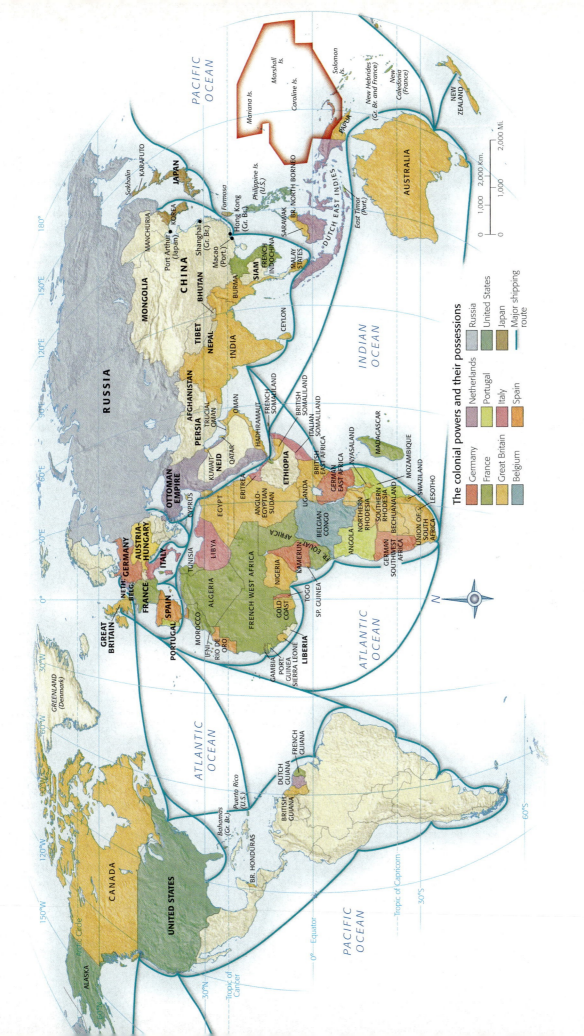

Map 19.4 The Great Powers and Their Colonial Possessions in 1913

By 1913 the British and French controlled huge empires, with colonies in Africa, southern Asia, the Caribbean zone, and the Pacific Basin. Russia ruled much of northern Eurasia, while the United States, Japan, and a half dozen European nations controlled smaller empires.

The colonial powers and their possessions

- Germany
- France
- Great Britain
- Belgium
- Netherlands
- Portugal
- Italy
- Spain
- Russia
- United States
- Japan
- Major shipping route

e Interactive Map

the survival of the fittest and applied this notion to the human world of social classes and nations. The industrialized peoples considered themselves the most fit and saw the poor or exploited as less fit. A German naval officer wrote in 1898 that "the struggle for life exists among individuals, provinces, parties and states. The latter wage it either by the use of arms or in the economic field. Those who don't want to, will perish."[23] Social Darwinists stereotyped the Asian and African societies as "backward" and held their own nations up as "superior" peoples who had the right to rule. As most Westerners took the innate inequality of peoples for granted, Western racism and arrogance toward other peoples increased. For example, whereas many Western observers had once admired the Chinese and Enlightenment thinkers had seen China as a model of secular and efficient government, by the 1800s Europeans and North Americans had developed scorn for "John Chinaman" and the "heathen Chinee." These stereotypes were popularized by intellectual and political leaders. Cecil Rhodes boasted, "I contend that we British are the finest race in the world, and that the more of the world we inhabit the better it is for the human race."[24]

This self-proclaimed superiority legitimized the effort to "improve" other people by bringing them Western culture and religion. The French proclaimed their "civilizing mission" in Africa and Indochina, the British in India claimed that they were "taking up the white man's burden," and the Americans colonized the Philippines claiming condescendingly to "uplift" their "little brown brothers." Western defenders argued that colonialism, despite much that was shameful, gave "stagnating" non-Western societies better government and drew them out of isolation into the world market. A British newspaper in 1896 claimed that "the advance of the Union Jack means protection for weaker races, justice for the oppressed, liberty for the down-trodden."[25] However, most people in Asia, Africa, and the Pacific opposed colonialism, seeing it only for the terrible toll it took on their lives. The Indian nationalist leader Mohandas Gandhi, educated in Britain, reflected the resentment. When asked what he thought about "Western civilization," he replied that civilizing the West would be a good idea.

SECTION SUMMARY

- Even after losing thirteen of its North American colonies, Britain continued to dominate the world economy through its other holdings and its technological advantages, but it gradually lost ground, especially to the United States.

- As Germany, France, and the United States became more competitive with Britain, the powers competed for colonies that could provide natural resources for their industries and power over their rivals.

- In the renewed scramble for colonial domination, many African, Asian, and Pacific peoples resisted Western imperialism, but the technological advantage of Western nations often proved insurmountable.

- Westerners rationalized imperialism and colonization as good for the colonized, who were offered the fruits of Western culture in exchange for their independence.

Chapter Summary

The years between 1750 and 1914 were an age of revolutions that reshaped economies, governments, and social systems in Europe and the Americas. Colonists in North America overthrew British rule and established a republic that included democratic institutions. The French Revolution ended the French monarchy and brought the middle classes to power. Although the Revolution was consumed in violence and then modified by Napoleon Bonaparte's dictatorship, the shock waves reverberated around Europe, carrying with them new ideas about liberty and equality. The American and French Revolutions also inspired peoples in the Caribbean and Latin America. Haitians ended slavery and forced out the French colonial regime and planters, and in South America creoles waged successful wars of independence against Spanish rule.

The Industrial Revolution, which began in Britain in the late 1700s, transformed societies profoundly, reorienting life to cities and factories and producing goods in unparalleled abundance. Until the 1850s Britain enjoyed unchallenged economic power. With the spread of industrialization, positions of world economic leadership began to change. New ideologies contributed to the creation of new states and government structures. Nationalism introduced new ideas of the nation and provided a glue to bind people within the same nation. Liberalism promoted increasing freedom and democracy. Socialism addressed the dislocations industrialization created and sought to improve life for the new working classes by forging a system of collective ownership of economic property. Capitalism, industrialization, and interstate rivalries in the West also generated a worldwide scramble for colonies and neocolonies in the later 1800s, allowing Western businesses to seek resources and markets abroad. This imperialism brought many more societies into a global system largely dominated by the West.

Of course, some day we [Americans] shall step in. We are bound to. We shall be giving the word for everything: industry, trade, law, journalism, art, politics, and religion. We shall run the world's business whether the world likes it or not. The world can't help it, and neither can we, I guess.

—AMERICAN MILLIONAIRE IN JOSEPH CONRAD'S NOVEL *NOSTROMO* (1904)[1]

FOCUS QUESTIONS

1. How and why did European social, cultural, and intellectual patterns change during this era?
2. What impact did westward expansion, immigration, and industrialization have on American society?
3. What political, economic, and social patterns shaped Latin America after independence?
4. Why did the foundations for nationhood differ in Canada and Oceania?

In 1871 a thirty-three-year-old Japanese samurai and Confucian scholar, Kume Kunitake (1839–1931), boarded an American steamship at Yokohama and began a three-week voyage to San Francisco as a member of an official information-gathering delegation sent from Japan to the United States and then Europe. Kume's delegation traveled around the country, visiting factories, museums, schools, churches, public parks, and scenic mountains. Kume faithfully recorded his perceptive impressions of Western life but also filtered them through the Japanese cultural lens, concluding that "the customs and characteristics of East and West are invariably different." Kume admired U.S. democracy but also saw its potential for disorder, since Americans were "careless about official authority, each person insisting on his own rights." Kume recorded the Americans' friendliness but also their brashness, ambition, and sense of destiny, attitudes satirized four decades later by the Polish-born British novelist Joseph Conrad through the words of his fictional American millionaire quoted above. Kume's delegation then traveled around Europe, where he noted how Europeans treasured and even imitated Japanese art. He loved the cafes, theaters, and art museums of Paris. But, as an ardent Confucian rationalist, he viewed Christianity as irrational and the Christian Bible as full of "absurd tales." Kume contrasted the splendor of the churches with the poverty of the people. But he preferred Europe's constitutional monarchies to the untidy U.S. republic and saw rapidly industrializing Germany as Japan's natural model. Returning by ship to Japan, Kume's delegation passed through Western colonies such as Ceylon, Singapore, and Hong Kong. Kume wrote that "Europeans treated the natives with arrogance and cruelty."[2] He later became a distinguished professor of history at Tokyo University.

Spurred by revolutions, industrialization, nation building, and overseas imperialism, Europeans reshaped their social, cultural, and intellectual patterns. By 1914 the United States, Canada, and Mexico occupied all of North America, while Latin America was divided into many countries large and small. Some Caribbean societies were independent, but many remained colonies of European nations. The Europeans also settled the Pacific region known today as Oceania, which comprises Australia and the two large islands of New Zealand, while colonizing the smaller Pacific islands. Although Europe, the Americas, and Oceania were separated from each other by vast distances and had unique characteristics, their societies were shaped by similar patterns of capitalism, migration, and nation building.

The United States, Canada, Australia, and New Zealand, but also Latin American countries such as Argentina, Uruguay, Brazil, and Chile, were settled chiefly by European immigrants who planted European institutions and ideas after the indigenous populations were largely displaced. These European traditions and institutions, while remaining influential,

e Visit the website and eBook for additional study materials and interactive tools:
www.cengage.com/history/lockard/globalsocnet2e

545

were modified by time, circumstances, and the cultures of ethnic minorities, either indigenous peoples, such as Native Americans and New Zealand Maori, or imported societies, such as Afro-Brazilians and Afro-Cubans. At the same time, the United States and Canada gradually diverged from the Latin American and Caribbean societies. By expanding its frontiers and rapidly industrializing in the 1800s, the United States became a world power, often extending its political and economic influence into Latin America and the Caribbean.

THE RESHAPING OF EUROPEAN SOCIETIES

How and why did European social, cultural, and intellectual patterns change during this era?

Thanks to destabilizing revolutions in political and economic life (see Chapter 19), modern Europeans lived in a world of cities, new forms of work, and rising populations, prompting millions of people to emigrate to the Americas, southern Africa, and Oceania in search of work and a better life. Industrialization transformed social structures and family systems. Thought, the arts, and science reflected and also shaped the new Europe, with the resulting innovations influencing peoples around the world.

Population Growth, Emigration, and Urbanization

Expanding economies, better public health, and new crops such as potatoes from the Americas lowered Europe's mortality rate and fostered population growth. People married earlier, increasing the birthrate, and more people married than in Early Modern times. Europe's population (including Russia) grew from 100 million in 1650 to 190 million in 1800 and to 420 million in 1900, creating new problems. Thomas Malthus, an English clergyman and economist, argued in 1798 that poverty, disease, war, and famine checked population growth, but if these problems were eliminated, population would outgrow its means of subsistence. Overpopulation did indeed bring bleak poverty and underemployment to many areas of Europe, problems accelerated by the replacement of small family farms by large farms that needed fewer workers. But the growth of cities and industries also provided new employment opportunities.

Population Movement

Population growth and poverty led to migration within Europe and emigration overseas. Many Poles, for example, moved to the mines of northern France and western Germany, and Irish immigrants built railroads, canals, and roads in England. Emigration cut Ireland's population by half between 1841 and 1911. As an identifiable, non-Christian minority, the Jews in eastern Europe and Russia became public scapegoats for unresolved problems and were sometimes subjected to violent, usually coordinated mob attacks known as *pogroms* (from the Russian word meaning "roundup"), prompting them to seek better lives in western Europe and the Americas. In total, some 45 million Europeans emigrated to the Americas, Australia, New Zealand, Algeria, and South Africa to escape their difficulties (see Map 20.1).

Growing Cities

Rural Europeans also moved to industrial cities. The population of Manchester, the British center of the cotton industry, grew tenfold between 1800 and 1900. By 1900 Britain had the world's most urban society, with 90 percent of its people living in towns and cities. Between 1800 and 1900 London increased from 900,000 to 4.7 million, Paris from 600,000 to 3.6 million, and Berlin from 170,000 to 2.7 million. Urbanization increased social problems. Rapidly expanding cities lacked social services such as sanitation, street cleaning, and water distribution. Huge numbers of people lived in poverty, crammed into overcrowded housing in crime-ridden slums with high disease rates, overflowing privies, and littered streets. As the English poet William Blake wrote: "Every night and every morn, some to misery are born." The standard of living did not rise much for most Europeans until the 1880s, when incomes began to improve and several countries, including Britain and Germany, began building a social safety net for their citizens. By 1900 British and French workers were earning nearly twice the wages of workers in 1850.

While cities grew dramatically, western European rural life also changed. Agricultural technology and practices developed rapidly, resulting in better yields, more mechanization, and improved animal breeding. Market agriculture largely displaced the subsistence production of earlier times. But peasants often earned low wages, and many small farmers frequently lost their land to more highly capitalized and mechanized operations. Occasional famines also occurred, notably in

CHRONOLOGY

	United States	Latin America	Canada and Oceania
1800	**1803** Louisiana Purchase **1846–1848** U.S.-Mexican War islands	**1823–1889** Abolition of slavery	**1840s–1890** Colonization of Pacific islands
1850	**1861–1865** Civil War **1898–1902** Spanish-American War	**1889** Brazilian republic	**1850** Treaty of Waitangi **1867** Canadian Confederation
1900		**1910–1920** Mexican Revolution **1914** Panama Canal	**1901** Australian Commonwealth

Ireland and Russia. In contrast to rural life in western Europe, some feudal traditions remained influential in eastern Europe, especially in Russia and Poland, where the landed gentry retained authority over peasant lives.

Social Life, Families, and Gender Relations

Europeans enjoyed wider social horizons than their ancestors. After 1870 the rise of mass-distribution newspapers, organized football (soccer) leagues, more widespread vacation travel, and other activities connected peoples within and between nations. The world's first cinema opened in Paris in 1896, launching a film industry that would produce one of the most popular entertainments in Europe and then the world. People enjoyed a growing range of options in areas of life once fixed by tradition, such as where to live, work, or worship and whom to marry. Choice brought more personal freedom but also more social instability. Some observers viewed these changes as liberation, while others concluded that they fostered anxious uncertainty.

Industrialization also reshaped sexual attitudes, particularly in Britain. The middle class, who considered unbridled passion a sign of bad character, increasingly discouraged sexual activity before marriage and limited sexual intercourse within marriage. In contrast, the working classes experienced higher rates of illegitimacy and more frequent sexual relations than ever before. Marital infidelity became common in the urban slums, fostering negative middle-class stereotypes of the poor. Thus, a British factory girl in 1909 complained, "I wanted no one to know that I was a factory girl because I was ashamed at my position. I was always hearing people say that factory girls were loose-living and corrupt."[3] Thanks to improved diets, children of all classes reached sexual maturity at a younger age, making it more difficult to maintain boys' choirs as male voices changed earlier.

Changing Sexual Attitudes

Home life and families underwent changes. During the Early Modern Era people in England and the Low Countries began to marry later and live in nuclear families, which usually included just parents and their children. During the 1800s the nuclear pattern became common in most of northern Europe, especially among the middle classes, while large extended families remained the norm in southern and eastern Europe. Families now included fewer nonrelated members, such as servants and apprentices, than had been usual in earlier centuries. In the 1700s western Europeans began to adopt the notion that people should have the freedom to choose their partner and marry for love rather than to meet family demands or economic need, but critics argued that love matches would lead to marital instability and divorce when romance faded. Married men and women often spent more time with their same-sex friends than their spouses, and sometimes the line between these friendships and homosexual relationships was murky.

Family Life

People also began to redefine family life. By the later 1800s some men and women criticized marriage as stifling and old-fashioned, living out of wedlock with lovers. Prominent people in the artistic and political worlds, such as the popular French actress Sarah Bernhardt, openly had affairs or, like the fiery German socialist Rosa Luxemburg, lived openly with same-sex partners. Homosexuals occupied all levels of society, but they often faced discrimination and persecution. The Irish poet, novelist, and playwright Oscar Wilde (1854–1900), the married father of two, was tried and imprisoned in 1895 for engaging in homosexual relationships, known as sodomy. The increasing attention to homosexuality and the first scientific studies of it sparked heated and ongoing debates as to whether the behavior was rooted in nature or perversion.

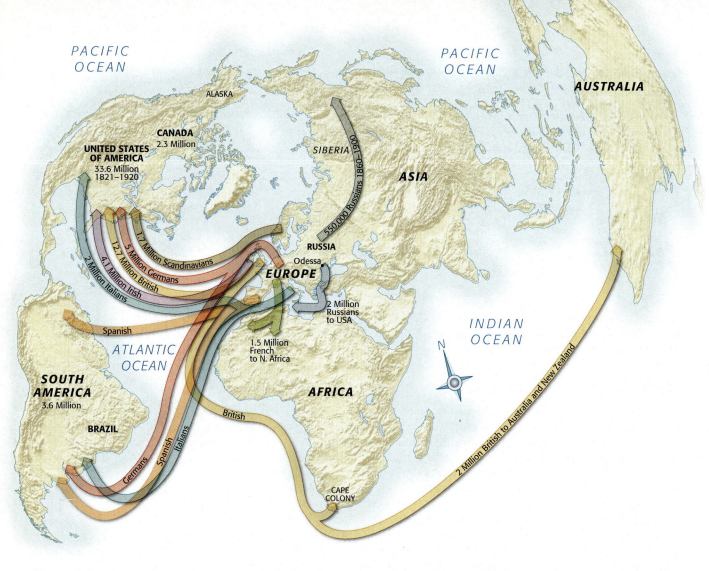

PACIFIC OCEAN

PACIFIC OCEAN

AUSTRALIA

ALASKA

CANADA
2.3 Million

UNITED STATES OF AMERICA
33.6 Million
1821–1920

SIBERIA

ASIA

550,000 Russians 1860–1900

RUSSIA

Odessa

EUROPE

1.7 Million Scandinavians
5 Million Germans
12.7 Million British
4.1 Million Irish
2 Million Italians

2 Million Russians to USA

1.5 Million French to N. Africa

Spanish

ATLANTIC OCEAN

INDIAN OCEAN

N

SOUTH AMERICA
3.6 Million

AFRICA

BRAZIL

Germans
Spanish
Italians

British

2 Million British to Australia and New Zealand

CAPE COLONY

Map 20.1   European Emigration, 1820–1910

Pushed by rapid population growth and poverty, millions of Europeans left their homes to settle in the Americas (especially the United States), North and South Africa, Siberia, Australia, and New Zealand. The British and Irish accounted for the largest numbers of emigrants, nearly 17 million combined.

e Interactive Map

Reprinted by permission of HarperCollins Publishers, Ltd. © *Times Atlas of World History*, 3rd. ed. Some data from Eric Hobsbawm, *The Age of Empire, 1875–1914* (New York: Pantheon, 1987)

Gender Relations

The industrial economy was hard on families, particularly on women and children. Seldom viewed as breadwinners, women typically earned only 25 percent of men's wages. Single mothers found it especially difficult to earn a living, and some were forced to turn to prostitution for survival. Women and children often did hard manual labor in cotton mills and mines. In 1838 a liberal member of the British Parliament reported: "I saw a cotton mill, a sight that froze my blood, full of women, young, all of them, some large with child, and obliged to stand twelve hours each day. The heat was excessive in some of the rooms, the stink pestiferous. I nearly fainted."[4] By the early 1900s, when machines did more of the factory work, fewer women and far fewer children worked full-time in the industrial sector.

The Industrial Revolution reshaped life for both genders, putting men and women into separate work worlds and lowering women's status by increasing their dependence on men. Moving the workplace from the home to the factory increased men's power over their wives. No longer needed in economic production, middle-class women lost their roles as direct producers, becoming instead home managers ("housewives") charged with keeping the house clean. Middle-class men assumed that women belonged at home as submissive helpmates and encouraged them to cultivate their beauty and social graces to please their menfolk. Men remained dominant in the political, social, economic, and religious spheres, and women's roles were increasingly restricted to marriage, motherhood, and child rearing. Moreover, often women had no legal standing and could not divorce their husbands. Upper- and middle-class women practiced artificial birth control and had fewer children than in earlier eras. By 1900, however, women enjoyed longer life expectancies and devoted fewer years to childbearing and rearing.

In the later 1800s European women gained more legal rights and economic opportunities. Some European women took new jobs as secretaries, telephone operators, or department store sales clerks, and occasionally doors opened to professional jobs. The Netherlands had Europe's first woman physician in 1870, and France the first woman lawyer in 1903. Leading professional women such as the Italian educator Maria Montessori **(mon-ti-SAWR-ee)** (1870–1952), who devised innovative schools allowing children to develop at their own pace; the Polish-born French scientist Marie Curie (1867–1934), who won a Nobel Prize in physics in 1903; the influential German composer and pianist Clara Schumann (1819–1896); and the British nurse Florence Nightingale (1820–1910), who revolutionized nursing practices, provided role models. In 1867 the University of Zurich in Switzerland became the first university to admit women, and it was soon followed by universities in France, Sweden, and Finland.

In quest of more rights, some women espoused views later known as **feminism**, a philosophy promoting political, social, and economic equality for women with men. Inspired by pioneers such as Mary Wollstonecraft in the late 1700s, the first feminist movements emerged in Britain and Scandinavia, with some activists, later known as **suffragettes**, pressing for the same voting rights as men. In 1896 Finland became the first European nation to accept female suffrage (see Chronology: European Society and Culture, 1750–1914). In Britain suffragettes led by Emily Pankhurst (1858–1928) campaigned for the right to vote by giving speeches, canvassing door-to-door, and demonstrating. In southern and eastern Europe feminists had only a small following.

CHRONOLOGY
European Society and Culture, 1750–1914

1859 Publication of Charles Darwin's *On the Origin of Species*

1860s Beginning of impressionist artistic movement in France

1896 Women's suffrage in Finland

1905 Publication of Albert Einstein's special theory of relativity

feminism A philosophy promoting political, social, and economic equality for women with men.

suffragettes Women who press for the same voting rights as men.

Thought, Religion, and Culture

The industrial and political revolutions, and the social changes they sparked, fostered new directions in European thought and culture. Philosophers such as the Germans Immanuel Kant (1724–1804) and Friedrich Nietzsche **(NEE-chuh)** (1844–1890) debated the values of the Enlightenment. An Enlightenment thinker, Kant believed that experience alone was inadequate for understanding because the perceptions it fosters are ultimately shaped by the mind, which imposes a structure on the sensations we see. Kant doubted that a perfect society could ever be achieved, arguing that "man wishes concord, but nature, knowing better what is good for his species, wishes discord."[5] Nietzsche rejected the Enlightenment notions of progress, perceiving a growing decadence in European culture that he blamed on Christian values and democratic ideas. To Nietzsche, there was no fundamental moral and scientific truth, as the Enlightenment philosophers had thought, but rather misconceptions developed by each culture as its members tried to understand the world. With no absolute truth, absolute good and evil cannot exist. In the twentieth century extreme nationalists and racists distorted Nietzsche's ideas to persecute ethnic minorities, while many European and North American intellectuals used Nietzsche's notion that truth is relative to argue that all knowledge was culturally constructed.

"Convicts and Lunatics" The movement for women's right to vote, or suffrage, was particularly strong in Britain. This poster, "Convicts and Lunatics," designed by the artist Emily Harding Andrews for the Artist's Suffrage League around 1908, shows a woman graduate, deprived of basic political rights, treated similarly to a convict and a mentally disturbed woman.

Religion

Religion also changed with the times. Gradually Protestants and Catholics learned to tolerate each other. In the later 1700s and early 1800s a religious revival inspired many European Protestants to move to the United States. Evangelicals stressed personal relations with God, favored missionary activity, and condemned behavior they considered sinful, such as social dancing and drinking. Soon new churches appeared. The charismatic British Anglican preacher John Wesley (1703–1791), seeking a more emotional faith, founded the Methodist movement, which later formed its own church. The Society of Friends, better known as Quakers, who believed in nonviolence, human dignity, and individual conscience, fought against slavery and for social and political freedom and humanitarian causes.

Many middle-class Protestants sought a liberalized faith stressing social tolerance rather than the hellfire and damnation preached by some evangelicals. As the relevance of religion declined, by 1851 only half of the English population attended church. The divide between the more liberal and the more devout resulted in public debates across Europe about the role of religion in society. In Britain evangelicals sought to impose their values on the increasingly secular society by trying to ban alcohol and gambling and by requiring all businesses to close on Sunday, moves fiercely opposed by many Protestants and Catholics.

The Roman Catholic and Greek Orthodox Churches also faced challenges. Spurred by the French Revolution, the Catholic clergy in France and Belgium lost the privileged status they had enjoyed for centuries. France opened a public school system in the 1890s and mandated state neutrality toward religion in 1905. At the same time, the Catholic Church generally strengthened church dogma and organization, and popes reasserted their theological infallibility and announced new doctrines such as the Immaculate Conception of the Virgin Mary. The church also remained a major spiritual force and landowner in Austria, southern Germany, Poland, Spain, Portugal, and Italy. Meanwhile, the Greek Orthodox world fragmented into national churches in Greece, Serbia, Romania, and Bulgaria.

Literature and the Arts

The growth of a literate public eager and able to consume cultural products liberated writers, composers, and artists from dependence on wealthy patrons. Imbibing various movements, European classical music enjoyed a golden age, and the compositions of this era are still enjoyed by audiences around the world. The Austrian Wolfgang Amadeus Mozart (MOTE-sahrt) (1756–1791) wrote thirty-five symphonies, eight operas, and many concertos. Inspired by the Age of Revolution, some thinkers and artists adopted **romanticism**, a philosophical, literary, artistic, and musical movement that questioned the Enlightenment's rationalist values and instead glorified emotions, individual imagination, and heroism. Some romantics celebrated great figures such as Napoleon Bonaparte. The German writer Friedrich Schiller (1759–1805) offered intense romantic images with a nationalist tinge, such as a poem that turned the story of William Tell, a legendary hero of Swiss resistance against foreign invasion, into a manifesto for German political freedom. Romanticism also inspired the German composer Ludvig von Beethoven (1770–1827), whose much-admired Ninth Symphony set Schiller's poem, "Ode to Joy," to music.

romanticism A philosophical, literary, artistic, and musical movement that questioned the Enlightenment's rationalist values and instead glorified emotions, individual imagination, and heroism.

In contrast, writers and artists embracing another movement, realism, portrayed a grimy industrial world filled with uncertainty and conflict. For example, the liberal Spanish painter Francisco de Goya's (1746–1828) moving series on the Napoleonic invasion of Spain portrayed not warfare's heroism but its horrors: orphans, pain, rape, blood, and despair. The British realist novelist and former factory worker Charles Dickens (1812–1870) revealed the hardships of industrial life, the injustices of capitalism, and the miseries of the poor.

modernism A cultural trend that embraced progress and welcomed the future.

impressionism An artistic movement that sought to express the immediate impression aroused by momentary scenes that were bathed in light and color.

Several significant movements shaped the visual arts in the later 1800s and reflected influences from Asian, African, and Pacific art. **Modernism** embraced progress and welcomed the future. Realistic landscape paintings, the appearance of photography, and the introduction of Japanese prints contributed to the rise in France of **impressionism**, an artistic movement that expressed the immediate impression aroused in momentary scenes, bathed in changing light and color. Impressionists painters such as Claude Monet (moe-NAY) (1840–1926) and Pierre Renoir (ren-WAH) (1841–1919) achieved worldwide fame. Some French artists rebelled against impressionism, returning to familiar shapes and compositions. The most influential included Paul Cezanne (say-ZAN) (1839–1906), famous for his landscapes, still lifes, and portraits; the prolific Dutch-born Vincent Van Gogh (van GO) (1853–1890), who introduced intense primary colors and thick brushstrokes; and Paul Gauguin (go-GAN) (1848–1903), a former stockbroker whose richly colored paintings often featured idyllic scenes of Polynesian life based on his long residence there, stimulating European interest in the wider world. Pablo Picasso (1881–1973), a young Spaniard who settled in Paris, revolutionized Western art by integrating ideas from African sculpture and masks. The new European art bore little resemblance to medieval European art.

Science and Technology

The Modern Era saw spectacular achievements in science and technology. The British naturalist Charles Darwin (1809–1882), after years spent traveling around the world studying plants, animals, and fossils in many lands, formulated the theory of evolution emphasizing the natural selection of species. In his book, *On the Origin of Species*, Darwin argued that all existing species of plants and animals, including humans, had evolved into their present forms over millions of years. Species either adapted to their environment or died out. Eventually evolution became the foundation for the modern biological sciences, confirmed by many studies and accepted by most scientists, but it generated opposition from many churches, whose leaders saw Darwin's evolutionary ideas as a degradation of humans and a negation of religious faith.

Darwin

The German-born Jewish physicist Albert Einstein (1879–1955) ranks with Galileo, Newton, and Darwin as a pathbreaking European scientist. His papers on the theory of relativity, published in the early 1900s, provided the basis for modern physics, our understanding of the universe, and the atomic age. Einstein offered a new view of space and time, showing that distances and durations are not, as Newton thought, absolute but are affected by one's motion. He also proved that matter can be converted into energy and that everything is composed of atoms, insights that provided the basis for atomic energy. Einstein's papers electrified the scientific world. He taught in Swiss, Czech, and German universities before immigrating to the United States in 1934.

Einstein

New and rapid health and technological discoveries all over Europe also characterized the age, improving people's lives. Physicians introduced the first effective vaccines against deadly diseases such as smallpox that had ravaged the world for centuries, and drugs and medical technologies improved. In 1895 the German physicist Wilhelm Rontgen (RUNT-guhn) (1845–1923) discovered x-rays, spurring progress in diagnosis and surgery. Medical advances and improved sanitation also led to better public health. Thanks to cleaner water, cholera was eradicated from Europe's industrial cities. Electric batteries, motors, and generators emerged as new sources of power. The Italian Guglielmo Marconi (1874–1937) introduced wireless telegraphy, and in 1901 he used his invention to communicate between England and Canada, opening another network connecting the world. Two Germans, Gottlieb Daimler and Karl Benz, became the "fathers of the automobile," producing the first petroleum-powered vehicle in the 1880s.

Meanwhile, some scientists worried about the effects of industrial pollution on the environment. The observation that carbon dioxide emissions from coal-burning factories heated the atmosphere led the Swedish scientist Svante Arrhenius to speak of a "greenhouse effect" that potentially threatened modern societies. Scientific studies over the next century confirmed his fears. The world still struggles with the promise but also the perils of the technologies and industrial processes developed in this era.

SECTION SUMMARY

- In Europe, better crops and health care produced larger populations, which led to increasing urbanization, impoverishment, and emigration.

- As Europe became more industrialized and interconnected, the nuclear family and love marriages became increasingly common, and some began to question the institution of marriage itself.

- Industrialization made men more powerful and relegated women to the home, but in the late nineteenth century women began to gain legal rights and economic opportunities.

- While some Protestants attempted to stamp out behavior they considered sinful, Europeans as a whole became more secular and the Catholic Church's influence declined.

- Artists, writers, and composers became dependent on the public marketplace rather than wealthy patrons, and artistic trends such as romanticism, realism, modernism, and impressionism became dominant.

- Advances in science and technology led to the theory of evolution, greater understanding of the physical world, improved medical care, new sources of energy, and new concerns about pollution and its effects.

THE RISE OF THE UNITED STATES

What impact did westward expansion, immigration, and industrialization have on American society?

After the American Revolution, the former colonists turned to building their new nation. During the early republic Americans established new forms of government, reshaped economic patterns, fostered a new culture, and began the movement westward, conquering Native Americans, acquiring Mexican territory, and becoming involved in the wider world. Then between 1860 and 1914 the United States changed dramatically. The Civil War maintained the territorial unity of the nation, ended slavery, and led to the increased centralization of the federal government, which, combined with economic protectionism, allowed the United States to duplicate the economic and political growth that was spurred by mercantilism in Early Modern western Europe. Industrialization created more wealth, supported U.S. power, and reshaped American society. By 1900 the United States had a larger population than all but one European nation, boasted the world's most productive economy, owned half a continent, enjoyed a powerful, stable, democratic government, and exercised its power abroad, all sustained by an abundance of natural resources.

The Early Republic and American Society

The new American republic, weak and surrounded by hostile neighbors in British Canada and the Spanish American Empire, found nation building a challenge. Unity was fragile, and Americans faced the daunting task of establishing principles to unite the diverse states. Ultimately they forged a new distinctive form of representative democracy and constructed an economic framework to preserve independence and encourage free enterprise capitalism. The Constitution and Bill of Rights established a relatively powerful central government, elected by voters in each state, within a federal system that recognized the lawmaking powers of each member state (see Chronology: The United States and the World, 1750–1914). By the mid-1800s all white adult males enjoyed the right to vote, but the government maintained slavery and excluded Native Americans and women from political activity.

Professing a love for freedom, Americans have had to constantly redefine the balance between the rights of the state and the individual, and of the majority and the minority. The U.S. political system reflected a mix of liberalism, which underpinned the Bill of Rights, and fear of disorder. The founders made tyranny difficult through the separation of powers into executive and legislative branches and an independent judiciary. But, wary of radicalism and shocked by the French Revolution's excesses, American leaders also discouraged attacks on the upper classes by limiting voting rights, such as through property and literacy qualifications for voting and the indirect election for the presidency through the Electoral College, in which each state chose electors to cast their votes, producing results that did not always reflect the popular vote.

American leaders also had to establish a sound economic foundation for the new nation. The southern plantation interests favored free trade to market their crops abroad without obstacles. But many founders insisted that economic independence was necessary to safeguard political independence and thus preferred self-reliance and **protectionism**, the use of trade barriers to shield local industries from foreign competition. The first treasury secretary, the West Indian–born Alexander Hamilton (1757–1804), established a national bank, favored tariffs to exclude competitive foreign goods, and provided government support for manufacturing. Continued conflicts with Britain brought about a U.S. decision in 1807 to temporarily embargo all foreign trade, which stimulated domestic manufacturing to offset the lost imports.

Trade and border conflicts between Britain and the United States led to the War of 1812 (1812–1814), during which the British captured Washington, burned down the White House, and repulsed a U.S. invasion of Canada. After some U.S. victories, however, the two sides negotiated peace. Industrialization proceeded in the U.S. northeast, and the first large textile mills to convert raw cotton into finished cloth opened in New England. The northern industrialists who favored protectionist policies soon prevailed over the southern planters who wanted free trade. Meanwhile, to move resources and products, Americans also built over 3,300 miles of canals, including the Erie Canal across New York State, linking the markets and resources of the Midwest to New York City.

Gradually Americans forged a society distinct from Britain's. The French writer Alexis de Tocqueville (1805–1859), who visited the United States in the early 1830s, noted the American commitment to democracy and individualism and Americans' "unbounded desire for riches."[6] But he also condemned slavery and feared that too much individualism and greed undermined community. De Tocqueville was fascinated by America's gender relations, admiring the independence of single American women, the tendency to view marriage as a voluntary contract between loving equals, and the resulting influence of married women in

protectionism Use of trade barriers to shield local industries from foreign competition.

CHRONOLOGY
The United States and the World, 1750–1914

1787 U.S. Constitution

1803 Louisiana Purchase

1812–1814 U.S.-British War of 1812

1823 Monroe Doctrine

1825 Completion of Erie Canal

1846–1848 U.S.-Mexican War

1848 U.S. acquisition of Texas, California, and New Mexico

1849 California gold rush

1861–1865 Civil War

1862 Lincoln's Emancipation Proclamation

1867 U.S. purchase of Alaska from Russia

1869 Completion of transcontinental railroad

1898 U.S. incorporation of Hawaii

1898–1902 Spanish-American War

1902 U.S. colonization of Philippines

1903 First powered flight by Wright Brothers

the family. Nonetheless, unmarried women and many wives were still under the strong control of men who believed that women's place was centered on the home.

African Americans

Enslaved African Americans, mostly plantation workers, were the majority in many southern districts, constantly replenished by new arrivals from Africa. They created music, including spirituals, that was based in part on African rhythms and song styles and that used Christian images to indirectly express a longing for freedom. In "Go Down Moses," for example, the refrain emphasized "let my people go," a clear call for emancipation, just as the Hebrews in Egypt were led to freedom by Moses. Many white Americans also wanted to eliminate slavery and other social ills. The abolitionists Sojourner Truth (ca. 1797–1883) and Frederick Douglas (1818–1895), both former slaves, also eloquently advocated gender equality and women's suffrage. Sarah Grimke (1792–1873), a Quaker from a South Carolina slaveholding family, became an active abolitionist and one of the first American feminists, rejecting the notion of different male and female natures (see Witness to the Past: Protesting Sexism and Slavery). Discovering that their deceased brother had fathered two sons with one of his slaves, Sarah and her sister Angelina flouted custom and laws by raising and educating their nephews.

This period also saw the development of distinctively American religious and cultural beliefs that often ignored rigid doctrines and dogmatic church leaders. Many Americans embraced secular values, showing tolerance for diverse ideas and indifference to organized religion. Others actively sought a personal and intense religious experience. Religious dissenters, such as Quakers and Methodists, had long flocked to North America, and Protestant denominations there multiplied, reinforced by the religious revivals that periodically swept the country. Yet, Puritan and Calvinist values remained influential, promoting a dedication to hard work and criticism of music, dancing, and reading for pleasure.

Religion

Manifest Destiny and Expansion

The nation gradually expanded westward, acquiring abundant fertile land and rich mineral deposits, thus providing a counterpart to European imperialism in Asia and Africa (see Chapter 19). As pioneers began moving across the Appalachian Mountains in search of new economic opportunities, they developed the potent notion of their **Manifest Destiny**, the conviction that their country's unmatched institutions and culture gave them a God-given right to take over the land. Manifest Destiny offered a religious sanction for U.S. nationalism and the thrust outward. In 1823 Secretary of State John Quincy Adams set a goal of transforming the United States into "a nation, coextensive with the North American continent, destined by God and nature to be the most populous and powerful people ever combined under one social compact."[7]

Manifest Destiny Americans' conviction that their country's unmatched institutions and culture gave them a God-given right to take over the land.

American Progress
This 1893 painting by the American artist John Gast extols progress and shows Americans, guided by divine providence, expanding across, and bringing civilization to, the forests and prairies of the Midwest and West. The painting reflects views held by many Americans of their destiny and special role in the world.

Library of Congress

Map 20.2 U.S. Expansion Through 1867

The United States expanded in stages after independence, gaining land from Spain, France, Britain, and Mexico until the nation stretched from the Atlantic to the Gulf and Pacific coasts by 1867. During the same period Canadians expanded westward from Quebec to British Columbia.

e Interactive Map

Territorial Expansion

After acquiring the Ohio territory, in 1787 the new nation extended from the Atlantic to the Mississippi River. In 1803 President Thomas Jefferson (g. 1800–1809) astutely bought from France, in the Louisiana Purchase, a huge section of the Midwest and South that doubled the size of the country. Then the United States acquired Florida and the Pacific Northwest. While many Americans moved into the Midwest, others continued on to Oregon by wagon train, crossing vast prairies, deserts, and mountains. In 1848, as a result of the U.S.-Mexican War, the United States obtained Texas, California, and New Mexico from Mexico. Then the discovery of gold near Sacramento in 1849 prompted over 100,000 Americans, known as "49ers," to board sailing ships or covered wagons and head for California from the distant east, hoping to strike it rich. In California the "49ers" sometimes clashed with the long-settled Mexicans and immigrant Chinese. The 1867 purchase of Alaska from Russia eliminated all European rivals from North America (see Map 20.2). By 1913 the United States had grown to forty-eight states.

Frontier Life

The vast North American frontier offered conditions where settlers could develop new ways of life and ideas. The rise of cattle ranching on the Great Plains fostered a new occupation, that of

Protesting Sexism and Slavery

Sarah Grimke and her younger sister, Angelina, were the daughters of a wealthy slaveholding family in Charleston, South Carolina. Adopting the Quaker faith, which emphasized human dignity, and rejecting their positions as members of the state's elite, they dedicated their lives to advocating women's rights and the abolition of slavery. In 1837 they moved north and began giving lectures before large audiences. Because they spoke out so publicly, they were often criticized by churches for violating gender expectations. Sarah Grimke responded in 1838 by writing letters to her critics that often used Christian arguments to defend women's right and obligation to voice their views. When the letters were published together in one volume, they became the first American feminist treatise on women's rights. The following excerpts convey some of Grimke's arguments.

Here then I plant myself. God created us equal; he created us free agents; he is our Lawgiver, our King and our Judge, and to him alone is woman bound to be in subjection, and to him alone is she accountable for the use of those talents with which her Heavenly Father has entrusted her. . . . As I am unable to learn from sacred writ when woman was deprived by God of her equality with man, I shall touch upon a few points in the Scriptures, which demonstrate that no supremacy was granted to man. . . . [In the Bible] we find the commands of God invariably the same to man and woman; and not the slightest intimation is given in a single passage, that God designed woman to point to man as her instructor. . . .

I hope that the principles I have asserted will claim the attention of some of my sex, who may be able to bring into view, more thoroughly than I have done, the situation and degradation of women. . . . During the early part of my life, my lot was cast among the butterflies of the *fashionable* world; and of this class of women, I am constrained to say, both from experience and observation, that their education is miserably deficient; that they are taught to regard marriage as the one

thing needful, the only notice of distinction; hence to attract the notice and win the attentions of men, by their external charms, is the chief business of fashionable girls. They seldom think that men will be allured by intellectual acquirements, because they find, that where any mental superiority exists, a woman is generally shunned and regarded as stepping out of her "appropriate sphere," which, in their view, is to dress, to dance, to set out to the best possible advantage her person. . . . To be married is too often held up to the view of girls as [necessary for] human happiness and human existence. For this purpose . . . the majority of girls are trained. . . . [In education] the improvement of their intellectual capacities is only a secondary consideration. . . . Our education consists almost exclusively of culinary and other manual operations. . . .

There is another class of women in this country, to whom I cannot refer, without feelings of the deepest shame and sorrow. I allude to our female slaves. . . . The virtue of female slaves is wholly at the mercy of irresponsible tyrants, and women are bought and sold in our slave markets, to gratify the brutal lust of those who bear the name of Christians. . . . If she dares resist her seducer, her life by the laws of some of the slave States may be . . . sacrificed to the fury of disappointed passion. . . . The female slaves suffer every species of degradation and cruelty, which the most wanton barbarity can inflict; they are indecently divested of their clothing, sometimes tied up and severely whipped. . . . Can any American woman look at these scenes of shocking . . . cruelty, and fold her hands in apathy, and say, "I have nothing to do with slavery"? *She cannot and be guiltless.*

THINKING ABOUT THE READING

1. What do the letters tell us about the social expectations and education for white women from affluent families?

2. In what way do Grimke's letters address the issue of slavery?

Source: Sarah M. Grimke, *Letters on the Equality of the Sexes, and the Condition of Woman* (Boston: Issac Knapp, 1838).

---

cowboys on horseback, who were needed to guide herds of several thousand cattle on long, lonely drives to railroad towns for shipment east. These cowboys—whites, Mexicans, African Americans, and men of mixed descent—often learned survival skills and knowledge of horses from Native Americans. Individualists sought adventure, social equality, and a better life in the West. Life on the frontier was often hard, especially on women. An Illinois farm wife, Sara Price, lamented her hardship in poetry, writing that "life is a toil and love is a trouble. Beauty will fade and riches will flee. Pleasures will dwindle and prices they double, And nothing is as I would wish it to be."[8]

Westward expansion came at the expense of the Mexicans, Spaniards, and Native Americans already there. Indians saw whites as invaders and often resisted violently. To whites, Indians represented an alien culture and needed to be restricted to reservations. The U.S. Supreme Court ruled in 1831 that the Indians' "relation to the United States resembles that of a ward to his guardian."[9] Over time many Indians, even tribes who lived in peace with whites, were removed from their native lands. The Cherokee, farmers of Georgia and the Carolinas who had developed an alphabet, published a newspaper, written a constitution, and had long cultivated good relations with their white

Westward Expansion and Native Americans

neighbors, were forced into concentration camps and then in 1838 sent on a forced march of 1,200 miles, the "Trail of Tears," to Oklahoma. Four thousand Cherokee died from starvation or exposure on the journey. Other tribes were broken up in coerced relocations. Some tribes also resisted removal. The Seminole (SEM-uh-nole) in Florida, led by Chief Osceola (os-ee-OH-luh) (ca. 1804–1838), fought two wars with the U.S. army, attacking with guerrilla tactics and then retreating into the Everglades swamps. Finally Osceola was captured, after which the Seminole resistance faded and many of the tribe were exiled to Oklahoma.

United States and Latin America

sphere of interest An area in which one great power assumes responsibility for maintaining peace and monopolizes the area's resources.

The Americans' quest for resources and markets led ultimately to territorial expansion into Latin America and the formation of a new kind of empire. In 1823 President James Monroe (1758–1831) authored one of the major principles of U.S. foreign policy. The Monroe Doctrine was a unilateral statement warning European nations against interfering in the Western Hemisphere and affirming U.S. commitment to shape the Latin American political future after the overthrow of Spanish colonialism. The doctrine effectively marked off Latin America as an American **sphere of interest**, an area in which one great power assumes responsibility for maintaining peace and monopolizes the resources of that area. The Monroe Doctrine forged complex links between the United States and the rest of the Americas, often provoking hostility in Latin America, and set the stage for the rise of the United States as a world power.

As a result of the U.S.-Mexican War of 1846–1848, the United States greatly expanded its national territory. Some 35,000 Americans and their slaves had settled in the Mexican province of Texas. Chafing at Mexican rule and its antislavery policies, in 1836 the Americans rebelled and pushed the Mexican forces out, declaring themselves an independent republic. Soon the Texans sought annexation to the United States, a move favored by the proslavery southern states and opposed by the antislavery northern states. After Texans talked of alliance with Britain, the U.S. president and Congress moved to admit Texas to statehood in 1844, provoking the pride of Mexicans, who had never recognized Texan independence and now reasserted their claims. The war that followed stirred divisive and passionate debate in the United States, where many people opposed the conflict. After President James Polk (1795–1849) ordered military action, a Massachusetts legislative resolution proclaimed "that such a war of conquest, so hateful, unjust and unconstitutional in its origin and character, must be regarded as a war against freedom, against humanity, against justice, against the Union."[10] The war ended when 14,000 U.S. troops invaded Mexico and captured Mexico City. This victory allowed the United States to permanently annex Mexican territories from Texas to California. However, the conflict had killed 13,000 Americans and 50,000 Mexicans, and it had also fostered an enduring Mexican distrust of the United States.

United States and Asia

Many Americans supported the extension of Manifest Destiny to Latin America and Asia. Polk wanted to seize California and its harbors to increase the profitable commerce with China. In 1853 Senator William Seward placed expansion in global perspective, advising Americans: "You are already the great continental power. But does that content you? I trust that it does not. You want the commerce of the world. The nation that draws the most from the earth and fabricates most, and sells the most to foreign nations, must be and will be the great power of the earth."[11] American traders participated in the lucrative China trade, including opium smuggling, while the United States Navy opened up reclusive Japan. Hence, after the American revolution, merchants from New England ports such as Salem (Massachusetts) established, and grew rich from, operations in Asian ports such as Macao and Madras. U.S. traders, missionaries, adventurers, diplomats, and soldiers flocked to Asia (see Chapters 22–23).

During the nineteenth century the United States began to build, not a territorial empire like the British and Spanish, but chiefly an "informal" empire based on extending U.S. power through financial controls, trade, and military operations. American naval forces intervened in Southeast Asia almost annually from the 1830s through the 1860s. For example, in 1832 a U.S. naval expedition bombarded a port on the Indonesian island of Sumatra, whose officials had seized a private U.S. ship for illegal activities; U.S. officials boasted that the demolition of the port had "struck terror" into the Sumatrans, forcing them to release the ship. Some American leaders advocated military action to gain trade agreements, an aggressive attitude that increasingly influenced U.S. policies during the century. Presidents also sought to obtain nearby Cuba from Spain, even financing Cuban revolts.

The Civil War, Abolition, and Industrialization

North-South Conflict

The Civil War (1861–1865) reshaped U.S. society by ending slavery. Like Sarah Grimke, many Americans had believed that slavery mocked liberal democracy. By the early 1800s it had largely disappeared from northern states, and in 1810 the U.S. government outlawed the slave trade.

Thousands of free blacks occupied a precarious position in the southern states. The Civil War was a last gasp for the slavery-based southern plantation society, which desperately tried to break free from the urbanization, industrialization, and social change percolating in the northern states. By 1860, the North was the home of industry, banks, and great ports such as New York, Boston, and Philadelphia. By contrast, the South was largely a monocultural plantation economy, inhabited by 350,000 white families and 3 million black slaves, which depended on exports to survive.

In 1860–1861 eleven southern states seceded from the union, forming the proslavery Confederate States of America. President Abraham Lincoln (1809–1865), a lawyer from Illinois who wanted to end slavery and preserve the union, mobilized the military forces of the remaining states to resist the secession. In 1862 he issued the Emancipation Proclamation, freeing all slaves in the Confederacy. After four years of war the North defeated the South, mainly because the North's dynamic economy better mobilized resources for war and the North also had a population advantage of nearly 4 to 1.

The northern victory ultimately displaced the southern plantation system, crushed the southern struggle for self-determination, destroyed the South's economic link to Britain, firmly established protectionism as economic policy, and fostered a much stronger federal government. The war resulted in more American deaths than all other wars fought by Americans combined, killing 360,000 Union and 258,000 Confederate troops. The South began to enjoy balanced economic development only with the growth of industry in the mid-twentieth century, largely paid for by northern investors.

Although the Civil War emancipated African Americans, it did not eliminate the disadvantages faced by them and other ethnic minorities. Many former slaves taught themselves to read, and some opened schools to expand opportunities for young blacks. Many African Americans left the plantations, but their job prospects were chiefly limited to sharecropping or physical labor. Long after slavery ended, African Americans also faced laws restricting their rights and barriers to voting. The southern states and some northern states had rigid laws against intermarriage and, unlike Latin America, little separate recognition for people of mixed ancestry, who were lumped with African Americans and treated as such. Any trace of African ancestry meant automatic relegation to inferior status. Skin color became the major determinant of social class, and racial segregation of schools, housing, and public facilities remained the norm in the South until the 1960s. Those who violated these laws and customs faced jail, beatings, or even executions by white vigilantes. The journalist Ida B. Wells (1862–1931), born into slavery, sparked a long movement to end mob violence, including hangings (known as "lynchings").

African Americans

As peace brought a resumption of expansion into central and western North America, more Native Americans lost control of their destinies. Whites subdued the Great Plains with new technology, including the six-shooter, the steel plough, and the barbed-wire fence. Settlers, railroad builders, and fur traders massacred 15 million bison, the chief source of subsistence for Great Plains tribes, while farmers and ranchers reshaped the environment of the prairies and northern woodlands. Indians resisted but eventually faced defeat. In 1890, the United States Army's massacre of three hundred Lakota Sioux followers of the Ghost Dance, an Indian spiritual revival movement, at Wounded Knee in South Dakota marked the triumph of U.S. colonization of the west. Defeated and impoverished, Indians were put on government-controlled reservations. Their children, prohibited from speaking their native languages or practicing tribal traditions in boarding and public schools, were stripped of their cultural heritage.

Resurgent Expansion

The northern victory in the Civil War and protectionism spurred the improved material life and great industrial growth in the later 1800s, with the rise of the food processing, textile, iron, and steel industries and growing coal, mineral, and oil production. In 1860 the United States ranked fourth among industrial nations, but by 1894 it ranked first; American exports had tripled, and the nation was second only to Britain as a world trader. Technological innovations changed economic life. Electricity as a power source, combined with improved production methods, turned out goods faster, more cheaply, and in greater quantities than ever before, increasing U.S. competitiveness. New inventions by Americans such as the typewriter, cash register, adding machine, telegraph, and telephone increased business productivity, while American and European inventions such as water-tube boilers, steam-powered forging hammers, portable steam engines, and the internal combustion engine revolutionized industry. Thomas Edison (1847–1931) benefited the public and industry by perfecting the light bulb.

Industrial Growth

Improved transportation and communication networks reshaped American life and population patterns. The transcontinental railroad, completed in 1869, opened western lands for settlement. Many of the workers who drove the spikes and blasted the passages through rocks and mountains for the railroad tracks were African Americans, Chinese, or Irish. Henry Ford (1863–1947) started a motor company in 1903, turning out the first affordable cars and refining the

Women Textile Workers In both Europe and North America women became the largest part of the work force in the textile industry. These women, working in a New England spinning mill around 1850, endured harsh work conditions and the boring, often dangerous, job of tending machines.

mass-production assembly line. Orville and Wilber Wright became the first men to achieve powered flight in 1903, launching the age of aviation.

Capitalists and Workers

But industrialization also led to a monopolistic concentration of industrial and financial resources similar to Europe's that worsened the inequitable distribution of wealth. A few fabulously wealthy tycoons such as John D. Rockefeller and J. P. Morgan, known to their critics as the Robber Barons, influenced politicians, controlled much of the economy, and expected workers to labor at subsistence wages. The Social Darwinist Rockefeller claimed that "the growth of large business is merely survival of the fittest and a law of God."[12] The wealthy flaunted their success, and many less-affluent Americans also valued and hoped to acquire wealth, believing that the United States was a land of opportunity where anyone could succeed with hard work regardless of social background.

Industrialization fostered industrial workers, who often experienced a hard life. In the coal mines of the southern Appalachians and Ohio River Valley, the work was dangerous, the hours long, and the wages low. Children worked alongside their parents, and miners often died young from breathing coal dust. Before the Civil War the textile industry, centered in New England, was based on exploitation of women and children. Companies recruited teenage girls from poor rural families to work in dark, hot mill rooms filled with cotton dust. They labored fourteen hours a day, six days a week, and were housed in company dormitories, six to eight girls per room. By the 1880s the textile industry had moved south to Virginia and the Carolinas, where wages were lower and people even more desperate for jobs.

Social Change, Thought, and Culture

Immigration

This era was also marked by social change. Some 25 million Europeans immigrated to the United States between 1870 and 1916. At first they came largely from northwestern Europe, especially

English, Irish, Germans, and Scandinavians. Later many arrived from southern and eastern Europe, including Italians, Greeks, Serbs, and Poles. Many Jews fleeing persecution in Europe saw the United States as the Promised Land, and by 1927 the Jewish population totaled 4 million. Meanwhile, thousands of Chinese, Japanese, and Filipino immigrants landed on the Pacific Coast. Most of these European and Asian newcomers faced discrimination. Some businesses posted signs saying, "No Irish need apply." Chinese and Japanese immigrants, mostly living in the western states, faced harsher restrictions and sometimes violence.

In less than a century the United States went from a mostly rural nation along the Atlantic coast to a transcontinental powerhouse. The federal government encouraged migration westward by giving free land to settlers in the Midwest for farming. The United States also became urbanized, with half of the people living in cities, including metropolises such as New York and Chicago.

These decades also saw movements seeking economic and social change. Since factories poured out more goods than Americans could consume, by the 1890s economic depression, panics, and bloody labor conflicts fostered working-class radicalism. Farmers and workers resented the wealth of the Robber Barons and the power of large corporations and railroads. Even while the United States became the world's leading agricultural producer, many farmers went bankrupt, losing their land to banks, and popular movements, some led by women, fought those with power and privilege. Labor unions had first appeared in the 1820s, and by midcentury mill girls were campaigning for better conditions and a shorter workday in New England textile mills. Eugene Debs (1855–1926), the socialist leader of the railway union, explained in 1893 that "the capitalists refer to you as mill hands, farm hands, factory hands. The trouble is he owns your head and your hands."[13] By the early 1900s the radical, Marxist-influenced International Workers of the World (better known as the Wobblies) gained influence among industrial workers, miners, and longshoremen. Union militants such as Mary Harris ("Mother") Jones (1830–1930), an Irish immigrant who called herself a hellraiser and organized coal miners and railroad workers, fought the power of big business. Employers and their political allies disparaged union members as communists and fought their demands.

Women also struggled for their civil rights. During the 1800s, although large numbers of women worked in factories, shops, and offices while also managing their homes, religious leaders urged women to be more pious, self-sacrificing, and obedient to men. They wore stiff, uncomfortable whalebone corsets that constrained movement and accentuated their figure, a symbol of their submission to male expectations. Many women wanted more options; the banners carried by striking factory workers in 1912 read, "We want bread and roses too." But women gained basic privileges on a par with men only after a long, nonviolent suffrage movement for the vote that declared that "all men and women are created equal." Suffragettes opposed a system in which women had no rights to property or even to their own children in case of divorce. After seven decades of marching, publicizing their cause, and lobbying male politicians, they convinced Congress to give women the right to vote in 1920.

Some Americans increasingly created their own distinctive literary and intellectual traditions. Walt Whitman (1819–1892), a journalist influenced by European romanticism, celebrated democracy, the working class, and both heterosexual and homosexual affection while addressing the transformations of the Industrial Revolution. Whitman described his ethnically diverse and dynamic nation as "a newer garden of creation, dense, joyous, modern, populous millions, cities and farms. By all the world contributed."[14] Mark Twain (1835–1910), a former printer and riverboat pilot from Missouri turned journalist, was inspired by European realism and sought material all over the country and the world. Twain emphasized the underside of American life and character, was skeptical about technology's value, and opposed the increasing U.S. imperial thrust in the world.

American philosophy and religion also went in new directions. The leading American philosophers, such as William James and John Dewey, broke with the European tradition by claiming that ideas had little value unless they enlarged people's concrete knowledge of reality, an approach known as pragmatism. While many Americans embraced secular and humanist views, many others sought inspiration in religion. The Protestant missionary impulse fostered religious and moral fervor, and Americans became active as Christian missionaries around the world. The nation itself became more religiously diverse. In 1776 most Americans were Protestant, often Calvinist, but by 1914 the United States contained followers of many faiths, including some Buddhist and Muslim immigrants from Asia.

Americans also produced unique music, largely the result of mixing black and white traditions. In the South, blues and jazz music developed in the early 1900s out of African American culture. The blues grew out of the plantation economy, the songs detailing personal woes in a world

Economic and Social Movements

Struggle for Women's Rights

Literature and Culture

of harsh reality and racism. Bluesmen sang of lost love, the brutality of police, jail, joblessness, and oppression. Some songs celebrated black heroes such as the legendary hand driller John Henry, who allegedly died competing against a steam drill to build a railroad tunnel in the later 1800s. The blending of black blues with white folk music and popular music provided a foundation for several forms of American popular music in the twentieth century, including rock, rhythm and blues, and soul, which spread around the world.

American Capitalism and Empire

Imperialism

As in Europe, industrial capitalism fostered imperialism and warfare. A series of economic depressions from the 1870s through the 1890s spurred public demand for foreign markets, as many American businessmen, farmers, and workers favored acquiring territories overseas to improve national economic prospects. Others hoped to spread American conceptions of freedom and a capitalist marketplace economy. Many argued that since domestic problems, such as the wide rich-poor gap, were not easily resolved, only acquiring resources and markets by directly or indirectly controlling other societies could generate enough wealth to avoid domestic turmoil. These pressures led to military interventions. The United States sent military forces to at least twenty-seven countries and territories between 1833 and 1898 to protect American economic interests or to suppress the piracy that threatened U.S. shipping. Troops were dispatched to many Latin American nations, China, Indonesia, Korea, and North Africa, and for decades U.S. gunships patrolled several of China's rivers to protect American businessmen and missionaries from Chinese who resented Western imperialism.

Colonization of Hawaii

U.S. forces also brought the Hawaiian Islands, a Polynesian kingdom where Americans had long settled as traders, whalers, planters, and missionaries, into the U.S. empire. The growing American population resented the Hawaiian monarchy. In 1891 Liliuokalani **(luh-lee-uh-oh-kuh-LAH-nee)** (1838–1917), a Hawaiian nationalist who wanted to restrict settler political influence, became queen. Although strong and resolute and beloved by her people as a songwriter, she faced economic disaster when the U.S. Congress abandoned preferential treatment for Hawaiian sugar imports. In 1893 American settlers, aided by 150 U.S. troops, overthrew the monarchy, formed a provisional government, and announced that they would seek affiliation with the United States. A heated debate in the United States on the advantages and disadvantages of direct colonization delayed annexation of the islands until 1898. The end of the monarchy also transformed the islands socially, as thousands of Japanese, Chinese, Korean, and Filipino immigrants become the main labor force, mostly working on plantations owned by American settlers and companies. By the 1930s, Asians constituted the large majority of Hawaii's population.

Spanish-American War

The major conflict involving the United States was the Spanish-American War (1898–1902), which pitted American against Spanish forces in several Spanish colonies. The war helped make the United States a major world power and empire and was motivated by President William McKinley's (1843–1901) desire to obtain foreign markets for America's surplus production. To that end, the United States fought with Spain over that country's remaining, restless colonies: Cuba, Puerto Rico, Guam, and the Philippines. The war unleashed American nationalist fervor, one observer describing patriotism as oozing out of every boy old enough to feed the pigs. While the United States quickly triumphed against the hopelessly outmatched Spanish, 5,500 Americans died in Cuba, mostly of disease; a surgeon who labored among the survivors wrote of pale faces, sunken eyes, staggering gaits, and emaciated forms.

The war also changed Americans' outlook on the world. A future president, Woodrow Wilson, boasted about America's emergence as a major power: "No war ever transformed us quite as the war with Spain. No previous years ever ran with so swift a change as the years since 1898. We have witnessed a new revolution, the transformation of America completed."[15] However, to colonize the Philippines, the United States had to brutally suppress a fierce nationalist resistance by Filipinos opposed to U.S. occupation, resulting in the deaths of thousands of Filipinos and Americans and indicating the costs of exercising power in the world. Many Americans protested the bloody U.S. invasion of the distant islands (see Chapter 22). The colonization of the Philippines, Puerto Rico, and Guam, as well as economic and political domination over nominally independent Cuba, also transformed the United States from an informal into a territorial empire much like the Netherlands and Portugal.

SECTION SUMMARY

- Americans were more individualistic and offered more independence to women than Europeans, and a struggle raged between supporters and opponents of slavery.

- Americans gradually pushed toward the West Coast, taking advantage of abundant natural resources and inflicting great suffering on Native Americans.

- The Monroe Doctrine announced that the United States saw Latin America as its own sphere of interest, off-limits to European powers.

- The bloody and divisive U.S.-Mexican War brought a large chunk of Mexican territory under American control.

- The Civil War killed hundreds of thousands, did tremendous damage to the South's economy, and freed the slaves, though discrimination and segregation continued for at least another century.

- American industry advanced rapidly, producing immense wealth for a small number of tycoons, helping others to prosper, and creating difficult, hazardous work for many.

- Millions of immigrants poured into the United States, seeking opportunity and often finding discrimination, while social movements seeking better treatment for workers and greater rights for women came into being.

- A distinctive American culture developed that celebrated democracy and practicality and that reflected the diverse origins of the American people.

- In the interests of promoting and protecting American business interests, the U.S. military intervened in the affairs of many foreign countries and territories, most notably in the Spanish-American War, which brought the United States its first formal colonies.

LATIN AMERICA AND THE CARIBBEAN IN THE GLOBAL SYSTEM

What political, economic, and social patterns shaped Latin America after independence?

Brazil and most of Spain's Latin American colonies won their independence in the early 1800s, although the Caribbean islands mostly remained colonies (see Chapter 19). But the new states did not forge the enduring democracy of their northern neighbors or foster significant economic change; instead most Latin Americans experienced political instability and regional conflicts. By the 1870s conditions stabilized as expanding European markets created a greater demand for Latin American exports, though free-trade policies also deepened the economic monocultures. Black slaves gained their freedom, waves of European immigrants changed the social landscape, and the United States increasingly exercised power in the region.

New Latin American Nations

Latin Americans faced new political and economic challenges. Some countries, such as Argentina, Brazil, and Mexico, were large and unwieldy, while others, such as El Salvador and the Dominican Republic, were small and had limited resources. Creating stable republics and political unity proved to be a struggle because the new governments did not always win the allegiance of all the people, and civil wars often pitted those favoring federalism and regionalism against partisans of a strong centralized government. In addition, various frontier disputes fostered occasional wars. Chile fought Peru and Bolivia in 1837 and again in 1879–1884, acquiring territory from those two countries as a result (see Chronology: Latin America and the Caribbean, 1750–1914).

Political Instability

Political instability often led to military dictatorships, since Spain and Portugal had never fostered democratic conditions in their colonies. Thus although most of the Latin American countries adopted elections and U.S.-style constitutions, authoritarian governments often ignored their provisions. Tensions between central governments and remote regions also became chronic. For example, the Argentine government did not impose its authority on the southernmost provinces until the 1870s.

Economic and Political Power

Despite political independence, most leaders did not favor dramatic social and economic change. The wealthy upper class, mostly creoles, owned large businesses, plantations, and haciendas; mestizos and mulattos dominated the small middle class of shopkeepers, teachers, and skilled artisans; and over half of the population, including most Indians and blacks, were lower class. Economies based chiefly on plantation agriculture or mining had similar, highly unequal social structures and offered limited educational opportunities. Planters, ranchers, mine owners, merchants, and military officers dominated politics and often restricted the political participation of the poor nonwhite majority. To contain or prevent unrest, military strongmen, known as **caudillos**, who acquired and maintained power through force, governed many Latin American countries. Some of these, such as the dictator Juan Manuel de Rosas **(huan man-WELL deh ROH-sas)** (1793-1877) in Argentina, were tyrants. Rosas's police and thugs beat up, tortured, or murdered opponents, often poor peasants. For their armies, caudillos and regional leaders sometimes recruited local cowboys, known as **gauchos** in Argentina and Uruguay, who worked on large ranches and were skilled horsemen and fighters.

caudillos Latin American military strongmen who acquired and maintained power through force.

gauchos Cowboys in Argentina and Uruguay who worked on large ranches and were skilled horsemen and fighters.

Despite these problems, most Latin American nations established some stability by the 1850s. Many countries sought both "progress and order," which usually meant caudillo rule, but a few fostered multiparty systems in which competing parties sought access to national power. Liberals generally favored federalism, free trade, and the separation of church and state; often irreligious, they opposed the institutional power of the Catholic Church as contrary to individual liberty. Conservatives sought centralization, trade protectionism, and maintenance of church power. Conflicts between these groups were sometimes violent.

Political Changes

Brazil was the only Latin American nation governed by a monarchy, which seemed unwilling to consider popular aspirations toward abolishing slavery and forming a republic. As tensions simmered, the army seized power in 1889, exiled Emperor Dom Pedro II, and replaced the monarchy with a republic. However, although a federal system emerged, suffrage was highly restricted, the majority of Brazilians gained neither property nor civil rights, and many remained desperately poor. In the end Brazil maintained an authoritarian tradition, but rebellions and regionalism constantly challenged the government.

Social and economic inequalities in Latin American countries often led to reforms and sometimes to revolutions. The birth of the Mexican republic in 1824 did not bring stability to the vast country, which stretched from northern deserts to southern rain forests. Between 1833 and 1855 a caudillo, General Antonio Lopez de Santa Anna (1797-1876), led a series of dictatorships punctuated by civil war. Santa Anna also lost half of Mexico's territory, including Texas and California, in the disastrous U.S.-Mexican War (1846-1848), a humiliation that is still felt by Mexicans today. Growing social problems and Santa Anna's misadventures sparked upheaval. In 1861 Mexican liberals led by Benito Juarez **(WAHR-ez)** (1806-1872), a pragmatic lawyer and Zapotec Indian, defeated the conservatives and suspended repayment of the foreign debt, provoking a short-lived occupation by France that made a member of the Habsburg family, Maximilian of Austria (1832-1867), emperor of Mexico. However, France withdrew its troops and Maximilian's regime collapsed in 1867. Juarez again served as president until his death in 1872, seeking social justice, fighting corruption, subordinating the church to the secular state, and assigning church and communal lands to individual families to create free peasants. His reformist policies and his Indian ancestry made Juarez Mexico's most honored leader and a symbol of the nation.

In 1876 Mexico came under the dictatorship of Porfirio Diaz **(DEE-ahs)** (1830-1915), a mestizo caudillo. Diaz brought stability and economic progress but also allowed foreign business interests and investors to take over much of Mexico's economy, doing little to help the poor majority. Under his free enterprise policies many Indians sold their land to large haciendas and land companies to pay off debts. The Diaz regime ended in civil war and the Mexican Revolution (1910-1920). One of several revolutionary factions was led by the liberal creole Francisco Madero (1873-1913), a landowner's son educated in France and the United States. Another rebel leader, Pancho Villa **(VEE-uh)** (1877-1923), a former cowboy, attracted support chiefly from ranchers in northern Mexico. In the south, the charismatic mestizo former peasant Emiliano Zapata **(zeh-PAH-teh)** (1879-1919) organized a peasant army that seized haciendas and fought the federal army.

CHRONOLOGY

Latin America and the Caribbean, 1750–1914

1861–1872 Benito Juarez president of Mexico

1876–1911 Diaz dictatorship in Mexico

1842 End of trans-Atlantic slave trade by most nations

1862–1867 French occupation of Mexico

1886 Abolition of slavery in Cuba

1889 Abolition of slavery in Brazil

1889 Brazilian republic

1879–1884 War between Chile and Peru-Bolivia

1895–1898 Cuban revolt against Spain

1898–1902 Spanish-American War

1901 Platt Amendment to Cuban constitution

1910–1920 Mexican Revolution

1912 U.S. intervention in Nicaragua

1914 Completion of Panama Canal

With the defeat of Diaz, largely by Zapata's forces, the idealistic Madero was elected president but, unable to hold the revolutionary movement together, was murdered by a rival, generating a free-for-all between the armies of Madero, Villa, Zapata, and other leaders. Mexico was engulfed in sporadic violence, all factions used ruthless tactics, and alliances formed and collapsed. A novel recorded the confusion: "thinkers prepare the Revolution; bandits carry it out. At the moment no one can say with any assurance: 'So-and-so is a revolutionary and What's-his-name is a bandit.' Tomorrow, perhaps, it will be clearer."[16] Zapata was assassinated by a rival in 1919, but his reputation lived on after death, making him the most celebrated revolutionary hero.

The fighting had raised expectations for social change and fostered a yearning for peace. Women played a critical revolutionary role. They cooked and commanded troops, served as spies and couriers, shot carbines and pistols, and fought disguised as men. Some of their hopes for more rights seemed realized in a constitution introduced in 1917, which set forth progressive goals such as an eight-hour work day and paid maternity leave. In 1920 the conflict wound down after claiming 1 million lives. While most Mexicans remained impoverished, a new party led by former revolutionaries formed a government and brought political stability while also opening some space for women to enter the business world and state governments.

Spanish-ruled Cuba also experienced revolt. By the later 1800s an independence movement had developed led by the journalist Jose Marti (1853–1895), who had traveled and lived in Europe, the United States, and various Latin American nations. Marti's writings promoting freedom, equality, and social justice helped inspire a Cuban revolt in 1895. Marti welcomed Afro-Cubans and women, who became the backbone of the struggle. However, Marti was killed in the fighting, and eventually the revolution was side-tracked by U.S. intervention during the Spanish-American War. Americans soon dominated the economy and strongly influenced the Cuban government.

Women Revolutionaries in Mexico
Women joined men in fighting, and sometimes dying, for one or another faction during the Mexican Revolution. Many women hoped that the revolution would bring social change and a greater emphasis on improving women's political and economic rights.

Latin American Economic and Social Change

Like North Americans, Latin Americans debated free trade and heavy involvement in the world economy as opposed to protectionism and self-sufficiency. But, as exports and investments declined, Latin American leaders, unlike U.S. leaders, decided to maintain the monoculture based on plantations, mines, and ranches, concentrating on the export, mainly to the United States and Europe, of raw materials such as Ecuadorian cocoa, Brazilian coffee, Argentine beef, Cuban sugar, and Bolivian and Chilean ores. The decision left Latin American societies economically vulnerable because earnings from minerals and cash crops ebbed and flowed with the fall or rise of world commodity prices. By the twentieth century economic conditions in Latin America were closely tied to fluctuating, "boom or bust" world prices for those countries' exports. Hence, the politically unstable Central American countries, whose economies depended on tropical agriculture, were derisively called "banana republics."

Because Latin American economic policies fostered growth but not development, the majority of people saw few benefits and the gap between the rich and the poor widened. The impoverished state of most Indians and blacks gave them little purchasing power to support any local industries that might be developed. Efforts to industrialize in Brazil, Colombia, and Mexico in the 1830s and 1840s failed because of competition from European imports. Independence also opened Latin America to North American, French, and especially British merchants and financiers, who used their economic power to dominate banking and the import trade for industrial goods while also investing in mines and plantations. By the mid-1800s British businessmen and bankers controlled the imports and exports of both Brazil and Argentina. Argentina was sometimes called an informal member of the British Empire, and an Argentine nationalist complained that "English capital has done what English armies could not do. Today our country is tributary to England."[17] After 1890 the United States also became a powerful economic influence in Latin America.

Growth Without Development

Foreign economic domination had several consequences. First, foreign corporations increasingly owned the plantations and mines. For example, the U.S.-based United Fruit Company dominated Central American banana growing. Latin America became a major contributor to world commodity markets, producing some 62 percent of the world's coffee, 38 percent of the sugar, and 25 percent of the rubber by World War I. Although growing U.S. demand for markets and raw materials fostered economic expansion, inequalities grew. In some rural areas of Brazil, for example, powerful landed families maintained the peasantry in what was essentially bondage through private armies and gunmen. Throughout Latin America powerful families or foreign corporations increasingly owned the usable land, fostering social and economic imbalances that produced political unrest in the twentieth century.

Abolition of Slavery

Yet, the abolition of slavery opened the door to social change. Some of the leaders who overthrew Spanish rule freed slaves who fought in the wars of independence. Between 1823 and 1854 slavery was legally abolished in most of Latin America and the Caribbean, and most European and American countries outlawed the trans-Atlantic slave trade. The Spanish rulers finally granted Cuban slaves their freedom in 1886, and abolitionists became more outspoken in Brazil. Increasing resistance by slaves, growing opposition by educated Brazilians, and the desire to promote European immigration led finally to abolition in 1889. However, as in the United States, emancipation did not dramatically improve economic conditions. Many Latin American and Caribbean blacks shifted from being slaves to low-status sharecroppers, tenant farmers, and laborers. As a popular Brazilian verse lamented: "Everything in this world changes; Only the life of the Negro [black] remains the same. He works to die of hunger."[18]

Immigration and Class System

While life for most blacks changed little, the immigration of millions of Europeans and Asians reshaped many Latin American societies. Latin America's population doubled between 1850 and 1900 to over 60 million. Italians, Spaniards, Germans, Russians, and Irish sought better economic prospects, especially in Argentina, Brazil, Chile, Uruguay, and Venezuela. The majority of people in Buenos Aires, Argentina, trace their roots to Italy. The continued immigration generated a long-term market for European products and fashions.

People from overcrowded lands in Asia and the Middle East also immigrated to the Americas. In Trinidad, British Guiana, and Dutch Guiana, the abolition of slavery prompted labor-short planters to import workers from India, with the result that Indians eventually accounted for around half of the population in these colonies. Japanese settled in Brazil, Peru, and Paraguay as farmers and traders, Arab immigrants from Lebanon and Syria developed trade diasporas throughout Latin America, and Indonesians moved to Dutch Guiana as plantation workers. Chinese flocked to Peru and Cuba and, in smaller numbers, to Jamaica, Trinidad, and the Guianas. Much cultural mixing occurred as a result. For example, an Afro-Trinidadian might have a Spanish surname, belong to the Presbyterian Church, possess a Hindu love charm, enjoy English literature, and favor Chinese food. People of Asian or Middle Eastern ancestry have sometimes headed Latin American or Caribbean governments.

Despite the newcomers, Latin American society remained more conservative than North America. The creole elite dominated most countries, while European and Asian immigrants and mixed-descent people constituted the middle class. Many mulattos and most blacks and Indians remained in the lower class. Indians often withdrew into their village communities and limited contact with the national society. In 1865 a Mexican described the wide gap between whites and Indians: "The white is the proprietor; the Indian the worker. The white is rich; the Indian poor and miserable."[19] In Brazil, large populations of European, African, and mixed-descent people fostered a unique, multiracial society. Unlike in the United States, economic class and skin color did not always coincide, and intermarriage and cultural mixing were common. Millions of Brazilians of all backgrounds blended African religions with Catholicism, creating new sects. Yet blacks were also more likely than whites to experience prejudice and to be poor, a fact reflected in Rio de Janeiro's largely black hillside shantytowns.

Latin American and Caribbean Cultures

Literature

Latin Americans struggled to reconcile indigenous with imported European and African cultural traditions. Rejecting European models, novelists focused on social themes. Euclides da Cunha **(KOO-nyuh)** (1866–1909) helped create a realistic Brazilian literature that described the life of the country's poor (see Profile: Euclides da Cunha, Brazilian Writer). The radical Chilean essayist Francisco Bilbao praised freedom and rationalism while denouncing slavery, Catholicism, and U.S. expansionism. In contrast, the well-traveled Nicaraguan poet Ruben Dario (1867–1916) favored escapist and fantastic images while stressing beauty as an end in itself.

Especially creative cultural innovations came in music and dance. The sensuous dance called the tango emerged in the working-class bars and clubs of Buenos Aires, becoming the most popular music in Argentina and Uruguay. The tango mixed African and European traditions, since its rhythms were derived from African drumming and the music featured the accordion-like *bandoneon*, carried to Argentina by Italian immigrants. The tango became a symbol of lower-class identity, and by the early 1900s it had also become popular in the ballrooms and nightclubs of Europe. Brazil's unique music also blended European melody and African rhythms. The migration of Afro-Brazilians from the poor northeast to Rio de Janeiro fostered **samba**, a popular music and dance developed by Bahian women who settled in Rio's hillside shantytowns. Popular with all classes, samba became integral to Carnival, the three-day celebration before the long Christian period of fasting and penitence known as Lent.

Caribbean peoples also mixed African and European influences to produce distinctive cultures. On Trinidad, the British officials, who feared the black majority, prohibited African-based musical forms. Two traditions emerged to reflect Afro-Trinidadian identity and defiance of British rule. The first, **calypso**, a song style featuring lyrics addressing daily life and topical subjects, eventually became the major popular music in the English-speaking eastern Caribbean islands. The second tradition, the pre-Lent Carnival already mentioned, became a major festival. Calypso songs performed during Carnival often questioned colonial policies. A song in the 1880s protested colonial restrictions on music during Carnival: "Can't beat my drum, In my own native land. Can't have Carnival, In my native land."[20] Informal calypso presentations in makeshift theaters evolved by the 1920s into elaborate, heavily rehearsed shows.

The United States in Latin America

Latin Americans both envied and feared the increasingly powerful United States, whose military forces occasionally intervened in Central America and the Caribbean. In 1856 William Walker, an American adventurer financed by influential U.S. businessmen, invaded Nicaragua with a well-armed American mercenary force and proclaimed himself president. Despite opposition by Central American leaders, the United States granted his government diplomatic recognition. Walker introduced slavery before being forced out in 1857, becoming a hated symbol in Central America of what Latin Americans often called Yankee imperialism.

Cuba was another example of U.S. interference. The Spanish-American War turned Cuba into a U.S.-dominated neocolony, and the Platt Amendment to the Cuban constitution, imposed by the United States in 1901, integrated the Cuban and U.S. economies and required that the U.S. Congress approve any treaties negotiated by Cuban leaders. The American military governor summarized the situation: "There is little or no real independence left to Cuba. She is absolutely in our hands, a practical dependency of the United States."[21] U.S. businessmen soon owned much of Cuba's economy, including railroads, banks, and mills, and the United States acquired a naval base at Guantanamo Bay. Later Cuban nationalists blamed Cuba's squalid condition not on the often despotic Cuban governments but on the United States. The Platt Amendment was finally repealed in 1934.

The United States became deeply involved in some parts of Central America and the Caribbean. To build a canal across Central America linking the Pacific and Atlantic Oceans, the United States helped Panama secede from Colombia in 1903. Now essentially a U.S. protectorate, Panama then leased a 10-mile-wide zone across the isthmus in perpetuity to the United States for the canal. Several thousand workers from Panama and various Caribbean islands died in the ten arduous years of construction. In 1914 the Panama Canal, 51 miles long, was completed, one of the great engineering feats of history. U.S. and other ships could now sail between the Atlantic and Pacific Oceans safely and conveniently. In 1912 Americans also overthrew the president of Nicaragua, whom they suspected of inviting the British to build a rival canal across his country. But unrest followed, prompting the United States to send in a military force, which remained until 1933. U.S. soldiers also occupied Haiti (1915–1933) and the Dominican Republic (1916–1924) to quell unrest or maintain friendly governments. These interventions set the stage for a more active U.S. imperial policy in Latin America and the Caribbean.

Musics

samba A Brazilian popular music and dance.

calypso A song style in Trinidad that featured lyrics addressing daily life and topical subjects.

United States and Cuba

United States and Central America

EUCLIDES DA CUNHA, BRAZILIAN WRITER

Euclides da Cunha (1866–1909) was one of Latin America's greatest writers, respected for his prose style, and the spokesman for a rising Brazilian nationalism. Born near Rio de Janeiro to a family originally from Bahia in the northeast, Cunha grew up at a time of great social change and political turmoil, when Brazilians abolished slavery and the Brazilian empire became a republic. He attended a military college to study engineering but rebelled against the rigid discipline. After angrily hurling down his sword in front of the Minister of War, he left the college before graduating to work as a journalist. Cunha was also a scientist interested in geography and a sociologist interested in people. A man of many skills, later in life he worked as a sanitary engineer and surveyor as well as a professor of logic. He lived most of his life in Rio de Janeiro and São Paulo.

Cunha's generation of urban Brazilian intellectuals, influenced by European writers, sought political democracy, national unity, and an end to violence and racial prejudice. A voracious reader, Cunha came to passionately share these progressive views. He also wanted Brazilians to free themselves from slavish imitation of European philosophical and intellectual trends and make Brazil rather than Europe their spiritual home. Perhaps because of his unhappy military school experience, he became antimilitarist, writing that war is "a monstrous thing, utterly illogical." Nonetheless, Cunha rejoined the army for a while to defend the new republican government that had replaced the conservative imperial state. But the republic's inability to maintain democracy proved demoralizing, and he left the army to work as a civil engineer before returning to writing.

Cunha's greatest literary contribution was his book *Rebellion in the Backlands*, published in 1902, which is often called the bible of Brazilian nationality and a major work of world literature. Cunha's book challenged the nation's conscience and stimulated other authors to question accepted political wisdom. The book examined a rebellion, the Canudos War of 1896–1897, in an impoverished and parched rural region of Bahia State in the northeast, where most people worked on cattle ranches. Cunha's somber book recounted the powerful story of a rural mystic, Antonio Conselheiro, who, preaching a primitive Christianity that rejected private property, gathered a fanatic group, numbering in the thousands, to oppose Brazil's republican government. Federal officials responded with force, brutally crushing the uprising and killing most of the rebels. The book was a sociological analysis that reads like fiction.

Cunha called his searing account of the struggle a "cry of protest" against an "act of madness" by the government, an attack on the barbarity of the "civilized" against the weak. He portrayed sympathetically the mestizo backwoods people, detailing their customs, occupations, joys, diversions, and sorrows. For example, he described their "multitude of extravagant" beliefs, a mix of Christian and African traditions, and their ceremonies to revere the dead: "It is a charming sight to see a backwoods family at nightfall kneeling before their rude altar, by the dim light of oil lamps, praying for the souls of their loved ones who have died or seeking courage against the storms of this life."

Few urbanites knew anything about the northeast backlands people, who were alien to urban Brazilians. "It was not an ocean which separates us from them," Cunha wrote, "but three whole centuries." Cunha portrayed the confrontation between two cultures, the coast and interior, a theme that became popular in Latin American literature. The deeply religious backlanders could not comprehend the antireligious, rationalist ideas popular in the major cities, while the urbanites could not understand why rural people did not want the modern vision of political and social progress offered them. Cunha admired the rural men who had thrown off European culture and desired to be left alone, finding in the northeastern cowboy "the very core of our nationality." He believed that mestizos, blacks, and Indians were all part of the nation but that bringing the urban and rural people together in one nation would take many years.

Cunha's writing laid the groundwork for artists, writers, and scholars in Brazil and the rest of Latin America to explore new topics. Sadly, Cunha himself would not live to see his influence spread. In 1909 he was a victim of the violence he deplored. Discovering that his wife was having an affair with an army officer, Cunha rashly confronted the rival and was mortally wounded in the ensuing exchange of gunfire.

THINKING ABOUT THE PROFILE

1. How did Cunha's ideas reflect the Brazil of his era?
2. How did he view the backlanders and their role in the Brazilian nation?

Note: Quotations from Euclides da Cunha, *Rebellion in the Backlands*, translated by Samuel Putnam (Chicago: University of Chicago Press, 1957), xiii, v, iii, 112, 161, xvi.

Euclides da Cunha Euclides da Cunha was one of the major writers and social critics of late-nineteenth-century Brazil.

Courtesy, Fundacao Biblioteca Nacional, Rio de Janeiro

SECTION SUMMARY

- After gaining independence from Spain, Latin American nations were plagued by instability, undemocratic governments, and socioeconomic inequality along racial lines.

- After a disastrous period as a republic, a brief occupation by the French, and a probusiness dictatorship, a long, violent revolution finally led to political stability in Mexico.

- Latin American economies tended to focus on the export of one or two natural resources, which created instability and made them susceptible to foreign domination.

- The abolition of slavery in Latin America did not greatly improve the economic conditions of former slaves, and millions of immigrants from Europe, India, Japan, and elsewhere flowed into Latin American countries.

- The tango developed in lower-class Buenos Aires, and samba was a result of cultural mixing in Rio de Janiero, while Caribbean calypso was a legacy of resistance to British efforts to stamp out African-based music on Trinidad.

- The United States repeatedly intervened in Latin American affairs, most directly in Cuba, whose diplomatic affairs it dominated for three decades, and Panama, through which it built the Panama Canal.

NEW SOCIETIES IN CANADA AND THE PACIFIC BASIN

Why did the foundations for nationhood differ in Canada and Oceania?

The United States became the most powerful and prosperous of the societies founded in the Americas and Oceania by European settlers, but it was not the only one to build a democratic nation and foster growing economies. Canada also expanded across North America to the Pacific. Western nations also colonized the island societies scattered around the Pacific Basin. In Australia and New Zealand, Britain established settler colonies, the British immigrants bringing with them their traditions and transforming these South Pacific territories.

Making a Canadian Nation

By 1763 the British had defeated the French and gained control of eastern Canada, including the main French colony, Quebec (see Chronology: Canada and the Pacific Basin, 1750–1914). The victorious British had to forge a stable relationship with French Canadians, who maintained their language, culture, and identity, and by 1774 the British pragmatically recognized the influential role of the Catholic Church and French civil law in Quebec. Meanwhile, British colonists settled chiefly in the Maritimes along the Atlantic coast, as well as west of Quebec in Ontario. Although the British governed Quebec and the English-speaking regions separately until 1841, relations between British and French Canadians remained uneasy, causing a British official in the 1830s to conclude that Canada was "two nations warring in the bosom of a single state."[22] The influence of France in North America ended in 1803, when the United States acquired the vast Louisiana territory, including the Mississippi River Basin long coveted by Americans.

English and French Canadians

Canada's peoples had to deal with the ambitions of the United States, whose leaders hoped that Canada might eventually join the Union. In a U.S.-British treaty in 1783, the United States recognized British control north of the Great Lakes and the Saint Lawrence River. After the American Revolution, many pro-British Loyalists moved to Canada, increasing the English-speaking population, especially in Ontario. Loyalists promoted democratic reforms and representative assemblies in Canada. The relations between the United States and Canada remained tense for years. Americans feared that their northern neighbors were aiding the Native Americans who resisted U.S. expansion in the Ohio region, such as the powerful and charismatic Shawnee chief Tecumseh (1768–1813), who gathered a large alliance of tribes to drive the white settlers out of Ohio and reinvigorate Indian ways. During the War of 1812 Americans repeatedly invaded Canada but were repulsed. The war ended U.S. attempts to expand north and also laid the seeds for a Canadian identity separate from the United States and Britain. In 1846 another treaty fixed the U.S.-Canada boundary in the west.

Canada and the United States

dominion A country having autonomy but owing allegiance to the British crown.

Along the Canadian Pacific Railroad During the late nineteenth century both native-born Canadians and immigrants from many lands—British, Dutch, Germans, Poles, Russians, Scandinavians—followed the Canadian Pacific Railroad to settle the newly opened lands of the midwestern prairies and western mountains. Some people set up temporary tent villages by railroad stops before taking up farming, mining, logging, trade, or fishing.

Canadians could now turn to building a democratic nation in peace while working to modify British control. Between 1815 and 1850 Canada welcomed 800,000 British immigrants, and gradually the British approved reforms that fostered a unified Canada, an elected national parliament, and waning British influence over the Canadian government. But Canadians rejected complete independence in favor of self-rule within the British Empire as a strategy to resist U.S. power. In 1867 leaders from Ontario, Quebec, and New Brunswick and Nova Scotia in the Maritimes negotiated a Canadian Confederation that guaranteed strong provincial rights and preservation of the French language wherever it was spoken. Canada then became a **dominion**, a country having autonomy but owing allegiance to the British crown.

However, expansion of white settlement and political power to the west fired resentment among Indians and people of mixed French-Indian descent, the French-speaking Metis **(may-TEES)**. The combative Metis leader, Louis Riel **(ree-EL)** (1844–1885), who had once studied to be a Catholic priest, led two rebellions before being executed for treason. Eventually, however, Manitoba and British Columbia joined the confederation and the federal government promised to build a transcontinental railroad, which Canada's first prime minister, Scottish-born John MacDonald (g. 1867–1873, 1878–1891), hoped would transform the 4 million Canadians into a unified nation. Crossing over 2,000 miles of forests, prairies, and high mountains, the railroad was completed in 1885. The government also negotiated treaties with Native Americans, allocating reservations to many of them as white settlers moved to the western provinces. By 1905 Canada included all the present provinces except Newfoundland.

The Canadian economy and ethnic structure were transformed between the 1860s and 1914. Beaver fur and fish had been the major exports since the 1600s, but now wheat grown in the Great Plains became the major export. Gold strikes in the Yukon and the offering of free land in western Canada attracted several million immigrants from many lands, including many from eastern and southern Europe as well as China and Japan, enriching the ethnic mosaic. By 1911 Canadians took control of their own foreign affairs and diplomacy. Over the next several decades Canada fostered increased industrialization and established warmer relations with the United States while maintaining the British monarch as symbolic head of state.

Exploration and Colonization of the Pacific Islands

The peoples who lived on the small mountainous islands and flat atolls scattered across thousands of miles in the vast Pacific Ocean Basin were the last to experience European expansion, but when it came, the impact was significant. The Spanish colonized Guam, in the Marianas, in 1663, but otherwise there had been little European contact with Pacific islanders. By the mid-

Library and Archives Canada, #PA 38667

1700s, however, the British and French had begun a race to explore what they considered the last frontier, eventually colonizing, along with Spain, Germany, Russia, and the United States, all the inhabited islands. The English captain James Cook (1728–1779), the son of an agricultural laborer, led some of the most extensive explorations. Cook reached the eastern Polynesian island of Tahiti in 1769, where he recruited a Polynesian high priest, Tupaia (ca. 1725–1771), whose skills as a navigator and speaker of several Polynesian languages greatly aided the expedition. Tupaia drew up the charts that helped Cook map Polynesia, including New Zealand, and the coast of Australia. Cook made two more expeditions to the Pacific in the 1770s, locating the Hawaiian Islands in 1778. His early reports created an image of the South Sea islands as a "Garden of Eden" with amiable people, an image that still survives in popular culture, but Cook himself was killed in Hawaii after antagonizing local leaders.

European explorations eventually led to economic exploitation and Christian missionary activity. In the late 1700s the Russians established a foothold in Alaska and the Aleutian Islands as a base for hunting seals and sea otters for their fur. Both animals were hunted to near extinction, and thousands of Aleuts died from exposure to European diseases. Deep-sea whaling lasted longer, attracting Western sailors. Western traders also visited the Pacific islands, seeking resources such as sandalwood, greatly valued in Asia for building furniture. Soon all of Fiji's sandalwood was gone. Meanwhile, Protestant and Catholic missionaries went to the islands, with varied results. The Samoans welcomed the missionaries, often adopting Christianity, and the Fijians initially rejected missionaries but later tolerated them, often pragmatically mixing Christianity with their own traditions. One chief, Ratu Tui Levuka, reportedly said that his right hand was Methodist, his left hand Catholic, and his body heathen. Some peoples were hostile to outside influences. For instance, the New Hebrides people killed the first missionaries who reached the islands.

Traders and missionaries opened the way for colonization, and between the 1840s and 1900 Western powers colonized all of the Pacific societies. The French gained domination over many island chains, such as the Society Islands, which included Tahiti, while the British colonized various others, among them Fiji. The Germans and Americans divided up Samoa. The Germans also acquired most of Micronesia, and Britain and France controlled much of Melanesia. By 1875 the smallpox, measles, and venereal diseases introduced by Western visitors and settlers to Hawaii had reduced the population from 150,000 to 50,000. Hawaii remained a Polynesian kingdom until 1893, when American settlers seized control.

Exploring and Colonizing the Pacific

The Rise of Australia and New Zealand

The British colonized the continent they named Australia and the two large islands they called New Zealand (see Map 20.3 and Chapter 9). European settlement in Australia began when the British began transporting convicts, often Irish, from overcrowded British jails to a penal colony they founded on the southeast coast in 1788. As more penal colonies were founded, settlements formed around the fine harbor at Sydney, and former convicts and discharged soldiers began settling the land. Agriculture, ranching, and mining became the basis for the modern economy. The British divided the continent into six colonies, with New South Wales and Victoria in the southeast having the largest populations.

British colonization came at the expense of the Aborigines, peoples completely different from the Pacific islanders in language, culture, and ways of life whose ancestors had lived on the continent for thousands of years. Divided into hundreds of scattered tribes, Aborigines lived chiefly by fishing and nomadic hunting and gathering, and the European settlers considered them to be an inferior people with a primitive way of life. Many Aborigines resisted encroachments on their land by raiding British settlements. While early British settlers killed as many as 20,000 Aborigines, diseases brought by Europeans such as smallpox and influenza were responsible for killing the majority of the Aboriginal population. By 1875 only 150,000 Aborigines remained, and whites forcibly settled their land. Eventually many Aborigines had little choice but to move to cities or to work on European cattle and sheep ranches. However, large numbers remained on tribal reservations, where they maintained many of their traditions and beliefs.

Britain and Australia

Creating a common Australian identity and nationhood took over a century. Throughout the 1800s Europeans clung to the coastal regions suitable for farming and ranching and avoided the inhospitable desert interior. The discovery of gold in southeastern Australia in 1851 attracted settlers from Europe and also prompted Chinese and other Asians to seek their fortunes in Australia, creating resentments among the Europeans. Violence between Europeans and Asians, especially in the mining camps, led to laws restricting Asian immigration. Meanwhile, white women struggled for influence in the male-dominated Australian society. By the 1880s women's movements were

Building an Australian Nation

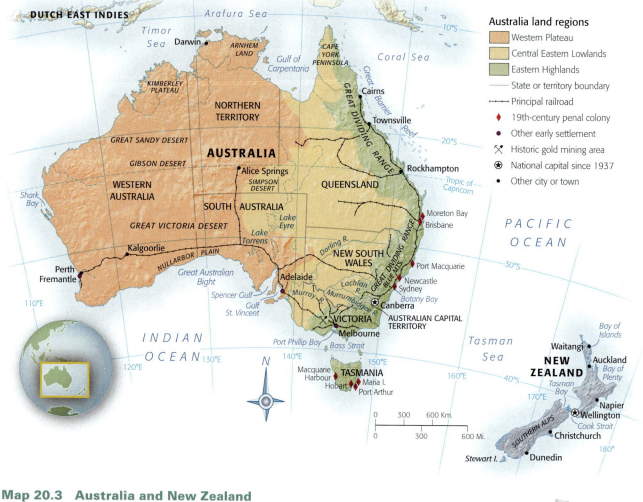

Map 20.3   Australia and New Zealand

The British colonized and gradually settled Australia and New Zealand between the late 1700s and 1914. In 1901 the six Australian colonies became a federation, with a capital eventually built in Canberra.

e   Interactive Map

pressing for moral reform and suffrage, and white women gained the right to vote in 1902. However, Aborigines only gained the right to vote in 1962.

Gradually Australia became a nation. By 1890 Britain had turned all six of its Australian colonies into self-governing states, which formed the Commonwealth of Australia in 1901 (see Map 20.3). Like Canada, Australia became a self-governing, democratic dominion and maintained close political links with Britain, but it gradually formed its own identity. A transcontinental railroad system, completed in 1917, connected the vast country. Yet the majority of white Australians lived in or near five coastal cities. Distance from European supplies fostered some local manufacturing, including steel production.

Colonizing New Zealand

The British also colonized the two large mountainous islands of New Zealand, 1,200 miles east of Australia, at the expense of the Polynesian Maori people. The Maori had lived on the islands, which they called Aotearoa, for a millennium, gradually dividing into sometimes warring tribes headed by chiefs. In 1792, when the first British settlers arrived, the Maori numbered around 100,000. Some Maori took advantage of the British newcomers for their own purposes. One chief, Hongi Hika (ca. 1772–1828), befriended a Protestant missionary, who took him to England. Returning with guns, Hongi and his warriors raided rival tribes. Maori intertribal warfare became more deadly and made it harder for the rival tribes to cooperate against the British.

As more British settlers came, territorial disputes with the Maori increased. The Treaty of Waitangi in 1850 between the British and five hundred Maori chiefs seemingly confirmed the Maori's right to their land while acknowledging British sovereignty. But the English-language and Maori-language versions differed. While Maori chiefs thought they still had authority over their lands and people, the British asserted that the treaty gave them political and legal power. Disagreement over the treaty provisions and occupation of more Maori land by British settlers led to deadly wars that ended only in the 1870s. The British skillfully exploited Maori tribal rivalries and had the military advantage of heavy artillery and armored steamships. Eventually Maori resistance subsided, leading to an 1881 peace agreement that accorded Maori control over some districts.

Gradually British identity in New Zealand grew stronger. The discovery of gold in 1861 stimulated British immigration, so that by 1881 the Maori accounted for only 10 percent of the half-million population. Immigrants were attracted by high living standards, a colonial economy based on farming and sheep raising, and a growing government welfare system. New Zealand prospered after 1882, when steamships acquired refrigerated holds to carry lamb and dairy products from the islands to Europe. A parliamentary government including Maori representatives was formed in 1852, and by 1893 both men and women of all communities enjoyed universal suffrage. New Zealand gained self-government as a British dominion in 1907, but it continued a close alliance with Britain as a guarantee of security and proudly remained an outpost of the British Empire well into the twentieth century.

SECTION SUMMARY

- Canada had to contend with the challenge of forming a unified country that included French and English speakers, as well as with the threat of the neighboring United States.

- Over time, Canada became increasingly independent of Britain and stretched across the continent, and wheat eventually surpassed beaver fur as the country's top export.

- Western nations, starting with Britain and France but later including Russia, the United States, and Germany, colonized the Pacific islands and exploited their natural resources.

- Starting as penal colonies, British settlements in Australia expanded and pushed the native Aborigines off their land and then clashed with Asians who came to mine gold.

- British colonizers of New Zealand clashed repeatedly with the native Maori, ultimately deceiving them into signing away the rights to their land in the Treaty of Waitangi, which led to a series of wars that ended only in the late nineteenth century.

Chapter Summary

During the Modern Era European populations grew and millions of people emigrated to the Americas and Oceania. More people lived in cities, where social problems and poverty increased. The industrial system influenced the relations between men and women, as family life changed and European women lost status, fostering feminist movements. Reacting to political and social turbulence, some European thinkers abandoned Enlightenment ideas. The pace of scientific and technological innovation also increased.

Across the Atlantic, the new democratic republic in the United States gradually became a regional and then world power with a diversified economy and distinctive culture. The United States expanded westward, eventually incorporating large sections of North America, some of it acquired after war with Mexico. As Americans settled the frontier, they subdued Native Americans and fostered new social patterns. The Civil War temporarily divided the nation and ended slavery. In the aftermath, economic growth and industrialization spurred massive immigration from Europe and social movements to improve the lives of workers and women. Industrial capitalism also motivated Americans to increase their influence in the wider world, eventually leading to the Spanish-American War. The U.S. victory in that conflict made the United States a world power.

Other new nations arose in the Americas and Oceania during the Modern Era. After Latin Americas gained independence from Spain and Portugal, the new governments remained authoritarian and fostered little economic or social change. Latin American and Caribbean economies remained monocultures geared to the export of raw materials and under foreign domination. While millions of European immigrants arrived, most blacks and Indians remained poor. Social inequalities produced tensions and, in Mexico, a revolution. Latin American and Caribbean societies created unique cultures that reflected the mix of peoples from around the world. The United States also played an increasing role in the region, fostering resentments that have lingered into the present.

Despite a division between French and English speakers, Canada expanded to the Pacific and became a nation with a self-governing democracy. Meanwhile European powers colonized the Pacific islands. Europeans settled in Australia and New Zealand and, like Canadians, elected to remain tied to Britain even while developing their own democratic nations.

KEY TERMS

feminism	impressionism	sphere of interest	samba
suffragettes	protectionism	caudillos	calypso
romanticism	Manifest Destiny	gauchos	dominion
modernism			

EBOOK AND WEBSITE RESOURCES

℮ INTERACTIVE MAPS

Map 20.1 European Emigration, 1820–1910
Map 20.2 U.S. Expansion Through 1867
Map 20.3 Australia and New Zealand

LINKS

WWW-VL: History: United States (http://vlib.iue.it/history/USA/). A virtual library that contains links to hundreds of sites.

Internet Resources for Latin America (http://lib.nmsu.edu/subject/bord/laguia/). An outstanding site with links to many resources.

Latin American Resources (http://www.oberlin.edu/faculty/svolk/latinam/htm). An excellent collection of resources and links on history, politics, and culture.

Modern History Sourcebook (http://www.fordham.edu/halsall/mod/modsbook.html). A very extensive online collection of historical documents and secondary materials.

The World of 1898: The Spanish-American War (http://www.loc.gov/rr/hispanic/1898). A Library of Congress site that provides excellent documents and resources.

Plus flashcards, practice quizzes, and more. Go to: www.cengage.com/history/lockard/globalsocnet2e.

SUGGESTED READING

Christensen, Carol and Thomas. *The U.S.-Mexican War.* San Francisco: Bay Books, 1998. A well-illustrated survey for the general public.

Clayton, Lawrence A. and Michael L. Conniff, *A History of Modern Latin America*, 2nd ed. Boston: Wadsworth, 2005. Good discussion of this era.

Costa, Emilia Viotti da. *The Brazilian Empire: Myths and Histories.* Chicago: The Dorsey Press, 1985. A study of the nineteenth century by a Brazilian historian.

Davies, Edward . *The United States in World History.* New York: Routledge, 2006. Access review of U.S. history and world connections.

Dubofsky, Melvyn. *Industrialization and the American Worker, 1865–1920*, 3rd ed. Wheeling, IL: Harlan Davidson, 1996. A good summary of the Industrial Revolution and its impact.

Fischer, Steven R. *A History of the Pacific Islands.* New York: Palgrave, 2002. A recent overview including New Zealand.

Foner, Eric. *The Story of American Freedom.* New York: W.W. Norton, 1998. A provocative examination of how Americans have pursued the dream of a free society.

Gonzalez, Michael J. *The Mexican Revolution, 1910–1940.* Albuquerque: University of New Mexico Press, 2002. Scholarly study of the conflict.

Keen, Benjamin, and Keith Haynes. *A History of Latin America*, 8th ed. Boston: Houghton Mifflin, 2009. A good general survey.

Knight, Alan. *The Mexican Revolution.* Cambridge: Cambridge University Press, 1986. A readable synthesis of this major uprising.

Kraut, Alan M. *The Huddled Masses: The Immigrant in American Society, 1840–1921*, 2nd ed. Wheeling, IL: Harlan Davidson, 2001. A brief survey.

Longley, Lester D. *The Americas in the Modern Age.* New Haven: Yale University Press, 2004. Relates recent relationships to developments around the hemisphere since the mid-1800s.

Nile, Richard, and Christian Clerk. *Cultural Atlas of Australia, New Zealand, and the South Pacific.* New York: Facts on File, 1996. A comprehensive and readable overview of history and cultures.

Paterson, Thomas G., et al. *American Foreign Relations: A History*, 6th ed. Boston: Wadsworth, 2005. A fine survey.

Riendeau, Roger E. *A Brief History of Canada.* Toronto: Fitzhenry and Whiteside, 2000. A short work covering 400 years of Canadian development.

Smith, Bonnie G. *Changing Lives: Women in European History Since 1700.* Lexington, MA: D.C. Heath, 1989. A comprehensive study of women's lives and their roles in public life.

Stearns, Peter N., and Herrick Chapman. *European Society in Upheaval: Social History Since 1750*, 3rd ed. New York: St. Martin's, 1991. A readable survey with lively material.

Stephanson, Anders. *Manifest Destiny: American Expansion and the Empire of Right.* New York: Hill and Wang, 1995. A readable brief analysis of this important American doctrine and its consequences.

Tyrrell, Ian. *Transnational Nation: United States History in Global Perspective Since 1789.* London: Palgrave, 2007. Study by an Australian scholar places U.S. history in a global context.

AFRICA, THE MIDDLE EAST, AND IMPERIALISM, 1750–1914

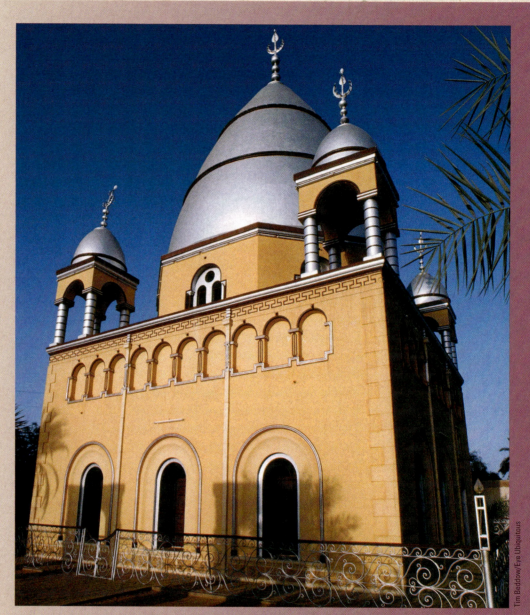

Tim Beddow/Eye Ubiquitous

Tomb of Muhammad Ahmad in Khartoum
Muhammad Ahmad ibn 'Abd Allah, known to history as the Mahdi ("Divinely Guided One"), used Islamic appeals to recruit a large army and lead opposition to the joint British and Egyptian rule in Sudan. He died soon after routing the British forces in 1885, but his tomb remains a popular place of pilgrimage and a symbol of Muslim resistance to Western power.

The power of these Europeans has advanced to a shocking degree and has manifested itself in an unparalleled manner. Indeed, we are on the brink of a time of [complete] corruption. As for knowing what tomorrow holds, I am blind.

—Moroccan historian Ahmad Ibn Khalid al-Nasri, 1860[1]

Fresh from his victories in Italy and Austria, in 1798 the French general Napoleon Bonaparte vowed to join the illustrious European conquerors who had achieved glory before him in the Middle East. Alexander the Great had conquered Egypt and Persia, Roman and Byzantine emperors had controlled the eastern Mediterranean, and medieval Christian crusaders had established temporary footholds in western Asia. Bonaparte admired the earlier military commanders and coveted the rich lands they had gained. In his mind, Europe was hardly a match for his talents when the rich Muslim world beckoned. He planned to invade Egypt and then reduce the Ottoman Turks and Persians to French vassals. With four hundred ships carrying 50,000 soldiers, Bonaparte quickly established control over northern Egypt. He also brought some five hundred French scholars to gather valuable information on Egyptian history, society, language, and environment. In the Nile River Delta they discovered the multilanguage Rosetta stone, a tablet made in 196 B.C.E. that allowed scholars for the first time to translate ancient Egyptian hieroglyphics. In a bid for popular support, the French general confidently announced: "People of Egypt, I come to restore your rights; I respect God, His Prophet and the Quran. We are friends of all true Muslims. Happiness to the People!"[2] He also claimed to have liberated the people from Egypt's repressive Mamluk rulers. But Bonaparte's policies soon alienated Egyptians, who came to see the French as even worse. The French army, small and ill-equipped, withered in the desert heat. An attempt to conquer Syria having failed, Bonaparte left for Paris in 1799, becoming just another example of westerners unsuccessfully attempting to control and change Muslim societies.

The unsuccessful French invasion of Egypt provided a harbinger of more conflicts, as the Moroccan historian Ahmad ibn Khalid al-Nasri had feared. Bonaparte's expedition was the cutting edge of a European imperial thrust in sub-Saharan Africa and the Middle East. Industrializing Europe's accelerating need for natural resources and new markets, combined with European political rivalries and a powerful military technology, launched ruthless colonization. European colonialism generally lasted for only a century or less, and sub-Saharan and North Africans often resisted Western power. Yet the power of Western governments, technologies, and ideas reshaped African societies and their economies, cultures, and political systems while linking them more closely to a European-dominated world economy. While western Asian societies experienced less disruption, the Ottomans lost their North African and European territories, and the Ottoman and Persian states struggled to meet the challenges posed by increased European power.

FOCUS QUESTIONS

1. How did various Western nations obtain colonies in sub-Saharan Africa?
2. What were some of the major consequences of colonialism in Africa?
3. What political and economic impact did Europe have on the Middle East?
4. How did Middle Eastern thought and culture respond to the Western challenge?

e Visit the website and eBook for additional study materials and interactive tools:
www.cengage.com/history/lockard/globalsocnet2e

575

THE COLONIZATION OF SUB-SAHARAN AFRICA

How did various Western nations obtain colonies in sub-Saharan Africa?

Between the later 1700s and later 1800s the diminishing importance of the trans-Atlantic slave trade gradually changed the relationship between Africans and Europeans. The Western impact on Africa had been uneven during the slave trade, which had integrated Africa into the world economy chiefly as a supplier of human beings while impeding most other trade between Europeans and Africans. But, as the demand for slaves waned, Europeans became more interested in acquiring African agricultural and mineral resources and more territories. Thus the full-blown quest for colonies, what a British newspaper called the "scramble for Africa," began only with the end of the trans-Atlantic slave trade and the spread of the Industrial Revolution in Europe in the mid-1800s. The European powers divided up the African continent among themselves, often against fierce resistance, and accelerated economic penetration of the continent. By 1914 the colonization process was complete.

The End of the Slave Trade and African Societies

For over three centuries the trans-Atlantic slave trade (1520–1870) dominated relations between Africa, Europe, and the Americas, but humanitarian opposition and economic concerns spurred an abolitionist movement. British abolitionists hoped to open Africa to both Christian missionaries and trade in commodities other than slaves. Many abolitionists were Christians prompted largely by moral outrage at slavery, while others were influenced by the Enlightenment vision of human equality. One sympathizer wrote that people "are not objects. Everyone has his rights, property, dignity. Africa will have its day."[3]

Africans and African Americans also struggled against slavery. Olaudah Equiano (1745–1797), an Igbo taken from Nigeria to Barbados and then Virginia, eventually purchased his freedom and then actively campaigned in Europe for abolition. Equiano published a best-selling book chronicling his own horrific experiences and pointing out the contradiction in self-proclaimed devout Christians mistreating their slaves. Slave revolts in the Americas, including the successful revolution in Haiti (see Chapter 19), indicated the willingness of many slaves to risk their lives for freedom. American and European opposition to slavery was also fueled by the widely read poetry and Christian writings of Phyllis Wheatley (ca. 1753–1785), a Senegal-born slave in Boston who learned Latin and Greek and eventually won her freedom. Her published writings undermined the widespread notion that Africans were incapable of sophisticated thought.

The Industrial Revolution made slavery uneconomical as overseas markets for factory-made goods became more desirable than cheap labor for plantations. So many colonies produced sugar that the market was flooded, making the plantations less profitable while African states charged more to provide slaves. Investing in manufacturing proved more profitable. As a result of these moral and economic factors, the slave trade and slavery came to an end in the Atlantic world in the nineteenth century. Denmark outlawed the slave trade in 1804, followed by Britain in 1807, and then all British-controlled territories, including their plantation-rich Caribbean colonies, in 1833 (see Chronology: Sub-Saharan Africa, 1750–1914). The British government declared war on the slave traders, intercepting slave ships in the Atlantic and returning the slaves to Africa. By 1842 most European and American countries had made it illegal to transport slaves across the Atlantic. The Civil War ended slavery in the United States in 1865, and in the later 1880s Brazil and Cuba also finally outlawed slavery.

The East African trade that sent slaves to the Middle East and the Indian Ocean islands, run chiefly by Arabs from Oman, continued longer. In 1835 the Omani leader, Sayyid Sa'id (**SIGH-id SIGH-eed**) (r. 1806–1856), moved his capital to Zanzibar, an island just off the coast of Tanzania, and built a commercial empire shipping ivory to India, China, and Europe and slaves to India, the Persian Gulf, and South Arabia. The Omanis also profited from growing Indonesian cloves on slave plantations on Zanzibar. To obtain slaves and ivory, Omani and Swahili merchants expanded over-

CHRONOLOGY

Sub-Saharan Africa, 1750–1914

1804 Launching of Fulani jihads by Uthman dan Fodio

1804 Abolition of slave trade by Denmark

1806 British seizure of Cape region from Dutch

1807–1833 Abolition of slave trade in Britain and its territories

1816 Beginning of Shaka's Zulu Empire

1838 Great Trek by South African Boers

1842 Ending of trans-Atlantic slave trade by most European nations

1847 First American freed slave settlement in Liberia

1874–1901 British-Ashante wars

1878 Belgian colonization in Congo

1884–1885 Berlin Conference

1884–1885 Discovery of gold in South Africa

1898 French defeat of Samory Toure

1899–1902 Boer (South African) War

1905 Maji Maji Rebellion in Tanganyika

1912 Founding of African National Congress in South Africa

CHRONOLOGY

	Sub-Saharan Africa	The Middle East
1800		**1805–1848** Rule of Muhammad Ali in Egypt **1830** French colonization of Algeria
1850	**1870** Ending of trans-Atlantic slave trade **1874–1901** British-Ashante wars **1884–1885** Berlin Conference on colonialism **1899–1902** Boer War	**1859–1869** Building of Suez Canal **1882** British colonization of Egypt

land trade routes through Tanzania into the eastern Congo River Basin. In 1873 the British convinced the Zanzibar sultan to close the island's slave market, and as compensation imported vast amounts of ivory. But slavers still raided African villages to acquire the labor needed to carry the huge ivory tusks to the coast for export. Although the British gained control of Zanzibar in 1890, some slave trading continued on a modest scale in parts of East and Central Africa until the early 1900s.

Even before abolition, freed slaves who chose, or were pressured, to return to Africa from the Americas had established several West African states and port cities. The black founders and white financers of these states wanted to give the freed slaves opportunities to run their own lives while also setting up new centers of Western trade. The two largest settlements of freed slaves emerged in Sierra Leone and Liberia. In 1787 the British settled four hundred former slaves around the fort at Freetown, which became the core of their colony of Sierra Leone. The British also shipped more former slaves to Freetown from their West Indian colonies and from British-ruled Canada, where they had fled for supporting the Loyalist cause during the American Revolution. Freed slaves from the United States were first shipped to Liberia in 1847 and then were joined by others after the Civil War. One of the first African nationalists, West Indian–born Edward Blyden (1832–1912), emigrated to Liberia after being denied admission to universities in the United States because he was black. Blyden believed that, given the racism in the Americas and Europe, people of African ancestry could realize their potential only in Africa.

New States

However, some problems remained. Although Liberia remained an independent state governed by the descendants of former slaves, its economy was dominated by U.S.-owned rubber plantations. In addition, in both Sierra Leone and Liberia, the local Africans often resented the freed slave settlers, mostly English-speaking Christians, because they occupied valuable land, dominated commerce, and held political power. In recent decades conflicts between the two groups have torn apart both countries.

The decline of the trans-Atlantic slave trade also made Africa more accessible to Western explorers who wanted to discover whether the great African rivers were navigable for commercial purposes. The Scottish explorer Mungo Park (1771–1806), a doctor for an English trading company in West Africa who traveled along the Niger, hoped to open to British industry new sources of wealth. Adventurers were obsessed with finding the source of Africa's greatest river, the Nile, and they finally located Lake Victoria in 1860. David Livingstone (1813–1873), a Scottish cotton mill worker turned medical missionary, spent over two decades traveling in eastern Africa, where he collected information and opened the region to Christian missionary activity and trade with the West. The European adventurers claimed to have "discovered" inland African societies and geographical features, but they discovered little that Africans and Arabs did not already know and usually followed long-established trading routes using local guides. The ethnocentric stereotype of intrepid white explorers struggling in hardship through virgin territories is a myth, but it shaped Western views. Explorers spread the notion of "Darkest Africa" awaiting salvation by Christian missionaries and Western traders.

Western Explorers

In the 1800s European traders began to obtain various raw materials needed by the West, such as peanuts, palm oil, gold, timber, and cotton. They had to contend with dynamic West African merchants who, with the end of the slave trade, had set up cash crop plantations, many producing palm oil, the main lubricant for industrial machinery in Europe before the development of petroleum. To avoid the African middlemen on the coast, British traders traveled up Nigeria's rivers to buy palm oil directly from the Igbo **(EE-boh)** producers. With superior financial resources and support from their governments, European companies eventually undermined African merchants and states that were reluctant to grant trade concessions, and by 1890 in the trading port of Lagos only one African merchant was still able to compete with British merchants.

European Traders

From John H. Hanson, *Migration, Jihad, and Muslim Authority in West Africa* (Bloomington and Indianapolis: Indiana University Press)

African Muslim Warrior While Western pressure on coastal societies increased, several Muslim peoples expanded their influence in the West African interior. Some military forces, having acquired Western arms in exchange for slaves and gold, conquered regional empires that flourished for a century or more.

Some major developments derived largely from forces within African societies rather than from relations with the West. For example, tensions within the Islamic societies of the Sudan fostered militancy and political expansion, and conflicts between those who wanted to purge Islamic practice of pre-Islamic customs and those who mixed Muslim and African traditions broke out sporadically in West Africa. By the 1790s these conflicts had spread to the Fulani, a pastoral and trading people scattered across the Sudan from Senegal east to Chad. Some Fulani were devout Muslims, some nominal Muslims, and some animists.

One Fulani, Uthman dan Fodio (AHTH-mun dahn FOH-dee-oh) (1754–1817), a respected Muslim scholar and ardent follower of Sufi mysticism who lived in the prosperous Hausa states of northern Nigeria, began criticizing the religious tolerance of Hausa rulers, called for the conversion of non-Muslim Fulani, and advocated making Islam central to Sudanic life. His magnetic personality and Islamic zeal soon attracted a Fulani and Hausa following. Uthman's attacks on high taxes and social injustice and his promise to build an Islamic government alarmed Hausa rulers, who feared the unrest he was causing. After an attempt on his life, Uthman launched a jihad (holy war) in 1804. He conquered the Hausa states and created a caliphate based in the city of Sokoto (SOH-kuh-toh), ruling much of northern Nigeria. Uthman divided his empire into small, Fulani-led states led by governors, known as *emirs*.

Uthman's jihad and his vision of a purified Islam sparked others to take up his cause, and several other jihadist states, often led by Fulani religious scholars, formed in the Sudan. The Islamic revival, which continued into the 1880s, allowed a more orthodox Islam to spread widely just as Western influence was increasing in Africa. But by the later 1800s, the Fulani states declined and Sokoto's power waned. The Fulani resisted French and British expansion but eventually were unable to stop it; however, Islam remained a vital force in the Sudanic zone.

European Conquest and Partition

Britain, France, Germany, Spain, Belgium, and Italy all acquired African colonies in the late 1800s, often by intimidating African leaders through warfare or the threat of force (see Map 21.1). Several factors made this possible. Western companies sought their government's help to pressure states to admit Western merchants; advances in tropical medicine, especially the use of quinine for malaria, freed Europeans from high tropical mortality rates; and the invention of more powerful weapons gave Europeans a huge military advantage over African forces armed only with rifles or spears. When possible, Europeans achieved conquest peacefully by using deceptive treaties, offering bribes, dividing up states, and convincing African leaders that resistance was futile. When faced with resistance, however, Europeans used ruthless force.

King Leopold of Belgium took the lead in colonization. In 1878 he hired Henry Stanley (1841–1904), a Welsh-born American and former Confederate soldier and journalist who had earlier searched successfully in East Africa to find David Livingstone. Stanley then explored the Congo River Basin, which King Leopold now commissioned him to acquire for Belgium. Soon other European powers joined the scramble to obtain colonies, and in 1884–1885 the colonizing nations held a conference in Berlin to set the ground rules for colonization. For a claim to be recognized, the colonizer had to first give notice of its intent and then occupy the territory with a military presence. Agents of European governments such as Stanley asked African chiefs, who knew no Western languages, to sign treaties of friendship or protection that actually gave the land to European countries. African chiefs usually had no right to sign over land, since it was owned by their people. If chiefs refused to sign, they were threatened with war. Fearing a slaughter or war with their neighbors, many chiefs signed. The king of Buganda reflected the Africans' distress when he concluded that the Europeans were coming to eat his country.

European Advantages   Europeans achieved domination for several other reasons. The colonial scramble came at a time of famine when rains failed and while epidemics of smallpox and cholera were killing mil-

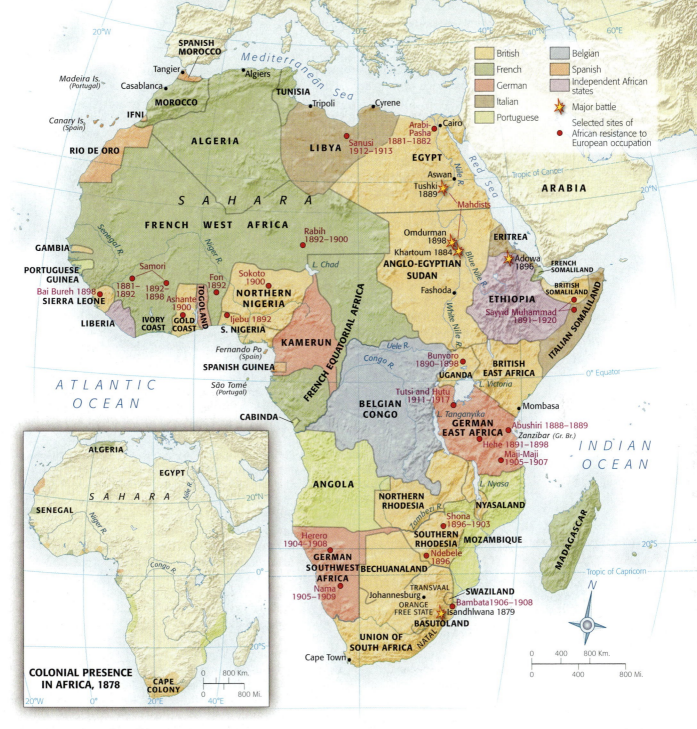

Map 21.1   Africa in 1914
Before 1878 the European powers held only a few coastal territories in Africa, but in that year they turned to expanding their power through colonization. By 1914 the British, French, Belgians, Germans, Italians, Portuguese, and Spanish controlled all of the continent except for Ethiopia and Liberia.

e Interactive Map

Map legend:
- British
- French
- German
- Italian
- Portuguese
- Belgian
- Spanish
- Independent African states
- ★ Major battle
- ● Selected sites of African resistance to European occupation

Inset map: **COLONIAL PRESENCE IN AFRICA, 1878**

lions. One French missionary reflected the despair: "wars, drought, famine, pestilence, locusts, cattle-plague! Why so many calamities in succession? Why?"[4] For most Africans these were bitter years indeed. In addition, the military disparity in weapons and tactics, already mentioned, played a major role. The British had the hand-cranked Gatling gun, which could fire hundreds of rounds per minute, and then the Maxim gun, a totally automatic machine gun invented in 1884. Europeans willingly slaughtered thousands. In Southwest Africa (today's Namibia), the Germans killed all but 15,000 of the 80,000 Herero (hair-AIR-oh) people after a rebellion in 1904. In Kenya, British military expeditions attacked villages for chasing away tax collectors or ambushing Western military patrols sent to intimidate potential resisters. A British officer in Kenya in 1902 boasted of giving orders that every living thing in a Gikuyu village, except children, should be killed without mercy because an

Englishman had been killed nearby. The British then burned all the huts and destroyed the banana farms. They called their policy of establishing law and order, often by force, the "Pax Britannica," or British peace.

After centuries of rivalries and slave wars, Africans could not unite for common defense, and Europeans took advantage of this weakness by pitting state against state and ethnic group against ethnic group. The region that became Nigeria had been the home of various independent kingdoms and village-based stateless societies. Thanks to the slave trade, some of these societies were already unstable, and the Yoruba had engaged in a bitter civil war for much of the 1800s. Between 1887 and 1903 the British conquered or annexed these diverse societies, creating the colony they called Nigeria because it occupied both sides of the lower Niger River.

Partitioning the Continent

By 1914 European powers, by drawing boundaries and staking claims, had divided up the entire continent except for Ethiopia and Liberia. The French empire was concentrated in North, West, and Central Africa, extending across the Sahara from Senegal to Lake Chad. The British had four colonies in West Africa, including Nigeria, but built most of their empire in eastern and southern Africa. The four German colonies were scattered, while Italy concentrated on the Horn region of Northeast Africa, including Somalia and Eritrea, and on Libya in North Africa.

European nations competed fiercely for territories, sometimes coming to the brink of war over rival claims. Britain wanted to control the whole eastern region from Cairo in the north to the Cape of Good Hope, while the Germans dreamed of an empire in Central Africa. German colonization of Tanganyika spurred Britain to move into Kenya, Uganda, and Zanzibar. In South Africa, the brash British imperialist Cecil Rhodes (1853–1902), a clergyman's son who had made millions in the South African diamond mining industry, was largely responsible for extending British influence into the territory he arrogantly named Northern and Southern Rhodesia to outflank Germany and Portugal. British settlers migrated to Southern Rhodesia (today's Zimbabwe) and Kenya, solidifying the British hold on the region.

African Resistance

Although outgunned, many Africans offered spirited resistance to European conquest. The Mandinka leader Samory Toure, in the western Sudan, resisted for decades (see Profile: Samory Toure, Mandinka King and Resistance Leader). In 1903 many people in Fulani-ruled Sokoto chose to die in battle against the British rather than surrender. In Muslim West Africa, the mystical Sufi brotherhoods sometimes rallied opposition to the French or British. In Senegal, when the French tried to rule the Wolof people through their kings and chiefs, Wolof resisters turned to Muslim clerics, especially Amadu Bamba Mbacke (AH-mah-doo BOM-ba um-BACK-ee) (ca. 1853–1927), who had founded a peaceful Sufi order, the *Murids* ("learners seeking God"). The French exiled him for many years but eventually realized that they could only rule Senegal with the cooperation of the Murids. Amadu Bamba acknowledged French administration but was free to expand the Murids. The only decisive African military triumph over Western forces, however, came in Ethiopia. In 1896, under the reforming Emperor Menelik (MEN-uh-lik) II (1844–1914), Ethiopia, fortified in high mountains difficult to penetrate, defeated an invasion force of 10,000 Italian troops with his French-trained army of 80,000 men.

In the Gold Coast (today's Ghana), the Ashante kingdom offered particularly strong political and military resistance. The British, seeking to protect their coastal forts, repeatedly clashed with the prosperous, powerful, expanding Ashante. In 1874 the British dispatched a large force against Ashante and secured the coast, but effective Ashante resistance prevented them from pushing into the interior. The British then deliberately fomented a civil war in the Ashante territories, but the Ashante king refused British ultimatums to surrender. In 1896 three thousand well-armed British troops finally occupied the Ashante capital, Kumasi, and exiled the king. However, resistance continued, often spurred by royal women such as the queen-mother Yaa Asantewa, who offered to lead Ashante forces if the men would not. Not until 1901 did the British manage to incorporate the Ashante into their Gold Coast colony.

SECTION SUMMARY

- Opposed by many Europeans on humanitarian and religious grounds, African slavery became less profitable than manufacturing as the Industrial Revolution gained momentum, and it was phased out by the end of the nineteenth century.

- With the end of the slave trade, Europeans began to explore Africa's interior and to take advantage of its vast store of natural resources.

- At the same time, tensions increased between purist and moderate West African Muslims, and Uthman dan Fodio, who led the Fulani jihads, established the Sokoto Caliphate, under which Islam became a strong presence in the Sudan.

- European nations rapidly colonized Africa by engaging in deceptive negotiations, by threatening and often carrying out acts of violence, and by exploiting existing rivalries among groups of Africans.

- By 1914, all but a small portion of Africa had been divided up among the European powers, which sometimes feuded over control of various territories and sometimes met fierce resistance from Africans such as the Ashante.

SAMORY TOURE, MANDINKA KING AND RESISTANCE LEADER

Samory Toure (1830–1900) was an effective resistance leader in West Africa and a powerful empire builder. He grew up an animist in a Mandinka village in what is today Guinea. Samory's mother was an animist Mandinka, and his father was a farmer descended from the Dyula, a Muslim merchant caste with branches throughout West Africa. His father's family had earlier abandoned Islam, but their connections to the Dyula trading world gave Samory links to a broader community and an understanding of both merchant and farmer concerns. The growing Atlantic trade brought prosperity to the Dyula and firearms to the interior, at a time when regional Islamic movements were energizing Muslims and fomenting conflict between varied Muslim and animist groups.

Samory began his career as a foot soldier and eventually became an inspirational military commander. By 1870 he had recruited a large, well-armed, well-trained, and intensely loyal force from many Mandinka groups. Skillfully exploiting divisions among his opponents while maintaining connections to both Muslims and animists, Samory built a large state, Kankan, in the Guinea highlands and western Niger River Basin. He personally adopted Islam, perhaps chiefly for political reasons, and earned Dyula support by keeping open the trade routes. Islamic revivalism in West Africa influenced Samory to view Islam as a unifying force that could hold his ethnically diverse empire together, and in 1884 he transformed the kingdom into an Islamic state. However, the required conversion of animists led to rebellion. In a pragmatic move that showed his willingness to ignore Islamic scruples to further his political goals and personal ambitions, Samory abolished the theocracy and replaced it with a state based not on Islam but on personal loyalty and national unity.

A political rather than a religious figure, Samory was aware of the traditions of Mandinka empires going back to the great Mali Empire founded by Sundiata in the thirteenth century, and he became the architect of a revived Mandinka Empire modeled on Mali. His later admirers viewed him as an early nationalist trying to maintain a Mandinka state. Samory recruited friends and relatives to form an advisory council, and its members became ministers responsible for specialized tasks such as supervising the treasury, the system of justice, religious affairs, and relations with Europeans. At the same time, Samory also respected the authority of local chiefs. In addition, he gained merchant support by seeking a stable and crime-free order where, as he said, "a woman alone should be able to travel as far as Freetown" in Sierra Leone without facing assaults or robberies.

Samory spent his last ten years defending his state against the French. He had long avoided conflict with Europeans, but his state posed a barrier to French expansion into the interior, and in the 1880s French forces began to move into the gold-rich area. After being defeated by Samory's army, they sent a larger force but again faced stiff resistance and were forced to negotiate a truce. During the 1890s the two sides fought a war for seven years. To oppose the French effort, the British in Sierra Leone gave Samory firearms in exchange for slaves and gold, and Samory built workshops to maintain and make muskets and rifles. His army of 30,000 men included mostly foot soldiers and an elite core of cavalry. A clever military strategist who made good use of guerrilla tactics, Samory also developed an effective system of intelligence throughout the villages to detect French movements. Asked how he repeatedly discovered French movements without giving away his own, he replied, "It is because I eat alone" (thus keeping his secrets).

But the French had more and better weapons, including heavy artillery and machine guns. Samory was also disadvantaged by not being able to unite with rival African states after years of conflict. The French gradually pushed Samory eastward, where he forged a new empire in today's northern Ivory Coast and Ghana. As they retreated into the interior, Samory's forces carried out a scorched earth policy that devastated the inhabitants and cost him popular support. In 1898 the French finally defeated Samory's brave but exhausted and hungry army, captured the ruler, and exiled him to the new French colony of Gabon in South-Central Africa, where he died.

THINKING ABOUT THE PROFILE

1. What does Samory's career tell us about Sudanic politics in this era?
2. How was Samory able to resist the French for decades?

Note: Quotations from *The Horizon History of Africa* (New York: American Heritage, 1971), 431; and Robert W. July, *A History of the African People,* 5th ed. (Prospect Heights, IL: Waveland, 1998), 207.

Roger-Viollet/Getty Images

Samory Toure Samory Toure, the ruler of a Mandinka state, led a military force that resisted French incursion into their West African region in the late nineteenth century, but he was eventually captured by the French. This photo shows him (front, left) in custody.

THE COLONIAL RESHAPING OF SUB-SAHARAN AFRICA

What were some of the major consequences of colonialism in Africa?

The experience of living under Western colonial domination from the 1880s to the 1960s reshaped sub-Saharan Africans' politics, society, culture, and economy. The trans-Atlantic and East African slave trades had devastated parts of Africa for four centuries, but the colonial conquests undermined the autonomy of all African societies. Colonialism created artificial states and transformed Africans into subject peoples who enjoyed few political rights. Europeans also took over large tracts of land as settlers. The largest settler colony, South Africa, experienced an unusual history: over three centuries of white supremacy introduced by the Dutch colonizers and perpetuated by the British. South Africa's political, social, and economic system reshaped life for both Europeans and Africans. European immigrants also settled in British East Africa, the Rhodesias, and the Portuguese colonies. Asian migrants joined them, often as traders. Colonialism also allowed Western business interests to penetrate the continent and integrate Africa into the global system as a supplier of valuable raw materials.

Colonial States and African Societies

Colonial Governments

The colonial policies devised in London, Paris, Berlin, Lisbon, and Brussels introduced new kinds of governments in Africa, as each colonizing power sought the best way to achieve maximum control at minimum expense. The French grouped their colonies into large federations such as French West Africa that were headed by one governor, while the British preferred to handle each colony, such as the Gold Coast and Nigeria, separately. Despite little understanding of or interest in African cultures, Europeans always held ultimate political authority and usually supervised administration, and Africans had to abide by decisions made by European bureaucrats. Under **direct rule** the administration was largely European, even down to the local level, and chiefs or kings were reduced to symbolic roles. Under **indirect rule** the Europeans gave the traditional kings or chiefs considerable local power but kept them subject to colonial officials. Indirect rule, which left much of the original society intact, caused less disruption than direct rule, but African leaders were required to consult with the local European adviser on many matters. Since Europeans lacked enough officials to administer a large colony such as Nigeria , indirect rule was inspired by pragmatism. In order to work with local leaders, Europeans sometimes strengthened chiefs or appointed chiefs where none previously existed, undermining village democracy.

direct rule A method of ruling colonies whereby a largely European colonial administration supervised all activity, even down to the local level, and native chiefs or kings were reduced to symbolic roles.

indirect rule A method of ruling colonies whereby districts were administered by traditional (native) leaders, who had considerable local power but were subject to European officials.

Nigeria, a huge unwieldy colony that contained some 250 distinct African ethnic groups, provided an example of both kinds of administration. As the British struggled to keep the largely Muslim north pacified, they needed the collaboration of the Hausa and Fulani emirs. Lord Lugard, the British governor, proclaimed that every emir "will rule over the people as of old time but will obey the laws of the [British] Governor."[5] The British also left the traditional Hausa-Fulani courts and social structure largely undisturbed. By contrast, they governed southern Nigeria chiefly through direct rule, with the result that greater change occurred in the south, including the introduction of Christian missions and cash crop farming. Peoples such as the Igbo and Yoruba adapted to these changes. The Igbo, particularly receptive to Christianity, became prominent in Nigeria's educated middle class. The Yoruba blended their rich artistic tradition and polytheism with imported English literary forms and Christianity, maintaining tolerance for divergent views. Rejecting fate and helplessness, the Yoruba described their culture as a river that is never at rest, caught up within swift-moving currents that can either run deep and quietly or be turbulent and overpowering.

However, many policies politically handicapped the Africans. Supporters of Western colonialism claimed it provided "a school for democracy," but by 1945 only a few Africans enjoyed political rights or access to democratic institutions. A few thousand urban merchants and professionals in British Nigeria and the Gold Coast could vote for and serve on city councils, while males in French Senegal elected members of the colonial council and a representative to the French parliament. Meanwhile, the traditional African chiefs and kings, to keep their positions, implemented colonial policies, such as by supervising cash crop agriculture and recruiting people for labor and war. Africans often viewed these privileged and wealthy leaders as little better than paid agents of colonialism.

Fostering "Tribalism"

Misunderstanding African ethnic complexities, to simplify administration colonizers identified people of similar culture and language as "tribes," such as the Yoruba of Nigeria and Gikuyu of

Kenya, even though these peoples were actually collections of subgroups without much historical unity. In reality, African peoples such as the Yoruba, Gikuyu, Igbo, Xhosa, and Mandinka were ethnic groups, not unlike the politically divided Italians, Irish, and Poles of early-nineteenth-century Europe. Thus the boundaries drawn up to partition Africa into colonies created artificial countries that often ignored traditional ethnic relationships. Countries such as Nigeria, Ghana (the former Gold Coast), Congo, and Mozambique were colonial creations, not nations built on shared culture and identity. Colonizers ignored the interests of local people, sometimes dividing ethnic groups between two or more colonial systems. The Kongolese, once masters of a great kingdom, were split between Portuguese Angola and the Belgian and French Congos. Rival societies were also sometimes joined, creating a basis for later political instability. In Nigeria the tensions between the Igbo, Yoruba, Hausa-Fulani, and other groups have fostered chronic conflict since the end of British rule. Other countries have also experienced ethnic conflicts that have sometimes led to violence.

Several colonies restricted African civil and economic rights, particularly South Africa, Portuguese-ruled Angola, and British-ruled Kenya and Southern Rhodesia. They reserved for immigrant white farmers not only the best land, such as the fertile Kenyan highlands once dominated by the Gikuyu people, but also the most lucrative crops, such as coffee. African farmers also faced barriers in obtaining bank loans. The whites participated in government and perpetuated white supremacy, and the settler colonies erected rigid color bars to limit contact between whites and Africans except as employers and hired workers.

European and Asian Immigrants

To Europeans, African culture was irrational and static, having no history of achievement. An ethnocentric British scholar argued in 1920 that "the chief distinction between the backward and forward peoples is that the former are of colored skin."[6] This prejudice translated into the demeaning idea that Africans were unfit to rule themselves and badly in need of Western leadership. Racist ideology spawned the French and Belgian idea of the "civilizing mission," which viewed Africans as children who could attain adulthood only by adopting French language, religion, and culture. Europeans also imposed a color bar that kept Africans out of clubs, schools, and jobs reserved for Europeans.

Asian minorities also became part of colonial societies. Beginning in the 1890s Indians arrived to build railroads, work on sugar plantations, or become middle-level retail traders. Indians became the commercial middle class of East Africa and occupied a key economic niche in South Africa, the Rhodesias, Mozambique, and Madagascar. Cities such as Nairobi in Kenya, Kampala in Uganda, and Durban in South Africa had substantial Indian populations, their downtowns dominated by Indian stores and Hindu temples. In West and Central Africa, Lebanese became shopkeepers in cities and towns. The Asians' growing influence and wealth, resented by black Africans, led after independence to many governments restricting Asian economic power. However, Europeans recognized Asians' value in perpetuating divide-and-rule tactics, since Africans often focused their resentment on the Asian traders they dealt with rather than European officials.

Europeans and Africans in South Africa

South Africa was shaped by conflicts between European settlers and the Bantu-speaking African peoples. The first Dutch settlement, Cape Town, was established at the Cape of Good Hope in 1652. As they expanded, the Dutch settlers, known as Boers (Dutch for "farmers"), established a system based on white rule over nonwhites that enforced physical separation of the groups in all areas of life. The system of white supremacy became even more rigid in the late 1700s and early 1800s among Boers who boarded wagon trains and migrated east along the coast and into the interior, a journey they called trekking, to find good farming land and to escape government restrictions on their freedom of action.

White Supremacy and Conflict

Trekking led to chronic conflict between the Boers and the Xhosa (KHO-sa) farmers and pastoralists who lived in the eastern Cape region. The two groups fought for nearly half a century, and many Xhosa died. When fearing attack, trekkers pulled their wagons into a circle, known as a **laager**, a tradition that symbolized Boer resistance to new ideas and their desire for separation from other peoples. In 1806 the British annexed the Cape Colony, giving Boers even more reason to migrate into the interior. Boers viewed white supremacy as sanctioned by their strict, puritanical Calvinist Christian beliefs, and the system also ensured them a cheap labor supply for their farms and ranches. By ending South African slavery, the British harmed the Boer economy, which depended on thousands of slaves of African and Asian origin. The Boers were also outraged when later the British granted the right to vote to Africans and mixed-descent people, known as coloreds.

laager A defensive arrangement of wagons in a circle. Used by the Boers in South Africa in the eighteenth and nineteenth centuries to guard against attacks by native Africans.

The migrating Boers had to contend with the largest Bantu people, the Zulus. In the early 1800s some Zulus began a military expansion under an ambitious military genius, Shaka (ca. 1787–1828),

Zulu Expansion

who overcame the disadvantage of being born out of wedlock to gain fame as a courageous warrior and become a powerful chief. Shaka united various Zulu clans in Natal (**nuh-TALL**), the region along South Africa's Indian Ocean coast, into a powerful nation. Soil exhaustion, severe drought, population growth, and fears of potential Boer migration may all have been factors provoking Zulu expansion. Shaka organized a disciplined army of some 40,000 warriors and invented effective new military tactics, such as dividing his troops into regiments armed with short, stabbing spears. In 1816 he began invading other groups' territories, and the resulting wars killed thousands of Zulus and non-Zulus while wreaking widespread disruption. After conquering much of the interior plateau, Shaka grew more despotic and was assassinated by his brother, and eventually the Zulu empire fell to the Boers. Ironically, by depopulating large areas of the mineral-rich interior plateau, the wars made it easier for the Boers to later move in.

The Sotho Kingdom

Some Bantu leaders avoided conquest by the Zulus and Boers. For example, Moshoeshoe (**MOE-shoo-shoo**) (b. ca. 1786) created a kingdom for his branch of the Sotho (**SOO-too**) people. With the region in turmoil because of the Zulu and Boer expansion, Moshoeshoe moved his people to an easily defended flat-top mountain in 1824, taking in African refugees regardless of their ethnic origin. The king preferred peaceful negotiation to warfare; he offered tribute, such as cattle, to his African rivals and cultivated friendship with the British as a counterweight to the Boers. He also invited Christian missionaries to his state and used them to acquire guns and horses. British support for Moshoeshoe allowed his Sotho kingdom to remain independent until 1871, when it was absorbed into the British-ruled Cape Colony.

Conflict between the Boers and the expanding British intensified. In 1838 a large minority of Boers began what they called the Great Trek, heading in well-armed wagon caravans of several hundred families with their sheep and cattle into the interior. After many hardships and fighting with Zulus, they moved into the high plateau and formed two independent Boer republics, Transvaal (**TRANS-vahl**) and the Orange Free State. After conquering the Africans, the Boers seized their cattle and forced them to work on Boer farms. As they consolidated control over Africans, their ideas of keeping themselves separate, preserving their culture, and upholding what one Boer leader called the proper relations between white "master" and African "servant" grew stronger. Boers despised the British and considered black Africans an "inferior race" hostile to European values.

The Great Trek
Many Boers migrated into the South African interior in wagon trains. These migrants, known as trekkers, endured hardships but also eventually subjugated the local African peoples, taking their land for farming, pasturing, and mining.

However, the discovery in the Boer republics of diamonds and gold spurred the British to seek control over the Boer republics, leading to the South African War (1899–1902), often called the Boer War. The war culminated in British victory but also intensified Boer resentment of the British. To eradicate local support for the Boer fighters, the British burned farms, destroyed towns, and interned thousands of Boers, including women and children, in concentration camps, where 26,000 died of disease and starvation. Moreover, the British relied on African troops, thousands of whom died fighting in hopes that the British would be less oppressive.

But Africans found they had merely exchanged one set of white masters for another. British and Boer leaders worked out a compromise in which the South African government, now a collaboration

WAGGON ASCENDING THE UNCOMMOSS HILL, NATAL.

Mansell/Time & Life Pictures/Getty Images

between the two groups, extended discriminatory Boer laws, restricting African civil and political rights and putting many Africans on reserves, rural lands with few resources from which workers desperate for jobs could be recruited. Africans were valued chiefly as cheap unskilled labor for the white-owned economy, and laws limited their movement and reserved the more desirable neighborhoods and jobs only for whites. Continued African resistance led the government to build a police state to enforce their racial policies. Furthermore, British-Boer tensions simmered as thousands of British settlers arrived, eventually becoming a third of the white population. The Boers began to call themselves Afrikaners (people of Africa) and their Dutch-derived language Afrikaans.

Christian Missions and African Culture

Supported by colonial governments, Christian missionaries, whose primary goal was to reshape African culture and religious life, established most of Africa's modern hospitals and schools. Mission doctors practiced Western medicine and denounced African folk medicine, and mission schools taught new agricultural methods, mathematics, reading, writing, and Western languages, giving a small group of Africans valuable skills in the colonial economy and administration. Critics complained that the mission schools not only taught Western values and European history but also ignored African history and derided African beliefs as superstition. Some African nationalists, themselves products of mission schools, charged that these schools, as an Igbo writer put it, "miseducated" and "de-Africanized" them, perpetuating their status as "hewers of wood and haulers of water."[7] The Africans who attended mission schools and adopted individualistic Western ways often became divorced from their village traditions, loosening the social glue of African communities. Yet, before 1945 only 5 percent of children attended any government or mission school. The first modern African college was established in Sierra Leone in 1827, but before 1940 the few Africans who could attend a university had to do so usually in Europe or the United States.

Mission Schools

Millions of Africans adopted Christianity. Some Africans became devout Catholics or Protestants, while others only accepted those beliefs they liked while rejecting others. Africans often emphasized Bible passages that called for justice and equality. Some African churches combined Christian doctrines with African practices and beliefs, such as condoning men having more than one wife. Yorubas often just added the Christian and Muslim gods to their polytheistic pantheon. Christianity also marginalized the female deities and shamans who had been influential, reducing women's religious roles. Moreover, when Christian leaders sometimes asked men to give up multiple wives, these women were left without support or their children. Yet, women often welcomed monogamy and favored Christian social values such as promoting education for girls.

Spreading Christianity

Africans in the World Economy

The transformation of African economic life was at least as significant as the political reorganization. Extracting wealth from a colony required tying its economy closely to that of the colonizer. European businessmen now controlled the top level of the economies, including the banks, import-export companies, mines, and plantations. Colonial policies transformed Africans into producers for the world market, replacing the subsistence agriculture, which could not produce enough revenues for the government or investors. Requiring taxes to be paid in cash promoted a shift from growing food to growing cash crops such as cotton, cocoa, rubber, and palm oil or mining copper, gold, oil, chrome, cobalt, and diamonds. If taxation did not spur the changes, authorities resorted to forced labor, most notoriously in the Belgian Congo, where much of the population was required to grow rubber for Belgian planters. An American missionary reported in 1895 that the Belgian policies "reduced the people to a state of utter despair. Each town is forced to bring a certain quality [of rubber]. The soldiers drive the people into the bush. If they will not go they are shot down, and their left hands cut off. The soldiers often shoot poor helpless women and harmless children."[8] Over half of the Congo's population died from overwork or brutality over a twenty-year period.

Colonial Economies

Colonial Africa became linked to the West and the world economy, often leaving Africans vulnerable as their livelihoods became subject to the fluctuations in the world price for the commodities they produced, a price determined by the whims of Western consumers and corporations. Colonies also became markets for Western industrial products, which displaced village handicrafts. Africans became exporters of cash crops they did not consume, such as cocoa and rubber, and importers of goods they did not produce. Many of the cash crops that dominated African lives had been

IN THE RUBBER COILS.

SCENE—*The Congo "Free" State.*

Punch Cartoon Library & Archive

Rubber Coils in Belgian Congo The Belgians colonized the Congo hoping to exploit its resources. This critical cartoon, published in the British satirical magazine *Punch* in 1906, shows a Congolese ensnared in the rubber coils of the Belgian king Leopold in the guise of a serpent. Rubber was the major cash crop, introduced by the Belgians to generate profits.

introduced from outside. Peanuts and rubber were brought from South America, and cocoa from Mexico. With the growth of an automobile culture in the West, an oil-drilling industry also emerged along the West African coast, making these societies dependent on oil exports. Colonies often became economic monocultures. Hence Northern Rhodesia (now Zambia) mostly exported copper, Senegal peanuts, and the Gold Coast cocoa. The dependence of Ghanaians on growing and selling cocoa was well described in a local popular song from the 1960s: "If you want to send your children to school, build your house, marry, buy cloth [or] a truck, it is cocoa. Whatever you want to do in this world, it is with cocoa money that you do it."[9]

The opportunities and demands of the colonial economy profoundly affected the lives of both men and women. As men were recruited or forced to migrate to other districts or colonies for mining or industrial labor, a permanent pattern of labor migration became established. Hence, the white-owned farms and mines of South Africa recruited thousands of workers from Mozambique and British Central Africa on renewable one-year contracts, and men from the Sahel migrated to the cocoa estates of the Ivory Coast and Gold Coast. This migration disrupted family and village life. The male migrants lived in crowded dormitories or huts that offered little privacy, enjoyed few amenities other than drinking beer in makeshift bars, and were able to visit their families back home for only a few days a year.

Africans were heavily recruited into the white-owned South African economy. Many thousands moved to cities, especially the Transvaal mining center of Johannesburg, thus becoming temporarily or permanently removed from their farming villages. They experienced dreadful work conditions on white-owned factories and farms, and even worse in the mines, where safety regulations were few and hundreds of miners died each year. The Zulu poet B. W. Vilakezi described the miner's life in the early 1900s: "Roar, without rest, machines of the mines, Roar from dawn till darkness falls. To black men groaning as they labor, Tortured by their aching muscles, Gasping in the fetid air, Reeking from the dirt and sweat. The earth will swallow us who burrow. And, if I die there, underground, What does it matter? All round me, every day, I see men stumble, fall and die."[10]

In many African societies women had long played a major role as traders and farmers. As men migrated for work or took up cash crop farming, women became responsible for the less lucrative food production, increasing their workload. The agricultural workweek for women in the German-ruled Cameroons went from forty-five to seventy hours. The Baule women of the Ivory Coast, who had long profited from growing cotton and spinning it into thread, lost their position to Baule men when cotton became a cash crop and textiles an export item. Women traders who had dominated town markets now faced competition from Indians or Lebanese. Some women responded with self-help organizations. Ashante market women in Kumasi organized themselves under elected leaders later known as market queens to promote cooperation and settle disputes among themselves. Thanks to education, self-help, and ambition, some African women also gained skills to support themselves as teachers, nurses, and traders. But many poor women were overwhelmed by the challenges of trying to preserve their families while fulfilling their new responsibilities.

African Responses and the Colonial Legacy

Cultural Resistance Africans responded to colonialism in various ways. In South Africa the small educated middle class of professionals and traders found ways to oppose white supremacy. One of these, the

[9]Song lyrics by Fred Sarpong as seen in Dennis Austen, *Politics in Ghana* (London: Oxford University Press, 1964).

Johannesburg lawyer Pixley ka Isaka Seme (PIX-ley ka I-sa-ka-SE-me), a graduate of Columbia University in New York, helped found the African National Congress in 1912 to promote African rights and cultural regeneration. In Nigeria many educated Igbos became cash crop farmers, merchants, professionals, or clerks. Other Africans dealt with change by enriching traditional ways. The imaginative Yoruba artist Olowe of Ise (oh-LO-way of ee-SAY) (ca. 1875–1938) emphasized Yoruba themes and ideals in the woodcarvings and elaborately carved doors he sculpted for Yoruba kings but creatively added richly textured surfaces and the illusion of movement. Some Africans mixed Western and African ideas. The Black Zion movement in South Africa had Christian overtones, claiming that Jesus was African, but also promoted African traditions such as faith healing.

Africans also used their traditional cultural forms to express their sentiments. Igbo women used a combination of dance and theater to influence their individualistic but patriarchal society, dancing and singing their grievances in a strategy known as "sitting on a man." The dance performances sometimes encouraged noncooperation with colonial demands, such as increased taxes, or with excessive male Igbo chauvinism. When local leaders ignored the dance messages of dissatisfaction, the women took stronger action, including rioting. In South Africa Zulu workers reworked dance tunes and turned them into songs to protest white domination. The Sotho people transformed their poetry praising influential people and ancestors into songs expressing the experiences of male migrants working in the mines and the women left behind in the villages. Some South African composers mixed Christian hymns with traditional Xhosa or Zulu choral music. The African National Congress adopted one such hymn, "God Bless Africa," as their official anthem. Later the song, with its uplifting message of hope, became the anthem of black empowerment:

Bless the youth, that they may carry the land with patience. Bless the wives and young girls. Bless agriculture and stock raising. Banish all famine and diseases. Fill the land with good health. Bless our effort, of union and self uplift, of education and mutual understanding.[11]

Many Africans chose noncooperation. Tax evasion and passive protest were rampant, especially in rural areas. Others chose a more activist strategy and formed labor unions, usually illegal in colonial systems that protected Western-owned businesses. Strikes were common, especially among mine workers, but governments arrested strike leaders and added them to the political prisoners rotting away in colonial prisons. Rebellions sparked by unpopular policies, such as new taxes or forced labor, also punctuated colonial rule. The Maji Maji Rebellion, which broke out in German-ruled Tanganyika in 1905, began as a peasant protest against a new cotton-growing scheme that forced people to work in the cotton fields for only 35 cents a month. Africans' preference to grow their own food rather than be commercial farmers led to a new religious cult known as Maji Maji ("water medicine"), which used magic water in hopes of better crops. In their uprising, the rebels occupied towns and sprinkled their bodies with magic water in hopes it would make them immune from bullets. The Germans, using machine guns, soon regained the towns and in 1907 defeated the Maji Maji at the cost of 26,000 African lives. However, the resistance caused the Germans to end forced labor.

Noncooperation

Some historians contend that colonialism increased the productive capacity of the land, built cities and transportation networks, brought advances in technology, and stimulated Africans to produce more wealth than they ever had before. Other historians argue that colonial rulers stole land, exploited labor, gained profitable access to raw materials, shifted profits back to Europe, limited Africa's economic growth, and created artificial, unstable countries. While profits from Africa supported European industrialization and enriched European businesses, colonial Africa enjoyed little balanced economic growth that benefited the majority of the people. One observer in the early 1900s noted that in Portuguese-ruled Mozambique a man "works . . . all his life under horrible conditions to buy scanty clothing for his wife and daughters. The men and boys can rarely afford proper clothing."[12] Moreover, many former colonies are economically vulnerable monocultures today. As for progress, seventy-five years of Belgian colonialism in the Congo failed to build any paved road system linking the major cities or to establish more than a handful of schools and medical clinics for the millions of Congolese. As a result sub-Saharan Africa was the most impoverished region of the world at the end of the colonial era, a legacy difficult to overcome.

Colonial Legacies

SECTION SUMMARY

- African colonial governments served the interests of the colonizers, though the colonizers' involvement in local affairs varied between direct and indirect rule.

- Colonizers divided Africa into countries with artificial boundaries, sometimes splitting an ethnic group into more than one country and sometimes throwing rival groups into a single country, thus creating lasting tensions.

- Dutch settlers of South Africa, called Boers, pursued a policy of white supremacy in spite of more liberal British policies.

- South Africa was also shaped by the conquests of Shaka, a Zulu leader.

- The Boers fled inland to escape British control, but when diamonds and gold were discovered in the Boer republics, the British won the South African War, after which they agreed to enforce white supremacist policies to gain Boer cooperation.

- In several colonies whites reserved the best resources and all political power for themselves, while Indians and Lebanese came to form the middle class in many African societies.

- Christian missionary schools provided a small minority of Africans with skills they could use in the colonial world but largely ignored and often damaged the native African culture.

- As African economies came to depend on a single commodity desired by Europeans, colonized Africans lost their subsistence skills and were often forced to work far from home.

- Blacks suffered greatly in white-dominated South Africa, but many resisted through poetry, music, dance, and political organizations such as the African National Congress.

- Some Africans took advantage of opportunities offered by colonization, others enriched their traditional ways, and a few, such as the Maji Maji, openly rebelled, though never successfully.

- While some historians think that colonization brought beneficial development to Africans, economic growth benefited mainly the colonizers, did little to materially improve African lives, and prevented Africans from building diversified and strong economies.

IMPERIALISM, REFORM, AND THE MIDDLE EASTERN SOCIETIES

What political and economic impact did Europe have on the Middle East?

Between 1750 and 1914 most Muslim societies suffered repeated challenges from western Europe and Russia. The Ottoman Empire remained the only significant Muslim power and, despite a remarkable ability to rejuvenate itself, fell behind the industrializing West. Expanding European empires ate at the fringes of Persia and the shrinking Ottoman domain, and European economic penetration and cultural influences forced responses that differed from society to society.

Challenges to the Ottoman Empire

Russian Expansion

During the Early Modern Era the Ottoman Turks forged a huge empire in southeastern Europe and western Asia, as well as gaining a strong influence across North Africa. Many Muslims viewed the Ottoman sultan as the caliph, the successor to the Prophet and leader of the Islamic community, giving Ottoman leaders enormous prestige. But by 1750, as a result of both Western pressure and internal problems, the Ottoman power had diminished. In the nineteenth century rising pressure from European nations, especially Russia, undermined the Ottoman Empire and its more than 60 million people (see Map 21.2). Since the 1500s the Russians had expanded south toward the Black Sea, and in 1768 they defeated Ottoman forces and gained control over part of the northern Black Sea coast. They extended this control to include the Crimean peninsula, and in 1829 they took over the largely Christian Caucasus state of Georgia (see Chronology: The Middle East, 1750–1914). In 1853 Czar Nicholas I characterized the weakening Ottoman Empire as "the sick man of Europe," a reputation that would stick.

Revolts

The European powers schemed to outflank each other while building up their influence in the weakening empire. With European support, the Greeks, Serbs, Romanians, and Bulgarians threw off Ottoman rule in the 1800s, revealing Ottoman weaknesses (see Chapter 19). An Anglo-French fleet and the Russian army intervened to aid the Greeks, shifting the military balance. The 1830 treaty ending the war recognized Greek independence and gave autonomy to Serbia and Moldavia.

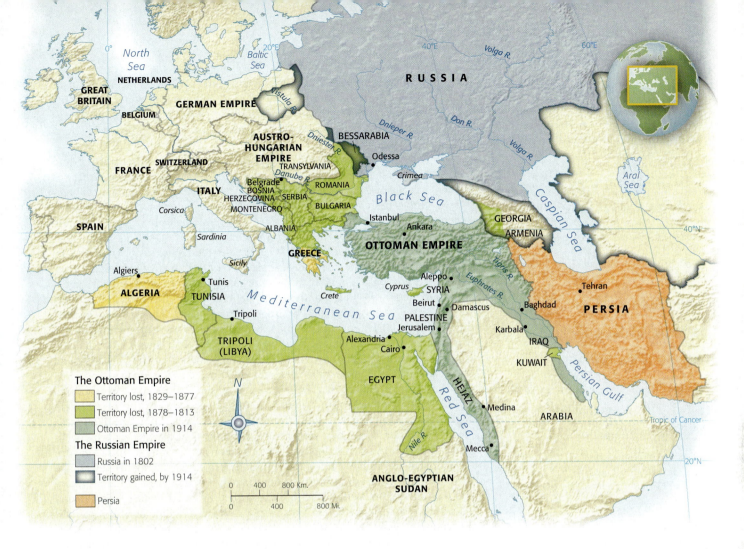

Map 21.2 includes labels: North Sea, Baltic Sea, Volga R., RUSSIA, 0°, 20°E, 40°E, 60°E, GREAT BRITAIN, NETHERLANDS, GERMAN EMPIRE, Vistula R., BELGIUM, Dnieper R., Don R., BESSARABIA, Dniester R., AUSTRO-HUNGARIAN EMPIRE, TRANSYLVANIA, Odessa, Volga R., FRANCE, SWITZERLAND, Danube R., ROMANIA, Crimea, Aral Sea, ITALY, Belgrade, BOSNIA, SERBIA, BULGARIA, Black Sea, Caspian Sea, 40°N, HERZEGOVINA, MONTENEGRO, Istanbul, Ankara, GEORGIA, Corsica, ALBANIA, ARMENIA, SPAIN, Sardinia, GREECE, OTTOMAN EMPIRE, Tigris R., Sicily, Crete, Cyprus, Aleppo, SYRIA, Euphrates R., Tehran, Algiers, Tunis, Mediterranean Sea, Beirut, Damascus, Baghdad, PERSIA, ALGERIA, TUNISIA, Tripoli, PALESTINE, Karbala, IRAQ, TRIPOLI (LIBYA), Alexandria, Jerusalem, KUWAIT, Cairo, Persian Gulf, EGYPT, HEJAZ, Red Sea, Medina, ARABIA, Tropic of Cancer, Nile R., Mecca, ANGLO-EGYPTIAN SUDAN, 20°N

Legend:
The Ottoman Empire
- Territory lost, 1829–1877
- Territory lost, 1878–1813
- Ottoman Empire in 1914
The Russian Empire
- Russia in 1802
- Territory gained, by 1914
- Persia

Scale: 0 400 800 Km. / 0 400 800 Mi.

Map 21.2   The Ottoman Empire and Persia, 1914

The Ottoman Empire once included much of southeastern Europe, western Asia, and North Africa. By 1914, after losing most of its European, Caucasian, and North African territories, it was restricted largely to parts of western Asia.

e Interactive Map

Ethnic Minorities

Weakened by military losses, the central government had difficulty satisfying the empire's multiethnic population. Because the Turks had long benefited from tapping the empire's varied peoples to enrich their state, non-Muslim minorities played major roles in commerce, the professions, and government. The Ottomans had generally been tolerant of minorities such as Kurds (mostly Sunni Muslims), Jews, and Arab Christians, allowing each group to basically rule itself through its own religious establishment, such as the Greek Orthodox Church. Christians and Jews felt particularly secure in the major Ottoman cities, and Jews generally enjoyed more rights and prosperity than they did in Europe. Multiethnic Istanbul was described in 1873 as "a city not of one nation but of many. Eight or nine languages are constantly spoken in the streets and five or six appear on the shop fronts."[13] Various religious sects also settled in the Lebanon mountains, maintaining their traditions.

But some ethnic minorities became restless, especially in eastern Turkey and the Caucasus, where Turkish relations with the Christian Armenians deteriorated. Armenians had generally remained loyal Ottoman subjects, and some held high government positions, but the nationalist and socialist ideas percolating in Europe influenced some to want their own state. Armenians founded their own schools, colleges, libraries, hospitals, presses, and charitable organizations and looked to Europe and North America for financial and moral support. In the 1890s and early 1900s the Ottoman government responded to increasing Armenian assertiveness, including terrorist attacks, by seizing Armenian property, killing over 100,000 Armenians, and exiling thousands more. Many moved to North America to escape the persecution. Then in 1915, during World War I, the government charged Armenians with supporting Russia and began removing Armenians from eastern Anatolia, where in response Armenian nationalists declared a republic. During the turmoil the Ottoman army, aided by local Turks and Kurds, killed around a million Armenians. Many

CHRONOLOGY
The Middle East, 1750–1914

1768–1829 Russians gain control of northern Black Sea lands and Georgia

1794–1925 Qajar dynasty in Persia

1798–1799 French occupation of Egypt

1805–1848 Rule of Muhammad Ali in Egypt

1830 Greek independence from Ottoman Empire

1830 French colonization of Algeria

1859–1869 Building of Suez Canal

1882 British colonization of Egypt

1890s–1915 Turkish genocide against Armenians

1897 First Zionist conference

1899 British protectorate over Kuwait

1905–1911 Constitutional revolution in Persia

1907–1921 Russian and British spheres of influence in Persia

1908 Young Turk government in Ottoman Turkey

1908 Discovery of oil in Persia

1911–1912 Colonization of Libya and Morocco

Young Turks A modernizing group in Ottoman Turkey that promoted a national identity and that gained power in the early twentieth century.

historians consider the violent assault a genocide, the singling out of one group for mass killing, but Turkish nationalists view it as an incidental side effect of war. The mass killings still complicate Armenian-Turkish relations. The surviving Armenians formed a small republic in the Caucasus, Armenia, that was absorbed by Russia in 1920.

To survive and match Western power, Ottoman sultans tried hard to reform and modernize, building a more secular and centralized government. However, this was no easy task because the Islamic religious leaders, the privileged Janissary military force, and governors of distant Arab provinces, who were virtually independent, benefited from weak central authority. Gradually Ottoman leaders and thinkers recognized the need to obtain knowledge and aid from the West. The reformist sultan Mahmud II **(MACH-mood)** (r. 1808–1839) tried to reestablish central authority by eliminating the Janissaries, once an effective fighting force but now resisting change and a costly burden. Mahmud recruited a new military force that crushed the Janissaries and then slowly built a modern army trained by Prussian officers. His successors set up new schools that taught European learning and languages, and by 1900 the University of Istanbul had become the Muslim world's first modern institution of higher education. The Ottomans also replaced many older Islamic laws with laws based on French revolutionary codes. Increasingly the rulers marginalized Islam and treated Islamic knowledge as irrelevant, demoralizing conservatives.

The growth of a more centralized government and a modern, secular Ottoman nationality continued through the 1800s. To foster a national identity, the Ottoman sultans declared all citizens equal before the law, announcing that "the differences of religion and sect among the subjects is something not affecting their rights of citizenship. It is wrong to make discriminations among us."[14] But attempts to involve the people in government largely failed, and the reforms proved inadequate. In the 1880s a modernizing group known as the **Young Turks** emerged in the military and the universities. With a goal to make Turkey a modern nation with a liberal constitution, in 1908 the Young Turks, espousing Turkish nationalism, led a military coup that deposed the old sultan. Under the facade of parliamentary government, they ruled as autocrats and military modernizers. During World War I, as an ally of Germany and Austria-Hungary, the Young Turks embraced a Turkish ethnic identity, secularization, and closer ties to the Western world. After their defeat in World War I, the Ottoman Empire was dissolved and the Arab peoples once ruled by the Ottomans fell under British or French rule. By 1920 the Turks were struggling to hold on to their Anatolian heartland.

Egypt: Modernization and Occupation

The most extensive effort to deflect Western pressure through modernization came in Egypt, but only after Ottoman influence was minimized. The Ottomans had governed the province through the Mamluks, a Muslim caste of Turkish origin whose corruption and repression gave French general Napoleon Bonaparte an excuse to invade the country. When Bonaparte abandoned his Egyptian adventure, Egypt came under the rule of Muhammad Ali (r. 1805–1848), a Turkish-speaking Albanian who had led the Ottoman forces that helped eject the French. After being appointed viceroy by the Ottoman sultan, Muhammad Ali made Egypt effectively independent but was forced by the European powers to remain loosely bound to the weakening Ottoman state. The charming sultan impressed Europeans with his talents: "If ever a man had an eye that denoted genius, [he] was the person. Never dead nor quiescent, it was fascinating like that of a gazelle; or, in the hour of storm, fierce as an eagle's."[15]

Muhammad Ali's Reforms

Muhammad Ali introduced ambitious reforms to transform Egypt into a European-style industrial nation. He used government revenues from increased agricultural exports to establish foundries, shipyards, and textile, sugar, and glass factories, as well as a conscript army trained by Western instructors, a navy, and an arms industry. He also replaced Islamic with French legal codes, sent Egyptians to study technical subjects in Europe, fostered the first Arab newspapers, and laid the foundation for a state educational system to train people for the military and bureaucracy. However, Muhammad Ali's programs did not ultimately protect Egyptian independence and foster development, a failure that invited British interference. Unlike European nations, Egypt lacked iron and coal, and the work force was not used to industrial regimentation. As Muhammad Ali and his successors welcomed Western investment, they became more shackled to European finance, and an influx of cheap British commodities also stifled Egypt's textile and handicraft manufacturing. Europeans were more interested in procuring Egyptian raw cotton for processing in their own mills than they were in buying finished textiles.

Following the European model, Muhammad Ali turned to seeking resources and markets through conquest. Egyptian armies moved south into the Sudanic lands along the Nile River, which they made into an Egyptian colony, and also into Ottoman-ruled Arabia, Palestine, Syria, and Greece. But this aggression alarmed the European powers, who intervened to push the Egyptians back. The British sought to undermine Egypt in order to have more influence in the region and to gain control of the Suez Canal, built as a French-Egyptian collaboration between 1859 and 1869. The 100-mile-long canal, a magnificent technological achievement whose construction had cost the lives of thousands of Egyptian workers, linked the Mediterranean and Red Seas, greatly decreasing the shipping time between Europe and Asia. British merchant and naval ships became the canal's major users, and Britain then gained control of the canal by capitalizing on Muhammad Ali's failure to transform Egypt. In 1875 Muhammad Ali's grandson was forced by skyrocketing national debt to sell Egypt's share of canal ownership to the British government.

To preempt the ambitions of other European powers, the British decided to seize Egypt using military force. Egypt was bankrupt and deeply in debt to European financiers and governments, while the country's political and commercial elite, including many Coptic Christians, were committed to modernization. But most Egyptians, influenced by conservative Islamic ideas and leaders, opposed the growing Western influence. In 1882 local unrest and threats to European residents provided an excuse for the British to invade the country. Egypt became part of Britain's growing worldwide empire.

British Occupation

Soon the British had to deal with a challenge coming from the Sudanic region to Egypt's south (today the nation of Sudan). In 1881 a militant Arab Muslim in the Sudan, Muhammad Ahmad (1846–1885), declared that he was the Mahdi **(MAH-dee)** ("the Guided One") sent to restore Islam's purity and destroy the corrupt Egyptian-imposed government. He recruited an army that defeated the Egyptian forces and their British officers, then formed an Islamic state. However, the Mahdist government wasted money in wars, and in 1898 British and Egyptian forces defeated it and formed a new state known as the Anglo-Egyptian Sudan, which was effectively a British colony.

Persia: Challenges and Reforms

Persia, increasingly known as Iran, faced many problems. After the Safavid collapse in 1736 and the following decades of turmoil, in 1794 one Persian tribe, the Qajars **(KAH-jars)**, established control from their base in Tehran and ruled uneasily until 1925. The early Qajar rulers were unable to resolve most of Persia's problems and became noted instead for greed, corruption, and

Qajar Rule

Muhammad Ali Meets European Representatives
Muhammad Ali, the Egyptian sultan who tried to modernize his state, cultivated ties with Western nations. This painting shows the sultan in 1839 meeting with representatives from several European governments.

Mary Evans Picture Library

lavish living. One particularly extravagant shah married 158 wives, fathering nearly 100 children, and was survived by some 600 grandchildren. Qajar Persia was more a diverse collection of tribes, ethnic groups, and religious sects than a nation, fostering conflict. The majority of Persia's people, including the Turkish-speaking Azeri minority in the northwest, were Shi'ites, but Christian Armenians, Jews, Zoroastrians, and Sunni Kurds all sought increased autonomy. Shi'ite clerics controlled education, law, and welfare and enjoyed vast wealth from landholdings and tithes, and the top Shi'ite clerics engaged in power struggles with the Qajar shahs. Shi'ites also persecuted as heretical the **Bahai** (buh-HI) religion. Founded in 1867 by the Persian Bahaullah **(bah-hah-oo-LAH)** (1817–1892) as an offshoot of Shi'ism, Bahai called for universal peace, the unity of all religions, and service to others. Shi'ites killed many Bahais and forced their leaders into exile.

Bahai An offshoot of Persian Shi'ism that was founded in 1867; Bahai preached universal peace, the unity of all religions, and service to others.

Persia also faced continuous pressure from Russia and Britain. By the 1870s Russia had gained territory on both sides of the Caspian Sea, including the Caucasus, and between 1907 and 1921 it asserted a sphere of influence in northern Persia. British power also steadily grew in the Persian Gulf and along Arabia's Indian Ocean coast. The British, who wanted to keep the Russians away from the Persian Gulf and India, asserted a sphere of influence in southeastern Persia, which gave them a foothold at the entrance to the Persian Gulf. British entrepreneurs gained a monopoly on Persian railroad construction and banking, and the Anglo-Persian Oil Company (later British Petroleum), which struck oil in 1908, became Persia's dominant economic enterprise, with profits going chiefly to Britain. Persians considered the powerful British economic role a humiliation. A weak government combined with foreign pressure led to reforms, as some Qajar shahs attempted to restore central government power, rebuilt an army, set up a Western-style college, introduced a telegraph system, and allowed Christian missionaries to establish schools and hospitals. While some celebrated the reforms, they threatened the conservative Shi'ite clergy, who hoped to thwart modernization.

Foreign Pressures

From 1905 to 1911 Persia enjoyed a constitutional revolution and a brief period of democracy, unique in the Middle East. The more liberal Shi'ite clergy, allied with Tehran merchants, Armenians, and Western-educated radicals, imposed a democratic constitution that curbed royal power by setting up an elected parliament and granting freedom of the press. When a conservative, pro-Russian shah took power and attempted to weaken the parliament, liberal newspapers, writers, and musicians lampooned him and his allies, with troubadours singing songs about the love of country, democracy, freedom, justice, and equality. However, Britain and Russia pressured Persia to grant them more influence, straining the progressive leadership. The constitutionalist forces soon split into pro-Western nationalists seeking separation of religious and civil power, land reform, and universal education, and Shi'ite clerics who, alarmed at the secular direction, favored slower change. As violence increased in 1911, the royal government closed down the parliament and ended the democratic experiment. Aref Qazvini, a popular prorevolution songwriter, lamented the setback: "O let not Iran thus be lost, if ye be men of truth."[16] By then, Britain and Russia, stationing troops in Persia, had reduced Persia's political and economic independence.

Constitutional Revolution

Western Asia, Northwest Africa, and Europe

Declining Ottoman power and growing Western activity eventually reshaped the Arab provinces of the eastern Ottoman Empire, especially Syria and Lebanon, which the Ottomans governed as one province. Despite their diverse ethnic and religious mosaic, including Arab and Armenian Christians, Sunni and Shi'ite Arabs, and Sunni Kurds, the peoples had mostly lived in peace. By recognizing each community's autonomy, the Ottoman government promoted religious tolerance. A British writer reported that under Lebanon's generally stable conditions, "every man lives in a perfect security of life and property. The peasant is not richer than in other countries, but he is free."[17] However, in the 1850s poverty and a stagnant economy fostered occasional conflicts, and the densely populated region around Mount Lebanon came under the influence of several Western powers. The French developed a special relationship with the Maronites **(MAR-uh-nite)**, Arab Christians who sought a closer connection with the Roman Catholic Church, and American Protestant missionaries established a college in the main Lebanese city, Beirut, that spread modern ideas. The weak economy also encouraged emigration, especially of Lebanese Christians to the United States. Other Lebanese Christians and Muslims moved to West Africa, Latin America, or the Caribbean. By 1914 perhaps 350,000 Syrians and Lebanese had emigrated to the Americas.

Syria and Lebanon

Under Ottoman rule, Iraq, the heart of ancient Mesopotamia, lacked political unity and had not prospered. The Ottomans divided Iraq into three provinces: a largely Sunni Arab and Kurdish north, a chiefly Sunni Arab center, and a Shi'ite Arab–dominated south. Iraqis suffered from major floods and repeated plague and cholera epidemics. A British official described Iraq as "a country of extremes, either dying of thirst or of being drowned."[18] Iraq also lacked order, foreign capital, and a transportation system such as railroads or steamships. Pirates attacked Persian Gulf shipping, and Bedouin tribes raided land caravans. The literacy rate remained extremely low. Yet, Western interest in this Ottoman backwater's economic potential and strategic location grew. In 1899 the British established a protectorate over the small neighboring kingdom of Kuwait (koo-WAIT) at the west end of the Persian Gulf, which allowed them to station troops and agents. But both the British and Germans came to believe that Iraq might have considerable oil, and in the early 1900s the Ottomans and foreign investors poured money into Iraq.

Iraq

The Arabic-speaking societies along Africa's Mediterranean coast from Libya to Algeria had never been under firm Ottoman control, and their proximity to Europe made them natural targets for colonization. In 1830 the French embarked on full-scale colonization of Algeria. Abd al-Qadir (AB dul-KA-deer), a Muslim cleric, used Islamic appeals to unite Arab and Berber opposition to the French. His resourceful followers quickly learned how to make guns. Facing years of determined resistance, the French attempted to demoralize the Algerians by driving peasants off the best land and selling it to European settlers while also relocating and breaking up tribes. Yet anti-French revolts, often spurred by appeals to Islam, erupted until the 1880s. The ruthless French conquest cost tens of thousands of French and hundreds of thousands of Algerian lives.

France and Algeria

The French intended to impose French culture, settlers, and economic priorities on the Algerians. General Bugeaud, the conqueror of Algeria, conceded in 1849 that "the Arabs with great insight understand very well the cruel revolution we have brought them; it is as radical for them as socialism would be for us."[19] Between the 1840s and 1914 over a million immigrants from France, Italy, and Spain poured into Algeria, erecting a racist society similar to South Africa. The European settlers eventually elected representatives to the French parliament as Algeria was incorporated into the French state. Vineyard cultivation and wine production displaced food crops and pasture, an economic change that mocked Islamic values prohibiting alcoholic beverages.

Gradually European power in Northwest Africa increased. In Morocco, Sultan Mawlay Hassan (r. 1873–1895) skillfully worked to preserve the country's independence by playing the rival European powers off against each other. However, the French and Spanish, attracted by Morocco's economic potential and strategic position, had divided the country between them by 1912. Tunisia, just east of Algeria, had long enjoyed considerable autonomy under Ottoman rule, and the port city of Tunis prospered as a center of trade and piracy. Coveting this trade, in 1881 France sent in troops to occupy Tunisia. Libya, a sparsely populated, mostly desert land between Tunisia and Egypt, was conquered by the Italians in 1911 and 1912. The country's Islamic orders led repeated resistance efforts, and the resulting conflicts killed one-third of Libya's people. European colonialism now dominated the whole of North Africa.

Colonizing North Africa

SECTION SUMMARY

- After 1750, the Ottoman Empire's power began to wane under pressure from Russia and western Europe and also from the Armenians, who exerted pressure from within the empire for greater autonomy.

- The Ottomans modernized their army, adopted French-style laws, and became increasingly secular, but their decline continued until the empire was broken apart after World War I.

- After Napoleon left Egypt, an Ottoman-appointed governor, Muhammad Ali, attempted an ambitious and somewhat successful program of modernization; ultimately, however, Britain gained control of the Suez Canal and made Egypt a colony.

- Persia, fragmented under the rule of the Qajars, came to be dominated economically by Britain, and interference by both Britain and Russia helped to end a brief period of progressive rule.

- Westerners became increasingly influential in Syria and Lebanon, as well as in Iraq, which was backward and undeveloped but attracted Western attention because of its economic potential.

- Europeans colonized Northwest Africa: first Algeria, where settlers established a racist society; then Morocco, which was shared by France and Spain; and finally Tunisia and Libya.

MIDDLE EASTERN THOUGHT AND CULTURE

How did Middle Eastern thought and culture respond to the Western challenge?

West Asians and North Africans responded to the challenges facing them in three ways. Some formed vibrant Islamic revivalist movements that promoted a purer version of Islamic practice rooted in early Muslim tradition. Others mounted reform movements that combined Islam with modernization and secularization. The early stirrings of Arab nationalism constituted a third response. While governments stagnated or struggled, revivalist, reform, and nationalist movements pumped fresh vitality into Islamic culture and religious life, influencing social and cultural patterns. But none of these movements offered an effective resistance to Western economic and military power.

Islamic Revivalism

Islamic revivalism Arab movements that sought to purify Islamic practices by reviving what they considered to be a purer vision of Islamic society.

Influential movements of **Islamic revivalism** sought to purify Islamic practices by reviving what they considered a purer vision of Islamic society rooted in the earliest form of Islam, embracing what they regarded as God's word in the Quran and the sayings of the Prophet Muhammad. They also reaffirmed the ideal of the theocratic state of the early caliphs in Mecca, which blended religion and government. The revivalists criticized as corrupt the scholarly and mystical additions that had resulted from encounters with Persian, Hindu, Indonesian, African, and European cultures over the centuries. In many African and Southeast Asian societies, Muslims still consulted shamans skilled in magic and healing, revered Sufi saints, and permitted women to engage in trade and reject veiling. Muslim revivalists despised Sufism and its mystical practices, such as music and dance, and in response several Sufi brotherhoods eventually moved away from mystical beliefs toward an emphasis on the original teachings of the Prophet Muhammad.

Religious Leaders

While political leaders lost prestige and authority, religious leaders allied to merchant and tribal groups seized the initiative to spread revivalist thought. Revivalists such as Othman dan Fodio in West Africa and the Mahdist Army in Sudan interpreted the early Muslim idea of jihad, or struggle for the faith, as a call to wage holy war against other Muslims who disagreed with them. Carried by scholars, merchants, and missionaries, revivalist Islam spread from the Middle East to every other part of the Islamic world. Many sub-Saharan African, Indian, and Southeast Asian Muslims visited, studied, or sojourned in the Middle East, often embracing the revivalist ideas. Revivalist movements stiffened resistance against French colonization in Algeria and West Africa and Dutch colonization in Indonesia.

Wahhabism A militant Islamic revivalist movement founded in Arabia in the eighteenth century.

Revivalism had its greatest impact in Arabia, spurring a militant movement in the 1700s known as **Wahhabism** (wah-HAH-bi-zuhm). The movement's founder, Muhammad Abd al-Wahhab (al-wah-HAHB) (1703–1792), led a long campaign to purify Arabian Islam. Al-Wahhab studied Islamic theology in Medina and Iraq, adopting a strict interpretation of Islamic law and promoting intolerance toward all alternative views, such as Sufism and Shi'ism, and those lax in their faith. In 1744 his campaign gained a key ally, Muhammad Ibn Saud (sah-OOD), a tribal chief, and together they put together a fighting force to expand their influence. During the later 1700s the Wahhabis used military force to take over parts of Arabia and then advanced into Syria and Iraq, occupying the city of Karbala, the major Shi'ite holy site, which they destroyed. By 1805 the Wahhabis controlled Mecca and Medina, Islam's two holiest cities, where they horrified non-Wahhabis by massacring the residents and trying to destroy all sacred tombs to prevent saint worship. Muhammad Ali, the governor of Egypt, used his European-style army and modern weapons to push the Wahhabis back from the holy cities. However, Wahhabi ideas, puritanism, and zeal spread widely during the 1800s as Western power undermined Middle Eastern governments. Yet many Muslims condemned Wahhabi intolerance, extremism, and such practices as the forced veiling of women.

Forming Saudi Arabia

In 1902 the descendants of al-Wahhab and Ibn Saud launched a second great expansion. The head of the Saud family, Abdul Aziz Ibn Saud (1880–1953), sent Wahhabi clergy among the Bedouins to convince them to abandon their nomadic ways and join self-sufficient farming communities that adopted extreme asceticism and a literal interpretation of the Islamic legal code, the Shari'a. Wahhabi clergy beat men for arriving late for prayers, and Wahhabi men pledged to die fighting for their beliefs. In 1925 the Saud family established Saudi Arabia, a state based on the Shari'a, and discovery of oil in 1938 gave the Saud family and their Wahhabi allies the wealth to maintain their control.

Primary Source: The History and Doctrines of Wahhabis Read Abdullah Wahhab's response to critics about the beliefs of the Wahhabis.

Modernist Islamic Thought

Some reformist Muslim thinkers, rejecting a rigid, backward-looking vision of Islam such as Wahhabism, promoted modernization as a strategy for transforming Islamic society and meeting the Western challenges. Intellectuals argued that Muslims should reject blind faith and welcome fresh ideas, social change, and religious moderation. Modernists detested many conservative traditions. Qasim Amin **(KA-sim AH-mean)**, a French-educated Egyptian lawyer, argued that the liberation of women was essential to the liberation of Egypt, that acquiring their "share of intellectual and moral development, happiness, and authority would prove to be the most significant development in Egyptian history." Women reformers such as Bahithat al-Badiya **(buh-TEE-that al-buh-DEE-ya)** echoed these sentiments (see Witness to the Past: Egyptian Women and Their Rights). The radical male Iraqi poet Jamil Sidqi az-Zahawi **(ja-MILL SID-key az-za-HA-wi)** identified the veil as the symbol of female exclusion, imploring women to "unveil yourself for life needs transformation. Tear it away, burn it, do not hesitate. It has only given you false protection!"[20]

Modernist Visions

Muslim modernists believed that introducing change would be a straightforward process, that by buying weapons and machines they could strengthen their armies and industries to deflect Western pressure, enrich their countries, and avoid domestic unrest. But their dreams proved impractical because the visionaries were ahead of their largely conservative populations. The challenges increased as Western technical and economic capabilities grew. Like European Enlightenment thinkers, some Muslim modernists struggled with how to reconcile faith and reason. They worried that modernization required adopting Western philosophical and scientific theories, which were often contrary to Islamic beliefs about society, God, and nature. Belief in equality contradicted the low status of Muslim women, and the Western notions of popular sovereignty and the nation troubled those who believed that only God could make laws or establish standards, which the state must then administer. Some reformers also doubted whether Islam, with its universalistic idea of a multiethnic community guided by God, was compatible with nationalism, which emphasized the unity of one group of people defined by a common state. The Moroccan historian Ahmad ibn Khalid al-Nasri, writing of military cadets being trained in Western weapons and tactics, worried that "they want to learn to fight to protect the faith, but they lose the faith in the process of learning how."[21] What role, the modernizers wondered, could clerics and the Shari'a have in a world of machines and nations?

Egyptian Thinkers

Egypt-based thinkers especially argued the compatibility of Islam with modernization. The Persia-born teacher Jamal al-Din al-Afghani (1838–1895) favored modern knowledge and believed that reason and science were not contrary to Islam, arguing that rigid interpretations of Islam and the weight of local traditions contributed to Arab backwardness. He lamented that, intolerant of new ideas, "the Arab world still remains buried in profound darkness,"[22] while rational interpretations of Islam would free Muslims for positive change. But his strong criticisms of British activity in Egypt and Persia as well as of Arab leaders he viewed as puppets led to his exile to Paris, where he

17 CAIRO. — 'Opera Square. — LL.

Hulton/Getty Images

Cairo Opera House Hoping to demonstrate modernization, Egyptian leaders built an opera house in Cairo in the 1860s. One of the first pieces staged was an opera by Italian composer Giuseppe Verdi to celebrate the opening of the Suez Canal in 1869.

Egyptian Women and Their Rights

One of the leading women writers and thinkers in early-twentieth-century Egypt, Bahithat al-Badiya (buh-TEE-that al-buh-DEE-ya) (1886–1918), advocated greater economic and educational rights for women in a rapidly changing society. She wrote at a time when Egyptian nationalists were demanding independence from Britain and a modern state and intellectuals were debating the merits of modernity as opposed to tradition. In 1909, in a lecture to an Egyptian women's club associated with a nationalist organization, Bahithat offered a program for improving women's lives. Struggling against male and Islamic opposition to women's rights, she sought a middle ground between Islamic conservatism and European secular liberalization.

Ladies, I greet you as a sister who feels what you feel, suffers what you suffer, and rejoices in what you rejoice. . . . Complaints about both men and women are rife. . . . This mutual blame which has deepened the antagonism between the sexes is something to be regretted and feared. God did not create man and women to hate each other but to love each other and to live together so the world would be populated. . . . Men say when we become educated we shall push them out of work and abandon the role for which God has created us. But isn't it rather men who have pushed women out of work? Before, women used to spin and to weave cloth for clothes, . . . but men invented machines for spinning and weaving. . . . In the past, women sewed clothes . . . but men invented the sewing machine. . . . Women . . . [made bread] with their own hands. Then men invented bakeries employing men. . . . I do not mean to denigrate these useful inventions which do a lot of our work. . . . Since male inventors and workers have taken away our work should we waste our time in idleness or seek other work to occupy us? Of course, we should do the latter. . . .

Men say to us categorically, "You women have been created for the house and we have been created to be breadwinners." Is this a God-given dictate? . . . No holy book has spelled it out. . . . Women in villages . . . help their men till the land and plant crops. Some women do the fertilizing, haul crops, lead animals, draw water for irrigation, and other chores. . . . Specialized work for each sex is a matter of convention, . . . not mandatory. . . . Women may not have to their credit great inventions but women have excelled in learning and the arts and politics. . . . Nothing irritates me more than when men claim they do not wish us to work because they wish to spare us the burden. We do not want condescension, we want respect. . . .

If we had been raised from childhood to go unveiled and if our men were ready for it I would approve of unveiling those who want it. But the nation is not ready for it now. . . . The imprisonment in the home of the Egyptian woman of the past is detrimental while the current freedom of the European is excessive. I cannot find a better model [than] today's Turkish woman. She falls between the two extremes and does not violate what Islam prescribes. She is a good example of decorum and modesty. . . . We should get a sound education, not merely acquire the trappings of a foreign language and rudiments of music. Our education should also include home management, health care, and childcare. . . . We shall advance when we give up idleness.

THINKING ABOUT THE READING

1. How does Bahithat evaluate women's roles and gender relations in Egypt?
2. What does her moderate advice to Egyptian women suggest about Egyptian society and the power of patriarchy?

Source: Bahithat al-Badiya, "A Lecture in the Club of the Umma Party, 1909," trans. by Ali Badran and Margot Badran, in *Opening the Gate: A Century of Arab Feminist Writing,* ed. by Margot Badran and Miriam Cooke, (Bloomington: Indiana University Press, 1990), pp. 228–238. Copyright © 1990 by Indiana University Press. Reprinted with permission of Indiana University Press.

published a weekly newspaper that promoted his views. Another major and well-traveled thinker, Muhammad Abduh (AHB-doo) (1849–1905), wanted to reform his native Egypt and rejuvenate Islam. Although opposed to wholesale Westernization, Abduh admired major European thinkers and contended that no knowledge, whatever its origin, was incompatible with Islam. Occupying a top Islamic legal position, he promoted modernist Islam at Al-Azhar University, the most influential institution of higher education in the Middle East.

The Roots of Arab Nationalism and the Zionist Quest

Challenges to Nationhood

During the 1800s an Arab national consciousness developed in response to domination by the Ottoman Turks and then by the British and French. Some proposed a pan-Arab movement uniting Arabs from Morocco to Iraq in a common struggle for political and cultural independence. But Arabs were divided by different religious and group affiliations. Most were Sunni Muslims, while others, particularly in the Persian Gulf and southern Iraq, were Shi'ites. Some in Egypt, Lebanon, and Syria were Christians. Arabs were also divided into feuding patriarchal tribes that sometimes disliked rival tribes as much as they disliked Ottoman or European overlords. Many Arabs remained loyal to Ottoman rule, and in 1876, hoping to defuse ethnic nationalism, the Ottomans gave the Arabs seats in the national legislature based on their large population in the empire.

Yet, some thoughtful Arabs envisioned self-governing Arab nations. Arab nationalism emerged from a Syrian literary and cultural movement in the later 1800s that included Lebanese Christians, one of whom published a poem calling on Arabs to "arise and awake." Modernist Muslim writings were also influential. The witty books of Abd-al-Rahman al-Kawabiki **(AB-dul RAH-man al-KA-wa-BIK-ee)** (1849–1903), a Syrian who had studied in Egypt and Mecca and hated intolerance and injustice, criticized Ottoman despotism as contrary to Islam and promoted Arab politics. Arab nationalist groups formed all over the Ottoman Empire, but before World War I they were small and had little public influence.

Syrian Roots

While Islamic societies struggled to respond to Western power, the Zionist movement (see Chapter 19) introduced another challenge. In the Jewish ghettoes of eastern Europe, especially Poland and Russia, some thinkers began a quest for a state for their long persecuted and widely scattered people. Prayers in Jewish synagogues for worshiping "next year in Jerusalem," the ancient Hebrew capital in Palestine, had endured for centuries. Few European Jews spoke Hebrew, and many rejected Zionism, identifying with the country where they lived. But for others, Zionism functioned like nationalism. The first Zionist conference, held in Basel, Switzerland, in 1897, identified Palestine, then under Ottoman rule, as the potential Jewish homeland. Jews had long visited or settled in Palestine, and perhaps 20,000 lived there in 1870, but the Ottomans refused Zionist leaders permission to organize a massive settlement of Jews, prompting the Zionist leader, the Hungarian-born journalist Theodor Herzl (1860–1904), to propose accepting a British offer for a temporary home in East Africa.

Zionism and Jewish Immigration

Soon militant Zionists promoted Jewish migration to Palestine without Ottoman permission or support from European governments. By 1914 some 85,000 Jews, many of them newcomers from Russia and Poland, lived in Palestine alongside some 700,000 Arabs. Committed to creating a socialist society, the immigrants established Jewish collective farms, each known as a **kibbutz**, whose members shared their wealth and promoted Hebrew rather than the German-based Yiddish widely spoken by central and east European Jews. Settlement in Palestine was funded by international Zionist organizations, who bought land from absentee Arab and Turkish landowners. The Zionists had a flag, an anthem, and an active Jewish press. However, since Jewish institutions had no legal recognition in Palestine, the stage was set for future conflict with Palestinian Arabs, who resented the newcomers and their plans to acquire more land for a Jewish state

kibbutz A Jewish collective farm in Palestine that stressed the sharing of wealth.

SECTION SUMMARY

- One response to European pressure was Islamic revivalism, which advocated a pure form of Islam, favored a theocratic state, and sometimes used violence.

- Revivalism was most influential in Arabia, where militant followers of al-Wahhab and Ibn Saud took over a number of cities and eventually formed Saudi Arabia.

- Some intellectuals tried to modernize their religion, but modern European ideas such as equality continued to clash with Islamic practices such as the subjugation of women, and Western nationalism was at odds with the idea of a universal brotherhood under God.

- Some tried to inspire Arab nationalism, but religious divisions and rivalries made this a difficult task.

- Muslims were also challenged by European Zionists, who moved to Palestine in spite of Ottoman objections and also in spite of the Palestinian Arabs, setting the stage for future conflict.

CHAPTER SUMMARY

Sub-Saharan Africa underwent extensive changes between 1750 and 1914. The ending of the trans-Atlantic slave trade opened Africa to exploration and trade by Europeans, and industrial Europe's need for resources and markets fostered a "scramble for Africa" as various Western nations colonized African societies, sometimes by military force against protracted resistance. The French colonized a vast area of West and Central Africa; Britain forged a large empire in West, Central, and East Africa; and the Germans, Belgians, and Italians also acquired African colonies. European settlers flocked to colonies in southern and eastern Africa, most notably South Africa, where they established white supremacist societies. Colonialism created artificial, multiethnic countries. It replaced subsistence agriculture with cash crop farming, plantations, and mineral exploitation while enmeshing Africa in the world economy as a supplier of natural resources. Africans mounted strikes and rebellions against colonialism, but all such efforts were eventually defeated.

The Middle East also experienced European imperialism. The Ottoman Empire attempted to stall its decline with Western-style reforms, but it still lost territory and influence. Egypt attempted an ambitious modernization program, but it proved inadequate to prevent British colonization. In Persia, Western economic and political influence sparked reforms that were later rejected by Persian conservatives. France and Italy colonized North Africa, and French settlers displaced Algerians from valuable land. In response, some Muslims, most notably the Wahhabis, pursued a revivalist strategy to purify the religion and reject Western influence, while modernist reformers sought to adapt secular Western ideas to Islam in order to energize Muslim societies. Arab nationalist movements also arose but remained weak before World War I. Finally, Jewish Zionists posed a threat to Palestinian Arabs by beginning to settle in Palestine, where they hoped to build a Jewish state.

KEY TERMS

direct rule	**laager**	**Bahai**	**Wahhabism**
indirect rule	**Young Turks**	**Islamic revivalism**	**kibbutz**

EBOOK AND WEBSITE RESOURCES

e PRIMARY SOURCE
The History and Doctrines of Wahhabis

e INTERACTIVE MAPS
Map 21.1 Africa in 1914
Map 21.2 The Ottoman Empire and Persia, 1914

LINKS

Africa South of the Sahara (http://www-sul.stanford.edu/depts/ssrg/africa/). A valuable site that contains links relevant to African history.

History and Cultures of Africa (http://www.columbia.edu/cu/lweb/indiv/africa/cuvl/cult/html). Provides valuable links to relevant websites on African history.

Internet African History Sourcebook (http://www.fordham.edu/halsall/africa/africasbook.html). Contains useful information and documentary material on Africa.

Internet Islamic History Sourcebook (http://www.fordham.edu/halsall/islam/islamsbook.html). A comprehensive examination of Islamic history and culture.

Middle East Studies Internet Resources (http://www.columbia.edu/cu/lweb/indiv/mideast/cuvlm/index.html). A useful collection of links.

Plus flashcards, practice quizzes, and more. Go to: www.cengage.com/history/lockard/globalsocnet2e.

SUGGESTED READING

Cleveland, William L. *A History of the Modern Middle East*, 4th ed. Boulder: Westview, 2008. One of the best surveys of the era.

Esposito, John L. *Islam: The Straight Path*. Revised 3rd ed. New York: Oxford University Press, 2005. Good discussion of Islamic thought in this era.

Goldschmidt, Arthur and Lawrence Davidson. *A Concise History of the Middle East*. 9th ed. Boulder: Westview, 2008. Well-written, up-to-date survey.

Hochschild, Adam. *King Leopold's Ghost: A Story of Greed, Terror, and Heroism in Colonial Africa*. Boston: Houghton Mifflin, 1998. A study of the Belgian Congo.

MacKinnon, Aran S. *The Making of South Africa: Culture and Politics*. Upper Saddle River, NJ: Prentice-Hall, 2003. A comprehensive, readable survey.

Marsot, Afaf Lufti al-Sayyid. *Egypt in the Reign of Muhammad Ali*. New York: Cambridge University Press, 1984. An excellent study.

Northrup, David. *Africa's Discovery of Europe, 1450–1850*. New York: Oxford University Press, 2002. A sweeping survey.

Palmer, Alan. *The Decline and Fall of the Ottoman Empire*. New York: Barnes and Noble, 1992. A readable narrative.

Quataert, Donald. *The Ottoman Empire, 1700–1922*, 2nd ed. New York: Cambridge University Press, 2005. Fine survey of major trends.

Robinson, Francis. *The Cultural Atlas of the Islamic World Since 1500*. Oxford: Stonehenge, 1992. A useful compilation of materials.

Rodney, Walter. *How Europe Underdeveloped Africa*. Washington, DC: Howard University Press, 1982. An influential and controversial critique of the West in Africa by a Guyanese scholar.

Shillington, Kevin. *History of Africa,* rev. 2nd ed. New York: Palgrave Macmillan, 2005. A standard text with good coverage of this era.

Wheatcroft, Andrew. *The Ottomans*. New York: Viking, 1993. A lively discussion with particular attention to the governing elites.

SOUTH ASIA, SOUTHEAST ASIA, AND COLONIZATION, 1750–1914

Universiteits-Bibliotheek, Leiden. Snouk Hurgronje Collection, Codex Orientales 7398

Dipenegara
This painting shows Prince Dipenegara, a Javanese aristocrat who led a revolt against the Dutch colonizers in the 1820s, reading, with several attendants at hand.

> *Rice fields are littered with our battle-killed; blood flows or lies in pools, stains hills and streams. [French] Troops . . . grab our land, our towns, roaring and stirring dust to dim the skies. A scholar with no talent and no power, could I redress a world turned upside down?*
>
> —Protest by Vietnamese poet Nguyen Dinh Chieu against French Conquest, late nineteenth century[1]

Frustrated by the Vietnamese emperor's refusal to liberalize trade relations with Western nations and protect Christian missionaries, the French, seeking to expand their empire, attacked Vietnam with military force in 1858 and over the next three decades conquered the country against determined resistance. A blind poet, Nguyen Dinh Chieu **(NEW-yin dinh chew)** (1822–1888), symbolized the Vietnamese resistance when he wrote an oration honoring the fallen Vietnamese soldiers after a heroic defense in a battle in 1862: "You preferred to die fighting the enemy, and return to our ancestors in glory rather than survive in submission to the [Westerners] and share your miserable life with barbarians."

FOCUS QUESTIONS

1. How and why did Britain extend its control throughout India?
2. How did colonialism transform the Indian economy and foster new ideas in India?
3. How did the Western nations expand their control of Southeast Asia?
4. What were the major political, economic, and social consequences of colonialism in Southeast Asia?

The French retaliated by seizing Chieu's land and property. The poet, unbowed, refused to use Western products and forbade his children to learn the romanized Vietnamese alphabet developed by French Catholic missionaries. In verse spread by word of mouth and painstakingly copied manuscripts distributed throughout the land, Chieu heaped scorn on his countrymen who collaborated with the French occupiers and promoted the struggle: "I had rather face unending darkness, Than see the country tortured. Everyone will rejoice in seeing the West wind [colonialism],Vanish from [Vietnam's] mountains and rivers."[2] The son of a mandarin in southern Vietnam, Chieu overcame blindness to become a physician, scholar, teacher, and writer famous for his epic poems sung in the streets extolling the love of country, friendship, marital fidelity, family loyalty, scholarship, and the military arts. He rejected the French offer of a financial subsidy and the return of his family land if he would rally to their cause. The Vietnamese continue to revere his stirring poems.

With enhanced military, economic, and technological power provided by the Industrial Revolution (see Chapters 19–20), Britain, France, the Netherlands, and the United States colonized all of South and Southeast Asia except Thailand. Western domination destroyed traditional political systems, reoriented economies, and posed challenges for societies and their world-views, including the Vietnamese whom Nguyen Dinh Chieu attempted to rally. Since Western domination occurred while western Europeans were at the high point of their military and industrial development and cultural arrogance, colonialism proved a transforming experience. It linked these regions more closely than ever to a European-dominated world economy and transmitted to the colonies the ideas and technologies of Western life. In turn, Asian workers produced resources that spurred Western economic growth. But the exchange of ideas was not all one way: Asian religions and arts attracted interest in the West and even developed a small following there. The unyielding resistance to imperialism exemplified by Nguyen Dinh Chieu also gave hope to colonized people in Africa and the Middle East. Resentment against colonialism simmered for decades, and eventually the Indians and Filipinos, among others, asserted the rights of their peoples for self-determination.

e Visit the website and eBook for additional study materials and interactive tools:
www.cengage.com/history/lockard/globalsocnet2e

601

FORMING BRITISH INDIA

How and why did Britain extend its control throughout India?

By the early 1700s the Muslim Mughals who ruled much of India (see Chapter 18) were in steep decline, challenged by both Indians and Europeans. The splendor of the Mughal court and India's valuable exports had earlier attracted the Portuguese, Dutch, and British. As the Mughals lost power, the British took advantage of a fragmented India and began their conquest of the subcontinent in the mid-1700s. By the mid-1800s Britain controlled both India and the island of Sri Lanka. India had often been conquered by outsiders from Western and Central Asia, but unlike those invaders, who often became assimilated into Indian society, the British maintained their own separate traditions.

Mughal Decline and the British

Europeans had long coveted South Asia for its spices and textiles. Even today, small, single-masted sailing barges ply the coastline between western India, the Persian Gulf, and East Africa, continuing the ancient exchange of merchandise with the coming and going of monsoon winds. Between 1500 and 1750 European powers controlled some of the Indian Ocean maritime trade but conquered only a few scattered outposts in South Asia. The Dutch, who destroyed Portuguese power in South and Southeast Asia, concentrated on Sri Lanka and Indonesia. By 1696 the British possessed three fortified trading stations in India: Calcutta (now Kolkata) in Bengal, Madras (today known as Chennai) on the southeastern coast, and Bombay (today called Mumbai) on the west coast.

By 1750 the Mughals were corrupt and weak, since many Indians had already broken away from Mughal control. Emperors might sit on the spectacular Peacock Throne in Delhi's spectacular Red Fort, but they had little actual power much beyond Delhi, often consoling themselves with the large royal harem or smoking opium. Mughal factions quarreled while the countryside became increasingly disorderly. Without a powerful imperial state to unite it, Indian society, with its diverse cultures, castes, languages, regions, and religions, was unable to effectively resist European encroachments. Mughal governors whose allegiance to the emperor was nominal formed new Muslim states. The **Marathas (muh-RAH-tuhs)**, a loosely knit confederacy led by Hindu warriors from west-central India, and the Sikhs, a religious minority in northwest India, built powerful new states. By 1800 the Marathas ruled much of western India, and the Sikhs, under the dynamic Ranjit Singh **(RUN-ji SING)** (1780–1839), had conquered the Punjab and Kashmir in the northwest. Mounted on sturdy ponies, the Marathas became feared for their plundering raids deep into central India against helpless Mughal armies. In southern India, the Mughal collapse left a power vacuum that both Britain and France attempted to fill by supporting their respective Indian allies in the struggle for regional advantage. Ultimately, none of the rising Indian states gained enough power or acquired enough weapons to repulse the West.

The British posed the gravest challenge. Bengal, India's richest and most populous region, was ruled by Muslim governors who mostly ignored the Mughal government. The Bengali ruler, Aliverdi Khan (r. 1740–1756), had left British trade unmolested. But his successor, Siraja Dowlah **(see-RAH-ja DOW-luh)** (ca. 1732–1757), considered the British bothersome leeches on his land's riches. Dowlah alienated Western merchants and in 1757 rashly attacked British trading stations. After capturing Calcutta, Dowlah's forces placed 146 captured British men, women, and children in a crowded jail known as the **Black Hole of Calcutta**. The next day only 23 staggered out, the rest having died from suffocation and dehydration. The enraged British blamed Siraja Dowlah for the atrocity and dispatched a force under Robert Clive (1725–1774) to regain Britain's holdings. A former clerk turned into a daring war strategist, the ambitious Clive and his 3,200 soldiers defeated 50,000 Bengali troops at the Battle of Plassey in 1757 and recaptured Calcutta (see Chronology: South Asia, 1750–1914). Clive allied with Hindu bankers and Muslim nobles unhappy with Siraja Dowlah, who was executed, and by 1764 he controlled Bengal.

Marathas A loosely knit confederacy led by Hindu warriors from west-central India; one of several groups that challenged British domination after the decline of the Mughals.

Black Hole of Calcutta A crowded jail in India where over a hundred British prisoners of a hostile Bengali ruler died from suffocation and dehydration in 1757. This event precipitated the beginning of British use of force in India.

CHRONOLOGY
South Asia, 1750–1914

1744–1761 Anglo-French struggle for Coromandel coast

1757 Battle of Plassey

1764 British acquisition of Bengal

1774–1784 Warren Hastings governor of Bengal

1793 New land policy in Bengal

1799 British defeat of Mysore

1796–1815 British colonization of Sri Lanka

1816 British protectorate over Nepal

1819 British occupation of all Maratha lands

1820s Beginning of British Westernization policy

1839–1842 First Anglo-Afghan War

1849 British defeat of Sikhs in Punjab

1850 Completion of British India

1857–1858 Indian rebellion

1858 Introduction of colonial system in India

1877 Founding of Muslim college at Aligarh

1878–1880 Second Anglo-Afghan War

1885 Formation of Indian National Congress

1903 British invasion of Tibet

1906 Formation of All-India Muslim League

CHRONOLOGY

	South Asia	Southeast Asia
1750	**1757** Battle of Plassey	**1788–1802** Tayson rule in Vietnam
1796–1815	**1802** British colonization of Sri Lanka	**1819** British colony in Singapore **1824–1886** Anglo-Burman Wars
1850	**1850** Completion of British India **1857–1858** Indian Rebellion	**1858–1884** French conquest of Vietnam **1898–1902** United States conquest of Philippines
1900	**1885** Indian National Congress	

The British government, following a policy of mercantilism to acquire wealth for the state, allowed the British East India Company (often known as "the Company") to govern Indian districts as they were acquired and to exploit the inhabitants while sharing the profits with the British government. As they acquired more Indian territory, the British, much like the former Mughal rulers, expected the Indians to serve them. They also showed a lust for riches equal to that of the Spanish conquistadors in the 1500s. As governor of Bengal (1758–1760, 1764–1767), Clive launched an era of organized plunder, allowing British merchants and officials to drain Bengal of its wealth while Company officials, including Clive, lived like kings. Praised by British leaders and celebrated in the press and schoolboy stories, Clive became the idol of every young Englishman who dreamed of marching to glory and wealth via India's battlefields and bazaars. The cry of "Go East," inspired by Clive's rags-to-riches story, fueled British imperialist ambitions. Eventually accused and later cleared of corruption and fraud charges, a depressed Clive committed suicide at the age of forty-nine.

To undo the economic chaos left by Clive and consolidate the British position, the Company appointed Warren Hastings to serve as governor-general (1774–1784) of Bengal. Hastings redesigned the revenue system, made treaty alliances, and annexed nearby districts to safeguard the British bases. A scholarly man influenced by Enlightenment thought, Hastings respected the people he governed, in contrast to other British officials, and, he claimed, hoped to never see the whole of India colonized. Like the English, he argued, many Indians had intellect and integrity and should enjoy the same equal rights as the English colonizers. His successors, however, often disregarded his advice. Hastings himself was accused of corruption and forced out of office, living the rest of his life in disgrace.

British Ambitions

Expanding British India

Success in Bengal fueled further British expansion in the subcontinent. The British government gave the Company authority to administer all British-controlled Indian territories while also seeking profit, but it forbade further annexation. Despite the ban, governor-generals after Hastings authorized the occupation of more areas, often against opposition, to prevent trade disruption or to counteract rival European nations. Some imperialists talked about Britain's sacred trust to reshape the world, viewing the extension of British authority, culture, religion, and free trade policies a great blessing for Asians. The reality, however, was often different. In expanding its territory, the British mixed military force, extortion, bribery, and manipulation of India's diversity. British agents and merchants could play one region off against another and Hindu against Muslim, aided by Indian collaborators, especially businessmen eager to increase their connections to the world market. Employing superior weapons and disciplined military forces, the British overcame spirited resistance. They recruited mercenary soldiers, known as **sepoys**, under the command of British officers, and by 1857 the Company forces comprised nearly 200,000 sepoy troops and 10,000 British officers and soldiers.

The French provided a serious roadblock to British expansion, and European wars involving the British and French were extended into a contest for India's southeastern Coromandel coast. Victory there over the French in 1761 soon led the British into actions against other Indian states, including formidable Mysore in south-central India led by Haidar Ali Khan (r. 1761–1782), a devout Muslim who modeled his army on Western lines. A brilliant military strategist, Haidar warned the British, "I will march your troops until their legs swell to the size of their bodies. You shall not have a blade of grass, nor a drop of water."[3] Only in 1799, after twenty years of bloody wars, was Mysore defeated.

Company Rule

sepoys Mercenary soldiers recruited among the warrior and peasant castes by the British in India.

Clive Meets Indian Leaders In this painting, Robert Clive meets the new Bengali official, Mir Jafir, after the British victory in the 1757 Battle of Plassey. Clive supported Mir Jafir's seizure of power from the anti-British leader, Siraja Dowlah.

National Portrait Gallery, London

Gradually the British imposed their control over western, central, and northern India. The Maratha confederacy was divided by rivalries, and in 1805 the British occupied the Marathas' northern territories and entered Delhi, where they deposed the aged Mughal emperor. After taking the remaining Maratha lands in 1819, they turned their attention to northwest India, dominated by Rajputs, a declining Hindu warrior caste, and Sikhs. The Rajputs, aware of their weakness, now signed treaties giving Britain claims on their lands. The death of the Sikh leader, Ranjit Singh, in 1839 shattered the Sikhs' unity and undermined their powerful military state. In 1849, after a series of bloody British-Sikh wars, Britain finally triumphed. Britain then stationed troops in the many small independent principalities scattered around India. By 1850, the British ruled all Indians directly or through princes who collaborated with them (see Map 22.1).

British expansion in India eventually led to interventions in neighboring societies, including Sri Lanka (Ceylon), the large, fertile island just south of India. Fearing that the French might establish a base there, in 1796 the British acquired the territory the Dutch had held since the 1630s, and by 1815, after conquering the last remaining Sri Lankan kingdom, Kandy, they controlled the entire island. The British seized rice-growing land from peasants to set up coffee, tea, and rubber plantations and recruited Tamil-speaking workers from southeast India as laborers. By 1911 the poorly paid Tamil laborers and their families made up 11 percent of the Sri Lankan population, maintaining their own customs, language, and Hindu religion and having little contact with Sri Lanka's majority population, the Buddhist Sinhalese. Since many Sinhalese considered both the British and the Tamils unwanted aliens, Sinhalese-Tamil tensions simmered and, after independence, led to a long civil war in Sri Lanka.

Britain and Sri Lanka

Fearing that the Russians, who were conquering Muslim Central Asia, intended to expand into South Asia, the British also attempted to secure India's land borders. First they invaded Nepal, a kingdom in the Himalayan Mountains, defeated Nepal's Hindu ruling caste and fierce fighters, the Gurkhas (GORE-kuhz), in 1814–1816, and turned Nepal into a British protectorate. Soldiers later recruited from Nepal, also known as gurkhas, were employed on battlefields around the world in support of British objectives. Mountainous Afghanistan, an ethnically diverse but Muslim region that had enjoyed only short periods of political unity, seemed the most vulnerable to Russian expansion. However, the Pashtun tribes in the south possessed the fighting skills to oppose Europeans bent on conquest. The British twice invaded Afghanistan and occupied the major eastern city, Kabul, but faltered against fierce Pashtun resistance. In the first Afghan War (1839–1842), Pashtuns massacred most of the 12,000 retreating British and sepoy troops and the British civilians, including women and children, who had accompanied them. Undeterred, the British fought the second Afghan War (1878–1880). Concluding that Afghanistan could not be annexed by military force, they

Nepal and Afghanistan

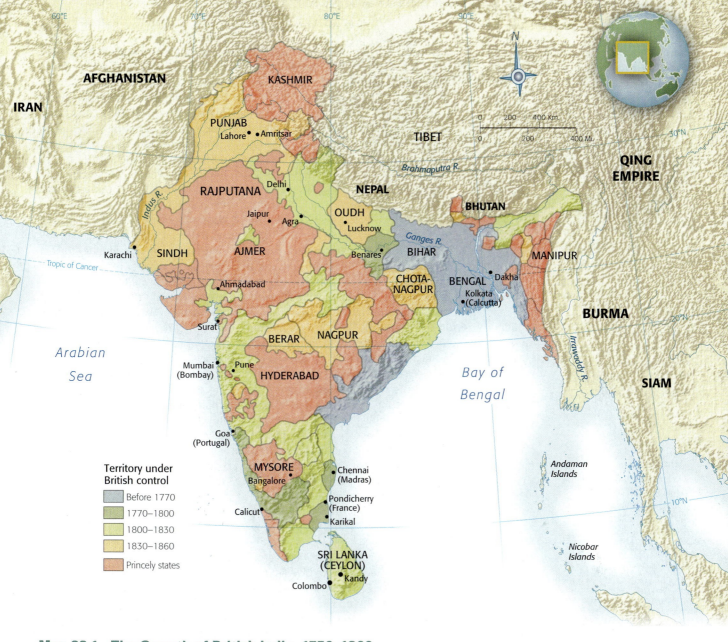

Map 22.1   The Growth of British India, 1750–1860
Gradually expanding control from their bases at Calcutta, Madras, and Bombay, the
British completed their military conquest of the final holdout states by the 1850s.

e **Interactive Map**

replaced a Pashtun leader who favored the Russians with one who was pro-British and who gave
Britain control of Afghanistan's foreign affairs.

India Under the East India Company

The British East India Company gradually tightened its control of India and shifted from sharing
government with local rulers to administering India through British officials. In arrogant colonial language, Sir Thomas Munro, governor of Madras from 1820 to 1827, explained the imperial mission, claiming that the British must maintain their rule until the Indians, sometime in
the distant future, abandoned their "superstitions" and became "enlightened" enough to govern
themselves. In the 1820s, the Company began promoting a policy of **Westernization**, a deliberate attempt to spread Western culture and ideas. Protestant evangelism, then strong in Britain, influenced the reform ideas. One devout Company director argued that Britain must diffuse
Christian teachings among Indians, whom he described as sunk in darkness and misery. British officials, often disregarding Indian traditions, encouraged Christian missions and tried to
ban customs they disliked. Many Indians rejoiced when they banned *sati*, the custom of widows

Reforming India

Westernization A
deliberate attempt to spread
Western culture and ideas.

British East India Company Court This painted wood model shows an Indian court presided over by an official of the British East India Company.

Orientalism A scholarly interest among British officials in India and its history that prompted some to rediscover the Hindu classical age.

Economic Policies

zamindars Mughal revenue collectors that the British turned into landlords who were given the rights to buy and sell land.

throwing themselves on their husband's funeral pyre, but there was less enthusiasm for British attempts to tinker with Muslim and Hindu law codes.

The British also established schools that taught in English. Lord Macaulay (1800–1859), a reformer and firm believer in Western cultural superiority, considered it pointless to teach Indian languages, declaring in 1832 that "a single shelf of a good European library is worth the whole native literature of India and Arabia." Consequently, Macaulay, reflecting Western racist views, proposed creating "a class of persons Indian in blood and color but English in taste, opinions, morals and intellect."[4] While many Indians considered English-medium schools a threat to both Hindu and Muslim customs, some welcomed the schools because they opened Indian students to a wider world. Indians themselves formed the first English-medium institution of higher education, the Hindu College in Calcutta, in 1818.

Yet, some British, reflecting what came to be called **Orientalism**, showed a scholarly interest in India and its history. Warren Hastings, who encouraged the study of Indian culture, languages, and literature, preferred reading the European and Asian languages he had mastered—Greek, Latin, Persian, and Urdu—to pursuing his official duties. One of his officials, William Jones (1746–1794), who mastered Arabic, Persian, and Sanskrit, became the most influential Orientalist scholar, but his views often reflected an attempt to fit India into Western concepts of history and religion. Just as Christians and Jews believed the Bible reflected historical truth, Jones treated ancient Vedic texts as accurate historical records rather than religious teachings and claimed that the classical Greeks, such as the mathematician Pythagoras and the philosopher Plato, derived their theories from the same ancient source as the classical Indian sages. Jones's ideas shaped scholarly understanding of Indian history. Several religious movements based on Hindu concepts, such as reincarnation, also gained a small following in the West. Yet by the later 1800s Orientalist respect for India had largely been replaced by British nationalism and intolerance.

The encounter between India and the West also fostered a Hindu social reform movement and philosophical renaissance led by the brilliant Bengali scholar Ram Mohan Roy (1772–1833). After seeing his sister burn to death on a funeral pyre, and concerned that customs such as *sati* and caste divisions were harmful, Roy hoped to adopt certain Western ways to reform and strengthen Hinduism. To better understand the world by studying non-Hindu religions, Roy mastered their source languages—Hebrew, Greek, Arabic, and Persian—and thus became the world's first modern scholar of comparative religion. Roy and his followers attempted to create a synthesis of the best in Hinduism and Christianity; he also founded secondary schools, newspapers, and a Hindu reform organization. Viewing the British as promoters of knowledge and liberty, Roy wanted Britain to promote modernization while also seeking Indian advice.

In order to make India more profitable, the British East India Company built roads, railroads, and irrigation systems; most significantly for rural Indians, it revised the land revenue collection, the principal source of public finance. The British viewed Indian rural society as stagnant, unable to provide the tax revenues needed to support British administration. In precolonial times, most Indians, living in self-sufficient villages that were governed by the family and caste, had enjoyed a measure of social stability and had the hereditary right to use the land. One British observer wrote that "the village communities [have] everything they want within themselves. They seem to last when nothing else lasts. Dynasty after dynasty tumbles down; but the village communities remain the same."[5]

Yet, Company officials, seeking higher revenues, began collecting taxes from farmers in money rather than, as had long been common, a portion of the crop. In 1793 British officials in Bengal converted the Mughal revenue collectors, or **zamindars**, into landlords, who, in addition to collecting taxes, were given the rights to buy and sell land if they paid additional high taxes whenever they did so. Under this system, peasant farmers became tenants to landlords, losing their hereditary rights to land. Many landlords sold their land rights to businessmen who became absentee landlords growing rich from the crops grown by the peasants. In Madras, however, the governor, Munro, mistakenly believed that the peasants were or could be converted into profit-seeking individualists like English farmers. In his system the peasant farmer dealt directly with the government but had to pay tax in cash and could be evicted for nonpayment. Under both systems a barter economy, in which villagers agreed to exchange their services or products with each other, was changed to a money economy. Since some villagers earned more money, the cash-based system undermined the stability and security peasants had once enjoyed and benefited a moneylender caste that came to control much of the land. The Company also encouraged a switch from food crops to cash crops such as opium, coffee, rubber, tea, and cotton, often grown on plantations rather than peasant farms.

Resistance: The 1857 Revolt

In spite of Indian reform movements such as Roy's, most Indians resented the Company's Westernization and economic policies. Many once-prosperous families lost land or become indebted, and the courts enforced laws based on British traditions, fueling hostility. As a result of such grievances, local revolts were common. Furthermore, sepoys increasingly resented the aggressive attempts of British officers to convert them to Christianity. Those stationed in Bengal were particularly outraged by new army rifle cartridges, which had to be bitten off with the teeth before being rammed down the gun barrel. A rumor, probably true, spread that the cartridges were greased with beef and pork fat, violating the religious dietary prohibitions of both cow-revering Hindus and pork-avoiding Muslims.

Roots of Revolt

In 1857 one revolt, which the British called the Indian Mutiny and Indian nationalists later termed the first War of Independence, spread rapidly and offered a serious challenge to British authority. The revolt began among sepoys and was soon supported by peasant and Muslim uprisings. A few members of princely families also joined the rebel cause, including the widow of the Maratha ruler of Jhansi, who led her troops into battle dressed as a man. The revolt was confined largely to north and northeast India. Because no rebel leaders envisioned a unified Indian nation, British observers argued that the rebels had limited and selfish goals, but many Indians perceived their customs and religions threatened by British policies. Some rebel leaders attempted to unite Hindus and Muslims against their common British enemy. A few wanted to restore the Mughal order.

British-Indian Conflict

The rebels captured Delhi and besieged several cities. Both sides used ruthless tactics and committed massacres. Rebels murdered a thousand British residents when they occupied the city of Kanpur, and, when British troops recaptured Delhi, they engaged in widespread raping, pillaging, and killing. The Muslim poet Ghalib mourned: "Here is a vast ocean of blood before me. Thousands of my friends are dead. Perhaps none is left even to shed tears upon my death."[6] The anti-British sentiment was not widespread enough, however, to overcome the rebels' problems: inadequate arms, weak communications, and lack of a unified command structure or strategy. In addition, the rebels received no support from people in other parts of India. Linguistic, religious, cultural, and regional fragmentation made a united Indian opposition impossible. When the British captured the last rebel fort, held by the rani (queen) of Jhansi, in 1858, she was killed and the rebellion collapsed, although a few small rebel groups fought skirmishes with the British until 1860.

Indian Railroad Train   The railroads built during British rule carried both resources and passengers. This lithograph shows a Sikh signalman at the station and a train conveying Indian women and a European.

SECTION SUMMARY

- Fragmented after the decline of the Mughals, India was unable to resist encroachment by the Portuguese, Dutch, British, and French.

- In reaction to the Black Hole of Calcutta, the British under Robert Clive took over Bengal and proceeded to plunder its riches; though his successor, Warren Hastings, was more respectful, many governor-generals disregarded Indians' rights.

- Though initially opposed by the French, the British East India Company gradually expanded its control over India by employing local collaborators and playing groups off against each other, and by 1850 Britain controlled all of India.

- The British expanded into Sri Lanka, where they imported Tamils to work on the tea plantations; into Nepal, where they recruited effective soldiers; and into Afghanistan, where they met fierce resistance but ultimately installed a friendly ruler.

- Many British tried to make Indians more Western by abolishing customs they considered backward, while others became interested in studying traditional Indian teachings.

- By having peasants pay their taxes in cash rather than in crops, the British began to shift India from a barter economy to a money economy, a change that undermined centuries of rural stability.

- Though some Indians supported Westernization, periodic revolts occurred, and in 1857 the sepoys began a large rebellion that led to much bloodshed and eventually Indian defeat.

THE RESHAPING OF INDIAN SOCIETY

How did colonialism transform the Indian economy and foster new ideas in India?

The 1857 revolt prompted the British to replace the British East India Company government with direct colonial rule. The British felt betrayed by the rebels, but some officials viewed the troubles as symptoms of deeper discontents that needed to be addressed. To move in that direction, the 1858 Government of India Act transferred sovereignty to the British monarch. In 1876 Queen Victoria was proclaimed Empress of India, head of the government known as the British *Raj*, named for the ancient title of Hindu kings. India became the brightest "jewel in the imperial crown," a source of fabulous wealth. The policies pursued by the British Raj reshaped economic, intellectual, and social patterns and eventually inspired movements reflecting a new sense of the Indian nation.

Colonial Government and Education

Colonial Rule

The British Raj bore many similarities to the Mughal system. The top British officials, the viceroys, lived, like Mughal emperors, in splendor in Delhi, enjoying pomp and circumstance, including Mughal-style ceremonies, and building a new capital at New Delhi next to the old Mughal capital of Delhi, with gigantic architecture. The British built palatial mansions, museums, schools, universities, and city halls but also faced health problems from the tropical heat and diseases such as malaria. They also connected India with a network of roads, bridges, and railways, so that by 1900 India had over 25,000 miles of track, the world's fourth largest rail system.

Although British officials mistrusted Indians after 1857, they allowed the traditional princes to keep their privileges and palaces in exchange for promoting acceptance of British policies. The British also deliberately pitted the Hindu majority against the Muslim minority by favoring one or the other group in law, language, and custom. For example, Hindus protested that the main Muslim language, Urdu, was used in many north Indian courts, exacerbating hatreds that remain today. To promote security, local revenue supported a huge army of 200,000 men, mostly Indian volunteers, who were needed to keep the peace in India and fight British battles abroad. As part of what Kipling called the "Great Game" of strategic rivalry with Russia, Britain invaded Tibet in 1903, prompting Tibetan leaders to agree not to concede territory to Russia or any other foreign power.

The British typically believed that Western colonialism improved Asian and African societies. Rudyard Kipling (1865–1936), a Bombay-born, Britain-educated English poet and novelist, reflected this view in his writings: "Take up the White Man's burden—Send forth the best ye breed—Go, bind your sons in exile. To serve your captives' need."[7] Some policies reflected racism. Much like colonized Africans, Indians were excluded from European-only clubs and parks as well as high positions in the bureaucracy, enjoying no real power or influence. The Raj continued the Westernization policy, promoting British and often Christian values through an expanded English-medium education system. English became the common language for educated Indians; however, only a privileged minority, mostly drawn from higher-caste Hindus, could afford to send their children, mostly boys, to the English schools. By 1911 only 11 percent of men and 1 percent of women were literate in any language. Although only a tiny minority of Indians converted to Christianity, an English-educated middle class emerged, with a taste for European products and ideas. They sent their sons and a few daughters to British universities, where they learned about notions like "freedom" and "self-determination of peoples" that stood in sharp contrast to nondemocratic conditions in India. This growing British-educated professional class organized social, professional, and political bodies concerned with improving Indian life and acquiring more influence in government.

Westernization

Economic Transformation

The British also transformed the Indian economy. Long an economic powerhouse and the world leader in producing cotton textiles, India still produced a quarter of all world manufactured goods in 1750. However, two centuries later, conditions had changed. Many historians believe that British policies, designed to drain India of its wealth to benefit Britain, harmed the Indian economy. British land policies commercialized agriculture, while tax and tariff policies diminished the existing manufacturing. The Company's land tax system exploited the peasantry, planting the roots of one of contemporary India's greatest dilemmas, inequitable land ownership. Many fell hopelessly into debt, and as peasants had to grow cash crops such as cotton, jute, pepper, or opium rather than food, famine became more common, killing millions as food supplies and distribution became more uncertain.

Rural Policies

Other changes also affected rural life. The introduction of steamships freed shipping from the vagaries of monsoon winds, and the opening of the Suez Canal in 1869 made it easier and much faster to ship raw materials from India to Europe. The return ships brought to India cheap machine goods, which undermined the role of village craftsmen such as weavers and tinkers. In addition, the quest for revenues, which included felling forests and ploughing grassland to grow more cash crops, placed massive pressure on the physical environment.

Many historians argue that British rule fostered the decline of Indian manufacturing. Hoping to find new markets abroad for its own industrial products, the British denied India tariff protection for its more expensive handmade products, excluded Indian manufactured goods from Britain, and prohibited the import of industrial machinery by Indians. Meanwhile British products flooded India, destroying the livelihood of many skilled craftsmen. Textile imports increased sixfold between 1854 and 1913, ruining millions of Indian weavers, who, along with metalworkers and glass blowers, often became farm laborers. Yet, industrial activity did not disappear completely from India, and a few Indians found ways to prosper. Some Indians continued to compete with British imports by manufacturing cotton textiles and initiated a modern iron and steel sector. For example, the Gujerati industrialist Jamsetji N. Tata (JAM-set-gee TA-ta) (1839–1904) built cotton mills, while his son, Sir Dorabji Tata (DOR-ab-ji TA-ta) (1859–1932), founded the Indian steel industry in 1907. Unable to get British funding, they raised money among Indian investors and used their wealth to promote scientific education and found technical colleges.

Industrial Decline

By the late 1800s the limits on India's industries became a subject of heated controversy. Indian critics alleged that tariffs protected British industries while strangling Indian competition. The gap between British and Indian wealth grew. By 1895 the per capita income in Britain was fifteen times higher than India's, a much greater gap than existed two hundred years earlier. Britain's defenders contended that British rule brought investment, imported goods, railroads, and law and order. But critics questioned whether these innovations benefited most Indians as it enriched the British merchants, industrialists, and collaborating Indian businessmen and landlords. Indian scholars attacked what one called "The Drain" of wealth and argued that British policies gave India "peace but not prosperity; the manufacturers lost their industries; the cultivators were ground down by a heavy and variable taxation; the revenues were to a large extent diverted to England."[8] By 1948, after two centuries of British influence, most Indians remained poor.

Population Growth and Indian Emigration

Population growth worsened the plight of the peasantry. As a result of peace and improved sanitation and health, the Indian population rose from perhaps 100 million in 1700 to 300 million by 1920. While encouraging agricultural productivity, the British also provided economic incentives to have more children to help in the fields. Although a similar population increase occurred in Europe at the same time, the growing numbers could be absorbed by industrialization or emigration to the Americas and Australia. India enjoyed neither an industrial revolution nor an increase in food growing. Moreover, Indian landlords had a stake in the cash crop system and discouraged innovation. As a result, population numbers far outstripped the amount of available food and land, creating dire poverty and widespread hunger.

Leaving India

As these problems mounted, millions of desperately poor Indians were recruited to emigrate to other lands. After the abolition of slavery in the Americas, African American workers often left the plantations. The need to replace them created a market for Indian labor in Trinidad, British Guiana (today's Guyana), and Dutch Guiana (now Suriname). Plantations in Sri Lanka, Malaya, Fiji, the Indian Ocean island of Mauritius, and South Africa also wanted Indian labor. But travel was hazardous. For example, in 1884 a family of low-caste landless laborers facing starvation in Bihar state boarded a sailing ship at Calcutta bound for the distant Fiji Islands in the South Pacific. The family was led by Somerea, a fifty-year-old widow, and included her two sons, a daughter-in-law, and four grandchildren. After three months the ship arrived in the islands, but, thanks to cholera, dysentery, typhoid, and a shipwreck, 56 of the 497 passengers had died during the trip. Somerea's family apparently survived the journey.

Indian Diaspora

Most Indian emigrants, including Somerea's family, were destined for plantations and were indentured, meaning they had signed contracts that obligated them to work for a period of years (usually three to five) to repay their passage. Somerea's family probably worked on a sugar plantation. The indenture contracts also stipulated the number of days per week (six) and hours per day (usually nine to ten) that must be worked. Many Indian merchants, moneylenders, and laborers also emigrated, flocking to British Burma, Singapore, Malaya, and East Africa. Between 1880 and 1930 around a quarter million people a year left India. Few returned. The mortality rates were so high and the indenture terms so unfavorable that critics considered the system another form of slavery. Moreover, the pay was so low that many Indians could never pay off their contracts.

Indians now had key economic roles in many countries. Cities such as Nairobi in Kenya, Rangoon in Burma, and Port of Spain in Trinidad had large Indian neighborhoods, and Indian trade networks reached around the Indian Ocean and Pacific Rim. The future leader of the Indian nationalist movement, Mohandas Gandhi (GAHN-dee), experimented with his ideas of nonviolent resistance to illegitimate power while working among Indians in South Africa. Today people of Indian ancestry make up half or more of the populations of Mauritius, Trinidad, Guyana, Suriname, and Fiji and are substantial minorities in Sri Lanka, Malaysia, Singapore, Burma, Kenya, and South Africa. However, although many Indian emigrants succeeded in business or the professions, the majority still labor on plantations growing cocoa, rubber, tea, or sugar.

Indian Thought, Literature, and Society

Indian intellectuals responded to British rule and ideas in several ways. A small group of well-educated Indians, like Ram Mohan Roy mentioned earlier, wanted to combine the best of East and West while reforming customs, such as the ban on widow remarriage, that they saw as corruptions of Hinduism. But their influence waned after 1900. Another group, hostile to Western ways, sought to revive Hindu culture, emphasizing the glories of the past and arguing that India needed nothing from the West. Swami Vivekananda (SWAH-me VIH-vee-keh-NAHN-da) (1863–1902) was an influential proponent of ending British cultural and political domination: "O India, this is your terrible danger. The spell of imitating the West is getting such a strong hold upon you. Be proud that thou art an Indian, and proudly proclaim: 'I am an Indian, every Indian is my brother.'"9

Hindu Reform and Revival

Swami Vivekananda was also a reformer, condemning the oppression of untouchables and the conditions of the poor. His writings and lectures gave Indians great pride in their own culture and also helped spread Hindu thought to the West. In 1893, on a visit to New York, he formed the Vedanta Society, which promoted a philosophical view of Hinduism based on the ancient *Upanishads*. Vedanta thought portrayed the Hindu holy books, the Vedas, compiled over 2,500 years ago, as the supreme source of religious knowledge, although not necessarily authored by either God or humans. Vedanta ideas had contributed to another movement, **Theosophy**, that attracted some

Theosophy A nineteenth-century North American and European movement that blended Hindu thought with Western spiritualist and scientific ideas.

Western followers by blending Hindu notions with Western spiritualist and scientific ideas. Theosophy promoted the idea that India was more spiritual than other societies.

Like Hindus, Muslims were forced to rethink their values and prospects. Although the British left many Muslim institutions untouched, Muslims resented the Christian missionary activity supported by British officials openly critical of Islam. To them, India seemed increasingly dominated by European and Hindu values. In response, some Muslims traveled to the Middle East to pursue Islamic knowledge and came home with Islamic revivalist ideas, some opening schools. In the northwest frontier and Bengal, dogmatic Wahhabism (see Chapter 21) gained a following. Opposed to modernization, the revivalists clashed with other Muslims, Christians, Sikhs, and Hindus.

In contrast, Muslim modernists, led by the cosmopolitan Sayyid Ahmad Khan (1817–1898), wanted Muslims to gain strength, suggesting that "the more worldly progress we make, the more glory Islam gains." Khan believed that Islam was compatible with modern science, and in 1877 he founded a college at Aligarh **(AL-ee-GAHR)** that offered Western learning within a Muslim context. Trained for jobs in government service, Aligarh students, often not devout, studied many subjects in English, and typically learned how to play the British game of cricket. Many went on to study at top British universities. A satirist observed the secular atmosphere at Aligarh, whose leaders "neither believe in God, nor yet in prayer. They say they do, but it is plain to see, What they believe in is the powers that be."[10] Aligarh graduates dominated Muslim political activity in India until independence.

Indian literature took on a more nationalist flavor. The Tagore family, Hindus from Calcutta, pioneered the movement to awaken national pride and expand literary expression. The hugely influential Rabindranath Tagore **(RAH-bin-drah-NATH ta-GORE)** (1861–1941) was a poet, educator, patriot, and internationalist whose writings won him the Nobel Prize for literature in 1913 (see Witness to the Past: Challenging British Imperialism with Spiritual Virtues). His wealthy family, he wrote, adopted foreign customs but also nurtured a pride in the Indian nation. Tagore sought a new and freer India, "where the mind is without fear and the head is held high; Where knowledge is free; where the clear stream of reason has not lost its way into the dreary desert sand of dead habit; Into that heaven of freedom, let my country awake."[11]

British policies also affected society, including the caste system. Historians debate whether the elaborate caste system of modern times had existed for centuries as an active, continually changing part of Indian life, or whether the modern system was shaped by the views of colonial era officials seeking to classify Indians for administrative and census purposes. Before the colonial era, Hindus in Bengal, Punjab, and south India generally saw the formal differences among varied castes as of only moderate importance. But British policies sharpened caste identities by classifying people largely through their caste affiliations, thus making the system more rigid and favoring the higher castes. Furthermore, as different Indians increasingly came into contact with one another, some Indians sought firmer social boundaries by further dividing castes from each other. In the nineteenth century, much of India became more caste conscious than ever before, with upper castes stressing their uniqueness and lower castes wanting to emulate the upper castes to improve their social status. Envying the highest caste, brahmans (priests), other castes adopted brahman rituals and ideas, such as vegetarianism. For example, some untouchable leather workers joined a movement that opposed the caste system but, like brahmans, avoided eating meat. For their part, higher castes tried to preserve their privileged positions by demanding that members of lower castes be excluded from government jobs. Hindu thinkers were divided about the caste system. Some reformers called for abolishing caste, while defenders praised the system's ideals of conduct and morality.

Gender relations also changed. Traditionally women and men had performed separate but interdependent roles within a patriarchal household. Ploughing was men's work; transplanting and weeding were shared duties; and women tended the house and garden. But both men and women lost work as absentee landlords emphasized growing cash crops rather than food. Lower-caste men emulated the upper castes, often forcing women into seclusion. But new opportunities also arose for women. More girls attended school, becoming teachers, nurses, midwives, and even doctors, and by the 1870s women published biographies of their experiences and struggles. For centuries girls had been married early with little choice of husband. Now a small minority of "new women" in Indian cities led more independent lives and married later, in their twenties or thirties, or sometimes not at all.

Indian and British reformers also sought to improve the lives of Indian women and foster greater gender equality. For example, a controversial new marriage act in 1872 provided for both civil marriage and marriage across caste lines. The British tried incremental reforms, such as allowing widow remarriage and raising the age of female consent from ten to twelve. But although

Muslim Revival and Reform

Literature

Caste and Gender Relations

Challenging British Imperialism with Spiritual Virtues

On the last day of the nineteenth century Rabindranath Tagore wrote a poem in Bengali protesting the brutal imperialism of the war Britain was waging against the Boers in South Africa, driven, Tagore believed, by British nationalism. The poem suggested that the patient cultivation of the "spiritual virtues" of India and the East would become a force in the world after the reckless power of Western imperialism, sparked by nationalism, had lost its control over humankind. In this, he echoed the views of many Hindu nationalists and reformers that Hinduism and India had a special devotion to peace and spiritual insights that could benefit the Western world. For this poem and other influential writings, Tagore won the Noble Prize for literature in 1913.

The last sun of the century sets amidst the blood-red clouds of the West and the whirlwind of hatred.
The naked passion of self-love of Nations, in its drunken delirium of greed, is dancing to the clash of steel and the howling verses of vengeance.
The hungry self of the Nation shall burst in a violence of fury from its own shameless feeding, for it has made the world its food.
And licking it, crunching it, and swallowing it in big morsels, It swells and swells,
Till in the midst of its unholy feast descends the sudden shaft of heaven piercing its heart of grossness.

The crimson glow of light on the horizon is not the light of thy dawn of peace, my Motherland.
It is the glimmer of the funeral pyre burning to ashes the vast flesh—the self-love of the Nation—dead under its own excess.
The morning waits behind the patient dark of the East, Meek and silent.
Keep watch, India.
Bring your offerings of worship for that sacred sunrise.
Let the first hymn of its welcome sound in your voice and sing
"Come, Peace, thou daughter of God's own great suffering.
Come with thy treasure of contentment, the sword of fortitude,
And meekness crowning thy forehead."
Be not ashamed, my brothers, to stand before the proud and the powerful, With your white robe of simpleness.
Let your crown be of humility, your freedom the freedom of the soul.
Build God's throne daily upon the ample barrenness of your poverty.
And know that what is huge is not great and pride is not everlasting.

THINKING ABOUT THE READING

1. How does Tagore perceive nationalism?
2. How does he believe India should respond to Western power?

Source: From *Sources of Indian Tradition, Vol. 2,* William Theodore de Bary, ed. Copyright © 1958 Columbia University Press. Reprinted with permission of the publisher.

---

reformers often supported the idea of marriage based on love, they also encouraged wives to show their husbands and children self-sacrificing devotion. This was not enough progress for some women. Pandita Ramabai (1858–1922) urged women to take control of their lives. Her father, a noted reformer, declined to marry her off as a child, and her knowledge of Sanskrit won her the reputation of *Saraswati*, after the Hindu goddess of wisdom. She married a lawyer of low-caste background, a shocking move for a brahman woman, and then traveled to England, where she became a Christian. Upon returning, Ramabai opened a school for girls, especially child widows, and later a refuge for female famine victims.

The Rise of Nationalism

National Feeling

British rule inevitably produced a nationalist reaction. The Western idea of the "nation," defined by a feeling of inclusiveness among people living within the same state (see Chapter 19), was new for Indians, who thought of themselves as joined by a common Hindu or Muslim culture rather than a centralized state. By establishing political unity in India, educating Indians in European ideas but then largely excluding Indians from administration, Britain fostered national feelings but also bitterness toward the colonizers. Furthermore, by 1900, Indians were publishing six hundred newspapers, which reported on world events such as the Irish struggle for independence from England, the Japanese defeat of Russia in war, and the U.S. conquest of the Philippines, all of which inspired Indians to oppose British rule. In 1885 nationalists formed the Indian National Congress, which worked for peaceful progress toward self-government. But the Congress mostly attracted well-educated professionals and merchants, especially Bengalis, of brahman backgrounds. British officials heaped scorn on the Congress, and constitutional reforms in 1909 brought a measure of representative government but no true legislative and financial power.

By 1907 a radical nationalist group led by a former journalist, Bal Gangadhar Tilak **(BAL GAGN-ga-DAR TEA-lak)** (1856–1920), transformed the Congress from a gentleman's pressure group into the spearhead of an active independence movement. Tilak fiercely defended Hindu orthodoxy and custom; however, many Indians disliked Tilak and remained wary of the Congress, while Muslims perceived the Hindu-dominated Congress, particularly radical leaders like Tilak, as anti-Muslim. As Hindu-Muslim tensions increased, the All-India Muslim League was founded in 1906 with the goal of uniting Muslims scattered all over the country. Hindus constituted 80 percent of India's population; Muslims were a majority only in eastern Bengal, Sind, north Punjab, and the mountain districts west of the Indus Valley. The influential Muslim reformer and educator Sayyid Ahmad Khan opposed potential Hindu majority rule, arguing that "it would be like a game of dice, in which one man has four dice and the other only one."[12] The Muslim League's first great victory came in 1909, when British reforms guaranteed some seats in representative councils to Muslims. The Congress was enraged, charging divide and rule. Hindu-Muslim rivalries continued to complicate the nationalist movement throughout the twentieth century, eventually leading to separate Hindu and Muslim-majority nations, India and Pakistan, in 1949.

Rise of the Congress

SECTION SUMMARY

- After 1857, the British monarchy ruled India through the British Raj, which built palatial buildings, a large railroad system, and an expanded English-language school system, thereby educating Indians about Western ideals such as nationalism and sowing the seeds for an Indian revolution against Britain.

- Britain stifled Indian industry by using India as a market for British industrial products, and it turned Indian peasants into tenants who had to grow cash crops for Britain rather than their own food, thus destroying the centuries-old village economy and exacerbating famine and poverty.

- As the Indian population increased, many poor Indians were driven to work abroad in indentured servitude, while other Indians emigrated to work as laborers, merchants, and moneylenders.

- While some Hindus wanted to combine the best in British and Indian culture, others, such as Vivekananda and Tagore, sought to revive more traditional Hindu traditions, while a Muslim college at Aligarh trained Muslims in English government and science.

- The caste system became more rigid under British rule, with lower castes imitating upper castes, upper castes trying to strengthen their privileges, and women facing greater restrictions in some cases and expanded opportunity in others.

- As Indian nationalists began to unite in their opposition to the British, members of the Hindu majority formed the Indian National Congress in 1885, but it was opposed by many Muslims, who formed the All-India Muslim League in 1906.

SOUTHEAST ASIA AND COLONIZATION

> How did the Western nations expand their control of Southeast Asia?

Like Indians, Southeast Asians also had colonization imposed on them by Western military force. During the 1800s the Western challenges became more threatening, and by 1914 all the major Southeast Asian societies except the Siamese had come under Western colonial control. The major changes came in Indonesia, Vietnam, and Burma, where the Dutch, French, and British, respectively, increased their power, and in the Philippines, which by 1902 was controlled by the United States. Thus Southeast Asian societies became tied, more than ever before, to the larger world but lost their political and economic independence.

Colonialism in Indonesia and Malaya

The Dutch expanded their power in the Indonesian archipelago. The Dutch East India Company already controlled the Spice Islands (Maluku) and Java, territories that supplied them with great wealth. In 1799 the Dutch government abolished the Company because of debts and corruption and replaced it with a formal colonial government that concentrated its economic exploitation in Java and Sumatra (see Chronology: Southeast Asia, 1750–1914). In 1830 the Dutch introduced the **cultivation system**, an agricultural policy that forced farmers on Java to grow sugar on

Dutch Expansion

cultivation system An agricultural policy imposed by the Dutch in Java that forced Javanese farmers to grow sugar on rice land.

their rice land and allowed the government to set a low fixed price to pay peasants for sugar, even when world prices were high, enriching the Dutch but ultimately impoverishing many peasants. A Dutch critic described the results: "If anyone should ask whether the man who grows the products receives a reward proportionate to the yields, the answer must be in the negative. The Government compels him to grow on *his* land what pleases *it*; it punishes him when he sells the crop to anyone else but *it*."[13] Dutch-owned plantations growing sugar and other cash crops replaced the cultivation system in the 1870s.

In the later 1800s the Dutch turned their attention to gaining control, and exploiting the resources, of the other Indonesian islands, such as Borneo and Sulawesi (see Map 22.2). In some areas they used violence to impose their rule and suppress resistance. For example, between 1906 and 1908 they crushed the small kingdoms on Bali, an island just east of Java. After the valiant Balinese resistance failed, the royal family of the largest kingdom committed collective suicide, walking into the guns of the Dutch forces rather than surrendering, shaming the Dutch and depriving them of any sense of victory. The Dutch also united the thousands of scattered societies and dozens of states of the vast Indonesian archipelago into the Dutch East Indies. But the diverse colony, governed from Batavia (now Jakarta) on Java, promoted little common national feeling, making it difficult later to build an Indonesian nation with a shared identity.

Meanwhile the British became more active in Malaya and eventually subjugated the varied Malay states. Seeking a naval base, the British East India Company purchased Penang **(puh-NANG)** Island, off Malaya's northwest coast, from a cash-strapped sultan in 1786. Then in 1819 a visionary British East India Company agent, Jamaica-born Thomas Stamford Raffles (1781–1826), capitalized on local political unrest to acquire sparsely populated Singapore Island, at the tip of the Malay Peninsula. A fine harbor and strategic location on the Straits of Melaka, the midpoint for shipping between China and India, made Singapore a valuable base and a great source of profit to both British businessmen and government treasuries. As the British welcomed Chinese immigrants, Singapore became the major hub for both British and Chinese economic activity and networks in Southeast Asia. By the 1860s Singapore, with a mostly Chinese population, had become the key crossroads of Southeast Asian commerce. Finally, after obtaining Melaka from the Dutch in 1824, Britain governed the three Malayan ports as one colony, the Straits Settlements.

British Expansion

Pressured by British merchants in the Straits Settlements, the British soon extended their influence into the Malay states. For some time Chinese had been immigrating to western Malaya, where they contracted with local Malay rulers to mine tin and gold. Growing demand for metals in industrializing Europe spurred British merchants, competitors of the Chinese, to seek control of the mining. By the 1870s the British used order and security as their rationale for threatening or forcing the Malay sultans to accept British advisers and then British domination. Britain soon achieved formal or informal control over nine sultanates, which, together with the Straits Settlements, became British Malaya. The British also colonized the northern third of Borneo, creating the states of Sabah (British North Borneo) and Sarawak and imposing a protectorate over the old sultanate of Brunei.

British rule changed Malaya, encouraging the planting of pepper, tobacco, oil palm, and especially rubber on the west coast while attracting many more Chinese and Indian immigrants. Malayan tin was shipped to Europe and North America for making household utensils, tin cans, and barrels for storage of food and oil. Malay villagers, pressured by British taxes to take up rubber planting, lost their self-sufficiency, while the British maintained the Malay sultans and aristocracy as symbolic and privileged leaders of the Malay states. Thus a **plural society** developed, a medley of peoples—Malays, Chinese, and Indians—that mixed but did not blend. The different groups generally maintained their own cultures, religions, languages, and customs, confirming a Malay proverb : "raven with raven, sparrow with sparrow."

plural society A medley of peoples who mix but do not blend, maintaining their own cultures, religions, languages, and customs.

Vietnam and Burma: Colonization and Resistance

The Taysons

Vietnam fell to French colonialism after a bitter struggle. In 1771 three brothers from Tayson, a village in southern Vietnam, launched the Tayson Rebellion. Social revolutionaries committed to a unified Vietnamese nation and fed up with corruption and misrule, the Taysons fought against the Vietnamese emperors and their French allies, using the slogan "seize the property

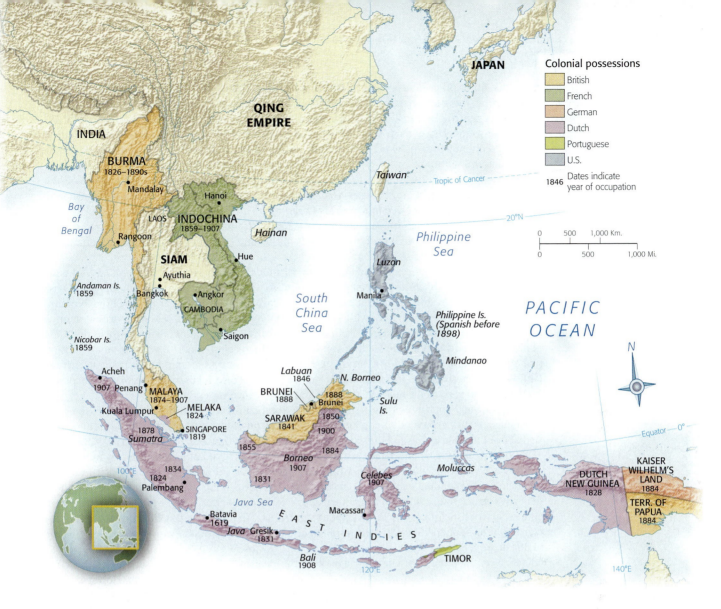

Map 22.2   The Colonization of Southeast Asia

Between 1800 and 1914 the European powers gradually conquered or gained control over the Southeast Asian societies that had not been colonized in the Early Modern Era. Only Siam remained independent.

e Interactive Map

of the rich and redistribute it to the poor."[14] In 1788 the Taysons defeated their foes and reestablished national unity, after which they sponsored economic expansion and rallied the people against a Chinese invasion.

In 1802, Nguyen Anh **(NEW-yin ahn)** (1761–1820), the leader of a princely family based in Hue, defeated the Taysons with French assistance and established a new imperial dynasty. But the Nguyen dynasty proved unpopular and unable to address the inequalities that had inspired the Tayson Rebellion. *The Tale of Kieu*, a 3,300-line poem cherished by the Vietnamese even today, sympathetically portrays an intelligent and beautiful young woman, Kieu, forced by poverty to become a concubine and then a prostitute but who keeps her sense of honor. Kieu symbolized the Vietnamese people mistreated by the upper-class Vietnamese and their French allies. Another critic of the imperial court and of patriarchal Confucianism, the outspoken woman poet Ho Xuan Huong **(ho swan wan),** had been a concubine to several high officials. Using wit and sarcasm, she wrote freely about sex, championed women's rights, and attacked polygamy: "One wife gets quilts, the other wife must freeze. To share a husband . . . what a fate! I labor as a wageless maid."[15]

In 1858 the militarily powerful French, hoping to control the Mekong and Red River trade routes to China, began what they arrogantly called a "civilizing mission" to spread French culture and Christianity, launching a bloody campaign of conquest against a determined but badly outgunned Vietnamese resistance. The French first conquered the south and then moved north, facing Vietnamese opposition the whole way. By 1884 the French were victorious but still faced prolonged

Nguyen Dynasty

French Conquest

can vuong ("aid-the-king") Rebel groups who waged guerrilla warfare for fifteen years against the French occupation of Vietnam.

resistance for another fifteen years against the heroic efforts of thousands of poorly armed rebels known as the **can vuong (kan voo-AHN)** ("aid-the-king"), who waged guerrilla warfare throughout the country, just as their ancestors had resisted the Chinese and Mongol invaders, often against hopeless odds. One of the rebel leaders rejected any compromise with the French: "Please do not mention the word *surrender* any more. You cannot give any good counsel to a man who is determined to die." As a French witness admitted, the Vietnamese resisted fiercely: "We have had enormous difficulties in imposing our authority. Rebel bands disturb the country everywhere, appear from nowhere, arrive in large numbers, destroy everything, and then disappear into nowhere."[16] The rebels received food and shelter from the local population. In suppressing the can vuong struggle, the French massacred thousands and executed surrendered or captured rebels. The can vuong rebels became powerful symbols of resistance for later generations of Vietnamese fighting colonialism and foreign invasion.

Federation of Indochina

In 1887 the French created the Federation of Indochina, an artificial unit linking Vietnam, which the French broke into three separate colonies, with newly acquired Cambodia and Laos, all of which had very different social, cultural, political, and historical legacies. The French maintained their rule by force while allowing French commercial interests and settlers to exploit natural resources and markets. The colonial regime also destroyed the traditional autonomy of the Vietnamese villages by appointing leaders and by greatly increasing the tax burden to finance colonial administrative costs. Many peasants lost their land or access to communal lands to private landowners, investors, and rubber planters, mostly French. Powerful French enterprises prospered even if Indochina proved a financial drain for the French government.

Britain and Burma

As with the French in Vietnam, it took decades for the British to colonize Burma and overcome resistance. As they expanded their power in India, the British coveted Burma's rich lands and worried about Burmese claims to border regions. In three wars—between 1824–1826, 1851–1852, and 1885–1886—the British conquered Burma (today Myanmar), with both sides suffering huge casualties. Vastly differing cultures and clashing strategic interests produced violent British-Burmese conflict, and the gradual loss of independence proved devastating to the Burmans, the country's majority ethnic group. As they lost territory, they felt an impending doom, expressed in a frenzied cultural activity, including drama, love poetry, and music. The court, fearing that the Burmese heritage might disappear if the British triumphed, also compiled *The Glass Palace Chronicle*, a history of Burma from earliest times.

Between 1853 and 1878 a new Burmese king, the idealistic Mindon, tried to salvage his country's prospects by pursuing modernization and seeking good relations with the British. However, worried that he might succeed, the British tried to humiliate Mindon, and in 1886, after completing their conquest, they exiled the royal family. When some Burmese resisted British rule, the British, calling it "pacification," destroyed whole villages and executed rebel leaders. The Burman aristocracy and royal system were abolished as Burma became a province of British India, a humiliating fate. For the next fifty years the British undermined Burmese Buddhism and cultural values, established Christian mission schools, and recruited non-Burman hill peoples into the government and army.

Bastille Day Parade in Vietnam This painting, by an unknown Vietnamese scholar, subtly criticizes the unpopular French colonization by satirizing the annual French holiday. A French man is shown with his arm around a Vietnamese woman while unarmed Vietnamese lantern-bearers are being commanded by a French official.

Siamese Modernization

Burma's traditional enemies, the Siamese (Thai), were the only Southeast Asians who retained their independence. In the early 1800s Siam was a strong state under the vigorous new Bangkok-based Chakri dynasty. Seeing Burma's dilemma, able Chakri kings mounted a successful strategy to resist Western pressures. With Britain and France, which both coveted Siam, preoccupied with controlling Malaya, Burma, and Indochina, Siamese leaders had time to strengthen government institutions, improve their economic infrastructure, cultivate a long-standing alliance with China, and broaden their popular support. The farsighted Siamese kings understood the changes in Southeast Asian politics and the rise of Western power, and they promoted a modernization policy, yielding to the West when necessary and consolidating what remained. Siamese leaders agreed to commercial agreements that opened the country to Western businesses. Recognizing Siamese determination and pressed to maintain their control of restless Burma and Indochina, Britain and France decided that conquering Siam would be too costly and left Siam as a buffer between British Burma and French Indochina.

Two kings and their advisers were most responsible for Siam's success. The first, the scholarly, peace-loving Mongkut **(MAHN-kut)** (r. 1851–1868), had served as a Buddhist monk and teacher for several decades, studying science and learning to read Latin. Rather than inviting invasion, he signed treaties with various Western powers, often with terms unfavorable for Siam, invited Western aid to modernize his kingdom, and hired the wives of Christian missionaries to teach English to his wives and sons. Mongkut's widely traveled son and successor, Chulalong-korn **(CHOO-lah-LONG-corn)** (r. 1868–1910), emphasized diplomacy and modernization. His reforms abolished slavery, centralized government services, strengthened the bureaucracy, and established a Western-style government education system. He also stimulated economic growth by encouraging Chinese immigration and opening new land for rice production, making Siam one of the world's leading rice exporters. As a result, Siam's economic development generally kept pace with that of its colonized neighbors but under Siamese rather than colonial direction. When Chulalongkorn died in 1910, Siam (today Thailand) was still independent, and the Western appetite for new colonies had waned.

Modernizing Kings

The Philippines, Spain, and the United States

As in Latin America (see Chapter 19), hostility toward the corrupt, repressive, and economically stagnant rule of Spain had simmered for decades in the Philippines. Many educated Filipinos of Spanish, indigenous, and mixed (mestizo) background resented colonial power, the privileged immigrants from Spain, and the Catholic Church's domination. Writers such as the poet and novelist Jose Rizal **(ri-ZAHL)** (1861–1896), who had lived for a time in Spain and Germany, encouraged anti-Spanish feeling. Rizal's novels satirized the government and the church, earning him official condemnation as a subversive heretic, and he was publicly executed for alleged treason against the colonial government in 1896. Rizal's death united varied opposition groups and turned nationalists toward revolution. One nationalist leader, Emilio Aguinaldo **(AH-gee-NAHL-doe)** (1870–1964), called on the Filipinos to rebel: "Filipinos! Open your eyes! Lovers of their native land, rise up in arms, to proclaim their liberty and independence."[17] Women played active roles in the movement, serving as soldiers, couriers, spies, and nurses. Despite the revolutionary's heroic efforts, however, the Spanish had contained the revolution by 1897, though they failed to crush scattered resistance.

Revolt Against Spain

The situation changed dramatically in 1898 when a U.S. fleet sailed into Manila Bay and destroyed the Spanish navy. Americans had engaged in occasional naval skirmishes in Southeast Asia throughout the 1800s, and they now sought control of resources and markets. The United States intervened in the Philippines as an episode of the Spanish-American War (see Chapter 20), the first of four ground wars that it would fight in East and Southeast Asia over the next eight decades. The U.S. attack on Manila rejuvenated the revolutionaries, who received American support and soon controlled much of the country. The revolutionaries declared independence and established a semidemocratic republican government. But the factionalized leaders disagreed in their objectives, and U.S. leaders had other plans for the country.

U.S. Intervention

The decision by the United States to remain in the Philippines as a colonizer led to its suppression of the nationalist revolution. U.S. president William McKinley answered Rudyard Kipling's call to assume "the white man's burden" and reflected the American idea of Manifest Destiny, the notion that God supported U.S. expansion. Ignoring centuries of Filipino history and deep desire for independence, McKinley proclaimed: "It is our duty to uplift and civilize and Christianize and by God's Will do our very best by [the Filipinos]."[18]

Philippine-U.S. War

But McKinley underestimated the Filipino opposition to the U.S. occupation. Some 125,000 American troops fought during the four-year Philippine-American War, with over 5,000 Americans and some 16,000 Filipinos dying in battle. Another 200,000 Filipinos perished either in guarded compounds the Americans set up to keep villagers from helping the revolutionaries or from famine and disease generated by the conflict. Since Filipino soldiers often enjoyed the active support of the local population, Americans had to fight for every town. The elusive revolutionaries' guerrilla warfare demoralized the American soldiers, who had expected a quick victory. While Americans controlled the towns, the revolutionaries controlled the countryside. Both sides committed atrocities, including torture. Americans destroyed whole villages and looted Catholic churches, while Filipinos killed captured Americans. Angered by American deaths, U.S. general Jacob Smith ordered his men to turn Samar Island into a "howling wilderness," to "kill and burn. The more you kill and burn the better you will please me."[19]

The war also divided Americans. Strong supporters coveted Philippine resources and markets, and U.S. newspapers urged the slaughter of all Filipinos who resisted. But an organized protest movement opposed the war. The writer Mark Twain satirized American economic motives in his 1900 rewriting of "The Battle Hymn of the Republic": "Mine eyes have seen the orgy of the launching of the Sword; He is searching out the hoardings where the strangers' wealth is stored; He hath loosed his fateful lightnings, and with woe and death has scored; His lust is marching on." American critics also rejected the imperialism: "We've taken up the white man's burden, of ebony and brown; Now will you tell us, Rudyard [Kipling], how we may put it down."[20]

U.S. Colonialism

By 1902, with the revolutionaries defeated and many wealthy Filipinos, to protect their interests, supporting U.S. rule, the Philippines became an American colony. Americans reshaped the society of those they paternalistically called "our little brown brothers," establishing an elected legislature filled mostly by Filipinos. The colonial government fostered modern health care and education, and the schools produced many Filipinos fluent in English. But American rule ignored peasant needs while perpetuating the power of the Filipino landowners, who controlled the lives of millions of impoverished peasant tenants, and reinforcing the cash crop economy now linked to American economic needs.

SECTION SUMMARY

- As the Dutch expanded their control over the Indonesian archipelago, they joined together vastly disparate cultures and disrupted the traditional economy, such as by forcing Javanese farmers to grow sugar on rice land and to sell it at unfairly low prices.

- The British expanded control over the Malay Peninsula, which they used to supply raw materials such as tin and rubber, and Singapore, which became a key crossroads of Southeast Asian and India-China trade.

- After conquering Vietnam, the French faced fierce resistance from can vuong rebels, but they ultimately conquered the rebels and opened the country to exploitation by French commercial interests.

- As the British gradually conquered Burma, native Burmans attempted to preserve their culture, but after the British victory in 1886 the Burmese traditions were largely undermined.

- Unlike the rest of Southeast Asia, Siam (now Thailand) avoided colonization because of its fortunate geographical location and its farseeing leaders, who gave in to some Western demands and consolidated popular support.

- After defeating the Spanish in the Philippines and supporting local rebels, the U.S. government turned against the Filipinos and, after a bloody struggle, established a colony geared toward American economic needs.

THE RESHAPING OF SOUTHEAST ASIA

What were the major political, economic, and social consequences of colonialism in Southeast Asia?

Colonialism in Southeast Asia had many parallels to that in India and Africa. Although some Southeast Asians benefited, many others experienced worsening living conditions. A chant popular among Vietnamese peasants lamented the seizure of Vietnamese resources by the French: "Ill fortune, indeed, for power has been seized by the French invaders. It's criminal to set out the food tray and find that one has nothing but roots and greens to eat."[21] From a global perspective, colonialism linked Southeast Asia more firmly to a Western-dominated world economy. But colonial policies also affected local political, social, intellectual, and cultural life. Like Indians, Southeast Asians responded to the challenges of colonialism in creative ways.

Colonial Governments and Economies

Colonialism proved a shattering experience. The only colony with much self-government, the U.S.-ruled Philippines, had an elected legislature, but its decisions had to be approved by U.S. officials. The British allowed some influential Malayans participation in local government and, in 1935, formed a legislature in Burma that included both elected and appointed members. But France and the Netherlands allowed little democracy, and colonialism often meant government by stodgy, autocratic European bureaucrats.

Colonial governments varied widely. As in sub-Saharan Africa (see Chapter 21), direct rule, which removed traditional leaders, such as the Burmese kings, or made them symbolic only, as with the Vietnamese emperors, was used in Burma, the Philippines, and parts of Vietnam and Indonesia. Europeans mostly applied indirect rule in Malaya, Cambodia, Laos, and some parts of Indonesia, governing a district through the traditional leaders, such as Malay sultans or Javanese aristocrats. The traditional leaders frequently supported colonial rule and enjoyed considerable local power. Colonial authorities also played one ethnic group or one region off against another, creating problems that persisted after independence and made national unity difficult. Also as in Africa, colonial boundaries sometimes ignored traditional ethnic relationships and rivalries, laying a basis for political instability. Countries such as Burma, Indonesia, and Laos were artificial creations of European colonialism rather than organic unities with culturally similar populations.

As in India, colonialism transformed economic life. Since subsistence food farming could not produce enough revenues for colonial governments or investors, it was replaced by cash crop farming, plantations, and mines, tying the colony's economy more closely to that of the colonizer. Western businessmen mostly controlled the banks, import-export companies, mines, wells, and plantations. As a result, Southeast Asia became one of the world's most valuable economic areas. Colonial taxation policies encouraged people to grow rubber, pepper, sugar, coffee, tea, opium, and palm oil; cut timber; mine gold and tin; and drill oil. Some key cash crops, such as rubber from

Colonial Governments

Economic Change

Java Coffee Plantation This painting from the nineteenth century shows a European manager supervising barefoot laborers who are raking and drying coffee beans, a major Javanese cash crop.

British Library

Brazil and coffee from the Middle East, originated elsewhere. Many colonies became specialized monocultures emphasizing one or two major commodities, such as rubber and tin from Malaya, or rubber and rice from Vietnam, but the world price for these exports fluctuated with unstable global demand. Moreover, these economic activities often harmed the natural environment, as forests were cleared for plantations or logged for timber to be shipped out of the region.

Many Southeast Asians now depended on rubber growing for their livelihood. The invention of bicycles and then automobiles opened up markets for rubber tires. To meet this need, the British introduced rubber to Malaya, from where it spread to Sumatra, Borneo, southern Thailand, Vietnam, and Cambodia, grown mostly on European-owned plantations. Malaya supplied over half of the world's natural rubber by 1920. Plantation workers endured long hours, strict discipline, monotonous routine, and poor food, generally arising before dawn to tend the rubber trees and replace the buckets that collected the sap, trying to finish their labor before the blazing tropical sun made hard physical work unhealthy. A Vietnamese writer described rubber estate workers: "every day one was worn down a bit more, cheeks sunken, eyes hollow. Everyone appeared almost dead."[22]

Economic growth did not benefit all equally. The European colonizers and the local officials and merchants who cooperated with them gained wealth, and the peasants on Java who grew sugar and coffee for the Dutch initially earned new income. But costs also rose faster than the compensation earned, forcing the peasants to grow more and work longer hours to earn the same profit as before. The peasants now depended on sugar or coffee profits for survival but often became impoverished because of the rising costs. They also faced disaster when world prices for sugar and coffee declined and then, in the 1930s, collapsed altogether.

Social Change

As in India, colonial policies also sparked rapid population growth. In 1800 perhaps 30 to 35 million people lived in Southeast Asia, but by the late 1930s it was around 140 or 150 million. The greatest increases came on Java, where the population in 1800 was some 10 million but increased to 30 million by 1900 and 48 million by 1940, creating a burden for contemporary Indonesia. As Dutch policies fostered better health care, people lived longer, while economic incentives encouraged larger families to provide more labor for the fields. However, women faced not only more hours working in the fields but also increased expectations for bearing more children. Fast-growing populations, especially in Java, Vietnam, and the Philippines, resulted in smaller farm plots and more landless people.

Population Growth and Immigration

Between 1800 and 1941 millions of Chinese and Indians immigrated to Southeast Asia to work as laborers, miners, planters, and merchants. The Chinese chiefly came from poor, overcrowded coastal provinces in southeast China. Although some established businesses or joined relatives, the majority immigrated under the indenture system, which obligated them to work for years in mines, plantations, or enterprises. Chinese immigrants, mostly males, hoped to make enough money to return to their native village wealthy and respected, but some remained poor, spending their lives as laborers, miners, or plantation workers. Many other Chinese prospered as merchants, planters, and mine owners, and often decided to remain in Southeast Asia. Dominating retail trade, they become the commercial middle class, operating general stores, specialty shops, and restaurants in every town. As a result, some cities, such as Kuala Lumpur (KWAW-luh loom-POOR) in Malaya and Singapore, became largely Chinese in population. Many Chinese married local women or brought families from China, their descendants often adopting aspects of local culture and language. By adjusting to local conditions, the Chinese became a permanent presence in Southeast Asian life.

British Malaya also attracted Indian settlers. Indian immigrants had long come to Malaya as traders, craftsmen, and workers. Beginning in the 1880s, the British imported Tamil-speaking people from southeast India to work on rubber plantations, and the Chinese and Indians together eventually outnumbered the Malays. The British governed the various communities through their own leaders: Malay chiefs, Chinese merchants, and urban Indian traders. But this strategy separated and discouraged cooperation between the three groups.

Gender Relations

The changes during the colonial era particularly affected women, who had traditionally played a major economic role as farmers, traders, and weavers. Now, as men took up cash crop farming, the responsibility for growing the family's food was often left to women, increasing their workload.

As Chinese, Indian, and sometimes Arab men increasingly took over small-scale trade in towns, many women also lost their role in the local marketplace and thus their status as income earners for the family. The expansion of textile imports also affected women's status. Women had previously dominated weaving, spinning, and dyeing. Although weaving was hard work, even drudgery, women could do it at home with friends and relatives while caring for children. But after 1850, as inexpensive factory-made textiles came from Europe, people stopped buying local handwoven cloth, slowly forcing women out of the textile business. A Javanese noblewoman wrote in a 1909 essay that "little by little [women] feel that their life is no longer of such value, considered by men only as ornaments as they are no longer contributing to the household coffers."[23] Women had to find other income sources, which often took them away from the home and children.

Some women joined movements to assert their rights, as European feminist movements had some influence in Southeast Asia in the late nineteenth and early twentieth centuries. For example, Siamese feminists opposed polygamy and supported girls' education. Today many Indonesians honor an inspirational Javanese woman, Raden Adjeng Kartini, as a heroine whose writings and life influenced the rise of Indonesian feminism and nationalism (see Profile: Kartini, Indonesian Feminist and Teacher). Although she died young, the schools for girls she founded in 1900 multiplied. Like Kartini, other women struggled to cope with the changing world.

Urbanization

Southeast Asia already had large cities, but Western rule encouraged more rapid urbanization. Cities such as Manila, Jakarta, Rangoon (today known as Yangon), Singapore, Kuala Lumpur, and Saigon (today Ho Chi Minh City) grew as colonial capitals. Cities attracted immigrants, such as the Chinese, and migrants from nearby districts. Most colonial towns and cities offered a diverse assortment of food stalls and restaurants, schools that catered to different ethnic groups, as well as Muslim mosques, Buddhist, Hindu, and Chinese temples, and Christian churches. While most people remained attached to their own culture, some descendants of Chinese and Indian immigrants assimilated into the surrounding culture; friendships and even marriages crossed ethnic lines. For example, much of Thailand's political and economic leadership has some mix of Chinese and Siamese ancestry.

Cultural Change

Religion and Education

Colonial governments differed in educating people and fostering indigenous cultures. Most colonies left education to the Christian missions. Some Vietnamese, Indonesians, and Chinese became Christian, and hill peoples frequently did so, but few Theravada Buddhists or Muslims abandoned their faiths. A few colonies set up government schools. The U.S.-ruled Philippines had the best record, enrolling 75 percent of children in elementary schools. Independent Siam also opened public schools that made education widely available for both boys and girls. At the other extreme, French Indochina spent little public money on schools. Some communities developed alternatives to Western education. Buddhist and Muslim groups expanded their schools and taught from a non-Western perspective, while other schools mixed Eastern and Western ideas. Schools opened by a mystical Javanese religious organization provided an alternative to both Islamic and Christian instruction, emphasizing Indonesian arts such as music and dance but also Western ideas such as expressing one's own ideas and social equality.

New Cultural Forms

Southeast Asians also developed new cultural forms. On Java, musicians mixed European string instruments with the rhythms of the largely percussion Javanese gamelan orchestra to create a romantic new popular music, *kronchong*. In the 1800s the sentimental songs were particularly favored by Indonesian sailors and soldiers, as well as by disreputable young men, known as kronchong crocodiles, who dressed flamboyantly, gambled, and drank heavily. By the early 1900s kronchong became respectable, and it was eventually embraced by Indonesian nationalists as an artistic weapon against the Dutch, offering songs on topical and nationalist themes.

The cultural exchange was not one-way. Western composers who observed performances by Javanese and Balinese gamelan orchestras incorporated gamelan influences into their music. In most colonies, a modern literature also developed that reflected alienation from colonialism and an awareness of rapid change. But since criticism of the colonial regime was suppressed, authors made their points indirectly to avoid censorship or arrest. Vietnamese writers used historical themes or critiques of Vietnamese society to discuss contemporary conditions, and Indonesian writers explored characters experiencing despair and disorientation because of the colonial system.

Guangzhou During the eighteenth century, the Western traders in China were restricted to one riverside district in Guangzhou (Canton), where they built their warehouses, businesses, and homes in European style.

Photograph Courtesy Peabody Essex Museum, E79708 View of Guangzhou ca. 1800

Primary Source: Letter to Queen Victoria, 1839 On behalf of the emperor, Lin Zexu implores Queen Victoria to halt the British opium trade in China.

appealed to bored officials, wealthy women cooped up at home, busy clerks, anxious merchants, nervous soldiers, and overworked peasants. Highly addictive, it also produced severe withdrawal symptoms such as cramps and nausea.

The British, who began to grow opium as a cash crop in Bengal, soon found foreign markets around Asia. In fact, the sale of opium, chiefly obtained from the British, became an important revenue source for all the European colonial governments in Southeast Asia. As British and American traders began smuggling opium into China, reaping huge profits, they were indifferent to the terrible moral and social consequences of their enterprise. Between 1800 and 1838 opium imports to China increased sixfold, and 5 to 10 million Chinese became addicts. As the opium trade undermined Chinese society and impoverished families, one Chinese official concluded that "opium is nothing else but a flowing poison [which] utterly ruins the minds and morals of the people, a dreadful calamity."[4] Another argued that opium smokers should be strangled and the pushers and producers beheaded.

Repressing the Opium Trade

After the Qing emperor issued decrees forbidding the marketing, smuggling, and consumption of opium, British, American, and other Western traders were forced officially to trade through the Co-hong merchant's guild in Guangzhou. But the British found that officials could be bribed to overlook opium smuggling. The British doubled opium imports during the 1830s while also pressing for reform of the trading system. Chinese leaders responded by further isolating the Western traders and attacking the opium trade. The emperor appointed the mandarin Lin Zexu **(lin tsay-shoe)** (1785–1850) to go to Guangzhou and end the opium trade. Lin, an incorruptible Confucian moralist, wrote to Britain's Queen Victoria: "Suppose there were people from another country who carried opium for sale to England and seduced your people into buying and smoking it. Certainly you would be bitterly aroused."[5] Lin ordered his officials to raid the Western settlement, where they seized and destroyed 20,000 chests of opium worth millions of dollars.

Opium War

Lin's seizure of opium outraged Western traders, and Britain declared war. In the Opium War (1839–1842), as the British called it, the British fleet raided up and down the Chinese coast, blockading and bombarding ports, including Guangzhou. The Chinese fought back, often resisting against hopeless odds, but they lacked the weapons to triumph. Although China had formidable military forces in 1600, Europeans had now greatly surpassed China in naval and military technology. A few alarmed officials were concerned with the inadequacy of Chinese military technology. Lin Zezu wrote to a friend that China badly needed ships and guns like the British had, but most officials rejected such ideas, detesting the British and remaining scornful of all things Western. Average Chinese reacted with rage. One placard in Canton in 1841 was addressed to "rebellious barbarian dogs. If we do not completely exterminate you we will not be manly Chinese able to support the sky over our heads. We are definitely going to kill you, cut your heads off, and burn your bodies in the trash."[6]

Treaty of Nanjing

When the British prepared to blow down the walls of the major city of Nanjing, the Qing were forced to negotiate for peace, and in 1842 they signed the Treaty of Nanjing, the first of a series of humiliatingly unequal treaties that nibbled away at Chinese sovereignty. The treaty gave Britain permanent possession of Hong Kong, a sparsely populated coastal island downriver from Guangzhou; opened five ports to British trade; abolished the Co-hong and its trade monopoly; set fixed tariffs so that China no longer controlled its economic policy; and gave the British **extraterrito-**

extraterritoriality Freedom from local laws for foreign subjects.

CHRONOLOGY

	China	Japan and Korea	Russia and Central Asia
1800	**1839–1842** Opium War		
1850	**1850–1864** Taiping Rebellion	**1853** Opening of Japan by Perry **1867–1868** Meiji Restoration	**1800–1870s** Russian conquest of Turkestan and Caucasus
1900	**1911** Chinese Revolution	**1910** Japanese colonization of Korea and Taiwan	**1905** First Russian Revolution

English traders were granted permission to trade at the southern port of Guangzhou (gwahng-jo) (known to the British as Canton).

Chinese merchants in coastal cities, who had long traded with Southeast Asia, often supported contact with the West because they could make fortunes by trading with the Europeans. For example, some merchants specialized in **Chinoiserie (chin-WAH-zur-ee)**, a Western vogue for Chinese ceramics, painting, lacquerware, and decorative furniture whose quality Europeans could not duplicate. Western merchants and diplomats also commissioned Chinese artists to paint Chinese people, costumes, and city scenes using Western artistic techniques. In the early 1800s a merchant's guild, the **Co-hong**, had a monopoly on Guangzhou's trade with the West, and its head, Howqua (how-kwah) (1769–1843), became one of the world's richest men. Howqua was famous in China for his spectacular pleasure garden and lavish mansion, which employed five hundred servants.

Nevertheless, largely self-sufficient in food and resources, China did not need foreign trade, and Qing emperors were unwilling to make concessions to the more open trade system desired by the Europeans. They restricted trade to a few ports such as Guangzhou and refused diplomatic relations on an equal basis with the West. The Chinese knew little of the Western world and were confused by the diverse European nationalities. Moreover, Chinese leaders viewed European merchants as barbarians bearing tribute, and they required visiting diplomats to perform the humiliating custom of prostrating themselves before the emperor. But the British righteously saw themselves as benefiting China by opening the country to free trade. China's attitude toward foreign trade and the outside world was well exemplified in a letter written by the Qing emperor Qianlong (chee-YEN-loong) (r. 1736–1795) to King George III of Britain following a British trade mission in 1793 requesting more access. The emperor denied Britain permission to establish an embassy but commended the king for his respectful spirit of submission and humility in sending tribute: "Our dynasty's majestic virtue has penetrated into every country under heaven. Our celestial empire possesses all things in prolific abundance. It behooves you, O king, to display ever greater devotion and loyalty in the future, so that by perpetual submission to our throne, you may secure peace and prosperity for your country hereafter."[3]

The Opium Trade and War

Half a century after Emperor Qianlong blithely dismissed the British request, the tables were turned. Two wars in the mid-1800s, in which Qing China suffered humiliating defeats, forcibly jarred the Chinese from their complacency and made clear that the world was changing. The British badly wanted more Chinese silk and tea, which had become valued revenue sources for British merchants. But China, desiring little from the West, accepted only precious gold and silver bullion as payment. Between the 1760s and 1780s the import of silver into China increased over 500 percent, presenting a serious balance of payments problem for Western economies. Seeking a marketable product that would solve this unfavorable trade disparity, the British found it in opium, an addictive drug that was grown in India and the Middle East.

The Chinese had used opium as a painkiller since the 1600s and then discovered that they could smoke opium for pleasure by mixing it in a pipe with tobacco. By the later 1700s opium dens, where people could buy and use opium, began to appear. The drug gave users a dreamy, relaxed experience that temporarily relieved boredom, stress, physical pain, and depression. Opium

CHRONOLOGY
China, 1750–1915

1644–1912 Qing dynasty

1839–1842 Opium War

1842 Treaty of Nanjing

1856–1860 Arrow War

1850–1864 Taiping Rebellion

1894–1895 Sino-Japanese War

1898 100 Days of Reform

1900 Boxer Rebellion

1911 Chinese Revolution

1912 Formation of Chinese Republic

1915 Japan's 21 Demands on China

Chinoiserie An eighteenth- and nineteenth-century Western vogue for Chinese painting, ceramics, lacquerware, and decorative furniture.

Co-hong A nineteenth-century Chinese merchant's guild that had a monopoly on Guangzhou's trade with the West.

Guangzhou During the eighteenth century, the Western traders in China were restricted to one riverside district in Guangzhou (Canton), where they built their warehouses, businesses, and homes in European style.

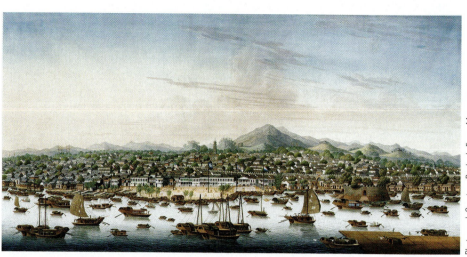

Photograph Courtesy Peabody Essex Museum, E79708 View of Guangzhou ca. 1800

Primary Source: Letter to Queen Victoria, 1839 On behalf of the emperor, Lin Zexu implores Queen Victoria to halt the British opium trade in China.

appealed to bored officials, wealthy women cooped up at home, busy clerks, anxious merchants, nervous soldiers, and overworked peasants. Highly addictive, it also produced severe withdrawal symptoms such as cramps and nausea.

The British, who began to grow opium as a cash crop in Bengal, soon found foreign markets around Asia. In fact, the sale of opium, chiefly obtained from the British, became an important revenue source for all the European colonial governments in Southeast Asia. As British and American traders began smuggling opium into China, reaping huge profits, they were indifferent to the terrible moral and social consequences of their enterprise. Between 1800 and 1838 opium imports to China increased sixfold, and 5 to 10 million Chinese became addicts. As the opium trade undermined Chinese society and impoverished families, one Chinese official concluded that "opium is nothing else but a flowing poison [which] utterly ruins the minds and morals of the people, a dreadful calamity."[4] Another argued that opium smokers should be strangled and the pushers and producers beheaded.

Repressing the Opium Trade

After the Qing emperor issued decrees forbidding the marketing, smuggling, and consumption of opium, British, American, and other Western traders were forced officially to trade through the Co-hong merchant's guild in Guangzhou. But the British found that officials could be bribed to overlook opium smuggling. The British doubled opium imports during the 1830s while also pressing for reform of the trading system. Chinese leaders responded by further isolating the Western traders and attacking the opium trade. The emperor appointed the mandarin Lin Zexu **(lin tsay-shoe)** (1785–1850) to go to Guangzhou and end the opium trade. Lin, an incorruptible Confucian moralist, wrote to Britain's Queen Victoria: "Suppose there were people from another country who carried opium for sale to England and seduced your people into buying and smoking it. Certainly you would be bitterly aroused."[5] Lin ordered his officials to raid the Western settlement, where they seized and destroyed 20,000 chests of opium worth millions of dollars.

Opium War

Lin's seizure of opium outraged Western traders, and Britain declared war. In the Opium War (1839–1842), as the British called it, the British fleet raided up and down the Chinese coast, blockading and bombarding ports, including Guangzhou. The Chinese fought back, often resisting against hopeless odds, but they lacked the weapons to triumph. Although China had formidable military forces in 1600, Europeans had now greatly surpassed China in naval and military technology. A few alarmed officials were concerned with the inadequacy of Chinese military technology. Lin Zezu wrote to a friend that China badly needed ships and guns like the British had, but most officials rejected such ideas, detesting the British and remaining scornful of all things Western. Average Chinese reacted with rage. One placard in Canton in 1841 was addressed to "rebellious barbarian dogs. If we do not completely exterminate you we will not be manly Chinese able to support the sky over our heads. We are definitely going to kill you, cut your heads off, and burn your bodies in the trash."[6]

Treaty of Nanjing

When the British prepared to blow down the walls of the major city of Nanjing, the Qing were forced to negotiate for peace, and in 1842 they signed the Treaty of Nanjing, the first of a series of humiliatingly unequal treaties that nibbled away at Chinese sovereignty. The treaty gave Britain permanent possession of Hong Kong, a sparsely populated coastal island downriver from Guangzhou; opened five ports to British trade; abolished the Co-hong and its trade monopoly; set fixed tariffs so that China no longer controlled its economic policy; and gave the British **extraterrito-**

extraterritoriality Freedom from local laws for foreign subjects.

East and Central Asia, also became a factor in Asian politics by expanding across Siberia to the Pacific. After it became dominant in parts of eastern Europe, pushed its borders southward into Ottoman territories, and conquered the Central Asian states, Russia was the largest territorial power in Eurasia.

THE ZENITH AND DECLINE OF QING CHINA

> What were the causes and consequences of the Opium War?

Established by the Manchus, the Qing **(ching)** (1644–1912) was the last dynasty in China's 2,000-year-old imperial history (see Chronology: China, 1750–1915). After reaching its zenith in the eighteenth century, Qing China experienced decay in the nineteenth as several catastrophic wars resulted in unequal treaties that increased Western penetration and fostered major rebellions. Meanwhile, China's economy underwent changes, and increasing poverty prompted millions of Chinese to seek their fortunes abroad. Qing decline had as much to do with Europe's rise as with China's failures.

Qing China in an Imperial World

Eighteenth-century China was still one of the world's most powerful, prosperous, and technologically sophisticated societies, self-sufficient and self-centered. But although the Manchus had followed the political example of earlier Chinese dynasties, they were more despotic and forbade intermarriage with the Chinese. While the Chinese accepted Manchu rule, as they had tolerated alien rule in the past, they resented the ethnic discrimination. The Qing had built a great empire by occupying predominantly Muslim Xinjiang **(shin-jee-yahng)**, a mostly desert region just west of China; conquering the Mongols; annexing Tibet; and adding the fertile island of Taiwan, known in the West as Formosa, to which many Chinese migrated. This expansion stretched Qing military power and proved economically costly.

Manchu Rule and Economy

Yet the Qing generally maintained prosperity for nearly two centuries. New crops from the Americas, such as corn, sweet potatoes, and peanuts, provided additional food sources. Cash cropping of cotton, tea, and American tobacco expanded but also led to a growing concentration of land ownership. In 1830 China, with growing domestic trade, new textile factories, and increased copper mining, remained the world's largest commercial economy and still accounted for a third of world manufacturing. Some historians suggest that the mid-Qing commercialized economy resembled the patterns that sparked economic change in Early Modern western Europe. For example, China's population nearly tripled from 150 million in 1700 to 432 million by 1850. Peasants responded to population pressure by farming marginal land and expanding their use of irrigation and fertilizer.

But population growth still outstripped the growth of the food supply, straining resources and fostering corruption and Chinese resentment of the Qing government. Although in the 1700s living standards in the more developed regions of China were probably comparable to those of the more affluent parts of western Europe, they deteriorated in the 1800s. Chinese culture and society also became more conservative, as the Qing government prohibited books and plays that it considered treasonable or subversive to traditional Chinese values. Some scholars, arguing that moral laxness caused the fall of dynasties, applauded the crackdown. The Qing also introduced harsher laws against homosexuality, which Chinese governments had generally tolerated, and increased social pressures on women to conform to such gender expectations as refusing to remarry after they became widows. Imperial edicts read in monthly public meetings emphasized Confucian notions of moral virtue, heaping honor on filial sons, loyal officials, and faithful wives. The government also published instructional books containing historical writings on female obligations such as not laughing aloud, talking loudly, or swaying their skirts. Yet, women also read popular literature, such as the satirical novel *Flowers in a Mirror*. And, in a few districts in central China, peasant women wrote their communications in a secret script, *nüxu* **(noo-shoe)**, that was perhaps developed by and for women centuries earlier.

Society and Culture

China's problems resulted from both internal decay and foreign pressure. Greedy officials took bribes to allow the smuggling and sale of narcotic drugs, and local rebellions against the Qing were suppressed, but at great cost. As conditions deteriorated at home, European nations demanded more privileges, including freedom to travel inside China. The Portuguese had established a base at Macao on the southern coast and gradually turned it into a colony, and in the 1700s Dutch and

China and Europe

*T*he sacred traditions of our ancestors have fallen into oblivion. Those who watch attentively the march of events feel a dark and wonderful presentiment. We are on the eve of an immense revolution. But will the impulse come from within or without?

—A Chinese official, 1846[1]

FOCUS QUESTIONS

1. **What were the causes and consequences of the Opium War?**
2. **Why did Chinese efforts at modernization fail?**
3. **How did the Meiji government transform Japan and Korea?**
4. **What factors explain the expansion of the Russian Empire?**

In 1820 Li Ruzhen (LEE ju-chen) (1763–1830) published a satiric novel that boldly attacked Chinese social conditions. Set in the Tang dynasty, *Flowers in the Mirror* explored, among other themes, a sensitive topic only superficially discussed by earlier male Chinese writers: the relationship between the sexes. Li described a trip by three men to a country in which all the gender roles followed in China for centuries have been reversed, where men suffered the pain of ear piercing and footbinding and endured hours every day putting on makeup, all to please the women who run the country. One of the men, Merchant Lin, is conscripted as a court "lady" by the female "king":

His [bound] feet lost much of their original shape. Blood and flesh were squeezed into a pulp and little remained of feet but dry bones and skin, shrunk to a dainty size. Responding to daily anointing [with oil], his hair became shiny and smooth. With blood-red lipstick, and powder adorning his face, and jade and pearl adorning his coiffure and ears, Merchant Lin assumed a not unappealing appearance.[2]

Li seemed an unlikely man to address so sympathetically the daily challenges faced by women. A conventionally educated Confucian scholar who had failed the civil service examinations, Li became a writer on language, political philosophy, mathematics, and astrology. But growing Western pressure to open China's borders to foreign trade, unchecked population growth, domestic unrest, political corruption, and growing opium addiction spurred Chinese scholars such as Li to reassess the relevance of Chinese traditions, such as outmoded civil service examinations and women's footbinding. Li addressed the social inequities that kept women from actively participating in China's regeneration. The growing dissatisfaction with China's practices that Li's provocative book represented, combined with Western intervention in China, set the stage for the immense revolution that would eventually transform this ancient society.

China was still powerful in the late 1700s, but in the 1800s it experienced three military defeats, a devastating rebellion, and increasing poverty for millions of Chinese. In response, the imperial government supported some reforms, but these did not foster the modernization that China needed to control foreign influence, and eventually revolutionary movements overthrew the imperial system. Like the Chinese, the Japanese also faced challenges, even before Western ships forced the nation open in the 1850s. Soon the old system fell, and Japan's new leaders began an all-out program of modernization to prevent Western domination. By 1900 the Japanese had heavy industry, a modern military, and a comprehensive educational system; they also sought their own resources and markets abroad and were soon colonizing their neighbor, Korea. Although historically linked more closely to Europe than to Asia, Russia, perched on the borders of Europe, East Asia, and the Islamic Middle

e Visit the website and eBook for additional study materials and interactive tools:
www.cengage.com/history/lockard/globalsocnet2e

627

EAST ASIA AND THE RUSSIAN EMPIRE FACE NEW CHALLENGES, 1750–1914

Visual Connection Archive

Treaty Between Japan and China
After an industrializing Japan defeated a declining China in a war over Japanese encroachments in Korea (1894–1895), diplomats from both nations met to negoti-ate a peace treaty. This painting shows the Chinese and Japanese representa-tives, easily identified by their different clothing styles, discussing the terms.

Karnow, Stanley. *In Our Image: America's Empire in the Philippines.* New York: Ballantine, 1989. A readable survey.

Larkin, John. *Sugar and the Origins of Modern Philippine Society.* Berkeley: University of California Press, 1993. Study of the sugar industry's impact on the colonial Philippines.

Marr, David G. *Vietnamese Anticolonialism, 1885–1925.* Berkeley: University of California Press, 1971. A scholarly examination of the resistance to French colonization.

Metcalf, Thomas R. *Imperial Connections: India in the Indian Ocean Arena, 1860–1920.* Berkeley: University of California Press, 2007. Studies the crucial role of Indians in the British Empire.

Owen, Norman G., et al. *The Emergence of Modern Southeast Asia: A New History.* Honolulu: University of Hawaii Press, 2005. The best survey, comprehensive and readable.

Tandon, Prakash. *Punjabi Century, 1857–1947.* Berkeley: University of California Press, 1968. A personal view of a century of change.

Tarling, Nicholas, ed. *The Cambridge History of Southeast Asia*, vol. 2. New York: Cambridge University Press, 1992. Contains interpretive essays on varied topics by major scholars.

Wyatt, David K. *Thailand: A Short History*, 2nd ed. New Haven: Yale University Press, 2003. The best general survey.

The Americans displaced the Spanish as the colonial power in the Philippines after suppressing a nationalist revolution. While they maintained the cash crop economic system, they also fostered some political participation. Only Siam, led by perceptive kings, avoided colonization. Colonialism reshaped social patterns, undermining the economic activities of women, fostering urbanization, and promoting the immigration of Chinese, who later became the commercial class. Southeast Asians responded by forming creative schools and unique cultural activities.

KEY TERMS

Marathas	**Westernization**	**Theosophy**	**plural society**
Black Hole of Calcutta	**Orientalism**	**cultivation system**	**can vuong**
sepoys	**zamindars**		

EBOOK AND WEBSITE RESOURCES

e INTERACTIVE MAPS
Map 22.1 The Growth of British India, 1750–1860
Map 22.2 The Colonization of Southeast Asia

LINKS

Asian Studies (http://coombs.anu.edu.au/ WWWVLAsianStudies.html). A vast Australian metasite.
East and Southeast Asia: An Annotated Directory of Internet Resources (http://newton.uor.edu/ Departments&Programs/AsianStudies-Dept/general .html). This site offers many links.
Internet Indian History Sourcebook (http://www .fordham.edu/halsall/india/indiasbook.html). An invaluable collection.

Virtual Library: South Asia (http://www.columbia.edu/ cu/libraries/indiv/area/sarai/). A major site on India.
WWW Southeast Asia Guide (http://www.library.wisc .edu/guides/SEAsia/). An easy-to-use site.

Plus flashcards, practice quizzes, and more. Go to: www.cengage.com/history/lockard/globalsocnet2e.

SUGGESTED READING

Bayly, C. A. *Indian Society and the Making of the British Empire.* New York: Cambridge University Press, 1988. A masterly scholarly synthesis of research on the Company era.

Bayly, Susan. *Caste, Society and Politics in India from the Eighteenth Century to the Modern Age.* New York: Cambridge University Press, 1999. A major scholarly study.

Bose, Sugata. *A Hundred Horizons: The Indian Ocean in the Age of Global Empire.* Cambridge: Harvard University Press, 2006. Examines British India's connections to the wider world.

Bose, Sugata, and Ayesha Jalal. *Modern South Asia: History, Culture, Political Economy,* 2nd ed. New York: Routledge, 2004. A recent brief survey text.

Brown, Ian. *Economic History in South-East Asia, c. 1830–1980.* Kuala Lumpur: Oxford University Press, 1997. A detailed but readable scholarly assessment.

Brown, Judith M. *Modern India: The Origins of an Asian Democracy,* 2nd ed. New York: Oxford University Press, 1994. A detailed study of India since 1750, especially strong on politics.

Crossette, Barbara. *The Great Hill Stations of Asia.* New York: Basic Books, 1999. Entertaining study of Western colonialism through hill towns.

Forbes, Geraldine. *Women in Modern India,* rev. ed. New York: Cambridge University Press, 1999. A scholarly study since 1750.

women in order to give them more options in life. Eventually Kartini bowed to her parents' demands and entered an arranged marriage with a man she scarcely knew who already had two other wives, but who agreed to support her plan to open a school for girls. Kartini sent a memorandum to the colonial government entitled "Educate the Javanese," and then, at twenty, she opened Indonesia's first girls' school, which combined Javanese and Western values.

Kartini wrote a series of fascinating letters to Dutch friends in Java and Holland that reveal much about her thinking. Her correspondents were often nonconformist career women with socialist leanings, known in Holland as "modern girls," who encouraged Kartini's educational plans and thirst for knowledge. In 1899 she told a pen-friend, the radical feminist Stella Zeehandelaar: "I have been longing to make the acquaintance of a 'modern girl,' that proud independent girl who has all my sympathy." Mixing her Dutch friends' ideas with her own, Kartini's letters asserted women's right to education and freedom from polygamy and child marriage.

Like European feminists, in her letters Kartini criticized the constraints of marriage, family, and society. She had serious doubts about the advantages of marriage in her own society: "But we must marry, must, must. Not to marry is the greatest sin which the Muslim women can commit. And marriage among us? Miserable is too feeble an expression for it. How can it be otherwise, when the laws have made everything for the man and nothing for the woman. When law and convention both are for the man; when everything is allowed to him." She thought women repressed: "The ideal Javanese girl is silent and expressionless as a wooden doll, speaking only when it is necessary." She also condemned religious prejudice, whether by Muslims or Christians: "We feel that the kernel of all religion is right living, and that all religion is good and

beautiful. But, o ye peoples, what have you made of it?" But she had hope for change: "I glow with enthusiasm toward the new time which has come. My thoughts and sympathies are with my sisters who are struggling forward in the distant West."

Kartini died in childbirth at age twenty-five. Her Dutch friends, such as Zeehandelaar, later published Kartini's letters, ensuring her fame. Thanks partly to the royalties from her published letters, the schools Kartini founded multiplied after her death, educating thousands of Indonesian girls in the twentieth century. But Kartini left a controversial legacy for Indonesians. Her schools filled a great need, for which many Indonesians are grateful, and although Kartini had criticized Javanese culture and admired Western ideals, in 1964 the Indonesian president named her a national heroine and honored her as the nation's *ibu*, or "mother." But conservatives accused her of abandoning Islam and Javanese culture. Because of her close ties to Dutch friends, her detractors labeled Kartini an apologist for colonialism, and some contrasted her unfavorably to Rahma El-Yunusiah, a devout Muslim woman from Sumatra who taught Arabic and the Quran and who refused any contact with the Dutch. Nonetheless, today Kartini is honored as a proponent of Indonesian women's rights and a precursor of Indonesian nationalist sentiment.

THINKING ABOUT THE PROFILE

1. What does Kartini's life tell us about the challenges that faced Javanese women of her day?
2. How do Kartini's thoughts reflect the meeting of East and West?

Note: Quotations from Raden Adjeng Kartini, *Letters of a Javanese Princess*, edited with an introduction by Hildred Geertz (New York: W. W. Norton, 1964), 31, 34, 42, 45, 73.

Chapter Summary

Change was more obvious than continuity in South and Southeast Asia. Gradually Britain extended its control over the Indian subcontinent, using military force but also outmaneuvering rivals, forging alliances, and intimidating small states into accepting British domination. By 1850 the British East India Company controlled all of India directly or indirectly. The Company introduced policies to reshape India's economy and culture, including a Westernizing education system. The rebellion of 1857, suppressed with great difficulty, shocked the British into replacing the Company with colonial government rule. The new British Raj allowed little Indian participation in government. British policies transformed the Indian economy by favoring landlords at the expense of peasants and by suffocating traditional industries to benefit British manufactures. Population growth and poverty fostered emigration. The encounter with the West also prompted Indian thinkers to reassess their cultural traditions. Some Indians adopted Western influences, some rejected them, and others tried to mix East and West. Finally, unpopular British policies generated a nationalist movement that challenged British rule.

The European powers finished colonizing Southeast Asia. Using military force or threats, the Dutch became dominant throughout the Indonesian archipelago, reaping its wealth in part by compelling Javanese to grow cash crops. Britain gained control of Burma through warfare but needed less force in Malaya, which proved profitable as a source of minerals and cash crops. Against strong resistance the French occupied Vietnam, exploiting and reshaping rural Vietnamese society.

As Chinese, Indian, and sometimes Arab men increasingly took over small-scale trade in towns, many women also lost their role in the local marketplace and thus their status as income earners for the family. The expansion of textile imports also affected women's status. Women had previously dominated weaving, spinning, and dyeing. Although weaving was hard work, even drudgery, women could do it at home with friends and relatives while caring for children. But after 1850, as inexpensive factory-made textiles came from Europe, people stopped buying local handwoven cloth, slowly forcing women out of the textile business. A Javanese noblewoman wrote in a 1909 essay that "little by little [women] feel that their life is no longer of such value, considered by men only as ornaments as they are no longer contributing to the household coffers."[23] Women had to find other income sources, which often took them away from the home and children.

Some women joined movements to assert their rights, as European feminist movements had some influence in Southeast Asia in the late nineteenth and early twentieth centuries. For example, Siamese feminists opposed polygamy and supported girls' education. Today many Indonesians honor an inspirational Javanese woman, Raden Adjeng Kartini, as a heroine whose writings and life influenced the rise of Indonesian feminism and nationalism (see Profile: Kartini, Indonesian Feminist and Teacher). Although she died young, the schools for girls she founded in 1900 multiplied. Like Kartini, other women struggled to cope with the changing world.

Southeast Asia already had large cities, but Western rule encouraged more rapid urbanization. Cities such as Manila, Jakarta, Rangoon (today known as Yangon), Singapore, Kuala Lumpur, and Saigon (today Ho Chi Minh City) grew as colonial capitals. Cities attracted immigrants, such as the Chinese, and migrants from nearby districts. Most colonial towns and cities offered a diverse assortment of food stalls and restaurants, schools that catered to different ethnic groups, as well as Muslim mosques, Buddhist, Hindu, and Chinese temples, and Christian churches. While most people remained attached to their own culture, some descendants of Chinese and Indian immigrants assimilated into the surrounding culture; friendships and even marriages crossed ethnic lines. For example, much of Thailand's political and economic leadership has some mix of Chinese and Siamese ancestry.

Urbanization

Cultural Change

Colonial governments differed in educating people and fostering indigenous cultures. Most colonies left education to the Christian missions. Some Vietnamese, Indonesians, and Chinese became Christian, and hill peoples frequently did so, but few Theravada Buddhists or Muslims abandoned their faiths. A few colonies set up government schools. The U.S.-ruled Philippines had the best record, enrolling 75 percent of children in elementary schools. Independent Siam also opened public schools that made education widely available for both boys and girls. At the other extreme, French Indochina spent little public money on schools. Some communities developed alternatives to Western education. Buddhist and Muslim groups expanded their schools and taught from a non-Western perspective, while other schools mixed Eastern and Western ideas. Schools opened by a mystical Javanese religious organization provided an alternative to both Islamic and Christian instruction, emphasizing Indonesian arts such as music and dance but also Western ideas such as expressing one's own ideas and social equality.

Religion and Education

Southeast Asians also developed new cultural forms. On Java, musicians mixed European string instruments with the rhythms of the largely percussion Javanese gamelan orchestra to create a romantic new popular music, *kronchong*. In the 1800s the sentimental songs were particularly favored by Indonesian sailors and soldiers, as well as by disreputable young men, known as kronchong crocodiles, who dressed flamboyantly, gambled, and drank heavily. By the early 1900s kronchong became respectable, and it was eventually embraced by Indonesian nationalists as an artistic weapon against the Dutch, offering songs on topical and nationalist themes.

New Cultural Forms

The cultural exchange was not one-way. Western composers who observed performances by Javanese and Balinese gamelan orchestras incorporated gamelan influences into their music. In most colonies, a modern literature also developed that reflected alienation from colonialism and an awareness of rapid change. But since criticism of the colonial regime was suppressed, authors made their points indirectly to avoid censorship or arrest. Vietnamese writers used historical themes or critiques of Vietnamese society to discuss contemporary conditions, and Indonesian writers explored characters experiencing despair and disorientation because of the colonial system.

KARTINI, INDONESIAN FEMINIST AND TEACHER

The inspirational social activist and teacher Raden Adjeng Kartini **(RAH-den AH-jeng KAR-teen-ee)** (1879–1905), usually known to Indonesians simply as Kartini, represented a feminist consciousness new to Indonesia. In her life, she shared the problems and faced the prejudices Indonesian women encountered in the colonial system and their own societies. The daughter of a Javanese aristocrat, she chafed against the confined lives of her social class, which expected young women to obey men, especially their fathers, without question, stay home, and train for marriage. However, Kartini's parents were unusually liberal, subscribing to Dutch-language newspapers and hiring Dutch tutors for their sons and daughters. Kartini's progressive father sent her and her siblings to a Dutch-language primary school. Her brothers later moved on to a Dutch-language high school, and one even attended a university in Holland. A good student, Kartini also keenly wanted to complete high school and then study in Holland, but attending high school or a Dutch university would have required her to leave home. Since Javanese customs discouraged aristocratic women from traveling without their families, her father would not permit it. In conformity with aristocratic custom, at puberty Kartini was restricted to the family's house and ordered to prepare herself for an arranged marriage by learning domestic skills.

But Kartini had larger ambitions. From her experience in Dutch-language school and friendships with Dutch women, she drew a model of personal freedom contrary to that of her Javanese society, including a commitment to educate Javanese

Raden Adjeng Kartini   This painting, completed decades after Kartini's death, honors the young Javanese woman who founded girls' schools.

Courtesy, Photo Gallery, Indonesian Embassy, London

SECTION SUMMARY

- Colonized Southeast Asian peoples were allowed very little autonomy and were frequently combined into countries with little ethnic or cultural unity.

- Economic life in colonies was reshaped to serve Western nations' needs for raw materials, especially rubber, and for markets for their goods, and in many cases it led to destruction of the natural environment and the impoverishment of local people.

- Millions of Chinese immigrated to Southeast Asia, where many prospered as merchants and retailers, while Indians came to work in Malayan rubber plantations.

- Economic changes due to colonization forced women to grow food for their families and eliminated the market for their handmade textiles, thus taking away their traditional ability to earn an income.

- Education in colonies included both Western-style and more traditional schools, and cultural and artistic interchange between Westerners and colonized peoples produced new cultural forms, such as kronchong music.

riality, or freedom from local laws. The Chinese were also forced to pay Britain the war costs. Soon other Western countries signed treaties with China that gave them the same rights as the British. Each successive treaty expanded foreign privileges. The Opium War became to the Chinese a permanent symbol of Western imperialism.

The Treaty System and Rebellion

The debacle of the Opium War soon led to other wars, a treaty system that opened China to the West, and rebellions. The British remained dissatisfied with the amount of trade, and the Chinese sought to evade their obligations, ensuring that another conflict would develop. China had imprisoned some Chinese sailors for suspected piracy aboard a Chinese ship, *The Arrow*, registered in Hong Kong, giving Britain a pretext to attack China and generating the Arrow War (1856–1860). France also entered the war. China was again defeated and forced to sign a new unequal treaty that opened more coastal and interior ports to Western traders, established foreign embassies in Beijing, and permitted Christian missionaries to enter the Chinese interior. Again forced to pay the war costs, China fell deeper into debt. It was also forced to give up its claim to Vietnam, a longtime vassal state being colonized by France, and to acquiesce in the Russian takeover of eastern Siberia.

Unequal Treaties

By restricting control of China's economy and power to make rules for Western residents, the treaty system deprived China of some of its autonomy. It also led to **international settlements**, zones in major Chinese port cities, such as Guangzhou and Shanghai, that were set aside for foreigners and in which most Chinese were not allowed. For example, a small island on the riverfront adjacent to downtown Guangzhou, and accessible only by a footbridge, became the home of Western merchants, officials, and missionaries. It boasted mansions, warehouses, clubs, and churches built by and serving the largely British, American, and French population. Chinese were clearly unwelcome except as servants and businessmen.

international settlements Special zones in major Chinese cities set aside for foreigners, where most Chinese were not allowed; arose as a result of China's defeat in the Opium and Arrow Wars.

The Opium and Arrow Wars and the treaty system forced the Chinese to debate how best to respond to the new dangers. Some Chinese officials understood the need for China to learn from the West, to examine Western books, build modern ships and guns, and study science, mathematics, and foreign languages. These views influenced the provincial official and reformer Zeng Guofan **(zung gwoh-FAN)** (1811–1872), who recommended making modern weapons and steamships. But, failing to see the magnitude of the challenges, few mandarins showed interest, one conservative rejecting Western knowledge as based largely on earlier Chinese discoveries.

China's Challenges

While scholars debated, China's problems multiplied, especially in the coastal provinces. To pay for the wars, the government had to raise taxes, causing many peasants to lose their land, and some turned to begging or banditry. Natural disasters also demoralized the country. Between 1800 and 1850 the Yellow River flooded twenty times and then changed course, wiping out hundreds of towns and villages. Western cultural influence increased, as Christian missionaries from the United States and Britain opened most of China's Western-type schools and hospitals, providing educational and health benefits to those Chinese who had access to them. By the 1920s there were 2,500 American missionaries in China and thirteen American-operated colleges. However, Christian missionaries, who often lived well and were protected by Western military power, challenged Chinese religions and provoked negative opinions. Western residents, often ethnocentric and seeing themselves as representing a superior Western civilization, tended to view the Chinese as depraved heathens and mocked their culture. Chinese generally distrusted the several hundred thousand Chinese who became Christian.

Deteriorating conditions eventually generated the Taiping Rebellion (1850–1864), the most critical of several midcentury upheavals against the Qing (see Map 23.1). Guangdong **(GWAHNG-dong)** province, on the southeast coast, experienced particularly severe social and economic dislocations that increased popular unrest. Many peasant families had no food surplus and were reduced to eating the chaff of the wheat. The rebellion was fueled by economic insecurity, famine, loss of faith in government, and a desire for social change. The leader, Hong Xiuquan **(hoong shee-OH-chew-an)** (1813–1864), who had failed to pass the civil service examinations and had also studied with Christian missionaries, believed that God had appointed him the new Son of Heaven to exterminate evil. Impressed by Western military power but also proudly Chinese, Hong preached a doctrine blending Christianity and Chinese thought, a mixing of local and Western ideas that was typical in Asia and Africa as a response to Western disruption.

Taiping Rebellion

Hong promoted a new form of government, equal distribution of goods, communal property, and equality between men and women. The puritanical Hong also prohibited opium use, polygamy, footbinding, prostitution, concubinage, and arranged marriages. He established a sect, the

Taipings (Heavenly Kingdom of Great Peace), that rejected Confucian traditions and envisioned a God-oriented utopia where all people would be equal. Many of the Taiping men and women were, like Hong himself, Hakkas, a dialect group in south China whose assertive women never bound their feet. Hong organized an army and in 1850 launched a rebellion, invoking Chinese nationalism: "We raise the army of righteousness to liberate the masses for the sake of China."[7] Soon he had attracted millions of supporters from among the poor and disaffected.

Taiping Defeat

Taiping armies conquered large parts of central and southern China, but the Taipings suffered from leadership conflicts, and their hostility to traditional Chinese culture cost them popular support. Conservative Confucians disliked the Taipings' espousal of women's rights, which threatened the patriarchal family system, and intellectuals accused them of opening China to Westernization. Thus most of the educated elite rallied to the Qing and organized provincial armies to oppose the Taipings. Westerners often sympathized with the progressive Taiping social message but knew that a weak Manchu government meant more Western ability to continue exploiting China. Hence, various Western nations aided the Qing with money, arms, mercenary soldiers, and military advisers. The Taipings were defeated, and the process of dynastic renewal was aborted. The conflict left

Map 23.1   Conflicts in Qing China, 1839–1870

During the mid-1800s Qing China experienced repeated unrest, including several major rebellions. The largest and most destructive, the Taiping Rebellion, engulfed a large part of southern and central China between 1850 and 1864.

Interactive Map

China in shambles, with provinces devastated and 20 million Chinese killed. An American missionary described the destruction: "Ruined cities, desolated towns and heaps of rubble still mark their path. The hum of busy populations had ceased and weeds and jungle cover the land."[8] The Qing were now deeper in debt to the West and compelled to adopt even more conciliatory attitudes.

Economic Change and Emigration

China's encounters with the West generated several economic changes. The extension of Western businesses into the interior stimulated the growth of the Chinese merchant class and small-scale Chinese-owned industries, such as match factories and flour mills, but the merchants disliked Western economic domination and the weak Qing government. Gradually a new working class formed that labored in mines, factories, railways, and docks. The gulf between peasants in the interior and the merchants and workers in the coastal cities was vast. The unequal treaties enabled Western economic penetration into China, and China's economy became increasingly geared to Western needs. Westerners often ran Qing government agencies, banks, railroads, factories, and mines and guarded them with Western police. By 1920 foreign companies controlled most of China's iron ore, coal, railroads, and steamships, and Western businessmen became inspired by the notion of the vast China market. One U.S. firm launched an advertising campaign to put a cigarette in the mouth of every Chinese man, woman, and child. Finally, women were harmed by imported British textiles, which frequently displaced Chinese women from textile production. Although women continued to weave, they earned lower incomes than before.

Some scholars view Western economic imperialism as a spur to the growth of China's domestic economy. Others argue that Western competition ruined Chinese industries such as cotton spinning and iron and steel production, hurting China's ability to compete with the West. Western businesses succeeded because they had greater capital and the support of Western governments and military power. China's traditional exports also declined because of competition with other Asian countries. By 1900 India and Sri Lanka had become the world's largest producers of tea and Japan the largest producer of silk. The Qing, already deeply in debt, had little money left for building China's economic institutions.

From the 1840s through the 1920s, deteriorating economic, social, and political conditions in hard-hit coastal provinces, combined with natural disasters, prompted millions of Chinese to

Western Economic Influence

Chinese Emigration

Courtesy, Daniel Wolf Collection, NY

Rattan Factory in Guangzhou This photo, taken around 1875, shows Chinese men and women workers, mostly of peasant background, in a factory making rattan, along with the factory's European owners.

emigrate, usually to places where Western colonialism and capitalism were opening new economic opportunities. Several hundred thousand people a year left from southern ports, usually headed for Southeast Asia but, in many cases, bound for Pacific islands such as Hawaii and Tahiti or for Australia, Peru, Cuba, North America, and South Africa (see Chapters 20 and 22). The Chinese emigrants who joined or opened businesses in these new countries formed the basis for local middle-class Chinese communities. But many left China as part of the notorious "coolie trade." Under this labor system, desperate Chinese were recruited or coerced to become indentured workers in faraway places, signing contracts that required them to labor for years in harsh conditions on plantations or in mines or to build railroads.

Chinese Diaspora

As a result of this emigration, the societies where Chinese settled, especially in Southeast Asia, became more closely connected to China through economic and social networks than ever before. Chinese businesses overseas often had branches in China, and families in China maintained ties to family members abroad. While Chinese emigrants often returned to their native villages with wealth earned abroad, others never earned enough money to return to China, and many settled permanently abroad. The emigrants and their descendants, while often sustaining Chinese culture and language, often mixed Chinese and local customs. Today some 30 million people of Chinese ancestry live outside of China, the large majority in Southeast Asia. Some finance businesses, industries, and educational institutions in China.

SECTION SUMMARY

- In the eighteenth century, Qing China was still thriving on the strength of its agriculture, trade, and manufacturing, but its rapidly growing population began to intensify internal problems such as poverty and corruption.

- In the nineteenth century, China faced increasing problems as well as pressure from Westerners for greater trade opportunities, but the Qing refused to allow an open trading system, thus creating a severe trade imbalance between the West and the East.

- To solve this imbalance, the British began smuggling opium into China, and when China resisted the British defeated China in the Opium War and forced the Chinese to agree to highly unfavorable terms that allowed the British to trade in China.

- After another war, China was forced to set aside special areas exclusively for Westerners, called international settlements, and to also allow Christian missionaries into the country.

- Economic insecurity, famine, and Western interference eventually led to the Taiping Rebellion, a widespread and devastating revolt that was ultimately put down by the Qing with help from Western powers.

- China's economy was increasingly penetrated and transformed by Western powers, and millions of Chinese emigrated throughout the world, some to be indentured workers and others to go into business.

FROM IMPERIAL TO REPUBLICAN CHINA

> Why did Chinese efforts at modernization fail?

The rebellions, government stagnation, poverty, and growing Western demands brought about a crisis for the Qing. Some Chinese still concluded that China should reaffirm its traditional ways and reject the West. But just as for centuries China had absorbed invaders to survive, a growing number of reformers wanted to adapt useful Western technologies to Chinese ways. As challenges and setbacks mounted, some gave up on reform and organized revolutionary movements. Eventually revolutionaries overthrew the imperial system, but these developments did not solve China's problems.

Chinese Debates and New Challenges

Conservatives and Liberals

China's elite divided over how much China should modernize its society. The conservatives, who dominated the bureaucracy, advised that China hold fast to Confucian traditions. Believing China could learn nothing from Westerners, they opposed railroads, underground mines, and other innovations because these disrupted the harmony between humanity and nature and put boatmen and cart drivers out of work. One conservative wrote that it was "better to see the nation die than its way of life change."[9] Conservatives believed that new technologies inevitably under-

mined social, economic, and even political values. Liberals, believing China had to adopt certain Western ideas to survive, sponsored impressive government innovations. They streamlined central and regional governments, set up a foreign ministry, formed a college to train diplomats, and sent some students to schools in the West, especially to the United States. A few argued that Confucius favored democracy and gender equality. Few liberals, however, wanted radical transformation, preferring to simply graft on some technological innovations. To most reformers, Western ideas such as political democracy and nationalism were too foreign to easily adapt to China's family-centered society. As one noted, "China should acquire the West's superiority in arms and machinery, but retain China's superiority in Confucian virtue."[10]

Meanwhile, reformers in the provinces, calling themselves "self strengtheners," aimed to strengthen China by building arsenals and shipyards. By 1894 China had a better-trained army and sixty-five warships. But this was still insufficient against a fully industrialized enemy. The reforms also failed to save the Qing because the technological innovations generated new problems. The new warships required coal to make steam to power them, which meant improving coal-mining technology. Railroads had to be built to move the coal, and they in turn required telegraphs to communicate train movements. Training workers for these new enterprises required technical schools. In addition, the new working class did not fit into Confucian social categories, which divided society into scholars, peasants, artisans, and merchants. China also employed Western advisers to help set up and run the new industries and government departments. But the new enterprises were often poorly run. The innovations were also expensive, further complicating the economic problems of a Chinese government financing a growing debt to Western nations and banks.

China's problems grew less manageable. China was too large, overpopulated, and saddled with a poorly led, bureaucratic, and overly conservative government. From 1861 to 1908 the Empress Dowager Ci Xi **(zoo shee)** (1835–1908), a concubine of the old emperor who had become the regent of the new child emperor, dominated the imperial government. Forceful and intelligent, she was also covetous and irresponsible. She diverted money intended to build a modern navy to construct the magnificent Summer Palace, just outside Beijing, for her imperial retreat. China's inability to deflect the growing challenges fostered escapism among many thoughtful Chinese, expressed by a poet official: "I'll drink myself merry, Thrash out a wild song from my lute, And let the storms rage at will."[11]

Self-Strengtheners

Empress Dowager

Chinese Study Maxim Gun After the Taiping Rebellion, the Qing emperor sent two Chinese mandarins to England to examine and purchase new weapons. In this photo, they examine a Maxim gun, one of the first machine guns that gave Western nations a great military advantage.

Peter Newark's Military Pictures

China and the West

In addition to these problems, foreign economic and political pressures placed constraints on what China could accomplish, putting Chinese leaders into a siege mentality. By the late 1800s Western gunboats patrolled China's rivers, international settlements existed in the major cities, Christian missionaries challenged Chinese values, and Westerners influenced the imperial government and the economy. Some foreign powers dominated particular regions as spheres of influence, such as Britain in Guangdong and the Germans in Shandong, acquiring resources, establishing enterprises, and manipulating local governments.

gunboat diplomacy The Western countries' use of superior firepower to impose their will on local populations and governments in the nineteenth century.

The United States, Britain, France, and Germany exercised power over China through **gunboat diplomacy**, the use of superior firepower to impose a country's will on local populations and governments. Western gunboats patrolled some of China's rivers and seacoasts in the late 1800s and early 1900s, interceding to protect Western businessmen, missionaries, and diplomats whose activities generated Chinese hostility. A notorious U.S. naval force, the Yangzi Patrol, comprising shallow-draft gunboats, destroyers, and cruisers, patrolled the hundreds of miles of the Yangzi River in order "to make every American feel perfectly safe in coming to live or to transact business, until such time as the Chinese themselves are able to afford these guarantees."[12] Sovereign Chinese rights and the people's outrage at foreign intrusion counted for little. Americans also promoted free trade, generously funded Christian missionaries, and donated to humanitarian causes such as flood relief and orphanages. Yet China never became a full Western colony such as India or Vietnam, perhaps because too many foreign powers were involved. The United States discouraged full colonization by promoting an "Open Door" policy that allowed equal access by all the foreign powers to China's vast markets and resources. The Open Door enabled the industrialized nations to avoid conflict and acquire wealth without the high political and military costs of conquering and governing China.

Wars, Reforms, and Nationalism

New Conflicts

The growing foreign challenge soon included rapidly industrializing Japan. In search of resources and markets, in the 1890s Japan began intervening in Korea, long a vassal state of China. The Koreans pleaded for help from China, and the resulting Sino-Japanese War (1894–1895) ended in a humiliating Chinese defeat. China was forced to pay an indemnity to Japan and to recognize Korean independence, and in 1910 Korea became a Japanese colony. The Qing were also forced to cede the large island of Taiwan, populated largely by Chinese, to Japan. The Manchus had already lost influence over other tributary states, such as Vietnam (to France) and Burma (to Britain). The defeat by Japan proved a blow to Chinese pride and to the credibility of the Qing rulers.

These crises brought a group of progressive reformers to the attention of the young Manchu emperor, Guangxu, and in 1898 he called for dramatic changes, later known as the 100 Days of Reform, including a crash program of economic modernization. But the Empress Dowager Xi Ci and her conservative allies blocked the proposals, arrested the reformers, placed the emperor under house arrest, promoted an antiforeign atmosphere, and encouraged the Chinese to organize antiforeign militias. The ensuing tensions led to the Boxer Rebellion, a popular movement in 1900 that aimed to drive the foreigners out of China but resulted in an even stronger Western presence. The Qing strongly backed the Boxers ("Righteous Harmony Fists"), an anti-Western, anti-Christian secret society comprising mostly poor peasants. While the Boxers attacked foreigners in north China, occupied Beijing, and besieged the foreign embassies, the Qing declared war on the foreign powers. In response, the British, Americans, and French organized an international force that routed the Boxers, occupied Beijing, and forced the Qing to pay another huge indemnity and to permit foreign military forces to stay in China. The Europeans talked openly of dismantling China, and the Russians used the rebellion as an excuse to occupy Manchuria.

Reformist Efforts

The string of defeats generated final frantic efforts at reform and modernization, setting the stage for more dramatic transitions. Fearing China might soon be divided into colonies, the chastened Manchus now looked to Japan for models. They abolished the 2,000-year-old Confucian examination system, set up modern, Western-style schools, and sent 10,000 students to Japan. But the 57,000 state schools enrolled only a fraction of China's school-age children. The Qing also allocated more money to the military and strengthened provincial governments.

Reformist ideas also sparked movements among women. Some women studying in Japan formed the Encompassing Love Society, with the goal of making Chinese women full participants in society. Other women worked to raise female literacy and expand economic opportunities. The feminist Qin Jin (chin jin) (1877–1907) left her arranged marriage for study in Japan and then started a women's magazine and pursued political activity. Later she was executed as a revolutionary. She wrote in a poem, "Our women's world is sunk so deep, who can help us? Unbinding my feet I clear out a thousand years of poison."[13] She expressed the hope that one day China would see free women "blooming like fields of flowers."

Liberals who had criticized the Qing reformers for going too slowly now became more influential. Many reformers had read and even translated European literature and scholarship and were deeply impressed by Japan's modernization. The leading liberal reformer, Liang Qichao (Li-ANG chi-CHAO) (1871–1929), a scholar and journalist, promoted a modernization that blended Confucian values and Western learning. He also believed China should industrialize, form a constitutional government, and focus on the idea of nation instead of culture. Liang's colleague, Kang Youwei (KANG yoo-WAY) (1858–1928), envisioned a world government, the end of nationalist strife and gender discrimination, and a welfare state. He also began a movement against footbinding, the long-time Chinese practice that severely hampered women; as a song passed among illiterate women put it, "Your body is so heavy a burden for your feet that you fear you may stumble in the wind."[14]

For some Chinese inspired by nationalism, most importantly Sun Zhong Shan, better known as Sun Yat-Sen (soon yot-SEN), the fiasco of the Boxer Rebellion showed the futility of trying to change China by reform from above and prompted them to organize a revolution from below. Sun (1866–1925) mixed tradition and modernity. Unlike the liberal reformers such as Liang and Kang, Sun did not come from an upper-class mandarin background and had no commitment to the traditional system. He identified with the poor and downtrodden. Born near Guangzhou to a peasant family that had supported the Taipings, Sun moved to Hawaii at age thirteen to join an elder brother. There he studied in an Anglican high school and became a semi-Christian. He then received a medical degree in British-ruled Hong Kong. He began dressing in Western clothes and visited England, where he learned that Westerners often criticized their own systems.

Sun Yat-Sen and Nationalism

Convinced that the Qing system was hopeless, Sun decided to devote his life to politics and became the chief architect of the Chinese Revolution. In 1895 he founded a secret society dedicated to replacing the imperial system with a Western-style republic, setting up branches in China, Japan, and Hawaii (see Witness to the Past: Planning a Revolutionary New China). Facing arrest in China for treason, Sun traveled extensively, recruiting support among Chinese merchants in Southeast Asia, North America, and the treaty ports; Chinese students in Japan; and sympathetic military officers. Sun and his followers thought of themselves as nationalists, more interested in China as a nation than as a culture.

Sun also began to develop his program, which he termed the "Three Principles of the People." The first principle, nationalism, involved overthrowing the Manchus, restoring ethnic Chinese to power, and reclaiming China's historical greatness. His second principle, republicanism, proposed a constitutional democracy with an elected representative government rather than the constitutional monarchy sought by the liberal reformers. The third principle, people's livelihood, envisioned an equitable economic status for all. Sun was vague on the details but favored partial state control of the economy and the reshaping of China into a modern, wealthy, powerful nation. Sun did not necessarily want to imitate Europe and the United States, but eventually the day would come, he hoped, when the Chinese could look over their shoulder and find the West lagging far behind.

Sun's Program

Chinese Revolution and Republic

Sun was traveling in the United States raising money for his cause when, on October 10, 1911, some of his followers began the uprising. Soldiers in the Yangzi River city of Wuhan (WOO-HAHN) mutinied and were soon joined by sympathizers in other cities. Within two months the revolutionary soldiers controlled provinces in central and southern China. As Qing authority quickly crumbled outside the north, Sun returned to China for the first time in sixteen years. The revolution had wide popular support, and Sun's nationalist message spread rapidly, especially among students, military officers, and Chinese in the treaty ports. Sun now reorganized his anti-Manchu secret society into a political party, the Guomindang (gwo-min-dong) (Chinese Nationalist Party), which gathered together varied nationalists and liberal reformers. However, Sun was not a forceful leader, and the revolutionaries could agree only on opposing the Manchus. Meanwhile, from Beijing, the Manchus asked an ambitious general, Yuan Shikai (yoo-AHN shee-KAI) (1859–1916), to deal with the revolutionaries. In control of a large army, Yuan decided to replace the dynasty with his own rule by playing the Manchus off against the revolutionaries.

Outbreak of Revolution

Two centers of power now existed. While General Yuan held the dominant position in the north and influence over the Qing leaders, the revolutionaries, who controlled the Yangzi Valley and parts of south China, made plans to establish a provisional government. Sun sought a compromise to save China from civil war, offering to make Yuan president if Yuan arranged for the abdication of

Planning a Revolutionary New China

In 1905 various radical Chinese groups met in Japan and merged into one revolutionary organization, the *Tongmen Hui* (Chinese Alliance Association), led by Sun Yat-Sen, then based in Tokyo. Most of the members were drawn from among the 10,000 Chinese students enrolled in Japanese universities. Unhappy with the Qing government and impressed by modernizing Japan, they sought to change China through revolution. In their founding proclamation, which was influenced by Western thought, they set out their agenda, visionary but vague, for a three-stage passage from military to constitutional government and a more equitable society.

Since the beginning of China as a nation, we Chinese have governed our own country despite occasional interruptions. When China was occasionally occupied by a foreign race, our ancestors could always . . . drive these foreigners out . . . and preserve China for future generations. . . . There is a difference, however, between our revolution and the revolutions of our ancestors. The purpose of past revolutions . . . was to restore China to the Chinese, and nothing else. We, on the other hand, strive not only to expel the ruling aliens [Manchus] . . . but also to change basically the political and economic structure of our country. . . . The revolutions of yesterday were revolutions by and for the heroes; our revolution, on the other hand, is a revolution by and for the people. . . . everyone who believes in the principles of liberty, equality, and fraternity has an obligation to participate in it. . . .

At this juncture we wish to express candidly and fully how to make our revolution today and how to govern the country tomorrow.

1. Expulsion of the Manchus from China. . . . We shall quickly overthrow the Manchu government so as to restore the sovereignty of China to the Chinese.
2. Restoration of China to the Chinese. China belongs to the Chinese who have the right to govern themselves. . . .

3. Establishment of a Republic. Since one of the principles of our revolution is equality, we intend to establish a republic. . . . all citizens will have the right to participate in the government, the president of the republic will be elected by the people, and the parliament will have deputies elected by and responsible to their respective constituencies. . . .
4. Equalization of land ownership. The social and economic structure of China must be so reconstructed that the fruits of labor will be shared by all Chinese on an equal basis. . . .

To attain the four goals . . . , we propose a procedure of three stages. The first . . . is that of military rule . . . [in which] the Military Government, in cooperation with the people, will eradicate all the abuses of the past; with the arrival of the second stage the Military Government will hand over local administration to the people while reserving for itself the right of jurisdiction over all matters that concern the nation as a whole; during the . . . final stage the Military Government will cease to exist and all governmental power will be invested in organs as prescribed in a national constitution. This orderly procedure is necessary because our people need time to acquaint themselves with the idea of liberty and equality . . . , the basis on which the republic of China rests. . . . On . . . restoring China to her own people, we urge everyone to step forward and to do the best he can. . . . Whatever our station in society is, rich or poor, we are all equal in our determination to safeguard the security of China as a nation and to preserve the Chinese people.

THINKING ABOUT THE READING

1. How does the proclamation use Western revolutionary and nationalist ideas?
2. How will revolution build a new China?

Source: Pei-Kai Cheng and Michael Lestz with Jonathan D. Spence, eds., *The Search for Modern China: A Documentary Collection* (New York: W.W. Norton, 1999), 202–206.

Republican Government

the five-year-old Qing emperor. In February 1912 the Qing dynasty, and with it the 2,000-year-old imperial system, was ended, and a republic was established in Nanjing. Symbolizing a change of direction, the new government adopted the Western calendar. But Sun had underestimated Yuan's ambitions. Hoping to restore an autocratic system with himself at the top, Yuan moved the capital back to Beijing.

During the first year, the republic's leaders established liberal institutions, including a constitution written by Sun that provided for a two-chamber parliament and a president, and in 1913, in the first general election in China's long history, a restricted electorate chose a national assembly and provincial assemblies. A new women's suffrage movement, influenced by its counterparts in Europe, also pressed for equal rights for women. But although Sun's Guomindang won a majority of seats in the election, it lacked a consensus about the directions of change, and the republican system failed to bring stability and liberty, dashing Sun's hopes. Convinced that China needed a strong leader, Yuan had Guomindang leaders assassinated, bought off, or, in Sun's case, forced into exile. Supported by much of the army, the imperial bureaucracy, and the foreign powers, who preferred a strongman to the democratic uncertainties of Sun, Yuan soon outlawed the Guomindang, suspended parliament, and banned the women's suffrage movement. Sun and his closest followers moved to Japan, embittered and demoralized, and Yuan became increasingly autocratic and announced plans to found a new dynasty.

Yuan's plans, however, were put on hold by financial problems, constant pressure from foreign powers, and the secession of regions occupied largely by non-Chinese. Although growing nationalism made concessions to foreign powers unpopular, China was bankrupt, and Yuan was forced to borrow heavily from foreign governments to keep the country afloat. In 1911 much of Mongolia declared independence and later became allied with Russia. Tibet also expelled the Chinese administration. Although China remained neutral during World War I, Japan, allied with Britain, occupied the German sphere of influence in the Shandong peninsula. Then in 1915 Japan presented Yuan with 21 Demands, including control of Shandong, more rights in Manchuria, and the appointment of Japanese advisers to the Chinese government. The 21 Demands set off huge Chinese protests and boycotts against Japan and Yuan's inability to protect China's interests. His imperial restoration plans aborted, a humiliated Yuan died in 1916. Yuan's years in power had wrecked the republican institutions, and his submission to Japan's 21 Demands suggested that China was even weaker than before. After Yuan's death, China fell into the abyss of prolonged civil war.

New Challenges

SECTION SUMMARY

- In the debate over what China should do next, conservatives thought China should stick to its traditions, while liberals tried to modernize China, but their reforms failed to bring it to the technological and military level of the West.

- By the late 1800s, China's autonomy had been all but eliminated by gunboat diplomacy, under which Western powers ensured the safety of Westerners in China through the use of force.

- After China lost its influence over Korea in the Sino-Japanese War and the Boxer Rebellion failed to rid China of foreigners, liberals moved to modernize and Westernize Chinese education and culture.

- Sun Yat-Sen, born to Chinese peasants but educated in Western schools, formed a secret society devoted to replacing imperial rule with a Western-style republic and set out three principles: nationalism, republicanism, and economic equality.

- A revolution inspired by Sun Yat-Sen succeeded in toppling the Qing dynasty with the assistance of General Yuan Shikai.

- Yuan seized power after Sun Yat-Sen's party won the republic's first election, but he was weakened by Japanese encroachment and the loss of influence over areas such as Mongolia and Tibet, and after his death China entered a period of civil war.

THE REMAKING OF JAPAN AND KOREA

How did the Meiji government transform Japan and Korea?

In the later nineteenth century Japan met the Western challenge more successfully than China, rapidly transforming itself into a powerful industrialized nation. Despite serious internal problems, Japan possessed significant strengths that fostered success. The shoguns, military dictators from the Tokugawa family, had governed Japan since 1600 and tightly controlled Japanese society (see Chronology: Japan and Korea, 1750–1914). When the first Western ships arrived demanding to open Japan, the Japanese, largely shut off from the outside world, were just as far behind the West in military and industrial technology as other Asian societies. Yet, the ultimate Japanese response to Western intrusion was radically different from China's, allowing Japan to avoid the shackles of colonialism and become the only non-Western nation to successfully industrialize before World War II. This transition owed much to a revolution that ended Tokugawa rule and created a new government that fostered dramatic reforms that helped Japan resist the West. Across the straits, Korea had also chosen a seclusion policy, and it, too, faced severe challenges, eventually becoming a Japanese colony.

Late Tokugawa Japan

Like China, Japan faced foreign pressures that led to change, but Japan successfully met the challenge of the Western intrusion while China, failing to rally, gradually lost some of its autonomy. The differences between these two ancient neighbors help explain the different outcomes. Japan,

Japanese-Chinese Contrasts

being geographically compact and linguistically homogeneous, had a strong loyalty to the emperor as a national symbol, whereas China's vastness created difficulties, and Chinese loyalties were restricted largely to the family. While new ideas, such as Buddhism, reached China over the centuries, their assimilation was a slow process, whereas Japan had a long tradition of readily borrowing from outside. Hence, Japanese leaders could more easily decide to import and adopt new ideas, technologies, and institutions.

The two neighbors also differed in economic, political, and military systems. The Japanese merchant class was assertive and rapidly expanding its scope and power, whereas in China the government restricted commercial energies. In contrast to China's centralized empire, the Tokugawa shoguns, based in Edo (today's Tokyo), had to balance the interests of the influential leaders (daimyo) of regional landowning families while keeping the Kyoto-based emperor powerless. Although the samurai had lost their fighting edge under the long-enforced Tokugawa peace, they still held a respected position and power in society. Never having been successfully invaded, the Japanese also felt vulnerable when they encountered the well-armed Westerners. Unlike the Chinese, they prized political independence far more than cultural purity. Thus Japanese leaders, learning of Western intentions and capabilities through the Dutch traders at the southern port of Nagasaki, were far more sensitive to the Western threat than the Chinese elite.

Japanese Borrowing

Japan also benefited from an openness to new ideas. Its many schools fostered high literacy rates, and Western knowledge acquired from Dutch traders included sciences such as medicine, physics, and chemistry. One reformer argued that "Dutch [Western] learning is not perfect, but if we choose the good points, what harm could come? What is more ridiculous than to refuse to discuss its merits?"[15] Even some women, who generally suffered a low status, gained an education. For example, the poet and painter Ema Saiko (1787–1861) compared her reading with her father's: "My father deciphers Dutch books; His daughter reads Chinese poetry. Divided by a single lamp, We each follow our own course."[16] The Japanese also valued hard work, thrift, saving, and cooperation—attributes that lent themselves to modernization. Cities such as Edo and Osaka, already among the world's largest, offered a flourishing commerce and diverse entertainments. A description of a carnival in Edo in 1865 recorded the following amusements, services, and vendors: kabuki theater, archery booths, fortunetellers, wandering balladeers, massage healers, barbershops, and peddlers of chilled water, sushi (raw fish), confectionery, stuffed fritters, dumplings, fried eel livers, toys, and lanterns.

Tokugawa Arts

Vigorous Tokugawa arts produced creations that achieved renown worldwide and were prized in the West, such as ceramics, jewelry, and furniture, enriching the Dutch traders at Nagasaki. This was also a great age for painting and woodblock prints, with the two greatest artists blending Japanese and imported art styles. Katsushika Hokusai **(HO-koo-sie)** (1760–1849) produced thousands of paintings, but he was most famous for landscape prints such as the *Thirty-six Views of Mount Fuji*. He strove to improve his craft, predicting that "by ninety I will surely have penetrated the mystery of life. At one hundred, I will have attained a magnificent level and at one hundred and ten, each dot of my work will vibrate with life."[17] Ando Hiroshige **(AN-do hir-o-SHEE-gee)** (1797–1858) concentrated on Tokyo scenes and landscapes emphasizing nature (see Profile: Ando Hiroshige, Japanese Artist). The treatment of atmosphere and light in Japanese color prints influenced the French impressionist painters of the later 1800s (see Chapter 20), especially the influential Dutch artist Vincent van Gogh. Both Japanese prints and French impressionism asked the viewer to look at an everyday scene in a new way.

Growing Problems and the Opening of Japan

Tokugawa Decline

By the early 1800s many Japanese blamed the Tokugawa for growing problems: inflation, increasing taxes, social disorder, and the gradual impoverishment of the samurai. As daimyo families, burdened with heavy expenses, had to cut samurai salaries, the samurai borrowed money from merchants to support their families. In the 1830s Japan also experienced widespread famine. The growing social tensions fostered urban riots, peasant revolts, and various plots to depose the Tokugawa shogun. Japanese officials were even more concerned about the growing Western presence in the region. They knew that Russians had been active in Siberia and the North Pacific and that British ships had sailed along Japan's coast. The shogun ordered samurai to fire on foreign ships approaching the coast, and after China's defeat in the Opium War, Japan's shocked leaders encouraged the samurai to develop more effective weapons. The Japanese considered the Westerners money-grasping barbarians who did not understand the proper rules of social

ANDO HIROSHIGE, JAPANESE ARTIST

The nineteenth-century Japanese artist Ando Hiroshige (1797–1858) gained a worldwide reputation for work that reflected a distinctly Japanese vision of landscape and urban life. His work,

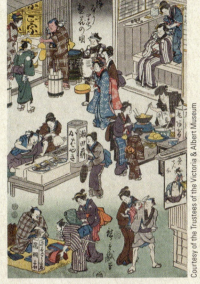

Street Stalls and Tradesmen in Joruricho This print by Hiroshige portraying the street life in Edo reveals the artist's sympathy for common people, such as the peddlers, barbers, and food-sellers shown at work and their customers.

along with that of his four-decades-older contemporary, Katsushika Hokusai, portrayed old Japan on the eve of dramatic change, a Japan of rice fields, small shops, traveling peddlers, sedan chairs, samurai warriors, and dirt roads rather than the later Japan of factories, conglomerates, railroads, and steamships. By portraying scenery and diverse urban scenes, Hiroshige and Hokusai carried printmaking far beyond the early Tokugawa tradition, which emphasized life in the restaurants, teahouses, theaters, and bordellos of the "Floating World" entertainment districts.

Hiroshige was born into a samurai family in Edo (Tokyo) in 1797. His father was a member of the fire brigade, and the family lived at the fire station. As a child, Hiroshige learned to read, write, and master martial arts, and he also developed a talent for poetry. Like other young samurai, he probably visited the Floating World to enjoy kabuki theater and to patronize courtesans. In 1809 the twelve-year-old youngster succeeded to his father's position as a fireman. Underpaid and enjoying art more than firefighting, he began studying with several famous artists. From this time on he used the name Utagawa Hiroshige, a tribute to the Utagawa school of art in which he had been trained. Dutch traders at Nagasaki had introduced Western art to Japan, and Hiroshige probably assimilated ideas from imported Dutch etchings. Inspired by mountains, rivers, rocks, and trees, the young artist gained a working knowledge of different modes and the techniques to use in depicting them. Influenced by Hokusai's pioneering work, Hiroshige began favoring rural landscapes and Edo scenes. At the age of twenty-seven he passed on his fire brigade post to his son and pursued art full time.

Although having much in common, Hokusai and Hiroshige had different outlooks. Hokusai's landscapes divided attention between the setting and the people in it, usually workers such as weavers, carpenters, and spinners. By contrast, Hiroshige subordinated everything to the setting, especially to the mood established by weather, season, time of day, and angle of view. Influenced by Chinese art, Hiroshige portrayed the insignificance of humans against the vastness of nature. His rain and snow scenes are marvels of mood, showing mastery of light and subtle harmony, mixing fact with imagination.

Hiroshige's art often reflected his personal experiences. In 1832, while accompanying an embassy of the Tokugawa shogun to the imperial court in Kyoto, Hiroshige gathered material for his famous work, *The 53 Stations of the Tokaido,* which depicts scenes of villages, inns, and lakes along the Tokaido (Eastern Sea Route) highway connecting Tokyo and Kyoto. Hiroshige immortalized the highway, which skirted the Pacific coast of Honshu Island, where mountains sweep down to the sea, and then traversed inland through majestic snowcapped mountains and past beautiful Lake Biwa. A continued stream of people—daimyo and their processions, couriers, monks, pilgrims, merchants, adventurers, entertainers—traveled the well-maintained Tokaido to and from the shogun's court. Stations with inns, restaurants, brothels, and bathhouses flourished as rest stops for the bustling traffic.

Since many Japanese had money to indulge in art, Hiroshige's later collections of prints sold thousands of copies, and he remained a very popular artist. Townspeople loved this art reflecting daily life or the worldly dreams of the merchant class. Hiroshige produced some 5,500 different prints, sold individually or in collections such as the *53 Stations of the Tokaido* and *One Hundred Views of Famous Places in Edo.* However, his personal life was often troubled. Hiroshige never prospered financially and was often pressed to finance his beloved nightly cup of rice wine. He married several times and sired several children. His eldest daughter's husband, known as Hiroshige II (1826–1869), continued Hiroshige's artistic tradition. At the age of sixty Hiroshige became a Buddhist monk, not an unusual step for aging Japanese men. He died at age sixty-two in 1858 of cholera during a great epidemic. On his deathbed, he discouraged his family from holding a lavish funeral by reciting an old verse: "When I die, Cremate me not nor bury me. Just lay me in the fields, to fill the belly of some starving dog."

Hiroshige was the last of the major Japanese print masters. Shortly after he died, Westerners opened up Japan, ending the secluded world that had nourished the woodblock prints and the artists who produced them. But Hiroshige prints continued to be traded around the world, giving foreigners their most vivid impressions of Japan. When Europeans imported the pictures in the late 1800s, they proved a revelation to artists looking for new ways to portray landscapes. Hence woodblock prints, born of isolation, became one of the first major cultural links between Japan and the outside world.

THINKING ABOUT THE PROFILE

1. How did Hokusai and Hiroshige's prints differ from earlier Japanese prints?

2. What do Hiroshige's life and art tell us about late Tokugawa Japan?

Note: Quotation from Julian Bicknell, *Hiroshige in Tokyo: The Floating World of Edo* (San Francisco: Pomegranate Artbooks, 1994), 50.

behavior. Samurai, vowing to fight to the death to resist Western invasion, put pressure on the shogun to deal firmly with the threat.

The Tokugawa responded with reforms at the national level, such as establishing a bureau to translate Western books and reducing the number of government officials to save money, but they failed to energize the system. Some provincial governments in the southwest attempted more daring changes, recruiting talented men to their administrations, emphasizing "Dutch studies," and even sponsoring industrial experiments, including an electric steam engine. Some samurai also learned how to cast better guns and iron suitable for making modern cannon.

Opening Japan

The need for change was made urgent by external threats that arose in the 1850s. The most dramatic attempt to break down Japanese seclusion came from the Americans. American ships had occasionally visited the Dutch base at Nagasaki to trade, and U.S. leaders also wanted Japan to protect shipwrecked sailors and provide fresh water and coal to ships making the long trip between California and China. In 1853 a fleet of eleven U.S. warships commanded by Commodore Matthew Perry sailed into Tokyo Bay and delivered a letter from the U.S. president, Millard Fillmore, to the shogun, demanding that the Japanese sign a treaty opening the country or face war when Perry returned the following year. The three U.S. steamships with the expedition shocked the Japanese with their ability to move against the wind and tide.

The shogun, more realistic than his critics, granted Perry's demands in the Treaty of Kanagawa (1854) and then accepted the blame for the nation's humiliation. The treaty opened two ports to U.S. trade and allowed for the stationing of a U.S. consul. Soon, American diplomats demanded a stronger treaty, the opening of more ports, extraterritoriality, and the admission of Christian missionaries. The shogun reluctantly agreed and soon signed similar treaties with the Dutch, British, French, and Russians. Although the changes still limited the Westerners' movement, most Japanese leaders saw Japan as the loser. As they had done earlier in China and India, Western merchants flooded the nation with cheap industrial goods to create a market and destroy the native industries. International settlements restricted to foreigners arose in major port cities, and Westerners enjoyed ever-increasing economic and legal privileges.

Government Crisis

Western encroachment provoked a government crisis and a national debate about how Japan should respond. Some Japanese believed accommodation was preferable to war and favored opening to the West. One prominent Westernizer, Fukuzawa Yukichi (FOO-koo-ZAH-wa you-KEE-chee) (1835–1901), traveled in the West and became a strong proponent of liberalism, rationalism, and political freedom. Another group advocated complete defiance and the use of force to expel the intruders, arguing that the Americans had dishonored and might enslave Japan. Turning against the ineffective Tokugawa shoguns but not the powerless emperor who symbolized the nation, one faction proclaimed, "Revere the Emperor, Expel the Barbarians."

Shaken, the Tokugawa government launched efforts at modernization. It established a shipbuilding industry, promoted manufacturing, hired two hundred Western teachers, sent a few Japanese students abroad, established an institute of Western studies, and expanded the study of foreign languages. The Japanese who had already become interested in Western science and technology, however, saw these innovations as too little and too late. Despite the reforms, the shogun was now widely perceived as weak. Aware of Japan's military disadvantage, the shogun always chose negotiation, even when the Westerners badly misused their power and retaliated for any attacks on Western residents. The shogun's strategy of avoiding confrontation led a respected poet to complain angrily: "You, whose ancestors in the mighty days, Roared at the skies and swept the earth, Stand now helpless to drive off wrangling foreigners—How empty your title, 'Queller of the Barbarians.'"[18] By the 1860s the Japanese seemed to be repeating the experience of China, gradually losing control of their political and economic future.

Tokugawa Defeat and the Meiji Restoration

Meiji Restoration A revolution against the Tokugawa Shogunate in Japan in 1867–1868, carried out in the name of the Meiji emperor; led to the successful modernization of Japan.

The deteriorating situation in Japan led to a revolution against the Tokugawa Shogunate, known as the **Meiji Restoration** (1867–1868) because it was carried out in the name of the emperor, whose reign name was Meiji (MAY-gee). The revolution resulted from a conspiracy by progressive daimyo and younger samurai from southwestern Japan, united by their hatred of the status quo, but with varied goals. Generally pragmatic, some were avid Westernizers, others extreme nationalists. Although from privileged families, they allied with commoners, especially merchants.

As an alternative to the discredited shogun, Japanese dissidents turned to the relatively powerless Meiji emperor who lived in seclusion in Kyoto. In 1868 anti-Tokugawa leaders, backed by military force, seized the imperial palace and convinced the emperor to decree the restoration of his own rule. The decree ousted the Tokugawa family from their land and positions, opened the government to men of talent, appointed the rebels as imperial advisers, and announced that "the evil customs of the past shall be broken off. Knowledge shall be sought throughout the world."[19] The Tokugawa fought back, sparking a bloody one-year civil war. The rebel forces crushed all armed resistance.

The Meiji regime's crash modernization program lasted for thirty years. Under the new regime, Japan joined the world community and agreed to honor all treaties. As a symbolic attack on tradition, the imperial residence was moved from Kyoto to Tokyo (formerly Edo), a much larger and more dynamic city. Perceiving change as a necessary evil, the Meiji leaders pragmatically sought ways to achieve national unity, wealth, defense, and equality with the West. Although influenced by Western political and economic models, Meiji reformers also incorporated Japanese traditions in building a distinctive form of industrial society, defusing the Western threat. Despite its flaws, the Meiji system proved productive for Japan and, in recent decades, an attractive model for the rapidly industrializing nations in East and Southeast Asia.

Crash Modernization

To establish an effective governmental structure and secure popular loyalty, the Meiji leaders formed a State Council to advise and control the emperor. To defuse potential opposition, they recruited both samurais and commoners into the new bureaucracy while convincing the daimyos to give up control of their land, in exchange for generous financial settlements and often for appointment as regional governors. Many newly freed peasants moved to cities in search of manufacturing or service work. The government also employed thousands of Western advisers, teachers, and workers, who were required to train Japanese assistants to replace them when their contracts expired. By financing these programs through tax revenues, Meiji Japan did not need foreign loans, hence avoiding the debt trap that ensnared most Latin American and Middle Eastern societies as well as China.

The new political system had some democratic trappings, but the Japanese, with no tradition of political freedom, had to invent a new word for the concept. A small group of men made most of the key decisions. Nonetheless, responding to a growing movement for more popular participation in decision making, in 1889 the Meiji leaders wrote the first constitution in Japanese history, forming a constitutional monarchy symbolically headed by the emperor. The constitution introduced an independent judiciary and a two-house parliament, elected by the 450,000 men who were tax-paying property holders, that chose members for the policy-making cabinet. Former samurai formed the first political parties, but they remained factionalized and weak as a political force.

Political Change

Using the slogan "rich country, strong army," the government stressed industrial development and built railroads and telegraphs. Anxious about Western imperialism, the Japanese also built up the armed forces, including a modern navy, by drafting commoners as soldiers, once a profession

First Commercial Bank in Edo   During the Meiji era the banking industry grew. This bank, built in Western style in Edo, was owned by the Mitsui family, which also owned large stores, breweries, factories, coal mines, and other enterprises. Mitsui was one of the major business conglomerates in Japan, with branches all over Asia.

limited to samurai. By breaking down the distinction between samurai, merchant, and peasant, the military draft promoted social leveling. Military service also fostered literacy and nationalism. Since pressure from the West gradually diminished, the Meiji leaders enjoyed more freedom of action compared with China to strengthen the nation. Japan was also a much less inviting target for the West, since it had few natural resources that could be profitably exploited. Although Westerners viewed Japan as a market for their goods, China had many more potential consumers. The various Western powers, largely preoccupied elsewhere, saw Japan mainly as a potential ally against each other.

Meiji Economy and Society

state capitalism An economic system in which the state takes a leading role in supporting business and industrial enterprises; introduced by the Meiji government in Japan.

In building a modern economic foundation, the Meiji created **state capitalism**, an economic system in which the state takes a leading role in supporting business and industrial enterprises and then regulates and closely monitors the economy once it is privatized. The state subsidized or purchased stock in light industries such as textiles and in heavy industries such as mines and steel mills. Sometimes it also formed new corporations that were sold to a few companies with political connections, such as Mitsui (MIT-soo-ee), a family-owned business from Tokugawa times. The most powerful corporations, the **zaibatsu**, maintained especially close ties to the government.

zaibatsu The most powerful Japanese corporations that dominated the national economy beginning during the Meiji regime and that maintained an especially close relationship to the government.

State capitalism and industrial growth often favored city people over the rural peasantry, and capital for industrialization was obtained by squeezing the peasants through the land tax. In exchange, the government spurred agricultural productivity by providing new seeds, improving land use, and supplying better irrigation. However, public investment favored the cities, prompting one liberal scholar to complain that "steel bridges glisten in the capital, and horse-drawn carriages run on the streets, but in the country the wooden bridges are so rotten one cannot cross them."[20]

Industrialization

The new economic structure perpetuated the traditional group orientation and social controls of Japanese society. Most Japanese identified closely with the company that employed them, and the economy flourished by exploiting Japanese workers. The government kept wages low so that scarce capital could be devoted to building factories, shipyards, and railroads, ultimately creating new jobs and fostering national wealth, but life in the Meiji era was not easy. As in the United States and Europe, the textile mills mainly employed women, half of them below the age of twenty and 15 percent younger than fourteen, chiefly recruited from rural villages. The young factory women, paid half the salary of male workers, lived in crowded, often locked dormitories and worked twelve-hour shifts, interrupted only by one half-hour meal break. Mill workers experienced high death rates from overwork, physical abuse from supervisors, and diseases such as tuberculosis caused by crowded working conditions.

Social Reforms

Meiji reforms also attacked the rigid Tokugawa class system. New laws allowed people to change occupations and travel or move freely. Losing their monopoly on military occupations, some samurai became lawyers, teachers, or journalists, while disgruntled samurai joined opposition political movements. To involve all Japanese in modernization, the regime emphasized mass education and constructed a universal school system paid for by both taxes and tuition, adopting the examination-based educational system of European nations such as Germany. It also opened technical schools and universities and dispatched students to Europe and the United States. By 1900 Japan was training its own scientists, engineers, and technicians.

Meiji policies stimulated debate about Japanese society. Some reformers blamed the patriarchal family for discouraging personal independence, while conservatives worried that the individual was replacing the family. To preserve gender roles and female obedience to men, Meiji policies promoted the idea of "Good Wife, Wise Mother" to strengthen families by having mothers stay at home with their children. Thus married women, with little income, had a low social status. Some women struggled to improve their position and change society. For example, Fukuda Hideko founded a magazine in 1907 to promote feminist and socialist thought, writing that "virtually everything [for women] is coercive and oppressive, making it imperative that we women rise up and develop our own social movement."[21]

Burakumin ("Hamlet people") A despised Japanese subgroup who traditionally performed jobs considered unclean and undignified.

But it proved difficult to completely eradicate old social prejudices. For instance, the **Burakumin** (boo-ROCK-uh-min), or "hamlet people," a poor, despised subgroup who performed jobs considered unclean and undignified, such as meat processing and leatherworking, remained subject to discrimination. Despite Meiji laws giving the Burakumin legal equality, Japanese still discouraged intermarriage with Burakumin and banned them from temples and shrines.

Westernization, Expansion, and the Meiji Legacy

The Japanese became acquainted with Western philosophy, social theory, economic thought, literature, and fashions, all of which influenced Japanese society. During the peak of Westernization in the 1870s, the Japanese adopted the Western calendar, added European words to the Japanese language, became familiar with chairs and couches, began eating more meat, wore leather shoes, attended fancy dress balls, carried umbrellas, sported watches, wore trousers, shook hands rather than bowed, and often married in the Western style. The Meiji also ended the prohibition on Christianity, though missionaries never converted more than a few thousand Japanese. Writers found that Western literary styles such as realism and romanticism allowed them freer expression. For example, Futabatei Shimei **(FOO-ta-BA-tay shi-MAI)** (1864–1909) wrote the first modern Japanese novels, in colloquial language rather than the highly formal language of tradition.

Synthesizing East and West

Many Westerners were amazed at Japan's dramatic transformation. A German doctor wrote that he felt lucky to be an eyewitness to the interesting experiment as Japan tried to make, in one great leap, the changes toward industrial society that took Europeans five centuries to complete. But in 1911 a Japanese novelist worried about a "nervous collapse" that would devastate the society as a result of cultural confusion. Japan seemed neither traditional nor Western.

By the later 1880s the mania for Western fads had abated. Hoping to keep Westernization from overwhelming Japan, the Meiji leaders carefully fostered a synthesis of old and new, reemphasizing traditional values, including ancient myths and the divinity of the emperor. Although the Japanese were never slavish imitators of the West, the dramatic changes created tensions between Japan and other nations that ultimately fostered a more imperialistic foreign policy, and some samurai advocated an invasion of Korea as a way for them to serve their nation in glory. But the Meiji leaders, fearful of antagonizing the Western powers, followed a cautious foreign policy. Nonetheless, they sponsored a vast colonization of the large northern island of Hokkaido **(ho-KIE-do)** to protect the country from potential Russian aggression.

Eventually Meiji Japan fought two wars (see Map 23.2). In the first one, the Sino-Japanese War (1894–1895), China and Japan battled each other over their competing influence in Korea, which Japan had long coveted for its fertile land but now also viewed as a market for Japanese products. After a smashing military victory, Japan dominated Korea as well as the Chinese island of Taiwan, and in 1910 it transformed both into colonies. Impressed, Britain forged an alliance with Japan that endured through the Meiji era. Britain's rival, Russia, had ambitions in Korea and had acquired a foothold in China's resource-rich Manchuria region, which Japan wanted to exploit. The rising tensions led to the Russo-Japanese War (1904–1905). During the conflict the Japanese seized a Russian-held Manchurian port and then destroyed the Russian fleet sent out from Europe. The Japanese victory electrified the world. A non-Western nation had defeated a major European power, giving hope to societies under Western domination and spurring Asian nationalisms. The triumph in the war further enhanced the pride of the Japanese people in their nation and confirmed that Japan had, in three decades, become a world power. Among the fruits of victory was the transfer to Japan of some Russian holdings in Manchuria and control of the southern half of Sakhalin island, off the Siberian coast.

Wars with China and Russia

The Meiji era, which came to an official end with the death of the Meiji emperor in 1912, had achieved stunning successes, giving Japan national security and a position as a powerful regional power. Although Japan's wealth and influence were still less than that of the major industrial powers—the United States, Britain, France, and Germany—Japan was now an industrial nation with 50 million people, on a par with countries such as Russia and Italy.

The Meiji changes have provoked debate. Some historians view the Meiji policies as a political and social revolution, not unlike the French Revolution in uprooting the old society. Others emphasize the longtime Japanese willingness to modify culture to strengthen the country. Some Japanese found the changes shattering, while others took them in stride. One supporter proclaimed Japan's "marvelous fortune. I feel as though in a dream and can only weep tears of joy." Another enthusiast wrote that "we are no longer ashamed to stand before the world as Japanese, known by the world."[22] But concerned that the growing military power would corrupt his country, one writer called on his people to open their eyes to the dangers ahead. His fears were realized three decades later in World War II, when Japan's conquest of an Asian and Pacific empire provoked U.S. retaliation, ultimately leading to Japanese military defeat and occupation by U.S. forces.

The Meiji Legacy

Map 23.2   Japanese Modernization and Expansion, 1868–1913
Japan undertook a crash modernization in the later 1800s. By 1910 its military power had increased, and it had won a war with Russia and colonized Korea, Taiwan, and Sakhalin (then known as Karafutu).

e Interactive Map

Korean Transitions

Late Yi Dynasty

The last of the Korean dynasties, the Yi **(YEE)** (1392–1910), who ruled the state they called Choson **(choh-SAN)** for over five centuries, had chosen seclusion from the outside world, earning Korea the label of "the Hermit Kingdom." However, Korea still had relations with China. Korean scholars who visited China, where some met Westerners, later criticized Korea's overly rigid and inequitable social system. Yet, several strong kings in the 1700s fostered learning, printing encyclopedias and historical records. Aristocratic women wrote memoirs, diaries, and stories of court life, and even some commoners wrote stories and novels.

However, by the early 1800s Choson, like Qing China and Tokugawa Japan, began to succumb to stress. The rigid social structure crumbled as the economy and population grew, increasing pressure on the land. With Buddhism losing influence, some Koreans turned to Christianity, and although officially prohibited, a few French and Chinese Christian missionaries had illegally entered Korea. Korea also experienced recurrent famines and peasant uprisings, for which the Choson government blamed and hence persecuted Christians and Western missionaries. Korean intellectuals debated the value of Western learning, and some pushed for reforms of the traditional system. With the Yi refusing direct commercial negotiations with the West, Korean military forces drove away French and American ships seeking to open Korea to Western trade. The Yi also worried about Russian expansion in eastern Siberia. By the later 1800s Korea seemed in need of rejuvenation.

Opening Korea

In 1876, Meiji Japan, adopting the model used by the United States to open Japan, sent a naval expedition to Korea that forced the Yi government to open five ports and sign unequal treaties that gave Japan a strong role in Korea's economy, sparking changes within Korea. Impressed by Meiji modernization, the Yi government introduced reforms, such as toleration of Christianity, and signed trade agreements with Western nations. In 1886 Christians opened Korea's first modern girls' school, whose graduates later promoted women's rights. Many Korean peasants joined the Tonghak ("Eastern Learning"), a protest movement not unlike the Taipings in China that mixed Confucianism, Buddhism, Christianity, and hatred of Japan and the West. Spurred by famine, the movement grew into the nationwide Tonghak Rebellion against the Yi government in 1894. When Korea's longtime ally, China, sent in troops to help repress the rebellion, Japan responded by sending in a force and capturing the Korean capital, Seoul, holding the Yi royal family hostage. This led to the Sino-Japanese War, which resulted in a humiliating Chinese withdrawal, a stronger Japanese presence, and an end to the decrepit Yi dynasty. Some 18,000 Koreans died in fighting the Japanese.

Japanese Colonization

In 1910 Japan forcibly transformed Korea into a Japanese colony and Korea remained a heavily exploited, harshly ruled Japanese colony until 1945, enduring brutal suppression of Korean nationalism and culture, although the Japanese also increased educational opportunities and built a modern economy. The Japanese seized Korean land for Japanese companies and restricted civil liberties, and in 1919 the Japanese police brutally crushed peaceful demonstrations calling for independence, killing or injuring some 24,000 demonstrators and arresting 47,000. Resentment simmered as repressive measures, such as forcing students to speak only Japanese, increased. Some Koreans found solace in Christianity, and perhaps a fifth became Catholics or Protestants. Others turned toward Marxism and joined an underground Communist Party founded by Korean workers in China and Russia. Many Koreans, however, rejected Western ideas, believing the best strategy was to strengthen Confucianism. Japanese relations with Koreans became even more exploitative during World War II. Korean men were conscripted as soldiers and workers, and young Korean women, termed by the Japanese "comfort women," were forced to serve as sex slaves for Japanese soldiers. Even today many Koreans have a deep antipathy for Japan as a result of colonial repression and exploitation.

SECTION SUMMARY

- Japan was better able than China to deal with foreign pressures because of its compactness and homogeneity, its openness to outside ideas, its balance of power between groups of elites, its strong merchant class, and its sensitivity to the threat posed by foreigners.

- Late Tokugawa Japanese culture was vigorous, open to Western learning, and marked by thriving urban centers and ambitious artists.

- Internal decay in Japan led to riots and revolts, but officials, more concerned with external threats, embarked on reforms designed to strengthen the country and enable it to withstand pressure from Westerners. However, when faced with a choice between war and opening Japan to American trade, the Japanese shogun chose trade, which led to trade agreements with other Western nations, a flood of cheap manufactured goods, and special privileges for Westerners in Japan.

- After the Meiji Restoration, which overthrew the Tokugawa Shogunate, Japanese samurai and others frustrated with the Tokugawa Shogunate established a regime that was dedicated to making Japan open to and competitive with the rest of the world.

- The Meiji regime modernized Japan by breaking down social distinctions, pursuing industrial and military strength, and establishing a constitutional monarchy.

- The Meiji state supported and closely regulated industry, gave workers new rights to change occupation and travel freely but kept wages deliberately low, stripped samurai of their traditional privileges, and attempted to preserve traditional gender roles.

- In the late 1800s, Meiji leaders worked to balance traditional practices with newly adopted Western ones and, while there was debate over how to conduct foreign policy, Japan fought successful wars against both China and Russia.

- Historians debate whether the Meiji era was a fundamental transformation or a continuation of Japan's ability to change with the times.

- The Yi dynasty had closed Korea off from the rest of the world, earning for itself the label "the Hermit Kingdom," and when Korea experienced famine and instability in the 1800s, its leaders blamed the influence of Christian missionaries.

- Meiji Japan forced Korea to accept unequal trade agreements and, after defeating China in the Sino-Japanese War, turned Korea into a colony and ruled it extremely harshly, brutally suppressing dissent and exploiting its men and women during World War II.

Russia's Eurasian Empire

What factors explain the expansion of the Russian Empire?

Between 1750 and 1914 Russia built a vast Eurasian empire stretching 3,200 miles from the Baltic Sea to the Bering Straits, creating more intensive ties to Asian societies. Russians continued to push their frontiers across Siberia and into Central Asia and south toward the Black Sea, making Russia a hemispheric power bordering Europe, Central Asia, and the Middle East. Shaped by autocratic governments, a rural system with some resemblance to medieval feudalism, and chronic discontent, Russia played an increasing role in both Asian and European politics.

Europeanization, Despotism, and Expansionism

Russian Government

Russians had long debated whether they belonged to the European tradition or had a unique heritage; Russian politics reflected these debates. Western European influence was particularly strong during the long reign of Catherine the Great (r. 1762–1796), who carried on Peter the Great's Europeanization campaign (see Chronology: Russia and Central Asia, 1750–1914). Influenced by the Enlightenment, Catherine denounced slavery, hailed liberty, and presided over a golden age of opulence for the nobility. Wearing sumptuous gowns, the czarina gave elegant private parties and masked balls and, like many European kings, had a series of lovers, some twenty-one in all. The Russian elite copied royal France and learned French, increasing the huge gulf between them and the peasants bound to estates as serfs. Despite her liberal views, Catherine could not encourage freedom among the disgruntled common people because she needed support from the landed aristocracy. To gain their favor, she extended serfdom to Ukraine and denounced the French Revolution as irreligious and immoral. Continuing Russian expansionism, Catherine's energetic foreign policy added Poland and Finland and extended the empire south to the Black Sea, annexing the Crimean peninsula in 1783.

To maintain order and their own power, the czars who followed Catherine often relied on the brutal despotism common in Russian history. Alarmed by the social changes in western Europe, the aristocracy opposed industrialization, which they worried might upset serfdom. Czar Nicholas I (r. 1825–1855) feared alienating the aristocracy and instead suppressed the restless Poles and formed a secret police force with wide powers to harass, imprison, or eliminate opponents. Nicholas also invaded Hungary and sought dominance over the Ottomans to secure Russia's grain exports through the Black Sea to the Mediterranean. His attempts to absorb the Ottoman-held Balkans by encouraging rebellion and occupying several Ottoman provinces provoked Britain and France, leading to the bloody Crimean War of 1854, which pitted Russia against a British-French-Ottoman alliance. Armies of conscripted Russian serfs were no match for modern British and French forces, and Russia had to withdraw from Ottoman territory. Nicholas's successor, Czar Alexander II (r. 1855–1881), was more oriented to western Europe and followed a reformist domestic policy, emancipating the serfs in 1861 and decentralizing government. But many serfs were unable to pay the landowners for the lands they wanted to use, and discontent grew.

Expansion in Asia

The Russians became more engaged with Asia, expanding their power in Siberia, the Caucasus, and Central Asia to form the largest contiguous land empire in the world (see Map 23.3). In search of imperial glory, markets, and resources such as sable fur, Russia had expanded across Siberia and reached the Pacific coast in the 1600s before losing to the Chinese forces and pulling back from the fertile Amur River Basin. By the early 1800s the Russians occupied the Amur Basin and in 1860 gained official Chinese recognition of their claims in exchange for helping negotiate the end of the Arrow War. They also acquired a coastal zone on Siberia's Pacific shore, building the port city of Vladivostok ("Ruler of the East") as a base for commercial and military activity in the Pacific Basin.

For several centuries the Russians had expanded around the Black Sea, seeking an outlet to the Mediterranean Sea. Between 1800 and the 1870s they expanded their control south through the mountainous Caucasus, absorbing Armenia and Georgia, both largely Christian, as well as Muslim Azerbaijan (az-uhr-bye-JAHN). Sometimes facing fierce resistance, they needed four decades to conquer the strongly Islamic Chechens (CHECH-uhnz). The Russians triumphed in 1859 by ravaging Chechen lands, herds, and crops and beheading their captives, fostering a Chechen hatred of Russian rule.

CHRONOLOGY
Russia and Central Asia, 1750–1914

1762–1796 Reign of Catherine the Great

1861 Emancipation of Russian serfs

1800–1870s Russian conquest of Caucasus and Turkestan

1891–1915 Building of Trans-Siberian Railroad

1904–1905 Russo-Japanese War

1905 First Russian Revolution

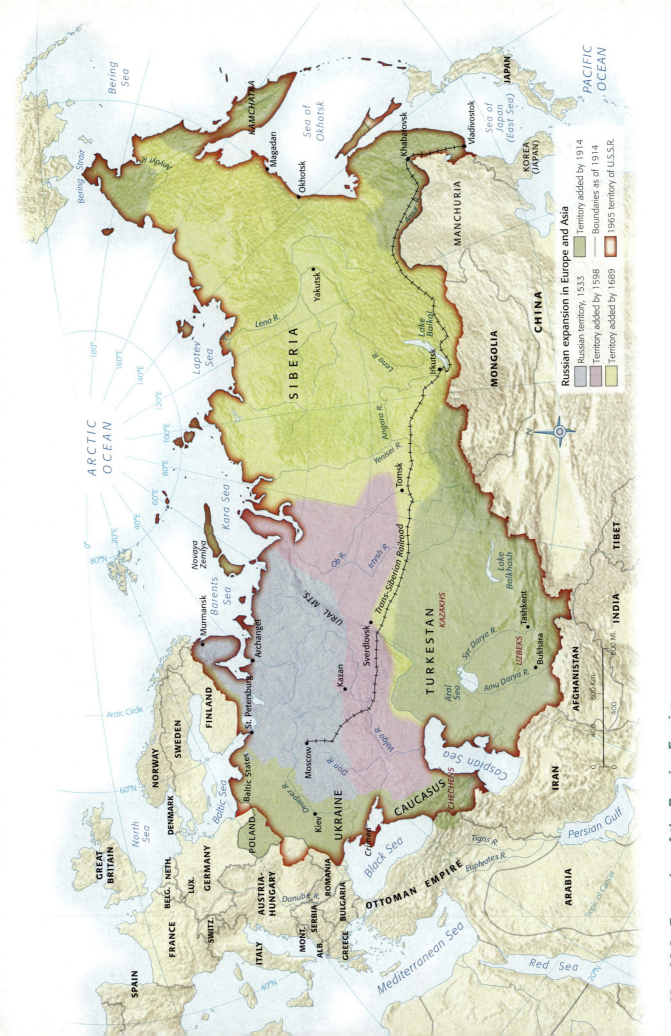

Map 23.3 Expansion of the Russian Empire
Between the 1500s and 1914 Russia gradually gained control of Siberia, Turkestan, the Caucasus, Ukraine, Poland, the Baltic states, and Finland, becoming the world's largest contiguous territorial empire.

Russian expansion in Europe and Asia

Russian territory, 1533
Territory added by 1598
Territory added by 1689
Territory added by 1914
Boundaries as of 1914
1965 territory of U.S.S.R.

e **Interactive Map**

Catherine the Great Resplendent in her royal robes, Catherine the Great triumphantly enters one of the ports of the Crimean peninsula recently captured from the Turks. Catherine presided over an expansion of the Russian Empire and efforts at modernization.

Giraudon/The Bridgeman Art Library International

Colonizing Muslim Central Asia

The Russians also colonized Muslim Central Asia, the first step in gaining direct access to the Indian Ocean trade and countering British influence in the region. By 1864 the Russians controlled all the Kazakh **(KAH-zahk)** lands east of the Caspian Sea and looked south to Turkestan's old and declining Silk Road cities. Although the cities remained vigorous centers of Islamic learning and Sufism, only Bukhara, a strong Uzbek **(OOZ-bek)**–dominated state, maintained a thriving trade. By the 1870s Russia dominated Turkestan. Russia now coveted Afghanistan, but the forbidding terrain and formidable reputation of Afghan warriors discouraged occupation. Eventually Afghanistan became a buffer between British India and Russian Central Asia.

Russification A czarist policy in the nineteenth century that promoted Russian language and culture for non-Russian peoples; created resentment among many Muslims.

Czarist policy in Central Asia and the Caucasus promoted changes that chiefly benefited Russians, as some Central Asian land suitable for growing cotton was given to several hundred thousand Russian farmers. The czars also gradually introduced a policy of **Russification**, the promotion of Russian language and culture for the non-Russian peoples, sparking resentment and spiritual revival among many Muslims. But Russian expansion brought problems along with the gains. The mighty empire's sheer size hindered governance, fostered corruption, and prevented the ready exploitation of the vast resources. Moreover, colonization of non-Russian lands made Russian leaders permanently fear rebellion and build a huge army to maintain security. The world's longest railroad, the Trans-Siberian, built between 1891 and 1915 and linking St. Petersburg with Vladivostok, fostered Russian settlement of eastern Siberia and helped Russian traders penetrate Manchuria and Korea. But expansion brought conflict with Japan, generating the Russo-Japanese War (1904–1905), in which Russia's humiliating defeat undermined its last czar, Nicholas II (r. 1894–1917).

Russian Economy, Society, and Revolution

Economic Growth

Territorial expansion and political developments created changes in many areas of Russian life. Spurred by acquiring Caucasus and Central Asian markets, the Russian economy grew. Russia enjoyed increased industrialization, financed largely by western European capital and by local bankers and businessmen of German or Jewish origin, and by 1914 Russia ranked fifth in the world as an industrial power. The factory workers, who increased in number fivefold between 1860 and 1914, resented the exploitation they faced when housed in crowded dormitories and expected to work thirteen hours a day. However, most Russians still lived in villages, dominated by the local nobility.

Gender Relations

Some Russian women sought to improve their status. While noblewomen frequently enjoyed some public influence, most commoner women had little power. Some were beaten and abused by husbands, since the laws gave men the right to control their wives and children. Peasants often spent their entire lives in the village where they were born. Even when some elite women became scholars and writers, they still had fewer rights than men. By the mid-nineteenth century, however, a women's movement had emerged that emphasized access to higher education. Thanks to these efforts, more women earned degrees and worked as doctors, midwives, and teachers.

Russian thinkers tormented themselves over their national identity and goals. Many were Westernizers who admired the efforts of rulers such as Catherine the Great to promote modernization, and some wanted to abolish serfdom and the nobility. The work of some Russian writers, such as Russia's beloved poet Alexander Pushkin **(POOSH-kin)** (1799–1837), reflected familiarity with western European literature and thought. In contrast, the **Slavophiles** rejected Western models and defended Russian culture, such as respect for the Russian Orthodox Church, which remained a dominant force. Slavophiles often advocated that Russians unite with other Slavs in eastern Europe and the Balkans to confront the West.

Whether Westernizers or Slavophiles, Russians were proud of their rich literary and artistic tradition. The novels of Fyodor Dostoyevsky **(dos-tuh-YEF-skee)** (1821–1881), reflecting his experiences as an exile in Siberia for revolutionary activities and his travels in Europe, were shaped by his awareness of poverty and the troubled human soul. Leo Tolstoy **(tuhl-STOI)** (1828–1910), master of the psychological novel, fought in the Crimean War. His epic work, *War and Peace* (1869), which profiled two noble families during war, portrayed people as mere victims of chance. One of Russia's most honored composers, Pyotr Tchaikovsky **(chi-KOF-skee)** (1840–1893), traveled widely in Europe and was criticized by Russian nationalists for his cosmopolitan approach to music and by conservatives for his homosexuality. He wrote operas as well as ballets of enduring popularity around the world, especially *Swan Lake* and *The Nutcracker*.

Increasing discontent with the autocratic system and the rising costs of empire building resulted in violent resistance. To crush opposition, the czars sent thousands of dissidents to remote Siberian prison camps, where many died of illness, starvation, overwork, or the harsh climate. Some dissidents joined the illegal Socialist Revolutionary Party, founded in 1898, that used terror to strike against the regime. After assassinating a minister of state, the party proclaimed that "the crack of the bullet is the only possible means to talk with our ministers, until they listen to the voice of the country."[23]

In 1905 the sacrifices imposed on common people by the Russo-Japanese War sparked a major socialist-led revolutionary movement involving both men and women and widespread violence. The unrest began when 100,000 factory workers in the capital, St. Petersburg, who were required to work longer hours to produce war supplies, went on strike and marched demanding equality before the law, freedom of speech, an eight-hour workday, social insurance, and other progressive goals. Russian troops opened fire on the peaceful marchers, killing some 200 and wounding hundreds more. The violence shattered public support for the czar and fueled outrage, which soon spread to the armed forces. The revolutionaries were split in their goals, enabling the government to crush the uprising, execute thousands of rebels, and burn pro-rebel villages. But the czar bowed to public demands and allowed an elected national assembly with limited powers. The socialist movement fractured into hostile factions; however, conflicts simmered, and in 1917 they produced the greatest upheaval in Russia's history, which ended the czarist system (see Chapter 24).

Russian Thought and Culture

Slavophiles Nineteenth-century Russians who emphasized Russia's unique culture and rejected Western models.

Dissent and Rebellion

SECTION SUMMARY

- The Russian leader Catherine the Great paid lip service to Enlightenment values, but she presided over an era of royal opulence, territorial expansion, and expanded serfdom, and she was followed by the despotic Nicholas I, who led the nation to defeat in the Crimean War.

- Russian expansion brought it control of eastern Siberia, Muslim Central Asia, and the Caucasus states, although some peoples, such as the Chechens, fiercely resisted.

- Russia's economy expanded along with its territory, creating a discontented proletariat; while many Russian thinkers embraced Western ideals, the Slavophiles argued for the superiority of traditional Russian culture.

- Russians increasingly discontented with the demands of empire building and autocratic rulers joined terrorist groups and supported a revolution in 1905, which, while put down, led to reforms.

WORLD WARS, EUROPEAN REVOLUTIONS, AND GLOBAL DEPRESSION, 1914–1945

Museum of the Revolution, Moscow/The Bridgeman Art Library International

Global Communism
The communist leaders of the Soviet Union hoped that their revolution in Russia in 1917 would inspire similar revolutions around the world, ending capitalism and imperialism. This poster reflects the dream of a triumphant communism.

SUGGESTED READING

Allworth, Edward, ed. *Central Asia: 130 Years of Russian Rule*, 2nd ed. Durham, NC: Duke University Press, 1994. A collection of essays.

Benson, John and Takao Matsumura. *Japan, 1868–1945: From Isolation to Occupation*. New York: Longman, 2001. Revisionist interpretation of political, economic, and social changes.

Chang, Hsin-Pao. *Commissioner Lin and the Opium War*. New York: W.W. Norton, 1964. The classic account.

Cumings, Bruce. *Korea's Place in the Sun: A Modern History*, 2nd ed. New York: W.W. Norton, 2005. Good coverage of this era.

Ebrey, Patricia Buckley, Anne Walthall, and James B. Palais. *East Asia: A Cultural, Social, and Political History*, 2nd ed. Boston: Houghton Mifflin, 2009. A recent, balanced survey.

Evtuhov, Catherine, et al. *A History of Russia: Peoples, Legends, Events, Forces*. Boston: Houghton Mifflin, 2004. A detailed survey.

Fahr-Becker, Gabriele, ed. *Japanese Prints*. New York: Barnes and Noble, 2003. A well-illustrated introduction to this wonderful art.

Madariaga, Isabel de. *Russia in the Age of Catherine the Great*. London: Phoenix Press, 1981. Reprint of a well-balanced and panoramic examination of Catherine and her era.

Matsunosuke, Nishiyama. *Edo Culture: Daily Life and Diversions in Urban Japan, 1600–1868*. Honolulu: University of Hawaii Press, 1997. A fascinating look at popular culture during the Tokugawa era.

McClain, James L. *Japan: A Modern History*. New York: W.W. Norton, 2002. An excellent survey of events since 1600.

Schirokauer, Conrad, and Donald N. Clark. *Modern East Asia: A Brief History*, 2nd ed. Belmont, CA: Wadsworth, 2007. A survey of China, Japan, and Korea in this era.

Schoppa, R. Keith. *Revolution and its Past: Identities and Change in Modern Chinese History*, 2nd ed. Upper Saddle River, NJ: Prentice-Hall, 2006. Well-written survey of continuity and change.

Smith, Richard J. *China's Cultural Heritage: The Ch'ing Dynasty, 1644–1913*, 2nd ed. Boulder, CO: Westview Press, 1994. A readable and comprehensive study.

Spence, Jonathan D. *The Search for Modern China*, 2nd ed. New York: W.W. Norton, 1999. A provocative examination.

WORLD WARS, EUROPEAN REVOLUTIONS, AND GLOBAL DEPRESSION, 1914–1945

Museum of the Revolution, Moscow/The Bridgeman Art Library International

Global Communism
The communist leaders of the Soviet Union hoped that their revolution in Russia in 1917 would inspire similar revolutions around the world, ending capitalism and imperialism. This poster reflects the dream of a triumphant communism.

spent their entire lives in the village where they were born. Even when some elite women became scholars and writers, they still had fewer rights than men. By the mid-nineteenth century, however, a women's movement had emerged that emphasized access to higher education. Thanks to these efforts, more women earned degrees and worked as doctors, midwives, and teachers.

Russian thinkers tormented themselves over their national identity and goals. Many were Westernizers who admired the efforts of rulers such as Catherine the Great to promote modernization, and some wanted to abolish serfdom and the nobility. The work of some Russian writers, such as Russia's beloved poet Alexander Pushkin **(POOSH-kin)** (1799–1837), reflected familiarity with western European literature and thought. In contrast, the **Slavophiles** rejected Western models and defended Russian culture, such as respect for the Russian Orthodox Church, which remained a dominant force. Slavophiles often advocated that Russians unite with other Slavs in eastern Europe and the Balkans to confront the West.

Whether Westernizers or Slavophiles, Russians were proud of their rich literary and artistic tradition. The novels of Fyodor Dostoyevsky **(dos-tuh-YEF-skee)** (1821–1881), reflecting his experiences as an exile in Siberia for revolutionary activities and his travels in Europe, were shaped by his awareness of poverty and the troubled human soul. Leo Tolstoy **(tuhl-STOI)** (1828–1910), master of the psychological novel, fought in the Crimean War. His epic work, *War and Peace* (1869), which profiled two noble families during war, portrayed people as mere victims of chance. One of Russia's most honored composers, Pyotr Tchaikovsky **(chi-KOF-skee)** (1840–1893), traveled widely in Europe and was criticized by Russian nationalists for his cosmopolitan approach to music and by conservatives for his homosexuality. He wrote operas as well as ballets of enduring popularity around the world, especially *Swan Lake* and *The Nutcracker*.

Increasing discontent with the autocratic system and the rising costs of empire building resulted in violent resistance. To crush opposition, the czars sent thousands of dissidents to remote Siberian prison camps, where many died of illness, starvation, overwork, or the harsh climate. Some dissidents joined the illegal Socialist Revolutionary Party, founded in 1898, that used terror to strike against the regime. After assassinating a minister of state, the party proclaimed that "the crack of the bullet is the only possible means to talk with our ministers, until they listen to the voice of the country."[23]

In 1905 the sacrifices imposed on common people by the Russo-Japanese War sparked a major socialist-led revolutionary movement involving both men and women and widespread violence. The unrest began when 100,000 factory workers in the capital, St. Petersburg, who were required to work longer hours to produce war supplies, went on strike and marched demanding equality before the law, freedom of speech, an eight-hour workday, social insurance, and other progressive goals. Russian troops opened fire on the peaceful marchers, killing some 200 and wounding hundreds more. The violence shattered public support for the czar and fueled outrage, which soon spread to the armed forces. The revolutionaries were split in their goals, enabling the government to crush the uprising, execute thousands of rebels, and burn pro-rebel villages. But the czar bowed to public demands and allowed an elected national assembly with limited powers. The socialist movement fractured into hostile factions; however, conflicts simmered, and in 1917 they produced the greatest upheaval in Russia's history, which ended the czarist system (see Chapter 24).

Russian Thought and Culture

Slavophiles Nineteenth-century Russians who emphasized Russia's unique culture and rejected Western models.

Dissent and Rebellion

SECTION SUMMARY

- The Russian leader Catherine the Great paid lip service to Enlightenment values, but she presided over an era of royal opulence, territorial expansion, and expanded serfdom, and she was followed by the despotic Nicholas I, who led the nation to defeat in the Crimean War.

- Russian expansion brought it control of eastern Siberia, Muslim Central Asia, and the Caucasus states, although some peoples, such as the Chechens, fiercely resisted.

- Russia's economy expanded along with its territory, creating a discontented proletariat; while many Russian thinkers embraced Western ideals, the Slavophiles argued for the superiority of traditional Russian culture.

- Russians increasingly discontented with the demands of empire building and autocratic rulers joined terrorist groups and supported a revolution in 1905, which, while put down, led to reforms.

CHAPTER SUMMARY

China faced daunting challenges from the Western powers. Qing China had long been able to rebuff Western demands for more trade, but the government and economy were declining by the early 1800s. China's attempts to halt British opium smuggling led to the Opium War, and its defeat in that war resulted in an unequal treaty system that gave Western nations greater access to China and its resources. Increasing poverty and rebellions further undermined Qing power. Attempts at modernization failed because of China's vast size, conservative opposition, and fears of radical culture change. In 1911 revolution ended the imperial system, but the new republic soon collapsed in civil war.

While the Western challenges progressively undermined China, they prompted Japan to transform its society. The arrival of American ships demanding that Japan open itself to the West forced the issue and undermined the shogunate, which then lost power in the 1868 Meiji Restoration. Capitalizing on dynamic merchants, high literacy rates, a tradition of cultural borrowing, and national loyalties, the Meiji government launched a crash program to modernize Japan's government, military, economy, and social patterns, importing Western ideas and institutions. By 1900 the Meiji had industrialized Japan, deflected Western ambitions, and turned Japan into a world power, able to defeat China and Russia in two wars and to colonize Korea.

Despotic Russian leaders pushed Russian control across Siberia and into eastern Europe and colonized Central Asia and the Caucasus. By the later 1800s Russia dominated large parts of Eurasia, forming the world's largest contiguous land empire. But maintaining an empire against restless colonized societies strained Russian capabilities. Russia also industrialized and promoted social change, but repression of the Russian peasants ultimately brought dissent and revolutionary movements.

KEY TERMS

Chinoiserie

Co-hong

extraterritoriality

international settlements

gunboat diplomacy

Meiji Restoration

state capitalism

zaibatsu

Burakumin

Russification

Slavophiles

EBOOK AND WEBSITE RESOURCES

PRIMARY SOURCE

Letter to Queen Victoria, 1839

INTERACTIVE MAPS

Map 23.1 Conflicts in Qing China, 1839–1870

Map 23.2 Japanese Modernization and Expansion, 1868–1913

Map 23.3 Expansion of the Russian Empire

LINKS

East and Southeast Asia: An Annotated Directory of Internet Resources (http://newton.uor.edu/Departments&Programs/AsianStudies-Dept/general.html). Links on history, culture, and politics.

The Floating World of Ukiyo-e: Shadow, Dreams, and Substance (http://www.loc.gov/exhibits/ukiyo-e/). Introduces the Japanese prints at the Library of Congress.

Internet Guide to Chinese Studies (http://www.sino.uni-heidelberg.de/igcs/). An excellent collection of links, maintained by a German university.

Internet East Asian History Sourcebook (http://www.fordham.edu/halsall/eastasia/eastasiasbook.html). Sources and links on China, Japan, and Korea.

Russian History Index: The World Wide Web Virtual Library (http://vlib.iue.it/hist-russia/Index.html). Useful links.

Plus flashcards, practice quizzes, and more. Go to: www.cengage.com/history/lockard/globalsocnet2e.

*M*y beautiful, pitiful era. With an insane smile you look back, cruel and weak, like an animal past its prime, at the prints of your own paws.

—Osip Mandelstam, Russian poet[1]

By April 1917 the French army had been fighting the Germans for over two and a half years during World War I. With growing casualty lists and tremendous hardship on soldiers, the French officers were divided over mounting a more aggressive strategy, likely to result in many more deaths, or a more defensive approach. Finally a new French commander, General Philippe Pétain **(peh-TANH)** (1856–1951), advocated a strategy to minimize French casualties. A peasant's son with an aristocratic demeanor, a sweeping white moustache, and many love affairs with other men's wives, Pétain regarded his soldiers as more than cannon fodder, endearing him to the fighting men. But Pétain was overruled, and the French launched another frontal assault on the well-fortified German lines, resulting in a military disaster that caused 120,000 deaths and broke the troops' fighting spirit. Mutinies broke out in the units, with the mutineers protesting the futile military strategy of suicidal assaults. Some soldiers proposed a protest march on Paris, and 20,000 deserted. In response, the army executed about 50 mutineers but also granted the frontline troops better food and more generous rations of wine. Mutinies and an overwhelming warweariness occurred among all the combatant nations. Pétain emerged from World War I as a hero but later lost his stature when he served as the nominal head of the French government under hated Nazi occupation in World War II. He died in prison, a broken man looking back on three tumultuous decades that had brought so much distress and destruction to the world.

Those decades included not only two great military struggles but also a mighty revolution in Russia, a terrible worldwide economic depression, and the rise of new ideologies. The Russian Jewish poet Osip Mandelstam described an era full of achievements and atrocities, heroism and hardship, as "beautiful [and] pitiful." Before World War I some Europeans believed that Western democracy might spread throughout the world and the horrors of war could be ended forever. Liberals even hoped World War I would be the war to end all wars. But the hopes of the idealists were dashed by two world wars, fought partly in Europe, that challenged the liberalism and rationalism spawned by the Enlightenment. Dictatorship in Russia, economic collapse, and organized slaughter shattered faith in progress. The disarray in Europe helped undermine Western political influence in the world, except for the rising Western power, the United States.

[1]Quoted in Anne Applebaum, *Gula: A History* (NY: Doubleday, 2003), p. 3.

FOCUS QUESTIONS

1. **What was the impact of World War I on the Western world?**

2. **How did communism prevail in Russia and transform that country?**

3. **How did the Great Depression reshape world politics and economies?**

4. **What were the main ideas and impacts of fascism?**

5. **What were the costs and consequences of World War II?**

Visit the website and eBook for additional study materials and interactive tools:
www.cengage.com/history/lockard/globalsocnet2e

THE ROOTS AND COURSE OF WORLD WAR I

What was the impact of World War I on the Western world?

In August 1914, as war broke out between the major powers of Europe, the British foreign secretary remarked, "The lights are going out all over Europe. We shall not see them again in our lifetime."[2] The conflict pitted two alliances. Britain, France, and Russia formed the Triple Entente, which later included Serbia, Japan, Italy, Portugal, Romania, Greece, and eventually the United States. These nations, also known as the Allies, faced the Central Powers: Germany, Austria-Hungary, the Ottoman Empire, and Bulgaria. Although most of the military action took place in and around Europe, the leaders of the countries involved saw the conflict as nothing short of a struggle to control the global system, with its industrial economies and colonial empires. The Great War, as many Europeans called it, was history's first total war, an armed conflict between industrialized powers that lasted four terrible years. The war brought down empires and dynasties, made the United States a world power, and weakened western Europe's hold over the colonial world. And the end of the conflict made a second major war almost inevitable.

Preludes to War

Early 20th Century Europe

In the early 1900s, Europeans enjoyed affluence, social stability, and growing democracy. The European economies benefited from their links to each other and their access to the world's resources and markets. Some thinkers believed nations tied by economic interdependence would never wage war against each other. European nations cooperated in many things. Treaties bound their nations to protect the right of workers to pensions and health insurance while restricting child labor. Whatever their nationality, educated Europeans loved the music of the Austrian composer Wolfgang Amadeus Mozart and the novels of the Russian writer Leo Tolstoy. Europeans frequently spoke two or three languages and traveled in other countries, and royal families intermarried across borders. In 1899 European nations agreed to limit armaments and create the International Court to settle disputes between nations. Although the court was seldom invoked, Europeans hoped it would discourage a sudden outburst of war. They looked to the future with confidence and felt superior to the rest of the world. Thanks to imperial expansion, rising populations, and expanded markets, Europeans consumed new products such as chocolate and rubber tires, while European emigration to the Americas and Australia increased markets there for European goods, and automobiles and large ships made it easier to move people, natural resources, and manufactured products over long distances. European capital financed South African gold and diamond mines, Malayan rubber plantations, Australian sheep stations, Russian railways, Canadian wheat fields, and every sector of the growing U.S. economy.

National Rivalries

However, the prosperity, interdependence, and idealism had their limits, and other conditions led to tensions and resentments. The quest for imperial glory increased competition between the European powers for economic and political influence outside of Europe, and each nation felt threatened in some way by competitors. Britain, France, and Germany were the wealthiest, most powerful nations and fierce rivals with large empires in Africa, Asia, the Pacific, and the Caribbean. Because they began empire building later than Britain and France, the Germans resented those nations' political control of much of the world. Britain, which generally commanded the seas, became concerned when Germany began building a naval fleet. As Germany challenged Britain for dominance in overseas markets, the two nations bolstered their military strength, stepping up the manufacture of heavier weapons and drafting more young men into the military. Still considering wars necessary struggles rather than terrible evils, by 1911 leaders began to plan for war. The chief of the German General Staff told the German chancellor, "I hold war to be inevitable, and the sooner the better. Everyone is preparing for the great war, which they all expect."[3]

As economic and military rivalries grew, alliances formed. Britain, France, and Russia were all wary of an aggressive Germany, which felt encircled by these three hostile powers, while Austria-Hungary and the Ottoman Empire shared German dislike of Russia. The growing nationalist agitation for self-determination by the many ethnic minorities within the multinational German, Russian, Austro-Hungarian, and Ottoman Empires added to the combustible mix. Austria-Hungary faced a particularly difficult challenge in governing the restless Czech, Slovak, and Balkan peoples within its empire. The Balkans, populated by feuding ethnic groups, was coveted by the Ottomans, Russia, and Austria-Hungary. In 1908 Austria-Hungary annexed Bosnia-Herzegovina **(boz-nee-uh-HERT-suh-go-vee-nuh)**, a territory containing Croats, Serbs, and Muslims that neighboring

CHRONOLOGY

	World War I and Aftermath	Era of Great Depression	World War II
1910	**1914–1918** World War I **1917** Russian Revolution		
1920	**1926** Fascist state in Italy	**1929–1941** Great Depression	**1939–1945** World War II
1930		**1933** Nazi triumph in Germany **1937** Japanese invasion of China	
1940			**1941** Japanese attack on Pearl Harbor **1944** Bretton Woods Conference

Serbia also wanted (see Chronology: World War I, 1914–1919). If their ally Germany could restrain Russia, Austria-Hungary's leaders thought war with Serbia might salvage their decaying empire, which once ruled large parts of Europe.

Historians often blame World War I on failures of diplomacy, breakdowns in communication among nations, and the personal ambitions of leaders. Although a grandson of Britain's Queen Victoria, the German monarch, Kaiser Wilhelm II (r. 1888–1918), who saw himself as a king answerable only to God, grew to envy British power. Political and military leaders also underestimated the human costs and long-term consequences of conflict. Although overstating the case, a key British leader later conceded that "the nations slithered over the brink into the boiling cauldron of war without a trace of apprehension or dismay."[4] Other issues also paved the road to war. Some governments hoped war might divert public attention from festering domestic problems, such as Irish resistance to English policies and growing German social ills. And while the general public did not pressure its governments for war, it did not try to restrain them. Feminists and socialists opposed war on principle, but, when war came, they often closed ranks. In the Austrian capital, Vienna, vast crowds paraded through the streets singing patriotic songs through the night, even though a local observer wrote that his people expected a nightmare. Meanwhile leaders, although believing war was preferable to maintaining a fragile peace, also feared their people would tire of it.

The Course of the European War

The pretext for war was the assassination of the Austrian archduke Franz Ferdinand (1863–1914), the heir to the Habsburg throne, and his wife, Sophie, while they rode through the crowded streets of Sarajevo (sar-uh-YAY-vo), Bosnia-Herzegovina's capital city, during an official visit. Although conciliatory toward the empire's Slavic minorities, to Serb nationalists in Bosnia the archduke symbolized continuing Austro-Hungarian domination. The Serb group behind the assassination, the Black Hand, wanted to merge Bosnia with Serbia. Austria-Hungary responded to the assassination by declaring war on Serbia, whose leaders they suspected of aiding the assassination. Germany supported Austria-Hungary, while Britain, France, and Russia entered the conflict against Germany. Soon Ottoman Turkey joined the Central Powers, closing off British and French access to the Black Sea. Germany planned a quick knockout blow against France, hoping that this would allow most troops to then be sent east to face Russia. These plans were thwarted.

European leaders expected a short war; instead they got a long, brutal conflict, the first war to be fought in three dimensions: air, sea, and land. It became a war of attrition and the first fully industrialized conflict as combatants employed more efficient and indiscriminate ways of killing, including long-range artillery, poison gas, flamethrowers, and aerial bombing. A generation of men was cut down by shrapnel that tore flesh to pieces, high explosives that pulverized bone, and gas that seared the lungs. The German soldier turned writer Erich Maria Remarque remembered the "great brotherhood [caused by] the desperate loyalty to one another of men condemned to die," while the British poet Wilfred Owen wrote: "By his dead [comrade's] smile I knew we stood in hell."[5] Many surviving soldiers were maimed mentally or physically, often suffering from shellshock, a

CHRONOLOGY
World War I, 1914–1919

1908 Austria-Hungarian annexation of Bosnia-Herzegovina

1914 Outbreak of conflict

1916 Battle of Verdun

June 1917 U.S. intervention

March 1917 Fall of czarist government in Russia

October 1917 Bolshevik revolution in Russia

March 1918 Brest-Litovsk Treaty

November 1918 End of conflict

1919 Paris Peace Conference

Renewed Conflict

Primary Source: Mud and Khaki: Memoirs of an Incomplete Soldier Read from the memoirs of a British soldier, and imagine the horrors of trench warfare and poison gas in World War I.

John Nash, *Over the Top* This painting, by the British artist John Nash, shows the trench warfare common on the western front during World War I. Here Allied soldiers leave their trenches to attack across "No Man's Land" on a snowy day.

Imperial War Museum/The Bridgeman Art Library International

horrific nervous condition that made normal life difficult or impossible. The war also generated disease and starvation among civilians.

Battlefronts

The war on the western front in Belgium and northern France largely involved soldiers huddling in muddy trenches, gas masks at hand, and using artillery and machine guns to pound the enemy troops in their trenches, combined with attacks across the barbed wire–filled ground, known as "No Man's Land," between the opposing trenches. This resulted in countless casualties. But for all the sacrifices, the front lines moved little in four years. The cataclysmic Battle of Verdun in northeastern France in 1916, during which the French stopped a surprise German assault, killed a million men, symbolizing the senseless slaughter. More soldiers may have been killed per square yard at Verdun than in any other battle in history. But despite the carnage, Verdun had little impact on the war itself. However, by 1917 the British had invented the first armored tank, "Big Willie," which was equipped with large guns and belted treads. Able to cross over No Man's Land and German trenches, it put more pressure on German lines.

The war had several fronts (see Map 24.1). In the east, Germany and its allies quickly overran Serbia and Romania and pushed deep into western Russia against poorly organized Russian armies. By 1917 the war had killed or wounded over 7 million Russians and caused Russian peasants to flee eastward, only to face hunger, disease, and homelessness. Originally a German ally, Italy switched sides in 1915 but lost heavily in unsuccessful battles. In the Middle East the Ottomans initially inflicted a heavy toll on the Allied troops that were sent to invade Turkey, including many soldiers from Australia and New Zealand. But an Arab uprising begun in 1916 and a British invasion of Ottoman-controlled Iraq forced the Ottoman forces eventually to retreat from that area. Some fighting also broke out in East Africa, as the British and South Africans invaded the German colony of Tanganyika. On the other side of the world, Japan, a British ally, occupied German-held territory in China and colonies in the Pacific islands.

Although the Germans won more battles than they lost, eventually the tide turned against them. Over time the Allies' superior wealth, better weapons, larger forces, and sea power proved decisive. Britain and Germany, possessing the world's two most powerful navies, with gigantic battleships known as dreadnoughts, engaged each other in the North Sea and the eastern Mediterranean. Eventually the Germans used their submarines to break Allied supply lines. Their attacks on British and U.S. shipping carrying supplies to Britain, however, enraged Americans and brought a reluctant United States into the war.

Turning Points

Two fateful developments in 1917—two Russian Revolutions and the intervention of the United States—altered the conflict. The first Russian Revolution overthrew the czarist government and the second, led by communists, took Russia out of the war. Freed from the eastern front, German armies made breakthroughs against the British and French forces in the west. But the U.S.

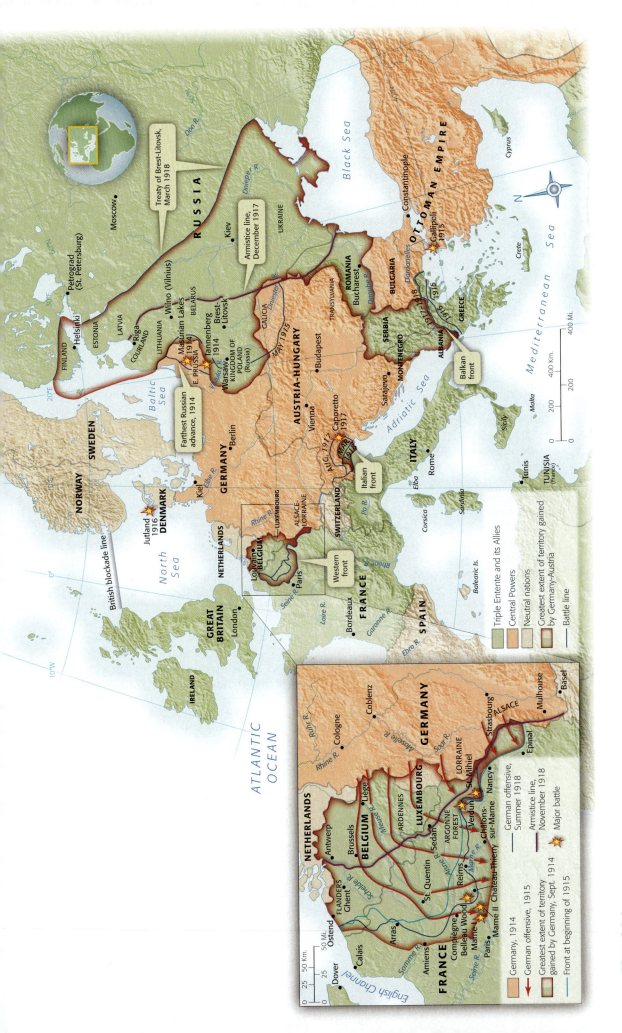

Interactive Map

Map 24.1
World War I

World War I pitted the Triple Entente of Britain, France, and Russia, and its allies, against the Central Powers: Germany, Austria-Hungary, and the Ottoman Empire. The worst fighting occurred along the western front and in eastern Europe and Russia. The intervention of the United States in 1917 against the Central Powers proved decisive.

659

intervention on the Allied side, the first major U.S. interference in European affairs, eventually offset German success. The United States had remained neutral, but, as a German victory seemed more likely, U.S. military leaders, munitions makers, politicians, and businessmen all pressed for intervention. U.S. companies and banks worried that an Allied defeat might prevent payment on orders for American products and investments in the British and French economies. Eventually President Woodrow Wilson committed the United States to war, linking the military commitment to idealistic American values when he told Congress that "the world must be made safe for democracy. We are the champions of the rights of mankind."[6]

Allied Victory

The U.S. intervention secured an Allied victory. Beginning in June 1917, American troops—ultimately over a million—arrived in Europe. Many of the young men, often from rural backgrounds, struggled to comprehend European ways; others developed a taste for European culture and a fondness for cities such as London and Paris. The United States helped the Allies blockade German ports, creating severe economic problems, and pushed the German forces back. Soon Germany's allies began surrendering. Demoralized, its overextended army in disarray, and suffering food and fuel shortages at home, Germany was forced to agree to peace in November 1918. Kaiser Wilhelm II and the Austro-Hungarian emperor both abdicated, ending two long-standing European monarchies. The Allies dictated the peace terms, which changed the old global order and began a new one.

Consequences of World War I

Reshaping Europe

World War I undermined German power and shifted more influence to Britain, France, and the United States. The Paris Peace Conference of 1919, held in the opulent former royal palace in the Paris suburb of Versailles **(vuhr-SIGH)**, reshaped Europe and resulted in the Treaty of Versailles. The U.S. president, Woodrow Wilson, hoped to use his prestige and his nation's growing power to sell an agenda, known as the Fourteen Points, to skeptical British and French leaders. Favoring political freedom and stability, Wilson proposed conciliatory treatment of Germany because he worried that a humiliated, crippled Germany would become chaotic. However, the hardline French wanted to divide Germany. The final treaty, a compromise, required Germany to partly dismantle its military; abandon its Asian, African, and Pacific colonies; and shift land to its European neighbors, leaving 3 million ethnic Germans in countries such as Czechoslovakia and Poland. The treaty also forced Germany to pay huge annual payments, known as reparations, to the Allies to compensate for their war costs. Ultimately the treaty failed to create a lasting settlement, left Germany virtually disarmed and bankrupt, and planted the roots for future problems, as Wilson had feared. The new German leader, Fridrich Ebert, saw a troubled future: "The armistice will not produce a just peace. The sacrifices imposed on us must lead to our people's doom."[7]

The war had taken an appalling human toll on both sides. Altogether 9 to 10 million soldiers died, including 2 million Russians, 2 million Germans, 1.5 million French, and 75,000 Americans. Since some 10 million civilians died, the total killed was around 20 million. The brutality and waste radicalized many workers and peasants, especially in eastern Europe, and leftist political parties—Socialists and Communists—gained strength. In 1914 Europeans had gone to war with patriotic enthusiasm, but by 1918 some philosophers and writers feared that the war meant the rejection of Enlightenment rationality; they also concluded that the slaughter had destroyed the Western claim to moral leadership in the world. Pacifist, antiwar sentiments grew. The French writer Henri Barbusse, a soldier himself, reflected these sentiments: "Shame on military glory, shame on armies, shame on the soldier's calling that changes men by turns into stupid victims and ignoble brutes."[8]

Imperial Consequences

The war destroyed several old states and created new ones. Four long-standing empires—the Russian, Ottoman, Austro-Hungarian, and German—collapsed, while Communists gained power in Russia, launching a new political and economic system. Elsewhere, Wilson, believing that ethnically homogeneous nation-states could prevent nationalist rivalries, promoted the self-determination of peoples in Europe. As a result, the Paris Peace Conference redrew national boundaries to give ethnic minorities their own states. Poland, Czechoslovakia, Yugoslavia, and Finland were carved out of the ruins of the German, Austro-Hungarian, and Russian Empires, but they later became pawns in the struggle between Germany and Russia that helped launch World War II. Many of the new states also placed various ethnic groups within arbitrary boundaries. For example, Yugoslavia included Orthodox Serbs, Catholic Croats and Slovenes, and Muslim Slavs and Albanians; these peoples had fought each other for centuries and did not share a common national identity.

The sacrifices of war, and the appeal of national independence, also led to changes within the British Empire. Britain faced uprisings and civil war in its longtime colony, Ireland, and in 1921 it was forced to grant most of the island special status within the British Empire as the self-governing

Irish Free State. In 1937 Ireland became completely independent of the British crown, finally realizing the centuries-old dream of Irish nationalists.

The victorious powers ignored the principle of self-determination for their colonies. In seeking to strengthen the main U.S. allies, Britain and France, Woodrow Wilson supported the preservation of their colonies in Asia, Africa, the Pacific, and the Caribbean. The peace settlement transferred Germany's African colonies to Britain, France, Belgium, and South Africa and its Asian and Pacific territories to Britain, France, Australia, New Zealand, and Japan. Britain and France also gained control of the Middle Eastern societies formerly ruled by Ottoman Turkey. The peace settlements, by ignoring the political struggles of colonized peoples, thus spurred opposition to the West. The death of thousands of Asian and African colonial subjects conscripted or recruited to fight for Britain, France, or Germany in World War I sparked even deeper resentments. Thus World War I was one of the key factors in the rise of nationalism, the desire to form politically independent nations, in the colonies between 1918 and 1941 (see Chapter 25).

Although the global system shaped by colonial empires and Western economic power survived after the war, European prestige and influence were weakened. The war undermined European economies, allowing the United States to leap ahead of Europe. Like British leaders in the nineteenth century, Wilson, heading the world's largest, most productive economy, wanted free trade and an open world in which American industry could assert its supremacy. Since European nations had borrowed from the United States to finance the war, they now owed the United States money, allowing the United States, long a debtor nation, to become a creditor nation. By 1919 it was producing 42 percent of all the world's industrial output, more than all of Europe combined, and had replaced Britain as the banker and workshop of the world. Wilson also helped form a League of Nations, the first organization of independent nations to work for peace and humanitarian concerns. But Wilson could not persuade the U.S. Congress, controlled by the largely isolationist Republican opposition, to approve U.S. membership in the league. Hence, the only nation with the power and stature to make the league work stayed outside, leaving Britain and France alone to deal with European and global issues.

A New Global System

SECTION SUMMARY

- The early 1900s in Europe were marked by great affluence and stability, expanding markets, and shared notions of culture, justice, and human rights.

- Many factors contributed to the start of World War I, including Germany's resentment of British and French colonial holdings, which led to a military buildup on both sides; competing claims on Bosnia-Herzegovina; and a few governments' desire to divert attention from domestic problems.

- Sparked by the assassination of Austrian archduke Franz Ferdinand in Sarajevo, the war soon involved Austro-Hungary, Germany, Britain, France, and Turkey, all of which employed unprecedented military technology that caused millions of deaths.

- In 1917 Germany seemed on the verge of victory when the United States entered the fighting, in part because of

pressure by business interests that provided goods to France and Britain and in part because of outrage over German submarine attacks on U.S. ships.

- The United States helped the French and British win the war, but U.S. president Woodrow Wilson could not prevent the French from dictating harsh settlement terms that required Germany to partially dismantle its military, abandon its colonies, give up some of its territory, and pay heavy reparations.

- The horrors of World War I led to the radicalization of many Europeans; a growth of antiwar sentiment; the breakup of the Ottoman and German Empires, much of which were colonized by Britain and France; the breakup of much of the Russian and Austro-Hungarian Empires, which were carved into new countries; and the world dominance of the United States.

THE REVOLUTIONARY PATH TO SOVIET COMMUNISM

How did communism prevail in Russia and transform that country?

The Russian Revolution, a major consequence of World War I, was a formative event of the twentieth century, shaping European and world history, politics, and beliefs. In the wake of the revolution, Russia provided a testing ground for a radical new ideology, communism, which fostered a powerful state that reshaped Russian society and provided an alternative to the capitalist democracy dominant in North America and western Europe.

The Roots of Revolution

The Russian Revolution had deep roots in Russian society and its history under the despotic czars (see Chapter 23). Controlling a huge Eurasian empire, Russia had enjoyed some industrialization, but the powerful landed aristocracy opposed further development. Socially and economically, Russia was still a somewhat feudalistic country, with peasants often remaining subject to the landowners and enjoying little social mobility or wealth. Growing discontent among intellectuals, the floundering middle class, underpaid industrial workers, and peasants, who hated the autocratic czarist system, fomented radical movements.

In 1905 a revolution broke out, only to be brutally crushed by the government, but it left a revolutionary heritage for the **Bolsheviks**, the most radical of Russia's antigovernment groups, who transformed the revolutionary socialist views promoted by Karl Marx into a dogmatic communist ideology. The Bolshevik founder and leader, Vladimir Lenin **(LEN-in)** (1870–1924), a lawyer from a middle-class family, was humorless and uncompromising but a clever political strategist who recruited supporters with his passionate beliefs and persuasive speeches. Influenced by the works of Karl Marx, he was further radicalized when the government executed his older brother for having joined an assassination plot against the czar. Most of the Bolshevik leaders, including Lenin, had spent time as political prisoners in harsh Siberian labor camps. To avoid another arrest Lenin had lived in exile elsewhere in Europe since 1907, organizing his movement.

The Bolsheviks espoused a goal of helping the downtrodden workers and peasants redress the wrongs inflicted upon them by the rich and privileged, claiming that revolutionary violence could bring about a new, classless communist society with a more equitable distribution of wealth and power. Lenin advocated a small, disciplined revolutionary organization that would work for workers' interests and whose leaders were full-time revolutionaries. All members had to abide by the decisions made by the leaders, a system known as the party line. When World War I broke out, the Russian people and even most opposition political parties rallied around the unpopular government, seeing it as a patriotic war of defense against the hated Germans. Only the Bolsheviks opposed the war, which they saw as an imperialistic struggle over markets and colonies. But the war soon lost its allure as Russian military forces collapsed in the face of stronger German armies.

By 1917 the demoralized Russian people were seeking change, sparking two revolutions. The first, in March, toppled the czar, imprisoned the imperial family, and set up a provisional government (see Chronology: Russia, 1917–1938). This unplanned revolution erupted while riots and strikes paralyzed the cities. Working women had begun the protests by swarming the streets of the capital, St. Petersburg, demanding relief and food, and they soon gained support from the soldiers sent to control them. The new provisional government leaders, such as the lawyer Aleksandr Kerensky (1881–1970), were well-meaning urban liberals who wanted reform and Western-style democracy, but they had no roots among the population. They failed because they refused to provide the two things most Russians wanted: peace and land. Because of their commitments

Bolsheviks The most radical of Russia's antigovernment groups at the turn of the twentieth century, who embraced a dogmatic form of Marxism.

Lenin The Bolshevik leader Vladimir Lenin stirred crowds with his fiery revolutionary rhetoric, helping to spread the communist message among Russians fed up with ineffective government, war, and poverty.

Sovfoto

to the Allies, they vowed to continue fighting the war, declining to redistribute land from the aristocracy to the peasantry until the war ended and elections could be held to form a new, more representative, government.

While the increasingly discredited provisional government asked for time, radicals organized **soviets**, local action councils that enlisted workers and soldiers to fight the factory owners and military officers. This grassroots movement for change undermined government authority. As the soviets and the government jockeyed for control of St. Petersburg, the Germans, hoping to weaken the Russian government, helped Lenin, in exile in Switzerland, to secretly return to Russia hidden in a railroad box car. Using the slogans of "peace, bread, and land" and "all power to the soviets," Lenin rapidly built up Bolshevik influence in the soviets. The provisional government tried to prevent the peasants from seizing land, and soldiers from deserting their units, but government control was weak.

The Bolshevik Seizure of Power and Civil War

In October 1917, the Bolsheviks and their 240,000 party members staged an uprising and grabbed power from Kerensky's crumbling provisional government. Aided by the soviets, they seized key government buildings in St. Petersburg. With a fragile hold on power, the Bolsheviks had to allow diverse parties to contest elections for an assembly, which met in January 1918. After the assembly refused to support a Bolshevik bid for leadership, however, the Bolsheviks used troops to take over the national and city governments, pushing other parties aside and terrorizing or executing opponents, including the moderate, prodemocracy socialists. Claiming that his goal was to transfer power to the working class, Lenin defended the violence, asserting that chefs cannot make an omelet without breaking eggs. The Bolsheviks then renamed themselves the Communist Party and gained popular support by pulling Russia out of the war. In the Treaty of Brest-Litovsk, negotiated with Germany in March 1918, Russia gave up some of its empire in the west to Germany, abandoning the Ukraine, eastern Poland, the Baltic states, and Finland. The Bolsheviks also moved the capital from St. Petersburg, which they renamed Leningrad, to Moscow.

Once in power, the communists had to develop a strategy for dealing with the wider world. In 1919, Lenin, hoping to protect Russia's revolution by promoting world revolution, organized the Communist International, often known as the Comintern, a collection of communist parties from around the world. However, the prospect of world revolution soon faded because of U.S. aid to Europe after the war.

The Russian Revolution sparked the Russian Civil War (1918–1921) (see Map 24.2). The leaders of the conservative, anticommunist forces, who called themselves White Russians in contrast to the communists' military force, the Red Army, included czarist aristocrats and generals who were angry at losing their dominance and a few pro-Western liberals favoring democracy. Heavily funded and armed by Western nations alarmed by the Revolution, the White Russians fought the communist forces for three years. However, the communists, with a cohesive party and brilliant military leadership, capitalized on the disunity among White Russian leaders and their Western backers. Most crucially, they received growing support from the working class and the peasants, who feared the return of the hated landowners with a White Russian victory. Although the communists initially looked vulnerable, they eventually gained the advantage, defeating the White Russians and even reclaiming some of the territory lost in the Brest-Litovsk Treaty, including the Ukraine.

Outside intervention by Japan, Britain, France, and the United States added an international flavor to the Russian Civil War. Japan, which concentrated on eastern Siberia, and Britain sent 60,000 and 40,000 troops, respectively, into Russia. The liberal idealist Wilson sent two separate American military forces to Russia to roll back the communist regime and, he claimed, spread democratic values. Five thousand American troops went to northern Russia to battle the Red Army for control of two port cities, but brutal winter weather, poor provisions, and high casualties drove the U.S. troops to near mutiny. Another contingent of 10,000 Americans entered eastern Siberia. Soon recognizing the intervention as a quagmire, Wilson lamented that it was harder to get out than it was to go in, and U.S. and other Western troops were finally removed in 1920. The Western intervention only helped solidify the communist government, widely seen by Russians as fighting a nationalist war against foreign powers seeking to restore the old discredited czarist order.

CHRONOLOGY
Russia, 1917–1938

1917 March revolution

1917 October revolution

March 1918 Brest-Litovsk Treaty

1918–1921 Russian Civil War

1922 Formation of Soviet Union

1924 Death of Lenin

1928 Beginning of Five-Year Plans

1929–1953 Stalin's dictatorship

1936–1938 Stalin's Great Purge

soviets Local action councils formed by Russian radicals before the 1917 Russian Revolution that enlisted workers and soldiers to fight the factory owners and military officers.

Russian Civil War

Foreign Interventions

Map 24.2 Civil War in Revolutionary Russia (1918–1921)

The communist seizure of power in Russia in 1917 sparked a counteroffensive, backed by varied Western nations and Japan, to reverse the Russian Revolution. The communists successfully defended the Russian heartland while pushing back the conservative offensive.

Interactive Map

Lenin, Stalin, and Dictatorship

By 1922 the Communist Party controlled much of the old Russian Empire, but the country was devastated and its people starving, and the civil war had made good relations with the capitalist democracies impossible, as well as reinforcing the paranoid, authoritarian, and militaristic attitudes of the communists. The party was forging the world's first state based on communist ideas, inspiring the growth of communist groups in other countries. Russia's leaders proclaimed their nation the Union of Soviet Socialist Republics (USSR), in theory a federation of all the empire's diverse peoples—such as Kazakhs, Uzbeks, Armenians, and Ukrainians—but largely controlled by Russians, and hence a continuation of the Russian Empire. Soon the USSR turned from world revolution to building "socialism in one country"—using coercion against reluctant citizens if necessary.

Building the Soviet Union

Since Soviet leaders had no model of a communist state, they experimented while using their secret police to eliminate opponents, among them liberals and moderate socialists. The basis for Soviet communism was **Marxism-Leninism**, a mix of socialism (collective ownership of the economy) and **Leninism**, a political system in which one party holds a monopoly on power. Lenin initially favored centralization of all economic activity, but he was forced by peasant opposition to adopt the **New Economic Policy** (NEP), a pragmatic approach that mixed capitalism and socialism, allowing peasants to sell their produce on the open market. The NEP brought economic recovery. However, with few consumer goods available, the peasants had no incentive to sell their produce for profit because there was little to buy with the money they earned.

Marxism-Leninism The basis for Soviet communism, a mix of socialism (collective ownership of the economy) and Leninism.

Leninism A political system in which one party holds a monopoly on power, excluding other parties from participation.

New Economic Policy Lenin's pragmatic approach to economic development, which mixed capitalism and socialism.

Lenin became dissatisfied with the results of the revolution, which he called socialist in appearance but not substance: "czarism slightly anointed with Soviet oil,"[9] and he criticized the bloated bureaucracy. Decades later, Lenin's assessment of his government's failures remained accurate, since the USSR never became the egalitarian communist society envisioned by Karl Marx. Lenin himself, who combined ruthless authoritarianism with concern for the exploited, deserves some of the blame. While Lenin constructed myths about mass support for the "dictatorship of the proletariat," led by the Communist Party, the ties between the political leaders and the Soviet people remained weak. The instability and divisions caused by World War I and the Russian Civil War made the communist leaders even less willing to trust the people or allow dissent, which they feared would provoke unrest.

The long czarist tradition of authoritarian, bureaucratic government and an obedient population fostered communist dictatorship. The communists were a small party, and most leaders were, like Lenin, intellectuals from urban middle-class backgrounds. To regenerate the economy, they eventually adopted not popular control of farms and enterprises by workers and peasants but a top-down managerial system staffed by officials chiefly of middle-class origin. The middle class was now largely composed of state employees, managers, and bureaucrats with salaries and privileges that were denied the masses and dedicated not to fostering social change but to maintaining their own power. Lenin hoped to reform the party but died in 1924.

Lenin's successor was a master bureaucrat, Joseph Stalin (STAH-lin) (1879–1953), who reshaped Soviet communism. Born in the Caucasus province of Georgia, he studied to be a Russian Orthodox priest before being expelled from the seminary. After joining the Bolsheviks, he adopted the name Stalin ("Man of Steel"). In control of the Communist Party apparatus, Stalin outmaneuvered his party rivals to succeed Lenin, coming to power as the peasants, no longer fearing landlords, increasingly turned away from the Communist Party. Stalin urged a hard line against those who resisted state policies, eliminated all his competition in the party, and became a dictator. The system he imposed, **Stalinism**, included state ownership of all property, such as lands and businesses, a planned economy, and one-man rule.

Stalin's Dictatorship

In 1928 Stalin ended Lenin's NEP and introduced an annual series of Five-Year Plans for future production, formulated by state bureaucrats. These plans produced basic industrial goods, such as steel and coal, but few consumer products. Stalin also launched a massive crash industrialization program and withdrew the country from the global system, mobilizing Russian resources and refusing foreign investment. In order to introduce tractors and harvesters to increase farm production, Stalin strengthened the party's grip and collectivized the land, turning private farms into commonly owned enterprises and destroying the wealthier small farmers, the *kulaks*, by exiling to Siberia those who refused to join the collective farms.

Stalinism Joseph Stalin's system of government, which included state ownership of all property, such as lands and businesses, a planned economy, and one-man rule.

The 1930s and 1940s were hard, terror-filled years for the Soviet people. Stalin ordered purges to eliminate actual or potential opponents; forced-labor camps for suspected dissidents; and the widespread use of the secret police (the KGB), which spied on and intimidated the people. When the collectivization of farming provoked a widespread famine, the growing dissent led to the Great

gulags Harsh forced-labor camps in Siberia.

Purge of 1936–1938, marked by well-publicized trials of some party leaders as traitors. Stalin also deported millions to the harsh forced labor camps in Siberia known as **gulags** (Russian shorthand for State Camp Administration). Some 4 to 5 million people were arrested and half a million executed for alleged subversion, and from 1929 until 1953 some 18 million people passed through the massive gulag system, 4.5 million of these never returning home. Gulag inmates toiled, starved, and died building railroads, cutting timber, or digging canals. Not even beloved artists were spared the repression, especially if they were Jewish. One of Russia's most revered poets, Osip Mandelstam **(MAHN-duhl-stuhm)** (1891–1938), died in the gulag in 1938. The total dead and jailed from Stalin's repression numbered around 40 million people. The Russian poet Anna Akhmatova **(uhk-MAH-tuh-vuh)** (1889–1966), in her requiem for a lost generation, summarized the horror: "Madness has already covered, Half my soul with its wing. And gives to drink of a fiery wine, And beckons into the dark valley."[10]

Economic Costs

The repression also came at a high economic cost. Peasants often destroyed their equipment and livestock as a protest, and agriculture suffered from these losses for decades. Peasants also adopted passive resistance, doing just the minimum to survive. As a result, Russia's annual food production between 1928 and 1980 was less than in 1924. Since the government could not use agricultural surplus to finance industrialization, it squeezed the urban workers, forced to labor long hours for low wages and few consumer goods. Workers in turn became alienated and passively resisted, voicing their feelings in the common expression: "The government pretends they are paying us so we pretend we are working." The economic system was hurt by a lack of initiative and creativity, as well as by high rates of alcoholism and theft.

Reshaping Russian Society

At the same time, the communists introduced modern ideas. The crash industrialization raised the gross national product (GNP), the annual total of all economic activities, to second in the world by 1932, and the Five-Year Plans mobilized the population for industrialization; as with Meiji Japan, the state, rather than private capital, was the main agent for change. The industrial work force nearly tripled between 1928 and 1937. In addition, mass education raised the literacy rate from 28 percent in 1900 to over 90 percent by the 1980s, and better medical care raised life expectancy from thirty-two in 1914 to seventy in 1960.

Communism also reshaped social patterns. Lenin wanted to promote social equality by breaking up traditional institutions, including the patriarchal family. In 1918 the Soviet official and feminist Alexandra Kollontai (1872–1952), arguing that the state should fund child care and domestic work, envisioned public kitchens, laundries, and nurseries so that women could work outside the home. Lenin also made divorce easier, legalized homosexuality, sanctioned free love and abortion, and forbade Muslim women from wearing the veil and men from having multiple wives. Stalin, however, reversed Lenin's policies, restoring the family, making divorce more difficult, banning abortion, and persecuting homosexuals. Kollontai, whose outspokenness on women's freedom antagonized party leaders, later became the Soviet ambassador to Sweden, the world's first female ambassador.

Unlike the atheistic Lenin, who considered religion a form of spiritual oppression by promoting a belief in a better life after death, Stalin moderated official atheism and pragmatically reached some accommodation with the Russian Orthodox Church, while keeping it subject to state control. While many Soviet citizens professed atheism, at least half identified themselves as religious in the 1936 census. Stalin also ordered literary and artistic works to depict Soviet life from a revolutionary perspective, a style known as **socialist realism**.

socialist realism Literary and artistic works that depicted life from a revolutionary perspective, a style first introduced in Stalin's Russia.

The USSR was the first society to leave the capitalist world order, industrialize rapidly under direct state control, and establish a socialist society. Although aimed at catching up to the West in a short time, it came at a high cost in human rights and lives, and its pervasive system of political repression and state control limited its appeal to other societies. Historians debate how much of the Soviet system was due to communism and how much to an autocratic Russian tradition that despised merchants and promoted deference to state power. The USSR combined Marxist ideology, czarist despotism, and the missionary impulse, derived from Christianity, to spread the "true faith" to the world.

SECTION SUMMARY

- The Bolsheviks, a group of Marxist revolutionaries led by Vladimir Lenin, were energized by the unsuccessful 1905 Russian revolution and organized a core of professional activists devoted to violent revolution and more equitable distribution of wealth and power.

- In March 1917, a spontaneous revolution overthrew the czar, but its urban liberal leaders could not satisfy the people's demand for reform and an end to the war, so radical soviets, allied with the Bolsheviks, organized, and in October they seized power and then removed Russia from the war.

- In the interest of spreading the revolution, Lenin founded the Communist International, but he was soon fighting the Russian Civil War against the White Russians, who included defenders of the aristocracy and were funded and armed by Western nations disturbed by the Bolshevik revolution.

- After winning the civil war, the Bolsheviks focused on establishing Marxism-Leninism in the USSR, a brand of socialism achieved through one-party rule that treated opponents ruthlessly and failed to achieve a true connection between the masses and the government.

- Lenin's successor, Joseph Stalin, sent millions to forced-labor camps called gulags and imposed state ownership of all property and a planned economy, which led to decreased harvests and widespread misery.

- Rapid industrialization made the USSR the second largest world economy by 1932, and other advances greatly increased the literacy rate and life expectancy, but at the cost of many lives and limitations of human rights even more severe than under the czars.

THE INTERWAR YEARS AND THE GREAT DEPRESSION

How did the Great Depression reshape world politics and economies?

Peace in Europe had brought a great questioning of the old order. By the early 1920s, however, western Europe had stabilized and most countries had democratically elected governments, while the United States enjoyed widespread prosperity. But Western affluence was dramatically undermined by the **Great Depression**, a collapse of the world economy that lasted in varying degrees of severity through the 1930s. The Depression's global reach illustrated the economic interdependence of societies. As the distress affected both industrialized nations and those countries and colonies supplying raw materials, it also fostered radical political movements.

Great Depression A collapse of the world economy that lasted in varying degrees of severity through the 1930s.

Postwar Europe and Japan

The 1920s was a decade of political, economic, and social change throughout western Europe and Japan. Europe's very slow and painful recovery fostered political opposition movements, placing conservatives on the defensive. Many European governments were weakened by political infighting, and conservative-dominated regimes usually rebuffed the demands of workers for better conditions or unions, causing socialist and social democratic parties, such as the British Labor Party, to grow stronger and try to extend workers' rights through legislation. Some countries remained politically and economically unstable. Under a new democratic government, the Weimar (VIE-mahr) Republic, Germany struggled with high unemployment and a devastated economy, and in 1923 France occupied the industrialized Ruhr district of western Germany to enforce reparations payments. The costly reparations caused hyperinflation in Germany, which in turn fostered extremist groups. Since German prosperity was essential for the European economy, the Allies reduced reparations and the United States extended loans, but the Weimar regime continued to face challenges. Multiethnic countries such as Poland, with its large German, Russian, and Ukrainian minorities, and a Czechoslovakia that mixed Czechs and Slovaks with Germans, Poles, Hungarians, and Ukrainians, also experienced tensions.

Political and Economic Changes

However, some countries enjoyed an economic recovery that curbed inflation and unemployment. After Europeans borrowed U.S. mass production processes, including the assembly lines pioneered at Ford Motor Company in Detroit, the growing middle classes could afford cars, radios, refrigerators, vacuum cleaners, and central heating. Although the urban white-collar class tended to oppose working-class socialism, labor unions also gained strength, helping some workers achieve an eight-hour day. Yet Europe's economies were more and more bound up with the world economy, losing ground to the United States and Japan.

Various forces fostered European unity to safeguard peace. To promote peace and unity among European nations, some leaders emphasized their common roots in classical Greece, Rome, and Christianity. The visionary French foreign minister, Aristide Briand **(bree-AHND)** (1862–1932), led efforts to renounce war among European nations, proposing a federal union and common market. His vision only came to fruition two decades later, with the formation of the European Common Market.

Cities and Gender Relations

Social change in the cities included new patterns of leisure and consumption. Affluent people found entertainment at nightclubs, cabarets, and dancehalls and shopped at large department stores, and U.S. culture, especially jazz, became widely popular. Religious observance declined because some Europeans felt abandoned by God on the battlefields or rejected Christianity as a patriarchal faith out of tune with their lives. Women's fashions emphasized short hair and a boyish figure, while the "new woman" sought financial independence through paid work. As the war had left fewer young men to marry or hire, women moved into office jobs, the female secretary replacing the male clerk. More women also became lawyers, physicians, and even members of parliaments. Finally, in many countries, women fought for and often achieved suffrage. Before the war only Norway and Finland had women's suffrage. Denmark gave women the vote in 1915 and Germany in 1919, while Britain extended it to women over thirty in 1918 and to all women over eighteen in 1928. But many countries, including France and Italy, ignored these demands.

As gender standards changed, once-shocking attitudes became common, including an openness about sexuality and a rejection of traditional marriage. Women now wore clothes that showed off their figure, and beauty contests featured women in revealing swimsuits that would have once been considered scandalous. Yet, official attitudes toward homosexuality shifted toward repression. In the nineteenth century, despite antisodomy laws on the books, courts had usually dismissed charges of homosexual relations, and Europeans understood that some men and women had same-sex relations or emotional ties. By the early 1900s, however, the media identified homosexuals as different in attitudes from heterosexuals. While gay men and lesbians lived openly in cities such as Paris and Berlin, they were often watched and suffered police raids on their clubs. Although Soviet Russia and Weimar Germany legalized homosexuality, these tolerant policies were later reversed. In 1934 Stalin defined homosexuality as a crime against the state, and in 1935 Nazi Germany prosecuted 50,000 men for homosexual activity. Many European nations also banned abortion and birth control.

Changing Japan

As in Europe, industrialization, democratic politics, and liberalization reshaped Japan during the 1920s, generating prosperity and new possibilities for the growing urban middle class. Japan's population tripled between 1860 and 1940 to 60 million, but lack of land forced many rural people to move to cities or emigrate to the Americas to find work. Cheap labor helped to gain foreign markets for Japanese consumer goods, especially textiles. Powerful business interests dominated the democratic system, and corrupt and volatile politics disillusioned many Japanese of all social classes.

Japan played a visible role in the world. Even before World War I, it had already colonized Taiwan and Korea and gained footholds in northern China, and during the war it acquired the German colonies in the Pacific and the German sphere of influence in eastern China. This assertive role created enemies. Tensions with the United States increased, fostered in part by the American racist laws restricting the rights of Japanese immigrants and in part by U.S. hostility to Japanese ambitions in Asia and the Pacific.

As in the 1870s, a wave of Western influence permeated Japan's cities. American popular culture influenced urban middle-class Japanese, and baseball became a popular sport. In Tokyo, young men and women, known as the "modern boy" and "modern girl," wore the latest imported styles while enjoying jazz, beer halls, and Western films. Young women avidly read mass women's magazines, many questioned the tradition of the submissive female and dominant male, and many young people sought freedom to choose their own marriage partners. Feminism also grew. For conservatives, nontraditional Japanese such as the openly lesbian writer Yoshiya Nobuko **(yo-SHE-ya no-BOO-ko)**, whose work had a large following among youth (see Profile: Yoshiya Nobuko: Japanese Writer and Gender Rebel), were leading Japan in the wrong direction. The feminist poet Yosano

Akiko celebrated the emerging women's movement: "All the sleeping women, Are now awake and moving."[11] Another leading feminist, Kato Shidzue **(KAH-to shid-ZOO-ee)** (1897–2001), sojourned in the United States and then advocated family planning and equal political rights for women. Japanese thinkers and artists also pondered the divide between traditional and modern values and cultural identity. The writer Akutagawa Ryunosuke (1892–1927), who combined Western and Japanese traditions, wrote an influential short story, *Rashoman*, that tells of a rape and murder from several eyewitness perceptions. However, the working classes and rural population were alienated from the Westernized middle class culture of the cities, seeing little benefit in either the liberalization of customs or individualistic Western thought. Nor did they share in the economic prosperity.

U.S. Society and Politics

In the United States, anticommunism prompted by the Russian Revolution and growing middle-class prosperity bolstered conservative forces. Americans were hostile to socialism of any kind and especially communist ideology, and hatred of Russians and communism replaced hatred of Germans. In 1919–1920 widespread public fear of communism, known as the "Red Scare," generated the first in a series of government crackdowns on dissidents that suppressed strikes, harassed labor unions, arrested political radicals, and deported foreigners (see Chronology: Europe, North America, and Japan, 1919–1940). The Red Scare froze attitudes toward communist movements for generations, as the United States pursued a policy of isolating the USSR. A U.S. senator and critic of this policy concluded in 1925, "So long as you have a hundred and fifty million people [in the U.S.S.R.] outlawed, it necessarily follows that you cannot have peace."[12] Not until 1933 would the United States soften its policy and extend diplomatic recognition.

Various forms of domestic unrest also existed. Desperate workers struck for better wages, while left-wing unions fought against the power of "big business." In response, alarmed federal, state, and local governments helped employers fight labor unions in the Appalachian coal fields, Detroit auto plants, and South Atlantic textile mills, sending police to break up strikes and arrest union organizers. There was also widespread resentment of the U.S. Congress for passing Prohibition, which outlawed alcohol production and made it harder to obtain liquor. In addition, World War I veterans protested when the government was slow in providing their back pay and they had trouble finding jobs. Federal government policies often made life worse for the less affluent, and political leaders ignored terrorism, including lynchings by white racists of African Americans in the South. To escape mistreatment and limited economic prospects, several million African Americans moved from southern states to the north and west in the 1920s, doubling the black populations of cities such as Chicago, Detroit, and New York. Dominating the federal government, the Republicans, oriented toward big business, neglected the country's natural and human resources, contributing to eroded croplands and fouled rivers.

For the top half of the U.S. population, however, including a growing middle class, these were the "Roarin' 20s," the hedonistic era when high society had few inhibitions. Affluent whites evaded Prohibition by buying illegally produced liquor. Gatsby, a character in a novel by the popular writer and playboy F. Scott Fitzgerald (1896–1940), exemplified the optimistic American values of the time: "Gatsby believed in the green light, the future that year by year recedes before us. It eluded us then, but that's no matter—tomorrow we will run faster, stretch out our arms farther, and one fine morning . . ."[13] Other changes affected all Americans. Jazz music, rooted in southern black culture, provided employment for black musicians and became so popular that the era was often known as "the Jazz Age." Women finally won the vote in 1920, allowing more of them to enjoy a larger public role. And all Americans celebrated the first nonstop flight between North America and Europe, made by Charles Lindbergh (1902–1974) in 1927, a feat demonstrating both heroism and advances in technology.

In contrast to Woodrow Wilson's idealistic globalism, American leaders proclaimed an isolationist foreign policy; in reality, however, they often practiced interventionism. Restless American citizens sought new Christian converts, commercial markets, and business investments, reflecting

The Roarin' 20s

Isolationism

CHRONOLOGY
Europe, North America, and Japan, 1919–1940

1919–1920 First Red Scare in United States

1921 Irish Free State

1921 Formation of Italian fascist movement

1926 Formation of fascist state in Italy

1929–1941 Great Depression

1931 Japanese occupation of Manchuria

1933–1945 Presidency of Franklin D. Roosevelt

1932 Nazi electoral victory in Germany

1933–1938 Anti-Jewish legislation in Germany

1935–1936 Italian conquest of Ethiopia

1936 Start of fascist government in Japan

October 1936 Hitler-Mussolini alliance

1936–1939 Spanish Civil War

1937 Japanese invasion of China

March 1938 Austrian merger with Germany

1938 German annexation of western Czechoslovakia

August 1939 Nazi-Soviet pact

September 1939 German invasion of Poland

1940 Tripartite Pact between Germany, Italy, and Japan

YOSHIYA NOBUKO, JAPANESE WRITER AND GENDER REBEL

Yoshiya Nobuko (1896–1973) was a popular, gender-bending writer who lived through major transitions as Japan moved from a parochial society through imperial power and world war to become an industrial powerhouse. She was born in the northern Honshu city of Niigata just after the Japanese victory over China in the Sino-Japanese War (1894–1895). Her middle-class, culturally conservative parents trained her for the "good wife, wise mother" role expected of women in Meiji Japan. Yoshiya observed that her mother encouraged her to adopt traditional roles of female domesticity and obedience to men while she herself remained in a loveless arranged marriage to Yoshiya's father.

Yoshiya, who began writing as a child, published her first short stories at age twelve. In 1915 she moved to Tokyo, where she began to diverge from Japanese society's career and gender expectations. Rising Japanese literacy was opening doors to literature aimed at a popular audience, allowing writers such as Yoshiya to make a living from their work. Between 1916 and 1924 Yoshiya's short stories were serialized in a popular magazine, *Girl's Illustrated*, aimed at young, chiefly female readers. The stories she published inspired a generation of women writers and made Yoshiya famous. They appealed to schoolgirls and to the growing group of women not yet committed to marriage and children. According to tradition, women were supposed to be married by age twenty-four, but many young women now worked in the public sector as clerks, cafe hostesses, ticket sellers, schoolteachers, typists, and telephone operators. Yoshiya's core audience came from this group, especially the so-called modern girl, a Westernized urban woman who avoided or postponed marriage. Critics accused these women of being un-Japanese and manly.

In her writing and life, the very modern Yoshiya took advantage of the new public sphere opened to women for redefining relations between them. She challenged the conventions of family life, openly avowing her lesbianism. Japanese had traditionally tolerated homosexuality, including public displays of affection by people of the same gender. Now more openly passionate friendships between females were becoming common among students, educators, civil servants, and actresses. Japanese society viewed female homosexuality as spiritual, in contrast to the popular image of the carnal male version, and gradually lesbianism developed from a phase of life among girls to an adult subculture. Despite laws requiring women to have long hair, Yoshiya was one of the first Japanese

Yoshiya Nobuko A prominent Japanese writer for popular audiences, especially for girls and young women, Yoshiya Nobuko represented the modern girl. She wore her hair short and usually dressed in a mannish style that defied gender expectations.

Kyoto News Photos

women to emulate Western fashion in the 1920s by cutting her hair short, symbolizing her maverick persona. In 1923 Yoshiya met her life partner, Monma Chiyo, a mathematics teacher at a Tokyo girls' school. They remained inseparable and openly lived together as a couple, writing steamy, often erotic, love letters to each other even when together. In 1957 Yoshiya adopted Monma, the only legal way for homosexual couples to share property and make medical decisions for each other. Yoshiya also flouted gender expectations in other ways. She designed her own house, was one of the first Japanese to own a car, and was the first Japanese woman to own a racehorse.

Yoshiya became one of Japan's most successful and highest-paid writers. A literary critic wrote in 1935 that "there isn't a [Japanese] woman alive who hasn't heard of Yoshiya." Her Japanese readership included many middle-class men and women, gay and straight, single and married. She published girls' fiction, social commentary, and autobiographical essays. Some literary critics criticized Yoshiya for seeking a mass audience, but her defenders argued that Yoshiya's writing broadened minds. She and Monma spent 1929 traveling in Russia, Europe, and the United States, where she was impressed by what she considered America's liberated women. After the trip, she vowed to no longer write about women "who cried a lot and simply endured their miserable lot in life."

While an ardent feminist, Yoshiya mistrusted political parties and never became active in the organized Japanese feminist movement. She also disliked the militaristic turn of the 1930s, which brought more censorship. To avoid political harassment or imprisonment, she joined a government writers' group that toured Southeast Asia and China during World War II and wrote stories and reports praising Japanese imperial ambitions. After the war she continued to publish fiction and nonfiction, winning numerous awards. She began to write historical novels to redress female stereotypes in male fiction, such as the dutiful wife, and to restore the voice of women to Japanese history. She died at home at age seventy-seven, holding Monma's hand. Yoshiya's writings remain popular in Japan today.

THINKING ABOUT THE PROFILE

1. How did Yoshiya's life reflect the social changes of the era in Japan?

2. Why might her writing have attracted a large audience?

Note: Quotations from Jennifer Robertson, "Yoshiya Nobuko: Out and Outspoken in Practice and Prose," in Anne Walthall , ed., *The Human Tradition in Modern Japan* (Wilmington, DE: SR Books, 2002), 156, 167.

the optimistic, unsettled character of American society, which emphasized free enterprise and the belief in America's political and economic model. In 1904 President Theodore Roosevelt had proclaimed that America should intervene as an international police power whenever a country, in his estimation, committed chronic wrongdoing. This view, adopted by later U.S. presidents, justified military interventions to punish opponents and reward allies in Latin America. U.S. Marines remained in Nicaragua for decades (1909–1933), and El Salvador, Haiti, Mexico, and the Dominican Republic all experienced major U.S. military incursions between 1914 and 1940.

The Great Depression

The major spur to change, the Great Depression, began in the United States in the fall of 1929, when prices on the New York Stock Exchange fell dramatically, ruining many investors. This crash ultimately precipitated a worldwide economic disaster unprecedented in intensity, longevity, and spread that lasted until 1941 and affected industrial and agricultural economies alike. The flow of wealth into the United States had intensified existing imbalances in world trade and investment. Generally self-sufficient, the U.S was less dependent on world trade than Britain had been when it was the world's leading economic power. While the British had invested profits abroad, Americans mostly invested and spent at home to satisfy a self-indulgent society. Meanwhile, stiff U.S. government tariff barriers against manufactured goods hurt European economies, and the nation refused to shift to an aggressive free trade position until well into the 1930s. Furthermore, the world banking and credit structure was very unstable, partly because the United States did not use its unmatched economic power to make the world economy work efficiently. Instead U.S. banks, too anxious for profits, became overextended in loans to Britain, France, and Germany. Conditions within the United States also generated the Great Depression. A "get-rich-quick" philosophy led to reckless financial practices, such as risky loans and investments. Income inequality was stark: by 1929 the top 20 percent of American families earned 54 percent of the income while the bottom 40 percent earned 12.5 percent. As more people fell into poverty, purchasing power declined, while more consumer products became available, causing a glut. As a result, many manufacturers could not sell enough products to stay in business or avoid layoffs.

These problems led to the stock market crash, followed later by bank failures. As U.S. banks faced ruin, they called in their debts from western European banks, triggering a chain reaction of bank failures. In the United States the GNP and industrial output fell by one-half in four years, and unemployment rose to 25 percent of the labor force by 1932. All areas of the U.S. economy were hurt, and the misery was widespread. President Herbert Hoover (g. 1929–1933), who opposed government intervention in the economy, failed to stem the collapse or the pain. Things were even

Roots of Disaster

Economic Collapse

WORLD'S HIGHEST STANDARD OF LIVING

There's no way like the American Way

Depression Breadline   During the Depression, breadlines, such as this one in New York City, were common in the United States as millions of unemployed and desperate people sought food from social service providers, including religious groups.

Time Life Pictures/Getty Images

worse in European nations. Some 30 percent of Germans were out of work by 1932, and German industrial output declined by half. A French politician summed up the disaster in his nation: "The oceans were deserted, the ships laid up in the silent ports, the factory smokestacks dead, long lines of workless in the towns, poverty throughout the countryside. Nations were economically cut off from one another, but they shared the common lot of poverty."[14] Many societies in Asia, Africa, Latin America, and the Caribbean were also devastated as demand for, and hence the price of, raw materials such as rubber, tin, and sugar plummeted. Only the USSR avoided major pain, since it was largely outside the world economy and hence somewhat insulated from the dislocations.

U.S. Distress

The Great Depression brought severe economic distress to the United States. Homeowners and farmers saw banks foreclose on their property, migrant workers moved around in a futile search for jobs, hungry Americans flocked to breadlines and soup kitchens for food and milk supplied by charitable organizations, and sidewalk vendors hoped to make a few pennies selling apples. Shantytowns known as "Hoovervilles" sprang up on the edges of cities to house the unemployed and dispossessed, and parts of the Midwest and Southwest became a **Dust Bowl**, as terrible drought and disappearing topsoil, caused by erosion and government neglect, put agriculture badly out of balance. Farm income dropped 50 percent, causing 3 to 4 million people, mostly farmers, to head to the West Coast after selling or losing their land. A witness in 1932 told a congressional committee: "The roads of the West and Southwest teem with hungry hitchhikers. The campfires of the homeless are seen along every railroad track."[15] The experiences of these impoverished migrants were chronicled in the novels of John Steinbeck (1902–1968), such as *The Grapes of Wrath*, and by the leftwing Oklahoma-born folksinger, Woody Guthrie (1912–1967), in songs such as "Pastures of Plenty": "I've worked in your orchards of peaches and prunes, Slept on the ground in the light of the moon, On the edge of your city you've seen us and then, We come with the dust and we go with the wind."[16]

Dust Bowl Parts of the U.S. Midwest and Southwest during the 1930s where disappearing topsoil and severe drought threw agriculture badly out of balance.

Panic, despair, and disillusionment seized the country. Unlike some western Europeans, Americans had no social security, unemployment insurance, or welfare system to turn to. In 1932, when ragged World War I veterans marched in Washington, D.C., demanding payment of the bonuses once promised them, President Hoover ordered federal troops to disperse them at gunpoint. As a result, the union movement and leftwing political parties such as the communists grew rapidly, and labor militancy and strikes led to confrontations between workers and the police. Women had to stay with their children in tent cities while their husbands looked for work. Jobless men lost status and often turned to drink. The Depression also intensified the poverty of African Americans, whose unemployment rate approached 70 percent.

Roosevelt's Presidency

The Depression caused a change of leadership and turnaround in U.S. government policy. Discontent against inaction drove the Republicans from office in 1933 and brought in a new president, Democrat Franklin Delano Roosevelt (1882–1945). Roosevelt expressed optimism, telling the nation that they had nothing to fear but fear itself. He introduced the **New Deal**, a new government policy of liberal reform within a democratic framework to alleviate the suffering. Roosevelt proposed what he called the "four freedoms"—freedom of speech and worship and freedom from want and fear. His reforms included regulations on banks and stock exchanges to prevent future depressions, public welfare programs, and social security, which guaranteed retirement income for workers. For the first time, the federal government took responsibility for providing pensions and other supportive help to citizens. Roosevelt also supported union organizing. Although it did not end the Depression, the New Deal made government popular and modified the pain. By defusing the appeal of socialism and communism, it also saved U.S. capitalism. In the later 1930s, when the recovery faltered, Roosevelt used the ideas of the British economist John Maynard Keynes (1883–1946), who advocated deficit spending by governments to spur economic growth. Keynes argued that free markets were not self-correcting and needed government regulation. The mobilization of military forces and manufacturing during World War II finally ended the Depression.

New Deal A new U.S. government program of liberal reform within a democratic framework introduced by President Franklin Roosevelt to alleviate suffering caused by the Great Depression.

European Distress

By devastating the economies of Europe and Japan, the Depression challenged the weaker democratic systems. A quarter to a third of Europeans became jobless. Germans often faced malnutrition, and hunger marches became common in Britain. A French observer described Paris as an "abyss of misery, suffering, and disorder, the theaters nearly empty, factories shut, businesses bankrupt; grey faces and bad news everywhere."[17] Countries developed public works programs to create jobs and also discouraged imports, further reducing international trade. However, some nations lacked the resources for a New Deal type of reform. To pay the World War I reparations, Germany had borrowed heavily, especially from the United States, and had no way to repay the loans.

A few nations gradually relieved the distress. Newer British industries such as motor and aircraft production and electronics showed rapid growth, and increased consumer demand gradually turned around the British economy. The Scandinavian nations of Denmark, Norway, and Sweden had the most success by pursuing "the Middle Way," a combination of undogmatic socialist economics with long-established democratic traditions based on community action. Social democratic parties, favoring a mix of free markets, a welfare state, and democratic politics, had come to power in Scandinavia in the 1920s. By increasing government intervention in the economy, the social democrats ensured full employment and protected people from hardship.

The Depression hit Japan even harder than Europe and the United States, making clear its nearly total dependence on foreign trade. As the world economy collapsed, many foreign markets closed, unemployment skyrocketed, and Japan's foreign trade was cut in half in two years, forcing Japan's 100 million people to dramatically reduce consumption of necessities such as food and fuel. Because Japan had no access to the resource-rich Western colonies in Southeast Asia, Japanese leaders, becoming more authoritarian, turned to radical solutions, including expansion abroad and building a heavy arms industry.

Japan in Crisis

Western Cultures, Thought, and Science

Tempered by the trauma of war and then the Depression, Western culture went in new directions, including the rise of mass culture, popular entertainments appealing to a wide segment of the population and disseminated by radio and motion pictures. Radio stations appeared and the recording industry grew. By 1930, 40 percent of U.S. families owned a radio; by 1940, 86 percent did. In North America and Europe the urban middle class found solace especially in popular music. American jazz musicians such as Louis Armstrong, Duke Ellington, and Billie Holiday had an international following, and songs written by New York City–based writers, known collectively as Tin Pan Alley, reached millions around the world through radios, records, movies, and musical theater. The sophisticated and romantic songs written by Americans like Richard Rodgers and Lorenz Hart, George and Ira Gershwin, Irving Berlin, Jerome Kern, and Cole Porter buoyed peoples' spirits. Porter's song, "Anything Goes" (1934), chronicled changing fashions: "In olden days a bit of [women's] stocking, was looked on as something shocking. Now, heaven knows, anything goes." By contrast, some popular songs of the 1930s, such as "The Boulevard of Broken Dreams" and "Brother, Can You Spare a Dime?," addressed harsh reality.

Rise of Mass Culture

Cultural vistas expanded. Painters, poets, and novelists settled in a few run-down Paris neighborhoods and produced work that vigorously broke from older traditions. The innovative and versatile painter Pablo Picasso (1881–1973), a Spaniard who settled in Paris, helped invent **cubism**, a form of painting that rejected visual reality and emphasized instead geometric shapes and forms that often suggested movement. Soon Picasso, who later joined the Communist Party, abandoned representational art entirely and sought visual experience as transformed by the artist in his mind. Literature explored the inner world of thought and feelings. The Irishman James Joyce (1882–1941), who had enjoyed no formal education, broke traditional rules of grammar, and his books were often banned for using obscenity. In England Virginia Woolf (1882–1941) converted the novel from a narrative story into a succession of images, thoughts, and emotions known as stream of consciousness. Her 1929 novel, *A Room of One's Own*, championed women's growing economic independence.

Arts and Science

cubism A form of painting that rejected visual reality and emphasized instead geometric shapes and forms that often suggested movement.

The social and natural sciences also brought a greater understanding of human behavior and the physical world. Sigmund Freud (FROID) (1856–1939), an Austrian Jewish physician, developed psychoanalysis, a combination of medical science and psychology, and shocked the world by arguing that sex was of great subconscious importance in shaping people's behavior. In physics, Albert Einstein (1879–1955) radically modified the Newtonian vision of physical nature and rejected the absolutes of space and time, arguing that time depended on the relative motion of the measurer and the thing measured. Einstein fled the anti-Jewish atmosphere of Nazi Germany for the United States, where he helped convince President Roosevelt to sponsor research on atomic weapons. He spent the rest of his life seeking a unifying theory to explain every physical process in the universe.

SECTION SUMMARY

- After the war Germany experienced rapid inflation because of its postwar debt, Europe lost economic ground to the United States and Japan, and women entered the work force and the political sphere.

- Many Japanese benefited from postwar economic growth, though some rural Japanese had to move to cities or emigrate, while Japan played a larger role in world affairs and clashed with the United States over its treatment of Japanese immigrants and Japanese ambitions in Asia.

- American fear of communism led to the "Red Scare," a harsh crackdown on dissidents and union organizers, while the split widened between the poor, who suffered under government policies, and the affluent, who enjoyed the "Roarin' 20s."

- Among the factors contributing to the Great Depression were America hoarding its profits, American tariffs against European imports, risky investment practices (which helped cause the stock market crash of 1929), and uneven distribution of income.

- With millions of Americans jobless, homeless, and hungry, radical movements grew in power and President Franklin Delano Roosevelt instituted the New Deal, a sweeping series of programs that put people to work, provided pensions, and protected against future depressions.

- The Great Depression hit Europe and Japan even harder than the United States, rendering Germany unable to pay its heavy debts and causing Japan to become more authoritarian and expansionist, while Scandinavian nations emerged in better condition by combining socialism, free markets, and democracy.

- The United States took the lead in developing the new mass media of radio and motion pictures, painters such as Picasso broke radically with earlier forms, and Freud and Einstein did pioneering work in psychoanalysis and physics.

THE RISE OF FASCISM AND THE RENEWAL OF CONFLICT

> What were the main ideas and impacts of fascism?

fascism An ideology that typically involved extreme nationalism, hatred of ethnic minorities, ruthless repression of opposition groups, violent anticommunism, glorification of the state, and authoritarian government.

By devastating the economies of Germany and Japan, the Great Depression helped spread a new ideology in these countries. This ideology, **fascism**, typically involved extreme nationalism, hatred of ethnic minorities, ruthless repression of opposition groups, violent anticommunism, glorification of the state, and authoritarian government. Fascist movements often included a party with a large membership, such as the German Nazis (National Socialist German Workers), that was headed by a charismatic leader and supported military expansion. Fascism, which assaulted liberal values and rational thinking, was embraced by Italy, Germany, and Japan and also influenced China and several eastern European and Latin American nations.

The March to Fascism

Fascism in Italy

First emerging in Italy in 1921, fascism was a response to political corruption, an economic slump, and the instability of democratic politics. Domestic unrest increased as peasants and workers demanded a fairer share of wealth, and fascism arose from a pragmatic alliance of upper-class conservatives in the military, bureaucracy, and industry with discouraged members of the middle class who faced economic hardships. Both groups feared communism. Benito Mussolini (1883–1945), a one-time teacher and journalist and former socialist and World War I veteran, founded the Italian fascist movement, which advocated national unity and strong government. A spellbinding orator, Mussolini aroused mass enthusiasm by promising a vigorous and disciplined Italy. He especially attracted war veterans with his nationalistic rhetoric, using an ancient Roman symbol, the *fasces*, a bundle of sticks wrapped around an ax handle and blade, to symbolize the unity he wanted to bring Italy. Landowners and industrialists funded his movement because it battered labor and peasant organizations, and the upper classes viewed Mussolini as a bulwark against the radical workers.

Mussolini also won the support of the Italian king, the Catholic Church, and the lower middle class, from which he organized a uniform-wearing paramilitary group, the Blackshirts, who violently attacked, intimidated, and sometimes murdered opponents. In 1922 the king asked Mus-

The Doctrine of Fascism

Benito Mussolini gradually developed an ideology for his movement that appealed to the Italian people's nationalistic emotions. The following excerpt comes from an essay under Mussolini's name that was published in an Italian encyclopedia in 1932. In fact, the true author was a Mussolini confidant, the philosopher Giovanni Gentile. The essay reflected Mussolini's vision of fascism as the wave of the future, in which the individual would subordinate her or his desires to the needs of the state.

Fascism, the more it considers and observes the future and the development of humanity quite apart from political considerations of the moment, believes neither in the possibility nor the utility of perpetual peace. It thus repudiates the doctrine of Pacifism—born of the renunciation of the struggle and an act of cowardice in the face of sacrifice. War alone brings up to its highest tension all human energy and puts the stamp of nobility upon the peoples who have the courage to meet it. . . . Fascism [is] the complete opposite of . . . Marxian Socialism, the materialist conception of history. . . . Above all Fascism denies that class-war can be the preponderant force in the transformation of society. . . .

After Socialism, Fascism combats the whole complex system of democratic ideology, and repudiates it, whether in its theoretical premises or in its practical application. Fascism denies that the majority, by the simple fact that it is a majority, can direct human society; it denies that numbers alone can govern by means of periodic consultation. . . . The democratic regime . . . [gives] the illusion of sovereignty, while the real effective sovereignty lies in the hands of other concealed and irresponsible forces. . . .

But the Fascist negation of Socialism, Democracy, and Liberalism must not be taken to mean that Fascism desires to lead the world back to the state of affairs before 1789 [the French Revolution]. . . . Given that the nineteenth century was the century of Socialism, of Liberalism, and of Democracy, it does not . . . follow that the twentieth century must also be the century of Socialism, Liberalism, and Democracy: political doctrines pass, but humanity remains. . . .

The foundation of Fascism is the conception of the State, its character, its duty, and its aim. Fascism conceives of the State as an absolute, in comparison with which all individuals or groups are relative, only to be conceived of in their relation to the State. . . . The Fascist state is itself conscious, and has itself a will and a personality. . . . The Fascist state is an embodied will to power and government, the Roman tradition is here an ideal of force in action. . . . Government is not so much a thing to be expressed in territorial or military terms as in terms of morality and the spirit. It must be thought of as an Empire—. . . a nation which directly or indirectly rules other nations. . . . For Fascism the growth of Empire, . . . the expansion of the nation, is an essential manifestation of vitality, and its opposite a sign of decadence. . . . But Empire demands discipline, the co-ordination of all forces and a deeply felt sense of duty and sacrifice; this fact explains many aspects of the practical working of the regime, the character of many forces in the State, and the necessarily severe measures which must be taken against those who would oppose this spontaneous and inevitable movement of Italy in the twentieth century, and would oppose it by recalling the outworn ideology of the nineteenth century.

THINKING ABOUT THE READING

1. Why does fascism reject pacifism, socialism, and liberal democracy?
2. What role does the state play under fascism?

Source: B. Mussolini, "The Political and Social Doctrine of Fascism," *Political Quarterly,* IV (July–September, 1933), pp. 341–356. Copyright © 1993 by Blackwell Publishing. Reprinted with permission by Blackwell Publishing.

solini to form a government, and by 1926 Mussolini had killed, arrested, or cowed his opponents, turned Italy into a one-party state with restricted civil liberties, and created a cult of personality around himself (see Witness to the Past: The Doctrine of Fascism). Many Italians believed Mussolini was restoring social order, and they appreciated that the government was efficient; the trains ran on time, a rare experience under democratic Italian regimes.

Fascism also became dominant in Germany after the Depression undermined the moderate, democratic Weimar Republic. Germany had no colonies to tap for resources and markets that might aid recovery from World War I, and Weimar leaders could not solve the severe problems. The German people, who had an authoritarian political tradition and an economy in shambles, resented the reparation payments imposed after World War I, which drained the treasury. Thus many Germans, preferring security to freedom, were willing to listen to a charismatic leader who offered simplistic answers to complex problems. The upper and middle classes also feared working-class socialism.

German Fascism

The Nazi (National Socialist) Party, led by Adolph Hitler (1889–1945), offered a strategy for regaining political and economic strength and for keeping workers under control. Hitler, an Austrian-born social misfit, had made a precarious living painting signs and doing odd jobs before joining the German army in World War I, at which time he already nurtured a hatred of Jews and labor unions. In 1920 Hitler helped form the Nazi Party, which promised to halt

Hitler's Motorcade
In this photo from 1938, Adolph Hitler, standing stiffly in his car, salutes members of a paramilitary Nazi group, the Brownshirts, who parade before him at a Nazi rally in Nuremburg.

Time Life Pictures/Getty Images

the unpopular reparations payments and capitalized on the Great Depression to increase their strength. With economic collapse, the industrial workers moved left toward the communists while the middle classes moved right toward the Nazi movement, financed by big industrialists. Thus Germany became a polarized society. Many Germans were willing to believe that Germany's problems could be blamed on unpopular minorities and foreign powers, and Hitler, understanding propaganda and how to use a few basic ideas, made up "facts" to gain support. In his book *Mein Kampf* (My Struggle), written in 1924, he argued that "all effective propaganda has to limit itself to a very few points and to use them like slogans. A political leader must not fear to speak a lie if this might be effective."[18] Hitler developed a catchy slogan: "one people, one government, one leader."

The Nazis won the largest number of seats in the 1932 elections, and Hitler became chancellor (the equivalent of prime minister) in 1933. Even though the Nazis won only 44 percent of the vote, Hitler tightened his grip on power and moved immediately to impose dramatic changes, including

Nazi Policies

a thorough purging of the schools, theater, cinema, literature, and press so that he could manipulate them. The Nazis outlawed leftist parties, suspended civil liberties, imposed heavy censorship, mobilized youth, told women to stay at home and take care of their husbands and children, and expanded the army. They also regeared the economy toward rearmament, thus solving the terrible unemployment problem. By 1939 Germany's GNP was 50 percent higher than it had been in 1929, mainly because of the manufacture of heavy machinery and armaments. The Nazi myth about maintaining a pure German people—what Hitler termed the Aryan race, after the ancient Indo-Europeans who settled Europe, Persia, and India—also led to anti-Semitic laws between 1933 and 1938. Hitler banned marriage and sexual relations between Jews and so-called Aryan Germans, and he excluded the Jews, many of them assimilated into German culture, from many occupations and citizenship, pushing them into ghettos in German cities, where they could be watched. The Nazis also enacted harsh laws against homosexuals and the Romany, or Gypsies, another unpopular minority.

During the 1930s Japan and Germany came to resemble each other fairly closely, even if their forms of fascism were very different. Although Japan never developed a mass-based Fascist Party,

Japanese Fascism

Japanese leaders blamed foreign nations, especially the United States and the USSR, for Japan's problems, and big business supported military expansion to gain resources and markets. To this end, military officers assassinated liberal politicians and fomented violence in the Chinese province of Manchuria, which was rich in natural resources and had open land on which to settle Japanese. In 1931 Japan invaded and occupied Manchuria, but the League of Nations imposed no stiff penalties on Japan, a failure that helped to discredit that organization. By 1936 the military, in alliance with big business and bureaucratic interests, controlled Japan and imposed a fascist government that promoted labor control, censorship, the glorification of war, police repression, and hatred of foreign powers. The schools and media indoctrinated the population in obedience, patriarchy, and the sacred origins of the Japanese people while attacking Western individualism and democracy. Then in 1937 a military skirmish outside Beijing provided an excuse for Japan to launch a full-scale invasion of China, and by 1938 Japan controlled most of eastern China. When Japan signed a pact with Germany and Italy in 1940, the United States and Britain introduced strong economic sanctions, including an oil embargo. Japan now faced economic collapse or war.

The Road to War

During the later 1930s the European nations moved toward war, forming various alliances. The United States, Britain, and France, known as the Allies, led democracies that wanted to preserve the European state structure, the global economy, and the colonial system in Asia and Africa. The fascist countries, led by Germany, Italy, and Japan, known as the Axis Powers, sought to change the political map of Europe and Asia and gain world economic dominance. The prelude to another world war was also marked by diplomatic problems caused in part by a massive arms buildup and the imperialism of the Axis nations. Hitler pursued an aggressive policy to dominate eastern Europe, arguing that Germany needed living space and colonies, and to unite the several million ethnic Germans living in eastern Europe. In 1936 Hitler's troops occupied the German territory west of the Rhine River that was demilitarized after World War I, and in 1935 Italy invaded and brutally conquered the last independent African kingdom, Ethiopia. The League of Nations voted ineffective sanctions against Italy. While Hitler and Mussolini forged a close alliance, the later Tripartite Pact of 1940, linking Germany and Italy with Japan, was a marriage of necessity, strained and wary. The Japanese pursued the pact partly to warn the United States that opposing Japanese expansion also meant facing the Germans and Italians.

Civil war in Spain heightened European tensions by drawing in foreign intervention. Liberals and conservatives had long struggled to shape Spanish politics, and Spain was polarized between left and right. During the 1936 elections, Spain's Republicans, a leftwing coalition of liberals, socialists, and communists promising reforms, edged out the National Front of conservatives, monarchists, and staunch Catholics. The right rallied around the fascist military forces led by General Francisco Franco (1892–1975), launching the Spanish Civil War (1936–1939). The Loyalist government, aided by the USSR, ultimately lost to Franco's fascists at a huge cost in lives. Germany and Italy helped the Spanish fascists with weapons and advice, and several thousand volunteers from North America and European nations fought for the Loyalist cause. But the Western Allies refused to support the Loyalists, viewing them as too radical. The German bombing of Guernica (GWAR-ni-kuh), a village in northern Spain, caused an international outcry and prompted Pablo Picasso to paint a celebrated testament to the atrocity. Spain endured Franco's fascist dictatorship until 1975.

In the late 1930s the Allies followed a policy of appeasement toward fascist aggression. They were not yet prepared for war, and the catastrophe of World War I led many to see another war as too terrible to contemplate, even the end of civilization. Historians debate whether the appeasement policy, generally supported by public opinion, was realistic, the best of the available options, or a shameful betrayal that only whetted fascist appetites and postponed the inevitable conflict. War did become inevitable. In 1938 Hitler succeeded through threats to merge German-speaking Austria, with many pro-Nazi citizens, into Germany, and then stimulated riots by German minorities in western Czechoslovakia, launching a claim to the territory. Czechoslovakia was handed over and occupied by German troops. Hitler declared: "We shall not capitulate—no never! We may be destroyed, but if we are, we shall drag a world with us—a world in flames."[19] In August 1939 Hitler and Stalin signed the Nazi-Soviet Pact, a nonaggression agreement, and in September, with the Soviet threat temporarily removed, Germany invaded Poland, forcing France and Britain to declare war against Germany (see Chronology: World War II, 1939–1945).

Spanish Civil War

German Aggression

CHRONOLOGY
World War II, 1939–1945

1939 Beginning of war in Europe

June 1941 German invasion of Soviet Union

December 1941 Japanese bombing of Pearl Harbor; invasion of Southeast Asia

1942 Battle of Midway

1944 Allied landing at Normandy

July 1944 Bretton Woods Conference

February 1945 Yalta Conference

April 1945 Allied invasion of Germany

August 1945 U.S. bombing of Hiroshima and Nagasaki

SECTION SUMMARY

- The Italian fascists, led by Benito Mussolini, appealed to those upset by instability, corruption, and economic problems and viciously fought communists and any others who opposed them.

- A new ideology, fascism, that developed out of economic collapse, stressed extreme nationalism, an authoritarian state, and hatred of minorities and leftists.

- Suffering from the Depression, resentful of post–World War I reparations, and fearful of socialism, many Germans supported Adolph Hitler's Nazi Party, which blamed problems on minorities such as the Jews and revived the economy through a military buildup.

- Japan became increasingly nationalistic and imperialistic, blamed its problems on foreigners, took over most of eastern China, and signed a pact with Germany and Italy.

- Tensions rose as Italy invaded Ethiopia, fascists took over Spain, and Germany took over Austria and Czechoslovakia; France and Britain declared war after Germany signed a nonaggression pact with the Soviet Union and invaded Poland.

WORLD WAR II: A GLOBAL TRANSITION

What were the costs and consequences of World War II?

Historians have sometimes viewed World War II as a continuation and amplification of World War I. Both wars shared some of the same causes, including nationalist rivalries, threats to the European balance of power, and a struggle to control the global economic system. But there were differences, too. World War II involved an ideological contest between democracy, fascism, and communism, and the trench warfare of World War I was superseded by the widespread aerial bombing and mobile armies used in World War II, with civilians now fair game. For the first two years, major battles were confined largely to Europe, the North Atlantic, and North Africa. Then the war spilled over to East and Southeast Asia and the western Pacific. The conflict, the most costly war in world history, brought staggering misery, 50 million deaths, one of history's worst genocides, and the use of the deadliest weapons ever known. It marked a major transition that reshaped world politics and international relations.

Cataclysmic War and Holocaust

Outbreak of War

In September 1939, Europe plunged into armed struggle. Germany and its allies overran nearly all of Europe except for valiant Britain and neutral Switzerland and Sweden (see Map 24.3). Germany then imposed puppet regimes in the conquered territories, including the Vichy **(VISH-ee)** government in France headed by World War I hero, General Philippe Pétain. The occupied countries had to send raw materials and food to Germany, and millions of civilians were enslaved to work on German farms and in factories. But Germany failed to achieve all of its strategic objectives. In a heroic resistance, Britain withstood a blitz of aerial bombing in 1940, prompting Prime Minister Winston Churchill (1874–1965) to boast that it was Britain's finest hour. Moreover, German submarines failed to sever Britain's maritime link with North America. Italian efforts to carve out a Mediterranean empire also faltered, as Greeks pushed the Italians back and the British seized parts of Italian North Africa and destroyed Italy's navy, compelling the Germans to divert military resources to confront British power in North Africa and Greece. Finally, underground movements emerged all over Europe to fight the Nazis. One of the major resistance heroes, the Swedish diplomat Raoul Wallenberg (1912–ca. 1947), stationed in occupied Hungary, risked death to save some 100,000 Jews by giving them Swedish passports and smuggling many out to safety.

German Invasion of Russia

In June 1941 Germany broke its nonaggression pact and invaded Russia. Top German officers opposed the invasion, but Hitler wanted the rich resources, especially Caucasus oil, and open lands for German colonization. Believing himself to be a military genius, he took control of all military operations and made many strategic blunders. Hitler also had an obsessive fear of communism. This invasion relieved pressure on Britain, since two-thirds of the German army was now committed to the eastern front. After misjudging German intentions and reeling from the invasion, the Soviet leader, Joseph Stalin, joined the anti-Axis alliance and received aid from the United States and Britain that helped the USSR resist, even though Western leaders, who mistrusted Stalin and still despised the Soviet system, expected Russia to remain a long-term threat to their interests. German forces reached the outskirts of Moscow and another major city, Stalingrad. But although German military forces were superior, they failed to capture the major Russian cities because the Red Army began an effective counterattack. Soon the German high command realized the folly of the invasion. The turning point came in February 1943, as the Soviet Red Army stopped the Germans at Stalingrad. By the summer, German forces, like the French army of Napoleon Bonaparte, began a long, humiliating retreat from Russia.

Map 24.3   World War II in Europe and North Africa

The Axis Powers, led by Germany and Italy, initially occupied much of Europe, and in 1941 they invaded the Soviet Union, but they were unable to hold their gains against the counteroffensive of the United States, Britain, the Soviet Union, and the Free French forces.

e Interactive Map

Legend:
- Hitler's Greater Germany
- Allied with Germany
- Occupied by Germany and its allies
- Grand Alliance
- Neutral nations
- ★ Major battle

Siege of Leningrad, Sept. 1941–Jan. 1944

Siege of Stalingrad, Aug. 21, 1942–Jan. 31, 1943

German surrender: Reims, May 7, 1945 Berlin, May 8, 1945

Battle of Britain, fall 1940

Rhine Crossing, March 7, 1945

Battle of the Bulge, Dec. 1944

Invasion of Normandy, June 6, 1944

Axis troops occupy Vichy France, Nov. 10 and 11, 1942

Allies land in Provence, Aug. 15, 1944

Rome (Liberated June 1944)

Monte Cassino, May 1944

Salerno, Sept. 1943

Allies invade Sicily and Italy, July–Sept. 1943

Sicily, July 1943

Casablanca, Nov. 1942

Rommel defeated in Tunisia; Axis troops evacuated, May 1943

El Alamein, summer 1942

Nazi Genocide

Holocaust The Nazis' deliberate murder of Jews and Romany (Gypsies), one of the worst genocides in world history.

German racist nationalism led to horrific campaigns of extermination against unpopular minorities and conquered peoples. Hitler ordered the "final solution" of the "Jewish Question," and the resulting **Holocaust**, the Nazis' deliberate murder of Jews and Romany (Gypsies), was one of the worst genocides in history, killing some three-quarters of Europe's Jews. During 1942 the Germans erected death camps, such as Bergen-Belsen (BUR-guhn-BEL-suhn) in Germany and Auschwitz (OUSH-vits) in Poland, targeting especially the large Jewish communities of Germany, Poland, and Ukraine. But Jews everywhere in Nazi-occupied Europe—Vichy France, the Netherlands, Hungary, Russia—were rounded up and put in death camps, to be killed in gas chambers, starved, or worked to death. In addition to the 6 million Jews and half a million Romany (Gypsies) murdered in the Holocaust, the Nazis were responsible for the deaths of 11 million Slavs (including over 3 million Poles) and many German communists, socialists, anti-Nazi Christians, homosexuals, children deemed physically or mentally unfit to serve the German nation, and prisoners of war.

Historians differ on how complicit the German people were in the Nazis' genocide. Some blame the grip of a terrorist dictatorship that suppressed information. Nazi police chief Heinrich Himmler told the murderous special force, the SS, that "among ourselves, we can speak openly about it [the Holocaust], though we can never speak of it in public. That is a page of glory in our history that never can be written."[20] Other historians also assign responsibility to the German people, many of them anti-Semitic. Only a few brave Germans dared to resist Nazi policies. Those who did, such as the Lutheran theologian Dietrich Bonhoeffer (BON-ho-fuhr) (1906–1945), a strong critic of anti-Semitism who supported the underground resistance, were executed.

Globalization of the War

U.S.-Japan Conflict

Conflict between Japan and the United States eventually globalized the war (see Map 24.4). Japanese leaders had a plan for a new economic order in the East led by Japan, and they knew that they had to eliminate both the Western colonial powers and the threat from the United States. On December 7, 1941, what President Franklin D. Roosevelt called "a date which will live in infamy," Japanese planes attacked the U.S. naval base at Pearl Harbor, Hawaii, destroying much of the U.S. Pacific fleet, killing 2,400 Americans, and ending U.S. neutrality. At the same time, Japanese military forces invaded Southeast Asia. Within several months they controlled most of the region, having forced the Americans out of the Philippines and jailed the British and Dutch residents of their respective colonies. However, already bogged down and unable to expand their occupation of China, Japan badly needed Southeast Asian resources, especially oil and rubber from the Dutch East Indies (Indonesia). Preoccupied with war in Europe, and with only modest military forces left in Asia, the Western powers were unable to resist the Japanese advance.

Japanese leaders disagreed about challenging U.S. power. Some top military officers argued against the Pearl Harbor attack, knowing that the superior U.S. military and economic power could defeat Japan if Americans geared up to do so. But other leaders, impressed by Hitler's quick victories in Europe, thought they could duplicate that success in the Pacific, immobilizing the U.S. fleet and gaining time to consolidate control of Asia and the Pacific. If Germany kept the United States focused on Europe, they thought Roosevelt might avoid a costly war in Asia. They also assumed that Americans, addicted to creature comforts, lacked the will to mobilize. But the surprise Pearl Harbor attack proved a strategic blunder, uniting Americans in support for war. Admiral Isoruku Yamamoto (EE-so-ROO-koo YAH-muh-MO-toe), the former university student in the United States who planned the attack, somberly told colleagues: "I fear all we have done is to awaken a sleeping giant and fill him with a terrible resolve."[21]

Roosevelt had been looking for ways to turn U.S. public opinion toward war and end his nation's isolationism, and Pearl Harbor served that purpose well. Historians remain divided about how much U.S. officials, including Roosevelt, knew about the forthcoming attack and whether they let it happen to shock the U.S. public into supporting the war. U.S. officials anticipated a military conflict with Japan but apparently expected an assault on the Philippines, an American colony, rather than on Hawaii, where Japanese Americans constituted over half of the population. The United States quickly mobilized and regeared the economy for war. A patriotic wave swept the country as America entered the war on both fronts.

Pacific War and U.S. Society

The war affected American society. Six million women joined the work force, replacing the men going off to fight. Although many men objected to the trend, by 1943 the government encouraged women as their "patriotic duty" to take up jobs once considered unladylike, such as on factory assembly lines. A popular song celebrated "Rosie the Riveter" who was "making history working for victory." The song could have described Sybil Lewis, an African American from Oklahoma, who

Map 24.4   World War II in Asia and the Pacific

After invading China in 1937, Japan disabled the U.S. fleet at Pearl Harbor in 1941 and in 1941–1942 occupied most of Southeast Asia and the western Pacific. The United States and its allies pushed back the Japanese forces from their bases in the Pacific and bombed Japan from those bases, but Japan did not surrender until 1945, when the United States dropped atomic bombs on Hiroshima and Nagasaki.

 Interactive Map

moved to Los Angeles to work as a waitress, became a riveter making airplane gas tanks for Lockheed Aircraft, and then worked as a shipyard welder. Anxious for workers, companies often hired African Americans, posing a challenge to prevailing racial attitudes, and millions of southern blacks found jobs in northern and western cities. When the war ended, over 19 million American women had full-time paid jobs, and the black population of many American cities had doubled. After defeating fascism, more white Americans were also sympathetic to black demands for democracy in the United States, especially in the segregated South.

But racism aimed at 110,000 Japanese Americans, many U.S.-born or naturalized citizens living in western states, fueled one of the greatest invasions of civil liberties in U.S. history. Many Japanese Americans joined U.S. military units to fight in Europe. Nevertheless, suspecting but offering little proof that some Japanese Americans might be spies or support the Japanese war effort, the U.S. government seized their property and sent them to sparse, remote internment camps, such as Manzanar in the harsh California desert, for the duration of the conflict. Their property was never returned. With a few exceptions, German and Italian Americans faced no similar treatment.

The End of the War

German Defeat

The U.S. entry changed the shape of the conflict. The Axis forces had been triumphant through 1942, as Germany dominated much of Europe and North Africa, and Japan controlled most of Asia east of India and large areas of the western Pacific. In 1943, however, the tide began to turn. The Germans were defeated in North Africa, and Allied landings in Italy knocked that country out of the war. In June 1944, British and American forces landed on five beaches at Normandy, on France's Atlantic coast. Although German defenses did not collapse, resulting in huge Allied casualties, the Allies, including the Free French forces under General Charles DeGaulle (1890–1970), finally began pushing the Germans back in France.

Germany was defeated only by massive Allied ground offensives and an aerial bombardment that demoralized the civilian German population. The British firebombed several German cities; in Hamburg, 30,000 civilians were killed in a firestorm. While the Soviet Red Army pushed the Germans back in the east, U.S. and British forces retook Italy, France, and other Nazi-occupied countries. By December 1944, Allied forces had reached Germany, and the Allies gained command of the skies. The German war economy collapsed. As the losses mounted, Hitler lost touch with reality, giving orders to nonexistent army divisions. In spring 1945, as British and U.S. armies moved into Germany from the west and the Soviet Red Army from the east, Hitler and his mistress, Eva Braun, went through a marriage ceremony and then committed suicide in their underground bunker in Berlin. Germany surrendered. Soon the liberation of the concentration camps revealed the full extent of Nazi atrocities to a shocked world.

A major reason for the Nazi defeat was Hitler's racist and imperialistic policies. Hitler believed that Germans were racially superior to all other peoples, including the conquered Slavs, and brutally exploited the occupied areas to supply Germany. Had the Germans patronized the east Europeans and Russians, they might have won their support. Some Ukrainians, Russians, Lithuanians, and Latvians worked with the Nazis because they hated the communists more, but they were hated as collaborators with the German occupiers and often pursued and punished after the war.

The Japanese defeat was more dramatic. In 1942, the United States stopped the Japanese advance at the battle of Midway Island, west of Hawaii, and began to isolate the Japanese bases in the Pacific. By mid-1944 they pushed the Japanese out of most of the western Pacific islands and began launching bombing raids on Japan. By early 1945, U.S., Australian, and British forces started to retake Southeast Asia and China. The invasion of Okinawa, in the Ryukyus Islands just south of Japan's main islands, cost the lives of 10,000 American troops and 80,000 Japanese civilians, warning what an invasion of the main Japanese islands might entail. U.S. and Japanese leaders could not agree on negotiations for peace, as Japan resisted American demands for total surrender.

Japanese Defeat

In August 1945, the United States forever changed warfare by dropping an atomic bomb on the Japanese city of Hiroshima, demolishing most of the city and killing 80,000 people; thousands more were maimed or died later from injuries or radiation. The Japanese cabinet, divided on surrender, debated whether the United States had more than one bomb. Three days later, a second bomb hit Nagasaki, killing 60,000 Japanese civilians. Japanese emperor Hirohito (1901–1989) opted for surrender, asking his people to "suffer the insufferable, endure the unendurable," and cooperate with the U.S. occupation. For the first time in its long history, Japan had been defeated and successfully invaded. Disgraced, more than five hundred military officers committed suicide. But a long-imprisoned Japanese leftist celebrated the defeat: "Ah, such happiness, At somehow living long enough, To see this rare day, When the fighting has ceased."[22] World War II had come to an end.

Historians debate whether it was necessary militarily to drop the atomic bombs on Japan, causing so many civilian deaths. Many contend that the Japanese would have fiercely resisted an invasion and hence the bombs saved many American and Japanese lives. Others argue that Japan was near surrender but U.S. leaders misread its intentions. Still others say that the United States rushed to defeat Japan because the Soviet Union was going to join the struggle against Japan and would demand territory or a role in the occupation. Soviet forces had already moved into Manchuria as Japanese resistance collapsed. The bomb warned the Soviet Union about U.S. capabilities to dissuade Stalin from expansionism.

Japan lost the war primarily because it overstretched its forces and failed to convert Southeast Asian resources into military and industrial products fast enough to defeat the larger, wealthier United States. Japan also imposed increasingly authoritarian, brutal policies on its subject peoples. Hence, Japanese troops, upon capturing China's capital in 1937, killed thousands of Chinese in an orgy of destruction that became known as "the Rape of Nanjing." In most cases Japan's military alienated the Chinese and Southeast Asians, and eventually most Southeast Asians looked on the Japanese as perhaps even worse than the Western colonizers.

The Costs and Consequences of Global War

World War II took a terrible toll in lives: approximately 15 million military and 35 million civilian deaths. Soviet Russia, which lost over 20 million people, or 10 percent of its population, now had one more bitter memory in a long history of threats and invasions by countries to the west. Poland and Yugoslavia both lost over 10 percent of their people. Britain lost 375,000 people and France 600,000, while strategic bombing blasted every major German city to rubble. Over 2 million Japanese military personnel and probably a million Japanese civilians died, and 7 million Chinese were killed or wounded. Fighting on both fronts, some 300,000 American military personnel died.

The European and Asian countries involved were also economically devastated, clearing the way for new global economic arrangements. In 1944 U.S. president Roosevelt summoned representatives of forty-four countries to a conference held in Bretton Woods, New Hampshire, to establish the postwar world economic order, including international monetary cooperation to prevent the financial crises that caused the Great Depression. The Bretton Woods Conference set up the U.S.-dominated World Bank and International Monetary Fund to provide credit to states requiring financial investment. Bretton Woods also fixed currency exchange rates and encouraged trade liberalization, benefiting the United States.

World War II also transformed world politics, first by removing the twin threats of German Nazism and Japanese militarism. Unlike in World War I, the victorious Allies were more generous toward the vanquished. Germany, Italy, and Japan lost their colonies and were required to adopt

democratic governments. In addition, U.S. forces occupied Japan for several years, while Germany was temporarily divided into sectors controlled by Russia, Britain, France, and the United States. But the Allies gave the defeated nations massive aid and guidance to speed recovery. Meanwhile, Chinese, Korean, and Vietnamese communists took advantage of Japanese occupation to gain support for their movements. In fact, Japanese occupation undermined Western colonial rule throughout Southeast Asia, while in India, nationalists who had been jailed for opposing the use of Indian troops in the war were even more embittered against British rule (see Chapter 25).

In February 1945, Roosevelt, Churchill, and Stalin met at a conference at Yalta (YAWL-tuh), in Russia's Crimean peninsula, to determine the postwar political order. They proposed goals, an institutional structure, and a voting system for the new world organization, the United Nations. The Yalta Conference also divided Europe into anticommunist and communist spheres of interest. Western leaders, drained by war and seeking postwar stability, reluctantly agreed that the Soviet Union could dominate eastern Europe by stationing troops and influencing governments.

A new rivalry between the two emerging superpowers, the United States and the USSR, complicated the new global political order. The United States, which had not fought on its own soil, emerged from the war much less devastated than other major combatants and politically and economically stronger. Now the dominant world power, it took the lead in protecting a global system in which it held the strongest cards. But the USSR emerged from the war as a military power with imperialist ambitions, and U.S. leaders realized that thwarting Soviet ambitions required reconstructing Europe and Japan to restore political stability.

Bombing of Nagasaki   This photo shows the awesome power of the atomic bomb dropped by the United States on the Japanese city of Nagasaki in August 1945, three days after the atomic bombing of Hiroshima. Some 60,000 Japanese died in the Nagasaki bombing.

U.S. Air Force/AP Images

U.S.-Soviet Conflict

The political history of the world between 1945 and 1989 revolved around the conflict between these two competing superpowers with very different governments and economies. The USSR replaced Germany as the dominant power in eastern Europe and installed communist governments, including one in the eastern part of Germany. World War II also increased the appeal of communism worldwide and led to communist regimes in Yugoslavia and North Korea and later in China and North Vietnam. Both Soviet and U.S. leaders tended to look at the world through the lens of their World War II experience. For the USSR that meant paranoia about any threat from the West, while Americans perceived a repeat of Hitler's aggression anywhere in the world where they experienced a political threat, such as a nationalist or communist-inspired revolution. The U.S.-Soviet rivalry created a world very different from that existing before World War II.

SECTION SUMMARY

- Germany rapidly took over most of Europe and used it as a source of raw materials, but the British withstood extended bombing and Germany wasted valuable resources on an ultimately unsuccessful invasion of the Soviet Union.

- Nazi Germany deliberately killed 6 million Jews and a half million Gypsies in death camps, along with millions of others; historians are divided on how much the German people knew about the death camps and how responsible they were for them.

- After Japan attacked Pearl Harbor, the United States entered the war in both Asia and Europe, and many women and blacks found work in professions that had until then been closed to them, while Japanese Americans were put in internment camps.

- After the United States entered the war, the Allies slowly began to win the war in Europe, and in the spring of 1945, with U.S. forces advancing from the west and the Soviets from the east, Hitler committed suicide and Germany surrendered.

- After Japan refused to agree to a total surrender despite serious setbacks, the United States dropped atomic bombs on Hiroshima and Nagasaki, killing, injuring, and sickening scores of thousands; historians still debate whether these bombs were necessary.

- World War II killed 50 million military personnel and civilians, but in its aftermath, Germany, Italy, and Japan were aided rather than punished, and the United States and the Soviet Union emerged as the world's dominant powers.

CHAPTER SUMMARY

War and its aftermath dominated the years between 1914 and 1929 in the industrialized Western nations. Growing tensions between European powers led to World War I, in which new weapons killed millions of civilians and soldiers alike. The terrible losses fostered widespread disillusionment and brought major political changes to Europe and the wider world. New nations were carved out of the German, Russian, Austro-Hungarian, and Russian Empires, while the United States emerged as a major world power. The communist Bolsheviks seized power in Russia and created the Soviet Union. Lenin forged a one-party state, and his successor, Stalin, imposed a brutal dictatorship under which he collectivized the economy, used Five-Year Plans to encourage industrialization, and modernized the society.

During the 1920s much of Europe, the United States, and Japan experienced liberal democracy and middle-class prosperity. However, in the 1930s, the Great Depression brought economic collapse, a sharp decline in world trade, and millions of unemployed workers. A few wealthy nations, especially the United States, pursued recovery through liberal reform and government spending, sustaining democracy despite the economic hardship. But for Germany, Italy, and Japan, economic disaster fostered fascism, an ideology that favored an authoritarian state, extreme nationalism, and repression of minorities. The increasing aggression of the fascist nations, in search of lands to exploit for their resources and markets, led to World War II. During the war, Nazi brutality perpetrated genocide against the Jews and other minorities. Germany initially occupied eastern Europe and much of western Europe, while Japan invaded China and Southeast Asia. With the entry of the United States into the war, the Allies eventually won. The war cost 50 million lives and devastated Europe and much of Asia. The United States emerged as the world's major superpower, with the Soviet Union as its major rival.

KEY TERMS

Bolsheviks

soviets

Marxism-Leninism

Leninism

New Economic Policy

Stalinism

gulags

socialist realism

Great Depression

Dust Bowl

New Deal

cubism

fascism

Holocaust

EBOOK AND WEBSITE RESOURCES

e PRIMARY SOURCE

Mud and Khaki: Memoirs of an Incomplete Soldier

e INTERACTIVE MAPS

Map 24.1 World War I

Map 24.2 Civil War in Revolutionary Russia
(1918–1921)

Map 24.3 World War II in Europe and North Africa

Map 24.4 World War II in Asia and the Pacific

LINKS

The Great War (http://www.pitt.edu/~pugachev/
greatwar/ww1.html). A useful site on World War I
with many essays and links.

WWW-VL: History: United States (http://vlib.iue.it/
history/USA/). A virtual library, maintained at the
University of Kansas, that contains links to hundreds
of sites.

Russian History Index: The World Wide Web Virtual
Library (http://vlib.iue.it/hist-russia/Index.html).
Contains useful essays and links on Russian history,
society, and politics.

Modern History Sourcebook (http://www.fordham.edu/
halsall/mod/modsbook.html). A very extensive online
collection of historical documents and secondary
materials.

**Plus flashcards, practice quizzes, and more. Go to:
www.cengage.com/history/lockard/globalsocnet2e.**

SUGGESTED READING

Boyle, John Hunter. *Modern Japan: The American Nexus.* Fort
Worth: Harcourt Brace Jovanovich, 1993. Good study of
U.S.-Japanese relations.

Brendon, Piers. *The Dark Valley: A Panorama of the 1930s.*
New York: Alfred A. Knopf, 2000. A readable account of this
decade in both Europe and North America.

Doughty, Robert A., et al. *World War II: Total Warfare Around
the Globe.* Lexington, MA: D.C. Heath, 1996. A brief account
emphasizing military history.

Dower, John. *War Without Mercy: Race and Power in the Pacific
War.* New York: Pantheon, 1986. A provocative look at the
U.S.-Japan conflict.

Fitzpatrick, Sheila. *The Russian Revolution*, 3rd ed. New York:
Oxford University Press, 2008. A provocative, concise, and readable account of developments from 1917 through the 1930s.

James, Harold. *Europe Reborn: A History, 1914–2000.* New
York: Longman, 2003. An excellent survey of the period.

Kitchen, Martin. *A World in Flames: A Short History of the Second World War in Europe and Asia, 1939–1945.* New York:
Longman, 1990. A readable narrative.

Kitchen, Martin. *Between the Wars*, 2nd ed. New York: Longman,
2006. Examines Europe's economic and international history.

Lee, Stephen J. *European Dictatorships, 1918–1945*, 2nd ed.
New York: Routledge, 2000. An interesting study of the major
dictatorships and their leaders.

Lewin, Moshe. *The Soviet Century.* New York: Verso, 2005. A
provocative and critical overview of the Soviet Union and
Soviet Communism.

Lyons, Michael J. *World War I: A Short History*, 2nd ed. Upper
Saddle River, NJ: Prentice-Hall, 2000. A readable and comprehensive overview.

Mann, Michael. *Fascists.* New York: Cambridge University
Press, 2004. A detailed but readable study of European fascism in this era.

Martin, Russell. *Picasso's War: The Destruction of Guernica and
the Masterpiece That Changed the World.* New York: Plume,
2002. Examines the era through the artist and his most
famous painting.

Mazower, Mark. *Hitler's Empire: How the Nazis Ruled Europe.*
New York: Penguin, 2008. Explores life under German
domination.

McClain, James L. *Japan: A Modern History.* New York: W.W.
Norton, 2002. A very readable recent account with good
coverage of these decades.

Moss, George Donelson. *America Since 1900*, 6th ed. Upper
Saddle River, NJ: Prentice-Hall, 2007. A readable survey of
the United States in this period.

Neiberg, Michael S. *Fighting the Great War: A Global History.*
Cambridge: Harvard University Press, 2005. A scholarly
analysis of the conflict.

Parrish, Michael E. *Anxious Decades: America in Prosperity
and Depression, 1920–1941.* New York: W.W. Norton, 1994.
An examination of this era in the United States.

Sato, Barbara. *The New Japanese Women: Modernity, Media,
and Women in Interwar Japan.* Durham: Duke University
Press, 2003. A fascinating scholarly study.

Wilkenson, James, and H. Stuart Hughes. *Contemporary
Europe: A History*, 10th ed. Upper Saddle River, NJ: Prentice-
Hall, 2004. A comprehensive general survey.

IMPERIALISM AND NATIONALISM IN ASIA, AFRICA, AND LATIN AMERICA, 1914–1945

Photo12 / The Image Works

Mao Zedong Organizing Communists in China
This later artist's rendition shows the young Mao Zedong, the future Chinese communist leader, organizing a communist group in his native province, Hunan, around 1921. A portrait of Karl Marx decorates the wall.

> *What* unhappiness strikes the poor, Who wear a single worn-out, torn cloth. Oh heaven, why are you not just? Some have abundance while others are in want.
>
> —Peasant folk song protesting colonialism in Vietnam[1]

In 1911 Nguyen Tat Thanh (NEW-win tat-tan), a young man from an impoverished village in French-ruled Vietnam, signed on as a merchant seaman on a French ship; he would not return to his homeland for another thirty years. Nguyen hated colonialism. The seaman visited North African and American ports, and he developed both a distaste for America's white racism and an admiration for its freedom. After working as a cook in London, Nguyen moved to Paris, where he worked chiefly as a photo retoucher while seeking to develop an anticolonial movement among the Vietnamese exiles in France. Adopting a new alias, Nguyen Ai Quoc (NEW-win eye-kwok) ("Nguyen the Patriot"), he spent his free time reading books on politics and working with Asian nationalists and French socialists to oppose colonialism.

FOCUS QUESTIONS

1. **What circumstances fostered nationalism in Asia, Africa, and Latin America?**
2. **How and why did the communist movement grow in China?**
3. **What were the main contributions of Mohandas Gandhi to the Indian struggle?**
4. **How did nationalism differ in Southeast Asia and sub-Saharan Africa?**
5. **What factors promoted change in the Middle East and Latin America?**

At the Paris Peace Conference after World War I, Nguyen Ai Quoc became famous among Vietnamese exiles for his efforts to address the delegates about the self-determination of colonized peoples. He attempted to enter the meetings and present a moderate eight-point plan for changes in France's treatment of its Southeast Asian colonies, including basic freedoms, representation in government, and release of political prisoners. But the Western powers refused to permit his entry. Disillusioned with Western democracy, the Vietnamese exile helped found the French Communist Party, which promised to abolish the French colonial system. He then moved to the Soviet Union and later, under a new name, Ho Chi Minh (ho chee-min) ("He Who Enlightens"), led the communist forces in Vietnam in their long struggle against French colonialism and then against the Americans. Concluding that communism was the most effective strategy for promoting nationalism, Ho became a worldwide symbol of opposition to Western imperialism and sympathy for peasants suffering under colonial policies in Vietnam and elsewhere.

Between 1914 and 1945 nationalistic Asians and Africans challenged the imperialism of the European powers, now weakened by World War I, that had reshaped Asian and African politics and economies. From Indonesia to Egypt to Senegal, but especially in India and Vietnam, rapid, often destabilizing change sparked nationalism aimed at escaping Western domination. Similar trends also influenced independent countries such as Siam (now Thailand), Persia (now Iran), and particularly China. The Great Depression and World War II unsettled the world even more, sometimes sending discontented people to join those seeking to overturn the status quo, such as Ho Chi Minh. Despite frequent uprisings and protests, the Western powers maintained their empires until after World War II. During and after that war, however, nationalist movements became even stronger, making a return to the world of the 1930s impossible.

e Visit the website and eBook for additional study materials and interactive tools: www.cengage.com/history/lockard/globalsocnet2e

687

WESTERN IMPERIALISM AND ITS CHALLENGERS

▎What circumstances fostered nationalism in Asia, Africa, and Latin America?

The events that rocked the industrialized nations—two world wars, the Russian Revolution, and the Great Depression—also affected the nonindustrialized societies of Asia, Africa, and Latin America. These societies, which enjoyed little power in the global system, also suffered from destabilizing social and economic changes resulting from colonialism. Many disenchanted Asians and Africans adopted nationalism and Marxism to struggle for power.

The Impact of Colonialism

World War I and the Colonies

Western colonialism had a major impact on Asians, Africans, and West Indians. The slaughter of millions of people during World War I undermined Western credibility and whatever moral authority Western peoples claimed to possess. Resentment also grew from the deaths of thousands of Asians and Africans conscripted as soldiers and workers to support the colonial powers in the war effort. Both France and Germany drafted men, often through harsh methods similar to forced labor, from their African colonies, while Britain sent Africans and Indians. Some 46,000 Kenyans died fighting for Britain, and at least 25,000 West Africans perished helping France on the front lines. Although British and French officials promised democratic reforms and special treatment for war veterans, these promises were not carried out, and few families of dead African soldiers ever received any compensation for their loss.

Colonial Systems

Colonialism also reshaped societies. As discussed in Chapters 21 and 22, colonization formed artificial states that often ignored social, economic, and historical realities in the region. Colonies such as Dutch-ruled Indonesia, British Nigeria, and the Belgian Congo incorporated diverse and often rival ethnic groups who had little sense of national unity. In addition, to cover the costs of managing the colonies, the colonial governments used a variety of methods, including higher taxes and forced labor, that increased resentment. In Portuguese-ruled Mozambique, men and women who had no cash to pay the required taxes were assigned to work on plantations or in mines in a system not unlike slavery. After months of labor they often received little more than a receipt saying they had met their tax obligation for the year. Among the worst abuses were the opium and alcohol monopolies that provided revenues for colonial governments in Southeast Asia. In French-ruled Vietnam all villages were required to purchase designated amounts of these products, so that by 1918 opium sales accounted for one-third of all colonial revenues in Vietnam, and some Vietnam-

Exporting Resources from Indonesia
Small boats brought cash crops grown in eastern Java, part of the Dutch East Indies, to the port of Surabaya, from where they were shipped to Europe.

CHRONOLOGY

	Asia	The Middle East and Africa	Latin America
1910	**1916–1927** Warlord Era in China		
1920	**1928–1937** Republic of China	**1920–1922** Nationalist unrest in Kenya **1922** Formation of Turkish republic **1925–1979** Pahlavi dynasty in Iran	
1930	**1930** Indochinese Communist Party **1935–1936** Chinese Communist Long March		**1930–1945** Estado Novo in Brazil **1934–1940** Cardenas presidency in Mexico
1940	**1941–1945** Japanese occupation of Southeast Asia **1942** Gandhi's Quit India campaign		

ese became addicted to opium. Moreover, villages that bought too little alcohol or were discovered making their own illicit alcoholic beverages were fined.

Among other problems, rising birth rates and declining death rates, abetted by colonial economic policies and, in some cases, improved health and sanitation, fostered rapid population growth in colonies such as India, Indonesia, the Philippines, and Vietnam. This population growth outstripped economic resources, exacerbating poverty and stimulating emigration. Furthermore, the production and export of one or two primary commodities, such as rice and rubber from Vietnam, sugar from Barbados and Fiji, copper from Northern Rhodesia, and oil from Trinidad and Iraq, put a brake on later economic diversification. Colonized peoples also disliked the arrogance of the Western colonizers. Assuming that their societies were superior, Europeans and North Americans had enshrined their racist attitude in the Covenant for the new League of Nations formed after World War I, which considered the colonized peoples not yet able to govern themselves in the modern world. Finally, Western officials, businessmen, and planters in the colonies lived in luxury—with mansions, servants, and private clubs—while many local people lived in dire poverty, often underfed and underemployed.

At the same time, colonial governments built a modern communications and economic infrastructure that often spurred economic growth. British India, Dutch Indonesia, and British East Africa built railroads that facilitated the movement of goods and people. Colonialism also fostered the growth of cities. For example, in 1890, to service their new East African Railroad from the Kenyan coast to Uganda, the British opened a settlement with a hotel and bar at Nairobi, a Gikuyu village in the Kenyan highlands. Nairobi, with its cool climate, later became the colonial capital. Port cities founded by Western colonizers, such as Hong Kong on the China coast, Jakarta in Indonesia, Singapore at the tip of Malaya, Bombay (today's Mumbai) in India, and Cape Town in South Africa, became key hubs of world trade. However, critics questioned how much these developments benefited Asians and Africans.

Colonial Economies

The capitalism introduced by the West also spurred resentment. Some non-European merchants, such as the Chinese in Southeast Asia and the Lebanese in West Africa, profited from the growing economic opportunities. But colonial policies that promoted the spread of the capitalist market, expanded communications, and eroded traditional political authority also destabilized rural villages, laying the groundwork for the rise of revolutionary responses in countries like Vietnam. The commercialization of agriculture transformed traditional, often communal, landowning arrangements into money-based private property systems with competitive values and policies that converted land into a commodity to be exploited on the free market. In many colonies, among them British India, French Vietnam, and Portuguese Angola, a powerful landlord class now flourished at the expense of once-self-sufficient peasant farmers. The remaining peasant farmers had no control over the constantly fluctuating prices paid for their crops. Lacking money or connections to influential people, many peasants fell into dire poverty. A Vietnamese peasant later recalled the bitter years of hardship under French colonization: "My father was very poor. He and my mother, and all of my brothers and sisters, had to pull the plow. In the old days, people did the work of water buffalo."[2]

The Great Depression

The Great Depression of the 1930s brought economic catastrophe to many nonindustrialized societies as demand for their resources in the industrialized nations plummeted. In Southeast Asia and Africa, prices for rubber, sugar, and coffee fell, in Argentina livestock and wheat prices collapsed, and Brazilians threw their nearly worthless sacks of coffee beans into the sea. To protect Western investors during this time, international agreements restricted rubber growing to large plantations, causing distress to small farmers, rubber workers, and the shopkeepers who serviced them in Malaya, Sri Lanka, and the Belgian Congo. As these exports declined, colonial revenues fell. Because rubber and tin provided the bulk of tax revenues in British Malaya, price collapse necessitated huge budget cuts, undermining such activities as education and road building.

Unequal landowning, growing mass poverty, few economic opportunities for displaced peasants, and foreign control of the economy produced political unrest. For example, on the Caribbean island of Trinidad, a British colony, the depression led to strikes and labor unrest. The calypso singer Growling Tiger implored the colonial government not to ignore human suffering: "The authorities should deal much more leniently with the many unemployed in the colony; work is nowhere to be found but there is rent to pay while the money circulation decreases by the day."[3] But most colonial regimes harassed and jailed protest leaders.

Nationalism, Marxism, and Imperial Expansion

Nationalism and Radical Movements

As a result of these hardships, ideologies of resistance, including nationalism and Marxism, became influential in the colonized world, fostering movements for independence. Since colonial governments jailed or exiled dissenters, nationalists had to organize underground. Nationalism appealed especially to the educated middle class—lawyers, teachers, merchants, and military officers—who faced white racism. The few existing universities in the colonies offered a venue for nationalist-government conflicts and campus protests. In British Burma (today's Myanmar) during the 1920s and 1930s, students, both men and women, at the University of Rangoon repeatedly went on strike to protest British policies. After a major strike in 1936, student leaders were expelled, but the administration also met some student demands such as introducing scholarships for poor students.

Nationalism promoted a sense of belonging to a nation, such as Indonesia or Nigeria, that transcended parochial differences such as social class and religion. Whereas colonialism had uprooted people from their villages, families, customs, and traditions, nationalists sought to foster stability and help the poor, often linking capitalism with foreign control. But the "nation" sometimes existed only in people's imagination: in the multiethnic colonies of Africa, Southeast Asia, and the Caribbean, ethnic rivalries hindered a feeling of nationhood.

Some Asians, Africans, and Latin Americans who sought radical change, such as Ho Chi Minh, mixed nationalism with Marxism, which provided an alternative vision to colonialism, capitalism, and discredited local traditions and leaders. Young Asians, Africans, and West Indians studying in Europe and North America often adopted Marxism after facing racism in the West and bleak employment prospects and political repression back at home. Some of them gravitated to the communism imposed on and practiced in the Soviet Union (see Chapter 24), which addressed social inequality and political powerlessness under the leadership of a centralized revolutionary party. Many found persuasive the theories of the Russian communist leader, Vladimir Lenin, who blamed the poverty of the colonial and neocolonial societies on the industrialized nations that had imposed a capitalist system on subject peoples. Lenin saw the world as divided between imperial countries (the exploiters) and dominated countries (the exploited). An Indian nationalist observed in the 1930s that younger Indian men and women who used to admire Western democracies now found inspiration in Soviet Russia. Although the Soviet Union also proved capable of blatantly imperialistic policies, many viewed Lenin's theory of capitalism-based imperialism as valid.

Asserting Western Power

At the same time that anti-imperialist feelings were rising, powerful nations expanded their imperial reach and intervened in less-powerful countries. Britain and France took control of the former Ottoman colonies in western Asia and the German colonies in Africa, some of which had valuable resources, while Australia and Japan occupied the German-ruled Pacific islands. Supported by colonial governments, Europeans continued to settle in Algeria, Angola, Kenya, South Africa, and Southern Rhodesia, dispossessing local people from their land. Moreover, Western military conquests in Africa had not ended. In 1935–1936 Italy invaded and brutally conquered the last independent African state, Ethiopia, killing some 200,000 Ethiopians. Despite their spirited defense, they succumbed to superior Italian aerial bombing and firepower.

Meanwhile, the United States exercised influence in the Americas. During the Mexican Revolution, President Woodrow Wilson sent thousands of U.S. troops into Mexico to restore order. Americans also owned a large share of the Mexican economy, including most of the oil industry. The longest U.S. intervention came in Nicaragua, where U.S. Marines overthrew a government hostile to the United States and then remained there from 1909 to 1933, often fighting a peasant resistance led by Augusto César Sandino (san-DEE-no) (1895–1934), who became a hero to nationalist Central Americans. In its desire to protect U.S. investments in Central America, the United States often supported governments led by landowners and generals, such as the notoriously corrupt Nicaraguan dictator, Anastasio Somoza (1896–1956). President Franklin D. Roosevelt defended this policy by maintaining that "they may be SOBs, but they're our SOBs."[4] These repeated U.S. interventions in the region left an aftertaste of local resentment against what Central Americans called "Yankee imperialism."

SECTION SUMMARY

- World War I affected colonies in Asia, Africa, and the Caribbean as thousands of colonial subjects were forced to fight and die for France, Germany, and Britain, and promises of democratic reforms and special treatment for war veterans were not carried out.

- Colonial governments imposed heavy taxes and hard labor on the colonial peoples, who often lived in poverty while their Western counterparts lived in luxury, a state of affairs that was defended by the Western idea that the colonial peoples could not yet govern themselves.

- Western capitalism disrupted traditional rural life in many colonies, placing formerly self-sufficient farmers at the mercy of landowners and the world economy, which led to misery, political unrest, and activism during the Great Depression.

- Nationalism appealed to many frustrated colonial subjects, though many multiethnic colonies struggled to develop a sense of nationhood, and Marxism appealed to many, such as Vietnam's Ho Chi Minh, as an alternative to exploitative capitalism.

- Despite local opposition, Western nations expanded their colonial reach between 1900 and 1945: Italy brutally conquered Ethiopia, France and Britain took over former Ottoman colonies, and the United States continued to meddle in Central America.

NATIONALISM AND COMMUNISM IN CHINA

| How and why did the communist movement grow in China?

The Chinese Revolution of 1911–1912, which ended the 2,000-year-old imperial system (see Chapter 23), had led to a republic that Chinese hoped would foster renewed strength in the world, but these hopes were soon dashed (see Chronology: China, 1911–1945). China lapsed into warlordism and civil war, nominally independent but subject to pressure from the West and Japan. Alarm at China's domestic failures and continuing Western imperialism sparked a resurgent nationalism more influential than in most nonindustrialized countries, as well as the formation of a communist party and China's eventual reunification.

Warlords, New Cultures, and Nationalism

During the demoralizing Warlord Era (1916–1927), China was divided into territories controlled by rival **warlords**, local political leaders who had their own armies, taxing and terrorizing the population. Some warlords called themselves reformers interested in promoting education and industry. Still others took bribes to carry out policies favoring merchants or foreign governments. High taxes, inflation, famine, accelerating social tensions, and banditry made life difficult for most Chinese, increasing frustration.

    One result was that cities became enclaves of new intellectual, social, cultural, and economic thought. New schools and universities opened, and by 1919 4.5 million girls were in school, although vastly more boys enjoyed access to formal education. By the 1920s many women worked as nurses, teachers, and civil servants, but few rural women became literate or enjoyed these new opportunities. Exposure to Western ideas in universities, especially those run by Christian groups, led some Chinese students to question their own cultural traditions. Women activists and sympathetic men

warlords Local political leaders with their own armies.

Radical Currents

CHRONOLOGY
China, 1911–1945

1911–1912 Chinese Revolution

1915 Beginning of New Culture Movement

1916–1927 Warlord Era

1919 May Fourth Movement

1926–1928 Northern Expedition to reunify China

1927 Guomindang suppression of communists

1927–1934 Mao Zedong's Jiangxi Soviet

1928–1937 Republic of China in Nanjing

1931 Japanese occupation of Manchuria

1935–1936 Long March by Chinese communists

1937–1945 Japanese invasion of China

**New Culture Move-
ment** A movement of
Chinese intellectuals started in
1915 that sought to wash away
the discredited past and sprout
a literary revival.

**May Fourth Move-
ment** A radical nationalist
resurgence in China in 1919
that opposed imperialism and
the ineffective, warlord-
controlled Chinese
government.

campaigned against footbinding, which largely disappeared except in remote rural areas by 1930. Chambers of commerce and labor unions also appeared.

Many Chinese intellectuals supported the **New Culture Movement**, which sought to wash away the discredited past and sprout a literary revival. The movement originated in 1915 at Beijing University, China's intellectual mecca that hired radical professors and that encouraged a mixing of Chinese and Western thought. University professors published the literary magazine *New Youth,* which became the chief vehicle for attacking China's traditions, including Confucianism, which they believed kept China backward by promoting conformity and discouraging critical thinking. The magazine's editor, Chen Duxiu **(chen too-shoe)** (1879–1942), promoted republican government and science. Contributors to the magazine, while detesting Western imperialism, admired the liberal, open intellectual atmosphere in Western nations and viewed modern science as liberation from superstition. Essays derided the traditional Chinese family system as contrary to individual rights and advised women to seek equality with men.

Chinese rage against Western and Japanese imperialism increased in the aftermath of World War I. China had remained neutral until 1917, but Japan had occupied the German sphere of influence in the Shandong peninsula of eastern China, and in 1915 it presented China with 21 Demands, including control of Shandong, increased rights in Manchuria, and appointment of Japanese advisers to the Chinese government. The decision by the Western allies to allow Japan to take over Shandong provoked a radical nationalist resurgence in 1919, known as the **May Fourth Movement**, that opposed imperialism and the ineffective, warlord-controlled Chinese government. Decrying social injustice and government inaction, students and workers, many of them women, mounted mass demonstrations, strikes, and boycotts of Japanese goods. Merchants closed their businesses in sympathy. Capitulating to the protests, the Chinese government refused to sign the Versailles treaty. The new Soviet Union sided with China and renounced the special privileges that had been obtained by the czars, winning admiration among the Chinese.

In 1921 professors and students at Beijing University, many of them active in the New Culture and May Fourth Movements, organized the Chinese Communist Party (CCP). Some of the party founders, such as the *New Youth* editor, Chen Duxiu, were Europe- or Japan-educated reformers who admired Western science and culture. Others were nationalists who despised Western models and believed the Chinese people could liberate China if they were mobilized for revolution. Soviet advisers, while encouraging the party to organize among the urban working class, considered the Chinese communists unlikely to become influential. But the communists formed peasant associations, labor unions, women's groups, and youth clubs, and by 1927 the party had some 60,000 members.

The Communist Party was only one strand of a resurgent nationalism. Sun Zhongshan, better known as Sun Yat-sen (1866–1925), whose revolutionary ideas helped overthrow the Qing dynasty (see Chapter 23), began to rebuild his Guomindang, or Nationalist Party. Receiving no help from the Western nations, who benefited from China's disarray, Sun accepted advisers and military aid from the Soviet Union. In the mid-1920s Sun's Guomindang and the Chinese communists worked together, in an alliance known as the United Front, to defeat warlordism. However, Sun's ideology grew more authoritarian, as he concluded that China's 400 million people—in his view just "loose sand"—were not ready for democracy. Sun died in 1925, and the new Guomindang leader, Sun's brother-in-law, Jiang Jieshi (better known in the West as Chiang Kai-shek **(CHANG kai-shek)**) (1887–1975), was more conservative. Chiang, who came from a wealthy landowning family, was a pro-business soldier and a patriot, but indifferent to social change. He began building a modern military force.

The Republic of China

Northern Expedition

Between 1926 and 1928 the Guomindang forces and their communist allies reunified China with a military drive, the Northern Expedition, that defeated or co-opted the warlords. The foreign powers recognized Chiang's new Republic of China. However, during the drive, tensions had grown between leftwing and rightwing factions. Whereas communists and leftist Guomindang leaders sought social change and mobilization of workers, the right wing, led by Chiang, was allied with the antiprogressive Shanghai business community. In 1927 Chiang expelled the communists from the United Front and began a reign of terror, killing thousands of leftists; those who survived went into hiding or fled into the rural interior or abroad.

From 1928 to 1937 Chiang's Republic of China, based at Nanjing (nahn-JING) along the Yangzi River, launched a modernization program. The Republic's leaders, many of them Western-educated Christians, built railroads, factories, a banking system, and a modern army, streamlined the government, fostered public health and education, and adopted new legal codes. New laws promoted monogamy and equal inheritance rights for women, though Chiang's government had little power to carry them out. The regime also negotiated an end to most of the unequal international treaties imposed by the Western nations and Japan in the 1800s. The U.S. government, closely allied with Chiang's regime, and private Americans provided generous political and financial support for Chiang's modernization efforts. Feeling a paternalistic responsibility for China, Americans funded schools, hospitals, orphanages, and Christian missions. In 1940 a prominent U.S. senator, reflecting the notion that Americans could enrich and Westernize China, proclaimed: "We will lift Shanghai up, ever up, until it is just like Kansas City."[5]

Yet the Republic faced daunting challenges. While the urban elite in big coastal cities prospered, Chiang was unable or unwilling to deal with the growing poverty of the peasantry. Commercialization of agriculture shifted more land to landlords, and half of China's peasants lacked enough land to support their families. Chiang also tolerated government corruption and rewarded his financial backers in the merchant and banking sector. As antigovernment sentiment grew, Chiang, influenced by European fascism, built an authoritarian police state that brutally repressed dissent. China also faced problems with Japan. In 1931 Japanese forces seized Manchuria, the large northeastern region rich in mineral resources and fertile farmland, and set up a puppet government under the last Manchu emperor, Henry Pu Yi (1906–1967) (see Map 25.1). As Japan gradually extended its military and political influence southward, Chiang, unable to match Japanese military power, followed a policy of appeasement. His attempts to strengthen the Chinese military diverted scarce resources from economic development, and his reluctance to fight Japan left him open to charges that he was unpatriotic.

China's challenges were reflected in cultural life. Disillusioned by China's weakness in the world and continued despotism, many intellectuals lost faith in both Chiang's regime and Chinese traditions. The writer Lu Xun (LOO shun) (1881–1936), who had studied in Japan and became proficient in several foreign languages, published satires on Chinese failures to meet the challenges of the modern world. Lu Xun later formed a leftist writers' group and supported the communists. In criticizing both imperialism and greedy Chinese leaders, he argued, "Our vaunted Chinese civilization is only a feast of human flesh prepared for the rich and mighty, and China is only a kitchen where these feasts are prepared."[6] Ding Ling (1904–1985), one of China's first feminist writers, had fled her native village to avoid an arranged marriage, participated in the May Fourth Movement, and lived a liberated city life. Her early novels and short stories focused on women's issues and featured independent women unable to find emotional or sexual satisfaction. After the Guomindang killed her politically activist husband, she dedicated her writing to the revolutionary cause but was later persecuted by the communists for her feminism and reluctance to follow the party line.

The Rise of Chinese Communism

As the communists who survived Chiang's terror worked to rebuild their movement, one of the younger party leaders, Mao Zedong (maow dzuh-dong) (1893–1976), pursued his own strategy to mount the revolution to reshape China. From a peasant family dominated by a father who abused Mao's mother, Mao had run away from home to attend high school. Moving to Beijing, he found work in the Beijing University Library, where he embraced communism. He then edited a radical magazine, became an elementary school principal, and organized workers and peasants. In 1927, as Chiang eliminated communists, Mao fled to the rugged mountains of Jiangxi (kee-ON-see) province in south-central China, where he set up a revolutionary base, known as the **Jiangxi Soviet**, and organized a guerrilla army out of peasants, bandits, and former Guomindang soldiers to fight the Guomindang. Rejecting the advice of Soviet advisers to depend on support from the urban working class, Mao opted instead to rely on China's huge peasantry.

Jiangxi Soviet A revolutionary base, established in 1927 in south-central China, where Mao Zedong organized a guerrilla force to fight the Guomindang.

Mao believed that violence was necessary to oppose Chiang, writing that "a revolution is not a dinner party, or writing an essay, or painting a picture, or doing embroidery; it cannot be so refined, so leisurely and gentle. A revolution is an act of violence by which one class overthrows another."[7] Between 1928 and 1934 Mao expanded the Jiangxi Soviet, redistributing land from the rich to the poor. As Chiang's repression intensified, top Chinese Communist Party leaders, who had once scorned Mao, moved to the Jiangxi Soviet.

Map 25.1 Chinese Communist Movement and Chinese-Japanese War

Japan occupied much of northern and eastern China by 1939. In 1935–1936 the Chinese communists made the famous 6,000-mile Long March from their base in Jiangxi in southern China to Yan'an in northwest China.

e Interactive Map

Long March An epic journey, full of hardship, in which Mao Zedong's Red Army fought their way 6,000 miles on foot and horseback through eleven Chinese provinces to establish a safe base.

Increasingly alarmed by Mao's growing base, Chiang had his army blockade the Jiangxi Soviet to keep out essential supplies, forcing Mao to reluctantly abandon his base. In 1935 Mao and 100,000 soldiers and followers broke through the blockade and, in search of a safer base, began the **Long March**, an epic journey, full of hardship, in which Mao's Red Army fought their way 6,000 miles on foot and horseback through eleven provinces. The communists crossed eighteen mountain ranges, forded twenty-four rivers, and slogged through swamps, losing 90 percent of their people to death or desertion. Finally in late 1936 the ragtag survivors arrived in a poor northwestern prov-

Private Collection

The Long March
This painting glorifies the crossing, over an old iron chain bridge, of the Dadu River in western Sichuan province by the communist Red Army during the Long March. This successful crossing, against fierce attacks by Guomindang forces, was a key event in the communists' successful journey to northwest China.

ince, where they moved into cavelike homes carved into the hills around the dusty city of Yan'an **(YEH-nan)**. The Long March saved the communists from elimination by Chiang, making Mao the unchallenged party leader. Mao celebrated the achievement: "The Long March is the first of its kind in the annals of history [and has] proclaimed that the Red Army is an army of heroes."[8] But the communists were still vulnerable to Chiang's larger, better-equipped forces and would be saved only by the Japanese invasion of China in 1937, which forced Chiang to shift his military priorities to fighting the Japanese. These developments allowed the communists to regroup and spread their message of change in wartime China.

Japanese Invasion and Communist Revolution

The Japanese invasion and the disastrous Chinese-Japanese war that followed altered China's politics as Chiang had to divert money from modernization to the military. Mao captured the patriotic mood of the country by proposing a united front against Japan, and Chiang had little choice but to agree. The Japanese soon occupied the major cities of north China and the coast, and by the end of 1938 Japanese forces controlled most of eastern China, including the best farmland and the major industrial cities, but became bogged down and unable to expand their control. War and occupation undermined Chiang's government and enabled the communists to recruit support, thus setting the stage for major changes in Chinese politics in the later 1940s.

Nationalist Retreat

Chiang's government relocated inland to Chongqing **(CHUNG-king)**, a city protected by high mountains on the Yangzi River. This move was followed by a mass migration of Chinese fleeing the Japanese. Unlike the cosmopolitan coastal cities, Chongqing offered no bright lights or French restaurants and had a depressing climate of fog and humidity. Fatigue, cynicism, and inflation discouraged the Guomindang's followers. Virtually broke, Chiang's government squeezed the peasants in the areas they still controlled for tax revenues to support an army of 4 to 5 million men. But it gradually lost support. Militarily ineffective, politically repressive, and economically corrupt, it offered limited resistance to the Japanese, killed and imprisoned opponents, and put the personal gain of its leaders above the economic well-being of China's people. Although the United States supported Chiang as an ally against imperial Japan, it was able to supply the Guomindang-held areas only by difficult, mountainous routes from Burma and India. Moreover, Chiang often ignored U.S. advice in military and political matters. As the war wore on, he lost much of his popular support.

Meanwhile, the communists at Yan'an were able to improve their prospects. Used to poverty, they had a more disciplined army with a higher morale. While Chiang's much larger forces had the main responsibility to fight the Japanese, the communists mobilized the people by forging a close relationship with the peasantry in north China and by mounting guerrilla bands to harass the Japanese. Their unconventional struggle, which Mao called "**people's war**," combined military action and political recruitment. In Mao's military strategy, "the enemy advances, we retreat; the enemy halts, we harass; the enemy retreats, we pursue."[9] In the political strategy, communist activists set up village governments and peasant associations and encouraged women's rights, punishing abusive husbands. The communist message of social revolution and nationalism offered hope to the downtrodden. Thousands of Chinese, students, intellectuals, and writers such as Ding Ling flocked to Yan'an to join the communist cause. By 1945 the party had 1.2 million members.

The communist experiences at Yan'an fostered what later came to be known as **Maoism**, an ideology promoted by Mao that mixed ideas from Chinese tradition with Marxist-Leninism from

Communist Resurgence

people's war An unconventional struggle combining military action and political recruitment, formulated by Mao Zedong in China.

Maoism An ideology promoted by Mao Zedong that mixed ideas from Chinese tradition with Marxist-Leninist ideas from the Soviet Union.

the Soviet Union. Mao emphasized the subordination of the individual to the needs of the group (a traditional Chinese notion), the superiority of political values over technical and artistic ones, and belief in the human will as a social force. To combat elitism, Mao introduced mass campaigns in which everyone engaged in physical labor, such as building dams and roads. The communists sent intellectuals into villages to teach literacy and learn from the peasants. Mao expressed faith that the Chinese people, armed with political understanding, had the collective power to triumph over nature, poverty, and exploitation to build a new society.

During the Japanese occupation the communists gained domination over much of rural north China, where Mao's ideas on social change and economic justice had gained support. Hence, when the war ended in 1945, the communists had improved their prospects while Chiang's Guomindang, although still a superior military force, was beset with problems resulting from its inability to defeat the Japanese and maintain popular support. In 1949 the communists won a bitter civil war and established a government.

SECTION SUMMARY

- After the end of the imperial system, rival warlords controlled China during a period of civil war, and intellectuals formed the New Culture Movement, which called for a modernized China that fostered individualism and equality rather than traditions such as Confucianism.

- Japan's aggressive demands after World War I enraged the Chinese, and some were attracted to communism, but Sun Yat-sen's successor, the probusiness Chiang Kai-shek, allied the nationalist movement with the United States.

- Chiang Kai-shek's Republic of China launched a modernization program, but it was hampered by a split with the communists, persistent rural poverty, and the Japanese seizure of Manchuria.

- Mao Zedong organized peasants into a communist revolutionary army and then led them on the punishing Long March in search of safety from Chiang Kai-shek's far-stronger army, which might have triumphed had it not been diverted by a 1937 Japanese invasion.

- The Chinese people lost faith in Chiang's government as it squeezed them for taxes to support a failing war against Japan, while Mao's communists instilled hope through guerrilla attacks on the Japanese and a promise of equality and progress through shared sacrifice.

BRITISH COLONIALISM AND THE INDIAN RESPONSE

What were the main contributions of Mohandas Gandhi to the Indian struggle?

In India, resentment of British colonialism and an inequitable social order sparked a powerful nationalist movement. Those Indians who hoped that World War I would bring them self-determination could see that the British rhetoric about democracy did not apply to India. Growing opposition to British rule, spurred by the Indian National Congress, led to unrest that forced the British to modify some of their policies. Nationalism also set the stage for the turmoil that eventually created separate Hindu and Muslim nations after World War II.

The Nationalist Upsurge and Gandhi

The severe dislocations caused by World War I spurred nationalist opposition to the British Raj. To pay for the war, the British raised taxes and customs duties on Indians, sparking several armed uprisings. Over 1 million Indians fought for Britain in France and the Middle East, and 60,000 were killed. Many Indians expected a better future because of their sacrifices in a war they did not start—perhaps a self-government similar to that of Australia and Canada, both former colonies. But the British dashed these hopes by declaring that they would maintain India as an integral part of their empire. However, the losses in World War I showed that British power was no longer unchallengeable.

Indian Discontent

A severe economic slump heightened Indian discontent, causing the alarmed British to clamp down on dissent and maintain the harsh wartime laws. In 1919, in the Punjab city of Amritsar, British officers, fearing a mass uprising, ordered their Indian soldiers to open fire on an unarmed crowd at an unauthorized rally held in a walled field where escape was difficult (see Chronology: South Asia, 1914–1945). The attack killed 400 protesters and wounded 1,000, including women and children. Throughout India, the Amritsar massacre was greeted with outrage. The anger intensified when the British hailed the officer in command, General Dyer, as a national hero. Prominent Indians, many once pro-British, were appalled at the cruelty. The Nobel Prize–winning writer Rabindranath Tagore (tuh-GAWR) (1861–1941) wrote, "The enormity of the measures taken up for quelling some local disturbances had, with a rude shock, revealed to our minds the helplessness of our position as British subjects in India."[10]

The unrest brought to the fore new Indian nationalist leaders, the most outstanding of whom was Mohandas K. Gandhi (GAHN-dee) (1869–1948) (see Profile: Mohandas Gandhi, Indian Nationalist). After getting his law degree in Britain, Gandhi lived for twenty-two years in South Africa, where the British colonial regime practiced racial segregation and white supremacy (see Chapter 21). To assert the rights of the Indian immigrants in South Africa, Gandhi developed tactics of **nonviolent resistance**, noncooperation with unjust laws and peaceful confrontation with illegitimate authority. Influenced by his pacifist wife, Kasturbai, Gandhi adopted ideas against taking life that had been introduced 2,500 years earlier by the Jains and Buddhists and also promoted by the Quakers, a pacifist Christian movement Gandhi had encountered in England. Nonviolence—Gandhi often called it passive resistance—was, he wrote, "a method of securing rights by personal suffering; it is the reverse of resistance by arms."[11] Gandhi believed that violence was never justified. The enemy was to be met with reason, and if he responded with violence, this had to be endured in good spirit.

After returning to India, in 1920 Gandhi became the president of the Indian National Congress. His message of resisting nonviolently led him to mount mass campaigns against British political and economic institutions. Inspired by his example, huge numbers of ordinary people—factory workers, peasants, estate laborers—joined his movement, shaking the foundations of British colonial rule. Gandhi made mass civil disobedience, involving marches, sit-ins, hunger strikes, peaceful violation of law, refusal to pay taxes, and boycotts of government and businesses, the most effective expression of nonviolence. Gandhi's Congress colleague, Jawaharlal Nehru (JAH-wa-HAR-lahl NAY-roo), placed Gandhi's strategy in perspective: "Gandhi was like a powerful current of fresh air that made us stretch ourselves and take deep breaths, like a Whirlwind that upset many things but most of all the working of people's minds."[12]

Yet, some of Gandhi's ideas were outside the mainstream of nationalist thought, confounding allies. Gandhi opposed the global economic system because it involved competitive capitalism and trade between societies with unequal power and wealth. He believed that India should reject Western models and return to the self-sufficient, village-based precolonial economy, where everyone could spin their own cloth. He called industrialization "a machinery which has impoverished India. India's salvation consists in unlearning what she has learned during the past fifty years. The railways, telegraphs, hospitals, [and] lawyers have all to go."[13] Critics considered Gandhi's ideal of self-sufficient villages living in simplicity a utopian fantasy that was impractical and out of touch with the modern world, unable to improve people's lives. Gandhi also insisted that Indian society's lowest social group, the untouchables, be included in political actions, much to the distress of high-caste Hindus. He coined the term *harijans* (children of God) as a more dignified label to replace *pariahs,* the centuries-old name for untouchables. Gandhi did not entirely reject the caste system, but he wanted all people to enjoy the same dignity. In his conception, harijan toilet cleaners would have the same status as members of the priestly caste but would go on cleaning toilets. Even untouchable leaders often considered Gandhi's views unrealistic and patronizing.

Thanks to Gandhi's efforts, during the 1920s the Congress developed a mass base that was supported by people from all of India's cultures, religions, regions, and social backgrounds. His tactics bewildered the British, who, while claiming to uphold law, order, and Christian values, clubbed hunger strikers, used horses to trample nonviolent protesters, and arrested Gandhi and other leaders. One Indian observer told British officials in 1930 that the Congress "has undoubtedly acquired a great hold on the popular imagination. On roadside stations where until a few months ago I could hardly have suspected that people had any politics, I have seen demonstrations and heard Congress slogans."[14] Each campaign led to British concessions and a growing realization that Britain could not hold India forever.

The Great Depression lowered the standard of living for most Indians, collapsing prices for India's cash crops and rural credit, causing distress and suffering, and sparking a new Gandhi-led campaign in 1930, the Great Salt March. Gandhi and several dozen followers marched to the west coast, where they produced salt from the Indian Ocean seawater. In doing so they broke British laws,

CHRONOLOGY
South Asia, 1914–1945

1919 Amritsar massacre

1930 Gandhi's Great Salt March

1931 London Conference

1935 Government of India Act

1937 Provincial elections

1942 Gandhi's Quit India campaign

nonviolent resistance Noncooperation with unjust laws and peaceful confrontation with illegitimate authority, pursued by Mohandas Gandhi in India.

Gandhi and His Strategies

Rising Congress Influence

MOHANDAS GANDHI, INDIAN NATIONALIST

Few individuals have had as much impact on history as Mohandas Gandhi (1869–1948), who became the leading figure of Indian nationalism in the 1920s by formulating ideas of nonviolent opposition to repressive colonial rule that influenced millions both inside and outside India. Gandhi was born into a well-to-do family of the vaisya caste in the western state of Gujerat; although vaisyas were commonly involved in commerce, his father was a government official. His parents maintained traditional attitudes, and his mother was a devout Hindu. Like many Hindu families, they arranged for him to marry young. The thirteen-year-old Mohandas married Kasturbai Kapada (KAST-er-by ka-PO-da) (1869–1948), the daughter of a rich merchant. Kasturbai proved a courageous helpmate in his later political activities.

Gandhi wanted to study law in London, but his family feared he would be corrupted there because his young wife, now with a son, had to stay in India. To gain their approval, he vowed to live a celibate life in England and never to touch meat or wine. In England he expanded his knowledge by reading Indian works such as the *Bhagavad Gita* and Western books such as the Christian Bible. His three years in London also gave him contact with Western nationalism and democracy, as well as a law degree.

At first unable to find a suitable position back in India, in 1893 Gandhi was hired by a large Indian law firm to work in South Africa, where the racist government and white minority mistreated not only Africans but also the thousands of Indians who had been recruited as laborers and plantation workers. With his wife's encouragement, he turned to helping the local

Gandhi Addressing Calcutta Meeting Mohandas Gandhi addressed some of his followers—many women as well as men—on a lawn following a meeting with British officials in Calcutta in 1931.

Indians assert their rights, for which he was jailed, beaten by mobs, and almost killed by angry opponents, both white and Indian. The British who ruled South Africa raised taxes on Indians, shut down Indian gatherings, and refused official recognition of Hindu marriages. In response, and influenced by Kasturbai's advocacy of justice and nonviolence, Gandhi began developing his strategy of nonviolent resistance against oppressive rule, ideas that later inspired admirers throughout the world and that were used by Dr. Martin Luther King, Jr., in the U.S. civil rights movement of the 1950s and 1960s.

since salt production was a lucrative government monopoly. Gandhi's action and arrest caught the popular imagination, setting off a wave of demonstrations, strikes, and boycotts. In quelling the unrest, the British killed 103, injured 420, and imprisoned 60,000 resisters. They released Gandhi a few months later, and he agreed to halt civil disobedience campaigns if the British would promote Indian-made goods and hold a conference to discuss India's political future.

Social Change: Caste and Gender Relations

These events took place against a backdrop of nationalist politics, economic dislocations, and rapid population growth that affected India's social structure. India's population grew from 255 million in 1871 to 390 million in 1940. The trends reshaping the caste system in the 1800s continued, including the adoption by lower castes of high-caste practices such as vegetarianism and more awareness of caste identities. Although Gandhi urged fair treatment for all groups, increasing attention to caste identities led to more discrimination against untouchables, the most disadvantaged group and perhaps a fifth of India's population. As a result, untouchables mounted movements promoting their rights. Dr. Bhimrao Ramji Ambedkar (BIM-rao RAM-jee am-BED-car) (1893–1956), who rose from one of the lowest groups, the sweepers who cleaned village streets, to earn a Ph.D. and a law degree from major U.S. and British universities, started schools, newspapers, and political parties. He rejected Gandhi's policies as inadequate for real change and successfully lobbied the government to offer untouchables government jobs and scholarships for higher education. Later in life, believing untouchables could never flourish within Hinduism, Ambedkar led thousands of followers to adopt Buddhism, which by then had only a small following in India.

Caste System

Between 1906 and 1914 Gandhi carried on his fight for justice for Indians in South Africa, spreading ideas of nonviolence. He led hunger strikes, public demonstrations, and mass marches, in which thousands of Indians resisted oppression by willingly risking beating or arrest for their cause. In 1914 the colonial regime bowed to the constant pressure and lifted the worst legal injustices against the Indians. Gandhi was forty-five years old when the triumph in South Africa earned him fame and the respected title of *Mahatma* (Great Soul) among Indians in South Africa and at home.

With the outbreak of World War I in Europe, Gandhi, Kasturbai, and their four children left South Africa to return to India. In 1915 he established a spiritual center near the Gujerat capital, Ahmedebad, where he trained followers in his ideas of nonviolence. Though Gandhi was deeply religious, he also believed that everyone had to reach truth in his or her own way, writing that "there are innumerable definitions of God, because His manifestations are innumerable. But I worship God as Truth only. I have not yet found Him, but I am seeking after Him." Moved by the poverty and suffering of the Indian masses, he also took up their cause. To identify with their plight, the high-caste Gandhi adopted the dress of the simple peasant and always traveled third class.

The British massacre of Indian protesters at Amritsar in 1919 shook Gandhi's faith in British justice. In 1920 he became the leader of India's major nationalist organization, the Indian National Congress, and over the next three decades he was at times a religious figure and at other times the consummate politician, crafty and practical. Needing mass support to build a policy of massive noncooperation, he launched three great campaigns of civil disobedience, in 1920, 1930, and 1942. Each time the British jailed him for long periods. His self-discipline was reflected in his practice of fasting to protest oppression, which added to his saintly image.

In his personal life, Gandhi was also troubled. His wife, Kasturbai, aided in his campaigns, but Gandhi was gone for long periods, neglecting her and their four children. One embittered son rejected his father entirely. When Gandhi took a life-long vow of chastity in 1906, Kasturbai did also. Both kept their vows. Although both were born into affluent families, the Gandhis agreed to live simply. Critics accused Gandhi of sometimes humiliating his wife by, for example, asking her to do menial tasks such as cleaning toilets. Arrested during Gandhi's "Quit India" campaign, Kasturbai, in failing health, died in her husband's lap in prison in 1944. Before she passed away, she noted that they had shared many joys and sorrows and asked that she be cremated in a sari (dress) made from yarn he had spun.

Gandhi helped lead India to independence from Britain. Shortly thereafter, when trying to end accelerating Hindu-Muslim violence in 1948, he was assassinated by a Hindu fanatic who opposed Gandhi's tolerant approach (see Chapter 31). India's first prime minister, Jawaharlal Nehru, called Gandhi's death the loss of India's soul: "The light has gone out of our lives and there is darkness everywhere."

THINKING ABOUT THE PROFILE

1. How did Gandhi's South African experiences shape his political strategies?
2. How did Gandhi's ideas and activities have a great influence in the world?

Note: Quotations from Judith M. Brown, *Modern India: The Origins of an Asian Democracy*, 2nd ed. (New York: Oxford University Press, 1994), 211; and Rhoads Murphey, *A History of Asia*, 4th ed. (New York: Longman, 2003), 437.

Attitudes toward women were also changing. Hindus increasingly favored widow remarriage, once forbidden, to help offset the higher Muslim birthrate. But greater emphasis on what traditionalists considered proper female conduct largely favored male authority. Yet, while the feminist movement remained weak, many women joined the Congress, and some demanded a vote equal to men for representative institutions. With British assent, all the provincial legislatures granted women the franchise between 1923 and 1930. Educated women published magazines. Rokeya Hossain (1880–1932), a Bengali Muslim raised in seclusion who had opened girls' schools and campaigned for equal rights, published a utopian short story, "Sultana's Dream," that portrayed men confined to seclusion because of their uncontrolled sexual desires while women governed. Gandhi's views on women were mixed. He advocated gender equality, encouraged women's participation in public life, and also urged women to abandon seclusion and join a nationalist women's corps. But women were usually offered the more menial tasks such as picketing and cooking. Gandhi promoted women's traditional roles as wives, mothers, and supporters of men and believed women were especially suited to passive resistance. Some women with a more militant vision joined men in terrorist organizations. Pritilata Waddedar (1911–1932), a brilliant Bengali university graduate, led and died in an armed raid on a British club that reportedly boasted a sign: "Dogs and Indians not allowed."

Gender Relations

Hindu-Muslim Division

A growing Hindu-Muslim division posed a problem for Indian nationalism. Although some Muslims supported the Congress, its largely Hindu membership sparked concerns among Muslims about their role in India. While Gandhi respected all religions and welcomed Muslim support,

Congress and the Muslims

Muslim leaders, fearing that independence would mean Hindu domination, mounted their own nationalist organizations to work for a potential Muslim country of their own. In 1930 student activists in Britain called their proposed Muslim nation Pakistan, meaning "Land of the Pure" in the Urdu language spoken by many Indian Muslims. Accounting for some 20 percent of British India's population and largely concentrated in the northwest and Bengal, Muslims occupied all niches of society but were divided by social status, ancestry, language, and sect. The great majority were Sunni, but some were Shi'a.

While Muslim leaders often focused on the need for a state that enshrined their religious values, Congress leaders were chiefly Western-oriented Hindu intellectuals. Jawaharlal Nehru (1889–1964), who succeeded Gandhi as Congress leader in 1929, wanted a secular state that was neutral toward religion and, in contrast with Gandhi, a modern India. Born into a wealthy brahman family and endowed with unusual charisma and rare public speaking skills, Nehru was a Marxist-influenced product of an elite Western education with a passion for the welfare of the common people. But while Gandhi wanted to reshape colonial society, Nehru and other Congress leaders focused more on political independence. Few of the Indian nationalists shared the Chinese communist goal of radical social transformation.

The Muslim League

By the 1930s the main rival to the Congress was the Muslim League, led by the Western-educated Bombay lawyer Muhammed Ali Jinnah (jee-NAH) (1876–1948), a dapper figure in his tailored suits who always spoke English and never learned Urdu. Jinnah argued that Islam and Hinduism were different social orders and that it was a naive dream that the two groups could ever forge a common nationality. Jinnah developed the Muslim League into a mass political movement in competition with the Congress. His claim to speak for all Muslims outraged the Congress, which had over a hundred thousand Muslim members and saw itself as a national party representing all religions and castes. But Jinnah cultivated good relations with the British and convinced regional Muslim leaders to support the Muslim League. The Congress tried to marginalize the Muslim League and refused to form a coalition with it, which proved a mistake in the long run.

Competing Visions

The competing visions of the Congress and the Muslim League complicated British efforts to introduce representative government institutions. The two rival organizations clashed in 1931, when Indian leaders and British officials met in London to discuss expanded elections. Representatives of various minorities, including Muslims, Sikhs, and untouchables, demanded separate electorates to ensure that their groups gained representation. Seeing this as a tactic that would allow the British to divide and rule, Congress objected, but the minorities won electoral rights in India's many provinces. The electoral agreement also did not end anticolonial unrest and counterviolence by the British. However, in the Government of India Act of 1935 the British introduced a new constitution that allowed some 35 million Indians who owned property to vote for newly formed provincial legislatures. In the first provincial elections, in 1937, the Congress won 70 percent of the popular vote and the majority of seats, defeating the Muslim League even for seats reserved for Muslims. More Indians also rose to leadership positions in the army, police, and civil service. However, British officials argued that the communal divisions necessitated the continuation of British rule to maintain order, and Jinnah redoubled his efforts to unite Muslims against the Congress.

World War II and India

World War II reshaped the nationalist dialogue by increasing the Hindu-Muslim divide. The British committed Indian troops without consulting Congress leaders, and in 1942 Gandhi, fearing that the British had no intention of ending their colonial rule, mounted a campaign calling on the British to "Quit India." The British arrested the entire Congress leadership and 60,000 party activists, jailing many of them for the duration of the war. During World War II, the rural poor and urban workers suffered as prices for essential goods soared, and famine in Bengal killed 3 to 4 million people. In response to these hardships, Nehru's main rival for Congress leadership, the militant Bengali Marxist Subhas Chandra Bose (1895–1945), allied with imperial Japan. With Japanese backing, Bose organized an Indian National Army, recruited largely from the British Indian army and Indian emigrants in Southeast Asia, that invaded India from Japan-held Burma. The invasion failed, but many Indians saw Bose as a national hero.

Meanwhile, the arrest of Congress leaders left a vacuum that allowed Jinnah to strengthen his Muslim League. The British cultivated Jinnah, who joined the government and demanded the creation of a separate Muslim state based on the provinces where Muslims were the majority. Rejecting Muslim separatism, the jailed Gandhi unsuccessfully urged Muslims to resist what he termed the suicide of partition. After World War II, the struggle between Indian nationalists and the British, and between Hindus and Muslims, resumed, leading to the end of British rule and the creation of two separate independent nations, predominantly Hindu India and a chiefly Muslim Pakistan.

SECTION SUMMARY

- In the aftermath of World War I Indians were angry that Britain denied them greater autonomy and imposed higher taxes to pay for the war, and resentment peaked with the massacre of hundreds of peaceful protesters at Amritsar.

- Mohandas Gandhi, the foremost Indian nationalist leader, promoted nonviolent resistance to British rule, including strikes, boycotts, and refusal to pay taxes, and won a massive popular following for the Indian National Congress.

- While even his Indian supporters considered some of Gandhi's ideas naive and utopian, campaigns such as the Great Salt March were highly effective in winning concessions from the British.

- Leaders of the untouchables, the lowest Hindu caste, pushed for and obtained greater opportunities, and women were allowed somewhat more freedom, though many Indian men, including Gandhi, did not see them as entirely equal to men.

- Feeling threatened by the predominantly Hindu National Congress, the Muslim League, led by Jinnah, argued that Indian Muslims should have a country of their own, which they called Pakistan.

- The British jailed tens of thousands of Indian National Congress activists after Gandhi objected to Indian troops being forced to fight in World War II, a Bengali Marxist led a failed invasion of India, the Muslim League grew increasingly independent, and eventually, after the end of World War II, both Pakistan and India gained independence from Britain.

NATIONALIST STIRRINGS IN SOUTHEAST ASIA AND SUB-SAHARAN AFRICA

How did nationalism differ in Southeast Asia and sub-Saharan Africa?

The challenges posed by European colonialism were also addressed by nationalist movements and protests in Southeast Asia and sub-Saharan Africa, though none were as influential as the Indian National Congress. In 1930 the Indonesian Nationalist Party, struggling against Dutch colonialism, urged Indonesians to be zealous in the cause of national freedom. The plea symbolized nationalist assertions in Southeast Asian colonies, especially French-ruled Vietnam. In sub-Saharan Africa nationalist movements, often based on ethnicity, were weaker.

Nationalism in Southeast Asia

The first stirrings of Southeast Asian nationalism came in the Philippines in the late 1800s, but the revolution was thwarted by the American occupation. The U.S. promise of eventual independence and its co-optation of nationalist leaders into the colonial administration reduced radical sentiments. By 1941 nationalists had a large following in Vietnam, British Burma, and Indonesia, all of which experienced oppressive colonial rule. In French-ruled Cambodia and Laos and in British Malaya and Borneo, all colonies that had experienced less social, economic, and political disruption, nationalism was weaker.

In Burma (today's Myanmar), despite limited self-government by the 1930s, the colony's majority ethnic group, the Burmans, hated British rule and resented British favoritism toward Christian ethnic minorities and the large, often wealthy Indian community, who dominated the economy. The colony's schools encouraged their students to adopt Western ways, including Western clothing styles, and devalued Buddhist traditions. The nationalist leaders, mostly graduates of these schools, used Theravada Buddhism as a rallying cry to press for reform, and some favored women's rights. When the Japanese invaded Burma in 1941, many Burmans welcomed them as liberators.

Burma and Siam

Although Siam (today's Thailand) was not a colony, nationalism emerged from tensions between the aristocratic elite and the rising middle class of civil servants, military officers, and professionals, who resented political domination by the royal family and aristocracy. Middle-class discontent was further fueled by the Great Depression, which forced salary and budget cuts. In 1932 military officers who called themselves nationalists took power in a coup against the royal government (see Chronology: Southeast Asia and Africa, 1912–1945), and the Siamese king agreed under pressure to become a constitutional, mostly symbolic monarch. Military leaders then ran the government through the 1930s, pursuing nationalist policies, renaming the country Thailand

CHRONOLOGY

Southeast Asia and Africa, 1912–1945

1912 Formation of African National Congress in South Africa

1912 Formation of Islamic Union in Indonesia

1920 Formation of Indonesian Communist Party

1920–1922 Nationalist unrest in Kenya

1926–1927 Communist uprising in Indonesia

1927 Formation of Indonesian Nationalist Party

1928–1931 Peasant rebellions in the Congo region

1930 Founding of Indochinese Communist Party

1932 Nationalist coup in Thailand

1935–1936 Conquest of Ethiopia by Italy

1941 Formation of Viet Minh in Vietnam by Ho Chi Minh

1941–1945 Japanese occupation of Southeast Asia

Viet Minh The Vietnamese Independence League, a coalition of anti-French groups established by Ho Chi Minh in 1941 that waged war against both the French and the Japanese.

lingua franca A language widely used as a common tongue among diverse groups with different languages.

Sukarno and Indonesian Nationalism

("Land of Free People"), and urging the Thais to live modern lives, including dressing in a modern Western fashion, with hats and shoes. Thailand forged an alliance with imperial Japan and introduced fascist policies, militarizing the schools and suppressing dissent.

The most powerful nationalist movement in Southeast Asia emerged in Vietnam, which was destabilized by French rule. The earliest leader was the passionately revolutionary Phan Boi Chau **(FAN boy chow)** (1867–1940), born into a mandarin family and educated in Confucian learning. By the time of his death in a French prison, Phan had inspired Vietnamese patriotism and resistance. As he wrote in his prison diaries, "It has been but a yearning to purchase my freedom even at the cost of spilling my blood, to exchange my fate of slavery for the right of self-determination."[15] But the older Confucian scholars gradually lost influence to the younger, urban, French-educated intellectuals of the Vietnamese Nationalist Party, which had few options other than terrorism: they assassinated colonial officials and bombed French buildings. A premature uprising in 1930 sparked greater French repression that destroyed the major nationalist groups except for the communists, thus becoming a turning point in Vietnamese history.

The rise of Vietnamese communism owed much to Ho Chi Minh, a mandarin's son and former sailor turned political activist who had spent many years organizing the communist movement among Vietnamese exiles in Thailand and China. Ho believed that revolution was the answer to economic exploitation and political repression in Vietnam, and he favored equality for women and improving the lives of the peasants and plantation workers. In 1930 Ho established the Indochinese Communist Party, which united anticolonial radicals from Vietnam, Cambodia, and Laos. Vietnamese Marxists linked themselves to the patriotic traditions of the Vietnamese rebels who for 2,000 years resisted Chinese, Mongol, and French conquerors. As one Vietnamese Marxist said: "Behind us we have the immense history of our people. There [are] still spiritual cords attaching us."[16] Vietnamese communism took on a strongly nationalist flavor. In 1941 Ho established the **Viet Minh**, or Vietnamese Independence League, a coalition of anti-French groups that waged war against both the French colonizers and the Japanese, who occupied Vietnam during World War II.

Nationalist activity also emerged in the Dutch East Indies in the early twentieth century. Diverse organizations sought freedom from Dutch control while seeking ways to unite the colony's hundreds of ethnic groups. One strategy was to adopt a unifying language. Malay was the mother tongue for many peoples in the western Indonesian islands, and elsewhere it served as a trading language. Malay was thus a **lingua franca**, a language widely used as a common tongue among diverse groups that also had their own languages. Nationalist intellectuals began using Malay and called it Indonesian, which gradually became the language of magazines, newspapers, books, and education. Indonesian religious traditions were also reshaped. Some Muslims, impressed with but also resenting Western power, sought to reform and purify their faith by purging it of practices based on older pre-Islamic influences, such as mysticism, which they believed held Indonesians back. *Muhammadiyah* ("Way of Muhammad") and its allied women's organization, *Aisyah*, criticized local customs, promoted the goal of an Islamic state, stressed the five pillars of Islam, and favored the segregation of men and women in public, a custom long ignored by most Indonesians.

In 1912 Javanese batik merchants who mixed reformist religious ideas with nationalism established the colony's first true political movement, the Islamic Union, which by 1919 had recruited 2 million members. As Marxism became influential in Indonesia after the Russian Revolution, the colonial government responded by arresting Marxists. The more radical Marxists established the Indonesian Communist Party in 1920, which grew rapidly by attracting support from nondevout Muslim peasants and labor union members in Java. Overestimating their strength, the communists sparked a poorly planned uprising in 1926. The Dutch crushed the uprising and executed the communist leaders.

The destruction of the communists left an opening for other nationalists. The Indonesian Nationalist Party, led mostly by Javanese aristocrats who rejected Islamic reform ideas, was established in 1927 and promoted a new national identity. Sukarno **(soo-KAHR-no)** (1902–1970), the key founder, was born into a wealthy aristocratic Javanese family. After studying engineering, he dedicated his life to politics and a free Indonesia. Sukarno loved the shadow puppet stories that had been popular on Java for centuries. Like the characters in those stories, Sukarno (who had no first name) brought together contradictory ideas, such as Islamic faith and atheistic Marxism. The mass popularizer of Indonesian nationalism, he created a slogan: "one nation—Indonesia, one people—Indonesian, one language—Indonesian." He even designed a flag and wrote a national anthem. The

Sukarno Indicts Dutch Colonialism

Sukarno, the fiery Indonesian nationalist, was skilled at articulating his criticisms of colonialism. A splendid orator, he attracted a large following through his use of Indonesian, especially Javanese, religious and cultural symbols and frequent historical references in his speeches. Arrested by the Dutch in 1930, Sukarno delivered a passionate defense speech, known as "Indonesia Accuses," at his trial that became one of the most inspiring documents of Indonesian nationalism. Sukarno stressed the greatness of Indonesia's past as a building block for the future.

The word "imperialism" . . designates a . . . tendency . . . to dominate or influence the affairs of another nation, . . . a system . . . of economic control. . . . As long as a nation does not wield political power in its own country, part of its potential, economic, social or political, will be used for interests which are not its interests, but contrary to them. . . . A colonial nation is a nation that cannot be itself, a nation that in almost all its branches, in all of its life, bears the mark of imperialism. There is no community of interests between the subject and the object of imperialism. Between the two there is only a contrast of interests and a conflict of needs. All interests of imperialism, social, economic, political, or cultural, are opposed to the interests of the Indonesian people. The imperialists desire the continuation of imperialism, the Indonesians desire its abolition. . . .

What are the roads to promote Indonesian nationalism? . . . First: we point out to the people that they have had a great past. Second: we reinforce the consciousness of the people that the present is dark. Third: we show the people the pure and brightly shining light of the future and the roads which lead to this future so full of promises. . . . The P.N.I. [Indonesian Nationalist Party] awakens and reinforces the people's consciousness of its "grandiose past," its "dark present" and the promises of a shining, beckoning future.

Our grandiose past? Oh, what Indonesian does not feel his heart shrink with sorrow when he hears the stories about the beautiful past, does not regret the disappearance of that departed glory! What Indonesian does not feel his national heart beat with joy when he hears about the greatness of the [Intermediate Era] empires of Melayu and Srivijaya, about the greatness of the empire of Mataram and Madjapahit. . . . A nation with such a grandiose past must surely have sufficient natural aptitude to have a beautiful future. . . . Among the people . . . again conscious of their great past, national feeling is revived, and the fire of hope blazes in their hearts.

THINKING ABOUT THE READING

1. What is Sukarno's evaluation of imperialism?
2. How does he think Indonesians should capitalize on their past?

Source: Harry J. Benda and John A. Larkin, eds., *The World of Southeast Asia: Selected Historical Readings* (New York: Harper and Row, 1967), pp. 190–193. Copyright © 1967 Harper and Row. Reprinted with permission of John A. Larkin.

Dutch authorities arrested Sukarno in 1929 and exiled him to a remote island prison for the next decade, making him a nationalist symbol (see Witness to the Past: Sukarno Indicts Dutch Colonialism). With Sukarno in jail, the Indonesian Nationalist Party and the nationalist vision grew slowly throughout the 1930s.

The Japanese Occupation and Its Consequences

The occupation of Southeast Asia by Japanese forces from 1941 to 1945 boosted nationalism and weakened colonialism. Before 1941 colonial authority had remained strong, with only Vietnamese nationalism posing a serious threat. Then everything changed. Japan had already bullied Thailand and the Vichy-controlled French colonial regime in Vietnam to allow the stationing of Japanese troops. Then the bombing of Pearl Harbor in 1941 was quickly followed by a rapid Japanese invasion of Southeast Asia. The Japanese easily overwhelmed the colonial forces, and within four months they controlled major cities and heavily populated regions, shattering the mystique of Western invincibility. As an Indonesian writer later remembered, the Japanese occupation "destroyed a whole set of illusions and left man as naked as when he was created."[17] European and American officials, businessmen, planters, and missionaries were either in retreat or confined in prison camps. The Japanese talked of "Asia for the Asians," and some Japanese officers with anticolonial sentiments sympathized with Southeast Asian nationalists. But this rhetoric also masked the Japanese desire for resources, especially the rubber, oil, and timber of Indonesia, British Borneo, and Malaya.

Japanese Invasion

Japanese domination was brief, less than four years, yet it led to significant changes. Conflicts between ethnic groups often increased because of selective repression. In Malaya, Japanese policy allowed Malay government officials to keep their jobs while the Chinese minority often faced

Japanese Rule

703

property seizures and arrest, creating antagonisms that persisted long after the war. By destroying the link to the world economy, the occupation also caused hardship. Western companies closed, while Japanese forces seized natural resources and food. By 1944 living standards, crippled by severe shortages of food and clothing, were in steep decline. Southeast Asians also suffered from harassment by the Japanese police, who treated even minor violators of occupation regulations with brutality. The Japanese forcibly conscripted thousands of Southeast Asians: Javanese men became slave laborers, and Filipinas, called "comfort women" by the Japanese, served the sexual needs of Japanese soldiers. As their war effort faltered, the desperate Japanese resorted to even more repressive policies.

Japan and Southeast Asian Nationalism

Japanese rule also offered some political benefits for Southeast Asians. Since they needed experienced local help, the Japanese promoted Southeast Asians into government positions once reserved for Westerners. To purge the area of Western cultural influences, they closed Christian mission schools, encouraged Islamic or Buddhist leaders, and fostered a renaissance of indigenous culture and local literature. This policy also promoted Southeast Asian nationalism, at least indirectly. Whereas under colonialism most nationalists had been in jail or exile and hence powerless, the Japanese freed nationalist leaders such as Sukarno and gave them official positions, if little actual power. The nationalists now enjoyed a new role in public life and used radio and newspapers to foster their beliefs. The Japanese also recruited young people into armed paramilitary forces, which became the basis for later nationalist armies in Indonesia and Burma that resisted the return of Western colonialism.

Opposing Japan

Some Southeast Asians actively opposed Japanese rule, especially in Vietnam. Vietnamese communism might never have achieved power so quickly had it not been for the Japanese occupation, which discredited the French administration and imposed great hardship on most of the population. The Viet Minh, led by Ho Chi Minh, were now armed and trained by American advisers, who had been sent to help anti-Japanese forces. In 1944 the Viet Minh moved out of their bases along the Chinese border and expanded their influence in northern Vietnam, attracting peasant support while attacking the Japanese occupiers with guerrilla tactics. When a famine killed 2 million Vietnamese, the Viet Minh gained popular backing and recruits because the Japanese exported scarce food to Japan. The Viet Minh organized local village administrations led by peasants who sympathized with their movement.

Japanese fortunes waned as the United States gained the upper hand and bombed Japanese installations in Southeast Asia. Fearful, the Japanese encouraged Southeast Asians to resist Western attempts to reestablish colonial control. Japanese officials helped Indonesian nationalists prepare for Indonesian independence and Burmese nationalists to establish a government. Some nationalists began secretly working with the Western Allies. Changing sides, the Burmese nationalist army helped push Japanese forces out of Burma. Tired of economic deprivation and repression, few Southeast Asians regretted Japan's defeat, and some, especially in Malaya, British Borneo, and the Philippines, even welcomed the return of Western forces. The United States granted independence to the Philippines under pro-U.S. leaders in 1946. But often the returning Westerners faced volatility, setting the stage for dramatic political change in Vietnam, Indonesia, and Burma as nationalist forces successfully struggled for independence in the late 1940s and early 1950s.

Nationalism in Colonial Africa

The roots of the African nationalist struggle were planted in the interwar years, although African nationalists lacked the mass base of the Vietnamese and Indians. African nationalists tried with limited success to overcome major barriers to widespread popular support. Few regimes prepared their colonies for political and economic independence by permitting African participation in government or producing a large educated class that could assume the responsibilities and burdens of nationhood. The artificial division of Africa was also a major hindrance to nationalist organizing. Colonial regimes, by using divide-and-rule strategies to govern the diverse ethnic groups living within artificial national boundaries, made creating viable national identities and uniting all people within a colony difficult. For example, Nigeria resulted from the British colonization of often-rival ethnic groups. While some Pan-Nigerian nationalists sought unity, most Nigerian nationalists found their greatest support only among particular regions or ethnic groups. In the 1940s a prominent Yoruba leader expressed the common fear that no Nigerian nation was really possible:

Challenges to Nationalism

> Nigeria is not a nation [but] a mere geographical expression. There are no "Nigerians" in the same sense as there are "English" or "French." The word "Nigerian" merely distinguish[es] those who live within the boundaries of Nigeria from those who do not.[18]

World War I and the unfulfilled expectations for better lives in its aftermath spurred nationalism. The British, French, and Germans had all drafted or recruited Africans to fight on European battlefields, where many thousands died. When the survivors returned home, the promises made to them about land or jobs proved empty, while taxes were raised. Returning Kenyan soldiers found that British settlers had seized their land. In response Harry Thuku **(THOO-koo)** (ca. 1895–1970), a Gikuyu, created an alliance of diverse Kenyans to confront the British. When the British arrested Thuku, rioting broke out led by Gikuyu women. The British fired on the rioters, killing many. Anticolonial protests were also common in the Belgian Congo, leading to rebellions by peasant farmers upset at Belgian demands for unpaid labor. Women often led resistance. Aline Sitoe Diatta (1920–1944), who led an uprising in Senegal when the French conscripted her village's rice supplies, was exiled and later executed. In Nigeria in 1929, tens of thousands of Igbo women, particularly the palm oil traders, rioted to protest taxes on them. After the British opened fire, killing thirty-two of them, the protests escalated and it took months to restore order.

In the 1920s urban-based nationalist organizations developed to press for African participation in local government. They were led by Western-educated Africans such as J. E. Casely Hayford (1866–1930), a lawyer and journalist in the British Gold Coast (today's Ghana) who was influenced by Gandhi. Some Africans, including Hayford, favored a Pan-African approach and sought support across colonial borders, which they did not view as the basis for nations. But both nationalists and Pan-Africanists were unable to overcome ethnic divisions and, unlike the Indian and Vietnamese nationalists, the gap between the cities and the villages. Furthermore, some African merchants, chiefs, and kings profited from their links to the colonizers and discouraged protests.

The nationalists, unable to capitalize on the brutal Italian invasion and occupation of Ethiopia in 1935–1936, had modest influence before World War II. West African nationalist currents were strongest in the multiethnic capital cities, which became the breeding grounds of new ideas. City life encouraged trade union movements, which sponsored occasional strikes to protest colonial policies or economic exploitation. Hence, market women in Lagos, Nigeria, protested taxation and demanded the right to vote. During World War II they refused to cooperate with price controls, forcing the British to back down. Rural people also asserted their rights. During the 1930s cocoa growers in the British-ruled Gold Coast held back their crops to protest low prices.

Colonial rule generated new cultural trends that allowed people to express their views, often critical, about colonial life. During the 1930s a musical style arose in the Gold Coast and soon spread into other British West African colonies, carried chiefly by guitar-playing Africans and West Indian sailors. **Highlife** was a mix of Christian hymns, West Indian calypso songs, and African dance rhythms. Later West African musicians added influences from Cuba, Brazil, and the United States, especially jazz, indicating the continuing cultural links between West Africa and the Americas. Although closely tied to dance bands and parties, some highlife musicians addressed social and political issues and the problems of everyday life. The very term *highlife* signified both an envy and disapproval of the Western colonizers and rich Africans, who lived in luxury in mansions staffed by servants. Many highlife songs were sung in **pidgin English**, the form of broken English that

Resistance to Colonialism

Nationalist Organizations

Cultural Nationalism

highlife An urban-based West African musical style mixing Christian hymns, West Indian calypso songs, and African dance rhythms.

pidgin English The form of broken English that developed in Africa during the colonial era.

African Jazz Band Jazz from the United States had a wide following in the world in the 1920s, 1930s, and 1940s. Jazz especially influenced the music of black South Africans, some of whom formed jazz groups such as the Harmony Kings.

Courtesy, National Library of South Africa

developed during the colonial era. This mix of African and English words and grammar spread throughout British West Africa as a marketplace lingua franca among diverse urban populations.

South African Resistance

Racial inequality and white supremacy sparked nationalism and resistance to oppression in South Africa. The early South African nationalists, such as the founders of the African National Congress (usually known as the ANC, established in 1912), came from the urban middle class. The ANC encouraged education and preached African independence from white rule but did not directly confront the government until the 1950s. More militant African resistance flourished in the mining industry, where strikes were endemic despite severe government repression. Resistance was often subtle, involving noncooperation or affirmation of African cultural forms. Protest was often expressed in music, although usually veiled to avoid arrest. Knowing that few whites understood lyrics sung in African languages, African workers filled the mining camps with political music, offering messages such as "we demand freedom" and "workers unite." For decades, road gangs worked to songs such as "We Say: Oh, the White Man's Bad." Zulu and Swazi workers blended their own traditions with Western influences to create new dances. Virile, stamping dancers laced their performances with provocative songs: "Who has taken our land from us? Come out! Let us fight! The land was ours. Now it is taken. Fight! Fight!"[19]

Music and Protest

In South African cities jazz became a form of resistance. A potent vehicle for protest, this music, adapted from African Americans, reflected the African rejection of the racist Afrikaner culture. African American musicians such as the trumpeter Louis Armstrong (1901–1971) and the pianist Duke Ellington (1898–1974) were particularly popular in the 1930s, influencing South African jazz bands and new jazz-based musical styles. Educated urban Africans envisioned a modern African culture and sometimes rejected African traditions, as one Johannesburg resident proclaimed:

> *Tribal music! Chiefs! We don't care about chiefs! Give us jazz and film stars, man! We want Ellington, Satchmo [Louis Armstrong], and hot dames! Yes, brother, anything American. You can cut out this junk about [rural homesteads] and folk-tales—forget it! You're just trying to keep us backward!*[20]

The preferred music of the small black professional and business class, jazz ultimately became a symbol of black nationalism in South Africa.

SECTION SUMMARY

- Southeast Asian nationalism was strong in places such as Burma, which experienced harsh colonial rule, and even emerged as a rallying cry in Siam, which was never colonized but where a military coup overthrew the royal government.

- Vietnamese resistance to French rule was continued by the terrorist Vietnamese Nationalist Party, which the French harshly repressed, and the Viet Minh, a coalition led by the communist Ho Chi Minh.

- A variety of groups representing Muslims, women, and communists worked toward independence for the Dutch East Indies; the Indonesian Nationalist Party, which was led by Sukarno and incorporated both Islam and Marxism, was most influential.

- Southeast Asians suffered greatly under Japanese occupation, but Japanese control also showed that Westerners could be defeated and primed the colonized peoples to resist recolonization by Westerners after the war was over.

- Although African nationalist movements were hampered by the existence of rival ethnic groups within artificial colonies, anger over the poor treatment of Africans who had fought in World War I inspired many, especially in cities, to work for independence.

- In South Africa, nationalists opposed the repressive white supremacist government through education, strikes, and, most pervasively, music.

REMAKING THE MIDDLE EAST AND LATIN AMERICA

What factors promoted change in the Middle East and Latin America?

The peoples of both the Middle East and Latin America were also influenced by nationalism. While North Africans experienced Western colonial rule, Arabs in western Asian territories controlled by the Ottoman Turks stagnated economically. After World War I the Ottoman-ruled

Arab territories were transferred to Britain and France, sparking nationalist resentment, while Turkey remained independent. In Latin America, two world wars and the Great Depression caused turmoil, fostered dictatorships, and spurred feelings of nationalism.

Reshaping the Ottoman Territories

World War I led to a dismantling of the Turkish-dominated Ottoman Empire and a reshaping of Arab politics. The Turks were allies of Germany, which shared their hatred of expansionist Russia. The Ottomans also dreamed of liberating Russian-controlled lands in the Caucasus and Central Asia, inhabited largely by peoples speaking languages related to Turkish. However, the Caucasus peoples, especially the Christian Armenians, desired independence. Suspecting them of aiding Russia, the Turks turned on the Armenians in eastern Anatolia (see Chapter 21). More than a million Armenians were deported, chiefly to Syria and Iraq, while perhaps another million died of thirst, starvation, or systematic slaughter by the Ottoman army. These sufferings created a permanent Turkish-Armenian hostility.

The hardships during World War I also spurred Arab nationalism against Ottoman rule. Hunger and disease affected millions of Arabs, with 200,000 dying in Syria alone during the war. Unrest in Syria brought on fierce repression, with dissidents sent into exile or hanged for treason. The most serious challenge came in Arabia, where Sharif Hussein ibn Ali (1856–1931), the Arab ruler of the Hejaz in western Arabia, which included Mecca and Medina, shifted his loyalties from the Ottomans to the British, who promised to support Arab independence. In 1916, at British urging, Sharif Hussein launched an Arab revolt (see Chronology: The Middle East, 1914–1945). British officers, including the flamboyant Lt. T. E. Lawrence (famous as "Lawrence of Arabia"), advised Sharif Hussein's tribal forces as they attacked Ottoman bases and communications. The British also invaded and occupied southern Iraq, an Ottoman province, which had a strategic position and was thought to have oil.

The end of World War I brought crushed dreams and turmoil. The Arab nationalists such as Sharif Hussein did not know that Britain, France, and Russia had made secret agreements that ignored Arab interests. The czarist Russians had planned to incorporate Istanbul and nearby territories into their empire, while Britain and France agreed to partition the Ottoman provinces in western Asia between them. The Russian plans had to be modified after the communists took power and signed a peace treaty with Germany that allowed the Caucasus region, occupied by the Russians in the 1800s, to be returned to Germany's Ottoman ally. When the war ended with Ottoman defeat, British troops occupied much of Iraq and Palestine, French troops controlled the Syrian coast, and the Russians regained control of the Caucasus, including Armenia.

European Colonialism

The Versailles treaty dismembered the Ottoman Empire (see Map 25.2). Turkey's neighbors—the Greeks, Italians, and Armenians—made claims on Anatolia and adjacent islands, and European Zionists asked for a Jewish national home in Palestine (see Chapter 21). The Allies promised eventual independence to the Kurds, a Sunni Muslim people, distinct from both Arabs and Turks, who inhabited a large, mountainous region of western Asia, including southeast Turkey. Both Syria and Iraq declared their independence. However, the League of Nations, dominated by Western countries, awarded France control over Syria and Lebanon, and Britain control over Iraq, Palestine, and Transjordan (today Jordan), under what the League called mandates, in theory less onerous than colonies because they were not considered permanent. Viewing mandates as a new form of colonialism, Arab nationalists in Syria proposed a democratic government, and some favored granting women the vote, which few Western nations had done. Ignoring Arab views, French forces quickly occupied Syria and, after facing armed resistance, exiled nationalist leaders. Despite promises, the Allies also ignored Kurdish desires for their own nation. The Kurds remained divided between Turkey, Persia (Iran), Iraq, and Syria, thus becoming the world's largest ethnic group without their own state.

The heart of the Ottoman Empire, Turkey, saw the most revolutionary changes. The disastrous defeat of the war and the humiliating agreements that followed left the Turks helpless, bitter, and facing a Greek invasion and Arab secession. But under the leadership of the daring war hero and ardent nationalist later known as Kemal Ataturk **(kuh-MAHL AT-uh-turk)** (1881–1938), the Turks enjoyed a spectacular resurgence. In 1919 Ataturk began mobilizing military forces in eastern Anatolia into a revolutionary organization to oppose the Ottoman sultan, discredited by defeats,

Ataturk and Modern Turkey

CHRONOLOGY
The Middle East, 1914–1945

1916 Arab revolt against the Turks

1917 Balfour Declaration

1919–1922 Turkish Revolution by Ataturk

1921 Formation of Iranian republic by Reza Khan

1922 Formation of Turkish republic

1922 End of British protectorate in Egypt

1925 Formation of Pahlavi dynasty by Reza Khan

1928 Formation of Muslim Brotherhood in Egypt

1930 Independence for Iraq

1932 Formation of Saudi Arabia

1935 Discovery of oil in Saudi Arabia

1936 Britain-Egypt alliance

1936–1939 Civil war in Palestine

Map 25.2 Partition of the Ottoman Empire

Before 1914 the Ottoman Turks controlled much of western Asia, including western Arabia. After World War II the League of Nations awarded Iraq, Transjordan, and Palestine to Britain. Syria and Lebanon were given to France, and western Arabia was ruled by Arabs. Eventually the Saudi family, rulers of the Najd, expanded their rule into western Arabia and created Saudi Arabia.

e Interactive Map

and to restore Turkish dignity and preserve the Turkish majority areas and the Kurdish districts in eastern Anatolia. After establishing a rival Turkish government in the central Anatolia city of Ankara, Ataturk's forces fought both the sultan's government in Istanbul and the Greek forces that had moved deep into Anatolia. Ataturk finally pushed the Greeks back, and Turkey and Greece eventually agreed to a population transfer in which many Greeks living in Turkey moved to Greece and most Turks dwelling in Greece moved to Turkey. In 1922 Ataturk deposed the Ottoman sultan and set up a republic with himself as president.

Ataturk was a controversial figure among Turks. A religious agnostic, he violated Muslim customs by pursuing sexual promiscuity and drinking heavily in public. As a Turkish nationalist who glorified the pre-Islamic Turkish past, Ataturk dismissed Islamic culture as outdated. He favored modernization, announcing that "our eyes are turned westward. We shall transplant Western institutions to Asiatic soil. We wish to be a modern nation with our mind open, and yet to remain ourselves."[21] Ataturk claimed that secularization and the emancipation of women were the Turkish tradition. In the 1920s these ideas were put in action through reforms that challenged Muslim traditions. Ataturk revamped the legal system along Western lines, replaced Arabic-based script with a Western alphabet, prohibited polygamy, abolished Islamic schools and courts, removed reference to Islam as the state religion from the constitution, and granted women equal rights in divorce, child custody, and inheritance. While his government resembled a parliamentary democracy, he exercised near-dictatorial power and alienated the Kurds by suppressing their language and culture. Ataturk left a deeply changed nation. While many of his reforms never reached the villages, where Islam remained a strong influence, his secular approach remained popular with Turkish nationalists, including military officers, influencing Turkish politics today.

Hulton Archive/Getty Images

Ataturk Wedding Dance The Turkish leader Kemal Ataturk promoted and adopted Western fashions while defying Muslim customs. In this photo from around 1925, Ataturk dances with his daughter at her Western-style wedding.

Modern Iran, Egypt, and Iraq

Major changes also occurred in the other major Middle Eastern countries. The end of the war left Britain with the power to impose a protectorate over Persia, forcing the government to accept British loans, financial controls, advisers, and military forces. Growing Persian opposition prompted the British in 1921 to support General Reza Khan **(REE-za kahn)** (1877–1944), a soldier who wanted to end the corrupt, ineffective royal dynasty, establish a secular republic, and address economic underdevelopment. Reza Khan drew support from secular Shi'ites, who had long struggled for a more democratic society that could reduce the powerful Shi'ite clergy's domination. But in 1925, at the urging of Shi'ite clerics, Reza Khan abandoned the republican government and formed the Pahlavi **(PAH-lah-vee)** dynasty, with himself as king (known in Persia as a shah).

Reza Khan, like Ataturk, promoted modernization and, in 1935, renamed his nation Iran, a symbolic break with the past. The shah created a large national army through conscription, built railroads, established government factories to produce textiles, sugar, cement, and steel, and took control over the oil industry. The regime also made social changes that outraged Muslim conservatives, such as introducing a Western law code, encouraging men to wear Western hats and clothes, and outlawing the veiling of women in public. This had the unintended effect of forcing women who wanted to wear the veil to stay home. But while the modernists, merchants, and middle class supported Reza Khan's policies, poor Iranians saw little improvement, especially as Reza Khan expanded the landlord class at peasant expense. The shah lacked Ataturk's charisma and had less success in transforming Iran. When during World War II he favored Germany, Anglo-Russian forces occupied Iran. Humiliated, Reza Shah abdicated in favor of his son, Muhammad Reza Pahlavi **(REH-zah PAH-lah-vee)** (1919–1980), who ruled until 1979.

British control of Egypt and Iraq also fostered nationalist feeling. In Egypt during World War I the British imposed martial law and drafted peasants to build roads and railroads and dig trenches in war zones, breeding resentment. A song of the period pleaded to be left alone and castigated British officials for carrying off the peasants' corn, camels, and cattle. After the war nationalists unsuccessfully sought an end to British domination. The leading nationalist party, the secular *Wafd*, led by Saad Zaghlul **(sod ZOG-lool)** (ca. 1857–1927), who had studied theology under Islamic

Egyptian Nationalism

modernists and then earned a French law degree, sought independence, representative government, civil liberties, and curtailed powers for the pro-British monarchy.

In 1919 the British arrested Wafd leaders. Enraged Egyptians—rich and poor, Muslims and Coptic Christians, men and women—responded with strikes, student demonstrations, sabotage of railroads, and the murder of British soldiers. The turmoil forced the British to release Zaghlul, who then went to the Paris Peace Conference to plead for national self-determination but, like Vietnam's Ho Chi Minh, was ignored. Upon returning, Zaghlul was arrested again, but the resulting unrest forced Britain to grant Egypt limited independence in 1922. Nationalists saw this agreement as a sham, since Britain still controlled Egypt's defense and foreign affairs. In 1936 Britain officially ended its occupation but still kept thousands of troops along the Suez Canal. It also shared with Egypt the administration of Sudan to the south. Resentment of the continuing British presence increased during World War II.

Britain and Iraq

The British also struggled to control Iraq, an artificial creation that united three Ottoman provinces, each dominated by a different group: Sunni Kurds, Sunni Arabs, and Shi'ite Arabs. Describing their occupation as a "liberation," the British promised the Iraqis an efficient administration, honest finance, impartial justice, and security. Planning to discourage self-government but wanting to give the appearance of popular support, they held a plebiscite but manipulated the results to suggest pro-British sympathies. Hating occupation, in 1920 Shi'ite clerics seeking an Islamic state proclaimed a holy war against the British, and various Shi'a and Sunni tribes rose in rebellion. The British, relying heavily on aerial bombing, suppressed the rebellion at a great cost, suffering 400 casualties themselves, killing some 10,000 Iraqis, and and flattening whole villages.

Shaken by the fierce resistance, the British changed direction and introducing limited self-government through an appointed Council of State. The skilled diplomacy of a pro-Arab British archaeologist, writer, and diplomat, Lady Gertrude Bell (1868–1926), defused tensions. Seeking a king for Iraq who would "reign but not govern, " in 1921 Britain installed a member of the Hashemite **(HASH-uh-mite)** royal family of Mecca, Sharif Hussein's son Faisal (1885–1935). In 1930 Faisal convinced Britain to grant Iraq independence after he agreed to accept continued British military bases and government advisers. By then the British had found oil, making them unwilling to cut their ties. Many Arabs considered Faisal and his successors to be British puppets, but a series of Sunni Arab military autocrats influenced government policies more than the kings.

Islam and Zionism

Debating Westernization

The stranglehold of European power and Western culture remained concerns of most Middle Eastern societies. Although various colonized peoples struggled to free themselves, nationalist success came slowly. Thinkers debated over how or whether to emulate the Western nations. While envying Western industrialization and consumer goods, they disagreed about how many Western patterns, such as freethinking, parliamentary democracy, and women's rights, should be adopted. Some sought wholesale transformation; some favored Islamic tradition; and still others sought a mixing of Western and Islamic traditions. Egypt, Iraq, Lebanon, Transjordan, and Syria adopted Western-style constitutions, providing for civil liberties and elected parliaments. But these parliaments were limited and unrepresentative. Real power remained with European officials or powerful kings who had little respect for civil liberties.

Inspired by Western modernity, Arabs made progress in education, public health, industrialization, and communications, but change came slowly. The Egyptian literacy rate rose from 9 percent in 1917 to only 15 percent in 1937. Some women asserted their rights, including Huda Shaarawi **(HOO-da sha-RAH-we)** (1879–1947). From a wealthy Cairo family, Huda had been married off at age thirteen to a much older cousin. Finding the marriage confining, she organized nonviolent anti-British demonstrations by women after World War I and then publicly removed her veil in 1923, shocking Egyptians. She also founded the Egyptian feminist movement, which succeeded in raising the minimum marriage age for girls to sixteen and increasing women's educational opportunities.

Islamic Thought

The debates over Westernization fostered new intellectual currents, some pro-Western, others anti-Western. A blind Egyptian, Taha Husayn (1889–1973), educated in traditional Islamic schools but also at the Sorbonne in Paris, became the key figure of Egyptian literature. He challenged orthodox Islam and, in 1938, proclaimed that Westernizing Arab culture would fit with Egypt's traditions, saying, "I want our new life to harmonize with our ancient glory." In contrast, the **Muslim Brotherhood**, founded in 1928 by schoolteacher Hasan al-Banna (1906–1949), reflected the popular reaction against Westernization. Al-Banna despised Western values, arguing that it "would be inexcusable for us to turn aside from the path of truth—Islam—and so follow the path of fleshly desires

Muslim Brotherhood
An Egyptian religious movement founded in 1928 that expressed popular Arab reaction to Westernization.

and vanities—the path of Europe."[22] The Brotherhood followed a strict interpretation of the Quran, though it also accepted modern technology and was open to a more active public role for women. Expressing a widespread resentment against Western films, bars, and figure-revealing women's fashions, the Brotherhood developed a following in Sudan and western Asia.

The most extreme anti-Western reaction, the puritanical Wahhabi movement, which eventually dominated Arabia, sought a return to a supposedly pristine Islam uncorrupted by centuries of change. The Wahhabis opposed shaving beards, smoking tobacco, and drinking alcohol. Wahhabi influence grew when a tribal chief, Abdul Aziz Ibn Saud (sah-OOD) (1902–1969), expanded the power of the Saudi family in central and eastern Arabia (see Chapter 21). By 1932 his forces had taken western Arabia and the holy cities from the Hashemites and formed the country of Saudi Arabia. As king, Abdul Aziz strictly enforced Islamic law by establishing Committees for the Commendation of Virtue and the Condemnation of Vice to mentor personal behavior. Policemen used long canes to enforce attendance at the five daily prayers, punish alcohol use and listening to music, and harass unveiled women. Yet, the Saudis also welcomed material innovations from the West, such as automobiles, medicine, and telephones. In 1935 it was discovered that Saudi Arabia contained the world's richest oil reserves. The oil wealth chiefly benefited the royal family and the Wahhabi clergy.

The roots of a long-term problem for Arab nationalists were planted in Palestine, part of Ottoman-ruled Syria that had a largely Arab population. The British took over Palestine after World War I. Meanwhile, the Zionist movement, which sought a homeland for the Jewish people, had been formed in the Jewish ghettoes of Europe (see Chapters 19 and 21). The Zionist slogan—"a land without a people for a people without a land"—offered a compelling vision: take the long-persecuted Jewish minorities and return them to Palestine, from where they had been expelled by the Romans two millennia earlier. Zionist leaders cultivated the British government, which in 1917 issued the **Balfour Declaration**, a letter from the British foreign minister to Zionist leaders giving British support for the establishment of Palestine as a national home for the Jewish people. But Palestine was not a land without a people. Arabs had lived there for many centuries, building cities, cultivating orchards, and herding livestock. In Arab eyes, Jewish immigrants were European colonizers planning to dispossess them.

In the interwar years, thousands of European Jews migrated to Palestine with British support, some fleeing Nazi Germany, so that by 1939 the Palestine population of 1.5 million was one-third Jewish. Although Jewish settlers contributed by establishing businesses, industries, and productive farms, Arabs feared becoming a vulnerable minority in their own land. Land became a contentious issue. Zionist organizations began buying up the best land from absentee Arab landlords who disregarded the customary rights of villagers to use it, uprooting thousands of Arab peasants. As tensions increased, violence spread, bewildering the British. Sometimes hundreds of Arabs and Jews were killed in armed clashes, and in 1936 an Arab rebellion fostered a three-year civil war, with Arabs demanding an end to Jewish immigration, land sales to Jews, and plans for an independent Palestine. In response, Britain proposed a partition into two states and the removal of thousands of Arabs from the Jewish side, but both groups rejected the proposal. Then in 1939 Britain limited Jewish immigration and banned land transfers; however, the Holocaust against the Jews during World War II spurred a more militant Jewish desire for a homeland where they could govern themselves.

Politics and Modernization in Latin America

Latin America, with economies reliant on a few natural resource exports such as beef, copper, coffee, and sugar, became more vulnerable to global political and economic crises. Sometimes this weakness resulted in foreign interventions, as when military forces from the United States occupied Nicaragua from 1909 to 1933 and Haiti from 1915 to 1934. During the Great Depression, as foreign investment fell and foreign markets closed, the foreign trade of some countries was cut by 90 percent, and by 1932 Latin America as a whole exported 65 percent less than it had in 1929. These economic downturns led to political instability and the rule of military dictators, known as caudillos, all over the region (see Map 25.3).

In 1930–1931 armed forces overthrew governments in a dozen Latin American nations (see Chronology: Latin America and the Caribbean, 1909–1945). Some of the new governments, such as those in Argentina and Brazil, were influenced by European fascism. Dictators often increased their governments' role in the economy, beginning industries to provide products normally imported. They also amassed huge fortunes and repressed dissent. In El Salvador President Maximiliano Hernandez Martinez massacred 30,000 protesting Indian peasants while putting a "positive spin" on poverty by saying that people who went barefoot could better receive the "beneficial

The Wahhabis and Saudi Arabia

Britain, Palestine, and the Jews

Balfour Declaration A letter from the British foreign minister to Zionist leaders in 1917 giving British support for the establishment of Palestine as a national home for the Jewish people.

Rising Dictatorships

N

ATLANTIC OCEAN

Gulf of Mexico

MEXICO

Mexico City•

Bahamas (Gr. Br.)

CUBA

HAITI
DOMINICAN REPUBLIC

Puerto Rico (U.S.)

20°N

BRITISH
HONDURAS

100°W

GUATEMALA
EL SALVADOR

HONDURAS

NICARAGUA

COSTA RICA

PANAMA

Jamaica (Gr. Br.)

Caribbean Sea

Panama•

Caracas•

Trinidad (Gr. Br.)

VENEZUELA

•Bogotá

COLOMBIA

BRITISH GUIANA
Georgetown•
•Paramaribo
FRENCH GUIANA

DUTCH
GUIANA

Orinoco R.

Equator 0°

Galápagos Islands (Ecuador)

Quito•

ECUADOR

Negro R.

Amazon R.

•Belém

PACIFIC OCEAN

PERU

Lima•

Lake Titicaca
•La Paz

BOLIVIA

Madeira R.

BRAZIL

Tocantins R.

São Francisco R.

•Salvador

Paraguay R.

20°S

CHACO

Paraná R.

PARAGUAY
•Asunción

•Río de Janeiro
São Paulo•

CHILE

Paraná R.

Santiago•

ARGENTINA

Buenos Aires•

URUGUAY
•Montevideo

40°W

40°S

| 0 | 500 | 1000 Km. |
| 0 | 500 | 1000 Mi. |

Falkland Islands (Gr. Br.)

80°W

60°W

Territory in dispute
Colony

Map 25.3   South and Central America in 1930

By 1930 Latin America had achieved its present political configuration, except that Britain, France, and Holland still had colonies in the Guianas region of South America, and Britain controlled British Honduras (today's Belize) in Central America.

e Interactive Map

vibrations" of the earth than those with shoes. Some dictatorships continued for years. The repressive Cuban rightwinger Gerardo Machado (r. 1925–1933) was forced out of office when the collapse of sugar prices generated a massive strike, temporarily bringing leftwing nationalists and socialists to power. But the United States disliked the new government because it implemented reforms that hurt influential American business interests. In 1934 the United States encouraged a coup by Sgt. Fulgencio Batista (fool-HEN-see-o bah-TEES-ta) (1901–1973), who dominated Cuba for the next twenty-five years as a rightwing dictator.

The challenges also affected Chile, one of the most open Latin American nations. Although the military had occasionally seized power for short periods, Chile had generally enjoyed elected democratic governments and competitive elections involving several parties. The Great Depression helped reformist parties and social movements to gain support, and the squabbling leftist and centrist parties united in a Popular Front that came to power in the 1939 elections. Their reformist government, supported by labor unions, sponsored industrialization. In addition, a growing women's movement allied with Chile's political left brought once-forbidden ideas into the patriarchal, strongly Catholic country. Demanding respect for Chilean women and an end to "compulsory motherhood," women lobbied for prenatal health care, child-care subsidies, birth control, and the right to abortion, which was illegal but widely practiced. But while women won some basic legal rights, they still struggled for voting rights and could not get most of their social agenda approved.

Brazil experienced political change tinged with nationalism. In the 1920s middle-class reformers challenged a corrupt ruling class that did not listen to the common people or assert Brazil's national interests in the world. Their proposals for a more liberal society included official recognition of labor unions, a minimum wage, restraints on child labor, land reform, universal suffrage, and expansion of education to poor children. Worker unrest aided the growth of labor unions. But the Great Depression prompted a civilian-military coup by Getulio Vargas **(jay-TOO-lee-oh VAR-gus)** (1883–1954) in 1930. A former soldier, lawyer, and government minister, Vargas launched the **Estado Novo** ("New State"), a fascist-influenced, modernizing dictatorship that ruled until 1945. An anti-Vargas businessman described him as "intelligent, extremely perceptive, but also a demagogue who knew how to manipulate the masses."[23] While Vargas used torture and censorship to repress opponents, the Estado Novo also sponsored modernizing reforms that made Vargas popular with the lower classes. He nationalized the banks, financed industrialization, and introduced social security, an eight-hour workday, a minimum wage, the right to strike, and the vote for literate eighteen-year-olds and working women. Gradually the dictator became more populist and nationalist. After he was deposed by the army in 1945, tensions between rightwing and leftwing Brazilians remained.

Progressive and nationalist ideas also emerged in Mexico. After the decade-long Mexican Revolution (see Chapter 20), which ended only in 1920, Mexico badly needed reconstruction funds but faced sharply reduced export earnings and a deepening economic slump. A popular song noted the hardship on common Mexicans: "The scramble to be president is one of our oldest haunts. But to eat a peaceful tortilla is all the poor man wants."[24] President Plutarcho Elias Calles **(KAH-yays)** (r. 1924–1928) put the political system on a solid footing by creating a new party that brought together various factions. Yet many Mexicans saw little improvement in their lives, and women remained largely excluded from public life. In 1934 Mexicans elected Lazaro Cardenas **(car-DAYN-es)** (r. 1934–1940), an army officer with socialist leanings, as president. Peasants had grown cynical about the promises by political leaders to supply them with land, but Cardenas fulfilled this dream for some by assigning land ownership to the *ejidos* **(eh-HEE-dos)**, the traditional agricultural cooperatives, who now apportioned land to their members. Cardenas hoped the ejidos would build schools and hospitals and supply credit to farmers, uplifting Mexico's poorest social class. But agricultural production fell, and promised government aid never materialized.

Cardenas also introduced reforms that made him popular. He encouraged the formation of a large labor confederation, allowing the working class to enjoy a higher standard of living and more dignity. He also followed a nationalist economic policy. After U.S.-owned oil companies ignored a Mexican Supreme Court order to improve worker pay, Cardenas nationalized the industry, spurring celebrations in Mexico and outraging U.S. leaders. The president also supported women's rights. In addition, Cardenas reorganized the ruling Party of Revolutionary Institutions around four functional groups: peasants, organized labor, the military, and the middle class. Cardenas gave the Mexican Revolution new life, while the wealthy Mexican landowners and merchants, as well as U.S. political and business leaders, hated him.

However, Cardenas was followed by more moderate leaders who reversed support for the ejidos, favoring instead individual farmers. They also ignored women's rights—Mexican women could not vote until 1953—and cooperated with the United States on immigration issues. While poor Mexicans had long moved to the United States, during World War II a Mexico–United States agreement sent more Mexican workers north to fill jobs in industry, agriculture, and the service sector left vacant by drafted American men. The flow northward of poor Mexicans became a flood-tide after the war.

Estado Novo ("New State") A fascist-influenced and modernizing dictatorship in Brazil led by Getulio Vargas between 1930 and 1945.

Politics in Mexico

e **Primary Source: Speech to the Nation** In this excerpt from a radio address given in 1938, President Lazaro Cardenas announces his decision to nationalize the Mexican oil industry.

Cultural Nationalism in Latin America and the Caribbean

Cultural nationalism greatly affected Latin American and Caribbean societies. A Brazilian literary trend, Modernism, explored the country's rich cultural heritage. Rather than emulating European literary trends, modernist writers reflected Brazil's uniqueness. For example, the poet, novelist, and critic Mario de Andrade (1893–1945) mixed words from regional dialects and Native American, African, and Portuguese folklore into his work. The more internationalist Oswald de Andrade (1890–1954) saw Brazil as a creative consumer of world culture, arguing that Brazilians should mix ideas from all over the world and turn them into something distinctively Brazilian. Meanwhile, nationalism shaped Brazilian music. The unconventional composer Heitor Villa-Lobos (1890–1959) was inspired by Afro-Brazilian and Indian religious rites and urban popular music, and the popular *samba* music and dance became not only a symbol of Brazilian society but also a way for the Afro-Brazilian lower classes to express themselves. Samba began as a street music associated with the annual pre-Lenten carnival in Rio de Janeiro. Professional samba groups competed for prizes awarded by a jury, making samba a major social activity of the city's shantytowns. Annual carnival processions grew increasingly extravagant, featuring elaborate floats, flamboyant costumes, and intricate group choreography.

Literature and Art

The progressive spirit spurred literary and artistic movements throughout Latin America. The work of Marxist-influenced Chilean writers such as the poet Pablo Neruda (**ne-ROO-duh**) (1904–1973) bristled with anger over economic inequalities. Sometimes governments retaliated against dissident artists, and Neruda wrote some of his greatest poetry while in hiding or exile. Mexican culture glorified the country's mixed-descent, or mestizo, heritage and addressed the poverty and powerlessness of the remaining Native American communities. In this tradition, several great artists painted, usually on walls of public buildings, magnificent murals showing the life of Mexico's people, most notably Diego Rivera (1885–1957), a Marxist who became one of the world's most famous artists. His huge, realistic murals depicted peasants and workers struggling for dignity or emphasized the conflicts between Indians and the Spanish colonizers. His wife, Frida Kahlo (1907–1954), the daughter of a German Jewish immigrant, specialized in vivid paintings expressing women's physical and psychological pain, reflecting her own health problems and stormy personal relationships.

Caribbean Thought

Caribbean intellectuals' search for an authentic West Indian identity involved overcoming the elite's reluctance to acknowledge influences from Africa. Adopting British and French stereotypes, West Indians had often associated Africa with the uncivilized. In contrast, some Afro-Caribbean intellectuals such as the Trinidadian Marxist C. L. R. James (1901–1989) sought to rebuild Afro-Caribbean pride by celebrating African roots and to use literature, art, and music to challenge Western colonialism. James was a well-traveled historian, prolific writer, political theorist, critic, skillful cricket player, and activist in Trinidad politics, equally at home in the Caribbean, Europe, Africa, and North America, who inspired intellectuals around the world.

Candido Portinari, _Coffee_ Portinari, one of the finest Brazilian painters of the 1930s and 1940s, often portrayed urban and rural labor, reflecting his leftwing political views. He had grown up the son of Italian immigrants on a coffee plantation near Sao Paulo. This painting from 1935 shows plantation workers carrying heavy bags of coffee, much of which will be exported.

Museo Nacional Bellas Artes, Rio de Janeiro/Art Resource, NY

SECTION SUMMARY

- In the post–World War I breakup of the Ottoman Empire, lands such as Iraq, Syria, and Lebanon that sought freedom were instead colonized by Britain and France, but Turkey revived under the leadership of Ataturk, who modernized the country and minimized the role of Islam.

- Reza Khan, the British-supported shah of Persia, attempted to modernize his country as Ataturk had Turkey, though with less success, while Britain, in reaction to violent opposition, granted Egypt and Iraq increasing measures of autonomy and independence.

- Arab leaders debated how to balance modernization with Islam; the most puritanical form of Islam, Wahhabism, came to dominate Saudi Arabia; and the return of Jews to Palestine caused great tensions with the Arabs who had lived there for centuries.

- Vulnerable Latin American economies were greatly damaged during the Great Depression, which led to instability and the rise of military dictators in many countries, while in Chile, instability led to a progressive, prolabor government.

- Impoverished and frustrated after a long revolution, many Mexicans were pleased by the rule of Lazaro Cardenas, who gave land to agricultural cooperatives, nationalized industries, and supported women's rights, but who was followed by less-progressive leaders.

- Latin American and Caribbean artists, musicians, and writers worked to produce art that expressed their unique cultural perspectives.

CHAPTER SUMMARY

During this era, nationalism became a strong force in the Western colonies and other dominated societies of Asia, Africa, and Latin America. Two world wars and the Great Depression destabilized local economies, capitalism reshaped rural life for millions of peasants, and many Asians and Africans resented the Western powers. Nationalism, often blended with Marxism, gained support as a strategy to oppose Western domination. Nationalists reunified China after two decades of warlord violence but could not improve rural life or halt Japanese expansion, providing an opening for the Chinese communists under Mao Zedong to gain support by offering a program to transform society. In India, nationalism opposing repressive British colonialism gained a mass following. Mohandas Gandhi mounted massive, nonviolent campaigns of civil disobedience, which undermined British rule. But Gandhi and other nationalist leaders, mostly Hindus, could not prevent the minority Muslims from seeking a separate nation.

Nationalism had an uneven history in Southeast Asia, sub-Saharan Africa, and the Middle East. In Vietnam, Ho Chi Minh organized an effective communist resistance to the French, while in Indonesia, Sukarno led opposition to Dutch rule. During World War II nationalists in Vietnam, Indonesia, and Burma organized to oppose a resumption of Western colonialism when the war ended. While political nationalist organizations developed in Africa and black South Africans resisted white domination, nationalism was often more influential as a cultural force, especially in music. World War I left the Middle East in turmoil, as Britain and France extended their power into Arab societies once ruled by the Ottoman Empire. But the Turks, led by Kemal Ataturk, and Iran developed modern states open to Western influences. Muslim intellectuals debated whether to adopt Western ideas or maintain Islamic traditions. Arab conservatives, including the Wahhabis, used Islam to oppose any social or cultural changes. The rise of Zionist immigration to Palestine posed another challenge to the Arabs. In many Latin American nations, while progressive social and literary movements proliferated, economic problems intensified and dictators gained power. Nationalism permeated literary, musical, and artistic expression in both Latin America and the Caribbean.

KEY TERMS

warlords	Long March	Viet Minh	Muslim Brotherhood
New Culture Movement	people's war	lingua franca	Balfour Declaration
May Fourth Movement	Maoism	highlife	Estado Novo
Jiangxi Soviet	nonviolent resistance	pidgin English	

EBOOK AND WEBSITE RESOURCES

e PRIMARY SOURCE
Speech to the Nation

e INTERACTIVE MAPS
Map 25.1 Chinese Communist Movement and Chinese-Japanese War
Map 25.2 Partition of the Ottoman Empire
Map 25.3 South and Central America in 1930

LINKS

History of the Middle East Database (http://www
.nmhschool.org/tthornton/mehistorydatabase/
mideastindex.php). A useful site on history, politics,
and culture.

Internet African History Sourcebook (http://www
.fordham.edu/halsall/africa/africasbook.html). This
site contains useful information and documentary
material on Africa.

Internet East Asian History Sourcebook (http://www
.fordham.edu/halsall/eastasia/eastasiasbook.html).
An invaluable collection of sources and links on
China, Japan, and Korea from ancient to modern
times.

Internet Indian History Sourcebook (http://www
.fordham.edu/halsall/india/indiasbook.html). An
invaluable collection of sources and links on India
from ancient to modern times.

Internet Islamic History Sourcebook (http://www
.fordham.edu/halsall/islam/islamsbook.html). A
comprehensive examination of Islamic societies and
their long history, with many useful links and source
materials.

Internet Modern History Sourcebook (http://www
.fordham.edu/halsall/mod/modsbook.html). An extensive online collection of historical documents and
secondary materials.

Latin American Resources (http://www.oberlin.edu/
faculty/svolk/latinam.htm). An excellent collection of
resources and links on history, politics, and culture.

WWW Southeast Asia Guide (http://www.library.Wisc
.edu/guides/SEAsia/). An easy-to-use site.

**Plus flashcards, practice quizzes, and more. Go to:
www.cengage.com/history/lockard/globalsocnet2e.**

SUGGESTED READING

Bogle, Emory C. *The Modern Middle East: From Imperialism to Freedom, 1800–1958.* Upper Saddle River, NJ: Prentice-Hall, 1996. An overview of the region during this era.

Brown, Judith M. *Gandhi: Prisoner of Hope.* New Haven: Yale University Press, 1991. One of the key studies of this seminal nationalist leader and thinker.

Brown, Judith M. *Modern India: The Origins of an Asian Democracy,* 2nd ed. New York: Oxford University Press, 1995. A strong introduction to modern Indian history.

Clayton, Lawrence A. and Michael L. Conniff, *A History of Modern Latin America,* 2nd ed. Boston: Wadsworth, 2005. Good coverage of this era.

Cleveland, William L. *A History of the Modern Middle East,* 4th ed. Boulder: Westview Press, 2008. One of the best surveys.

Erlmann, Veit. *African Stars: Studies in Black South African Performance.* Chicago: University of Chicago Press, 1991. Essays on South African music and nationalism in this era.

Findley, Carter Vaughn, and John A. M. Rothney. *Twentieth Century World,* 6th ed. Boston: Houghton Mifflin, 2006. A comprehensive survey of this era.

Freund, Bill. *The Making of Contemporary Africa: The Development of African Society Since 1800,* 2nd ed. Bloomington: Indiana University Press, 1999. An excellent discussion of the colonial era and the changes it brought.

Gonzalez, Michael J. *The Mexican Revolution, 1910–1940.* Albuquerque: University of New Mexico Press, 2002. Good scholarly study of this period.

Huynh Kim Khanh. *Vietnamese Communism, 1925–1945.* Ithaca: Cornell University Press, 1982. A valuable scholarly study of this topic.

Keen, Benjamin, and Keith Haynes. *A History of Latin America,* 8th ed. Boston: Houghton Mifflin, 2009. A comprehensive account with considerable coverage of these decades.

Lary, Diane, *China's Republic.* New York: Cambridge University Press, 2007. Well-written survey of China from 1912–1949.

Marlay, Ross, and Clark Neher. *Patriots and Tyrants: Ten Asian Leaders.* Lanham, MD: Rowman and Littlefield, 1999. Sketches of Asian nationalists such as Gandhi, Nehru, Ho, Mao, and Sukarno.

Martin, Cheryl E., and Mark Wasserman. *Latin America and Its People,* 2nd ed. New York: Longman, 2007. A readable introduction with much on this era.

Owen, Norman G., et al. *The Emergence of Modern Southeast Asia: A New History.* Honolulu: University of Hawai'i Press, 2005. The best survey of modern Southeast Asian history, comprehensive and readable.

Sheridan, James E. *China in Disintegration: The Republican Era in Chinese History, 1912–1949.* New York: Free Press, 1975. Dated but still a standard work on this period in China.

Spence, Jonathan D. *The Gate of Heavenly Peace: The Chinese and Their Revolution, 1895–1980.* New York: Penguin, 1982. A masterful account of China in this era through the eyes of artists, thinkers, and writers.

Stavrianos, Leften S. *Global Rift: The Third World Comes of Age.* New York: William Morrow, 1971. A provocative, innovative, and readable study that provides a global context.

Wolf, Eric R. *Peasant Wars of the Twentieth Century.* New York: Harper and Row, 1969. A pathbreaking study of the revolutions in China, Vietnam, Algeria, Cuba, and Mexico.

Historical Controversy

Modernization or World-System?

Historians and social scientists in the West have vigorously debated which theories best explain the modern world, especially how it became interconnected. One influential approach uses the concept of modernization and focuses on individual societies. The other approach, world-system analysis, emphasizes the links between societies. This second approach has often interested world historians.

THE PROBLEM

Historians and historically oriented social scientists have sought to understand societies and their changes over time. These efforts have spawned new intellectual approaches in the past several decades. Scholars have asked why some societies in the modern world, such as the United States, Britain, and Japan, became rich and powerful while others, such as Mozambique, Haiti, and Laos, remained poor and weak. Have societies developed as they did because of their own traditions or because of their connections to the larger world? Should we study societies as separate units, as the modernization approach advocates? Or should societies be examined as part of a larger system of exchange and power, or a world-system? Or are both of these approaches inadequate?

THE DEBATE

During the 1950s and 1960s modernization theory was developed in the United States by scholars such as C. E. Black and W. W. Rostow. In their classification, most societies were traditional, retaining centuries-old political and economic institutions and social and cultural values. These societies had despotic governments, extended family systems, and fatalistic attitudes. In contrast, a few dynamic societies became modern by adopting liberal democracy, secularism, flexible social systems, high-consumption lifestyles, and free market capitalism. This modernization began in Europe between 1500 and 1750 and reached its fullest development in the United States by the mid-twentieth century. All societies, these theorists asserted, were moving, rapidly or slowly, in the same direction toward U.S.-style modernization—some enthusiastically, others reluctantly—and this modernization was desirable.

Modernization theory was influential in the United States for several decades, but by the 1970s it began losing considerable support among historians. While the notion of modernity seemed helpful, critics found many flaws in the theory of modernization. They argued that it centered history on the West as the dynamic nursery of modernization and neglected other politically and economically successful societies, such as Qing China, Tokugawa Japan, Siam (today's Thailand), Ottoman Turkey, Morocco, and the Ashante kingdom in Africa. Although these societies had all either collapsed or struggled against Western imperialism during the nineteenth century, they had once flourished and fostered economic growth despite having few of the characteristics associated with modernity. Further-

more, by emphasizing the individual trees (societies) at the expense of the larger forest (the global context), the theory failed to explain the interconnections of societies through various international networks and processes that created global imbalances, such as the transfer of wealth and resources—Indonesian coffee, Iraqi oil, West African cocoa, Latin American silver, Caribbean sugar—from colonies to colonizers.

Modernization theory generally reflects the views of scholars who believe that U.S.-style individualism, democratic government, and free enterprise capitalism are the best strategies to promote personal freedom and economic growth, and who want to export these ideas to the world. Modernization theorists such as Rostow have considered challenges to U.S. influence and to capitalism, from Marxists and radical nationalists, to be diversions leading to despotic governments and an economic dead end. While agreeing that political and economic freedom were valuable ideas that generally benefited Western peoples, critics doubt these are the foundation of modernity or applicable everywhere. By characterizing traditional societies as "backward" and blaming them for being this way, modernization theory, critics contend, reflects Western prejudices about the world, such as the French "civilizing mission" and the U.S. notion of "Manifest Destiny, " and supports the expansion of Western political power and economic investment into Asia and Africa on the grounds that it fosters "progress." Furthermore, critics argue, most societies are a mix of "traditional" and "modern" traits. For example, the "modern" United States has been a highly religious society from its beginning, arguably less secular than "traditional" China. Nor have Asians and Africans always found Western social and cultural models, such as nuclear families and Christianity, to be more appealing or useful than their own traditions; some, often inspired by Western ideas, have hoped to reform Muslim, Hindu, Confucian, or Buddhist traditions, but most continued to find meaning in the beliefs and customs of their ancestors.

Challenging modernization theory's neglect of connections, scholars led by the American sociologist Immanuel Wallerstein developed the concept of the "world-system," a network of interlinked economic, political, and social relationships spanning the globe. To Wallerstein the world-system, originating in Europe in the 1400s and based on a capitalist world economy, rival European states, and imperialism, explains growing Western global dominance after 1500. By 1914 Western military expansion, colonialism, and industrialization had enriched Europe and brought other societies into the modern world-system. An Africa specialist, Wallerstein views the modern world-system as more widely spread than the more limited networks, such as those of the Mongols and Arabs, that linked Afro-Eurasian societies prior to the 1400s.

In this view, modernization involves not only changes within societies but also their changing relationship to the dominant political powers and the world economy. For example, the Ashante kingdom became a West African power in the 1700s by trading slaves to the West, but, in the late 1800s, it was conquered and absorbed into the British colony of the Gold

Coast (modern Ghana). Under British rule, the Ashante chiefly grew cocoa for export and thus were dependent on the fluctuations of the world price for cocoa. To understand modern Ghana, then, requires knowledge of the Ashante relations to both British colonialism and the world economy.

To describe the world political and economic structure, Wallerstein divided the world-system into three broad zones, or categories of countries: the *core, semiperiphery*, and *periphery*. In 1914 the core included the rich and powerful nations such as Britain, France, and the United States, which all benefited from industrialization, growing middle classes, democracy, a strong sense of nationhood, and political stability. They sometimes used their armies and financial clout to assert power over other societies, even independent ones such as China, where Western powers established spheres of interest patrolled by their gunboats. By 1914 Wallerstein's middle category, the semiperiphery, included countries such as Japan, Russia, and Italy, which were partially industrialized, politically independent nation-states but less prosperous and powerful than the core nations. Finally, the largest group in 1914, the periphery, comprised the colonized societies, such as French Vietnam, British Nigeria, and the U.S.-ruled Philippines, and the neocolonies such as Brazil, Thailand (Siam), and Iran (Persia). These societies were burdened with export economies based on natural resources, little or no industrialization, massive poverty, little democracy, and domination by more powerful core nations. Colonialism transferred wealth from the periphery to the core, which used the wealth for its own economic development. As Wallerstein acknowledges, the world-system is not rigid, and a few societies shifted categories over the centuries. For example, the United States was semiperipheral in 1800, but by 1900 industrialization and territorial expansion had propelled it into the core. By contrast, once-powerful China fell into peripheral status after 1800. But even with some movement up or down, Wallerstein argues, the core-semiperiphery-periphery structure still characterizes the world-system today.

If modernization theory predicts an increasing standardization around the world toward a Western-influenced pattern, world-system analysis suggests that the core and periphery, serving different functions in the world economy, have moved in opposite directions, toward wealth on the one hand and poverty on the other. Since the economic exchange between them was unequal, the periphery became dependent on the core for goods, services, investment, and resource markets, giving core societies, which exploited the resources of the periphery, great influence. For example, the Gold Coast's cocoa growers needed British markets, and British companies provided consumer goods to the shopkeepers, often Lebanese immigrants, who served these communities. The wealth and power of a country, then, reflect its political and economic position in the world-system.

Like modernization theory, world-system analysis has provoked controversy. Some scholars embrace a world-system approach but disagree with Wallerstein's version. Whereas Wallerstein believes a world-system began only around 1500, Christopher Chase-Dunn and Thomas Hall emphasize a longer history with diverse intersocietal networks that can be called world-systems beginning in ancient times. Andre Gunder Frank and Barry Gills identify one single world-system

Private Collection

A Japanese View of America   This Japanese print records the impression of the United States and its wealth and power by a Japanese trade mission in 1860. It shows an American man and woman posing with symbols of modern technology, a pocket watch and a sewing machine.

existing for 5,000 years, since, they argue, some form of capitalism began with the earliest states, such as Sumeria, in Afro-Eurasia. Some critics accuse Wallerstein, like the modernization theorists, of overemphasizing the West and underestimating the key roles played by Asians in the Afro-Eurasian economy.

Other critics are harsher. Some charge that Wallerstein's stress on exchange between countries downplays inequitable economies and class structures within countries—such as rapacious landowners, privileged aristocrats, tyrannical chiefs, and greedy merchants—hence shifting the blame for poverty to the world economy. Others, such as Daniel Chirot, question whether exploitation of the periphery explains the economic growth of the core. Critics also wonder whether terms such as *core* and *periphery* constitute a more sophisticated version of "modernity" and "tradition, " marginalizing and perhaps demeaning poor societies. Finally, some think Wallerstein's focus on economic factors neglects politics and cultures, including religion, and places so much stress on the forest that it misses the trees.

EVALUATING THE DEBATE

The modernization and world-system theorists launched an ongoing debate about how world history can be understood, but neither approach fully explains modern history. World historians widely agree that the once-dominant modernization theory is inadequate for understanding the world as a whole. Some are attracted to one or another version of world-system analysis. While many details of Wallerstein's approach are open to challenge, the general concept of a global system, divided into several categories of countries each with common features, helps understand relations between societies and the exchanges within the world economy. Situating societies within an interlinked world helps explain the impact of colonialism, the background to military interventions by more powerful countries, and the political turbulence of the poorer states today. While each society has unique characteristics that shape its history, perceiving some sort of global system or systems that rise and fall over time helps us understand large-scale, long-term change and explains how thousands of small hunting and gathering bands 12,000 years ago became the contemporary global community of nation-states.

THINKING ABOUT THE CONTROVERSY

1. How do modernization and world-system approaches explain the modern world and its diverse societies differently?
2. What are the major advantages and problems of each of the two approaches?

EXPLORING THE CONTROVERSY

Among the major works of modernization theory are C. E. Black, *The Dynamics of Modernization: A Study in Comparative History* (New York: Harper and Row, 1966); and W. W. Rostow, *The Stages of Economic Growth: A Non-Communist Manifesto* (Cambridge: Cambridge University Press, 1960). Immanuel Wallerstein has summarized his ideas in *The Capitalist World-Economy* (New York: Cambridge University Press, 1979) and *World-Systems Analysis: An Introduction* (Durham, NC: Duke University Press, 2004). Alternative versions of the world-system concept include Christopher Chase-Dunn and Thomas D. Hall, *Rise and Demise: Comparing World-Systems* (Boulder, CO: Westview Press, 1997); and Andre Gunder Frank and Barry K. Gills, eds., *The World System: Five Hundred Years or Five Thousand?* (New York: Routledge, 1996). Daniel Chirot takes issue with much of world-system analysis in *Social Change in the Modern Era* (New York: Harcourt Brace Jovanovich, 1986). Excellent summaries and critiques of world-system analysis and competing ideas can be found in Thomas R. Shannon, *An Introduction to the World-System Perspective* (Boulder, CO: Westview Press, 1989); Alvin Y. So, *Social Change and Development: Modernization, Dependency, and World-System Theories* (Newbury Park, CA: Sage, 1990); Stephen K. Sanderson, ed., *Civilizations and World Systems: Studying World-Historical Change* (Walnut Creek, CA: Altamira Press, 1995); Pamela Kyle Crossley, *What Is Global History?* (Malden, MA.: Polity Press, 2008); and Thomas D. Hall, ed., *A World-Systems Reader: New Perspectives on Gender, Urbanism, Cultures, Indigenous Peoples, and Ecology* (Lanham, MD: Rowman and Littlfield, 2000). For a provocative critique of these debates and the rise of the world economy by an Indian scholar, see Amiya Kumar Bagchi, *Perilous Passage: Mankind and the Global Ascendancy*

Global Imbalances in the Modern World, 1750–1945

of Capital (Lanham, MD: Rowman and Littlefield, 2005).

A world traveler in the nineteenth century could not help but notice the imbalances in wealth and power between the world's societies, imbalances that became even wider in the early twentieth century. One of these travelers, the American writer Mark Twain, author of beloved novels about Tom Sawyer and Huckleberry Finn, became a critic of the imperialism that increased these imbalances. Returning to the United States after lengthy travels in the South Pacific, Asia, Africa, and Europe, Twain blasted U.S. policies in Asia, including the costly military occupation of the Philippines as part of the Spanish-American War, writing in 1900 that "I left these [American] shores a red-hot imperialist. I wanted the American eagle to go screaming into the Pacific. But I have thought more, since then. [Now] I am opposed to having the eagle put its talons on any other hand."[1] His travels had convinced him that, despite Western stereotypes, most peoples, including Filipinos, were capable of governing themselves and that efforts to impose U.S. models on others were doomed to failure.

The imbalances that Twain had observed in his travels or gleaned from news accounts were part of the modern world, which was shaped in part by revolutions and innovations in western Europe and North America. In these Western societies, capitalism and industrialization fostered wealth and inspired new technologies, such as the steamships and railroads that conveyed travelers like Twain, resources, and products over great distances. But the new technologies also included deadly new weapons, such as repeating rifles and machine guns, that enabled the Western conquest of Asian and African societies, reshaping the world's political and economic configuration. Just as Spain and Portugal controlled Latin America until the early 1800s, a half-dozen Western nations ruled, or influenced the governments of, most Asian, African, and Caribbean peoples by 1914. Western domination of the global economy fostered investment but also facilitated a transfer of vast wealth to the West.

While several Western societies exercised disproportionate power in this era, other societies were not passive actors, simply responding to the West. In whatever part of the world they lived, people were linked to a global system that, however imbalanced in terms of political and economic power, promoted often-useful exchanges between distant societies. Societies borrowed ideas, institutions, and technologies from each other, though redefining them to meet their own needs. Societies such as Siam (later Thailand), Persia (later Iran), Turkey, and, most spectacularly, Japan successfully resisted colonialism and, borrowing Western models, introduced some modernization. In fact, resistance to Western power was endemic in the global system. Even in colonized societies such as Vietnam, Indonesia, India, and South Africa, local peoples actively resisted domination and asserted their own interests. The movement of products, thought, and people, on a larger scale than ever before, transcended political boundaries, connecting distant societies. Europeans avidly imported Asian arts, Africans embraced Christianity, and peasants from India settled in the South Pacific and the West Indies. By the 1930s people around the world, often using borrowed Western ideas such as nationalism and Marxism, were challenging Western political and economic power.

Imperialism, States, and the Global System

The world's governments changed greatly during the Modern Era, fostering new types of empires and states. A more integrated international order, dominated by a few Western nations and, eventually, also by Japan, was built on the foundation of the varied Western and Asian empires that had been the main power centers during the Early Modern Era. Societies worldwide grappled with the global political trends that affected people's well-being and livelihoods.

Global Empires

Powerful societies had formed empires since ancient times, but over the centuries successive empires grew larger and more complex. In the mid-1700s over two-thirds of the world's people lived in one of several large, multiethnic empires whose economies were based largely on peasant agriculture. These empires stretched across the Eastern Hemisphere from Qing China and the Western colonies in Southeast Asia, such as Dutch Java and the Spanish Philippines, to the Ottoman, Russian, and Habsburg Empires. In the Americas the huge Spanish Empire, Portuguese Brazil, and British North America all resembled the Eurasian empires in their multiethnic populations and agrarian base, although much of the agriculture was done by unfree labor. In addition to empires but smaller, there were also strong states such as Tokugawa Japan, Siam, and the Ashante kingdom in West Africa. All empires and states depended on a command of military power, especially gunpowder weapons. Great Britain and the Netherlands differed from the other strong states mainly in their greater reliance on world trade.

Many of the empires of the mid-1700s had crumbled by the early twentieth century. The Spanish, Portuguese, and British lost most of their territories in the Americas, and the Habsburg and Ottoman Empires were dismantled after World War I. In their place, modern empires had emerged. Between 1870 and 1914, Britain and France established overseas empires on a grander scale than ever before in history, ruling colonies in Africa, Asia, and the Pacific, and Russia now controlled a vast expanse of Eurasia. On a smaller scale, Germany, Japan, and the United States also forged territorial empires. A huge portion of the globe, divided up into colonies or spheres of influence by the West, was incorporated into a Western-dominated world economic system. The influential British imperialist

Queen Victoria as Seen by a Nigerian Carver This wood effigy of the British monarch was made by a Yoruba artist in just-colonized Nigeria in the late nineteenth century.

Pitt Rivers Museum, Oxford University

and author Rudyard Kipling summarized the rationale for exercising imperial power: "That they should take who have the power, And they should keep who can."[2]

Like empires throughout history, modern imperial states, whatever their democratic forms at home, punished dissent in their colonies. Sometimes protests, such as those led by Mohandas Gandhi in India, forced Western colonizers to modify their policies; more commonly, protest leaders, such as Gandhi, Harry Thuku in Kenya, and Sukarno in Indonesia, were jailed or exiled. Some observers recognized the failure of democratic countries to encourage democracy in their own colonies. For example, British critics condemned the repressive colonial policies of their government, especially the harsh treatment designed to discourage rebellion in Ireland against Britain. A nineteenth-century English wit charged that "the moment the very name of Ireland is mentioned, the English seem to bid adieu to common feelings, common prudence and common sense, and to act with the barbarity of tyrants and the fatuity of idiots."[3]

Nations and Nationalisms

Whether parts of empires or not, all over the world societies struggled to become nations, enjoying self-government and a common identity. But Western peoples formed the most powerful nations. Many European nations were formidable forces because of their strong government structures and democratic practices that fostered debate; they also enjoyed economic dynamism, possessed advanced weapons, and engaged in fierce rivalries with each other. Across the Atlantic most Latin American nations struggled to achieve prosperity and internal unity, but the United States matched European capabilities and shared similar imperial ambitions by the later 1800s, much to the disgust of anti-imperialists such as Mark Twain. Americans believed in the tenets of Manifest Destiny, articulated by an influential U.S. politician: "God has marked the American people as his chosen nation to finally lead in the regeneration of the world."[4] By contrast, few people in the colonies shared any sense of common identity, let alone a national mission; colonial governments were unpopular and usually viewed by the colonized as illegitimate. By drawing up arbitrary colonial borders, often without regard to ethnic connections or economic networks, the British created Nigeria, the Dutch created Indonesia, the French created Laos, and the Belgians created the Congo, all colonies lacking any national cohesion.

The ethnic diversity of most colonies—Indonesia and the Congo each contained several hundred ethnic groups—inhibited nationalist feeling and thus the formation of nationalist movements.

Still, despite the barriers, nationalism spread, often encouraged by travel, exile, or education. Giuseppi Garibaldi (gee-you-SEP-ee gare-a-BALL-dee) (1807–1882), for instance, who helped unify Italy, was born in France of Italian parents and nursed a love for his ancestral homeland during his years living in South America and then the United States before he returned to Italy. The Venezuelan Simon Bolivar, the Filipino Jose Rizal (rih-ZALL) (1861–1896), and the Vietnamese Ho Chi Minh (1890–1969), all disenchanted with colonial restrictions, embraced a nationalist agenda while living in Europe. Indian students discovered the writings of the English-born American revolutionary and exponent of liberty Tom Paine and wondered why their British rulers had ignored Paine's "rights of man" in India. Yan Fu, a Chinese student living in England in the 1870s, recalled spending "whole days and nights discussing differences and similarities in Chinese and Western thought and political institutions."[5] He perceived how Europeans became powerful by combining military aggression, well-defined national states, growing commerce, and a culture approving of political and religious debate. Back in China, Yan Fu translated the work of liberal British thinkers and used it to spread nationalism and other Western ideas in China. But nationalists seeking to confront Western power did not all look to the West for inspiration. By 1900 Japan was a role model of nationalism and modernization for many Asians, and the Vietnamese anticolonial leader Phan Boi Chau (fan boy CHOW) (1867–1940) advised his countrymen to look east to Japan.

But nationalism was not always an imported sentiment. Many Asians had a sense of identity similar to nationalism long before the nineteenth century. People in Korea, Japan, and Vietnam, for example, had long enjoyed some national feeling based on shared religion, a common language, bureaucratic government, and the perception of one or more common enemies. African kingdoms such as Ashante, Oyo, and Buganda enjoyed some attributes of nationhood. Reflecting such national feeling, in 1898, Hawaii's last monarch, Queen Liliuokalani (luh-lee-uh-ohkuh-LAH-nee), pleaded with the United States not to colonize the islands, since her people's "form of government is as dear to them as yours is precious to you. Quite as warmly as you love your country, so they love theirs."[6] U.S. leaders ignored her pleas and annexed Hawaii. To protect their position, colonizers labored hard to crush these traditions and to counter anticolonial nationalism through the use of divide-and-rule strategies, such as the British encouragement of the Hindu-Muslim divide in India. Formerly well-defined states, such as Ashante and Buganda in Africa, lost their traditional cohesion as they now became parts of larger colonies. To resist colonial strategies, nationalists sought ways to regain the initiative and achieve sovereignty. The Indian nationalist Jawaharlal Nehru expressed the search for a successful anticolonial strategy: "What could we do? How could we pull India out of this quagmire of poverty and defeatism, which sucked her in?"[7]

Nationhood Through Revolutions

Some societies needed major rebellions and revolutions to transform old discredited orders and create new nations. The American and French Revolutions of the later 1700s began an Age of Revolution and inspired people elsewhere to take up arms against unjust or outdated governments. In the U.S. case, disgruntled colonists overthrew British rule, and key American revolutionaries, such as Thomas Jefferson and English-born Tom Paine, became known around the world as exponents of political freedom. During the mid-nineteenth century the Taiping (TIE-ping) Rebellion against China's Qing dynasty and the Indian Rebellion against the British East India Company, although they ultimately failed, provided fierce challenges to established governments in the world's two most populous societies. Like these upheavals, the rebellion by the southern states of the United States against the federal government, which resulted in some 600,000 deaths during the American Civil War, did not succeed. Nonetheless, the struggle reshaped American society by allowing President Abraham Lincoln to abolish slavery and forge a stronger national government. Early in the twentieth century, other revolutions overturned old governments and built nations in Mexico, Turkey, and China; the Chinese revolution ended 2,000 years of imperial control and established the foundation for a modern republic. The Russian Revolution of 1917 installed the world's first communist government, inspiring communist movements and revolutionary nationalists around the world.

The aftermath of World War I brought new revolutionary upheavals and ideologies. Old states collapsed in eastern Europe, fascism spread in Germany and Japan in the economic shambles caused by the Great Depression, and Spain erupted in civil war. In 1914 Marxism, the revolutionary socialist vision developed by Karl Marx (1818–1883), had relatively little influence outside of Germany and Russia, but by 1945 the ideology had mass support in many societies. Communist revolutionary movements percolated in China, Korea, Indonesia, and Vietnam. Karl Marx had supplied the critique of the old society, which he saw as shaped by class struggle and capitalism. Now the Russian leader, Vladimir Lenin (1870–1924), forged a revolutionary party and strategy to overthrow that society, and the Chinese communist leader Mao Zedong (maow dzuh-dong) (1893–1976) contributed a vision of a new, unselfish socialist society. Unlike Lenin, Mao believed that revolutionaries must work closely with the local people, writing that "the people are the sea, we [communists] are the fish, so long as we can swim in that sea, we will survive."[8] By combining communism with nationalism, the Vietnamese revolutionary Ho Chi Minh provided a workable model to overthrow colonialism. The ideas of Lenin, Mao, and Ho made Marxism a major vehicle for change after World War II.

Change in the Global System

During the Modern Era the global system expanded and changed as Western influence increased. Networks of trade and communication linking distant societies grew in number and extent. However, because some Western nations came to enjoy more political and military power than other societies, they benefited more from their exchanges with the rest of the world. Aided by this power, Western culture dominated local traditions, especially in Western colonies. For example, textbooks in French colonial schools, where the students were of African, Afro-Caribbean, Asian, or Pacific islander descent, celebrated the history of the French—"our ancestors the Gauls"—while children in the U.S.-ruled Philippines, a tropical and predominantly Catholic land, learned English from books showing American youngsters throwing snowballs, playing baseball, and attending Protestant church services. In some cases this deliberate Westernization reshaped beliefs and ways of life, as occurred among the Filipinos and the Igbos of southern Nigeria. However, Western cultural influence was weak in other colonized societies, especially Muslim ones such as Egypt, the Hausa of northern Nigeria, and the Achehnese of Indonesia.

Countries gained or lost power in the global system, depending on their wealth, type of government, and access to military power (see Historical Controversy: Modernization or World-System?). In 1750, Western overseas expansion, including military conquests, had already reshaped the Americas and some regions of Africa and southern Asia. Chinese, Indians, and western Europeans were the richest peoples at this time, the Chinese accounting for a third and India and western Europe each accounting for a fourth of the world's total economic production. Collectively they accounted for 70 percent of all the world's economic activity and 80 percent of its manufacturing. China remained the greatest engine of the world economy. Britain was the rising political and economic European power, but it faced challenges from France, Russia, Spain, and the Ottoman Empire. The more economically developed districts and the major cities within the two wealthiest countries, Britain and China, apparently enjoyed similar living standards, such as abundant food and long life spans, until at least 1800. As late as the 1830s British observers reported that residents of Britain's capital, London, and the key Chinese trading city of Guangzhou had a roughly comparable material life.

By 1914, however, after a century and a half of Western industrialization, imperial expansion, and colonization, the global system had become more divided than ever before into rich and poor societies. India was now among the poorer countries, and China had succumbed to Western military and economic influence, falling well behind the West. Meanwhile, a few Western nation-states—especially Great Britain, the United States, Germany, and France—had grown rich and powerful, enjoying substantial influence around the world and over the global economy. Because of their unparalleled military power, all four of these nations ruled colonial empires, from which they extracted valuable resources; played a leading role in world trade; and tried to spread, with some success, their cultures and ideas. Also among the richest nations, but having less international power, were a few other western European countries, including the Netherlands, Belgium, and Switzerland. A middle category of countries—Canada, Japan, and European nations such as Russia, Italy, Portugal, and Spain—had a weaker economic base and less military power than those of the richest nations, but they still enjoyed eco-

nomic and political autonomy. A third category of countries were those that were economically poor and militarily weak, either ruled directly as Western colonies, such as India, Indonesia, Nigeria, or Jamaica, or under strong political and economic influence as neocolonies, such as China, Thailand, and Iran. Economically, Latin American countries, relative to the rich North American and western European nations, were also poor.

Living conditions and governments in the rich countries differed dramatically in 1914 from those in the poor societies. Capitalism fostered growth in Europe and North America, although it took many decades for the benefits to reach the common people. The rich countries, such as Britain and the United States, were highly industrialized and enjoyed well-diversified economies and large middle classes. Many of their people lived in cities and, owing to mass education systems, became literate. These countries also boasted efficient, well-financed, constitutional governments. Rich countries were typically democratic, with their governments being chosen by voters (though usually only men) through regular elections. These governments generally tolerated an independent mass media, including newspapers and magazines, and diverse political opinions, such as those represented by socialist and feminist movements. These patterns were also common in the less-powerful Western nations and in Japan.

By contrast, the poor societies, especially Western colonies in Asia and Africa, where many people worked the lands owned by foreign landlords or planters, were not industrialized and people earned meager wages. Economic growth was often determined by foreign investment and markets rather than by local needs. For example, rather than growing food for the local community, farmers in Honduras, in Central America, grew bananas for the U.S. market while farmers in French-ruled Senegal, in West Africa, raised peanuts for export. Politically, a small upper class—African chiefs, Indian princes, Javanese aristocrats—played a political role by cooperating with Western rulers. Only a small minority of people had access to formal education. A tiny middle class and low rates of literacy made democracy difficult, even if it had been allowed, but most Western colonies also prohibited or limited voting or officeholding by anyone who was not white and European.

Their general poverty and lack of economic and political options did not mean that people in poor societies were always miserable. For many generations, and through successive governments, they had learned how to make the best of poverty. Celebrating their survival skills in the early 1900s, the Indian writer and thinker Rabindranath Tagore (rah-BIN-dra-NATH TUH-gore) (1861–1941) found both triumphs and tragedies in Indian peasant life through the ages, which "with its everyday contentment and misery, has always been there in the peasants' fields and village festivals, manifesting their very simple and abiding humanity across all of history—sometimes under Mughal rule, sometimes under British rule."[9]

In the colonies, heavy Western cultural influence, such as the policies the French called their "civilizing mission" in Vietnam and West Africa, by which they tried to impose French ways on people they regarded as culturally inferior, was combined with psychological trauma as once-proud peoples succumbed to foreign rule and its racist restrictions. An anti-imperialist African organization complained in 1927 that colonialism had abruptly cut short "the development of the African people. These nations were later declared pagan and savage, an inferior race."[10] Although Western Christian missionaries often found eager converts, as in Vietnam, Nigeria, and Uganda, nationalists frequently criticized the well-funded Christian missions, accusing them of undermining traditional beliefs. Western domination, however, did not preclude cultural and scientific achievements by colonized people. For example, although their country was a British colony, various Indian mathematicians, biochemists, and astrophysicists won international renown. In Calcutta the experiments of Sir Chandrasekhara Raman (CHAHN-dra-SEE-ker-ah RAH-man) (1888–1970) led to significant advances in the theory of the diffusion of light, for which he won the Noble Prize for physics in 1930.

Between 1914 and 1945 the global system underwent further changes. Wars were now sometimes world wars, titanic struggles that reshaped world politics, fought on a greater scale than ever before and on battlefields thousands of miles apart. World Wars I and II were the deadliest conflicts in history. The United States became the world's richest, most powerful nation. Because of its military defeat in World War I, Germany temporarily lost wealth and power. Germany, Italy, and Japan—all middle-ranking nations by the 1930s—challenged the rich nations—Britain, France, and the United States—during World War II. Several Latin American nations and Turkey enjoyed enough economic growth and stability of government to move into the middle-ranking category by the 1940s. Yet most of the societies of Asia, Africa, Latin America, and the Caribbean remained poor colonies or neocolonies, exercising little diplomatic and economic influence in the global system.

The World Economy

Even before the Western overseas expansion that occurred between 1500 and 1914, trade had taken place over vast distances. Chinese, Indian, Arab, and Armenian merchants had long dominated the vigorous Asian trade, and for centuries Chinese silks and porcelains and Southeast Asian and Indian spices had reached Europe, the Middle East, and parts of sub-Saharan Africa. European explorers wished to locate the source of these riches, and after 1500 the Portuguese, Dutch, and British played key roles in this trade, beginning the rise of the world economy. European influence on the world economy increased in the 1700s and 1800s when Western traders, supported by their governments, sought new natural resources and markets in the tropical world, thereby creating a truly global economic exchange. By 1914 the entire world was enmeshed in a vast economic exchange that particularly benefited the more powerful nations. People often produced resources or manufactured goods—Middle Eastern oil, Indonesian coffee, British textiles—for markets thousands of miles away. Europe's Industrial Revolution, which provided manufactured goods to trade for resources, dramatically reshaped the Western economies in the 1800s but only slowly spread to other regions.

The Inequality of Global Economic Exchange

Economic exchange between societies within the world economy did not proceed on an even playing field. As had been the case for empires throughout history—Assyrian, Roman, Chinese, Inca, Spanish, Dutch—imperialism and colonialism remained the means for transferring wealth to the imperial nations, which used that wealth to finance their own development. The imperial powers, seeking to enhance the value of their colonial economies, also used their control of world trade to shift cash crops indigenous to one part of the world to another. For example, Europeans introduced South American peanuts and rubber to colonized Africa, and coffee from Arabia became a major cash crop in Brazil and Indonesia. This transfer benefited colonial treasuries and plantation owners but also sometimes earned income for the small farmers who started growing these crops.

Gearing economic growth chiefly to the needs of the imperial powers impeded economic development that might have benefited everyone. Many colonies developed economies that produced and exported only one or two primary resources, such as rice and rubber from French Vietnam, sugar from Spanish Cuba, and cocoa from the British Gold Coast. Most of these resource exports were transformed into consumer goods, such as rubber tires and chocolate candies, and sold in stores in Western nations, to the profit of their merchants. For instance, chocolate, whose use for over two millennia was confined to elites in Mexico, became popular among wealthy Europeans after 1500. During the nineteenth century European chemists figured out how to produce chocolate bars, and soon chocolate products gained an eager market among all classes throughout the Western world. Meanwhile, the Western manufactured goods exchanged for these resources, especially textiles, found markets in Africa, Asia, and Latin America. Although much of this exchange was largely at the expense of the colonized peoples, some of them, including a few women, managed to capitalize on it. For example, Omu Okwei (OH-moo AWK-way) (1872–1943), an Igbo, made a fortune trading palm oil for European imported goods, which she distributed widely in Nigeria through a vast network of women traders.

Societies specializing in producing one or two natural resources were especially vulnerable to a changing world economy. To take one case, British Malaya was a major rubber exporter, but most of its rubber plantations, worked chiefly by poorly paid Indian immigrants, were British-owned, and Malayans had little influence over the world price of rubber, which was determined largely by demand in the West. And the prices of agricultural and mineral exports fluctuated more than the prices for industrial goods, which were produced largely in the West. Furthermore, the rise and fall of rubber prices affected not only the rubber tappers and their families but also the shops, often owned by Chinese immigrants, who sold them goods or extended credit to them. Thus the livelihoods of people all over the world increasingly became subject to chronic fluctuations in the world prices of the resources they grew or mined. These prices rose or fell depending on the whims of Western consumers and decisions by the corporations who controlled the international trade.

The world economy widened the wealth gap between societies. In 1500 the differences in per capita income and living standards between people in the richer regions—China, Japan, Southeast Asia, India, Ottoman Turkey, and western Europe—had probably been minor. And these peoples were roughly only two to three times better off materially than the farmers and city folk of the world's poorest farming societies. By 1750, however, while China, western Europe, and British North America enjoyed similar levels of economic production, the wealth gap between them and others was increasing. By 1900 the wealth gap between the richest and poorest societies had grown to about 10 to 1. This trend accelerated throughout the twentieth century, in part because the wealth produced in Western colonies seldom contributed to local development. For example, by the 1950s, after seventy-five years of Belgian colonialism that produced vast wealth for Belgian corporations, mine owners, and rubber planters, the Belgian Congo still lacked all-weather roads linking the major cities and had only a few schools and health clinics for its millions of people.

Unequal economic exchange also fostered conflict. Wars erupted as one country threatened another's access to markets and resources. For example, British free trade policies caused the Opium War with China in the mid-1800s. The Qing government worked to end both the legal and illegal opium trade, but, as the leading opium supplier, Britain needed to protect the opium exports to China from British India, which earned 20 percent of its colonial revenues from charging duty on opium. Britain's defeat of China hastened Chinese decline. In the first half of the twentieth century, World War I was at least partly caused by the bitter competition between European nations for resources in Asia and Africa.

The Spread of Industrialization

The Industrial Revolution, which began in Britain in the late 1700s, was not just a Western development. China and India had once been the world's leading manufacturing countries, and knowledge of Chinese mechanical devices probably stimulated several British inventions. Between 1750 and 1850, however, Britain took the lead in industrialization, and by the mid-1800s it produced about half of the world's manufactured goods while China and India fell behind. Various other European nations, the United States, and Japan industrialized in the later 1800s. Only these few nations increased their resources and weapons as a result of industrialization, and hence only a few became world powers. Some of the profits from colonialism and other overseas activities stimulated or furthered European industrialization. For instance, the Dutch based some of their industrial and transportation growth on profits earned from selling coffee and sugar grown by peasants in their Indonesian colony. But even in Europe agriculture and other nonindustrial activities, such as trade, remained economically important. By 1881 only 44 percent of the British, 36 percent of the German, and 20 percent of the American labor force were employed in industrial or industry-related occupations.

Industrialization gradually spread beyond Europe and North America, but it was highly uneven in its impact and pace. Western policies commonly discouraged other societies, especially colonies, from maintaining or opening industries

that might compete with Western manufacturers. For instance, India had been the world's greatest textile manufacturer for centuries, but British colonization gradually diminished the industry through tax and tariff policies, opening the way for British-made textiles to dominate the Indian market. The British saw India not only as a market for their goods but also as a source of cash crops, such as jute and opium. Hence, in 1840 a British official boasted that his nation had "succeeded in converting India from a manufacturing country into a country exporting raw materials."[11] The once-flourishing Indian textile center of Calcutta lost two-thirds of its population between 1750 and 1850 as its manufacturing declined.

Several nations sought to foster development by setting up manufacturing operations. China, Persia, Egypt, the Ottoman Empire, and Mexico introduced textile industries in the nineteenth century. However, the British, nominally proponents of free trade, used tariffs, or stiff duties on imports to Britain, to stifle many of these industries, thereby opening doors for the export of British fabrics and clothing to these countries. Between 1900 and 1945 there was resurgence of efforts at industrialization in various nations—China, Argentina, Brazil, and Australia—but agriculture remained the economic foundation for most of their population.

Before 1880 few industrial cities had emerged outside of northwestern Europe and North America, but, in a global economy, several cities far from factories had grown dependent on the Industrial Revolution for their livelihood, becoming hubs for the distribution of imported industrial products. For example, Shanghai thrived as the commercial gateway to central China's interior, Singapore served as the economic hub for much of Southeast Asia, and Alexandria was the import-export center for Egypt and the upper Nile basin.

Frontiers and Migrations

People have always been pushed to relocate by necessity or drawn to new lands by opportunity. But the rise of a modern world economy, and its constant quest for resources, markets, and labor, accelerated migration. Modern transportation networks, linked by larger and faster ships and later airplanes, facilitated the movement not only of commodities but also of people. Rapid population growth also spurred migration. Between 1800 and 1900 the world population grew from 900 million to 1,500 million, with two-thirds of these people living in Asia. While some people escaped poverty and overcrowding by moving into nearby frontier regions, many others, more than 100 million between 1830 and 1914, left for distant lands. Some, such as enslaved Africans transported to the Americas, were taken from their homes unwillingly. In contrast, millions of Europeans and Asians sought, and often found, a better life in other countries.

Settling Frontiers

From ancient times people left overcrowded lands to move into sparsely settled frontiers. Bantu-speaking Africans, for instance, took their ironworking and farming technologies from West Africa into the sparsely populated grasslands and forests of central, eastern, and southern Africa, and Chinese expanded from north China into central and south China. Similar movements continued in modern times. For example, millions of Russians migrated east into Siberia and Turkestan to settle what they wrongly considered virgin lands. White Americans and Canadians moved westward across the North American continent, subduing, marginalizing, and killing off the Native American peoples and seizing their land. In Australia, New Zealand, and South Africa, European colonists also settled the land at the expense of local peoples. In South America, Brazilians moved from the Atlantic coast westward into the rain forests and grasslands, setting up farms or ranches after pushing out or killing local Indians, and Argentines settled the vast interior grasslands they called the Pampas. Generally the frontier settlers thought they were bringing "progress" to a "wild" area. An influential leader in the United States, Benjamin Franklin, ignoring the native peoples who still inhabited America, wrote in 1784 about the "vast quantity of forest land we have yet to clear, and put in order for civilization."[12]

Remote from central government controls and traditional social structures, the frontier fostered innovations. Frontier social conditions were often freer and more fluid and flexible, promoting new ideas and offering new opportunities. Cultures met and mixed, and people of different groups intermarried, such as white backwoods hunters, trappers, and itinerant traders with Native Americans. Cultural blending produced hybrid social groups such as the Russian Cossacks, western American cowboys, and Argentine gauchos. The cowboys and gauchos, who chiefly herded cattle for ranchers, combined European and self-sufficient Native American customs, and many were themselves of mixed white and Native American ancestry. Eventually, however, as farmers, ranchers, towns, and states gradually replaced the frontier pioneers, the nearby states incorporated the frontier territories. In this way, for example, the settlers in frontier territories, such as Kentucky, Kansas, and Oregon, were gradually absorbed into the larger U.S. society, and the prairie provinces and British Columbia joined Canada.

African and European Population Movements

The largest population movements of the era involved the involuntary transport of African slaves across the Atlantic to the Americas and the chiefly voluntary migration of European emigrants to the Americas, southern Africa, Australia, and New Zealand. The Africans, shipped in chains and filth, were forced to work for whoever purchased them in the Americas. They typically faced lives shortened by harsh conditions. In contrast, most of the Europeans chose to leave their homelands to seek a better life, and often succeeded.

The major movement of Africans resulted from the transAtlantic slave trade, which reached its height between 1760 and 1800. During these years over 70,000 people a year were herded onto crowded slave ships and shipped from Africa. Between 1800 and 1850 the annual export of Africans to the Americas ranged between 36,000 and 66,000. The great majority of Africans were landed in Brazil and the Caribbean islands, where people of African ancestry today account for a large part of the population. But the gradual abolition of slavery in the Americas eroded the trade. Between 1851 and 1867 the flow of human cargo dropped dramatically. However, the longtime slave trade from East and Central Africa to the Middle East continued until the end of the nineteenth century. By the early 1900s slavery had declined significantly or been abolished in Africa, the Middle East, and Southeast Asia. Abolition resulted in part from the efforts of Western colonial governments, often prompted by humanitarian organizations and Christian missionaries, and both Western and local abolitionists. Some had themselves been slaves, such as Mary Prince, a slave from the British West Indies who was taken to London, freed, and became an active abolitionist, arguing eloquently in 1831: "All slaves want to be free. They work night and day, sick or well, till we are quite done up."[13] The end of plantation slavery in the Americas opened the doors to recruitment of impoverished workers from Asia, who chiefly came voluntarily but under restrictive contracts that limited their rights by requiring them to work for years under harsh conditions.

During the Modern Era the European migration across oceans to the Americas and the South Pacific dwarfed other population movements (see map). Unlike the African slaves, many European emigrants were escaping poverty or political repression and expected to improve their lives abroad. While the ships carrying the emigrants were often crowded and unhealthy and the emigrants sometimes struggled to find jobs that could support their families, Europeans did not arrive in chains, with no possibility of freedom. Some of them received free land upon arrival. The emigrants represented Europe's ethnic diversity but came largely from the British Isles, Germany, Italy, Spain, Poland, and Russia.

Between 1500 and 1940 some 68 million people left Europe, creating new societies in the Americas, Australia, New Zealand, and southern Africa. The largest movement came in the nineteenth and early twentieth centuries. For example, between 1820 and 1930 some 32 million Europeans moved to the United States, the major destination. In the same period another 20 million shipped off to Argentina, Canada, Brazil, and Australia. Not all movement was by ship, however; some 14 million Russians moved overland to the Asian regions of their empire. The result of this large population movement was a Europeanization of societies, as European cultures were implanted far from their ancestral homes. The tendency to look toward Europe for inspiration was especially strong in Argentina, Chile, Canada, Australia, and New Zealand. In these societies many immigrants and their descendants tended to maintain their native languages, churches, and social customs and to identify with their homeland. As a result, the numerous Italians in Argentina's capital, Buenos Aires, often spoke Italian, while Anglo-Argentines sent their children to private English-medium schools. Similarly, Canadians, Australians, and New Zealanders commonly revered the British crown. Immigrants contributed much to their new lands. For example, in the United States, the Scottish-born Andrew Carnegie (1835–1919) helped build the iron and steel industry and with his philanthropy sponsored libraries. Others found different ways to improve their new societies, such as working for social change. The controversial Lithuanian-born leftwing activist Emma Goldman

(1869–1940) was one of these individuals. Goldman had moved with her family to Russia and then to Germany fleeing anti-Semitism. She finally reached the United States in 1885, where she was later arrested and deported for being an advocate for slum-dwellers and for opposing U.S. entry into World War I.

Asian Migrations

During this era, peoples from eastern and southern Asia also emigrated in large numbers, usually by ship to distant shores. They went in response to the demand among Western colonies and American nations for a labor force for the mines and plantations that supplied their wealth. As a result, Chinese mined tin in Southeast Asia and gold in California and Australia, while Indians worked on rubber plantations in British Malaya and sugar plantations in South Africa, Fiji in the South Pacific, and the Guianas in South America. Immigrants often died from overwork or ill health and, as happened with Chinese in California, sometimes suffered from violent attacks by local people who resented their presence. Yet, many Asians survived to raise families in their new homes. Today approximately 40 to 45 million Asians live outside, and often thousands of miles away from, their ancestral homelands. Chinese and Indians constituted the great majority of Asian migrants, settling in Southeast Asia while also establishing communities, often large, in the Americas, the Pacific islands, and parts of Africa. Their descendants became a vital presence in the world economy as merchants, miners, and plantation workers.

Although most moved as poor contract laborers, Asian emigrants often found success abroad, chiefly as merchants. Through hard work, organization, and cooperation many Chinese in Southeast Asia became part of a prosperous, urban middle class that controlled retail trade, operating everything from small general stores and coffee shops to large import-export firms and banks. Today the majority of Chinese in Southeast Asia, the South Pacific and Indian Ocean islands, the Caribbean, and Latin America are engaged in commerce. A Chinese man who settled in New Zealand in the 1920s recalled the hard work that brought him success: "My generation really worked for a living. We had to open the shop at 7 A.M. and we closed [at] 1 A.M. Then we had to clean the shop. It was seldom before 2 A.M. before we got to bed."[14] The descendants of Chinese immigrants have constituted the most dynamic economic sector in Southeast Asia, with their money and initiative spurring the dynamic economic growth since 1970. Indian merchants also prospered in the diaspora. Many were linked to Indian trade networks that moved capital and products around the Indian Ocean and Pacific Rim as well as into Central Asia and Russia. Lebanese and Syrians became merchants in the Americas and West Africa.

Pushed by poverty, overpopulation, or war, people also emigrated from Northeast and Southeast Asia, forming cohesive communities in new lands. Numerous Japanese and Koreans left their homelands between 1850 and 1940. Some settled in Hawaii to work on pineapple plantations or in the canning industry. Many Japanese migrated to the Pacific Coast of the United States and Canada, some taking up farming. In response to growing local prejudice against all Asian

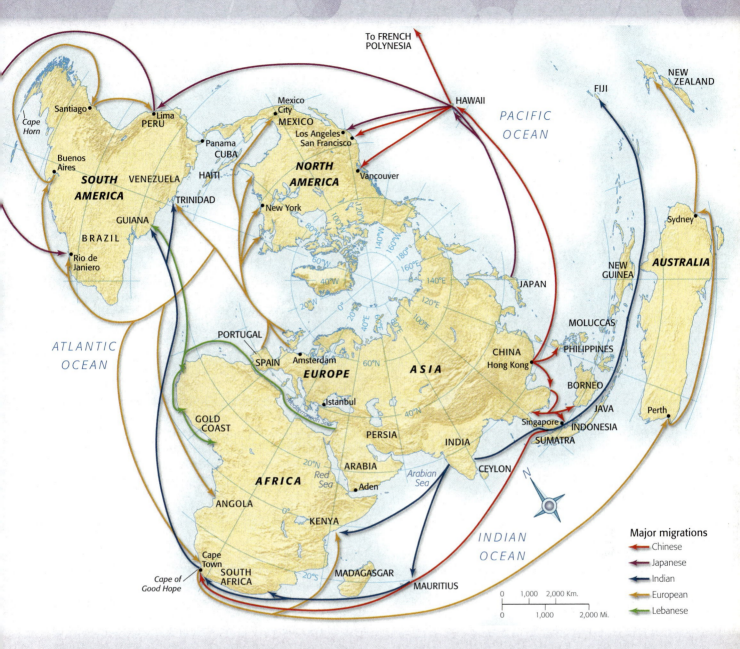

Asian and European Migration, 1750–1940

During this era millions of Europeans emigrated to the Americas, South Africa, Australia, and New Zealand. Millions of Asians, especially Chinese and Indians, left their homes to work or settle in Southeast Asia, Africa, the Pacific islands, and the Americas.

Major migrations
- Chinese
- Japanese
- Indian
- European
- Lebanese

e **Interactive Map**

immigrants, the United States and Canada restricted Japanese immigration in the early 1900s. As a result, the Japanese emigrant flow turned to Latin America, especially Peru and Brazil. Southeast Asians also departed from their homelands to live abroad. Between 1875 and 1940 Indonesians, mostly Javanese, were recruited to work on plantations in Malaya and British North Borneo but also in Dutch Guiana (today's Suriname), in South America, and on the French-ruled South Pacific island of New Caledonia. Some 50,000 Javanese today live in Suriname. After the United States colonized the Philippines, Filipinos began migrating to Hawaii and the U.S. Pacific coast as factory workers or farm laborers. Today one and a half million Filipinos live in the United States.

The Spread of Technology and Mass Culture

The modern global system owed much to innovations in technology. Improved methods of communication and transportation allowed people, ideas, and products to travel farther and faster than ever before, enhancing networks of power and

Courtesy, Singapore History Museum

Singapore's Chinatown   By the early 1900s Singapore, a major Southeast Asian port and commercial crossroads, was predominantly Chinese in population. The bustling streets were lined by shops, workers' quarters, theaters, and brothels.

exchange. More effective military technologies enabled a few societies to gain control of other societies and to combat rival powers. Finally, the increasing connections around the world enabled cultural ideas and products to spread across national and regional borders.

Communication and Transportation

For much of history, communication over long distances had been slow, depending largely on beasts of burden carrying riders or pulling wagons, and later on sailing ships. In 500 B.C.E. a message carried by successive riders on horses could travel the 1,800-mile length of the Persian Empire in nine days. Two millennia later, in the 1600s, it took Dutch ships some nine months to sail from Amsterdam to Dutch-ruled Java to deliver news and orders. Then in the nineteenth century, thanks to the Industrial Revolution, communications changed dramatically. In 1844 the first telegraph messages were exchanged between Washington and Baltimore. By 1861 submarine telegraph cables linked Britain to North America, prompting a poet to write: "Two mighty lands have shaken hands, Across the deep blue sea; the world looks forward with new hope, Of better times to be."[15] By 1870 the cables had reached from Britain to India. The invention of the telephone in 1876 and radio in 1895 further increased the potential for communications. In

1906 a Canadian scientist, Reginald Fessenden, broadcast the first experimental entertainment program on radio, featuring Christmas carols and speeches. As the possibilities and advantages of broadcasting over great distances became apparent, the New Zealand premier proposed in 1911 that Britain build an empirewide radio network because of "the great importance of radio for social, commercial, and defensive purposes."[16] World War I postponed the scheme, but radio technology improved. By the 1920s radio transmissions had become commonplace in industrial nations and British broadcasts could reach Canada, South Africa, India, and Australia.

Some technologies conveyed people and commodities as well as messages, transforming peoples' lives around the world. Railroads were built all over the world to carry goods and passengers, and as trains reached stations, telegraph messages smoothed their journeys by passing on traffic and weather information. By 1869 railroads connected the Pacific and Atlantic coasts of North America, and by 1903 anyone determined to make the long journey could ride the 9,000 miles between Paris and Siberia's Pacific coast. While railroads extended land networks, shipping lines that employed steamships linked the world. The opening of the 105-mile-long Suez Canal in 1869 and the 51-mile Panama Canal in 1914, both of which cost the lives of thousands of workers during their construction, greatly reduced travel times for many sea journeys and also made it easier and cheaper to ship resources from Asia and Latin America to Europe and North America. Now it only took a few weeks to sail from China or Singapore to New York or London. Political and economic leaders took advantage of the new travel opportunities. For instance, seeking to forge diplomatic alliances and recruit laborers for his islands' plantations, in 1880–1881 Hawaii's king, David Kalakaua **(KAH-la-COW-ah)** (r. 1874–1891), sailed around the world by steamship and in the course of his journey met the Japanese emperor, the Siamese king, the pope, and Britain's Queen Victoria, among other dignitaries. In Japan, he signed an agreement to import thousands of Japanese laborers to his kingdom.

In the early 1900s motor cars and buses continued the revolution in land transportation begun by railroads, allowing people to more easily commute to city jobs and downtown stores or to travel between cities. After World War I thousands of middle-class Europeans and North Americans owned their own cars, and in the 1930s the first commercial air flights began, making long-distance journeys even faster. Transportation depended increasingly on fossil fuels, first coal and then oil. The use of vehicles fueled by oil increased the strategic importance of oil-rich regions such as the Middle East, Indonesia, Mexico, and the Gulf Coast of the United States.

Technologies of Warfare
New technologies included those devoted to warfare that made it easier to kill more people and at a greater distance. Most of these weapons remained largely a monopoly of Western nations and Japan during this era, and thus contributed to the imbalances in global power. White adventurers and settlers used the rifle invented by the American Philo Remington (1816–1889), which was effective at 1,500 yards, to defeat, and seize the lands of, the Native Americans and the Australian Aborigines. In 1878 an Argentinean observed that the Remington rifle has left "the land strewn with the bodies of those [local Indians] who dared to oppose it."[17] Effective rifles also proved devastating in Africa against warriors armed only with spears and arrows. The British-born American explorer Henry Morton Stanley boasted of his use of repeating rifles and terrorism to destroy a hostile Congo village that had greeted him with spears and arrows: "I skirmish in their streets, drive them pell-mell into the woods beyond; with frantic haste I fire the huts, and end the scene by towing their canoes into midstream and setting them adrift."[18]

Military weaponry quickly improved, including more powerful repeating guns. In 1861 an American doctor, Richard Gatling (1818–1903), invented what quickly came to be known as the Gatling gun, which could fire up to 3,000 rounds of ammunition a minute. The Gatling gun was quickly adopted by Western armies. The first totally automatic machine gun, spitting out 11 bullets a second, was invented in 1884 by Hiram Maxim (1840–1916), an American working in Britain, and gave the British an unparalleled military advantage. The Western powers used the Maxim gun and similar repeating weapons to subdue resistance to colonialism in Africa and Asia. During World War I, since most Western armies had an array of repeating weapons and field artillery, the two rival

alliances in that war inflicted terrible casualties on each other. The Western nations had also by this time developed the first armored tanks and increasingly relied on battleships at sea. Air power was introduced to combat in World War I but did not become central to wars until the Spanish Civil War and World War II. The methods of warfare were now more indiscriminate in their targets and more lethal than ever before in history. In 1945 the United States used the most deadly weapon in history, the atomic bomb, to force Japanese surrender and end World War II.

The Spread of Mass Cultures
The revolution in communications and transportation technologies contributed to the creation and spread of mass cultures, popular entertainments appealing to a large audience that often crossed class divisions and national borders. People were increasingly exposed to cultural products, such as films and music, and pastimes, such as sports, that were common in other regions of their countries or imported from abroad. Mass cultures percolated into and spread outward from the major cities, where the emerging mass media, such as newspapers and radio, were centered. These media disseminated mass culture, reporting on film stars and sports events or playing popular music. The influence of Paris on the rest of France, Berlin on Germany, Tokyo on Japan, Istanbul on Turkey, Buenos Aires on Argentina, and New York City on the United States grew. As literacy rates rose, the print media gained particular influence. Between 1828 and 1900 the number of newspapers published around the world grew from 3,100 to 31,000, making available news and opinions in hundreds of languages. India alone supported 600 different newspapers in several dozen languages in 1900. Popular books, from Arab detective novels to romances written in South Africa's Xhosa **(KHO-sa)** language, competed with classic works of philosophy and religion for the hearts and minds of readers.

By spreading cultural influences into other societies, mass communications and increased travel sometimes fostered Westernization. Reflecting Westernization, orchestras playing Western classical music appeared in various Asian societies, including India, China, and Japan, by the early 1900s. Like Europeans, many educated Asians enjoyed the music of Beethoven, Bach, and Mozart. Films and popular music from the United States had an even larger international audience. American film stars such as Charlie Chaplin, born in Britain, became known throughout the world, and U.S.-born jazz musicians often made a living playing the nightclubs of Europe and Asia, where they inspired local musicians to take up jazz. Many societies adopted and excelled in Western sports. For example, Indians became skilled in British cricket; India's Prince Ranjitsinhji **(RAHN-jeet-SING-jee)** (1872–1933) became one of the world's best players. India's field hockey team remained unbeaten in the Olympics from 1932 through 1960. European football, also known as soccer, became an international sport that was played and watched all over the world.

But Westernization was only part of the story. Influences from non-Western cultures also spread, contributing to a creative cultural mixing. For example, in the eighteenth and nineteenth centuries the growing Western interest in Chinese painting, Japanese prints, Indonesian gamelan music, and African woodcarvings influenced Western arts. Later, in the 1930s, Indian films and Indian popular music became popular in Southeast Asia and the Middle East, and Cuban music, a mix of African and Western traditions, developed a large following in West and Central Africa, where it blended with local styles. Hawaiian music, which mixed Polynesian and Western influences, became popular in the continental United States in the 1920s and later developed a following in Southeast Asia. People found ways to combine imported ideas, whatever their source, with their own traditions. For instance, in his lyrical suite, *Bachianas Brasileiras*, of 1930, the Brazilian composer Heitor Villa-Lobos (1887–1959) adapted the Baroque influences of German composer Johann Sebastian Bach (1685–1750) to Brazilian folk and popular music.

The reach of organizations and social movements expanded, as did awareness of the world. Some organizations developed a global focus. For example, the Red Cross, a Christian organization formed in nineteenth-century Switzerland to alleviate human suffering by helping war victims, eventually became an international movement devoted to humanitarian aid around the globe. Its global reach encouraged it to adapt to non-Christian cultures; in the Islamic world it became the Red Crescent. Social movements also crossed borders. For instance, women in China, Japan, Indonesia, Egypt, and Chile, inspired in part by feminist movements in Europe and North America, sought to adapt the notions of women's rights and education to their own societies. The winning of women's suffrage resulted from the efforts of women worldwide. Thus, in the United States, Susan B. Anthony (1820–1906) began campaigning at age seventeen for equal pay for female teachers and later cofounded the key national and international organizations working for women's suffrage. Across the Pacific, Ichikawa Fusae (ITCH-ee-KAH-wa foo-SIGH) (1893–1918) fought for the rights of women to attend political meetings and, in 1924, formed the major women's suffrage group in Japan, which won the right to vote in 1945.

Global crises now became more widely known, and people followed world events in newspapers and radio newscasts. An avid news follower, the Trinidad calypso singer who humorously called himself Atilla the Hun, appraised the devastation in the world of the later 1930s:

All we can hear is of unrest, riots, revolutions; There is war in Spain and China. Man using all his skill and ingenuity making weapons to destroy humanity. In the [Italian invasion of Ethiopia] it is said, over six hundred thousand maimed and dead. The grim reaper has taken a gigantic toll. Why all the bloodshed and devastation, Decimating the earth's population? Why can't this warfare cease? All that the tortured world needs is peace.[19]

Soon after Atilla's plea, World War II raised the level of violence even further, providing a fitting end to a turbulent, violent era during which the world's people had become more closely linked into a common global system.

Suggested Reading

Books

Abernathy, David B., *The Dynamics of Global Dominance: European Overseas Empires, 1415–1980*. New Haven: Yale University Press, 2002. One of the best studies of European imperialism.

Bayly, C. A. *The Birth of the Modern World, 1780–1914*. Malden, MA: Blackwell, 2004. A brilliant, detailed study.

Cohen, Robin. *Global Diasporas: An Introduction*. Seattle: University of Washington Press, 1997. A brief, valuable survey.

Cook, Scott B. *Colonial Encounters in the Age of High Imperialism*. New York: Longman, 1996. Examines Western imperialism.

Curtin, Philip D. *The World and the West: The European Challenge and the Overseas Response in the Age of Empire*. New York: Cambridge University Press, 2000. An interesting study of reactions to European imperialism.

Hobsbawm, Eric. *The Age of Extremes: A History of the World, 1914–1991*. New York: Pantheon, 1994. A masterful overview, especially strong on social and cultural history.

Hoerder, Dirk. *Cultures in Contact: World Migrations in the Second Millennium*. Durham, NC: Duke University Press, 2003. A comprehensive, detailed summary of migrations and diasporas.

Marks, Robert B. *The Origins of the Modern World: A Global and Ecological Narrative*, 2nd ed. Lanham, MD: Rowman and Littlefield, 2007. A concise, readable examination of some major themes.

Neiberg, Michael S. W*arfare in World History*. New York: Routledge, 2001. Good coverage of this era.

Ponting, Clive. *The Twentieth Century: A World History*. New York: Henry Holt and Company, 1998. A thematic study.

Stavrianos, Leften S. *Global Rift: The Third World Comes of Age*. New York: William Morrow, 1971. A provocative, innovative study.

Stearns, Peter N., *The Industrial Revolution in World History*, 3rd ed. Boulder: Westview Press, 2007. Useful comparative study with much on this era.

Wesseling, H. L. *The European Colonial Empires, 1815–1919*. Harlow, United Kingdom: Pearson, 2004. A useful overview of the entire colonial enterprise by a Dutch scholar.

Wolf, Eric R. *Europe and the People Without History*. Berkeley: University of California Press, 1982. A thought-provoking analysis of the Western impact on the wider world from 1400 to 1914.

WEBSITES

Modern History Sourcebook (*http://www.fordham.edu/halsall/*). An extensive online collection of historical documents and secondary materials.

Modern World History Links (*http://www.loeser.us/mhist.html*). A quirky site with links to various useful information sources.

Modern World History Resources (*http://www.historesearch.com/modworld.html*). Has links to sites on many topics and regions.

GLOBAL SYSTEM: INTERDEPENDENCE AND CONFLICT IN THE CONTEMPORARY WORLD, SINCE 1945

The key events of the first half of the twentieth century, including the rise of communism in Russia, the growth of anti-Western nationalism in Africa and Asia, the economic disaster of the Great Depression, and the traumas of World Wars I and II, laid a foundation for a new global system. Yet the world of today has also been shaped by the trends marking the decades since World War II, what historians often term the Contemporary Era. During this era, political and economic power in the world passed from huge Western colonial empires to Russia, Japan, China, and especially the United States. Meanwhile, the world's nations became more closely linked through trade, cooperation, and worldwide movements.

A key feature of world politics until the end of the 1980s was the conflict known as the Cold War. Marking this conflict was a competition for influence between the United States and its allies and the Soviet Union and its allies. Another major political trend was the ending of Western colonial control in Asia, Africa, and most of the Caribbean and Pacific islands by the 1970s. Nationalist movements in these colonized areas demanded and gained political independence but sometimes achieved their goals only through violent resistance, including revolutions in countries such as Indonesia, Algeria, and Mozambique. While the Soviet Union imposed communism on eastern Europe, communist-led movements came to power through revolution in countries such as China, Vietnam, and Cuba. Despite fierce competition between the major powers, new international organizations, among them the United Nations, fostered cooperation among nations on issues of common concern, such as women's rights, proliferating nuclear weapons, and threats to public health.

The world has also seen significant economic change since 1945. Western Europe and Japan recovered quickly from World War II, regaining prosperity. Economic links between nations became much stronger, greatly enlarging the world economy. A trend known as globalization spread, facilitating the flow of investment, jobs, resources, and products, not to mention information and ideas, around the world. New or improved technologies, from home appliances and automobiles to cell phones and computers, made life more convenient while fostering economic change. Capitalizing on globalization, several industrializing Asian nations, including India, South Korea, Malaysia, and especially China, grew economically, reshaping world trade. But Japan and the western nations, led by the United States, have controlled much of the world's wealth and have had the most productive economies. The gap between these industrialized countries and the world's poorest countries has grown even wider.

Furthermore, economic growth has come at a huge cost in environmental destruction, from the cutting down of forests to the polluting of the world's air, land, and water. Skyrocketing population growth has harmed the environment, diminished natural resources, and fostered poverty. While people in several

Corbis

dozen nations have enjoyed unprecedented affluence and longer, healthier lives, a fifth of the world's people live in desperate poverty, unable to meet their basic needs for food and shelter.

Social and cultural change has also characterized recent decades. Spurred by war or the quest for a better life, for example, people have left their homelands to settle in other lands. As a result, millions of Africans, Arabs, Turks, and South Asians live in Europe while Latin Americans and Asians have moved to North America. In many countries women have gained better job opportunities and political rights, and ethnic minorities have struggled for social equality. Popular culture products, such as Hollywood films, Caribbean reggae music, and Japanese video games, have spread around the world. Although secular thought has enjoyed increased influence, especially in western Europe and East Asia, Christianity and Islam have rapidly gained followers and influence in many lands. These social and cultural changes, however, are balanced by continuities. While people often enjoy the latest entertainment and gadgets, in many ways they remain like their ancestors, devoted to their families, faiths, and customs. Most societies are a mix of old and new, the traditional and the contemporary.

Since the collapse of European communist regimes and the Soviet Union at the end of the 1980s, which left the United States as the sole global superpower, the world's nations have faced other challenges. These include international terrorism, deadly diseases, food and energy shortages, weapons of mass destruction, global warming, unstable nations engulfed in conflict, and the growing inequality between rich and poor countries. How nations, working together, deal with these and other problems will determine the shape of the future.

NORTH AND CENTRAL AMERICA
The United States became the world's richest nation and greatest political, economic, and military power. It led the Western alliance against the Soviet Union, fighting major wars in Korea and Vietnam and intervening in other nations. After 1990 the United States had no major rival but confronted international terrorism, which prompted it to send military forces into Afghanistan and Iraq. Mexico's economic growth lagged, fostering emigration to the United States, while the Cuban Revolution brought communists to power, provoking U.S. hostility.

SOUTH AMERICA
The South American nations, often troubled by tensions between the political left and right, struggled to achieve political stability and economic growth. Some nations, such as Brazil, Argentina, and Chile, alternated between democratic, reformist regimes and brutal military dictatorships. U.S. intervention helped overthrow several leftist governments. After 1990 Argentina faced economic collapse; Brazil and Chile, mixing capitalism and socialism, enjoyed growth; and Venezuela turned to the left.

EUROPE

Although western Europe recovered quickly from World War II, the imperial Western states were unable to maintain control of their colonies. The western European nations forged stable welfare states, providing a social safety net, and moved toward close cooperation and economic unity among themselves. The Soviet Union became a global superpower, controlling eastern Europe, but at the end of the 1980s it and its communist satellites collapsed. Germany, divided after World War II, was reunified, and Russia sought a new role in the world.

WESTERN ASIA

Nationalists gained control of the western Asian nations but faced new challenges. Israel, a new Jewish state in Palestine, won wars against Arab neighbors, and Arab-Israeli hostilities have remained a source of tension. Some nations, such as Turkey, pursued modernization. An Islamic revolution reshaped oil-rich Iran, which fought oil-rich Iraq in the 1980s. Saudi Arabia and several Persian Gulf states flourished from oil wealth. After 2001 U.S.-led forces invaded and occupied Afghanistan and Iraq but, while removing despotic governments, struggled to restore stability.

EASTERN ASIA

Coming to power through revolution in 1949, communists transformed China, creating a socialist society and fighting the United States during the Korean War. After 1978 new communist leaders mixed free markets with socialism and fostered modernization, turning China into an economic powerhouse. Japan recovered rapidly from World War II, embracing democracy and becoming an economic giant. Borrowing Japanese models, South Korea and Taiwan industrialized. North Korea remained a repressive communist state.

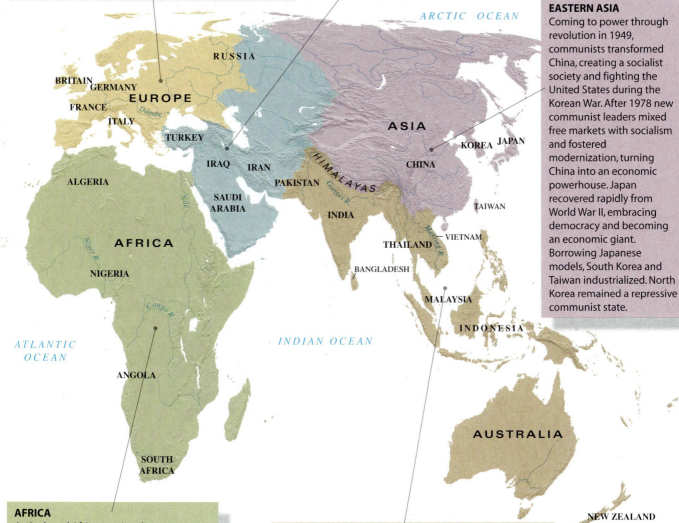

AFRICA

As Arab and African nationalism grew stronger, colonies became independent nations, sometimes, as in Algeria and Angola, through revolution. In North Africa, Egypt promoted Arab nationalism and became a regional power but faced economic problems. Most of the new sub-Saharan African nations, which were artificial creations of colonialism, struggled to maintain political stability and foster economic development, but South Africans finally achieved black majority rule.

SOUTHERN ASIA AND OCEANIA

Britain granted independence to predominantly Hindu India but also to largely Muslim Pakistan, which eventually split when Bangladesh seceded. India enjoyed democracy and economic progress, but Pakistan and Bangladesh often fell under military rule. In Southeast Asia, the U.S. and British colonies gained independence peacefully while Indonesians triumphed through revolution. Vietnamese communists first defeated the French and then the United States. Malaysia, Singapore, and Thailand developed economically. Australia and New Zealand established closer links to Asia, and most of the Pacific islands gained independence from Western colonialism.

THE REMAKING OF THE GLOBAL SYSTEM, SINCE 1945

AP/Wide World Photos

"Our World Is Not for Sale"
In 2004 tens of thousands of activists from all over the world, under the banner of "Our World Is Not for Sale," marched on the streets of Mumbai (formerly Bombay), India's largest city, to protest economic globalization, racial and caste oppression, and the U.S.-led war in Iraq. The march reflected the globalization of social movements and political protests in the contemporary world.

One heart, one destiny. Peace and love for all mankind. And Africa for Africans.

—BOB MARLEY, REGGAE SUPERSTAR[1]

In 1980, when the new African nation of Zimbabwe (formerly Southern Rhodesia) celebrated its independence from British rule, Bob Marley, a Jamaican reggae music star and a symbol of black empowerment, performed at Zimbabwe's national stadium. Marley's experience there reflected many late-twentieth-century politcal and cultural trends. He had been invited in part because his songs often dealt with issues such as poverty, racial prejudice, and asserting one's rights, realities for Zimbabweans, who had lived under an uncaring British colonial and then white supremacist government. But Marley's concert was disrupted by the local police, mostly whites fearing a riot and vandalism, who used tear gas to disperse thousands of black Zimbabweans, often poor, who gathered outside the overcrowded stadium. The next night Marley ignored threats of violence against him by local white racists and gave a free concert for 40,000 Zimbabweans. The violence of the previous night and the threats to his life showed Marley that the social ills and ethnic hatreds he knew in Jamaica also occurred elsewhere in the world. In Zimbabwe they would not be solved by a black majority government.

Marley's career reflected a world interconnected as never before. An eloquent advocate of political and cultural freedom whose music was enjoyed around the world, Marley came from the slums of a small island of barely 2 million people, yet his music touched hearts and minds across racial, political, religious, class, and cultural barriers. Reggae was a truly world music, an intoxicating mix of African, Caribbean, and North American traditions. To the world, Marley personified reggae's progressive politics and spiritual quest.

Some 2,500 years ago ancient thinkers such as the Buddha in India, Daoists in China, and the Greek philosopher Heraclitus had argued that nothing was permanent except change. Never was this more true than in the second half of the twentieth century and the early twenty-first. Since World War II the pace of change quickened and the global economy grew dramatically. Economic and cultural networks linked societies ever more closely while ideas, technologies, and products flowed across porous borders, affecting the lives of people everywhere. World politics were turbulent, reflecting the conflict between the United States and the Soviet Union (USSR) and the struggle of African, Asian, and Latin American countries for decolonization and development. Since 1989, when the Soviet bloc collapsed, the world has groped toward a new political configuration while dealing with mounting economic and environmental problems.

FOCUS QUESTIONS

1. How did decolonization change the global system?
2. What roles did the Cold War and superpower rivalry play in world politics?
3. What were some of the main consequences of a globalizing world economy?
4. How did growing networks linking societies influence social, political, and economic life?

DECOLONIZATION, NEW STATES, AND THE GLOBAL SYSTEM

How did decolonization change the global system?

The contemporary world derived both from Western imperialism and from the resistance waged against it. After World War II Asia, Africa, and Latin America became major battle-grounds between the United States and the Soviet Union, which had so much military, political, and economic might in comparison to other countries that they were known as superpowers. The struggle of Asian, African, and Latin American societies to end Western domination and to develop economically also shaped the postwar era. Nationalist movements proliferated, some-times leading to interventions by Western powers or the USSR, which were anxious to preserve their political and economic influence. The former colonies now became part of a global system marked by continued imbalances in wealth and power.

Nationalism and Decolonization

Types of Nationalism

Nationalism became a powerful force in the colonized world by the mid-1900s (see Chapter 25). Three basic types of nationalist movements developed. In the first type, which occurred in most colonized societies, the goal was the end of colonial rule, but not necessarily major social and economic change. Colonial powers were often willing to grant independence where nationalist leaders, in countries such as Nigeria and the Philippines, accepted continued Western control of mines, plantations, and other resources. The second type of nationalist movement, mounted by social revolutionaries inspired by Marxism, wanted not only political independence but also a new social order free of Western economic domination. In China the communist movement led by Mao Zedong reorganized Chinese society while limiting contact with the world economy and the United States. Making up a third type were the nationalist movements by long-repressed nonwhite majorities in white settler colonies such as Algeria and Zimbabwe, which struggled against domination by the minority whites, who owned most of the land and resources.

Dismantling Empires

The dislocations caused by the Great Depression and World War II intensified anticolonial feelings. In the three decades after World War II, colonialism gradually crumbled, often after nationalist resistance led by charismatic figures such as Mohandas Gandhi in India and Sukarno in Indonesia. Most of the Western colonizers realized that the increased military force required to maintain their control was too expensive. In 1946 the United States began the decolonization trend, granting independence to the Philippines (see Chronology: Global Politics, 1945–1989). Weary of suppressing nationalist resistance, the British gave up their rule in India and Burma, and the Dutch left Indonesia. Between 1946 and 1975 most of the Western colonies in Asia, Africa, and the Carib-bean achieved independence (see Map 26.1).

Some colonizers accepted decolonization only after failing to quell nationalist uprisings. The Dutch planned to regain Indonesia, a source of immense wealth, but the struggle against a nationalist army proved bloody and demoralizing. Similarly, the French had no plans to abandon their profitable colonies in Vietnam and Algeria, but uprisings by revolutionaries forced them to leave. In Vietnam, heavy U.S. aid could not prevent a humiliating French defeat by communist forces led by Ho Chi Minh in 1954. The ultimately successful anticolonial struggles by the Indonesian, Vietnamese, and Algerian nationalists had electrifying global effects, giving hope to colonized peoples elsewhere and warning the Western powers that they would pay a heavy cost for opposing decolonization.

Nationalism and the Superpowers

Both superpowers sought to capitalize on the nationalist surge. The Soviet Union generally supported nationalist movements, sometimes supplying arms to revolutionaries. The Soviets also offered economic aid and diplomatic support to Asian and African countries that achieved inde-pendence and had strategic value because of their size, location, or valuable resources, such as India, Egypt, and Indonesia. The United States followed a mixed policy on decolonization. Want-ing access to trade and outlets for investment in Asia and Africa, the United States encouraged the Dutch to leave Indonesia and urged independence for some British colonies in Africa. But Ameri-cans also opposed communism and Soviet influence. Thus where nationalism had a leftist orienta-tion, as in French-ruled Vietnam and Portuguese-ruled Mozambique, the United States supported continued colonial power, no matter how unpopular, and helped finance the French and Portu-guese military efforts to suppress the revolutionaries. Portugal stubbornly resisted decolonization until festering African rebellions, growing demoralization at home, and the toppling of its fascist dictator forced it to abandon its African empire in 1975.

CHRONOLOGY

	International	Eurasia	The Americas
1940	**1945** Formation of the United Nations **1946–1975** Decolonization in Asia, Africa, and Caribbean **1946–1989** Cold War	**1950–1953** Korean War **1959–1975** U.S.-Vietnam War	
1960	**1968** Widespread political protests		**1962** Cuban Missile Crisis
1980		**1989–1991** Dismantling of Soviet bloc and Soviet Union	
2000			**2001** Al Qaeda attack on United States

Colonialism did not completely disappear. By the 1980s one major territorial empire, the USSR, remained, and it strained to repress the nationalist demands of the Baltic, Caucasus, and Central Asian peoples it ruled. The Soviet Empire was largely dismantled between 1989 and 1991, when the communist system collapsed, although Russians still controlled some unwilling subjects, such as the Muslim Chechens in southern Russia. Britain, France, and the United States still control small empires. Britain and France retain direct control of a few islands, mostly in the South Pacific, South Atlantic, and Caribbean, and some outposts such as French Guiana in South America. The territories, mostly self-governing, that are linked to the United States include Puerto Rico and the Virgin Islands in the Caribbean and a few Pacific islands such as American Samoa and Guam.

Decolonization often resulted in neocolonialism, a continuing Western political and economic influence. In the Philippines, Americans maintained a major role in the economy, Philippine governments loyally supported U.S. foreign policies, and Filipinos avidly consumed American products and popular culture such as music, films, and fashions. Similarly, the French controlled much of the economy and advised the government in Cote d'Ivoire **(COAT dee-VWAHR)** (Ivory Coast), and many Ivoirians favored French cuisine, literature, and language. A West Indian–born writer offered a radical nationalist but oversimplified view of why most former colonies accepted neocolonialism: "The colonial power says, 'Since you want independence, take it and starve' [after economic aid ends]. Other countries refuse to undergo this ordeal and agree to [accept] the conditions of the former guardian power."[2] Some Asian and African intellectuals advocated "decolonizing the mind," to escape what Bob Marley called "mental slavery" that kept formerly colonized people in awe of Western power, wealth, and culture. This sometimes meant building a nationalist culture reflecting local traditions or abandoning the use of Western languages in literature. For example, the Kenyan novelist Ngugi wa Thiongo **(en-GOO-gey wah they-ON-go)** switched from writing in English to his native Gikuyu.

African Independence   In 1961 the British monarch, Queen Elizabeth II, made an official visit to newly independent Ghana, the former British colony of the Gold Coast. Here she walks under a ceremonial umbrella with the Ghanian president, Kwame Nkrumah.

UPI/Bettmann/Corbis

Map 26.1 Decolonization

Between 1946 and 1975 most of the Western colonies in Asia, Africa, and the Caribbean won their independence, with the greatest number achieving independence in the 1960s. The decolonization reshaped the political map, particularly of Africa, South Asia, and Southeast Asia.

 Interactive Map

1960 Year independence achieved

Former ruler

Great Britain	Belgium
France	Portugal
Netherlands	United States
Italy	Other

PACIFIC OCEAN

ATLANTIC OCEAN

INDIAN OCEAN

Bay of Bengal

Arabian Sea

Caspian Sea

Black Sea

Mediterranean Sea

Tropic of Cancer

Equator 0°

Tropic of Capricorn

GREAT BRITAIN
FRANCE
SPAIN
PORTUGAL
NETHERLANDS
BELGIUM
ITALY
JAPAN

NORTH KOREA 1948
SOUTH KOREA 1948 (From Japan)

PHILIPPINES 1946

NORTH VIETNAM 1954 (Unified 1975)
SOUTH VIETNAM 1954
CAMBODIA 1953
LAOS 1949
MYANMAR (BURMA) 1947
BRUNEI 1984 (From Gr. Br.)
MALAYSIA 1963
SINGAPORE 1965 (From Malaysia)
INDONESIA 1949
TIMOR-LESTE 1999 (From Indonesia)
PAPUA NEW GUINEA 1975 (from Australia)

PAKISTAN 1947, BANGLADESH 1973
INDIA 1947
PAKISTAN 1947
SRI LANKA (CEYLON) 1948
MALDIVES 1975 (From Gr. Br.)

IRAQ 1932
KUWAIT 1961
BAHRAIN 1971
QATAR 1971
UNITED ARAB EMIRATES 1971
OMAN 1971
P.D.R. OF YEMEN 1967 (Unified 1990) YEMEN
SYRIA 1944
JORDAN 1946
CYPRUS 1960
LEBANON 1944
ISRAEL 1948
EGYPT 1922
ERITREA 1993 (From Ethiopia)
SUDAN 1956
DJIBOUTI 1977
ETHIOPIA
SOMALIA 1960
SEYCHELLES 1976 (From Gr. Br.)
COMOROS 1975 (From France)
MAURITIUS 1968 (From Gr. Br.)

MOROCCO 1956
WESTERN SAHARA 1975 (Morocco) (From Spain)
CAPE VERDE 1975 (From Port.)
MAURITANIA 1960
SENEGAL 1960
GAMBIA 1965
GUINEA-BISSAU 1974
GUINEA 1958
SIERRA LEONE 1961
LIBERIA 1820s
ALGERIA 1962
MALI 1960
NIGER 1960
BURKINA FASO 1960
CÔTE D'IVOIRE 1960
GHANA 1957
TOGO 1960
BENIN 1960
NIGERIA 1960
EQUATORIAL GUINEA 1968 (From Spain)
SÃO TOMÉ AND PRÍNCIPE 1975 (From Port.)
CAMEROON 1960
GABON 1960
REPUBLIC OF CONGO 1960
CENTRAL AFRICAN REPUBLIC 1960
CHAD 1960
TUNISIA 1957
MALTA 1964 (From Gr. Br.)
LIBYA 1951
DEM. REP. OF CONGO 1960
RWANDA 1962
BURUNDI 1962
UGANDA 1962
KENYA 1963
TANZANIA 1964
ANGOLA 1975
ZAMBIA 1964
MALAWI 1964
MOZAMBIQUE 1974
MADAGASCAR 1960
ZIMBABWE 1980
NAMIBIA 1990 (From South Africa)
BOTSWANA 1966
SWAZILAND 1968
LESOTHO 1966
SOUTH AFRICA (Republic 1961)

N

0   1,000   2,000 Mi.
0   1,000   2,000 Km.

Social Revolutionary States

During the twentieth century, revolutionary activity erupted in Asia, Africa, and Latin America, intensified by the drive to end Western domination. This revolutionary activity often engaged peasants impoverished by the loss of their lands or the declining prices for their crops. Revolutionary intellectuals spurred by a Marxist vision mobilized support. Amilcar Cabral **(AM-ill-car ka-BRAWL)** (1924–1973), the revolutionary leader in Portugal's colony of Guinea Bissau **(GIN-ee bi-SOW)**, advised his Marxist colleagues to "always bear in mind that the people are not fighting for ideas, for the things in anyone's head. They are fighting to live better, and in peace, to guarantee the future of their children."[3] Between 1949 and 1980 social revolutionary regimes came to power through force of arms in China, Vietnam, Algeria, Cuba, Nicaragua, Angola, and Mozambique. Opposed by the United States, they necessarily looked to the USSR for political, economic, and military support. Revolutionary movements were also active, although ultimately frustrated, in various other Latin American and Southeast Asian countries.

Thinkers and activists around the world, such as the West Indian–born psychiatrist and writer Frantz Fanon (1925–1961), who joined the anti-French movement while working in colonial Algeria, often romanticized the revolutionaries' promise to create more just societies. Yet scholars of politics disagreed as to whether revolutions ultimately improved lives and righted injustice or instead generated tyranny and economic stagnation. While social revolutionary governments often raised the status and living standards of the poor, they also became bureaucratic, despotic, and intolerant of dissent, frequently compiling poor human rights records. Influenced by Stalinism, they had uneven relations with the capitalist nations. In order to rebuff outside interference, renounce foreign debts, and assume control of their economic direction, these states usually limited their involvement with the world economy, instead creating planned economies in which economic decisions, such as allocation of investment capital, were made by governments rather than through free markets. Nevertheless, many people welcomed the end of the uncaring, often repressive governments the revolutions replaced.

Social revolutionary approaches brought mixed results. Some countries saw their goals sidetracked by civil wars or rebellions. South Africa and the United States supported rebels in Angola who fought the Marxist-dominated government for over two decades, costing over 200,000 lives, ruining much of the country, and diverting resources to the military. In contrast to Angola's woes, between 1949 and 1978 communist-run China was able to increase its economic potential and address social problems, but at a heavy cost in limiting personal freedom. After 1978 China sparked even more rapid growth by modifying its socialist economy with foreign investment and free enterprise. The shift of China, followed by Vietnam, toward market economies and greater participation in the world economy suggested that revolution may have helped nations gain control of their resources but was insufficient to raise living standards to the levels of the richer nations. Yet, China and Vietnam also found that although free markets could create more wealth than socialism, they did not necessarily lead to an equitable distribution of wealth, breeding explosive social tensions.

A New Global System

A new global system emerged after 1945. The prewar world had been dominated by a few great Western powers, led by Britain and France, ruling over vast empires in Asia, Africa, and the Caribbean, but decolonization and the rise of the United States and Soviet Union to superpower status modified this pattern. Many observers now divided the world into three categories of countries, each one having a different level of economic development. The **First World** comprised the industrialized democracies of western Europe, North America, Australia–New Zealand, and Japan. The **Second World** referred to the communist nations, led by the USSR and China. The **Third World** was made up of most societies in Asia, Africa, Latin America, and the Caribbean that were marked by mass poverty and a legacy of Western colonization or neocolonialism. Some experts added a fourth category, the **Fourth World**, which included the poorest societies with very small economies and few exploitable resources, such as Laos, Afghanistan, Haiti, and Mali. However, critics argued that lumping the world's societies—with their very different histories,

CHRONOLOGY
Global Politics, 1945–1989

1945 Formation of United Nations

1946–1975 Decolonization in Asia, Africa, Caribbean

1946–1989 Cold War

1949 Communist victory in China

1950–1953 Korean War

1954 Vietnamese defeat of French

1955 Bandung Conference

1959–1975 U.S.-Vietnam War

1959 Communist victory in Cuba

1962 Cuban Missile Crisis

1968 Widespread political protests

1975 End of Portuguese Empire

1979-1989 Soviet War in Afghanistan

First World The industrialized democracies of western Europe, North America, Australia–New Zealand, and Japan.

Second World The communist nations, led by the USSR and China.

Third World Societies in Asia, Africa, Latin America, and the Caribbean, which were shaped by mass poverty and a legacy of colonization or neocolonialism.

Fourth World The poorest societies, with very small economies and few exploitable resources.

cultures, and global connections—into a few categories was highly misleading. Furthermore, after the 1970s the global system changed. Countries such as Malaysia, South Korea, Dubai (doo-BYE), and Chile, once grouped with the Third World, achieved rapid economic growth, and the communist systems that had defined the Second World often collapsed.

Rich and Poor Nations

At the developed end of the global system, most Western nations and Japan enjoyed new heights of prosperity from the 1960s through the 1980s. After World War II the dominant world power, the United States, offered generous aid and investment to its allies, restarting further economic growth in industrialized, diversified countries that already had literate, skilled, and mostly urban populations. Hence, western Europe and Japan recovered from the ashes of World War II and prospered. Japan's economy increased fivefold between 1953 and 1973, the fastest economic growth in world history. As Western and Japanese businesses invested heavily around the world, international trade soared. Japan and West Germany became the second and third largest capitalist economies. By the 1970s several Western nations, such as West Germany, Sweden, Canada, and Australia, had standards of living similar to those in the United States but far more income equality.

Although economic growth rates often slowed after 1990, Western prosperity relative to the rest of the world continued. Every year the United Nations issues a Human Development Report that rates the quality of life of the world's nations by examining per capita income, health, and literacy. Generally Norway, Sweden, Australia, Canada, and the Netherlands are rated as the most livable nations. A hundred years earlier Norway and Sweden were among the poorest European countries. Now Sweden has achieved the world's lowest poverty rate, largely because the Swedish state provides each citizen with free education, subsidized health care, and other welfare benefits, and the Swedish economy has grown steadily. The reports rank several dozen nations, mostly in sub-Saharan Africa, as having a low quality of life—massive poverty, inadequate health care, and low rates of literacy. Tanzanian president Julius Nyerere (nye-RE-re) put the gap between rich and poor nations in perspective: "While the United States is trying to reach the moon, Tanzania is trying to reach its villages."[4]

Some nations had more political stability and resources to secure their citizens' lives. Richer nations usually benefited from democracy and were nation-states where the large majority shared a common culture and language. Some of these nations did contain restless ethnic or religious minorities. For example, the Basques in northern Spain, whose language and identity differ completely from the Spanish majority, sought autonomy or independence. But democratic governments mostly diminished social tensions, while generous welfare systems prevented mass poverty. Many western European states, Canada, and New Zealand adopted ambitious welfare systems, including comprehensive national health insurance, which promoted social justice and equality. Poorer nations, often with highly diverse populations, small budgets, and limited resources, faced greater challenges in building stable nation-states. Violence, such as the repeated ethnic conflicts in Yugoslavia, occurred in nations that had abandoned communism and its safety net. The fighting between Yugoslavs sometimes resulted in brutal atrocities and the forced expulsion of minorities. Only a few non-European nations, such as Sri Lanka and oil-rich Brunei and Saudi Arabia, tried to mount welfare states with free education and health care, but they struggled to pay for them.

SECTION SUMMARY

- Between 1946 and 1975, most Western colonies achieved independence, in many cases as a result of violent opposition movements, though the United States continued to oppose leftist movements and the Soviet Union's vast colonial empire endured until 1989.

- Western nations maintained a great deal of influence over the economy and culture of many of their former colonies, which led some intellectuals to call for "decolonizing the mind."

- Revolutionary regimes, often inspired by Marxism, came to power in a number of Asian, African, and Latin American nations, though they met with mixed economic success and in some cases were embroiled in long-term civil war.

- The division of the world's nations into First, Second, and Third Worlds grew blurry as some Third World nations developed First-World-level economies and the Soviet Union collapsed, though democratic countries tended to be more stable and offer more support to their citizens.

COLD WAR, HOT WARS, AND WORLD POLITICS

What roles did the Cold War and superpower rivalry play in world politics?

Cold War A conflict lasting from 1946 to 1989 in which the United States and the USSR competed for allies and engaged in occasional warfare against their rival's allies rather than against each other directly.

A new global political configuration emerged after World War II. From 1946 to 1989 the two major superpowers, the United States and the USSR, engaged in the **Cold War**, a conflict in which they competed for allies and engaged in occasional warfare against their rival's allies rather than with each other directly. The United States enjoyed much greater influence and boasted more allies. While the Cold War did not lead to a military conflict in which U.S. and

Soviet military forces fought each other, it produced chronic tensions and led to covert and military interventions by each of the superpowers seeking to block gains by the other.

The Cold War: A Divided World

The world took on a bipolar political character. Nations practicing capitalism and often democracy, led by the United States, were on one side, while those marked by socialist authoritarianism, led by the USSR and known as the Soviet bloc, were on the other. For over four decades U.S.-USSR relations were a major factor in international affairs. The United States sought to contain communism, while the USSR worked to spread communism and undercut American influence. Leaders of nations such as Egypt, India, and Indonesia promoted nonalignment with either superpower. In 1955 leaders from twenty-nine nonaligned Asian and African countries held a conference in Bandung, Indonesia, to gain recognition for what they called a Third World bloc, but they had trouble maintaining unity in the decades to follow.

The United States became the world's most powerful nation, enjoying far greater wealth, military force, and cultural influence than any other nation, including the USSR. In 1945, the United States already had the atomic bomb, produced half of the world's industrial output, and held two-thirds of the gold. Americans seemed willing to bear a heavy financial and military burden to sustain their leading role in world affairs and to promote U.S. economic growth by obtaining raw materials and preserving profitable markets.

By 1948 the Soviets controlled all of eastern Europe and were allied with communist governments in Mongolia and North Korea. After World War II, therefore, U.S. concern shifted to countering the USSR, which Americans perceived as a rival for influence in the world. Americans tried to prevent communists from gaining control of China; then they became involved in the Korean War (1950–1953) to fight successfully the North Korean effort to forcibly reunify the Korean peninsula. Yet, in spite of U.S. efforts, communist regimes came to power in China in 1949, North Vietnam in 1954, and Cuba in 1959. Furthermore, waging the Cold War and using military force to contain communism, including a long war in Vietnam, cost the United States $4 trillion or $5 trillion and some 113,000 American lives, mostly soldiers, between 1946 and 1989.

Historians debate whether the USSR ever posed a serious military threat to the United States and how much both sides misinterpreted their rival's motives and actions. Remembering centuries of invasions from the west, the USSR occupied eastern Europe as a buffer zone and considered the United States and its western European allies a lethal danger whose combined military power greatly exceeded that of the USSR. For their part, Americans mistrusted Soviet leaders and despised communism. While Americans viewed themselves as protecting freedom, the Soviets claimed that they were helping the world's exploited masses and fighting imperialism.

Primary Source: The Long Telegram This critique of the Soviet Union's ideology, authored by an American diplomat in 1946, profoundly influenced the foreign policy of the United States.

Some historians believe the Cold War brought stability, while others point to some eighty wars between 1945 and 1989, resulting in 20 million deaths and perhaps 20 million refugees. The Cold War rivalries also dragged in emerging nations, already damaged by their long, humiliating subservience to Western power, and led to upheavals that bankrupted economies and devastated entire peoples. A series of small conflicts involved surrogates, governments, or movements allied to one superpower and fighting the troops from the other superpower. In Korea and Vietnam U.S. troops battled not Soviet armies but Soviet-supported communist forces. Similarly, the Soviets sent military supplies and advisers to help the Vietnamese communists fight first the French and then the United States, which had supported a pro-Western government in South Vietnam after the French defeat. The communists gained control of the entire country in 1975. Americans also used surrogates, such as when they supplied Islamic groups fighting the Soviets in Afghanistan in the 1980s. Insurgencies using unconventional warfare, such as sniping, sabotaging power plants, and planting roadside bombs, also became common. Insurgents often resorted to **guerrilla warfare**, an unconventional military strategy of avoiding full-scale direct confrontations in favor of small-scale skirmishes. For example, Vietnamese communist guerrillas staged hit-and-run attacks on American patrols and field bases and planted land mines on trails used by American troops.

Cold War Conflicts

guerrilla warfare An unconventional military strategy of avoiding full-scale direct confrontations in favor of small-scale skirmishes.

The Cold War fostered interventions—both covert and military—by both superpowers to protect their interests. The USSR sent military forces into Poland, Hungary, and Czechoslovakia to crush anti-Soviet movements and into Afghanistan to support a pro-Soviet government. Sometimes Soviet invasions proved disastrous; the heavy Soviet losses and humiliating withdrawal from Afghanistan in 1989 contributed to the collapse of the Soviet system. Communist parties established a strong presence in nations such as Indonesia, India, and Chile, where they participated openly in politics, but they also launched unsuccessful insurgencies against governments in

U.S. Interventions

countries such as Peru, Malaysia, and the Philippines. The United States actively sought to shape the political and economic direction of Asian, African, and Latin American societies, often giving generous aid and promoting human rights. Americans generously donated food, disaster and medical assistance, offered technical advice, and supported the growth of democratic organizations. But other efforts destabilized or helped overthrow governments deemed unfriendly to U.S. business and political interests, including left-leaning but democratically elected regimes in Brazil, Chile, and Guatemala.

One of the earliest U.S. interventions came in 1953 in oil-rich Iran, which was governed by a nationalist but noncommunist regime that had angered the Americans and British by nationalizing British- and U.S.-owned oil companies that sent most of their huge profits abroad and paid their Iranian workers less than fifty cents a day. Britain and the United States imposed an economic boycott, making it hard for Iran to sell its oil abroad. American agents also recruited disaffected military officers and paid Iranians to spread rumors and spark riots that paralyzed the capital, forcing the nationalists from power and leading to a pro-U.S. but despotic government. For the first time ever the United States had overthrown a foreign government outside the Western Hemisphere. One result was the long-term hatred of the United States by many ordinary Iranians.

To critics, the U.S. interventions constituted a new form of imperialism. The interventions often proved costly as well. In Vietnam the communist-led forces achieved a military stalemate that cost the United States vast sums of money, killed some 58,000 Americans, and forced it to negotiate for peace and withdraw, harming U.S. prestige in the world. The war also created economic problems in the United States and reduced the U.S. willingness to exercise military power. But the Vietnam conflict also cost the lives of several million Vietnamese on all sides and required the USSR and China to spend scarce resources supplying their communist allies.

The Nuclear Arms Race and Global Militarization

nuclear weapons Explosive devices that owe their destructive power to the energy released by either splitting or fusing atoms.

The superpower arms race and increasing militarization around the world became major components of the Cold War. Both superpowers developed first atomic and then **nuclear weapons**, explosive devices that owe their destructive power to the energy released by either splitting or fusing atoms. These weapons were the most deadly result of the technological surge that can be traced back through Albert Einstein to Sir Isaac Newton and the scientific revolution. A nuclear explosion produces a powerful blast, intense heat, and deadly radiation over a wide area. The United States dropped the first atomic bombs on the Japanese cities of Hiroshima and Nagasaki to end World War II, and both the United States and the USSR eventually developed even more deadly nuclear warheads that could be placed on the tips of missiles. The growth of nuclear arsenals was only the most dangerous part of a larger trend toward the expansion of war-making ability by many nations.

Threats of Mass Destruction

Since 1945 the world has lived in the shadow of nuclear weapons; a small number of them could reduce whole countries to radioactive rubble and, many scientists believe, radically alter global weather patterns. Einstein fretted that the unleashed power of the atom would change everything except peoples' ways of thinking, and he worried that leaders would create a global catastrophe by rashly using the new technologies. Fortunately these weapons were never used after 1945, although the world was close to a nuclear confrontation on several occasions. For example, in 1962, after discovering that the USSR had secretly placed nuclear missiles in Cuba, just 90 miles from Florida, President John F. Kennedy (1917–1963) demanded they be removed but vetoed a U.S. invasion that might have sparked all-out nuclear war. Kennedy rejected attacking Cuba with nuclear weapons, but his firm stance created a tense crisis, ultimately forcing the Soviets to withdraw them. However, before that withdrawal, in response to a U.S. attack on his boat, a Soviet submarine commander armed but did not fire a nuclear missile aimed at Florida, averting catastophe.

The Cold War fostered a balance of terror, with both superpowers unwilling to use their weapons for fear the other would retaliate. Historians debate whether the nuclear arms race preserved the peace by discouraging an all-out U.S.-USSR military confrontation or unsettled international politics and wasted trillions of dollars. Britain, France, China, India, and Pakistan also constructed or acquired nuclear bombs, while countries like Israel, Iran, and North Korea began programs to do the same. Although in 1987 the two superpowers negotiated their first treaty to reduce their nuclear arms, concerns grew about nuclear proliferation, especially that North Korea or Pakistan could sell bombs to other countries or terrorist groups. But some outside the West argued that the monopoly on such weapons by a few powerful nations was unfair.

Costs of Militarization

The proportion of total world production and spending devoted to militaries grew dramatically during the Cold War. By 1985, the world was spending more on military forces and weapons than the combined income of the poorest 50 percent of the world's countries. The two superpowers together, with 11 percent of the world population, accounted for 60 percent of military spending, 25 percent of the world's armed forces, and 97 percent of its nuclear weapons. They also sold conventional weapons to other countries with which they had friendly relations.

The varied wars since 1945 caused enormous casualties, with civilians accounting for some three-fourths of the casualties. Two million people died during the Chinese civil war (1945–1949), 800,000 during the violent partition of India (1948), 2 million during the American-Vietnamese War, 1 million during the Nigerian civil war (1967), and more than 2 million in the Cambodian violence from 1970 to 1978. Millions of these deaths resulted from genocide. For example, in the 1990s members of the Hutu majority slaughtered people belonging to the Tutsi minority in Rwanda (roo-AHN-duh), while extremist Serbs killed Bosnian and Albanian Muslims in Yugoslavia, in a policy they called "ethnic cleansing." The Yugoslav killings were finally stopped when the United States and western European nations sent in troops to restore order and punish the worst human rights violators.

Global Organizations and Activism

During the Cold War, more than ever before in history, public and private organizations with a global reach and mission promoted political cooperation and addressed various social, political, economc, and environmental issues. The largest effort to cooperate for the common good, the United Nations, was founded in 1945 with fifty-one members, becoming a key forum for global debate and an agency for improving global conditions. The United Nations Charter enumerated the founding principles: "To develop friendly relations among nations based on respect for the principle of equal rights and self-determination of peoples and to take other appropriate measures to strengthen universal peace." The founding members aimed to "save succeeding generations from the scourge of war, reaffirm faith in fundamental rights, and respect international law."[5] As colonies gained independence and joined, the organization grew to nearly two hundred member states. The United Nations sponsored humanitarian agencies such as the World Health Organization, which monitored diseases, funded and fostered medical research, and promoted public health, and the United Nations Children Fund (UNICEF), which promoted children's welfare and education around the world. Such U.N.-sponsored programs helped increase average life expectancy from 45 in 1900 to 75 in 2000, as well as greatly reducing the risk of mothers dying in childbirth. Yet, critics believed that political differences often obstructed the United Nation's work.

The five major powers of 1945 (the United States, China, Britain, France, and the USSR) enjoyed permanent seats with veto power in the policy-making U.N. Security Council, and both superpowers vetoed decisions that challenged their national interests. Hence, the United States often vetoed resolutions aimed at penalizing Israel, and it also blocked the communist government from occupying China's seat in the United Nations. The Security Council also sometimes sent peacekeeping troops into troubled countries. However, the United Nations discouraged, but could not prevent, states from resorting to force. To gain support for a possible military action, nations often felt it necessary to make their case before the Security Council; sometimes they received support, as when a United States–led U.N. military force repulsed a North Korean invasion of South Korea. However, nations often ignored widespread disapproval by the organization's members, as the United States did when it invaded Iraq in 2003.

Nations also forged international agreements and treaties, such as an agreement in 1972 banning biological weapons. In 1997, 132 nations signed an international treaty to ban the production, use, and export of land mines, which kill and injure civilians years after the end of conflicts. In 1997 most nations also signed the Kyoto Protocol, pledging to reduce the harmful gases that contribute to global warming. In 2002 a treaty established an International Criminal Court to prosecute the perpetrators of genocide, war crimes, and crimes against humanity. But the United States and several other industrial nations refused to ratify these modest efforts to reduce weapons, promote environmental stability, and establish accountability for international crimes.

Private organizations and activists also worked for issues of peace, social justice, health, refugees, famine, conflict resolution, and environmental protection. For example, Doctors Without Borders offered medical personnel, and Amnesty International worked to free political prisoners. Some religious leaders promoted world peace, justice, and humanitarian issues. The Dalai Lama (b. 1935), the highest Tibetan Buddhist spiritual leader, won the Nobel Peace Prize in 1989 for his efforts to promote human rights, nonviolent conflict resolution, and understanding among different religions. In 1997 the Dalai Lama pleaded, "We all have a special responsibility to create

The United Nations

International Agreements

U.N. Peacekeepers in Congo   The United Nations has regularly sent peacekeepers into troubled countries such as the Congo. This photo, from 2003, shows U.N. troops from Uruguay guarding a U.N. office while a Congolese woman and her four children, displaced from her village by factional fighting, seek U.N. help.

AP/World Wide Photos

a better world. No one loses, and everyone gains by a shared universal sense of responsibility to this planet and all living things on it."[6] Similarly, the Aga Khan IV (b. 1936), the spiritual leader of a largely Indian Shi'ite Muslim sect, funded schools and clinics all over the world. The World Council of Churches, supported by diverse Protestant and Eastern Orthodox churches, encouraged interfaith cooperation and understanding, and several Catholic popes favored interfaith dialogue and denounced war and capital punishment.

World Politics Since 1989

U.S. as Sole Superpower

Between 1989 and 1991 the Soviet bloc disintegrated and the communist regimes in eastern Europe and the USSR collapsed, ending the Cold War and the bipolar world it had defined (see Chronology: Global Politics Since 1989). Longtime State Department official George Kennan (1904–2004), the architect of the U.S. policy to contain communism in the 1940s, concluded that no country or person "won" the Cold War because it was fueled by misconceptions and nearly bankrupted both sides. Other nations, especially Japan and West Germany, both protected by U.S. military bases, had gained the most economically from the conflict by investing heavily in economic growth. As both U.S. and Soviet leaders deescalated tensions in the later 1980s, the United States became the sole superpower. By 2008 it spent as much on defense as all other countries combined and was the world's major supplier of arms. Yet some observers perceived a tripolar system in which the United States had to share political and economic leadership with western Europe and several Asian nations, especially China, Japan, and India.

The first major post–Cold War challenge for the United States came from Iraq's brutal dictator, Saddam Hussein (1937–2006), whose army invaded and occupied Iraq's small, oil-rich neighbor, Kuwait, in 1990. Since the United States opposed the Islamic government of Iran, it had supported Saddam's military with weapons in the 1980s, when Iraq was fighting Iran. Now the United States organized an international coalition and, in 1991, quickly defeated the Iraqis, pushing them out of Kuwait. In the aftermath, U.S. president George H. W. Bush proclaimed a "new world order" led by the United States and based on American values, envisioning the United States as a world policeman.

New World Disorder

The end of the long, costly Cold War did not result in universal peace or the triumph of American political values. Instead, the 1990s saw a new world disorder. Ethnic and nationalist conflicts exploded in violence in Yugoslavia, eastern Europe, Sri Lanka, west Africa, and Rwanda, and states with weak or dysfunctional governments, such as Haiti, Liberia, Sierra Leone, Congo, and Somalia, experienced chronic fighting and civil war. In addition, rising tides of religious militancy or conflict between rival faiths complicated politics in countries such a s India, Indonesia, Algeria, Egypt, and Nigeria. In particular, militant Islam demonstrated its potency in Iran, Sudan, and Afghanistan and led some extremists to form terrorist groups to fight moderate Islamic regimes, Israel, and Western nations. By the early 2000s Islamic radicals posed a greater challenge in Southeast Asia and the Middle East than the declining communist movements. The ambitions of aggressive dictators, such as Iraq's Saddam Hussein, and the communist regime in North Korea, which limited contact with the outside world, also fostered regional tensions. Then in 2008 a severe global recession added to the problems as businesses closed, world trade declined, and national economies floundered. The new world order promise of a peaceful world moving, with U.S. support, toward democracy foundered on the shoals of proliferating regional, nationalist, religious, and ethnic conflicts that, combined with economic collapse, produced a context for violence.

CHRONOLOGY
Global Politics, Since 1999

1989–1991 Dismantling of Soviet bloc and empire

1997 Kyoto Protocol on climate change

2001 Al Qaeda attack on United States

2003 U.S. invasion of Iraq

2008–2009 Global recession

SECTION SUMMARY

- During the Cold War, the United States and the USSR struggled for world control, with the United States generally favoring democracy and capitalism but also seeking access to resources and foreign markets, and the USSR supporting emerging communist regimes and movements.

- Though the United States and the USSR never fought directly, they were involved in wars in other countries, such as Vietnam, Korea, and Afghanistan, in which millions died, and they intervened in countries such as Guatemala, Iran, Poland, Hungary, and Czechoslovakia.

- The United States and the USSR participated in a massive arms race, spending trillions of dollars on nuclear weapons, which led to widespread fear of mass destruction, though some argue that this fear helped prevent all-out war.

- The United Nations was formed with the goal of promoting world peace and human rights, and various agreements have been signed to ban biological weapons and land mines, to prevent global warming, and to facilitate an international justice system, though they have encountered opposition by the United States and some other industrial nations.

- When the Soviet Union collapsed, the United States was the sole superpower, with a military budget dwarfing that of other countries and dreams of a peaceful democratic world, but religious extremism and ethnic and nationalist conflicts have ensured continuing conflict.

GLOBALIZING ECONOMIES, UNDERDEVELOPMENT, AND ENVIRONMENTAL CHANGE

What were some of the main consequences of a globalizing world economy?

The world economy was increasingly characterized by **globalization**, a pattern in which economic, political, and cultural processes reach beyond national boundaries. This trend reduced barriers between countries, allowing for more collaboration, and turned the world into a more closely integrated whole through worldwide commercial markets, finance, telecommunications, and the exchange of ideas. However, globalization also generated a widening inequality of nations and negative environmental consequences from industrialization and economic growth, including ever-increasing pollution and a warming climate. In response to population growth, people expanded agriculture into semidesert areas and cut down rain forests, causing environmental deterioration.

globalization A pattern in which economic, political, and cultural processes reach beyond nation-state boundaries.

The Transnational Economy

A world economy that links distant societies has been developing over the past 2,500 years, but after World War II globalization rapidly spread market capitalism as well as flows of capital, goods, services, and people. The world's production of goods and services was 120 times higher in 2000 than it had been in 1500, and average personal income grew fourfold between 1900 and

Economic Growth

2000. As the interconnectedness between societies has increased, events occurring or decisions taken in one part of the world affect societies far away. Rising or falling prices on the Tokyo or New York stock exchanges quickly reverberate around the world, influencing stock markets elsewhere. Similarly, the decision by Western governments to sell supplies of stockpiled rubber, hence depressing world prices, affects the livelihood of rubber growers, and the businesses that supply them, in Malaysia, Sri Lanka, Brazil, and the Congo. Not all the transnational economic activity has been legal, especially the flow of narcotics. Heroin and cocaine sold in North America and Europe, creating millions of addicts, originates largely in Asia and Latin America and is smuggled by transnational criminal syndicates.

Changing World Economy

Americans have been the major proponent of globalization, arguing that open markets, investment, and trade foster prosperity. By 2000 the United States produced nearly a third of the world's goods and services; Japan, with the next largest economy, accounted for around a sixth. International observers described U.S. leadership metaphorically: when the United States sneezes, the rest of the world catches cold. However, economic growth does not necessarily improve the living conditions for all people; well-functioning governments, legal and political rights, and health and education services are also required. Moreover, critics charge that globalization promises riches it does not always deliver, distributing the benefits unequally. By the 1990s the United States and China were gaining the most from removing trade barriers and fostering competitive markets worldwide. Both sucked in investment capital, aggressively acquired natural resources from around the globe, and supplied diverse products to foreign markets. China surpassed Germany to become the world's third largest economy as Chinese factories turned out clothing, housewares, and other consumer goods. The Chinese also began investing in Africa, Latin America, and the Middle East and buying U.S.-based companies. However, not all Chinese benefited. China's less-efficient state-owned enterprises often closed down, while peasants protested as their farmland was bulldozed to build foreign-owned factories, private housing developments, and golf courses for affluent Chinese.

A few other nations, such as India, Ireland, Singapore, and South Korea, also capitalized on globalization, fostering economic growth and becoming centers of high technology. But not all countries enjoyed such success. By the 1990s Japan and some European nations struggled to compete in the globalizing economy, while many Asian, African, and Caribbean nations fell deeper into poverty. Many people in developing nations—Mexican corn growers, West African wheat growers, Pakistani textile workers—faced trade barriers and well-funded, technologically superior Western competitors. As U.N. Secretary General Kofi Annan (KO-fee AN-uhn), a Ghanaian, put it in 2002: "Our challenge today is to make globalization an engine that lifts people out of hardship and misery, not a force that holds them down."[7]

Although experiencing occasional setbacks, the Western industrial nations and Japan have generally maintained a favorable position in the global economy. They control most of the capital, markets, and institutions of international finance, such as banks, and their corporations also own assets in other nations. For example, U.S. citizens control businesses, mines, and plantations in Latin America, Japanese operate factories in Southeast Asia, and the French maintain a large economic stake in West Africa. The capitalist systems in the industrialized nations have ranged from limited government interference, common in the United States, to the mix of free markets and welfare states in western Europe, to the closely linked government-business relationship in Japan and South Korea. These contrast with the economies in many former colonies where power holders, often closely tied to foreign or domestic business interests, preside over largely poor populations. Hence, in the Congo, corrupt leaders protect Belgian-owned and local corporations who fund them.

Newly Industrializing Nations

Some once-poor countries have used the transnational economy to their advantage, achieving spectacular growth. If revenues are not stolen by corrupt leaders, as has happened in Iraq and Nigeria, possession of oil can enhance national wealth. A few oil-rich nations, such as Kuwait and the United Arab Emirates, use oil revenues to improve their citizens' lives. Various Asian countries, much like Japan in the late 1800s, have combined market economies, cheap labor, and powerful governments to promote industrialization. By repressing opposition, they have ensured political stability and attracted foreign investment. These countries have favored export-oriented growth, producing consumer goods—clothing, toys, housewares—for sale abroad, especially in Europe and North America, and fostering high growth rates and the import of industrial jobs from other, often Western, countries. Beginning in the 1980s China, South Korea, Taiwan, Malaysia, Thailand, Singapore, and eventually Vietnam created the world's fastest-growing economies and considerable prosperity, their major cities boasting well-stocked malls, freeways, diverse restaurants, and luxury condominiums.

Often the growing middle class and labor leaders have demanded a larger voice in government and political liberalization. By the 1990s Indonesians, South Koreans, Taiwanese, and Thais had replaced dictatorships with democratic governments. The Asian systems became development models by mixing capitalism, which creates wealth, with socialism, which can distribute wealth equitably. With this combination, the Asian economic resurgence seemed to have the potential to restore the leading role some Asian societies had enjoyed in the world economy for many centuries before 1800. But in the late 1990s the economies of many Asian nations crashed and only slowly rebounded, only to be damaged again in 2008–2009 as the U.S. economic crisis affected Asia and the rest of the world. Factories closed and revenues declined, causing massive unemployment and hardship. By later 2009 some Asian nations, including China and India, re-established strong growth.

Various institutions shaped the transnational economy, especially the international lending agencies formed by the Allies in 1944 to aid postwar reconstruction. The World Bank funded development projects such as dams and agricultural schemes, and the International Monetary Fund (IMF) regulated currency dealings and addressed financial problems. Many Asian, African, Caribbean, and Latin American nations did not earn enough income from selling natural resources to buy food and medicine, import luxuries, or finance projects such as building dams and improving ports. Hence, they took out loans from the IMF or the World Bank, closely linked to the United States. Some Latin American and African countries fell deeply in debt. Moreover, the IMF, which had the right to dictate economic policies to borrowing countries, favored Western investment and free markets at the expense of social services.

Trade agreements and trading blocs have also reflected an economic connectedness unprecedented in world history. Formed in 1947, the General Agreements on Trade and Tariffs (GATT) set general guidelines for world trade and rules for establishing tariffs and trade regulations (see Chronology: The Global Economy and New Technologies). The World Trade Organization (WTO), founded by 124 nations in 1995, marked a new phase in the postwar economic system. The WTO had stronger dispute-resolution capabilities than GATT. Regional trading blocs also formed. The European Common Market (now the European Union) eventually included most European nations. The major industrial nations also cooperated to manage the global economy. By the 1990s leading economic officials in the seven richest industrial countries met regularly as the G7 (Group of 7) to discuss common concerns, later joined by Russia to form the G8. But China, India, and other newly industrialized nations sought more input. Thanks to the 2008–2009 economic crisis and the need for concerted action on a world scale, by late 2009 the G8 leaders agreed to permanently expand the discussion to include 12 other countries with large economies, such as China, India, Brazil, Indonesia, South Korea, and Argentina. This new G20 grouping confirmed the changing world economic leadership and especially the key role of China.

Another development is the growth of giant business enterprises, known as **multinational corporations** because they operate all over the world, which have gained a leading role in the

CHRONOLOGY
The Global Economy and New Technologies

1947 Formation of GATT

1947 Invention of transistor

1958 Invention of silicon microchips

1995 Formation of World Trade Organization

1997 Asian economic collapse

2008–2009 Global recession

Trade Agreements and Blocs

multinational corporations Giant business enterprises that operate all over the world, gaining a leading role in the global marketplace.

The Global Economy
Cambodian Buddhist monks, following ancient traditions, collect their food from the devout in the capital city, Phnom Penh, while advertising for American cigarettes entices Cambodians into the global economy, despite government concerns about the health danger posed by tobacco products.

AP/World Wide Photos

global marketplace. Some 300 to 400 companies, two-thirds of them U.S.-owned, dominate world production and trade. These are now the world's third largest economic force, with great influence on governments. The multinationals set the world price for various commodities, such as coffee, copper, or oil; can play one country off against another to get the best deal; and can switch manufacturing jobs from one country to another. Multinationals have also created millions of jobs in poor countries. Increasingly women provide the majority of the labor force in the global assembly lines of factories producing for export. Supporters argue that outsourcing—moving jobs from high-wage to low-wage countries—creates a middle class of managers and technicians and offers work to people with few other job prospects. Critics reply that most of these jobs pay low wages, require long hours, and offer little future. For example, the U.S.-based Nike Corporation, praised for creating needed jobs in Vietnam, is also criticized because the Vietnamese employees, mainly women, work in unhealthy conditions, face sexual harassment, and are fired if they complain.

The Spread of Industrialization

Industrial Growth

During the later twentieth century, industrialization spread to other parts of the world, especially to Asia and Latin America. Entrepreneurs or state agencies in countries such as China, India, South Korea, Brazil, and Mexico built textile mills, steel mills, and automobile plants, and Chinese textiles, Indian steel, and South Korean cars found markets around the world. Meanwhile, the U.S. share of world industrial production fell from 50 percent in 1950 to 30 percent in the 1980s; whereas Americans built over 75 percent of all cars in 1950, by the early 1990s they built less than 20 percent. Malaysians could now drive Volvos made in Sweden, Hyundais made in South Korea, Toyotas made in Japan, and Proton Sagas manufactured locally.

Third Industrial Revolution The creation of unprecedented scientific knowledge and new technologies.

Technological innovations spurred economic growth. The so-called **Third Industrial Revolution** created unprecedented scientific knowledge and new technologies that made the creations of the first and second Industrial Revolutions seem obsolete. Traditional smokestack industries such as steel mills were displaced by nuclear power, computers, automation, and robotry. The technological surge also brought rocketry, genetic engineering, silicon chips, and lasers. Space technology produced the first manned trips to the moon and unmanned crafts exploring the solar system. In 2005 a probe from one of these crafts landed on Saturn's large, mysterious moon, Titan, sending back photographs of the surface. More powerful telescopes increased knowledge of the solar system and the universe, including the discovery of several hundred planets circling other stars. The British poet Archibald MacLeish observed that the astronauts on the space capsules circling the planet did not perceive national boundaries or international rivalries, but only oceans and lands containing people with a common planetary home: "To see the Earth as we now see it, small and blue and beautiful in that eternal silence [of space] where it floats, is to see ourselves as rulers on the Earth together."[8]

Green Revolution Increased agricultural output through the use of new high-yield seeds and mechanized farming.

The Third Industrial Revolution has had potentially dramatic consequences for people around the world. Part of it, the **Green Revolution**, has fostered increased agricultural output through the use of new high-yield seeds and mechanized farming. Farmers able to afford these innovations can shorten the growing season, thus raising more crops a year. Between 1965 and 1978, one village in India increased its food output by 300 percent. But not all farmers benefited. In countries such as India, the Philippines, and Mexico, the Green Revolution, which requires more capital for seeds and machines but fewer people to work the land, has often harmed poor peasants who could not afford the investment. And in many industries, such as automobile manufacturing, automation has taken over production, allowing companies to fire workers.

Globalizing Industry

Industry also became globalized. By the 1990s over two hundred industrial parks, occupied largely by foreign-owned factories paying low taxes and wages, existed around the world. For example, factories in northern Mexico, usually U.S.-owned, made goods largely for the U.S. market and employed nearly half a million workers, mainly women. The service and information exchange industries also grew. More people worked in service enterprises, such as fast-food restaurants, while others established transnational computer networks, such as AOL and Google, to help people use the Internet for communication and knowledge acquisition. Responding to these trends, India graduated each year thousands of people fluent in English and skilled in computer technology, becoming a world center for offshore information and technical services. Increasingly consumers calling North American companies for computer technical support, product information, or billing questions reached Indians working in cubicles in cities such as Bangalore and Bombay (Mumbai).

Yet, industrialization and its globalization have come with risks. Hoping to better compete, businesses have moved factories to countries with low wages and costs. Some Western and Japanese businesses have shifted operations to South Korea or Taiwan, where the average worker earns in a month what a U.S. or German worker earns in a week or ten days, yet produces as much. Others have established operations in Asian, African, Latin American, or eastern European nations where workers earn even less. In 1990 the U.S. clothing maker Levi Strauss closed its plant in San Antonio, Texas; laid off 1,150 workers, most of them Mexican American women; and relocated the operation to Costa Rica. Viola Casares, one of the fired workers, expressed the despair: "As long as I live I'll never forget how the white man in the suit said they had to shut us down to stay competitive."[9] Levi Strauss closed fifty-eight U.S. plants with over 10,000 workers while shifting half of its production overseas.

Underdevelopment and Development

Uneven economic growth has contributed to a growing gap between rich nations and poor undeveloped nations. The gap was already wide in 1945, since colonialism seldom raised people's general living standards. As a Guyanese historian concluded, "the vast majority of Africans went into colonialism with a hoe and came out with a hoe."[10] But fluctuation in the world economy has also caused hardships. Many Asian, African, and Latin American economies grew rapidly in the 1950s and 1960s, when the world economy boomed. Then in the 1970s and 1980s, as the world economy soured and the world prices for many exports collapsed, the growth rates of these economies declined. Then the world economy revived for a few years, only to experience a dramatic downturn in the later 1990s and early 2000s. In 2008–2009 the world economy went into the worst crisis since the Great Depression, affecting many nations severely, but some Asian and European countries began to recover in later 2009.

Moreover, economic growth has not always fostered development that benefits the majority of the population. With globalization, rich countries encourage other nations to open their economies to foreign investment. Some Asian nations have prospered from this investment, building schools, hospitals, and highways, but elsewhere Western investment often has done little to foster locally owned businesses. In Nigeria, for example, British-owned enterprises have controlled banking, importing, and exporting, and foreign investment has gone mainly into cash crops and oil production, controlled largely by Western companies. Outraged that they gain little from the polluting oil wells around them, local people in Nigeria's main oil-producing region have sabotaged operations and kidnapped foreign oil workers. Some resorted to armed insurgency against government targets. Furthermore, foreign investment and aid has often been siphoned off to line the pockets of corrupt leaders, bureaucrats, and military officers.

Scholars debate how poor countries can better profit from their connections to the world economy and spur local efforts at development. One of the most influential economists, the Indian Amartya Sen (b. 1933), had helped run evening schools for illiterate rural children as a youth. This experience laid a foundation for his studies of global poverty, for which he won the Nobel Prize in economics in 1998. Sen believes that the main challenges are how to use trade and technology to help the poorest people by addressing famine, poverty, and social and gender inequality. Influenced by his first wife, a prominent Indian writer and political activist, Sen focused on women in development. Sen argues that women's literacy and employment are the best predictors of both child survival and fertility rate reduction, prerequisites for development in poor villages. His views on poverty and gender inequality influenced the United Nations when, in 2000, they developed an agenda to address the world's pressing problems by 2020 (see Witness to the Past: An Agenda for the New Millennium). However, without outside financial support, few poor countries have sufficient resources to seriously combat widespread poverty or promote women's empowerment.

While some nations have become richer, others have become poorer. Most poor nations have suffered from some combination of rapid population growth, high unemployment, illiteracy, hunger, disease, corrupt or ineffective governments, and reliance on only a few exports. By the 1990s the richest fifth of the world's people received 80 percent of the total income

Growing Rich–Poor Gap

Rich and Poor in Brazil   The stark contrast between the wealthy and the poor in many nations can be seen in the Brazilian city of Rio de Janeiro. Seeking jobs in expanding industries, millions of migrants flock to the city, building shanty-town slums and squatter settlements in view of luxury high-rise apartment and office buildings.

Stephanie Maze/Woodfin Camp & Associates

An Agenda for the New Millennium

In 2000 the United Nations called together the 188 member states for a summit at its headquarters in New York City to discuss the issues facing the world during the new millennium. In the following document, distributed before the summit, the United Nations secretary general, Kofi Annan of Ghana (GAH-nuh), laid out his vision for the organization and the challenges it faced in a world that had changed dramatically since the organization's formation over five decades earlier.

If one word encapsulates the changes we are living through, it is "globalization." We live in a world that is interconnected as never before—one in which groups and individuals interact more and more directly across State frontiers. . . . This has its dangers, of course. Crime, narcotics, terrorism, disease, weapons—all these move back and forth faster, and in greater numbers, than in the past. People feel threatened by events far away. But the benefits of globalization are obvious too: faster growth, higher living standards, and new opportunities—not only for individuals but also for better understanding between nations, and for common action.

One problem is that, at present, these opportunities are far from equally distributed. How can we say that the half of the human race which has yet to make or receive a phone call, let alone use a computer, is taking part in globalization? We cannot, without insulting their poverty. A second problem is that, even where the global market does reach, it is not yet underpinned by rules based on shared social objectives. In the absence of such rules, globalization makes many people feel they are at the mercy of unpredictable forces. So, . . . the overarching challenge of our times is to make globalization mean more than bigger markets. To make a success of this great upheaval we must learn how to govern better, and . . . how to govern together. . . . We need to get [our nations] working together on global issues—all pulling their weight and all having their say.

What are these global issues? . . . First, freedom from want. How can we call human beings free and equal in dignity when over a billion of them are struggling to survive on less than one dollar a day, without safe drinking water, and when half of all humanity lacks adequate sanitation? Some of us are worrying about whether the stock market will crash, or struggling to master our latest computer, while more than half our fellow men and women have much more basic worries, such as where their children's next meal is coming from. . . . I believe we can halve the population of people living in extreme poverty; ensure that all children—girls and boys alike, particularly the girls—receive a full primary education; and . . . transform the lives of one hundred million slum dwellers around the world.

The second main [issue] is freedom from fear. Wars between States are mercifully less frequent than they used to be. But in the last decade internal wars have claimed more than five million lives, and driven many times that number of people from their homes. . . . We must do more to prevent conflicts from happening. Most conflicts happen in poor countries, especially those which are badly governed or where power and wealth are very unfairly distributed between ethnic or religious groups. So the best way to prevent conflict is to promote [fair representation of all groups in government], human rights, and broad-based economic development.

The third [issue] is . . . the freedom of future generations to sustain their lives on this planet. Even now, many of us have not understood how seriously that freedom is threatened. We are plundering our children's heritage to pay for our present unsustainable practices. We must stop. We must reduce emissions of . . . "greenhouse gases," to put a stop to global warming. . . . We must face the implications of a steadily shrinking surface of cultivable land, at a time when every year brings many millions of new mouths to feed. . . . We must preserve our forests, fisheries, and the diversity of living species, all of which are close to collapsing under the pressure of human consumption and destruction. . . . We need a new ethic of stewardship to encourage environment-friendly practices. . . . Above all we need to remember the old African wisdom which I learned as a child—that the earth is not ours. It is a treasure we hold in trust for our descendants.

THINKING ABOUT THE READING

1. What does Annan see as the major global issues of the new millennium?

2. How are the problems he outlined connected to each other?

Source: United Nations, *The Millennium Report* (*http://www.un.org/millennium/sg/report/state.htm*). Reprinted with permission of the United Nations.

while the poorest fifth earned less than 2 percent. For example, in Guatemala, 90 percent of people lived below the official poverty line, and nearly half had no access to health care, indoor plumbing, piped water, or formal education. A fifth of the world's people earned less than $1 per day. By 2000 the world's three richest persons owned more assets than the forty-eight poorest nations together, and 358 billionaires had a combined net worth equal to that of the bottom 45 percent of the world's population combined. The United Nations estimated that one billion people suffered from hunger in 2009, a problem made worse by the global recession. Furthermore, despite preaching the benefits of free trade, rich nations have often blocked or restricted food and fiber exports from poor nations into their own markets while heavily subsidizing their own farmers. Hence, wheat farmers in Mali, however industrious, cannot compete with French or U.S. wheat farmers, who can sell their crops at much lower prices because of the financial support from their governments.

Yet, the nations outside of Europe and North America can boast of achievements. Between 1960 and 2000 they reduced infant mortality by half and doubled adult literacy rates. China, Sri Lanka, Malaysia, and Tanzania have been particularly successful in providing social services, such as schools and clinics, to rural areas. Various countries have developed their own locally based development strategies. In sub-Saharan Africa, for instance, some countries, such as Burkina Faso (buhr-KEE-nuh FAH-so) and Niger (nee-jer), have moved away from big, expensive prestige projects—such as building large dams to supply hydroelectric power—to small-scale labor-intensive projects that aid the environment, such as tree-planting campaigns, while local cooperative banks have provided credit to farmers. However, severe drought can still cause widespread starvation.

Improving Lives

Women and their children have faced the harshest problems. Economic change has not only undermined the handicrafts that once provided incomes for women, but it has also fragmented families: many men have to find work in other districts or countries, leaving their wives to support and raise the children. In Africa, men migrate each year from Burkina Faso to the Ivory Coast's cocoa plantations and logging camps, and from Mozambique to South African mines. Meanwhile, women leave India, Sri Lanka, and the Philippines to work as domestic servants in the Persian Gulf states and Saudi Arabia, some facing sexual harassment or cruel employers. Asian and Latin American women work in homes and sweatshops in North America and Europe.

Economic Change and Gender Relations

Development often leaves women behind because of their inferior social status and relative invisibility in national economic statistics. For example, women often face social customs that accord them little influence and, in case of divorce, award their children to the father. An Indian folk song expressed the bitterness of village women who, after marriage, have no claim on their birth family's property: "To my brother belong your green fields, O father, while I am banished afar."[11] While women do 60 percent of the world's work and produce 50 to 75 percent of the world's food, they own only 1 percent of the world's property and earn 10 percent of the world's income. Most of poor women's labor—food preparation, cleaning, child rearing—is unpaid, done at home, and often demanding. In Senegal a typical rural woman, married at a young age, gets up at 5 A.M. to pound millet, the staple food, for an hour. She then walks a few hundred yards or perhaps several miles to get water from a well, makes breakfast for the family, goes to the village shop, makes the family lunch, takes food to family members working in the fields, does laundry, makes supper, and then pounds millet again before bed. Some women combine all this with farm work.

Some nations help women and children through bottom-up policies relying on grassroots action. The Grameen (GRAH-mean) Bank in Bangladesh, which promotes a philosophy of self-help, provides an outstanding model. After meeting a woman matmaker who earned only four cents a day, the economist Muhammad Yunus (b. 1940) concluded that conventional economics ignored the poverty and struggles occurring in his nation's villages. Learning that few banks made loans to the poor, in 1983 Yunus opened the Grameen Bank, which makes loans under $100 on cheap terms to peasants, especially women, for buying the tools they needed to earn a living. A borrower might buy a cell phone that villagers could use to make business or personal calls, paying the owner for each call, or purchase bamboo to make chairs. Less than 2 percent of borrowers defaulted. The women earning an income now enjoyed higher social status and many began using contraceptives, helping lower the Bangladesh birthrate from 3 to 2 percent a year. For his vision and efforts, Muhammad Yunus won the Nobel Peace Prize in 2006.

Population, Urbanization, and Environmental Change

Rapid population growth and overcrowded cities have become manifestations of global imbalance. Since 1945 the world's population has grown faster than ever before in history (see Map 26.2). Two thousand years ago the earth had between 125 and 250 million people; it took roughly 10,000 generations for the world to reach 1 billion in 1830. At the end of World War II the population had risen to 2.5 billion, and by 2008 it had more than doubled to 6.7 billion. Some experts talked of a "population bomb" overwhelming the world's water, food sources, forests, and minerals and a population of perhaps 12 billion by 2100, which the earth's resources could not support. But fertility rates began dropping in much of the world, especially in industrialized nations, thanks to the widespread use of artificial birth control, such as contraceptive pills, better health care, and larger numbers of women entering the paid work force. By 1990 over half of the world's couples practiced some form of contraception to prevent births. As a result, demographers now envision a world population of some 9 billion by 2050, which will still impose a heavy burden on food supplies and services and intensify social, economic, and environmental problems. For example, overpopulation, and the ensuing competition for limited resources, probably contributed to violence in crowded countries such as Ethiopia,

Rising Population

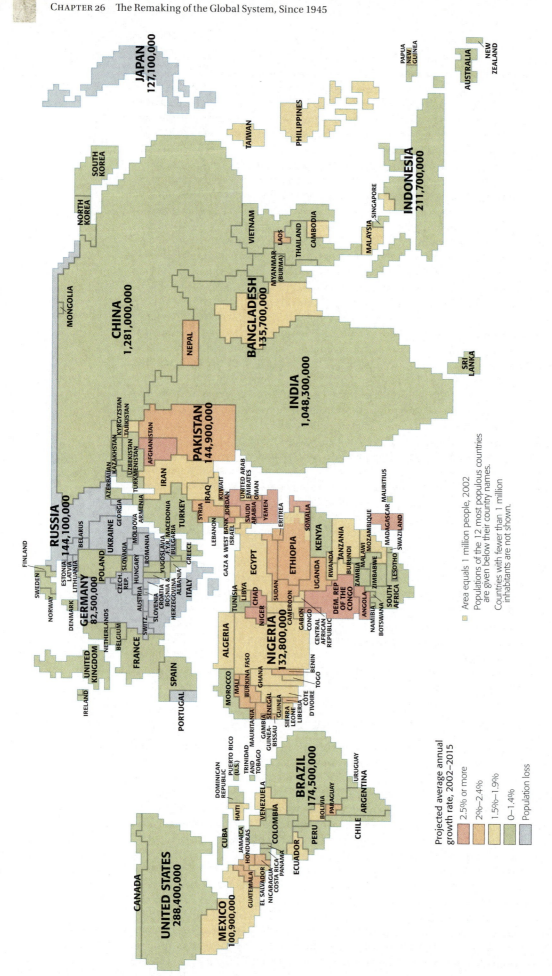

Interactive Map

Map 26.2 World Population Growth

This map shows dramatically which nations have the largest populations: China, India, the United States, Indonesia, and Brazil. It also shows which regions experience the most rapid population growth: Africa, South Asia, and Central America.

Projected average annual growth rate, 2002–2015

- 2.5% or more
- 2%–2.4%
- 1.5%–1.9%
- 0–1.4%
- Population loss

Area equals 1 million people, 2002

Populations of the 12 most populous countries are given below their country names.

Countries with fewer than 1 million inhabitants are not shown.

JAPAN 127,100,000

CHINA 1,281,000,000

INDONESIA 211,700,000

RUSSIA 144,100,000

GERMANY 82,500,000

BANGLADESH 135,700,000

INDIA 1,048,300,000

PAKISTAN 144,900,000

NIGERIA 132,800,000

BRAZIL 174,500,000

UNITED STATES 288,400,000

MEXICO 100,900,000

Rwanda, and El Salvador. Several British studies in 2009 predicted a worldwide 50 percent rise in demand for food, 30 percent for water, and 50 percent for energy by 2030.

Population growth has been more rapid in some regions. Most of it has occurred in Asia, Africa, and Latin America. By 2000, China and India had the largest populations, with around a billion people each. While Asia has continued, as it has for millennia, to house at least 60 percent of humanity, Europe's share of population fell from a quarter in 1900 to an eighth. Because of their falling birthrates, various European nations, Russia, China, and Japan have declining and aging populations, which puts a growing burden on those of working age to produce more wealth to support elderly populations. Italy and Spain, both predominantly Roman Catholic nations that once had high birthrates, now have the world's lowest fertility rates. North American birthrates have also dropped, but the decline has been offset by immigration.

Nonetheless, the Western nations, Japan, and recently China, enjoying high rates of resource consumption, including fossil fuels, have done more harm to the environment than countries with large populations but low consumption rates. Owing to heavy use of energy and metals-dependent innovations—air conditioners, central heating systems, gasoline-powered vehicles, refrigerators—the average American or Canadian consumes some twenty times, and the average Australian, German, or Japanese ten to fifteen times, the resources of the average Pakistani or Peruvian.

Population growth has diminished the possibility for economic development in overcrowded nations already struggling with a scarcity of food, health care, housing, and education. In countries such as the Philippines, Pakistan, and Uganda, the population of school-age children has expanded faster than the resources needed to build new schools and hire teachers. Many countries cannot afford compulsory education. By 2000, over 1 billion people around the world were desperately poor and unable to obtain basic essentials, such as adequate food. The Green Revolution, sparking dramatic increases in food production, averted mass famine, but by the 1990s harvests reached a plateau, producing only small food increases or sometimes even decreases in food supplies. Furthermore, fish catches have declined steeply, partly because of overfishing by Western and Japanese fleets using high-technology equipment. Feeding the new mouths has also required massive clearing of forests for new cropland.

For all these reasons, twentieth-century advances in health and welfare could be reversed unless nations find ways to slow population growth and reduce poverty. Predominantly Islamic and Roman Catholic nations often discourage birth control and outlaw abortion as contrary to their religious beliefs. But other nations have pursued vigorous population control programs, increasing their economic potential. Thailand cut its birthrate by a fifth between 1980 and 2000. Using harsher means, overcrowded China dramatically reduced fertility by mandating only one child per family; couples who flouted the laws faced stiff fines or, sometimes, forced abortions. The most successful campaigns have targeted women by giving them better education, health care, and a sense of dignity independent of their roles as mothers. In the past, many parents viewed having many children as insurance for their old age; for example, in Mali the average woman had seven children, of which four survived to adulthood. Economic development, including better health care to lower infant mortality, often changed these attitudes. Increasing affluence also reduces birthrates. Thus, as women in Bangladesh opened small businesses, they had fewer children.

Rural folk have often had to abandon the livelihoods that had sustained their ancestors, usually ending up in crowded cities—Jakarta in Indonesia, Calcutta in India, Cairo in Egypt, Mexico City—where they often live in shantytowns or on the sidewalks. Whereas cities held some 10 percent of the world population in 1900, they held 50 percent in 2000. Cairo grew from 900,000 in 1897 to 2.8 million in 1947 and 13 million in 1995. In 1950 Western cities, headed by New York, accounted for most of the world's ten largest metropolitan areas; fifty years later Asian and Latin American cities dominated the list. Tokyo, with 28 million people, was followed by Mexico City, Bombay (India), São Paulo (Brazil), and Shanghai (China). Huge traffic jams make driving in Bangkok, Tokyo, Mexico City, and Lagos a nightmare. Struggling to provide needed services, cities usually dump raw sewage into bays and rivers. Today cities are responsible for 75 percent of the world's resource consumption and produce 75 percent of its trash. City life has also reshaped traditional ways. In a pop song from Peru, a boy who migrated to Lima complained that his girlfriend had abandoned rural values: "You came as a country girl. Now you are in Lima you comb your hair in a city way. You even say, 'I'm going to dance the twist' [a popular dance from the United States]."[12]

Industrialization, population growth, and urbanization have posed unprecedented environmental challenges and increased competition for limited resources such as oil, timber, and tin while contributing to a warmer, drier global climate. Over the twentieth century societies increased their industrial output twentyfold and their energy use fourteenfold. Industrialized nations as well as once-poor nations that became richer, such as China, South Korea, and Malaysia, paid the cost in noxious air, toxic waste, stripped forests, water pollution, and hotter climates. Some environmental disasters

Population Growth and Poverty

Migration to Cities

Environmental Challenges

WANGARI MAATHAI, KENYAN ENVIRONMENTAL ACTIVIST

Wangari Maathai (wahn-GAHR-ee muh-THIGH), who won the 2004 Nobel Peace Prize for her environmental activism, was born in 1940 and grew up in Nyeri, a small village in Kenya, East Africa. As a young girl, Wangari fetched water from a small stream. She grew fascinated by the creatures living in the stream and loved the lush trees and shrubs around her village. But over the years the stream dried up, silt choked nearby rivers, and the once green land grew barren. She lamented the assault on nature. Girls in rural Kenya in the 1940s and 1950s commonly spent their youth preparing for marriage and children. But a brother convinced Wangari's parents to send the inquisitive girl to the primary school he attended.

After graduating from a Roman Catholic high school, Wangari was awarded a scholarship to study in the United States, where she earned a B.A. in biology from a small Kansas college in 1964 and then completed an M.A. at the University of Pittsburgh in 1966. She credited her U.S. experience, including her observations of anti–Vietnam War protests, with encouraging her interest in democracy and free speech. Returning home, she earned a Ph.D. at Nairobi University in 1971, the first East African woman to achieve that degree, and then joined the faculty to teach biological sciences. She became a dean and joined a local organization that coordinated United Nations environmental programs.

Throughout her life Wangari has faced and overcome gender barriers, including in her marriage. Wangari married Mwangi Maathai and had three children, but their relation-

Wangari Maathai Wangari Maathai, winner of the 2004 Nobel Prize for peace, plants a tree outside the United Nations headquarters in New York in 2005. Earlier that day she challenged world leaders to dirty their hands by planting trees and working to stop the destruction of forests worldwide.

ship soured and they divorced after he was elected to parliament in 1974. She attributed the breakup to gender prejudice:

have affected large populations. In 1957 an explosion in a Russian nuclear waste dump killed some 10,000 people, contaminated 150 square miles of land, and forced the evacuation of 270,000 people. A massive die-off among varieties of frogs and some ocean species, a catastrophe perhaps due to pollution and ecological instability, suggested that diverse environments are increasingly dangerous to life. Sea turtle populations decreased drastically in regions as far apart as Southeast Asia, the Persian Gulf, and Central America.

Deforestation

Deforestation provides one sign of environmental destruction. In the twentieth century half of the world's rain forests were cut down, as commercial loggers obtained wood for housing, farmers converted forests into farms, and poor people collected firewood. This destruction continues at a furious pace today; an area larger than Hungary is cleared each year. Between 1975 and 2000 a quarter of the Central American rain forest was turned into grasslands, where beef cattle, raised chiefly to supply North American fast-food restaurants, now graze. Most of the world's tropical rain forest survives in only three nations: Brazil, Congo, and Indonesia. In tropical regions clearing the land exposes the thin topsoil to leaching of the nutrients by rains, so that often the cleared land can be farmed only for a few years before it becomes unusable desert. Deforestation has had enormous long-term consequences, ranging from decreasing rainfall to loss of valuable pharmaceuticals that might cure cancer or other illnesses. Millions of species of plants and animals have disappeared in recent decades, and by 2000 more than 11,000 species of plants and animals were threatened with extinction. A quarter to half of all current species could disappear by 2100. The destruction of forests, which absorb the carbon dioxide that heats up the atmosphere, has contributed, along with carbon dioxide–producing fossil fuels and industrial pollution, to the accelerating global warming. Scientists worry that this will raise ocean levels as glaciers and polar ice melts, flooding lowlands, river deltas, and small islands, ruin good farmland as drought increases, and make tropical regions unlivable as temperatures rise.

"I think my activism may have contributed to my being perceived as an [un]conventional [woman]. And that puts pressure on the man you live with, because he is then perceived as if he is not controlling you properly."

To stop the spread of desert in Kenya by planting trees, the dogged Wangari founded the Greenbelt Movement on Earth Day, 1977. She got the idea for the movement from talking to women when she served on the National Council of Women. Women told her they needed clean drinking water, nutritious food, and energy, and she realized trees could provide for all these needs: they stop soil erosion, help water conservation, bear fruit, provide fuel and building materials, offer shade, and also enhance the beauty of the landscape. Over 10,000 Kenyans, largely women, became involved, planting and nurturing more than 30 million trees. For each tree planted, the members earned a small income. The movement showed Kenyans that the health of their forests and rivers mattered for both their immediate well-being and their future.

Realizing that logging contracts enriched leaders of corrupt governments, including Kenya's repressive regime, Wangari began to see the link between environmental health and good governance. As a result, the Greenbelt Movement launched programs of civic education, linking human rights, ecology, and individual activism and helping thousands of women gain more control of their lives. Women took on local leadership roles, running tree nurseries and planning community-based projects. Thanks to the movement, she said, "women have become aware that planting trees or fighting to save forests from being chopped down is part of a larger mission to create a society that respects democracy, the rule of law, human rights, and the rights of women."

Wangari and her campaign to empower and educate rural women had many critics in Kenya, including the country's dictatorial president. She was threatened by violence, harassed,

sometimes severely beaten, arrested over a dozen times, and had her public appearances broken up by police. When she led protests against the building of a 62-story tower that would destroy much of Nairobi's main public park in the mid-1970s, the police killed seven of her associates. Still, she continued to protest illegal forest clearing and the Kenya government's holding of political prisoners. Wangari's efforts inspired similar Greenbelt movements in the United States, Haiti, and over thirty other African countries, and she became an international environmental spokesperson. In 2002, during the first fair elections in years, Wangari ran for the Kenyan parliament as a Green Party member and gained election by a huge majority. In 2003 a reformist president appointed her to his cabinet as an Assistant Minister for Environment, Natural Resources, and Wildlife. In awarding her the Noble Peace Prize, the Nobel committee praised Wangari for taking a comprehensive "approach to sustainable development that embraces democracy, human relations, and women's rights," saying that she "thinks globally and acts locally." She celebrated winning the Noble Prize by planting a tree on the slopes of Mount Kenya, near her childhood home, and recommitting herself to the struggle for a better world.

THINKING ABOUT THE PROFILE

1. How did Wangari's activities help Kenyan women?
2. How did Wangari's efforts to protect the environment also foster change in the political and social realms?

Note: Quotations from Friends of the Greenbelt Movement North America website (*http://gbmna.org/a.php?id*).

Desertification, the transformation of once productive land into useless desert, has increased with government, market, and population pressure to expand agriculture onto marginal land. During the past half century in Africa, some 20,000 square miles of land became desert every year. To combat the resulting farming failures, Africans used more pesticides, fertilizers, and irrigation, but these often have negative consequences. Drier climates diminish water supplies. One of Africa's largest lakes, Lake Chad, has lost 90 percent of its water since 1975. Deforestation and desertification also undermine farming by causing soil erosion, since, with less vegetation to absorb water, rains wash away fertile topsoil and cause severe flooding. Drought has become a regular reality in Africa, forcing millions to become refugees in other lands. With less rain to feed it, the Niger River in West Africa, once the location of great trading cities, no longer supports farming on a level of five centuries ago. The problems are not confined to Africa. In Nepal, farmers have stripped the once-lush Himalayan mountainsides for wood. The rain has then washed unimpeded down the slopes into the rivers, causing, along with melting Himalayan glaciers, ever more destructive floods downstream in India and Bangladesh, while reducing fresh water supplies in the region.

desertification The transformation by which productive land is transformed into mostly useless desert.

Movements to counter environmental decay have emerged. Some, such as the Sierra Club in the United States and the Malaysian Nature Society, appeal chiefly to middle-class people. Others, such as the Chipko tree protection movement in India and the Greenbelt movement in Kenya, bring middle-class urbanites and rural peasants together in a common cause. In 2004 the Greenbelt leader and global environmental activist, Wangari Maathai, won the Noble Peace Prize (see Profile: Wangari Maathai, Kenyan Environmental Activist). The United Nations established an environmental program that issues regular reports warning that environmental destruction, combined with poverty and population growth, threatens the long-term health of the planet and its people.

Environmental Movements

SECTION SUMMARY

- Globalization has boosted world economies and has reaped great rewards for countries such as the United States and China, but it has not always benefited the lives of poor people and has also led to continued foreign domination of some groups and nations by others.

- The World Bank and the International Monetary Fund have lent money to developing nations but sometimes dictate economic policies to borrowers, while multinational corporations have become so large that they exert great influence over governments and set the world prices for some commodities.

- Industrialization has spread throughout Asia and Latin America, the Third Industrial Revolution has created powerful new technologies, the Green Revolution has allowed for increased agricultural production, and the service and information industries have grown rapidly; but some globalization practices, such as outsourcing jobs to countries with cheaper labor, have produced hardships.

- Despite worldwide economic growth, some countries remain underdeveloped and the gap between the wealthiest and poorest people is striking; however, the developing world has made great improvements in infant mortality and adult literacy.

- Women have faced great problems in the modern economy as they have been drastically underpaid for their contributions, but grassroots programs such as the Grameen Bank have offered some increased economic opportunity.

- Over the past fifty years, the world population has exploded, especially in Asia, Africa, and Latin America, prompting fears that it will eventually outstrip available resources; while in more developed countries, fertility rates have dropped and populations have grown older.

- Industrialization and population growth have led to increased pollution and deforestation, which have led to massive extinction of plant and animal species, global warming, and the rise of environmental groups.

NEW GLOBAL NETWORKS AND THEIR CONSEQUENCES

How did growing networks linking societies influence social, political, and economic life?

global village An interconnected world community in which all people, regardless of their nationality, share a common fate.

During the late twentieth century the world became connected in unprecedented ways, leading to talk of a "spaceship earth" or a **global village**, an interconnected world community in which all people, regardless of nationality, share a common fate. A study of the interconnectedness contended that "the boundaries of the 'global village' are fluid, the inhabitants are highly mobile. Each street has its own problems, but each problem impinges increasingly on the population as a whole. The 'tyranny of distance' has been overcome; isolation has been eliminated."[13] Globalization has reshaped politics and cultures, fostering the movement of people, diseases, cultures, and religions. Increasingly the world is marked by both unity and diversity, common influences mixing with local traditions.

The Global Spread of Migrants, Refugees, and Disease

Population Movement

Today, many people live in nations filled with immigrants and their descendants from the four corners of the globe. Forty percent of Australians are immigrants or the children of immigrants. Thirty million people moved to labor-short western Europe between 1945 and 1975, chiefly from North Africa, West Africa, Turkey, South Asia, and the Caribbean. Similarly, 4 million Mexicans legally entered the United States, many filling low-wage jobs. Immigrants rapidly transformed cities such as Vancouver, Los Angeles, Sydney, and Paris into internationalized hubs of world culture and commerce. The many educated people who have moved to Western nations constitute a "brain drain" from poor countries. For example, doctors from India and nurses from the Philippines have played key roles in North American health care. Cosmopolitanism—a blending of peoples and cultures—flavors cities closely linked to the world economy, such as Hong Kong, Singapore, São Paulo (POU-lo), London, Dubai, and New York.

Immigrants often trigger tensions and debates as local people feel threatened by the newcomers and resent their continuing attachment to their own languages and traditions. While the globalization of trade and jobs dissolves economic boundaries, governments increasingly impose tighter border controls to discourage illegal immigration. For example, the United States has devoted more resources to patrolling the long border with Mexico, even building a high fence hundreds of miles long, but has been unable to stop the flow of Latin Americans flocking north.

The world contains over 100 million voluntary migrants to foreign countries, the great majority moving for economic rather than political reasons. Many migrants—some from impoverished regions such as Central America and South Asia, others from more prosperous nations such as South Korea and Taiwan—have sought better economic opportunities in the industrialized West. Small Indian- and Pakistani-run sundry goods and grocery stores, known as corner shops, have become a fixture in British cities. Millions of Asians and Africans have moved to the Middle East seeking work. Filipinos are an especially mobile people, migrating for short periods to other Southeast Asian nations and the Middle East and more permanently to North America. Some 8 million Filipinos now live abroad. Moving to a faraway, alien society is often traumatic. A poem by a Moroccan woman whose husband worked in Europe and rarely returned home captured her distress: "Germany, Belgium, France and Netherlands, Where are you situated? I have never seen your countries, I do not speak your language. I am afraid my love forgets me in your paradise. I ask you, give him back to me."[14]

Political turbulence, wars, genocides, government repression, and famine have also created some 20 million refugees. Desperate people have fled nations engulfed in political violence, such as Sudan, Guatemala, Afghanistan, Somalia, and Cambodia, and drought-plagued states such as Ethiopia and Mali. Over 2 million African Muslims from the Darfur region of Sudan fled genocidal attacks by Arab militias for refuge in Chad, an equally impoverished nation. Cubans, Chinese, Laotians **(lao-OH-shuhnz)**, and Vietnamese have fled communist-run states that restricted their freedoms. Others, such as Haitians, Chileans, Iranians, and Congolese, have escaped brutal rightwing dictatorships or corrupt despotisms. Millions of refugees have remained for decades, even generations, in squalid refugee camps, often fed and housed by international aid organizations. Many Palestinians who fled conflict in Israel have lived in refugee camps in Egypt, Jordan, and Lebanon for over six decades. Many refugees have nurtured resentments against the governments whose policies they escaped from or who forced them out, and citizens in countries offering refuge have often resented the refugees. Moreover, by the 1990s many nations, especially in Europe, became more cautious in granting political asylum.

Diseases traveling the routes of trade and migration have produced major pandemics, or massive disease outbreaks, throughout history. Today, although modern medicine has eliminated diseases that had long plagued humanity, such as smallpox, leprosy, and polio, other diseases, such as cholera and malaria, still bedevil people with little access to health care. Cholera, a bacterial disease that easily crosses borders, still kills several thousand people a year in poor countries, and malaria, spread by mosquitoes, debilitates millions of people in tropical regions. In the early twenty-first century, experts worried about a possible global spread of several viral diseases, perhaps killing millions of people, that passed from birds, poultry, and pigs to humans. Both United Nations agencies and private organizations have worked to reduce health threats and treat victims. But the travel of migrants, tourists, business people, armies, truck drivers, sailors, and others continues to spread diseases.

Spreading Diseases

The most deadly contemporary scourge affecting nations rich and poor, autoimmune deficiency syndrome (AIDS), caused by a virus known as HIV, is partly spread through the increased trade and travel associated with globalization. The disease spreads through sexual contact, needle sharing by drug addicts, and selling or receiving blood. Long-distance truck drivers who visit prostitutes along their routes spread the infection, especially in Africa and India. By 2005 some 42 million people around the world were infected with either HIV or AIDS, and 3.1 million died annually, a fifth of them children and one-third of them adult women, infected by husbands or lovers, leaving millions of orphans. As much as 30 percent of the adult population of some African nations was HIV positive. The disease is less catastrophic in richer countries. Only 0.2 percent of Americans were infected, and the rate was even lower in Europe. Although the pandemic undermines economic development in Africa and parts of Asia, only a few African and Asian governments have mounted education campaigns to convince people to take precautions or to seek treatment. Treating AIDS patients stresses health care resources, and AIDS victims are often rejected by their families and communities, dying alone and neglected by society.

Cultures and Religions Across Borders

The spread of cultural products and religions across national borders and the creative mixing of these with local traditions have been hallmarks of the modern world. Popular culture, commonly produced for commercial purposes and spread by the mass media, such as radio, television, and

Popular Cultures

films, has become a part of everyday life for billions of people. In recent decades, Western influences have been pervasive, although often superficial. Western videos, pop music recordings, jeans, and shopping malls have attracted some youth in Asia, Africa, and Latin America, but their influence on the broader society, especially in the rural areas, is often more limited. No common world culture has emerged, and Western technologies sometimes serve local needs. India developed the world's largest film industry, producing some 1,000 films a year by 2002, three times more films than the next largest producers, the United States and Japan. And cheap, often pirated, audio cassettes in the 1970s, videocassettes in the 1980s, and DVDs in the 1990s enabled even many more people to enjoy music and films while also enabling political or religious groups to spread their messages. Modern media have reshaped people's lives, especially in cities. One observer in the 1990s noted the global popularity of television:

Take a walk down any street, in any city or village, as the twilight fades and the darkness comes. Whether you are in London or Tokyo, Cairo or New York, Buenos Aires or Singapore, a small blue light will flicker at you from the unshuttered windows. These lights are the tiny knots in the seamless web of modern media.[15]

Popular Musics

Popular musics reflect the mixing of cultures and the increasing role of the mass media. Some popular styles, such as American jazz and Brazilian samba, emerged well before World War II, but most appeared after 1945. Rock, jazz, and rap, all African American forms with African roots, have found audiences all over the world. Vaclav Havel **(VAH-slav HAH-vel)**, the leader of the movement that overthrew Czech communism, credited the songs of the U.S. rock musician Frank Zappa with inspiring him to become an activist. Havel had once written songs for a Czech rock group. Rebellious youth in Manila and São Paulo use rap to express their feelings. The sudden death in 2009 of American pop musician Michael Jackson, known equally for his spectacular musical talents and bizarre lifestyle, illustrated the global influence of U.S. popular culture. His passing and legacy dominated the mass media in many nations for weeks, a star-studded memorial tribute was televised around the world, and millions of fans bought his recordings and memorabilia. Through the global reputations they often enjoy, pop stars also mount concerts to address issues such as racism, political prisoners, famine, and African poverty. Bono, the lead singer for the Irish rock band U2, uses his fame to campaign among world leaders for causes such as debt relief for poor nations.

Many musicians have mixed indigenous and imported influences, often from outside the West. For example, Congolese popular music, which borrowed Latin American dance rhythms, gained audiences throughout Africa and Europe. Indian film music and Arab folk music have influenced the popular music of Southeast Asia and East Africa. Even pop music that does not cross many borders can reflect a creative blending. *Dangdut*, an Indonesian popular music, originated as a fusion of Western rock, Indian film music, and local folk music. The major dangdut star, Rhoma Irama **(ROW-muh ih-RAH-muh)**, sometimes faced arrest for offering political protests in songs that address poverty, human rights abuses, the struggle of the underdog, and the betrayal of the nationalist promise. Beginning in the 1970s he developed a huge following among poor rural folk and urban youth, who agree with the message of one of his more famous songs: "The rich get richer and the poor get poorer." Rhoma's music, which has a strong Islamic quality and promotes Muslim moral teachings, helped inspire the Islamic revival in Indonesia, but conservative Muslims have often condemned other dangdut singers for their erotic lyrics and suggestive performances.

Religions

Although secular thought has become more popular than ever before in history, over three-quarters of the world's people identify with one or another universal religion with roots deep in the past. The world contains over 2 billion Christians, 1.5 billion Muslims, 900 million Hindus, 375 million Buddhists, and 14 million Jews. Well over 1.5 billion practice a local faith, such as animism or Daoism, or profess no religion (see Map 26.3). Religion sometimes provides the basis for national identity, as in Roman Catholic Poland and Ireland and in Muslim Bangladesh and Pakistan. Religious leaders have debated how much, if at all, their faiths need to change to better engage the contemporary world. Pope John XXIII (pope 1958–1963) liberalized church practices, such as having the mass in a vernacular language rather than Latin, and encouraged a more active dialogue with other churches and religions. Meanwhile, a controversial movement arose among Catholic clergy and laypeople in Latin America, called liberation theology, that cooperated with socialist and communist groups to improve the lives of the poor. Muslim liberals and militants confronted each other over such issues as the role of women, relations with non-Muslims, and whether Muslim majority states should base their legal systems on Islamic law. In sub-Saharan Africa and Southeast Asia, where many Sunni Muslims are tolerant toward other beliefs, some people have become more devout, and more men have studied in the Middle East, often returning with more militant views.

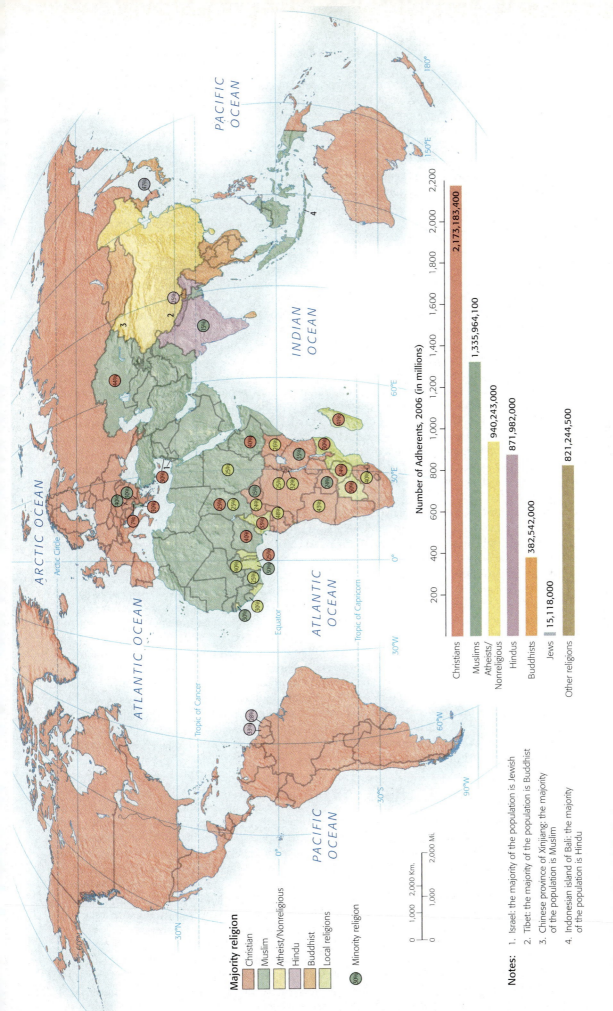

Map 26.3 World Religions

Christianity has the most believers and is the dominant faith in the Americas, Oceania, Europe, Russia, and central and southern Africa. Most people in the northern half of Africa, western Asia, and Central Asia embrace Islam. Hindus are concentrated in India, and Buddhists in East and Southeast Asia.

Majority religion

- Christian
- Muslim
- Atheist/Nonreligious
- Hindu
- Buddhist
- Local religions

Minority religion

Number of Adherents, 2006 (in millions)

Religion	Number
Christians	2,173,183,400
Muslims	1,335,964,100
Atheists/Nonreligious	940,243,000
Hindus	871,982,000
Buddhists	382,542,000
Jews	15,118,000
Other religions	821,244,500

Notes:
1. Israel: the majority of the population is Jewish
2. Tibet: the majority of the population is Buddhist
3. Chinese province of Xinjiang: the majority of the population is Muslim
4. Indonesian island of Bali: the majority of the population is Hindu

 **Interactive Map**

The easy spread of ideas in the globalized world has worked to the advantage of portable creeds not dependent on one culture or setting. In Africa, polytheism and animism have faded while Christianity and Islam, promoted by missionary activity, have gained wider followings. Protestants have evangelized and gained ground in predominantly Catholic Latin America, and Pentacostalism, an American-born Christian tradition that promotes charismatic worship and faith healing, has developed a large following. Protestants and Catholics have competed with each other, and often with Muslims, for followers in Africa, Southeast Asia, and East Asia. Christianity has increasingly become a non-Western faith, with far more believers in Africa, Asia, and Latin America than in Europe and North America. Christian and Muslim missionaries have appealed to the downtrodden, suggesting that adopting their faith could lead not only to spiritual health but also to material wealth, and have recast their messages to recognize local cultural traditions.

Religious Tensions and Militancy

Yet, organized religion has declined in East Asia and much of the West. Communist regimes discouraged religious observance, and many Japanese found neither their traditional faiths nor imported religions relevant to their lives. Church attendance and membership in Europe, Canada, and Australia fell dramatically after 1960. Traditional church attitudes have also competed with changing social attitudes. Even predominantly Catholic European nations have legalized abortion and moved toward equal rights for homosexuals, policies opposed by the Catholic Church. Both the Netherlands, once a center for puritanical Protestantism, and Spain, once one of the staunchest Catholic nations, have approved same-sex marriage, as have Belgium, Canada, South Africa, Mexico City, and several U.S. states.

Tensions remain between different faiths. Sparked by political differences, some Christians and Muslims have violently attacked each other in Indonesia, the Philippines, Lebanon, Yugoslavia, and Nigeria, causing many casualties. Conflicts between Muslims and Hindus generated sporadic violence in India, Catholics and Protestants opposed each other in Northern Ireland and Uganda, and Sunni and Shi'ite Muslims occasionally fought in Pakistan and western Asia. Some Sunni Muslim regimes discriminated against or persecuted Shi'ites. In Iraq, where some 60 percent of the population is Shi'ite, the Sunni dictator, Saddam Hussein, restricted Shi'ite religious holidays and executed Shi'ites who opposed his regime. After his removal by the U.S. invasion, Shi'ite and Sunni conflict erupted, complicating U.S. efforts to restore stability.

Religious militancy has also grown. Some Muslim militants have turned the notion of *jihad*, or struggle within believers to strengthen their faith, into a campaign for holy war against unbelievers, secular Muslims, and countries or groups they consider anti-Muslim, and for turning secular states into Islamic ones. The militants, often known as Islamists or jihadis, appeal especially to the young and poor, often unemployed and embittered. Many Muslims oppose market capitalism and Western cultural influence, and the more puritanical Muslims despise the revealing clothing styles, open romantic behavior, independent women, and rebellious youth portrayed in Western television programs and movies. Similarly, some Christians, especially in the United States, Latin America, and Africa, have turned to literal, fundamentalist interpretations of the Bible and fund proselytizing efforts. Some Nigerian Protestant churches have even sent missionaries to the United States and Europe, while South Korean Protestants evangelize in China. Conservative churches have often opposed secular culture, rejected scientific findings they deem incompatible with biblical accounts, and condemned leftwing political and social movements, particularly those promoting socialism, feminism, legalized abortion, and homosexual rights. Christian and Islamic militancy has sparked similar movements in Buddhism, Hinduism, and Judaism, pitting the zealous believers against those with moderate, tolerant views.

Global Communications and Movements

A worldwide communications network has been a chief engine of globalization. The introduction of radio in the early 1900s was followed by tape recording, television, and then the transistor, which allowed for the miniaturization of electronics. In 1953 portable transistor radios became available and soon reached even remote villages, opening them to world news and culture. Even villages without electricity could use transistor radios and cassette players. By the 1960s in central Borneo, a densely forested island divided between Indonesia and Malaysia, isolated villagers listened to radio broadcasts from the United States, Britain, and Australia and could often sing the songs of Western pop musicians such as the British rock group the Beatles.

Technological Breakthroughs

Technological breakthroughs provided the foundation for more rapid and widespread communications. The first general-purpose computers were built in 1948, and in 1958 the first silicon microchips began a computer revolution that led to the first personal computers. By 2008 the world had nearly 800 million personal computers with 1.6 billion Internet users as well as countless web pages and blogs, all part of a vast network often termed the information superhighway. E-mail allows people in different countries, such as Canada and Malaysia, to communicate instantly with each other, and every minute millions of e-mails are dispatched via computer. An interested reader in Hong Kong, Ghana, or Finland can also access online versions of newspapers, such as the *New York Times*, *Al Ahram* in Cairo, or the *Deccan Herald* in India. Finally, the rise of 24-hour cable news networks able to reach worldwide audiences, such as U.S.-based CNN (Cable News Network) and the Arab-language Al Jazeera, based in the Persian Gulf state of Qatar, widened access to diverse views, enriching people's understanding of the wider world. Technologically literate people can send music, video, and photos around the world via computers and cell phones.

A Networked World

The rapid evolution of media and information technology has had many consequences. Through fax communications, orbiting communications satellites, portable phones, electronic mail, and the worldwide computer web, information can be transmitted outside the reach of governments, diminishing their power to shape their citizens' thinking. For this reason, repressive states seeking to limit information flow, such as Iran, Cuba, Burma, and China, have banned satellite dish receivers and tried to jam access to controversial and dissident websites, but these efforts have been only partly successful. In 2009, protesters in nations like China and Iran used cellphones, Twitter, and YouTube to coordinate their activities, spread their message, and circumvent government control of the mass media. The U.S.-based social media site Facebook claims 250 million members, seventy percent of them outside the U.S. Technologies, especially the World Wide Web, have enhanced the value of education and of English, which has gradually become a world language, like Latin in the Mediterranean zone 2,000 years ago and Arabic in the Islamic world 1,000 years ago. By 2005 some three-quarters of all websites were in English. Perhaps a quarter of the world's people know some English, and Asian countries with many educated people fluent in English, such as India and Singapore, have an advantage in competing for high-technology industries. But in the poorest nations, only a lucky few have access to satellite dishes, fax machines, and networked computers. Furthermore, many nations resent the strong U.S. influence over the Internet.

Social and Political Movements

The increasing links between far-flung peoples have allowed for social and political movements originating in different countries to transcend borders and link to similar movements elsewhere. A wide variety of transnational organizations promote issues such as the treatment of political prisoners, women's rights, and antiracism. Amnesty International, based in Britain, publicizes the plight of people imprisoned solely for their political views and activities, such as the Burmese opposition leader Aung San Suu Kyi (AWNG sahn soo CHEE) and, during the Cold War, the Soviet dissident scientist Andrei Sakharov (SAH-kuh-RAWF), organizing letter writing and pressure campaigns to seek their release. The World Social Forum, formed in 2001 and meeting annually in Brazil, brings together nongovernment organizations and activists who oppose globalizing free market capitalism and imperialism. They believe globalization undermines workers' rights and environmental protection.

Movements or upheavals in one nation or region sometimes spread widely. During the 1960s, students, workers, and political radicals in many nations organized protests against the U.S. war

Internet Cafe in Thailand In this photo, a waiter at a cyberspace café, operated by the Swiss multinational ice cream company, Häagen Dazs, in Bangkok, Thailand, helps a young Thai woman navigate one of the café's computers.

AP/Wide World Photos

in Vietnam, racism, unresponsive governments, capitalism, and other concerns. In 1968 demonstrations, marches, and strikes intensified around the world. Although these movements were not coordinated, young protesters were often influenced by the same writers, music, and ideas. The more radical protesters wore t-shirts celebrating Che Guevara (guh-VAHR-uh) (1928–1967), an Argentinean-born revolutionary who helped Fidel Castro take power in Cuba and who became a communist martyr when he was killed in Bolivia. The 1968 turbulence affected over a dozen countries, from the United States and Mexico to France, Czechoslovakia, and Japan. However, other protesters have looked to noncommunists or even anticommunists, such as the dissidents—often devout Catholics—who opposed the communist regime in Poland. In the wake of the 1968 activism, environmental, peace, workers' rights, homosexual rights, and feminist movements grew, chiefly but not only in industrialized nations.

Women's Movements

Women have been particularly active in seeking to expand their rights, and some activists have placed women's issues on the international agenda. The United Nations periodically sponsors global conferences on women's issues such as gender equality. However, women who attend international conferences, divided by culture and nationality, do not always agree on goals and strategies. In the United Nation's fourth World Conference on Women, held in China in 1995, the 40,000 delegates disagreed sharply on priorities. Delegates from rich nations wanted to expand women's employment options, social freedom, and control over their bodies, while Asian, African, and Latin American delegates emphasized making their families more healthy and economically secure. One Indian delegate described the goals of U.S. delegates as irrelevant to Indian women: "They ask for abortion rights. We ask for safe drinking water and basic health care."[16] While abortion remained a controversial issue in most of the world, it became legal in most Western and many Asian nations.

Despite disagreements, women have worked across borders on issues such as preventing violence against women. For example, women activists and their male supporters from Muslim and Western nations have fought the tradition common in some conservative Muslim societies of jailing or killing women for adultery while exonerating the man responsible. In 2005 Mukhtaran Bibi (MOOK-tahr-an BIH-bee), an illiterate woman from an impoverished Pakistani village without electricity, gained worldwide sympathy for her resistance to male brutality. The tribal council had ruled that she be gang-raped to punish her family, which had been involved in a village dispute. Instead of following custom by ending the "disgrace" through suicide, she bravely pursued the rapists in court. They were convicted, and she used the money awarded her by the court to start two village schools, one for boys and one for girls. When a higher court then overturned the men's convictions, her courageous refusal to accept the verdict caused an international outcry. While the Pakistani government tried to suppress the controversy, men and women around the world, alerted by news accounts and Internet appeals, donated money and made her a symbol of the need for women's rights. Mukhtaran Bibi inspired millions everywhere with her courage and faith in education and justice.

Global Terrorism

terrorism Small-scale but violent attacks aimed at undermining a government or demoralizing a population.

Terrorism, small-scale but violent attacks, often on civilian targets, aimed at undermining a government or demoralizing a population, intensified in the late twentieth and early twenty-first century, expanding to global dimensions and reshaping world politics. Terrorism has a long history, going back many centuries. After 1945 Palestinians under Israeli control, Basque nationalists in Spain, and Irish nationalists in Britain, among others, engaged in terrorism for their causes. Some states also carried out or sponsored terrorism against unfriendly governments or political movements. South Africa's white minority government financed insurgencies that opposed the Marxist governments of Angola and Mozambique, resulting in thousands of civilian deaths. Similarly, the United States sponsored terrorism against leftist-ruled Nicaragua in the 1980s, helping form a military force, known as the *Contras,* that often attacked civilian targets, such as rural schools, day-care centers, and clinics operated by the government. An increasingly interconnected world has spurred some terrorist organizations to operate on a global level, forming networks with branches in many countries. The most active of these networks, formed by militant Islamists, has capitalized on widespread Muslim anger at Israel, their own governments, and U.S. foreign policies. Muslim terrorist groups have become increasingly active in Egypt, Algeria, Lebanon, and Pakistan, attacking politicians, police, Western residents and tourists, and Israeli and U.S. targets.

Terrorism became a growing threat to life in the Middle East. For example, the *Hezbollah* movement in Lebanon, formed by Shi'ite Arabs opposed to the U.S.-backed Lebanese government and to U.S. support for Israel, used suicide bombers driving explosive-filled trucks to destroy the U.S. Embassy and a Marine Corps base in Beirut in 1983, killing several hundred Americans. Later, to oppose Israeli occupation of Arab lands and demoralize Israelis, Palestinian militants strapped explosives to their bodies and detonated them in Israeli buses and businesses. Outraged by these murderous attacks, the Israelis responded with force, killing or arresting Palestinians and expelling families of suspected militants from their homes, often bulldozing the houses into rubble. Divided by politics, Israelis and Palestinians have shared the bitter experience of grieving for those lost in the chronic violence, among them innocent women and children.

Middle Eastern Terrorism

The Soviet military intervention in 1979 to support a pro-Soviet government in Afghanistan provided the spark for forming a global network of Islamist terrorists. Militants from the Middle East and Pakistan flocked to Afghanistan to assist the Muslim Afghan insurgents resisting the Soviets. In 1988 the most extreme of the foreign fighters came together in a jihadi organization known as *Al Qaeda* ("The Base"). Al Qaeda's main leader, the Saudi Osama bin Laden (b. 1957), came from an extremely wealthy family and had been trained as an engineer. Bin Laden used his wealth to support the Afghan rebels, who were also funded and armed by the United States as part of its Cold War rivalry with the USSR. After the Soviets abandoned Afghanistan in 1989, bin Laden set up Al Qaeda cells in Saudi Arabia, whose government he viewed as corrupt, and aimed to target Egypt and Iraq, whose secular regimes suppressed Islamic militants. To recruit, support, and communicate with members, Al Qaeda used the information superhighway, setting up websites, using e-mail and satellite phones, and releasing videotapes to cable news networks of bin Laden's messages. Eventually Al Qaeda looked beyond the Middle East for targets. The Afghanistan-based bin Laden, a ruthless man willing to kill innocent people in pursuit of his goals, plotted terrorist efforts against his former ally in the Afghan resistance, the United States, whose military bases in Saudi Arabia, support for repressive Arab governments, and close alliance with Israel enraged many Arabs. Al Qaeda or related groups sponsored attacks on U.S. targets, such as the embassies in Kenya and Tanzania, causing hundreds of casualties.

Al Qaeda

On September 11, 2001, Al Qaeda members hijacked four U.S. commercial airliners and crashed two of them into New York's World Trade Center and another into the Pentagon near Washington, D.C., killing over 3,000 people, mostly civilians. A fourth airliner crashed into a Pennsylvania farm field before reaching Washington, D.C. The attacks shocked Americans and people everywhere who opposed indiscriminate killing and prompted U.S. president George W. Bush to declare a war on terrorism. U.S. forces attacked Al Qaeda bases in Afghanistan and then occupied the country, whose government, controlled by Islamists who had fought the Soviets, shielded bin Laden; but although they installed a new pro-U.S. government, the Americans failed to capture bin Laden and still faced resistance from Islamic militants.

In 2003 the United States, claiming that Saddam Hussein's Iraq was closely linked to Al Qaeda and possessed weapons of mass destruction, invaded Iraq, removed Saddam's brutal government, and imposed a U.S. military occupation supported chiefly by Britain. However, the U.S. troops found no evidence of any Saddam ties to Al Qaeda or any weapons of mass destruction, and the occupation sparked an insurgency, including suicide bombings, and unleashed sectarian divisions that hindered the U.S. efforts to stabilize and rebuild Iraq. While most of the insurgents were Sunni Iraqis fearing domination by the Shi'ite majority, Islamists from other countries also flocked to Iraq to attack Americans and destabilize the country. The U.S. invasion and occupation, and the resistance to it, killed over 100,000 Iraqis, resulted in 4,300 U.S. deaths and tens of thousands of wounded, and kept a large U.S. military force tied down in Iraq.

United States and Iraq

Eventually violence diminished. Whether the war in Iraq helped or harmed the U.S.-led war against terrorism remained subject to debate. The war alienated many U.S. allies and, like the earlier U.S. conflict in Vietnam, was unpopular around the world. Transferring U.S. troops and funds from Afghanistan to Iraq allowed the Islamic militants to regroup and fight the U.S.-backed Afghan government. Meanwhile, capitalizing on anti-U.S. sentiments among Muslims, Al Qaeda spawned loosely affiliated terrorist groups, often operating without direct Al Qaeda guidance, that launched terrorist attacks on several continents, from Spain and Britain to Indonesia, Kenya, and Morocco. Nations with despotic governments, such as China, Egypt, and Uzbekistan, also invoked terrorism as a reason to restrict civil liberties. In 1993 a German historian had perceptively predicted the challenges ahead in the post–Cold War world: "We are at the beginning of a new era, characterized by great insecurity, permanent crisis and the absence of any kind of *status quo*. We must realize that we find ourselves in one of those crises of world history."[17]

EAST ASIAN RESURGENCE, SINCE 1945

Wally McNamee/Corbis

The China Stock Exchange
The East Asian nations enjoyed an economic resurgence in this era. Since the 1980s, China has boasted the world's fastest-growing economy and a booming stock exchange.

EBOOK AND WEBSITE RESOURCES

e PRIMARY SOURCE
The Long Telegram

e INTERACTIVE MAPS
Map 26.1 Decolonization
Map 26.2 World Population Growth
Map 26.3 World Religions

LINKS

Global Problems and the Culture of Capitalism (http://faculty.plattsburgh.edu/richard.robbins/legacy/). An outstanding site, aimed at undergraduates, with a wealth of resources.
The Globalization Website (http://www.emory.edu/SOC/globalization/). A useful site with many resources and essays on globalization.
Human Rights Watch (http://www.hrw.org/wr2k3/introduction.html). The website of a major human rights organization that reports on the entire world.

Modern History Sourcebook (http://www.fordham.edu/halsall/mod/modsbook.html). A very extensive online collection of historical documents and secondary materials.
United Nations Environment Program (http://www.unep.org/geo2000/ov-e/index.htm). Provides access to United Nations reports on the world's environmental problems.

Plus flashcards, practice quizzes, and more. Go to: www.cengage.com/history/lockard/globalsocnet2e.

SUGGESTED READING

Ali, Tariq. *The Clash of Fundamentalisms: Crusades, Jihads and Modernity*. London: Verso, 2003. A controversial but powerful examination, by a London-based Indian writer, of Western policies and Islamic movements around the world.

Axford, Barrie. *The Global System: Economics, Politics and Culture*. New York: St. Martin's, 1995. A comprehensive, thoughtful review by a British scholar of approaches to understanding the global system.

Crossley, Pamela Kyle, et al. *Global Society: The World Since 1900*, 2nd ed. Boston: Houghton Mifflin, 2008. A comprehensive survey.

DeFronzo, James. *Revolutions and Revolutionary Movements*. Boulder, CO: Westview Press, 1991. Useful surveys of revolutions and the societies they made, with case studies of Russia, China, Vietnam, Cuba, Nicaragua, Iran, and South Africa.

Enloe, Cynthia. *Bananas, Beaches and Bases: Making Feminist Sense of International Relations*, 2nd ed. Berkeley: University of California Press, 2001. A provocative examination of women's experiences in global politics.

Ehrenreich, Barbara, and Arlie Russell Hochschild, eds. *Global Women: Nannies, Maids, and Sex Workers in the New Economy*. New York: Henry Holt, 2002. A provocative look at the feminization of the migrant work force.

Eriksen, Thomas Hylland. *Globalization: The Key Concepts*. New York: Berg, 2007. Useful introduction by a Norwegian scholar.

Frieden, Jeffrey A. *Global Capitalism: Its Fall and Rise in the Twentieth Century*. New York: W.W. Norton, 2006. Provocative examination of globalization and capitalism.

Hunt, Michael H. *The World Transformed, 1945 to the Present*. Boston: Bedford/St. Martin's, 2004. A readable and up-to-date survey.

Kechner, Frank J., and John Boli. *World Culture: Origins and Consequences*. Malden, MA: Blackwell, 2005. Examines the impact of globalization on world culture.

Khanna, Parag. *The Second World: Empires and Influence in the New Global Order*. New York: W.W. Norton, 2008. Exploration of world politics by India-born scholar.

LaFeber, Walter. *America, Russia and the Cold War, 1945–2006*, 10th ed. New York: McGraw-Hill, 2006. An excellent examination of the Cold War around the world.

Mazlish, Bruce, and Akira Iriye, eds. *The Global History Reader*. New York: Routledge, 2005. A provocative set of essays on global trends in the twentieth century, from the information revolution and environmental change to human rights and terrorism.

McNeill, J. R. *Something New Under the Sun: An Environmental History of the Twentieth-Century World*. New York: W.W. Norton, 2000. An outstanding examination of the interface between societies and environmental change.

Ponting, Clive. *The Twentieth Century: A World History*. New York: Henry Holt, 1999. A valuable thematic examination by a British scholar.

Reynolds, David. *One World Divisible: A Global History Since 1945*. New York: W.W. Norton, 2001. A comprehensive survey.

Sen, Amartya. *Identity and Violence: The Illusion of Destiny*. New York: Norton, 2006. An influential Indian economist's views on globalization, freedom, violence, and other global issues.

Stearns, Peter N. *The Industrial Revolution in World History*, 3rd ed. Boulder, CO: Westview Press, 2007. Useful comparative study.

Wang, Gungwu, ed. *Global History and Migrants*. Boulder, CO: Westview Press, 1997. Essays on recent population movements.

Weiss, Thomas G., et al. *The United Nations and Changing World Politics*, 5th ed. Boulder, CO: Westview Press, 2006. Examines the history and roles of the United Nations.

Westad, Odd Arne. *The Global Cold War*. New York: Cambridge University Press, 2005. A provocative study by a Norwegian scholar.

EAST ASIAN RESURGENCE, SINCE 1945

Wally McNamee/Corbis

The China Stock Exchange
The East Asian nations enjoyed an economic resurgence in this era. Since the 1980s, China has boasted the world's fastest-growing economy and a booming stock exchange.

Terrorism became a growing threat to life in the Middle East. For example, the *Hezbollah* movement in Lebanon, formed by Shi'ite Arabs opposed to the U.S.-backed Lebanese government and to U.S. support for Israel, used suicide bombers driving explosive-filled trucks to destroy the U.S. Embassy and a Marine Corps base in Beirut in 1983, killing several hundred Americans. Later, to oppose Israeli occupation of Arab lands and demoralize Israelis, Palestinian militants strapped explosives to their bodies and detonated them in Israeli buses and businesses. Outraged by these murderous attacks, the Israelis responded with force, killing or arresting Palestinians and expelling families of suspected militants from their homes, often bulldozing the houses into rubble. Divided by politics, Israelis and Palestinians have shared the bitter experience of grieving for those lost in the chronic violence, among them innocent women and children.

Middle Eastern Terrorism

The Soviet military intervention in 1979 to support a pro-Soviet government in Afghanistan provided the spark for forming a global network of Islamist terrorists. Militants from the Middle East and Pakistan flocked to Afghanistan to assist the Muslim Afghan insurgents resisting the Soviets. In 1988 the most extreme of the foreign fighters came together in a jihadi organization known as *Al Qaeda* ("The Base"). Al Qaeda's main leader, the Saudi Osama bin Laden (b. 1957), came from an extremely wealthy family and had been trained as an engineer. Bin Laden used his wealth to support the Afghan rebels, who were also funded and armed by the United States as part of its Cold War rivalry with the USSR. After the Soviets abandoned Afghanistan in 1989, bin Laden set up Al Qaeda cells in Saudi Arabia, whose government he viewed as corrupt, and aimed to target Egypt and Iraq, whose secular regimes suppressed Islamic militants. To recruit, support, and communicate with members, Al Qaeda used the information superhighway, setting up websites, using e-mail and satellite phones, and releasing videotapes to cable news networks of bin Laden's messages. Eventually Al Qaeda looked beyond the Middle East for targets. The Afghanistan-based bin Laden, a ruthless man willing to kill innocent people in pursuit of his goals, plotted terrorist efforts against his former ally in the Afghan resistance, the United States, whose military bases in Saudi Arabia, support for repressive Arab governments, and close alliance with Israel enraged many Arabs. Al Qaeda or related groups sponsored attacks on U.S. targets, such as the embassies in Kenya and Tanzania, causing hundreds of casualties.

Al Qaeda

On September 11, 2001, Al Qaeda members hijacked four U.S. commercial airliners and crashed two of them into New York's World Trade Center and another into the Pentagon near Washington, D.C., killing over 3,000 people, mostly civilians. A fourth airliner crashed into a Pennsylvania farm field before reaching Washington, D.C. The attacks shocked Americans and people everywhere who opposed indiscriminate killing and prompted U.S. president George W. Bush to declare a war on terrorism. U.S. forces attacked Al Qaeda bases in Afghanistan and then occupied the country, whose government, controlled by Islamists who had fought the Soviets, shielded bin Laden; but although they installed a new pro-U.S. government, the Americans failed to capture bin Laden and still faced resistance from Islamic militants.

In 2003 the United States, claiming that Saddam Hussein's Iraq was closely linked to Al Qaeda and possessed weapons of mass destruction, invaded Iraq, removed Saddam's brutal government, and imposed a U.S. military occupation supported chiefly by Britain. However, the U.S. troops found no evidence of any Saddam ties to Al Qaeda or any weapons of mass destruction, and the occupation sparked an insurgency, including suicide bombings, and unleashed sectarian divisions that hindered the U.S. efforts to stabilize and rebuild Iraq. While most of the insurgents were Sunni Iraqis fearing domination by the Shi'ite majority, Islamists from other countries also flocked to Iraq to attack Americans and destabilize the country. The U.S. invasion and occupation, and the resistance to it, killed over 100,000 Iraqis, resulted in 4,300 U.S. deaths and tens of thousands of wounded, and kept a large U.S. military force tied down in Iraq.

United States and Iraq

Eventually violence diminished. Whether the war in Iraq helped or harmed the U.S.-led war against terrorism remained subject to debate. The war alienated many U.S. allies and, like the earlier U.S. conflict in Vietnam, was unpopular around the world. Transferring U.S. troops and funds from Afghanistan to Iraq allowed the Islamic militants to regroup and fight the U.S.-backed Afghan government. Meanwhile, capitalizing on anti-U.S. sentiments among Muslims, Al Qaeda spawned loosely affiliated terrorist groups, often operating without direct Al Qaeda guidance, that launched terrorist attacks on several continents, from Spain and Britain to Indonesia, Kenya, and Morocco. Nations with despotic governments, such as China, Egypt, and Uzbekistan, also invoked terrorism as a reason to restrict civil liberties. In 1993 a German historian had perceptively predicted the challenges ahead in the post–Cold War world: "We are at the beginning of a new era, characterized by great insecurity, permanent crisis and the absence of any kind of *status quo*. We must realize that we find ourselves in one of those crises of world history."[17]

SECTION SUMMARY

- In the new global village, millions of people have immigrated to foreign countries seeking greater economic opportunity or an escape from insufferable conditions at home, including political repression, famine, and civil war.

- Modern medicine has eliminated many diseases, but cholera and malaria are still serious problems, and AIDS has seriously affected India, Southeast Asia, and especially Africa.

- Western consumer culture has spread around the world, while musical forms from different cultures have mingled and musicians and performers have expressed political and often controversial views.

- The world's major religious traditions have remained numerically strong, and some have worked to adapt to the modern world, while representatives of rival religions have fought for control of various areas and many Muslims and Christians have grown more fundamentalist.

- Worldwide communication was facilitated by technologies such as radio, television, and the Internet, making a vast array of information available, even in countries such as China, Iran, and Cuba, whose governments attempted to limit its availability.

- Increased global communication led to political movements that transcended conventional borders, such as Amnesty International, the 1968 youth protests, and women's rights movements.

- Terrorism, which had been used throughout the twentieth century by groups such as the Palestinians, the Basques, and the Irish, became more deadly, culminating in the radical Muslim group Al Qaeda's 2001 attack on the United States.

CHAPTER SUMMARY

The later twentieth century proved turbulent. Nationalism spread in Asia and Africa, leading to decolonization. During the 1950s and 1960s most of the Western colonies gained their independence through negotiations, the threat of violence, or armed struggle, and social revolutionaries gained power in some nations. However, the West maintained a strong economic presence in many former colonies. The rivalry between the United States and the USSR also shaped the global system, generating a Cold War in which the two superpowers faced each other indirectly or through surrogates. The powerful United States had a large group of allies and sometimes intervened in Asian and Latin American nations, while the USSR occupied eastern Europe. The collapse of the Communist bloc and then the USSR allowed the United States to become the world's lone superpower.

The world was also shaped by globalization, with its unprecedented flow of money, products, information, and ideas across national borders. The global economy grew rapidly but did not spread its benefits equally. As industrialization spread, most Western and some Asian and Latin American nations prospered, but many poor nations struggled to escape underdevelopment and raise living standards. A billion people remained mired in deep poverty. Meanwhile millions of people migrated, social and political movements addressed local and global problems, universal religions gained new converts, and the information superhighway and other technological innovations linked millions of people in new ways. New international terrorist networks also challenged governments and reshaped world politics.

KEY TERMS

First World	Cold War	multinational corporations	global village
Second World	guerrilla warfare	Third Industrial Revolution	terrorism
Third World	nuclear weapons	Green Revolution	
Fourth World	globalization	desertification	

> *O*nce China's destiny is in the hands of the people, China, like the sun rising in the east, will illuminate every corner with a brilliant flame, and build a new, powerful and prosperous [society].
>
> —MAO ZEDONG, CHINESE COMMUNIST LEADER[1]

*O*n October 1, 1949, Mao Zedong (1893–1976), the Chinese communist leader, was driven into Beijing accompanied by soldiers from the communist military force, the People's Liberation Army. Mao, fifty-five years old and a peasant's son, had never been out of China and had spent the previous twenty-two years living in remote rural areas while directing brutal warfare against the Japanese invaders and the Chinese government. Ahead of Mao's car rolled a Sherman tank, originally donated by the United States to the Republic of China government, headed by Jiang Jieshi (better known in the West as Chiang Kai-shek) (1887–1975), to help crush Mao's communist forces. But Chiang's army had lost, and the president had fled to the large offshore island of Taiwan. Wearing a new suit, Mao climbed to the top of the Gate of Heavenly Peace, the entrance to the Forbidden City of the Qing emperors overlooking spacious Tiananmen Square. He and his comrades had sacrificed much to reach this pinnacle of power. Chinese jammed the square to hear their new ruler announce the founding of a new communist government, the People's Republic of China. Referring to a century of corrupt governments and humiliation and domination by Western nations and Japan, Mao thanked all those who, starting with the Opium War, had "laid down their lives in the many struggles against domestic and foreign enemies," finally proclaiming: "The Chinese people have stood up. Nobody will insult us again."[2]

The formation of the People's Republic marked a watershed in the history of China and the world, bringing to an end a century of severe social and political instability, caused in part by China's inability to defend itself against foreign imperialism. Its communist leaders were committed to the revolutionary transformation of the society while making China respected abroad once again. Given China's size and a population of 1.3 billion by 2008, greater than that of North America, Europe, and Russia combined, any major transition there had global significance. By the early twenty-first century Mao was long gone and many of his policies discarded, but China, with a booming economy, had reclaimed some of the political and economic status it had lost two centuries earlier.

The Chinese were not the only East Asians to enjoy a resurgence. By the 1980s observers referred to the **Pacific Rim**, the economically dynamic Asian countries on the edge of the Pacific Basin: China, Japan, South Korea, Taiwan, and several Southeast Asian nations. Many predicted that the twenty-first century would be the **Pacific Century**, marked by a shift of global economic power from Europe and North America to the Pacific Rim, whose export-driven nations seemed poised to dominate a post–Cold War world where economic power might outweigh military might. The center of gravity of world economic life, for centuries located in the eastern half of Eurasia, had shifted to Europe and North America, and then in the 1990s had moved back toward a resurgent Asia. Although changing world

FOCUS QUESTIONS

1. How did Maoism transform Chinese society?
2. What factors explain the dramatic rise of Chinese economic power in the world since 1978?
3. How did Japan rise from the ashes of defeat in World War II to become a global economic powerhouse?
4. What policies led to the rise of the "Little Dragon" nations and their dynamic economies?

Pacific Rim The economically dynamic Asian countries on the edge of the Pacific Basin: China, Japan, South Korea, Taiwan, and several Southeast Asian nations.

Pacific Century The possible shift of global economic power from Europe and North America to the Pacific Rim in the twenty-first century.

e Visit the website and eBook for additional study materials and interactive tools: www.cengage.com/history/lockard/globalsocnet2e

767

politics and economic crises, especially an Asian financial collapse in 1997 and a severe global recession in 2008–2009, have challenged the Pacific Century concept, China, Japan, and their neighbors have remained major players in the global system.

MAO'S REVOLUTIONARY CHINA

How did Maoism transform Chinese society?

The Chinese Revolution that brought the Chinese communists to power was one of the three greatest upheavals in modern world history. The French Revolution (1789) destroyed the remnants of feudalism throughout western Europe, with its leaders extolling the rights of the common people, and the Russian Revolution (1917) charted a noncapitalist path to industrialization. Both events swept away old social classes and ruling elites. China's revolution remade a major world society while restoring its international status. The communists built a strong government that made China the most experimental nation on earth, veering from one innovative policy to another in an attempt to renovate Chinese life and overcome underdevelopment. In the process, the People's Republic created a new model of economic development different from both Western-dominated capitalism and highly centralized Soviet communism. But the path was littered with conflict and repression. Furthermore, the Chinese, like all societies, were products of their history. China remained partly an ancient empire and partly a modern nation, and its leaders often behaved much like the emperors of old in their autocratic exercise of power.

CHRONOLOGY

China Since 1945

1945–1949 Chinese civil war

1949 Chinese communist triumph

1949–1957 Stalinist model

1950 Occupation of Tibet

1950 New marriage law

1950–1953 Korean War

1957–1961 First use of Maoist model

1958–1961 Great Leap Forward

1960 Sino-Soviet split

1966–1976 Great Proletarian Cultural Revolution

1972 Nixon's trip to Beijing

1976 Death of Mao Zedong

1976 Arrest of Gang of Four

1978 Four Modernizations policy

1978 Normalization of U.S.-China diplomatic relations

1978–1989 Market socialism

1978–1997 Deng Xiaoping era

1989 Tiananmen Massacre

1989 Introduction of market Leninism

1997 Return of Hong Kong to China

The Communist Triumph and the New China

The U.S. defeat of Japan in 1945 sparked a fierce civil war between Mao's communists and Chiang Kai-shek's nationalist government for control of China. While Mao and Chiang despised each other, both men were patriotic, autocratic, and hungry for power. Chiang's 3.7-million-man army vastly outnumbered the 900,000 communist troops, and the United States lavished military aid on Chiang, providing planes and trucks to transport his soldiers so they could occupy as much territory as possible. The communists, aided by the Soviet Union (USSR), concentrated on north China and Manchuria. In trying to block Mao's forces, however, Chiang overstretched his supply lines. In addition, Chiang's Republic experienced corruption and a rapid decline in the value of Chinese currency that demoralized the population. Seeking change, many came to view the communist movement as a more honest alternative to Chiang's Nationalist Party.

Meanwhile, in the villages that they controlled, the communists promoted a social revolution, known as the "turning over," by encouraging villagers to denounce local landlords, transferring land from richer to poorer peasants, replacing government-appointed leaders with elected village councils, and protecting battered wives. Encouraged to air their grievances by "speaking pains to recall pains" in village meetings, women warned abusive men to mend their ways or face punishment or arrest. However, inevitably the release of pent-up rage against violent husbands or greedy landlords who mistreated tenants led to excesses, such as angry crowds beating them to death.

The military and political tide turned against the Republic, and in 1948 Chiang's troops in Manchuria surrendered to the communists. To revive Chiang's prospects, the United States pressured him unsuccessfully to broaden his political base with democratic reforms. Some American leaders demanded that the United States send troops to help Chiang, but others concluded that his regime had lost too much popular support to win the conflict. Through 1949 the communists took the major cities of north China and pushed Chiang's army south. Finally Chiang fled to the island of Taiwan, along with thousands of troops and 2 million supporters. On Taiwan, with massive U.S. aid and military protection, the leaders of the relocated Republic of China developed a successful capitalist strategy for economic growth. Meanwhile, mainland China's history now moved in a direction very different from that of Chiang's Republic of China.

CHRONOLOGY

	China	Japan	Korea and Taiwan
1940	**1945–1949** Chinese civil war **1949** Chinese communist triumph	**1946–1952** U.S. occupation of Japan	**1950–1953** Korean War
1960	**1960** Sino-Soviet split **1966–1976** Great Proletarian Cultural Revolution **1978** Four Modernizations policy	**1960s–1989** Rapid economic growth	
1980			**1997** Asian financial collapse

The key question confronting the Chinese communists after 1949 was how to achieve rapid economic development in an overpopulated, battered country. Two decades of war had ruined the economy, leaving little capital for industrialization. China had no overseas empire to exploit for economic resources, and the communists did not want loans and foreign investment that might reduce their independence. Furthermore, they faced a powerful enemy: propelled by alarm at Mao's policies and anticommunist Cold War concerns, the United States launched an economic boycott to shut China off from international trade, refused diplomatic recognition, and surrounded China with military bases. Isolated, China created its own models of economic and political development.

China's Challenges

Between 1949 and 1976 China followed two different models of economic development, each with its own priorities and consequences. The first, Stalinism, a system based on the Soviet model of central planning, heavy industry, a powerful bureaucracy, and a managerial system, dominated the early years (1949–1957) (see Chronology: China Since 1945). China received some Soviet aid but otherwise financed development before the late 1970s through self-reliance, limiting contact with the global system. As in Meiji Japan and the Soviet Union, the state took the lead, emphasizing austerity and making people work hard for low wages in hopes that future generations would live better. The communists also abolished private ownership of business and industry and transferred land to poor peasants. Soon they began collectivizing the rural economy into cooperatives, in which peasants helped each other and shared tools. As in the Soviet Union, new privileged elite emerged in the government and the ruling Communist Party, which cracked down on dissent.

Stalinism and Maoism

By the late 1950s Mao, disenchanted with Stalinism, reintroduced Maoism, a unique synthesis of Marxism and Chinese thought that emphasized the mass mobilization of the population. Under Maoism, China's guiding ideology from 1957 to 1961 and then again from 1966 to 1976, people were mobilized for development projects, such as building dams and pest elimination. Everyone was issued fly swatters and asked to kill as many flies as possible in hopes of reducing disease, and the party introduced tree-planting campaigns to reverse the ecological instability of recent centuries. Mao also reorganized the rural economy into **communes**, large agricultural units that combined many families and villages into a common administrative system for pooling resources and labor. A commune could build and operate a factory, secondary school, and hospital, tasks that would be impractical for a single village. The communes raised agricultural productivity, eliminated landlords, and promoted social and economic equality. Mao also located industry in rural areas, keeping the peasants at home rather than fostering movement to cities.

communes Large agricultural units introduced by Mao Zedong that combined many families and villages into a common system for pooling resources and labor.

The most radical Maoist policy was the **Great Leap Forward** (1958–1961), an ambitious attempt to industrialize China rapidly and end poverty through collective efforts. Farmers and workers built small iron furnaces in their backyards, courtyards, and gardens and spent their free time turning everything from cutlery to old bicycles into steel. But the poorly conceived campaign, pushing the people too hard, nearly wrecked the economy and, along with disastrous weather, caused 30 million people to starve. One of Mao's critics in the leadership charged: "Grains scattered on the ground, potato leaves withered; Strong young people have left to smelt iron, only children and old women reaped the crops; How can they pass the coming year?"[3] These failures diminished Mao's influence, bringing moderate policies in the early 1960s.

Great Leap Forward Mao Zedong's ambitious attempt to industrialize China rapidly and end poverty through collective efforts.

Chinese Politics and the World

Communist Rule

The Communist Party, led by Mao as chairman, dominated the political system; party members occupied all key positions in the government and military. Using the slogan "Politics Takes Command," the communists emphasized ideology, making political values pervasive and requiring all Chinese to become members of political discussion groups. Party activists monitored the discussions and reported dissenters, and political education was integrated into the schools, work units, and even leisure activities. The party also sought to eradicate inequalities and to alter thought patterns and attitudes, emphasizing the interests of the group over those of the individual. To eliminate class distinctions, officials and intellectuals had to perform physical labor, such as laying bricks for house construction or spreading manure to fertilize farm fields, so that they would understand the experience of the workers and peasants. The system required massive social control, enabled by a vast police apparatus; millions suspected of opposing the communists were harassed, jailed, exiled, or killed. Even communist sympathizers, such as the outspoken feminist writer Ding Ling (1902–1986), were purged after falling out of official favor. In exchange for accepting its policies, the state promised everyone the "five guarantees" of food, clothes, fuel, education, and a decent burial. But over the years thousands of people fled to British-ruled Hong Kong.

Despite these problems, the communists restored China's status as a major world power (see Map 27.1) and pursued a foreign policy that maximized stability at home. Mao reasserted Chinese sovereignty in outlying areas and in 1950 sent armies to occupy Tibet, once a Qing province, whose people were culturally and historically distinct from the Chinese and had broken away in 1912. Most Tibetans, however, opposed Chinese rule, sparking periodic unrest. The Chinese suppression of a Tibetan revolt led the highest Tibetan Buddhist leader, the Dalai Lama (b. 1935), to flee to India in 1959. Revered by devout Tibetans as both a spiritual and political leader, he became a defiant symbol of Tibetan resistance to Chinese rule, traveling the world to rally support for the Tibetan cause while promoting Buddhist ethics and world peace. China failed to reclaim another former Qing-ruled territory, Mongolia, which in 1924 had become a communist state allied to, and protected by, the USSR.

China and the World

China faced major challenges in foreign affairs. In 1950 China, which supported the communist North Korean government installed in 1948, was drawn into the Korean War between the USSR-backed North Korea and United Nations forces led by the United States, sent to defend pro-U.S. South Korea. When the U.N. forces pushed the North Korean army toward China's border and the U.S. commander, General Douglas MacArthur, talked recklessly of carrying the offensive across the Yalu River into China, the Chinese entered the conflict and pushed U.N. troops back south. The war produced huge casualties on both sides, including several hundred thousand Chinese, and reinforced the hostility and mutual fear between China and the United States. The Korean War

Honoring Chairman Mao Since the beginning of communist rule in China in 1949, this giant portrait of Mao Zedong, the chairman of the Chinese Communist Party, has hung on the Gate of Heavenly Peace, the entrance to the Forbidden City of the Qing dynasty emperors, in the heart of Beijing.

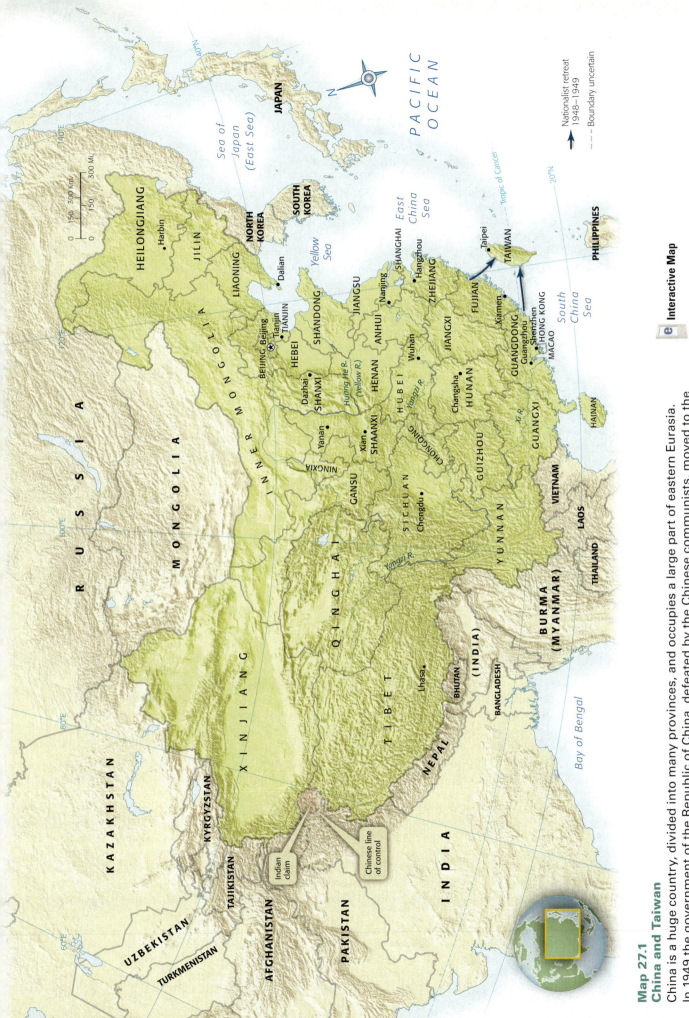

Map 27.1
China and Taiwan

China is a huge country, divided into many provinces, and occupies a large part of eastern Eurasia. In 1949 the government of the Republic of China, defeated by the Chinese communists, moved to the island of Taiwan, off China's Pacific coast.

PACIFIC OCEAN

⬆ Nationalist retreat 1948–1949
- - - Boundary uncertain

e Interactive Map

RUSSIA

KAZAKHSTAN

KYRGYZSTAN

TAJIKISTAN

UZBEKISTAN

TURKMENISTAN

AFGHANISTAN

PAKISTAN

MONGOLIA

INNER MONGOLIA

XINJIANG

TIBET

QINGHAI

NINGXIA

GANSU

SHAANXI
- Yanan
- Xian

SICHUAN
- Chengdu

CHONGQING

YUNNAN

GUIZHOU

GUANGXI

Xi R.

HAINAN

GUANGDONG
- Guangzhou
- Shenzhen
HONG KONG
MACAO

South China Sea

VIETNAM

LAOS

THAILAND

BURMA (MYANMAR)

BANGLADESH

NEPAL

BHUTAN

INDIA

(INDIA)

Indian claim

Chinese line of control

Lhasa

Bay of Bengal

HEILONGJIANG
- Harbin

JILIN

LIAONING
- Dalian

NORTH KOREA

SOUTH KOREA

JAPAN

Sea of Japan (East Sea)

HEBEI

BEIJING Beijing ✪
Tianjin TIANJIN

SHANXI
- Dazhai

SHANDONG

Huang He R. (Yellow R.)

HENAN

Yellow Sea

JIANGSU
- Nanjing

SHANGHAI

ANHUI

HUBEI
- Wuhan

Yangzi R.

HUNAN
- Changsha

ZHEJIANG
- Hangzhou

East China Sea

JIANGXI

FUJIAN
- Xiamen

TAIWAN
- Taipei

Tropic of Cancer

20°N

PHILIPPINES

300 Mi.
0 150 300 Km
0 150

N

ended in a stalemate in 1953, and the United States signed a mutual defense treaty with Chiang Kai-shek's regime on Taiwan. The substantial U.S. forces stationed in Taiwan and South Korea joined the thousands of U.S. troops that had remained in Japan, Okinawa, and the Philippines after World War II, while the U.S. Navy patrolled the waters off China. But Mao used paranoia about this formidable U.S. military presence to mobilize the Chinese around his programs, and the ability to achieve a Korean stalemate with the powerful Americans improved China's international position. Many countries allied to the United States recognized the Republic of China, now based on Taiwan, as the official government of China, even while the United States continued to veto the Chinese communist effort to gain China's United Nations seat.

Relations with Russia and the United States

In the late 1950s tensions between China and the USSR grew. The Soviet policy of "peaceful coexistence" with the West enraged Mao, who labeled the United States "a paper tiger." Mao also opposed the 1956 decision of the Soviet leader, Nikita Khrushchev **(KROOSH-chef)**, to reveal the excesses of Stalinist police-state rule in Russia. By 1960 the Sino-Soviet split was official; the USSR withdrew advisers, technicians, and even the spare parts for the industries they had helped build. The Chinese built up their military strength, tested their first atomic bomb, and occasionally clashed with Soviet forces on their border. To counterbalance the power of the United States and the USSR, China sought allies and influence in Asia and Africa. Yet, despite fierce anti-U.S. and anti-Soviet rhetoric, Chinese leaders generally followed a cautious foreign policy.

During the 1970s Chinese foreign policy changed dramatically, symbolized by U.S. president Richard Nixon's trip to Beijing in 1972. The two nations shared a hostility toward the USSR; moreover, the bitter U.S. experience in Vietnam had opened the door to foreign policy rethinking in both the United States and China. Chinese leaders perceived the Americans as stepping back from Asian commitments, and hence a diminishing threat. The United States quit blocking Chinese membership in the United Nations and, in 1978, normalized diplomatic relations with China. Meanwhile, the Chinese developed better relations with noncommunist nations in Southeast Asia and Africa.

Cultural Revolution and Maoist Society

Mao was a complex figure, a self-proclaimed feminist who promoted women's rights but also a sexually promiscuous man who married several times and had many lovers, but who also seldom bathed or brushed his teeth. A poor public speaker, he could nevertheless inspire millions to follow his lead. A poet and philosopher but also power hungry and ruthless, he made many enemies, even within the leadership. Although many of his initiatives ultimately failed or resulted in misery for millions of people, he played a powerful role in modern world history, leading the communists to victory, reunifying China, focusing public attention on rural people, and placing his stamp on the world's most populous nation.

Primary Source: "One Hundred Items for Destroying the Old and Establishing the New" Read this document of support for Mao's socialist ideology and commitment to destroy the old ways of Chinese thinking by a student group of Red Guards.

Dissatisfied with China's development and his eclipse by the early 1960s, in the mid-1960s Mao regained his dominant status by resurrecting Maoism and its vision of a new society comprising unselfish, politically conscious citizens. In Mao's vision, individuals inspired by the slogan "Serve the People" subordinated their own needs to the broader social order. His allies emphasized the cult of Mao, and newspapers reported that, illuminated by Mao's revolutionary ideas, factory workers would discover better techniques for galvanizing, the manager of a food store would double his sales of watermelons, and farmers would learn to judge exactly the right amount of manure to fertilize their plots. Following these ideas, between 1966 and 1976 a radical movement generated by Mao convulsed and reshaped China like a whirlwind. The **Great Proletarian Cultural Revolution** represented Mao's attempt to implant his vision, destroy his enemies, crush the stifling bureaucracy, and renew the revolution's vigor. Workers and students known as **Red Guards** roamed around cities and the countryside in groups, attacking and arresting anti-Mao leaders and smashing temples, churches, and party and government headquarters. Mao's supporters also created revolutionary committees, led by students, workers, and soldiers, to run cities, factories, and schools. The Red Guards carried copies of a little red book containing short quotations from Mao's writings, such as his claim that Marxism cannot be understood through books alone but also requires contact with the workers and peasants. One observer noted that "giant portraits of [Mao] now hung in the streets, busts were in every chamber, his books and photographs were everywhere on display."[4]

Great Proletarian Cultural Revolution
A radical movement in China between 1966 and 1976 that represented Mao Zedong's attempt to implant his vision, destroy his enemies, crush the stifling bureaucracy, and renew the revolution's vigor.

Red Guards Young workers and students who were the major supporters of the Cultural Revolution in Mao's China.

The turmoil disrupted industrial and agricultural production, closed most schools for two years, and resulted in thousands killed, jailed, or removed from official positions. Millions of others were sent to remote rural areas to experience peasant life, and anti-Mao officials, intellectuals, and people with upper-class backgrounds faced public criticism and often punishment. A Chinese journalist whose grandparents were capitalists remembered the attacks on her family: "Red Guards swarming all over the house and a great fire in our court-yard onto which were thrown my father's books, my grand-parent's precious traditional furniture and my toys."[5] Soon even Mao was dampening the radical fervor.

The communists reshaped Chinese society in many ways. Mao promoted a model of social equality, known as the **Iron Rice Bowl**, in which the people, especially in villages, shared resources—food, draft animals, farm equipment—and the peasants enjoyed dignity. As a result, Maoism generally improved life for the poorer Chinese. An emphasis on preventive medicine included the training of villagers as paramedics, known as barefoot doctors, who addressed everyday health care, such as distributing medi-cation and setting broken bones. Where once famine and disease were common, most Chinese now enjoyed decent health care. In addition, mass education raised literacy rates to the levels of industrialized nations. Many peasants appreciated the changes. In 1971 an elderly peasant told visiting Western scholars what he had gained: "Now we are free to work full-time, have a secure home, eat enough food, have complete medical care, receive education—and take our future in our hands."[6]

The communists also tried to overturn Confucian-influenced patriarchy by raising the status of women. Mao praised women, who he said "held up half the sky," as a force in production. A new marriage law abolished arranged marriages, forbade men from taking concubines, and made divorce easier, while a land reform empowered women economically by expanding their property rights. Women now enjoyed legal equality with men and greater access to education, often worked for wages, and played a stronger public role, often leading local organizations. In

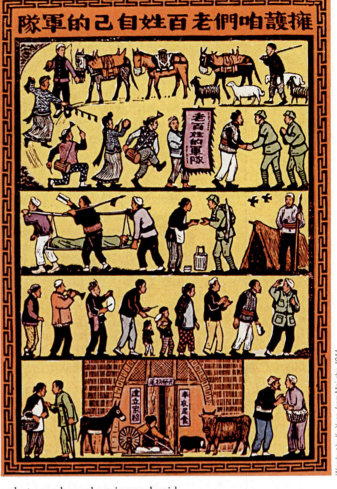

Woodcut by Ku Yuan, from Mei-shu, 1944

conferences and periodicals, women debated the proper balance between housekeeping and paid work and whether they should devote their energies to the revolution as well as to their husbands and children. Women activists worked to build a democratic family, emphasizing love matches rather than arranged marriages, fostering closer emotional ties between husbands, wives, and chil-dren, and lessening male domination. But the rural areas remained more conservative than the cit-ies. Moreover, few women held high national positions. Mao's last wife, Jiang Qing **(chang ching)** (1914–1991), a former film actress, wielded great power during the Cultural Revolution but was unpopular because of her radical policies. In 1976, after Mao's death, Jiang and her top party allies, the "Gang of Four," lost a power struggle and were imprisoned.

The communists often undermined traditional beliefs and culture. Calling religion a bond enslaving people, Mao moved to control religious behavior and marginalize Christian churches, Buddhist monasteries, and Islamic mosques, and by the 1970s only a small minority openly prac-ticed religion. Only religious leaders who cooperated with the state maintained their positions. Mao also sought to use the arts as a weapon in the class struggle, fostering a "people's art" cre-ated by and for the common people. He wrote, "In the world today all culture, all literature and art belongs to definite political lines. Art for art's sake, art that stands above the class and party do not exist in reality."[7] During the Great Leap Forward, party activists collected literature written by com-mon people and encouraged peasants and workers to compose poetry and songs. Peasants painted scenes of people at work, often in bright, cheerful colors conveying an optimistic tone, and part-time writers got a day off from the factory to work on literary projects. A 1958 poem proclaimed: "Labor is joy, how joyful it is, Bathed in sweat and two hands full of mud. Like sweet rain, my sweat waters the land."[8] However, critics argued that art serving revolutionary goals was reduced to politi-cal propaganda.

The politicization of the arts reached its peak levels during the Cultural Revolution, when elit-ism came under fierce attack. Red Guards sang new songs in praise of change and Chairman Mao, such as "The East is red, the sun has risen. China has produced a Mao Zedong; He is the great savior of the people."[9] Militant operas had a strong revolutionary message, such as the dignity of peas-ant life or Communist Party history. Rejecting Western-style ballet as decadent, dancers composed

Chinese Political Art This woodcut, carved during the Chinese civil war of the late 1940s, was typical of the politi-cal art made by the com-munists to rally popular support for their cause, a hallmark of Mao's era. Entitled "Support Our Common People's Own Army," the woodcut shows Chinese peasants working together with the communist military forces.

Iron Rice Bowl A model of social equality in Mao's China in which the people, especially in the villages, shared resources and the peasants enjoyed status and dignity.

revolutionary ballets that integrated Chinese martial arts, such as kung fu, folk dances, and Russian ballet. For example, *The Red Detachment of Women* portrayed the experiences of a company of women soldiers during the civil war against Chiang's Republic.

Mao's Legacy

After Mao died in 1976, the Chinese took stock of Mao's legacy. The communists had restored China to great power status and renewed the people's confidence after a century of imperialistic exploitation and invasion. China was no longer a doormat; it even had nuclear weapons. Once again, the Chinese envisioned themselves as the Middle Kingdom exercising influence in the world. Whereas a generation earlier begging or prostitution had been common, now most Chinese, though enjoying little material surplus, could satisfy their basic food, housing, and clothing needs. The economy was also healthier and more broadly based than in 1949.

Mao's policies, however, had also resulted in failures and political repression. Although China may have gained control of its economic destiny, it was still poor by world standards. In addition, Mao had discouraged free enterprise and individual initiative, so that few private cars interfered with the bicycles that most Chinese used to get to work or go shopping. Chinese wanted better housing and more consumer goods now rather than in a distant future. With few luxuries or diversions available, life was dull. In addition, the fierce punishment of dissenters and the turmoil of the Great Leap Forward and Cultural Revolution had ruined numerous lives. People were disillusioned by government coercion, unfulfilled promises, and the chaos of the Cultural Revolution, and bitter disagreements had ripped the Communist Party leadership apart. Many blamed Mao and his radicalism for the problems, and reformers in the party charged that, in his later years, Mao had lost touch with common people's lives. The often erratic policies made people cynical, willing to give only passive cooperation and avoiding commitment to a particular line. Many Chinese were ready for change.

SECTION SUMMARY

- After Japan was defeated in World War II, Chinese communists and nationalists fought a civil war in which Mao Zedong's communists triumphed by appealing to people's frustration with the corruption of Chiang Kai-shek's nationalists.

- To develop its economy, China first employed Stalinism, which featured central planning dominated by a bureaucratic elite, and then shifted to Maoism, which emphasized mass mobilization of the people to industrialize and maximize output, but under Maoism millions starved to death and many suffered under political repression.

- China reasserted itself as a world power, reclaiming Tibet, becoming involved in the Korean War, ultimately splitting with the USSR, and only reestablishing formal relations with the United States in the 1970s.

- Frustrated with China's development, Mao led a decade-long cultural revolution, a period of radical upheaval in which young Red Guards attempted to destroy Mao's enemies and obstacles to progress, which caused great economic problems and brought misery to many.

- Mao reshaped Chinese society, improving literacy rates and health care, especially for rural people, expanding the rights of women, opposing traditional religious institutions and elitism, and encouraging the people to produce their own literature and art, but at the cost of many human rights abuses.

- While Mao restored China as a world power and brought many out of poverty, after his death in 1976 many Chinese wanted to join the modern world and gain increased access to material benefits.

CHINESE MODERNIZATION

What factors explain the dramatic rise of Chinese economic power in the world since 1978?

Deng Xiaoping (dung shee-yao-ping) (1904–1997), a longtime Communist Party leader who had often clashed with Mao, came to power in 1978 and changed China's direction. Deng and his allies rejected Mao's view of a self-sufficient, ideologically pure China outside the world economy, concluding that collectivized agriculture had failed to raise productivity enough to finance a jump into the high technology and industry needed to make China a major power. In 1978 Deng, portraying China as at a turning point in history, announced the policy of Four Modernizations: the development of agriculture, industry, military, and science and technology to turn China into a powerful nation by 2000. Deng's successors generally followed his pragmatic policies, which transformed China into an economic powerhouse and modified Maoist society.

Market Socialism and Repression

From 1978 to 1989 Chinese leaders pursued **market socialism**, a mix of free enterprise, economic liberalization, and state controls that produced economic dynamism. This pragmatic approach, unlike Mao's, was more concerned with economic results than socialist values. Twice purged for opposing Mao, Deng was fond of a Chinese proverb: "It doesn't matter whether a cat is black or white, only if it catches mice." Deng used the market to stimulate productivity, and China reentered the world economy to obtain capital investment to spur manufacturing. Like Meiji Japan, China now imported technology, foreign expertise, and capitalist ideas. Deng believed that China had reached a plateau; to move to the next levels required wider international participation. Hence, he improved ties with the United States, Japan, western Europe, and non-communist Southeast Asia. Dazzled by China's huge potential market of, as Western experts put it, 1 billion toothbrushes (for toothpaste) and 2 billion armpits (for deodorant), Western companies promoted increased trade.

Introducing capitalist ideas, such as offering workers material incentives rather than ideological slogans, Deng's reforms sparked dramatic changes. The government first allowed small private enterprises, then larger ones; ultimately both private and state-owned enterprises competed with each other. In agriculture, Deng replaced Mao's communes with the contract system in which peasants could lease (but could not buy) land to work privately. In many districts this free market led to soaring productivity, with rural per capita incomes rising fourfold in the first decade. Tapping a skilled, industrious, but cheap labor force, hundreds of Western and Asian companies set up manufacturing operations, producing goods such as shirts, underwear, and toys chiefly for export. In the 1980s, China became a consumer society; even in small cities, shops stocked Japanese televisions and Western soft drinks. Over the next twenty-five years the economy quadrupled in size and foreign trade increased ten times over.

Deng also loosened political and cultural controls. Intellectuals and artists enjoyed greater freedom; people long silenced or imprisoned were heard from again. The press was enlivened and the scope for public debate widened. Deng also increasingly tolerated organized religion. Western popular culture, especially films, rock music, and discos, won a huge audience; books and magazines from around the world became available; and foreign travelers backpacked in remote areas. The sentimental recordings of Taiwan's top female singer, Deng Lijun (deyn lee-choong), better known to her millions of fans in Hong Kong, Japan, and Southeast Asia as Teresa Teng, were so widely played in Chinese homes and restaurants that people said that "the day belongs to Deng Xiaoping but the night belongs to Deng Lijun."[10] At the same time, novels and short stories revealed the depth of suffering during the Cultural Revolution, and popular writers developed huge audiences for stories daring to use sexual themes. Chinese-made films won international acclaim, while creative directors associated with semi-independent film studios skirmished with wary government censors. Their films portrayed China as anything but a communist paradise. Rock musicians, especially Cui Jian (sway jen), a former trumpeter with the Beijing Symphony, became a major voice for alienated urban youth. Dressed in battered army fatigues and a coat style favored by Mao, Cui sang: "This guitar in my hands is like a knife. I want to cut at your hypocrisy till I see some truth." Cui's songs were indirect, focusing more on bureaucratic corruption, social problems, and young people's frustrations than on politics, but Chinese youth easily read between the lines for the hidden meanings. One fan commented that "Cui Jian says things we all feel, but cannot say."[11]

Although many Chinese applauded the ideological loosening and the growing economic options, market socialism hid a dark underside. Many districts had seen few benefits from the reorganization of rural life. Chinese authorities imposed one policy for the vast nation rather than allowing districts and villages to find a policy that worked for them. Some villagers, because of their better land, political connections, or entrepreneurial skills, benefited more than others, opening a gap between newly rich and poor villagers. Prices rose rapidly, and corruption increased as bureaucrats and Communist Party officials lined their own pockets. Moreover, tension increased within the party, with Stalinists and Maoists viewing economic liberalization as undermining one-party rule and communism. The fall of communism in eastern Europe and the USSR in 1989 alarmed hardliners. But dissidents and some reformers, seeing strong controls as inhibiting initiative, pushed democracy as "the fifth modernization." In response, party hardliners called for cracking down, arresting dissidents.

In 1989 the tensions in Deng's China reached a boiling point, generating massive protests and government repression. Thousands of protesters, led by university students and workers, took over Tiananmen Square in downtown Beijing, demanding the resignation of the most unpopular leaders, an end to government corruption, and a transition to a fully open system. The party hardliners, in alliance with Deng, purged the moderate party leaders and ordered the army to clear out the demonstrators. In what became known as the Tiananmen Massacre, the army killed hundreds and arrested thousands, while millions around the world watched the violence on television. The courageous

market socialism A Chinese economic program used between 1978 and 1989 that mixed free enterprise, economic liberalization, and state controls and that produced economic dynamism in China.

Spurring Economic Growth

Cultural Life

Tensions and Government Crackdown

Beijing protesters had overestimated their popular support. Since many Chinese outside the cities valued stability more than vague promises of a better world, the protesters had also miscalculated the prospects of democracy in a country with an authoritarian political tradition.

Economic Change and Politics Since 1989

market Leninism A policy followed after the Tiananmen Massacre in 1989 whereby the Chinese communist state asserted more power over society while also fostering an even stronger market orientation in the economy than had existed under market socialism.

After the Tiananmen Massacre the communists modified market socialism into **market Leninism**, a policy whereby the Chinese state, obsessed with stability, asserted more power over society while also fostering an even stronger market orientation in the economy. The communist leadership reestablished control in political, social, and cultural life, tolerating less dissent than in the 1980s, but the economy became further privatized. Remembering the chaos of the Cultural Revolution and the 1989 unrest, Chinese often valued political stability over individual rights, such as unfettered free speech and participation in government, especially at a time of overheated economic growth. For 2000 years Chinese governments have promoted social and political harmony to discourage conflict.

Social Unrest

However, the control of the one-party state was not absolute. In some local elections communist officials permitted competition between candidates, and some dissenters still spoke out. Opponents of the environmentally damaging Three Gorges Dam project, constructed to control the Yangzi (yahng-zeh) River and provide electrical power, publicized their views but could not halt the expensive project, which forced several million people to move from their homes. However, the Chinese state, often arbitrary in its actions, used the military and police to intimidate dissidents. Assertive dissidents faced arrest, and public debate was dampened. China executed thousands of people a year, mostly criminals but including some accused of economic misbehavior or political opposition. Anxious to preserve national unity, China's leaders also suppressed dissent in Tibet and among Muslim Turkish groups in Xinjiang (shinjee-yahng), in far western China, where people sought autonomy, greater religious freedom, and limits on large-scale Chinese immigration. In Tibet in 2008 and Xinjiang in 2009, the seething resentment against the government and Han Chinese newcomers led to riots and inter-ethnic violence, leaving hundreds of people dead or injured.

Rapid Economic Growth

After 1980 China enjoyed the fastest economic growth in the world, often 10 percent a year, abetted by a "get-rich-quick" mentality among many Chinese. Deng claimed that to get rich is glorious. China's exports increased fifteenfold between 1980 and 2000, and the communist leadership sought popular support by offering consumer goods and wealth rather than political reform, providing shops with ample consumer goods and households with spending money. In the early days of reform people aspired to the "three bigs": bicycle, wristwatch, and sewing machine. Now they wanted televisions, washing machines, and video recorders. The urban middle class grew rapidly, and by 2009 China had moved ahead of Germany into third place in world economic strength. China also clearly benefited from the mobility of capital and products with globalization. If the economy maintains high annual growth rates, China may eventually have the world's largest economy.

Although the economic reforms have improved living standards for many Chinese, they have also produced numerous downsides. For example, economic dynamism is concentrated in a few coastal provinces and special economic zones, where living standards approach those of Taiwan and South Korea. Cities such as Shanghai and Shenzen boast towering skyscrapers and huge shopping malls with upscale shops. Elsewhere, conditions have often deteriorated. Unemployment grows dramatically as state enterprises close or become uncompetitive and inflation skyrockets. Although laws discourage migration to another district without government permission, millions of peasants seeking jobs or a less rustic life have nonetheless moved to cities, where they struggle. Their precarious position became clear in 2008, when the global economic crisis began to affect China as overseas markets collapsed. Thousands of factories closed, leaving millions of disillusioned workers without incomes. Many had little choice but to return to their home villages. Yet, unlike the Western nations and Japan, China's economy still grew, albeit at about half the rate of 2007. By later 2009, thanks to a huge government stimulus package and autocratic decision-making, China's economy began a recovery and many workers found jobs.

Resource and Energy Consumption

The Chinese have also become even greater users of world resources, such as oil and coal, and major polluters of the atmosphere. China has become the number two producer of greenhouse gases that cause global warming, although its output is only half that of the the United States. Mindful of the unhealthy air pollution of China's cities and fouled rivers and lakes fostered by industrialization, by 2009 Chinese leaders placed more emphasis than Americans do on developing cleaner, greener, and renewable energy sources such as wind and solar. Yet, China still relies heavily on coal-based power sources and now leads the world in carbon emissions. Water supplies have become badly overstretched, and, with private cars clogging the city streets where bicycles once dominated, smog blankets the cities. Land and energy grow more expensive.

Political and economic changes have influenced other areas of Chinese life. In the cities, the newly rich entrepreneurs enjoy luxury cars, access to golf courses, and vacations abroad. China has several hundred thousand millionaires and some billionaires. Even the middle class, numbering over 200 million and chiefly working in business, can enjoy a comfortable life. With money concentrated in the private sector, teachers, professors, and doctors leave their low-paying state jobs to open businesses or join foreign corporations, and some village leaders use their power to amass wealth and power. The wealthy flaunt their affluence, and the poor resent it. Street songs often mock the powerful: "I'm a big official, so I eat and drink, and I've got the potbelly to prove it. Beer, spirits, rice wine, love potions—I drink it all."[12] By 2005 peasant protests against seizure of village land to build polluting factories, luxury housing, and golf courses had become frequent, numbering in the thousands annually and resulting in the arrests of protest leaders. Meanwhile, the shift to market forces leaves millions unable to afford medical care and schooling for their children. Thanks to the decline in health care, especially in rural areas, between half a million and 1.5 million Chinese have HIV or AIDS. Some poorer Chinese long fondly for Mao and the dismantled Iron Rice Bowl. Yet, despite reduced job security and social services, people are now freer than before to travel, change jobs, enjoy leisure, and even complain.

The Communist Party has faced problems Mao could never have anticipated. Once viewing itself as the protector of the working class and poor peasants, it now welcomes wealthy businessmen and professionals into its ranks. Many who have little faith in the communist vision still see party membership as helpful to their career prospects. And most young Chinese, preoccupied with seeking wealth, know little about the Tienanmen Massacre. Yet, powerful provincial leaders whose first priority is economic growth increasingly ignore Beijing. The rapid economic growth raises questions as to whether Chinese leaders can resolve the increasing inequalities and spread wealth more equitably to check the growth of social tensions. Some pessimists forecast more conflicts between rich and poor Chinese, or civil war between rich and poor regions.

Chinese Society and Culture Since 1989

The government struggles to maintain social stability. Mao's China had been one of the world's safest countries, but economic growth and the quest for wealth generated a rapid increase in crime. The close connection between government and business corruption, underworld activity, and financial success led to Chinese talking about the "Five Colors," or surest roads to riches: Communist Party connections, prostitution, smuggling, illegal drug dealing, and criminal gangs. Drug dealing became rampant once again, serving the growing number of people using narcotics for escape. Maintaining Confucian and Maoist attitudes, many Chinese view wealth as corrupting and mistrust rich business interests.

Although women's economic status has often improved, many still face restricted gender expectations. While the feminist journalist Xue Xinran **(shoe shin-rahn)** wrote that "Chinese women had always thought that their lives should be full of misery. Many had no idea what happiness was, other than having a son for the family"[13] (see Profile: Xue Xinran, a Chinese Voice for Women), many scholars consider the stereotype of the long-suffering, submissive Chinese woman misleading, noting that modern women are often strong-willed and resourceful. But many rural women may feel intimidated by men. Women now receive little support because government policies are aimed at economic growth, not gender equality. Millions of rural women migrate to the cities for industrial and service jobs, providing much of the labor force for the new factories that have helped turn China into an economic giant. Wherever they live, women commonly work long hours, and few women occupy high positions in the government, Communist Party, or top business enterprises.

Since China already had 1 billion people, a fifth of humankind, Deng Xiaoping introduced a one-child-per-family policy to try to stabilize the population. Critics complained that children without siblings were pampered and self-centered. The policy also encouraged and sometimes mandated abortion and, since traditional attitudes favoring sons remained, resulted in widespread killing of female babies. With more boys than girls being born and raised, an imbalance in numbers between the sexes developed, with serious social consequences as men cannot find wives.

Global entertainment and consumer culture also affect China, with Western popular culture becoming a powerful force among youth. Cui Jian and other rock musicians, some of whom had participated in the Beijing student protest movement, now compete with heavy metal, punk, and rap musicians. Every city has clubs offering Western music, and Chinese imitators of Anglo-American boy bands and girl groups have found a vast teen audience. In 2005 more than 8 million Chinese voted for three finalists in a hugely popular Chinese television program, *Super Girl*, a local version of the popular U.S. television program, *American Idol*. Television offers U.S. series dubbed in Chinese, such as *The X-Files* and *Baywatch*, and in Shanghai a theme park very similar to Disney

World features a Wild West Town. Chinese consumers are served by numerous McDonald's outlets (one near Mao's mausoleum), Hard Rock Cafes, Wal-Marts, and some 85,000 Avon agents selling American cosmetics and beauty products. Homosexuals, who faced condemnation and discrimination under Mao, have been slowly coming out, especially in the cities, where gay bars are common, and even have hundreds of their own websites. But South Korean popular culture and consumer products—music, clothing, television dramas, movies, cosmetics—also became very fashionable among young Chinese. Much of the conversion of millions of Chinese to evangelical Christianity is due to the thousands of South Korean Protestant missionaries in the country.

China and the Information Superhighway

Those Chinese able to afford satellite dishes, fax machines, and personal computers linked to the Internet have gained access to ideas from around the world. More than 300 million Chinese are Internet users, and 53 million own personal computers. E-commerce is becoming much more popular and China's biggest on-line auction site had some 145 million registered members in 2009. To restrict the free flow of information, officials crack down on cyberspace, sometimes closing down Internet cafes and preventing Internet providers—local and Western—from allowing access to banned websites. But websites and blogs proliferate rapidly, making complete monitoring difficult. By 2009 the government sought even stricter controls over the Internet and electronic tools such as Twitter, Facebook, and YouTube. The government also sometimes shuts down newspapers and magazines whose reporting is too daring, but brave journalists and officials have risked punishment by openly criticizing micromanagement of the media. Some liberal party members and intellectuals sign petitions and write articles calling for more attention to human rights abuses, actions that may cost them their jobs or invite police surveillance. Yet, several hundred thousand Chinese, including the children of high officials, have studied in Western universities.

Policies toward religion have been inconsistent. After 1978 the government tolerated millions of Chinese returning to their ancestral faith, but it has cracked down on movements deemed a threat or that refuse to accept official restrictions. Officials arrest and sometimes execute leaders and members of the assertive, missionary *Falun Gong* meditation sect, a mix of Daoist, Buddhist, and Christian influences, and have tried to close down rapidly proliferating independent Christian churches that do not seek government approval.

China in the Global System

China's relations with the wider world have been colored by humiliation from the lost wars and foreign gunboats of the nineteenth century and by civil wars and Japanese invasions in the twentieth. Eventually the Chinese saw their nation once again stand tall, strong, and increasingly rich. In 1997 they celebrated the peaceful return of Hong Kong from British colonial control, rectifying the loss of that territory during the Opium War. Hong Kong, a prosperous enclave whose towering skyscrapers, dazzling neon-lit waterfront, bustling shopping malls, and dynamic film industry made it a symbol of East Asian capitalism, was incorporated under the policy of "one nation, two systems." At the same time, a vocal and popular pro-democracy movement in Hong Kong charges that China's occasional interference in Hong Kong politics threatens political freedoms. Another loss was rectified when in 1999 Portugal returned its small coastal colony of Macao to Chinese control. Macao's economy is based on gambling casinos, a lucrative enterprise the once-puritanical communists now seem happy to tolerate.

Reclaiming Hong Kong and Macao

China and Global Power

Since 1976 China has pursued a pragmatic foreign policy designed to win friends and trading partners but to also avoid entangling alliances. China gradually improved relations with the United States and USSR, cultivated diplomatic ties with other nations, and became increasingly active in the world community, joining international institutions such as the World Trade Organization. To enhance China's competitive stance, some 200 million children study English. China now enjoys tremendous influence in the world economy, importing vast amounts of capital and natural resources, such as Zambian copper and Venezuelan oil, while exporting industrial products of every kind. Thousands of foreign investors have come from the West, Japan, Southeast Asia, South Korea, and even Taiwan, opening factories and negotiating joint ventures with Chinese firms. Meanwhile, China has supported the U.S. economy, becoming the major buyer of the treasury bonds that financed the growing U.S. national debt in the early 2000s. Chinese enterprises have also begun buying up companies in other nations. Hundreds of Chinese companies operate in Africa and Latin America. Many thousands of Chinese have followed them as workers or to open small enterprises. In addition, China provides investment and loans to governments but expects cooperation in return. Thus China has become the world's most successful newly industrializing economy, buttressed by a vast resource base, a huge domestic market, and a resourceful labor force.

Yet China has met roadblocks in enhancing its global power. The government continues to threaten forced unification if Taiwan, which enjoys a defense agreement with the United States,

XUE XINRAN, A CHINESE VOICE FOR WOMEN

In the 1980s Xue Xinran **(shoe shin-rahn)**, known professionally as Xinran, began working for a radio network and went on to become one of China's most successful and innovative journalists. A radio call-in show that she launched in 1989 featured hundreds of poignant and haunting stories by women. The huge audience the show attracted and her sensitive handling of the callers made Xinran a role model and heroine for Chinese women. Her own life and career also revealed women's experiences in contemporary China.

Born in Beijing in 1958, Xinran had a difficult childhood that was complicated by the turmoil of the Cultural Revolution. Her mother came from a capitalist, property-owning family. But Xinran's grandfather, although he cooperated with the communists, lost his property and was imprisoned during the Cultural Revolution. Her mother joined the Communist Party and army at sixteen but was occasionally jailed or demoted in purges of those from capitalist class backgrounds. Xinran's father was a national expert in mechanics and computing but, like her mother, also from a once wealthy family. He too had been imprisoned. Xinran had been sent to live with a grandmother when she was one month old and seldom saw her parents during her childhood. Reflecting on her family, she wrote that, like many Chinese, her parents endured an unhappy marriage: "Did [my parents] love each other? I have never dared to ask." While working as an army administrator, Xinran married, had a son, PanPan, and later divorced.

Eventually Xinran became a radio journalist. But she had to persuade the station to let her begin a nightly call-in program, *Words on the Night Breeze*. Since 1949 the media had been the mouthpiece of the Communist Party, ensuring that it spoke with one identical voice. However, Xinran said, "I was trying to open a little window, a tiny hole, so that people would allow their spirits to cry out and breathe after the gunpowder-laden atmosphere of the previous forty years." In starting her call-in program, the question that obsessed her was, What is a woman's life really worth in a China where footbinding was a recent memory but women now lived and worked alongside men? Xinran's compassion and ability encouraged callers to talk freely about feelings. For eight groundbreaking years, women called in and discussed their lives, and Xinran was shocked by much of what they said. Broadcast all over China, the program offered an unflinching portrait of what it meant to be a woman in modern China, including the expectations of obedience to fathers, husbands, and sons. Women from every social status—daughters of wealthy families, wives of party officials, children of Cultural Revolution survivors, homeless street scavengers, isolated mountain villagers—called in stories, often heartbreaking tales of sexual abuse, gang rape, forced marriages, and enforced separation of families.

The stories Xinran heard did not fit the image promoted by the Communist Party of a happy, harmonious society. She told, for instance, of Jingyi and her boyfriend, Gu Da, university classmates who fell passionately in love but were sent by the government to work in different parts of the country. They had

Xue Xinran The Chinese journalist, Xue Xinran, explored the lives of Chinese women on her radio program and in her writings.

planned to eventually marry but lost touch during the chaos of the Cultural Revolution. For forty-five years Jingyi had first longed for and then searched for Gu Da. When they finally had a reunion in 1994, Jingyi was devastated to discover that Gu Da, despairing of ever seeing Jingyi again, had married another woman. Their saga provided a window on the disrupted personal and family lives common in China after 1949.

In Xinran's view, "When China started to open up [to the outside world], it was like a starving child devouring everything without much discrimination. But China's brain had not yet grown the cells to absorb truth and freedom." In 1997 the conflict between what Xinran knew and what she was permitted to say caused her to give up her career and leave for Britain, where she hoped to find a freer life and reach a global audience. In Britain, after mastering English, she first taught at the University of London and then became a columnist for a national newspaper, *The Guardian*. She published several nonfiction books based on the stories she learned in China. In *The Good Women of China: Hidden Voices* (2002), she opened a window revealing the lives of Chinese women to the outside world. Her reports revealed strong, resourceful characters who offered insights into China's past and present. Another book, *The Sky Burial* (2004), told the extraordinary story of an intrepid Chinese woman who spent thirty years searching rugged Tibet, a thousand miles from her home city, for her beloved husband, an army doctor who was reported killed. In *China Witness* (2008), Xinran traced China's traumatic modern history through candid interviews with aging Chinese. In 2002 Xinran married an Englishman, the literary agent Toby Eady. Every year she returns to China for visits and reporting, and also sponsors a charity, The Mother's Bridge of Love, that helps disadvantaged children.

THINKING ABOUT THE PROFILE

1. Why did Xinran achieve such fame in China?

2. What does her journalism tell us about the experiences of Chinese women?

Note: Quotations from Xue Xinran, *The Good Women of China: Hidden Voices* (New York: Anchor, 2002), 3, 126, 227.   **779**

tries to declare a permanent break from China. Although economic and social links between China and Taiwan have increased, few in the island nation, which enjoys democracy and a much higher standard of living, want a merger with the mainland in the near future. Meanwhile, Chinese relations with Japan ebb and flow. The two nations have close economic ties—thousands of Japanese businessmen are based in China—but are also natural rivals, the Chinese remaining resentful of Japanese brutality during World War II and antagonistic to contemporary Japanese nationalism. However, China has improved political and economic relations with once-bitter enemies such as South Korea and anticommunist countries such as Malaysia, the Philippines, and Australia, which view China as the future regional power and hence seek friendly relations. In many Asian and some African and Latin American countries, large numbers of people are learning Chinese, and some 90,000 foreign students study in China. Nonetheless, historical resentment of Japan and the West stokes Chinese nationalism, sometimes resulting in anti-Japan or anti-U.S. protest demonstrations. In addition, although by the early 2000s China only ranked fifth among the world's nations in defense spending, its neighbors have feared Chinese military power.

China's Prospects

China's tremendous size, population, natural resources, military strength, national confidence, and sense of history have placed it in an unusual position of being a major global power while still having a much lower overall standard of living and far more poverty than North America, western Europe, Japan, and several industrializing Asian nations. Nonetheless, China, rather than the United States, led global recovery from the 2008–2009 recession, suggesting that the world's economic center of gravity may be shifting to East Asia. Perhaps China has been returning to its historical leadership as the Asian dragon and a major engine of the global economy. Experts debated whether either China or India might replace the United States as the major world power by 2050 or 2100. Some argued that India had advantages, such as democracy, a free press, and a sounder financial system, while others thought China had the better prospects, especially if the growing middle class fosters a more open political system. Still others doubted that a decline of U.S. power was imminent. As during the long period of Chinese power and prosperity between 600 and 1800, China is once again a major force in world affairs.

SECTION SUMMARY

- Under Deng Xiaoping, China opened up to Western economic ideas and investment, gradually introducing private ownership and competition, as well as to political, religious, and cultural currents that had been suppressed under Mao.

- Although many supported Deng's reforms, they led to increasing corruption and a growing gap between rich and poor, especially in rural areas, and, in 1989, a violent suppression of prodemocracy dissidents in the Tiananmen Massacre.

- Under market Leninism, the Chinese state increased political and social control while continuing to privatize the economy, which grew briskly, though there was stagnation in many rural areas and environmental damage in others.

- The growth of China's economy has improved access to consumer goods but has also led to increased crime and drug use, and an effort to limit population has led to many abortions and the killing of female babies.

- China has become more open to Western culture, though its government has attempted to restrict the free flow of information.

- China has enjoyed a great recovery and return to world prominence in recent decades, though it still has uncertain relations with Taiwan and Japan, and its living standard remains much lower than many of its rivals.

THE REMAKING OF JAPAN

> How did Japan rise from the ashes of defeat in World War II to become a global economic powerhouse?

In August 1945, Japan lay in ruins, its major cities largely destroyed by U.S. bombing and its economy ruined (see Map 27.2). Having no concept of military defeat, the Japanese people were psychologically devastated. Yet, within a decade the country had recovered from the disaster of World War II. After several decades of the highest economic growth rates in world history, Japan became one of the world's major economic powers, and by the 1980s it was challenging the United States for world economic leadership. A system stressing cooperation rather than individualism provided the basis for economic and social stability in an overcrowded land. But beginning in the 1990s Japan experienced political and economic uncertainty.

Map 27.2
Japan and the Little Dragons

Japan fostered the strongest Asian economy through the second half of the twentieth century, but in recent decades the Little Dragons—South Korea, Taiwan, Hong Kong, and Singapore—also have had rapid economic growth.

Interactive Map

Occupation, Recovery, and Politics

The post–World War II occupation by the United States aided Japan's recovery. The emperor, Hirohito (here-o-HEE-to) (1901–1989), still a revered figure, asked them to cooperate with the Allied occupation forces, and by and large they did. Japan was placed under a U.S.-dominated military administration, the Supreme Command of Allied Powers (SCAP), that was tasked with rebuilding rather than punishing Japan. Japan also lost Korea, Taiwan, and Manchuria, while the United States took control of the Ryukyu Islands, which were returned to Japan in the 1970s,

U.S. Occupation

781

and Micronesia. SCAP hoped to demilitarize and democratize Japan, using the United States as the model, and to aid economic recovery. It dismantled the Japanese military, removed some civilian politicians, and tried and hanged seven wartime leaders as war criminals. Fearing that punishing the emperor, a member of an imperial family over 1,500 years old, would destabilize Japan, U.S. officials did not charge Hirohito with war crimes, but he was forced to renounce his god-like aura and become a more public figure.

SCAP fostered political and social changes. Sustaining democracy required a more egalitarian society in which once-disadvantaged people shared in the progress. A new constitution guaranteed civil liberties and forever renounced war as the nation's sovereign right. The first democratic elections, held in 1946, involved various competing political parties. All adult citizens, including women, could vote. Women gained legal equality in society and marriage but were only partly freed from the expectations of a patriarchal society. New universities opened, giving Japanese youth greater access than ever before to higher education. The economy also gradually recovered, using the same mix of government intervention and free markets that Japan had introduced in the Meiji era. Land reform subsidized the peasantry, making them strong government supporters and bringing prosperity to rural areas. Although SCAP attempted to break up entrenched economic power, large industrial-commercial-banking conglomerates still dominated manufacturing and foreign trade, making Japan more competitive in the world economy. But workers gained the right to unionize.

After the Chinese communist victory and the outbreak of the Korean War, the United States shifted its emphasis from restructuring Japanese society to integrating Japan into the anticommunist Western alliance, symbolized by the signing in 1951 of a formal U.S.-Japan peace treaty. U.S. military bases have remained in Japan ever since as part of a mutual defense pact. The policies implemented during the SCAP occupation, which officially ended in 1952, were most successful where U.S. and Japanese desires coincided or when the policies fit with the nation's traditions (see Chronology: Japan Since 1945). Democratic government fit both criteria. The Japanese had enjoyed several decades of democracy before the Great Depression, and borrowing from abroad also fit with Japanese tradition. They were again receptive to importing Western culture. With conditions stabilized, Japanese leaders embarked on a strategy of capitalizing on peace to strengthen the nation.

Japanese Politics

Despite stresses, Japan's democratic political system has endured. A variety of political parties—socialists, communists, liberals, Buddhists, and rightwing nationalists—have competed for parliamentary seats. But one major party, the center-right Liberal Democratic Party (LDP), has dominated politics, applying generally conservative, probusiness, and pro-U.S. policies. The SCAP-imposed electoral system gave greater weight to rural voters, the backbone of LDP support. But although prime ministers learned to negotiate with opposition parties as well as with the diverse LDP factions, critics believed that a political system dominated by one party and a few wealthy kingmakers, who faced little criticism from media largely owned by huge corporations, was at best a partial democracy.

Indeed, the need to finance political careers and raise money for elections from powerful corporations and criminal gangs has fostered political corruption. Bribery scandals have sometimes forced political leaders to resign, and a few have gone to prison. In 1993 the LDP fragmented in factional disputes, and various opposition parties gained support. But the LDP soon returned to power under a reform leader, though it faced challenges from opposition parties, and it has lost support for failing to resolve economic crises. Finally, in 2009, with Japan mired in severe recession and facing a huge national debt, the LDP experienced a huge defeat in national elections, losing power to the center-left Democratic Party, which promised reforms.

Japan and the United States

For self-protection, Japanese leaders forged a military alliance with the United States that allowed U.S. bases in Japan. As a result, Japan's military spending has long remained meager compared to that of the United States and the USSR, and Japan has been able to devote more resources to the civilian economy to help propel rapid economic growth. While the Cold War superpowers invested in weapons and armies, Japan devoted its economic surplus largely to industrial development. However, leftist parties, labor unions, and militant student groups long opposed the U.S. military presence as neocolonialism. Japanese also feared that the U.S. military interventions in places such as Vietnam and Iraq made Japan a potential target. Remembering the horrors of World War II, especially the atomic bombings that killed some 200,000 Japanese, many Japanese favored pacifism and believed that Japan's economic strength protected them from attack. Yet, with U.S. support, Japan began increasing military spending in the 1980s, and by 2009 it had the fourth largest military budget in the world, ahead of China but still much below that of the United States.

The Japanese decision to send soldiers to support, in noncombat activities, the U.S. war in Iraq was widely unpopular and, to critics, violated the constitutional ban against engaging in war.

The Japanese Economy and Growth

Adapting capitalism to its own traditions, Japan achieved phenomenal economic growth, its goods in demand on every continent only a century after it opened to the outside world. Wartime destruction required the rebuilding of basic industries using the latest innovations. Investing in new industries and high-tech fields, the Japanese became the world leaders in manufacturing products such as pianos, oil tankers, and automobiles, as well as electronics products such as watches, televisions, and cameras. As a result, from the 1960s through the 1980s Japan's annual growth rate was three times higher than that of other industrialized nations. Now an industrial giant possessing an advanced technology and distinctive economic and industrial structure, in 2000 Japan produced some 16 percent of the world's goods and services, half the U.S. percentage but twice that of third-place Germany. What observers often called an economic miracle was particularly impressive considering that the country has few mineral resources, limited productive farmland, and no major rivers to produce hydroelectric power. Consequently, the Japanese must import minerals needed for industry, such as iron ore, tin, and copper. Oil obtained from Alaska, Southeast Asia, and the Middle East powers Japan's transportation.

Getty Images

Japanese Protest
Political demonstrations are common in Japanese cities. During this protest in 2001, liberals and leftists criticized new middle-school textbooks, approved by the Education Ministry, that, the critics claimed, distorted history by emphasizing nationalist viewpoints and downplaying Japanese atrocities in World War II.

Japan became known for innovative technologies and high-quality products. A magnificent mass transit system included the state-of-the-art bullet trains that whisked passengers around the country at 125 to 150 miles per hour and were always on time. Electronics manufacturers such as Sony, Atari, and Nintendo invented entertainment-oriented products, among them video and handheld game systems that became part of life on every continent, especially for youth. Millions of people, from Boston to Bogotá, Barcelona to Bombay, drove Toyotas, Hondas, and other Japanese-made cars. Enjoying living standards equal to those of most western Europeans, the Japanese themselves became Western-style consumers; everyone now sought to own cars, televisions, washing machines, and air conditioners. The Japanese also enjoyed the world's highest average life expectancy: seventy-nine or eighty years; in addition, a more varied diet, including more meat and dairy products, produced taller, healthier children. Western foods and beverages became popular, and Western fast-food outlets such as McDonald's proved a great success, serving the same items popular in the West as well as dishes adapted to local taste, such as teriyaki burgers and Chinese fried rice. The rural areas shared in the prosperity. However, most rural youth left their villages for the cities, and many workers had to make do with part-time jobs offering few benefits, and a small but growing underclass had no permanent jobs or homes.

Japan's capitalist economy has differed in fundamental ways from those of other industrial nations. The national government and big business work together in a cooperative relationship that became known as **Japan, Inc.** (Japan Incorporated). The government regulates business, setting overall guidelines, sponsoring research and development, and leasing the resulting products or technologies to private enterprise. Most Japanese businesses have accepted the guidelines because they take a longer-term view of profitability than was common among Western business leaders. But government-business cooperation has occurred chiefly in international trade, the country's lifeblood, and is made easier by the dominance of large Japanese conglomerates that own diverse enterprises such as factories, banks, and department stores. The government aids Japanese businesses by erecting protectionist barriers and bureaucratic hurdles that impede foreign businesses in the Japanese market.

Economic growth has generated new problems. As in the West, industrialization has fostered wealth but also harmed the environment. Pollution of rivers and bays has wiped out coastal

Japan, Inc. The cooperative relationship between government and big business that has existed in Japan after 1945.

Environmental Problems

fishing, and smoggy air is so bad that city residents sometimes cover their noses and mouths with masks to avert respiratory difficulties. Thousands of people have died or been made ill by toxic waste dumped by factories. In addition, many younger people resent the long hours and sacrifices expected of both white-collar and blue-collar employees, especially since a high standard of living has already been achieved.

Industrial System

Japan's business and factory life has contributed to success. The system takes advantage of Japanese cultural values, such as conformity, hard work, cooperation, thrift, and foresight, while adding innovations. The 30 percent of workers employed in larger Japanese companies have often enjoyed lifetime job security and access to generous welfare benefits offered by their employer, such as health insurance, recreation, housing, and car loans. Some companies sponsor group tours abroad or own vacation retreats for their employees. When a corporation has faced financial trouble, top managers often accept responsibility for the problems, cutting their own pay rather than firing workers. Most workers remain with the same employer for life, though, by the 1980s, it became more common to change jobs. To encourage workers to feel a part of the corporate family, employers often gather the employees together to sing the company anthem each morning before they head for their workstations. Yet, many employees in smaller businesses, as well as temporary workers, do not enjoy generous benefits and are vulnerable to layoffs. Japanese companies also emphasize working in teams and "bottom-up" decision making through quality control circles and work groups, such as a factory team that installs a car engine; these groups decide how best to undertake their tasks. Business offices tend to be organized around large tables, where white-collar employees work collaboratively, rather than around the small cubicles common in North America. Businesses and factories have also expected their employees to put company over personal interests, including regularly working overtime.

Japanese Society, Culture, and Thought

City Life

Urbanization and affluence have contributed to social change. Sixty percent of Japanese now live in cities of over 100,000. With 35 million people, Tokyo is the world's largest metropolitan area by far. Some of Tokyo's legendary traffic jams take police several days to untangle. The city subways are convenient but overcrowded, and rush hour has evolved into "crush hour," with city employees equipped with padded poles pushing commuters into overflowing cars to enable subway train doors to close. Yet, despite Mafia-like organized crime syndicates, Japan's cities are the safest in the world; experts attribute low rates of violent crime in part to strict gun control.

salaryman An Japanese urban middle-class male business employee who commits his energies and soul to the company, accepts assignments without complaint, and takes few vacations.

The economy has changed men's lives. Most university-educated men want to become white-collar office workers for major corporations. Japanese observers describe the **salaryman**, an urban middle-class male business employee who commits his energies and soul to the company, accepts assignments without complaint, and takes few vacations. The cover of a local book on the salaryman pictures a harried middle-aged man eying the sundry items that define his work life: a computer, newspaper, lunch box, demanding boss, and subway strap. Many men working in white-collar jobs are also known as "7-11 husbands" because they leave for work at 7 A.M. and do not return until 11 P.M. After work they and their office mates socialize in restaurants, bars, and nightclubs while their wives take care of the home. In the 1980s one wife complained, "I don't know why Japanese men marry if they are never going to be home."[14]

Women's Roles

Meanwhile, while earning more money, gaining legal protections, and enjoying greater freedom, women still struggle for full social and economic equality in a hierarchical society obsessed with patriarchy and seniority. Most women are expected to marry and then retire from the work force to raise children, even though they often remain in paid work. According to one young woman, when she and other women graduated from a top Japanese university, "our bright appearance [for the graduation ceremonies] in vividly colored kimonos [traditional robes] was deceiving. Deep in our hearts we knew that our opportunities to use our professional education would be few."[15] As single women often discovered they could support themselves, the average age of marriage for women rose from twenty-two in the 1950s to twenty-seven in the 1990s. Indeed, in recent years, many women have avoided marriage altogether, preferring to concentrate on their careers or leisure interests. Accordingly, marriage rates have declined, alarming politicians.

Despite the popular image of the timid Japanese female, women have become more assertive. Feminist organizations and leaders have publicized women's issues, and working women have lobbied companies for equal treatment and pay. Some women have moved into middle management or prestige occupations, such as law, journalism, college teaching, and diplomacy. Yet, women also largely remain outside political and economic power, and only a few attain positions of political leadership. Women aspiring to gender equality admire activists such as Ichikawa Fusae **(ee-CHEE-**

kah-wah foo-SIGH) (1893–1981), a former schoolteacher and journalist who organized the women's suffrage movement in the 1920s and served in the parliament as a political independent for twenty-five years after World War II, campaigning for women's equality and human rights. At the same time, family life has gradually changed. Although the traditional arranged marriage remains common, many men and women select their own spouse, and more Japanese get married late or opt to end unhappy marriages in divorce. The decline of marriage has made it easier for homosexuals to find social acceptance. Japanese society has always tolerated homosexual behavior, but now more have become open about their sexual orientation.

Urban housing remains cramped, and the elderly complain of neglect by their children, who have no room for them in their small homes. Birth control and abortion had been widely practiced in overcrowded Japan for centuries; the renewal of these practices after World War II, along with lower marriage rates, stabilized the population at 120 million for several decades. Yet, by 2000 Japan had a birthrate well below replacement standards and a rapidly aging population that placed a heavy burden on a shrinking work force to pay for retiree's benefits and a generous health care system. Despite this problem, the government has discouraged immigration to provide new workers. Thousands of Brazil-born Japanese who have returned to their ancestral homeland, mostly to work in factories, often face resentment, and those who became unemployed were encouraged to return to Brazil. In 2005, foreigners, mostly Chinese and Koreans, numbered less than 2 percent of the population; by contrast, the foreign-born accounted for 5 percent in Britain, 10 percent in Germany, 12 percent in the United States, and 22 percent in Australia. Despite laws banning discrimination, the Japanese have also largely failed to end prejudice against the *Burakumin,* a despised underclass for centuries, who number some 1 to 3 million people and traditionally did jobs considered unclean, such as leatherworking.

Youth face their own kinds of pressures. Young people take difficult exams to get into the better kindergartens, grade schools, and secondary schools, and the entrance exam for the top universities is so rigorous it is known as "exam hell." These varied pressures, and the expectations of conforming to the values of mainstream society, have encouraged youth rebellion. Indifferent students sometimes drop out and join motorcycle gangs that roar along the highways by day and neighborhood streets by night, annoying middle-class families trying to sleep. University students have often supported leftwing political organizations that protest issues such as U.S. military bases or the destruction of farmland to build new airports or business developments, but student activism has waned in recent years (see Witness to the Past: A Japanese Generation Gap). Eventually, however, most young people return to the mainstream upon graduation and take jobs in the corporate or industrial world. Some who cannot conform emigrate to North America, Europe, or Latin America in search of a more free-spirited life.

The Japanese, while continuing to blend traditional and modern cultures and beliefs, East and West, debate this blending and its effect on cultural identity. Artists and writers ponder whether synthesizing foreign and local ideas has been the nation's salvation or its bane. Some worry that

Social Problems

Japanese Youth

Arts and Film

Japanese Women Commuters A female passenger boards a train compartment reserved for women in a subway station in Tokyo. Tokyo's subways are usually jammed with passengers, and special cars allow women to travel without fear of possible sexual harassment.

Getty Images

A Japanese Generation Gap

The rapid pace of change since World War II has fostered growing generation gaps in many nations. In 1993 the Japanese essayist Yoshioka Shinobu (born in 1948) discussed the differences in perceptions between his "baby boomer" cohort born in the decade after 1945 and those Japanese of the next generation. Yoshioka's experiences reflected the exciting era of social experimentation during his teenage years in the 1960s. By contrast, young people in the 1970s faced a tighter economy and less official tolerance of radical ideas and organized political protests.

Whenever I hear someone mention Japan's baby boomers, . . . I think back to a conversation I had . . . [in] 1976 at a rock concert. . . . The band had the latest sound equipment, but its talent was no match for its technology. Bored, . . . I struck up a conversation with two young girls. . . . They had run away from home . . . because they were sick of school, and had come to Tokyo in search of adventure. . . . They had lied about their ages to get part-time jobs, were sharing a tiny apartment, and from time to time went out to concerts. . . . I told them I thought they must be having the time of their lives.

"Your generation had it good," one of the girls answered. "When you ran away from home, there was rock music, underground theater, demonstrations, all kinds of things— you could do whatever you wanted. Our generation has to walk a tightrope, . . . and there's nothing to catch us if we fall. We lose our balance, we die. You guys might have walked a tightrope too, but you had a safety net below. If you didn't like it up on the rope, you could always dive down and let yourself be caught in midair. You could do whatever you wanted to."

She had hit home. So that's how we look in the eyes of someone ten years younger, I thought. My generation . . . had an entirely different understanding of itself. [We] . . . had many names . . . : the baby boomers, the Beatles generation, the anti-Vietnam [War] generation. . . . [Our radical student movements] did much to discredit the established political system, but our generation was more than just a new political

force. We began new trends in music, theater, art, and social customs . . . that defied the existing structure of authority and social conventions. In those days, nothing was worse than a willingness to capitulate to the "system" and adopt its narrow conventions.

Consequently, we tried our hands at everything. Singers of traditional [music], who had put in years of hard work climbing the rigid, hierarchical ladder before they were allowed to perform publicly, suddenly found themselves displaced by our barely rehearsed bands and spontaneous concerts. Some put on plays in . . . tents set up in vacant lots, ridiculing the empty and imitative formalism of Japan's commercial theater. Others . . . took off nearly penniless to wander about in foreign countries—their adventureousness helped make travel abroad commonplace.

The two girls were saying that these experiences . . . were only possible because we had a safety net underneath us. . . . The girls had a point. When [my] generation was growing up, the . . . confusion of the early postwar years had given way to spectacular economic growth. . . . This . . . engendered confidence in liberal politics and democratic government, and it also created a willingness to forgive the unruliness of the younger generation. . . . If we were arrested [in antiwar demonstrations] it did not worry us much. . . . The runaway girls told me that the age of such optimism was over. . . . Between my generation and the next, attitudes toward change took a 180-degree turn. For us, changes in society and the individual were exciting and intrinsically valuable. For the younger generation, however, change is frightening and the source of insecurity.

THINKING ABOUT THE READING

1. How did Yoshioka's generation contribute to change?
2. What does the essay tell us about Japan's connection to the wider world?

Source: Shinobu Yoshioka, "Talkin' 'bout My Generation," in Merry L. White and Sylvan Barnet, eds., *Comparing Cultures: Readings on Contemporary Japan for American Writers* (Boston: Bedford Books of St. Martin's Press, 1995), pp. 119–122. Reprinted with permission by Yoshioka Shinobu.

Japan's adoption of foreign culture has imperiled its own distinctive culture. Others contend that the Japanese needed to become more global-minded, even encouraging immigration that would make Japan a multicultural nation.

The questions about Japanese identity and problems facing society are often analyzed in films that have achieved worldwide recognition. While the Japanese film industry, the world's third largest, produces escapist films, such as those portraying samurai warriors and gigantic city-wrecking monsters, it also makes thought-provoking masterpieces, especially grand historical epics and introspective psychological or sociological studies. One of the most skillful directors, Kurosawa Akira (kur-o-SAH-wa a-KEER-a) (1910–1998), mixed a distinctive Japanese style and setting with a theme appealing to viewers in other cultures. *Rashomon* (1950), for example, deals with the relativity of truth by examining one event, the killing of a feudal lord and the violation of his wife by a bandit, through varied eyes. Another Kurosawa film, *Ikuru*, or "To Live" (1952), explores the meaning of life through the story of a Japanese bureaucrat dying of cancer who overcomes endless red tape to facilitate the building of a small neighborhood park.

The Japanese have the world's highest literacy rate (99.9 percent) and the largest numbers of newspaper readers, magazine subscribers, and bookstores per capita, which have fostered both popular and serious literature. Kawabata Yasunari (ka-wa-BAH-ta yah-suh-NAHR-ee) (1899–1972) became the first Japanese novelist, in 1968, to receive the Nobel Prize for literature. Directly addressing Japanese identity, the writings of Mishima Yukio (me-SHE-mah YOO-kee-oh) (1925–1970) portray an effete, decadent "nation of shopkeepers" that need a return to the martial values of the Tokugawa period. His best novel concerns a disturbed young man torn, like Mishima himself, between old samurai and modern Westernized values. For Mishima, a conflicted homosexual and avid body builder, life became art; in 1970 he publicly committed suicide in samurai style in front of his private army to sacrifice himself for what he called the "old beautiful tradition of Japan, which is disappearing day by day."[16] His action shocked the Japanese, but his message died with him; the Japanese continued to develop a consumer society.

Continuity has long characterized Japanese popular culture. Every sport, art form, and religion that has appeared in the past 1,500 years in Japan still attracts practitioners or followers. Japanese remain passionate about sumo wrestling, a sport, going back centuries, in which two large, paunchy Japanese men attempt to push each other out of a small ring. Yet, while performances of kabuki or bunraku, theatrical forms that appeared in the 1600s, still attract devoted audiences, and young Japanese women preparing for marriage often master the even older tea ceremony, many more Japanese follow professional baseball teams; consume Japanese comics, or *manga* (mahn-gah), and animated films, or *anime*, that are popular worldwide; and flock to Japanese or Western films, discos, pinball palaces, and video-game arcades. Modern Japanese, especially young people, have avidly adopted cultural forms from around the world. Japanese also frequent nightclubs featuring many musical styles, including both local and imported versions of rock, jazz, reggae, country western, rap, and salsa.

Organized religion continues to decline, although some Japanese remain deeply religious. Militant Buddhist groups claim several million followers, and various new religions based on Buddhist or Shinto traditions, or a mix of the two, have flourished by addressing material prosperity and family problems. Nonetheless, the contemporary Japanese are a largely secular people. In census questionnaires, less than 15 percent reported any formal religious affiliation by 2000. Although Japan's Christian population is tiny, millions of non-Christians ardently celebrate Christmas as an opportunity to give and receive gifts, and Japanese department stores often feature elaborate Christmas displays, complete with Santa Claus and brightly decorated Christmas trees. However, the weak influence of religions has not resulted in social breakdown. Japanese remain among the world's most law-abiding, peaceful citizens, with a morality that mostly derives from the fear of bringing shame on the family or group rather than fear of retribution by gods or ancestors. The reluctance to disgrace the family suggests that Confucianism remains important. Yet the emphasis on conforming to the group and its rules has a downside. Criticizing the attitudes expressed by an old saying—"the nail that sticks up gets hammered down"—Japanese liberals have sought a less-conformist society that would nourish rather than inhibit individual genius.

Popular Culture

Religion

Japan in the Global System

The Japanese have had to readjust their views of the economy and international relations over the past several decades. Like their North American and European counterparts, Japanese companies have sought cheaper labor by setting up factories in Southeast Asia, South Korea, and China, costing Japan jobs. In 1989 the Japanese economy went into a severe downturn, due in part to overvalued stocks that caused a crisis on the Tokyo Stock Exchange but also to global recession and competition from the newly industrializing nations of Southeast Asia. Only in the early 2000s did Japanese leaders introduce policies that fostered higher growth rates and renewed business confidence, but the recovery remained incomplete. The global economic crisis of 2008–2009 undermined export-oriented Japan, causing recession, bank failures, bankruptcies, and a huge drop in consumer spending abroad that even affected automobile manufacturers like Toyota. As in the United States, Japanese corporations have reacted to foreign competition and crises by slashing salaries, cutting benefits, and even firing employees, modifying the business system that brought Japan prosperity for a half century. Many newly unemployed men, especially office workers, ashamed to admit their humiliation to friends and families, spend each work day on park benches or in coffee houses. The economic problems caused disenchanted voters to turn the long-ruling Liberal Democratic Party out of office

Economic Challenges

While comfortable as an economic powerhouse, the Japanese remain reluctant to assert their political and military power in the world, remembering how the attempt to dominate eastern Asia brought them disaster during World War II. Japan's main concerns are the continued health of the

Japanese Power in the World

world economy and continuing access to overseas resources and markets. To this end, the Japanese prefer that the country seek peaceful rather than military solutions to world problems. Japan has maintained a strategic alliance with its major trading partner, the United States, but the two nations have also remained keen economic rivals and have sometimes engaged in trade disputes. Japanese leaders have also worked to promote peaceful exchange with China and South Korea, two countries with long memories of Japanese imperialism during the first half of the twentieth century. Relations with China have often been strained, as the Chinese have demanded that Japan accept responsibility for World War II atrocities in China. Resurgent Japanese and Chinese nationalisms clash. As China and several other Asian nations rise economically, Japan faces more competition and the challenge of maintaining its position in the world economy.

SECTION SUMMARY

- After World War II, a U.S.-led occupation of Japan (SCAP) worked to rebuild Japan's economy while demilitarizing the country and encouraging the return of democracy, much of which was successful; however, it was difficult to break up large business conglomerates.

- The Liberal Democratic Party dominated Japanese politics for decades, with a brief break in the 1990s, and the presence of U.S. military bases within Japan was seen by some as neocolonialism but freed up resources to help fuel the economy.

- Relying on innovation and collaboration between government and big business, Japan's economy has grown at a phenomenal rate, though it has caused environmental problems and great personal sacrifices on the part of workers.

- Japan's cities have become increasingly congested, men are expected to devote all their energy to work, women struggle for equality and increasingly choose work over marriage, arranged marriages have become less common, and students face the pressure of an arduous education system.

- Japanese have managed to blend their traditions with modern and foreign influences and have maintained a high degree of social order in spite of low participation in organized religion, but some criticize Japanese society as too conformist.

- In the early 2000s, Japan's economy began to recover from a decade-long downturn, while in world politics, Japan has played an important role, though it has been hesitant to assert its power too forcefully.

THE LITTLE DRAGONS IN THE ASIAN RESURGENCE

What policies led to the rise of the "Little Dragon" nations and their dynamic economies?

Little Dragons South Korea, Taiwan, Singapore, and Hong Kong, which were strongly influenced by Chinese culture and built rapidly growing, industrializing economies.

While China and Japan were rising to regional and global power, a few of their East Asian neighbors also achieved economic development. Known as the **Little Dragons** because they were strongly influenced by Chinese culture, South Korea, Taiwan, Singapore, and Hong Kong built rapidly growing, industrializing economies. Except for Hong Kong, a British colony until 1997 and a bastion of free enterprise, these societies largely followed the Meiji Japan model of state-directed capitalism. They were also inspired by Japan's resurgence after World War II, which depended on participation in the world economy. All the Little Dragons shared a Confucian cultural heritage that emphasized hard work, discipline, cooperation, and tolerance for authoritarian governments. They all achieved an export-oriented industrialization that raised incomes, reduced poverty, and forged high standards in health and education. For South Korea, however, this development came only after a brutal war that left a hostile, rigidly communist North Korea on the border. Taiwan had to find its own path in the shadow of China, while Singapore (see Chapter 31) and Hong Kong (now part of China) are city-states with largely Chinese populations.

Korean Independence and War

Japanese Colonialism

The Korean War (1950–1953) was rooted in the Korean nationalism that, despite fierce repression, simmered during a half century of harsh Japanese colonial rule (see Chapters 23 and 24). While introducing some economic modernization, the Japanese arrested or executed Korean nationalists, conscripted Korean women to serve Japanese soldiers, relocated thousands of Korean workers to Japan, and manipulated the divisions within Korean society. Christians constituted one influential group, growing in numbers, and by the 1940s a fifth of Koreans had become Catholics or Protestants. Another group of Koreans had gravitated toward communism, some escaping to the USSR to form a revolutionary movement. In contrast, a majority of Koreans maintained their adherence to Buddhism and Confucianism as central to Korean identity. Although Christians, communists, and traditionalists all hated Japanese rule and worked underground to oppose it, they could not cooperate, and no unified nationalist movement emerged.

Japan's crushing defeat by the United States in 1945 meant political liberation for Korea and a chance to reestablish the nation free of foreign interference. But the United States quickly occupied the southern half of the peninsula and the Soviet Union the north, bisecting Korea and making it a hostage to the Cold War. As the USSR and the United States imposed rival governments, unification quickly became impossible. With Soviet help, communists led by the ruthless Kim Il-Sung **(KIM ill-soon)** (1912–1994) formed a government in North Korea (see Chronology: The Little Dragons Since 1945). A clever strategist from a Christian family, Kim quickly built a brutal communist system, eliminated his opponents, and reorganized rural society. But the impatient Kim disastrously overestimated the revolutionary potential of the south and also misjudged the Americans, who were determined to stop the spread of Soviet influence. The United States helped create and then supported a South Korean state headed by Rhee Syngman **(REE SING-man)** (1865–1965). A politically conservative Christian from a powerful landlord family, Rhee had lived in exile in the United States for over two decades. Unpopular with the majority non-Christians, the autocratic Rhee imprisoned or eliminated his opponents and sparked a leftist rebellion supported by many factory workers and peasants, which United States troops helped crush. Although less repressive than Kim's North Korean regime, Rhee's South Korea held some 30,000 political prisoners.

These developments set the stage for the Korean War (see Map 27.3), a result of mixing revolution and nationalism into a Cold War–driven stew. Both Korean states, threatening to reunify Korea with military force, had initiated border skirmishes. In this highly charged context, North Korea, with Soviet and Chinese approval, invaded the South in 1950. The Western-dominated United Nations agreed to let the United States lead a military intervention to support South Korea, thus turning a Korean crisis into a Cold War confrontation; the United States made the major commitment of troops, war materials, and funding. U.S. president Harry Truman secretly planned to strike North Korea with atomic weapons if the USSR entered the war. But while the Soviets gave military supplies and advice, they sent no combat troops.

Korean War

U.N. troops, aided by U.S. air power, quickly pushed the North Koreans back across the north-south border. But the U.N. move into North Korea and push toward the Chinese border sparked a massive Chinese intervention that drove back U.N. troops and turned a likely victory into a bitter stalemate. U.S. leaders had misjudged the Chinese willingness to fight and had underestimated Chinese military capabilities. When the war ended in 1953 with peace talks, the boundary between the Koreas remained roughly in the same place it was before the war but was now a heavily fortified zone where North and South Korean troops glared at each other across the barbed wire. The war left 400,000 Korean troops and 1 or 2 million civilians dead, and some 400,000 Chinese and 43,000 U.N. forces, 90 percent of them American, were killed. The fighting also generated millions of Korean refugees who wandered the countryside, seeking food and shelter. Both Koreas were left in economic shambles.

The Two Koreas

The postwar rise of South Korea was nearly as dramatic as that of Japan. Closely allied to the United States, the South Korean governments ranged from highly repressive military dictatorships from the 1950s through the mid-1980s, to moderate semidemocracies in the later 1980s, and then to liberal democracies with free elections since the early 1990s. All regimes aimed at economic development. The dictator Park Chung Hee (1917–1979) argued in 1970, "My chief concern was economic revolution. One must eat and breathe before concerning himself with politics, social affairs, and culture."[17] The United States protected the South Korean regimes by permanently stationing troops and supplying generous economic and military aid. A half-century after the war, some 40,000 U.S. troops remained in South Korea.

Rise of South Korea

CHRONOLOGY
The Little Dragons Since 1945

1948–1994 Kim Il-Sung's leadership of North Korea

1950–1953 Korean War

1954 U.S.-Taiwan mutual defense treaty

1980s South Korean democratization movement

1989 First democratic elections in Taiwan

1989–1991 Collapse of Soviet bloc and Soviet Union

1997 Asian financial collapse

1998 Beginning of South Korean "sunshine policy"

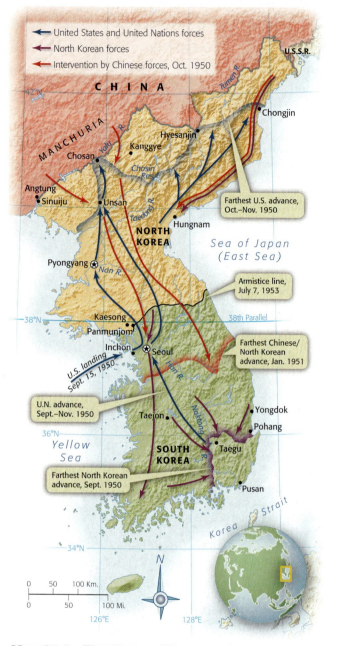

Map 27.3 The Korean War
In 1950, North Korean forces crossed the 38th parallel and invaded South Korea, but they were then pushed back north by United Nations forces led by the United States. The intervention of China in support of North Korea pushed the United Nations forces south and produced a military stalemate, preserving the border between North and South Korea at the 38th parallel.

e **Interactive Map**

South Korea has enjoyed enormous economic growth, investing heavily in the Middle East, Southeast Asia, and Russia, while exporting automobiles and electronic products. By the 1990s South Korea had joined the ranks of advanced industrial nations, the first non-Western nation to make that transition since Japan in the late nineteenth century, and became a proud member of the G-20 grouping of major industrial nations. Having acquired a standard of living South Koreans could only dream of two decades earlier, with nearly full employment and universal literacy, South Koreans now enjoy the highest rate of high-speed Internet access in the world: some 75 percent of households are wired, far more than in North America and Europe, and 35 percent of the population play computer games online. The country became a high-technology model. Both boys and girls received free education through age twelve. South Korean women benefited from new job options in the professions and business. With more women in the work force and self-supporting, marriage rates declined and average births per woman fell dramatically from 6 in 1990 to 1.6 in 2005.

Economic growth has also fostered political change. Democracy movements had begun in the 1960s, but they often faced government repression. In 1980 the dictatorship brutally crushed an uprising in a southern province that began when some five hundred people demonstrated, demanding an end of martial law; paratroopers landed and slaughtered the protesters and local people. Hundreds of thousands of enraged people then drove the troops out of the city, only to face a much larger force, which shot their way into the city, killing over 2,000 people. Eventually, however, political tensions diminished. Governments fostered more liberalization, tolerated a freer press, and made overtures toward former enemies in the USSR and China. By the early 1990s, with the growth of the middle class and organized labor, democracy flowered, though it was sometimes sullied by political corruption. South Koreans took pride in their freedom, bustling cities, and the influence of their popular culture in both China and Japan.

But while the country clearly outshined repressive North Korea, problems arose. Many rural people and unskilled workers did not share in the prosperity, and factories expected long hours from poorly paid workers. Frustrated at their prospects, thousands of Koreans, many of them middle class, emigrated to the United States. Discontent also grew with the economic slowdown beginning in 1997, and then with the 2008–2009 global economic crisis, which cost many jobs. Furthermore, while many South Koreans welcomed U.S. bases, others viewed them as an affront to nationalism. Koreans yearned for reunification and an end to the peninsular cold war. After years of hostility, and owing partly to South Korean efforts to improve relations, North and South Korea finally achieved a wary peaceful coexistence. A dialogue known as the "sunshine policy," begun in 1998, resulted in limited cross-border trade and allowed a few South Koreans to visit family members in North Korea they had not seen since the early 1950s. Televised images of South Koreans tearfully embracing aging parents or siblings mesmerized the nation. Then in 2000 South Korean president Kim Dae-jung **(kim day-chung)** (1925–2009), a liberal reformer, visited North Korea, an event unthinkable a decade earlier. Yet national reconciliation still remains a dream, and South Koreans worry about North Korean military capabilities and its quest to build nuclear weapons. Tensions increased again in 2009 over these issues.

North Korea   North Korea's leaders chose a completely different path from that taken by South Korea. The Korean War devastated the country, though North Korea quickly recovered with aid from China

Tony Stone/Getty Images

and the USSR. From 1948 until his death in 1994, Kim Il-Sung was the nation's president, creating a personality cult around himself as the "Great Leader." North Koreans were taught that they owed everything—jobs, goods, schooling, food, military security—to Kim. To ensure loyalty and deflect blame for failures, Kim purged many communist officials and jailed or executed thousands of dissidents. He also mixed Stalinism and Maoism to shape the economy and society, with Soviet-style economic planning and central direction emphasizing heavy industry and weapons at the expense of consumer goods. Hence, North Koreans did not enjoy the rising living standards of South Koreans. Kim invented a political philosophy of self-reliance that was heavily influenced by Mao Zedong's policies. Although North Korea contained most of Korea's factories and mines, built during Japanese colonial times, the huge military establishment drained resources as North Korea concentrated on deterring enemies and intimidating South Korea.

North Korea stressed group loyalty, ultranationalism, and independence from foreign influence, following the model of the Yi dynasty and Confucian bureaucracy in the nineteenth century. A small political and military elite, isolated from the bleak existence of the peasants and workers, enjoyed comfortable apartments and sufficient food, while controlling the people through regimentation and restricting information. To monitor activities and thoughts, the government required each citizen to register at a public security office and urged people to spy on their families and neighbors. To prevent people from hearing contrary views, radios were fixed to receive only the government station. Political prisoners and people caught trying to flee to China or South Korea faced long terms in harsh concentration camps or execution. As a result, the regime faced increasing international isolation. The economy declined rapidly, thanks to poor management, commodity shortages, and rigid policies. Satellite photos of the Korean peninsula at night revealed the stark differences in electrical power between a brilliantly lit South Korea and a completely dark North Korea. Even in the capital city nearly all lights are turned off each night by 9 P.M. U.S. diplomatic and economic pressure isolated the regime, making North Korea totally reliant economically on the Soviet bloc. Various efforts to strike back, such as assassination attempts on South Korean leaders, earned North Korea a reputation as an unpredictable terrorist state. When the Soviet bloc collapsed in 1989, Russia and China demanded that North Korea pay cash for oil and other imports.

North Korea's problems increased after Kim Jong-Il (chong-ill) (b. 1942), known as the "Dear Leader," succeeded his deceased father in 1995. When the nation soon faced mass starvation, South Korea, Japan, and the United States, anxious to discourage any desperate military action, sent food aid to North Korea. Even with the aid, many people died or were malnourished, and thousands of North Koreans fled to China to find food and work. Yet the regime avoided collapse. Thanks to

South Korean Economic Growth One of South Korea's major, most diverse enterprises, the Hyundai Corporation, formed in 1976, engages in shipping, manufacturing, and trade, producing, among other products, chemicals, machinery, and information and telecommunications equipment. The ships in this company dry dock are being readied to carry Hyundai-made cars to distant markets around the world.

isolation and tight information control, few North Koreans traveled abroad, studied foreign languages, met foreigners, or encountered foreign publications, films, and music. Meanwhile, a small dissident movement, risking harsh reprisals, smuggled in food from China and videotapes, books, and music from South Korea.

North Korea and the World

North Korea became a concern in both regional and world politics. Its military force was twice as large as South Korea's and was capable of building nuclear weapons. But with both Koreas possessing lethal military forces, and U.S. nuclear weapons in South Korea, war became less likely. This perception encouraged the search for common ground. The economic disasters, especially food shortages, softened the North Korean position, and after 1998 South Korea actively sought better relations to reduce the threat from its dangerous northern neighbor and its unpredictable leader. North Korea's neighbors and the United States also sought diplomatic ways to eliminate the possibility of a conventional war or a nuclear confrontation, but by 2008 tensions returned as North Korea continued to sporadically test nuclear weapons and missiles, unsettling the region.

Taiwan and China

The Chinese communist triumph on the mainland in 1949 led to the relocation of Chiang Kai-shek and his Nationalist government to the mountainous, subtropical Taiwan island, where he reestablished the Republic of China. Taiwan had only become a part of Chinese territory in the seventeenth and eighteenth centuries, and in 1910 it became a Japanese colony. Japan ruled Taiwan less harshly than it did Korea, financing industrialization that produced a higher standard of living than that known in mainland China. After World War II China reclaimed the island, but in 1947 local resentment of Chiang's heavy-handed regime led to an island-wide uprising. Chiang dispatched 100,000 troops from the mainland, who killed 30,000 to 40,000 Taiwanese, including many local leaders, in quelling the unrest.

Nationalist Government

As Chiang's Republic of China collapsed in 1948–1949, Chiang and 2 million mainlanders moved to Taiwan, taking with them their government, the Nationalist Party, the remaining military forces, the priceless art collections of the national museum, and China's national treasury. These mainlanders and their descendants eventually constituted some 15 to 20 percent of the total island population, which numbered 23 million by 2008. Because the minority mainlanders dominated politics, the economy, and the military, the majority Taiwanese, although Chinese in culture and language, often considered the mainlanders colonizers. Chiang viewed Taiwan as a temporary refuge, since he hoped to reconquer the mainland. But after his death in 1975, many mainlanders (and their children) realized that, with a return to the mainland unlikely, Taiwan might be their permanent home. They then cultivated better relations with the Taiwanese. However, two governments claiming to represent China created a long-term diplomatic problem for the world community. Both the governments of the People's Republic and of the Republic on Taiwan regarded the island as an integral part of China rather than a separate nation; this "one China policy" was endorsed by most of the world.

Economic Growth

Learning from their defeat in China, and using generous U.S. aid, the Republic's leaders promoted rapid industrial and agricultural growth, a more equitable distribution of wealth, and land reform. With land ownership and access to credit facilities, the peasantry prospered. As in South Korea and Meiji Japan, the economy mixed capitalism and foreign investment with government planning and investment. Light industry and manufacturing eventually accounted for half of Taiwan's economic production and the bulk of exports. Taiwan became the world's third largest producer, after the United States and Japan, of computer hardware. Between the early 1970s and the late 1990s it enjoyed more years of double-digit growth than any other nation. Taiwanese companies set up operations in Southeast Asia, China, Africa, and Latin America. The economic indicators far surpassed those on the mainland, including a per capita annual income of $8,000, 99 percent of households owning a color television, 92 percent literacy, and a life expectancy of seventy-five. In the 1990s Taiwan businessmen built the world's tallest skyscraper, 1,667 feet high, in the capital city, Taipei. Rapid development, however, brought environmental destruction, traffic congestion, political corruption, and a severe economic slowdown in 1997 and 2008–2009. Concrete high-rise buildings increasingly displace the lush greenery of the mountains around Taipei.

Modernization has challenged Chinese values and traditions. The small roadside cafés selling noodle soup and meat dumplings often close, unable to compete with U.S. fast-food restaurants and convenience stores selling Coca-Cola, hamburgers, and ice cream. Rampant materialism concerns those who believe life should offer more than the quest for luxury goods and money. While Confucian values have fostered material success, some Taiwanese have worried that Confucian ethics, including respect for parents and concern for the community rather than the individual, are threatened. Despite the modernization, traditional Chinese culture remains stronger in Taiwan than the mainland. Over 90 percent of the people describe themselves as Buddhists, Daoists, Confucianists, or a mix of the three ancient traditions. Some 5 percent of Taiwan's people have adopted Christianity, while several million others infrequently attend temples or churches.

Like South Korea, Taiwan until the later 1980s followed the authoritarian Little Dragon political model, with Chiang Kai-shek and his family implementing a police state that held numerous political prisoners. Chiang made it illegal to advocate making Taiwan permanently independent of China, and the communists on the mainland also opposed those who advocated two separate Chinese nations. For four decades Chiang's Nationalist Party ruled, but in 1989, nudged by a growing middle class seeking liberalization, they permitted opposition candidates to run in elections. Gradually the regime recognized civil liberties, including the freedom of speech and press. The 2000 elections swept into office the Democratic Progressive Party (DPP), largely supported by the native Taiwanese; many party leaders advocated that Taiwan become a separate nation, a stance that angered both the Nationalist leaders on Taiwan and the communist leaders on the mainland. However, Taiwan's voters seemed less eager to confront China and in 2008 replaced the DPP government, beset by corruption, with the Nationalists, who sought friendlier ties with China.

Taiwan Politics

China has remained Taiwan's permanent challenge. Fearing an invasion to forcibly annex the island, Taiwan lavishly funded its military, kept a large standing army, and bought the latest fighter jets and gunboats, at the same time maintaining after 1954 a defense alliance with the United States and allowing U.S. bases. But in 1978 the United States recognized the People's Republic as China's only government and withdrew diplomatic recognition from the Republic of China. However, it has maintained a strong informal economic presence and repeatedly reaffirms a commitment to defend the island from attack. In the later 1980s Taiwan and China began informal talks about improving relations. As a result, informal trade between the two countries has grown substantially, and many people from Taiwan have visited the mainland to do business or look up relatives. However, doubts about whether China will move toward political liberalization and democracy, as well as alarm at occasional Chinese military exercises being conducted near Taiwan, have precluded any serious negotiations on reunification. China's leaders have threatened military action to prevent any move by Taiwan for permanent independence. Such action would alarm Japan, and might draw in the United States. Thus Taiwan's political future remains an open question, fiercely debated by Taiwanese and their several competing political parties.

Taiwan and China

The Little Dragons in the Global System

The rise of the Pacific Rim, including China, Japan, and the Little Dragons, in the late twentieth century reshaped the global system. The quarter of the world's population living along the western edge of the Pacific Basin outpaced the West and the rest of the world in economic growth while maintaining political stability. A global economy that had been based on the tripod of the United States, western Europe, and Japan now has to accommodate China and the Little Dragons. The Little Dragons industrialized and then diversified into high technology, making computers and other electronics products and thereby posing an economic challenge to Japan and the West. They successfully used the Meiji Japan model to develop and compete with Japan and the West.

Some trends suggested that the Pacific Rim nations were becoming an Asian counterpart to the European Community, the free-trade zone formed by western European nations, thus foreshadowing the possible Pacific Century in which Asian nations might dominate the world economy. Many East and Southeast Asian nations forged closer economic cooperation, with Japan and China forming the hubs. But in 1997 and again in 2008–2009 a severe economic meltdown hit South Korea, Taiwan, Japan, and the industrializing economies of Southeast Asia. As businesses closed, unemployment soared and economies went into deep recession. Thus both the Pacific Rim and the United States face uncertain futures, and China, Japan, and the United States will undoubtedly play major roles in the years to come. Yet in many respects, East Asia had returned to its historical role as a key engine of the world economy.

SECTION SUMMARY

- After World War II, communist North Korea, assisted by the USSR and China, fought a war with South Korea, assisted by a U.S.-dominated United Nations force, that caused thousands of deaths and economic devastation and ended with roughly the same border that existed at the start of the war.

- South Korean governments have grown more tolerant of internal dissent and more open to relations with former enemies such as communist North Korea and China, though their primary emphasis has been on economic growth.

- After the Korean War, North Korea recovered with support from the USSR and China and was ruled as a repressive communist dictatorship with a centrally planned economy whose shortcomings led to widespread food shortages in the 1990s.

- With the communists ruling mainland China, the nationalists took over Taiwan, which they ruled as a police state and turned into an economic powerhouse, but relations with mainland China have continued to be tense.

- China and the "Little Dragons" (Taiwan, South Korea, Singapore, and Hong Kong) grew rapidly in the late twentieth century, leading to predictions of a coming "Pacific Century," but several slowdowns dampened such expectations.

REBUILDING EUROPE AND RUSSIA, SINCE 1945

AP/Wide World Photos

Fall of the Berlin Wall
In 1989, as communist governments collapsed in eastern Europe, peaceful protesters climbed on top of the Berlin Wall, which had already been decorated with
graffiti. The wall, which divided communist East and democratic West Berlin, was
soon torn down.

SUGGESTED READING

Benson, Linda. *China Since 1949*. New York: Longman, 2002. A brief overview.

Cheek, Timothy. *Living With Reform: China Since 1989*. New York: Zed Press, 2006. Lively and balanced review of post-Mao China.

Cumings, Bruce. *Korea's Place in the Sun: A Modern History*, 2nd ed. New York: W.W. Norton, 2005. A provocative and readable account emphasizing the years since World War II.

Dietrich, Craig. *People's China: A Brief History*, 3rd ed. New York: Oxford University Press, 1998. A fine study of China's Communist era.

Dower, John W. *Embracing Defeat: Japan in the Wake of World War II*. New York: W.W. Norton, 1999. Detailed look at the postwar U.S. occupation and its consequences.

Dreyer, June Teufel. *China's Political System: Modernization and Tradition*, 5th ed. New York: Longman, 2005. One of the best surveys of contemporary China.

Ebrey, Patricia Buckley, Anne Walthall, and James B. Palais. *East Asia: A Cultural, Social, and Political History*, 2nd ed. Boston: Houghton Mifflin, 2009. A readable, comprehensive survey.

Gamer, Robert E., ed. *Understanding Contemporary China*, 3rd ed. Boulder, CO: Lynne Rienner, 2008. An excellent collection of essays on all aspects of Chinese society.

Kingston, Jeffrey. *Japan in Transformation, 1952–2000*. New York: Longman, 2001. A useful study of Japan's recent history.

McCargo, Duncan. *Contemporary Japan,* 2nd ed. New York: Palgrave, 2004. A provocative survey by a British scholar.

Peerenboom, Randall. *China Modernizes: Threat to the West or Model for the Rest?* New York: Oxford University Press, 2007. Scholarly study of China's recent development.

Reischauer, Edwin O., and Marius B. Jansen. *The Japanese Today: Change and Continuity*, 2nd ed., enlarged. Cambridge: Harvard University Press, 2004. A classic examination of Japanese society.

Schirokauer, Conrad, and Donald N. Clark. *Modern East Asia: A Brief History*, 2nd ed. Belmont, CA: Wadsworth, 2007. Extensive coverage of China, Japan, and Korea in this era.

Schoppa, R. Keith. *Revolution and Its Past: Identities and Change in Modern Chinese History*, 2nd ed. Upper Saddle River, NJ: Prentice-Hall, 2006. A recent study offering a historical perspective.

Spence, Jonathan. *Mao Zedong*. New York: Viking, 1999. One of the best, most readable biographies of this major Chinese leader.

Stueck, William, ed. *The Korean War in World History*. Lexington: The University Press of Kentucky, 2004. A recent reassessment from multiple perspectives.

Tao Jie, et al., eds. *Holding Up Half the Sky: Chinese Women Past, Present, and Future*. New York: Feminist Press, 2004. Interesting essays on many aspects of women's lives in China today.

Terrill, Ross. *The New Chinese Empire*. New York: Basic Books, 2003. A readable recent study that places China's rise in historical context.

Yahuda, Michael. *The International Politics of the Asia-Pacific*, 2nd ed. New York: Routledge Curzon, 2005. A comprehensive study of the changing roles of China, Japan, Russia, and the United States in East Asia and the world.

REBUILDING EUROPE AND RUSSIA, SINCE 1945

AP/Wide World Photos

Fall of the Berlin Wall
In 1989, as communist governments collapsed in eastern Europe, peaceful protesters climbed on top of the Berlin Wall, which had already been decorated with graffiti. The wall, which divided communist East and democratic West Berlin, was soon torn down.

than the mainland. Over 90 percent of the people describe themselves as Buddhists, Daoists, Confucianists, or a mix of the three ancient traditions. Some 5 percent of Taiwan's people have adopted Christianity, while several million others infrequently attend temples or churches.

Like South Korea, Taiwan until the later 1980s followed the authoritarian Little Dragon political model, with Chiang Kai-shek and his family implementing a police state that held numerous political prisoners. Chiang made it illegal to advocate making Taiwan permanently independent of China, and the communists on the mainland also opposed those who advocated two separate Chinese nations. For four decades Chiang's Nationalist Party ruled, but in 1989, nudged by a growing middle class seeking liberalization, they permitted opposition candidates to run in elections. Gradually the regime recognized civil liberties, including the freedom of speech and press. The 2000 elections swept into office the Democratic Progressive Party (DPP), largely supported by the native Taiwanese; many party leaders advocated that Taiwan become a separate nation, a stance that angered both the Nationalist leaders on Taiwan and the communist leaders on the mainland. However, Taiwan's voters seemed less eager to confront China and in 2008 replaced the DPP government, beset by corruption, with the Nationalists, who sought friendlier ties with China.

Taiwan Politics

China has remained Taiwan's permanent challenge. Fearing an invasion to forcibly annex the island, Taiwan lavishly funded its military, kept a large standing army, and bought the latest fighter jets and gunboats, at the same time maintaining after 1954 a defense alliance with the United States and allowing U.S. bases. But in 1978 the United States recognized the People's Republic as China's only government and withdrew diplomatic recognition from the Republic of China. However, it has maintained a strong informal economic presence and repeatedly reaffirms a commitment to defend the island from attack. In the later 1980s Taiwan and China began informal talks about improving relations. As a result, informal trade between the two countries has grown substantially, and many people from Taiwan have visited the mainland to do business or look up relatives. However, doubts about whether China will move toward political liberalization and democracy, as well as alarm at occasional Chinese military exercises being conducted near Taiwan, have precluded any serious negotiations on reunification. China's leaders have threatened military action to prevent any move by Taiwan for permanent independence. Such action would alarm Japan, and might draw in the United States. Thus Taiwan's political future remains an open question, fiercely debated by Taiwanese and their several competing political parties.

Taiwan and China

The Little Dragons in the Global System

The rise of the Pacific Rim, including China, Japan, and the Little Dragons, in the late twentieth century reshaped the global system. The quarter of the world's population living along the western edge of the Pacific Basin outpaced the West and the rest of the world in economic growth while maintaining political stability. A global economy that had been based on the tripod of the United States, western Europe, and Japan now has to accommodate China and the Little Dragons. The Little Dragons industrialized and then diversified into high technology, making computers and other electronics products and thereby posing an economic challenge to Japan and the West. They successfully used the Meiji Japan model to develop and compete with Japan and the West.

Some trends suggested that the Pacific Rim nations were becoming an Asian counterpart to the European Community, the free-trade zone formed by western European nations, thus foreshadowing the possible Pacific Century in which Asian nations might dominate the world economy. Many East and Southeast Asian nations forged closer economic cooperation, with Japan and China forming the hubs. But in 1997 and again in 2008–2009 a severe economic meltdown hit South Korea, Taiwan, Japan, and the industrializing economies of Southeast Asia. As businesses closed, unemployment soared and economies went into deep recession. Thus both the Pacific Rim and the United States face uncertain futures, and China, Japan, and the United States will undoubtedly play major roles in the years to come. Yet in many respects, East Asia had returned to its historical role as a key engine of the world economy.

SECTION SUMMARY

- After World War II, communist North Korea, assisted by the USSR and China, fought a war with South Korea, assisted by a U.S.-dominated United Nations force, that caused thousands of deaths and economic devastation and ended with roughly the same border that existed at the start of the war.

- South Korean governments have grown more tolerant of internal dissent and more open to relations with former enemies such as communist North Korea and China, though their primary emphasis has been on economic growth.

- After the Korean War, North Korea recovered with support from the USSR and China and was ruled as a repressive communist dictatorship with a centrally planned economy whose shortcomings led to widespread food shortages in the 1990s.

- With the communists ruling mainland China, the nationalists took over Taiwan, which they ruled as a police state and turned into an economic powerhouse, but relations with mainland China have continued to be tense.

- China and the "Little Dragons" (Taiwan, South Korea, Singapore, and Hong Kong) grew rapidly in the late twentieth century, leading to predictions of a coming "Pacific Century," but several slowdowns dampened such expectations.

CHAPTER SUMMARY

I n the decades after World War II, East Asia experienced revolutionary upheavals and dramatic economic development that led to a resurgence of the region's influence in the world. The communist triumph in China began the process of change. After experimenting with a Soviet-style Stalinist development model, China's leader, Mao Zedong, imposed his own version of communism. Emphasizing collective efforts, political values, and mass mobilization, Mao reorganized the rural economy into communes. He also sparked the Cultural Revolution, which attacked the bureaucracy and those who opposed his political and economic vision but also created turmoil. After Mao's death, Deng Xiaoping led China in a new direction; his market socialism energized the economy but led to tensions and then repression. During the 1990s market Leninism continued the economic reforms, providing a basis for rapid growth. China became a world economic power, but the growing inequalities of wealth have threatened to destabilize the nation.

The experiences of Japan and the Little Dragons differed from those of China. After the World War II defeat and U.S. occupation of Japan, the nation rapidly rose to become an economic powerhouse, based on a system mixing political democracy and a form of capitalism in which government and business worked together. The Japanese rebuilt their industries and fostered new forms of business and production. But social change came slowly, leaving Japan hierarchical. The Little Dragon nations of South Korea and Taiwan achieved industrial growth and prosperity by borrowing the Japanese model and mixing free markets with government intervention, eventually fostering democracy, while North Korea chose Stalinism and isolation from the world. The dynamism of most East Asian nations suggests that they have recovered from the disasters they experienced from the mid-1800s to the mid-1900s as a result of Western imperialism, Japanese expansion, and war, but their overall role remains unclear for the twenty-first century.

KEY TERMS

Pacific Rim
Pacific Century
communes
Great Leap Forward

Great Proletarian Cultural Revolution
Red Guards
Iron Rice Bowl

market socialism
market Leninism
Japan, Inc.

salaryman
Little Dragons

EBOOK AND WEBSITE RESOURCES

e **PRIMARY SOURCE**
"One Hundred Items for Destroying the Old and Establishing the New"

e **INTERACTIVE MAPS**
Map 27.1 China and Taiwan
Map 27.2 Japan and the Little Dragons
Map 27.3 The Korean War

LINKS

Asian Studies (http://coombs.anu.edu.au/WWWVL-AsianStudies.html). A vast metasite maintained at Australian National University, with links to hundreds of sites.

China-Profile: Facts, Figures, and Analyses (http://www.china-profile.com). Offers useful information on China today.

East and Southeast Asia: An Annotated Directory of Internet Resources (http://www.newton.uor.edu/Departments&Programs/AsianStudies-Dept/asianam.html). A superb set of links, maintained at the University of Redlands.

Internet East Asian History Sourcebook (http://www.fordham.edu/halsall/eastasia/eastasiasbook.html). An invaluable collection of sources and links on China, Japan, and Korea from ancient to modern times.

Internet Guide to Chinese Studies (http://www.sino.uni-heidelberg.de/igcs/). An excellent collection of links, maintained at a German university.

Plus flashcards, practice quizzes, and more. Go to: www.cengage.com/history/lockard/globalsocnet2e.

> This [united] Europe must be born. And she will, when Spaniards say "our Chartres," Englishmen "our Cracow," Italians "our Copenhagen," and Germans "our Bruges." Then Europe will live.
>
> —SPANISH WRITER SALVADOR DE MADARIAGA, 1948[1]

Jacques Delors (deh-LOW-er) faced a challenge. This French banker's son turned socialist politician had lived through a tumultuous history, including the Great Depression, World War II, and the Cold War. Now, after holding high positions in the French government, he had dedicated himself to building a united Europe. In 1985 he became president of the European Commission, established to reconcile national loyalties with more political cooperation. In 1991, Delors convened the leaders of twelve closely linked European nations in the Dutch city of Maastricht, full of historic buildings, where, calling on all his diplomatic skills, he prodded them to conclude a historic agreement for increased cooperation. The Maastricht meeting affirmed a dream of European unity that had been percolating among European visionaries. Now Europeans, chastened by centuries of conflict, seemed ready to subordinate national interests to a common good. Delors asked the national leaders to transform the economic and political alliance begun in the late 1940s and expanded in the 1950s into a more comprehensive union.

This meeting took place in the same month that the Soviet Union (USSR) dissolved. With their biggest communist rival no longer a threat, European leaders hoped to link their countries to ensure a stable and peaceful future. In theory the European Union, as the grouping was called, would stretch from the Atlantic to the western frontier of Russia, allow goods and people to freely cross borders between member states, and use a single currency, the *euro*. Persuaded by Delors, conference leaders signed the Maastricht Treaty, and it was later ratified by voters in all member nations, though debates contin ued as new members joined. While facing bumps in the road, the European Union, given the centuries of European strife, was a huge achievement.

From 1945 until 1990 three themes dominated European history: (1) the Cold War shaped by the United States and the USSR, each with a political and military power vastly exceeding that of other nations; (2) the rebirth of western European wealth and power; and (3) the movement toward European unity represented by the Maastricht Treaty. After World War II, which had left most countries in shambles, Europe became divided into mutually hostile political and military blocs. While eastern Europe came under Soviet domination, enduring authoritarian communist governments, much of western Europe recovered its prosperity, ensuring freedom, peace, and the well-being of citizens. The trauma of two world wars had fostered a drive for unity involving consensus rather than military might. After 1989, when the communist governments collapsed, this movement accelerated, opening the way for a new, interconnected Europe.

FOCUS QUESTIONS

1. What factors fostered the movement toward unity in western Europe?
2. How did the rise of welfare states transform western European societies?
3. What factors contributed to political crises in the Soviet Union and eastern Europe?
4. How did the demise of the communist system contribute to a new Europe?

e Visit the website and eBook for additional study materials and interactive tools:
www.cengage.com/history/lockard/globalsocnet2e

797

WESTERN EUROPE: REVIVAL AND UNITY

What factors fostered the movement toward unity in western Europe?

Western Europe, emerging from the ashes of World War II economically bankrupt, made a rapid recovery with aid from the United States. Most western Europeans reestablished working multiparty democracies that accorded personal freedom to their citizens. Beginning in 1947, however, Europe was split into two mutually hostile camps with rival military forces—western and eastern Europe—each with a different model of postwar reconstruction. Gradually West Germany, France, and Britain served as the core of a rebuilt, increasingly unified western Europe and were able to regain influence in the world, while economic prosperity blunted the appeal of radicalism.

The Remaking of European Nations

World War II had cost some 50 million lives, reduced major cities to rubble, and destroyed bridges, tunnels, and roads. Transportation, food, housing, and fuel were in short supply. The chaos and the redrawing of political boundaries after the war had displaced people from their home countries, including 10 million Germans who were forced to leave eastern Europe and move to Germany. Emotionally traumatized by the war and the atrocities, Europeans also saw their prestige in tatters. War crimes trials held in Nuremberg, Germany, in 1946 condemned Nazi leaders to death and declared crimes against humanity, especially genocide, indefensible. A fresh start was needed.

Economic Recovery

Economic growth provided the foundation for a new Europe. In 1947 the U.S. secretary of state, World War II general George Marshall (1880-1959), proposed that, to achieve stability and guarantee peace, the United States assist in restoring Europe's economic health. This initiative, the **Marshall Plan**, created a recovery program aimed at preventing communist expansion and spreading liberal economic principles, such as free markets. Between 1948 and 1952 the United States offered $13 billion in aid, about half going to Britain, France, and West Germany. In exchange, American business enjoyed greater access to European markets. The Marshall Plan restored agricultural and industrial production while bolstering international trade. The rapid economic resurgence from 1948 to 1965, unmatched in world history except for Japan's recovery in the same years (see Chapter 27), also owed much to liberal democracy, modern production and managerial techniques, and advances in science, technology, transportation, and agriculture.

Marshall Plan A recovery program created for western Europe by the United States that aimed to prevent communist expansion and to spread liberal economic principles.

Promoting Unity

The British leader Winston Churchill (1874-1965), who served twice as prime minister (1940-1945, 1951-1955), prophesied the new trends for Europe. Churchill warned that the Soviet Union was expansionist and that "an iron curtain" had descended across Europe, dividing western Europe from eastern Europe and pro-Western, capitalist West Germany from communist East Germany. This Cold War division stimulated western European cooperation. When eight hundred delegates met at the Hague, in Holland, in 1948, where they called for a democratic European economic union, Churchill urged them to "design a United Europe, where men and women of every country will think of being European as of belonging to their native land, and wherever they go in this wide domain they will truly feel 'Here I am at home'"[2] (see Chronology: Western Europe, 1945-1989). The Hague Congress, which created a European assembly and a court of human rights, generated what soon became the "European Movement."

Western Europeans also committed to sustaining parliamentary democracy. This was true even for the surviving constitutional monarchies, including Belgium, Britain, the Netherlands, and the Scandinavian nations, where kings and queens remained symbols of their people but enjoyed little power. In the 1970s longtime dictators opposed to change were overthrown and replaced by democrats in Spain, Portugal, and Greece. Britain, France, Italy, and West Germany became the most influential European nations.

New political alignments also emerged. Political stability in western Europe depended on improved relations between France and Germany, as well as on German recovery from war. Although Charles De Gaulle (1890-1970), the crusty general and proud nationalist who dominated French politics between 1947 and 1969, imagined France "like the princess in the fairy stories, as dedicated to an exalted and exceptional destiny,"[3] he made French-German reconciliation the cornerstone

CHRONOLOGY

	Western Europe	Russia	Eastern Europe
1940	**1946–1989** Cold War **1949** Formation of NATO **1957** European Common Market	**1955** Warsaw Pact	**1945–1948** Formation of communist governments
1960		**1979–1989** Soviet war in Afghanistan	
1980	**1991** Maastricht Treaty	**1991** Breakup of Soviet Union	**1989** End of communist governments

of French policy. Similarly, the West German leader, Konrad Adenauer (ODD-en-HOUR) (1876–1967), sought a cooperative relationship with France. Germany's reconciliation with its neighbors was furthered in the 1960s by West German chancellor Willy Brandt (1913–1992), a fervent anti-Nazi who had fled Adolph Hitler's government. Brandt accepted German responsibilities for the war and the new borders imposed after the war, which awarded a large chunk of German territory to Poland. Economic growth also improved French-German relations. Because of its sheer size and central location, West Germany's economy lay at the heart of western European recovery, and by 1960 West Germany, now firmly allied with France, accounted for a fifth of the world's trade in manufactured goods, surpassing Britain.

New political parties and movements took shape. On the right, Christian Democrats, who, aligned with the Catholic Church, emphasized Christian values and protecting the traditional family, either formed governments or led the opposition in a half dozen countries, including West Germany and Italy. But Christian Democratic corruption scandals erupted in West Germany and Italy, and by the 1990s the parties had lost considerable support. Parties on the left competed for support. The social democratic parties, which favored generous welfare programs to provide a safety net for all citizens, acquired more clout than they had enjoyed in the prewar years. Social democratic governments came to power in several countries, including Britain and France, and moved toward state ownership of large industries such as steel and railroads. Eventually most of the social democratic parties, such as the British Labor Party, abandoned state ownership and economic planning for free markets.

Political Parties

AP/Wide World Photos

Basque Terrorism   The extremist Basque nationalist movement, the ETA, has waged a terrorist campaign against the Spanish government for decades, assassinating dozens of people and exploding bombs at government targets in cities and towns. The result is the sort of destruction shown here after one attack.

Eurocommunism
A form of communism in western Europe that embraced political democracy and free elections and that rejected Soviet domination.

Greens A political movement in western Europe that rejected militarism and heavy industry and favored environmental protection over economic growth.

Meanwhile, the western European communist parties declined rapidly, maintaining a large following only in France, Italy, Portugal, and Spain. Seeking popular support, some adopted **Eurocommunism**, a form of communism that embraced political democracy and free elections and that rejected Soviet domination. Despite Eurocommunism, the communist parties lost most of their support in the 1990s, fragmenting into small feuding parties. By the 1980s a new political movement had an impact. The **Greens** rejected militarism and heavy industry and favored environmental protection over economic growth. Women such as Petra Kelly (1947–1992) were prominent in the West German Green Party leadership, helping it appeal to women voters and win seats in the West German parliament.

Ethnic and Religious Conflicts

However, western Europe was not immune to political unrest. Between 1946 and 1949 a civil war raged in Greece, where conservatives supporting the monarchy, aided by the United States, defeated revolutionaries who wanted to end the monarchy and establish a communist state. Elsewhere, the desire of ethnic minorities for their own nations spurred violence and sometimes terrorism. For example, a chronic ethnic conflict embroiled Spain, where the Basque people, who live mostly in the north and speak a language completely different from Spanish, have long sought either autonomy within, or independence from, Spain. An underground Basque independence movement, known as ETA (for "Basque Homeland and Freedom"), has carried out assassinations and bombings against people linked to the Spanish government. Similarly, for decades in Northern Ireland (Ulster), which remains part of Great Britain, the Catholic minority, often less affluent, have sought freedom from British rule and a merger with the largely Catholic Irish Republic, while the majority Protestants have wanted to remain a British province. For decades extremist Catholic and Protestant paramilitary groups attacked each other and the British army, causing thousands of civilian deaths, but violence ebbed as relations between Britain and Ireland improved.

Decolonization and the Cold War

Dismantling Empires

Both the end of colonial empires and the Cold War affected Europe. Most European colonizers gradually abandoned their efforts to quell nationalist movements in Asia and Africa and started to leave their colonial territories. The British, whose empire had occupied an area 125 times larger than Great Britain, realized that imperial glory was only memory. In 1947 they recognized the independence of India and in 1948 of Burma. The Dutch, facing a determined nationalist resistance, reluctantly abandoned their lucrative colony, Indonesia, in 1950. By the mid-1960s the British had also turned over most of their colonies in Africa, Asia, and the Caribbean to local leaders, retaining control of only a few tiny outposts, such as Gibraltar, a strategically valuable peninsula on the southern coast of Spain, and a few Caribbean, South Atlantic, and South Pacific islands. While postimperial Britain sought to balance a special relationship to the United States with closer links to Europe, it also continued economic ties to many former colonies. A more formal connection was maintained through the British **Commonwealth of Nations**, established in 1931 and comprising fifty-three states by 2009, which provided a forum for cooperating and discussing issues of mutual interest.

Commonwealth of Nations A forum, established by Britain in 1931, for discussing issues of mutual interest with its former colonies.

By contrast, the French and Portuguese only grudgingly recognized the inevitable. In the 1940s nationalist rebellions broke out in Algeria and Vietnam, which France attempted to quell at the cost of much bloodshed. In his criticism of torture used against rebels in Algeria, the French philosopher Jean-Paul Sartre, an outspoken opponent of colonialism, wrote: "We are sick, very sick. Feverish and prostrate, obsessed by old dreams of glory and the foreboding of its shame, France is struggling in the grip of a nightmare it is unable either to flee or to decipher."[4] In 1954, unable to defeat communist-led revolutionaries, the French withdrew from Vietnam. Then in 1962 they left Algeria, causing 800,000 European settlers, many embittered toward the French government, to flee to France. France retained a few small Caribbean, Pacific, and Indian Ocean islands and French Guiana, and eventually it established close relations with most of its former colonies, including an enduring economic connection that critics considered a form of neocolonialism, since French business interests and advisers remained prominent. Portugal wasted lives and wealth violently resisting African nationalist movements but, after democrats overthrew the long-standing fascist dictatorship, granted its African colonies independence in 1975.

Europe and the Cold War

Beginning in 1946, the Cold War shaped the European roles in the world. The USSR helped install communist governments in eastern Europe and East Germany, while the United States assumed the burden for protecting western Europe militarily. In 1947 the U.S. president, Harry Truman (president 1945–1953), introduced a policy, known as the **Truman Doctrine**, that asserted that the United States, as the leader of the free world, was charged with defending countries that were threatened by communist movements or Soviet pressure. Then in 1949 strong European and

Truman Doctrine
A policy formed in 1947 that asserted that the United States, as the leader of the free world, was charged with protecting countries from communism.

U.S. fears of possible Soviet attack led to the formation of the North Atlantic Treaty Organization, **NATO**, a military alliance that linked nine western European countries with the United States and Canada. NATO allowed coordination of defense policies against the USSR and its communist allies, known as the **Soviet bloc**, with the aim of repulsing any potential Soviet military attack across the "iron curtain" frontier. Permanent U.S. military bases were set up in NATO countries, especially West Germany. The Soviets responded in 1955 by forming the **Warsaw Pact**, a defense alliance that linked the communist-ruled eastern European countries with the USSR (see Map 28.1). By the 1980s senior officers in NATO and the Warsaw Pact had spent their careers preparing for a war that, partly because both sides possessed nuclear weapons, never came. Western Europeans were alarmed by nuclear weapons, which could obliterate their cities in minutes, and worried that a nuclear conflict between the United States and the USSR would inevitably destroy Europe as well.

The Cold War and NATO were partly a response to the postwar division of Germany. Each of the four World War II allies—the United States, Britain, France, and the USSR—had an occupation zone in Germany and had also divided up the German capital, Berlin. In 1948 the three Western powers united their occupation zones. Angered, the USSR blockaded Berlin to prevent supplies from reaching the city's Western-administered zone by land through Soviet-controlled East Germany. For a year the allies supplied the city with food and fuel by airlift. In 1949 the USSR stopped the blockade and allowed the creation of the Federal Republic of Germany, or West Germany, while forming its own allied government, the German Democratic Republic, or East Germany. West Germany later joined NATO.

Cold War fears gradually slackened as the danger of actual war faded, leading western Europeans to reappraise their policies toward both of the two superpowers. Some, especially in Britain, promoted the U.S. alliance, while many Europeans, resenting what they considered irresponsible U.S. foreign policies, wanted weaker ties. Most opposed the American war in Vietnam, as well as U.S. interventions to overthrow left-leaning governments in Latin America, such as Guatemala (1954) and Chile (1973). In 1969 the West German chancellor Willy Brandt, a Social Democrat and strong anticommunist, introduced his policy of **ostpolitik** ("eastern politics"), which sought a reconciliation between West and East Germany and an expanded western European dialogue with the USSR. This stance led to a thaw between West Germany and the Soviet bloc and gave hope to eastern Europeans who wanted more freedom. Gradually western Europeans, by building their own military forces, became less reliant on U.S. power. Despite the differences, however, the Western alliance and NATO remained strong because of mutual interests during the Cold War.

From Cooperation to European Community

Western Europe's role in the global system changed. Between the two world wars Europeans owned enterprises all over the globe, including Indian tea plantations, Malayan rubber estates, African mines, and South American railroads. But during the 1940s Europeans lost influence to the United States. The Bretton Woods agreement on international monetary cooperation in 1944 made the U.S. dollar, pegged to the price of gold, the staple currency of the Western nations. Europeans concluded they had no choice but to cooperate with each other. In 1949 ten nations formed the Council of Europe, which operated on the basis of a shared cultural heritage and democratic principles. In 1950 the Council produced the European Convention on Human Rights, the root of a Europe-wide justice system and court. But some leaders wanted more. Jean Monnet (MOAN-ay) (1888–1979), a French economist, financier, and former League of Nations official who is often called the "Father of United Europe," and French prime minister Robert Schuman (1886–1963), a strong proponent of French-German reconciliation, wanted to make war not only unthinkable but impossible. To encourage better economic coordination, they proposed a European Coal and Steel Community (ECSC), which finally formed in 1951. They hoped that the ECSC, which brought together six nations, would be a first step for unity and peace. But some nations, including Britain, fearing loss of economic independence, declined to join.

Building on the ECSC, the Common Market, later known as the European Community (EC), was formed in 1957 with six members: France, Italy, West Germany, the Netherlands, Belgium, and Luxembourg. By removing tariff barriers, it opened frontiers to the free movement of capital and labor. The members called upon other Europeans to join in their efforts and added Britain, Ireland, and Denmark in 1973. The EC created unprecedented economic unity in the world's largest free trade zone.

Monnet and Schuman dreamed of a Europe united politically: societies that depend on one another, they reasoned, won't go to war. But European nationalism occasionally flared up. The EC weathered many disagreements as the member nations squabbled to get the best deal for their own farmers or businesses, and the British, an island people proud of their distinctive traditions,

NATO A military alliance, formed in 1949, that linked nine western European countries with the United States and Canada.

Soviet bloc The Soviet Union and the communist states allied with it.

Warsaw Pact A defense alliance formed in 1955 that linked the communist-ruled eastern European countries with the USSR.

Reducing Tensions

ostpolitik A West German policy, promoted by Chancellor Willy Brandt, that sought a reconciliation between West and East Germany and an expanded dialogue with the USSR.

Increasing Cooperation

The European Community

Map 28.1
Military Alliances and Multinational Economic Groupings, 1949–1989

Post–World War II Europe was divided by Cold War politics into communist and noncommunist blocs. Most western European nations joined the NATO defense alliance. Western Europeans also cooperated in economic matters. By 1989 the Common Market had expanded from six to eleven members. The Soviet bloc counterpart, COMECON, had eight members.

Interactive Map

Map legend:

$ Participants in the Marshall Plan

Member of NATO,* formed in 1949

Member of COMECON,** formed in 1949, and the Warsaw Pact, organized in 1955

Member of the European Common Market, formed in 1958

Iron Curtain

* North Atlantic Treaty Organization
** Council for Mutual Economic Assistance

Map 28.2

Europe's Gross Domestic Product

The gross domestic product, or the official measure of the output of goods and services in a national economy, provides a good summary of a nation's economic production. In the early twenty-first century, Norway, Ireland, and Switzerland were the most productive European countries on a per capita basis, while former Soviet bloc nations had the weakest performance.

GDP per capita

- Over $40,000
- $30,000–40,000
- $25,000–29,999
- $20,000–24,999
- $15,000–19,999
- $10,000–14,999
- Under $10,000

e Interactive Map

periodically threatened to quit the grouping. While every member economy had to adapt to the marketplace, dumping uncompetitive industries, some doubters, the "Euro-skeptics," believed cooperation had gone too far. Yet the EC greatly reduced old national tensions. The members eventually established an elected European Parliament, based in Brussels, Belgium, to discuss shared issues and to make policies that encouraged cooperation and standardization.

The European Community spurred growth, creating a consumer society in western Europe (see Map 28.2). With higher wages, greater purchasing power, and more available consumer products, families bought automobiles, washing machines, refrigerators, and televisions. More people worked in the service sector and fewer in agriculture, and the middle classes grew rapidly, while blue-collar workers shared middle-class aspirations. Consumer markets reached from Europe's sprawling cities into remote villages. A journalist's description of an old French village in 1973 revealed the change: "The last horse trod its streets in 1968. The water mill closed down in 1952.

Growing Prosperity

SECTION SUMMARY

- World War II devastated western Europe's population, infrastructure, and economy, but it enjoyed a remarkable period of growth, aided by extensive U.S. funding under the Marshall Plan.

- After World War II, Germany and France overcame centuries of mutual hatred, rightwing Christian Democrat parties competed with leftist social democrats, and the Greens agitated for environmental protection over economic growth.

- A wave of decolonization followed World War II, though the British Commonwealth maintained connections between Great Britain and its former colonies, and France, after struggling to maintain its colonies, maintained economic ties with its former holdings.

- The Cold War shaped European politics, with eastern Europe allied with the USSR and western Europe allied with the United States, but over time some European leaders distanced themselves from U.S. policies and advocated dialogue with the USSR.

- Having been surpassed economically by the United States, European countries joined together in the European Community, which became the world's largest free-trade zone and led to increased prosperity; however, the 1970s brought hard times, and European unity sometimes threatened to give way.

The washing machine replaced the wash house—and broke up the community of women—in the 1960s."[5] Europeans invested in high-speed railroads and turnpikes to link peoples together, as well as mass transit—subways and commuter trains—to make city life more convenient. Yet prosperity did not eliminate all poverty or regional disparities. For example, industrialized northern Italy remained much wealthier than largely agricultural southern Italy.

Despite the growing cooperation and successes, western Europe still faced economic problems. For one thing, Europeans were hurt by U.S. decisions that led to the dismantling of the Bretton Woods international monetary system. In 1971, with the U.S. economy undermined by the war in Vietnam, President Richard Nixon devalued the U.S. dollar, the staple currency of the Western nations, and ended its parity with gold. These moves destabilized world trade, triggering soaring prices and trade deficits. Then in 1973 European economies were brought to a standstill by a quadrupling of oil prices, followed by a short embargo on oil exports, by the major oil-producing nations, which were angered by Western support of Israel. The frustrated motorists waiting in long lines at gas stations showed how vulnerable prosperity could be in the global system. Western Europe also faced the environmental problems common to all industrial societies, such as noxious air, toxic waste, and lakes and forests dying from acid rain, the apparent price of industrialization.

The end of cheap energy and growing competition from industrializing Asian nations and Japan also hurt European industries and workers. Factories built a century or more earlier, often decaying and inefficient, scaled back operations or closed, causing high unemployment in industrial cities such as Birmingham and Manchester in England. Jobless young people, living in bleak row houses or apartments and surviving on welfare payments, hung out on street corners, some turning to drugs or crime. By 1983 unemployment rates in western Europe had risen to 10 percent, posing a special problem to women, immigrants, and those just out of school. As some blamed their problems on immigrant workers, especially the Arabs and Turks who competed with local people for jobs, these feelings gave a boost to rightwing, anti-immigrant parties. As a result, free market conservatives often regained political power, penalizing striking workers and weakening labor unions.

WESTERN EUROPEAN SOCIETIES AND CULTURES

How did the rise of welfare states transform western European societies?

In the ashes of World War II the wartime British prime minister, Winston Churchill, wrote, "What is Europe? A rubble heap, a charnel house, a breeding ground for pestilence and hate."[6] Seeing the need for change, western European nations embarked on reshaping their societies and improving the quality of life for all their citizens, often blending capitalism and socialism. The economic boom from the late 1940s to the 1970s allowed most western European states, influenced by socialism, to construct welfare programs that fostered political stability, ensured public health, and eliminated poverty for most citizens. Gender relations, family life, and sexual attitudes were also reshaped, while musicians, philosophers, and churches addressed the changes of the times.

Social Democracy and Welfare States

welfare states Government systems that offer their citizens a range of state-subsidized health, education, and social service benefits; adopted by western European nations after World War II.

The rise of western European **welfare states**, government systems that offer their citizens a range of state-subsidized health, education, and social service benefits, and the high quality of life they fostered, owed much to an influential political philosophy called social democracy. Social democracy derived from socialists in the early 1900s who favored evolutionary rather than revolutionary change, eventually promoting a mixing of liberal democracy, market economies, and a safety net for workers. Since 1945 social democratic parties have governed or been the dominant opposition in many Western countries. They have usually controlled the governments in the Scandinavian nations of Denmark, Finland, Norway, and Sweden and have often governed in several other nations, including Britain, France, Netherlands, West Germany, and Spain. They have also been influential in Australia, Canada, and New Zealand.

Social democracy has fostered welfare programs, a mix of free markets and government regulation, a commitment to parliamentary democracy and civil liberties, support for labor unions, and the goal of moderating the extremes of wealth and poverty. As a result, workers in northern and central Europe have gained more rights and protections than workers enjoy anywhere else in the world. In West Germany, for example, they received generous pensions and gained seats on the boards of directors of the enterprises that employed them. Often valuing leisure at the expense of work, Europeans boasted that they work to live while Americans, who on average earn more, live to work. By the 1990s both white-collar and blue-collar Europeans worked many fewer hours each year than their counterparts in the United States and Japan. The 35-hour workweek became the norm in France and West Germany, and by 2000 the average German spent around 400 fewer hours a year on the job than the average American. Moreover, the average paid vacation has been four to six weeks a year. During the most popular vacation month, August, the beach and mountain resorts are jammed, and, with many employees gone, stores often offer limited services.

Social Democratic Policies

Citizens in nations influenced by social democracy have received generous taxpayer-funded benefits from the state. Europeans tend to define welfare not just as assistance to the poor, as Americans do, but also as ensuring that everyone enjoys better living standards and opportunities. Free education through the university level (but with stiff university entrance exams) has helped people from working-class and farming backgrounds to move into the middle and upper classes, and generous unemployment insurance removes the pain of job loss. Governments also subsidize housing for the elderly, while inexpensive, widely available day care allows mothers to work outside the home for wages. Whether married or single, custodial parents receive child support payments from the welfare state. While extensive mass transit makes travel and commuting affordable for all, universal health coverage has removed the fear of serious illness, providing inexpensive prescription drugs and guaranteeing medical care to all citizens. These benefits have greatly improved public health. Most Western European nations spend less than Americans do on health care yet often see better outcomes. Using statistical methods the World Health Organization identified France as having the world's best health care system, with the lowest per capita number of avoidable deaths and a life expectancy three years longer than Americans. Where Europeans had once looked to the extended family for support in the early 1900s, now they expect the welfare state to care for the elderly and incapacitated. In addition, northern European nations have the most equitable distributions of income in the world and have nearly eliminated slums and deep poverty.

The Scandinavian nations, poor a century ago, have elected the strongest social democratic governments and become the world's most prosperous societies. Norway has achieved the highest standard of living in the Western world, thanks to North Sea oil and a generous welfare state.

Scandinavian Welfare States

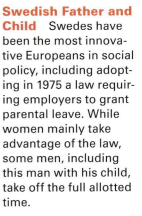

Swedish Father and Child   Swedes have been the most innovative Europeans in social policy, including adopting in 1975 a law requiring employers to grant parental leave. While women mainly take advantage of the law, some men, including this man with his child, take off the full allotted time.

B.O. Olsson, photographer

The annual Human Development Report, issued by the United Nations, usually ranks Norway and Sweden as having the highest quality of life in the world, along with several other countries in which social democracy has been influential, such as Australia, Canada, Iceland, and the Netherlands. The Scandinavian nations are also ranked, along with Ireland, the Netherlands, and Switzerland, as having the most press freedom in the world, with the least government interference in the free flow of information. In Sweden, which has been Europe's most creative country in experimenting with social change, women, youth, and even animals have more rights and protections than elsewhere. Swedish citizens enjoy housing subsidies, free hospitalization, and a pension that pays two-thirds of their salary upon retirement. By providing child care in kindergartens and preschools, the Swedes also attract women into the work force. Nor have the world's most level playing field and lowest poverty rate dampened economic growth. In recent decades, Sweden has often enjoyed the most dynamic economy in Europe. And, thanks to the social safety net and wise investment of oil revenues, Norway even thrived during the 2008–2009 global economic crisis that undermined most European economies.

Challenges to Welfare States

All welfare states have problems, however. Although they foster social stability, funding them has required high taxes, often half of a citizen's annual income. There are also some workplace consequences. Worker protections make it hard for companies to fire workers, prompting companies to hire fewer people. The shift in emphasis from work to leisure has given workers so much security that they may not need to strive harder, which has economic costs. Losing a job is less disastrous than for Americans, since the welfare state insulates people from many effects of economic slumps. Yet, many people with modest incomes, especially immigrants, live in drab apartment blocks or houses, often far from potential jobs and the best schools.

Beginning in the 1980s the welfare states experienced more problems related to sporadic downturns in the world economy. For decades governments had paid for social services by borrowing against future exports, a strategy known as deficit spending. Falling export profits, and hence revenues, placed the welfare systems under strain, forcing cutbacks in benefits, and also prompted nations to cut spending for military defense. Companies downsized, thus putting pressure on generous unemployment programs. As a result, in some countries conservative parties gained power and began to modify the welfare systems. For example, in Britain, the government led by Prime Minister Margaret Thatcher (governed 1979–1990), a free market enthusiast, reduced health services, with the result that people had to wait longer to receive medical attention. But the conservative regimes did not dismantle welfare state institutions such as national health insurance, which remained hugely popular.

Political and Economic Stability

Unlike in the 1930s, the economic problems did not bring serious violence or political instability. While occasionally a political party with an anti-immigrant or anti–European Union platform has gained a following, extremist rightwing and ultranationalist forces have remained weak in most countries. For example, the French National Front, led by the paratrooper turned lawyer Jean-Marie Le Pen (b. 1928), won 10 percent of the national vote in 1986 by calling for expulsion of Arab and African immigrants and secession from the European Community, but Le Pen's appeal faded. The welfare state, which allows even the unemployed to receive their basic necessities such as health care, provides stability because it diminishes workers' fear of job competition from immigrants. Hence, even most free market conservatives have accepted the broad framework of the welfare state, although they want to make it more efficient and cost-effective.

Social Activism, Reform, and Gender Relations

Social Protests and Problems

Although most people have seemed satisfied with their lives, occasional student and worker protests against capitalism and materialism have erupted. A serious challenge to mainstream society came in 1968, when youth protests broke out in France that were aimed at the aging, autocratic president Charles De Gaulle, an antiquated university education system, and the unpopular U.S. war in Vietnam, France's former colony. Protest posters urged students to "be realistic—ask for the impossible." University students went on strike, police beat hundreds of them, protesters blocked traffic, and activists fought pitched battles in the streets with police, who responded with teargas. As public sentiment shifted toward the protesters, industrial workers called a general strike, bringing some 10 million workers into the streets. Although De Gaulle outmaneuvered the protesters by rallying conservatives, raising workers' wages, and calling for a new national election, the protests begun in Paris soon spread to Italy and West Germany, where students resented conservative governments, staid bureaucracies, rigid university systems, and powerful business interests. Lacking strong public support, however, Europe's student protests soon fizzled; governments did not fall or need troops to restore order. However, De Gaulle resigned a year later after the public rejected, in a referendum, his proposals to reorganize the French government.

Europeans also dealt with social problems common to all industrialized nations, such as drug and alcohol abuse and high divorce rates. But European attitudes to the problems were often different from those in the United States. For example, while Americans harshly punished drug use and trafficking, by the 1980s many western Europeans generally treated drug use and minor drug sales as social and medical issues rather than criminal ones. Some European countries even decriminalized use of marijuana. Other laws in Europe also differed from those elsewhere. European nations generally abolished capital punishment, and most enacted strict gun control laws, often banning handguns. The scarcity of guns fostered low rates of violent crime.

Attitudes toward marriage and gender relations also shifted. After World War II, governments tried to revitalize traditional marriage and family patterns, such as the view that women were chiefly homemakers and should have many children. But in the 1960s and 1970s the changing attitudes toward sexual activity, often known as the sexual revolution, facilitated by general access to birth control, undermined conventional practices. The contraceptive pill, which remained illegal in some Catholic countries until much later, gave women control over their reproduction and sexuality. The sexual revolution upset those with traditional values, such as the rural Spanish woman who ruefully observed the ease of pursuing sex outside of marriage: "If a boy wants to be alone with a girl there's no problem; they go off alone and whatever fires they have can burn."[7]

Gender Relations

Changing social attitudes also eliminated or moderated the social shame of divorce, extramarital sex, and unmarried cohabitation. All these activities now became open, a challenge to cultural taboos. Although sex scandals involving politicians are not unknown, especially in Britain, most political leaders have little fear of public criticism for openly having extramarital relationships or children out of wedlock, and such practices are common in France and Italy. Pornography and obscenity laws were relaxed, allowing long banned work to be published, such as the racy 1920s novel *Lady Chatterly's Lover* by the British author D. H. Lawrence. British poet Philip Larkin satirized the changes: "Sexual intercourse began, in nineteen sixty-three (Which was rather late for me)—Between the end of the *Chatterly* ban, And the Beatles' first LP."[8]

Inspired by feminist thinkers such as the French philosopher Simone de Beauvoir (bo-VWAHR) (see Profile: Simone de Beauvoir, French Feminist and Philosopher), women's movements grew in strength and, by the 1970s, pressed their agendas more effectively. An English women's group hoped that "a world freed from the economic, social and psychological bonds of patriarchy would be a world turned upside down, creating a human potential we can hardly dream of now,"[9] benefiting both men and women. Feminists wanted legal divorce, easier access to birth control, the right to abortion, and reform of family laws to give wives more influence. They had their most success in Protestant countries, which often adopted their agenda. In 1973 Denmark became the first nation to allow abortion on request. The feminist movements also made headway in Catholic nations. Although Pope John Paul II (pope 1978–2005) reiterated the long-standing church ban on contraception, abortion, and divorce, many Catholics ignored the conservative teachings of their church, and during the 1970s and 1980s most Catholic nations, including Italy and Spain, followed the earlier examples of France, Britain, and Germany and legalized both divorce and abortion.

Women's Movements

The lives of both men and women were affected by changes in work, politics, and family life. Men and women now shared responsibility for financially supporting their families. By the 1980s women were half the work force in Sweden, a third in France and Italy, and a quarter in conservative Ireland. Women also moved into the professions, business, and even politics. Having won the right to vote, they constituted a majority of the electorate. In some nations, such as Belgium, France, and Italy, female suffrage came only in 1945, but as once-powerful male-dominated institutions such as the military and church declined in influence, more and more women voted for socialist and liberal parties supportive of the welfare state that guaranteed them and their children health care and education. At various times women headed governments in nations such as Britain, France, Germany, Iceland, and Norway. Even Ireland, where patriarchy remained strong, in 1991 elected its first woman president, social democrat Mary Robinson (b. 1944), an outspoken law professor, feminist, single parent, and supporter of homosexual rights.

Women political activists made their voices heard. In 1976 two Northern Ireland mothers, Mairead Corrigan (b. 1944) and Betty Williams (b. 1943), jointly shared the Nobel Peace Prize for their efforts to bridge the Catholic-Protestant divide and bring peace to their troubled land. Women wage earners became less dependent on men. Yet, some changes came slowly. So few women had been able to achieve high business and industry positions that, in 2006, Norway's social democratic government outraged corporate leaders by requiring that 40 percent of the board members of large private companies must be women.

Less-rigid gender roles affected marriage patterns. In the 1970s the model of the married heterosexual couple remained the norm, and even rock stars known for their live-in girlfriends, such

Marriage Patterns

as Mick Jagger of the Rolling Stones, a popular British group, got married, surrounded by celebrities. Some celebrities, such as French rock star Johnny Halliday, changed spouses frequently. But by the 1980s more men and women remained single and lived on their own. In Scandinavia and Germany, the singles accounted for between a quarter and a third of the adult population. Increasing personal independence and mobility fostered small nuclear families instead of the large extended families of old. As unhappy couples no longer needed to stay married, divorce rates more than doubled between 1960 and 1990.

Homosexuality

Homosexuals also began to enjoy equal rights. Homosexual subcultures in European cities had been active for decades. Organizing to change discriminatory laws and attitudes, reform movements began in several countries. Yet, in the 1950s many governments still prosecuted homosexuals, some of them respected figures in the arts, for consensual sexual activity. In West Germany between 1953 and 1965 some 99,000 men were convicted, and frequently jailed, under still-existing Nazi-era laws prohibiting homosexual activity. Although governments began to eliminate laws opposing homosexual behavior by the 1960s, combating prejudice took longer. Hence, in 1974 a conservative Christian Democrat leader in Italy warned that "if divorce is allowed, it will be possible to have marriages between homosexuals, and perhaps your wife will run off with some pretty young girl."[10] However, most societies developed more tolerant attitudes. Denmark recognized domestic partnerships in 1989, and by 2001 most of northern Europe had such laws providing legal protection, while discrimination against homosexuals had ebbed. Several nations, including the Netherlands, Belgium, and Spain, legalized homosexual marriage in the early twenty-first century. At the same time, openly homosexual men and women served as high government officials or political leaders in nations as socially different as the liberal Netherlands and conservative Ireland. In 2009 Iceland, engulfed in economic collapse, chose the openly lesbian Johanna Sigurdarlottir, a leftwing former flight attendant and trade unionist, as prime minister.

Immigration: Questions of Identity

In the later twentieth century several million immigrants settled in various European countries as "guest workers." In response to labor shortages in northern Europe and Britain in the 1950s and 1960s, poorer southern Europeans, especially Italians, Greeks, and Portuguese, migrated north in search of better jobs and pay. They were soon joined by Turks, Algerians, Moroccans, and people from West Africa and the Caribbean, fleeing even harsher poverty. At first many were single men who were brought for factory work and often housed in bleak shantytowns. Later entire families arrived. Many Indians, Pakistanis, and Bangladeshis sought a better life in their former imperial power, Britain, while people left the former Dutch colonies of Indonesia and Suriname for the Netherlands. By the early twenty-first century immigrants constituted 10 percent of the population in Germany, 6 percent in France, and 5 percent in Britain. Major European cities such as Berlin, London, and Paris took on an international flavor. By 2006 London's population was 40 percent nonwhite, and Islamic culture flourished in cities such as Hamburg (Germany) and Marseilles (France), where Arab- and Turkish-language radio stations had large audiences.

Immigrant Life

Immigrants contributed much to European societies. Paris became a center of Arab and African culture, including a large recording industry churning out music by Arab and African musicians, often for export to their homelands. Small Arab-run neighborhood grocery stores served vital functions in French urban life, and the Indian and Pakistani sundry goods and grocery shops and restaurants became features of English and Irish city life. Observers remarked that the favorite British food was now Indian curry, while in Ireland Chinese carry-out restaurants opened in nearly every town. In Britain many immigrants served as mayors, officials, doctors, professors, writers, and entertainers, and people of Asian, Middle Eastern, and African descent were elected to parliaments in countries such as Britain, France, and the Netherlands. In 2007 two Muslim women, of Algerian and Senegalese background respectively, were named to the French cabinet.

The immigration also posed problems of absorption into European society, fostering tensions between whites and the nonwhite immigrants. Over the years, as Turks, Arabs, Africans, and Pakistanis arrived to do the low-paying jobs nobody else wanted and then settled down, they and even their local-born children faced discrimination and sometimes violent attack by rightwing youth gangs. Neo-Nazis in Germany sometimes set fire to immigrant apartment buildings, and young toughs in England boasted of "Paki-bashing," or beating up people from the Indian subcontinent. In response, many immigrants retreated into their own cultures. While older immigrants often clung to the cultures and attitudes they brought from their Asian or Middle Eastern village, such as a husband's authority over his wife and the preference for arranged marriages, their children struggled to reconcile the contrasting expectations of their conservative parents and religious traditions with the materialistic, individualistic, secular societies of Europe.

SIMONE DE BEAUVOIR, FRENCH FEMINIST AND PHILOSOPHER

Few thinkers have had more influence on the study of women and on contemporary women's movements than Simone de Beauvoir (1908–1986), the first systematic feminist philosopher and a prolific writer of novels, essays, and autobiographical works. She was born in Paris to a middle-class family. Her father, a lawyer, and a devout mother with very traditional values sent her to fashionable Roman Catholic girls' schools that taught her, she remembered, "the habit of obedience." She believed that God expected her "to be dutiful." Her classmates aimed at marriage rather than careers. But when World War I impoverished de Beauvoir's family, Simone was pushed toward a career. During her teens she battled her parents for more freedom to leave the house on her own and alarmed her parents by becoming an atheist.

Simone loved the liberating intellectual atmosphere at the Sorbonne in Paris, the most prestigious French university, but found that, to succeed in her studies there, she had to overcome gender stereotypes: "My upbringing had convinced me of my sex's intellectual inferiority. I flattered myself that I had a woman's heart and a man's brain." Graduating at the top of her class, she then supported herself, first as a high school teacher and then as a writer. De Beauvoir began a romantic and intellectual partnership with Jean Paul Sartre, later to become Europe's most acclaimed philosopher, whom she had met at the Sorbonne, and became a vital contributor to Sartre's ideas and books. The two maintained an intense free union, and their lifelong connection provided a model of an adult relationship between a man and a woman without wedlock or exclusive commitment. Both had lovers on the side.

De Beauvoir's life reflected the transformation of a privileged woman into a feminist icon. By the late 1940s she was the most famous female intellectual of the day. Throughout her life she enjoyed the new opportunities gained by women as French society liberalized, offering women legal equality, educational opportunities, the vote, and diverse economic roles, but she also saw the limits to these freedoms. Sartre suggested she write about what difference being a woman had made in her life. The result was the pioneering 1,200-page study *The Second Sex* (1949), which challenged conventional thinking on women's issues, becoming perhaps the most influential book on women ever written. The study ranged through biology, history, mythology, sociology, and Marxist and Freudian theory to conclude that all women were oppressed by the attitudes of society. It critically analyzed Western culture as dominated by males and argued that women are not born inferior but are made to view themselves as such. De Beauvoir showed how girls saw their future different from that of boys and had their choices, such as in careers, restricted. Men took themselves as the model: "There is an absolute human type, the masculine. He is the Absolute—she is the Other." In her view, marriage denied women's individuality, becoming a contract of subjugation rather than an equal partnership. Her writings greatly influenced the North American and European feminist movements. Later she addressed aging, including the way society dictated roles for the elderly.

Disillusioned by the slow pace of change in gender relations, in 1972 de Beauvoir became a feminist activist, acknowledging her solidarity with other women and arguing that they had to fight for an improvement in their social condition. She became president of the French League of Women's Rights and editor of journals that called attention to problems of violence, sexual assault, and lack of easily available contraception in Europe and the world. In 1976 she addressed the International Tribunal of Crimes against Women, noting, "You are gathered here to denounce the oppression to which women are subjected. Talk to the world, bring to light the shameful truths that half of humanity is trying to cover up." Admired by millions, de Beauvoir died in 1986 at age seventy-eight.

THINKING ABOUT THE PROFILE

1. How did de Beauvoir's personal life affect her ideas?
2. What were de Beauvoir's main arguments about how history and society shaped perceptions of gender?

Note: Quotations from Bonnie S. Anderson and Judith P. Zinsser, *A History of Their Own: Women in Europe from Prehistory to the Present*, vol. 2 (New York: Harper, 1988), 240, 169, 422; and Bonnie G. Smith, *Changing Lives: Women in European History Since 1700* (Lexington, MA: D.C. Heath, 1989), 519.

Time Life Pictures/Getty Images

Simone de Beauvoir and Jean Paul Sartre The French feminist thinker Simone de Beauvoir and her partner, the philosopher Jean Paul Sartre, were frequent visitors to the cafés of European cities and influential participants in the lively intellectual life of post–World War II Europe.

Tensions mounted further after 1989. Vanishing jobs put both the immigrants and the local people on the unemployment rolls or in competition for scarce work. Illegal immigration also increased as people fled extreme poverty or harsh repression. Boarding rickety boats, desperate Albanians headed to Italy and Africans tried to reach Spain. As a result, anti-immigrant (especially anti-Muslim) movements have emerged even in famously tolerant countries like Denmark and the Netherlands, especially after the terrorist attacks against the United States in 2001, which shocked Europeans. To express their alienation from European society, young people of Middle Eastern, South Asian, and African-Caribbean background have often turned to musical forms from their countries of origin, such as Algerian *rai* for Arabs and Jamaican dancehall and reggae for Afro-Caribbeans. Some immigrant youth have adapted African American rap to their needs, writing lyrics in their own languages. Hence, in France the Senegal-born M. C. Solaar achieved popularity for songs commenting on the lives of young people of African ancestry. Facing particular hostility since 2001, some young Muslims, rejecting Western culture as immoral and criticizing the Islam brought by their parents from North African, Turkish, or South Asian villages as corrupted by Sufi mysticism, have become more devout and rigidly orthodox than their parents. The most alienated have turned to militant Islamic groups for direction.

Rising Tensions

Reshaping Cultures, Thought, and Religion

Popular Culture

Enriched by imports from societies around the world, western Europeans enjoyed a resilient cultural and intellectual life. Mass culture from the United States became widespread. American cigarettes, Coca-Cola, and chewing gum symbolized postwar fashions, while American films and music reshaped cultural horizons. African American jazz musicians often settled in Europe, especially in France and Scandinavia, to escape racism at home. European governments tried to protect their languages and culture industries from the powerful American challenge by mandating how much foreign music could be played on government radio stations. Young people also enjoyed popular entertainments from outside of North America, such as Caribbean reggae music, Latin American dances, and Japanese animated films. Yet Europeans often treasured entertainers who reflected local culture, such as the waiflike French singer Edith Piaf (1915–1963), known for her sad, nostalgic songs of lost love and lost youth.

Rock, an exciting, edgy music that parents often disliked, helped define youth cultures. After rock emerged in the United States in the mid-1950s, it rapidly gained a huge following in Europe, with American rock stars such as Bill Haley, Buddy Holly, Elvis Presley, and Chuck Berry enjoying massive popularity. By the 1960s European musicians inspired by U.S. rock and blues, such as Francois Hardy in France and the Beatles and Rolling Stones in Britain, had reshaped the local music scenes. The Beatles, young working-class men from Liverpool, a gritty but cosmopolitan port city, matured as musicians while playing clubs in West Germany. Beatlemania, as their impact was called, reached around the world. Rock became known as "yeah yeah" music in nations as different as Brazil and Malaysia, after the Beatles lyric "she loves you yeah yeah yeah." The music and fashion, such as clothing and hair length, of the Beatles and other rockers represented an assertion of youth identity. But eventually rock music introduced more personal reflection and social commentary, as reflected in such top-selling Beatles albums as *Revolver* (1966), which lambasted the taxman, greedy for revenues, and introduced Eleanor Rigby, a fictive woman who died alone, ignored by society. The Beatles 1967 album, *Sgt. Pepper's Lonely Hearts Club Band*, became the prototype of the concept album, with a linking theme, cross-cultural musical explorations (including use of Indian instruments), and provocative lyrics, influencing popular musicians around the world for decades after.

By the mid-1970s a new style of rock, punk, appeared that expressed social protest. Although it gained a presence in North America and continental Europe, punk became especially influential in Britain, where working-class youth faced limited job options. The provocative songs of a leading British punk group, the Sex Pistols, deliberately insulted the monarchy and offended the deeper values of British society, much to the delight of their fans. As a leading punk magazine asserted: "[Punk] music is a perfect medium for shoving two fingers up at the establishment."[11] As punk's energy dissipated, it was largely replaced in the 1980s by escapist dance music. But punk provided a foundation for creative new forms of rock in the 1990s in Europe and North America.

Cultural forms from Asia and Africa also influenced European culture. For example, in Britain the popular **bhangra** music emerged from a blending of Indian folk songs with Caribbean reggae and Anglo-American styles, such as rock, hip hop, and disco. Using a mix of Indian and Western instruments, bhangra became a lively dance music, popular with both white and Indian youth in Britain. By the 1980s bhangra had spread to the Indian diaspora communities in North America,

bhangra A popular music that emerged in Britain from a blending of traditional folk songs brought by Indian immigrants with Caribbean reggae and Anglo-American styles, such as rock, hip hop, and disco.

the Caribbean, and to India and Pakistan, sustaining Indian identity and encouraging Indian youth to have fun.

Cultural life was influenced not only by the wave of cultural imports but also by local developments, especially political liberalism and a growing mass media such as television and cinema. The creative cinema of France, Italy, and Sweden developed a global audience by depicting the humblest lives and psychological and social dilemmas common to people in a rapidly changing world. Literature also reflected political change. Writers known as postcolonialists sought to escape the world-view shaped by Western dominance. The India-born British writer Salman Rushdie (b. 1947), a Cambridge University–educated former actor and advertising copywriter from a Muslim family, confronted Western ethnocentrism. Remembering the prejudice he faced in British schools, Rushdie criticized Western society but also challenged what he considered the antimodern sensibilities of Islamic culture. His books *Shame* (1983), a satire on Pakistan's history, and especially *The Satanic Verses* (1988), a critical look at Islamic history, created an uproar among conservative Muslims and earned him death threats.

As Europeans struggled to understand the horrors of World War II, which seemed to contradict the rational thought and tolerance that had been building in Europe since the Enlightenment, some turned to new philosophies. **Existentialism**, a philosophy whose speculation on the nature of reality reflects disillusionment with Europe's violent history and doubt that objectivity is possible, and Marxism, which envisions a noncapitalist future for societies, became the most influential schools of secular thought. At the same time organized religion declined as churches struggled to remain relevant in an increasingly secular society.

The French philosopher Jean Paul Sartre **(SAHRT)** (1905–1980) and the French feminist thinker Simone de Beauvoir (1908–1986), his longtime partner, transformed existentialism from a little-known Scandinavian and German approach into a philosophy with wide appeal. Sartre argued that women and men are defined by a reality that they view as fate or imposed by others. He advised people not to let others determine their lives, but find their own meaning. They cannot banish uncertainty about the world and their place in it, but they can overcome it. People must accept responsibility for their actions, and this should lead to political engagement to create a better society. Sartre himself became active in leftwing movements promoting world peace and banning nuclear weapons, thus providing a philosophy that every individual could act upon and that reached across political boundaries. Sartre achieved fame unusual for a philosopher; when he died in 1980, thousands attended his funeral.

Other influential philosophies debated the nature of reality. Marxism emphasized social class and gender inequality, but as a political philosophy it lost many followers after the 1960s. In contrast to Marxism's certitude about truth, an approach called deconstruction, pursued by the Algeria-born Frenchman Jacques Derrida **(DER-i-dah)** (1930–2004), claimed that all rational thought could be taken apart and shown to be meaningless. Derrida questioned the entire Western philosophical tradition and the notion that Western civilization was superior to other cultures. Inspired by Derrida, by the 1990s literature and scholarship were influenced by **postmodernism**, which contends that truth is not absolute but constructed by people according to their society's beliefs. Hence, notions of different male and female aptitudes or of the superiority of one literary work over another are not objective but merely subjective attitudes acquired by people as they grow up in a society. Even scholars, postmodernists argue, cannot completely escape the prejudices of their gender, social class, ethnicity, and culture. Some thinkers, however, rejected the postmodernist notion that truth is relative and objectivity impossible.

Organized religious life went into decline, partly because the horrors of World War II and postwar materialism had destroyed many people's faith. Churchgoing ceased to be the social convention it once was, often leaving churches semideserted. Polls in the 1990s showed that, whereas some two-thirds of Americans had a moderate or strong religious faith, less than half of western Europeans did, and while 40 percent of Americans regularly attended church, only 10 percent of western Europeans did. Meanwhile, conflicts between rival Christian churches lost their intensity. Protestants and Catholics no longer lived in separate worlds, and ecumenical cooperation increased. Formed in 1948, the World Council of Churches, based in Switzerland, brought together the main Protestant and Eastern Orthodox churches. Appalled by the Holocaust, Christian thinkers began acknowledging their faiths' relationship to Judaism by referring, for the first time in history, to Europe's *Judeo-Christian* heritage. Although the Jewish population in Europe decreased sharply because of the Holocaust and post–World War II emigration to Israel and the Americas, Jews remained a key religious minority and active in public life. Christians also had to deal with another faith: by 2000 immigration and conversions had made Islam the second largest religion after Catholicism in France, Belgium, and Spain.

Cinema and Literature

Philosophy

existentialism A philosophy, influential in post–World War II western Europe, whose speculation on the nature of reality reflects disillusionment with Europe's violent history and doubt that objectivity is possible.

postmodernism A European intellectual approach contending that truth is not absolute but constructed by people according to their society's beliefs.

Religion

Protestant churches struggled to maintain their influence in increasingly secular societies, with churches often paying a price for their close ties to the state. Governments often subsidized state churches, as in Scandinavia and Britain, and church-operated schools, but many observers believed this only undermined religious devotion as people found traditional values irrelevant. Because churches funded partly by the state did not need to actively solicit support, they were unable to generate religious passion. This truth was expressed by a popular joke about a young British man joining the army, who wrote on his enlistment form "no religion" and was told, "We'll put you down as Church of England [Anglican] then."

The Roman Catholic Church also had to address the changes. Pope John XXIII (pope 1958–1963) began a comprehensive reform with the convocations of church leaders known as the Second Vatican Council (1962–1965), or Vatican II, which launched the most radical church changes since the Council of Trent in the 1500s. Vatican II officially ended the campaign against Protestantism sparked at Trent and reconciled the church with modernity, while giving the laity greater responsibility in worship; it no longer required Latin in the liturgy and removed blame from the Jews for the death of Jesus. Even after Vatican II, many Catholics ignored church teachings they disliked, such as the ban on artificial birth control, while some conservative Catholics turned to more traditionalist movements opposing Vatican II. Some Catholic women sought more influence and advocated allowing women to become priests, and every year fewer European and North American men and women entered Catholic religious vocations. Meanwhile, the church evangelized in Asia and Africa, and Asians, Africans, and Latin Americans made up a growing share of the priesthood and religious orders. As a result, Catholic churches in Europe and North America increasingly imported parish priests from countries such as Nigeria or Mexico, and some observers talked about a Third World rather than a Western church of the future.

Primary Source: Vatican II: The Catholic Church Engages the Modern World Read how Pope John XXIII opened the Second Vatican Council, at which the Catholic Church reformed itself in significant ways.

SECTION SUMMARY

- Western European governments have generally instituted the welfare state, a mix of capitalism and socialism in which citizens pay high taxes in exchange for an extensive safety net, including national health coverage, generous pensions, and workers' rights.

- In 1968, a wave of radical protest swept Europe, and over the decades European society was changed by the sexual revolution; increasing divorce rates; acceptance of birth control, abortion, and homosexuals; and rising numbers of women in the work force.

- The large numbers of immigrants, legal and illegal, who have come to western Europe seeking work have given many of its cities an international flair but have also led to tensions and problems with assimilation.

- Rock music, originally imported from the United States, became extremely popular among European youth, as did punk, which expressed working-class frustrations, while other popular music showed Asian and African influences.

- Philosophies such as existentialism, which urged people to control their own lives, and postmodernism, which claimed that complete objectivity is impossible, became popular in postwar Europe.

- Organized religion became less influential in postwar Europe, while long-standing tensions among branches of Christianity faded, Roman Catholicism liberalized, and Muslims became a significant portion of the European population.

COMMUNISM IN THE SOVIET UNION AND EASTERN EUROPE

What factors contributed to political crises in the Soviet Union and eastern Europe?

Like western Europe, the Soviet Union changed after World War II. Western Europeans had struggled for centuries to understand Russia; Winston Churchill called Russia a riddle wrapped in a mystery inside an enigma. For several generations during the Cold War the USSR was the major political, military, and ideological rival to the North American and western European nations. The Soviets feared U.S. ambitions and NATO military power, viewing themselves as more threatened than threatening. The USSR was the last great territorial empire and enjoyed substantial natural resources while maintaining a powerful state and a planned economy. But while the communists had modernized society, by the 1980s the Soviet system was showing signs of decay.

Soviet Politics and Economy

The USSR emerged from World War II as the world's number two military and economic power, no mean achievement given the ravages of war: 20 million killed, millions left homeless, cities blasted into rubble, the countryside laid waste. The trauma of that war helps explain the hostility toward the West: Russians resented the sacrifices they had been forced to make because of Germany's conflict with Britain and France. These experiences reinforced traditional Russian paranoia, fostered by two centuries of invasions by Germany or France, and led Russians to maintain a huge defense establishment and their power in eastern Europe, keeping the region as a buffer zone between them and western Europe. While the Soviet political system was rigid, it was also subject to stresses that fostered some change over the decades.

The early postwar USSR reflected the policies of Josef Stalin (STAH-lin) (1879–1953), who believed that, because of their key role in the victory over Nazism and the Russian occupation of eastern Europe, the Soviets could deal as equals with the West. Soviet armies remained in eastern Europe and helped establish communist governments there, while Stalin also kept control of the Baltic states of Estonia, Latvia, and Lithuania, formerly independent nations that the Soviets occupied in World War II. Thus was created the Soviet bloc of nations, divided from the West by heavily fortified borders. In 1949 the USSR gained a key ally with the communist victory in China (see Chapter 27). By 1949 Soviet scientists, helped by information collected by spies in the United States, had built and tested an atomic bomb, enabling them to keep pace with the United States in the emerging arms race.

Stalin's years in power had been brutal. The paranoid dictator, imagining potential enemies everywhere, maintained an iron grip on power. Millions of Soviet citizens were exiled to Siberia, and hundreds of others, including top Communist Party officials and military officers Stalin suspected of disloyalty, were convicted of treason in show trials and then executed. The Communist Party also maintained a tight rein on the arts, education, and science. For instance, party officials banned the poetry of Anna Akhmatova (uhk-MAH-tuh-vuh) (1888–1966), who had courageously recorded the agonies of Stalin's purge victims, and detained her in a filthy hospital; they also imprisoned scientists whose research questioned theories favored by party-approved scientists in fields such as plant genetics, resulting in flawed studies. Stalin's government also stepped up the effort to spread Russian language and culture in the non-Russian parts of the empire, especially Muslim Central Asia.

The death of Stalin in 1953 sparked rethinking and modest political change (see Chronology: The Soviet Union and Eastern Europe, 1945–1989). The Russian poet Evgeni Evtushenko remembered that "all Russia wept tears of grief—and perhaps tears of fear for the future."[12] Stalin's successor, Nikita Khrushchev (KROOSH-chef) (1894–1971), courageously began de-Stalinization in 1956 with a secret speech to party leaders critical of Stalin's dictatorial ruling style and crimes. Khrushchev sought to cleanse communism of the brutal Stalinist stain in order to legitimize the system among the Soviet people and around the world. The speech circulated underground throughout the Soviet bloc, stirring up dissent in eastern Europe. In Poland workers went on strike, and hundreds died or were wounded when the government suppressed it with force. Twenty thousand Hungarians died in an abortive uprising against Soviet domination.

De-Stalinization

While it began a political thaw at home, de-Stalinization opened a split in the communist world, leading eventually to China breaking its alliance with the USSR in 1960, and perhaps planted the seed for the unraveling of the Soviet Empire and system three decades later. Khrushchev promised that the Soviet standard of living would eventually equal that of the United States. It never happened, but Khrushchev produced some achievements. In 1957 the USSR shocked the world by launching *Sputnik,* the first artificial satellite to orbit earth, and in 1961 cosmonaut Yuri Gagaran (guh-GAHR-un) (1934–1968) became the first man to fly aboard a rocket ship into earth orbit, returning to land a hero. In 1963, cosmonaut Valentina Tereshkova (tare-esh-KO-va) (b. 1937), the daughter of a tractor driver and textile mill worker, defied the conventional wisdom and became the first woman to fly in space. Along with these achievements came some old-style Soviet repressiveness: in 1957 Khrushchev prevented novelist Boris Pasternak (PAS-ter-NAK) (1890–1960) from publishing the novel *Dr. Zhivago,* a critical look at the Bolsheviks during the Russian Civil War that had won a Nobel Prize in 1959 after being smuggled to the West.

CHRONOLOGY

The Soviet Union and Eastern Europe, 1945–1989

1945–1948 Formation of communist governments in eastern Europe

1948 Yugoslavia split from Soviet bloc

1953 Death of Stalin

1955 Formation of Warsaw Pact

1956 Khrushchev de-Stalinization policy

1956 Uprising in Hungary

1957 Launch of *Sputnik*

1960 Sino-Soviet split

1961 Building of Berlin Wall

1962 Cuban Missile Crisis

1968 Prague Spring in Czechoslovakia

1979–1989 Soviet war in Afghanistan

1980 Formation of Solidarity Trade Union in Poland

1985 Gorbachev new Soviet leader

Repression

In 1964 Khrushchev was deposed, replaced by Leonid Brezhnev (1906–1982), a cautious bureaucrat who imposed a Stalinist system in which the state had a hand in everything. Russians still found subtle ways to express their discontent. As they had cautiously during Stalin's time, average Russians addressed their political powerlessness by passing jokes along to friends and relatives. In a popular joke, a man arrested for shouting "Brezhnev is an idiot" in Moscow's Red Square received fifteen days for hooliganism and fifteen years for revealing a state secret. Brezhnev led the country for the next two decades (1964–1982). Under Brezhnev and his successors the Soviet state, run mostly in secret by a group of elderly, bureaucratic men, was intolerant of dissent, although less brutal than in Stalin's time. The secret police (KGB) monitored thought and behavior; most citizens accepted Communist Party control as inevitable; and Russians learned how to cooperate just enough to avoid trouble. Active dissidence came from a few intellectuals and artists, who were often deprived of jobs and benefits, and some dissidents found themselves in the remote prison camps of Siberia, where poorly fed inmates spent their regimented days in hard labor. Many died there.

Some of the intellectuals persecuted had made notable achievements. In 1970 the writer Alexander Solzhenitsyn **(SOL-zhuh-NEET-sin)** (1918-2008), a Red Army veteran imprisoned by Stalin, was forbidden to receive the Nobel Prize for literature because his novel, *One Day in the Life of Ivan Denisovich*, had exposed the harsh life in the labor camps. He later went into exile in the United States. Another well-known dissident, Andrei Sakharov **(SAH-kuh-rawf)** (1921–1989), a physicist who had helped develop the first Soviet atomic bomb but became disillusioned, was exiled to a remote city after championing human rights, democracy, and an end to the nuclear arms race. Sakharov won the Nobel Peace Prize in 1975 but was not allowed to attend the ceremonies. Milovan Djilas **(JIL-ahs)** (1911–1995), a Yugoslav communist leader turned dissident, described the contrast between the two great political movements of modern Europe: "Fascism is a nightmare and madness; communism is force and taboo. Fascism is temporary, communism is an enduring way of life."[13]

Economic and Environmental Problems

While the Soviets achieved notable successes, they also experienced severe economic problems. Stalin's Five-Year Plans had rapidly transformed the USSR from a backward to a fairly modern society. To encourage more economic progress, Soviet leaders had three tools: the Communist Party, the bureaucracy, and the military. By the 1980s all three had proved inadequate in directing a modern economy and society. The authoritarian party tolerated little dissent and fostered rigidity; the overcentralized bureaucracy often bungled the planning and management; and officials planned the number of industrial products needed—from steel beams to dish pans—for five years ahead when they didn't know precisely how many they had produced five years earlier. Soviet bureaucrats were cautious, anxious to preserve their perks and power, while the military, large but inefficient, was held together by brutal discipline, promoted incompetent officers, and wasted resources. In 1987 a West German college student deliberately exposed the flaws by piloting his small, single-engine plane unnoticed right through Soviet air security to land in Red Square, where he was arrested by astonished police.

Increasingly the economy struggled. The Soviets spent vast sums to achieve nuclear and military parity with the United States, building a massive defense establishment and arms industry that sucked money from other scientific and technological projects. As a result, Soviet factories were unable to supply consumer goods to meet growing demand, and people often bought food and clothes through the black market from illegal vendors. Paying workers regardless of effort also caused absenteeism and indifference; bored shop clerks seemed annoyed to have their frequent tea breaks and gossip sessions interrupted by shoppers. The Soviets also failed to innovate high technology, completely missing the personal computer revolution sweeping the West. By the 1990s few citizens or schools had yet acquired computers. Thus, although better off than most Asians, Africans, or Latin Americans, most Soviet citizens lived well below North American and western European standards.

Industrial pollution also ravaged the environment, producing dying forests and lakes, toxic farmland, and poisoned air. Diverting rivers for farming and power caused the Aral Sea, once nearly as large as Lake Michigan, to practically dry up, and it also diminished the world's largest inland body of water, the Caspian Sea. Then in 1986 the nuclear power station at Chernobyl in the Ukraine exploded, causing numerous deaths and injuries, releasing radiation over a wide area of Europe, and revealing the Soviet Union's inadequate environmental protections.

Communist Decline

When living standards were rising under Krushchev in the 1950s, Soviet people turned optimistic about communism. Even U.S. intelligence analysts estimated in 1960 that the total Soviet production of goods and services would be three times higher than that of the United States by 2000. But Soviet leaders responded slowly to change and papered over problems, and by the 1970s fewer Soviet citizens believed in the communist future. People joked cynically: "Under capitalism man exploits man; under communism it's the other way around." In a supposedly classless society, the contrast between the wealth of the party, government, and military elite and that of everyone else was striking. Communism had fostered a favored elite that Djilas called a new class, enjoying special privileges denied to average citizens, such as weekend retreats in the countryside. Social decay was evident everywhere: drab working-class lives, rampant corruption and bribery, the shortage of goods, high rates of alcoholism, and demoralized youth seeking access to Western popular culture and consumer goods.

The Soviet Union in the Cold War

United States–USSR tensions reached a height in the late 1940s through late 1950s. During the Korean War (1950–1953), the Soviets supplied communist North Koreans fighting the South Koreans and the United States. Then from the late 1950s through late 1970s, as Stalin's successors promoted a less aggressive policy, known as "peaceful coexistence," toward the West, the tensions eased somewhat, even though Soviet-backed forces took control of North Vietnam in 1954 and Cuba joined the communist camp in 1959. In 1961 the Soviet ally, East Germany, built a high, 27-mile-long wall around West Berlin to prevent disenchanted East Germans from fleeing to the West. However, the Berlin wall also symbolized the fears of exposing their people to Western culture and values. In 1962 a crisis caused by secretly placing Soviet nuclear missiles in Cuba, and by the U.S. demand that the missiles be removed, brought the two superpowers to the brink of nuclear war. The Soviets withdrew the missiles, easing tensions. The Soviets also helped arm the communist forces fighting U.S.-supported South Vietnam, Laos, and the Philippines in the 1950s and 1960s, conflicts that drew in U.S. advisers and troops.

United States-Soviet Relations

The Soviets generally subordinated the global crusade for communism to the normal pursuit of allies, security, and political influence. While they supported nationalist and revolutionary movements in Asia, Africa, and Latin America, often supplying weapons and advice, on the whole, the Soviets followed pragmatic policies, usually sending military force into another country only when their direct interests were threatened. After China broke with the USSR in 1960 and became a rival for influence in international communism, Soviet and Chinese troops watched each other warily along their common border. In contrast, they tolerated no opposition to Soviet power in the east European satellites and intervened to protect their allied governments. Hence the Soviets moved quickly to use military force to suppress revolts in Poland and Hungary in the 1950s, liberalizing tendencies in Czechoslovakia in 1968, and dissident movements in Poland in the 1970s and 1980s. The **Brezhnev Doctrine** asserted Moscow's right to interfere in the satellites to protect communist governments and maintain the Soviet bloc.

Soviet Foreign Policies

Eventually, military interventions proved costly. In 1979 Soviet armies invaded neighboring Afghanistan to prop up a pro-Soviet government. But the United States, along with Arab nations and Pakistan, actively aided the Afghan rebels, mostly militant Muslims, who were fighting the secular Afghan regime and the Soviet occupation. Ultimately Afghanistan, where the mountain and desert terrain made fighting difficult, proved a disaster, costing 13,000 Russian lives and billions of dollars, and the Soviets withdrew their forces in 1989. Economic problems, restless subject peoples,

Brezhnev Doctrine An assertion by Soviet leaders of Moscow's right to interfere in Soviet satellites to protect communist governments and the Soviet bloc.

Aral Sea As water from the rivers that supplied it was diverted for agriculture and industry, the Aral Sea in Soviet Central Asia lost over half its water between 1960 and 2000. This photo shows a stranded boat where rich lake fisheries once existed.

Gerd Ludwig/Corbis

and the cost of supporting a huge military and its widespread commitments contributed to a major reassessment by Soviet leaders in the later 1980s.

Soviet Society and Culture

Soviet society changed over the decades. Population growth surged, from 180 million in 1950 to 275 million by the late 1980s. The Soviet people were far healthier, better paid, and more educated than their predecessors in 1917. Citizens enjoyed social services unimaginable fifty years earlier, such as free medical care, old-age pensions, maternity leaves, guaranteed jobs, paid vacations, and day-care centers. Most people were grateful to the state for providing such economic and physical security. In exchange for the security, however, people knew they had to accept state power and the subordination of individual rights. The benefits provided by the state, often termed "cradle to grave socialism," meant that individuals were not responsible for their own lives.

Gender Relations

The experiences of Soviet women reflected the provision of education and social services. While few women served in the Soviet hierarchy, most women were in the paid work force, and among the highly skilled, some three-quarters of doctors were women. Many young rural women migrated to the cities in search of a better life. While rural women often faced a hard life—no running water, indoor plumbing, central heating, or access to nearby shops—urban women also faced challenges. In addition to their paid jobs, women of modest means stood in long lines to buy food and necessities, took their kids to and from school, washed clothes and dishes in the bathroom sink, and sometimes prepared meals in communal kitchens. Meanwhile, because women increasingly divorced abusive husbands and the state legalized abortion, the average family became smaller. Except in Central Asia, both the birthrate and life expectancy fell dramatically. Schools perpetuated the Russian stereotype that women were weak and passionate while men were strong and rational, and sometimes feminist activists were harassed, arrested, or even deported.

Ethnic Tensions

Relations between ethnic Russians and the diverse ethnic minorities deteriorated. Restless ethnic minorities chafed at domination by ethnic Russians, who constituted only about half of the Soviet population by the 1980s. In Central Asian Soviet republics such as Kazakhstan and Uzbekistan, the newly built industrial cities attracted millions of ethnic Russian migrants, who monopolized most of the managerial and professional positions. Compared to neighboring regions of Asia, communism brought relatively high living standards to Soviet Central Asia. But many Muslim peoples resented the Russification of their cultures and the weakening of Islamic practice. Most Baltic peoples hated Russian domination and the replacement of local languages with Russian, and some Jews sought the freedom to openly practice their religion or to emigrate to Israel or North America.

Religion and Culture

The state marginalized organized religion but did not eliminate it. Soviet leaders promoted atheism and denounced Christianity as superstition, and the Russian Orthodox Church became an informal state agent, with a the clergy that carefully avoided contesting the Communist Party. Still, Russians often attended church and nurtured their faith, and in the 1980s, when the state became more tolerant, millions returned to the church. Yet, many Russians remained skeptical of or indifferent to organized religion.

Soviet state policies forced most cultural creativity underground. Intellectuals exchanged copies of forbidden books and magazines in secret, and writers sent their work abroad illegally to be published. Anti-Stalinist poets explored the breathing space between the official line and prison. Soviet and east European authorities were often baffled by youth movements. Considering Western rock degenerate, the authorities subjected innovative musicians to restrictions, although few faced arrest. Russian Vladimir Vysotski **(VLAD-eh-meer vih-SOT-skee)** (1938–1980), an irreverent singer-songwriter-actor-poet, expressed political disenchantment without incurring arrest, although he was harassed. Vysotski maintained a large cult following among the urban intelligentsia for songs that exposed the Russian soul, extolled sex and liquor, and mocked Soviet corruption, hypocrisy, labor camps, and even politics: "But wait—let's have a smoke, better yet, let's drink to a time, when there will be no jails in Russia."[14] Cassette tapes of his unofficial concerts in small theaters enjoyed wide underground distribution. After his death from cancer, hundreds of mourners left flowers at his Moscow grave every month for years.

Young people wanted a cultural liberalization. By the 1960s some young Russians were modeling themselves on the Anglo-American "hippie" counterculture, wearing jeans, bell-bottom pants, miniskirts, and peace medallions and listening to the Beatles or their Soviet clones. For youth, rock music, often spread by illicit cassettes, remained the chief escape from an oppressive society, and some 160,000 underground rock and jazz bands existed by the 1980s. While few musicians dared to

RIA-Novosti

Soviet Rock Band For Soviet youth, rock music became a way of escaping the restrictions of Soviet life. This long-haired rocker from the 1980s wears a shirt with the communist symbol, the hammer and sickle, but the lyrics of rock bands often addressed the problems of Soviet life.

challenge the system directly, like Vysotski, they explored the fringes, mocking the bureaucracy or the absurdity of Soviet life. Rather than seeking to change the Soviet government, rock musicians and their audience sought to live beyond the police and the bureaucracy.

Eastern Europe in the Soviet System

During the late 1940s the Soviets installed communist governments in each eastern European nation, sealing the fate of eastern Europe for over forty years. Political parties were abolished, churches persecuted, and nationalistic leaders purged. In 1949 the communist nations formed COMECON (Council for Mutual Economic Assistance), which more closely integrated the Soviet and eastern European economies. Communism also fostered economic development in Romania and Bulgaria, which had little industrialization before World War II. But people in the more industrialized Czechoslovakia, Poland, and East Germany aspired to living standards closer to those in western Europe. To supply consumer goods and finance industrialization, the governments took out loans and built up huge debts. Increased industrial activity also had serious environmental side effects. Finally, while the Soviets treated the satellite countries as neocolonies, exploiting their resources, they also had to give them generous subsidies to maintain control.

Communist Rule

Yugoslavia followed the most independent path, breaking with the USSR entirely in 1948. In 1945 the Yugoslav Communist Party, led by Marshal Josip Broz Tito **(TEE-toe)** (1892–1980), the popular leader of the anti-Nazi resistance, won national elections. Tito wanted to avoid Soviet domination, and his Yugoslavia cooperated with the nonaligned nations while also maintaining friendly relations with the West. Tito's unique form of communism, which experimented with worker rather than manager control of factories, created enough prosperity and popular support to neutralize his nation's powerful ethnic divisions.

The resentment of Soviet domination fostered unrest. After the Soviets crushed protest demonstrations in Poland in the early 1950s, a Polish poet daringly wrote: "They [the communists] ran

Unrest and Revolt

to us shouting, 'Under socialism, a cut finger doesn't hurt.' But they [the people] felt pain [and] lost faith."[15] Poland, with its strong Catholic allegiances, was the most restless satellite, with its workers demanding more public input into the government. In 1956 Hungarian leaders tried to break with rigid communism by reinstating private property, inviting noncommunists into the government, and declaring the country neutral. In response, a Soviet bloc force occupied Hungary and executed the anti-Soviet leaders. But even under the new pro-Soviet leaders, Hungary remained open to the West and was more tolerant of dissent than other Soviet satellites. While the other satellites followed the Soviet pattern of highly centralized bureaucracies, Hungary's blend of state influence and free markets, known as market socialism, created the most prosperous Soviet bloc economy. Hungarians called it "goulash communism," after their favorite dish, a mix of pasta and meat.

Other disgruntled eastern Europeans later defied Soviet power. In Czechoslovakia in 1968 the reform-minded leader Alexander Dubček (DOOB-check) (1927–1993), during what was called the "Prague Spring," sought to shift to a more liberal "communism with a human face." Alarmed, the Soviets sent in Warsaw Pact troops and replaced Dubček and his supporters with repressive Soviet puppets. In Poland, the Soviets allowed Polish-born Pope John Paul II to make a triumphant visit in 1979 but were alarmed at the outpouring of religious and nationalist fervor. Then in 1980 shipyard workers led by Lech Walesa (leck wa-LEN-za) (b. 1943), an electrical engineer, went on strike. As food prices increased, thousands of women took to the streets, shouting, "We're hungry!" When the dissidents formed the Solidarity trade union, which aimed at economic liberalization, the government declared martial law and banned Solidarity. Even though illegal, Solidarity had 9.5 million members by 1981 and worked for political as well as economic goals. As one leader put it: "What we had in mind was not only bread, butter and sausage but also justice, democracy, truth, legality, human dignity, freedom of convicts, and the repair of the republic."[16]

Soviet Decline and Reform

Soviet Challenges Soviet problems mounted, forcing a reappraisal of the political and economic system and the nation's place in the world. The USSR had steadily lost ground in world affairs to the United States and economic ground to Japan and West Germany. China became a bitter rival, and the Afghanistan war and the subsidizing of the east European satellites drained Soviet wealth. By the mid-1980s the USSR had few close remaining allies outside the Soviet bloc, which was restless, and few Asian, African, or Latin American revolutionaries looked toward Moscow for inspiration. Soviet power in the world had always been mostly military, whereas the United States and its Western allies also had cultural, economic, technological, and even linguistic influence. All over the world people studied English or French, not Russian, and some observers found more power in rock music, videos, fast food, youth fashions, and global news networks than in the Soviet Red Army. Young people from Bangkok to Buenos Aires avidly sought blue jeans and flocked to American adventure films; few of them knew or cared much about Soviet life. Thus the Beatles, McDonald's, and the Cable News Network (CNN) were at least as crucial, some scholars concluded, in the West winning the Cold War as was U.S. military power.

This declining international influence, combined with spiraling social and economic problems and a stifling bureaucracy, ultimately led to the rise of younger, reform-minded Soviet leaders who introduced dramatic change. Soviet leaders now had more contact with the outside world and an appreciation of their growing technological backwardness. The planned economy that had powered a largely peasant society into a superpower now seemed a severe drag. In 1985 Mikhail Gorbachev (GORE-beh-CHOF) (b. 1931) became Soviet leader. Because of the escalating costs of militarization, he realized the nation could not win an arms race, and while hoping to preserve the basics of the Soviet system, he understood the need to liberalize the economy, decentralize decision making, and relax ideological controls. However, Gorbachev inherited a Communist Party that allowed no political competition and managed a planned economy, run from the top with little room for individual initiative. With such a rigid system, he concluded, the USSR could never match the United States as a superpower.

Gorbachev introduced a dazzling series of reforms to reenergize the Soviet Union, developing closer relations with the West and abandoning the ideological struggle with the liberal democracies. In 1987 a United States–USSR treaty lessened

Restructuring Soviet Society

In 1987 Mikhail Gorbachev, the head of the Soviet Communist Party and government, published a book, *Perestroika*, outlining his policy of economic restructuring. His goal was to transform the inefficient, stagnant Soviet economy into one based on a decentralized market orientation similar to the market socialism of Hungary and China. The new policy gave greater autonomy to local government officials and factory managers and attempted to democratize the Communist Party itself. Causing a sensation, the book was ranked by some observers as the most important publication of the late twentieth century. By the early 1990s, with Gorbachev himself removed from office, the policy was eclipsed, but the book remained a testimony to the problems that led to the Soviet system's collapse. In this excerpt, Gorbachev defines perestroika.

Perestroika means overcoming the stagnation process, breaking down the braking mechanism, creating a dependable and effective mechanism for acceleration of social and economic progress and giving it dynamism.

Perestroika means initiative. It is the comprehensive development of democracy, socialist self-government, encouragement of initiative and creative endeavor, improved order and discipline, more glasnost (openness), criticism and self-criticism in all spheres of our society. It is utmost respect for the individual and consideration for personal dignity.

Perestroika is the all-round intensification of the Soviet economy, the revival and development of the principles of democratic centralism in running the national economy, the universal introduction of economic methods, the renunciation of management by injunction and by administration methods, and the overall encouragement of innovation and socialist enterprise.

Perestroika means a resolute shift to scientific methods, an ability to provide a solid scientific basis for every new initiative. It means the combination of the achievements of the scientific and technological revolution with a planned economy.

Perestroika means priority development of the social sphere aimed at ever better satisfaction of the Soviet people's requirements for good living and working conditions, for good rest and recreation, education and health care. It means unceasing concern for cultural and spiritual wealth, for the culture of every individual and society as a whole.

Perestroika means the elimination from society of the distortions of social ethics, the consistent implementation of the principles of social justice. It means the unity of words and deeds, rights and duties. It is the elevation of honest, highly-qualified labor, the overcoming of leveling tendencies in pay and consumerism.

This is how we see perestroika today. This is how we see our tasks, and the substance and content of our work for the forthcoming period. It is difficult now to say how long that period will take. Of course, it will be much more than two or three years. We are ready for serious, strenuous and tedious work to ensure that our country reaches new heights by the end of the twentieth century.

THINKING ABOUT THE READING

1. What did Gorbachev mean by perestroika?
2. What problems did the policy aim to solve?

Source: Mikhail Gorbachev, *Perestroika* (New York: HarperCollins, 1987), pp. 34–35. Copyright © 1987 by Mikhail Gorbachev. Reprinted by permission of HarperCollins Publishers.

the threat of nuclear war by having both countries destroy their short- and long-range missiles. With his **glasnost** ("openness") policy, Gorbachev democratized the political system, including free elections, a real parliament that included noncommunist parties, the release of most political prisoners, and a deemphasis on the role of the Communist Party. Gorbachev also loosened state control of the media and the arts and invited scholars to talk truthfully about the Soviet past. Furthermore, realizing the ruinous financial cost of maintaining the unpopular eastern European governments, Gorbachev made clear he would not intervene to preserve them. They collapsed or were toppled in 1989 (see Chronology: Europe, 1989–Present).

Admitting the faults of Soviet communism, Gorbachev also liberalized the economy, using market mechanisms in a policy known as **perestroika** ("restructuring") (see Witness to the Past: Restructuring Soviet Society). But the economic changes failed to take off. While many in the intelligentsia wanted democratization, the working classes mostly preferred consumer goods, which did not come. Meanwhile, top bureaucrats, including the managers of state enterprises, resisted changes that might threaten their role. Conservatives in the Communist Party and the secret police also opposed reforms that might undermine their power. Soon the Soviet system collapsed.

glasnost The policy introduced in the Soviet Union by Mikhail Gorbachev to democratize the political system.

perestroika ("restructuring") Mikhail Gorbachev's policy to liberalize the Soviet economy using market mechanisms.

SECTION SUMMARY

- Under Stalin, the USSR ruthlessly suppressed dissent, while under Khruschev, it moderated somewhat and focused on competing with the United States economically and technologically; under Brezhnev, it became somewhat more repressive again.

- Although the Soviet economy grew under communism, it suffered from lack of innovation, inept planning, and an overemphasis on the military, and it created a privileged class of Communist Party and military insiders who lived much better than the common people.

- U.S.-USSR relations were strained by the Cuban Missile Crisis, the Berlin Wall, and Soviet support for communist Cuba and North Vietnam, but the USSR's foreign interventions were usually motivated by its national interest rather than a desire to spread communism.

- In exchange for limited freedom, Soviet citizens were offered extensive social services, but many non-Russians in Central Asia and the Baltics resented Russian domination and the devaluing of their own cultures, while Soviet youth turned to rock music to express their rebellion.

- Much of eastern Europe was effectively colonized by the USSR, though Yugoslavia pursued an independent communist course, and citizens of Poland, Hungary, and Czechoslovakia mounted periodic challenges to Soviet rule.

- With the USSR losing ground economically and culturally, Soviet leader Mikhail Gorbachev introduced reforms designed to democratize the USSR, to liberalize its economy, and to allow eastern European countries greater self-determination.

COMMUNIST COLLAPSE: A NEW RUSSIA AND EUROPE

How did the demise of the communist system contribute to a new Europe?

For over four decades the Cold War and the iron curtain had provided the context for both western and eastern European politics. The breakup of the communist bloc of nations in 1989 and the USSR in 1991 reshaped the political and economic face of Russia, the former Soviet territories, eastern Europe, and western Europe, creating hope but also uncertainties. Russia struggled to rebuild and to revive its power. While Yugoslavia was torn apart by wars and Germany was reunited, western Europe pushed toward unification, seeking to include some of eastern Europe as well, but it still faced the conflicting forces of nationalism and cooperation. Most Europeans now chose governments through multiparty elections. By the beginning of the twenty-first century, Europe, though no longer the world leader it had once been, still influenced the age of globalization.

A New Russia and New Post-Soviet Nations

Soviet Collapse

The sudden collapse of the Soviet empire and communism in Europe was a major development of twentieth-century history. In 1985 there had been 5 million Soviet soldiers stationed from East Germany to eastern Siberia's Pacific coast, symbolizing the reach of imperial Soviet power. Six years later the Soviet Union and its satellite nations had unraveled, without a shot being fired. Though the collapse was not a complete surprise, its pace was astonishing. While outside factors, including east European unrest and escalating U.S. defense spending that was hard for the Soviets to match, played a role, Soviet economic decline was probably the decisive cause. The collapse showed the failure of the Soviet system, founded on Leninism and strongly shaped by Stalinism. Democratic governments and decentralized capitalism had adjusted better to global changes than the communist-planned economies, and nationalist yearnings among non-Russians had sapped the empire's foundations.

Gorbachev's greatest contribution was to face up to failure. By 1991 Gorbachev, unable to control the forces unleashed, had lost his credibility and resigned, replaced as leader by Boris Yeltsin (b. 1931), a communist bureaucrat turned reformer with strong U.S. support. Yeltsin ended seven decades of communist rule by outlawing the Communist Party. Russians who welcomed the party's demise toppled statues of Lenin and restored czarist names to cities that had been renamed during the Soviet era. Leningrad once again became St. Petersburg.

Dismantling the Soviet Union

Yeltsin acquiesced in the breakup of the USSR itself, while maintaining the unity of the largest Soviet republic, Russia, which stretched from the Baltic Sea through ten time zones to the eastern tip of Siberia, only a few miles from Alaska (see Map 28.3). But glasnost had opened a Pandora's box.

Ethnic hatreds, long suppressed by military force or alleviated by the government-provided safety net, soon exploded to the surface. In 1991 all of the fourteen Soviet republics outside of Russia, from Lithuania and the Ukraine in the west to Kyrgyzstan (**KER-giz-STAN**) in eastern Turkestan, declared their independence, often under former communist officials whose autocratic ruling style and intolerance of dissent resembled the old Soviet system.

Most of the new nations have struggled to achieve economic self-sufficiency and political stability. Some have been engulfed in conflict between rival ethnic or nationalist groups or have fought each other over territorial claims, as did Christian Armenia and Muslim Azerbaijan. In three of the former Soviet republics—Georgia, Ukraine, and Kyrgyzstan—what observers called "colored revolutions" because their proponents symbolized their cause with a color, such as orange in the Ukraine, pro-democracy activists, with U.S. and western European encouragement, forced out dictatorial regimes. But the results of revolutions are usually unpredictable, and the leaders soon disappointed their supporters by becoming less democratic or antagonizing the Russians. In Central Asia, inhabited largely by Muslims, some nominal and others devout, militant Muslims launched insurgencies against the secular post-Soviet governments, and Islam gained support among the disenchanted and marginalized, especially jobless young men. Islamic fervor also forced or prompted many women to don the headscarf or veil and to dress and behave modestly. Meanwhile, millions of ethnic Russians in the former Soviet republics faced resentment for their relative affluence and ties to the former colonizer. In Latvia, for example, the indigenous Lett people make up only half the population: Russians constitute a third. The Latvian government now requires everyone to learn the Latvian language, which was marginalized under Soviet rule.

Former Soviet Republics

Map 28.3
The Dissolution of the Soviet Union
In 1991 the leaders of Russia, who had abandoned communism, allowed the other fourteen republics to leave the Soviet Union, bringing an end to a vast federation that had endured for over seven decades. Even without the fourteen republics, Russia remained the world's largest nation in geographical size, stretching across ten time zones from the Pacific Ocean to the Baltic Sea.

e Interactive Map

Shock Therapy

Yeltsin had difficulty solving Russia's problems. Taking the advice of Russian free market enthusiasts and of American advisers, who often knew little of Russian culture, he introduced a "shock therapy": rapid conversion of the stagnant planned economy to market capitalism, which produced more consumer goods and a growing middle class but created other problems. Party officials converted the enterprises they managed into their own private companies, becoming Russia's new capitalists, while organized crime groups and a few well-placed former communists, known as **oligarchs**, gained control of many economic assets. Yeltsin also faced secession movements within the Russian federation, especially in oil-rich Chechnya, a largely Muslim Caucasus region that declared independence in 1994. Yeltsin, fearing that Chechnya's independence would encourage other secession movements, tried to crush the separatists, sucking the Red Army into a quagmire with thousands of casualties.

oligarchs Well-placed former communists who amassed enough wealth to gain control of major segments of the post–Soviet Russian economy.

The economic pain in Russia was widespread. Millions of workers, the majority of them women, lost their jobs as inefficient, obsolete Soviet industries closed. Some leaders reemphasized the Soviet era ideal of men as soldiers and women as working mothers, and conservatives advocated that women stay at home and tend to family obligations. Moreover, with the end of free higher education, families preferred to devote their funds to their sons. Factory workers, miners, and state employees, such as teachers, were often not paid for years. As Yeltsin dismantled parts of the welfare state, health-care reductions, declining incomes, heavier drinking, and illegal drug use affected public health; men's life expectancy dropped from sixty-four in 1990 to fifty-nine in 2002. By 1992 inflation was 2,500 percent, devastating people who lived on pensions and fixed incomes. According to a popular local joke, "All the good things the communists said about communism were false, but all the bad things they said about capitalism were true."

Putin's Russia

In 2000, with the Russian economy near collapse and free markets discredited, Yeltsin resigned in disgrace and was replaced by Vladimir Putin (b. 1952), who ended shock therapy and brought back stability after fifteen years of turbulence. A former secret police colonel who kept a portrait of Peter the Great in his office, Putin espoused capitalism and democratic reforms, including multiparty elections, but also pursued more authoritarian and nationalist policies than Yeltsin. Political liberalism faded as Putin took control of much of the media, seizing or muffling opposition newspapers and television stations and prosecuting some oligarchs for alleged corruption The state also took over many large private companies, turning the economy into a form of state capitalism not unlike Meiji Japan. Eventually the economy made a substantial recovery because of improved tax collection and higher prices for two leading Russian exports, oil and natural gas, allowing Putin to assert Russian interests in the world. Through these measures Putin outmaneuvered the discredited pro-U.S. free market advocates, the rebuilt Communist Party, and extreme rightwing nationalists. However, the 2008–2009 global economic crisis brought a rapid decline in oil prices after Putin had committed oil to various trading partners, and drastic revenue declines brought cutbacks and recession, hurting Putin's prestige and fomenting dissent.

Putin's Russia mixed autocratic government with a more outward-looking attitude. The Russian Orthodox Church, for centuries closely connected to national identity and political power, regained influence, and even Putin claimed to be a believer. Within the church leadership, liberals promoted a tolerant and ecumenical view while conservatives denounced ecumenism, some even supporting anti-Semitic, anti-Muslim views and a return of the monarchy. Yet, in many places, Muslims—some 15 percent of the population—and Christians live in harmony. Putin also sought good relations with Germany, France, the United States, and China. In 2009 education officials announced that Alexander Solzhenitsyn"s long-banned book about Stalin-era Soviet labor camps, *The Gulag Archipelago*, would be taught in Russian secondary schools. However, while the middle class grew, the contrasts between rich and poor became stark. While elegantly dressed men and women in Moscow cavorted in fine restaurants and glitzy casinos, some remote towns went without heat and power. In addition, corruption, poverty, unaccountability, weak legal institutions, and the festering war in Chechnya stifled development. And while Russia still had a large military budget, it was only a fifth that of the United States. Some polls showed that a majority of Russians preferred the communist years to the new Russia, and many people expressed nostalgia for Stalin and Lenin. Future directions remained unclear.

The New Eastern Europe

Collapsing States

The changes in the USSR resonated throughout eastern Europe. In the late 1980s Mikhail Gorbachev, who admired Hungarian market socialism, promoted reform in eastern Europe. The USSR could no longer afford to subsidize these states, and when it became clear that the USSR was no longer willing to protect the largely unpopular eastern European governments, they began to fall like dominoes. Democratic movements once underground surfaced. Hungary adopted democracy, Solidarity came to power in Poland, and East Germans streamed across the border into West Germany. The world could watch on television as Berliners gleefully knocked down the Berlin Wall, the symbol of Cold War division, and carried off its bricks as souvenirs. Soon the East German regime and the other east European communist governments had collapsed or been overthrown. After massive demonstrations forced the communist leaders to resign in a largely peaceful "Velvet Revolution," Czechoslovaks elected as president the playwright and former rock group lyricist, Václav Havel (vax-LAV hah-VEL) (b. 1936), who had been frequently arrested for his prodemocracy activities. Havel announced, "Your government, my people, has been returned to you."[17]

The new democratic or semidemocratic governments replaced planned economies with market forces, and east Europeans took up voting enthusiastically. Yet, reformers did not anticipate the results of their policies. The end of communism uncorked ethnic hatreds and rivalries going back centuries. Slovaks seceded from the Czechs, forming their own country, while Romanians repressed the large Hungarian minority. Several countries persecuted or avoided providing services, such as schools, to the Romany (Gypsies), and prejudice against Jews intensified.

The rapid move to capitalism, while providing abundant consumer goods, also proved destabilizing. Critics wrote of shock without therapy. While millions were thrown out of work as obsolete factories closed, western European or North American companies bought many of the remaining enterprises. Dazzled by the Western consumer goods just over the border, east Europeans may have underestimated the risks that came with Western-style capitalism. Shops were full of attractive goods, but few people had the money to buy them. Only Poland and the Czech Republic enjoyed robust economic growth. Protections of the communist welfare system, such as free education, health care, and subsidized housing, were removed. While some economies gradually improved, pockets of high unemployment remained and the rich-poor gap widened.

The political environment changed as diverse political parties competed for power. Capitalizing on popular support for the social safety net, former Communist Party members who now called themselves reform communists won some national elections, competing for power with free market advocates, pro-Western liberals, and rightwing nationalists. In a striking repudiation of the Soviet legacy, reform communists often supported joining the European Union and even NATO. Few anticommunists regretted the changes, however jarring they were. Adam Michnik, a leader of Polish Solidarity, concluded that "without the slightest hesitation it is much better to live in a country that is democratic, prosperous and thus boring."[18]

The greatest instability came to Yugoslavia, an artificial federation of states that self-destructed in bloody civil wars between ethnic groups (see Map 28.4). Created for political convenience after World War I, Yugoslavia contained antagonistic ethnic and religious groups. The nationalistic Orthodox Serbs tried to dominate the federation, while the Catholic Croats and Slovenians and the Bosnian and Albanian Muslims wanted independence for their regions. After Marshal Tito, the product of a mixed Croat-Serb marriage whose autocratic policies kept the lid on ethnic hatreds, died in 1980, Yugoslavia became a seething cauldron of ethnic conflict. In 1991 the Serb-dominated Yugoslav army tried to stop Slovenia and Croatia from breaking away, but the United Nations sent in peacekeeping troops to secure their independence. Then in 1992 the Muslim majority in multi-ethnic Bosnia declared independence, a move opposed by the minority Serbs and Croats in the state. Bosnian Serb militias, aided covertly by the largest Yugoslav state, Serbia, massacred thousands of Muslims, using a new term for genocide, "ethnic cleansing." The United Nations sent more peacemakers, and U.S. air strikes under NATO auspices forced the Serbs to accept a peace treaty in 1995. The Bosnia conflict killed 200,000 people and generated 4 million refugees. In 1999 violence returned when the Albanian majority in Kosovo, the southern region of Serbia, revolted and the Serbs responded with ferocity, prompting another NATO-imposed settlement in 2000. Thousands of NATO troops remained in Bosnia and Kosovo, a symbol of eastern Europe's unresolved challenges.

New Governments and Economies

The Velvet Revolution Protesters took to the streets in Prague, Czechoslovakia, to protest communist government and demand democracy. These protests, known as the Velvet Revolution for their peaceful nature, were led by Václav Havel, pictured on the poster carried by a protester.

PRESIDENTEM

Map 28.4
Ethnic Conflicts in Eastern Europe
Many of the nations in central and eastern Europe contain substantial ethnic minorities, and tensions between various groups have often led to conflict. In Yugoslavia, the conflicts between the major ethnic groups—Serbs, Croats, Bosnian Muslims, and Albanians—led to violence and civil war at the end of the twentieth century.

e Interactive Map

Toward European Unity

The reunification of Germany and the unity movement have dominated western Europe in the years after 1989. The East German state collapsed and Germany was quickly reunified in 1990, but the results have satisfied neither West nor East Germans. For many East Germans, merging with the prosperous West Germany promised access to a materially comfortable life they could only dream of before. But reunification cost billions and threw the German economy into a tailspin. Before reunification West Germany had enjoyed a long boom, but a decade later, the reunified nation's 80 million people were stuck in deep recession. Since Germany has western Europe's largest economy, the German slump dragged down the rest of Europe. Many East German workers lost jobs as obsolete factories were closed or sold to West Germans, who often downsized the

German Reunification

work force. The unemployment rate in the east was twice as high as in the west and wages much lower. As a result, some angry youth turned to rightwing, often neo-Nazi, groups that favor heavy metal rock groups whose songs promote hatred of foreigners and immigrants.

Worried by Germany's problems, western European leaders believed that hastening unification would stabilize postcommunist Europe. The Maastricht Treaty, discussed in the chapter opening, set a goal of economic and monetary union that required budgetary and wage restraint as a prelude. Most signers of the treaty adopted the euro as their currency. Unity was aided by other factors as well. Millions of Europeans were multilingual, moving easily between cultures, and many studied in other countries. The cosmopolitanism also influenced the arts. For example, the popular Greek singer Nana Mouskeri (NA-na mouse-KUR-ee) gained a large international audience by recording in English, French, German, and Spanish. The Eurotunnel, which stretched ninety-four miles under the English Channel and made possible a three-hour train ride from London to Paris, symbolized the decline of both political and cultural borders.

Hastening Unity

The European Union (EU) doubled its membership from twelve nations in 1993 to twenty-seven by 2009, including ten former Soviet bloc states and republics. The Czech Republic, Poland, Hungary, and Estonia had joined in 2004. The Danish prime minister told prospective new EU members: "In 1989 brave and visionary people brought about the collapse of the Berlin Wall. They could no longer tolerate the forced division of Europe. Today we are giving life to their hopes."[19] With the new members the EU became a bloc of nearly 500 million people encompassing most of Europe and enjoying a combined economic power larger than that of the United States. Some of the members, such as Sweden and Ireland, the latter once one of Europe's poorest countries but soon known as the Celtic Tiger because its rapid growth, resembled that of the "Little Tiger" nations of Southeast Asia (see Chapter 31), becoming models for the world. Many thousands of migrants from Europe and Asia moved to Ireland for jobs, fostering multiethnic neighborhoods in Dublin.

Expanding the European Union

Conducting a quarter of the world's commerce and economic production, the EU became one of the world's three dominant economic forces, along with the U.S. and Japan. Some observers spoke of a tripolar world led by the United States, the EU, and East Asia (especially China and Japan). However, the European Union hit several major road bumps. Critics called the EU a faceless bureaucracy with innumerable rules that compromised national independence, and two of Europe's most prosperous nations, Norway and Switzerland, declined membership. The EU leaders have also been cautious in admitting former Soviet bloc states with weak economies and autocratic leaders. Turkey, a largely Muslim nation, has long sought membership, fostering an EU debate about how to define Europe. This debate spilled over into the effort to prepare an EU constitution. Amid much controversy, the proposed constitution rejected any mention of Europe's Christian heritage. But in 2005 voters in two of the most pro-unity countries, France and the Netherlands, fearing loss of control, shocked EU leaders by rejecting the constitution, raising questions about the EU's future. After the proposed constitution was modified into a treaty forming a stronger executive and European parliament while promising more democracy, transparency, and efficiency, it was approved by most member nations.

European Economic Power Business and political leaders from India and the European Union met in a summit in 2005 to increase trade relations, reflecting the growing economic power of both India and western Europe. This photo shows British Prime Minister Tony Blair and India's Prime Minister Manmohan Singh in conversation.

Increasing unity may have contributed to problems caused by the economic austerity policies of the 1990s, which unsettled welfare states. Social democrats, who had governed eleven of the sixteen western European nations in the early 1990s, now jockeyed with centrists, free market conservatives, Greens, anti-immigrant nationalists, and the fading communists for power. Attempts to roll back but not eliminate social benefits sometimes set off massive protests and long strikes. While many Europeans preferred to maintain what they termed the social market economy, even at the cost of slower economic growth, both the German and French governments replaced the 35-hour workweek with the 40-hour workweek to increase their competitiveness. Yet, some large companies continued to downsize or export jobs, and in 2006 thousands in France rioted against loosening job protections. Some observers compared Europe's sluggish social market economies unfavorably with the dynamic U.S. economy. Others disagreed, noting that many European nations have nearly as high a per capita income as the United States, less inequality, universal health insurance, a greater commitment to a high quality of life for all, and, collectively, a larger total production of goods and services. The 2008–2009 global economic crisis challenged both arguments. The crisis, the worst since the Great Depression, began in the United States with real estate, banking, and financial problems, discrediting the free-wheeling U.S. economic model. Yet, European economies also went into steep decline, greatly stressing welfare states and demonstrating government inadequacies in resolving the problems. Germany, saddled with an indecisive coalition government, reacted slowly as deficits mounted. The economy of Iceland collapsed from bank failures, while Ireland's economy plummeted so rapidly that many thousands of immigrants, losing jobs, returned home. Indeed, the grim job market prompted many Arabs, Africans, and East Europeans to leave western European countries. By later 2009 some economies, including France and Germany, were growing again but most East European economies remained deeply troubled

Europeans also faced other challenges. A century earlier overcrowded and the world's greatest exporter of people, Europe now has a declining population, due mainly to the world's lowest birthrate: 1.2 children per woman. Yet, Europeans became increasingly hostile to immigration from the Middle East. Tensions simmered, and in 2005 rioting and vandalism by young Arab and African residents in France, many of them unemployed and resenting discrimination and police harassment, caused much damage and raised the issue of what sort of integration into European societies was possible. The population decline also posed a long-term problem: with more people retiring from than entering the work force, younger workers had more responsibility for financing government services for the elderly. By the early twenty-first century, political disenchantment, an anti-incumbent mood, and stronger anti-U.S. sentiments often caused voters to reject the governing parties. Anti-immigrant parties became more influential, even in tolerant nations like Denmark and the Netherlands. Europeans still struggled to define their place in a changing world.

Europe and Russia in the Global System

With the end of the Cold War, Russia, western Europe, and the former Soviet bloc states searched for new roles in the world. Russia sought good relations with the EU, the United States, China, and the nearby Islamic nations, such as Iran, but also acted in its own self-interest, sometimes opposing U.S. or EU policies. NATO needed to redefine its mission as it added many of the former Warsaw Pact nations, discomforting Russia. After Russia warned NATO against admitting former Soviet republics such as Ukraine and Georgia, it reinforced its threat in 2008 by briefly invading Georgia, a small U.S. ally in the Caucasus, to protect pro-Russian enclaves. For their part, western Europeans seemed more reluctant than Americans to devote vast sums to the military or to send their armed forces into combat. The United States, not Europe, led the intervention to end the killing and restore order in Yugoslavia.

In the early twenty-first century, European relations with its military ally and main trading rival, the United States, became complicated. Various European nations, as part of NATO, sent troops to Afghanistan after the 2001 terrorist attacks on the United States and shared the goal of combating international terrorism. But most Europeans mistrusted the U.S. decision to invade oil-rich Iraq in 2003, believing it had little to do with fighting terrorism and fearing it would destabilize the Middle East. European nations such as France and Germany criticized the U.S. invasion and occupation. Although their people strongly opposed the war, some close U.S. allies, such as Italy, Poland, and Spain, sent small token forces, but only Britain had a sizable military presence in Iraq.

Europeans also disagreed on how best to respond to international terrorism and militant Islamic groups. The substantial Muslim immigrant populations complicated policies on the Islamic militancy that spread among some people of Arab or South Asian ancestry, especially unemployed youth. Some of the men who perpetrated the 2001 attacks on the United States had studied in Europe, where they were recruited by Islamic militants. Deadly terrorist attacks on commuter trains in Madrid in 2004 and the London subway in 2005, which killed several hundred people, showed the potential for terrorist violence but convinced many that military interventions in the Middle East might actually increase the terrorist threat. In 2006, shocked Europeans found how tense Muslim-Western relations had become when offensive cartoons insulting or satirizing the Islamic prophet Muhammad, published by a rightwing, anti-immigrant Danish newspaper, caused riots and demonstrations around the Muslim world and attacks on Danish embassies and business interests.

However, Europeans played key roles in resolving world problems. Before the 2008–2009 economic crisis, Europeans tended to identify global warming as the major world problem. Some nations strongly encouraged alternative energy strategies. Hence Denmark now imports no Middle Eastern oil. They also took the lead in developing international treaties on issues such as climate change, biological and chemical weapons, international criminal courts, and genocide. U.S. opposition to these treaties built resentment. Yet, by 2009, mired in recession, both European leaders and the new pro-environment Barack Obama administration in the U.S. struggled to develop joint policies to combat global warming. European workers also led movements against the economic globalization they saw as costing jobs and livelihoods. Saying the world is not for sale, French farmer José Bové drove a tractor into a McDonald's outlet and vandalized it to protest against the large global corporations that often displace local enterprises, becoming a hero to those Europeans opposed to globalization and the institutions that promote it.

With the move toward closer political and economic integration, Europe became much more than a geographical expression and a collection of separate countries sharing cultural traditions and history. A few European leaders have even envisioned a political federation, or united states of Europe, but many hurdles would have to be overcome first. While Europe is no longer the powerhouse it had been in the nineteenth century, its peoples are carving out a new place in the world.

SECTION SUMMARY

- The collapsing Soviet bloc and Soviet decay created problems for Mikhail Gorbachev, and he was replaced by Boris Yeltsin, who allowed independence for all the non-Russian Soviet republics, some of which ended up with authoritarian governments, and pursued a rapid shift to capitalism.

- However, as a result of this "shock therapy," a small group of former Communist Party officials became extremely wealthy while most Russians suffered economically, and Yeltsin was replaced by the more authoritarian Vladimir Putin, who brought back some stability and pursued good relations with Europe and the United States.

- With the fall of the USSR, formerly communist eastern Europe became more democratic, though many countries struggled economically and others suffered political upheaval, especially Yugoslavia, which experienced violent civil war and "ethnic cleansing."

- German reunification, celebrated at first, yielded mixed results, while the European Union grew to include many nations but faced questions over whether to admit non-Christian nations and over what form its constitution should take.

- European nations struggled to navigate the evolving world economy, to deal with Islamic terrorism, and to work out relations with each other and with the United States, whose 2003 invasion of Iraq was generally unpopular in most countries.

CHAPTER SUMMARY

Emerging shattered from World War II, western Europeans were determined to build a new Europe. Although the Cold War divided Europe, western Europeans rebuilt democracies and began a movement to foster unity. Sparked by French-German reconciliation, Europeans established institutions for economic cooperation. Eventually these became the European Union, which established a single currency and a European parliament. Stability also resulted from the rise of welfare states, which guaranteed all citizens fair access to housing, health care, and education. Social democratic parties took the lead in creating the safety net, but supporting it became more costly with growing economic problems and unemployment rates. Gradually family and gender relations changed, while millions of immigrants reshaped European societies.

After the war the Soviet Union maintained a communist-run government and economy, with a powerful state dominating life and work. The Soviets installed communist governments in eastern

Europe and brutally repressed opposition, but they failed to realize much economic dynamism and lost ground in the Cold War to a more powerful U.S.–western Europe alliance. By the 1980s the Soviet system and the Soviet bloc needed reform. Although communism generated modernization and improved living standards, ethnic minorities were restless, the bureaucracy was stifling, and the economy remained stagnant. Unsettling reforms resulted in the collapse of communism and the dismantling of the Soviet Empire in 1991. Since then the former communist nations have struggled to introduce capitalism and liberal democracy. Meanwhile, most of the European nations joined the European Union, the world's third largest economic power. Germany struggled to make reunification work, Russia debated a new role in the world, and the European Union sought the appropriate mix of cooperation and national sovereignty.

KEY TERMS

Marshall Plan	NATO	welfare states	Brezhnev Doctrine
Eurocommunism	Soviet bloc	bhangra	glasnost
Greens	Warsaw Pact	existentialism	perestroika
Commonwealth of Nations	ostpolitik	postmodernism	oligarchs
Truman Doctrine			

EBOOK AND WEBSITE RESOURCES

e PRIMARY SOURCE
Vatican II: The Catholic Church Engages the Modern World

e INTERACTIVE MAPS
Map 28.1 Military Alliances and Multinational Economic Groupings, 1949–1989
Map 28.2 Europe's Gross Domestic Product
Map 28.3 The Dissolution of the Soviet Union
Map 28.4 Ethnic Conflicts in Eastern Europe

LINKS

EUROPA—Gateway to the European Union (http://europa.eu.int/index_en.htm). Provides information on many topics.

European Union in the US (http://www.eurunion.org/states/home.htm). Provides a wealth of data on the European Union.

Internet Resources on Russia and the CIS (http://www.ssees.ac.uk/russia.htm). A British site with a collection of links on many aspects of Russia and the Soviet Union.

Internet Modern History Sourcebook (http://www.fordham.edu/halsall/mod/modsbook.html). A very extensive online collection of historical documents and secondary materials.

Russian History Index: The World Wide Web Virtual Library (http://vlib.iue.it/hist-russia/Index.html). Contains useful essays and links on Russian history, society, and politics.

Plus flashcards, practice quizzes, and more. Go to: www.cengage.com/history/lockard/globalsocnet2e.

SUGGESTED READING

Bridenthal, Renate, et al., eds. *Becoming Visible: Women in European History*, 3rd ed. Boston: Houghton Mifflin, 1998. Offers readable essays.

Crockatt, Richard. *The Fifty Years War: The United States and the Soviet Union in World Politics, 1941–1991*. New York: Routledge, 1995. A detailed study of the Cold War and U.S.-Soviet relations.

Evtuhov, Catherine, et al. *A History of Russia: Peoples, Legends, Events, Forces*. Boston: Wadsworth, 2004. A readable survey.

Gleason, Gregory. *The Central Asian States: Discovering Independence*. Boulder, CO: Westview Press, 1997. A study of the peoples and modern history of Turkestan.

James, Harold. *Europe Reborn: A History, 1914–2000*. New York: Longman, 2003. A survey of the period.

McCormick, John. *Understanding the European Union: A Concise Introduction*, 4th ed. New York: Palgrave Macmillan, 2008. A broad-ranging introduction to European integration.

Meyer, Michael. *The Year That Changed the World: The Untold Story Behind the Fall of the Berlin Wall*. New York: Scribner, 2009. Account of the dramatic changes in 1989.

Pagden, Anthony, ed. *The Idea of Europe: From Antiquity to the European Union*. New York: Cambridge University Press, 2002. An interesting collection of essays on European unity through the ages, including the contemporary era.

Reid, T.R. *The United States of Europe: The New Superpower and the End of American Supremacy*. New York: Penguin, 2005. Interesting examination of a predicted "European Century."

Rifkin, Jeremy. *The European Dream: How Europe's Vision of the Future Is Quietly Eclipsing the American Dream*. New York: Tarcher/Penguin, 2004. A provocative, sympathetic examination by an American scholar.

Roskin, Michael G. *The Rebirth of Eastern Europe*, 4th ed. Englewood Cliffs, NJ: Prentice-Hall, 2001. A provocative survey emphasizing politics and economics.

Ryback, Timothy W. *Rock Around the Bloc: A History of Rock Music in Eastern Europe and the Soviet Union*. New York: Oxford University Press, 1990. A fascinating examination of the role of rock music in the communist bloc.

Smith, Bonnie G. *Changing Lives: Women in European History Since 1700*. Lexington, MA: D.C. Heath, 1989. A readable introduction with good coverage of the twentieth century.

Strayer, Robert. *The Communist Experiment: Revolution, Socialism, and Global Conflict in the Twentieth Century*. New York: McGraw-Hill, 2007. Useful comparative study with much on the Soviet Bloc and Cold War.

Suny, Ronald Grigor. *The Soviet Experiment: Russia, the USSR, and the Successor States*. New York: Oxford University Press, 1998. An excellent overview of Soviet history and the aftermath.

Tipton, Frank B., and Robert Aldrich. *An Economic and Social History of Europe: From 1939 to the Present*. Baltimore: Johns Hopkins University, 1987. An accessible and comprehensive introduction.

Vinen, Richard. *A History in Fragments: Europe in the Twentieth Century*. Cambridge: Da Capo Press, 2000. A provocative, wide-ranging narrative by a British historian.

Wilkenson, James, and H. Stuart Hughes. *Contemporary Europe: A History*, 10th ed. Upper Saddle River, NJ: Prentice-Hall, 2004. One of the best, most comprehensive general surveys.

THE AMERICAS AND THE PACIFIC BASIN: NEW ROLES IN THE CONTEMPORARY WORLD, SINCE 1945

A Naturalization Ceremony
Seeking political freedom or economic opportunities, immigrants flock to the United States, and many become citizens. At this ceremony, 800 residents, representing 88 countries, took the oath of citizenship in Columbus, Ohio, in April 2005.

> It's curious. Our generals listen to the [U.S.] Pentagon. They learn the ideology of National Security and commit all these crimes [against the Argentine people]. Then the same [American] people who gave us this gift come and ask, "How did these terrible things happen?"
>
> —PRESIDENT RAUL ALFONSIN OF ARGENTINA, 1984[1]

The women appeared one day in 1977 in the historic Plaza de Mayo, adjacent to the presidential palace in downtown Buenos Aires, Argentina. For several years the military government had waged a bloody campaign to eliminate dissidents, killing or abducting some 30,000 people and arresting and torturing thousands more. Some of those targeted may have belonged to outlawed leftist groups, but many simply held progressive ideas or were friends with regime critics. Initially only the feared secret police paid attention to the dozen or so frightened women who came once a week, standing in silent protest. But soon the women's ranks swelled to over a hundred, and a year later the peaceful protesters numbered more than a thousand. Wearing kerchiefs on their heads and sensible flat shoes, the mothers and grandmothers pinned to their chests photographs of missing family members, victims of the state's terror. They all asked the same question: Where were their missing children, husbands, pregnant daughters, and grandchildren? The "Mothers and Grandmothers of the Plaza de Mayo" challenged one of Latin America's most brutal tyrannies. Whether rich, poor, or middle class, most were housewives fighting, as one put it, vicious armed forces, spineless politicians, complicit clergy, muzzled press, and co-opted labor unions. Their courageous protest inspired others in Argentina and around the world with hope and moral outrage at military repression. The gatherings continued weekly until 1983, when the regime fell and a civilian government could investigate the disappearances. Most of the women never learned the fates of their loved ones.

The Plaza de Mayo protest illustrates how some Latin Americans addressed the authoritarian governments under which they lived, sometimes for decades. Latin American countries often shifted back and forth between dictatorship and democracy, neither of which fostered widespread economic prosperity amid the stark contrasts between rich and poor. Many Latin Americans also resented the United States, which, as Raul Alfonsin (1927–2009), the democratically elected Argentine president who replaced the military dictatorship, noted, often supported the Latin American dictatorships that welcomed U.S. investment. The United States remained the hemisphere's dominant power while expanding its global influence. Wars in Korea and Vietnam were part of the U.S. effort to oppose the expansion of communism. U.S. president Harry Truman (president 1945–1953) argued in 1947 that American political and business practices could thrive at home only if foreign countries also embraced similar practices. Following this logic, the United States became the global workshop and banker, preacher and teacher, umpire and policeman. Between 1946 and 1989, it enjoyed unrivaled supremacy, a combination of military might, economic power, and political-ideological leadership, contested only by the Soviet Union. Meanwhile, U.S. society increasingly differed from its North American neighbor, Canada, and the Pacific Basin countries of Australia and New Zealand.

FOCUS QUESTIONS

1. How did the Cold War shape U.S. foreign policies?
2. How and why are the societies of the United States, Canada, and Australia similar to and different from each other?
3. Why have democracy and economic development proved to be difficult goals in Latin America?
4. How have Latin American and Caribbean cultures been dynamic?

e Visit the website and eBook for additional study materials and interactive tools:
www.cengage.com/history/lockard/globalsocnet2e

831

THE UNITED STATES AS A SUPERPOWER

How did the Cold War shape U.S. foreign policies?

By virtue of its size, power, and wealth, the United States has played a major world role. The Americans helped Europe and Japan to recover from World War II, espoused and often promoted human rights and freedom, lavished aid on allies, and provided leadership in a politically fragmented world. During the Cold War, competition with the Soviet bloc for allies and strategic advantage shaped U.S. policies, and these policies influenced the world's perceptions of the United States (see Chronology: North America and the Pacific Basin, 1945–Present). Soviet domination of eastern Europe, the communist victory in China, and the Korean War all convinced Americans that communism was on the march. But while people around the world admired America's democratic ideals, prosperity, and technological ingenuity, the drive to oppose communist expansion led to wars, interventions, support for often authoritarian allies, frequent neglect of human rights, and the globalization of capitalism that fostered widespread hostility. After the Cold War, the United States and its allies faced new challenges.

The American Century and the Cold War

World War II was a watershed that forged Americans' vision of world politics. As a result of the war, acceleration of U.S. political centralization and economic growth encouraged Americans to accept international involvements, thus promoting an activist foreign policy. Observers began referring to both the United States and the USSR as superpowers. As the United States became the global powerbroker and policeman, the two superpowers sought to block each other from gaining influence in other countries. The victory over Nazism and Japanese militarism reinforced American confidence and sense of mission. In 1941, Henry Luce, the publisher of one of the most influential news magazines in the United States, *Time*, declared that the twentieth century would be the American Century, and that Americans must accept their duty and opportunity to influence the world. Luce believed that America's idealistic Bill of Rights, magnificent industrial products, and technological skills would be shared with all peoples. His view, while arrogant, reflected Americans' longtime belief in the exportability of their country's values and institutions, that their nation was the world's model. But U.S.-style capitalism and democracy proved difficult to implant where they had no roots.

In 1941 a conference of influential Americans recommended strengthening U.S. economic influence around the globe. After the war, therefore, the U.S. government rebuilt defeated Germany and Japan, established global financial networks, lavished aid on western Europe to help stabilize it under democratic governments, and used military forces to protect U.S. allies in Asia. It also opposed radical nationalist and communist-led movements in Asia, Africa, and Latin America. For several decades, as the U.S. economy soared, the notion of an American Century seemed realistic. But the economic superiority of the United States in the 1940s and 1950s was founded on unusual conditions. Among the great powers, only the United States had not been bombed or financially drained, and therefore it was able to keep intact a modern industrial system. The United States alone could produce, on a large scale, the consumer goods needed by others. In 1950, it accounted for 27 percent of total world economic output. By supplying the world, Americans experienced an economic boom that lasted until the late 1960s and helped finance an activist U.S. foreign policy.

As the United States became the engine of the world economy, it forged close trade links with Canada, western Europe, and Japan while sponsoring large-scale foreign aid programs and investment, especially in Asia and Latin America. Such aid and investment sparked an economic renaissance and promoted political stability in western Europe and Japan after World War II. However, in developing nations the aid and investment often supported cash crop agriculture and mining and thus reinforced dependence on export of natural resources, promoting unbal-

CHRONOLOGY
North America and the Pacific Basin, 1945–Present

1946–1989 Cold War

1947 Formation of CIA and National Security Council

1950–1953 Korean War

1954 U.S. Supreme Court invalidation of school segregation

1955 Sparking of Montgomery bus boycott by Rosa Parks

1960–1975 U.S. secret war in Laos

1962–1990 Decolonization of Pacific islands

1963 Assassination of U.S. president John F. Kennedy

1963–1975 U.S. war in Vietnam

1968 Assassination of Dr. Martin Luther King, Jr.

1969 Woodstock rock festival

1973 End of "white Australia" policy

1988 Canadian Multiculturalism Act

1991 Gulf War

1994 Formation of NAFTA

1999 Formation of Nunavut in northern Canada

2001 Al Qaeda terrorist attacks in United States

2003 U.S. invasion of Iraq

CHRONOLOGY

	North America	Pacific Basin	Latin America and the Caribbean
1940	**1946–1989** Cold War **1950–1953** Korean War		**1959** Cuban Revolution
1960	**1963–1975** U.S. war in Vietnam	**1962–1990** Decolonization of Pacific islands **1973** End of "white Australia" policy	**1964–1985** Military government in Brazil **1973–1989** Military government in Chile
1980	**1994** Formation of NAFTA		
2000	**2001** Al Qaeda terrorist attacks in United States		

anced growth. Later, U.S. investment developed light industry, especially textile factories, that utilized cheap labor in countries such as Mexico and Thailand. Asian, African, and Latin America countries became key U.S. markets, acquiring over a third of American exports by the 1990s and enriching U.S. corporations. However, American consumption of ever more foreign imports, from Japanese cars to Middle Eastern oil, contributed to a chronic trade imbalance, as Americans spent more for foreign products than they earned from exports. By 2005 imports were 57 percent larger than exports as Americans lived beyond their means and globalization led to outsourcing of manufacturing and jobs.

The Cold War produced long-term conflict between two competing ideologies: communism and capitalist democracy. For decades after World War II, U.S. foreign relations were shaped by the idea that the Soviet Union was pursuing global domination. Although they had good reason to worry about a Soviet state headed by dictators and possessing formidable military might, U.S. leaders and intelligence analysts often overestimated the Soviet threat. Two key U.S. institutions carrying out the anti-Soviet strategy, the Central Intelligence Agency (CIA) and the National Security Council, both established in 1947, operated in top secrecy, with little congressional oversight and ever larger budgets, reaching $40 billion per year for all intelligence agencies by the 1980s. In the early 1950s the **domino theory**, which envisioned countries falling one by one to communism, became a mainstay of U.S. policy.

Competing Ideologies

Anticommunism intensified after hard-drinking U.S. senator Joseph McCarthy (1909–1957) and his allies charged, without offering much proof, that communists had infiltrated the U.S. government and shaped foreign policy. During the early and mid-1950s a campaign, known as McCarthyism, to identify suspected communists in the government, the military, education, and the entertainment industry led to the firing or the blacklisting of thousands of Americans who held leftwing political views, which were condemned as "un-American." (Blacklisting prevented people from working.) For example, university experts on Asia lost their positions for criticizing U.S. Asian policies, forcing some to finish their careers overseas. McCarthy called hundreds of people, from movie actors to State Department officials, before his Senate committee, where he questioned them about their political activities or their friends' political views. In 1954 the U.S. Senate censured McCarthy for recklessly charging top military leaders with treason. To critics, McCarthy's investigation was a witch-hunt and a Cold-War-driven hysteria that violated the Bill of Rights.

domino theory A theory that envisioned countries falling one by one to communism and that became a mainstay of U.S. policy.

For much of the Cold War era, as a broad consensus emerged around opposing the spread of communism and Soviet power, most American leaders favored an activist foreign policy and the use of military power. However, they disagreed on the approach. Some leaders pursued **multilateralism**, in which the United States sought a common front and a coordination of foreign policies with allies in western Europe, Japan, and Canada, avoiding activities that might enflame world opinion against the United States. In contrast, most policymakers, and the presidents they served, favored **unilateralism**, whereby the United States acted alone in its own perceived national interest even if key allies disapproved, as they did with the U.S. war in Vietnam. Unilateralism often led to support of repressive allies such as the Philippines and the Congo, while consensus stifled those who questioned the rationale, tactics, and cost of an activist policy. Ultimately the costly interventions abroad, especially the frustrating war in Vietnam, generated a debate about the

multilateralism A foreign policy in which the United States sought a common front and a coordination of foreign policies with allies in western Europe, Japan, and Canada, avoiding activities that might enflame world opinion against the United States.

unilateralism A foreign policy in which the United States acted alone in its own perceived national interest even if key allies disapproved.

goals, operation, and impact of U.S. foreign policy. By the later 1960s, this debate had undermined the consensus and provoked increasing dissent.

containment The main U.S. strategy aimed at preventing communists from gaining power, and the USSR from getting political influence, in other nations during the Cold War.

The main U.S. strategy, known as **containment**, was aimed at preventing communists from gaining power, and the USSR from getting political influence, in other nations. Containment resulted in wars, as in Korea and later Vietnam, and in briefer interventions in countries that were gaining independence from Western colonialism or seeking to weaken Western economic domination. An influential, top secret government report, known as NSC-68, prepared by the National Security Council in 1950, provided the rationale for activist policies by painting a bleak picture of the USSR's search for world supremacy: "The issues that face us are momentous, involving the fulfillment or destruction not only of this [U.S.] Republic but of civilization itself."[2] NSC-68, which sanctioned any tactics in the anticommunism struggle, remained a key basis for U.S. military and intelligence policies abroad until the mid-1970s.

Defense Spending

NSC-68 had called for a huge defense budget and expansion of the nuclear weapons arsenal as a deterrent, to be paid for by tax increases and major reductions in social welfare spending. Thus security was to take precedence at the expense of all other priorities. The Soviets matched the U.S. military buildup, creating a constant and costly escalation of military spending and ever more sophisticated weapons on both sides. Under the policy of **Mutually Assured Destruction**, or MAD, the United States and the USSR used the fear of nuclear weapons to deter each other. Historians debate whether MAD prevented a direct military confrontation that might have sparked World War III. Americans reacted to the threat of nuclear war in the 1950s by often building bomb shelters in their basements or backyards and having schools hold mock air raid drills, during which students learned to "duck and cover," jumping under their desks to protect themselves from a hypothetical nuclear attack.

Mutually Assured Destruction A policy, known as MAD, in which the United States and the USSR used the fear of nuclear weapons to deter each other.

Defense spending reshaped the U.S. economy. Despite the warning of U.S. president and World War II commander Dwight Eisenhower (g. 1953–1961) about the growing influence of what he termed the "military-industrial complex," an alliance of military leaders and weapons producers, defense became an enormous business. By the 1960s it employed a fifth of the U.S. industrial work force and a third of scientists and engineers, while costing U.S. taxpayers hundreds of billions of dollars a year. The United States also sold weapons to allied nations, among them dictatorships such as Argentina and Thailand. Unfortunately, these nations sometimes used the weapons against their own populations, while their military officers and police forces often used the tactics they learned from U.S. forces to eliminate dissidents.

United States Power and the World

Between 1945 and 1975 U.S. power was unmatched in the world, and the United States maintained military bases on every inhabited continent and in dozens of countries (see Map 29.1). Both the United States and the USSR intervened directly or indirectly in civil wars and revolutions to outflank the other. Americans employed military force, as in the long war in Vietnam and the invasion of the Dominican Republic in 1965, and covertly aided governments to suppress opposition or helped overthrow governments considered unfriendly to U.S. economic or political interests, even if, as in Chile in 1973, these governments were democratic and freely elected. Some foreign observers applauded American efforts to suppress leftwing governments and movements, while others criticized the U.S. for superpower imperialism. The U.S.-U.S.S.R. rivalry persisted until the collapse of many communist regimes in 1989.

U.S. power was less dominant between the mid-1970s and the early 1990s. Reasons included the resurgence of western Europe and Japan, Soviet military strength, the economic challenge from industrializing nations such as South Korea and China, the damage done to the U.S. economy and prestige by the widely unpopular war in Vietnam, and the economic price Americans paid for global power. The extension and cost of military commitments caused the nation's economic creativity to sag and industries to become obsolete as defense spending diverted U.S. wealth from the domestic economy. Over four decades the Cold War cost the United States around $4 trillion, money that did not go to improving education and health care or meeting other needs. The growing U.S. defense budgets helped undermine the Soviet Union, unable to match the lavish spending on expensive, often unproven, weapons, but they also transformed the United States into the world's largest debtor nation, leaving ballooning federal deficits. In the 1990s, President Bill Clinton (g. 1993–2001) eliminated the budget deficits, but the debts skyrocketed under his successor, George W. Bush (g. 2001–2009).

The United States, Wars, and the Developing Nations

Korean War

The 1949 communist victory in China, a country long allied with and armed by the United States (see Chapter 27), escalated U.S. concern about communist expansion, leading to the Korean War

Map 29.1 U.S. Military Presence in the World, 1945–Present
As the major superpower, the United States maintained several dozen military bases outside of North America while engaging in military operations in Latin America, Africa, Asia, the Middle East, and Europe. This map shows some of the major U.S. bases and military conflicts.

Interactive Map

(1950–1953) (see Chapter 27). The decision to send U.S. troops to Korea signaled the U.S. adoption of an interventionist foreign policy, with the U.S. president, Harry S. Truman, viewing the North Korean invasion as a second coming of Nazi aggression. The anticommunist mood in the United States made it politically unthinkable for Truman not to oppose the North Korean invasion of South Korea. Truman never consulted the Congress, which had the constitutional responsibility to declare war, and his approach thereafter made presidents supreme in decisions to go to war without congressional approval, enhancing the power of the executive branch. Furthermore, the Soviet support of North Korea and the intervention of the Chinese on the North Korean side deepened American fear of an expanding communism. However, despite the 38,000 Americans killed and over 100,000 wounded, the war ended not in victory but in stalemate. For the first time since the War of 1812, the United States had failed to decisively win a major military conflict. The U.S. intervention in Korea also reflected the idealistic American desire to spread democracy and free market capitalism around the world. An American official reported sarcastically the hope of his more idealistic American colleagues that South Korea "will institute a whole series of necessary reforms which will so appeal to the North Koreans that their army

On Patrol in Vietnam
U.S. soldiers sought out National Liberation Front fighters and supporters in the villages, rice fields, and jungles of South Vietnam. They could not easily tell friend from foe and warily dealt with local people.

Corbis

will revolt, kill all the nasty communists, and create a lovely liberal democracy to the everlasting credit of the U.S.A.!"[3] North Korea, however, remained a rigid communist state, and South Korea did not become a democracy until the 1980s, over three decades after the war. By 2009 U.S. military bases and thousands of troops remained in South Korea.

War in Indochina

The domino theory, which predicted a communist sweep through Southeast Asia, as well as the desire to maintain military credibility and keep valuable Southeast Asian resources in friendly hands, also provided the rationale for financing the French effort to maintain colonial control (1946–1954) in Vietnam. When that effort failed, the U.S. military eventually fought Vietnamese communist forces armed by the USSR and China (see Chapter 31). But few U.S. leaders comprehended the historical and cultural factors that sparked, and generated much local support for, the Vietnamese communist movement. By the mid-1960s, as the unpopular U.S.-backed South Vietnamese regime lost support, the U.S. president, Lyndon B. Johnson (g. 1963–1969), committed military forces and launched an intensive air war against targets in North and South Vietnam and later in neighboring Cambodia and Laos. Using domino theory rhetoric that exaggerated the communist threat, Johnson asserted that "if we don't stop the [communists] in South Vietnam, tomorrow they will be in Hawaii and next week they will be in San Francisco,"[4] very unlikely scenarios. As a result, between 1963 and 1975, 2.5 million Americans served in Vietnam; 58,000 died and 300,000 were wounded there.

As support within the United States for the war ebbed with military stalemate and increasing casualties in what seemed a quagmire, Johnson's successor, President Richard Nixon (g. 1969–1973), placed more emphasis on South Vietnamese forces, negotiated a political settlement with North Vietnam, and gradually withdrew U.S. forces. But a wartime policy of spending lavishly on both "guns and butter"—military and domestic needs—generated huge deficits and other economic problems with which the United States struggled from the later 1960s into the 1990s. The war in Vietnam ultimately cost U.S. taxpayers around $1 trillion. Furthermore, the lack of a military victory made Americans temporarily wary of supporting other military interventions that might become quagmires.

United States and Decolonization

During the Cold War, decolonization, nationalism, the U.S.-Soviet struggle, and persistent poverty combined to make the Asian, African, and Latin American societies prone to crises. The United States often favored decolonization that presented opportunities to U.S. business; for example, it successfully pressured the Dutch to abandon Indonesia and the British to grant independence to most of their African colonies. However, it opposed independence for colonies, such as French-ruled Vietnam and Portuguese-ruled Mozambique, where communists or leftists dominated the nationalist movements. After decolonization, Americans offered generous aid to friendly nations and to victims of famine or natural catastrophes, and they also funded the Green Revolution in agriculture, which led to improved food production. However, Cold War challenges involved the United States in long-term confrontations with communist-led China, North Vietnam, and Cuba, as well as interventions, sometimes with military force, to help U.S. allies suppress leftist insurgencies and to oppose left-leaning governments. But some U.S.-supported governments lacked widespread popular support or lost their credibility, often surviving only by repressing and sometimes killing domestic opponents.

While U.S. leaders used the threat of communism as the rationale, some interventions removed democratic governments, as in Guatemala and Chile, or suppressed democratic movements. For example, President Lyndon Johnson, fearing another Cuba, dispatched 20,000 U.S. Marines into the Dominican Republic in 1965 to support a military government under attack by the democratically elected leaders they had recently overthrown. However, Johnson consulted no other Latin American governments, and the antimilitary leaders, while left-leaning, were mostly noncommunist reformers with wide popular support. Former Dominican president Juan Bosch (1909–2001) declared that "this was a democratic revolution smashed by the leading democracy in the world."[5] Instead of troops, the United States also provided friendly governments or antileftist groups with weapons, military advisers, intelligence agents, and funding. For example, during the 1970s and 1980s it aided a pro-Western but often repressive government combating a leftist insurgency in El Salvador. In Laos from 1960 to 1975, during the CIA's "secret war," kept hidden from Congress and the U.S. public, Americans recruited an army from among hill peoples to fight communist Laotian and North Vietnamese forces (see Chapter 31).

Interventions

A final type of intervention involved covert destabilization. American agents worked underground to help undermine or spark the overthrow of governments by spreading misinformation about government policies, subsidizing opposition political parties, providing weapons to the military, and arranging for assassinations of government leaders. U.S. clandestine activity undermined left-leaning democratic governments in Iran in the 1950s and Thailand and Chile in the 1970s, resulting in brutal dictatorships. Secretary of State Henry Kissinger defended the U.S.-supported military coup against the elected Chilean government, which respected civil liberties, by explaining, "I don't see why we [Americans] need to stand by and watch a country go communist due to the irresponsibility of its own people."[6] Only in the mid-1970s, with congressional hearings, did Americans learn of the U.S. role in Chile and other interventions, forcing debate on whether engaging in secret operations and foreign interventions unknown to the public is compatible with democracy and open, accountable government.

The United States in the Global System After 1989

The demise of the Soviet bloc in 1989 and the dissolution of the USSR in 1991 left the United States the dominant world power, although the European Union, Japan, and rising China and India also enjoyed great influence in the global system. But the lack of a rival superpower under what some called the *Pax Americana* ("American Peace") did not mean the end of challengers. The United States now struggled to find a new role in a world characterized by small, deadly conflicts. During the early 1990s, for example, it sent a small number of U.S. troops, under United Nations auspices, to stabilize Somalia, a famine-racked northeast African state involved in a civil war. The intervention turned out badly when the forces of a local warlord paraded the mutilated bodies of dead U.S. soldiers through the streets, forcing a U.S. withdrawal. In the aftermath, the United States declined to intervene to stop bloody ethnic conflicts and genocides in the African states of Rwanda, Liberia, and Sierra Leone. However, working with European allies, President Clinton sent U.S. forces to help end the deadly civil wars in the former Yugoslavia. The Clinton administration also established diplomatic ties and lifted the trade embargo that had been imposed on Vietnam after 1975, which it viewed as counterproductive, forging better relations with Vietnam.

Pax Americana

Cold War policies sometimes came back to haunt the United States. For example, Iranian resentment over the 1953 overthrow of their government still complicates U.S.-Iran relations. In the 1980s, when the United States gave military and financial aid to the Islamic rebels fighting Soviet troops and the pro-Soviet government in Afghanistan (see Chapter 30), some of this aid went to Arab volunteers fighting alongside the rebels, among them the Saudi militant Osama bin Laden (b. 1957). After the defeated Soviets left Afghanistan in 1989, Muslim extremists, the Taliban, ultimately took power, imposing a rigid Islamic state and offering a base for bin Laden to form the global terrorist network known as Al Qaeda ("the Base"). Al Qaeda now plotted terrorist attacks against the United States, sometimes using leftover U.S. weapons (see Chapters 26 and 30). Farther west, Iraq's ruthless dictator, Saddam Hussein, used weapons acquired from the United States, his ally against Iran in the 1980s, to threaten Iraq's neighbors and repress dissident groups. In 1991 the United States led a coalition of nations that pushed invading Iraqi forces out of Kuwait during the Gulf War and then later protected the Kurds in northern Iraq from Saddam's reprisals. The intervention in oil-rich Kuwait was part of a consistent U.S. policy over the decades to protect the flow of oil from the Middle East to the West.

United States and Middle East

International Terrorism

The terrorist attack carried out by Al Qaeda on the World Trade Center in New York and the Pentagon in Washington, D.C., in September 2001, which killed nearly 3,000 Americans, shocked the nation and led to a reshaping of both domestic and foreign policies. The new U.S. president, George W. Bush (g. 2001–2009), introduced policies, such as preventive detention, intercepting overseas phone calls, and monitoring of libraries, designed to prevent possible domestic terrorism but that critics believed infringed on civil liberties. The terrorists, young Muslim fanatics mostly from two close U.S. allies, Egypt and Saudi Arabia, attacked buildings that symbolized often-unpopular U.S. economic and military power to people around the world. However, people in most countries, even if they disliked U.S. power, deplored the bombings and the loss of innocent life.

As a result of September 2001, President Bush declared war on international terrorism. But unlike the USSR during the Cold War, whose leaders had to be cautious, terrorist networks had no clear command structure or military resources and could not be influenced by diplomacy. With international support, the United States invaded Afghanistan to destroy Al Qaeda terrorist bases and displace the Taliban government that tolerated their presence. Bush also announced a new doctrine of **preemptive war** that sanctioned unilateral military action against potential threats (see Witness to the Past: Justifying Preemptive Strikes), and he named Iraq, Iran, and North Korea as states at the core of an "axis of evil" that threatened their neighbors and world peace. The Bush doctrine advocated that the United States maintain overwhelming military superiority over all challengers. Critics perceived the Bush doctrine as a recipe for acquiring an American empire through military action, a violation, they charged, of international law and the United Nations charter.

preemptive war A U.S. doctrine, triggered by the 2001 terrorist attacks, that sanctioned unilateral military action against potential threats.

The U.S. and Iraq

The Bush administration's concern with international terrorism led to a resumption of unilateralist U.S. foreign policies. Rejecting opposition from the United Nations and key U.S. allies, among them Canada and Germany, in 2003 the Bush administration invaded and occupied Iraq, ending Saddam Hussein's brutal regime. On the basis of faulty or manipulated intelligence, Bush claimed that Iraq possessed weapons of mass destruction and aided Al Qaeda. But the U.S. forces found no such weapons or evidence of a Saddam–Al Qaeda link. Furthermore, the Bush administration had planned poorly for restoring stability in Iraq, a nation rich in oil but troubled by ethnic and religious divisions that threatened to explode into civil war and that frustrated U.S. attempts to foster democracy. A mounting insurgency by some Iraqi factions, as well as suicide bombings largely linked to foreign terrorists flocking to Iraq to fight Americans, caused many thousands of U.S. casualties and complicated political and economic reconstruction, making an early withdrawal of U.S. forces difficult. By 2007 oil production and basic services such as electricity had still not been restored to prewar levels, and the streets in many regions remained unsafe, demoralizing Iraqis. Only in 2008, after Bush dispatched more troops, did conditions stabilize, violence diminish, and political conditions improve, but over 130,000 U.S. troops remained in later 2009. The U.S.-led NATO force in Afghanistan also faced increased resistance from Islamist fighters led by a rejuvenated Taliban.

In both Afghanistan and Iraq, U.S. forces, although trained for conventional warfare relying heavily on air power, had to return to the counterinsurgency strategy they used in Vietnam. Moreover, the spiraling costs of the Iraq occupation and other expenses, combined with large tax cuts, ballooned U.S. budget deficits that damaged the U.S. economy. The ever-expanding appetite of Americans for oil also contributed to the Middle East interventions and support for dictatorial regimes; critics charged that the Iraq war was about oil. The Iraq war, unpopular in much of the world, the allegations that the U.S. tortured suspected terrorists, holding suspected enemies for years without trial, and the U.S. rejection of several international treaties, such as that on global warming, further alienated Western allies. Yet, the United States also earned praise for generous assistance to the victims of a catastrophic tidal wave in South and Southeast Asia in 2005.

The Price of World Power

Because of its unparalleled economic and military might, the United States had assumed heavy burdens, sending troops to Afghanistan, Iraq, and elsewhere while maintaining military bases around the world. By 2008 the U.S. accounted for some two thirds of arm sales to other nations, earning some $40 billion per year. While western Europeans and East Asians have generally concentrated on trade relations with other nations, Americans have attempted to balance trade with confronting the nations they perceive as dangerous. By 2008 the United States accounted for half of all military spending worldwide, devoting as much to its military and weapons as all other nations combined, and it also accounted for about half of all arms sales to the world's nations. While anti-U.S. sentiments grew steadily in the early twenty-first century, no coalition of nations has come together to oppose the U.S. role. However, the budget deficits that now pay for it, more than doubling the national debt between 2001 and 2008, are only possible because Asian investors, especially the Chinese, Japanese, and South Koreans, finance around half of the debt, giving these countries leverage with the United States.

The spiraling national debt, expensive global commitments, housing market crisis, and overly lax regulation of banks, corporations, and the stock market led to an economic meltdown in 2008–2009 that soon spread to the rest of the world. Millions of Americans lost their jobs and homes,

Justifying Preemptive Strikes

In the wake of the shocking terrorist attacks on the United States in September 2001, the administration of President George W. Bush produced a document, the National Security Strategy of the United States, that restated the U.S. desire to spread democracy and capitalism while announcing that the United States would act preemptively, striking first, unilaterally if necessary, against any hostile states that the Bush administration believed might be planning to attack U.S. targets. Depending on the observer, the document either reflected or exploited Americans' fear of terrorist attacks. In 2003 Bush used the preemptive strike rationale to order a military invasion and occupation of Iraq, which he claimed had weapons of mass destruction. After Saddam's fall, Bush offered a new mission: fostering democracy in Iraq as an example for the Middle East. To critics, however, the failure to find such weapons, the faulty intelligence about them, and the huge financial and human costs of the resulting occupation for both Americans and Iraqis all suggested the dangers of a preemptive strategy. Furthermore, they argued, many presidents before Bush had claimed to promote democracy abroad but had rarely done so, especially when they used military force to install a pro-U.S. government in another country.

The great struggles of the twentieth century between liberty and totalitarianism ended with a decisive victory for the forces of freedom—and a single sustainable model for national success: freedom, democracy, and free enterprise. . . . Only nations that share a commitment to protecting basic human rights and guaranteeing political and economic freedom will be able to unleash the potential of their people and assure their future prosperity. . . . Today the United States enjoys a position of unparalleled military strength and great economic and political influence. In keeping with our heritage and principles, we do not use our strength to press for unilateral advantage. We seek instead to create a balance of power that favors human freedom. . . . We will extend the peace by encouraging free and open societies on every continent.

Defending our Nation against its enemies is the first and fundamental commitment of the Federal Government. Today, that task has changed dramatically. Enemies in the past needed great armies and great industrial capabilities to endan-

ger America. Now, shadowy networks of individuals can bring great chaos and suffering to our shores for less than it costs to purchase a single tank. Terrorists are organized to penetrate open societies and to turn the power of modern technologies against us. To defeat this threat we must make use of every tool in our arsenal. . . . The war against terrorists of global reach is a global enterprise of uncertain duration. . . . America will hold to account nations that are compromised by terror, including those who harbor terrorists—because the allies of terror are the enemies of civilization. . . . Our enemies have openly declared that they are seeking weapons of mass destruction. . . . The United States will not allow these efforts to succeed. . . . And, as a matter of common sense and self-defense, America will act against such emerging threats before they are fully formed. . . . We must be prepared to defeat our enemies' plans. History will judge harshly those who saw this coming danger but failed to act. In the new world we have entered, the only path to peace and security is the path of action. . . .

The struggle against global terrorism is different from any other war in our history. It will be fought on many fronts against a particularly elusive enemy over an extended period of time. . . . New deadly challenges have emerged from rogue states and terrorists. . . . Rogue regimes seek nuclear, biological, and chemical weapons. . . . We must be prepared to stop rogue states and their terrorist clients before they are able to threaten or use weapons of mass destruction against the United States and our allies. . . . The United States can no longer solely rely on a reactive posture as we have in the past. . . . We cannot let our enemies strike first. . . . We must adapt the concept of imminent threat to the capabilities and objectives of today's adversaries. . . . The greater the threat, the greater the risk of inaction—and the more compelling the case for taking anticipatory action to defend ourselves, even if uncertainty remains as to the time and place of the enemy's attack. To forestall or prevent such hostile acts by our adversaries, the United States will, if necessary, act preemptively.

THINKING ABOUT THE READING

1. How does the document reflect the tendency of U.S. leaders to claim a national goal of spreading U.S. political and economic models in the world?
2. What does the document offer as the rationale for preemptive actions?

Source: The National Security Strategy of the United States (http://www.whitehouse.gov/nsc/print/nssall.html).

consumer spending dropped dramatically, stock prices plummeted, pension funds dwindled, and state and local governments faced severe budget cuts. The government was forced to bail out major banks, the distressed automobile industry, and revenue-starved states, adding to budget deficits. While the severe recession was not as catastrophic as the Great Depression, it did force debate on the continuing relevance of the free-wheeling U.S. economic model and on the heavy cost of the nation's obligations in the world. Whether the United States will retain its dominance in the years ahead or whether the growing burdens will reduce U.S. power as other nations, perhaps China or India, surge ahead, remains unclear. Due to the economic crisis, some experts perceived a transition underway toward a multi-polar economy less dependent on U.S. leadership and consumption. Whatever the case, since the Romans two millennia ago, no other nation has been as dominant in military, economic, political, and social realms as the United States has been after 1990, forcing Americans to debate, as the Romans and the Athenians did, whether democracy and imperial power are consistent.

SECTION SUMMARY

- For several decades after World War II, the United States enjoyed a period of economic growth and lavished economic aid on western Europe and Japan, where it helped those countries to recover, and later on developing nations, where it was not used as effectively.

- During the Cold War, McCarthyism led to the persecution of many U.S. citizens for supposed communist sympathies, U.S. presidents aimed to contain the spread of communism through unilateral action, the two superpowers followed the Mutually Assured Destruction policy, and defense spending became a key factor in the U.S. economy.

- On the basis of the domino theory, which argued that if communism wasn't stopped it would take over the world,

- the United States adopted an interventionist foreign policy and fought communists in Korea and Vietnam, but neither war achieved U.S. goals, and the Vietnam War severely crippled the U.S. economy.

- During the Cold War, the United States opposed not only communist movements but also noncommunist leftist movements in several countries, in many cases helping to replace them with brutal military dictatorships.

- In response to the terrorist attacks of September 11, 2001, U.S. president George W. Bush proclaimed a policy of pre-emptive war and led the country to war in Afghanistan and then in Iraq, the second of which was fought despite United Nations disapproval and has been very controversial.

THE CHANGING SOCIETIES OF NORTH AMERICA AND THE PACIFIC BASIN

How and why are the societies of the United States, Canada, and Australia similar to and different from each other?

The United States, Canada, Australia, and New Zealand, all originally settled by people from the British Isles, shared a general prosperity, stable democracies, similar social patterns, and many cultural traditions. Millions of immigrants also helped to globalize their cultures and link them more closely to other nations. But the United States played a different role than the other countries and exercised more power in the world.

Prosperity, Technology, and Inequality in the United States

Economic Growth

Living in the world's richest nation, many Americans benefited from a growing economy and widespread affluence. During the 1960s, as many Americans worked in new automobile, aerospace, service, and information technology industries, the production of goods and services doubled and per capita income rose by half. By 2000 the United States accounted for a third of the world's total production of goods and services, over twice as much as second-place Japan, and enjoyed a median annual family income of over $40,000. Americans also owned the majority of the giant multinational corporations, such as General Motors and Wal-Mart, that played ever larger roles in the globalizing world. However, there were downsides to this growth. With 6 percent of the world population, Americans consumed around 40 percent of all the world's resources, such as oil and iron ore, and produced a large share of the chemicals, gases, and toxic wastes that pollute the atmosphere, alter the climate, and destroy the land. At the same time, the United States lagged in environmental protection; in 2005 it ranked twenty-eighth in meeting sustainable environmental goals, well behind most of western Europe, Japan, Taiwan, and several developing nations. Americans also worked longer hours than any industrialized people except the Japanese.

New Technologies

The rise of high technology and the decline of smokestack industries, such as steel production, reshaped the economy and workplace. Americans made innovations in medicine, space research, transportation, and electronics. Space satellites greatly improved weather forecasting, communications, and intelligence gathering, and computers revolutionized life with their convenience and versatility, since these machines could, as *Time* magazine concluded, "send letters at the speed of light, diagnose a sick poodle [and] test recipes for beer."[7] By 2008 many Americans carried with them pocket-sized devices, once the stuff of science fiction novels, that could make telephone calls, send text messages, take photos, play music and films, and access news and weather.

Beginning in the 1970s, a growing economy improved the lot of some people, especially those trained in the new technologies, but hurt millions of unskilled workers, younger workers, and children in single-parent households. While computers and robots increased efficiency, they also replaced workers, and in the 1980s a third of industrial jobs disappeared. Industrialists won corporate bonuses for relocating factories and exporting jobs to Latin America or Asia, devastating factory-dependent American communities. By the early 2000s, although life for the majority of Americans remained comfortable compared to that in most other nations, unemployment for men was the highest it had been in five decades, and millions of men and women had to work two jobs to support their families. Moreover, the United States generally ranked behind several European nations, Canada, and Australia in overall quality of life in the annual United Nations Human Development Report. Some economists referred to a "winner-take-all economy" that produced ever more millionaires—over 2 million of them by 2005—but also a struggling middle class and, at the bottom of the social ladder, more homeless people sleeping in city streets and parks. Except for the richest 1 percent of Americans, whose earnings skyrocketed, average incomes fell between 2001 and 2008. Yet, most Americans identified themselves with the middle class rather than, as Europeans often did, with the working class.

In contrast to most industrialized nations, the United States never developed a comprehensive welfare state. Hence, despite sporadic government efforts at abolishing poverty, a widening gap separated the richest third and the poorest third of Americans. The inequality of wealth grew dramatically after 1980, and by 2004, 12.5 percent of Americans lived below the poverty line, the highest poverty rate in the industrialized world. Today the gap between the richest 20 percent and the poorest 20 percent of Americans is three times wider than in Japan, the Netherlands, Sweden, or Germany, and millions of Americans today have no health insurance, a striking contrast to western Europe and Canada. A devastating hurricane that caused massive damage and flooding in the Gulf Coast in 2005, ruining New Orleans, rendering millions homeless, and killing several thousand people, starkly revealed the gap; most of the people who died or were only rescued days later were black and poor, unable to afford transportation out of the area.

Economic changes went hand in hand with the suburbanization of American life, deepening the inequalities. Following World War II families with young children wanted affordable housing and sought a better life in suburbia, the bedroom communities on the edges of major cities. Suburbs, occupied typically by white Americans, built shopping malls, offered well-funded schools, and seemed immune from city violence. Governments supported the suburban trend by subsidizing real estate developers. William Leavitt, who built vast suburban tracts, known as Leavittown, around New York City, argued that no person who owned his or her own house and yard could be a communist because he or she was too busy keeping up, and working to pay for, the property. The two-car, multitelevision family symbolized affluence. The increasingly affordable automobile, combined with government-funded highway construction, made long commutes from the suburbs to jobs in the central city possible. Later, as the jobs often moved to the suburbs, the city cores were increasingly dominated by the local-born poor, often nonwhite, or immigrants. Furthermore, increasing use of fossil fuels for gasoline, electricity, and heating caused pollution, while clearing land for housing and business development harmed the environment. Most suburbs lacked ethnic and cultural diversity and isolated residents from the stimulation, as well as the problems, of big city life. Suburban living also intensified the trend, begun before World War II, toward two-parent, single-breadwinner nuclear families that lived apart from other relatives. Finally, moving people farther away from city jobs encouraged mothers to stay at home. Until the mid-1960s the image of the fashionably dressed, stay-at-home suburban housewife, smiling proudly as she served breakfast to her husband and children, remained ingrained in the culture, even as women increasingly found it necessary to undertake paid work. Critics lambasted the conformity of life in the standardized suburban tract houses, which, according to a song from the 1950s, resembled "little boxes. There's a green one, a pink one, a blue one and a yellow one. And they're all made out of ticky-tacky, And they all look just the same."[8]

American Political Life: Conservatism and Liberalism

Americans tended to alternate between political conservatism and liberalism. For most of the postwar years, political conservatives, allied with big business groups favoring low taxes and religious groups who disliked social and cultural liberalization, dominated the presidency and often the Congress and the judiciary. Liberals played a key role in U.S. politics chiefly in the 1960s, the 1990s, and after 2006. They were generally supported by labor unions, environmentalists, and groups that sought social change and a stronger government safety net, such as women's and civil rights organizations.

1950s Conservatism

The widespread desire for stability after the Great Depression and a calamitous world war encouraged political and social conservatism throughout the 1950s. Prosperous, the middle and upper classes rarely questioned their government or the prevailing social patterns. Americans who criticized U.S. foreign policy or favored extensive social change faced harassment, expulsion from job or school, arrest, or grillings by congressional committees. More Americans than ever before married, producing a "baby boom" of children born in the years following the war. The mass media portrayed women as obsessed with bleaching their clothes a purer white and defined by kitchen, bedroom, babies, and home. Society expected homosexuals to remain deep in the closet, and those who did not faced taunting, beatings, or arrest. The growing consumer economy also emphasized pleasure and leisure activities, such as cocktail parties, backyard barbecues, and baseball games. Like their parents, teenagers became consumers, creating a market for youth-oriented clothes and music.

1960s Liberalism

During the 1960s, Americans became open to new ideas and lifestyles as liberalism became influential. The era saw the first people to walk on the moon and the Peace Corps, an agency that sent idealistic young Americans to help developing nations as teachers, health workers, and agricultural specialists. Presidents John F. Kennedy (g. 1961–1963) and Lyndon B. Johnson (g. 1963–1969) launched programs to address poverty and racism. But the 1960s was also a decade of doubts, anger, and violence. Three national leaders were assassinated, including Kennedy, shot in the head while riding in a motorcade in 1963. The war in Vietnam, the civil rights movement for African Americans, and issues of environmental protection and women's empowerment divided the nation. The country's social fabric fragmented as prowar "hawks" and antiwar "doves" competed for support, and riots and demonstrations punctuated the decade.

Much of the commotion came from a large segment of young people, chiefly middle class, who rebelled against the values of their parents and established society. The popular folksinger Bob Dylan (b. 1941) sang: "Come, mothers and fathers, throughout the land, And don't criticize what you can't understand. Your sons and your daughters are beyond your command, Your old world is rapidly aging. Please get out of the new one if you can't lend your hand, For the times, they are a-changing."[9] Some youth, especially high school and university students, worked to change society and politics, registering voters, holding "teach-ins" to discuss national issues, and going door to door to spread their cause. Other youth forged a counterculture that often involved using illegal drugs, such as marijuana, and engaging in casual sex, with some emblazoning the slogan "Make love, not war" on bumper stickers, posters, and buttons. The Summer of Love in 1967, during which young people from North America and elsewhere gathered in San Francisco to hear rock music and share comradery, and the Woodstock rock music festival of 1969, which attracted over 300,000 young people to a New York farm to hear some of the most popular rock musicians, marked the zenith of both the youth counterculture and political activism.

Return to Conservatism

In the 1970s, with the winding down of the war, the nation returned to more conservative values and politics. With the exception of the 1990s, when the moderate Bill Clinton held the presidency, conservatives maintained their dominance of American politics and the social agenda until 2006, when Democrats reclaimed Congress, followed by the 2008 election of Democrat Barack Obama as president. President Ronald Reagan (g. 1981–1989), a former movie star and zealous anticommunist, symbolized conservative governance by weakening the labor movement and the welfare system while taking a hard line toward the Soviet Union. Religion has also remained a powerful force, with Americans more likely to attend churches and profess strong Christian beliefs than Canadians or most Europeans. While many Protestants, Catholics, and Jews supported liberal causes, by the 1980s conservative Catholics and evangelical Protestants became influential in public life, helping elect political conservatives to office. Some experts attributed Christian conservatism to a rejection of the Enlightenment emphasis on reason and tolerance as believers sought certainty and timeless rules. Others stressed the search for a personal spiritual experience. Many churches stressed membership in a supportive community or emphasized self-help. While Americans avidly consumed new technologies, such as cell phones and portable music players, polls showed that, because of religious conservatism, substantial numbers also mistrusted science, rejecting scientific explanations for the origins of the universe and human evolution in favor of biblical accounts.

Observers found much to deplore and much to praise in post-1960s U.S. politics. As money from big corporations and other special interests increasingly played a major role in politics, fostering corruption and political apathy, fewer Americans participated in the democratic process, with barely half of eligible voters bothering to vote in presidential elections—far lower numbers than in most other industrial democracies. However, a free media exposed government corruption,

President Obama
Villagers in Kogelo, Kenya, celebrate the inauguration of Barack Obama as president of the United States in early 2009. While many around the world watched the ceremony on television, the interest was was especially strong in Kogelo, where Obama's father was born.

including abuse of power by presidents. President Richard Nixon, facing impeachment, resigned in 1973 for sanctioning and then covering up illegal activities by his subordinates, and the presidencies of both Reagan and Clinton were marred by congressional hearings examining their misdeeds. After the controversial, bitter 2000 and 2004 elections, Americans were sharply divided between the two major political parties and the divergent policies they supported.

However, the apathy faded in 2008 during an exciting election campaign to replace a strongly conservative President George W. Bush, widely disliked for the unpopular Iraq war, an incompetent response to Hurricane Katrina, a spiraling national debt, controversial social and environmental policies, and the economic meltdown of 2008. Illinois Senator Barack Obama (b. 1961), the Hawaii-born son of a black Kenyan father and white mother from Kansas, won the Democratic nomination over New York Senator Hillary Rodham Clinton (b. 1947), a former First Lady. Obama had lived in Indonesia for a few years as a child. By mobilizing a coalition of racial minorities, women, youth, and labor unions, Obama went on to win the presidency over Arizona Senator and Vietnam War hero, Republican John McCain (b. 1936). Obama's victory as the first nonwhite president electrified the world, and suggested that U.S. society was changing. Obama urged global cooperation on pressing issues and many non-Americans hoped for a less unilateral and aggressive U.S. foreign policy than under Bush. Inheriting two wars and an economic crisis, and enjoying Democratic congressional majorities, Obama proposed New Deal–like policies to generate economic recovery, made plans to withdraw U.S. troops from Iraq, and promised to deliver universal health coverage and implement more environmentally friendly policies. However, while a government stimulus package averted a complete economic crash, reducing unemployment proved a challenge. Whether Obama had begun a new era of liberalism and economic resurgence remained to be seen.

The Obama Presidency

American Society and Popular Culture

The changing American society affected ethnic minorities, families, women, and men. As they had since the end of slavery, African Americans, over 10 percent of the population, experienced much higher rates of poverty than whites and faced various forms of discrimination. Until the 1960s the southern states maintained strict racial segregation, forcing blacks to attend separate schools and to even use different public drinking fountains than whites, while in northern industrial cities racism and poverty often encouraged African Americans to concentrate in run-down inner-city neighborhoods, known as ghettos.

African Americans and Civil Rights

The civil rights movement, organized by African Americans in the 1950s, eventually forced courts, states, and the federal government to introduce reforms. In 1954 the Supreme Court outlawed segregated schools. A year later, in Montgomery, Alabama, Rosa Parks (1913–2005), a seamstress and community activist, bravely refused to follow the local custom to give up her front seat on a bus to a white man, sparking a mass movement for change. A black minister, Reverend Martin

Luther King, Jr. (1929–1968), led a bus boycott to protest her arrest and fine. Using the strategy of nonviolent resistance pioneered by Mohandas Gandhi, King led a protest movement all over the South. While leading the 1963 March on Washington to demand equal rights, he presented his vision: "I have a dream. When we let freedom ring, all of God's children will be able to join hands and sing in the words of that old spiritual, 'Thank God almighty, we are free at last!'"[10] King's assassination by a white racist in 1968 shocked the nation, but by then the African American struggle had inspired similar struggles elsewhere in the world, including black South Africans, Afro-Brazilians, and Australian Aborigines. Thanks to the efforts of King, Parks, and many others, African Americans gradually gained legal equality, and many moved into the middle and upper classes, although African Americans were still far more likely than whites to live in poverty, face unemployment, and be imprisoned. While they celebrated Obama's presidential victory as a sign of progress, they were also more likely to lose jobs and homes in the 2008–2009 recession.

Multiracial Society

Americans have often boasted that they live in a "melting pot" where ethnic groups merge and lose their separate identity, which has often been the case for people of European ancestry. However, because members of many nonwhite ethnic groups have often maintained their separate identities and cultures, Americans have increasingly faced a multiracial, multicultural society. By 2008 the U.S. population of 300 million, the third largest in the world, was more diverse than ever, and over 10 percent were foreign-born. As a result, American life took on a cosmopolitan flavor: Spanish became widely spoken, and Latin American grocery stores, Asian restaurants, and African art galleries opened in communities throughout the country. Alaska and Hawaii, both with large nonwhite populations, became states in 1959, adding to the nation's diversity.

Ethnic groups grew through both legal and illegal immigration. By 2006 the Hispanic/Latino population alone totaled around 45 million, two-thirds of Mexican origin, outnumbering the 41 million African Americans. Several million Asians arrived, mostly from China, South Korea, India, and Southeast Asia, and immigrants also came from Europe, the Middle East, the Caribbean, and South Pacific islands, especially Samoa and Tonga. Some immigrants labored for meager wages in crowded sweatshops in big cities, where bosses often allowed workers only one or two breaks during their shift and ignored city safety regulations. Chinese sewed clothing in New York City, and Mexicans did the same in Los Angeles. At the same time, immigration marginalized Native Americans. While many lived in cities, others remained isolated on reservations. Some joined movements to assert their rights, often seeking a return of lands seized by white settlers generations earlier. While a few tribes achieved prosperity by operating gambling casinos, most Native Americans remained poor.

Gender Relations

After the 1960s women's issues became more prominent. In the 1950s few women worked for high pay, colleges imposed strict quotas on female applicants, married women could not borrow money in their own names, there was no legal concept of sexual harassment, and men often joked of keeping women "barefoot and pregnant." By the early twenty-first century conditions had changed dramatically, but it took a long struggle for gender equality. Beginning in the 1960s many women joined feminist movements demanding equal legal rights with men and improved economic status. In 1963 Betty Friedan's (1921–2006) passionate book, *The Feminine Mystique*, identified women's core problem as a stunting of their growth by a patriarchal society and unfulfilling housework. With slogans such as "Sisterhood Is Powerful," women came together in groups, such as the National Organization for Women (NOW), founded by Friedan in 1966, to fight for expanded opportunities. Thanks in part to feminists' efforts, the median income of women workers climbed to 70 percent of that of men, and the number of women with paid work more than doubled between 1960 and 2000. Women now held governorships and federal cabinet posts, served in Congress, sat on the Supreme Court, and, as Hillary Clinton's campaign demonstrated, were serious candidates for president. Clinton became Obama's Secretary of State, the third woman to hold that influential post. By the twenty-first century more women than men finished secondary school and attended universities, some joining highly paid, traditionally male occupations such as law, university teaching, engineering, and medicine. Women pursuing satisfying, well-paid careers, running for political office, and enjoying personal freedoms unimaginable to their great grandmothers owed their gains largely to the feminist movement and its male supporters. However, most employed women struggled to juggle work with family and housekeeping responsibilities. One young mother of two complained in the 1990s that "it's like twenty-four hours a day you're working. My day never ends."[11] Moreover, sexual harassment in the workplace, stalking, and rape remained serious problems. Scholars wrote of a "feminization of poverty" as many women headed single-parent families.

Social and legal changes affected both women and men. As divorce became easier and more common, by the 1990s over half of all marriages ended in divorce. Single-parent households grew more frequent, and increasingly, as in Europe, many men and women never married, often living with partners out of wedlock. Americans remained deeply divided on some women's issues, especially abortion, which was long common but illegal in the United States before being declared legal by the Supreme Court in 1973. Americans also disagreed about homosexuality. By the 1960s gay men and lesbians actively struggled to end harassment and legal discrimination, gaining greater acceptance in society, yet the growing numbers who openly acknowledged their sexual identity still faced hostility. During the early twenty-first century Americans quarreled over allowing homosexuals to serve openly in the armed forces, marry, or establish legal partnerships, a pattern of acceptance common in Europe and Canada but opposed by many Christian churches. By 2009 several states had legalized homosexual marriages, while many other states passed laws forbidding it.

Once importers of culture from Europe, Americans became the world's greatest exporters of popular culture products. U.S.-made films, television programs, books, magazines, and sports reached a global audience, and popular music had widespread influence. Various musical styles, including the Broadway musicals of songwriters such as Richard Rogers and Oscar Hammerstein, the blues of singer Billie Holiday and guitarist B. B. King, the jazz of saxophonist John Coltrane and trumpeter Miles Davis, and the country music of singer-songwriters Hank Williams and Dolly Parton, spread far and wide.

Popular Culture

But no music style had the power of rock, which in the 1950s and 1960s helped spark a cultural revolution, especially among youth, in the United States and gained a huge following abroad. The first exhilarating blasts of rock and roll, notably from the white singer Elvis Presley (1935–1977), whose suggestive, hip-swinging performances earned him the nickname "Elvis the Pelvis," and the inventive black guitarist Chuck Berry (b. 1926), defied the Eisenhower era's puritanical emphasis on social and political conformity, often alarming adults. Rock music broke down social barriers by challenging sexual and racial taboos. The first American popular music that appealed across social class boundaries, rock was inspired by black rhythm and blues but also by the country and gospel music of white southerners, and early rock made a powerful statement that young Americans were less divided by race than their parents. Rock became the heart of the youth movement of the 1960s, when albums by key rock musicians, such as the poetic American singer-songwriter Bob Dylan and the British group the Beatles, seemed infused with political meaning. Rock later lost its political edge but, evolving into forms such as punk, grunge, and heavy metal, remained at the heart of U.S. popular music.

The music created by African Americans has also addressed the problems of American life. The soul music in the 1960s, from artists like James Brown and Aretha Franklin, promoted black self-respect and unity, paralleling the messages of black pride movements. In the 1980s rap music emerged out of urban black ghettos to become the cutting-edge, politicized form of Western pop music. An eclectic mix of rock, soul, rhythm and blues, and Caribbean music, rap expresses the tensions of urban black youth. The boastful, often angry tone highlights conflict between white and black, rich and poor, and male and female. Rap musicians have outraged segments of both white society and the black middle class. Musicians in nations around the world have adopted the rap style, often integrating it into their own traditions.

The Canadian Experience

Although they share cultural traditions and a democratic spirit with Americans, Canadians have remained proudly independent of their powerful southern neighbor while nurturing differences from Americans, such as by maintaining two official languages—English and French. Two main parties, one liberal and one conservative, have dominated national elections, but, in contrast to the United States, smaller leftwing and rightwing parties also play key roles, often governing Canadian provinces. The French Canadian nationalist Party Québécois (KAY-be-KWAH) has often governed French-speaking Quebec, which contains a quarter of Canada's population, and periodically holds provincial votes on independence from Canada (see Map 29.2). In 1985 the federal parliament, hoping to preserve a united Canada, recognized Quebec as a distinct society within largely English-speaking Canada and granted it more provincial autonomy. Canadians still debate how much power to allocate to the provinces and how much to the federal government.

English and French Canadians

Canadians, 34 million strong by 2009, cannot ignore their proximity to the United States, which has almost ten times Canada's population and vastly more global power. Former prime minister Pierre Trudeau (troo-DOE) (g. 1968–1984), a French Canadian, complained that sharing a border with the United States was "like sleeping with an elephant. No matter how friendly or even-tempered the beast, one is affected by every twitch and grunt."[12] Most Canadians live within a hundred miles of the U.S. border and thus have easy access to the U.S. mass media. Moreover, Americans own some 20 percent of the Canadian economy. While some Canadians welcome U.S. investment as a spur to economic growth, others resent U.S. domination. In 1994 the North American Free

Canada and the United States

Map 29.2 Canada

The Canadian federation includes eleven provinces stretching from Newfoundland in the east to British Columbia and the Yukon in the west. In 1999 a large part of northern Canada, inhabited chiefly by the Inuit, became the self-governing region of Nunavut.

Interactive Map

Trade Agreement (NAFTA) further bound the Canadian, Mexican, and U.S. economies. Yet, despite usually friendly relations, Canadians have often opposed U.S. foreign policies, including the wars in Vietnam and Iraq.

Economy and Society

Canadians have generally enjoyed prosperity, which has fostered social stability. Agricultural, industrial, and natural resource exports have helped finance rising living standards, while vast oil reserves have enriched western provinces. As a result, Canada has consistently ranked among the top five nations in the annual United Nations Human Development Index of quality of life. Unlike the more individualistic Americans, Canada, influenced by social democratic ideals, built a strong social safety net, including national health insurance. Canadians have generally been more liberal on social and economic issues than Americans, approving same-sex marriage, banning the death penalty, and, in some provinces, decriminalizing marijuana use. Organized religion has had a declining influence in public life. The secularizing trend has been especially notable in Quebec, where the Catholic Church once enjoyed great influence. Even openly homosexual politicians have gained popular support, and Quebec's birth rate, one of the world's highest in the 1940s, has fallen by over half to become one of the world's lowest.

Canadian society has become increasingly diverse by welcoming several million immigrants from all over the world, many from Asia and the Caribbean. In 2005 one of those immigrants, Haitian-born Michaelle Jean, a television journalist in Quebec, became Canada's first female governor general, the official head of state as the representative of the British monarch. Rather than following the American "melting pot" ideal, Canadian laws, especially the Multiculturalism Act of 1988, allow ethnic minorities to maintain their cultures and languages. But some Canadians, resenting the recognition of Portuguese-Canadians or Chinese-Canadians, prefer unhyphenated Canadians. Canadians have also recognized the rights of the Native Americans, known as the "First Nations," who have pressed land claims. To address the desire for autonomy of the Inuit, or Eskimo, people of the Arctic region, in 1999 the federal government transformed much of northern Canada into the self-governing territory of Nunavut (NOO-nuh-voot). Canadians are still debating how much to think of themselves as English or French or Inuit Canadians and how much to live comfortably with multiple identities.

The Pacific Basin Societies

The diverse societies scattered around the Pacific Basin experienced major changes as they adjusted to a new world. In the two largest, most populous countries, Australia and New Zealand, the majority population, descended from European, mainly British and Irish, settlers, had long identified with western European society, building economies that closely resembled those of the industrial West. Australia became one of the world's most affluent nations, known to its people as the "lucky country" because of its abundant resources and high living standards. Thanks in part to a comprehensive system of social welfare, health care, and education, Australians forged a quality of life that usually places the nation near the top in the annual United Nations Human Development Reports. However, the nation has also faced a chronic high unemployment rate and areas of persisting poverty. In addition, feminists complain that men dominate government, business, and churches and that women are less influential than in most Western nations. Nonetheless, women's organizations have won considerable gender equity.

Australia's 22 million people are increasingly diverse. In 1973 the federal government, seeking better relations with Asian nations, abandoned restrictions on nonwhite immigration—known as the "white Australia" policy—that had been in place since 1901. The shift to a policy based on skills stimulated immigration from Asia and the Middle East; as a result, predominantly Asian neighborhoods developed in major cities. Newcomers from Europe also continued to arrive. For example, one of the major cities, Melbourne, boasted the world's largest Greek emigrant population. Eventually nearly a quarter of Australia's people were born abroad. Race relations also improved as Aborigines, often poor and facing discrimination, gained some self-determination and land rights for their tribal territories. As a result, one group was able to block a dam project in the 1990s that threatened tribal land. Yet, those Aborigines living in run-down city neighborhoods have struggled in the largely white-owned urban economy. Moreover, occasional attacks on Arab and Indian immigrants by drunken white youth showed that racism had not been eliminated.

Changing global conditions forced new economic thinking. With an economy based primarily on the export of minerals, wheat, beef, and wool, Australia needed secure outside markets. But the formation of the European Community and NAFTA threatened traditional markets in Europe and North America, raising questions about the nation's link to Britain. In a 1995 referendum, 55 percent of Australians supported remaining a constitutional monarchy under the British queen. Yet, Britain was far away, while Asia was, as Australians put it, the "near north." Australians therefore

Australian Society

Lion Dance In recent decades, many Asians have settled in Australia. This Chinese lion's dance, in Melbourne's large Chinatown, celebrates the Chinese New Year.

Glenn Hunt/AAP

established closer trade and investment links to Southeast Asia, East Asia, and the Pacific islands, so that, by 2000, Asian nations accounted for some 60 percent of Australia's export market.

New Zealand

New Zealanders had long cultivated their British heritage and British patronage, but they now had to forge strategic and economic connections within the Asia-Pacific region. The economy relied heavily on tourism and the export of agricultural products, mostly to Britain. Suffering from a stumbling economy and jolted by Britain's membership in the European Community, New Zealand cultivated close relations with the United States. However, these relations cooled after New Zealand refused to allow nuclear-armed U.S. ships to make visits to its ports. New Zealand then fostered economic cooperation with nearby Asian and Pacific countries, and by 2000 these countries accounted for one-third of the nation's trade. While experiencing rising unemployment, New Zealanders were supported by an elaborate social welfare system. Owing in part to expanded educational opportunities, women gained new economic roles and served in politics. In 1999 Helen Clark (b. 1950), a former university professor, became the nation's first female prime minister. Closer ties to the Pacific region also resulted in increased immigration from Asia and the Pacific islands. The government also recognized the land rights of, and worked to end discrimination against, the native Maori minority, who sought to maintain their Polynesian culture while adding modern economic skills.

The Pacific Islands

While Australians and New Zealanders had long enjoyed independence, the decolonization of the Pacific islands, spurred by the United Nations, had to wait until the 1960s. Between 1962 and 1980 nine independent Pacific nations were formed in Polynesia and Melanesia, and in 1990 the United States gave up control of some of its Micronesian territories. The new states ranged from republics such as Fiji to kingdoms like Tonga to groupings such as the Federated States of Micronesia. Not all Pacific islanders, however, became independent. Some French-ruled islands, such as Tahiti and New Caledonia, became semiautonomous French territories with representation in the French parliament, but many islanders resented what they considered a disguised French colonialism. Most independent islands retained close ties to their former colonizer, as Micronesia did with the United States. Pacific islanders usually remained dependent on fishing, tourism, and the export of mineral and agricultural products to Japan, the United States, Australia, and New Zealand.

Islanders cooperated on common issues. For example, they formed regional organizations to promote everything from duty-free trade to art festivals, and they fought high-technology fishing fleets from industrialized nations that threatened their own low-technology fishing. To oppose nuclear weapons testing, they joined with Australia and New Zealand to declare the Pacific a nuclear-free zone. The international Law of the Sea Treaty gave the islands more control of adjacent sea beds, and hence their minerals. However, some problems have defied solution. Thanks to rising sea levels, which threaten low-lying atolls and coastal plains, many islanders will have to relocate over the next century. The Tuvalo islands in the central Pacific, home to 11,000 people and on average only three feet above sea level, will be inundated by 2050.

The Pacific islanders have held on to some indigenous traditions while also adapting to social and political change. While most islanders have become Christian, some pre-Christian customs have remained important. For example, although Western Samoa, first ruled by Germany and then by New Zealand, has an elected parliament, adopted from the West, clan chiefs still govern the villages, as they have for centuries. But poverty has fostered migration to island cities, such as Suva in Fiji and Pago Pago in American Samoa, and emigration to Australia, New Zealand, Hawaii, and the mainland United States. More Samoans and Cook Islanders live abroad than at home, and thousands of Tongans reside in California. The money sent back by migrants has become a valuable source of income. Some islands have also experienced ethnic or regional conflict over political power and scarce land. Occasional military coups have rocked Fiji, resulting from ten-

SECTION SUMMARY

- On average, U.S. residents are among the wealthiest in the world, yet in recent decades many industrial jobs have been moved overseas and the gap between rich and poor has grown wider, with the former often living in suburbs and the latter left behind in inner cities.

- In the 1950s, political conservatism dominated the United States and a large number of children were born; in the 1960s, liberalism was prominent, especially among the rebellious youth; since the 1970s, conservatism has been generally dominant, though the country is sharply divided politically; and the 2008 election of Barack Obama launched a new era.

- After 1945 African Americans gained legal rights through the civil rights movement, immigrants made America more diverse, women increasingly entered the work force, and gays and lesbians became more visible but still struggled for equal rights.

- American culture became popular around the world, particularly music such as rock, which energized youth in the 1950s and 1960s, and rap, which initially expressed the radical political sentiments of African Americans but became watered down in the twenty-first century.

- While Canada's culture and economy are strongly influenced by the United States, in many ways Canada resembles western Europe, with a strong social safety net and a more liberal attitude on social issues.

- Australia and New Zealand have maintained their traditional ties with Britain but have also traded increasingly with their Asian neighbors, while many Pacific islands have gained independence from former colonizers but still face challenges such as rising sea levels, poverty, and ethnic conflict.

sions between the descendants of Indian immigrants, nearly half of the population, and the native Fijians, who fear that Indians want to diminish the role of traditional Fijian chiefs and challenge tribal rights to land.

POLITICAL CHANGE IN LATIN AMERICA AND THE CARIBBEAN

Why have democracy and economic development proved to be difficult goals in Latin America?

The Latin American and Caribbean peoples (see Map 29.3) had a different experience than North Americans and Pacific Basin societies. Social inequality, economic underdevelopment, and the demands for change often created a pressure cooker, generating revolutionary and progressive political movements in impoverished villages and shantytowns. Sometimes leftists gained power, launching reforms, though only in Cuba did they remain in power for decades. A few Latin American countries and most small Caribbean islands enjoyed a consistent democratic tradition; elsewhere, however, military leaders or autocratic civilians often dominated governments. Most governments, whether democratic or dictatorial, proved unable to eliminate their nation's major problems.

Despotisms, Democracies, and the United States

Latin American governments struggled to raise living standards and expand political participation. Some paternalistic but authoritarian reformers mobilized workers and peasants for change, but they also failed to empower the people or significantly improve their lives. The charismatic Juan Peron **(puh-RONE)** (1895–1974), a former army officer, admirer of Benito Mussolini, and hypnotic public speaker, who was elected Argentina's president in 1946, was a major autocratic reformer who marginalized the legislature and crushed opposition (see Chronology: Latin America and the Caribbean, 1945–Present). With help from his hugely popular wife, Evita Peron (1919–1952), a radio and stage actress from a poor family and a proponent of social justice, the nationalistic Peron's regime won the support of workers and the middle class by emphasizing industrialization and buying up banks, insurance companies, railroads, and shipping companies often owned by unpopular foreign interests. Evita promoted women's issues, including voting rights. After Evita's death in 1952, corruption, growing unemployment, inflation, strikes, and human rights abuses led to Peron's overthrow in 1955. Peron returned to power briefly in 1973–1974, but otherwise the military mostly ruled Argentina from the 1950s through 1983, often killing opponents. Yet Peron's followers sustained a Peronist movement with a working-class base that often governed the nation after the restoration of democracy.

Argentina

Rightwing and leftwing forces have jockeyed for power in Latin America. In the majority of countries from the 1950s through the late 1980s, rightwing military governments and despots ruled, suppressing labor unions, student protesters, and democracy activists to maintain stability. Some rightwing governments, especially in Central American countries such as El Salvador and Guatemala, organized death squads to assassinate dissident peasants, liberal clergy, teachers, and journalists deemed threats to the regime. Despite the repression, leftwing movements increased their strength. By 1979 the Sandinistas, a revolutionary movement led by Marxists, defeated the long-standing dictatorship and gained control of Nicaragua. In 1970 an even more radical movement, the Shining Path, emerged in Peru; its leaders, half of them women, mixed Maoist ideas with a call to emancipate the impoverished Indians. Their rebellion terrorized Peruvians and brought the country to its knees before finally being crushed in the early 1990s.

Left-Right Conflicts

During the later 1980s, with rightwing rule largely discredited by being unable or unwilling to address mass poverty, many nations turned to democracy and free markets under centrist or moderate leftist leaders. But in most cases they were unable to resolve the severe problems or diminish social equalities. Some nations also faced racial and ethnic tensions. The large Indian communities in Bolivia, Peru, Colombia, Mexico, and Guatemala, often allied with the left, increasingly sought equal rights, a fairer share of the wealth, and recognition of their cultures and aspirations. In 2005, for example, chronic resentment by Bolivia's Indian majority led to the election, as president, of Evo Morales (b. 1959), a former small-town soccer player of humble origins who had led a movement of coca farmers fighting a white-dominated government and U.S. opposition to coca growing. At the

Democratization

Map 29.3 Modern Latin America and the Caribbean

Latin America includes the nations of Central and South America and those Caribbean societies that are Spanish-speaking, including Cuba and the Dominican Republic. Brazil, Argentina, and Mexico are the largest Latin American nations. The peoples, mostly English or French speaking, of the small Caribbean islands also formed independent states.

Interactive Map

ruins of an ancient temple, Morales took part in a spiritual ceremony steeped in the pre-Inca traditions of his Aymara people. Walking barefoot up the pyramid steps, he donned a traditional tunic and cap and accepted a gold and silver baton from Aymara priests, then promised to "seek equality and justice" for the poor and do away with the vestiges of the Spanish colonial past. However, his efforts to redistribute wealth and power from the white minority, reshape the political system, and pursue nationalistic economic policies generated conflict within Bolivia and U.S. opposition.

Leftist Resurgence

By the later 1990s, as disillusionment with capitalism increased, the left regained the political initiative, working largely within a democratic context. Mobilizing workers and peasants, who had benefited little from the country's oil wealth, the former general Hugo Chavez (b. 1954) was elected president of oil-rich Venezuela and introduced socialist policies that alienated the wealthy and middle class, who organized mass protests against his regime. However, poor Venezuelans supported his marginalization of the congress and control of the courts. Chavez called his policies the Bolivaran Revolution, linking them to the nineteenth-century, Venezuelan-born liberator. But the United States moved to isolate the dictatorial, pro-Cuba Chavez regime and support the opposition. Chavez lambasted U.S. president George W. Bush, provided aid and oil to other Latin Americans, and tightened his grip on politics and the media, but declining oil prices in 2009 threatened his foreign policies and domestic support. Elsewhere, voters desperate for more equitable policies also elected pragmatic leftist leaders in countries such as Argentina, Brazil, Chile, Ecuador, Uruguay, and El Salvador. These leaders often began the process of prosecuting the human rights violations perpetrated under military rule. But whether imported economic ideas from the left or the right will work for Latin Americans remained unclear.

Latin Americans also had to deal with the United States, which has had a powerful presence in that area. Referring to longtime U.S. economic leverage, a leftist Nicaraguan leader lamented that his country's "function was to grow sugar, cocoa and coffee for the United States; we served the dessert at the imperialist dining table."[13] The United States served not only as the neighborhood bully at times but also as a leading trading partner, a major source of investment capital, a supplier of military and economic assistance, and an inspiration to the region's democrats and free market enthusiasts. Some Latin American leaders supported U.S. foreign policies, and U.S. popular culture, particularly films and music, reached a huge audience, influencing local cultures. Moreover, millions of people seeking a better life have moved to the United States legally or illegally. In 1999 the United States gained favor by transferring control over the Panama Canal to Panama, yet U.S. military bases remained along the canal, a symbol of U.S. regional power.

Under the banner of anticommunism, the United States often intervened in Latin American and Caribbean countries, arousing much local resentment. For example, in 1954 a force led by exiled Guatemalan military officers, covertly organized, armed, and trained by the U.S. Central Intelligence Agency (CIA), overthrew a democratically elected reformist government, led chiefly by liberals and socialists, that American leaders accused of being communist. The government angered U.S. business interests by implementing land reform and encouraging leftist labor unions. The powerful United Fruit Company controlled much of the Guatemalan economy, especially the banana plantations, and had close ties to officials in the Eisenhower administration. The removal of the democratic regime cheered wealthy Guatemalans and U.S. corporations, but the new Guatemalan leaders formed death squads that killed over 200,000 Guatemalans, especially poor Indian peasants and workers, over the next three decades. By 1990, when the repression diminished, 90 percent of Guatemalans still lived in poverty, and one-third of them lacked adequate food.

The successful ousting of the Guatemalan government encouraged U.S. leaders to use their power elsewhere, offering military assistance and advice to friendly governments against the challenge of revolutionary movements in El Salvador, Honduras, and Colombia. The United States also used covert operations to undermine or overthrow governments deemed too left-leaning in Brazil (1964), Chile (1973), and Nicaragua (1989). The American public was often unaware of the covert activities until years later. Sometimes the United States sent in military force, as in the Dominican Republic (1965) and Grenada (1982). Not all interventions were inspired by anticommunism. In 1990 U.S. troops invaded Panama to remove and arrest the dictator Manuel Noriega (b. 1940), a longtime U.S. ally and well-paid CIA informant who was also implicated in human rights abuses and smuggling narcotics into the United States. Then in 1994 U.S. troops were sent to Haiti to support a reform government that had replaced a brutal dictatorship. U.S. troops remained in Haiti promoting stability as leftwing and rightwing forces intermittently battled for control, leaving Haitians poorer and more desperate.

United States and Latin America

The Legacy of Revolution: Mexico and Cuba

The Mexican Revolution in the early twentieth century inspired hopes of reducing social inequality, but the nation's leaders soon turned to emphasizing economic growth over uplifting the poor

Mexico

CHRONOLOGY
Latin America and the Caribbean, 1945–Present

1946–1955 Government of Juan Peron in Argentina

1954 CIA overthrow of Guatemalan government

1959 Triumph of Fidel Castro in Cuba

1962 Cuban missile crisis

1964–1985 Military government in Brazil

1973 Overthrow of Chilean government

1973–1989 Military government in Chile

1979–1989 Sandinista government in Nicaragua

1983 Restoration of Argentina's democracy

1990 U.S. invasion of Panama

1994 Formation of NAFTA

1998 Economic collapse in many nations

2000 Election of President Vicente Fox in Mexico

2002 Election of President Lula da Silva in Brazil

majority. Even today, in southern states where revolutionaries once promised to bring liberty and justice, peasant men, wearing traditional white cotton pants and shirt, still use a machete to cultivate their tiny plots of corn. Although Mexico's limited democracy offered regular elections, one party, the Party of Revolutionary Institutions (PRI), controlled the elections, often resorting to voter fraud. A coalition of factions ranging from left to right and led by businessmen and bureaucrats, the PRI fostered stability for decades while deflecting challenges to its power monopoly. Although it usually co-opted or arrested opponents, in 1968 it ordered police to open fire on a large demonstration, killing hundreds of university students and other protesters.

By the 1980s the PRI began to falter as leftist and rightwing parties, which struggled to overcome the PRI's vast power and wealth, made some national gains. In the early 1990s a peasant revolt in a poor southern state, Chiapas, revealed starkly the PRI's failure to redress rural poverty, and in 2000 the election of a non-PRI president, Vicente Fox, a pro-U.S. rancher and free market conservative, ended the seven-decades-long PRI monopoly on federal power. However, Fox proved unable to foster much economic or social change, while the PRI still held power in many states and enjoyed a national power base. Gradually a more open and pluralistic political system emerged, with stronger leftist and rightwing parties contending with the PRI for support. In 2008 elections another conservative edged out a leftist for the presidency, solidifying a multiparty system.

Mexico's economic system also gradually opened, but without diminishing poverty. For decades the PRI had mixed capitalism with a strong government role. However, the collapse of world oil prices in the 1980s damaged development prospects, since oil was the major foreign revenue source, and led to replacing protectionist policies with open markets. In 1994, after the North American Free Trade Agreement (NAFTA) helped integrate the U.S. and Mexican economies, many U.S.-owned factories opened on the Mexican side of the border. The majority of the new workers were poorly paid young women, usually housed in crowded dormitories or flimsy shacks, who often complained of harassment or assault by male workers or managers. Elsewhere Mexicans have lost jobs; peasant corn farmers were unable to compete with highly subsidized U.S. farmers. By 2000 half of the 100 million Mexicans lived on $4 a day or less, and the bottom 20 percent of Mexicans earned only 3.5 percent of the country's personal income. Even the urban middle class has felt the economic pain as wages stagnate. Whereas in 1980 Mexico's economy was nearly four times larger than South Korea's, by 2005 a dynamic South Korea had pushed ahead. At the same time, Mexico's population quadrupled between 1940 and 2000. Because of poverty and overpopulation, thousands of desperate Mexicans continue to cross the border to the United States each year, legally or illegally, in search of a better life. Others have taken up growing or smuggling illegal drugs, and bloody wars between rival drug cartels have made life dangerous in many districts.

Castro and Cuba

Primary Source: Free Trade and the Decline of Democracy Read a cogent critique by Ralph Nader, a consumer advocate and political activist, of international free trade agreements.

Castroism Innovative socialist policies introduced by Fidel Castro to stimulate economic development in Cuba while tightly controlling its population.

In contrast to Mexico, Cuba, led by Fidel Castro (b. 1927), built a society dominated by a powerful communist government. Castro, a onetime amateur baseball star who was nearly signed by a U.S. professional team but instead became a lawyer, came to power in 1959, the victor of a revolution against a corrupt U.S.-supported dictator. Although the son of a rich sugar planter, Castro allied with the Cuban Communist Party and promised to introduce radical change, prompting many thousands of affluent Cubans to flee to the nearby United States. In 1961 the United States moved to isolate and then overthrow his regime by organizing a military force of Cuban exiles that landed on a Cuban beach known as the Bay of Pigs. But the invasion, poorly planned and enjoying little popular support in Cuba, was routed—a humiliation for the United States. Castro became a firm Soviet ally, igniting even more U.S. opposition and soon precipitating the Cuban missile crisis. In 1962 U.S. air surveillance of Cuba discovered Soviet ballistic missiles with a 2,000-mile range and capable of carrying nuclear warheads. The United States demanded that the missiles be removed, imposed a naval blockade on Cuba, and considered invading the island. With the threat of nuclear confrontation looming, however, the Soviets backed down and removed the missiles, defusing the crisis. In the aftermath, the United States imposed an economic boycott, strongly supported by Cuban exiles, that endured into the twenty-first century, cutting off Cuba from sources of trade and investment.

In the 1960s and 1970s Castro tried innovative socialist policies, often known as **Castroism**, to stimulate economic development while also tightly controlling its population. Castro called capitalism "repugnant, filthy, gross, alienating because it causes war, hypocrisy and competition"[14]; yet his own policies generated little surplus food and few consumer goods. Despite valiant efforts, Cubans also largely failed to diversify their sugar-based economy. Nonetheless, Castroism improved the life of the working classes by building schools and clinics, mounting literacy campaigns, and promoting equality for long-marginalized Afro-Cubans and women. By the mid-1980s Cuba had the lowest infant mortality and highest literacy rates and life expectancy in Latin America, with its citizens living as long as North Americans and ten years longer than Mexicans and Brazilians. Cuba also had nearly as many doctors per population as the United States. Moreover, in contrast to some Latin American dictatorships, the Cuban government did not form death squads

Castro Addressing Crowd A spellbinding orator, the Cuban leader, Fidel Castro, often recruited support for his government and policies by speaking at large rallies.

or murder dissidents. However, government agencies monitored citizens and their opinions, and Castro placed limits on free expression, jailing or harassing those who defied the ban, including brave writers, homosexuals, and human rights and free speech advocates. Seeking political freedom, better-paying jobs, or higher living standards, several hundred thousand Cubans have fled over the years to the United States.

Castro exchanged dependence on the United States for dependence on the USSR, which poured billions of dollars of aid into the country. With the collapse of the USSR, however, Castro lost his patron, and since then Cuba has struggled. With the country having few markets or sources of capital, the social welfare system cracked, and the economy crumbled despite introducing some market forces. Yet, frustrating his opponents, Castro remained in power for fifty years. However, in 2008 an ailing Castro turned over leadership to his brother Raul Castro (b. 1931), who offered some cautious reforms, including leasing some state-owned land to private farmers, and hinted at more flexibility in domestic and foreign affairs. Critics of U.S. policy, including most U.S. allies, have opposed the embargo, arguing that it helps Castro by reinforcing anti-U.S. feelings and discrediting dissidents. In 2009 new U.S. President Barack Obama made it easier for U.S.-based Cubans to visit the island. Remembering American domination from 1898 to 1959, many Cubans, while desiring a freer system, remain wary of the United States.

Dictatorship and Democracy: Brazil and Chile

Few Latin American nations have had as much promise and experienced as many problems as Brazil and Chile. Occupying half of the South American continent and with a population of nearly 200 million, Brazil is Latin America's colossus, with its largest economy. From the mid-1940s to the mid-1960s the nation, despite economic crises, maintained a democratic government. In 1961 Joao Goulart **(jao joo-LART)** (1918–1976), a populist reformer supported by leftists, assumed the presidency, but the economy stumbled, and efforts to organize the impoverished peasants and rural workers antagonized powerful landlords. Seeking to impose order, the military overthrew Goulart in 1964 and ruled for the next two decades under a harsh dictatorship, which arrested some 40,000 opponents. Fearing a communist takeover, the United States had encouraged the military coup, while Brazilian industrialists, businessmen, planters, and affluent urbanites welcomed the change. Between 1964 and 1985 U.S.-supported authoritarian governments gave priority to economic growth and national security. Relying on brutal repression, they imposed censorship, outlawed political parties, and banned strikes and collective bargaining. Rightwing vigilante groups and death squads killed up to 100 dissidents a month and tortured countless others, among them labor leaders and slum dwellers.

The generals imposed a capitalist economic model recommended by American advisers. For a decade the economy boomed, eliciting American praise of the "Brazilian miracle" as annual growth rates averaged 10 percent between 1968 and 1974 and exports soared. The policies promoted a

Brazilian Dictatorship

major shift in exports from natural resources, such as coffee, to manufactured goods, and the industrialization relied heavily on foreign investment, technology, and markets. The United States and international lending agencies also poured in $8 billion in aid. But the "miracle" depended on low wages and redistributing income upward to the rich and middle class, confirming the local saying that there is no justice for the poor. The top 10 percent of people enjoyed 75 percent of the income gain, while half of all households lived below the poverty line. While many people went barefoot and dressed in rags, Brazil made and exported shoes. Brazilian governments also encouraged land speculators and foreign corporations to open up the vast Amazon basin, the world's largest tropical rain forest and river system. The virgin forest was rapidly stripped for logging, farming, mining, and ranching, displacing many of the 200,000 Indians who lived off its resources and destabilizing the local environment.

Brazilian Democracy

By 1980 the "miracle" was fading as Brazil experienced an inflation rate of over 100 percent, a huge balance of payments deficit, a massive foreign debt, and sagging industrial production. Meanwhile, numerous Brazilians demanded democracy, and the Catholic Church criticized human rights violations and advocated for social justice. In 1985 democracy returned with the election of a civilian president. However, under the successive democratic governments led by moderate reformers, many problems remained unresolved, since leaders feared another military coup. Inflation soared to 2,500 percent by 1994. When landless peasants seized land, well-connected landowners hired gunmen to harass them. In addition, social inequities such as school dropout rates, malnutrition, bankrupt public health services, homelessness, and debt slavery grew. Brazil maintained one of the world's most unequal income distributions: the wealthiest 1 percent of people earned the same percentage of national income as the poorest 50 percent. As a result, many Brazilians became disillusioned with democracy.

Although the economy revived in the later 1990s, Brazilians, wanting further reform, turned to the political left. In 2002 they gave leftist candidates 80 percent of the vote and elected as president socialist labor leader Luis Ignacio da Silva (b. 1944), known as Lula, a former metalworker and longtime dissident. While Lula has fostered dramatic economic growth, and some observers compare Brazil to dynamic Southeast Asian nations such as Malaysia, Singapore, and Thailand, peasant and worker groups believe that Lula's moderate economic policies go too far in pleasing financial interests and international lenders, and that he has done too little for the poor and the environment. Yet, the booming economy, growing manufacturing, and discovery of offshore oil have given Brazil regional and international clout and restored national self-confidence. Brazil became a major player in the G-20 group of key industrial nations. Brazilians have often shared an optimistic outlook because of the nation's size and economic potential, reflected in the saying that "God is a Brazilian." But a perennial local joke reflects cynicism: "Brazil, Country of the Future, but the future never comes."[15]

Reform in Chile

Chileans, like Brazilians, tried a succession of strategies, from reform to dictatorship to democracy, to foster development. Chileans had enjoyed a long tradition, unusual in Latin America, of elected democratic governments sustained by a large middle class, high rates of literacy and urbanization, and multiple political parties. Nonetheless, a wealthy elite of businessmen, military officers, and landowners held political power and suppressed labor unrest. Chile depended on the export of minerals, especially copper. By the 1960s it was divided politically between the right, center, and left and had a stagnant economy, with two-thirds of Chileans earning under $200 a year. Chile shifted direction with the 1970 elections. Six liberal, socialist, and communist parties united in a coalition, the Popular Unity, supported by small businessmen, the urban working class, and peasants. Their winning presidential candidate, Salvador Allende (ah-YEN-dee) (1908–1973), promised a "Chilean road" to socialism, with red wine and meat pies, through constitutional means in a parliamentary democracy. His regime took over banks and a copper industry that had been dominated by powerful U.S. corporations, while land reform broke up underutilized ranches and divided the land among the peasant residents. Allende's government supported the labor unions and provided the urban shantytowns with health clinics and better schools. Both employment and economic production soared. The Popular Unity also fostered a Chilean cultural renaissance, arguing that American magazines, recordings, and films had overwhelmed Chilean-produced cultural products. A pro-Allende cultural organization protested that "Our folklore, our history, our customs, our way of living and thinking are being strangled [by] the uncontrolled invasion [of the U.S. media and popular culture]."[16]

Although democracy flourished and Allende enjoyed growing popularity, rapid reforms produced shortages of luxury goods, fostering middle-class resentment. Moreover, Allende's opponents controlled the mass media and judiciary and dominated the congress. The U.S. president, Richard Nixon, worried about Allende's friendship with Cuba's Fidel Castro and feared that Allende's socialism without revolution could spread, threatening U.S. power and economic interests. The United

States therefore mounted an international economic embargo on Chilean exports, while the CIA spread untrue rumors, helped assassinate pro-Allende military officers, and organized strikes to paralyze the economy.

In 1973 a U.S.-supported military coup overthrew Allende, who died while defending the presidential palace. The military imposed a brutal military dictatorship, led by General Agusto Pinochet (ah-GOOS-toh pin-oh-CHET) (b. 1915), that arrested some 150,000 Allende supporters and detained and tortured hundreds of political prisoners for years. The regime murdered thousands of dissidents, sometimes in front of other prisoners held in the national stadium. Thousands of Chileans fled the country. The junta forbade labor unions and strikes, prohibited free speech and political parties, restored nationalized U.S. property, and publicly burned books and records produced by leftist Chileans. Advised by U.S. economists, Pinochet shifted to a free enterprise economy, similar to military-ruled Brazil's, that generated growth and moderate middle-class prosperity purchased at the cost of a monumental foreign debt and environmental degradation. But little of this wealth trickled down to the poor, whose living standards deteriorated. By the later 1980s, unemployment had skyrocketed to 30 percent, and some 60 percent of people were poor. Two observers wrote that Pinochet's Chile "remained a dual society of winners and losers. The rich, roaring through traffic in their expensive sedans, seemed to mock those left behind, trapped in fuming buses."[17]

However, a severe economic crisis undermined the regime's legitimacy, and in 1989 escalating social tensions and political protests prompted the junta to hold an election. The resulting center-left governments, often headed by presidents from Allende's Socialist Party, retained free enterprise while boosting health, housing, education, and social spending. The poverty sector has been reduced by half, unemployment has plummeted, and tax increases and increased welfare have not stifled the annual economic growth of about 10 percent. Chile has become the most prosperous Latin American economy, enjoying a stable democratic system. While leaders have sought closer economic ties with the United States, many Chileans remain bitter toward the Americans for having helped perpetuate a brutal military regime.

Rise and Fall of Chilean Military Rule

SECTION SUMMARY

- In Latin America, rightwing and leftwing movements competed for power; rightwing movements were dominant from the 1950s through the 1980s, and moderates and leftists such as Venezuela's Hugo Chavez gained more power in the 1990s.

- Many Latin Americans resented U.S. interference in their economies and support for the overthrow of leftist governments, while others welcomed the U.S. example of democracy and free trade.

- The Mexican Revolution led to decades of single-party rule that failed to significantly help the poor, and a reformist president elected in 2000 also failed to improve their lot. Many Mexicans crossed the U.S. border in search of a better life.

- Under Castro, communist Cuba has attempted to control its people but has also provided excellent medical care and education; however, the withdrawal of aid from the USSR in 1991 and the U.S. embargo have left its economy struggling.

- Under a brutal U.S.-supported military dictatorship, Brazil enjoyed a period of impressive growth but then experienced extreme inflation and increasing gaps between rich and poor; democracy returned in the mid-1980s, and the economy recovered in the late 1990s.

- Alarmed by the popularity of a democratically elected leftist government in Chile, the United States supported a 1973 coup there as well as the brutal military dictatorship that resulted, which rewarded the wealthy and further impoverished the poor, and which was replaced by a democratic government in 1989.

CHANGING LATIN AMERICAN AND CARIBBEAN SOCIETIES

How have Latin American and Caribbean cultures been dynamic?

The societies of Latin America and the Caribbean, while facing daunting economic problems, have had social and cultural patterns different from those of North America and the Pacific Basin. Most have still emphasized export of traditional natural resources such as oil, sugar, coffee, bananas, wool, and copper. The Spanish-speaking nations, Portuguese-speaking Brazil, and the English-, Dutch-, and French-speaking Caribbean societies, being derived from varied mixes

U.S. Factory in Mexico   Since the 1980s growing numbers of U.S. companies have relocated industrial operations to Mexico, building many factories along the Rio Grande River that separates Mexico from Texas. In this factory, in Matamoros, Mexico, the mostly female labor force makes toys for the U.S. market.

Keith Dannemiller/Corbis

of peoples and traditions, often have little in common with each other but have fostered dynamic cultural forms that have gained international popularity.

Latin American Economies

Although often enjoying economic growth, no Latin American nations have achieved the affluence common in the industrialized West or eastern Asia. Latin Americans forged rising literacy rates and lowered infant mortality rates, and more people now own televisions, even in poor neighborhoods. Nonetheless, the world prices for most of their natural resource exports have declined over the years, leaving less money for development. As a result, most countries have experienced at best modest growth in per capita income and productivity. To pay the bills and import luxury items, governments have taken out loans, eventually owing billions to international lenders. Rapidly expanding populations, growing at 3 percent a year, add to the social burden and cause environmental problems. Governments have tried to satisfy land hunger, mineral prospecting, and timber exploitation by treating the rain forests as expendable resources.

Income Inequality

Latin America has also suffered severe income inequality. By 2000 the top 10 percent of the population earned half of all income, and 70 percent of the people lived in poverty. Often evading taxes, the small elite class drive Rolls Royces, while the poor lack bus service. In Brazil half of the people had no access to doctors in 2000, even while Rio de Janeiro became the world's plastic surgery capital, with hundreds of cosmetic surgeons catering to wealthy Brazilians and foreigners. In Caracas, Venezuela's capital, one shopping mall that serves the affluent boasts 450 stores, an amusement park, two movie theaters, and a McDonald's. But any customers coming from a slum of open sewers and tin shacks, perched a few miles away on unstable hillsides, would have to pay half a day's wage for a Big Mac. Such inequality fuels support for leftists like Hugo Chavez. To survive, poor peasants in some nations, especially after a decline of world coffee prices, have turned to growing coca and opium for making cocaine and heroin. But the drug trade, largely to the U.S. market, fosters political turbulence and government corruption and profits only a few drug kingpins. In recent years, violence between rival drug cartels has killed many people, and made life dangerous, in Colombia and Mexico.

Rural Economy

Agriculture has remained an economic mainstay, but landholding remains concentrated in a small group of aristocratic families and multinational corporations, such as the U.S.-based United Fruit Company. By the 1990s, 60 percent of all agricultural land was held in large estates and farmed inefficiently, contributing to food shortages. Although modern agriculture requires large investments for machinery, fertilizers, pesticides, and fuel, growing beans and corn to feed hungry peasants supplies inadequate revenue. Hence, vast tracts of rain forests and farms have been transformed into ranches that often raise beef cattle for fast-food outlets in North America and Europe. Latin America remains a food importer, mostly from North America, and malnutrition causes half of all child deaths. In Peru's major city, Lima, hundreds of poor children, known as "fruit birds," desperately compete with stray dogs for spoiled fruit. In Mexico, beef cattle consume more food than the poorest quarter of people.

Rural life has often been marked by hardship. A Brazilian novel captured the hopelessness in the drought-tortured northeast, where, in the 1980s, life expectancy was thirty years, and only two-thirds of children attended school. The herder Fabiano understands that everything prevents his escape from endless poverty: "If he could only put something aside for a few months, he would be able to get his head up. Oh, he had made plans, but that was all foolishness. Ground creepers were never meant to climb. Once the beans had been eaten and the ears of corn gnawed, there was no place to go but to the boss's cash drawer [for a loan]."[18] Unemployment and unprofitable farms generated migration to cities, so that by 2000 Latin America had become the world's most urbanized region, with 75 percent of people living in cities and towns. Living in festering shantytowns, migrants work as shoe-shine boys, cigarette vendors, car washers, or in other poorly paid work. Half the urban population lacks adequate water, housing, sanitation, and social services. But economic growth has also fostered growing middle classes, now a third of the population in Argentina, Chile, and Uruguay and a fifth in Brazil and Mexico.

Beginning in the 1980s many Latin American nations adopted **neoliberalism**, an economic model, encouraged by the United States, that promoted free markets, privatization, and Western investment. Neoliberalism generated growth for a decade, but more people than ever remained stuck in poverty because it failed to curb government corruption, install honest judicial systems, foster labor-intensive industries, or reduce the power of rich elites or the dependence on foreign loans and investment. Free markets have often meant that a few people enjoyed fabulous wealth while most people remained poor. The nation that most ardently adopted neoliberalism, Argentina, saw its economy collapse in 1998; unemployment soared, and by 2001 half of the people lived in poverty. The economy only revived after Argentineans elected pragmatic Peronist leftists into power in 2003. The economy grew by 9 percent a year, and in 2006 the nation paid back the money still owed to the International Monetary Fund, a symbol of recovery as well as of a turn to a more state-oriented economy. However, in 2008 Argentine economic growth dwindled and the Peronists lost some support. But although neoliberalism lost credibility, no other economic model, such as Cuban communism or Allende's socialism with democracy, had widespread support or a record of success in Latin America.

neoliberalism An economic model encouraged by the United States in the developing world that promoted free markets, privatization, and Western investment.

Latin American Societies and Religions

Political and economic change has reshaped gender relations and family life. Although men dominate governments, militaries, businesses, and the Catholic Church, women's movements have reduced gender inequality. Once considered helpless and groomed as girls to be a wife and mother, many women now go out to paid work, some in male-dominated trades. Millions of women earn money selling clothing, handicrafts, and food in small markets or from street stalls. Factories relocating from North America prefer young women, who accept lower wages and have been raised to obey. Family life has also undergone strains. By the 1990s far fewer people married, especially among the poor. But divorce, banned by the Catholic Church, has remained difficult or impossible in some nations, and men still enjoy a double standard in sexual behavior: men's extramarital affairs are tolerated while women's are condemned. Although abortion is illegal everywhere in the region, Latin America has one of the world's highest abortion rates. Homosexuality remains illegal and often punished in many nations, including Castro's Cuba, although Brazil and Costa Rica have fostered more tolerant climates, and liberal Mexico City legalized homosexual marriage in 2009.

Gender Relations

Women have become more active in politics. Between 1945 and 1961 women gained the right to vote, and in 1974 Isabel Peron (b. 1931) of Argentina, a former dancer who married Juan Peron after Evita's death, succeeded her late husband to become the region's first woman president; however, she was ousted in a military coup in 1976. In 1990 Violeta Chamorro (vee-oh-LET-ah cha-MORroe) (g. 1990-1996), a newspaper publisher, was elected president of Nicaragua, serving until 1996. Then in 2006 Chileans elected as president the pediatrician turned socialist politician Michelle Bachelet (BAH-she-let), a divorced mother of three and avowed agnostic whose father was murdered while she and her mother were jailed and tortured during the Pinochet years. Bachelet struck a blow for gender equity by filling half of her cabinet positions with women, including the key defense and economy ministries. Yet, men have often resented women's empowerment, and dictatorships have singled out women activists, such as Bachelet's mother, for torture. During military rule in Argentina, Brazil, and Chile, women political prisoners were kept naked and often raped. However, women have made gains in several areas. In Mexico, the feminist movement challenged inequitable laws and social practices, and in 1974 the Mexican legislature passed a law guaranteeing women equal rights for jobs, salaries, and legal standing. Meanwhile, in Argentina, Brazil, and Uruguay, liberal women's groups made loosening the antiabortion laws a top priority and gained more public support for their cause.

Religion

liberation theology A Latin American movement that developed in the 1960s to make Catholicism more relevant to contemporary society and to address the plight of the poor.

The religious landscape of Latin America has become increasingly diverse. In the 1960s progressive Latin American Roman Catholics developed **liberation theology**, a movement to make the church more relevant to contemporary society and address the plight of the poor. Until the Vatican prohibited the movement in the 1980s, priests favoring liberation theology, especially in Brazil, cooperated with Marxist and liberal groups in working for social justice. Meanwhile, the Roman Catholic hierarchy generally remained conservative. While fewer Catholics attended church, the popular Catholicism of fiestas, pilgrimages, and the family altar flourished. Protestantism, chiefly evangelical or pentecostal, grew rapidly with increased missionary efforts, attracting converts with its participatory, emotional services. By the 1990s Protestants numbered nearly 20 percent of the population in Guatemala and 8 percent in Brazil and Chile. But their active evangelization caused resentment among Catholic leaders.

Social Change and Popular Culture

Brazil has reflected both the region's social changes and its continuities. Between 1920 and 1980 Brazil's urban population grew from about a quarter to three-fifths of Brazilians. Migrants jammed into shantytowns, such as the notorious hillside shacks of Rio de Janeiro, and poverty remained pervasive. By the 1980s three-fourths of Brazilians were malnourished, a third of adults had tuberculosis, a quarter of the population suffered from parasitic diseases, and millions of abandoned or runaway children wandered city streets, living by their wits. Yet, the shantytowns were also well organized, led by community activists and filled with hard-working residents seeking a better future for their children.

Although Brazilians have increasingly tolerated racial and cultural diversity, race remains a central social category. Like the United States, Brazil has never become a true racial "melting pot." Afro-Brazilians often condemn what they view as a racist society steeped in prejudice. Race has often correlated with social status: whites dominate the top brackets, blacks the bottom, and mixed-descent Brazilians fall in between. The flexible Brazilian concept of race, however, differs from the biological concept that North Americans have. Dark-skinned people can aspire to social mobility by earning a good income, since, as a popular local saying claimed, "money lightens." Furthermore, Afro-Brazilian culture has increasingly influenced whites. Over a third of Brazilians, often devout Catholics, have adopted or been interested in one of the Afro-Brazilian faiths that link West African gods or other African traditions with Roman Catholic saints and ceremonies.

The mass media and professional sports have become popular entertainments and diversion from social problems. Immensely popular local television soap operas dominate prime time television viewing, with those from Brazil and Mexico enjoying the widest popularity and gaining a large market around the world. European football, or soccer, has been hugely popular, uniting people of all social backgrounds. From the late 1950s to late 1970s the storied career, fluid play, and magnetic personality of Brazilian superstar Pele (b. 1940), from a poor Afro-Brazilian family, did much to spread the popularity of soccer in the world. Brazilians are especially proud of the international success of their national team, which won the World Cup championships five times between 1958 and 2002 by employing a creative, teamwork-oriented strategy, known as "samba football." A playwright noted how Brazilians obsessively suspend their daily lives during the World Cup, held every four years: "The nation pauses, all of it. Robbers don't rob, ghosts don't haunt, no crimes, no embezzlements, no deaths, no adulteries."[19]

Latin American and Caribbean Cultures

Creative Latin American and Caribbean cultural forms have reached a global audience. Latin American literature flourished, with writers often describing social conditions and government failures. The popular Brazilian novelist Jorge Amado (HOR-hay ah-MAH-do) (1912–2001) blended fantasy, realism, and political commitment, providing insight into life in Brazil's impoverished northeast. Former journalist Gabriel García Márquez (MAHR-kez) (b. 1928), a Nobel Prize–winning Colombian novelist, developed an international audience for imaginative books full of "magic realism," the representation of possible events as if they were wonders and impossible events as commonplace. His most famous work, *One Hundred Years of Solitude* (1970), charts the history of a Colombian house, the family who live in it, and the town where it was located, through wars, changing politics, and economic crises. Some writers tested the tolerance of governments. In Chile, the greatest epic poem of the leftist writer and former diplomat Pablo

Latin American Literature

Neruda (neh-ROO-da) (1904–1973), *General Song,* published in 1950, portrays the history of the entire hemisphere, showing an innocent pre-Columbian America cruelly awakened by Spanish conquest. The poem romanticizes the Incas, extolls the liberators who ended Spanish rule, castigates foreign capitalists (often from the United States) as exploiters, and identifies an emerging mass struggle to establish government by and for the people rather than the rich. In 1971 Neruda won the Nobel Prize for literature, cheering his admirers and distressing those who considered his radical views a threat to society.

Other art forms also developed a social consciousness. The Brazilian New Cinema movement, launched in 1955, tried to replace Hollywood films with films reflecting Brazilian life. One of the movement's finest films, *Black Orpheus* (1959), which gained an international audience, employed a soundtrack of local popular music to examine the annual pre-Lenten Carnival in Rio de Janeiro's shantytowns and the extremes of wealth and poverty revealed in the different ways rich and poor celebrated Carnival. A musical style known as **New Song**, based chiefly on local folk music and closely tied to progressive politics and protest, gained popularity in a half-dozen countries in the 1960s and 1970s, becoming especially influential in Chile. Seeking an alternative to the Anglo-American popular culture favored by elite Chileans, Chilean musicians have used indigenous Andean instruments and tunes. For example, Chilean New Song pioneers such as Violeta Parra (1918–1967) and Victor Jara (HAR-a) (1932–1973) wrote or collected songs that addressed problems of Chilean society such as poverty and inequality (see Profile: Violeta Parra, Chilean New Song Pioneer). Jara put his goal of using music to promote his political goals in song: "I don't sing for the love of singing, Or to show off my voice, But for the statements, Made by my honest guitar."[20]

Because of its leftwing connections, New Song was vulnerable to changing political conditions. In 1970 Chilean New Song musicians had joined the electoral campaign of the leftist Popular Unity coalition. After Salvador Allende won the presidency, he encouraged the media to pay more attention to New Song and less to popular music from the United States. New Song musicians promoted the new government's programs, such as land reform, and some toured abroad to foster foreign support for Allende's government. In 1973, the Chilean military seized power and arrested, executed, or deported most of the New Song musicians while making it illegal to play or listen to New Song. Before thousands of other detainees held in the national stadium, soldiers publicly cut off Victor Jara's fingers, which he had used to play his guitar, and then executed him, symbolizing the death of free expression in Chile and the government's fear of the power of popular culture. New Song faded as a popular music in Latin America, replaced by local forms of rock and by distinctive dance-oriented hybrid musics such as *salsa* (originally from Cuba and Puerto Rico) and *meringue* from Colombia, both of which feature more of a big band sound.

With diverse populations of blacks, whites, and Asians, the Caribbean islands also offered an environment for creative cultural development, especially in religion and music. Jamaica proved particularly fertile soil. **Rastafarianism**, a religion mixing Christian, African, and local influences, arose in Jamaica in 1930 and attracted the urban and rural poor by preaching a return of black people to Africa. The believers revered the emperor Ras Tafari of Ethiopia, the sole uncolonized African state in 1930. Its followers, known as Rastas, adopted distinctive practices, including smoking ganja, an illegal drug, and sporting dreadlocked hair, that outraged Jamaica's elite. The return to Africa became more a spiritual than a physical quest and was mixed with black nationalism. Rastafarianism became identified as a movement of the black poor, seeking to redistribute wealth.

The most influential popular music to come out of the Caribbean had similar mixed origins. In the 1960s Jamaican musicians created **reggae**, a style blending North American rhythm and blues with Afro-Jamaican traditions and marked by a distinctive beat maintained by the bass guitar. The songs of reggae musicians, many of them Rastas, promoted social justice, economic equality, and the freedom of Rastas to live as they liked. The international popularity of reggae owed much to Bob Marley (1945–1981), a Rasta, and his group, the Wailers. Marley became the first international superstar from a developing nation (see Chapter 26). His perceptions were shaped by the status of blacks in Jamaica and the wider world and the degrading conditions of the nonwhite poor. His explosive performances and provocative lyrics offered clear messages: "Slave driver, the table is turned; Catch a fire, you gonna get burned."[21] Like New Song musicians in Chile, Marley and other reggae musicians became involved in politics. Many musicians supported socialist Michael Manley (1924–1997), whose antibusiness policies as prime minister (1972–1978) prompted crippling U.S. sanctions that caused the Jamaican people hardship. After Marley's death from cancer in 1981, many reggae musicians watered down their message. Raunchy party music soon dominated the Caribbean music scenes, but reggae was mixed with rock, rap, and Latin musics to create *reggaeton*, a hugely popular Spanish-language music around Latin America and among Hispanics in the United States.

Latin American Cinema and Music

New Song A Latin American musical movement based chiefly on local folk music and closely tied to progressive politics and protest; became popular in the 1960s and 1970s, especially in Chile.

Caribbean Culture

Rastafarianism A religion from Jamaica that arose in 1930 and that mixed Christian, African, and local influences; Rastafarianism attracted urban slum dwellers and the rural poor by preaching a return of black people to Africa.

reggae A popular music style that began in the 1960s and that blended North American rhythm and blues with Afro-Jamaican traditions; reggae is marked by a distinctive beat maintained by the bass guitar.

VIOLETA PARRA, CHILEAN NEW SONG PIONEER

Born in 1918 to a poor school-teaching family, Violeta Parra was the key figure in the early development of New Song, a Chilean music based chiefly on local folk music, and a multi-talented artist in many mediums, including poetry, filmmaking, tapestry, and painting. Despite her lower-middle-class background, the unconventional Parra lived and dressed like a peasant, wearing her hair long and almost uncombed. Restless and unsuited for marriage, she struggled to find the best outlet for her talents while supporting herself and her two children, Isabel and Angel (AHN-hell). After working as a commercial entertainer, she began collecting, writing, and singing folk music in the 1940s and eventually collected over 3,000 songs. She had clear musical goals: "Every artist must aspire to unite his/her work in a direct contact with the public. I am content to work with the people close to me, whom I can feel, touch, talk and incorporate into my soul." Yet, unlike her protégés, such as Victor Jara, who was deeply engaged in leftwing movements, she never became directly active in politics.

In the early 1950s Parra began Chile's first folk music radio program and recorded her debut album, with simple guitar-accompanied arrangements. She also taught briefly at a southern Chilean university. Parra and her children introduced Andean and African American folk music to Chile after a four-year sojourn in Paris, France, where they encountered musicians from various countries. Settling with her children in Chile's capital city, Santiago, she enjoyed cooking huge pots of beans for the young Chileans who gathered around her to drink wine, discuss Chilean affairs, and exchange songs and stories. A café the Parras opened in Santiago became a meeting place for performers and other Chileans interested in New Song and leftist politics. Parra greatly influenced younger urban musicians, who began learning from her how to play traditional Andean instruments while collecting or writing their own songs, and she provided a role model for other Latin American musicians. As Cuba's top New Song musician, Silvio Rodriguez, claimed: "Violeta is fundamental. Nothing would have been as it is had it not been for Violeta."

Parra's songs displayed two essential elements of later New Song: a base in folk music and concern with Chile's social, economic, and political problems. In "Look How They Tell Us About Freedom," she critiqued the Catholic Church establishment and her nation's ills: "look how the nation's religious and political leaders brag about freedom," she sang, "when they are actually keeping it from us; they boast about tranquility as their power tortures us." Her music attacked such issues as the brutality of the police, the inequalities of capitalism, the exploitation of Indians, and chronic conflict between Latin American governments. At the same time, her songs retained an intense, highly personal, and contemporary mood, which was both Chilean and universal.

Besides being held in contempt by the Chilean elite for her unconventional life and antiestablishment sympathies,

Parra was plagued by poverty and increasing personal problems, including depression. Even her closest friends found her strong, often unpredictable personality difficult, and younger musicians began gravitating to Victor Jara and other New Song figures. Her later songs took on a more philosophical spirit. On her last album in 1966 she recorded her famous farewell, "Gracias a la Vida" (I Give Thanks to Life), a prayerlike expression of gratitude for the richness of life: "I am grateful for the life that has benefited me so much; It has given me both laughter and tears; because of this I can differentiate happiness from sadness; everybody's song is my own song." Not overtly political, the song reflected her identification with the common people and became the underground anthem of many Latin Americans living under dictatorships. As Parra's depression deepened, she committed suicide in 1967. But her career had built a bridge between an older, peasant-based folk tradition and the developing interest of younger musicians. She may have gone, but New Song flowered in Chile and around Latin America.

THINKING ABOUT THE PROFILE

1. Why did her peers consider Parra fundamental to the evolution of New Song in Latin America?

2. How did Parra's life reflect Chilean social and political conditions?

Notes: Quotations from *Studies in Latin American Popular Culture* 2 (1983): 177–178, and 5 (1986): 117; and Nancy E. Morris, *Canto Porque es Necesario Cantar: The New Song Movement in Chile, 1973–1983* (Albuquerque: Latin American Institute, University of New Mexico, Research Paper Series No. 16, July 1984), 6.

Archivo, La Fundacion Violeta Parra

Violeta Parra An influential Chilean musician, folklorist, and artist, Violeta Parra is credited with founding the folk-music-oriented New Song movement, influencing many musicians in Chile and throughout Latin America.

Latin America and the Caribbean in the Global System

The peoples of Latin America and the Caribbean forged closer relations with one another and increased regional economic cooperation and trade, often through trade pacts. The Southern Cone Common Market, formed in 1996, included six South American nations with over 200 million people. Similarly, Caribbean countries cooperated in the Caribbean Community and Common Market, formed in 1973. Latin and North American leaders periodically met in summits to bolster hemispheric solidarity and enhance cooperation on immigration, tariff reduction, suppression of the illegal drug trade, and other issues. Some U.S.–Latin American issues remain contested. While people in the United States have blamed Latin American drug cartels for smuggling illegal drugs, Latin Americans have often resented the U.S. interventions and economic impositions they consider "Yankee imperialism." Latin American and Caribbean leaders have also feared being pushed aside in a world economy dominated by North American, European and, increasingly, Asian nations.

Regional Cooperation

Globalization has influenced Latin Americans and their economies. Asian nations, especially China, Japan, Taiwan, and South Korea, have captured a growing share of Latin America's traditional overseas markets while also investing in Latin America and the Caribbean. Energy-hungry China has been particularly active in seeking resources such as oil from countries like Brazil and Venezuela. In a globalized economy, a hiccup in Tokyo or New York causes a stomach ache in Ecuador or El Salvador. Since most Latin American and Caribbean economies have followed the track of the U.S. economy, they are particularly vulnerable to change in the United States. When the 2001 terrorist attacks diverted U.S. attention to the Middle East, the sudden U.S. disinterest in Latin America and its problems sparked a regional economic downturn that reduced demand for Latin American exports. The economic gains made in the mid-1990s slipped away, and the fifth of Latin America's 500 million people who lived in extreme poverty faced an even grimmer future, which leftists capitalized on to win elections and take power in many countries. Only a few nations, such as Brazil and Chile, had much hope of significantly improving their status in the global system. The 2008–2009 global economic crisis further damaged many Latin American and Caribbean economies as jobs disappeared, tourism declined, and many jobless migrants to North America returned home. Although U.S. exports to Latin America nearly matched those to Europe, by 2008, at the end of the George W. Bush presidency, U.S.–Latin American relations were at their lowest point since the Cold War.

Globalization

Buffeted by political changes and economic crises, Latin Americans search for their identity and role in a world dominated by other societies. Calling on leaders to recognize the needs of all the people, regardless of class, ethnicity, and gender, and for both North and Latin Americans to find common ground with each other, the Panamanian salsa music star, lawyer, and part-time U.S. resident Ruben Blades **(blayds)** pondered the hemisphere's destiny in song: "I'm searching for America and I fear I won't find her. Those who fear truth have hidden her. While there is no justice there can be no peace. If the dream of one is the dream of all let's break the chains and begin to walk. I'm calling you, America, our future awaits us, help me to find her."[22]

SECTION SUMMARY

- Latin American economies have been marked by over-dependence on natural resources, extreme inequality of income, agriculture that deemphasizes production of foodstuffs for domestic consumption, increasing urbanization, and failed experiments with free trade.

- Though men continue to dominate Latin American society, more women have entered the work force, and several have become national leaders, while liberation theology, a Catholic movement addressing the plight of the poor, became popular for a while but was outlawed by the Vatican; Protestantism also gained a following.

- Brazil, Latin America's largest nation, became increasingly urban and suffered widespread poverty, with a racial divide between lighter- and darker-skinned people, but Brazilians have found escape from their problems through popular sports such as soccer.

- Latin American culture has flourished, with writers employing magic realism to explore their region's experience, others airing political views through poetry and music, and many preferring to use local traditions and forms rather than foreign ones.

- In the Caribbean, the Jamaican religion of Rastafarianism promoted redistribution of wealth, while a closely related musical form, reggae, frequently included calls for social justice and freedom from police interference.

- Latin American and Caribbean nations forged closer relations, signed several trade pacts, and shared an uneasy economic relationship with the United States, while Asian nations also became important competitors with and investors in their economies.

CHAPTER SUMMARY

Having emerged from World War II as the dominant superpower, the United States soon engaged in a Cold War with the Soviet Union. The U.S. campaign to contain communism fostered the growth of a powerful military and a strong government. During the Cold War the United States lavished aid and investment on its allies and the developing nations and intervened in many nations, including some in Latin America and the Caribbean, to counter revolutionary movements or overthrow left-leaning governments. While the U.S. economy flourished for decades, American society and culture rapidly changed, as ethnic minorities and women struggled for equal rights. Although shaped, like the United States, by massive immigration from Europe, especially Britain, the societies of Canada, Australia, and New Zealand have more liberal attitudes on social issues and, unlike the United States, have extensive social welfare systems.

Latin American and Caribbean experiences differ from those in the United States and Canada and the Pacific Basin. Military dictatorships dominated many Latin American nations for decades. Most nations struggled to implement and sustain democracy, which became prevalent in the 1990s, and to find the right economic mix to foster economic development. Many people have remained in dire poverty. Women and nonwhites have worked to improve their status, with only modest success. The Latin American and Caribbean peoples have also fostered dynamic cultural forms, from innovative literatures to popular musical forms, that have often expressed protest and have gained worldwide audiences.

KEY TERMS

domino theory	Mutually Assured	Castroism	New Song
multilateralism	Destruction	neoliberalism	Rastafarianism
unilateralism	preemptive war	liberation theology	reggae
containment			

EBOOK AND WEBSITE RESOURCES

e PRIMARY SOURCE

Free Trade and the Decline of Democracy

e INTERACTIVE MAPS

Map 29.1 U.S.Military Presence in the World, 1945–Present
Map 29.2 Canada
Map 29.3 Modern Latin America and the Caribbean

LINKS

WWW-VL: History: United States (http://vlib.iue.it/history/USA/). A virtual library, maintained at the University of Kansas, that contains links to hundreds of sites.

Internet Modern History Sourcebook (http://www.fordham.edu/halsall/mod/modsbook.html). Extensive online collection of historical documents and secondary materials.

Internet Resources for Latin America (http://lib.nmsu.edu/subject/bord/laguia/). This outstanding site, from New Mexico State University, provides information and links.

Latin American Network Information Center (http://lanic.utexas.edu/). Very useful site on contemporary Latin America, maintained at the University of Texas.

Plus flashcards, practice quizzes, and more. Go to: www.cengage.com/history/lockard/globalsocnet2e.

SUGGESTED READING

Beezley, William, and Colin MacLachlan. *Latin America: The Peoples and Their History*, 2nd ed. Belmont, CA: Wadsworth, 2007. Comprehensive study.

Brown, D. Clayton. *Globalization and America Since 1945*. Wilmington, DE: Scholarly Resources, 2003. A brief but useful study of the U.S. role in a globalizing world.

Chafe, William H. *The Unfinished Journey: America Since World War II*, 5th ed. New York: Oxford University Press, 2003. An outstanding, readable survey of the era.

Clayton, Lawrence A., and Michael L. Conniff. *A History of Modern Latin America*, 2nd ed. Belmont, CA: Wadsworth, 2005. A readable general history, with much on the contemporary era.

DePalma, Anthony. *Here: A Biography of the New American Continent*. New York: Public Affairs, 2001. A U.S. jounalist's account of contemporary Canada, Mexico, and the United States.

Green, Duncan. *Faces of Latin America*, 3rd ed. New York: Monthly Review Press, 2006. An entertaining and provocative examination of Latin America's people and their vibrant cultures.

Guarneri, Carl. *America in the World: U.S. History in Global Context*. New York: McGraw-Hill, 2007. Places recent U.S. history in comparative perspective.

Hillman, Richard S., ed. *Understanding Contemporary Latin America*, 3rd ed. Boulder: Lynne Rienner, 2005. A valuable collection of essays.

Hillman, Richard S., ed. *Understanding the Contemporary Caribbean*, 2nd ed. Lynne Rienner, 2009. A valuable collection of essays.

Hobsbawm, Eric. *On Empire: America, War, and Global Supremacy*. New York: New Press, 2008. Provocative critique of U.S. role in the world by a British historian.

Hunt, Michael H. *The American Ascendancy: How the United States Gained and Wielded Global Dominance*. Chapel Hill: University of North Carolina Press, 2007. Tracks the factors behind the U.S. rise to global power.

Isserman, Maurice, and Michael Kazin. *America Divided: The Civil War of the 1960s*. New York: Oxford University Press, 2000. A comprehensive history of this important era.

Kinzer, Stephen. *Overthrow: America's Century of Regime Change from Hawaii to Iraq*. New York: Times Books, 2006. A critical examination of U.S. interventions and forced regime changes abroad over the past century.

Page, Joseph A. *The Brazilians*. Reading, MA: Addison-Wesley, 1995. A readable examination of Brazilian society and culture.

Paterson, Thomas, et al. *American Foreign Relations Since 1895*, 7th ed. Boston: Wadsworth, 2009. A readable survey with much on this era.

Rosen, Ruth. *The World Split Open: How the Modern Women's Movement Changed America*. New York: Viking, 2000. One of the best studies of the women's movement in the United States since World War II.

Schaller, Michael, et al. *Present Tense: The United States Since 1945*, 3rd ed. Boston: Houghton Mifflin, 2004. An informative survey.

Skidmore, Thomas E., and Peter H. Smith. *Modern Latin America*, 6th ed. New York: Oxford University Press, 2004. An excellent introduction to the recent history of the region and its nations.

Sullivan III, Michael J. *American Adventurism Abroad: Invasions, Interventions, and Regime Changes Since World War II*, revised and expanded ed. Malden, MA: Blackwell, 2008. Traces foreign policy from the 1940s to today.

Terrill, Ross. *The Australians*. New York: Touchstone, 1988. A readable introduction to Australian history and society.

Thompson, Roger C. *The Pacific Basin Since 1945*, 2nd ed. New York: Longman, 2001. An Australian scholar's broad examination of the East Asian, Pacific, Latin American, and North American societies and their relations.

Winn, Peter. *Americas: The Changing Face of Latin America and the Caribbean*, 3rd ed. Berkeley: University of California Press, 2006. A sweeping, highly readable examination of the region and its peoples.

THE MIDDLE EAST, SUB-SAHARAN AFRICA, AND NEW CONFLICTS IN THE CONTEMPORARY WORLD, SINCE 1945

AP/Wide World Photos

Modern vs. Traditional
Wearing traditional clothing, including veils and head scarves, Egyptian women walk through downtown Cairo in 1998 in front of billboards promoting popular entertainers. The scene illustrates the encounter between Islamic customs and modern ideas in many Middle Eastern nations.

> I saw the Berlin Wall fall, [Nelson] Mandela walk free. I saw a dream whose time has come change my history—so keep on dreaming. In the best of times and in the worst of times gotta keep looking at the skyline, not at the hole in the road.
>
> —"YOUR TIME WILL COME" BY SOUTH AFRICAN POP GROUP SAVUKA, 1993[1]

In 1987 the Nigerian writer Chinua Achebe (ah-CHAY-bay) (b. 1930) dissected the underside of African politics in a controversial novel, *Anthills of the Savannah*, about a military dictatorship like the one he had experienced in his own country. *Anthills* portrays the problems faced by average people and throughout much of Africa, mercilessly depicting the immorality, vanity, and destructiveness of dictatorship. Achebe did not have to look far for examples: the Nigerian military leaders who overthrew a civilian government in 1983 had first arrested people well-known as corrupt, but then proceeded to jail anyone who questioned the regime's own economic mismanagement and human rights abuses.

FOCUS QUESTIONS

1. How have Arab-Israeli tensions and oil shaped contemporary Middle Eastern politics?
2. What roles has Islam played in the contemporary Middle East?
3. What were the main political consequences of decolonization in sub-Saharan Africa?
4. What new economic, social, and cultural patterns have emerged in Africa?

Achebe's satire on moral bankruptcy illustrated the dangers of unaccountable, repressive power. Just as the black and white musicians in the South African pop group, Savuka, could sing of dreams changing history and a new era beginning with the end of white minority rule, Achebe also offered a powerful message about the need for people to struggle to attain a better life. Achebe has argued that the artist and society cannot be separated, that no novel is ever politically neutral because even saying nothing about politics is a political statement that says everything is OK. *Anthills* argues eloquently that, in Achebe's view, everything is not OK. Like various other creative writers, musicians, and artists who used their art to spur political and social change, Achebe has had to live in exile from intolerant governments.

The problems Achebe vividly described—corruption, economic stagnation, combustible social tensions, and failed promises of democracy—have applied to most other nations in sub-Saharan Africa and the Middle East. Between 1945 and 1975 country after country became independent or escaped from Western political domination. In contrast to various Asian and Latin American nations, however, African and Middle Eastern nations have often struggled just to survive. While innovative in areas such as music, literature, and other forms of culture, few of the nations have successfully resolved their social and economic problems or substantially raised living standards. For some nations, Islam has become a rallying cry to assert political interests and preserve cultures. To serve their own ends, global superpowers have manipulated governments and intervened to shape the regions.

[1]Written by Johnny Clegg. Publisher: HRBV Music/Thythm Safari

e Visit the website and eBook for additional study materials and interactive tools:
www.cengage.com/history/lockard/globalsocnet2e

865

THE MIDDLE EAST: NEW NATIONS AND OLD SOCIETIES

How have Arab-Israeli tensions and oil shaped contemporary Middle Eastern politics?

Few world regions have witnessed more turbulence in the past half-century than the predominantly Muslim nations stretching from Morocco eastward across North Africa and western Asia to Turkey, Iran, and Afghanistan. The Arabs have dominated most of these nations, but Turks, Iranians, Kurds, and Israeli Jews also influence the region. After World War II the Middle Eastern societies ended Western colonization and asserted their own political interests, often under modernizing leaders. But they have also endured dictatorial governments, chronic political instability, and centuries-old hostilities between Sunni and Shi'a Muslims. Meanwhile, containing much of the world's oil reserves, the Middle East became crucial to the global system.

CHRONOLOGY

The Middle East, 1945–Present

1948 Formation of Israel

1948–1949 First Arab-Israeli War

1951 Nationalist government in Iran

1954–1970 Nasser presidency in Egypt

1953 CIA overthrow of Iranian government

1954–1962 Algerian Revolution

1956 Suez crisis

1960 Formation of OPEC

1967 Arab-Israeli Six-Day War

1973 Arab-Israeli (Yom Kippur) War

1973 OPEC oil embargo

1978 Egypt-Israel peace treaty

1979 Islamic revolution in Iran

1979–1989 Soviet war in Afghanistan

1980–1988 Iran-Iraq War

1987 Beginning of Palestinian Intifada

1996–2001 Taliban government in Afghanistan

1993 Limited Palestinian self-government

2000 Renewed Israeli-Palestinian conflict

2001 U.S. invasion of Afghanistan

2003 U.S. invasion and occupation of Iraq

The Reshaping of the Middle East

In the decade after World War II nationalist governments replaced most of the remaining colonial regimes (see Chronology: The Middle East, 1945–Present). The French abandoned control of Morocco, Tunisia, Lebanon, and Syria, while the Italians left Libya. However, during the Algerian Revolution (1954–1962) nationalist guerrillas fought 500,000 French troops for eight years to bring independence to Algeria, which had a large European settler population. Some 250,000 Algerians died in the conflict. Seeing no clear end to the struggle, the French granted independence in 1962. Although some Middle Eastern nations, such as Egypt and Morocco, had a long history of national identity and unity, many states were fragile. For example, after World War I the British had formed the artificial states of Iraq, Jordan, and Palestine with arbitrary boundaries, while Afghanistan, Turkey, Lebanon, and Syria included diverse and often feuding ethnic and religious groups.

Iran and Turkey, which had never been colonized, sought influential roles in the region and built formidable military forces. Both also abused their citizens' human rights, arresting dissidents and restricting ethnic minorities. Turkey shifted from military-dominated to democratically elected governments by the 1980s, but the military remained powerful, and strict internal security laws resulted in the imprisonment of several thousand people for political offenses. Led largely by secular politicians, Turks looked increasingly westward, joining NATO (the North Atlantic Treaty Organization), hosting U.S. military bases, and applying for membership in the European Union. But Turkey's governments, while generally promoting a modern version of women's rights, have also suppressed the culture and language of the largest ethnic minority, the Kurds, who chiefly live in southeastern Turkey. Although the nation's 73 million people are largely Muslim, nationalist governments long limited political activity by groups favoring an Islamic state and discouraged conservative religious customs. However, the moderate Islamic Justice and Development Party, which came to power in 2002 and won successive elections, has loosened restrictions on Muslim practices, such as by allowing devout female students to wear head scarves, while pursuing a pro-Western policy and closer ties to Europe.

The hopes for development throughout the Middle East were soon dashed as vested interests, such as large landowners and most of the Muslim clergy, opposed significant changes. Many people also remained mired in illiteracy, poverty, and disease. But although freewheeling and enduring multiparty democracy has been hard to establish or maintain, some have made the effort. Lebanese could choose between many competing warlord or sectarian-based parties, and in recent years both men and women in the small Persian Gulf kingdoms of Bahrain **(BAH-rain)** and Kuwait have elected parliaments. In 2009 three Kuwaiti women won seats. Due to U.S. occupation, Iraq also now has an elected, although deeply factionalized, parliament with some women deputies. As another example, the Moroccan king,

CHRONOLOGY

	The Middle East	Sub-Saharan Africa
1940	**1948** Formation of Israel **1954–1962** Algerian Revolution	**1948** Apartheid in South Africa **1957–1975** African decolonization
1960	**1967** Arab-Israeli Six-Day War **1973** OPEC oil embargo **1979** Islamic revolution in Iran	**1975** Independence for Portuguese colonies
1990	**2003** United States invasion of Iraq	**1994** Black majority rule in South Africa

Muhammad VI, who claims descent from the prophet Muhammad, has used a tolerant interpretation of Islam to try to modernize his nation, granting new rights to women and strengthening civil liberties and the role of an elected parliament. Yet, the king still controls vast power. In most countries elections are rigged, parliaments are weak, or governments make it hard for opposition candidates to run. Furthermore, the United States and the Soviet Union, attracted by the region's oil and strategic location along vital waterways, including the Persian Gulf and Suez Canal, soon filled the power vacuum created by decolonization. Pan-Arab nationalism, based more on Arabs' shared cultural and linguistic background than political interests, was never able to overcome political rivalries and superpower meddling. Divided by rival Muslim sects and differing outlooks toward the West, Arabs floundered in their quest for unity. As a result, the Middle East became a highly combustible region subject to many strains.

Arab Nationalism and Egypt

During the 1960s and 1970s confrontation between Arab nationalism and the world's superpowers was acute in Egypt, which, with 82 million people by 2008, is the most populous Arab country. In 1954 a charismatic Egyptian leader, General Gamal Abdul Nasser (NAS-uhr) (1918–1970), became Egypt's leader after a military coup in 1952 that ended the corrupt pro-British monarchy. From the lower middle class in cosmopolitan Alexandria, Nasser's frequent visits to his parents' impoverished farming village had sparked his sympathy for the poor and his resentment of rich landlords. He also despised the British and their Egyptian collaborators. As a radical student and then army officer with a commanding personality, he developed a vision of a new Egypt, free of Western domination and social inequality.

Rise of Nasser

President Nasser preached modernization, socialism, and unity, promising to improve the lives of the poor and to implement land reform, making him a hero in the Arab world. To generate electric power and improve flood control, Nasser used Soviet aid to build the massive Aswan High Dam along the Nile, completed in 1970. But his nonaligned foreign policy antagonized a Cold War–obsessed United States, and his support of pan-Arab nationalism also generated wars. In 1956 Nasser's government took over the British-operated Suez Canal, a key artery of world commerce. To Egyptians, foreign ownership of the canal had symbolized their subjugation to foreign powers, but to Europeans, the canal was the lifeline that moved oil and resources to the West from Asia. Britain, France, and Israel sent in military forces to reclaim the canal from Egyptian troops, but diplomatic opposition by the United States, which disliked Nasser but feared regional instability, and by the USSR, forced their withdrawal. By standing up to the West, Nasser became an even greater Arab hero and a leader of the movement among developing nations for nonalignment, or neutrality, between the two rival superpowers. However, the Israeli defeat of Egypt and its allies in a brief 1967 war humiliated Nasser. Furthermore, Nasser's social and economic reforms fostered little economic development or military strength.

Nasser's successors followed pragmatic, pro-U.S. policies. In 1978 Anwar Sadat (g. 1970–1981) signed a peace treaty with Israel brokered by the U.S. president, Jimmy Carter (g. 1977–1981). For his efforts Sadat was assassinated by hardline military officers. Sadat and his successor, Hosni Mubarak, dismantled the socialist economy, allowing a few well-connected capitalists to become fabulously rich while the poorest became even poorer. In Cairo, the contrast has grown more dramatic between the glittering rich neighborhoods, featuring luxury apartments and mansions surrounded by high walls, and the poor, overcrowded neighborhoods, where the most desperate

Egypt after Nasser

families live in huts on top of ramshackle apartment buildings. As a result, millions of Egyptians have sought work in oil-rich Arab nations.

With little oil and few resources other than the fertile lands along the Nile, Egypt suffers from high malnutrition and unemployment, low rates of literacy and public health, and a huge national debt. In elections other candidates were able to run against the long-entrenched president Hosni Mubarak (r. 1981–present), but they were hampered in campaigning by limits on free speech, harassment, and the arrest of opposition leaders. While liberals seek more democracy, Islamic militants, feeding on these frustrations, challenge the secular but corrupt, repressive government.

Israel in Middle Eastern Politics

Birth of Israel

The conflict between Israel and the Arabs became the Middle East's most insurmountable problem, sustaining tensions for over half a century. Zionist Jews had been emigrating from Europe to Palestine since the late 1800s, building cities and forming productive socialist farming settlements. The growing Jewish presence triggered occasional conflicts with the Palestinian Arab majority. Then the Nazis' murder of 6 million Jews during World War II spurred a more militant Zionism and a Jewish desire for a homeland free of oppression, and in the later 1940s Jewish refugees poured into Palestine from Europe. Moderate Jewish leaders negotiated with the sympathetic British for a peaceful transfer of power to them in Palestine. However, Zionist extremists practiced "gun diplomacy," using bombings and assassinations against the British, Arabs, and moderate Jews, while Arabs, opposed to an Israeli state at their expense, attacked Jews. Unable to maintain order, Britain referred the Palestine question to the new Western-dominated United Nations. As the British withdrew in 1948, Jewish leaders proclaimed the establishment of Israel. By establishing a multiparty democracy and seeking to rebuild shattered Jewish lives, the Israelis gained the strong support of Western nations and especially the United States, which has pumped in generous aid ever since.

Arab-Israeli Conflicts

The establishment of a Jewish state led to full-scale war in 1948–1949 between Israel and its Arab neighbors, to whom Israel was a white settler state and a symbol of Western colonialism (see Map 30.1). As some 85 percent of Palestinian Arabs fled the fighting and attacks by Jewish extremists, or heeded the calls of opportunistic Arab leaders to leave, Israelis occupied their farms and houses. Through these means the Israelis won the war against the disorganized Arabs. Palestinian refugees settled in overcrowded, squalid refugee camps in Egypt, Lebanon, Jordan, and Syria. While some Palestinian exiles became a prosperous middle class throughout the Middle East, most remained in the camps, nursing their hatred of Israel. They supported the Palestine Liberation Organization (PLO), a coalition of Arab nationalist, Muslim, and Christian groups led by Yasser Arafat **(YA-sir AR-uh-fat)** (1929–2004), an engineer and journalist from a wealthy Jerusalem family. However, neither the Western nations nor Israel officially recognized or would negotiate with the PLO until the 1990s, prompting it to resort to terrorism, such as by attacking public buses and rural settlements.

Israel remained in a state of confrontation with its Arab neighbors and the PLO. The Palestinians still in Israel participated in democratic politics but were disproportionally poor and often saw themselves as second-class citizens. Meanwhile, thousands of Jewish immigrants arrived, many from Middle Eastern countries where they had faced discrimination or retribution. The immigration intensified the divisions in Israel between secular and devout Jews and between European and Middle Eastern Jews. Israeli, obsessed with military security, became well armed, especially by the United States, with half its total national budget going to the military. A cycle of violence followed as the PLO attacked and Israelis bombed a refugee camp in Lebanon in retaliation.

1967 War and Aftermath

An Arab-Israeli War in 1967 further complicated regional politics, heightening conflict and reshaping Israeli society. Responding to an ill-advised attack led by Egypt and Jordan, Israel gained control of the West Bank, that part of Jordan on the western side of the Jordan River; eastern Jerusalem, filled with both Jewish and Islamic holy places; the Gaza Strip, a small coastal enclave of Egypt; and the Golan Heights, a Syrian plateau overlooking northeast Israel. The Israeli victory greatly increased the amount of Israeli-controlled land but incorporated a large Arab population, a combustible situation. By 2005 Israel and the occupied territories contained some 5 million Jews and 4 million Arabs. Israel treated the occupied Palestinians as a colonized people, allowing them no political rights. In 1973 another Israeli war with Egypt and Syria proved costly to all sides.

Increasing Israeli control over the Palestinians exacerbated the conflict. Although many Israelis wanted to trade occupied land for a permanent peace settlement, others hoped to permanently annex the occupied lands as part of biblical Israel. Ultranationalist Israelis, with government support, began claiming and settling on Arab land, creating another problem: thousands of Jewish settlers, largely militant Zionists and religious conservatives, living amid hostile Arabs. Palestinians

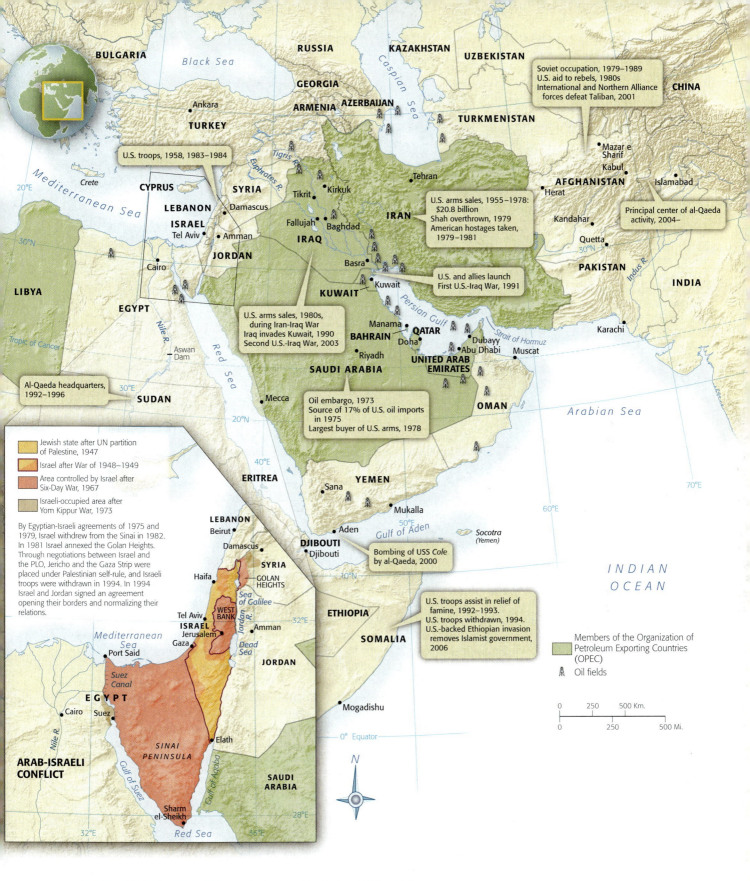

Map 30.1 Middle East Oil and the Arab-Israeli Conflict

Several Middle Eastern nations, including Saudi Arabia, Iran, Iraq, Libya, and the small Persian Gulf states, are rich in oil and active members of OPEC. Israel, founded in 1948, and the neighboring Arab countries of Egypt, Jordan, and Syria have been in chronic conflict that has resulted in four wars. Israel's victory in the 1967 war allowed it to take control of Gaza, the West Bank, and the Golan Heights.

Interactive Map

The following labels and callouts appear on the map:

Soviet occupation, 1979–1989
U.S. aid to rebels, 1980s
International and Northern Alliance forces defeat Taliban, 2001

U.S. troops, 1958, 1983–1984

U.S. arms sales, 1955–1978: $20.8 billion
Shah overthrown, 1979
American hostages taken, 1979–1981

Principal center of al-Qaeda activity, 2004–

U.S. and allies launch First U.S.-Iraq War, 1991

U.S. arms sales, 1980s, during Iran-Iraq War
Iraq invades Kuwait, 1990
Second U.S.-Iraq War, 2003

Al-Qaeda headquarters, 1992–1996

Oil embargo, 1973
Source of 17% of U.S. oil imports in 1975
Largest buyer of U.S. arms, 1978

Bombing of USS *Cole* by al-Qaeda, 2000

U.S. troops assist in relief of famine, 1992–1993.
U.S. troops withdrawn, 1994.
U.S.-backed Ethiopian invasion removes Islamist government, 2006

Members of the Organization of Petroleum Exporting Countries (OPEC)

Oil fields

ARAB-ISRAELI CONFLICT

Jewish state after UN partition of Palestine, 1947
Israel after War of 1948–1949
Area controlled by Israel after Six-Day War, 1967
Israeli-occupied area after Yom Kippur War, 1973

By Egyptian-Israeli agreements of 1975 and 1979, Israel withdrew from the Sinai in 1982. In 1981 Israel annexed the Golan Heights. Through negotiations between Israel and the PLO, Jericho and the Gaza Strip were placed under Palestinian self-rule, and Israeli troops were withdrawn in 1994. In 1994 Israel and Jordan signed an agreement opening their borders and normalizing their relations.

Dismantling Israeli Settlements

Palestinians have viewed the settlements built by ardent Zionists in the West Bank and Gaza as a provocation. Israeli troops have sometimes been ordered to dismantle settlements, which are expensive to protect, and remove the enraged settlers by force. In 2005 all the Israeli settlements were closed down in Gaza.

AP/Wide World Photos

Intifada ("Uprising") A resistance begun in 1987 by Palestinians against the Israeli occupation.

Recent Politics

Primary Source: Arab and Israeli Soccer Players Discuss Ethnic Relations in Israel, 2000
Learn how Arabs and Jews get along in the world of professional soccer in Israel.

resent the heavily fortified settlements, guarded by Israeli soldiers, that often overlook Palestinian cities and villages from nearby hilltops. Because Israel proper has remained a democracy with a vibrant free press, Israelis have heatedly debated these policies and the general treatment of Arabs. In 1987 desperate Palestinians began a resistance known as the **Intifada** ("Uprising") against the Israeli occupation. However, the turmoil spawned a rising Islamic militancy in the occupied territories that alarmed both the secular Fatah movement, the main party in the PLO, and the Israelis. Negotiations led in 1993 to limited self-government under the PLO in some parts of the occupied territories, the basis for a possible Palestinian state, and a peace agreement between Israel and Jordan. Optimists hoped a permanent peace agreement might be found to satisfy both sides. But the assassination in 1995 of Israeli president Yitzak Rabin by Jewish extremists proved a setback for peace talks.

In 2000 violence erupted again, returning the Israel-Palestine problem to center stage in Middle Eastern politics. Moderate Israelis and Palestinians lost hope as demoralizing Palestinian suicide bombings of civilian targets, such as restaurants and public buses, and Israeli reprisal attacks on Palestinian neighborhoods made life insecure for everyone. Israel also built a high security fence separating it from the West Bank that incorporated some occupied territory, enraging Palestinians. In a 2006 election promoted by the United States the Palestinians, tired of Fatah's ineffective and corrupt regime, unexpectedly gave the militant Islamic Hamas movement a majority of seats in the Palestinian parliament, alarming Israelis, since Hamas had sponsored terrorist attacks and refused to recognize Israel's right to exist. Soon Hamas seized Gaza, from where militants fired rockets into Israel, while Fatah controlled the West Bank. An inconclusive Israeli invasion of southern Lebanon in 2006 to stop terrorist attacks and a bloody military incursion in Gaza in 2008 that reduced some Gaza neighborhoods to rubble hardened Israeli and Palestinian attitudes and led to condemnation in the world community. As a hardline Israeli government took power in 2009, the future of Israeli-Palestinian relations remained uncertain. With only a third of the world's 14 million Jews living in Israel, the Zionist dream of a Greater Israel stretching from the Mediterranean coast through the West Bank to the Jordan River is fading. At the same time, with conflicting visions of how Israelis and Palestinians might coexist, no basis for ensuring long-term peace has yet emerged.

Islamic Revolution in Iran

Western Intervention

Rich in oil and strategically located along the Persian Gulf, Iran had been buffeted between rival European nations for a century. Outside interference continued after World War II, when internal politics revolved around a conflict between the young king, Shah Mohammed Pahlavi **(pah-LAH-vee)** (1919–1980), and nationalist reformers opposed to foreign domination. In 1951 nationalists came to power, reducing the shah to a ceremonial role. Because Iran had been receiving little of the oil revenue, the reformers also nationalized the British-dominated oil industry. Britain and its ally, the United States, which considered the nationalists sympathetic to the USSR, cut off aid and launched a boycott to close oil markets, bringing Iran to near bankruptcy and fostering unrest. Then in 1953, American CIA agents secretly organized opposition among military leaders and riots against the nationalist government. In the turmoil, royalists overthrew the government, imprisoned its leaders, and restored the unpopular shah to power, embittering many Iranians. Shah Pahlavi, a ruthless, pleasure-loving man who dreamed of restoring Persia as a great power, allied himself with the United States and allowed American companies to control the oil industry.

Along with the modernization, the shah's three and a half decades of rule also brought political repression and a huge military force built with oil revenues. What the shah termed his "white revolution," which promoted a market economy and women's rights while enlarging the middle class, was admired in the West but failed to improve living standards for most Iranians. While a corrupt elite siphoned off most of the development money, including generous U.S. aid, and the royal family lived extravagantly, 60 percent of peasants remained landless. As people flocked to the cities, choked in traffic and smog, the population of Tehran, the capital, increased fivefold between 1945 and 1977. To increase national pride and attract Western tourists, the shah spent billions to renovate the splendid palaces and tombs of Persepolis, a city built for Persian kings 2,400 years ago, but few Iranians had the money to visit the city. The absolute monarchy tolerated little dissent, and the shah's secret police eliminated opposition. Political prisoners numbered in the thousands. The poetess Faruq Farrukhzad **(fuh-ROOK fuh-ROOK-sad)** wrote of how the intellectuals, cowed into submission, retreated into "swamps of alcohol [while] the verminous mice gnawed through the pages of gilded books, stacked in ancient closets."[2] Conservative Shi'ite leaders opposed the modernization, such as the unveiled women and crowded bars, which they viewed as a threat to Muslim culture. Then in 1979, as the economy slumped, strikes and protests forced the shah into exile in the United States and turned the Americans and Iranians into bitter foes.

An Islamic revolution began to reshape Iran. While some Shi'ite thinkers discouraged the clergy from political activism, others promoted a clergy-governed Islamic state. Militant Shi'ite clerics, led by the long exiled Ayatollah Ruhollah Khomeini **(roo-HOLE-ah KOH-may-nee)** (1902–1989), took power, eliminated leftists and moderate nationalists, and overturned the shah's modernization. Khomeini had long criticized the shah's secular policies, urging that they be replaced by the Islamic Shari'a law codes. As Iran became an Islamic state, thousands of Iranians fled abroad, many to the United States. Women were forced to wear veils and prohibited from socializing with men from outside their families. The regime restricted other personal freedoms as well, as reflected in a popular joke: "We used to drink in public and pray in private. Now we pray in public and drink in private." Like the shah, the clerics ruled by terror, suppressed ethnic minorities, such as the mostly Sunni Kurds in the northwest, and executed opponents.

The Iranian Revolution fostered opposition from outside. The United States became a bitter enemy after Islamic militants, led by women students and driven by hatred of the United States for its long support of the shah, seized the U.S. Embassy in 1979 and held it and the U.S. diplomats for one year. Iran's Arab neighbors, who had always feared Iran's territorial size, large population (70 million in 2006), military strength, and regional ambitions, were also alarmed. Now they had to worry about Islamic militancy aimed at their more secular governments. Animosity between the mostly Sunni Arabs and the mostly Shi'ite Iranians also fueled tensions and led to war with Iraq. Finally, an Iranian program to develop nuclear power and perhaps nuclear weapons gave worry to the international community.

Eventually Iran mixed theocracy with the trappings of democracy. A more open electoral process allowed opposition parties to win seats in parliament. Beginning in 1997, reformers gained a share of power, fostering a power struggle between moderate reformers and the hardline clerics who controlled the judicial and electoral systems. With the economy floundering, the reformers sought closer ties to the outside world, democratization, and a loosening of harsh laws, but they found the United States unwilling to improve relations. Young people, resenting clerical leadership and Islamic laws, often supported reform and increasingly challenged restrictions on personal behavior. Young women, often unveiled or wearing fashionable head scarves, began socializing again with men. But the hardliners banned reformist newspapers and disqualified reformist candidates. Shirin Ebadi **(shih-RIN ee-BOD-ee)** (b. 1947), a feminist Iranian lawyer and human rights activist, won the Nobel Peace Prize in 2003 for bravely challenging the clerical leadership and favoring a reformist Islam, distressing the hardliners. But in 2005 Iranians lost faith in the ineffective reformist leaders and elected a hardline president, Mahmoud Ahmedinijad **(mah-MOOD ah-mah-DIH-nee-zhahd)** (b. 1956), who increased nuclear capabilities, restored conservative values, harassed dissidents, threatened Israel, and openly defied the United States. One of his first acts was to ban Western music from radio and television. However, as the economy declined, reformers and hardliners continued to struggle for

Iran under Shah Pahlavi

Islamic Revolution and the United States

Recent Iranian Politics

influence. In 2009, a victory by Ahmedinijad and the hardliners—in a disputed election that many Iranians considered rigged and that generated massive street protests—intensified repression of dissidents, and divided the clerical leadership, leaving the nation's political future uncertain.

Iraq and Regional Conflicts

Iraqi Dictatorship

Iraq proved a major source of regional instability. In 1958 the Iraqi army overthrew an unpopular monarchy and began over four decades of ruthless dictatorships that crushed all opposition. These governments also fostered secular policies and some economic development, making Iraq one of the most prosperous Arab societies by the 1980s. They were usually led by members of the **Ba'ath** ("Renaissance") Party, which favored socialism and Arab nationalism and strongly opposed Israel. Representing the Sunni Arab minority of 20 percent, the Ba'ath ruled a nation with a restless Arab Shi'ite majority, located mostly in the south, and a disaffected Sunni Kurdish minority in the north. In 1979 Saddam Hussein (1937–2006), a landless peasant's son, seized power and proved even more brutal than his predecessors.

Ba'ath ("Renaissance") A political party in the Middle East that favored socialism and Arab nationalism and strongly opposed Israel.

Alarmed by the Iranian Revolution, and hated by Ayatollah Khomeini, who considered Saddam's secular regime godless, in 1980 Saddam launched an invasion of Iran, using poison gas against Iranian soldiers, but he was unable to achieve victory. The war drew in outsiders because it threatened Persian Gulf shipping lanes and hence the world supply of oil. The United States, with its vested interest in Iraq's oil—the world's second largest proven reserves—and hostility toward Iran, sided with Iraq, attacking Iranian shipping and arming Saddam's military. As the casualties mounted, both Iran and Iraq drafted teenagers to fight. The costs of war were staggering: over 260,000 Iranian and 100,000 Iraqi dead and grave damage to the Iraqi economy.

Iraq and the United States

When the war ended in 1988 with no victor, Saddam's actions fostered regional tension. U.S. president George H. W. Bush (r. 1989–1993) viewed Saddam as a useful strategic ally and continued providing him with weapons. But Iraqi leaders had long claimed that Kuwait, a British protectorate until 1961 that sits atop oil riches and blocks Iraq from enjoying greater access to the Persian Gulf, should be part of Iraq. In 1990 Iraq invaded prosperous Kuwait, ruled by an Arab royal family. Bush, worried that oil-rich Saudi Arabia might be next, formed a coalition and launched the Persian Gulf War (1991), which drove Iraqis from Kuwait and killed perhaps 30,000 Iraqi soldiers. The war restored Americans' faith in their military, which had been undermined by the bitter defeat in Vietnam, but the euphoria proved short-lived. Saddam remained in power, persecuting dissidents and slaughtering Shi'ites and Kurds, who rebelled with U.S. encouragement. At least 30,000 Shi'ites and many thousands of Kurds died from the fighting. Nevertheless, Saddam's war-making capabilities had been badly damaged, and the United States and United Nations eventually gave the Kurds some military and police protection, allowing them to set up a government with democratic trappings in their northern region. Meanwhile, U.N. sanctions imposed to restrict Iraq's foreign income and ability to buy weapons undermined Iraq's economy. The Iraqi people struggled to acquire food and medical supplies, and thousands died from the resulting shortages.

Saudi Arabia, Oil, and the World

Saudi Society

The Persian Gulf War pointed out the close connection between Saudi Arabia and the United States, which had military bases and a strong economic stake in the kingdom. Mostly bleak desert, Saudi Arabia possesses the world's largest known oil reserves. The Saudis used oil revenues to fund modernization projects, building highways, hospitals, and universities, and by the 1980s they had achieved high health and literacy rates for the Middle East. Glittering shopping malls offer the latest Western fashions and electronic gadgets serve affluent urbanites, who reach the malls in luxury cars often driven by chauffeurs. Yet, outside the cities, poor Saudis often still travel by camel and sleep in tents.

Despite the modernization, Saudi political and social life has remained conservative, with the royal family exercising absolute power and living extravagantly while tolerating corruption and quashing dissent. They have used their power to maintain traditional customs and social patterns. Indeed, the country became a laboratory for the clash between modern institutions (like television) and a highly puritanical, patriarchal Islamic culture. With the acquiescence of the Saudi royal family, the Wahhabis, followers of the most rigid form of Islam, maintain a stranglehold on religious thought, life, and education. Wahhabis are hostile to Western and often any modern ideas; they believe, for example, that women should stay at home and be controlled by men. Hence, although some educated women wish to enjoy freedom, thanks to Wahhabi-influenced laws they still cannot legally drive or work or study alongside men. Armed with canes, a special police force patrols the

Bill Strode/Woodfin Camp & Associates

Oil Wealth Saudi Arabia contains the world's largest oil operations, mostly located on or near the Persian Gulf. A Saudi worker overlooks one of the nation's many refineries, which produces the oil exports that have brought the nation wealth.

streets, markets, and city malls to punish women for violating the strict dress codes, which require them to be covered head to foot. In the 1990s the religious police prevented unveiled female students from fleeing a school dormitory fire, causing dozens of the girls to burn to death. The Shi'ite minority, despised by the Wahhabis, have also enjoyed few rights. These conflicts have fostered tensions. Saudi and Western critics believe that what they see as the narrow Islam taught in Saudi schools promotes extremism and anti-Western feeling, and some Saudi men and women have called for a liberalization and women's empowerment.

Saudi Arabia's policies have strongly influenced world oil prices and availability. The kingdom was the major player in the formation in 1960 of **OPEC** (Organization of Petroleum Exporting Countries), a cartel designed to give the producers more power over the price of oil and leverage over consuming nations. OPEC's members range from Middle Eastern nations such as Algeria, Iran, and the United Arab Emirates to more distant countries such as Mexico, Nigeria, and Indonesia. In 1973 OPEC members, angry at Western support of Israel, reduced the world oil supply to raise prices, badly discomforting industrialized nations by causing long lines at gasoline stations. After the embargo ended, the world price remained high, enriching OPEC members. High prices also forced the United States and western Europe to find ways to conserve fuel, such as by designing more fuel-efficient cars. But in the 1980s reduced oil consumption broke OPEC's power and prices plummeted, damaging the economies of most OPEC members.

Saudi Arabia remained the world's largest exporter of oil, ensuring political support and profits from industrialized nations but not guaranteeing Saudi prosperity. Indeed, by the 1990s the Saudi economy had soured. Between 1980 and 2000 income levels fell by two-thirds, resulting in the cutting of government welfare benefits and climbing unemployment. Meanwhile, members of the royal family spent money lavishly and often violated Wahhabi restrictions with their high living abroad, cavorting in the nightclubs of Beirut and the casinos of Europe. Resentment of the royal family and its U.S. allies increased. Many Saudis oppose the U.S. military bases on Saudi soil, which symbolize U.S. support for the royal family and materialistic interest in the kingdom's oil. Seeing little future, frustrated young people often drink alcohol and have mixed-gender parties behind closed doors. Others have embraced militant Islam, a few joining terrorist groups such as Al Qaeda. Most of the young men who hijacked four U.S. airliners and crashed them into the Pentagon and World Trade Center in 2001 were Saudis, often well educated. The Al Qaeda leader, Osama bin Laden (b. 1957), a militant Wahhabi from a large, wealthy Saudi family, had long raged against the

Oil Wealth

OPEC (Organization of Petroleum Exporting Countries) A cartel formed in 1960 to give producers more power over the price of oil and leverage with the consuming nations.

presence of U.S. military bases in Saudi Arabia. Yet, Saudis also have been among the biggest investors in the U.S. and European economies, and many Saudis have studied in the West. Thanks to oil, Saudi Arabia and the industrialized nations have remained close allies despite vastly different social and political systems.

SECTION SUMMARY

- After World War II, nationalist governments replaced many colonial regimes in the Middle East, but the region has failed to develop many working multiparty democracies.

- Egyptian leader General Gamal Abdul Nasser became a hero when he threw off British influence, seized control of the Suez Canal, and pursued socialist policies, but neither Nasser nor his pro-American successors brought prosperity to Egypt.

- Traumatized by the Holocaust, many Jews moved to Palestine after World War II and established the state of Israel, which led to a war between Jews and Arabs, a mass exodus of Palestinians into refugee camps, and enduring tensions.

- After the 1967 Arab-Israeli War, Israel occupied lands with a large Arab population and severely limited Arabs' freedom, and, while Israelis debated how to achieve

peace, Palestinians became increasingly militant in their opposition.

- After nationalists overthrew the Iranian shah, the United States helped organize a coup that returned him to power, and he ruled ruthlessly until 1979, when he was overthrown by Islamic fundamentalists.

- From 1958 on, Iraq was ruled by ruthless military dictatorships dominated by the Sunni minority, and in 1979 Saddam Hussein came to power, launched a costly war against Iran, and then was attacked by the United States after invading Kuwait.

- Saudi Arabia grew extremely wealthy from oil sales, but many citizens have remained poor, and Saudi society is dominated by extremely conservative religious leaders, some of whose followers resent the close relationship the Saudi royal family has forged with the United States.

CHANGE AND CONFLICT IN THE MIDDLE EAST

> What roles has Islam played in the contemporary Middle East?

In 1979 the Islamic world celebrated thirteen centuries of Islamic history. For most of those centuries Muslims had made brilliant contributions to the world, fostering extensive trade networks, accommodating and introducing scientific knowledge, and founding powerful empires. By the mid-twentieth century the European powers dominated the political and economic life of these societies, though many older traditions remained relevant into the present. In recent decades new conflicts resulting from foreign interventions, Islamic militancy, and international terrorism unsettled the Middle East and world politics.

Social Change and Conflict

Divisions in Lebanon

In parts of the Middle East ethnic and religious hostilities have fostered long-term conflict. In Lebanon a series of political crises and a long civil war resulted from competition between a dozen rival factions, Christian, Sunni, and Sh'ia, for control of the small state. In this deeply fragmented land, a national government mostly existed only in name during the 1970s and 1980s. Beirut, once a prosperous, freewheeling mecca for trade, entertainment, and tourism, was devastated by factional fighting. Supporting various factions, Israel, Syria, and the United States were all sucked into the conflict. Syria stationed troops in the north and east, and Israel in the south. In the 1980s the United States intervened on behalf of a weak national government led by the largest, most pro-Western Christian faction. U.S. warships shelled areas around Beirut dominated by opposition, especially Shi'ite, factions while U.S. Marines secured the Beirut airport. The disastrous U.S. mission resulted in some five hundred U.S. deaths from suicide bombers and the holding of U.S. hostages. The intervention also made the United States a focus of Arab rage. In the 1990s the fighting ebbed, and Lebanon regained some stability but little national unity. However, the U.S. and Israeli interventions energized radical Shi'ites, who formed a militant Iran-backed organization, Hezbollah (HEZ-bo-LAH), which shelled Israel. The Israelis responded by invading Lebanon in 2006 to weaken Hezbollah, but the incursion was costly in lives on all sides and failed to destroy Hezbollah, which remained a strong force in the deeply polarized Lebanon politics.

In the Sudan, a huge country, the Arab Muslim-dominated government, which imposed an Islamic state, used military force to control the rebellious black African Christians and animists in the south, a conflict that resulted in 2 million deaths. In 2005 the two sides agreed to end the conflict, but by then a rebellion in Darfur, an impoverished western region where African Muslim farmers competed for scarce land with Arab pastoralists, had erupted. The government launched, with the aid of local Arab militias, a genocide against the Africans, earning condemnation from around the world. Thousands of people died from military assaults on their villages or from disease and starvation after they fled, many into neighboring Chad. By 2009, violence also resurfaced in the south.

Another longtime ethnic conflict concerned Kurds, a large ethnic group—over 20 million strong—inhabiting mountain districts in Iran, Iraq, Syria, and Turkey. Although deeply divided by clan and factional rivalries, Kurds had long sought either their own nation or self-government within their countries of residence, generating constant conflict with central governments. Kurdish rebel groups were especially active in eastern Turkey, where the Turkish government, hoping to build a national identity based on Turkish values and language, repressed Kurdish culture and language. Kurds were also restless in oil-rich northern Iraq, where the dictator, Saddam Hussein, made Kurds a special target of his repression, launching air raids and poison gas attacks against Kurdish villages.

Ethnic Conflicts

In almost all Arab countries, gender relations and family life have changed relatively little. Although women have been elected prime ministers in the predominantly Muslim nations of Bangladesh, Pakistan, Indonesia, and Turkey, no Arab or Iranian women have reached this goal. In Turkey, Iraq, Jordan, and Lebanon urban women have expanded their opportunities by running businesses and entering the professions. But many women have remained in the home, often secluded from the outside world, with their lives as daughters, wives, and mothers controlled by men. Liberals have advocated improving women's lives through education, and Turkey, Tunisia, and Iraq have adopted Western-influenced family laws allowing civil marriages that accord women rights in divorce and child custody. Blaming patriarchal cultural traditions for restrictions, some women activists have argued that the Quran supports women's rights, using such arguments to fight against controlling parents and spouses. But conservative Muslims have prevented the enactment of liberal laws in other Middle Eastern societies. Moreover, devout women have often opposed secular feminism, arguing that women are best protected by strict Islamic law. Zainab Al-Ghazali (1917–2005) in Egypt founded an organization that built mosques, trained female preachers, and promoted an active women's role in public life, but her staunch support of Islamic values upset not only liberal feminists but also Egypt's modernizing President Nasser, who had her jailed and tortured. The conflict between modernizers and traditionalists has often resulted in gender role confusion, as an Egyptian writer noted: "Our mothers understood their situation. We, however, are lost. We do not know whether or not we still belong to the harem, whether love is forbidden or permitted."[3]

Gender Relations

Liberal and conservative Muslims disagree on women's dress. Liberals often see the veil as symbolizing female subjugation, and many women from the urban middle and upper classes have adopted Western dress. However, traditionalists have praised the veil as essential to female modesty. In secular nations such as Turkey and Egypt, women influenced by revivalist Islam have lobbied to wear the full veil or the head scarf as a symbol of piety. In Turkey the secular government, wary of Islamic militancy, long banned head scarves from schools, a policy that has been recently modified. A young Egyptian reflected the views of many religious women when she claimed that "being totally covered saves me from the approaches of men and hungry looks. I feel more free, purer, and more respectable."[4] Indeed, many independent-minded, well-educated Muslim women have not wanted to uncritically adopt Western ways. The liberal Moroccan sociologist and Quranic scholar Fatema Mernissi, a frequent visitor to the West, argued that Western women face their own version of the veil through their obsession with physical appearance, limiting their ability to compete with men for power: "I thank you, Allah, for sparing me the tyranny of the 'size six harem.' I am so happy that the conservative male elite [in the Middle East] does not know about it. Imagine the [Muslim] fundamentalists switching from the veil to forcing women to fit size 6."[5]

Attitudes toward homosexuality have often become more repressive. For centuries many Muslim societies tolerated, although did not approve, homosexual activity, and writings sympathetically exploring homosexual experiences circulated widely. By the late 1800s this changed, forcing homosexuals into the closet. In the 1990s the taboo began to slowly diminish, at least in some cities. The strict gender segregation in countries such as Saudi Arabia, where people spend most of their time, and enjoy emotional bonds, with other people of the same sex, and where hand holding between same-sex friends is common, makes it easier for homosexual couples to escape notice.

Yet, in many countries homosexual behavior, when discovered, frequently results in jail terms or even execution.

Religion and Culture

Islamic Divisions

Islamists Antimodern, usually puritanical Islamic militants who seek an Islamic state.

The clash between tradition and modernity has provided a fertile environment for creativity in religion, music, and literature. Islam has remained at the heart of Middle Eastern life, but, despite its message of peace, social justice, and community, it has often proved divisive (see Map 30.2). Age-old divisions between Sunni and Shi'a, liberal and conservative, secular and devout, Sufi and anti-Sufi, remain powerful. Antimodern, usually puritanical militants known as **Islamists**, who seek an Islamic state and are bitter rivals of secular Muslims, have become increasingly influential, especially in Egypt, Sudan, Algeria, Turkey, and Iran. After World War I the Islamist Muslim Brotherhood spread around the region. The Iranian Ali Shariati **(SHAR-ee-AH-tee)** (1933–1977), educated in France but a critic of the West who influenced Shi'ites, castigated Western democracy as subverted by the power of money but also social justice and blamed Islamic tradition for reducing women to, as he put it, the level of a washing machine. Egyptian writer Sayyid Qutb **(SIGH-eed ka-TOOB)** (1906–1966) sparked political Sunni Islam and redefined *jihad* ("struggle") as violent opposition to the West rather than personal struggle to maintain faith. Qutb lived in the United States for two years; he found Americans friendly but was appalled by the antiblack racism and by the hedonism, such as heavy drinking and casual romantic relations between men and women, that he witnessed. Returning to Egypt, Qutb promoted an Islamic state and joined the Muslim Brotherhood. Inspired by thinkers like Qutb, the most extreme Islamists, known as *jihadists,* plotted violence against secular Muslims, Sufis, and non-Muslims they considered obstacles to imposing their rigid version of Islam.

Disillusionment with repressive and corrupt governments, dissatisfaction with lack of material improvement, and resentment of Western world power have prompted a growing turn to Islam. When elections are allowed, Islamic groups with their large followings tend to triumph over secular parties, as happened in Iraq, Egypt, and Palestine in 2005, a reason why pro-Western modernists often fear democracy. In a troubled world the Islamic revival satisfies for millions a need for personal solace, a yearning for tradition, and a dream of a just political system as propounded by the earliest Muslims. Islamic dress and practice became more common in Egypt after war losses to Israel, as well as in Iraq after the U.S. invasion of 2003, which overthrew Saddam Hussein and the secular Ba'athist government. Devout Muslims dominate the U.S.-installed Iraqi government. While activists in Iraq have closed bars, harassed unveiled women, and terrorized Christians, Sunni militants in various lands have attacked followers of Sufi mysticism as heretics. Islamist movements in Algeria, Egypt, and Saudi Arabia have also challenged their governments, sometimes using terrorism; some, frustrated at home, join international terrorist groups.

Popular Culture

While Islamic militants have condemned music, dance, and other pleasures, many people—both the secular and the devout—have been fans of popular culture, especially popular music. Musicians often hope to encourage national unity or shape society, usually in a more liberal direction. The Egyptian singer Oum Kulthum **(oom KAL-thoom)** (1904–1975) symbolized Arab people's feelings. Attracting a region-wide following with her emotional songs of love and abandonment, Kulthum dominated Middle Eastern popular music from the 1940s through the 1960s. At her height she was one of the two most popular figures among Arabs, the other being her friend, Egypt's president Nasser. Her concerts attracted huge crowds, and her recordings were always on the radio and in films. Popular music also created a sense of community. The songs of peace and coexistence sung by hugely popular Lebanese singer Fairuz **(fie-ROOZ)** were sometimes credited with being the major symbol of hope in that turbulent, civil war–plagued land. Similarly, Israelis revered Yemen-born Shoshana Damari (1923–2006), whose optimistic songs encouraged Israeli unity by extolling the nation and its military forces.

In religiously dogmatic or ethnically divided states, popular music has sometimes stirred controversy. The Islamic government of Iran, opposed to women performing in public, tried to silence all female singers, especially the vocalist and film star Googoosh **(GOO-goosh)**, whose melancholic Westernized pop music had a huge audience during the 1960s and 1970s. The clerics destroyed all her recordings, posters, and films, turning Googoosh into a popular symbol against clerical rule. The *arabesk* pop music of Turkey is rooted in the experiences of poor Arab and Kurdish migrants to Istanbul. One observer noted that "arabesk describes a decaying city in which poverty-stricken migrant workers are exploited and abused, and calls on its listeners to pour another glass of wine and curse fate and the world."[6] Some popular music styles blend Arab and

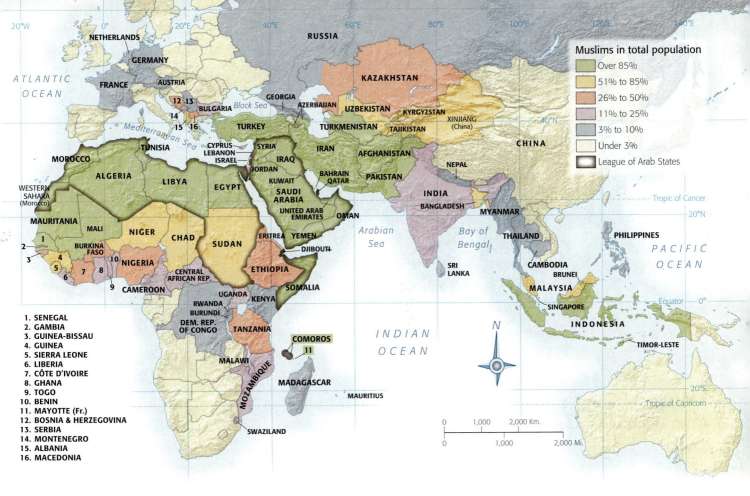

Muslims in total population
- Over 85%
- 51% to 85%
- 26% to 50%
- 11% to 25%
- 3% to 10%
- Under 3%
- League of Arab States

1. SENEGAL
2. GAMBIA
3. GUINEA-BISSAU
4. GUINEA
5. SIERRA LEONE
6. LIBERIA
7. CÔTE D'IVOIRE
8. GHANA
9. TOGO
10. BENIN
11. MAYOTTE (Fr.)
12. BOSNIA & HERZEGOVINA
13. SERBIA
14. MONTENEGRO
15. ALBANIA
16. MACEDONIA

Map 30.2   The Islamic World

The Islamic world includes not only the Middle East—Western Asia and North Africa—but also countries with Muslim majorities in sub-Saharan Africa, Central Asia, and South and Southeast Asia. In addition, Muslims live in most other Eastern Hemisphere nations and in the Americas.

e Interactive Map

foreign forms while addressing social problems. The **rai** ("opinion") pop music of Algeria is based on local Bedouin chants, Spanish flamenco, French café songs, Egyptian pop, and other influences, and its improvised lyrics often deal with forbidden themes of sex and alcohol. By the 1970s synthesizers, drum machines, and electric guitars were added to the exciting mix. Rai holds great appeal to urban working-class youth in North Africa and to the offspring of Arab immigrants in France, but it is anathema to puritanical Islamic militants in Algeria, who have frequently forced singers into exile or even assassinated them. Rai musicians have often moved their base to Paris.

Middle Eastern writers have also expressed ideas forbidden in politics and religion. The novels of the Egyptian Naguib Mahfuz **(nah-GEEB mah-FOOZ)** (b. 1911–2006), a merchant's son turned government official and journalist, have addressed social problems, such as poverty, and questioned conservative religious values and blind faith, which he believes keep individuals from realizing their full potential. Many of his writings have been banned in Egypt and other nations. But in 1988 Mahfuz, strongly influenced by both Western and Arab writers, became the first Arab writer to win a Nobel Prize for literature. Iranian writers have often risked punishment attacking religious hypocrisy while satirizing the failings of governments and business. One famous Iranian novel recommended opportunism for career success: "Try to establish connections with the holders of high offices. Agree with everybody, no matter what his opinion is."[7]

rai ("opinion") A pop music of Algeria based on local Bedouin chants, Spanish flamenco, French café songs, Egyptian pop, and other influences and featuring improvised lyrics that often deal with forbidden themes of sex and alcohol.

Literature

Turmoil in Afghanistan and Iraq

Afghanistan and Iraq have been two of the most troubled nations, and both were reshaped by foreign interventions. Violence and extreme militant Islamic movements generated instability in Afghanistan for three decades. Afghanistan's diverse Muslim ethnic groups, subdivided

Afghanistan and Russia

Monument to Revolution, Liberation Square, Baghdad. Artist: Jawad Salim

Arab Art   The large monument of Revolution, in Baghdad, sculpted by a major modern Iraqi artist, Jawad Salim (1920–1961), occupies a central place in the city. Commissioned in 1958 after the overthrow of the monarchy, it celebrates the Iraqi struggle for justice and freedom and often provided a motif for Iraqi poets.

into rival tribes, have little sense of national unity. From the early 1800s until 1978 kings from the largest ethnic group, the Pashtuns, loosely governed the territory. Some Afghan leaders advocated modernization, triggering revolts by conservative tribes. In 1978 procommunist generals seized power, forged close ties with the Soviet Union, and introduced radical social and economic reforms that challenged Islamic traditions. They implemented land reform, promoted women's education, and replaced Islamic law with a secular family law giving women more rights. When conservative Islamic rebels, known as **mujahidin** (moo-JAH-hi-deen) ("holy warriors"), rebelled against the pro-Soviet regime, the USSR invaded in 1979 to protect their allies, launching decades of turbulence. The mujahidin, while poorly armed and divided, won small victories against the 150,000 Soviet troops. Both sides were ruthless, attacking civilians suspected of aiding or supporting the enemy. Indiscriminate Soviet air attacks on the rebels created 5 million refugees and turned the population against the Soviet occupation. Meanwhile, the United States, Pakistan, and Arab nations sent military and financial aid to the rebels and to Islamic volunteers such as the wealthy Saudi Osama bin Laden (b. 1957). Afghanistan became an unwinnable quagmire for the Soviet forces, and they withdrew in 1989, a defeat that led to the ending of Soviet communism and the dismantling of the Soviet Empire. The pro-Soviet government collapsed, and rival mujahidin groups fought for control. With the USSR gone and the civil war over, the West offered little help to reconstruct the ruined country.

mujahidin ("holy warriors") Conservative Islamic rebels who rebelled against the pro-Soviet regime in Afghanistan in the 1970s and 1980s.

As conflict between rival militias continued, a group of Pashtun militants known as the **Taliban** ("Students"), many educated in Pakistani Islamic schools, organized a military force to impose order and stamp out what they considered immoral behavior among the tribal factions fighting each other. The Taliban conquered much of the Pashtun south, then seized the capital, Kabul, in 1996 and eventually extended their influence into the north. The puritanical Taliban introduced an especially harsh form of Islamic rule. Women in Kabul, who once wore jeans and T-shirts and attended universities, were now required to wear long black robes and stay at home. Education for women was banned and alcohol disappeared from stores. The Taliban also banned pleasures such as music and films as sinful and executed people for even minor infractions. Although the streets were safe, life offered no joy. Reflecting their disdain for Afghanistan's pre-Islamic past, the Taliban

Taliban ("Students") A group of Pashtun religious students who organized a military force in the 1980s to fight what they considered immorality and corruption and to impose order in Afghanistan.

also destroyed spectacular monumental Buddhas carved into a mountainside over a millennium ago, outraging the world.

Meanwhile, international terrorist groups with a jihadist agenda and hatred for the West and the Saudi royal family formed around radical Arab volunteers who had come to fight for the muja-hidin and then remained. Osama bin Laden, who became the leader and chief financial backer of the largest group, Al Qaeda, called on Muslims to take up arms against the United States and other Western regimes, whom he called "crusaders" after those Christian knights who fought Muslims during the Intermediate Era: "Tell the Muslims everywhere that the vanguards of the warriors who are fighting the enemies of Islam belong to them."[8] These Islamic terrorist groups made Taliban-controlled Afghanistan their base, building camps to train more terrorists.

Al Qaeda and the United States

After the Al Qaeda attacks on the United States in September 2001, Americans, with widespread world support, sent military forces into Afghanistan, where, with local anti-Taliban allies, they soon displaced the Taliban from government and the main cities, destroyed the Al Qaeda bases, and installed a fragile pro-Western government. Many Afghans and most Muslims outside Afghanistan applauded the Taliban's demise, but instability ensued: the major Taliban and Al Qaeda leaders, including bin Laden, went into hiding, and the victors struggled to foster development and support a fledgling democracy, especially after the United States shifted much of its military force and development aid to Iraq. In 2005 the Taliban regrouped and mounted an insurgency against the pro-Western regime and the U.S.-European forces that supported it. By 2009, using Pakistan tribal areas as a refuge and recruiting base, the Taliban controlled large sections of the Pashtun south, forcing the new Obama administration in the United States to send in more troops, expand development efforts, and pressure Pakistan to better police the porous border.

The Afghan war was followed by a larger conflict in Iraq. Charging that Saddam Hussein had weapons of mass destruction and was linked to Al Qaeda, the U.S. president George W. Bush ordered an invasion and occupation of Iraq in 2003 by U.S. troops and small forces from a few other nations. But Bush got no support from the United Nations, many Western allies, and regional allies such as Turkey and Egypt. Massive looting followed the quick U.S. victory, as museums, ancient historical sites, power plants, armories, and communications networks were plundered. U.S. credibility suffered after American claims about the Iraqi threat proved wrong. Nor had the Americans adequately planned for the problems of the postwar reconstruction, forcing them to shift troops and resources from Afghanistan to Iraq. While the Bush administration changed its goal to fostering democracy, containing factional divisions and restoring basic services such as electricity and clean water proved a challenge.

U.S. Occupation of Iraq

Although Saddam was captured and executed, American forces, lacking enough troops, also struggled to maintain order against a persistent resistance movement, supported by many Sunnis and some Shi'ites, and to defend against terrifying suicide bombings by newly arrived foreign jihadis linked to Al Qaeda. Between 2003 and 2008 over 100,000 Iraqis died, 2 million became refugees in neighboring countries, and many were forced from their neighborhoods by "ethnic cleansing." Many Iraqis, especially Shi'ites and Kurds, had hated Saddam's bloody regime and welcomed its demise, but Iraqis, remembering British colonization after World War I, often resented yet another Western occupation and feared potential U.S. control of their oil industry. While some Arab liberals hoped democracy would flower in Iraq and throughout the region, the occupation of an oil-rich Arab country, at a high cost in U.S. and Iraqi casualties, tied down the U.S. military in a quagmire and intensified anti-U.S. feeling around the world, probably increasing support for Islamic militancy in the Muslim world generally. However, Iraqis now elected their own government, one whose Shi'ite leaders were closely tied to Iran, that had to handle ethnic and tribal rivalries while trying to hold the nation together. By 2009 violence had diminshed but had not ended, and a large U.S. military presence remained.

The Middle East in the Global System

By the late twentieth century, many observers in the region argued that most Middle Eastern countries had adjusted poorly to a rapidly changing world, lagging behind much of Asia and Latin America in development. A Lebanese novelist wrote that the dictatorial Arab regimes succeeded in depriving people not only of dignity but also of air: the opportunity to discuss problems freely. In 2002 Arab thinkers issued an Arab Human Development Report that outlined economic and social failures, including the marginalization of women and the limited development in health and education (see Witness to the Past: Assessing Arab Development). Debate has been spurred by regional cable networks, such as Qatar-based Al Jazeera, that spread awareness of political and social developments while promoting a modern image, such as by using unveiled female

Confronting Modernity

news anchors. Some urban people have access to the Internet, often at cafés, and go online to access foreign news, shop, or arrange dates, and Arab and Turkish chat rooms and blogs abound. Religious and political groups also use the Web to recruit support, among them Al Qaeda and the Iraqi insurgents fighting the U.S. occupation.

Economic Problems

The region's economic record has been checkered. The Middle East has had the world's highest unemployment rate and, except for sub-Saharan Africa, the slowest economic growth and lowest productivity. Only Turkey has fostered much industrialization and high economic growth. Nations with oil, such as Algeria, Iran, and Libya, have remained dangerously dependent on oil revenues for survival. Some 10 million migrant workers from other Arab countries, South Asia, and Southeast Asia work in the Gulf states, though most are semiskilled or unskilled and often face abuse and discrimination. Oil wealth often leads to political corruption, spurs autocratic leaders to oppose democracy, and sometimes funds Islamist and terrorist groups. Yet several small Persian Gulf states have used their oil wealth to become centers of global commerce. For example, Dubai has become one of the world's most modern cities and the region's most globalized society, with luxury hotels, towering skyscrapers, futuristic architecture, the world's largest artificial port, local branches of Western universities, and thousands of businessmen and workers from all over the world. However, the 2008–2009 world economic crisis also hurt Dubai, and many foreigners left. Yet, the Western, Japanese, and new Chinese and Indian appetite for oil ensures that the profits will flow to oil-rich nations for years to come. Middle Eastern nations that are without oil and so must rely mostly on agriculture, such as Egypt and Lebanon, have struggled to build modern economies with limited resources.

Past and present, tradition and modernity, have been all jumbled in the contemporary Middle East, whose people have hoped to preserve revered traditional patterns while harmonizing them with the modern world. An Egyptian novelist wrote that a Cairo resident has a split personality: "Half of him believes, prays, fasts and makes the pilgrimage [to Mecca]. The other half renders his values void in banks and courts and in the streets, the cinemas, perhaps even at home among his family before the television set."[9] The recent history of the Middle East, like that of India and sub-Saharan Africa, challenges the notion that contact with the modern world automatically erodes all traditional cultures and steers people inevitably toward Western models. Older patterns of life and thought have persisted in much of the region. Observers disagree whether this constitutes a barrier to progress or gives the people an anchor to deal with the destabilizing effects of change.

Islamic Militancy

Islamic militancy has become a major force, tapping a strand of unease with Western ideas. Many Muslims reject what they see as the materialistic, hedonistic values of Western culture. The Iranian Revolution of 1979 was the first successful attempt by an Islamic country to become totally independent of Western political, economic, social, and cultural influence. Iranians and Arabs have often agreed with the Indian Muslim poet Muhammad Iqbal (ik-BALL) (1873–1938), who wrote in 1927: "Against Europe I protest, And the attraction of the West: Woe for Europe and her charm, Swift to capture and disarm! Earth awaits rebuilding; rise! Out of slumber deep, Arise!"[10] Militancy has emerged as a challenge to capitalism, secularism, failed governments, and Western-style democracy. Other Muslims have feared Islamic militancy, which has not delivered a better material life in the main countries it controls, Iran and Sudan. The hopes of modernist reformest Muslims for greater economic development, political freedom, and rights for women were expressed by Reza Aslan, an influential liberal Iranian based in the United States, who argued that a reformation has begun to cleanse Islam of the "false idols" of bigotry and fanaticism and return the faith to its roots as an egalitarian social reform movement.

The Middle East and the Superpowers

Interventions by outside powers, such as the USSR and the United States, reflected the global importance of the Middle East, especially its oil wealth and its strategic location among key waterways of world trade. Until cost-effective alternative power sources become common, all industrial economies need access to Middle Eastern oil, without which modern lifestyles would come to a screeching halt. The desires of some countries to control the oil flow have led to wars, since the world community will not tolerate anything that threatens the movement of oil tankers through the Persian Gulf. While U.S. leaders hope democracy will spread, many experts worry that instability in Iraq has unsettled the entire region, perhaps strengthening Iran and forcing the United States to maintain a large military presence. Furthermore, few conflicts or persistent problems, including the Arab-Israel conflict and Arab-Iranian tensions, seem resolvable anytime soon. These challenges make the Middle East a focus of world attention and, some fear, a potential tinderbox.

Assessing Arab Development

Under the auspices of the United Nations Development Programme, a group of Arab scholars and opinion makers from the twenty-two member states of the Arab League, a regional organization, met to consider the Arab condition. In 2002 they issued the first of four planned reports that offered both a description of the Arab condition and a prescription for change. Hailed by Arab and non-Arab observers as a pathbreaking effort by Arabs to foster a debate on the inadequacies of Arab development and local barriers to progress, the first document reported great strides in many areas but also unsolved problems. This excerpt is from the Executive Summary.

The Arab Human Development Report 2002 . . . places people squarely at the [center] of development in all its dimensions: economic, social, civil, political, and cultural. It provides a neutral forum to measure progress and deficits, propose strategies to policymakers, and draw attention to country problems that can benefit from regional solutions. It is guided by the conviction that solid analysis can contribute to the many efforts underway to mobilize the region's rich human potential. There has been considerable progress in laying the foundations for health, habitat, and education. Two notable achievements are the enormous quantitative expansion in educating the young and a conspicuous improvement in fighting death. For example, life expectancy has increased by 15 years over the last three decades, and infant mortality rates have dropped by two-thirds. Moreover, the region's growth has been "pro-poor": there is much less dire poverty (defined as an income of less than a dollar a day) than in any other developing region.

But there have been warning signs as well. Over the past twenty years, growth in per capita income was the lowest in the world except in sub-Saharan Africa. . . . If such trends continue [into] the future, it will take the average Arab citizen 140 years to double his or her income. . . . The decline in productivity has been accompanied by deterioration in real wages, which has accentuated poverty. It is evident that . . . Arab countries have not developed as quickly or as fully as other comparable regions. . . . The Arab region is richer than it is developed, . . . hobbled by a . . . poverty of capabilities and . . . opportunities. These have their roots in three deficits: freedom, women's empowerment, and knowledge. Growth alone will neither bridge these gaps nor set the region on the road to sustainable development.

The way forward involves tackling human capabilities and knowledge. It also involves promoting systems of good governance, those that promote, support and sustain human well-being, based on expanding human capabilities, choices, opportunities and freedoms, . . . especially for the poorest and most marginalized members of society. The empowerment of women must be addressed throughout. . . .

[The Report concludes that] People in most Arab countries live longer than the world average life expectancy of 67. However, disease and disability reduce life expectancy by between five and 11 years. Arab women have lower life expectancy than the world average. . . . Arab countries have made tangible progress in improving literacy: . . . female literacy rates tripled since 1970. Yet 65 million adults are illiterate, almost two-thirds of them women. . . . One out of every five Arabs lives on less than $2 per day . . . Arab countries had the lowest freedom score [in the world] in the late 1990s. . . . [Utilization] of Arab women's capabilities through political and economic participation remains the lowest in the world. . . . Serious knowledge deficits include weak systems of scientific research and development.

The Arab world is at a crossroads. The fundamental choice is whether its trajectory will remain marked by inertia, as reflected in much of the present institutional context, and by ineffective policies that have produced the substantial development challenges facing the region; or whether prospects for an Arab renaissance, anchored in human development will be actively pursued.

THINKING ABOUT THE READING

1. How have Arabs done in promoting freedom, women's empowerment, and knowledge?

2. What does the report consider the major improvements and the major failures and challenges of the Arab nations?

Source: Arab Human Development Report 2002: Creating Opportunities for Future Generations (UNDP, 2002), available online at http://www.rbas.undp.org/ahdr/press_kits2002/PRExecSummary.pdf. Reprinted with permission of the United Nations Development Program (UNDP).

SECTION SUMMARY

- For several decades, Lebanon was mired in civil war among a variety of factions supported by foreign governments, including the United States; in the Sudan, Arab Muslims fought with African Christians and launched a genocide against African Muslims; and the Kurds came into conflict with the governments of several Middle Eastern countries.

- Although some Middle Eastern women have attained greater freedom and adopted Western dress, many remain in the home and wear a veil, which some argue protects them from predatory men.

- Middle Eastern societies have been divided between Islamists and secular Muslims, and musicians and writers, popular among the people, have raised the ire of religious conservatives.

- In Afghanistan, U.S.-supported Islamic rebels and Soviet-assisted communists fought for a decade until the Soviets withdrew, after which the Taliban, led by extremely conservative, repressive Muslims, took over much of the country and allowed terrorist groups such as Al Qaeda to base themselves there.

- After Al Qaeda's September 2001 attack on the United States, a U.S.-led invasion overthrew the Taliban and set up a weak pro-Western government, and in 2003 the United States invaded Iraq, generating massive looting and persistent, violent opposition, even by Iraqis who hated life under Saddam Hussein.

- Middle Eastern societies have been torn between those who feel they have failed to adapt to the modern world and those who champion tradition and urge rejection of the modern, Western values, while the region has remained extremely important to outside powers, such as the United States, because of its oil reserves.

POLITICAL CHANGE IN SUB-SAHARAN AFRICA

What were the main political consequences of decolonization in sub-Saharan Africa?

As in the Middle East, the rise of nationalism and the consequent wave of decolonization in Africa between 1957 and 1975 reduced Western political influence, reshaping societies and politics (see Chronology: Sub-Saharan Africa, 1945–Present). Countries won political independence as the British, French, Belgians, Spanish, and eventually the Portuguese came to terms with rising nationalist activity. In the 1960s, as optimistic Africans celebrated their freedom and formed governments, some observers proclaimed that this was Africa's Age of Glamor. The times were electric with change, and hopes for a better future were high. The years since have been the most momentous and rapid time of change in all of Africa's history, though they have often been destabilizing. Africans still struggle to find the right mix of policies to resolve their problems.

Nationalism and Decolonization

Anti-Colonialism

Rising nationalism sparked decolonization. The European colonial powers did little to encourage national feeling among Africans and maintained control through divide and rule of the different ethnic groups. Nationalists also had to struggle to overcome the ethnic complexities within colonies whose boundaries were arbitrarily imposed by the colonialists. But the increasing nationalism often encouraged the Western colonizers to transfer power peacefully. World War II, during which Europeans slaughtered both one another and the Africans they drafted or recruited to fight in North Africa, Asia, and Europe, undermined Western credibility. Africans felt revulsion against the Western powers and their pretensions of superiority, represented by the British official in Nigeria who argued that Nigerian "barbarism" required maintaining the "civilizing mission" into the far future. While the British and French espoused freedom and democracy, Africans noticed that these values were seldom applied in the colonies. With Western vulnerability obvious, nationalist leaders negotiated for reforms in the 1940s. After the war the British encouraged African hopes by granting independence to India and Burma and by introducing local government in some African colonies. Yet most colonial governments did little to prepare their societies for true political and economic independence.

Independence Movements

The first change came in the British Gold Coast. In 1948 riots followed when small farmers boycotted European businesses they suspected of profiteering at their expense. A rising leader, Kwame

Nkrumah **(KWAH-mee nn-KROO-muh)** (1909–1972), who had graduated from both British and American universities, became convinced that only socialism could save Africa, and in 1949 he organized a political party. He was soon arrested by the British, who viewed Nkrumah as a dangerous leftist. However, because of the continued unrest the British allowed an election in 1951 for a legislative council, which was won by Nkrumah's party. After negotiations, in 1957 the Gold Coast became independent and was renamed Ghana, after the first great West African kingdom over a millennium earlier. Nkrumah became the nation's first prime minister and Africa's hero. His message was **pan-Africanism**, the dream that all Africans would cooperate to eventually form some sort of united states of the continent.

The anticolonial dam had now burst, and it was impossible to stem the tide. By 1963, after peaceful negotiations and workers' strikes, all the British colonies in West Africa had become independent. By contrast, the French had no plans to abandon their empire and fought brutal but unsuccessful wars in the 1950s to keep Vietnam and Algeria as colonies. Finally realizing that a peaceful transition might better maintain their economic influence, France gave its colonies the option of a complete break or autonomy within a French community of closely connected nations. Initially only Guinea opted to expel the French completely, prompting the French to withdraw all economic aid. Later all the French colonies became fully independent, though they usually maintained close political and economic ties to France.

Whereas peaceful power transfers succeeded in many colonies, widespread violence preceded or accompanied independence in others. Many British settlers had migrated to Kenya after both World War I and World War II, taking land from the Africans to establish farms. In 1952 many Gikuyu, Kenya's largest ethnic group, who had suffered the most land losses, began an eight-year uprising known as the **Mau Mau Rebellion**, during which they attacked British farmers and officials. The British sent thousands of troops and committed atrocities against pro–Mau Mau villages, ultimately killing 10,000 Gikuyu and detaining 90,000 others in harsh prison camps, where many died from disease or mistreatment. Finally realizing the futility of their cause, the British released from prison the leading nationalist leader, Jomo Kenyatta **(ken-YAH-tuh)** (ca. 1889–1978), a Gikuyu former herd boy who had studied anthropology in Britain. Negotiations resulted in Kenyan independence in 1963, and Kenyatta became the first freely elected prime minister. Britain also granted independence to its other East African colonies, Uganda and Tanzania. In Kenya white settlers who had strongly opposed political rights for the African majority often remained, sometimes serving in the Kenyan government.

Violence also engulfed the Belgian Congo, a vast, natural resource–rich territory containing some two hundred ethnic groups. The Belgians had failed to foster an educated leadership class, encourage national consciousness, or build adequate paved roads, bridges, and telephone systems. At independence the Congo had only a few university graduates. The only Congolese leader with any national following, the widely admired left-leaning visionary Patrice Lumumba **(loo-MOOM-buh)** (1925–1961), a former post office clerk and brewery director, opposed economic domination by Belgian business and mining interests. In 1959 riots broke out in Congolese cities, forcing the Belgians to announce the colony's first free elections, which were won by Lumumba's party. As Lumumba took power, some Congolese troops mutinied and attacked whites. Taking advantage of the chaos, Belgian-supported leaders in the mineral-rich Katanga region who opposed Lumumba announced their secession from the country. The United Nations sent in a peacekeeping force that restored order in the Congo. But Katanga leaders, with the complicity of Belgium and the United States, who feared that Lumumba favored the Soviet Union, abducted and murdered him in 1961. Both Belgium and the U.S. supported the Congo's new leader, General Joseph Mobuto **(mo-BOO-to)**, who became a dictator. In 1971 Mobuto, who had given his country a new name, Zaire, also changed his name to Mobuto Sese Seko, "Mobuto the All Powerful." He required his people to sing his praises every day at the workplace and in schools and to replace European names and values with African ones, including exchanging Western clothes, such as ties, for traditional garb. Wearing a tie then became an act of political resistance for men.

Portugal, ruled by a fascist dictator, had been reluctant to give up its empire. When revolts broke out in its three colonies—Angola, Guinea-Bissau, and Mozambique—in the 1960s, the Portuguese military struggled to crush them. Angola's liberation movement was divided into three rival

CHRONOLOGY
Sub-Saharan Africa, 1945–Present

1948 Introduction of apartheid in South Africa

1949 First mass-based political party in Gold Coast

1952–1960 Mau Mau uprising in Kenya

1957 Independence for Ghana

1957–1975 African decolonization

1961 Assassination of Patrice Lumumba in Congo

1965–1980 White government in Southern Rhodesia

1967–1970 Nigerian civil war

1975 Independence for Portuguese colonies

1991–1994 Civil war in Somalia

1994 Genocide in Rwanda

1994 Nelson Mandela first black president of South Africa

1997 End of Mobuto era in Congo

pan-Africanism The dream that all Africans would cooperate to eventually form some sort of united states of the continent.

Mau Mau Rebellion An eight-year uprising in the 1950s by the Gikuyu people in Kenya against British rule.

Dismantling Portuguese Rule

Hulton-Deutch Collection/Corbis

factions based on the country's major ethnic groupings, while Marxists led the major liberation movements in Mozambique and Guinea Bissau. The visionary Amilcar Cabral **(AH-mill-CAR kah-BRAHL)** (1924–1973), a university-educated agronomist who founded and led the Guinea-Bissau movement, emphasized educating the people to empower them, telling his followers: "Learn from life, people, books, the experiences of others, never stop learning."[11] Portuguese agents assassinated Cabral in 1973. In 1974, however, Portugal's war-weary army ended the dictatorship in Portugal, and the new democratic, socialist-led government granted the colonies their independence in 1975. In Angola, the nationalist factions fought each other for dominance for the next two decades, and Mozambique's revolutionary government faced a long insurgency supported by white-ruled South Africa.

Mau Mau   During the 1950s Africans in Kenya, especially the Gikuyu, rebelled against British colonial rule. The British responded by detaining some 90,000 suspected rebels and sympathizers in concentration camps such as this, where many died.

The British colonies of the Rhodesias and Nyasaland in southern Africa, all containing white settlers who bitterly resisted efforts at political and social equality for Africans, were among the last colonies to gain independence under black majority rule. After African nationalists launched largely nonviolent resistance campaigns, the British granted independence to Zambia (Northern Rhodesia) and Malawi (formerly Nyasaland), both of which had only small white minorities in 1963. But the large white settler population in Southern Rhodesia declared independence from Britain in 1965 and installed a white racist government that imposed stricter racial segregation and prohibited nonwhite political activity. Africans took up arms in two rival Marxist-led liberation movements. By 1980 the African resistance was so strong that the United States and Britain pressured the white government to allow elections, which were won by Robert Mugabe **(moo-GAH-bee)** (b. 1924), a guerrilla leader and former political prisoner. The country became independent as Zimbabwe.

Political Change and Conflict

New Nations   A West African scholar called the term *nation* "a magical word meant to exorcise ethnic quarrels and antagonisms—and as such very precious"[12]; but, as he conceded, the magic usually failed to overcome disunity. New African nations typically experienced political and economic challenges that fostered instability: coups, prolonged civil wars, and recurring famines (see Map 30.3). Although most new nations started as parliamentary democracies, only a few sustained democratic systems. Rule by the military or by one dominant party has been more common. Militaries have often been the only groups that can govern effectively, since they have a sense of superiority over civilians, good internal communications, and a tradition of discipline. But military officers enjoying a privileged existence are also often out of touch with the population; used to giving orders, they have ruled with a heavy hand and often looted treasuries. Civilian leaders have often favored one-party states because such parties can minimize ethnic divisions. While some of these one-party states, such as in the Congo (Zaire), have been despotisms, others have been relatively open, even allowing some choice among candidates for office. Some nations, such as Nigeria and Ghana, have shifted back and forth between authoritarian military dictatorships and ineffective, corrupt civilian governments. Some of the despotic governments have brutally mistreated their own people. During the 1970s in Uganda, then ruled by Idi Amin **(EE-dee AH-meen)** (1925–2004), a poorly educated former amateur boxing champion who rose to become a general, some 300,000 people were killed, and thousands more were jailed or fled into exile.

Western-style democracy has had little chance to flower in these artificial countries with a tiny middle class and numerous poor people. Given the often deteriorating economic conditions, governments have had little money to spend on containing ethnic tensions or for building schools,

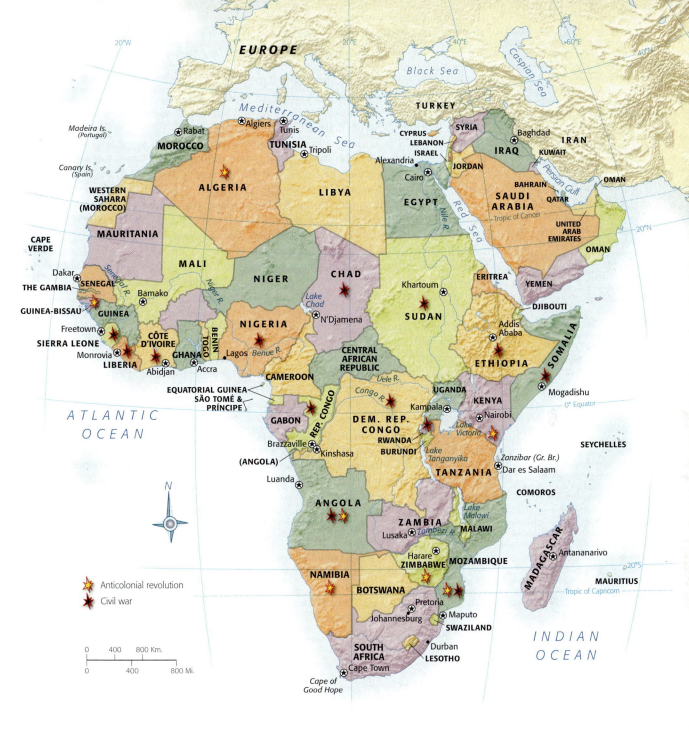

Map 30.3 Contemporary Africa and the Middle East
Sub-Saharan and North Africa contain over forty nations. Six sub-Saharan African nations and Algeria in North Africa experienced anticolonial revolutions, and a dozen sub-Saharan nations have been racked by civil wars since independence.

★ Anticolonial revolution
✹ Civil war

e Interactive Map

hospitals, and roads. As a result, the nationalist leaders and parties that governed the new nations often lost their credibility and mass support after a few years. For instance, Ghana's Kwame Nkrumah was overthrown for economic mismanagement and an autocratic governing style and died in exile. Some African leaders have been highly respected, farsighted visionaries, such as Tanzania's Julius Nyerere **(NEE-ya-RARE-y)** (g. 1962–1985) and Mozambique's Samora Machel (g. 1975–1986), and pragmatic problem solvers, such as South Africa's first black president, Nelson Mandela. While not all their initiatives succeeded, these leaders have used political office largely to improve society rather than enrich themselves. However, many leaders, emulating the despotic kings of old Africa, have too often been reluctant to give up their power, rigging elections or having compliant parliaments declare them presidents for life. Others have disappointed or brutalized their people. Some, such as the Congo (Zaire) dictator Mobuto (g. 1965–1997) and the Nigerian military dictator Sani Abacha (g. 1993–1998), have been ruthless crooks, arresting or murdering opponents and plundering the public treasury to amass multibillion-dollar fortunes. When Abacha, hopped up on Viagra, died of a heart attack while he engaged in an orgy with prostitutes, few Nigerians lamented.

Social Conflict

Political instability, conflict, and social unrest have grown as people have struggled for their share of the wealth. The blatant corruption, conspicuous consumption, and smuggling in government and the business sector have increased inequalities and deepened public frustrations. Sub-Saharan Africa has the world's highest income inequality. In some countries, government officials were known as "Mr. 10 Percent," a reference to the share of public budgets they grab. East Africans chastise the **wabenzi**—"people who drive a Mercedes Benz"—a privileged urban class of politicians, bureaucrats, professionals, military officers, and businessmen who manipulate their connections to amass wealth. These elites have often squandered scarce resources on importing luxuries, such as fancy cars and hard liquor, signs of the continuing hold of Western taste and consumer goods.

wabenzi ("people who drive a Mercedes Benz") A privileged urban class in Africa of politicians, bureaucrats, professionals, military officers, and businessmen who manipulate their connections to amass wealth.

On the other hand, in some societies relations between governments and the governed have improved. New grassroots nongovernmental organizations have addressed issues such as human rights and the environment, and ordinary people have demanded greater responsibility for improving their lives. For example, by 2000 some 25,000 local women's groups in Kenya had pushed for improved rights and other issues, such as environmental protection. The Kenyan women's rights and environmental activist, Wangari Maathai (wan-GAHR-ee MAH-thai), won the Nobel Peace Prize in 2005 (see Chapter 26). Since few Africans can afford health insurance, in countries such as Senegal poor people have come together to form small mutual health organizations, negotiating with local clinics to get an affordable group rate for health care. In Liberia, strong support from women voters helped economist Ellen Johnson-Sirleaf (b. 1939), a Harvard-trained banker and former United Nations official, become Africa's first woman president in 2005, as her country sought to recover from a long civil war and then a corrupt dictatorship. But she faced a monumental challenge to bring progress to a maimed nation with no piped water or electric grid and few functioning schools and hospitals.

Nigeria and Its Challenges

Africa's hopes and frustrations are mirrored in Nigeria, home to some 140 million people, about a fifth of Africa's total population. Nigeria's ethnic and religious diversity and natural wealth have been both a blessing and a curse. Among the 250 ethnic groups, about two-thirds of the people belong to the Hausa-Fulani, Igbo (Ibo), or Yoruba groups. Nigeria's oil wealth has produced 80 percent of the nation's total revenues but has also corrupted politics and increased social inequality. Once a food exporter, Nigeria neglected agriculture and is now a food importer. Nearly two thirds of the people have insufficient food. Moreover, Nigeria's history has frequently been punctuated by coups, countercoups, riots, political assassinations, and civil war rooted in regional and ethnic rivalries. Between 1967 and 1970 Nigeria endured a bloody civil war to prevent the secession of the Igbo-dominated oil-rich southeast region. The religious divide between Christians, who dominate the south, and Muslims, who control the northern states, also complicates politics. Following a Muslim revival among the Hausa-Fulani, many northern states imposed strict Islamic law, antagonizing non-Muslims. Several Muslim women were sentenced to death by stoning for adultery while the men involved were not punished, causing an outcry in Nigeria and around the world. Sometimes severe Christian-Muslim fighting causes the death of hundreds of people. The chaos has often led to corrupt military rule, which has brought stability by suppressing opposition but pushed the people hard, alternated with periods of corrupt civilian democracy, which has increased political freedom but often governed ineffectively.

The Nigerian oil industry, while creating some prosperity, has also made Nigeria dependent on oil exports. A few politicians, bureaucrats, and businessmen have monopolized oil profits, fostering corruption, sometimes outright plunder of public wealth, and inequitable wealth distribution. By 2005 the top 20 percent of Nigerians received 56 percent of all the country's wealth, while the bottom 20 percent got only 4.4 percent. People in the southern oil-producing districts see few benefits and watch sullenly as pipelines through their villages move oil to the coastal ports, from where tankers carry the oil to European and North American consumers. Their sporadic protests, including sabotage of the oil pipelines, have been met with military force and sometimes execution of protest leaders. Meanwhile, local rebel groups harass the oil industry and fight the army. Disenchanted Nigerians refer to a "republic of the privileged and rich" and a "moneytocracy." After oil money created high expectations in the 1970s, world oil prices collapsed in the 1980s, forcing the nation to take on massive foreign debt.

Political Turmoil

The combination of artificial boundaries, weak national identity, and economic collapse has produced chronic turmoil in several African nations, resulting in what one discouraged African observer called the "dark night of bloodshed and death." Liberia and Sierra Leone, once among the more stable countries, disintegrated in the 1990s as ethnic-based rebel groups challenged governments for power. In both countries thousands fled the slaughter and the maiming of civilians, causing African nations like Nigeria to send in troops to bring stability. In drought-plagued Somalia, when longtime military rule collapsed in 1991, the country divided into regions ruled by feuding

Somali clans with their own armies. As the Somali economy disintegrated, causing thousands to starve to death, the United Nations dispatched a humanitarian mission. But some Americans with the mission were killed and the U.N. withdrew in 1994, unable to achieve a unified government. Somalia remained a country in name only, controlled by warlords and, more recently, engulfed in civil war involving various Islamist militias, a weak central government, and the Ethiopian army. In the chaos, desperate young men in coastal villages turned to piracy, disrupting shipping and prompting an international naval force to police the nearby seas.

Hatreds led to genocide in impoverished, densely populated Rwanda, divided between majority Hutus and minority Tutsis. The Belgians had ruled through Tutsi kings, and soon after independence, the Hutus rebelled, slaughtering thousands of Tutsis and forcing others into exile. The remaining Tutsis faced discrimination and repression. In 1994 the extremist Hutu government began a genocide against the Tutsis and moderate Hutus, murdering over 500,000 people. Tutsi exiles based in Uganda then invaded Rwanda, forcing the Hutu leaders and their followers—over 2 million–into the neighboring Congo. As a result, the new Tutsi-led government continued to face militant Congo-based Hutu resistance groups, leading to Rwandan military incursions into the Congo and support for Congolese rebel groups.

The New South Africa

South Africa experienced a distinctive conflict and inequality for over three centuries. From World War II to the early 1990s, South Africa remained the last bastion of institutionalized white racism on a continent where white rule had once been widespread. The white population, in the 1990s some 15 percent of the total, and divided between an Afrikaner majority (descendants of Dutch settlers) and an English minority, ruled the black majority (74 percent) and the Indians (2 percent) and mixed-descent Coloreds (9 percent). Racial inequality became more systematic after 1948, when Afrikaner nationalists won the white-only elections and declared full independence from Britain. A top nationalist leader claimed: "We [whites] need [Africans] because they work for us but they can never claim political rights. Not now, nor in the future."[13] Their new policy, **apartheid** (uh-PAHRT-ate) ("separate development"), set up a ruthless police state to enforce racial separation; laws required all Africans to carry ID ("pass") cards specifying the locations where they could legally reside or visit. Interracial marriage and sexual relations were also outlawed. Apartheid created a nearly unparalleled cruelty, a chilling juxtaposition of comfort for whites and despair for blacks.

White Supremacy

apartheid ("separate development") A South African policy to set up a police state to enforce racial separation.

Apartheid expanded segregation to include designated residential areas, schools, recreational facilities, and public accommodations. Urban black men were commonly housed in crowded dormitories near the mines or factories where they worked or, often with their families, in shantytown suburbs, from where they commuted to their jobs. While most white families lived comfortably in well-furnished apartments or houses with swimming pools, a typical house in Soweto, a dusty African suburb of Johannesburg, was bleak, with the residents using candles or gas lamps for lighting and most having no running water. Demoralized blacks, especially men, found escape in alcohol, frequenting the informal bars that dotted African urban neighborhoods.

Apartheid also created what white leaders called tribal homelands, known as **bantustans**, rural reservations where black Africans were required to live if they were not needed in the modern economy. The system allocated whites 87 percent of the nation's land and nonwhites the other 13 percent. Every year thousands of Africans were forcibly resettled to the impoverished bantustans, which contained too little fertile land and too few jobs, hospitals, and secondary schools. Infant mortality rates in the bantustans were among the world's highest. Under this system black families were fractured as men and women were recruited on annual contracts for jobs outside the bantustans. Even if a husband and wife were both recruited for jobs in the same city, they could not legally visit each other if their ID cards restricted each of them to a different neighborhood.

bantustans Rural reservations in South Africa where black Africans under apartheid were required to live if they were not needed in the modern economy.

Rich in strategic minerals such as gold, diamonds, uranium, platinum, and chrome, South Africa became the most industrialized African nation. But while whites enjoyed one of the world's highest standards of living, with access to well-funded schools and medical centers, Africans and the Colored and Indian minorities enjoyed few benefits. Whites controlled over two-thirds of the nation's wealth and personal disposable income, while a third of Africans were unemployed. By 1994 the ratio of average black to white incomes stood at 1:10, the world's most inequitable income distribution. The government enjoyed the open or tacit support of several industrialized countries, including the United States, Britain, and Japan, who feared that unrest or black majority rule might threaten their billions in investments and access to lucrative resources.

Africans resisted and often paid a price for their defiance. The police state featured brutal treatment of dissidents and the world's highest rate of execution. Stephen Biko (1946–1977), a former medi-

African Resistance

cal student who led an organization that encouraged black pride and self-reliance, was beaten to death in police custody. Hundreds of Africans were arrested each day for "pass law" violations and held for a few days or weeks. The police violently repressed protests and imprisoned thousands of dissidents, including numerous children, often without trial. Off-duty policemen sometimes assassinated black leaders, such as Victoria Mxenge (ma-SEN-gee), a lawyer who defended anti-apartheid activists. Nevertheless, various forms of defiance, including strikes, work interruptions, and sabotage, became common. Resistance was often subtle, too; Nobel Prize–winning white South African novelist and apartheid critic Nadine Gordimer (b. 1923) described in her novel, *Something Out There*, how even domestic servants in white households could protest and assert their dignity in nonverbal ways:

> *Every household in the fine suburb had several black servants—a shifting population of pretty young housemaids whose long red nails and pertness not only asserted the indignity of being un- discovered fashion models but kept hoisted a cocky guerrilla pride against servitude to whites.*[14]

The African National Congress (ANC), the major opposition organization, remained multira- cial, with some whites, Coloreds, and Indians serving in its leadership. In 1955, despairing of peace- ful change, a more militant ANC leadership framed its inclusive vision in the Freedom Charter: "South Africa belongs to all who live in it, black and white."[15] But the government declared the ANC illegal and fierce repression forced it underground, where it adopted violent resistance. Several of its main leaders, including Nelson Mandela (b. 1918), spent almost thirty years in prison for their political activities (see Profile: Nelson and Winnie Mandela, South African Freedom Fighters). Women, among them Mandela's wife, Winnie Mandela, played an influential role in the ANC, often facing arrest and mistreatment.

Ultimately, international isolation, economic troubles, the need for more highly skilled black workers, and growing black unrest forced the government to relax apartheid and release Mandela from prison. The two parties agreed on a new constitution requiring "one man, one vote," and in 1994 an amazed world saw white supremacy come to an end in the first all-race elections in South African history, which installed Mandela as president and gave the ANC two-thirds of the seats in Parliament. The ANC government enjoyed massive goodwill but also faced daunting challenges in healing a deeply fragmented society while restoring the pride and spirits of Africans demoralized by apartheid. Mandela sought the right mix of racial reconciliation and major changes to benefit the disadvantaged black majority. In 1999 he voluntarily retired, a still-popular figure, and the ANC retained power in free elections. It improved services, such as electricity and water, in black com- munities, raised black living standards, and fostered a growing black upper and middle class.

Yet millions of other blacks have felt neglected, wanting better land and services and com- plaining about corruption and mismanagement. South Africa has one of the world's highest rates of HIV/AIDS, crime has rapidly increased, violent protests have broken out, and black unemploy- ment has remained high. In 2009 the election of a more radical ANC leader, Jacob Zuma (b. 1942), prompted some blacks to leave the ANC and form or join opposition parties. Zuma has faced widespread discontent and strikes. But while some of the goodwill of the Mandela years has faded, given the long history of repression and fear, the rapid transition to multiparty democracy has been impressive. People all over the continent hope that the nation of 50 million succeeds in healing racial wounds while spreading the wealth to all its citizens.

SECTION SUMMARY

- European colonial rulers had played rival ethnic groups in Africa against each other, but after World War II, pressures for independence became stronger and Ghana, under the leadership of Kwame Nkrumah, became the first colony to achieve independence.

- Most British colonies attained independence through peaceful means, but Kenya's transition was long and violent, as was that of the Belgian Congo, Angola, Guinea-Bissau, Mozambique, and Zimbabwe.

- After independence, many African nations were ruled by military dictatorships or corrupt civilians, many nationalist leaders lost favor over time, the gap between rich and poor widened, and some nations experienced ongoing violence, disorder, and genocide.

- Nigeria, home to rival ethnic and religious groups, has experienced civil war, coups, and corrupt military rule, and while its oil reserves have brought wealth to the elite, they have hardly benefited the poor, and dependence on them led to economic problems in the 1980s.

- Under apartheid, a white minority in South Africa viciously suppressed the black majority with laws restricting their political, economic, and physical freedom, but the African National Congress, led by Nelson Mandela, resisted fiercely and ultimately won control of the government in 1994.

NELSON AND WINNIE MANDELA, SOUTH AFRICAN FREEDOM FIGHTERS

Courageous symbols of unbroken black determination, Nelson Mandela (b. 1918) and Winnie Mandela (b. 1934) made a mark on history in the struggle against apartheid, South Africa's policy of rigid racial separation, despite severe white supremacist repression. The inspirational Mandelas represented African ambitions for several generations.

Nelson Mandela was born in the Transkei reserve near South Africa's southeast coast, the son of a Xhosa (KHO-sa) chief. His middle name, Rolihlahla (ROH-lee-la-la), meant "troublemaker." Mandela was groomed to succeed his father as chief, but, after years of hearing stories about the valor of his ancestors in war, he wanted to help with the freedom struggle. After attending a Methodist school and then earning a B.A. from the only college for black South Africans, he qualified as a lawyer and opened the country's first black legal practice. He also joined the African National Congress (ANC), which had, for half a century, followed a policy of promoting education for blacks and cautiously criticizing rather than confronting the government. Mandela and his young colleagues transformed the ANC into an activist mass movement. In 1958 he married Winnie Madikizela (MAH-dee-kee-ZEH-la), a Xhosa nurse, but they had only a short life together before political repression separated them.

The white government tolerated little opposition. In 1960, after police opened fire on 20,000 peaceful black protesters, killing 69 of them (including women and children), the government banned the ANC and arrested black leaders. The ANC then became an underground movement committed to violence. In 1964, found guilty of sabotage and treason, Mandela was sentenced to life in prison. In his stirring statement to the court, Mandela articulated his goals: "During my lifetime I have dedicated myself to this struggle of the African people. I have fought against [both] white and black domination. I have cherished the ideal of a democratic and free society in which all persons live together in harmony and with equal opportunities. It is an ideal for which I am prepared to die."

Mandela spent most of the next three decades in the notorious Robben Island prison off Cape Town, where he was joined by dozens of other ANC leaders and members. He turned the prison experience into an ANC school, leading political discussions and studying other freedom fighters, such as Mohandas Gandhi and Jawaharlal Nehru in India. Over the years Mandela grew into an international hero. During his imprisonment, although jailed for a short time herself and then confined to a remote settlement, Winnie Mandela kept her husband's flame burning, gaining an international reputation as a freedom fighter. Returning to Johannesburg in 1985, Winnie campaigned ceaselessly for black rights and her husband's release, earning a reputation for courage and skill in negotiating a male-dominated society.

In 1990, after secret negotiations, a realistic new South African president, F. W. de Klerk, legalized the ANC and released Nelson Mandela from prison, and in 1993 Nelson Mandela and de Klerk shared a Nobel Peace Prize. In 1994 the first all-race elections made Nelson Mandela the first black president of South Africa. At his inauguration, he told the people: "Out of the experience of an extraordinary human disaster that lasted too long must be born a society of which all humanity will be proud. Let there be justice [and] peace for all. We must act together as a united people, for the birth of a new world. God bless Africa!"

Forgiving and pragmatic, Mandela remained popular with most South Africans, white and black. His moderate, accommodationist style reassured whites but also disappointed some impatient blacks. Meanwhile, his marriage to Winnie

Nelson Mandela A symbol of black South African aspirations for nearly thirty years in prison, Mandela led the African National Congress after his release and, in 1994, was elected the nation's first black president.

Corbis

889

became strained, in part because of her controversial activities, legal problems, and political ambitions. Her popularity declined after 1988 when bodyguards she hired to protect her from black and white foes were implicated in the kidnapping and murder of a black youth; Winnie herself was convicted of involvement in the kidnapping, but her sentence was commuted. In 1996 Nelson and Winnie Mandela divorced. Winnie remained active in the ANC, supporting a militant faction that mistrusted Nelson's conciliatory policy of bringing white and black South Africans together. Nelson later married Grace Machel, the widow of the respected Mozambique president Samora Machel, who had been killed in an airplane crash.

In 1999, at the age of eighty-one, Mandela voluntarily retired from politics and moved to his native village. In his autobiography, he wrote, "I have walked a long road to free-dom. I have tried not to falter, I have made missteps along the way. After climbing a great hill, one only finds that there are many more hills to climb. With freedom come responsibilities. I dare not linger, for my long walk is not yet ended." The long walk taken by Nelson and Winnie Mandela changed history.

THINKING ABOUT THE PROFILE

1. Why did the Mandelas become international symbols of the freedom struggle?
2. How did the Mandelas change history?

Note: Quotations from Kevin Shillington, *History of Africa*, rev. ed. (New York: St. Martin's, 1995), 405; and Nelson Mandela, *Long Walk to Freedom: The Autobiography of Nelson Mandela* (Boston: Little, Brown, 1996), 620, 625.

AFRICAN ECONOMIES, SOCIETIES, AND CULTURES

What new economic, social, and cultural patterns have emerged in Africa?

Since the 1960s, for many sub-Saharan African nations, achieving economic development has seemed a desperate struggle rather than an exhilarating challenge. African nations have tried various strategies, including capitalism and socialism, to benefit the majority of people, but no strategy has proved effective over the long term. Economic problems have proliferated. But Africans have created new social and cultural forms to aid them in dealing with their problems.

Economic Change and Underdevelopment

Economic Problems

Africa has experienced severe economic problems. As during colonial times, Africans have mostly supplied agricultural and mineral resources, such as cocoa and copper, to the global economy, but this has not brought widespread wealth. For example, in Kenya, small farmers encouraged to abandon subsistence food growing and take up tobacco planting found that their new crops brought in little money, required cutting down adjacent forests, and leached nutrients from the soil. In 2004 one of the farmers, Jane Chacha, who still lived in the same two-room, mud-and-thatch house she and her husband built fifteen years earlier, complained that "this is a hopeless dream. Growing tobacco has been nothing but trouble."[16]

Only a few countries have enjoyed consistently robust economic growth, been able to escape reliance on producing one or two resources, or substantially raised living standards. As a result, sub-Saharan Africa contains most of the world's twenty poorest countries. With nearly 800 million people, this region accounts for only 1 percent of the world's production of goods and services, about the same as one of the smallest European nations, Belgium, with 10 million people. Most sub-Saharan African countries have annual per capita incomes of under $1,000 per year, and some are under $500. Half of the people earn less than $1 per day, the world's highest rate of desperate poverty. Sub-Saharan Africa has also had the world's highest infant mortality rates and lowest literacy rates and average life expectancies.

The economic doldrums are linked to other problems. The region's economies have generally grown by 1 to 2 percent a year, but its population increase is the world's highest, over 3 percent. Since 10 to 15 percent of babies die before their first birthday, parents have had an incentive to have many children to provide for old-age security. While the population may double by 2025, new jobs, classrooms, and food supplies will not keep pace. Only a few nations have enjoyed self-sufficiency in food production; most require food imports from Europe and North America. Women grow the bulk of the food, but the male farmers growing cash crops receive most of the government aid. Millions of people are chronically malnourished, and several million children die each year from hunger-related ailments. In addition, severe drought and the drying up of water sources results in numerous deaths from dehydration or starvation, or in migration in search of a better life. In Kenya some malnourished people are reduced to eating cactus. Some 25 million girls receive no elementary education, and less than half of school-age children attend school, while millions of others work in the labor force. Poverty means scraping by, physically and mentally exhausted by the struggle for survival.

As Africans have sought viable economic strategies to achieve economic development, neocolonial capitalism, involving close economic ties to the Western nations, foreign investment, and free markets, has became the most common model. Countries following this strategy have favored the cash crops and minerals that had dominated the colonial economy, and Westerners, especially British and French, have managed or owned a substantial portion of the economies. A few countries prospered with this strategy, but the political consequences were often negative. Ivory Coast (or Côte d'Ivoire) and Kenya were hospitable to a Western presence, and in the 1960s and 1970s they were rewarded with high growth and rising incomes. Ivory Coast remained a major exporter of coffee and cocoa, while Kenya, with world-famous game parks, lived from tourism and the export of coffee, tea, and minerals. By the 1980s both had per capita incomes about double the African average. That success came at some cost, however. The Ivory Coast rapidly logged the once-verdant forest, causing less rain, and more French lived there than during colonial times, owning, along with other non-Ivoireans, most of the economy. Both countries also eventually became one-party states that, while stable, grew despotic and corrupt. While the glittering major cities, Abidjan and Nairobi, had fancy restaurants, boutiques, and nightclubs, some rural people faced starvation. By the 1990s, as collapsing world prices for coffee and cocoa stressed their economies, protesters demanded more democracy, the delicate ecologies became dangerously unbalanced, and crime rates soared. Economic development became a fading memory. Ivory Coast became engulfed in civil war, while Kenyans forced out a dictator and elected a reformist government that, while spurring economic growth, failed to fulfill most of its promises. In 2008 a disputed Kenyan election led to riots, interethnic fighting, and hundreds of deaths.

The most disastrous neocolonial capitalist state was the Democratic Republic of the Congo (known as Zaire between 1971 and 1997). A huge country, with 66 million people, Congo enjoys a strategic location in the center of Africa and rich mineral resources, but it became Africa's biggest failure. The United States and Belgium poured in billions of investment and aid to support President Mobuto, who looted the treasury and foreign aid to amass a huge personal fortune—some 4 to 5 billion dollars—while repressing his opponents. Mobuto built palaces for himself all over the country and in Europe and hired top French chefs to prepare his food, spending little money on schools, roads, telephones, and hospitals. Hence, the Congo suffered one of the world's highest infant mortality rates, limited health care, and widespread malnutrition. In 1997 a long-festering rebellion gained strength, forcing Mobuto into exile, where he died. Rebels took over, but they have done little to foster democracy or development. The Congo soon fragmented in civil war and interethnic fighting that drew in armies from neighboring countries, and rebel groups controlled large sections of the sprawling country. Nearly 4 million Congolese died from the fighting and the collapse of medical care, causing a humanitarian crisis.

The most recent showcases for economic success have been Ghana and Botswana. Once a symbol of failure, Ghana has made steady progress. For several decades the country experienced a roller coaster of corrupt civilian governments interspersed with military regimes. But in the 1990s the leaders gradually strengthened democracy and adopted certain policies of the Asian Little Dragons, such as Taiwan and South Korea, by mixing capitalism and socialism. Ghana became increasingly prosperous: by 2009 it enjoyed one of the continent's highest annual per capital incomes, $2,700, a life expectancy of fifty-nine, democratic elections, and press freedom. In addition, investment in schools resulted in one of Africa's most educated populations. Botswana also made a turnaround. When it gained independence in 1966, it was one of the world's poorest countries, with an annual per capita income of $35. Gradually, however, using ethnic traditions as a foundation, Botswanans carved out a successful democracy; the economy, health care, education, and protection of resources all steadily improved, despite deadly droughts. By 2000 Botswanans had fostered living standards higher than those of most African and many Middle Eastern, Asian, and Latin American societies, boasting an annual per capita income of over $3,000, an economy growing by 11 percent a year, and a literacy rate of 70 percent. Unfortunately, the AIDs epidemic, which hit Botswana particularly hard, rapidly undermined economic and health gains and reduced life expectancy to thirty-four years.

Some African nationalists pursued revolutionary or reformist strategies. Since the political institutions, businesses, and plantations inherited from colonialism were geared to transfer wealth and resources to the West, the radicals argued that they could not spark economic development: after independence more wealth still flowed out of Africa than into it. To empower Africans, it was necessary to replace the colonial state with something entirely new. Thus various social revolutionary regimes emerged from the long wars of liberation against colonial or white minority governments. Looking toward China or the USSR for inspiration, Marxist revolutionary governments

Neocolonial Capitalism

Social Revolutionary States

came to power in Angola and Mozambique after the Portuguese left. To counter these governments, white-ruled South Africa sponsored opposition guerrilla movements, aided by an anticommunist United States, that kept these countries in civil war for several decades. During Angola's conflict, over 1.5 million people died. While the war eventually ended, Angola, blessed with coffee, diamonds, and especially oil but plagued with corruption, still struggled to foster development despite considerable Western investment. The civil war in Mozambique resulted in 1 million deaths and 5 million refugees. Since its war ended in 1992, the pragmatic Marxist leaders introduced multiparty elections and liberalized the economy, raising the per capita income to $1,500.

One social revolutionary state, Zimbabwe, at first became Africa's biggest success story. The Marxist-influenced government, led by the liberation hero Robert Mugabe, proved pragmatic for over a decade, largely respecting democracy and human rights, encouraging the white minority to stay, and raising living standards and opportunities for black Zimbabweans. The country became one of Africa's few food-exporting nations. But Zimbabwe eventually faced severe problems, including tensions between rival African ethnic groups. Blacks resented continuing white ownership of the best farmland, and during the 1990s Mugabe became more dictatorial and used land disputes to divide the nation. As his support waned, he rigged elections, harassed or jailed his opponents, and ordered the seizure of white-owned farms. Meanwhile, uncontrolled inflation made local currency worthless. Commercial agriculture collapsed, the country was gripped by drought and a cholera outbreak, life expectancy dropped sharply, food disappeared from shops, refugees fled to neighboring countries, and Mugabe's police demolished the homes and shops of poor blacks who favored the opposition, driving them out of the cities. As the nation veered toward catastrophe, African nations forced Mugabe to form a coalition government with the opposition party in 2009, but he still held most of the power.

African Socialism and Reform

Tanzania experimented with an "African" socialism compatible with African traditions, especially cooperation and mutual sharing of resources. Under its visionary president, Julius Nyerere (1922–1999), Tanzania reorganized agriculture into cooperative villages with the goal of achieving national self-sufficiency. Nyerere encouraged some democracy in his one-party state by holding regular elections and allowing multiple candidates to run for each office or parliamentary seat. His emphasis on building schools and clinics improved literacy to 68 percent and health to well above African norms. But Nyerere's dreams were dashed as the government became overly bureaucratic, the planning proved inadequate, and many people lost enthusiasm for socialism. Because Tanzania imported few luxury goods, life was austere compared to that available to affluent residents in capitalist Kenya. Peasants often preferred their small family farms to the collective villages they were encouraged, or forced, to join. As the economy slumped, Tanzania had to take more foreign loans. Still admired by his people, Nyerere retired in 1985, one of the few founding African leaders to voluntarily give up power. His successors dismantled much of the socialist structure, promoted free enterprise, welcomed foreign investment and loans, and fostered a multiparty system. Yet life for most Tanzanians has improved little, malnutrition has become widespread, and Tanzania remains a poor nation.

Social Change

City Life

Modern Africa has seen rapid social change. More people live in cosmopolitan cities where traditional and modern attitudes meet, mix, and clash. City life offers more variety—jobs, department stores, movie theaters, nightclubs—than village life and hence attracts rural people. The cities that developed under colonial auspices, such as Nairobi (Kenya), Lagos (Nigeria), and Dakar (Senegal), which have grown nearly 5 percent a year since 1980, serve as economic centers and seats of government. Between 1965 and 2000 the percentage of Africans living in urban areas doubled to 30 percent. Abidjan in Ivory Coast and Luanda in Angola each contain a quarter of their country's population. Cities have grown so fast that services such as buses, water, power, police, schools, and health centers cannot meet peoples' needs. These problems are exemplified by Nigeria's largest city, Lagos, which grew from less than a million in 1965 to a megalopolis of some 12 million by 2008. A journalist described the urban chaos:

> *Lagos is a vast laboratory of helter-skelter expansion, a fount of confusion and frenzy. A tiny minority of people live extremely well, in villas or plush apartments, and they go to work in gleaming skyscrapers that sit awkwardly next to traditional marketplaces. A vastly larger number of people live in appalling slums, where open sewers may run under disintegrating floorboards. The traffic jam, or "go-slow," is a fact of life. Much of the everyday commerce occurs in this city through the windows of cars, trucks, and other vehicles.*[17]

Social changes have been numerous in cities. Interethnic mixing, even marriage, has become more common. Neighborhoods have developed their own slang, hairstyles, music, dance, art, and poetry. They forge their own institutions such as football (soccer) leagues, labor unions, and women's clubs, helping migrants adjust by creating a new community to replace the village left behind. Small traders set up shop along the sidewalks, hawking everything from food and drinks to cheap clothes, religious items, and music cassettes. Various African nations have enjoyed international football success, and Ethiopians and Kenyans have dominated long-distance running. Africans have also played in the U.S. National Basketball Association and the National Football League.

The family has also changed. The extended family of the villages is often replaced in cities by the smaller nuclear family. Individualism increasingly challenges the village tradition, where marriages were largely arranged by elders. In the cities, love has become a major criterion for selecting a spouse. Traditionally village men had an economic incentive to take more than one wife, since women did most of the routine farm work, especially food crops, which gave rural women economic status. With no farming option, urban women have lost economic status and men no longer need several wives. Men enjoy more educational opportunities and hence dominate wage labor in business and transportation.

Gender roles have changed as women have become more independent, and a growing number have served in governments and parliaments. Indeed, sub-Saharan Africa ranks ahead of the rest of the developing world in the percentage of women in legislative positions. Some women have achieved positions as politicians, professors, lawyers, and company heads. The Kenyan Grace Ogot (OH-got) (b. 1930) served in parliament while writing short stories in which her heroines confronted traditional values and change. In addition to organizations for work, savings, or worship, women have formed groups to work for society's improvement. The Nigerian Eka Esu-Williams (b. 1950), the daughter of a midwife, earned a Ph.D. in immunology and pursued an academic career before forming Women Against AIDS in Africa in 1988. Her goal was to educate and empower women, more likely than men to get HIV, through workshops, schools, and support groups. Some women have also become teachers, nurses, and secretaries, but these are poorly paid occupations. Most women are left with self-employment in low-wage activity, such as the small-scale trade of hawking goods and keeping stalls in city markets, a female near monopoly for centuries; domestic work as maids, cooks, or nannies; or hairdressing. Meanwhile, many men spend long hours commuting to and from work and socializing with their friends after work in bars or at club meetings. Although homosexuals face severe intolerance in many African countries, homosexuality has been more open in South Africa, where the courts legalized homosexual marriage in 2005.

African Culture and Religion

In the area of culture, Africans have combined imported ideas with their own traditions, creating works that are loved around the world. As the Senegalese writer and president Leopold Senghor (sah-GAWR) (1906–2001) has asked, "Who else would teach rhythm to the world that has died of machines and cannons?"[18] Urbanization, the growth of mass media, and the mixing of ethnic groups and outside influences have all created a fertile ground for exciting new popular music styles that reflect social, economic, and political realities. Miriam Makeba (muh-KAY-ba) (1932–2008), the South African jazz and pop singer forced to spend decades in exile, described her mission as follows: "I live to sing about what I see and know. I don't sing politics, I sing truth."[19] Popular music styles that creatively blend local and imported influences have helped Africans adjust to change while affirming their spirit in the face of external influences and internal failures. For instance, the *juju* music of Nigeria reflects Yoruba traditions while adopting Western instruments, such as electric guitars.

African popular musicians also reach an international audience, performing and selling recordings around the world. Perhaps the greatest African superstar, the Senegalese Youssou N'Dour (YOO-soo en-DOOR) (b. 1959), often collaborates with leading Western and Arab musicians. Yet, he remains true to his roots, living in Dakar and following his tolerant Sufi Muslim faith. Some musicians are highly political. The Nigerian Fela Kuti (1938–1997), whose music mixed jazz, soul, rock, and Yoruba traditions, used his songs as a weapon to attack the Nigerian government and its Western sponsors, facing frequent arrests and beatings for his protests. Like Bob Marley, Bob Dylan, and Chile's Victor Jara, Fela gained worldwide fame for using music to attack injustice. Women have also expressed their views through music. For instance, Oumou Sangare of Mali had a massive hit with her account of a young woman torn between pleasing her parents and her loved one. In the Congo, a particularly influential (Zairean) pop music, known widely as **soukous** ("to shake"), was shaped by dance rhythms from Cuba and Brazil, created by the descendants of African slaves. Soukous depends heavily on the guitar as well as on traditional African songs and melodies. Congolese musicians, unable to make a living or speak freely in their troubled homeland, have often sought their fortunes elsewhere. Soukous became a major dance music throughout Africa and among African immigrants in Europe.

As with popular musicians, writers combined old traditions with new influences to comment on modern society, assert African identity, and influence political change and economic development.

Families and Gender Relations

Popular Musics

soukous ("to shake") A Congolese popular music that was shaped by dance rhythms from Cuba and Brazil.

Literature

Many write in English or French to reach an international audience. The Nigerian Wole Soyinka **(WOE-lay shaw-YING-kuh)** (b. 1934), a Yoruba poet, playwright, novelist, and sometime film-maker who won the 1986 Nobel Prize for literature, has mixed Yoruba mysticism with criticisms of Western capitalism, racism, and cultural imperialism and of African failures, including the bru-talities of Nigerian political life. A former political prisoner, Soyinka denounced repressive African leaders, chastising "Nigeria's self-engorgement at the banquet of highway robberies, public execu-tions, public floggings and other institutionalized sadisms, casual cruelties, wanton destruction."[20] The powerful criticism of governments offered by Soyinka and his Nigerian colleague Chinua Achebe has often forced both men to live in exile.

negritude A literary and philosophical movement to forge distinctively African views.

Writers and artists have also tried to find authentic African perspectives. **Negritude** is a literary and philosophical movement to forge distinctively African views that first developed in the 1930s. The Senegalese writer and later the first president of his country after independence, Leopold Senghor, attempted to balance the Western stress on rational thought with African approaches to knowledge, such as mysticism and animism, long disdained by Europeans as superstition. To Senghor, Africans needed to assert, rather than feel inferior about, their black skins and cultural traditions. Negritude influenced French artists and writers, and the philosopher Jean Paul Sartre praised it as a weapon against all forms of oppression.

One of the best-known writers in Francophone West Africa, Ousmane Sembene **(OOS-man sem-BEN-ee)** (b. 1923) of Senegal, was influenced more by Marxism than by negritude. Drafted into the French army during World War II, Sembene, the son of a poor fisherman, fought in Italy and Ger-many. After the war he worked in France as a dockworker and became a leader of the dockworkers' union, and his first novel portrayed the stevedore's hard life. After returning to Senegal, Sembene often wrote about the colonial period, showing African resistance to Western domination and social inequality while attacking Senegal's greedy businessmen and government officials. Sembene also achieved international acclaim for films satirizing corrupt bureaucrats and illustrating the exploita-tion of the poor by the rich.

English-language literature also flourished in South Africa and East Africa. Kenyan Ngugi Wa Thiongo **(en-GOO-gee wah thee-AHN-go)** (b. 1938), a journalist turned university professor, has written several novels that explore the relationship between colonialism and social fragmentation, showing Gikuyus struggling to retain their identity, culture, and traditions while adjusting to the modern world. Once a devout Christian, Ngugi later rejected Christianity, which he viewed as a legacy of colonialism. His 1979 novel, *Petals of Blood*, portrays a Kenya struggling to free itself from neocolonialism but also beset with corruption. His attacks on the privileged Kenyan elite allied with Western exploitation earned Ngugi several jail terms and later forced him into exile.

African Cultural Expression Africans have developed diverse and vibrant popular music, often by mixing Western and local tradi-tions. In Nigeria, juju music, played by bands such as Captain Jidi Oyo and his Yankee System in this 1982 photo, has been popular among the Yoruba people.

Religion has remained in constant flux. In general, Africans have maintained a triple religious her-itage: animism/polytheism, Islam, and Christianity. All these faiths have many followers, although the believers in animism now account for only a tenth of Africans. With their links to wider worlds, Chris-tianity and Islam are also globalizing influences, spreading Western or Middle Eastern political, social, and economic ideas. Africans often view religions in both theoretical and practical terms, adopting views that help them adjust to change while rejecting old ideas and adding new ones as needed.

Christianity has become Africa's largest religion, attracting some 46 percent of Africans by 2008, both the fervent and the nominal in faith. Some countries, such as Congo, South Africa, and Uganda, have become largely Christian. Christianity has proven a powerful force for social change, and mission schools have educated many African lead-ers, influencing their world-views. However, many Christian churches have prevented their followers from practicing traditional customs. Believers often favor the liberation of women, yet many criticize progressive social views common in the West such as tolerance for homosexuality. A growing number of independent churches, some blending African traditions into worship and theology, have no ties to the older Western-based denominations. By promis-ing to help members acquire wealth and happiness, some African churches have enjoyed spectacular growth, which has enabled them to build big urban churches that attract thousands of congregants each Sunday. In a reversal of historical patterns, several evangelical Nigerian churches even send mission-aries to revitalize Christianity in the West, establishing

Courtesy, Christopher Waterman, UCLA

branches in Europe and North America. Yet many other Africans have viewed Christianity as connected to Western imperialism. According to a popular nationalist saying: "When the missionaries came the Africans had the land and the Christians had the Bible. They taught us to pray with our eyes closed. When we opened them they had the land and we had the Bible."[21]

Some 40 percent of black Africans follow Islam, and about a fourth of all sub-Saharan countries have Muslim majorities. Some revivalist and Wahhabi movements have gained influence, especially in northern Nigeria, where some states have imposed Islamic law, sparking deadly clashes with Christian minorities that have left hundreds dead. But most Muslims and Christians remain moderate and inclusive. While politicians use religion as a wedge issue, and Christian-Muslim clashes have occurred in countries such as Ivory Coast and Sudan, relations among Christians, Muslims, and animists have more often been marked by tolerance. Among the Yoruba, for example, members of each group mix easily and even intermarry. One sect in Lagos even mixes Islam and Christianity into a blend called "Chrislam." Ethnicity often divides people more than religion.

Africa in the Global System

The Cold War rivalry between the USSR and the United States gained some countries aid but also fostered manipulation by superpowers. Countries such as Congo and Angola often became pawns as superpowers helped to support or remove leaders. But with the Cold War over, the Western world has largely ignored Africa, providing it with little aid and investment. Furthermore, the wealth gap between African countries and the Western industrialized nations has grown even wider than during colonial times. Today the gap between the richest Western nations and the poorest African countries is around 400 to 1. Only when the world economy boomed in the 1950s and 1960s did African economies show steady growth. Between the 1970s and 2000, however, as world prices for many African exports collapsed, African economic growth rates steadily dropped.

Africa and the World Economy

Western experts have encouraged a policy of "structural adjustment," in which international lenders, such as the International Monetary Fund (IMF) and the World Bank, loan nations money on the condition that these nations open their economies to private investment and, to balance national budgets, reduce government spending for health, education, and farmers. The resulting hardship on average people—from eliminating money for poor children to attend the village primary school to closing the local office that aids small farmers—increases resentment both of governments and of the Western nations that control the IMF and World Bank. This private investment also promotes a shift away from traditional farming to more productive modern agriculture that relies on tractors, chemical fertilizers, and new seeds. However, this kind of farming has a large environmental and social cost: marginal land is often turned into desert, and small farmers lack the means to buy the modern supplies.

To obtain the cars, fashionable clothes, and electronic gadgets desired by the urban middle and upper classes, African nations have taken out loans. As a percentage of total output, African countries have had the largest foreign debts in the world. Yet, the world prices for most of Africa's exports, such as coffee, cotton, and tobacco from Tanzania and cocoa from Ghana, have steadily dropped since the 1960s. Some exports now bring in a third of what they once did, leaving ever larger revenue gaps. And small farmers, such as the cotton growers in Mali, cannot compete with highly subsidized Western farmers and the tariff barriers erected in Europe, North America, and Japan against food and fiber imports from Africa. Increasingly desperate, countries such as Guinea-Bissau and Somalia have agreed to allow dangerous toxic waste, such as deadly but unwanted chemicals produced in the West, to be buried on their land in exchange for cash. Although prices for exports, especially minerals and oil, rebounded by 2000, spurring faster economic growth, the 2008–2009 global economic crisis lowered growth rates from 6.1 percent in 2007 to 2.8 percent in 2009. Taking advantage of Western disinterest, in the past decade China has made huge investments in African oil, refining, mining, timber, agriculture, and banking as well as constructing railroads, dams, bridges and other infrastructure projects. Bilateral trade quintupled between 2000–2006, and perhaps 750,000 Chinese now live and work in Africa. The Chinese activity may foreshadow a change of direction for many Africans.

Africa's economic problems have had diverse roots. Colonial economic policies caused severe environmental destruction, such as desertification and deforestation, while incorporating the people into the world economy as specialized producers of minerals or cash crops for export rather than food farmers. Hence, Zambia relies on exploiting copper (87 percent of exports), Uganda coffee (72 percent), Malawi tobacco (72 percent), and Nigeria oil (95 percent). In addition, the colonial regimes often failed to build roads, schools, and clinics. Bad policy decisions, poor leadership, corruption, unstable politics, and misguided advice from Western experts have also contributed to the economic challenges, while the rapid spread of HIV/AIDS has killed and affected millions (see Chapter 26). In some nations a third of the population has the HIV virus.

Colonial Legacies

African Successes

But although falling behind much of Asia and Latin America, Africans have had successes. Using foreign aid and their own resources, they have made rapid strides in literacy, social and medical services, including active birth control campaigns, and road construction. Some nations, such as South Africa, Ghana, and Uganda, have a feisty free press. Nations have also worked together to resolve problems. The African Union, formed in 2000 with fifty-four members, has sent peacekeeping troops into violence-torn countries such as Sudan. By the 1990s Africans had grown skeptical about the usefulness of Western models of development, which often depend on expensive high technology, and were also disillusioned with socialist governments controlling economic activity. Many nations have moved toward more democratic systems and private enterprise. However, political leadership has often failed to root out corruption and poverty and foster food production. Africa also suffers a particularly acute "brain drain" as academics, students, and professionals, seeking a better life, move to Europe or North America. Thus Africans have not enjoyed complete control of their destiny. The Ghanaian historian Jacob Ajayi (a-JAH-yee) laid out the challenge: "The vision of a new [African] society will need to be developed out of the African historical experience. The African is not yet master of his own fate, but neither is he completely at the mercy of fate."[22]

SECTION SUMMARY

- African countries have struggled economically, with many being forced to import food and others, like the Congo, to enter into neocolonial relationships with Western powers, but Ghana and Botswana have managed to significantly improve their economies.

- Marxist revolutionary governments, which appealed to many Africans who wanted to erase the colonial legacy, came to power in Angola and Mozambique, both of which then entered into long civil wars, as well as in Zimbabwe.

- African cities have grown rapidly and often lack necessary services, individualism has grown more common, and women have lost some of the economic value they had in agricultural villages, though some have become successful professionals.

- African musicians, writers, and artists have drawn on local traditions as well as influences from the West to create original forms, such as soukous, as well as works that criticize both Western encroachment and homegrown corruption.

- While animism has grown less influential in Africa, Christianity is the most popular religion and has undermined traditions and been seen by some as connected to Western imperialism, while Islam is followed by 40 percent of Africans.

- The economic gap between Africa and the industrialized West continues to grow larger, and Western attempts to help Africa through the IMF and the World Bank often include requirements that harm the environment and the poor and inspire resentment, as do tariffs against African imports and the enduring colonial legacy.

CHAPTER SUMMARY

The Middle East and sub-Saharan Africa have shared certain experiences, including decolonization, mass poverty, reliance on exporting natural resources, political instability, and intervention by Western powers. The Middle East was reshaped by diverse developments since 1945. Arab nationalism, especially strong in Egypt, generated conflict with the West and with Israel, which became the major Arab enemy. The Arab-Israeli conflict greatly destabilized the region, while ethnic and religious divisions fostered violent struggles within nations. Islam proved most potent as a revolutionary political force in Iran, long a battleground for international rivalries over its oil supplies. The Middle East, especially the Persian Gulf region, provided much of the world's oil, fostering wealth but also global attention as world consumption increased. Oil-rich Saudi Arabia forged an alliance with the United States. Most Middle Eastern societies remained conservative but also fostered cultural creativity. The rivalry between militants and secular Muslims has provided a major cleavage in many countries.

By the 1970s the long-colonized African nations had achieved independence under nationalist leaders. But the hopes for a better life were soon dashed. Artificially created multiethnic nations have found it difficult to sustain democracy, and dictatorial governments have often gained power. Most nations have remained dependent on exporting one or two resources. Ambitious development plans have given way to economic stagnation and, as commodity prices fall, increasing poverty. Neither capitalism nor socialism has proved able to both stimulate growth and raise living standards for Africa's majority. But South Africa was finally transformed from a racist state to a multiracial democracy. Societies urbanized, redefined family life and gender roles, and created new music and literature. Africans still search for the right mix of imported ideas and local traditions to create better lives.

KEY TERMS

Intifida
Ba'ath
OPEC
Islamists

rai
mujahidin
Taliban
pan-Africanism

Mau Mau Rebellion
wabenzi
apartheid
bantustans

soukous
negritude

EBOOK AND WEBSITE RESOURCES

e PRIMARY SOURCE

Arab and Israeli Soccer Players Discuss Ethnic Relations in Israel, 2000

e INTERACTIVE MAPS

Map 30.1 Middle East Oil and the Arab-Israeli Conflict
Map 30.2 The Islamic World
Map 30.3 Contemporary Africa and the Middle East

LINKS

Africa South of the Sahara (http://www-sul.stanford.edu/depts/ssrg/africa/guide.html). A valuable gateway for links on many topics in African studies.

African Studies Internet Resources (http://www.columbia.edu/cu/lweb/indiv/). Provides valuable links to relevant websites on contemporary Africa.

Arab Human Development Reports (http://www.un.org/Pubs). The general United Nations site contains links to the reports, issued annually beginning in 2002 and available online, that assess the successes and challenges facing the Arab nations.

History of the Middle East Database (http://www.nmhschool.org/tthornton/mehistorydatabase/mideastindex.php). A useful site on history, politics, and culture.

Internet African History Sourcebook (http://www.fordham.edu/halsall/africa/africasbook.html). Contains useful information and documentary material on Africa.

Internet Islamic History Sourcebook (http://www.fordham.edu/halsall/islam/islamsbook.html). A comprehensive examination of Islamic societies and their long history, with useful links and source materials.

Plus flashcards, practice quizzes, and more. Go to: www.cengage.com/history/lockard/globalsocnet2e.

SUGGESTED READING

Anderson, Roy R., et al. *Politics and Change in the Middle East: Sources of Conflict and Accommodation*, 9th ed. Upper Saddle River, NJ: Prentice-Hall, 2008. An introductory survey of politics and economies.

Bates, Daniel G., and Amal Rassam. *Peoples and Cultures of the Middle East*, 2nd ed. Upper Saddle River, NJ: Prentice-Hall, 2001. A readable introduction to the social and cultural patterns of the region.

Clark, Nancy L., and William H. Worger. *South Africa: The Rise and Fall of Apartheid*. New York: Longman, 2004. A brief survey with documents.

Cleveland, William L. *A History of the Modern Middle East*, 4th ed. Boulder, CO: Westview, 2008. A political overview of the region during this era.

Cooper, Frederick. *Africa Since 1940: The Past of the Present*. New York: Cambridge University Press, 2002. A brief overview of contemporary history.

Danielson, Virginia. *The Voice of Egypt: Umm Kulthum, Arabic Song, and Egyptian Society in the Twentieth Century*. Chicago: University of Chicago Press, 1997. A fascinating view of modern Egypt through the life and work of the Arab world's most famous pop singer.

Davidson, Basil. *The Black Man's Burden: Africa and the Curse of the Nation State*. New York: Times Books, 1992. Reflections on modern Africa and its challenges by an influential historian.

Esposito, John L. *Islam: The Straight Path*, 3rd ed. revised. New York: Oxford University Press, 2005. A detailed examination of modern Islam.

Gerges, Fawaz A. *The Far Enemy: Why Jihad Went Global*. New York: Cambridge University Press, 2005. A gripping account of the rise of Islamism, Al Qaeda, and terrorism by a Lebanon-born, U.S.-based scholar.

Gerner, Deborah J., and Jillian Schwedler, eds. *Understanding the Contemporary Middle East*, 3rd ed. Boulder, CO: Lynne Rienner, 2008. A useful collection of essays on varied aspects of the Middle East today.

Gordon, April A., and Donald L. Gordon, eds. *Understanding Contemporary Africa*, 4th ed. Boulder, CO: Lynne Rienner, 2006. An excellent collection of essays on aspects of Africa.

Keddie, Nikki R. *Modern Iran: Roots and Results of Revolution*, updated ed. New Haven: Yale University Press, 2006. Updating and revision of a major study.

Martin, Phyllis M., and Patrick O'Meara, eds. *Africa*, 3rd ed. Bloomington: Indiana University Press, 1995. Essays on African history, politics, culture, and economies.

Nugent, Paul. *Africa Since Independence: A Comparative History*. New York: Palgrave Macmillan, 2004. A recent, detailed survey.

Smith, Charles D. *Palestine and the Arab-Israeli Conflict: A History with Documents*, 7th ed. Boston: Bedford/St. Martin's, 2009. A comprehensive, balanced survey.

Tenaille, Frank. *Music Is the Weapon of the Future: Fifty Years of African Popular Music*. Chicago: Lawrence Hill, 2000. A recent overview of varied African pop musicians and musical styles.

SOUTH ASIA, SOUTHEAST ASIA, AND GLOBAL CONNECTIONS, SINCE 1945

Commuting to Work
Vietnam has largely recovered from its decades of war and has experienced increasing economic growth. These women in Hanoi are commuting to work by bicycle.

> This music sings the struggle of [humanity]. This music is my life. This is the revolution we have begun. But the revolution is only a means to attain freedom, and freedom is only a means to enrich the happiness and nobility of human life.
>
> —HAZIL, THE INDONESIAN REVOLUTIONARY NATIONALIST IN MOCHTAR LUBIS'S NOVEL *A ROAD WITH NO END* (1952)[1]

In 1950 an idealistic group of Indonesian writers published a moving declaration promoting universal human dignity: "We [Indonesians] are the heirs to the culture of the whole world, a culture which is ours to extend and develop in our own way [by] the discarding of old and outmoded values and their replacement by new ones. Our fundamental quest is [helping] humanity."[2] These writers, hoping that Indonesia could combine the most humane ideas of East and West to become a beacon to the world, open to all cultures, had been shaped by Western Enlightenment traditions, including the ideals of democracy, free thought, and tolerance. Having witnessed the Indonesian Revolution against the Dutch, a nationalist struggle that raged between 1945 and 1950 and finally led to Indonesian independence, the writers also warned against a narrow nationalism. They had been inspired by the irreverent Sumatran poet Chairul Anwar (CHAI-roll ON-war) (1922–1949), who believed that the revolution had made possible a new, open society. A true bohemian, undisciplined in his personal life, Anwar had risen from poverty—his family was too poor to send him to secondary school—to master the Dutch, English, Spanish, and French languages. Influenced both by Western books and by an Indonesian sensibility, Anwar excited Indonesians with his pathbreaking poems that stretched the possibilities of the Indonesian language. But Anwar had died at twenty-seven, sapped by his appetite for the pleasures of the flesh. His death left it to others, among them the liberal Sumatran novelist and journalist Mochtar Lubis (MOKE-tar LOO-bis) (b. 1920), to carry on the campaign. Their goal, as expressed in the writers' declaration, was to blend widely admired ideas from abroad with Indonesian ideas, fostering change while also preserving continuity.

The declaration's noble aspirations and recognition of Indonesia's connection to the wider world reflected a new sense of possibility as colonial walls were being knocked down. But the writers' idealism was soon dashed by the realities of the early post–World War II years. While South and Southeast Asians longed for human dignity, other, more immediate goals took precedence: securing independence, building a new nation, and addressing poverty and underdevelopment. The cosmopolitan values of Anwar, Lubis, and their colleagues even came to seem quaint and contrary to the dominant nationalist agenda. But despite false starts and conflicts, over the following decades Indonesians and other nations of South and Southeast Asia sought, and sometimes found, answers to their challenges while increasing their links to global networks. As a result, these societies changed dramatically without destroying tradition. Except for East Asia, southern Asia is the most densely populated part of the world: well over 2 billion people live in the lands stretching eastward from Pakistan and India to Indonesia and the Philippines. It is also very diverse, containing a wide array of languages, ethnic groups, religions, world-views, governments, and levels of

FOCUS QUESTIONS

1. What factors led to the political division of South Asia?
2. What have been the major achievements and disappointments of the South Asian nations?
3. What were the causes and consequences of the struggles in Southeast Asia?
4. What role do the Southeast Asian nations play in the global system?

e Visit the website and eBook for additional study materials and interactive tools:
www.cengage.com/history/lockard/globalsocnet2e

899

economic development. Some nations have experienced destabilizing conflict; others have achieved widespread prosperity. This region of contrasts between wealth and poverty has played an important role in the world for over four millennia and continues to be one of the cornerstones of the world economy.

THE RESHAPING OF SOUTH ASIA

What factors led to the political division of South Asia?

World War II undermined British colonialism and led to independence for South Asians. The British, economically drained by the war and realizing that continued control would come only at a great cost in wealth and perhaps lives, handed power over to local leaders. The first prime minister of independent India, Jawaharlal Nehru (JAH-wa HAR-lahl NAY-roo) (1889–1964), told his people: "A moment comes, which comes rarely in history, when we step from the old to the new, when an age ends and when the soul of a nation, long suppressed, finds utterance."[3] Yet Nehru's idealism was tempered by the realities of the challenges ahead. India's long struggle for independence, marked by the nonviolent philosophy of Mohandas Gandhi (1868–1948), had ironically ended with Gandhi assassinated and British India divided into two separate, often hostile countries, predominantly Hindu India and largely Muslim Pakistan. Mostly Buddhist Sri Lanka and, in the 1970s, largely Muslim Bangladesh also gained independence. Each nation had its achievements and failures, but the largest and most populous, India, has been the regional colossus and a major player in world affairs.

Decolonization and Partition

South Asia's religious divisions undermined regional unity. During World War II relations between the British and the mainly Hindu leadership of the Indian National Congress ruptured (see Chapter 25). Taking advantage, and fearing domination by the Hindu majority, the Muslim League pressed its case with the British for a separate Muslim nation, to be called Pakistan. Negotiations to bring the Congress and the Muslim League together broke down in 1946. As the tension increased, rioting broke out, and Muslims and Hindus began murdering each other, pulling victims from buses, shops, and homes. In Calcutta alone 5,000 people died. The rioting undermined any pretence of Hindu-Muslim unity, and the Muslim League leader, Mohammed Ali Jinnah (1876–1948), announced that if India were not divided it would be destroyed. As the rioting spread, the Congress leaders and British officials now realized that some sort of partition was inevitable. In 1947 the British, Congress, and Muslim League agreed to create two independent nations, India and a Pakistan formed out of the Muslim majority areas of eastern Bengal and the northwestern provinces along the Indus River (see Chronology: South Asia, 1945–Present).

In a speech to his new nation, Prime Minister Nehru proclaimed: "Long years ago we made a tryst with destiny, and now the time comes when we shall redeem our pledge. At the stroke of the midnight hour, when the world sleeps, India will awake to life and freedom."[4] A similar mood of renewal struck people in Pakistan. But the euphoria in both new nations proved short-lived as a bloodbath ensued. Muslims and Hindus had often lived side by side, but partition sparked hatreds between local members of the majority faith, who felt empowered, and religious minorities, who feared discrimination. As violence flared, Hindus and Sikhs fled Pakistan for India, and Muslims fled India for Pakistan. Altogether some 10 to 12 million refugees crossed the India-Pakistan borders. Perhaps 1 million died and 75,000 women were raped. Religious extremists sometimes attacked whole villages or whole trainloads of refugees.

The sixty-eight-year-old Mohandas Gandhi labored to stop the killing. Moving into the Muslim quarter of Delhi, he toured refugee camps without escort, read aloud from the scriptures of all religions, including the Quran, and confronted Hindu mobs attacking mosques. Finally, in desperation, and hoping to send a message to everyone, Gandhi, who weighed only 113 pounds, began a fast until all the violence

CHRONOLOGY

South Asia, 1945–Present

1947 Independence for India and Pakistan

1948 Assassination of Mohandas Gandhi

1948 Sri Lankan independence

1950 Indian republic

1948–1964 Nehru era in India

1959 Sri Lanka's Sirimavo Bandaranaike first woman prime minister

1962 India-China border war

1971 Formation of Bangladesh

1975–1977 State of emergency under Indira Gandhi

1984 Assassination of Indira Gandhi

1988–1990 First Benazir Bhutto government in Pakistan

1993–1996 Second Benazir Bhutto government

1999–2006 Military government led by Pervez Musharraf

2006 Assassination of Benazir Bhutto

CHRONOLOGY

	South Asia	Southeast Asia
1940	**1947** Independence for India and Pakistan **1948–1964** Nehru era in India	**1945–1950** Indonesian Revolution **1946–1954** First Indochina War **1948** Independence of Burma
1950		
1960	**1963–1975** U.S.-Vietnamese War	**1966–1998** New Order in Indonesia
1970	**1971** Formation of Bangladesh	**1975** Communist victories in Vietnam, Cambodia, Laos
1980	**1984** Assassination of Indira Gandhi	
1990		**1997** Asian economic crisis
2000		**2008–2009** World economic crisis

in the city had stopped or he died. He quickly fell ill, but Gandhi's effort worked, allowing him to break off his fast. After the violence subsided, a substantial Muslim and Sikh minority remained in India and a Hindu and Sikh minority in Pakistan. But partition had been shattering. A Muslim poet spoke for many disillusioned people: "This is not that long looked-for break of the day. Where did that fine breeze blow from—where has it fled?"[5] Gandhi's support for Muslim victims of Hindu violence outraged Hindu extremists, who regarded Gandhi as a traitor. In January 1948, one of them gunned down Gandhi as he walked to a meeting, shocking the whole country and the world.

Despite its bloody start, India was built on a solid political foundation. Britain bequeathed the basis for democracy, a trained civil service, a good communications system, and an educated if Westernized elite committed to modernization. India became a republic with a constitution based on the British model, led by a prime minister chosen by the majority party in an elected parliament. However, given its huge ethnic, religious, and linguistic diversity (fourteen major languages and hundreds of minor languages), India has had difficulty building national unity. To accommodate the many religious minorities, regions, and cultures, India adopted a federal system, with elected state governments, and was officially secular with complete separation of religion and state. Kashmir, a mountainous Himalayan state on the India-Pakistan border, presented a long-term problem because it had a Muslim majority but a Hindu ruler who opted to join India. Kashmir has remained a source of constant tension and sometimes war between India and Pakistan.

Two New Nations

The new Pakistan confronted numerous problems. It was an artificial country, with two wings separated by a thousand miles of India. The nation's founding leader, Jinnah, died soon after independence, and his successor was assassinated. Muslims had been overrepresented in the British Indian military, and the army now played a stronger role in Pakistan's politics than in India's. The loss of top civilian leaders, lack of a balanced economic base, massive poverty, and geographical division made Pakistan more vulnerable than India to political instability and military rule. Pakistan and India quarreled over issues from water use to trade to ownership of Kashmir.

Building a New India

India's first prime minister, Nehru, a close associate of Gandhi, dominated Indian politics for a decade and a half (1948–1964). A gifted speaker and brilliant thinker, Nehru was supported by the small middle class, who wanted a modern India, and by the lower-class majority who lived in overcrowded, unhealthy urban slums or dusty villages that lacked electricity and running water. Nehru promised to raise living standards and address the nation's overwhelming poverty. He believed firmly in democracy. While India lagged behind China in economic development, it preserved personal freedom. Believing in peaceful coexistence with neighbors, renouncing military aggression, and hoping to prevent a nuclear conflict between the superpowers, Nehru became a major figure on the world stage. He helped found the Non-Aligned Movement of nations, such as Egypt and Indonesia, that were unwilling to commit to either the U.S. or Soviet camps in the Cold War. As India's stature grew, Nehru led the Congress Party to three smashing electoral victories.

Nehru's India

Muslims Leaving India for Pakistan During Partition As India and Pakistan split into two new nations in 1947, millions of Muslims and Hindus fled their homes to escape violence. This photo shows displaced Muslims, carrying a few meager belongings, jamming a train headed from India to Pakistan.

Wide World Photos

Nehru's Policies

Nehru's policies derived from his complex ideals. Although the British-educated lawyer admired Western politics, literature, and dynamism, he also respected India's cultural heritage, speaking of its moral strength. Raised a Hindu brahman, Nehru was nevertheless a secularist who believed that Congress should represent and serve all religions and social groups. Perhaps his greatest contributions came in addressing social problems. Like Gandhi, he opposed the caste system and fought gender inequalities. Nehru convinced parliament to approve new laws on untouchability and women's rights that penalized discrimination. Untouchables, who have preferred the designation **Dalit** ("suppressed" or "ground down" people) since the 1970s, acquired special quotas in government services and universities, while Hindu women gained legal equality with men, including the right to divorce and inheritance. To discourage child marriage, Nehru set a minimum marriage age at eighteen for males and fifteen for females. But these laws challenging centuries of tradition were often ignored, especially in rural areas.

Dalit The designation commonly used for untouchables since the 1970s.

Nehru introduced a planning system to foster modern technology while mixing capitalism and socialism. He left established industries in private hands but set up public ventures to, for example, build power plants and dams, which doubled power production, and irrigation canals, which increased agricultural yields by 25 percent. In the 1960s the Green Revolution of new high-yield wheat and rice fostered a dramatic rise in food production. Thanks to Nehru's five-year plans, by the 1970s India produced many industrial products, including steel, and was nearly self-sufficient in food.

But some of Nehru's policies proved failures. Government control of the private sector through regulations gave bureaucrats great power, fostered corruption, and shackled private enterprise. Nehru also failed to cultivate good relations with Pakistan or with China, and in 1962 Chinese troops humiliated Indian forces during a border dispute. Moreover, Nehru did not recognize that a rapidly growing population, which rose from 389 million in 1941 to 434 million in 1961, would undermine most of India's economic gains; thus he only belatedly endorsed family planning. In addition, the government built schools and universities but failed to substantially raise literacy rates. Yet, when Nehru died in 1964, millions mourned the end of an idealistic era that had earned India respect in the world.

The Nehru Dynasty

Nehru also fostered a family political dynasty. With the sudden death of his respected successor in 1966, the Congress selected Nehru's daughter, Indira Gandhi (1917–1984), to be the nation's first woman prime minister. She had worked closely with her father while her husband (no relation to Mohandas Gandhi) served in parliament. Mrs. Gandhi enjoyed a decade and a half in power. When her support waned in the 1967 elections, she responded aggressively with policies to win back the poor. India's smashing military victory over archenemy Pakistan elevated her status. But

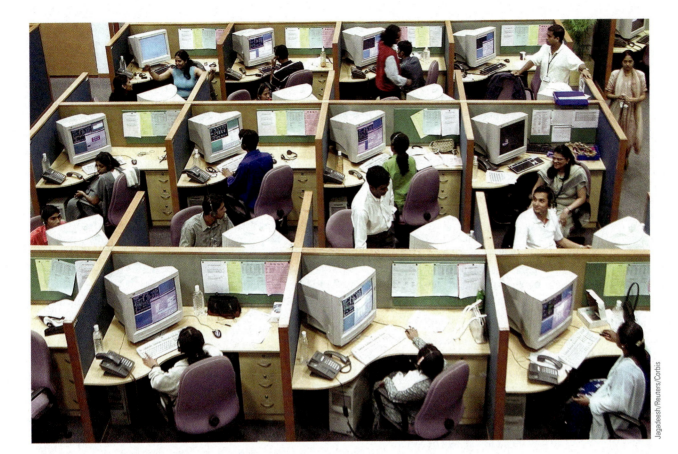

mounting domestic problems precipitated increasingly harsh policies, which often made matters worse. Powerful vested interests ignored her reforms, the economy faltered, and many Indians turned against the Congress. As a result, Indian democracy faltered. In 1975 Gandhi declared a state of emergency, suspending civil rights, closing state governments, and jailing some 10,000 opposition leaders and dissidents. While her actions were condemned, some of her policies improved the economy. Meanwhile, her youngest son, Sanjay Gandhi (1946–1980), launched a controversial birth control campaign to forcibly sterilize any man with more than three children, and also implemented a slum-clearance program that forced thousands out of sidewalk shanties. Both programs became deeply unpopular. In 1977 Indira lifted the emergency. After thirty years in power, the Congress Party, and with it Indira Gandhi, was voted out of office and replaced by an uneasy coalition of parties, including Hindu nationalists opposed to secularism. But the coalition government, which solved few problems, collapsed.

Indira Gandhi returned to power in the 1980 elections, restoring the Nehru dynasty. But Mrs. Gandhi faced voter apathy, growing unemployment, and unrest. In 1980 Sanjay Gandhi died in a plane crash, and Indira Gandhi elevated her eldest son Rajiv (1944–1991), an apolitical airline pilot, as her heir apparent. Violence in the Punjab, India's richest state, which had a heavy Sikh population, provoked Mrs. Gandhi's final crisis. Many Sikhs, whose religion mixes Hindu and Muslim ideas, desired autonomy from India. In 1983 armed Sikh extremists occupied the Golden Temple at Amritsar (**uhm-RIT-suhr**), the holiest Sikh shrine, and turned it into a fortress, calling for an independent Sikh homeland and murdering those, including moderate Sikhs, who opposed them. In 1984 the Indian army stormed the Golden Temple. When the fighting ended, the temple was reduced to rubble and over a thousand militants and soldiers lay dead.

Violence had returned to Indian political life. The destruction of their holiest temple shocked the Sikhs and led to the shooting death of Indira Gandhi by two of her Sikh bodyguards. In response, Hindu mobs roamed Delhi, burning Sikh shops and killing Sikhs, often by pouring gasoline over them and setting them ablaze. The dead numbered in the thousands. Meanwhile, Rajiv Gandhi succeeded his mother but proved ineffective, and in 1991, while campaigning in the southern city of Madras, he was blown up by a young Sri Lankan woman handing him flowers. The suicide bomber opposed India's support of the Sri Lankan government in its war against the Tamil secessionist group to which she belonged. Yet despite this tumult, India remained a functioning democracy and a thriving nation.

Global Communications   A workroom in one of the hundreds of call centers in Indian cities such as Bangalore and Mumbai (Bombay). The workers, mostly well-educated and fluent in English, field customer service calls from around the world for Western companies, many of them in the financial services, computer, and electronic businesses.

Political Violence

The Making of Pakistan and Bangladesh

Pakistan faced greater challenges than did India. Jinnah had pledged to make the nation happy and prosperous, but the leaders who followed him had only limited success, in part because of tensions between ethnic groups who shared an Islamic faith but often little else. Hostilities flared between the nationalistic Bengalis, who dominated the east, and the Punjabis and Sindhis, who dominated the west. The two regions differed in language, culture, and outlook. The factionalized Pakistani parliament, whose members chiefly represented regions and ethnic groups rather than rival ideologies, proved unworkable, providing an excuse for military leaders to take over the government in 1958. But by 1969 dissatisfaction with military dictatorship led to riots, prompting martial law. The Bengalis felt they did not get a fair share of the nation's resources and political power, and eventually ethnic tensions came to a boil. After the **Awami League**, a Bengali nationalist party, won a majority of East Pakistan's seats in national elections, in early 1971 Pakistani troops arrested the party leader, Sheikh Mujiber Rahman (shake MOO-jee-bur RAH-mun) (1920–1975). Hoping to crush Awami League support, troops opened fire on university dormitories and Hindu homes, causing hundreds of casualties.

Awami League A Bengali nationalist party that began the move for independence from West Pakistan.

Inspired by Sheikh Mujiber, who asked his supporters to carry his message to every rice field and mango grove, the Awami League then declared independence. In response, West Pakistani troops poured into East Pakistan, terrorizing the Bengali population with massacres, arson, and the raping of thousands of women. At least half a million Bengalis died. The civil war caused 10 million desperate, starving refugees to flee to India. World opinion turned against Pakistan. India appealed for support of East Pakistan, armed the Bengali guerrillas, and, after an ill-advised Pakistani attack on Indian airfields, sent troops into both West and East Pakistan, rapidly gaining the upper hand. Meanwhile, Pakistan received military aid from China and the United States, both of which it had courted. But while the U.S. administration of President Richard Nixon ignored the slaughter of Bengalis and China threatened to intervene on behalf of Pakistan, Soviet backing of India discouraged such a move. By the end of 1971 Pakistani troops in Bengal had surrendered to Indian forces, and the Awami League, led by Sheikh Mujibur, established a new nation, Bangladesh (Bengali Nation) (see Map 31.1).

SECTION SUMMARY

- After World War II, when majority Muslim Pakistan broke off from majority Hindu India, widespread religious violence broke out and a dispute over the territory of Kashmir set the stage for continued tension between the two countries.

- Nehru attempted to expand the rights of women and, through a mix of capitalism and socialism, vastly increased India's industrial and agricultural output, but the population expanded at a dangerously rapid rate and not all policies were successful.

- Nehru's daughter, Indira Gandhi, was prime minister for over a decade, but she treated her opposition harshly and was assassinated in the midst of clashes between Hindus and Sikhs, and her son and successor, Rajiv Gandhi, was also assassinated.

- East and West Pakistan were divided along ethnic lines, and a military crackdown on a Bengali nationalist party led to a bloody civil war in which India intervened on behalf of East Pakistan, which then became a separate country, Bangladesh.

SOUTH ASIAN POLITICS AND SOCIETIES

> What have been the major achievements and disappointments of the South Asian nations?

South Asian societies each forged their own political role in the region. With 1.2 billion people by 2009 and 65 percent of the land in the subcontinent, the Republic of India rose to regional dominance. Indian governments began to liberalize the economy, stimulating growth. But growing Hindu nationalism has challenged the domination of the Congress Party, threatening its secular vision. Meanwhile, India's neighbors have struggled to achieve stability and economic development. Both Pakistan and Sri Lanka have experienced persistent ethnic violence, while India and Pakistan remain wary, building up military forces and nuclear weapons to use against the other. In each South Asian nation ancient customs exist side by side with modern machines and ways of living.

Indian Politics and Economic Change

Indian Democracy

When India celebrated its fiftieth jubilee of independence in 1997, the nation's president reminded his people that India's challenge was to achieve economic growth with social justice. That goal remains elusive; India has been unable to mount the sort of concerted attack on mass poverty found in China. However, Indians can boast that they have maintained one of the few

Map 31.1 Modern South Asia

India, predominantly Hindu, is the largest South Asian nation and separates the two densely populated Islamic nations of Bangladesh and Pakistan. Buddhists are the majority in Sri Lanka, just off India's southeast coast. The small kingdoms of Bhutan and Nepal are located in the Himalayan mountain range.

e Interactive Map

working multiparty democracies outside the industrialized nation-states, one that fosters lively debate and forces candidates to appeal to voters. An Indian novelist described the campaign rhetoric leading up to elections: "The speeches were crammed with promises of every shape and size: promises of new schools, clean water, health care, land for landless peasants, powerful laws to punish any discrimination."[6] While such grandiose promises usually prove difficult to fulfill, millions of people vote in these elections, and changes in state and federal governments have regularly occurred.

To some observers, democracy fosters national unity by providing a flexible system for accommodating the diverse population. Others argue that democracy has intensified differences between groups. Certainly, tensions between Hindus and Muslims and between high-caste and low-caste Hindus, manipulated by opportunistic politicians, have complicated political life. While voting may give the poor an opportunity to put pressure on elites, elites can manipulate the system to preserve their privileges. Critics contend that democracy functions as a safety valve for popular frustration, creating the illusion of mass participation that prevents a frontal attack on caste and class inequalities. Yet, lower-caste voters sometimes force officials to meet their needs, such as by paving the pathways in their neighborhoods.

The Congress Party has remained nationally influential but has had to contend with rivals. On the left, several communist parties dominate politics in West Bengal and in Kerala in the southwest, repeatedly winning elections by promoting modernization and support for the poor. On the right are Hindu nationalist parties, which had limited success until the 1990s. In the southern states various parties representing regional interests have generally dominated state governments and joined federal coalitions. These regional parties, often led by stars of the local film industries, have protected local languages while preserving English, understood by educated people around the country, as a national language. All of India's parties have suffered from corruption.

Bharatha Janata The major Hindu nationalist party in India.

Since 1989 Indian politics has become more pluralistic. The major Hindu nationalist party, the **Bharatha Janata** (BJP), gained influence in north India by espousing hostility to Muslims and state support for Hindu issues, such as having schools teach Indian history in accordance with Hindu traditions and religious writings. The BJP slogan, "One Nation, One People, One Culture," confronts the Gandhi-Nehru vision of a tolerant multicultural state. By the late 1990s India, under a BJP-dominated government, suffered from rising political corruption, violent secessionist movements in border regions, caste conflict, religious hostilities, and fragmentation into several rival political factions. In 2002 major Hindu-Muslim violence broke out again, leaving over a thousand people dead and over 100,000 terrified Muslims, burned out of their cities, huddled in tent camps. In 2004 the Congress, led by Rajiv Gandhi's Italian-born, sari-wearing widow, Sonia Gandhi (b. 1946), a Roman Catholic who met Rajiv when both were students in England, capitalized on disenchantment among the poor and Muslims and, allied with leftist parties, unexpectedly defeated the ruling BJP-led coalition. A Pakistan-born Sikh economist, Manmohan Singh (b. 1932), became the first non-Hindu prime minister.

A free press monitors politics in India. In 2005 an investigation of corruption by a television station forced several members of parliament to resign, indicating the continued vibrancy of Indian democracy. Although India was rocked by a terrorist attack on Bombay by Pakistani militants and then by the global economic crisis, in 2009 the Congress and Singh won a big electoral victory with strong support from the poor, grateful for increased spending on rural health and education. While older politicians still dominated government, a quarter of the successful parliamentary candidates were younger than forty-five.

Economic Policies

India struggled to resolve economic backwardness, skyrocketing population growth, and crushing poverty for the majority. Nehru had sought to end ignorance, poverty, and inequality of opportunity. While his dream has not been fully realized, Indians can boast of many gains, especially after India changed directions economically in the 1970s. For example, in 1956 India had to import vital foodstuffs and manufactured goods. Twenty tears later it was a net exporter of grain and by 2000 was making and exporting its own cars, computers, and aircraft. To spur faster growth after 1991, Indian leaders began dismantling the socialist sector of the economy built by Nehru. Reform, deregulation, and liberalization contributed to an economic growth rate of 6 to 7 percent a year by the late 1990s, and several cities, especially Bangalore and Bombay, became high-tech centers closely linked to global communications. Hundreds of North American and European companies, taking advantage of a growing, educated Indian middle class, especially university graduates fluent in English, have moved information and technical service jobs, such as call-in customer service and computer programming, from North America and Europe to India. India's boom even prompted thousands of highly educated Indians living in North America and Europe to return and join its high-tech sector. These returnees often move into spacious, newly built California-style suburbs with names like Ozone and Lake Vista. Even greater progress has been made in agriculture. The nation now grows enough wheat and rice to feed the entire population.

However, persisting social, economic, and regional inequalities have prevented equitable food distribution. Hence, when inadequate monsoon rains caused a severe drought in 2009, millions of poor farmers lost income, perpetuating the cycle of rural poverty. Moreover, in spite of the economic revival and a growing middle class, many Indians have yet to enjoy its fruits. Compared to China, Malaysia, and South Korea, India's economy has been less able to deliver a better life to the majority. More than half of Indians still live below the poverty line, 25 percent lack an adequate diet, and nearly 80 percent earn less than $2.50 per day. While China nears universal literacy, only half of Indians can read and write. Meanwhile, population growth eats away at the national resources. Every year 30 million Indians are born, and by 2050 India will have 1.5 billion people, more than

China and four times more than the United States. Ironically, success in doubling life expectancy contributes to overpopulation, which causes overcrowded cities, a lack of pure drinking water and adequate sanitation, and insufficient primary health care. India has half as many physicians per population and over twice as much infant mortality as China; Chinese live twelve years longer than Indians. Millions of Indians sleep on city sidewalks for lack of money and housing. Many schools are inadequate, staffed by poorly-paid teachers. While affluent Indians increasingly buy fancy imported cars to drive along newly built highways, many commuters ride on the roofs of jammed buses and trains. India's greenhouse gas emissions are expected to triple in the next two decades.

The stark contrasts between the modern and traditional sectors have produced development amid underdevelopment and raised questions as to who benefits from the changes. The "haves" can afford to pay for services that strapped governments cannot provide—good schools, clean water, decent health care, efficient transport—while ambitious birth control campaigns enjoy success in cities but less in the countryside. The Green Revolution has increased output but mostly benefits the big landowners, who can afford the large investments in tractors and fertilizers, and per capita calorie consumption remains well below world averages. Because successive Indian governments have been largely unable or unwilling to challenge vested interests such as the powerful landlords, half the rural population has become landless. Poverty fosters growing urban crime and rural banditry. Maoist guerrillas challenge local police in some impoverished districts. Economic growth and poverty also ravage the environment as cities encroach on farmland and people cut down trees for firewood. As in China, poor peasants protest, often violently, the taking of their land for building factories, often foreign-owned, and highways. The Chipko forest conservation movement, based on traditional and Gandhian principles and led mostly by women, is one of many groups working to protect the environment. A Chipko leader, the globetrotting Sunderlal Bahugana (SUN-dur-LOLL ba-hoo-GAH-na), stresses the place of people in the larger web of nature.

Development and Underdevelopment

Indian Societies and Cultures

In his will, India's first prime minister, Jawaharlal Nehru, asked that his ashes be scattered in the Ganges River, not because of the river's religious significance to Hindus but because it symbolized to him India's millennia-old culture, ever changing and yet ever the same. Ancient traditions have persisted but have also been modified, especially in the cities. The contrast between the villages, where 80 percent of Indians live, and the often-modern cities remains stark. The growing urban middle class enjoys recreations and technologies, from golf to video games, that are available to the affluent around the world. As young people move around the country, often on the new national highway system, they identify less with their home region and more with India, becoming cosmopolitan. Whether they live in the Punjab, Calcutta, or Bangalore, educated urban young people often like the same music and buy the same consumer goods, which conservatives see as a threat to local cultures. Conservatives fumed but many urbanites cheered when Indian courts struck down laws against homosexuality in 2009.

Cities and Villages

Moreover, practices that ensure strict divisions between castes, such as avoiding physical contact or sharing food, are harder to maintain in cities than in villages. While city people often still pay attention to caste, their approach to preserving it is different. For instance, high-caste families often place classified ads in national newspapers seeking marriage partners from similar backgrounds for their children, as in this example: "Suitable Brahman bride for handsome Brahman boy completing Ph.D. (Physics). Write with biodata, photograph, horoscope."[7] Meanwhile, caste remains much more firmly rooted in the villages. At the bottom of the caste system, the untouchables (Dalits), some 20 percent of India's population, still live difficult lives, especially in the villages, even though government policies to improve their status have enabled some low-caste people to succeed in high-status occupations or politics. The grooves of tradition run deep, particularly in the rural areas, and changes can bring demoralization and disorientation as well as satisfaction.

Modern life has also hastened the breakup of the traditional joint families, where parents lived in large compounds with their married and unmarried children and grandchildren; some Indians now live in smaller, nuclear families. New forms of employment, which can cause family members to move to other districts or countries, have undermined family cohesion. A traditional preference for male babies, however, has continued. Today the ability of technology to determine the sex of a fetus has led many Indians who want male children to terminate pregnancies. Experts worry that a gender-imbalanced population will experience increasing social problems.

Families and Gender Relations

Nehru had believed that India could progress only if women played a full part, and new laws banned once-widespread customs such as polygamy, child marriage, and sati. In addition, female literacy has risen, from 1 percent in 1901 to 27 percent in 2000, though it is still only half the male rate. But some changing customs have penalized women. The practice of requiring new brides to provide generous dowries to their in-laws, once restricted to higher castes, has become common in all castes. As a result, some families banish, injure, or kill young brides whose own families failed to supply the promised dowries. Moreover, notions of women's rights, common in cities, are less known in villages. In some towns the police harass unmarried couples in public parks for public displays of affection, and even in Bangalore, where many educated women work in high-tech jobs, conservatives sometimes harass young women who go with friends to bars and discos.

Nevertheless, many Indian women have benefited from education, even becoming forceful leaders in such fields as journalism, business, trade unions, and the arts. Women have been elected to parliament and serve as chief ministers of states, especially in south India. In 2009 the Congress Party challenged tradition by naming a Dalit woman, former diplomat Meira Kumar, as Speaker of the Parliament. An antipatriarchy women's movement, growing for a century, has also become more active. The Self-Employed Women's Association, founded by Ela Bhatt in 1972, has provided low-cost credit and literacy training to some of the poorest city women, the ragpickers and sidewalk vendors. Outside the big cities, however, women have remained largely bound by tradition, expected to demonstrate submission, obedience, and absolute dedication to their husband. Women's organizations affiliated with the Hindu nationalist BJP emphasize women as mothers who produce sons and portray Muslim men as a threat to them. But a more concrete threat has come from AIDS, which has rapidly become a health problem, a result largely of women being forced into prostitution to serve the sexual needs of increasingly mobile male workers such as long-haul truckers.

Religion

Religion still plays a key role in Indian life. Although Hindus form a large majority, India's population also includes 140 million Muslims, over 20 million Sikhs, and nearly 20 million Christians. However, religious differences have become politicized. Some upper-caste Hindus, particularly in the BJP, have used the notion of a Hindu nation to marginalize Muslims and low-caste Hindus. Violent attacks on Muslims by militant Hindu nationalists, often fundamentalists who interpret the ancient Hindu religious texts literally, have caused political crises. At other times Muslims have initiated the violence. In 2006 Muslims protesting Danish cartoons offensive to Muslims rioted and attacked Hindu and Western targets. Tensions are fueled by mass poverty among all the religious groups. Yet, Muslims occupy high positions in India's government, business, and the professions and play a key role in cultural expression, such as films and music. India's most famous modern artist, Tyeb Mehta (1925–2009), was a Shi'ite Muslim whose works, much of which address the Hindu-Muslim divide, sell all over the world. Yet, art can stir controversy. Many Indian galleries refuse to show the works of another acclaimed Muslim artist, Maqbool Fida Husain, because some of them depict Hindu goddesses in the nude.

Literature and Popular Culture

Indians have also eagerly embraced modern cultural forms. While Indian-born novelists such as Arundhati Roy **(AH-roon-DAH-tee roy)** and Salman Rushdie have achieved worldwide fame, a more popular cultural form has been film. India has built the world's largest film industry, making about a thousand movies a year. Many films also find a huge audience among both Indian emigrants and non-Indians in Southeast Asia, the Middle East, Africa, Europe, and the Caribbean. The Mumbai film industry, known as "**Bollywood**," (see Profile: Raj Kapoor, Bollywood Film Star), churns out films in the major north Indian language, Hindi. But other regions make films in local languages, such as Tamil in southeast India. Many films, especially musicals, have portrayed a fantasy world that enables viewers to forget the problem-filled real world. As one fan explained: "I love to sit in the dark and dream about what I can never possibly have. I can listen to the music, learn all the songs and forget about my troubles."[8] Religious divisions are muted in Bollywood, and many leading directors, writers, and stars come from Muslim backgrounds. Because of their superstar status, film stars are often able to move into state and federal politics. For example, voters in southern India have long favored stars of the local film industries as state leaders. By the 1980s that trend had even spread to parts of north India.

Bollywood The Mumbai film industry.

Islamic Societies and Sri Lanka

Politics in Pakistan

South Asia's two densely populated Muslim countries, Pakistan and Bangladesh, struggled to develop and maintain stability while alternating between military dictatorships and elected civilian governments. Containing 170 million people, over 95 percent of them Sunni Muslims, Pakistan has had difficulty transforming its diverse ethnic and tribal groups into a unified nation. The longest-serving civilian leader, Zulkifar Ali Bhutto **(zool-KEE-far AH-lee BOO-toe)** (r. 1971–1977), a lawyer from a wealthy landowning family and educated at top universities in Britain and California, pursued socialist policies to help the poor. Accusing him of corruption, the army took power and later executed Bhutto. The Soviet occupation of Afghanistan in 1979 and the Pakistan-supported Islamic resistance to the Soviets that followed (see Chapter 30) distracted Pakistanis

RAJ KAPOOR, BOLLYWOOD FILM STAR

Raj Kapoor (1924–1988) was a true pioneer: the first real superstar of Indian film, an accomplished actor, director, producer, and all-round showman. Kapoor skillfully combined music, melodrama, and spectacle to create a cinema with huge popular, even international, appeal, especially among the poor. He was born in Peshawar, the son of one of India's most distinguished stage and film actors, Prithviraj Kapoor, among whose hundreds of roles was that of Alexander the Great. The family settled in Bombay in 1929, when the Hindi-language film industry was in a formative stage (Hindi is the major language spoken in north India). At age twenty-two Kapoor entered an arranged marriage to Krishnaji. Although he had romances with actresses, the marriage endured and the couple had five children.

Handsome and vigorous, with a talent for comedy, music, and self-promotion, the young Kapoor formed his own film company in 1948 with hopes of appealing to the common person. Over the next three decades he starred in or oversaw dozens of films, many of them commercially successful. Kapoor's greatest success came during the Nehru years from the late 1940s to mid-1960s, when Indians were optimistic and looked outward. His films, often subtitled in local languages, brought him celebrity all over South Asia and in Southeast Asia, East Africa, the Middle East, the Caribbean, and the Soviet Union. He was largely responsible for the recognition of Indian cinema in the world. Songs from his films were sung or hummed on streets of cities and small towns thousands of miles from India, and he and his female costars became popular pin-ups in the bazaars of the Arab world and folk heroes in the Soviet lands. Kapoor, like Nehru, believed that an Indian could be international, enjoying foreign products and influences, while also remaining deeply Indian. A song from his film *The Gentleman Cheat* in 1955 reflected the hero's transnational identity: "The shoes I'm wearing are made in Japan, My trousers fashioned in England. The red cap on my head is Russian. In spite of it all my heart is Indian."

Kapoor believed that some of his films achieved international success because "the young people of those countries saw in the films their own sufferings, the strivings to achieve, and their own triumph over a world in chaos." Fans saw in his characters youth, optimism about life, and revolt against authority, the little man straddling the great divides of wealth and poverty, city and village, sophistication and innocence. For example, in *The Vagabond* (1951) he portrays a rebellious youth and petty thief growing up on the streets, both daring and vulnerable, charming and reckless, surviving by his wits.

The themes of Kapoor's films often touched on social problems or politics and were filled with humanism and sensitivity. They cried out against destitution and unequal wealth, offering underdog heroes who were poor but also happy. These themes permeated some of his most popular films, such as *The Vagabond,* which broke box-office records in the USSR and the Middle East, where it was dubbed into Arabic, Persian, and Turkish. An ardent fan of American comedians, especially Charlie Chaplin, Kapoor, like Chaplin, often portrayed a deglamorized tramp, the little man at odds with the world and hiding his pain behind a smiling face, a figure he thought "had a greater identity with the common man."

Kapoor's romanticism was evident in his sympathetic treatment of women. The heroine, often played by the actress Nargis **(NAR-ghis)** (1929–1981), a Muslim whose mother was a famed singer, was always a central player in his films. Sometimes Kapoor's films presented women as strong and without flaws, as was his character's love interest, Nargis, in *The Vagabond;* at other times women were victims, exploited and tormented by religion and tradition. Kapoor argued, "We eulogize womankind as the embodiment of motherhood but we always give our women the worst treatment. They are burnt alive [in sati], treated as slaves [by men]." Yet, in spite of his concern for the sexual exploitation of women, Kapoor's films presented sensuous actresses and opened the way to more sexually explicit scenes, shocking social conservatives.

Kapoor's career faded in the 1970s, when his style of romantic hero became old-fashioned. The newer films focused on the angry young man, often a gangster, and turned away from Kapoor's adoring treatment of women. At the time of his death in 1988 he was making a film exploring the taboo subject of love across the India-Pakistan border, between a Hindu and a Muslim. His sons, all actors, tried to keep his banner alive, but Bollywood moved in new directions, centering stories on men and their challenges rather than balancing strong male-female roles as Kapoor had done.

Raj Kapoor As the most influential male lead and director in Indian films, Kapoor could attract the top actresses to star in his films. He made many films with Nargis, the two of them shown here in a 1948 musical, *Barsaat.*

Dinodia Picture Agency

THINKING ABOUT THE PROFILE

1. Why is Kapoor often credited with spreading Indian film to other countries?
2. What social viewpoints were expressed in his films?

Note: Quotations from Sumita S. Chakravarty, *National Identity in Indian Popular Cinema, 1947-1987* (Austin: University of Texas Press, 1993), 138, 30; and Malti Sahai, "Raj Kapoor and the Indianization of Charlie Chaplin," *East-West Film Journal* 2, no. 1 (December 1987): 64.

from their unpopular military regime and brought more U.S. military aid to Pakistan. Bhutto's daughter, Benazir Bhutto **(BEN-ah-ZEER BOO-toe)** (1953-2006), a graduate of Oxford University, put together a movement to challenge the military regime. As unrest increased in 1988, Benazir Bhutto became prime minister and later the first head of a modern Asian government to give birth to a child while in office. She was respected abroad but, accused of abuse of power, was dismissed in 1990. Although Bhutto returned to power after the 1993 elections, she failed to resolve critical problems, including growing fighting between ethnic factions and attacks by militant Sunnis on the small Shi'a Muslim and Christian minorities. In 1996 she was once again removed.

In 1999 the military took over, installing as president General Pervez Musharraf **(per-VEZ moo-SHAR-uff)** (b. 1943), whose family had fled to Pakistan during the partition of India in 1947. He faced and largely failed to meet the same challenge as his predecessors: to halt factional violence, punish corruption, collect taxes from the wealthy, restore economic growth, solve high unemployment, and balance the demands of both militant and secular Muslims. Although Musharraf allied with the United States after the 2001 terrorist attacks on the United States and the resulting U.S. invasion of Afghanistan, many Pakistanis resented the United States and the West. While seeking Pakistani help in the war on international terrorism, the United States was reluctant to remove high tariff barriers against Pakistani textiles, a major export that accounts for nearly half of all manufacturing jobs—Pakistanis make everything from shirts to sheets for Western companies. After popular unrest forced Musharraf out in 2006, Benazir Bhutto won free elections, but she was soon assassinated by a Muslim zealot. Since then the government has been besieged by the rise of a Pakistani Taliban, Muslim extremists seeking to impose a rigid theocracy, leading to terrorist attacks and Taliban-army fighting that has displaced several million refugees.

Pakistani Society and Culture

Pakistani society and culture have remained conservative and deeply divided between Sufis and secular urbanites, generally moderate, and those who favor strict Islamic laws and conduct. Pakistan's founding leader, Jinnah, a cosmopolitan British-educated lawyer, had favored more rights for women, arguing that it was a crime that most Pakistani women were shut up within the four walls of the house as prisoners. But national leaders who shared this view were reluctant to challenge the strong opposition to women's rights, especially in rural areas. In 1979 an Islamizing military government pushed through discriminatory laws that made women who were raped guilty of adultery, a serious offense. Women enjoyed far fewer legal rights than men and were more commonly jailed or punished for adultery. Women's groups who courageously protested in the streets were attacked by military force, prompting the feminist poet Saeeda Gazdar **(SIGH-ee-da GAZ-dar)** to write: "The flags of mourning were flapping, the hand-maidens had rebelled. Those two hundred women who came out on the streets, were surrounded on all sides, besieged by armed force, [repressed by] the enemies of truth, the murderers of love."[9] By the 1990s things had changed little: only 10 percent of adult women were employed outside the home, and fewer than 20 percent were literate. In some districts Islamic militants succeeded in restricting women from voting or from attending school with males.

Repression exists in other areas as well. The attempts by Islamic leaders to prohibit the broadcasting of music by popular singers, especially women such as London-based Nazia Hassan, set off an ongoing debate about the role of Westernized popular culture and women entertainers. Finally, Pakistan remains a land of villages dominated by large, politically influential landowners. Although life expectancy improved from forty-three to sixty-three years between 1960 and 2005, 40 percent of children suffered from malnutrition. With far too few public schools, many Pakistani youngsters attend Islamic madrassahs with narrow religious curriculums.

Politics and Society in Bangladesh

Bangladesh, overcrowded with 155 million people, has also encountered barriers to development. Mostly flat plains, the land is prone to devastating hurricanes, floods, tornados, famine, and rising sea levels due to global warming. The nation's founder, Sheikh Mujiber Rahman, had hoped that the nation he envisioned—secular, democratic, and socialist—would rapidly progress, but, after tightening his power, he was assassinated by the military. None of the succession of governments after him, whether military or civilian, have had much success in resolving problems, and all have suffered from corruption. Several leaders have been assassinated. After 1991 democracy became the main pattern, and the two largest parties have been led by women. The conservative Islamic and pro-capitalist Khaleda Zia **(ZEE-uh)** (b. 1945), the widow of an assassinated leader, heads one party while the left-leaning Sheikh Hasina Wajed **(shake ha-SEE-nah WAH-jed)** (b. 1947), the daughter of the assassinated Sheikh Mujiber Rahman, the nation's first prime minister, leads the Awami League. Sheikh Hasina herself escaped an assassination attempt in 2004. The two women, bitter rivals, have alternated as the nation's prime minister.

Despite political turbulence, however, Bangladesh has been a pioneer in programs to eliminate poverty and now provides some formal education to 60 percent of its children. The Grameen Bank, which loans small amounts of money, particularly to poor women for starting a village business, has helped millions of people, earning world attention (see Chapter 26). A visionary activist, Fazle Hasan Abed, also launched a movement to improve rural life through forming cooperatives. But the nation's per capita income remains $120 per year (35 cents per day), only 43 percent of adults are literate, and nearly half the population live below the official poverty line. Conflict and instability continue to plague the country.

As in Pakistan, social and cultural issues have divided Bangladesh. Bangladesh is officially a secular state and has a large Hindu minority (16 percent). Although over the centuries the Bengalis incorporated Hindu and Buddhist influences as well as Sufi mysticism, creating a tolerant Islam, militant Muslim political movements seeking an Islamic state gained strength in the 1990s, heightening divisions. The militants, allied with Khaleda Zia's party, succeeded in restricting women's rights. Public universities implemented a regulation to require women students to return to their dormitories by sunset to, as they put it, protect the women's chastity. Zia's government also prosecuted feminist writers such as the medical doctor-turned-novelist Taslima Nasreen (b. 1962), who criticized religion and a conservative culture for holding Bengali women back, arguing that the basic division was not between religions but between those favoring modern, rational values and those steeped in irrational, blind faith. Muslim militants condemned Nasreen's writing as blasphemy against Islam, a capital offense. Nasreen fled Europe to escape death threats.

Sri Lanka shares problems of ethnic conflict and poverty with its neighbors but has generally maintained a democracy. In 1948 the leaders of the Sinhalese, some 75 percent of the population and mostly Theravada Buddhists, negotiated independence from Britain, inheriting a colonial economy based on rubber and tea plantations. The Sinhalese-dominated government has also discriminated against the language and culture of the major ethnic minority, the Tamils, who are mostly Hindus. In 1959 Sirimavo Bandaranaike **(sree-MAH-vo BAN-dar-an-EYE-kee)** (1916–2004), the widow of an assassinated leader, led her party to victory and became the world's first woman prime minister. Her enemies derided her as a "kitchen woman," someone who knew all about cooking but nothing about running a country, yet she proved to be a strong leader and dominated politics in the 1960s and 1970s. The successive governments promoted Sinhalese nationalism while sponsoring textile and electronics manufacturing to reduce dependence on cash crop exports. While socialist policies discouraged free enterprise, they fostered the highest literacy rates (85 percent) and, by providing rice and free medical care to the poor, South Asia's longest life span (seventy-three). In 1983 some of the Tamils seeking independence for their northern and eastern region began a rebellion that has kept the island in a constant state of tension, resulting in assassinations of top political leaders and communal fighting. In 1994 Chandrika Kumaratunga **(CHAN-dree-ka koo-MAHR-a-TOON-ga)** (b. 1945), the University of Paris–educated daughter of Sirimavo Bandaranaike, led her left-leaning party to victory and became Sri Lanka's second woman leader. She sought both military victory over the Tamils and political peace but achieved neither, narrowly escaping an assassination attempt in 2000. Nearly 60,000 people, many innocent civilians, have died in twenty years of violence between Tamils and Sinhalese. The violence has also split the Buddhist clergy between those advocating peace and tolerance and those demanding defeat of the Hindu Tamils, whom they view as a threat to Buddhism. In 2009 the Sri Lankan military finally defeated the main Tamil insurgent group, bringing hope for peace. But national reconciliation has long proved elusive, and the future for multiethnic democracy remains unclear.

Sri Lankan Policies and Society

South Asia in the Global System

Since 1945 South Asian nations have grown in geopolitical and economic stature. Along with China and Brazil, India has become a major voice in the G-20 nations. Although Nehru strode the world stage as a major leader, seeking a middle ground between the United States and the USSR, his successors lacked his international influence. However, India has become a center of advanced technology, importing high-tech and service jobs from the West, and one of the most industrialized nations outside of Europe and North America, exporting heavy machinery, steel, and autos while producing abundant consumer goods for local consumption. Some Indian employees, such as those providing telephone technical support to users of U.S.-made computers, receive training in mastering an American or Australian accent to facilitate rapport. Even with the global recession of 2008–2009, outsourcing of jobs to India has continued. In addition, every year Indian universities, some of them world class, turn out thousands of talented engineers and computer scientists who have built up homegrown industries and also helped staff the high-tech "silicon valleys" of North America and Europe. As a result, experts have debated whether India or China might eventually compete for world economic leadership with the United States. Some point to India's large number of English-speakers, solid financial system, and vibrant democracy

Indian Economic Power

SECTION SUMMARY

- India's multiparty democracy has endured despite religious and caste tensions, and the Congress Party has been consistently influential, though communist parties have often governed in the northeast and south and Hindu nationalists have gained strength since 1989.

- Despite great advances in agricultural and industrial production, India still suffers from extensive poverty, and its rapidly growing population is likely to perpetuate this problem.

- While caste distinctions have remained strong in villages, they have broken down somewhat in cities; women have advanced in education and opportunity, though they are still less educated than men; and religion continues to be a source of tension.

- Pakistan has alternated between civilian and military governments and has been slow to grant women equal rights, while Bangladesh has combated poverty in spite of great challenges and has generally accepted religious minorities, though militant Muslim groups have gained influence in recent years.

- Since it became independent, Sri Lanka has been a democracy; it elected the world's first woman prime minister, and it has nurtured a well-educated, long-lived population, but since 1983 the minority Tamils have fought for independence from majority Sinhalese.

- India has produced talented engineers and computer scientists and made advances in technology, although its nuclear weaponry has prompted Pakistan to also develop nuclear arms and thus raised the worry of nuclear weapons in the hands of Islamic terrorists.

- Though women's rights are not universal in South Asia, more South Asian women have achieved positions of great power than in other areas of the world.

as advantages. However, the nation's boom has added few jobs, and to become a world power, India, like China, needs to contain social tensions and find ways to better share the wealth and reduce rural poverty.

South Asian technology and ingenuity have led to scientific achievements. In 1975 the Indian government launched into orbit its first satellite, named after Aryabhata (OUR-ya-BAH-ta), a major Indian scientist and mathematician who lived over fifteen hundred years ago. In 1998 India openly tested its first nuclear bomb. But these achievements have also triggered India-Pakistan rivalries. In response to the regional arms race with India, Pakistan also developed nuclear weapons. Since the late 1990s the weapons experts of many nations and international organizations have worried about Pakistan's nuclear abilities, since Islamic militants, some with possible links to global terrorist networks, have influence in Pakistan's military and play a key role in local and national politics. In 2004 a top Pakistani nuclear scientist admitted to selling nuclear secrets to other nations.

Global and regional politics have intensified Indian-Pakistani rivalries. After U.S. president George W. Bush, in the wake of the 2001 terrorist attacks on the United States, justified preemptive military attacks against potential threats and ordered U.S. forces into Afghanistan and Iraq, some Indians, adapting that justification to their own ends, wondered why India should not preemptively attack Pakistan: "If the United States can fly its bombs 10,000 miles to hit terrorist bases [in Afghanistan], why should India wait to knock out Pakistan's [military] bases?"[10] But while India-Pakistan relations have remained combustible, after 2000 Indian and Pakistani leaders promoted a thaw in relations, visiting each others' countries and giving hope that tensions might diminish. The thaw fostered cross-border visits and sports competitions. However, the Afghanistan conflict has spilled over into Pakistan. Islamist groups flourish among conservative Pashtuns in the tribal regions bordering Afghanistan, which have never been under firm government control. Over time the Islamists have extended their influence beyond the tribal areas, alarming moderate Muslims and the United States.

South Asians have made a distinctive contribution to world politics. Although maintaining traditional social patterns and cultural viewpoints, the four major South Asian nations, all democracies some or most of the time, have been led by women at various times, a striking difference from the preference for male leaders elsewhere in the world. Indeed, both Sri Lanka and Bangladesh elected two different women prime ministers. Hence, while women remain disadvantaged, they have enjoyed more high-level political power than in other nations. The political power of a few women is just part of the great complexity of this region.

REVOLUTION, DECOLONIZATION, AND NEW NATIONS IN SOUTHEAST ASIA

What were the causes and consequences of the struggles in Southeast Asia?

The nationalist thrust for independence from colonialism produced new nations in Southeast Asia after World War II (see Map 31.3). But the euphoria of independence proved short-lived, and the building of states capable of improving the lives of their people had only just begun. The peoples of Indochina experienced wrenching violence as two powerful Western nations—France and the United States—attempted to roll back revolutionary nationalism. During the First Indochina War (1946–1954), the French attempted to maintain their colonial control of Vietnam against communist-led opposition, a conflict that eventually ended in French defeat (see Chronology: Indochina, 1945–Present). The second and more destructive war, in which the United States and its Vietnamese allies waged an ultimately unsuccessful fight against communist-led Vietnamese forces, also dragged in Cambodia and Laos. Indonesia, the Philippines, Burma, and the other new nations, while often facing violent unrest, avoided the destructive warfare rocking Indochina but also had to overcome economic underdevelopment, promote national unity in ethnically divided societies, and deal with opposition to the new ruling groups. The years between 1945 and 1975 were marked by economic progress, but also by conflict and dictatorships. The leaders also had to forge new relationships with the former colonial powers and the new superpowers of a Cold War world—the United States and the Soviet Union—as well as with nearby China.

The First Indochina War and Two Vietnams

For Vietnam, the first decade after World War II included an anticolonial revolution. In 1945 the Japanese army in southern Vietnam had surrendered to British forces, which moved into southern Vietnam to prepare the ground for a French return to power. Meanwhile the Viet Minh, the communist-led, U.S.-armed anti-Japanese guerrilla force that had occupied much of rural northern and central Vietnam during the Japanese occupation, captured the capital of colonial Vietnam, Hanoi, and declared the end of French colonialism. Controlling northern Vietnam and parts of the center and south, the Viet Minh–led government, headed by Ho Chi Minh, became the first non-French regime in over eighty years. In his address to a half-million jubilant Vietnamese who gathered in Hanoi's main square, Ho quoted the U.S. Declaration of Independence and added: "It means: All the peoples on earth are equal from birth, all the peoples have a right to live and to be happy and free."[11] Both French and American observers on the scene noted that the majority of Vietnamese supported the Viet Minh.

However, the French, desperate to retain their empire in Southeast Asia, quickly regrouped and reoccupied southern Vietnam. Meanwhile, the Republic of China sent its troops to disarm the remaining Japanese soldiers in northern Vietnam. This provocative move made the Vietnamese fear a permanent presence by their traditional enemy, China. Using earthy language, Ho told his followers he had to patiently negotiate with the French because it was better to sniff French manure for a while than to eat China's all their lives. The United States, influenced by Cold War thinking and an ally of both France and China, was alarmed at Ho Chi Minh's association with the USSR and communism. Hence, the Americans shifted from supporting the Viet Minh during World War II to opposing all left-wing nationalists, including Ho and the Viet Minh.

Vietnam remained tense. The French, refusing to accept Ho's government, had allies among anticommunist Catholics and pro-Western nationalists. After Ho negotiated with the French for recognition of Vietnamese independence, the French arranged a Chinese troop withdrawal but refused to give up their claims. Ho also appealed to the U.S. president, Harry Truman, for political and economic support but received no answer. French leaders were determined to regain domination of all of Vietnam. In 1946 Ho warned a French diplomat that a war would be costly and unwinnable: "You will kill ten of my men while we will kill one of yours, but you will be the ones who will end up exhausted."[12] During the First Indochina War (1946–1954) the French attempted, with massive U.S. economic and military aid, to maintain their colonial grip. A large French military force pushed the Viet Minh out of the northern cities, but their brutal tactics alienated the population, while in the rural areas the Viet Minh won peasant support by transferring land to poor villagers. The French could not overcome an outgunned but determined foe with a nationalist message. As his forces became bogged down in what observers called a "quicksand war," a French general complained that fighting the Viet Minh was "like ridding a dog of its fleas. We can pick them, drown them, and poison them, but they will be back in a few days."[13] After a major military defeat in 1954, when Viet Minh forces overwhelmed a key French base in the mountains at Dien Bien Phu and took thousands of prisoners, the French abandoned their efforts and went home.

The peace agreements negotiated at a conference in Geneva, Switzerland, in 1954 divided the country into two Vietnams. But while northern and southern Vietnamese spoke different dialects and had some cultural differences, few Vietnamese wanted separate nations. The agreements left the Viet Minh in control of North Vietnam and provided that elections be held in 1956 to determine whether the South Vietnamese wanted to join in a unified country. Ignoring the Geneva agreements,

First Indochina War

North and South Vietnam

CHRONOLOGY
Indochina, 1945–Present

1945 Formation of Viet Minh government in Vietnam

1946–1954 First Indochina War

1953 Independence of Laos, Cambodia

1963 Assassination of South Vietnam president Ngo Dinh Diem

1963–1975 U.S.-Vietnamese War

1964 Gulf of Tonkin incident

1968 Tet Offensive

1970 Overthrow of Prince Sihanouk in Cambodia

1975 Communist victories in Vietnam, Cambodia, Laos

1978 Vietnamese invasion of Cambodia

which it had not signed, the United States quickly filled the political vacuum and helped install Ngo Dinh Diem (no dinh dee-EM) (1901–1963), an anticommunist and longtime U.S. resident, as president of South Vietnam. Concerned that Ho would easily win a free election, with U.S. support Diem refused to hold reunification elections. Some Vietnamese opposed communist ideology and backed Diem and the United States.

North and South Vietnam differed dramatically. Ho's government built a disciplined state that addressed the inequalities of the colonial period, redistributing land from powerful landlords to poor peasants. However, the government's authoritarian style and socialist policies prompted nearly a million North Vietnamese, including many Catholics, to move to South Vietnam, where President Diem, an ardent Catholic from a wealthy family, established a government based in Saigon. The United States poured in economic and military aid and, to stabilize Diem's increasingly unpopular regime, sent military advisers to aid the South Vietnamese army.

However, the rigid Diem alienated peasants by opposing most land reform. In 1960 dissidents in South Vietnam, including former Viet Minh soldiers, formed a communist-led revolutionary movement, the **National Liberation Front (NLF)**, often known as the Viet Cong. Armed by North Vietnam, the insurgency in South Vietnam grew. Diem responded with repression, murdering or imprisoning thousands of suspected rebels and other opponents. Buddhists resented the Diem government's pro-Catholic policies, and nationalists generally viewed Diem as an American puppet. Meanwhile, the NLF spread their influence in rural areas, often assassinating government officials.

By the early 1960s the NLF, supplied by North Vietnam, controlled large sections of South Vietnam, and thousands more American troops, still called military advisers, became more involved in combat. In 1963 U.S. leaders, judging Diem ineffective, sanctioned his overthrow by his own military officers, who killed him. As the situation deteriorated and North Vietnamese troops moved south, U.S. concerns about a possible communist sweep through Southeast Asia provided the rationale for action. The stage was set for what Americans called the Vietnam War (1963–1975) and what many Vietnamese termed the American War.

The American-Vietnamese War

Escalating United States Intervention

The United States escalated the conflict into a full-scale military commitment (see Map 31.2). U.S. president Lyndon Johnson's (g. 1963–1969) excuse was an alleged North Vietnamese attack on a U.S. ship in the Gulf of Tonkin in 1964, which probably never occurred. When Johnson said in 1965, "I want to leave the footprints of America there [Indochina]. We can turn the Mekong into [an economically developed] Tennessee Valley,"[14] he was reflecting a longtime American sense of mission to change the world and spread democracy and capitalism. However, Johnson and other U.S. leaders, civilian and military, had little understanding of the nationalism and spirited opposition to foreign occupation that had shaped Vietnam, a country with many historical reasons for mistrusting foreign powers—whether Chinese, French, or American—on "civilizing" missions. Soon the war intensified, drawing in a larger U.S. presence. In 1965 Johnson ordered an air war against targets in both South and North Vietnam and a massive intervention of ground troops, peaki ng at 550,000 Americans by 1968. However, a series of military regimes never achieved credibility with the South Vietnamese majority. Meanwhile, military supplies and North Vietnamese troops regularly moved south through the mountains of eastern Laos and Cambodia, along what came to be known as the Ho Chi Minh Trail.

Despite their technological superiority, U.S. forces struggled to find effective strategies to overcome the communists, often ignoring South Vietnamese leaders and the consequences of U.S. military actions. Since the South Vietnamese army, largely conscripts, suffered from low morale and high desertion and casualty rates, Americans did much of the fighting. U.S. strategists viewed Vietnam chiefly in military terms: they measured success by counting the enemy dead and creating free fire zones, areas where civilians were ordered to evacuate so that U.S. forces could attack any people remaining as the enemy. Such policies made it hard for the Americans to win Vietnamese "hearts and minds," a key doctrine of counterinsurgency strategies, and diminishh local support for the NLF. Vietnam also became the most heavily bombed nation in history, with the United States dropping twice the total bomb tonnage used in World War II. The use of chemical defoliants to clear forests and wetlands, and the countless bomb craters, caused massive environmental damage. Thanks in part to the toxic chemicals, Vietnam today has the world's highest rate of birth defects and one of the highest rates of cancer.

South Vietnamese Divisions

South Vietnamese had to choose sides. For procommunist Vietnamese, the American-Vietnamese War was a continuation of the First Indochina War to expel the French and rebuild a damaged society. When the Viet Minh humbled the hated French colonizers, they gained a

National Liberation Front (NLF) Often known as the Viet Cong, a communist-led revolutionary movement in South Vietnam that resisted American intervention in the American-Vietnamese War.

Legend:
- Main area of confrontation
- Viet Cong base areas
- Communist supply route
- U.S. forces
- Major battle

0   50   100 Km.
0   50   100 Mi.

CHINA

MYANMAR (BURMA)

Red R.

Black R.

Dien Bien Phu

U.S. air raids on Hanoi 1966, 1968, 1972

Hanoi
Haiphong

NORTH VIETNAM

20°N

Gulf of Tonkin

Hainan

PLAIN OF JARS

Ca R.

Gulf of Tonkin, 1964

LAOS

Mekong R.

Vientiane

Vinh

Keo Nua Pass

Mu Gia Pass

Demilitarized Zone

Demarcation Line, 1954

17°N

Hue Tet Offensive 1968

THAILAND

Da Nang

South China Sea

My Lai Massacre 1968

15°N

Mekong R.

Pleiku

Qui Nhon

Bangkok

CAMBODIA

Ho Chi Minh Trail

CENTRAL HIGHLANDS

110°E

Phnom Penh

SOUTH VIETNAM

Saigon

N

Gulf of Thailand

Tet Offensive 1968

10°N

CA MAU PENINSULA

Mekong Delta

100°E   105°E

Map 31.2 The U.S.-Vietnamese War

From the early 1960s until 1975 South Vietnam, aided by thousands of U.S. troops and air power, resisted a communist-led insurgency aided by North Vietnam, which sent troops and supplies down the Ho Chi Minh Trail through Laos and Cambodia.

e Interactive Map

popularity with many Vietnamese that the United States could not overcome. The communists also gained peasant support by advocating reform to help landless peasants. Moreover, some U.S. policies, especially the air war, which killed thousands of innocent people, backfired. One of the thousands of women who fought for the NLF reported: "The first days I felt ill at ease—marching in step, lobbing grenades, taking aim with my rifle, hitting the ground. But as soon as I saw the American planes come back [to bomb], my timidity left me."[15] However, some South Vietnamese supported the pro-U.S. government or rejected both sides. Pham Duy **(fam do-ee)**, a folksinger in South Vietnam who, like many South Vietnamese, disliked both the corrupt Saigon government and the often ruthless communists, wrote a song describing the war's impact on average Vietnamese: "The rain of the leaves is the tears of joy, Of the girl whose boy returns from the war. The rain on the leaves is bitter tears, When a mother hears her son is no more."[16]

Tet Offensive Communist attacks on major South Vietnamese cities in 1968, a turning point in the American-Vietnamese War.

By 1967 the U.S. military strategy had brought about a military stalemate, but a turning point came in 1968 with the **Tet Offensive**, when communist forces attacked the major South Vietnamese cities during the Vietnamese new year. Although the communists were pushed back and suffered high casualties, Tet proved a political and psychological setback for Americans, who watched on television as communist guerrillas attacked the U.S. embassy in Saigon and U.S. Marines fought their way, block by block, against fierce resistance into the old imperial capital of Hue.

The war bitterly divided Americans, and by the late 1960s a majority had turned against the commitment to a seemingly endless quagmire in which American soldiers were being killed or injured for uncertain goals. Even Ho Chi Minh's death in 1969 did not alter the situation. The United States began a gradual withdrawal of troops and negotiated peace agreements with North Vietnam. By 1973 U.S. ground forces had left Vietnam; the air war ended a year later; and in 1975 the NLF and North Vietnam defeated the South Vietnamese forces and reunified the country under communist leadership. As the victors marched into Saigon, many South Vietnamese fled the country, some 1.3 million eventually settling in the United States. General Maxwell Taylor, former U.S. ambassador to South Vietnam, later concluded that Americans lost because, never understanding the Vietnamese on either side, they overestimated the effectiveness of U.S. policies. The devastating war cost the United States 58,000 dead and 519,000 physically disabled. It cost the Vietnamese around 4 million killed or wounded—10 percent of the total population. After the fighting ended, Vietnam turned to reconstruction.

War in Laos and Cambodia

Laos and Cambodia became pawns in the larger conflict between the United States and the North Vietnamese. Anticolonial sentiment had grown during and after the Japanese occupation of World War II. In 1953 the French, wearying of their Indochinese experience, granted Laos independence under a conservative, pro-French government dominated by the ethnic Lao majority. Cambodia gained its independence under the young, charismatic, and widely popular Prince Norodom Sihanouk **(SEE-uh-nook)** (b. 1922), who won the first free election in 1955. However, both countries were eventually engulfed in the Vietnam conflict, in part because of U.S. military interventions.

Pathet Lao Revolutionary Laotian nationalists allied with North Vietnam during the American-Vietnamese War.

The U.S. intervention in Laos, which began in the late 1950s and continued until 1975, intensified conflict between U.S.-backed anticommunist rightwingers, people favoring neutrality between the superpowers, and the **Pathet Lao**, revolutionary Laotian nationalists allied with North Vietnam. In 1960 rightwing forces advised and equipped by the U.S. Central Intelligence Agency (CIA) seized the Laotian government. As fighting intensified, the Pathet Lao controlled the northern mountains while the government controlled the south and the Mekong Valley. Because the Laotian regime, bloated with corruption, had an ineffective U.S.-financed army, Americans turned to the hill peoples for recruits, among them a large faction of one group, the Hmong, that sought autonomy from the government. Promising them permanent U.S. support and protection, in 1960 the CIA recruited a secret army of some 45,000 soldiers, largely Hmong, that attacked North Vietnamese forces along the Ho Chi Minh Trail and fought the Pathet Lao. As a result, 10 percent of the Hmong population, some 30,000 people, died during a conflict that was largely unknown to the American public. U.S. bombing depopulated large areas, forcing many Laotians into refugee camps, and the war killed some 100,000 Laotians. After 1975, when the Pathet Lao took full control of a war-weary Laos, thousands of anticommunist Laotians fled into Thailand, many later moving to the United States and other Western nations.

Like Laos, Cambodia also became part of the Indochina conflict. Its first president, Prince Sihanouk, ruled as a benevolent autocrat while also writing sentimental popular songs, playing the saxophone, directing films, and publicizing his political views in foreign newspapers. Sihanouk diplomatically maintained Cambodian independence and peace. But both the Vietnamese communists, whose forces roamed the border area, and the United States, whose war planes bombed communist positions in Cambodian territory, violated Cambodian neutrality. Sihanouk faced other problems as well. The **Khmer Rouge (kmahr roozh)** ("Red Khmers"), a communist insurgent group seeking to overthrow the government and led by alienated intellectuals educated in French universities, built a small support base of impoverished peasants. Moreover, although Sihanouk remained popular among many peasants, military officers and big businessmen resented his dictatorial rule and desired to share in the U.S. money and arms flowing into neighboring South Vietnam, Laos, and Thailand.

In 1970 Sihanouk was overthrown by U.S.-backed generals and civilians. With Sihanouk in exile, U.S. and South Vietnamese forces soon invaded eastern Cambodia in search of Vietnamese communist bases, and the resulting instability created an opening for the Khmer Rouge to recruit mass support. The pro-U.S. government lacked legitimacy, becoming dependent on U.S. aid for virtually all supplies, and the ineffective Cambodian army suffered from corruption and low morale. Meanwhile, to attack the Khmer Rouge, U.S. planes launched an intensive, terrifying air assault through the heart of Cambodia's agricultural area, where most of the population lived, killing thousands of innocent civilians. Rice production declined by almost half, raising the possibility of massive starvation. Amid the destruction, the Khmer Rouge rapidly enlarged its forces, recruiting from among the displaced and shell-shocked peasantry. From 1970 through 1975, between 750,000 and 1 million Cambodians, mostly civilians, perished from the conflict between the Khmer Rouge, who were brutal toward their enemies, and the U.S.-backed government. In 1975 the Khmer Rouge seized the capital, Phnom Penh, and controlled the country until 1978 (discussed in next section).

Indonesia: The Quest for Freedom and Unity

Indonesian independence came through struggle. During the violent anti-Dutch resistance of the late 1940s, known as the Indonesian Revolution, the Dutch used massive force to suppress the nationalists, who fought back. In a short story about a brutal battle, a nationalist writer noted that, for the revolutionary soldiers, "everything blurred: the future and their heart-breaking struggle. They only knew that they had to murder to drive out the enemy and stop him trampling their liberated land. They killed [the Dutch soldiers] with great determination, spirit and hunger."[17] The United States, fearing regional instability, pressured the Dutch to grant independence in 1950 (see Chronology: Noncommunist Southeast Asia, 1945–Present).

Indonesia still faced the challenge of fostering a unified nation. Given the diversity of islands, peoples, and cultures, Indonesian leaders became obsessed with creating national unity and identity. Their national slogan, "unity in diversity," expressed more a goal than a solid reality. During the 1950s and early 1960s Indonesia was led by the charismatic but increasingly authoritarian president Sukarno **(soo-KAHR-no)** (1902–1970), an inspirational nationalist. A spell-binding orator able to rally popular support and bring different factions together, Sukarno worked to create national solidarity and unite a huge nation in which villagers on remote islands and cosmopolitan city dwellers on Java knew little about each other.

Despite his efforts, Sukarno proved unable to maintain stability. The multiparty parliamentary system became divisive. Regionalism also grew as outer islanders resented domination by the Javanese, who constituted over half of Indonesia's population and, many outer islanders believed, were favored by Sukarno. By the early 1960s Sukarno's nationalistic but poorly implemented economic policies had caused a severe economic crisis and deepened divisions between communist, Islamic, and military forces. A procommunist Javanese novelist described the economic failures: "Jakarta [the capital city] reveals a grandiose display with no relationship to reality. Great plans, enormous immorality. [There are] no screws, no nuts, no bolts, no valves, and no washers for the machinery we do have."[18]

By 1965 Indonesia had become a country of explosive social and political pressures and was experiencing its greatest crisis as an independent nation. After a failed attempt by a small military faction with communist sympathies to seize power, discontented generals arrested Sukarno, took power, and launched a brutal campaign to eliminate all leftists, especially members of the large Communist Party, influential among poor peasants in Java. The resulting bloodbath, led by the army and Muslim groups, killed perhaps half a million Indonesians, including members of the unpopular Chinese minority. Most communist leaders were killed or arrested, and thousands of leftists were held in remote prison camps for years. Sukarno died in disgrace in 1970.

Khmer Rouge ("Red Khmers") A communist insurgent group seeking to overthrow the government in Cambodia during the 1960s and 1970s.

CHRONOLOGY
Noncommunist Southeast Asia, 1945–Present

1945–1950 Indonesian Revolution

1948 Independence of Burma

1963 Formation of Malaysia

1965 Secession of Singapore from Malaysia

1965–1966 Turmoil in Indonesia

1966–1998 New Order in Indonesia

1997 Economic crisis in Southeast Asia

2008–2009 World economic crisis

Political and Economic Turmoil

Map 31.3 Modern Southeast Asia
Indonesia, covering thousands of islands, is the largest, most populous Southeast Asian nation. Southeast Asia also includes four other island nations (including the Philippines and Singapore), five nations on the mainland, and Malaysia, which sprawls from the Malay Peninsula to northern Borneo.

e Interactive Map

Making the Philippine and Malaysian Nations

Philippine Politics

The Philippines and Malaysia both became independent but troubled nations. The Philippines achieved independence from the United States on July 4, 1946, though the two countries remained bound by close political and economic links. The new nation soon faced problems sustaining democracy. A small group of landowners, industrialists, and businessmen who had prospered under U.S. rule manipulated elected governments to preserve their power and to protect U.S. economic interests. Free elections involved so much violence, bribery, and fraud that disillusioned Filipinos spoke of them as decided by "guns, goons, and gold." Furthermore, nationalists believed that continuing U.S. influence hindered a truly independent Filipino identity and culture. Several major U.S. military bases near Manila symbolized this influence, and the popular U.S. films, television programs, music, comics, and books helped to spread it. A prominent scholar wrote that her people "sing of White Christmases and of Manhattan. Their stereos reverberate with the American Top 40."[19] Outside influences—first Spanish and then American—on Filipino culture were often superficial, but Filipinos have struggled to create a clear national identity out of the diverse mosaic of local languages and regions.

Economic inequality and social divisions fueled conflict. A Filipino poet portrayed the gap between the rich and poor: "[For the affluent] there's pleasure and distraction, fiesta and dancing, night-long, day-long; who dares whisper that thousands have no roofs above their heads; that hunger stalks the town."[20] The communist-led Huk Rebellion from 1948 to 1954 capitalized on discontent among the rural poor and was suppressed only by heavy U.S. assistance. In the 1970s the communist New Peoples Army (NPA) controlled many rural districts. Like the Huks, the NPA's promise of radical social and economic change attracted support from rural tenant farmers and urban slum dwellers. Religious differences have also led to conflict. While most Filipinos became Christian in Spanish times, the southern islands have large Muslim populations, who have often resented domination by and favoritism toward Christians. Several Muslim groups have taken up arms to fight for autonomy. In 1972 President Ferdinand Marcos (1917–1989) used law and order as an excuse to suspend democracy, and from 1972 until 1986 he ruled as a dictator, resolving few problems.

Malayan governments proved more stable after independence. After World War II the British sought to dampen political unrest as communist-led insurgents kept the colony on edge for a decade. In 1957, with the insurgency crushed by the British, Malaya became independent as a federation of states under a government led by the main Malay party, **UMNO** (United Malays National Organization). However, the predominantly Chinese city-state of Singapore, a major trading center and military base, remained a British colony. In Malaya the majority ethnic group, the Malays, nearly all Muslim, dominated politics, but the Chinese, a third of the population, were granted liberal citizenship rights and maintained strong economic power. British leaders, seeing their colonial role in Singapore as well as in two northern Borneo states they controlled, Sabah and Sarawak, as burdensome, suggested joining them with Malaya in a larger federation, to be called Malaysia. This new, geographically divided Malaysia was formed in 1963.

Malaysians struggled to create national unity out of deep regional and ethnic divisions. Singapore withdrew in 1965 and became independent. Given the need to reduce political tensions, sustain rapid economic growth, and preserve stability, the leaders of the key ethnic groups in Malaya—Malays, Chinese, and Indians—cooperated through political parties that allied in an UMNO-dominated ruling coalition, but below the surface ethnic tensions simmered. Street fighting between Chinese and Malays following the heated 1969 election led to a nationwide state of emergency. After 1970 Malay-dominated governments pursued policies designed to reshape Malaysia's society and economy.

Building Malaysia

UMNO The main Malay political party in Malaysia.

Diversity and Dictatorship in Thailand and Burma

Thailand and Burma also struggled to create national unity and stability. Although historical rivals, the two countries have shared certain patterns. The majority Thais (Siamese) and the Burmans, both Theravada Buddhists, assert authority over diverse minorities, including various hill tribes, Malay Muslims, and Chinese. Both countries experienced insurgencies by disaffected ethnic, religious, or communist factions.

In Thailand, leaders sought to build a national culture based on Thai cultural values, including reverence for Buddhism and the monarchy, which symbolized the nation, respect for those in authority, and social harmony. However, this conservatism fostered authoritarian governments and bureaucratic inertia. Various communist and Islamic insurgent groups operated during the 1960s and 1970s in ethnic minority regions. Partly because of this unrest, Thailand's political history after 1945 was characterized by long periods of military rule, often corrupt and oppressive, followed by short-lived democratically elected or semidemocratic governments. Not until the 1970s would opposition movements challenge the long-entrenched military regime. Many Thais resented the United States, which supported the military regime and had military bases and some 50,000 troops in the country. The presence of free-spending American soldiers created a false prosperity, while staunch Buddhists were outraged by the sleazy bars, gaudy nightclubs, and brothels that often exploited poor Thai women and served the Americans but also attracted eager Thai men.

In 1973 antigovernment feelings boiled over and the military regime was overthrown following massive student-led demonstrations. The military strongman fled the country, having lost public support after his troops arrested protest leaders and killed or wounded over a thousand demonstrators. The collapse of military rule opened a brief era of political liberalization as democracy and debate flourished. The civilian government tolerated these activities but proved fragile and unable to resolve major problems. Meanwhile, rightwing military officers and bureaucrats resisted challenges to their power and privileges, and Thai society became polarized between liberals and conservatives. Finally, in 1976, bloody clashes between leftist students and rightwing youth gangs led to a military coup and martial law, which resulted in the killing or wounding of hundreds and the arrest of thousands of students and their supporters. The return of military power reestablished order, but the massacres discredited the military.

Burma emerged from the Japanese occupation devastated, whole cities blasted into rubble by Allied bombing. After the war the British returned to reestablish their colonial control. Facing a well-armed Burmese nationalist army and weary of conflict, they negotiated independence with the charismatic nationalist leader Aung San (1915–1947) and left in 1948. But newly elected Prime

Thailand Policies and Society

Burma's Politics and Society

Minister Aung San was assassinated by a political rival and replaced by his longtime colleague, U Nu (1907–1995), an idealistic Buddhist and democrat. Soon key ethnic minorities, fearful of domination by the majority Burmans, declared their secession and organized armies. For several decades the central government rarely controlled more than half the nation's territory as ethnic armies and communist insurgents, funded by opium revenues, battled the Burmese army. In 1962, however, the army deposed U Nu and seized control, suspended civil liberties, imposed censorship, and claimed most of the government budget. The military also took over industries, banks, and commerce and discouraged foreign investment. By the 1980s, economic stagnation and political repression had fostered dissent and the various secession movements continued, only to be largely suppressed in the 1990s.

SECTION SUMMARY

- After World War II, the communist Viet Minh, led by Ho Chi Minh, took partial control of Vietnam and declared independence, but the U.S.-supported French fought back in the First Indochina War, which ended in frustration for the French.

- Instead of allowing an election to determine the future of South Vietnam, the United States installed Diem as president, but he was opposed by the communist National Liberation Front, setting the stage for the Vietnam War.

- Using a questionable attack as a pretext, the United States went to war to rid Vietnam of communism, but despite vastly superior resources, the United States and its allies in South Vietnam could not triumph over the communists, who gained control of Vietnam two years after the United States pulled out its ground forces.

- In Laos the United States recruited Hmong hill people to fight the Pathet Lao revolutionaries, who took control of the country in 1975, while in Cambodia the United States

- bombed areas occupied by North Vietnamese and supported a weak, dependent government, which was overthrown in 1975 by the Khmer Rouge.

- After a difficult fight for independence from the Dutch, Indonesia's wildly diverse population struggled to attain unity under Sukarno, but different groups became more divided and a group of generals cracked down harshly on leftists and removed Sukarno from power.

- After attaining independence, the Philippines remained strongly influenced by the United States and struggled with economic inequality and a Muslim insurgency, while Malaysia experienced intermittent tensions between the politically dominant Malays and the economically strong Chinese.

- Thailand alternated between long periods of military rule and short periods of democratic or semidemocratic rule, while Burma endured decades of factional fighting and, since 1962, brutal military domination.

TIGERS, POLITICS, AND CHANGING SOUTHEAST ASIAN SOCIETIES

What role do the Southeast Asian nations play in the global system?

Southeast Asia changed dramatically after 1975, mixing influences from the past and from the wider world. The fast pace of change has reshaped life in both cities and villages. Indonesia, Malaysia, Singapore, and Thailand, with market economies geared to world commerce, have gained reputations as "tigers" because of their dynamism. At the same time, governments played a major role in stimulating economies and often became authoritarian to ensure social stability. When the fighting ended in Indochina, all the societies involved had to rebuild their societies and the lives shattered by the turmoil. Vietnam eventually developed a tiger economy.

The Resurgence of Southeast Asia

Economic Growth

A shift of economic direction allowed several Southeast Asian nations to develop and play a greater role in the world economy. In 1976, Indonesia, Burma, and Thailand were under military rule, the communist regimes in Indochina faced monumental reconstruction, a dictator governed in the Philippines, and only Malaysia and Singapore had semidemocracies. Few of the countries enjoyed impressive economic growth. But in the 1980s, the pace of change accelerated. Inspired by Japan's industrialization in the late nineteenth century and rapid recovery from World War II, leaders encouraged their people to "Look East" by mixing capitalism and activist government to spur economic expansion. Local entrepreneurs of Chinese ancestry provided much of the initiative and capital. Economic growth had drawbacks: for example, industrial activity and the expansion of agriculture, mining, and logging caused widespread environmental destruction. Yet, migrants crowding into cities rubbed elbows with other peoples, encouraging cultural mixing. Even though governments often squashed dissent and repressed personal liberties, an expanding education fostered larger middle classes, who sought more political influence. Experts identified a vibrant Pacific Rim that included the "tiger" nations as well as Japan, China, Taiwan, South Korea (see Chapter 27), and eventually Vietnam. Some forecast a Pacific Century in which these nations would lead the world economically and increase their political strength.

To promote growth and stability, Southeast Asian countries began cooperating as never before. Founded in 1967 by Malaysia, Indonesia, Thailand, Singapore, and the Philippines, **ASEAN** (Association of Southeast Asian Nations), a regional economic and political organization, promoted economic exchange among the noncommunist Southeast Asian nations and coordinated opposition to Vietnam. However, ASEAN's priorities shifted after the end of the Indochina wars. As Vietnam, Cambodia, Laos, Burma, and the tiny, oil-rich state of Brunei became members, ASEAN emerged as the world's fourth largest trading bloc. It also provided a forum for the members to work out their differences and deal with the wider world. Eventually ASEAN cultivated closer relations with China and Japan.

Many challenges remained. By 2008 there were some 580 million Southeast Asians. Population growth outstripped economic growth, placing a greater burden on limited resources such as food and water, especially in the Philippines, Indonesia, and Vietnam. These conditions sometimes generated riots or even full-blown insurgencies. But despite occasional violence and political upheavals, the destructive wars of the earlier years were not repeated. In some cases, dictatorships were eventually replaced by more open regimes. In 1997, however, most Southeast Asian countries faced a severe economic crisis, part of a broader collapse among Asian and world economies. The reasons for the troubles included poorly regulated banking systems, overconfident investments, and government favoritism toward well-placed business interests. The dislocations hit all social classes. The crisis eventually bottomed out, only to be rekindled in 2008–2009 by a larger world economic downturn that reduced demand for Southeast Asian products, caused massive job losses, and slowed foreign investment. The widespread dislocations called into question the prospect of a forthcoming Pacific Century. Southeast Asia is also one of the regions most threatened by global warming, which may foster erratic rains and will raise sea levels, flooding densely populated river deltas and lowlands.

New Orders in Indonesia and the Philippines

Indonesia, with more than seven hundred ethnic groups and a rapidly growing population of 240 million, struggled to preserve political stability while developing economically. Between 1966 and 1998 the government, known as the **New Order**, headed by general-turned-president Suharto (1921–2008), a Javanese, mixed military and civilian leadership to maintain law and order. Suharto used force to repress independence movements in East Timor, a small, former Portuguese colony with a mostly Christian population, north Sumatra, dominated by the fiercely Islamic Achehnese, and West Irian (western New Guinea). However, although it limited political opposition, the New Order improved Indonesia's economic position and fostered an educated urban middle class. Per capita income, life expectancy, and adult literacy increased, aided by an annual economic growth rate of nearly 5 percent by the 1990s, though a third of the population remained desperately poor, earning less than a dollar a day. Creative musicians, writers, artists, and filmmakers shaped a vibrant popular culture.

Yet, the New Order also started some negative trends. Indonesia became dependent on exporting oil, which represented 80 percent of foreign earnings. As a result, whenever world oil prices decline and reduce the national budget, Indonesia adds to an enormous foreign debt. The rapid development of mining, forestry, and cash crop agriculture also has taken a toll on the environment. Rain forests were clear-cut so rapidly for timber and plantations that forest fires became common, polluting the air and creating a thick, unhealthy haze that spread into neighboring nations. Furthermore, income disparities between classes and regions widened while political and business corruption thrived. One Indonesian fiction writer criticized a society in which government officials and predatory businessmen solicited bribes and grabbed public funds for themselves: "Indonesia, Land of Robbers. My true homeland stiff with thieves. In the future, I shall plunder while my wife shall seize."[21] The wealthy frolicked in nightclubs, casinos, and golf courses built across the street from slums or on land appropriated from powerless villages. Suharto, the son of poor peasants, became one of the world's most corrupt leaders, and he and his family acquired over $15 billion in assets from their business enterprises and access to public coffers.

Many Indonesians disliked the New Order, with Islam providing the chief vehicle for opposition. Some 87 percent of Indonesians are either devout or nominal Muslims, but few have

ASEAN A regional economic and political organization formed in 1967 to promote cooperation among the noncommunist Southeast Asian nations; eventually became a major trading bloc.

New Challenges

Indonesia under Suharto

New Order The Indonesian government headed by President Suharto from 1966 to 1998, which mixed military and civilian leadership.

Indonesian Islam

supported militant Islamist movements. Suharto discouraged Islamic radicalism as a threat to national unity in a country that includes many Christians and Hindus. However, devout Muslims have often opposed secular policies and desired a more Islamic approach to social, cultural, and legal matters. Muslim conservatives denounce gambling casinos, racy magazines and films, and scantily clad female pop singers. At the same time, a progressive, democratic strand of Islamic thought has favored liberal social and political reform. Muslim liberals tap into the Javanese emphasis on harmony, consensus, and tolerance that was incorporated into Indonesian Islam, offering a stark contrast to the more dogmatic Islam common in Pakistan and Saudi Arabia. Nevertheless, Muslims blamed the New Order government for poor living standards and massive corruption.

Post-Suharto Politics

By the 1990s Indonesian society suffered from increasing class and ethnic tensions, student protests, and labor unrest, setting the stage for dramatic changes. When the economy collapsed in 1997, throwing millions out of work and raising prices for essential goods, widespread rioting resulted in Suharto's resignation. The country fell into turmoil, and protests and ethnic clashes proliferated. Many among the urban middle class wanted to strengthen democracy, and in 1999 free elections were held. Later, Megawati Soekarnoputri (MEH-ga-WHA-tee soo-KAR-no-POO-tri), the daughter of Indonesia's first president, Sukarno, became Indonesia's first woman president. Like her father, Megawati followed secular, nationalist policies but also showed little faith in grassroots democracy and resolved few problems. By 2004 popular support for her regime had ebbed and she was defeated for reelection by a retired Javanese general, who was reelected in 2009.

The disorderly democracy that replaced the New Order brought unprecedented freedom of the press and speech. But removing New Order restrictions allowed long-simmering ethnic hostilities to reemerge. East Timor, which had endured a long, unpopular occupation by Indonesia, finally achieved independence in 1999, but only after thousands of its people were killed by Indonesian troops and militias. Muslim-Christian conflicts also resulted in numerous deaths, with Islamic militants capitalizing on the instability to recruit support. Several terrorist bombings of popular tourist venues, most recently in 2009, added to the growing tensions. Then in 2005 over 100,000 Indonesians perished from earthquakes and a deadly tidal wave, or tsunami, that destroyed cities and washed away coastal villages on Sumatra. These setbacks raised questions about the long-term viability of Indonesian democracy. Yet, in 2009 voters decisively rejected anti-Western Islamist parties and reelected the centrist, secular government.

Marcos Dictatorship

Like Indonesia, the Philippines also experienced political turbulence and social instability, lagging well behind the most prosperous Southeast Asian nations in economic development. When Ferdinand Marcos ruled as a dictator, economic conditions worsened, rural poverty became more widespread, the population grew rapidly, and political opposition was limited by the murder or detention of dissidents, censorship, and rigged elections. The dictator, his family, and cronies looted the country, amassing billions. The regime built high walls along city freeways so that affluent motorists would not have to view slums along the route. A tiny minority lived in palatial homes surrounded by high walls topped with broken glass and barbed wire, and with gates manned by armed guards. Across the street from the glittering pavilions of Manila's Cultural Center, whose landscaped gardens were a gaudy monument to Marcos splendor, homeless families slept in bushes. The majority of rural families were landless, and child malnutrition increased. A Filipino novelist described rural society and its poverty, with villagers eking out a living on unproductive land: "Nothing in the countryside had changed, not the thatched houses, not the ragged vegetation, not the stolid people. Changeless land, burning sun."[22] To escape poverty, Filipinos often migrated, temporarily or permanently, to other Asian nations, the United States, or the Middle East. Some 10 million Filipinos lived abroad by 2009, with many women working as nurses, maids, or entertainers. About 2,500 Filipinos leave the country every day for overseas work.

The failures of the Marcos years led to massive public protests in 1986 that restored democracy. The opposition rallied around U.S.-educated Corazon Aquino (ah-KEE-no) (1933–2009), a descendant of a Chinese immigrant, whose popular politician husband had been assassinated by Marcos henchmen. In a spectacular nonviolent "people's power" revolution, street demonstrations involving students, workers, businessmen, housewives, and clergy demanded justice and freedom. Marcos and his family fled into exile in the United States, which had long supported his regime. As Marcos and his family escaped by helicopter, thousands of demonstrators who broke into the presidential palace found that the dictator's wife, Imelda Marcos, a former beauty queen, had acquired thousands of pairs of shoes and vast stores of undergarments, symbolizing the Marcoses' waste of public resources. Mrs. Aquino became president and reestablished democracy.

Recent Politics

Yet the hopes that the Philippines could resolve its problems proved illusory. The new government, while open to dissenting voices, was, as had been true since independence, dominated

People's Power Demonstration in the Philippines In 1986 the simmering opposition to the dicta-torial government of Fer-dinand Marcos reached a boiling point, resulting in massive demonstra-tions in Manila. Under the banner of "people's power," business-people, professionals, housewives, soldiers, students, and cultural figures rallied to topple the regime.

by the wealthiest Filipinos, mostly members of the hundred or so landowning families who were favored during U.S. colonial rule. Mrs. Aquino, herself a member of one of these families, volun-tarily declined reelection in 1992. Her successors had rocky presidencies; one of these men, a for-mer film star with a reputation for heavy drinking, gambling, and womanizing, was impeached for corruption and vote-rigging. In 2001 another woman, Gloria Macapagal-Arroyo (b. 1947), a Ph.D. economist and the daughter of a former president, became president but also faced corruption allegations; however, she was reelected in 2005.

Two decades after the overthrow of Marcos the public seems disillusioned with the results. Many Filipinos also have resented the continuing close ties to, and influence from, the United States. A best-selling pop song reflected the opposition to what nationalists considered neocolonialism: "You just want my natural resources, And then you leave me poor and in misery. American Junk, Get it out of my bloodstream. Got to get back to who I am."[23] While democracy has returned, a free press flourishes, and the economy has improved, much of the economic growth has been eaten up by rapid population growth; the nation now has 85 million people. And none of the governments have successfully addressed poverty or seemed willing to curb the activities of influential com-panies exploiting marine, mineral, and timber resources, often harming the environment. A local Catholic priest noted how economic exploitation and environmental destruction have remained common: "A plunder economy, that's the post World War II Philippine history: plunder of seas, plunder of mines, plunder of forests."[24] At the same time, differences in access to health care, wel-fare, and related services have continued to reflect the great gaps in income between social classes and regions.

Politics and Society in Thailand and Burma

The striking contrasts between prosperous Thailand and stagnant Burma have increased. In the 1950s both nations had economies of similar size and growth rates, but the gap between them has become vast. While both nations have had a long history of military dictatorship, only the Thais, finding the repressive atmosphere chilling, made a transition to more open government. By the 1980s Thailand developed a semidemocratic system combining order and hierarchy, sym-bolized by the monarchy, with representative, accountable government. While most successful political candidates came from wealthy families, often of Chinese ancestry, the rapidly expand-ing urban middle class generally supported an expansion of democracy that would give them more influence. A new constitution adopted in 1997 guaranteed civil liberties and reformed the electoral system, and a lively free press emerged.

Thailand generally has enjoyed high rates of economic growth. Despite a growing manufacturing sector, the export of rice, rubber, tin, and timber remains significant. Although the Chinese minor-ity of some 10 percent controls much wealth, Thais enjoy high per capita incomes and standards of

Thailand's Economy and Politics

A Thai Poet's Plea for Saving the Environment

Angkhan Kalayanaphong (AHN-kan KALL-a-YAWN-a-fong), born in 1926, the most popular poet in Thailand for decades, also gained fame as an accomplished graphic artist and painter. His poems often addressed social, Buddhist, and environmental themes. In his long poem, "Bangkok-Thailand," he examines Thailand and its problems in the 1970s and 1980s. The author pulls no punches in condemning Thai society for neglecting its heritage; he skewers politicians, government institutions, big business, and the entertainment industry. In this section, Angkhan pleads for Thais to save the forest environment being destroyed by commercial logging.

Oh, I do not imagine the forest like that
So deep, so beautiful, everything so special.
It pertains to dreams that are beyond truth. . . .
Dense woods in dense forests; slowly
The rays of half a day mix with the night.
Strange atmosphere causing admiration.
Loneliness up to the clouds, stillness and beauty.
Rays of gold play upon, penetrate the tree-tops
rays displayed in stripes, the brightness of the sun.
I stretch out my hand drawing down clouds mixing them with
*   brandy.*
This is supreme happiness. . . .
The lofty trees do not think of reward for the scent of their
*   blossoms. . . .*

Men kill the wood because they venerate money as in all the
*   world. . . .*
The lofty trees contribute much to morals.
They should be infinitely lauded for it.
The trace of the ax kills. Blood runs in streams. . . .
You, trees, give the flattering pollen attended by scents.
You make the sacrifice again and again.
Do you ever respond angrily? You have accepted your fate which
*   is contemptuous of all that is beautiful.*
But troublesome are the murderers, the doers of future sins.
Greedy after money, they are blind to divine work.
Their hearts are black to large extent, instead of being honest and
*   upright.*
They have no breeding, are lawless. . . .
Thailand in particular is in a very bad way.
Because of their [commercial] value parks are "purified," i.e.,
*   destroyed.*
Man's blood is depraved, cursed and base.
His ancestors are swine and dogs. It is madness to say they are
*   Thai.*

THINKING ABOUT THE READING

1. What qualities does the poet attribute to the forest?
2. What motives does he attribute to the loggers and businessmen who exploit the forest environment?

Source: Klaus Wenk, *Thai Literature: An Introduction* (Bangkok: White Lotus, 1995), pp. 95–98. Copyright © 1995 Klaus Wenk. Reprinted with permission.

---

public health by Asian standards. Indeed, thousands of people from North America and Europe come to Thailand each year for medical treatment. Yet perhaps a quarter of Thais are very poor, especially in rural areas. The economic "miracle" has, in many respects, been built on the backs of women and children, many from rural districts, who work in urban factories, the service sector, and the sex industry. Millions of Thai women have identified with the songs of popular singer Pompuang Duangjian (POM-poo-ahn DWONG-chen) (1961–1992), herself the product of a poor village, that often deal with the harshness of the lives of poor female migrants to the city: "So lousy poor, I just have to risk my luck. Dozing on the bus, this guy starts chatting me up. Say's he'll get me a good job."[25] Pompuang herself had only two years of primary school education and worked as a sugar-cane cutter before starting a music career. With much of her money stolen by lovers, managers, and promoters, she died at age thirty-one unable to afford treatment for a blood disorder.

The economic collapses of 1997 and 2008–2009 threw many Thais out of work. The overcrowded capital, Bangkok, is one of Asia's most polluted cities, drenched in toxic matter from factories and automobiles despite efforts by local environmental groups to clean up the air. The nation's once-abundant rain forests disappear at a rapid rate, a fact lamented by Thai musicians and poets (see Witness to the Past: A Thai Poet's Plea for Saving the Environment). The AIDs rate skyrockets. And, in recent years, massive street protests, political turmoil between rival factions, and a return of military influence have divided the country and weakened democracy. Yet, Thais possess a talent for political compromise, and Buddhism teaches moderation, tolerance, respect for nature, and a belief in individual worth. Thus Thais have the basis for a democratic spirit, a more equitable distribution of wealth, and an environmental ethic.

Burma's Economy and Politics

Whatever Thailand's problems, they seem dwarfed by a Burma ruled by a harsh, corrupt military regime. Few outside the ruling group have prospered, despite the country's natural riches of timber, oil, gems, and rice. As a result, Burma is now one of Asia's poorest nations. Sparked by economic decline and political repression, mass protests in 1988, led by students and Buddhist monks, demanded civil liberties, but the protests ended when soldiers killed hundreds and jailed thousands of demonstrators. In 1990 Burma (now renamed Myanmar (my-ahn-MAH), under international pressure, allowed elections. Although most of its leaders were in jail, the opposition quickly organized and won a landslide victory. Aung San Suu Kyi (AWNG sahn soo CHEE) (b. 1945), daughter of the founding president and an eloquent orator, returned from a long exile in England to lead the democratic forces. But the military refused to hand over power, put Aung San Suu Kyi under house arrest, and jailed thousands of opposition supporters. Aung San Suu Kyi refused to compromise in exchange for the regime ending her house arrest. A courageous symbol of principled leadership, she won the Nobel Peace Prize in 1991.

Meanwhile, the military regime remains in power, detaining opposition leaders. Although many Burmese still dream of democracy, and illicit cassettes of protest music and opposition messages are exchanged from hand to hand, others have accommodated themselves to military rule, valuing stability and fearing civil war. To increase its own revenues, the government began welcoming some limited foreign investment. But investments by Western, Japanese, and Southeast Asian corporations in Burma, especially in the timber and oil industries, diminish the willingness of other countries to punish Burma for gross human rights violations. In recent years the brutal suppression of Buddhist-led protests, a refusal of foreign assistance for the victims of a devastating hurricane, and increased military assaults on ethnic minority settlements, made clear that the generals would not relax their grip or modify their isolation from the world.

Diversity and Prosperity in Malaysia and Singapore

Malaysia and Singapore, both open to the world, have achieved the most political stability and economic progress. Both countries have successfully diversified their economies and stimulated development while raising living standards and spreading the wealth. The two nations, once joined in the same federation, have shared a similar mix of ethnic groups, though while Malays constitute slightly over half, Chinese a third, and Indians a tenth of the Malaysian population, around three-quarters of Singaporeans are Chinese. Malaysia and Singapore have maintained limited democracies, holding regular elections in which the ruling parties control the voting and most of the mass media. While opposition leaders sometimes face arrest or harassment, dissidents use the Internet to spread their views. By 2008 an opposition coalition overcame obstacles and made electoral gains against the ruling alliance in Malaysia, possibly foreshadowing a more open system.

In Malaysia religion has often divided the Muslim majority from the Christian, Hindu, Buddhist, and animist minority. Conflict also occurs within religious traditions. Islamic movements with dogmatic, sometimes militant views have gained support among some young Malays, especially rural migrants to the city alienated by a Westernized, materialistic society and looking for an anchor in an uncertain world. These movements, which encourage women to dress modestly and sometimes reject modern technology or products, often alarm secular Malays and non-Muslims who oppose taking Malaysia backward. In response, Malay women's rights groups use Islamic arguments to oppose restrictions favored by conservatives. Hence, Sisters in Islam, founded by the academic Zainab Anwar (ZEYE-nab AN-war), espouses freedom, justice, and equality and fights strict interpretations of Muslim family law. Numerous women also hold high government positions. At the other extreme, aimless Malay youth mock the conventions of mainstream society, wearing long hair and listening to heavy metal and hip hop music.

Malaysian Society and Economy

Supported by abundant natural resources, such as oil and tin, economic diversification, and entrepreneurial talent, Malaysia has surpassed European nations like Portugal and Hungary in national wealth. High annual growth rates have enabled it to achieve a relatively high per capita income and to build export industries that employ cheap, often female, labor to make shoes, toys, and other consumer goods. The manufacturing sector has continued to grow rapidly—Malaysians even build their own automobiles—and timber and oil have become valuable export commodities. But economic growth comes at the price of toxic waste problems, severe deforestation, and air pollution. In 1969 violence between Chinese and Malays resulted in the New Economic Policy; aimed at redistributing more wealth to Malays, it has fostered a substantial Malay middle class. Televisions, stereos, cell phones, and videocassette recorders became nearly universal in the cities and increasingly common in the rural areas. Many Malaysians have personal computers or access to Internet cafés, and official poverty rates dropped from some 50 percent in 1970 to around 20 percent by 2000. Nevertheless, the gap between rich and poor remains and may have widened. In the bustling capital city, Kuala Lumpur, jammed freeways, glittering malls, and high-rise luxury condominiums contrast with shantytown squatter settlements and shabbily dressed street hawkers hoping to sell enough of their cheap wares to buy a meal.

Kuala Lumpur Dominated by new skyscrapers, including some of the world's tallest buildings, and a spectacular mosque, the Malaysian capital city, Kuala Lumpur, has become a prosperous center for Asian commerce and industry. Modern buildings gradually replace the older shophouses built decades ago. Yet, poor shantytowns have also grown apace to house the poor.

Singapore Politics and Society

Restricted to a tiny island, Singapore, despite few resources, has joined the world's most prosperous nations, with a standard of living second only to Japan in Asia. The numerical and political predominance of ethnic Chinese makes Singapore unique in Southeast Asia. The government has mixed freewheeling economic policies with an autocratic leadership that tightly controls the 5 million people and limits dissent. Singapore is run like a giant corporation, efficient and ruthless. People pay a stiff fine if caught spitting, littering, or even tossing used chewing gum on the street. Yet it is also one of the healthiest societies, enjoying the world's lowest rate of infant mortality. Singapore devotes more of its national budget to education than other nations, everyone studies English in school, and world-class universities attract international faculties. In the vanguard of the information revolution, the city has also become a hub of light industry, high technology, and computer networking. Businesspeople and professionals from around the world have flocked to this globalized city, just as they had flocked to the trading states of Srivijaya and Melaka centuries ago.

Conflict and Reconstruction in Indochina

After years of war and destruction, Vietnam, Laos, and Cambodia began to rebuild and deal with lingering tensions. In Vietnam, socialist policies failed to revitalize the economy, and the reunification of North and South Vietnam proved harsh. Because of mismanagement, natural disasters, a long U.S. economic embargo, and the devastation of the war, between 1978 and 1985 half a million refugees, known as "boat people," risked their lives to escape Vietnam in rickety boats, becoming easy targets for pirates. After spending months or years in crowded refugee camps in Southeast Asia, most of the refugees were resettled in North America, Australia, or France.

Vietnam's Politics and Economy

In the 1980s the government recognized its failures and introduced market-oriented reforms similar to those in China favoring private enterprise and foreign investment. These reforms increased productivity, fostered some prosperity in the cities, and ended the refugee flow. Emphasis on education also more than doubled the 1945 literacy rates to 85 percent of adults. But the shift from rigid socialism also widened economic inequalities, leaving most farmers living just above the poverty line. The Vietnamese have debated the appropriate balance between socialist and free market policies to resolve the rural problems. With the global recession of 2008, the Vietnamese experienced the full effects of globalization. Hundreds of villages which had shifted from farming to producing handicrafts for export saw their income collapse as foreign consumers cut spending.

Politically, Vietnam, like China, has remained an authoritarian one-party state, with little democracy, but restrictions on cultural expression have loosened. Several former soldiers became rock or disco stars, and many writers addressed contemporary problems and the war's legacy in fiction. For example, "The General Retires," a short story by a former North Vietnamese soldier, caused a sensation by depicting the despair of an old soldier contemplating the emptiness of the new society. However, the communists expanded ties to the West and the world economy, the United

States and Vietnam resumed diplomatic relations, and U.S. president Bill Clinton lifted the U.S. economic embargo. Urban streets are now jammed with motor scooters, and bustling Saigon, renamed Ho Chi Minh City, has enjoyed especially dynamic economic growth and prosperity. Consumers in the United States now buy shrimp and underwear imported from Vietnam, while many Americans, including former soldiers and Vietnamese refugees, visit Vietnam. Hundreds of American veterans operate businesses or social service agencies in Vietnam, sometimes in partnership with former communist soldiers. Still, the ruling communists have to satisfy the expectations of the 80 million Vietnamese struggling to overcome the devastation wrought by decades of war.

Laotians also needed to deal with the divisions and destruction caused by the war. Many Laotians fled into exile, among them over 300,000 Hmongs who settled in the United States. The Laotian government persecuted some remaining Hmong who they believed were supporting anti-communist guerillas. While Laotian leaders sought warmer relations with neighboring Thailand, China, and the United States, they failed to foster a more open society or energize the economy. Rigid communists still dominate the one-party state. While several places have attracted Western tourists, most Laotians remain poor. Looking across the Mekong at the busy freeways, neon lights, and high-rise buildings in Thailand, Laotians see a more successful development model.

Cambodia has faced a far more difficult challenge because war was followed by fierce repression and mass murder. Agriculture had been badly disrupted, raising the specter of widespread starvation. When the communist Khmer Rouge, hardened by years of brutal war, achieved power in 1975, they turned on the urban population with a fury, driving everyone into the rural areas to farm. The Khmer Rouge's radical vision of a propertyless, classless peasant society, combined with violence against suspected dissenters and resisters, led thousands to flee into neighboring countries. Even worse were the "killing fields": the Khmer Rouge executed thousands of victims in death camps and shot or starved many others, including both common people, such as peasants and taxi drivers, and Westernized and educated people. Ultimately the Khmer Rouge and their brutal leader, Pol Pot (1925–1998), in their attempt to create a new communist society, were responsible for 1.5 to 2 million deaths. Perhaps 500,000 were executed, and the rest died from illness, hunger, and overwork, sparking comparisons with Nazi Germany.

The situation changed in 1978, leading to a new government. The Vietnamese, alarmed at Khmer Rouge territorial claims and the murder of thousands of ethnic Vietnamese in Cambodia, allied with an exile army of disaffected former Khmer Rouge, invaded Cambodia, and rapidly pushed the Khmer Rouge to the Thailand border. The Vietnamese invasion liberated the Cambodian people from tyranny and installed a less brutal communist government. But military conflict continued for years as a Khmer Rouge–dominated resistance, subsidized chiefly by China and the United States, which both wanted to weaken Vietnam, controlled some sections of the country. Cambodia proved to be for Vietnam what Vietnam had been for the United States, an endless sinkhole of conflict that drained scarce wealth and complicated Vietnam's relations with the West.

In the early 1990s a coalition government was formed under United Nations sponsorship. The Khmer Rouge, which refused to take part, splintered and collapsed as a movement. While the

AP/Wide World Photos

Honoring Ho Chi Minh These schoolgirls, dressed in traditional clothing and parading before Ho Chi Minh's mausoleum in Hanoi, are part of an annual festival to honor the leading figure of Vietnamese communism.

Cambodian Political Change

resulting peace was welcomed by all, the government remained repressive and corrupt, tolerating some opposition but controlling the vote. Sihanouk returned from exile to become king but had little power and served largely as a symbol of Cambodia's link to its past. Life for many Cambodians remained grim as they faced everything from the high price of fuel to poor education, problems that have spurred some people to demand more democracy and attention to social problems. Nevertheless, the new government has transformed Cambodia, while still haunted by past horrors, from a traumatized to a functioning society, kept afloat largely by Western tourism and aid.

Southeast Asia in the Global System

Economic Models

Although Southeast Asians still export the natural resources they did in colonial times, some nations have seen major economic growth through industrialization and exploitation of other resources. The gold, pepper, and spice exports of earlier centuries have been largely replaced by oil, timber, rubber, rice, tin, sugar, and palm oil. The region's role in the world has also changed, fostering some of the fastest-growing economies. Malaysia, Thailand, Singapore, and, to some extent, Indonesia and Vietnam have become major recipients of foreign investment. Meanwhile, workers produce manufactured goods like shoes, clothing, computer chips, and sports equipment for European and North American markets. Several countries elsewhere in Asia, Africa, and Latin America now borrow economic models from the Southeast Asian "tigers." Recently Southeast Asians began shifting their focus from the United States to China, which they viewed as the rising world power with which they must cooperate.

Southeast Asia and Global Influences

Southeast Asians also influenced politics worldwide. The Indonesian Revolution, for instance, forced a major colonial power to abandon its control, giving hope to colonized Africans. Similarly, Vietnamese communists under Ho Chi Minh, in their ultimately successful fifty-year fight against French colonialism, Japanese occupation, and then U.S. intervention, stimulated a wave of revolutionary efforts, from Nicaragua to Mozambique, to overthrow Western domination. The Vietnamese struggle for independence also inspired student activists in Europe and North America; in the 1960s, while protesting against war and inequality, a few of the more radical shouted slogans in praise of the Vietnamese communist leader, Ho Chi Minh. Women have long played an influential role in Southeast Asia, and the political leaders Megawati Soekarnoputri in Indonesia, Corazon Aquino in the Philippines, and Aung San Suu Kyi in Burma have become inspirations to women worldwide.

Global influences and economic development have increasingly modified lives. For example, the resident of an upscale suburb of Kuala Lumpur, Bangkok, or Manila, connected through her home computer to the information superhighway and working in a high-rise, air-conditioned office reached by driving a late-model sports car along the crowded freeways, has a way of life vastly different from that of the peasant villager whose life revolves around traditional society. The modern cities boast malls, supermarkets, boutiques, Hard Rock Cafes, and Planet Hollywoods. Indonesian television now features many U.S.-style reality shows, which have replaced local soap operas in the ratings. Even rural areas have become more connected to wider networks by televisions, outboard motors, motor scooters, and telephones. Yet change has often been superficial. In poor-city neighborhoods restaurants may have compact disc players and cold beer, but they may also feature traditional music and dance and serve up fiery hot curries. For every youngster who joins the fan club for a Western or local pop star, another identifies with an Islamic, Buddhist, or Christian organization, sometimes a militant one. Many people find themselves perched uneasily between the cooperative village values of the past and the competitive, materialistic modern world.

SECTION SUMMARY

- Beginning in the late 1970s, Southeast Asia experienced rapid economic growth through a Japanese-style mix of capitalism and active government involvement, though a severe economic crisis hit the region in 1997.

- Under Suharto, the Indonesian New Order government repressed regional opposition and improved the economy, but Suharto was extravagantly corrupt and was forced to resign in 1997 amid widespread unrest and economic collapse.

- Under Marcos, the Philippines was divided between the very rich and the poor; Marcos was forced out after massive protests, and the democratically elected governments that followed were more open to dissent but still dominated by the wealthy.

- Since the 1980s, Thailand has developed a semidemocratic system and has grown economically, though it has endured widespread poverty and sexual exploitation, while Burma has been burdened with a corrupt regime that has failed to take advantage of ample natural resources and stifled its opposition.

- Malaysia has taken advantage of abundant natural resources to become highly successful, surpassing some European nations in wealth, while Singapore, with fewer resources, has been even more successful through a combination of economic freedom and political restriction.

- Vietnam struggled after the war, but in the 1980s it opened up its economy and by the 1990s had reestablished ties with the rest of the world, including the United States.

- Many Laotians fled into exile, while the communist-dominated government has opened somewhat to the world economy, and Cambodia endured vicious repression under the Khmer Rouge, who continued to wreak havoc even after a Vietnamese invasion pushed them out of power.

- With their rapidly growing economies, the Southeast Asian "tigers" have inspired developing nations around the world, and while most of the region has joined the modern world, tradition thrives in them as well.

CHAPTER SUMMARY

After decolonization, the societies of southern Asia struggled to shape their futures. Since Hindu and Muslim leaders could not agree on a formula for unity after independence, British India fragmented into two rival nations, predominantly Hindu India and mostly Muslim Pakistan. Under Nehru, India adopted democratic practices and modernizing policies. Indians generally sustained multiparty democracy, raised the legal status of untouchables and women, achieved a dramatic rise in food production, industrialized, and fostered high-technology enterprises. But they failed to transform rural society, distribute the fruits of economic growth equitably, and eradicate Hindu-Muslim conflict. Muslim-dominated Pakistan divided when Bangladesh broke away, and both Pakistan and Bangladesh have had difficulty maintaining democracy and generating economic development. India and Pakistan, both armed with nuclear weapons, have remained hostile neighbors.

Like South Asians, Southeast Asians also regained the independence they had lost under Western colonialism. Vietnamese communists led by Ho Chi Minh launched a revolutionary war that eventually forced the French to leave, giving the communists control of North Vietnam. The United States, influenced by Cold War thinking, supported anticommunist South Vietnam and, in response to a growing communist insurgency, sent American troops to South Vietnam. But the United States withdrew in 1975, unable to triumph over a determined foe. The conflict caused several million casualties and major environmental damage. With the war over, Vietnam, Cambodia, and Laos, all under communist control, struggled for reconstruction. Meanwhile Indonesia and Malaysia worked to build national unity in a complex mosaic of peoples and cultures. Burma, Thailand, and the Philippines experienced chronic unrest that often led to military or civilian dictatorships. But eventually Malaysia, Singapore, Thailand, Indonesia, and Vietnam achieved rapid economic growth, supplying natural resources and manufactured goods to the world.

KEY TERMS

Dalit	Bollywood	Tet Offensive	UMNO
Awami League	National Liberation Front	Pathet Lao	ASEAN
Bharatha Janata	(NLF)	Khmer Rouge	New Order

EBOOK AND WEBSITE RESOURCES

e **INTERACTIVE MAPS**

Map 31.1 Modern South Asia
Map 31.2 The U.S.-Vietnamese War
Map 31.3 Modern Southeast Asia

LINKS

Asian Studies: WWW Virtual Library (http://coombs.anu
.edu.au/WWWVL-AsianStudies.html). A vast metasite
maintained at Australian National University, with
links to hundreds of sites.

East and Southeast Asia: An Annotated Directory of Internet Resources (http://newton.uor.edu/
Departments&Programs/AsianStudies-Dept/). A
superb set of links on Southeast Asia, maintained at
the University of Redlands.

Internet Indian History Sourcebook (http://www
.fordham.edu/halsall/india/indiasbook.html). An
invaluable collection of sources and links on India
from ancient to modern times.

Virtual Library: South Asia (http://www.columbia.edu/
cu/libraries/indiv/area/sarai/). A major site maintained
by Columbia University.

WWW Southeast Asia Guide (http://www.library.wisc
.edu/guides/SEAsia/). An easy-to-use site.

**Plus flashcards, practice quizzes, and more. Go to:
www.cengage.com/history/lockard/globalsocnet2e.**

SUGGESTED READING

Abinales, Patricio N., and Donna J. Amoroso. *State and Society in the Philippines.* Lanham, MD: Rowman and Littlefield, 2005. A readable study with much on recent politics.

Beeson, Mark, ed. *Contemporary Southeast Asia: Regional Dynamics, National Differences.* New York: Palgrave Macmillan, 2004. Essays on varied topics.

Brown, Judith M. *Nehru.* New York: Longman, 1999. A readable biography of an important Asian leader.

Chalmers, Ian. *Indonesia: An Introduction to Contemporary Traditions.* New York: Oxford University Press, 2006. Explores social and cultural life.

Chandler, David, 4th ed. *A History of Cambodia.* Boulder: Westview, 2008. Extensive coverage of contemporary era.

Ganguly, Sumit, ed. *South Asia.* New York: New York University Press, 2006. Recent essays on the South Asian countries.

Ganguly, Sumit, and Neal DeVotta, eds. *Understanding Contemporary India.* Boulder, CO: Lynne Rienner, 2003. An accessible collection covering most aspects of Indian society.

Guha, Ramachandra. *India After Gandhi: The History of the World's Largest Democracy.* New York: Harper, 2008. Explains factors behind India's recent rise.

Harrison, Selig S., et al., eds. *India and Pakistan: The First Fifty Years.* New York: Cambridge University Press, 1999. An excellent collection of essays covering many topics.

Karnow, Stanley. *Vietnam: A History,* 2nd ed. New York: Penguin, 1997. One of the better introductions to modern history and the American-Vietnamese War.

Kingsbury, Damien. *South-East Asia: A Political Profile,* 2nd ed. New York: Oxford University Press, 2005. A comprehensive, up-to-date survey by an Australian scholar.

Lockard, Craig A. *"Dance of Life": Popular Music and Politics in Southeast Asia.* Honolulu: University of Hawaii Press, 1998. An examination of politics and societies through popular culture.

Luce, Edward. *In Spite of the Gods: The Rise of Modern India.* New York: Anchor, 2008. Journalistic account of India today.

Marlay, Ross, and Clark Neher. *Patriots and Tyrants: Ten Asian Leaders.* Lanham, MD: Rowman and Littlefield, 1999. Sketches of Asian nationalists, such as Gandhi, Nehru, Ho, and Sukarno.

Neher, Clark D. *Southeast Asia: Crossroads of the World,* 2nd ed. DeKalb: Center for Southeast Asian Studies, Northern Illinois University, 2004. A general, readable introduction to cultures and politics.

Olson, James S., and Randy Roberts. *Where the Domino Fell: America and Vietnam, 1945–2006,* 5th ed. St. James, NY: Wiley-Blackwell, 2006. An outstanding survey with an emphasis on U.S. policies and actions.

Stein, Burton. *A History of India.* Malden, MA: Blackwell, 1998. A detailed history with good coverage of the contemporary era.

Varshney, Ashutosh. *Ethnic Conflict and Civic Life: Hindus and Muslims in India,* 2nd ed. New Haven, CT: Yale University Press, 2003. A key study of Hindu-Muslim relations in three cities, including peacemaking and violence.

Vickers, Adrian. *A History of Modern Indonesia.* New York: Cambridge University Press, 2005. A quirky but fascinating study.

Globalization: For and Against

The first pictures taken from the moon in 1969, which showed the earth as a blue oasis in the middle of nowhere, made clear that humans share a single home. The pictures also suggested that this home is shared by an interlinked future. Different kinds of networks have increasingly connected peoples across distance and borders, and globalization—the interconnections between societies, the rise in cross-border exchanges, and the creation of one world—has become a major subject of debate. Often used vaguely and inconsistently, the concept became a metaphor to explain capitalism spreading throughout the world. But to many observers, the concept has deeper meanings, describing a process that both unites and divides, creates winners and losers, and brings both new possibilities and new risks. The debates on globalization cut across political leanings and national divisions.

THE PROBLEM

Globalization inspires passionate support and bitter opposition, generating immense discussion and disagreement. The debate focuses on four questions: When did globalization begin? What are the arguments in favor of it? What are some of the major opposing views? Is the trend leading the world into a troubled era of increasing conflict or greater cooperation?

THE DEBATE

The first question, the roots of globalization, remains disputed. Some scholars argue that its origins lie deep in the past, going back to the interconnections that slowly enveloped people from the dawn of cities and states. The German historians Jurgen Osterhammel and Niels Petersson, for example, trace it back a millennium or two to the silk trade between China and the Mediterranean region, the sea trade between the Middle East and India, and the caravans crossing the deserts of Africa, all activities that moved people, ideas, artwork, natural resources, goods, and coins. By contrast, Robbie Robertson, an Australian, argues that history changed dramatically only five hundred years ago, when the gradual linking of the world by European voyages of discovery transformed societies and economic activities. Still other scholars trace it no further back than the mid-nineteenth century, pointing to the first permanent transoceanic telegraph cable in 1866, global social movements such as feminism, and global regulatory bodies such as the Universal Postal Union. Some other writers claim that globalization did not affect most of humanity until the 1960s or later. Whatever the roots, by 2000 a global system—defined by market capitalism, over two hundred nation-states, some four hundred international organizations, and 40,000 transnational corporations—existed with no central authority.

On the second and third questions, whether the effects are positive or negative, the debate has raged for years. Among the benefits attributed to globalization are higher living standards and the worldwide sharing of culture. British sociologist John Giddens identifies a worldwide trend toward democracy and intellectual freedom. Walter Anderson praises the opening of societies to one another, as reflected in communications satellites and the fiber-optic submarine cable system winding its way around the world. As a result, he notes, the Inuit people living in northern Alaska watch twenty-eight channels of satellite television, take courses through the Internet, and stay in touch with their families by cell phones. Free market enthusiasts, such as Indian-born, U.S.-based economist Jagdish Bhagwati, stress the fostering of economic freedom. Opposing antiglobalization movements as the misguided enemy of progress, all these thinkers complain that newspapers and television reports focus more on shuttered textile factories, as jobs move overseas, than on the African child at the computer. Bhagwati claims that when properly governed, globalization becomes a powerful force for social good, bringing prosperity to underdeveloped nations, reducing child labor, increasing literacy, and helping women by creating jobs that increase their income and status. Another enthusiast, Thomas Friedman, considers globalization the principal trend of the post-Cold War world, symbolized by the Lexus, a Japanese-made luxury car sold around the world. Yet, he argues, people often prefer to hold on to meaningful traditions, symbolized by the olive tree often found at the center of an Arab village, rather than embrace new ideas. The world, he argues, has gotten flat, and this level playing field has allowed over 2 billion Chinese, Indians, and Russians to contemplate eventually owning a car, house, refrigerator, and toaster, increasing competition and dramatically raising the demand for the world's resources.

The contrary views on globalization stress negative consequences. These consequences include a concentration of economic power, more poverty, and less cultural diversity. The challengers of economic globalization argue that powerful governments and multinational corporations bully the marketplace, control politics, and stack the deck in their favor. Walter LaFeber shows how U.S. basketball star Michael Jordan, whose games were broadcast all over the world, became an international phenomenon of great commercial appeal, benefiting the international corporations who used Jordan to create a demand for their expensive products, such as sneakers, often at the expense of local manufacturers making the same product. To LaFeber, the terrorist attacks on the United States, especially the World Trade Center in New York in 2001, must also be understood in the context of the growing opposition to globalization around the world as the rich become richer and the poor become poorer. Joseph Stiglitz, an ardent fan of capitalism and former World Bank official, believes that globalization can be positive but that misguided policies and the economic power of industrial nations have made free trade unfair for developing nations. Looking at other aspects of globalization, Cynthia Enloe explores the often-negative effects of tourism and U.S. military bases on women, who, enjoying fewer economic options than men, often need to sell their bodies to male tourists and soldiers to survive. James Mittelman argues that, experienced from below, globalization fosters the loss of local political control as power shifts upward and also a devaluation of a society's cultural achievements as foreign

Kuwaiti Stock Exchange

Capitalism has spread widely in the world, and with it financial institutions such as investment banks and stock exchanges. The oil-rich, politically stable Persian Gulf sultanate of Kuwait has one of the most active stock exchanges.

Corbis

cultural products, such as music and films, become influential. All of these globalizing trends spur angry resistance, reflected in antiglobalization movements.

Experts also disagree about the fourth question, where globalization is taking the world. Some predict a growing divide both between and within societies. Benjamin Barber, for example, analyzes the conflict between consumerist capitalism (what he calls McWorld, after McDonald's) and tribalism or religious fundamentalism (what he terms jihad, after Islamic militants). Barber dislikes both trends: the dull homogeneity of McWorld, in which everyone, moved by capitalism and advertising, has the same tastes and ideas; and the balkanized world of jihad in which rival cultures, convinced of their own superior values and disdainful of others, struggle for dominance. Other scholars also predict tensions. John Giddens argues that the globalization of information, symbolized by the World Wide Web, that puts people in touch with others who think differently will promote a more cosmopolitan world-view respecting cultural differences but will also generate a backlash among narrow nationalists and religious fundamentalists who see only one path to truth. Preventing conflict between the factions and lessening the growing divide between rich and poor nations require cooperation between nations. Bhagwati, for example, supports managed rather than unfettered globalization, with world leaders discussing how to foster equality as well as growth. Taking a different approach, Mittelman doubts that globalization can be managed and calls for people around the world, rather than leaders and governments, to work together to decentralize political and economic power to build a future of greater equity.

EVALUATING THE DEBATE

The globalization discussion, much more than an academic debate, is a disagreement about profound transformations in the world and about what ethical and institutional principles should be applied to better organize human affairs for a brighter future. Some authors engaged in the debate have proposed catchy ideas, such as the Lexus and the olive tree, jihad and McWorld, but the reality of globalization is usually more complex. Both proponents and opponents make convincing points about the consequences of globalization; the truth may lie somewhere between. Globalization may indeed bring great benefits, at least to a section of the world's people. While the free flow of ideas inspires some people to demand more political rights or social inequality, many young women working long hours for low wages in foreign-owned factories may often prefer that life to the dead end of rural poverty. But improving the lives of those who do not benefit, as even globalization proponents Bhagwati and Friedman concede, will probably require action such as land reform to help poor peasants, more funding for schools, and stiffer environmental and worker protection laws to smooth the impacts on societies, cultures, and environments. Yet, the relations between business interests and their political supporters prompting globalization and the antiglobalization activists, often from worker or peasant backgrounds, remain tense. Local, national, regional, and global forces are intermingling in new and complex ways that may necessitate not just actions to remedy inequalities but also new ways of thinking.

THINKING ABOUT THE CONTROVERSY

1. When did globalization begin?
2. What are the positive arguments for globalization?
3. What main points do opponents make?

EXPLORING THE CONTROVERSY

Among the key historical studies are Robbie Robertson, *The Three Waves of Globalization: A History of a Developing Global Consciousness* (New York: Zed Books, 2003), and Jurgen Osterhammel and Niels P. Petersson, *Globalization: A Short History* (Princeton: Princeton University Press, 2005). Some of the major proponents are John Giddens, *Runaway World: How Globalization Is Reshaping Our Lives* (London: Routledge, 2000); Walter Truett Anderson, *All Connected Now: Life in the First Global Civilization* (Boulder, CO: Westview Press, 2001); Jagdish Bhagwati, *In Defense of Globalization* (New York: Oxford University Press, 2004); and Thomas L. Friedman, *The Lexus and the Olive Tree: Understanding Globalization* (New York: Anchor, 2000) and *The World Is Flat: A Brief History of the Twenty-First Century* (New York: Farrar, Straus, and Giroux, 2005). Writers questioning the benefits include Walter LaFeber, *Michael Jordan and the New Global Capitalism*, new and expanded ed. (New York: W.W. Norton, 2002); Joseph E. Stiglitz, *Globalization and Its Discontents* (New York: W.W. Norton, 1993); Cynthia Enloe, *Bananas, Beaches and Bases: Making Feminist Sense of International Politics*, updated ed. (Berkeley: University of California Press, 2001); and James H. Mittelman, *The Globalization Syndrome: Transformation and Resistance* (Princeton: Princeton University Press, 2000). For one view of future trends, see Benjamin R. Barber, *Jihad vs. McWorld* (New York: Times Books, 1995). On globalization generally, see Thomas Hyland Eriksen, *Globalization: The Key Concepts* (New York: Berg, 2007); David Held, ed., *A Globalizing World? Culture, Economics, Politics* (New York: Routledge, 2000); Mark Kesselman, ed., *The Politics of Globalization: A Reader* (Boston: Houghton Mifflin, 2007); George Ritzer, *Globalization: A Basic Text* (Hoboken, N.J.: John Wiley, 2009); Robert K. Schaeffer, *Understanding Globalization: The Social Consequences of Political, Economic, and Environmental Change* (Lanham, MD: Rowman and Littlefield, 1997); and Manfred B. Steger, *Globalization: A Very Short Introduction* (New York: Oxford University Press, 2003).

The Contemporary World, Since 1945

The world has changed dramatically since 1945. Some observers have described these years as the most revolutionary age in history, reshaping whole ways of life and world-views. All regions of the world, opening to ideas and products from everywhere, have become, as some experts put it, part of a global village or global system. The Indonesian thinker Soedjatmoko (so-jat-MOH-ko), summing up the era's trends, described a world of collapsing "national boundaries and horrifying destructive power, expanding technological capacity and instant communication [in which] we live in imperfect intimacy with all our fellow human beings."[1] This interconnected and rapidly changing global society, and the people who shape it, have produced both great good and indescribable horrors.

The contemporary world has become a global unity within a larger diversity. Globalization has fostered or intensified networks of exchange and communication: international trade pacts and electronic fund transfers, jet-speed travel and fax machines. These networks link distant societies. Yet, even as they have become more closely linked, nations have not been able to work together to meet the challenges facing humanity, such as poverty and environmental distress. No clear international consensus has emerged on maintaining strong local cultures in the face of global influences, correcting the widening gap between rich and poor nations, and achieving a better balance between environmental preservation and economic development. Solving these problems requires complex strategies and the joint efforts of many nations. Ensuring a brighter future also requires examining how the patterns of the past and the trends of the present may shape the years to come.

Globalization and Cultures

Over recent centuries the world's people have built a human web, or networked society—a global system that today encompasses most of the world's 6.8 billion people. All these terms imply transnational connections and the institutions that foster them, such as the World Bank, the Internet, and religious missionaries. Around the world people speak, with fear or enthusiasm, of globalization. Some observers see the trend as dangerous folly, others as a boon, and still others have mixed feelings. In recent decades, people have experienced global influences not only by, for some, frequent travel abroad but also because these influences have reshaped the cities, towns, and villages where they live. The interaction between global influences and local traditions, such as religion and music, has become a force in the world, helping to shape cultures.

Globalization and Its Impacts

The roots of globalization go deep into the past. During the first millennium of the Common Era trade networks such as the Silk Road, which linked China and Europe across Central Asia and the Middle East, and the spread of religions such as Buddhism, Christianity, and Islam, connected distant societies. A thousand years ago an Eastern Hemisphere–wide economy based in Asia and anchored by Chinese and Indian manufacturing and Islamic trade networks represented an early form of globalization. The links between the hemispheres forged after 1492, during which Europeans competed with each other and with Asians for a share of the growing trade in raw materials, expanded the reach of this economy. In the nineteenth century the Industrial Revolution, which produced desirable trade goods, and European imperialism, which led to the Western colonization of large parts of the world, extended the connections even further, aided by technological innovations such as steamships and transoceanic cables.

The integration of commerce and financial services today is more developed than ever before. As the global system has become increasingly linked, societies have become more dependent on each other for everything from consumer goods and entertainments to fuels and technological innovations. For example, all over the world people consume Chinese textiles, U.S. films, Persian Gulf oil, Indian yoga, and Japanese electronics. Videoconferencing allows business partners in Los Angeles, Berlin, and Hong Kong to confer instantaneously with one another. During the early twenty-first century the world's most powerful nation, the United States, has become increasingly reliant on Asian nations, especially China, to finance its skyrocketing national debt. The debt has grown in part because of a costly U.S. military engagement in Iraq and an increasing economic imbalance as Americans import more from abroad than they export. Such interdependence, as well as the reach of political, cultural, and social events across distances, has had an increasing impact in a shrinking world. This reality was demonstrated in 2005 when some faraway African societies were affected indirectly by Hurricane Katrina, which devastated the Gulf Coast of the United States, disrupting the export of corn from the U.S. Midwest through the port of New Orleans. Japan, a major consumer of that corn, then turned to South Africa for supplies, which deprived people in Malawi of South African corn, causing widespread starvation in Malawi. Yet, while globalization affects every country to some degree, the great bulk of world trade and financial flow and activity is concentrated in, and has the largest impact on, the peoples of three huge interlinked blocs: North America, Europe, and a group of Asian nations stretching from Japan to India.

Furthermore, many observers believe that globalization is unmanageable. U.S. journalist Thomas Friedman writes:

> Globalization isn't a choice. It's a reality, and no one is in charge. You keep looking for someone to complain to, to take the heat off your markets. Well guess what, there's no one on the other end of the phone. The global market today is an electronic herd of anonymous stock, bond and currency traders sitting behind computer screens. Sure, this is unfair [but] there's nobody to call.[2]

If governments are often somewhat powerless in the face of global economic trends, they need to adapt by educating their citizens, especially their young people, for a new, more competitive world. Various Asian nations, such as India, Taiwan, and

Singapore, have adapted to these changes more rapidly than North American and European nations, pouring money into education, science, and high technology. The Western nations that have successfully adjusted to globalization are mainly those, especially in Scandinavia, that have combined open markets with strong societal and environmental protections.

This impersonal globalization, operating independent of governments, has had major impacts on societies, politics, economies, cultures, and environments. Whether they are seen as positive or negative consequences depends on the observer. For example, some Western free market enthusiasts celebrate a new global order in which everybody on the planet is in the same economy, offering entrepreneurs unparalleled opportunities for profit. But graffiti by disillusioned Poles in the 1990s took a different view, complaining that when Poland abandoned communism it asked for democracy but ended up with the bond market and domination by transnational corporations. Scholars and others energetically debate the value and scope of globalization (see Historical Controversy: Globalization: For and Against).

Global forces, symbolized by advertising for foreign-made goods and satellites miles up in the sky relaying information around the world, interact with local cultures, raising questions about national and local identity. As a result, local traditions and products sometimes get replaced, and imported and local cultures blend. An example of blending comes from France, where, with its large Arab immigrant population, Arab entrepreneurs have prospered by selling fast-food hamburgers and pizza prepared according to Muslim requirements and adapted to Arab taste. People around the world consume global products, from fast food to fashionable footwear to action films, but still enjoy cultural traditions that are distinctly local and popular with earlier generations. Examples include the unique Thai style of boxing in which combatants can attack with both hands and feet, sumo wrestling in Japan, and the African-influenced martial arts of Brazil.

To adapt and flourish in an interconnected world, people have had to become aware of international conditions. In North America, activists seeking to fight inequality or preserve the environment have urged people to think globally but act locally. Thinking globally, for example, would include understanding how rapid deforestation in the tropics—especially in the Amazon and Congo Basins, where rain forests recycle vast amounts of water into the air—diminishes rainfall around the world. Acting locally, Brazilian environmental and citizens' groups work to save their rain forests, while environmentally conscious North Americans and Europeans support organizations, businesses, and political leaders committed to improving the global environment. Others wonder, however, if this is enough, arguing that, since the world is so interlinked, people must think and act both globally and locally—to embrace both a global citizenship and a local citizenship. But, despite greatly increased travel and migration, only a small minority of people have become true citizens of the world, comfortable everywhere. Few people have gone as far toward an ecumenical view as Australian Aboriginal writer Colin Johnson, who both embraced Hinduism, imported from India, and dedicated his first novel to the Jamaican reggae star Bob Marley and his Rastafarian faith. Moreover, world government remains a distant prospect at the beginning of the twenty-first century.

Cultural Imperialism: The Globalization of Culture

The inequitable relationship between the dominant West and the developing nations has compelled observers to examine global change. Arising from this effort has been the concept of cultural imperialism, in which the economic and political power of Western nations, especially the United States, enables their cultural products to spread widely. Some African writers have called this pattern a "cultural bomb" because, they believe, Western products and entertainments destroy local cultures. In this view, the developed countries export popular music, disco dancing, skimpy women's clothing, and sex-drenched films and publications reflecting these countries' own values and experiences. Other societies adopt these products, which modify or suffocate their own traditions. For instance, big budget Hollywood films attract large audiences while local films, made on small budgets, cannot compete, and the local film industries often die as a result. To survive, local filmmakers adopt the formulas used by successful Hollywood filmmakers: sex and violence. Critics of Western power argue that cultural exchange has been common throughout history but in the modern world has become largely a one-way street, leading to domination by Western, especially Anglo-American, culture.

Popular culture produced in the United States, entertaining but also challenging to traditional values, has emerged as the closest thing available to a global entertainment. The Monroe Doctrine—the early-nineteenth-century declaration by Congress that the United States would interfere in Latin American political developments—has now become, in the view of certain wags, the "Marilyn Monroe Doctrine," after the famous American actress who, for many non-Americans, symbolized U.S. culture in the 1950s. Other examples of American cultural influence were popular U.S. television programs, such as the drama series *Dallas,* the racy *Desperate Housewives,* and *The Muppet Show,* a variety show, which have been broadcast in dozens of nations.

Some American icons, from basketball star Michael Jordan to McDonald's, have become symbols of a new global modernity and capitalism. In 1989 two young East Germans crossed the Berlin Wall and discovered their first McDonald's restaurant. One of them remembered, "It was all so modern, the windows were so amazing. I felt like a lost convict who'd just spent twenty-five years in prison. I was in a state of shock."[3] Not even the Chinese, with one of the world's most admired cuisines, were immune to the appeal of modern U.S. marketing techniques and convenience for harried urbanites. In 1993 a famous roast duck restaurant in China's capital, Beijing, sent its management staff to study the McDonald's operation in British-ruled Hong Kong and then introduced its customers to "roast duck fast food." The restaurant also faced a challenge from the growing number of McDonald's franchises in Beijing. Yet, Chinese restaurants flourish around the world.

Still, popular American entertainments often face opposition. Governments, from the Islamic clerics running Iran to the more democratic leaders of India, have attempted to halt or control the influx of what they consider destabilizing, immoral pop culture. In 1995 an Islamic political party in Pakistan even demanded, unsuccessfully, that the United States turn over to them American pop stars Madonna and Michael Jackson so that they could be placed on trial as "cultural terrorists" destroying humanity. In 2005, representatives of many nations, meeting under the auspices of the United Nations cultural organization, agreed that all nations had the right to restrict cultural imports, outraging American political and entertainment leaders. To maintain their cultural traditions and boost local artists many nations have mandated, as Portugal did in 2006, that a set percentage of music on radio and television must be locally made.

Forming New World Cultures

Whatever the real scope of cultural imperialism, a new world culture appears to be on the rise. The world is becoming one vast network of relationships as ideas, people, and goods move between its different regions. Similar cultural forms, often Anglo-American in origin, develop across national boundaries, transcending any one territory, society, or tradition. Yet the rising world culture is not uniform. No total homogenization of expression and meaning has occurred.

Anglo-American cultural forms are not the only ones to reach a global audience. Mexican and Brazilian soap operas, Indian (Bollywood) films, Nigerian novels, Arab, African, and Caribbean pop music, and Japanese comics and electronic games have been popular all over the globe. For example, thanks in part to the popularity of Jamaican singer/songwriter Bob Marley, reggae music spread around the world, as one observer marveled in the 1980s:

> In Papeete, Tahiti, the buses all have speakers the size of foot lockers, making them moving sound systems. Their routes are jumping with the rhythms of [reggae groups] Steel Pulse, Black Uhuru, and Bob Marley. Four thousand miles away in Tokyo, there is a reggae night spot called Club 69, where local youth wear dreadlocks and dance to the beats of the Wailers. Africa has its own reggae styles and hundreds of bands.[4]

The cultural traffic flow is not one-way. In North America, western Europe, and Australia, people take up Indian yoga, Chinese *tai qi*, and other Asian spiritual disciplines; patronize Thai, Indian, Chinese, and Japanese restaurants; enjoy Brazilian and African pop music; learn Latin American dances; and master Asian martial arts, such as karate and judo. Even classical musicians in the West have embraced foreign influences. For instance, in 1998 the Chinese cellist Yo Yo Ma, born in Paris and later a U.S. resident, founded the Silk Road Ensemble, which brings together Western, East Asian, and Middle Eastern musicians to tour the world playing music that mixes the instruments and traditions of both East and West.

The meeting of global and local cultures fosters hybridization, the blending of two cultures, a process that can be either enriching or impoverishing. Record stores in Western cities set aside some of their display space to sell a hybrid form called "world music," popular music originating largely outside of the West that mixes Western influences with local and other traditions. Some experts contend that world music reflects Western cultural imperialism, since Western influence—rock beats and electric instruments, for example—are often strong, and Anglo-American rock stars such as Peter Gabriel, Paul Simon, and Sting have promoted and sometimes appropriated some of the music. Yet world music has introduced Western and global audiences to a rich variety of sounds, often rooted in Asian, African, Caribbean, and Latin American traditions. While reshaping music for a global market, world music has also given Asian, African, and Latin American musicians a larger audience. Just like Western pop stars, some world musicians such as the Brazilian singer-songwriter Caetano Veloso, the Indian film diva Asha Bhosle (the most recorded artist in history: 20,000 songs in over a dozen languages), and the Senegalese Youssou N'Dour, the descendant of griots, who mixes guitars with West African talking drums, perform around the world.

Inequality and Development

Globalization, resulting from interconnections transcending the boundaries of nations, benefits some people but not all equally. The gap between rich and poor nations, and rich and poor people within nations, has grown and remains one of the world's major problems. In 1960 the richest fifth of the world's population had a total income thirty times the poorest fifth; by 2000 the ratio had more than doubled. The former Soviet leader Mikhail Gorbachev, a keen student of world affairs, has asked: "Will the whole world turn into one big Brazil, into countries with complete inequality and [gated communities] for the rich elite?"[5] International and national leaders have addressed the challenges of development, considering a more equitable sharing of the world's diminishing resources.

The North-South Gap

With the changes in the global system since World War II, nations on every continent have improved their living standards, lowered poverty rates, and increased their stake in the global economy, which has more than quintupled in size since 1950. The average per capita income in the world grew 2.6 times in the same period, to some $5,000 per year. But the rising tide of the world economy has not lifted all ships, leaving some nations, especially in the southern lands near or below the equator, poor relative to the northern countries. The economies of these nations, known as underdeveloped nations, have stagnated or enjoyed only very modest growth, leaving the majority of their people in poverty. Over 1 billion people live in extreme poverty, with an income of less than $1 per day. Using a popular term for an underdeveloped nation, Jamaican reggae star Pato Banton reflected on the harshness of poverty in a 1989 song, "Third World Country":

> In a Third World country, the plants are green, it's a beautiful scene. Seems like a nice place for human beings. But there's people on the streets, no shoes on their feet. They gotta hustle to get a little food to eat. Things shouldn't be this way.[6]

The gap between the richest and poorest countries, often known as the North-South gap, has widened steadily (see map). For instance, the difference in average per capita incomes between industrialized and nonindustrialized nations grew from 2:1 in 1850 to 10:1 in 1950 to 30:1 by 2000. Today the industrialized North contains a quarter of the world's population but accounts for over three-quarters of its production of goods and services. Meanwhile, poor nations from Haiti to Sierra Leone have experienced civil war or insurgency as rival factions fight to control their limited resources and revenues.

The growing North-South gap has many aspects all documented in dry statistics that, however, represent real people. The disparity in consumption is striking. For example, while Americans, 5 percent of the world's population, consume 40 percent of the world's resources, people in a Bolivian valley consume few resources and experience an impoverished material life. According to a study of the valley: "In a man's lifetime, he will buy one suit, one white shirt, perhaps a hat and a pair of rubber boots. The only things which have to be purchased in the market are a small radio-record player, the batteries to run it, plaster religious figures, a bicycle, and some cutlery."[7] Food consumption also differs dramatically. On average, North Americans consume twice as many calories each day as Haitians and Bangladeshis. While overeating contributes to widespread obesity in industrialized nations, a sixth of the world's people are chronically malnourished, often suffering permanent brain damage because of it, and lack access to clean water. Fifteen million children die each year from hunger-related ailments.

There are also other indicators of difference in wealth. The 10 percent of people who live in the most industrialized nations consume two-thirds of the world's energy. Literacy rates range from a low of 14 percent in Niger, in West Africa, to a high of 99 percent in some twenty wealthy countries. Life expectancy ranges from a high of eighty in Japan to a low of thirty-seven in Sierra Leone, in West Africa. Over 60 percent of the world's poorest people are women, who often struggle to compete with men for resources or are often prevented by local custom from working outside the home.

Challenges of Development

Of course, the experiences of the Asian, African, and Latin American nations involve more than the bleak story of poverty and underdevelopment. Life expectancy worldwide has grown by nearly half, and infant mortality has dropped by two-thirds since 1955. Some Asian and Latin American nations have achieved literacy rates comparable to those of some European nations, and the number of countries the United Nations considers to have "high human development" grew from sixteen to fifty-five between 1960 and 2004. The rapidly industrializing nations of East and Southeast Asia have led the way: Singapore and South Korea achieved similar world economic rankings with such European nations as Italy, Greece, and Portugal. Several Latin American nations, Caribbean islands, and small oil-rich Persian Gulf states joined the top development category. Many rising nations—such as Malaysia, Thailand, India, and Brazil—formed a growing group of newly industrializing countries (NICs) which, since the 1960s, have enjoyed high economic growth rates. Malaysia, for example, has dramatically reduced poverty rates, while India and Singapore have become centers of high technology. Nor is technological innovation restricted to the well educated. In India, for example, creative farmers have made their work easier by inventing cotton-stripping machines and modifying motorcycles into tractors.

While some countries are on the rise, however, others struggle to spur economic growth that benefits all the population. Valiant efforts have failed to substantially raise living standards or create wealth for everyone. For instance, in much of Latin America the wealthiest 20 percent have enjoyed huge income increases while the poorest 40 percent have lost income. Capitalism supported by Western investment has helped a few countries, especially those that combine strong governments with social and economic reform, as in South Korea, Malaysia, and Thailand. But reliance on free markets and Western investment has often failed to sustain development. Little of the trickle down of wealth from the rich to the poor, predicted by Western economists who favor free enterprise, has occurred. Instead, the result has often been trickle out: the loss of a country's wealth to multinational corporations and international banks. Throughout the Contemporary Era, for example, more wealth has flowed out of Africa and Latin America in the form of resources and profits than has flowed in through aid and investment.

At the same time, alternatives to capitalism have not necessarily brought improvement. Communist and other social revolutionary countries have experienced severe problems. Some of these countries, such as Fidel Castro's Cuba and Mao Zedong's China, did a good job of delivering education and health care but were unable to create much wealth. Some communist countries, such as Angola and Vietnam, also sometimes faced civil wars and trade embargoes imposed by the West that drained their economies. Since in most cases neither capitalism nor socialism by itself proved the answer, most communist regimes eventually introduced economic liberalization, such as allowing private companies and Western investment while still maintaining strong, centralized governments. Since adopting this model after the end of the Maoist era, China, for example, has generated the world's most rapid economic growth; in recent years Vietnam has tried to follow the same path. However, economic liberalization that dismantles government services has deprived millions of Chinese and Vietnamese, especially peasants, of the free education and health care they enjoyed under socialism, fostering unrest. Meanwhile, the formula of mixing capitalism and socialism has worked well in much of East and Southeast Asia. In these regions, a dynamic, largely unfettered private sector has evolved along with government investment, planning, land reform, investment in education, and other public policies to benefit the common people.

Envisioning a New World Order

The challenge of development is only a part of a larger contemporary question: how societies, working together, can forge a new, more equitable world order. The old world order, built in the nineteenth century when powerful Western nations conquered much of Asia and Africa, was one in which a few rich nations politically and economically dominated most of the others. Even after World War II, decolonization, and the rise of revolutionary states such as China, a few nations, mostly in the West and East Asia, still held disproportionate power and influence. The United States has played the key role and borne the major costs in managing the global system through military alliances (such as NATO), trade pacts (such as GATT), and international organizations (such as the World Bank). However, since the 1960s experts and, often, leaders of underdeveloped nations have argued that fostering widespread economic development also requires addressing the inequalities within the global system, including adjusting power relations

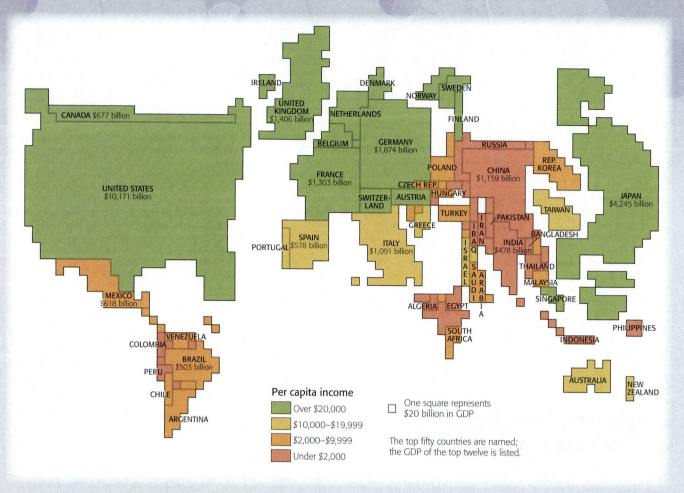

Per capita income

- Over $20,000
- $10,000–$19,999
- $2,000–$9,999
- Under $2,000

☐ One square represents $20 billion in GDP

The top fifty countries are named; the GDP of the top twelve is listed.

Global Distribution of Wealth

The countries of North America, northern Europe, and Japan have the most wealth and the world's highest per capita incomes, averaging over $20,000 per year. At the other extreme, many people in South America and most people in the poor countries of sub-Saharan Africa, South Asia, and the Middle East earn under $2,000 per year.

e Interactive Map

between the North and South, and spurring cooperation on international issues. The United Nations has been one major attempt at global cooperation but has had a mixed record.

The current world order contains many problems. The tensions resulting from governments unable significantly to raise living standards for the majority, to deal successfully with mounting social and economic problems, or to sustain hope for a better future have often led to political instability: coups, rebellions, and interventions by foreign powers. Conflicts in one nation then often spill over into neighboring nations, complicating international relations. Furthermore, people have experienced feelings of powerlessness in a world dominated by the governments, businesses, armies, and cultural influences of a few industrialized nations and the impersonal force of global markets. Leaders in the West have also expressed doubts about globalization. French president Jacques Chirac (g. 1995–present), for example, is suspicious of globalization, arguing that democracies "must tame it, accommodate it, humanize it, civilize it."[8]

The prospect of fostering a more equitable sharing of world resources raises questions about the availability of resources. Experts worry that the world's resources and environment could not support a Western standard of living for all the world. If every

Chinese, Indian, Egyptian, and Peruvian, they argue, consumed the same products and calories as Americans, Swedes, or Japanese, world resources would quickly diminish. For all 6.8 billion people in today's world to live at a western European standard of living would require a 140-fold increase in the consumption of resources and energy. Present oil supplies would run out in one or two decades, assuming the oil could be pumped and refined into petroleum that fast. Furthermore, the world population is growing rapidly—4.4 people born every second—and most of the growth is occurring in the developing nations, putting even more pressure on diminishing resources.

China's recent economic success shows the challenges ahead. By the early twenty-first century a China rushing toward development had become a huge consumer of the world's industrial, agricultural, and natural resources, energizing global trade but causing shortages elsewhere. For example, world oil prices have soared since 2000 in part because of China's increasing energy appetite as Chinese switch from bicycles to cars. If the Chinese consumed as much oil per capita as Americans, their demand would exceed the present world production. By 2006 the Chinese consumed nearly twice as much meat and more than twice as much steel as Americans.

China's living standards remain far below those of Japan and South Korea. Should they rise to that level, however, in the next decade or two, China will import vastly more resources than it does today, further stressing supplies. Assuming China does not experience a revolution, civil war, or economic collapse, all of which are possible, experts expect it to surpass Japan in the next few years and to have the world's largest economy by 2035 or 2040, eclipsing the United States. As occurred in the industrializing West earlier, rapid Chinese development, including the growing use of polluting fossil fuels, has also led to environmental degradation, including dangerous air pollution. People in nations once poor but becoming developed, such as China, India, and Brazil, do not believe that the industrialized Western peoples have any more right to consume the world's resources than they do, and they want their fair share.

Resolving problems of underdevelopment, and the poverty it brings, requires change within individual countries, such as implementing land reform, curbing corruption, and reducing bureaucratic obstacles to enterprise. Many experts have advocated "bottom up" development that involves peasants, workers, and women, rather than bureaucratic elites, in decision making. Such decisions would include shaping policies that provide families with adequate economic security, hence reducing the desire among parents for many children to ensure their support in old age. The Grameen Bank in Bangladesh, which loans money to poor women, is an outstanding example of such a "bottom up" policy. The visionary Tanzanian leader Julius Nyerere argued that people cannot be developed by outsiders but must develop themselves, using their own efforts and visions to improve their lives. Self-development, however, requires more social and economic equality within societies so that the wealth can be shared more equitably.

International cooperation is hobbled because the leaders of rich and poor nations often disagree on how to address global inequality. For economic and strategic reasons, Western nations want to protect their access to and heavy consumption of resources such as oil and copper and also worry about trade competition from NICs. In democratic nations these leaders have had to answer to voters, who fear compromising their own prosperity. Beginning in the 1970s various conferences and movements have debated modifying the world economic order by, for example, stabilizing world prices for natural resource exports, which chiefly come from developing nations, so that governments could better anticipate annual revenues. Responding to a worldwide campaign to help poor nations, in 2005 the industrialized nations canceled the burdensome debts of the poorest nations. Yet critics wondered whether poor nations with corrupt, often dictatorial, governments would use increased revenues or aid wisely. Furthermore, several Western nations, including the United States, Britain, and France, have often opposed efforts to build a new economic order because such an order could threaten their powerful position in the world economy and transfer wealth to poor nations. Yet, the world demand for food, water, and energy may increase between 30 and 50 percent by 2030.

Sustainable Environments

The decades since the mid-twentieth century were unusual for the intensity of environmental deterioration and the central-

ity of human effort in sparking it. The industrialized nations especially had become used to rapid economic growth and were dependent on abundant cheap energy and fresh water, needs that led to environmental destruction on an unparalleled scale. By the dawn of the twenty-first century the challenge of a changing environment became obvious. On every continent, but especially in Eurasia and North America, gas-guzzling vehicles, smoky factories, coal-fired power plants, and large farming operations produce large amounts of carbon dioxide and other pollutants, contributing to rising average temperatures that scientists call global warming. This climate change, if it continues, may have a greater impact—possibly catastrophic—on human life than any conventional war or other destructive human activities. Problems such as global warming raise the question of whether in the long term the natural environment can maintain itself and support plant, animal, and human life—a pattern known as sustainability.

Societies and Environmental Change

Experts have wondered whether the world's resources—minerals, wild plants, food crops, fresh water—could sustain present living standards on a long-term basis. For the past several decades scientists have been alarmed at the human consumption of natural resources faster than nature can replenish them. A major scientific study in the 1990s concluded that a devastating environmental crash would occur during the twenty-first century as resources become exhausted, forests disappear, plant and animal species die off, a warming climate makes certain regions uninhabitable, and pollution increases.

Human activity has altered environments since prehistory, sometimes with catastrophic results. Environmental collapse triggered by agricultural practices or deforestation helped undermine the Mesopotamians, Romans, and Maya, among others. But modern industrial societies and rapidly growing populations encroach on their natural settings even more heavily than did earlier societies. In the twentieth century people used more energy than had been used in all previous history. Between the 1890s and the 1990s the world economy grew fourteen times larger, industrial output twenty times, energy use fourteen times, carbon dioxide emissions seventeen times, water use nine times, and marine fish catches thirty-five times. These increases contributed to, among other pressing problems, air and water pollution, disposal of hazardous waste, declining genetic diversity in crops, and a mass extinction of plant and animal species. With their heavy economic production and consumption, people today are borrowing from tomorrow.

The atmosphere faces particular dangers, including a measurable warming. Earth's climate changed little, with only minor fluctuations, between the last Ice Age, which ended 10,000 years ago, and the end of the eighteenth century, when the Industrial Revolution began in Europe, but it has been changing fast over the past two centuries. The global temperature rose by one degree during the twentieth century. Since 1985, the world has experienced the highest average annual temperatures on record and unprecedented droughts. Scientists now largely agree that global warming has been increasing, although they debate its causes and dangers. Without major efforts to curb warming, scientists forecast a rise of somewhere between an alarming 2.5 and a catastrophic 10.4 degrees by 2100, which, if it happens, will change human life

Protesting Global Warming People in societies around the world became alarmed at the increasing environmental damage brought by modern economic activity and exploitation of resources. This demonstration by environmental activists concerned with global warming, a potentially dangerous trend caused by burning fossil fuels such as coal that produces more carbon dioxide, took place in Turkey.

AP/Wide World Photos

dramatically. Referring to the enclosed buildings where warm-weather plants are raised in cold climates, scientists speak of a Greenhouse Effect, the overheating of earth from human-made pollutants. The main culprits are gases such as carbon dioxide, chlorofluorocarbons, and methane that accumulate in the atmosphere and trap heat. The amount of heat-trapping carbon dioxide in the atmosphere increased by a third between 1900 and 2000, mostly from burning coal and oil. The greenhouse gases come largely from factory smokestacks, coal-fired power plants, and gasoline-powered vehicle exhausts. The most industrialized nation, the United States, has become the major producer, accounting for some 25 percent of the carbon dioxide and up to 50 percent of the other polluting chemicals. Europe, Russia, Japan, and China produce much of the rest. Some pollutants also destroy the ozone layer, a gaseous region in the upper atmosphere that protects humans from the cancer-causing ultraviolet rays of the sun. Scientists discovered that the ozone depletion rate in the 1990s was twice as fast as was thought a decade earlier.

In the pessimistic scenarios, the consequences of rising temperatures for many of the world's peoples are devastating. Earth gets baked, rich farmland turns to desert, and forests wilt. Fresh water, already scarce, becomes even harder to find as lakes and streams dry up. Rising ocean temperatures damage fisheries and kill most protective coral reefs while also increasing the intensity of hurricanes, making them more often like the catastrophic storm that devastated New Orleans and the U.S. Gulf Coast in 2005. Tropical and subtropical nations find agriculture and life generally more difficult. In North America farming becomes tougher in the southern United States, though more productive in a warming Canada. As the ice on Greenland melts, pouring fresh water into the North Atlantic, the warming Gulf Stream may shift southward and bring harsher winters to Europe and eastern North America.

Some peoples might face even more daunting challenges. Global warming has reduced the ice covering the Arctic Ocean

by half in recent years while thawing the adjacent land; these developments diminish the habitat for cold-adapted animals, such as polar bears, and threaten the livelihood and settlements of Arctic peoples. At the other end of the world, the West Antarctic ice shelf holds a vast amount of water and in some places has already begun to melt. If this trend accelerates, it will raise sea levels enough over the next two centuries to cover much low-lying coastal land. This will have disastrous consequences for regions such as the U.S. Gulf Coast and Florida, the Low Countries of northwest Europe, Bangladesh and eastern India, the Southeast Asian river deltas, and small island nations already now barely above sea level, including Tonga, Tuvalu, the Bahamas, and the Maldives.

Environmental Issues and Movements

The environmental challenges, such as diminishing resources, global warming, and deforestation, reinforce the scientific concept, first popularized in the 1970s, of global ecology—of the world, including human societies, as a complex web in which all living things interact with each other and their surroundings. From earliest times, societies have had complex relations with the environment, including interdependence with it. The Industrial Revolution, which has reshaped the world over the past two centuries, often for the better, came at great costs to the environment. Yet the world's leaders cannot agree on ways to better balance economic growth, which all nations desire, with environmental protection.

The exploitation of the earth's resources for human benefit, which has accelerated since 1945, has undermined sustainability. While soil, forests, and fisheries are renewable resources if properly managed, which they often were not in the past century, mineral resources such as oil and copper cannot be replaced once used up. Oil experts disagree as to when all known recoverable oil reserves will become exhausted. Optimists think oil supplies will be adequate through much of this century, and perhaps longer, before becoming scarce. Pessimists, noting the increased demand by countries such as China and India, believe all easily exploitable sources will be gone within two or three decades, causing conflict as nations scramble for oil supplies. Anticipating future resource and energy shortages, experts have for years recommended that industrial nations conserve oil by reducing dependence on it as the main fuel while developing renewable energy resources, such as solar, tidal, and wind power. Some nations have turned toward building more nuclear power plants, which are expensive and potentially dangerous but do less damage to the climate than burning fossil fuels. So far a few developing nations and some European countries have shown the most commitment to conservation and developing renewable energies.

Scientific conclusions about global warming and the need to reduce dependence on oil have often challenged powerful economic interests and upset governments that favor economic growth and worry about economic competition from rival nations. For example, since the 1970s U.S. presidents and Congress, fearing possible negative effects on U.S. business, have often opposed environmental agreements, such as the Kyoto Treaty of 1997, which was an effort, supported by most of the world's nations, to begin reducing greenhouse gases, as well as a European proposal seeking a 15 percent alternative energy use by 2010 (versus 1 percent today). Leaders of a few other powerful nations, including Japan, Russia, Britain, and China, have also been reluctant to cooperate with the world community on environmental issues. In 2005, 150 nations met in Montreal, Canada, and reaffirmed their commitment to the Kyoto treaty. Another international conference, scheduled for 2009 in Denmark, will determine whether heavy contributors to global warming will make binding commitments and cooperate on a common program. To sustain environmental health, a Canadian statesman has argued, requires a "revolution in [our] thinking as basic as the one introduced by Copernicus who [in the 1500s] first pointed out that the earth was not the center of the universe."[9]

An environmental movement began in the West in the late nineteenth century, eventually sparking similar movements around the world. Yet environmental awareness grew slowly. In the 1940s, the American environmentalist Aldo Leopold called for an ethic that treats the land with respect because all life belongs to a community of interdependent relationships: "Land is a fountain of energy flowing through a circuit of soils, plants, and animals, a sustained circuit, like a slowly augmented revolving fund of life."[10] Such ideas did not gain a large following. By the 1970s, however, views had changed; organizations such as Greenpeace, Earth First!, and the Rainforest Action Network pressed for a global commitment to stop environmental destruction. In 1992 a United Nations–sponsored global conference in Rio de Janeiro issued a proclamation urging sustainable development: "Human beings are entitled to a healthy and productive life in harmony with nature."[11] But the realities of modern politics, national rivalries, and fierce economic competition continue to make such a change difficult.

Global Pasts and Futures

The study of history helps us understand today's news and views as they are reported in daily newspapers, broadcast on radio and television, and disseminated on the World Wide Web. Historians often describe their work as involving a dialogue between past, present, and future. A few years ago French scientist René Dubos argued: "The past is not dead history. It is living material out of which makes the present and builds the future."[12] Current global problems have their roots in the patterns of world history: the rise of cities, states, and organized religions; the expansion of trade and capitalism to global dimensions; the unprecedented mastery and altering of nature represented by the scientific, industrial, and technological revolutions; the proliferation of competitive, unequal nations; and the myriad of social, economic, political, and cultural connections between peoples encompassed in the expanding global system. While seeking to understand how the past shaped the present, historians also speculate on how current trends may shape the future.

Understanding the Global Past

World historians offer several ways of understanding the world of yesterday, today, and tomorrow. One view is that contacts and collisions between different societies produce change. Whether through peaceful exchange or warfare or perhaps both, when societies encounter other societies they are exposed to different customs and ideas. For millennia after the transition to agriculture most of those contacts were with nearby peoples, but around two thousand years ago, thanks to advances in transportation and growing economies, increasingly mobile peoples began to encounter others much farther away, laying the roots for a global system to emerge after 1450. Historians also emphasize continuity, the persistence of social, cultural, political, and religious ideas and patterns, as well as change, the transformations in ways of life, work, and thought. Continuities are common. For example, many Christians, Muslims, Jews, Buddhists, and Hindus still look at the world through the prism of traditional religious values forged millennia ago and still meaningful today. Hence, in 2004 over 400,000 Christian missionaries—many from countries like Nigeria, the Philippines, and South Korea—were spreading the gospel around the world, at an annual cost of some $11 billion. Islam increased its following from 400 million people in 1960 to 1.3 billion by 2004. Yet changes, too, are everywhere. Thus most people, among them the devout followers of the old religions, also engage in activities, face challenges, and use forms of transportation and communication nonexistent a few generations ago. As a result, missionaries and clerics often use radio, television, and the Internet to spread their message. Another insight offered by global historians is that great transitions, such as the agricultural and industrial revolutions or, more recently, the rise of high technology, can turn history in new directions. Hence, thousands of years ago farming largely displaced hunting and gathering, two centuries ago industry transformed the world economy, and today instant communication and information bring distant peoples closer together. For instance, youngsters in Wisconsin can watch Australian-rules football matches from Melbourne on cable television while fans of Chinese rock and rap groups can hear their music on websites accessible from around the world.

As an example of the contacts and collisions that foster change, some scholars explain the changes of the past five hundred years in terms of the larger world's exposure and accommodation to the West, which led in turn to the political, economic, and military triumph of the West and often the adoption of its values and institutions. As a result of the spread of Western cultural influences, market economies, economic consumption practices, and individualistic values, they see a growing standardization of the world's societies. Many people welcome this standardization as a sign of progress, while others perceive it as a threat to local traditions. Still others consider the claim that societies and cultures are standardizing inaccurate, seeing instead a real increase in differences, especially the growing gap between rich and poor nations. In fact, living standards in the world have not been standardized. While people in the rich countries usually own several expensive electrical appliances, from washing machines to plasma televisions, millions of people in the poor nations do not even have electricity. Still, thanks to contacts between distant societies, the Western value of materialistic indulgence has become common, even if often out of reach for the poorest half of the world's people.

The experiences of most societies over the past half century reveal a mix of change and continuity. For example, Western ideas have gained even greater influence in the world since 1945 than they had before. People in different lands have adopted Western ideas of government, such as constitutions and elections, although not necessarily the substance of democracy, along with Western-rooted ideologies and faiths: capitalism, socialism, nationalism, and Christianity. Western pop culture, from rock music to soft drinks and blue jeans, has spread widely, leading to the "Coca-Colazation" of the world stemming from Western economic power, including advertising. Yet influences from the West are usually strongest in large cities and penetrate less deeply into the villages in Africa, Asia, and the Middle East, where traditional ways reflect continuity with the past. As a result, city youth in Malaysia or Tanzania may follow the latest recordings from Western pop stars, but these recordings may be unknown to their rural counterparts. Yet the urban youth may also share with rural youth traditional views about family and faith, and rural youth may, like their city counterparts, own motorcycles, boom boxes, and cell phones that make their lives different from those of their parents.

As a result of the transition to globalizing technology, culture, and commerce, the contacts between societies and their interdependence have vastly increased since 1945. In different ways nuclear weapons, multinational corporations, earth-circling satellites, World Cup soccer, and cable news networks draw people together, willingly or not. Imperialists once claimed proudly that "the sun never set on the British Empire." By the 1990s observers noted that "the sun never sets on McDonald's." Closer contact, of course, does not necessarily mean friendly relations and a less dangerous world; it can also bring collisions. Guided missiles and planes carrying bombs can reach 10,000 miles from their base. Over the past several decades over 60,000 Americans have died fighting in Vietnam, Afghanistan, and Iraq in support of U.S. efforts to reshape distant nations. On the other side, terrorist plots hatched in Afghanistan by Islamic militants who blame the United States for Middle Eastern problems killed Americans in New York City and Washington, D.C., in 2001. Some of the terrorists involved in planning or carrying out those and other attacks were once secular Muslims who went to Europe or the United States for college and, culturally disoriented and resentful of Western policies, became Islamic

militants and then joined a terrorist organization with global reach and access to high technology such as satellite phones, computers, and the Internet. Experts also speak of cyberspace terrorism, in which political or religious extremists advertise their violent goals and deeds on websites. The same technologies that allow people to instantly access and share information around the world also allow governments to spy on citizens and criminals to use cyberspace for their own purposes. Meanwhile, hackers can live anywhere and disrupt computer operations all over the world. Technology also threatens governments. In 2005 the search engine company, Google, made available a program, Google Earth, that can be freely downloaded and allows a user anywhere to see aerial and satellite photos of any location in the world. Governments from Algeria to India to Russia protested unsuccessfully that this violated their laws and revealed data, such as the layout of military bases, that they did not want available to the general public.

The contacts, changes, and transitions since 1945 have created a global village, a single community of exchange and interaction. In some regions, such as Southeast Asia, even remote villages have become part of this global village. By the 1960s, for example, people living in the once-isolated interior of the island of Borneo, divided between Indonesia and Malaysia, could access the outside world through battery-powered transistor radios and cassette players, and also by means of visiting traders, Christian missionaries, and government officials. Borneo's interior people also often left their remote villages to find work at logging camps, oil wells, or plantations as their rain forest environment and small farms rapidly disappeared, destroyed by international timber and mining operations that cut forests and stripped land to procure resources to ship to distant countries. As once-remote peoples, like those in the Borneo interior, are brought into the global system, and ethnic minorities are incorporated into nations, they find it harder to maintain their cultures and languages. Half of all languages are in danger of dying out over the next several decades, and less than 1 percent of languages are used on the Internet.

Toward the Future

Women and men created the present world from the materials of the past and are now laying the foundation for the future. As a Belgian scholar wrote a few years ago, "We cannot predict the future, but we can prepare it."[13] But this raises the question of what kind of future. In 1974 the American economic historian Robert Heilbroner, asking what promise the future holds, doubted the permanence of modern industrial society and even democracy in the face of population explosion, environmental degradation, resource depletion, militarization, and the increasing economic desperation of people in the poorest countries. His question remains highly relevant in the early twenty-first century. For example, as industrialization spreads to other nations, the world requires more use of fossil fuels, which spurs more global warming. Heilbroner drew a gloomy picture of the future. He believed most people are not willing to sacrifice for the good of future generations. Like him, other experts often despair. The world's long history of war, inequality, and exploitation, even when seemingly offset by progress, does not foster optimism. Indeed, some respected experts predict human extinction if people do not adopt more sustainable ways, and scientific studies are more frequently pessimistic than optimistic about the future. Worried that we face environment collapse, one study concludes: "Our generation is the first to be faced with decisions that will determine whether the earth our children inherit will be habitable."[14]

Yet, since World War II humanity has produced many green shoots of hope. Western Europe moved rapidly to political and economic unity, defusing centuries of conflict. Eastern Europeans and Russians overturned dogmatic communist regimes, ending the long Cold War between the superpowers. The Scandinavian nations, a hundred years ago among the poorest European societies, have virtually eliminated poverty, achieving the world's highest quality of life. Several Asian nations rapidly developed, dramatically improving living standards and national wealth. A century ago desperately poor, China has become not only able to feed and clothe its huge population but also to export industrial products to the world. Thanks in part to global efforts, black majority rule came to South Africa. Over two dozen nations, including some in Asia, Latin America, and the Caribbean, have elected women presidents or prime ministers, and women, making their voices heard, have increasingly gained more power over their lives in many countries. Despite some notable conflicts, wars have become less common than before. Unlike the Cold War years between 1946 and 1992, when fighting between and within nations was frequent, between 1992 and 2005 the number of wars with over 1,000 battle deaths a year declined by 80 percent.

Hopeful developments have also resulted from international cooperation. A large majority of nations have signed agreements to ban weapons of mass destruction, punish genocide, and reduce gases contributing to global warming. Drastic reductions in the arms race have diminished the threat of nuclear war. United Nations agencies have improved lives for children and women in many countries and spurred cooperation on environmental issues. Local nongovernmental organizations, often with international connections, have also become active, working for the rights of women, children, workers, and peasants and for a healthier environment. Human rights groups with chapters around the world have worked courageously to promote civil liberties and the release of political prisoners. Encouraged by environmental activists abroad, brave tribal groups in tropical rain forests have resisted the logging and mining destroying their habitats. Not least in its effects, the growing information superhighway now instantly links millions of office or home computers with people, libraries, and other information sources around the world.

A history not only of cruelty and exploitation but also of compassion and sacrifice provides hope in navigating troubled times. Remembering when people behaved magnificently may foster inspiration to answer the challenges. The contemporary age offers ample examples of inspiring people: democracy activists such as Nelson Mandela, Vaclav Havel, Mohandas Gandhi, and Aung San Suu Kyi; social activists such as Wangari Maathai, Dr. Martin Luther King, Jr., Shirin Ebadi, and Mukhtaran Bibi; cultural figures such as Wole Soyinka, Violeta Parra, Simone de Beauvoir, and Cui Jian; and figures who have built links between societies such as Jean Monnet, Bono, and the Dalai Lama. Historians sometimes view the past as a stream with banks. The stream is filled with people killing, bullying, enslaving, and doing other things historians usually record, while on the banks, unnoticed, women and men build homes,

International Women's Day 2005 Women around the world became more willing to assert their rights. Activists from diverse Indian nongovernmental organizations interested in women's rights marched in New Delhi, India's capital, in 2005 to mark International Women's Day.

raise children, tend farms, settle disputes, sing songs, whittle statues, trade with their neighbors, and chat with travelers from other lands. Historians often ignore the banks for the stream, but what happens on the banks may be more reassuring.

Some observers, believing that cultural differences will increasingly drive international politics, forecast a clash of civilizations, such as between the Christian West and Islam, which are seen as irreconcilably opposed in world-views. But simplistic formulas miss the complexity of the global order. None of the great religions and the cultures that they shaped are monolithic, the divisions among Christians or Muslims, Westerners or Middle Easterners, being as great as their differences with other traditions. No cultures or religions have a monopoly on values such as peace, justice, charity, tolerance, public discussion, and goodwill. In any case, nations generally shape their foreign policies according to their national interests rather than ideology. Wars over resources, such as oil and water, some observers claim, are more likely to occur than wars over cultural differences. Other observers doubt that, whatever the tensions, any titanic military struggle like the two world wars of the twentieth century is inevitable; they expect that the world will cooperate on major issues and tolerate different concepts of economics, government, God, morality, and society for years to come. Furthermore, thanks to the many available information sources, people can become informed about why past societies, such as the Mesopotamians and Maya, destroyed their environments and collapsed, and how countries blundered into wars or failed to develop cooperative relations with their neighbors that maintained peace. These insights, if acquired, may help people today to avoid repeating the mistakes of the past and construct a better future.

Four centuries ago, the English playwright William Shakespeare wrote that the past is prologue to the present. The study of world history allows us to ask questions about the global future because we understand the changing patterns of the global past, including the building of societies, their interactions through networks, and the great transitions that reshaped humanity. These have led to an increasingly connected world in the past 1,500 years. The contemporary age has been marked by a complex mix of dividing and unifying forces, unique societies differing greatly in standards of living but linked into a global system of exchange. People today cannot yet know with certainty where the path will lead, but they can help build it. Nineteenth-century British novelist Lewis Carroll (1832–1898) suggested a way of looking at the problem in his novel *Through the Looking Glass*, about Alice in Wonderland. Lost and perplexed in Wonderland, Alice asked the Cheshire Cat: "Would you tell me, please, which way I ought to go from here?" The enigmatic cat pondered the query for a few moments and then replied: "That depends a great deal on where you want to get to."[15] Societies, working together, must chart that course into the future.

Suggested Reading

Books

Baylis, John, et al., eds. *The Globalization of World Politics: An Introduction to International Relations,* 4th ed. New York: Oxford University Press, 2008. Essays on world politics by British scholars.

Brown, Lester. *Plan B 2.0: Rescuing a Planet Under Stress and a Civilization in Trouble*, 3rd ed. New York: W.W. Norton, 2008. A survey of the world's environmental and resource challenges and some possible solutions.

Eriksen, Thomas Hylland. *Globalization: The Key Concepts.* New York: Berg, 2007. A Norwegian scholar's provocative introduction to the debates.

Hannerz, Ulf. *Transnational Connections: Culture, People, Places.* New York: Routledge, 1996. Interesting essays on cultures and networks in the age of globalization by a Swedish scholar.

Held, David, ed. *A Globalizing World? Culture, Economics, Politics*, 2nd ed. New York: Routledge, 2004. An excellent collection of essays and readings on various aspects of globalization, compiled by British scholars.

Hobsbawm, Eric. *On the Edge of the New Century.* New York: The New Press, 1999. Thoughts on the past, present, and future by a British historian.

Kennedy, Paul. *Preparing for the Twenty-First Century.* New York: Random House, 1994. A study of how population, technology, and the environment shaped the contemporary world and various regions.

Mayor, Federico, and Jerome Bindé. *The World Ahead: Our Future in the Making.* New York: Zed Books, 2001. A comprehensive study, prepared by European scholars for the United Nations, of political, economic, social, cultural, and environmental trends.

Mazrui, Ali. *Cultural Forces in World Politics.* London: Heinemann, 1990. A challenging examination of world-views and patterns by a distinguished African scholar.

Newland, Kathleen, and Kamala Chandrakirana Soedjatmoko, eds. *Transforming Humanity: The Visionary Writings of Soedjatmoko.* West Hartford, CT: Kumarian Press, 1994. Thoughtful essays on development, violence, religion, and other issues in the contemporary world by an influential Indonesian thinker.

Pieterse, Jan Nederveen, ed. *Global Futures: Shaping Globalization.* London: Zed Books, 2000. Provocative essays on world trends by scholars from around the world.

Pieterse, Jan Nederveen. *Globalization and Culture: Global Melange*, 2nd ed. Armonk, NY: Rowman and Littlefield, 2009. A study of cultural hybridization.

Sachs, Jeffrey. *The End of Poverty: Economic Possibilities for Our Time.* New York: Penguin, 2005. A controversial but stimulating discussion of global poverty issues.

Seager, Joni. *The Penguin Atlas of Women in the World,* 4th ed. New York: Penguin, 2008. A creative, indispensable examination of women around the world.

Sen, Amartya. *Identity and Violence: The Illusion of Destiny.* New York: W.W. Norton, 2006. A provocative critique by an India-born economist of the clash-of-civilizations idea.

Smith, Dan, and Ane Braein. *Penguin State of the World Atlas,* 8th ed. New York: Penguin, 2008. The latest edition of an invaluable map-based reference providing an overview of world conditions.

Worldwatch Institute. *State of the World.* New York: W.W. Norton. Informative annual surveys of the world's environmental health that are published annually by the Worldwatch Institute in Washington, D.C.

Taylor, Timothy D. *Global Pop: World Music, World Markets.* New York: Routledge, 1997. A fine study of the world music industry and major musicians.

WEBSITES

Global Problems and the Culture of Capitalism (*http://faculty.plattsburgh.edu/richard.robbins/legacy/*). An outstanding site, aimed at undergraduates, with a wealth of resources on many topics.

Globalization Guide (*http://www.globalisationguide.org*). A useful collection of essays and links.

The Globalization Website (*http://www.sociology.emory.edu/globalization/*). A very useful site with many resources and essays related to globalization.

United Nations (*http://www.un.org*). The pathway to the websites of the many United Nations agencies, operations, and ongoing projects.

The WWW Virtual Library (*http://vlib.org/*). The homepage of a vast and indispensable British-based network of links on many topics and issues.

Notes

Chapter 19 Modern Transitions: Revolutions, Industries, Ideologies, Empires, 1750–1914

1. Quoted in Eric Hobsbawm, *The Age of Revolution, 1789–1848* (New York: New American Library, 1962), 44.
2. From Charles Dickens, *A Tale of Two Cities* (New York: Bantam, 1989), 1.
3. From David A. Hollinger and Charles Capper, eds., *The American Intellectual Tradition: A Sourcebook,* vol. 1, 2nd ed. (New York: Oxford University Press, 1993), 131.
4. Quoted in William Appleman Williams, *America Confronts a Revolutionary World, 1775–1976* (New York: William Morrow, 1976), 15, 25.
5. Quoted in Peter N. Stearns, *Life and Society in the West: The Modern Centuries* (San Diego: Harcourt Brace Jovanovich, 1988), 164.
6. Quoted in Eric Hobsbawm, *Workers: World of Labor* (New York: Pantheon), 34.
7. Quoted in Michael Elliott-Bateman et al., *Revolt to Revolution: Studies in the 19th and 20th Century European Experience* (Manchester, England: Manchester University Press, 1974), 87.
8. Jose San Martin, quoted in Edwin Early, *The History Atlas of South America* (New York: Macmillan, 1998), 76.
9. Quoted in Carlos Fuentes, *The Buried Mirror: Reflections on Spain and the New World* (New York: Houghton Mifflin, 1992), 252.
10. Quoted in E. Bradford Burns and Julie A. Charlip, *Latin America: A Concise Interpretive History,* 7th ed. (Upper Saddle River, NJ: Prentice-Hall, 2002), 75.
11. Quoted in John R. Gillis, *A World of Their Own Making: Myth, Ritual, and the Quest for Family Values* (New York: Basic Books, 1996), 65.
12. Quoted in Fernand Braudel, *The Perspective of the World: Civilization and Capitalism, 15th–18th Century* (New York: Harper and Row, 1984), 553.
13. Quoted in Peter Gay, *Age of Enlightenment* (New York: Time, Inc., 1966), 105–106.
14. Quoted in Peter Hall, *Cities in Civilization* (New York: Fromm International, 1998), 310.
15. Quoted in Oliver Zimmer, *A Contested Nation: History, Memory and Nationalism in Switzerland, 1761–1891* (Cambridge: Cambridge University Press, 2003), 119.
16. Quoted in W. Raymond Duncan et al., *World Politics in the 21st Century,* 2nd ed. (New York: Longman, 2004), 311.
17. Quoted in Patrick Galvin, *Irish Songs of Resistance* (New York: Folklore Press, n.d.), 84.
18. Quoted in S. C. Burchell, *The Age of Progress* (New York: Time, Inc., 1966), 120.
19. Quoted in Reginald Nettel, *Sing a Song of England: A Social History of Traditional Song* (London: Phoenix House, 1969), 183.
20. Quoted in Robert A. Huttenback, *The British Imperial Experience* (New York: Harper and Row, 1966), 101.
21. Hillaire Beloc, quoted in Eric Hobsbawm, *The Age of Empire, 1875–1914* (New York: Vintage, 1987), 20.
22. Quoted in John Steele Gordon, *A Thread Across the Ocean: The Heroic Story of the Transatlantic Cable* (New York: Perennial, 2003), 215.
23. Quoted in Winnifred Baumgart, *Imperialism: The Idea and Reality of British and French Colonial Expansion, 1880–1914* (New York: Oxford University Press, 1986), 88.
24. Quoted in L. S. Stavrianos, *Global Reach: The Third World Comes of Age* (New York: William Morrow, 1981), 263.
25. Quoted in Baumgart, *Imperialism,* 52.

Chapter 20 Changing Societies in Europe, the Americas, and Oceania, 1750–1914

1. *Nostromo* (Garden City, NY: Doubleday, Page, and Company, 1924), 77.

2. The Kume quotes are from Donald Keene, *Modern Japanese Diaries: The Japanese at Home and Abroad as Revealed Through Their Diaries* (New York: Columbia University Press, 1998), 90–115.
3. Quoted in Frederic Delouche et al., *Illustrated History of Europe* (New York: Barnes and Noble, 2001), 312.
4. Quoted in Louise A. Tilly and Joan W. Scott, *Women, Work and Family* (New York: Holt, Rinehart and Winston, 1978), 64.
5. Quoted in T. W. C. Blanning, "The Commercialization and Sacralization of European Culture in the Nineteenth Century," in *The Oxford Illustrated History of Modern Europe,* ed. T. W. C. Blanning (Oxford: Oxford University Press, 1996), 147.
6. From Alexis De Tocqueville, *Democracy in America and Two Essays on America* (New York: Penguin, 2003), xxxiii.
7. Quoted in James Chase and Caleb Carr, *America Invulnerable: The Quest for Absolute Security from 1812 to Star Wars* (New York: Summit, 1988), 46.
8. From Peter Blood-Patterson, *Rise Up Singing* (Bethlehem, PA: Sing Out Publications, 1988), 246.
9. Quoted in Walter L. Williams, "American Imperialism and the Indians," in *Indians in American History: An Introduction,* ed. Frederick E. Hoxie (Arlington Heights, IL: Harlan Davidson, 1988), 233.
10. Quoted in Simon Serfaty, *The Elusive Enemy: American Foreign Policy Since World War II* (Boston: Little, Brown, 1972), 13.
11. Quoted in William Appleman Williams, *The Contours of American History* (Chicago: Quadrangle, 1966), 284.
12. Quoted in Robert Heilbroner and Aaron Singer, *The Economic Transformation of America, 1600 to the Present,* 3rd ed. (Fort Worth, TX: Harcourt Brace, 1994), 163.
13. Quoted in Juliet Haines Mofford, ed., *Talkin' Union: The American Labor Movement* (Carlisle, MA: Discovery Enterprises, 1997), 24.
14. From Mark Van Doren, ed., *The Portable Walt Whitman* (New York: Penguin, 1973), 210.
15. Quoted in Lloyd Gardner, *Safe for Democracy: The Anglo-American Response to Revolution, 1913–1923* (New York: Oxford University Press, 1984), 26.
16. From Mariano Azuela's novel *The Flies,* quoted in Lesley Byrd Simpson, *Many Mexicos,* 4th ed. rev. (Berkeley: University of California Press, 1967), 298.
17. Quoted in Stanley J. Stein and Barbara H. Stein, *The Colonial Heritage of Latin America: Essays on Economic Dependence in Perspective* (New York: Oxford University Press, 1970), 151.
18. Quoted in E. Bradford Burns, *Latin America: A Concise Interpretive History,* 5th ed. (Englewood Cliffs, NJ: Prentice-Hall, 1990), 213.
19. Quoted in Michael C. Meyer and William L. Sherman, *The Course of Mexican History,* 2nd ed. (New York: Oxford University Press, 1983), 416.
20. Quoted in Lloyd Braithwaite, "The Problem of Cultural Integration in Trinidad," in *Consequences of Class and Color: West Indian Perspectives,* ed. David Lowenthal and Lambors Comitas (Garden City, NY: Anchor, 1973), 248.
21. General Leonard Wood, quoted in Saul Landau, *The Dangerous Doctrine: National Security and U.S. Foreign Policy* (Boulder, CO: Westview Press, 1988), 80–81.
22. Quoted in Louis Hartz, *The Founding of New Societies* (New York: Harcourt, Brace and World, 1964), 248.

Chapter 21 Africa, the Middle East, and Imperialism, 1750–1914

1. Quoted in Edmund Burke III, *Prelude to Protectorate in Morocco: Precolonial Protest and Resistance, 1860–1912* (Chicago: University of Chicago Press, 1976), xi.
2. Quoted in Alan Palmer, *The Decline and Fall of the Ottoman Empire* (New York: Barnes and Noble, 1992), 58.

3. Quoted in John Iliffe, "Tanzania Under German and British Rule," in *Zamani: A Survey of East African History*, ed. B. A. Ogot, new ed. (Nairobi: Longman Kenya, 1974), 301.

4. Francois Coillard, quoted in John Iliffe, *Africans: The History of a Continent* (New York: Cambridge University Press, 1995), 208.

5. Quoted in ibid., 200–201.

6. H. H. Johnston, quoted in M. E. Chamberlain, *The Scramble for Africa* (Harlow, UK: Longman, 1974), 96.

7. Nnamdi Azikiwe, quoted in Minton F. Goldman, "Political Change in a Multi-National Setting," In David Schmitt, ed., *Dynamics of the Third World: Political and Social Change* (Cambridge: Winthrop, 1974), 172.

8. Rev. J. B. Murphy, quoted in Kevin Shillington, *History of Africa*, rev. ed. (New York: St. Martin's, 1995), 333–334.

9. Quoted in Dennis Austin, *Politics in Ghana* (London: Oxford University Press, 1964), 275.

10. Quoted in Tom Hopkinson, *South Africa* (New York: Time Inc., 1964), 93.

11. The lyrics are in David B. Coplan, *In Township Tonite: South Africa's Black City Music and Theater* (London: Longman, 1985), 44–45.

12. Quoted in Leroy Vail, "The Political Economy of East-Central Africa," in *History of Central Africa*, ed. David Birmingham and Phyllis M. Martin, vol. 2 (New York: Longman, 1983), 233.

13. Quoted in Andrew Wheatcroft, *The Ottomans* (New York: Viking, 1993), 146.

14. Quoted in Halil Inalcik, "Turkey," in *Political Modernization in Japan and Turkey*, ed. Robert E. Ward and Dankwart A. Rostow (Princeton: Princeton University Press, 1964), 57–58.

15. Quoted in Afaf Lufti al-Sayyid Marsot, *Egypt in the Reign of Muhammad Ali* (New York: Cambridge University Press, 1994), 28.

16. Quoted in Yahya Armajani and Thomas M. Ricks, *Middle East: Past and Present*, 2nd ed. (Englewood Cliffs, NJ: Prentice-Hall, 1986), 221.

17. Quoted in Charles Issawi, *The Middle East Economy: Decline and Recovery* (Princeton: Markus Wiener, 1995), 126.

18. Gertrude Bell, quoted in Emory C. Bogle, *The Modern Middle East: From Imperialism to Freedom, 1800–1958* (Upper Saddle River, NJ: Prentice-Hall, 1996), 103.

19. Quoted in Eric R. Wolf, *Peasant Wars of the Twentieth Century* (New York: Harper and Row, 1969), 209.

20. The quotes are from Akram Fouad Khater, ed., *Sources in the History of the Modern Middle East* (Boston: Houghton Mifflin, 2004), 75; Wiebke Walther, *Women in Islam* (Princeton: Markus Wiener, 1993), 221.

21. Quoted in Burke, *Prelude to Protectorate*, 38.

22. From Khater, *Sources*, 34.

Chapter 22 South Asia, Southeast Asia, and Colonization, 1750–1914

1. From Huynh Sanh Thong, *An Anthology of Vietnamese Poems from the Eleventh Through the Twentieth Centuries* (New Haven, CT: Yale University Press, 1996), 88.

2. The poem excerpts are in Helen B. Lamb, *Vietnam's Will to Live: Resistance to Foreign Aggression from Early Times Through the Nineteenth Century* (New York: Monthly Review Press, 1972), 134, 152.

3. Quoted in Sinharaja Tammita-Delgoda, *A Traveller's History of India*, 2nd ed. (New York: Interlink, 1999), 154.

4. The quotes are in Burton Stein, *A History of India* (Malden, Mass.: Blackwell, 1998), 265–266.

5. Charles Metcalfe, quoted in David Ludden, *An Agrarian History of South Asia* (New York: Cambridge University Press, 1999), 161.

6. Quoted in Tammita-Delgoda, *Traveller's History*, 167.

7. Quoted in ibid., 173.

8. Dadabhai Naoroji and R.C. Dutt, quoted in Ainslee T. Embree, *India's Search for National Identity* (New York: Alfred A. Knopf, 1972), 48–49.

9. Quoted in Clark D. Moore and David Eldridge, eds., *India Yesterday and Today* (New York: Bantam, 1970), 154–155.

10. The quotes are in Francis Robinson, *The Cultural Atlas of the Islamic World Since 1500* (Oxford: Stonehenge, 1992), 148–149.

11. From Rabindranath Tagore, *Gitanjali: A Collection of Indian Songs* (New York: Macmillan, 1973), 49–50.

12. Quoted in John McLane, ed., *The Political Awakening of India* (Englewood Cliffs, NJ: Prentice-Hall, 1970), 46.

13. Douwes Dekker, from Harry J. Benda and John A. Larkin, eds., *The World of Southeast Asia: Selected Historical Readings* (New York: Harper and Row, 1967), 127.

14. Quoted in Truong Buu Lam, *Resistance, Rebellion, Revolution: Popular Movements in Vietnamese History* (Singapore: Institute of Southeast Asian Studies, 1984), 11.

15. From Huynh, *Anthology of Vietnamese Poems*, 214.

16. The quotes are in Lamb, *Vietnam's Will to Live*, 229; and Truong Buu Lam, *Patterns of Vietnamese Response to Foreign Intervention, 1858–1900*, Monograph Series No. 11, Southeast Asia Studies (New Haven, CT: Yale University Press, 1967), 8.

17. Quoted in Teodoro A. Agoncillo, *A Short History of the Philippines* (New York: Mentor, 1969), 93.

18. Quoted in David Joel Steinberg et al., *In Search of Southeast Asia: A Modern History*, rev. ed. (Honolulu: University of Hawaii Press, 1987), 274.

19. Quoted in Daniel B. Schirmer, *Republic or Empire: American Resistance to the Philippine War* (Cambridge: Schenkman, 1972), 237.

20. The quotes are in David Howard Bain, *Sitting in Darkness: Americans in the Philippines* (Baltimore: Penguin, 1986), 2; and Gary R. Hess, *Vietnam and United States: Origins and Legacy of War* (Boston: Twayne, 1990), 25.

21. Quoted in Ngo Vinh Long, *Before the Revolution: The Vietnamese Peasants Under the French* (New York: Columbia University Press, 1991), v.

22. Tran Tu Binh, *The Red Earth: A Vietnamese Memoir of Life on a Colonial Rubber Plantation*, translated by John Spragens, Jr. (Athens, OH: Center for International Studies, Ohio University, 1985), 26.

23. Raden Ajoe Mangkoedimedjo, quoted in Norman Owen et al., *The Emergence of Modern Southeast Asia: A New History* (Honolulu: University of Hawaii Press, 2005), 197.

Chapter 23 East Asia and the Russian Empire Face New Challenges, 1750–1914

1. Quoted in Frederic Wakeman, Jr., *Strangers at the Gate: Social Disorder in South China, 1839–1861* (Berkeley: University of California Press, 1966), p. 126.

2. Quoted in Jonathan D. Spence, *The Search for Modern China*, 2nd ed. (New York: W.W. Norton, 1999), 148.

3. Quoted in Derk Bodde, *China's Cultural Tradition: What and Whither?* (New York: Holt, Rinehart and Winston, 1957), 62–63.

4. Chu Tsun, quoted in Hsin-Pao Chang, *Commissioner Lin and the Opium War* (New York: W.W. Norton, 1970), 89.

5. Quoted in Mark Borthwick, *Pacific Century: The Emergence of Modern East Asia* (Boulder, CO: Westview Press, 1992), 97.

6. Ssu-Yu Teng and John K. Fairbank, eds., *China's Response to the West: A Documentary Survey, 1839–1923* (New York: Atheneum, 1963), 26.

7. Quoted in Jean Chesneaux et al., *China: From the Opium Wars to the 1911 Revolution* (New York: Pantheon, 1976), 123.

8. S. Wells Williams, quoted in John A. Harrison, *China Since 1800* (New York: Harcourt, Brace and World, 1967), 42.

9. Hsu Tung, quoted in Joseph R. Levenson, *Confucian China and Its Modern Fate: A Trilogy* (Berkeley: University of California Press, 1968), 105.

10. Quoted in Earl Swisher, "Chinese Intellectuals and the Western Impact, 1838–1900," *Comparative Studies in Society and History* 1 (October 1958): 35.

11. Wang Pengyun, from Cyril Birch, ed., *Anthology of Chinese Literature* (New York: Grove Press, 1972), 294.

12. Quoted in Lloyd Gardner, *Safe for Democracy: The Anglo-American Response to Revolution, 1913–1923* (New York: Oxford University Press, 1984), 318.

13. Quoted in Jonathan D. Spence, *The Gate of Heavenly Peace: The Chinese and Their Revolution, 1895–1980* (New York: Viking, 1981), 52.

14. Quoted in Ono Kazuko, *Chinese Women in a Century of Revolution* (Stanford, CA: Stanford University Press, 1989), 30.
15. Otsuki Gentaku, quoted in Mikiso Hane, *Modern Japan: A Historical Survey*, 2nd ed. (Boulder, CO: Westview Press, 1992), 59.
16. Quoted in Patricia Fister, "Female *Bunjin*: The Life of Poet-Painter Ema Saiko," in *Recreating Japanese Women, 1600-1945*, ed. Gail Lee Bernstein (Berkeley: University of California Press, 1991), 109.
17. Quoted in Matthi Ferrer, *Hokusai* (New York: Barnes and Noble, 2002), 9.
18. Yanagawa Seigan, quoted in H. D. Hartoonian, *Toward Restoration: The Growth of Political Consciousness in Tokugawa Japan* (Berkeley: University of California Press, 1970), 1-2.
19. Quoted in Paul Varley, *Japanese Culture*, 4th ed. (Honolulu: University of Hawaii Press, 2000), 238.
20. Fukuzawa Yukichi, quoted in Mikiso Hane, *Peasants, Rebels, and Outcasts: The Underside of Modern Japan* (New York: Pantheon, 1982), 33.
21. Quoted in Conrad Totman, *A History of Japan* (Malden, MA: Blackwell, 2000), 341.
22. The quotes are from Varley, *Japanese Culture*, 272.
23. Quoted in L. S. Stavrianos, *Global Rift: The Third World Comes of Age* (New York: William Morrow, 1981), 344.

Chapter 24 World Wars, European Revolutions, and Global Depression, 1914-1945

1. Quoted in Anne Applebaum, *Gulag: A History* (New York: Doubleday, 2003), 3.
2. Quoted in S. L. Marshall, *World War I* (Boston: Houghton Mifflin, 1987), 53.
3. Quoted in Sir Michael Howard, "Europe 1914," in *The Great War: Perspectives on the First World War*, ed. Robert Cowley (New York: Random House, 2003), 3.
4. David Lloyd George, quoted in Holger H. Herwig, ed., *The Outbreak of World War I*, 6th ed. (Boston: Houghton Mifflin, 1997), 12.
5. The quotes are in Michael J. Lyons, *World War I: A Short History*, 2nd ed. (Upper Saddle River, NJ: Prentice-Hall, 2000), 195; and Ian Barnes and Robert Hudson, *The History Atlas of Europe: From Tribal Societies to a New European Unity* (New York: Macmillan, 1998), 131.
6. From L. S. Stavrianos, ed., *The Epic of Modern Man: A Collection of Readings* (Englewood Cliffs, NJ: Prentice-Hall, 1966), 354.
7. Quoted in A. J. Nicholls, *Weimar and the Rise of Hitler*, 2nd ed. (New York: St. Martin's, 1979), 11.
8. Quoted in Piers Brendon, *Dark Valley: A Panorama of the 1930s* (New York: Alfred A. Knopf, 2000), 6.
9. Quoted in L. S. Stavrianos, *Global Rift: The Third World Comes of Age* (New York: William Morrow, 1981), 499.
10. Quoted in Brendon, *Dark Valley*, 493.
11. Quoted in Kenneth B. Pyle, *The Making of Modern Japan*, 2nd ed. (Lexington, MA: D.C. Heath, 1996), 173.
12. Senator William Borah, quoted in William Appleman Williams, *American-Russian Relations, 1781-1947* (New York: Rinehart, 1952), 164.
13. *The Great Gatsby* (New York: Scribner's, 1925), 182.
14. Paul Reynaud, quoted in Brendon, *Dark Valley*, 153-154.
15. Quoted in Robert Heilbroner and Aaron Singer, *The Economic Transformation of America, 1600 to the Present* (Fort Worth: Harcourt Brace, 1994), 289.
16. From Harold Leventhal and Marjorie Guthrie, eds., *The Woody Guthrie Songbook* (New York: Grosset and Dunlap, 1976), 180-181.
17. Maurice Sachs, quoted in Brendon, *Dark Valley*, 168.
18. Quoted in Felix Gilbert with David Clay Large, *The End of the European Era, 1890 to the Present*, 4th ed. (New York: W.W. Norton, 1991), 263.
19. Quoted in Martin Kitchen, *A World in Flames: A Short History of the Second World War in Europe and Asia, 1939-1945* (London: Longman, 1990), vi.
20. Quoted in Stephen J. Lee, *European Dictatorships, 1918-1945*, 2nd ed. (London: Routledge, 2000), 207.
21. Quoted in George Donelson Moss, *America in the Twentieth Century*, 4th ed. (Upper Saddle River, NJ: Prentice-Hall, 2000), 257.
22. Quoted in James L. McClain, *Japan: A Modern History* (New York: W.W. Norton, 2002), 515.

Chapter 25 Imperialism and Nationalism in Asia, Africa, and Latin America, 1914-1945

1. Quoted in James C. Scott, *The Moral Economy of the Peasant: Rebellion and Subsistence in Southeast Asia* (New Haven: Yale University Press, 1976), 236.
2. Quoted in James W. Trullinger, *Village at War: An Account of Conflict in Vietnam* (Stanford, Calif.: Stanford University Press, 1994), 18.
3. Dick Spottswood, liner notes to the album *Calypsos from Trinidad: Politics, Intrigue and Violence in the 1930s* (Arhoolie 7004, 1991).
4. Quoted in Lester Langley, *Central America: The Real Stakes: Understanding Central America Before It's Too Late* (New York: Dorsey, 1985), 23.
5. Kenneth Wherry of Nebraska, quoted in John Brooks, *The Great Leap: The Past Twenty-five Years in America* (New York: Harper and Row, 1966), 327.
6. Quoted in *A Pictorial Biography of Luxun* (Beijing: Peoples Fine Arts Publishing House, n.d.), 157.
7. "Report on an Investigation of the Peasant Movement in Hunan," in *Selected Works of Mao Tse-Tung*, vol. 1 (Peking: Foreign Languages Press, 1965), 28.
8. Quoted in Stephen Uhalley, Jr., *Mao Tse-Tung: A Critical Biography* (New York: New Viewpoints, 1975), 55.
9. Quoted in John Meskill, "History of China," in *An Introduction to Chinese Civilization*, ed. John Meskill (Lexington, MA: D.C. Heath, 1973), 302.
10. Quoted in Sinharaja Tammita-Delgoda, *A Traveller's History of India*, 2nd ed. (New York: Interlink, 1999), 189.
11. From Clark D. Moore and David Eldridge, eds., *India Yesterday and Today* (New York: Bantam, 1970), 174.
12. Quoted in Martin Deming Lewis, ed., *Gandhi: Maker of Modern India?* (Lexington, MA: D.C. Heath, 1965), xii.
13. Quoted in Hermann Kulke and Dietmar Rothermund, *History of India*, 3rd ed. (New York: Routledge, 1998), 135-136.
14. Sir T.P. Sapru, quoted in Judith M. Brown, *Modern India: The Origins of an Asian Democracy*, 2nd ed. (New York: Oxford University Press, 1994), 280.
15. "Phan Boi Chau's Prison Reflections, 1914," in *Major Problems in the History of the Vietnam War: Documents and Essays*, ed. Robert J. McMahon (Lexington, MA: D.C. Heath, 1990), 32.
16. Hoai Thanh, quoted in David Marr, "Vietnamese Historical Reassessment, 1900-1944," in *Perceptions of the Past in Southeast Asia*, ed. Anthony Reid and David Marr (Singapore: Heinemann, 1979), 337-338.
17. Sitor Situmorang, quoted in Harry Aveling, ed., *From Surabaya to Armageddon: Indonesian Short Stories* (Singapore: Heinemann, 1976), vii.
18. Obafemi Awolowo, quoted in Chester L. Hunt and Lewis Walker, *Ethnic Dynamics: Patterns of Intergroup Relations in Various Societies*, 2nd ed. (Holmes Beach, FL: Learning Publications, 1979), 277.
19. Quoted in Veit Erlmann, *African Stars: Studies in Black South African Performance* (Chicago: University of Chicago Press, 1991), 95-96.
20. Quoted in Charles Hamm, " 'The Constant Companion of Man': Separate Development, Radio Bantu and Music," *Popular Music* 10, no. (May 1991): 161.
21. Quoted in Hans Kohn, *A History of Nationalism in the East* (New York: Harcourt, 1929), 257.
22. The quotes are from Akram Fouad Khater, ed., *Sources in the History of the Modern Middle East* (Boston: Houghton Mifflin, 2004), 167, 176.
23. Severino Fama, quoted in Robert M. Levine, *The History of Brazil* (New York: Palgrave, 1999), 107.
24. From Frederick B. Pike, ed., *Latin American History: Select Problems. Identity, Integration, and Nationhood* (New York: Harcourt, Brace and World, 1969), 319.

Societies, Networks, Transitions: Global Imbalances in the Modern World, 1750-1945

1. From Jim Zwick, ed., *Mark Twain's Weapons of Satire: Anti-Imperialist Writings on the Philippine-American War* (Syracuse, NY: Syracuse University Press, 1992), 3-5.

2. Quoted in L. S. Stavrianos, *Lifelines from Our Past: A New World History*, rev. ed. (Armonk, NY: M.E. Sharpe, 1997), 114.

3. Rev. Sydney Smith, quoted in Frederic Delouche et al., *Illustrated History of Europe: A Unique Portrait of Europe's Common People* (New York: Barnes and Noble, 2001), 289.

4. Senator Albert Beveridge of Indiana, quoted in Henry Allen, *What It Felt Like Living in the American Century* (New York: Pantheon, 2000), 7.

5. Quoted in Benjamin Schwartz, *In Search of Wealth and Power: Yen Fu and the West* (New York: Harper Torchbooks, 1964), 29.

6. Quoted in Scott B. Cook, *Colonial Encounters in the Age of High Imperialism* (New York: Longman, 1996), 100.

7. From Clark D. Moore and David Eldridge, eds., *India Yesterday and Today* (New York: Bantam, 1970), 170.

8. Quoted in John A. Harrison, *China Since 1800* (New York: Harcourt, Brace and World, 1967), 161.

9. Quoted in Ranajit Guha, *History at the Limit of World-History* (New York: Columbia University Press, 2002), 91.

10. International Congress of the League Against Imperialism and Colonial Oppression, quoted in Clive Ponting, *The Twentieth Century: A World History* (New York: Henry Holt, 1998), 197.

11. Quoted in Richard H. Robbins, *Global Problems and the Culture of Capitalism* (Boston: Allyn and Bacon, 1999), 90.

12. Quoted in "Introduction," in *The Frontier in Perspective*, ed. Walter D. Wyman and Clifton B. Kroeber (Madison: University of Wisconsin Press, 1965), xviii.

13. Quoted in Pamela Scully, "Race and Ethnicity in Women's and Gender History in Global Perspective," in *Women's History in Global Perspective*, ed, Bonnie G. Smith, vol. 1 (Urbana: University of Illinois Press, 2004), 207.

14. Quoted in Ng Bickleen Fong, *The Chinese in New Zealand* (Hong Kong: Hong Kong University Press, 1959), 96.

15. Quoted in J. R. McNeill and William H. McNeill, *The Human Web: A Bird's-Eye View of World History* (New York: W. W. Norton, 2003), 217.

16. Quoted in Daniel R. Headrick, *The Tentacles of Progress: Technology Transfer in the Age of Imperialism, 1850–1940* (New York: Oxford University Press, 1988), 127.

17. Quoted in L. S. Stavrianos, "The Global Redistribution of Man," in *World Migration in Modern Times*, ed. Franklin D. Scott (Englewood Cliffs, NJ: Prentice-Hall, 1968), 170.

18. Quoted in Daniel R. Headrick, *The Tools of Empire: Technology and European Imperialism in the Nineteenth Century* (New York: Oxford University Press, 1981), 116.

19. Quoted in Gordon Rohlehr, *Calypso and Society in Pre-Independence Trinidad* (Port of Spain: Gordon Rohlehr, 1990), 80–81.

Chapter 26 The Remaking of the Global System, Since 1945

1. Quoted in Adrian Boot and Chris Salewicz with Rita Marley as Senior Editor, *Bob Marley: Songs of Freedom* (London: Bloomsbury, 1995), 278.

2. Frantz Fanon, *The Wretched of the Earth* (New York: Grove, 1968), 97–98.

3. Quoted in Goran Hyden, *Beyond Ujamaa in Tanzania: Underdevelopment and an Uncaptured Peasantry* (Berkeley: University of California Press, 1980), 202.

4. Quoted in Jennifer Seymour Whitaker, *How Can Africa Survive?* (New York: Harper and Row, 1988), 13.

5. The quotes are in Choi Chatterjee et al., *The 20th Century: A Retrospective* (Boulder, CO: Westview Press, 2002), 153, 306.

6. Dalai Lama, *My Land and My People* (New York: Warner Books, 1997), x.

7. Quoted in Peter Singer, "Navigating the Ethics of Globalization," *Chronicle of Higher Education*, October 11, 2002, B8.

8. Quoted in J. Donald Hughes, *An Environmental History of the World: Mankind's Changing Role in the Community of Life* (New York: Routledge, 2002), 206.

9. Quoted in Miriam Ching Louie, "Life on the Line," *The New Internationalist* (http://www.newint.org/issue302/sweat.html)

10. Walter Rodney, *How Europe Underdeveloped Africa* (London: Bogle-L'Ouverture, 1972), 162.

11. Quoted in Michael H. Hunt, *The World Transformed, 1945 to the Present* (Boston: Bedford/St. Martin's), 428.

12. Quoted in Eric Hobsbawm, *The Age of Extremes: A History of the World, 1914–1991* (New York: Pantheon, 1994), 365.

13. A. G. Hopkins, "Globalization: An Agenda for Historians," in *Globalization in World History*, ed. A. G. Hopkins (New York: W.W. Norton, 2002), 11.

14. From Hazel Johnson and Henry Bernstein, eds., *Third World Lives of Struggle* (London: Heinemann Educational, 1982), 173.

15. J. R. McLeod, "The Seamless Web: Media and Power in the Post-Modern Global Village," *Journal of Popular Culture* 15, no. 2 (Fall 1991): 69.

16. Quoted in David Reynolds, *One World Divisible: A Global History Since 1945* (New York: W.W. Norton, 2000), 491.

17. Michael Sturmer, quoted in Hobsbawm, *Age of Extremes*, 558.

Chapter 27 East Asian Resurgence, Since 1945

1. Quoted in Jerome Chen, *Mao and the Chinese Revolution* (New York: Oxford University Press, 1967), 6.

2. The quotes are from Ross Terrill, *Mao: A Biography* (New York: Harper, 1980), 198.

3. Peng Dehuai, quoted in Craig Dietrich, *People's China: A Brief History*, 3rd ed. (New York: Oxford University Press, 1998), 130.

4. Quoted in Maurice Meisner, *Mao's China and After: A History of the People's Republic*, 3rd ed. (New York: The Free Press, 1999), 281.

5. Xue Xinran, *The Good Women of China: Hidden Voices* (New York: Anchor, 2002), 175.

6. Quoted in the Committee of Concerned Asian Scholars, *China! Inside the Peoples Republic* (New York: Bantam, 1972), 34.

7. From Timothy Cheek, *Mao Zedong and China's Revolutions: A Brief History with Documents* (Boston: Bedford/St. Martin's, 2002), 116.

8. Quoted in Hu Kai-Yu, *The Chinese Literary Scene: A Writer's Visit to the People's Republic* (New York: Vintage, 1975), 227.

9. Quoted in Orville Schell, *Discos and Democracy: China in the Throes of Reform* (New York: Anchor, 1989), 101.

10. Quoted in June Teufel Dreyer, *China's Political System: Modernization and Tradition* (New York: Paragon House, 1993), 345.

11. The quotes are in Andrew F. Jones, *Like a Knife: Ideology and Genre in Contemporary Chinese Popular Music* (Ithaca, NY: East Asia Program, Cornell University, 1992), 97, 148.

12. Quoted in R. Keith Schoppa, *Revolution and Its Past: Identities and Change in Modern Chinese History* (Upper Saddle River, NJ: Prentice-Hall, 2002), 433.

13. Xue Xinran, author interview in *Random House: Reading Group for the Good Women of China* (http://www.randomhouse.co.uk/offthepage/guide.htm?command=Search&db=catalog/mai)

14. Quoted in James L. McClain, *Japan: A Modern History* (New York: W.W. Norton, 2002), 585.

15. Misuzu Hanikara, from Richard H. Minear, ed., *Through Japanese Eyes*, vol. 2 (New York: Praeger, 1974), 88.

16. Quoted in Mikiso Hane, *Modern Japan: A Historical Survey*, 2nd ed. (Boulder, CO: Westview Press, 1992), 371.

17. Quoted in Frank Gibney, *The Pacific Century: America and Asia in a Changing World* (New York: Charles Scribner's, 1992), 231.

Chapter 28 Rebuilding Europe and Russia, Since 1945

1. Quoted in Norman Davies, *Europe: A History* (New York: Harper, 1998), 1066.

2. Quoted in ibid.

3. Quoted in Felix Gilbert with David Clay Large, *The End of the European Era, 1890 to the Present*, 4th ed. (New York: W.W. Norton, 1991), 429.

4. Quoted in Harold James, *Europe Reborn: A History, 1914–2000* (New York: Longman, 2001), 248.

5. Quoted in Robert O. Paxton, *Europe in the Twentieth Century* (New York: Harcourt Brace Jovanovich, 1973), 576.

6. Quoted in Davies, *Europe*, 1065.

7. Quoted in Bonnie G. Smith, *Changing Lives: Women in European History Since 1700* (Lexington, MA: D.C. Heath, 1989), 509.

8. Quoted in Richard Vinen, *A History in Fragments: Europe in the Twentieth Century* (New York: Da Capo, 2000), 370.

9. Quoted in Bonnie S. Anderson and Judith P. Zinsser, *A History of Their Own: Women in Europe from Prehistory to the Present*, vol. 2 (New York: Harper Perennial, 1988), 334.

10. Amintore Fanfani, quoted in Vinen, *History in Fragments*, 493.

11. *Sniffin' Glue*, quoted in Peter Wicke, *Rock Music: Culture, Aesthetics and Sociology* (New York: Cambridge University Press, 1990), 148.

12. Quoted in Ronald Grigor Suny, *The Soviet Experiment: Russia, the USSR, and the Successor States* (New York: Oxford University Press, 1998), 387.

13. Quoted in James, *Europe Reborn*, 279.

14. Quoted in Timothy W. Ryback, *Rock Around the Bloc: A History of Rock Music in Eastern Europe and the Soviet Union* (New York: Oxford University Press, 1990), 35.

15. Quoted in Davies, *Europe*, 1102.

16. Quoted in James, *Europe Reborn*, 300.

17. Quoted in James Wilkenson and H. Stuart Hughes, *Contemporary Europe: A History*, 10th ed. (Upper Saddle River, NJ: Prentice-Hall, 2004), 559.

18. Quoted in Vinen, *History in Fragments*, 520.

19. Quoted in Wilkenson and Hughes, *Contemporary Europe*, 590.

Chapter 29   The Americas and the Pacific Basin: New Roles in the Contemporary World, Since 1945

1. Quoted in James D. Cockcroft, *Latin America: History, Politics, and U.S. Policy*, 2nd ed. (Chicago: Nelson-Hall, 1996), 567.

2. Quoted in Marilyn B. Young, *The Vietnam Wars, 1945–1990* (New York: HarperCollins, 1991), 25.

3. Quoted in James Matray, *The Reluctant Crusade: American Foreign Policy in Korea, 1941–1950* (Honolulu: University of Hawaii Press, 1985), 3.

4. Quoted in L. S. Stavrianos, *Global Rift: The Third World Comes of Age* (New York: William Morrow, 1981), 712.

5. Quoted in Walter LaFeber, *America, Russia and the Cold War: 1945–1992*, 7th ed. (New York: McGraw-Hill, 1993), 248.

6. Quoted in Cockcroft, *Latin America*, 531.

7. Quoted in Walter LaFeber et al., *The American Century: A History of the United States Since 1941*, 5th ed. (Boston: McGraw-Hill, 1998), 519.

8. Folksinger Malvina Reynolds, quoted in Richard O. Davies, "The Ambivalent Heritage: The City in Modern America," in *Paths to the Present: Interpretive Essays on American Society Since 1930*, ed. James T. Patterson (Minneapolis: Burgess, 1975), 163.

9. From Peter Blood-Patterson, ed., *Rise Up Singing* (Bethlehem, PA: Sing Out Publications, 1988), 219.

10. Quoted in George Donelson Moss, *America in the Twentieth Century*, 4th ed. (Upper Saddle River, NJ: Prentice-Hall, 2000), 409.

11. Quoted in James T. Patterson, *America Since 1941: A History*, 2nd ed. (Fort Worth, TX: Harcourt, 2000), 254.

12. Quoted in Wayne C. Thompson, *Canada 1997* (Harpers Ferry, VA: Stryker-Post, 1997), 1.

13. Jaime Wheelock, quoted in Kyle Longley, *In the Eagle's Shadow: The United States and Latin America* (Wheeling, IL: Harlan Davidson, 2002), 291.

14. Quoted in Sebastian Balfour, *Castro*, 2nd ed. (New York: Longman, 1995), 167.

15. The quotes are in Thomas E. Skidmore and Peter H. Smith, *Modern Latin America*, 4th ed. (New York: Oxford University Press, 1997), 147; Joseph A. Page, *The Brazilians* (Reading, MA: Addison-Wesley, 1995), 5.

16. Quoted in David J. Morris, *We Must Make Haste—Slowly: The Process of Revolution in Chile* (New York: Vintage, 1973), 270–271.

17. Pamela Constable and Arturo Valenzuela, *A Nation of Enemies: Chile Under Pinochet* (New York: W.W. Norton, 1991), 38.

18. Graciliano Ramos, *Barren Lives*, quoted in E. Bradford Burns, *Latin America: A Concise Interpretive History*, 5th ed. (Englewood Cliffs, NJ: Prentice-Hall, 1990), 231.

19. Nelson Rodrigues, quoted in Warren Hoge, "A Whole Nation More Agitated than Spike Lee," *New York Times*, June 5, 1994, A1.

20. From Jara's song "Manifiesto." The song and the translation can be found on Jara's album *Manifiesto: Chile September 1973* (XTRA 1143, 1974).

21. See Marley's album *Catch a Fire* (Island ILPS 9241, 1973).

22. Quoted in Jan Fairley, "New Song: Music and Politics in Latin America," in *Rhythms of the World*, ed. Francis Hanly and Tim May (London: BBC Books, 1989), 90.

Chapter 30   The Middle East, Sub-Saharan Africa, and New Conflicts in the Contemporary World, Since 1945

1. See Savuka's album *Heat, Dust and Dreams* (EMI 9777-7-98795, 1993)

2. Quoted in James Alban Bill, *The Politics of Iran: Groups, Classes and Modernization* (Columbus, OH: Charles E. Merrill, 1972), 76–77.

3. Latifa az-Zayyat, quoted in Wiebke Walther, *Women in Islam from Medieval to Modern Times* (Princeton: Markus Wiener, 1993), 235.

4. Quoted in Daniel Bates and Amal Rassam, *Peoples and Cultures of the Middle East*, 2nd ed. (Upper Saddle River, NJ: Prentice-Hall, 2001), 235.

5. Fatema Mernissi, *Scheherazade Goes West: Different Cultures, Different Harems* (New York: Washington Square Press, 2001), 219.

6. Martin Stokes, *The Arabesk Debate: Music and Musicians in Modern Turkey* (Oxford: Clarendon Press, 1992), 1.

7. Sadiq Hidayat, in *Hajji Aqa*, quoted in Bill, *Politics of Iran*, 105.

8. From Akram Fouad Khater, ed., *Sources in the History of the Modern Middle East* (Boston: Houghton Mifflin, 2004), 362.

9. Naguib Mahfuz, quoted in Bates and Rassam, *Peoples and Cultures*, 199.

10. Quoted in Frances Robinson, *The Cultural Atlas of the Islamic World Since 1500* (Alexandria, VA: Stonehenge, 1982), 158.

11. Quoted in Basil Davidson, *The People's Cause: A History of Guerrillas in Africa* (Burnt Mill, UK: Longman, 1981), 165.

12. A. Toure, quoted in Bill Freund, *The Making of Contemporary Africa: The Development of African Society Since 1800* (Bloomington: Indiana University Press, 1984), 192.

13. Prime Minister John Vorster in 1968, quoted in L. S. Stavrianos, *Global Rift: The Third World Comes of Age* (New York: William Morrow, 1981), 759.

14. Quoted in Jean Comaroff, *Body of Power, Spirit of Resistance: The Culture and History of a South African People* (Chicago: University of Chicago Press, 1985), vi.

15. Quoted in Gwendolen Carter, "The Republic of South Africa: White Political Control Within the African Continent," in *Africa*, ed. Phyllis Martin and Patrick O'Meara, 2nd ed. (Bloomington: Indiana University Press, 1986), 353.

16. Quoted in Joe Asila, "No Cash in This Crop," in *Global Studies: Africa*, ed. Wayne Edge, 2nd ed. (Guilford, CT: Dushkin, 2006), 285.

17. Sanford Unger, *Africa: The People and Politics of an Emerging Continent* (New York: Simon and Schuster, 1985), 131–132.

18. Quoted in Richard A. Fredland, *Understanding Africa: A Political Economy Perspective* (Chicago: Burnham, 2001), 139.

19. Quoted in John Follain, "Only the First Step for 'Mama Africa,'" *New Straits Times*, February 23, 1990.

20. Quoted in Tejumola Olaniyan, "Narrativizing Postcoloniality: Responsibilities," *Public Culture* 5, no. 1 (Fall 1992): 47.

21. Quoted in Chinweizu, *The West and the Rest of Us: White Predators, Black Slavers, and the African Elite* (New York: Vintage, 1975), 1.

22. Quoted in Jennifer Seymour Whitaker, *How Can Africa Survive?* (New York: Harper and Row, 1988), 197.

Chapter 31   South Asia, Southeast Asia, and Global Connections, Since 1945

1. Mochtar Lubis, *Road with No End*, translated by Anthony Johns from 1952 Indonesian edition (Chicago: Henry Regnery, 1968), 9.

2. Quoted in Anthony Johns, "Introduction," in ibid., 4.

3. Quoted in John R. McLane, ed., *The Political Awakening of India* (Englewood Cliffs, NJ: Prentice-Hall, 1970), 178.

4. Quoted in B. N. Pandey, *The Break-up of British India* (New York: St. Martin's, 1969), 209.

5. Faiz Ahmed Faiz, quoted in Sugata Bose and Ayesha Jalal, *Modern South Asia: History, Culture, Political Economy* (New York: Routledge, 1998), 200.

6. Rohinton Mistry, *A Fine Balance* (London: Faber, 1996), 143.

7. Quoted in Susan Bayly, *Caste, Society and Politics in India from the Eighteenth Century to the Modern Age* (New York: Cambridge University Press, 1999), 315.

8. Quoted in Jeremy Marre and Hannah Charlton, *Beats of the Heart: Popular Music of the World* (New York: Pantheon, 1985), 150.

9. Quoted in Bose and Jalal, *Modern South Asia*, 232.

10. Quoted in Stanley Wolpert, *A New History of India*, 7th ed. (New York: Oxford University Press, 2004), 462.

11. Quoted in William J. Duiker, *Ho Chi Minh: A Life* (New York: Hyperion, 2000), 323.

12. Quoted in George Donelson Moss, *Vietnam: An American Ordeal*, 4th ed. (Upper Saddle River, NJ: Prentice-Hall, 2002), 40.

13. Jacques Philippe Leclerc, quoted in James S. Olson and Randy Roberts, *Where the Domino Fell: America and Vietnam, 1945–1995*, 3rd ed. (St. James, NY: Brandywine, 1999), 28.

14. Quoted in Thomas G. Paterson et al., *American Foreign Policy: A History Since 1900*, 3rd ed. rev. (Lexington, MA: D.C. Heath, 1991), 553.

15. Anh Vien, quoted in Arleen Eisen Bergman, *Women of Vietnam*, rev. ed. (San Francisco: Peoples Press, 1975), 123.

16. Quoted in Neil L. Jamieson, *Understanding Vietnam* (Berkeley: University of California Press, 1993), 290.

17. From Idrus, "Surabaya," in *From Surabaya to Armageddon: Indonesian Short Stories,* ed. Harry Aveling (Singapore: Heinemann, 1976), 13.

18. From Pramoedya Ananta Toer, "Letter to a Friend in the Country," in Aveling, *From Surabaya*, 72.

19. Doreen Fernandez, "Mass Culture and Cultural Policy: The Philippine Experience," *Philippine Studies* 37 (4th Quarter, 1980): 492.

20. "The Kingdom of Mammon," in Amado V. Hernandez, *Rice Grains: Selected Poems* (New York: International Publishers, 1966), 31.

21. From Taufiq Ismail's story "Stop Thief!" in *Black Clouds over the Isle of Gods and Other Modern Indonesian Short Stories,* ed. David M. E. Roskies (Armonk, NY: M.E. Sharpe, 1997), 97.

22. F. Sionel Jose, quoted in David G. Timberman, *A Changeless Land: Continuity and Change in Philippine Politics* (New York: M.E. Sharpe, 1991), xi.

23. "American Junk," by the Apo Hiking Society, quoted in Craig A. Lockard, *Dance of Life: Popular Music and Politics in Southeast Asia* (Honolulu: University of Hawai'i Press, 1998), 156.

24. Quoted in Robin Broad and John Cavanaugh, *Plundering Paradise: The Struggle for the Environment in the Philippines* (Berkeley: University of California Press, 1993), xvii.

25. Quoted in Pasuk Phongpaichit and Chris Baker, *Thailand: Economy and Politics* (Kuala Lumpur: Oxford University Press, 1995), 413–415.

Societies, Networks, Transitions: The Contemporary World, Since 1945

1. Kathleen Newland and Kamala Chandrakirana Soedjatmoko, eds., *Transforming Humanity: The Visionary Writings of Soedjatmoko* (West Hartford, CT: Kumarian Press, 1994), 186–187.

2. Quoted in Jan Pronk, "Globalization: A Developmental Approach," in *Global Futures: Shaping Globalization*, ed. Jan Nederveen Pieterse (London: Zed Books, 2000), 46.

3. Daphne Berdahl, quoted in James L. Watson, ed., *Golden Arches East: McDonald's in East Asia* (Stanford, CA: Stanford University Press, 1997), xvii.

4. Billy Bergman, *Hot Sauces: Latin and Caribbean Pop* (New York: Quill, 1985), 18.

5. Quoted in Hans-Peter Martin and Harald Schumann, *The Global Trap: Globalization and the Assault on Democracy and Prosperity* (New York: Zed Books, 1996), 163.

6. From Banton's album, *Visions of the World* (IRSD-82003, 1989).

7. Frank Cajka, quoted in Peter Worsley, *The Three Worlds: Culture and World Development* (Chicago: University of Chicago Press, 1984), xi.

8. Quoted in Robbie Robertson, *The Three Waves of Globalization: A History of a Developing Global Consciousness* (New York: Zed Books, 2003), 263.

9. Lester Pearson, quoted in Lester R. Brown, *World Without Borders* (New York: Vintage, 1972), ix.

10. Aldo Leopold, *A Sand County Almanac* (New York: Ballantine, 1966), 253.

11. Quoted in J. Donald Hughes, *An Environmental History of the World: Humankind's Changing Role in the Community of Life* (New York: Routledge, 2001), 230.

12. Rene Dubos, *So Human an Animal* (New York: Scribner's, 1968), 270.

13. Ilya Prigogine, quoted in Federico Mayor and Jerome Bindé, *The World Ahead: Our Future in the Making* (New York: Zed Books, 2001), 1.

14. Lester Brown et al., "A World at Risk," in *State of the World 1989* (New York: W.W. Norton, 1989), 20.

15. Lewis Carroll, "Alice's Adventures in Wonderland," in *The Complete Works of Lewis Carroll* (New York: Modern Library), 71–72.

Index

Shakespeare, William, 944

Shamans: African, 585; Muslims and, 594

Shandong Peninsula (China): German control of, 636, 639, 692

Shanghai, 631, 725; business community in, 692; growth of, 753, 776; theme park in, 777–778

Sharecropping, 557, 564. *See also* Tenant farmers

Shar'ia. *See* Islamic law

Shariati, Ali (Indian thinker), 876

Shawnee Indians, 567

Sheep raising: in New Zealand, 571; in Australia, 569, 656

Sheffield, industrialization of, 530*(illus.)*

Shellshock, in World War I, 657–658

Shi'ite Islam, 908. *See also* Sunni-Shi'ite rivalry; Aga Khan IV and, 744; *Hezbollah* movement and, 763; in Iraq, 594, 710, 760; in Pakistan, 700; in Iran, 592, 709; in Saudi Arabia, 873

Shimei Futabatei (Japanese writer), 645

Shining Path (Peru), 849

Shinto, in Japan, 787

Shipping routes, 541*(map)*. *See also* Maritime trade

Ships and shipping (merchant marine): *See also* Navy (warships); Japanese, 642; canals and, 565; steamships, 529, 538, 571, 609, 642, 728; British, 591; South Korean, 791*(illus.)*

Shock therapy, in Russia, 822

Shoguns, in Japan, 639, 642. *See also specific shogunate*

Siam: Chinese in, 508; constitutional monarchy in, 701; diplomacy in, 617; France and, 510

Siberia: Russia and, 631, 640, 648, 649*(map)*; prison camps *(gulags)* in, 651, 662, 666, 813; railroad across, 649*(map)*, 650, 656, 728

Sidqi az-Zahawi, Jamil (Iraqi poet), 595

Sierra Club, 755

Sierra Leone, 577, 744; college in, 585; ethnic conflict in, 886; life expectancy in, 937

Sigurdarlottir, Johanna (Icelandic leader), 808

Sihanouk, Norodom (Cambodia), 916–917, 928

Sikhs, 908; Mughal India and, 602; British and, 604, 700; partition of India and, 900, 901; autonomy of, 903

Silk industry: Chinese, 629; Japanese, 633

Silk Road Ensemble (musical group), 936

Silk Road trade, 650, 934

Silver, in China trade, 629

Singapore, 689, 725; in ASEAN, 921; Chinese in, 614, 620, 728*(illus.)*, 788, 926; English language in, 761; independence of, 918*(map)*, 919; globalization and, 746, 756, 935; economic growth in, 746, 781*(map)*, 920; high technology in, 761

Singh, Manmohan (Indian leader), 825*(illus.)*, 906

Singh, Ranjit, 602, 604

Sinhalese: Buddhism and, 604; in Sri Lanka, 604, 911

Sinn Fein (Ireland), 535

Sino-Japanese War (1894-1895), 636, 647

Sisters in Islam, 925

Skin color, racism and. *See also* Racism; in Brazil, 858; in colonial Africa, 583; in United States, 557

Skyscrapers, in East Asia, 926*(illus.)*

Slave revolts, 576; in Haiti, 524

Slavery, abolition of, 726; in Britain, 576; in France, 520; in United States, 520, 556–557; Haitian Revolution and, 524; in Latin America, 564; Quakers and, 550, 553, 555; in United States, 520, 553, 555, 576, 722

Slaves (slavery). *See also* African slavery; in Nicaragua, 565

Slavophiles, 651

Slavs (Slavic peoples), 657, 660; Nazi Germany and, 680, 682; Slovaks, 667, 823, 824*(map)*

Slovenes (Slovenia), 660, 823, 824*(map)*

Smallpox, 578, 757; Aborigines and, 569; vaccines against, 551

Smith, Adam (British economist), 530

Smith, Jacob (American general), 618

Soccer (football), 729, 858

Social Darwinism, 540, 542, 558

Social Democrats, in Europe, 538, 667; welfare state and, 673, 799, 804–806, 826

Social diversity, cultural change and, 732

Socialism: utopian, 535–536; fascism and, 675; feminists and, 657; in Europe, 589; labor unions and, 667, 675; World War I and, 660; and capitalism, in Asia, 747; in Soviet Union, 816; in Venezuela, 851; in Cuba, 852; in Chile, 854, 855; in North Vietnam, 914; and capitalism in India, 902; in Africa, 883, 891, 892; in Jamaica, 859; in Sri Lanka, 911

"Socialism in one country," 665

Socialist realism, 666

Socialist Revolutionary Party (Russia), 651

Social market economy, in Europe, 826

Social revolution: in China, 767, 768; Marxism and, 739; nationalism and, 736; in Africa, 891–892; in Vietnam, 614

Social safety net (welfare): *See also* Welfare state; in Europe, 546, 799, 804–806

Social security, in United States, 672

Society Islands, 569

Society of Jesus. *See* Jesuit missionaries

Society (social structure): in British India, 610–611; Korean, 646; Latin American, 562; Qing China, 635; United States, 558–559, 669, 680; in colonial Africa, 582; Japanese, 644–645; colonial Southeast Asia, 620–621; in Europe (1920s), 668; Chinese, 777–778; Soviet Union, 816–817; Western Europe, 804–812; Latin America, 855–859; Indian, 907–908; in African cities, 892–893; environmental change and, 939–940

Soedjatmoko (Indonesian thinker), 934

Soekarnoputri, Megawati (Indonesian leader), 922, 928

Soil erosion, 672, 755

Sokoto Caliphate, 578, 580

Solaar, M. C., 810

Soldiers. *See* Armed forces; Infantry; Mercenaries; Military

Solidarity (Poland), 818, 823

Solzhenitsyn, Alexander, 814, 822

Somalia, 580, 886–887; civil war in, 744–745; refugees from, 757; toxic waste in, 895; United States' intervention in, 837; famine in, 887

Somerea family (India), 610

Something Out There (Gordimer), 888

Somoza Debayle, Anastasio (Nicaraguan leader), 691

Son of Heaven, in China, 631

Sotho kingdom, 584

Soukous (Congolese music), 893

South, United States: civil war in, 557, 722; plantation slavery in, 557; African American music in, 559–560; racist lynchings in, 557, 669; segregation in, 681, 843–844

South Africa (South Africans), 844; Angola and, 892; Asians in, 610, 634; Black Zion movement in, 587; Boer War (1899-1902), 584; Dutch colony in, 583; homosexuality in, 893; as British colony, 539, 583–585; Christianity in, 894; European immigrants in, 546, 690, 725; same-sex marriage in, 760; labor migration in, 586; music of, 705*(illus.)*, 706, 865, 893; nationalism in, 706; white supremacy in, 582, 583, 585, 586–587, 697, 698, 699; in World War I, 658; apartheid in, 887–888; black majority rule in, 888; diamond mining in, 580, 584, 656; Mandela in, 885, 888, 889–890 *and illus.*; Zulu expansion in, 583–584

South America. *See also* Latin America; in 1930, 712*(map)*; political stability in, 732

South Asia. *See also* Bangladesh; India; Pakistan; Sri Lanka; decolonization in, 738*(map)*, 900–901; labor migration from, 756, 757, 810; chronology (1919-1942), 697; reshaping of, 900–912; chronology (1947–2006), 900; diversity in, 899–900; politics and societies in, 904–912; in the global system, 911–912

Southeast Asia. *See also* Burma; Cambodia; Indonesia; Malaysia; Philippines; Thailand; Vietnam; Islamic militancy in, 745; European colonies in, 615*(map)*; Islam in, 510, 758, 759*(map)*, 877*(map)*; Chinese merchants in, 620, 634, 726; chronology (1786–1908), 614; colonization of, 613–623, 688; intermarriage in, 620; social and cultural change in, 620–621; Great Depression in, 690; Japanese occupation of, 680, 681*(map)*, 682–683; nationalism in, 701–704; transitions in, 733; revolution, decolonization and new nations in, 738*(map)*, 912–920, 918*(map)*; resurgence of, 920–921; economic "tigers" in, 920, 928; in global system, 928

Southern Cone Common Market, 861

Southern Rhodesia. *See* Zimbabwe

South Korea (South Koreans). *See also* Korea; democracy in, 746–747, 836; environmental destruction in, 753; globalization and, 746; government-business ties in, 746; labor migration from, 757, 790; China and, 778; Korean War and, 743, 770, 789, 790*(map)*, 835–836; economy of, 740, 781*(map)*, 790, 791*(illus.)*, 834, 852, 937; North Korea and, 788, 789, 790, 791; United States and, 789

South Vietnam, 741, 815, 836 *and illus.*, 913. *See also* Vietnam War; Diem regime in, 914

Soviet bloc, 815; economies of, 803*(map)*; North Korea and, 791; Stalin and, 813; United States and, 741, 832; Western Europe and, 801, 802*(map)*; collapse of (1989), 744, 820–821

Soviets (local councils), 663

Soviet Union (USSR), 672. *See also* Communist Party (Soviet Union); Superpowers, in Cold War; economic insulation of, 672; global communism and, 654*(illus.)*; roots of revolution in, 662–663; Comintern and civil war in, 663, 664*(map)*; industrialization in, 665, 666; Lenin's economic policy, 665; reshaping society in, 666; Spanish civil war and, 677; Stalinism in, 665–666; in World War II, 678–679 *and map*, 682, 813; aid to nationalists by, 736; Eastern Europe and, 683, 733, 741, 797, 817–818; Marxist-Leninism in, 665, 695–696; China and, 692, 693, 768, 772; chronology (1945–1985), 813; under Khrushchev, 772, 813–814; Korean War and, 789, 790*(map)*; military spending by, 743; expansion of, 682, 813; politics and economy, 813–815; rivalry with United States, 683, 740–741, 834; society and culture, 816–817 *and illus.*; war in Afghanistan, 741, 763, 815, 878, 908; Cuba and, 742, 815; decline and reform in, 818–820; collapse of, 737, 820–821 *and map*

Soyinka, Wole, 894

Space exploration, 748, 813

Space satellites, 813, 840, 912

Spain (Spanish): immigrants from, 564, 593; Inquisition in, 524; Picasso and, 550, 673; Napoleonic era, 522, 523*(map)*, 525, 550; agriculture in, 529; Catholicism in, 550, 753; United States and, 519, 560; civil war in, 677; Basque nationalism and, 740, 762, 799*(illus.)*, 800; low fertility in, 753; same-sex marriage in, 760, 808; in Common Market and NATO, 802*(map)*; terrorism in, 763, 799*(illus.)*, 800, 826; trade routes of, 504*(map)*